The Book of Jeremiah

The New International Commentary
on the
Old Testament

Series Editors

E. J. Young
(1965–1968)

R. K. Harrison
(1968–1993)

Robert L. Hubbard Jr.
(1994–   ·   )

Bill T. Arnold
(2020–   )

The Book of
JEREMIAH

John Goldingay

William B. Eerdmans Publishing Company
Grand Rapids, Michigan

Wm. B. Eerdmans Publishing Co.
4035 Park East Court SE, Grand Rapids, Michigan 49546
www.eerdmans.com

27 26 25 24 23 22 21   1 2 3 4 5 6 7

ISBN 978-0-8028-7584-6

Library of Congress Cataloging-in-Publication Data

Names: Goldingay, John, author.
Title: The Book of Jeremiah / John Goldingay.
Description: Grand Rapids, Michigan : William B. Eerdmans Publishing Company, 2021. |
    Series: The new international commentary on the Old Testament | Includes bibli-
    ographical references and index. | Summary: "A commentary for scholars and pastors
    on the biblical book of Jeremiah, with an emphasis on reading it as authoritative
    Christian Scripture"—Provided by publisher.
Identifiers: LCCN 2021007065 | ISBN 9780802875846 (hardcover)
Subjects: LCSH: Bible. Jeremiah—Commentaries.
Classification: LCC BS1525.53 .G649 2021 | DDC 224/.2077—dc23
LC record available at https://lccn.loc.gov/2021007065

Contents

CONTENTS

CONTENTS

Contents

CONTENTS

Series Editor's Preface

"Do you *understand* what you're *reading*?"

What a question!

With this opening line, Philip, one of Christianity's first evangelists, approached a seeker from Africa, who had been in Jerusalem to worship. Somewhere along the Gaza Road, on his return trip to Ethiopia, the stranger was reading a portion of the Old Testament. Philip asked the question when he heard him "reading" the ancient text, an activity that almost certainly involved verbalizing the text by reciting it aloud (*anaginōskō*; Acts 8:30). An "angel of the Lord" had sent Philip to meet the Ethiopian for this very opportunity (8:26–29).

Realizing that the seeker was reading a difficult text, and yet also realizing how vitally important it was to the stranger's faith, Philip distinguished between reading and comprehending. "Understanding" is different from simply pronouncing the text aloud; comprehension involves grasping the significance of what is read (*ginōskō*).

Such a deep-level understanding of ancient Israel's Scriptures has always been the goal of The New International Commentary on the Old Testament. Since 1965, the editors of this series—Edward J. Young, Roland K. Harrison, and Robert L. Hubbard Jr.—have guided the series and its authors with the sole purpose of aiding the reader to gain understanding of the text. They have left us a treasured gift. Today a wide readership of scholars, priests, pastors, rabbis, and other serious students of the Bible turn to NICOT volumes for assistance in reading the ancient text.

The aim of the series has always been "to publish biblical scholarship of the highest quality" (to quote the preface of my predecessor, Professor Hubbard) and to do so respectfully from a position of faith seeking understanding. The series appeals to readers across the entire spectrum of theological or philosophical perspectives, and always with the conviction that the Old Testament is more than great literature from the past. Its authors engage the range of traditional methodologies, always sensitive to newer innovations in recent scholarship, and always remembering that the books of the Old Testament constituted the first Bible for the earliest Christians.

Specifically, the NICOT authors believe the books they are writing about—ancient Israel's Scriptures—are God-breathed (*theopneustos*) or "inspired" and therefore "useful for teaching, for reproof, for correction, and for training in righteousness" (2 Timothy 3:16). This high regard of and respect for the authority of Scripture characterizes what has come to be known as "evangelicalism," together with conversionism, activism, and crucicentrism (according to noted historian David W. Bebbington). While the term "evangelical" today requires considerable qualification, the movement it denotes is of God and is still much needed in the Church universal. The authors of the NICOT come from diverse theological branches of the Church, and yet they hold firmly to this conviction that the Old Testament continues as God's means of grace for the Church today. In its pages, and by means of its message, God calls readers into an ever-deepening relational intimacy, inviting all who read (*anaginōskō*) to understand (*ginōskō*).

In response to Philip's question, the Ethiopian seeker admitted that he could not possibly read the ancient text with understanding "unless someone guides me" (Acts 8:31). He was aware of his need to have someone come alongside him to help him acquire the knowledge he desired. He invited Philip to join him in his chariot (and thus in his reading experience), and once he finally understood the Old Testament text, he immediately asked to be baptized (Acts 8:31–38).

This exchange illustrates the difficulty of reading for true understanding, the need for a faithful guide in one's reading, and the power of the ancient text to lead one into saving faith. The goal of each NICOT volume is to be such a guide. Readers around the world have invited the volumes of this series into their reading experience. The ancient text may seem obscure and distant. But God is still at work in its power, and reading it for understanding still makes a life-changing difference for the reader, as it did for Philip's new Ethiopian friend.

BILL T. ARNOLD

Abbreviations

AB	The Anchor Bible
AcT	*Acta Theologica*
AIIL	Ancient Israel and Its Literature
AJSL	*American Journal of Semitic Languages and Literatures*
AnBib	Analecta Biblica
ANET	*Ancient Near Eastern Texts Relating to the Old Testament.* Edited by James B. Pritchard. 3rd ed. Princeton: Princeton University Press, 1969
Aq	Aquila's Greek translation, as documented in F. Field, *Origenis Hexaplorum quae supersunt* (Oxford: Clarendon, 1867)
AUSS	*Andrews University Seminary Studies*
b.	(followed by the name of a tractate) Babylonian Talmud
BA	*Biblical Archaeologist*
BASOR	*Bulletin of the American Schools of Oriental Research*
BBB	Bonner biblische Beiträge
BBR	*Bulletin for Biblical Research*
BBRSup	Bulletin for Biblical Research, Supplements
BDB	Brown, F., S. R. Driver, and C. A. Briggs. *A Hebrew and English Lexicon of the Old Testament.* Reprinted with corrections. Oxford: Oxford University Press, 1962
BETL	Bibliotheca ephemeridum theologicarum Lovaniensium
BHS	*Biblia Hebraica Stuttgartensia.* Edited by K. Elliger and W. Rudolph. Stuttgart: Deutsche Bibelgesellschaft, 1983
BibInt	*Biblical Interpretation*
BibInt	Biblical Interpretation Series
Bib	*Biblica*
BSac	*Bibliotheca Sacra*
BWANT	Beiträge zur Wissenschaft vom Alten und Neuen Testament
BZ	*Biblische Zeitschrift*

BZAW	Beihefte zur Zeitschrift für die alttestamentliche Wissenschaft
CD	*Church Dogmatics*. K. Barth. 4 vols. Edinburgh: T&T Clark, 1936–1969
CHP	*Classical Hebrew Poetry: A Guide to Its Techniques*. W. G. E. Watson. JSOTSup 26. 2nd ed. Sheffield: JSOT Press, 1986
CTAT	*Critique textuelle de l'Ancien Testament*. D. Barthélemy. Vol. 2. Göttingen: Vandenhoeck & Ruprecht, 1986
CTJ	*Calvin Theological Journal*
CurBR	*Currents in Biblical Research* (formerly *Currents in Research: Biblical Studies*)
DCH	*Dictionary of Classical Hebrew*. Edited by D. J. A. Clines. 9 vols. Vols. 1–5, Sheffield: Sheffield Academic, 1993–2001; vols. 6–9, Sheffield: Sheffield Phoenix, 2007–2016
DDD	*Dictionary of Deities and Demons in the Bible*. Edited by K. van der Toorn, B. Becking, and P. W. van der Horst. 2nd rev. ed. Grand Rapids: Eerdmans, 1999
DG	*Davidson's Introductory Hebrew Grammar—Syntax*. J. C. L. Gibson. Edinburgh: T&T Clark, 1994
DSS	*The Dead Sea Scrolls*. Edited by F. García Martínez and E. J. C. Tigchelaar. Repr., Leiden: Brill, 2000
DTT	*A Dictionary of the Targumim, the Talmud Babli and Yerushalmi, and the Midrashic Literature*. M. Jastrow. New York: Choreb, 1926
ETL	*Ephemerides theologicae Lovanienses*
EvQ	*Evangelical Quarterly*
EvT	*Evangelische Theologie*
FAT	Forschungen zum Alten Testament
FRLANT	Forschungen zur Religion und Literatur des Alten und Neuen Testaments
GKC	*Gesenius' Hebrew Grammar*. Edited by E. Kautzsch. Translated by A. E. Cowley. 2nd ed. Oxford: Clarendon, 1910
HALOT	*The Hebrew and Aramaic Lexicon of the Old Testament*. L. Koehler, W. Baumgartner, and J. J. Stamm. Translated and edited under the supervision of M. E. J. Richardson. 4 vols. Leiden: Brill, 1994–1999
HAR	*Hebrew Annual Review*
HBT	*Horizons in Biblical Theology*
HSM	Harvard Semitic Monographs
HTS	Hervormde Teologiese Studies
HUBP	The Hebrew University Bible Project. C. Rabin. *The Book of Jeremiah*. Jerusalem: Magnes, 1997
IBHS	*An Introduction to Biblical Hebrew Syntax*. B. K. Waltke and M. O'Connor. Winona Lake, IN: Eisenbrauns, 1990

ICC	International Critical Commentary
Int	*Interpretation*
ITC	International Theological Commentary
JANES	*Journal of the Ancient Near Eastern Society*
JATS	*Journal of the Adventist Theological Society*
JBL	*Journal of Biblical Literature*
JETS	*Journal of the Evangelical Theological Society*
Joüon	Joüon, P. *A Grammar of Biblical Hebrew*. Translated and revised by T. Muraoka. 2 vols. Rome: Pontifical Biblical Institute, 1991
JNSL	*Journal of Northwest Semitic Languages*
JSJSup	Supplements to the Journal for the Study of Judaism
JSNTSup	Journal for the Study of the New Testament Supplement Series
JSOT	*Journal for the Study of the Old Testament*
JSOTSup	Journal for the Study of the Old Testament Supplement Series
JTISup	Journal for Theological Interpretation, Supplements
JTS	*Journal of Theological Studies*
LHBOTS	Library of Hebrew Bible/Old Testament Studies
LXX	*Septuaginta: Id est Vetus Testamentum graece iuxta LXX interpretes.* Edited by A. Rahlfs and R. Hanhart. Rev. ed. Stuttgart: Deutsche Bibelgesellschaft, 2006
MG	Miqraot Gedolot (the "Rabbinic Bible")
MT	Masoretic Text
MT^A	Aleppo Codex
MT^L	Leningrad Codex
NETS	*A New English Translation of the Septuagint*. Edited by A. Pietersma and B. G. Wright. New York: Oxford University Press, 2007
NICOT	The New International Commentary on the Old Testament
NJPS	*Tanakh: The Holy Scriptures: The New JPS Translation according to the Traditional Hebrew Text*
NPNF	*A Select Library of the Nicene and Post-Nicene Fathers of the Christian Church*. Repr., Grand Rapids: Eerdmans, 1988
OBO	Orbis Biblicus et Orientalis
OL	Old Latin text as reported in *BHS*
OTE	*Old Testament Essays*
OTL	The Old Testament Library
OTM	Old Testament Message
OTS	Oudtestamentische Studiën
PG	Patrologia Graeca [= *Patrologiae Cursus Completus: Series Graeca*]. Edited by J.-P. Migne. 162 vols. Paris, 1857–1886
PL	Patrologia Latina [= *Patrologiae Cursus Completus: Series Latina*]. Edited by J.-P. Migne. 217 vols. Paris, 1844–1864
RevExp	*Review and Expositor*

SBLDS	Society of Biblical Literature Dissertation Series
SBLStBL	Society of Biblical Literature Studies in Biblical Literature
SBT	Studies in Biblical Theology
SCS	Septuagint and Cognate Studies
SJOT	*Scandinavian Journal of the Old Testament*
SSN	Studia Semitica Neerlandica
StBibLit	Studies in Biblical Literature (Lang)
STDJ	Studies on the Texts of the Desert of Judah
Sym	Symmachus's Greek translation, as documented in F. Field, *Origenis Hexaplorum quae supersunt* (Oxford: Clarendon, 1867)
TDOT	*Theological Dictionary of the Old Testament*. Volumes 1–8 edited by G. J. Botterweck and H. Ringgren. Volumes 9–15 and volume 17 edited by G. J. Botterweck, Helmer Ringgren, and Heinz-Josef Fabry. Volume 16 edited by Holger Gzella. Translated by J. T. Willis et al. 17 vols. Grand Rapids: Eerdmans, 1974–2021
Tg	*The Latter Prophets According to Targum Jonathan*. A. Sperber. The Bible in Aramaic 3. Leiden: Brill, 1962
Theod	Theodotion's Greek translation, as documented in F. Field, *Origenis Hexaplorum quae supersunt* (Oxford: Clarendon, 1867)
TLOT	*Theological Lexicon of the Old Testament*. Edited by E. Jenni with assistance from C. Westermann. Translated by Mark E. Biddle. 3 vols. Peabody, MA: Hendrickson, 1997
TTH	*A Treatise on the Use of the Tenses in Hebrew and Some Other Syntactical Questions*. S. R. Driver. 3rd ed. Oxford: Oxford University Press, 1892
TynB	*Tyndale Bulletin*
Vg	*Biblia sacra iuxta vulgatam versionem*. Edited by R. Weber. 3rd ed. Stuttgart: Deutsche Bibelanstalt, 1983
VT	*Vetus Testamentum*
VTSup	Supplements to Vetus Testamentum
WBC	Word Biblical Commentary
WMANT	Wissenschaftliche Monographien zum Alten und Neuen Testament
WW	*Word and World*
ZABR	*Zeitschrift für altorientalische und biblische Rechtsgeschichte*
ZAW	*Zeitschrift für die alttestamentliche Wissenschaft*

Select Bibliography

Abravanel, I. *Commentary on the Latter Prophets*. [*pyrwš 'al nby'ym 'ḥrwnym*.] Jerusalem: Torah vaDa'at, [? 1955].

Achtemeier, E. R. *Jeremiah*. Knox Preaching Guides. Atlanta: John Knox, 1987.

Albertz, R. *Israel in Exile: The History and Literature of the Sixth Century B. C. E.* SBLStBL 3. Atlanta: Society of Biblical Literature, 2003.

Allen, L. C. *Jeremiah: A Commentary*. OTL. Louisville: Westminster John Knox, 2008.

Avioz, M. *"I Sat Alone": Jeremiah among the Prophets*. Piscataway, NJ: Gorgias, 2009.

Baillet, M. "Jérémie." Pages 62–69 in *Les "petites grottes" de Qumran*. Edited by M. Baillet, J. T. Milik, and R. De Vaux. Discoveries in the Judaean Desert 3. Oxford: Clarendon, 1962.

Barstad, H. M., and R. G. Kratz, eds. *Prophecy in the Book of Jeremiah*. BZAW 388. Berlin: de Gruyter, 2009.

Bauer, A. *Gender in the Book of Jeremiah: A Feminist-Literary Reading*. StBibLit 5. New York: Lang, 1999.

Berridge, J. M. *Prophet, People, and the Word of Yahweh: An Examination of Form and Content in the Proclamation of the Prophet Jeremiah*. Basel Studies of Theology 4. Zurich: EVZ, 1970.

Berrigan, D. *Jeremiah: The World, the Wound of God*. Minneapolis: Fortress, 1999.

Blayney, B. *Jeremiah and Lamentations*. 2nd ed. Edinburgh: Oliphant, 1810.

Boadt, L. *Jeremiah 1–25*. OTM 9. Wilmington, DE: Glazier, 1982.

———. *Jeremiah 26–52, Habakkuk, Zephaniah, Nahum*. OTM 10. Wilmington, DE: Glazier, 1982.

Bogaert, P.-M. *Le livre de Jérémie: Le prophète et son milieu, les oracles et leur transmission*. 2nd ed. BETL 54. Leuven: Peeters, 1997.

Bright, J. *Jeremiah: Introduction, Translation, and Notes*. AB 21. Garden City, NY: Doubleday, 1965.

Brown, M. L., and P. W. Ferris. *Jeremiah, Lamentations*. The Expositor's Bible Commentary. Grand Rapids: Zondervan, 2010.

Brueggemann, W. *Jeremiah 1–25*. ITC. Grand Rapids: Eerdmans, 1988.

———. *Jeremiah 26–52*. ITC. Grand Rapids: Eerdmans, 1991.

———. *Like Fire in the Bones: Listening for the Prophetic Word in Jeremiah*. Minneapolis: Fortress, 2006.

———. *The Theology of the Book of Jeremiah*. Old Testament Theology. Cambridge: Cambridge University Press, 2007.

Bugenhagen, J. *In Ieremiam Prophetam Commentarium*. Wittenberg: Seitz, 1546.

Calvin, J. *Commentary on Jeremiah and Lamentations*. Translated by J. Owen. 5 vols. Repr., Grand Rapids: Christian Classics Ethereal Library.

Carroll, R. P. *From Chaos to Covenant: Uses of Prophecy in the Book of Jeremiah*. London: SCM, 1981.

———. *Jeremiah: A Commentary*. OTL. London: SCM, 1986.

———. *Jeremiah*. Old Testament Guides. Sheffield: JSOT, 1989.

Clements, R. E. *Jeremiah*. Interpretation: A Bible Commentary for Teaching and Preaching. Atlanta: John Knox, 1988.

Cloete, W. T. W. *Versification and Syntax in Jeremiah 2–25: Syntactical Constraints in Hebrew Colometry*. SBLDS 117. Atlanta: Scholars, 1989.

Coulibaly, I. "Jeremiah." Pages 879–950 in *Africa Bible Commentary*. Edited by T. Adeyemo. Nairobi: Word Alive, 2006.

Craigie, P. C., P. H. Kelley, and J. F. Drinkard. *Jeremiah 1–25*. WBC 26. Dallas: Word, 1991.

Crouch, C. L. *An Introduction to the Study of Jeremiah*. T&T Clark Approaches to Biblical Studies. London: T&T Clark, 2017.

Cunliffe-Jones, H. *Jeremiah: God in History*. 2nd ed. Torch Bible Commentaries. London: SCM, 1966.

Curtis, A. H. W., and T. Römer, eds. *The Book of Jeremiah and Its Reception*. BETL 128. Leuven: Peeters, 1997.

Davidson, R. *Jeremiah*. 2 vols. The Daily Study Bible. Edinburgh: Saint Andrew, 1985.

Davidson, S. V. *Empire and Exile: Postcolonial Readings of the Book of Jeremiah*. LHBOTS 542. London: T&T Clark, 2011.

Dearman, J. A. *Jeremiah and Lamentations*. The NIV Application Commentary. Grand Rapids: Zondervan, 2002.

Dempsey, C. J. *Jeremiah: Preacher of Grace, Poet of Truth*. Interfaces. Collegeville: Liturgical, 2006.

Denis the Carthusian. *Enarratio in Jeremiam*. Pages 5–312 in *Opera Omnia*. Vol. 9. Montreuil: Typis Cartusiae S. M. de Pratis, 1900.

Diamond, A. R. P. *The Confessions of Jeremiah in Context: Scenes of Prophetic Drama*. JSOTSup 45. Sheffield: Sheffield Academic, 1987.

———. "Jeremiah." Pages 543–622 in *Eerdmans Commentary on the Bible*. Edited by J. D. G. Dunn and J. W. Rogerson. Grand Rapids: Eerdmans, 2003.

Diamond, A. R. P., K. M. O'Connor, and L. Stulman, eds. *Troubling Jeremiah.* JSOTSup 260. Sheffield: Sheffield Academic, 1999.

Diamond, A. R. P., and L. Stulman, eds. *Jeremiah (Dis)placed.* LHBOTS 529. London: T&T Clark, 2011.

Duhm, B. *Das Buch Jeremia.* Kurzer Hand-Commentar zum Alten Testament 11. Tübingen: Mohr Siebeck, 1901.

Ellison, H. L. "The Prophecy of Jeremiah." *EvQ* 31–40 (1959–68).

Eusebius Hieronymus. *Commentariorum in Jeremiam Prophetam Libri Sex.* PL 24:679–900.

Finsterbusch, K., and A. Lange, eds. *Texts and Contexts in Jeremiah.* Leuven: Peeters, 2016.

Fischer, G. *Jeremia.* 2 vols. Herders Theologischer Kommentar zum Alten Testament. Freiburg: Herder, 2005.

Fretheim, T. E. *Jeremiah.* Smith and Helwys Bible Commentary. Macon, GA: Smith and Helwys, 2002.

Glanz, O. *Understanding Participant-Reference Shifts in the Book of Jeremiah: A Study of Exegetical Method and Its Consequences for the Interpretation of Referential Incoherence.* SSN 60. Leiden: Brill, 2013.

Goldingay, J., ed. *Uprooting and Planting: Essays on Jeremiah for Leslie Allen.* LHBOTS 459. London: T&T Clark, 2007.

Green, B. *Jeremiah and God's Plans of Well-Being.* Studies on Personalities of the Old Testament. Columbia, SC: University of South Carolina, 2013.

Gross, W., ed. *Jeremia und die "deuteronomistische Bewegung."* BBB 98. Weinheim: Beltz Athenäum, 1995.

Harrelson, W. *Jeremiah: Prophet to the Nations.* Philadelphia: Judson, 1959.

Harrison, R. K. *Jeremiah and Lamentations: An Introduction and Commentary.* Tyndale Old Testament Commentaries. London: Tyndale, 1973.

Henderson, J. M. *Jeremiah under the Shadow of Duhm: A Critique of the Use of Poetic Form as a Criterion of Authenticity.* T&T Clark Biblical Studies. London: T&T Clark, 2019.

Herrmann, S. *Jeremia.* 2 fascicles. Biblischer Kommentar: Altes Testament. Neukirchen: Neukirchener, 1986–1990.

Hill, J. *Friend or Foe? The Figure of Babylon in the Book of Jeremiah MT.* BibInt 40. Leiden: Brill, 1999.

Holladay, W. L. *A Commentary on the Book of the Prophet Jeremiah.* 2 vols. Hermeneia. Philadelphia: Fortress, 1986; Minneapolis: Fortress, 1989.

———. *Jeremiah: Spokesman out of Time.* Philadelphia: United Church, 1974.

———. "Text Criticism and Beyond: The Case of Jeremiah." *Textus* 23 (2007): 173–210.

Holt, E. K., and C. J. Sharp, eds. *Jeremiah Invented: Constructions and Deconstructions of Jeremiah.* LHBOTS 595. London: T&T Clark, 2015.

Hugh of St. Cher. "Liber Jeremiae." Pages 175–282 in *Praedicatorum Tomus Quartus.* Venice: Pezanna, 1703.

Jerome. *Commentary on Jeremiah.* Translated by M. Graves. Ancient Christian Texts. Downers Grove, IL: InterVarsity, 2011.

Job, J. B. *Jeremiah's Kings: A Study of the Monarchy in Jeremiah.* Society for Old Testament Study Monographs. Aldershot: Ashgate, 2006.

Jones, D. R. *Jeremiah.* The New Century Bible Commentary. Grand Rapids: Eerdmans, 1992.

Kalmanovsky, A. *Terror All Around: The Rhetoric of Horror in the Book of Jeremiah.* LHBOTS 390. London: T&T Clark, 2008.

Keown, G. L., P. J. Scalise, and T. G. Smothers. *Jeremiah 26–52.* WBC 27. Dallas: Word, 1995.

Kessler, M., ed. *Reading the Book of Jeremiah: A Search for Coherence.* Winona Lake, IN: Eisenbrauns, 2004.

Kidner, D. *The Message of Jeremiah.* The Bible Speaks Today. Leicester, UK: InterVarsity, 1987.

King, P. J. *Jeremiah: An Archaeological Companion.* Louisville: Westminster John Knox, 1993.

Lalleman-de Winkel, H. *Jeremiah and Lamentations.* Tyndale Old Testament Commentaries. Nottingham: InterVarsity Press, 2013.

———. *Jeremiah in Prophetic Tradition.* Contributions to Biblical Exegesis and Theology 26. Leeuven: Peeters, 2000.

Leuchter, M. "Jeremiah." Pages 171–89 in *The Oxford Handbook of the Prophets.* Edited by C. J. Sharp. Oxford: Oxford University Press, 2016.

———. *The Polemics of Exile in Jeremiah 26–45.* Cambridge: Cambridge University Press, 2008.

Lipschits, O. *The Fall and Rise of Jerusalem: Judah under Babylonian Rule.* Winona Lake, IN: Eisenbrauns, 2005.

Longman, T. *Jeremiah.* New International Biblical Commentary. Peabody, MA: Hendrickson, 2008.

Lundbom, J. R. *Jeremiah 1–20: A New Translation with Introduction and Commentary.* AB 21A. New York: Doubleday, 1999.

———. *Jeremiah 21–36: A New Translation with Introduction and Commentary.* AB 21B. New York: Doubleday, 2004.

———. *Jeremiah 37–52: A New Translation with Introduction and Commentary.* AB 21C. New York: Doubleday, 2004.

———. *Jeremiah: A Study in Ancient Hebrew Rhetoric.* 2nd ed. Winona Lake, IN: Eisenbrauns, 1997.

———. *Jeremiah among the Prophets.* Cambridge: James Clarke, 2013.

———. *Jeremiah Closer Up: The Prophet and the Book.* Hebrew Bible Monographs 31. Sheffield: Sheffield Phoenix, 2010.

———. *Jeremiah: Prophet Like Moses.* Eugene: Cascade, 2015.

Lundbom, J. R., C. A. Evans, and B. A. Anderson, eds. *The Book of Jeremiah: Composition, Reception, and Interpretation.* VTSup 178. Leiden: Brill, 2018.

Maier, C. M. *Jeremia als Lehrer der Tora: Soziale Gebote des Deuteronomiums in Fortschreibungen des Jeremiabuches.* FRLANT 196. Göttingen: Vandenhoeck & Ruprecht, 2002.

Maier, C. M., and C. J. Sharp, eds. *Prophecy and Power: Jeremiah in Feminist and Postcolonial Perspective.* LHBOTS 577. London: T&T Clark, 2013.

Martens, E. A. *Jeremiah.* Believers Church Bible Commentary. Scottdale, PA: Herald, 1986.

Mayer, J. *A Commentary upon All the Prophets both Great and Small.* London: Millar and Cotes, 1652.

McConville, J. G. *Judgment and Promise: Interpretation of the Book of Jeremiah.* Leicester: Apollos, 1993.

McKane, W. *A Critical and Exegetical Commentary on Jeremiah.* 2 vols. ICC. Repr., London: T&T Clark, 2014.

Mein, A., E. K. Holt, and H. C. P. Kim, eds. *Concerning the Nations: Essays on the Oracles against the Nations in Isaiah, Jeremiah and Ezekiel.* LHBOTS 612. London: T&T Clark, 2015.

Michaelis, J. D. *Observationes philologicae et criticae in Jeremiae Vaticinia et Threnos.* Göttingen: Vandenhoeck & Ruprecht, 1793.

Miller, P. D. "Jeremiah." Pages 553–926 in *The New Interpreter's Bible.* Edited by L. E. Keck. Vol. 6. Nashville: Abingdon, 2001.

Mills, M. E. *Jeremiah: An Introduction and Study Guide; Prophecy in a Time of Crisis.* London: T&T Clark, 2015.

Mowinckel, S. *Zur Komposition des Buches Jeremia.* Kristiania: Dybward, 1914.

Najman, H., and K. Schmid, eds. *Jeremiah's Scriptures.* JSJSup 173. Leiden: Brill, 2016.

Nicholson, E. W. *Jeremiah 1–25.* The Cambridge Bible Commentary: New English Bible. Cambridge: Cambridge University Press, 1973.

———. *Jeremiah 26–52.* The Cambridge Bible Commentary: New English Bible. Cambridge: Cambridge University Press, 1973.

———. *Preaching to the Exiles.* Oxford: Blackwell, 1970.

Nicolai de Lira. *Secunda pars tractas super toto corpore biblie.* Strasbourg: Grüninger, 1492.

O'Connor, K. M. *The Confessions of Jeremiah: Their Interpretation and Role in Chapters 1–25.* SBLDS 94. Atlanta: Scholars, 1988.

———. "Jeremiah." Pages 487–528 in *The Oxford Bible Commentary.* Edited by J. Barton and J. Muddiman. Oxford: Oxford University Press, 2007.

———. *Jeremiah: Pain and Promise.* Minneapolis: Fortress, 2011.

Oecolampadius, J. *In Hieremiam prophetam.* Strasbourg: Apiarius, 1533.

Origen of Alexandria. *Homilies on Jeremiah and 1 Kings 28.* Translated by John Clark Smith. The Fathers of the Church 97. Washington: Catholic University of America, 1998.

Overholt, T. W. *The Threat of Falsehood: A Study in the Theology of the Book of Jeremiah.* SBT 2/16. London: SCM, 1970.

Pappus, J. *In Omnes Prophetas.* Frankfurt: Spiessius, 1593.

Perdue, L. G., and B. W Kovacs, eds. *A Prophet to the Nations: Essays in Jeremiah Studies.* Winona Lake, IN: Eisenbrauns, 1984.

Pixley, J. *Jeremiah.* Chalice Commentaries for Today. St. Louis, MO: Chalice, 2004.

Plant, R. J. R. *Good Figs, Bad Figs: Judicial Differentiation in the Book of Jeremiah.* LHBOTS 483. London: T&T Clark, 2008.

Pohlmann, K.-F. *Die Ferne Gottes: Studien zum Jeremiabuch.* BZAW 179. Berlin: de Gruyter, 1989.

———. *Studien zum Jeremiabuch: Ein Beitrag zur Frage nach der Entstehung des Jeremiabuches.* FRLANT 118. Göttingen: Vandenhoeck & Ruprecht, 1978.

Polk, T. *The Prophetic Persona: Jeremiah and the Language of the Self.* JSOTSup 32. Sheffield: JSOT, 1984.

Reventlow, H. G. *Liturgie und prophetisches Ich bei Jeremia.* Gütersloh: Mohn, 1963.

Rosenberg, A. J. *Jeremiah.* 2 vols. New York: Judaica, 1985.

Rudolph, W. *Jeremia.* 3rd ed. Handbuch zum Alten Testament 12. Tübingen: Mohr Siebeck, 1968.

Schmidt, W. H. *Das Buch Jeremia.* 2 vols. Das Alte Testament Deutsch. Göttingen: Vandenhoeck & Ruprecht, 2008–2013.

Schroeder, J. A. *The Book of Jeremiah.* The Bible in Medieval Tradition. Grand Rapids: Eerdmans, 2017.

Seitz, C. R. *Theology in Conflict: Reactions to the Exile in the Book of Jeremiah.* BZAW 176. Berlin: de Gruyter, 1989.

Sharp, C. J. "Jeremiah." Pages 223–35 in *Theological Bible Commentary.* Edited by D. L. Petersen and G. R. O'Day. Louisville: Westminster John Knox, 2009.

———. *Prophecy and Ideology in Jeremiah: Struggles for Authority in the Deutero-Jeremianic Prose.* Old Testament Studies. London: T&T Clark, 2003.

Shead, A. G. *A Mouth Full of Fire: The Word of God in the Words of Jeremiah.* New Studies in Biblical Theology 9. Nottingham: Apollos, 2013.

Skinner, J. *Prophecy and Religion: Studies in the Life of Jeremiah.* Cambridge: Cambridge University Press, 1922.

Smith, M. S. *The Laments of Jeremiah and Their Contexts.* Society of Biblical Literature Monograph Series 42. Atlanta: Scholars, 1990.

Stephen, D. *The Prophet of Hope.* Cambridge: Cambridge University Press, 1923.

Stipp, H.-J. *Das masoretische und alexandrinische Sondergut des Jeremiabuches.* OBO 136. Göttingen: Vandenhoeck & Ruprecht, 1994.

———. *Studien zum Jeremiabuch: Text und Redaktion.* FAT 96. Tübingen: Mohr Siebeck, 2015.

Stulman, L. *Jeremiah.* Nashville: Abingdon, 2005.

———. *Order amid Chaos: Jeremiah as Symbolic Tapestry.* The Biblical Seminar 57. Sheffield: Sheffield Academic, 1998.

———. *The Prose Sermons of the Book of Jeremiah: A Redescription of the Correspondences with Deuteronomistic Literature in the Light of Recent Text-Critical Research.* SBLDS 83. Atlanta: Scholars, 1986.

Theodoret of Cyrus. *Ermeneia tēs prophēteias tou Ieremiou.* PG 81:495–806.

Thiel, W. *Die deuteronomistische Redaktion von Jeremia 1–25.* WMANT 41. Neukirchen: Neukirchener, 1973.

———. *Die deuteronomistische Redaktion von Jeremia 26–45.* WMANT 52. Neukirchen: Neukirchener, 1981.

Thomas Aquinas. *In Jeremiam prophetam expositio.* Corpus thomisticum. Parma: Fiaccadori, 1863.

Thompson, J. A. *The Book of Jeremiah.* NICOT. Grand Rapids: Eerdmans, 1980.

Tov, E. "Jeremiah." Pages 145–207 in *Qumran Cave 4: X: The Prophets.* Edited by E. Tov. Discoveries in the Judaean Desert 15. Oxford: Clarendon, 1997.

———. "The Jeremiah Scrolls from Qumran." *Revue de Qumran* 14 (1989): 189–206.

Trapp, J. *A Commentary or Exposition upon These Following Books of Holy Scripture: Proverbs of Solomon, Ecclesiastes, the Song of Songs, Isaiah, Jeremiah, Lamentations, Ezekiel & Daniel.* Kidderminster: Simmons, 1660.

Tyler, J. J. *Jeremiah, Lamentations.* Reformation Commentary. Downers Grove, IL: InterVarsity, 2018.

Unterman, J. *From Repentance to Redemption: Jeremiah's Thought in Transition.* JSOTSup 54. Sheffield: Sheffield Academic, 1987.

Volz, P. *Der Prophet Jeremia.* Kommentar zum Alten Testament 10. 2nd ed. Leipzig: Deicher, 1928.

Walser, G. A. *Jeremiah: A Commentary Based on Ieremias in Codex Vaticanus.* Septuagint Commentary Series. Leiden: Brill, 2012.

Weippert, H. *Die Prosareden des Jeremiabuches.* BZAW 132. Berlin: de Gruyter, 1973.

Weiser, A. *Das Buch des Propheten Jeremia.* 2 vols. Das Alte Testament Deutsch. Göttingen: Vandenhoeck & Ruprecht, 1952.

Wenthe, D. O. *Jeremiah, Lamentations.* Ancient Christian Commentary on Scripture: Old Testament 12. Downers Grove, IL: InterVarsity, 2009.

Wright, C. J. H. *The Message of Jeremiah.* The Bible Speaks Today. Nottingham: InterVarsity Press, 2014.

Ziegler, J., ed. *Ieremias, Baruch, Threni, Epistula Ieremiae.* 2nd ed. Septuaginta: Vetus Testamentum Graecum 15. Göttingen: Vandenhoeck & Ruprecht, 1976.

Judah in Jeremiah's Day

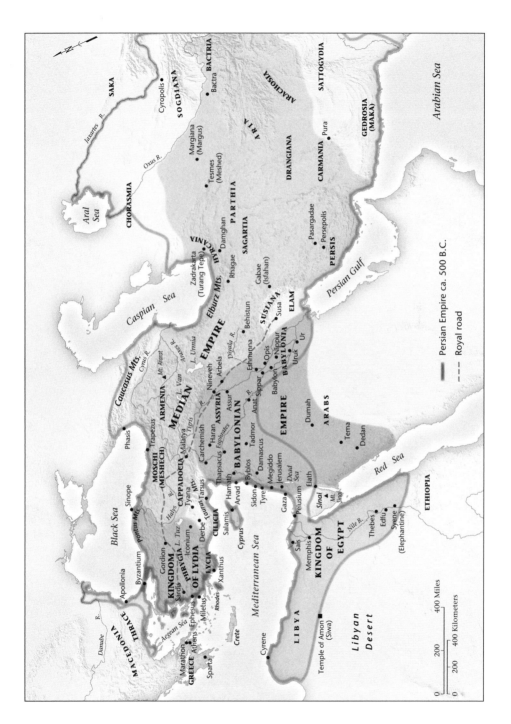

Empires of the 6th Century BC

Introduction

The Jeremiah scroll is a compilation of messages from Yahweh, stories about Jeremiah, and exchanges between Jeremiah and Yahweh. I use the word "scroll" since it's not a "book" in most senses of that word. The majority of the messages are in poetry, which makes the Jeremiah scroll resemble Isaiah, though many are in prose, which makes it resemble Ezekiel. The prominence of stories and exchanges as well as messages makes it unique and contributes to its being the longest of the prophetic scrolls. Further, whereas the Isaiah and Ezekiel scrolls incorporate many messages of an overtly hopeful kind, Jeremiah is dominated by threat and warning, which makes it more like shorter prophetic scrolls such as Hosea and Amos.

I. BACKGROUND

The introduction to the Jeremiah scroll (1:1–3) provides key information concerning its background:

> The words of Jeremiah ben Hilkiah, one of the priests who were in Anathoth in the territory of Benjamin, to whom Yahweh's message came in the time of Josiah ben Amon King of Judah, in the thirteenth year of his reign, and came in the time of Jehoiakim ben Josiah King of Judah, until the ending of the eleventh year of Zedekiah ben Josiah King of Judah, until the exile of Jerusalem in the fifth month.

A. JOSIAH, JEHOIAKIM, ZEDEKIAH, AND THE FALL OF JERUSALEM

Jeremiah was born during the reign of Manasseh in Judah (687–642 BC).[1] For a century, Judah and its neighbors had been the victims of Assyria's desire to control the Levant, the area bordering on the Mediterranean. Judah was an Assyrian tribute state and effectively part of the Assyrian Empire even though it still had its own monarchy. One consequence was that Manasseh allowed worship in Jerusalem to take account of Assyrian understandings of the gods and worship practices. In addition, traditional ("Canaanite") understandings of the gods and related aspects of spirituality continued to be influential in Jerusalem and in people's everyday lives. Manasseh's son Amon succeeded him and reigned for two years (642–640) before being assassinated, after which his son Josiah, still a boy, succeeded him.

Assyrian power was declining, and Josiah's mentors and Josiah himself were able to initiate changes in Judah that amounted to both religious reformation and assertion of political independence. Second Kings 22–23 relates how a "Torah scroll" came to light in 622 in the course of restoration work in the Jerusalem temple, and this discovery stimulated further reforms. Overlaps between these reforms and Deuteronomy suggest that the scroll was some form of what we know as Deuteronomy. The discovery came just after Yahweh's commission of Jeremiah in 626, which was also about the time when Ashurbanipal, the last great king of Assyria, died, and when Nabopolassar, the first great Neo-Babylonian king, asserted control of Babylon and initiated the process whereby Babylon would take over the Assyrian Empire.[2]

As Assyria declined, Babylon and Media grew in power, and 609 saw a key battle between these forces. The Egyptian king decided to join in, perceiving that a Babylonian victory would be a threat to him. Josiah thought that Assyria's losing was desirable, so it seemed in Judah's interest to back Babylon—ironically, in light of later events. Josiah therefore tried to stop the Egyptian army's advance but failed and lost his life.

His son Jehoahaz thus succeeded him in 609 but was swiftly deposed by the Egyptians (he is unmentioned in Jer 1:1–3) and replaced by his brother

---

1. Formulating dates for Israelite kings raises difficulties. Many kings appointed their successors to reign jointly with them, presumably in part to ensure the succession; thus, the dates of reigns can overlap. Manasseh had apparently reigned as co-king with Hezekiah since about 697. Date formulations in modern books may also vary by a year because the Jewish year starts at a different point from the Western year (and sometimes in the spring, sometimes in the fall; see the commentary on 36:9) and because formulations vary over whether a king's accession year counts as his first actual year.

2. For these events and the ones in the next paragraph, see, e.g., O. Lipschits, *The Fall and Rise of Jerusalem: Judah under Babylonian Rule* (Winona Lake, IN: Eisenbrauns, 2005), 11–35.

Jehoiakim, who encouraged the dismantling of Josiah's reformation. A key event during his reign was the Battle of Carchemish in 605, when Babylonian and Median forces again defeated the armies of Assyria and Egypt. This event had decisive implications for the future of Judah. Judah would thenceforth come under the domination of the Babylonians, who were from that time the people who wanted to control the Levant. The next year saw Nebuchadrezzar[3] campaigning there, and Jer 36 gives a dramatic account of Yahweh's telling Jeremiah to have his messages written down that year and read to Jehoiakim, only for Jehoiakim to dismiss them.

Jehoiakim died in 597 and was succeeded by his son Jehoiachin. Like Jehoahaz, he was swiftly deposed, this time by the Babylonians (he is also unmentioned in Jer 1:1–3). They plundered the temple, took Jehoiachin and many leading Judahites to Babylon, and replaced him with his uncle, Zedekiah, another son of Josiah, who continued the religious policies of Jehoiakim. He reigned from 597 to 587. During this decade, there were thus two Judahite communities, both with Davidic kings, one in Babylon and one in Judah, though we have no evidence of tension between them. In 589/588, Zedekiah led Judah in asserting independence from the Babylonians, who again invaded Judah, captured and devastated Jerusalem, and took Zedekiah into exile.

The political story that holds together the narrative implied by the Jeremiah scroll is thus the story of three kings, Josiah, Jehoiakim, and Zedekiah, followed by the fall of Jerusalem and the aftershocks in Mizpah, of which we will read in Jeremiah.

B. YAHWEH'S MESSAGE CAME

According to its introduction, the Jeremiah scroll comprises words of Jeremiah given in this historical context. The words of Jeremiah given in this historical context also comprise the "message," more literally the "word," of Yahweh that came to Jeremiah.[4] The introduction implies that the scroll's readers need to adopt the position of people who accept that presupposition if they are to understand the scroll.[5]

---

3. I will use this English form of the name, reflecting the Hebrew form that usually appears in Jeremiah, except in connection with Jer 27–29, where the form Nebuchadnezzar appears; see the translation note on 21:2.

4. A. G. Shead takes up this opening phrase of the scroll in his study of "The Word of God in the Words of Jeremiah," the subtitle of *A Mouth Full of Fire*, New Studies in Biblical Theology 9 (Nottingham: Apollos, 2012).

5. E. K. Holt, "Word of Jeremiah—Word of God," in *Uprooting and Planting: Essays on Jeremiah for Leslie Allen*, ed. J. Goldingay, LHBOTS 459 (London: T&T Clark 2007), 172–89.

More literally, the message "happened" (*hāyâ*) to Jeremiah. How did it do so? The introduction goes on to recount a conversation between Yahweh and Jeremiah (1:4–19). If we had been there, would we have heard Yahweh's voice? Surely not everyone who claims to have heard God's voice is crazy, and sometimes the Scriptures give a realistic report of God's speaking aloud: see 1 Sam 3 and the varying accounts of Yahweh's speaking at Sinai and of Jesus's appearing to Saul of Tarsus. Or did the conversation happen inside Jeremiah's head? Either way, Yahweh formulated words and spoke them to Jeremiah, and Jeremiah heard them.

The conversation includes Yahweh's declaring that he will be giving Jeremiah orders about what Jeremiah is to say. He will be dictating messages that Jeremiah will pass on. Many of the messages that we later read in the scroll presumably issued from such dictation. They came "from Yahweh's mouth," not from Jeremiah's mind (23:16).

Yahweh also touches Jeremiah's mouth and says he is putting his words in Jeremiah's mouth (1:9), which suggests a different model from dictation for the transmitting of a message. It implies that Jeremiah's lips may utter words he has not heard or consciously formulated; he will open his mouth and will himself listen to what comes out. In a promise of which Jeremiah might be understood as the fulfillment, Yahweh says of the prophet whom he will cause to arise, "I will put my words in his mouth" (Deut 18:18). On the other hand, on some occasions when someone puts words in another person's mouth (Exod 4:15; 2 Sam 14:19; Ezra 8:17), they seem to indicate the nature of the message, but they leave the messenger to formulate the actual words, like (one suspects) the Rabshakeh in 2 Kgs 18. Jeremiah can thus move between speaking as one directly uttering Yahweh's words, so that Yahweh is "I," and speaking about Yahweh as "he."[6] Modern preachers may be aware that there are insights and words that they are given and ways in which they themselves develop and formulate these insights and words. Jeremiah's messages also combined these two aspects.

Jeremiah later suggests yet another model for understanding how Yahweh's message comes to him. The difference between him and other prophets is that he has stood in Yahweh's cabinet (23:21–22). He has been in attendance on Yahweh there along with Yahweh's other aides (mostly supernatural ones), he has listened to debates, and he has taken part in them and in the making of decisions (cf. 1 Kgs 22:19–22). He then functions as someone sent by Yahweh with a role to play in the implementing of these decisions—by declaring Yahweh's message to people. In what sense did he attend these

---

6. In Jeremiah, "the means for marking DD [direct divine discourse] are the most varied, unpredictable, and . . . chaotic of any book in the Hebrew Bible" (S. A. Meier, *Speaking of Speaking: Marking Direct Discourse in the Hebrew Bible*, VTSup 46 [Leiden: Brill, 1992], 258).

meetings? When Ezekiel was transported to Jerusalem (Ezek 8–11), I imagine one would still have found him physically in Babylon, and when Paul was transported into the third heaven (2 Cor 12), one would still have found him wherever he had been before this experience began (though he interestingly expresses uncertainty about whether or not it was an out-of-body experience). One's body and spirit are sufficiently separable for body to be in one place and spirit in another (cf. 1 Cor 5:3–4). So it would be for Jeremiah.

A further element in Jeremiah's account of his commission deserves note as background to his work. In response to Yahweh's speaking to him, he says, in effect, "Not me, I'm only a kid." His attempt to resist Yahweh then becomes part of Yahweh's message in this scroll. Subsequently, he makes other comparable contributions to the message, not least as he protests about things that happen to him. A related possible ambiguity in the scroll's introduction deserves noting in this connection as background to the idea of the scroll as "Yahweh's message." The expression for "the words of Jeremiah" (*dibrê yirməyāhû*) could be understood to mean "the acts of Jeremiah" (the equivalent expression is applied to Jehoiakim in 2 Kgs 24:5).[7] A distinctive feature of the Jeremiah scroll is the extent to which it relates things that Jeremiah does and things that happen to him. Yahweh's message expresses itself in those actions and experiences.

II. UNITY OF COMPOSITION

The scroll's introduction indicates that it came into being sometime after the fall of Jerusalem in 587 but that the scroll will refer to events going back over the preceding forty years. Was it composed in one go, or does the story of its composition go back some time? Conversely, the scroll makes no reference to events beyond the immediate aftermath of 587 (except in 52:31–34), but this fact need not imply that it came into being in those immediate years or decades. Does the story of its composition go on for some time? What can we say about its composition and unity?

A. THE THREE HORIZONS

The scroll directly suggests three horizons[8] for reading it; they correspond roughly to three horizons implied by the introduction.

---

7. R. Davidson, *Jeremiah*, The Daily Study Bible (Edinburgh: Saint Andrew, 1985), 1:1.

8. With apologies to A. C. Thiselton, *The Two Horizons* (Grand Rapids: Eerdmans,

(1)   There is the series of particular contexts in which Jeremiah delivered his messages, to which the scroll sometimes refers (e.g., 3:6;
21:1; 25:1).

(2)   There is Jeremiah's dictation of his entire message up to that point
to Baruch in 604, to which 36:1–4, 32 refers (30:1–2 also refers to
his writing, as does 51:59–64—with a date, 594).

(3)   There is the production of an expanded scroll sometime after 587
(to judge from 1:1–3) and of its final form as we have it not before
562 (to judge from 52:31–34).

As the scroll reports it, then, Jeremiah uttered his words to Judahite people during the reigns of the kings it names and in the aftermath of the fall of
Jerusalem, between the 620s and the 580s. When it reports that Yahweh said
something to Jeremiah in the reign of one or another of the kings, it invites
us to listen to its words against that context.

Yet the scroll as a whole sets Jeremiah's individual messages in the context
of the history that continues until the fall of Jerusalem and its aftermath.
They would have a nuanced significance once the catastrophe had actually
happened, after which Jeremiah continued to embody Yahweh's straightness
and mercy as he was taken off to Egypt. The scroll itself thus came into being
to speak to people some while after the events it threatens and then relates.
So we read it against two horizons: the context in which Jeremiah spoke a
particular message and the context from which people can look back on his
message and on the events surrounding it and ask about their significance.
By 562, Jeremiah would have been at least eighty, and he might have still
been alive, but the last we hear of him is around 585, in Egypt. After that
date, no one preserved any messages he received or told any stories about
him that made it into the scroll. In effect, his work and life come to an end
about 585.

In between the initial speaking and the final composition, Jer 36 suggests
an intervening horizon by telling the story of Jeremiah having his message
transcribed by Baruch. The original production of this 604 scroll was designed to bring home in that context the message Jeremiah had been delivering for two decades: "Yahweh is bringing catastrophe on Judah; you
must turn back to him." In that scroll and context, Jeremiah need not have
been concerned to anchor individual messages in their original settings. They
became part of a message designed to speak in 604. "The mind of Jeremiah
is fixed on the situation in 604 BC and he calls the old prophecies to mind
entirely in terms of this situation." He is not aiming to repeat them as he
might have uttered them years previously but to speak them as "the divine

1980), though he adapted the image from H.-G. Gadamer, *Truth and Method* (New York:
Crossroad, 1975).

word to Jehoiakim and his cabinet" now.[9] Actually, something similar is true about the Jeremiah scroll that eventually emerged after 587. It aims to bring Yahweh's word to Judah *now*.

Although messages in Jer 1–20 indicate that they speak to concrete settings and events in the decades beginning in 626, only once (3:6) do they mention the reign of a particular king. Jeremiah and the scroll's compilers apparently saw no reason to preserve his messages in a way that would enable people reading the scroll to place each of them in particular contexts in the time of a particular king. Actually, Jeremiah implies that he has been saying the same thing all through, so what difference would it make? While we might like to set each message in its specific context, and while commentators have sought to do so, it is simply a matter of guesswork, and in this commentary I will not make the attempt.

On the other hand, if Jeremiah got Baruch to put a collection of his messages into writing in 604, I am going to guess that Jer 2–6 represents Baruch's subsequent rewritten scroll and keep that possibility in mind as a heuristic device—an aid to imagination. But the Jeremiah scroll does not privilege any one of the three horizons, and interpreters may properly vary over which context they focus on. In connection with any section of the scroll, it is worth asking which context illuminates it.

The Jeremiah scroll is one work, but its contents suggest that its composition reflects the contributions of more than one person. One indication is that it incorporates first-person speech ("Yahweh's word came to me") and third-person speech ("Yahweh's word came to Jeremiah"). While first-person speech may mean that these words are Jeremiah's own, it need not carry that implication; Ecclesiastes uses the "I" form, as ghostwriters and speech writers do. Conversely, while third-person speech may mean that the words come from someone speaking about Jeremiah, this speech form also need not carry the obvious implication; writers sometimes refer to themselves in the third person (Robert Carroll did so in his writings on Jeremiah[10]). Rhetorically, the two forms of speech have different affects, but a move between first person and third person need not signify a change in speaker or writer.

Likewise, a move between poetry and prose need not signify a change in speaker or writer.[11] The English author Philip Larkin published both poetry and prose. Nor can one infer from someone's poetic style what their prose

9. D. R. Jones, *Jeremiah*, The New Century Bible Commentary (Grand Rapids: Eerdmans, 1992), 96.

10. E.g., R. P. Carroll, "Radical Clashes of Will and Style," *JSOT* 45 (1989): 99–100; "Arguing about Jeremiah," in *Congress Volume: Leuven 1989*, ed. J. A. Emerton, VTSup 43 (Leiden: Brill, 1991), 229–33.

11. Cf. F. Lippke, "Ancient Editing and the Coherence of Traditions within the Book of Jeremiah and throughout the *nby'im*," in *Jeremiah's Scriptures*, ed. H. Najman and K. Schmid, JSJSup 173 (Leiden: Brill, 2016), 49–52.

style would be or vice versa. Nor does a change of subject signify a change of author: Larkin wrote extensively on jazz in his prose, but not in his poetry. In the Jeremiah scroll, only the prose speaks of the "temple" (as the *hêkāl*) and of the (old) "covenant"; this difference may signify nothing about whether or not the prose came from the author of the poetry. A difference between the convictions or message expressed in the prose and poetry would be more significant, but the Jeremiah scroll does not manifest divergences of this kind. It is (for instance) capable of speaking both as if the fall of Jerusalem is inevitable and as if people need to turn so that they may avert this catastrophe, but such tensions appear within the poetry and within the prose, not just between them. More significant is, again, the fact that the two forms of speech or writing have different rhetorical affects.[12]

I do assume that there is material in the scroll conveying Jeremiah's own words and also material produced by people who wanted to write about him. One may think of these people as his disciples, though the scroll never says that he had any, and the word's meaning is vague. One may think of them as his editors, though editors are somewhat distanced from the object of their work, and they may not agree with it. One may think of them as his secretaries or scribes, which is at least a word that comes in the scroll, and it has the advantage and disadvantage of being much used in current scholarly writing on Jeremiah;[13] it thus carries some freight. One may think of them as preachers aiming to interpret Jeremiah to their contemporaries.[14] Calvin sees them as priests and Levites.[15]

12. I thus do not work with the assumption that distinguishing between poetry and prose, and then between prose messages and narratives, is key to studying the scroll—an assumption that has been basic to Jeremiah scholarship since Duhm's commentary (*Das Buch Jeremia*, Kurzer Hand-Commentar zum Alten Testament 11 [Tübingen: Mohr Siebeck, 1901]) and S. Mowinckel's *Zur Komposition des Buches Jeremia* (Kristiania: Dybward, 1914). Indeed, L. Stulman has noted that, in effect, though the world of scholarship has concluded that the twentieth-century framework for the study of Jeremiah was fundamentally flawed, it has carried on using it all the same ("Reflections on the Prose Sermons in the Book of Jeremiah," in *Bible Through the Lens of Trauma*, ed. E. Boase and C. G. Frechete, Semeia Studies 38 [Atlanta: SCM, 2016], 127–30). See further J. M. Henderson, *Jeremiah under the Shadow of Duhm: A Critique of the Use of Poetic Form as a Criterion of Authenticity*, T&T Clark Biblical Studies (London: T&T Clark, 2019); D. Rom-Shiloni, "From Prophetic Words to Prophetic Literature: Challenging Paradigms That Control Our Academic Thought on Jeremiah and Ezekiel," *JBL* 138 (2019), 565–86.

13. See the survey in B. E. Kelle, "The Phenomenon of Israelite Prophecy in Contemporary Scholarship," *CurBR* 12 (2013): 296–300.

14. E. W. Nicholson, *Preaching to the Exiles: A Study of the Prose Tradition in the Book of Jeremiah* (Oxford: Blackwell, 1970).

15. J. Calvin, *Commentary on Jeremiah and Lamentations*, trans. John Owen, 5 vols. (repr., Grand Rapids: Christian Classics Ethereal Library), 4:3.

I will refer to them as the scroll's curators and storytellers. Storytellers use imagination to generate a narrative with form and drama that makes it possible for people to appreciate and respond to it; it may be more factual or more fictional. Curators conserve things so as to look after them and make them available, selecting, arranging, and thus enabling them to say what they have to say. If we wish to think more concretely about these storytellers and curators, we could imagine them as embodied in the person of Baruch. The scroll calls him Jeremiah's scribe, though it never implies that he did the work of storyteller or curator except in compiling the 604 scroll, nor that he thus had anything like the creative role in generating the Jeremiah scroll that has sometimes been imagined for him. Scholarly study has thought of these curators and storytellers as "the Deuteronomists," the people whose work lies behind the "Deuteronomistic History," especially 2 Kings, though scholarly thinking about their relationship with the thought and language of Jeremiah has been fraught.[16] Nor is it clear whether the Deuteronomists will survive the ferment over the origin of Genesis to Kings that now characterizes First Testament scholarship,[17] though this difficulty does not terminate discussion of intertextual and other forms of relationship between Jeremiah and Deuteronomy or 2 Kings.[18]

Scholars traditionally describe the material in the scroll that they think came from Jeremiah as "authentic," though they sometimes put scare quotes around this word.[19] Material that came from a curator or storyteller is thus "inauthentic."[20] The two words imply an inappropriate value judgment. Storyteller and curator may be just as authentic messengers of Yahweh and interpreters of Jeremiah as Jeremiah himself. The word "authentic" also gets us into trouble if we cannot distinguish between material that came directly from Jeremiah and material that did not—if this uncertainty leaves us uncer-

16. See, e.g., a number of the papers in Najman and Schmid, *Jeremiah's Scriptures*; C. J. Sharp, *Prophecy and Ideology in Jeremiah: Struggles for Authority in the Deutero-Jeremianic Prose*, Old Testament Studies (London: T&T Clark, 2003), esp. 1–39; W. L. Holladay, "Elusive Deuteronomists, Jeremiah, and Proto-Deuteronomy," *CBQ* 66 (2004): 55–77; M. J. Williams, "An Investigation of the Legitimacy of Source Distinctions for the Prose Material in Jeremiah," *JBL* 112 (1993): 193–210.

17. Cf. C. L. Crouch, *An Introduction to the Study of Jeremiah* (London: T&T Clark, 2017), 48.

18. See, e.g., N. Mastnjak, *Deuteronomy and the Emergence of Textual Authority in Jeremiah*, FAT 2/87 (Tübingen: Mohr Siebeck, 2016).

19. E.g., J. A. Thompson, *The Book of Jeremiah*, NICOT (Grand Rapids: Eerdmans, 1980), 37, 38; S.-M. Kang, "The Authentic Sermon on Jeremiah in Jeremiah 7:1–20," in *Texts, Temples, and Traditions: Tribute to Menahem Haran*, ed. M. V. Fox et al. (Winona Lake, IN: Eisenbrauns, 1996), 147–62; Sharp, *Prophecy and Ideology in Jeremiah*, 8, 45, 106.

20. E.g., W. L. Holladay, *A Commentary on the Book of the Prophet Jeremiah*, 2 vols., Hermeneia (Philadelphia: Fortress, 1986; Minneapolis: Fortress, 1989), 2:165.

tain of the material's value. Further, the value judgment pushes people who want to affirm that the material is valuable into arguing that it must therefore come directly from Jeremiah. Actually, we do not know which material came from Jeremiah, but this fact does not stop the entire scroll being authentic in the sense of the product of people who worked under God to bring his message to Judah.

Therefore, as I pay little attention to establishing the dates of messages that the scroll leaves undated, I also do not pay much attention to determining whether messages came from Jeremiah or a curator or where the boundary lies between fact and imagination in the stories.

If Jeremiah and Baruch produced a scroll comprising messages delivered by Jeremiah over twenty-three years, it would be surprising if Jeremiah or Baruch did not have it in their backpack in 587. In keeping with a pattern that one can infer in regard to Hosea and Amos in connection with the fall of Samaria in 722, one may imagine that the confirmation of Jeremiah's message by the fall of Jerusalem in 587 led some people in Jerusalem or in locations such as Mizpah, Bethel, Babylon, and Egypt to think more about his message, to make sure it was preserved, to ask what implications it had for the future, and to develop it in a way that provided answers to that question. The people I am calling Jeremiah's storytellers and curators are such people. In principle, then, one might seek to discern ways in which they have done their work.

In Mizpah and then in Egypt, Jeremiah himself would surely have been involved in that reflection, while the storytellers and curators will have generated the narratives within Jer 26 to 36 and the complex into which they were incorporated, as well as the longer complex comprising Jer 37–44. While most people in Jeremiah's day might have had some basic literacy, only a tiny number would be able to write stories such as appear in the Jeremiah scroll or to compile it or read it (as Jer 36 implies).[21] One can imagine collections of Jeremiah's sayings like the 604 scroll and of stories involving him being read "by small groups of trained scribes" or "in acts of public confession and worship"[22] in the period following the catastrophe of 587. Treating scribal and liturgical as alternatives may involve a false antithesis if Levites could be scribes and vice versa.[23]

21. See, e.g., J. M. Bos, "The 'Literarization' of the Biblical Prophecy of Doom," in *Contextualizing Israel's Sacred Writing: Ancient Literacy, Orality, and Literary Production*, ed. B. B. Schmidt, AIIL 22 (Atlanta: Society of Biblical Literature, 2015), 263–65; M. Nissinen, "How Prophecy Became Literature," *SJOT* 19 (2005): 153–72.

22. R. E. Clements, "Jeremiah 1–25 and the Deuteronomistic History," in *Understanding Poets and Prophets: Essays in Honour of George Wishart Anderson*, ed. A. G. Auld, JSOTSup 152 (Sheffield: JSOT, 1993), 93.

23. See, e.g., K. van der Toorn, *Scribal Culture and the Making of the Hebrew Bible* (Cambridge, MA: Harvard University Press, 2007).

Could something like the Jeremiah scroll have been produced in a context like the aftermath of 587 and before the Persian period, or does its production imply a setting where there is a leisured class who can settle down and write books, as some argue?[24] That argument works in connection with writing books about the Jeremiah scroll, but writing the scroll itself seems at least as likely to be a response to a religious and social crisis (the picture that Jer 36 gives) or to a community trauma like that of the fall of Jerusalem and the experience of exile. A prophet or a curator needs no great infrastructure in this connection, only a scroll, a pen, a dark evening, and a candle. Accumulating evidence of a significant ongoing community in Judah (outside the devastated capital) in the Babylonian period[25] provides a plausible context for such reflection and work—if it did not take place in Egypt. Conversely, there is no direct evidence that Judahites in the Persian period possessed infrastructure for writing a scroll in a way that Judahites in the Babylonian period did not.

One possible aim of the curators' and storytellers' work is thus to provide a rationale for the sad state of Judah and its people, which reflects their abandonment of Yahweh.[26] In this respect, the Jeremiah scroll complements the books of Kings.[27] As German theology flourished (in a way that may seem surprising) after the catastrophe of the First World War and again after the catastrophe of the Second World War, it would not be difficult to imagine that the calamity that came upon Jerusalem in 587 issued in creativity among Judahites in subsequent decades. The scroll itself is then "a 'thick' response to disaster. . . . It names the disaster, interprets the disaster, and portrays the prophet as a survivor of disaster."[28] It is "a kind of survival manual."[29]

24. Carroll, "Arguing about Jeremiah," 234.

25. See Lipschits, *Fall and Rise of Jerusalem*; E. Meyers, "Exile and Restoration in Light of Recent Archaeology and Demographic Studies," in *Exile and Restoration Revisited: Essays on the Babylonian and Persian Periods in Memory of Peter R. Ackroyd*, ed. G. N. Knoppers, L. L. Grabbe, and D. Fulton, The Library of Second Temple Studies 73 (London: T&T Clark, 2009), 166–73.

26. The word "theodicy" is often used in this connection: the word comes about eighteen times in A. R. P. Diamond's commentary on Jer 1–10 ("Jeremiah," in *Eerdmans Commentary on the Bible*, ed. J. D. G. Dunn and J. W. Rogerson [Grand Rapids: Eerdmans, 2003], 548–65); see also A. R. P. Diamond, *The Confessions of Jeremiah in Context: Scenes of Prophetic Drama*, JSOTSup 45 (Sheffield: Sheffield Academic, 1987), e.g., 189–91 on Jer 11–20. See my introductory comment on 11:1–13:22 below.

27. Cf. T. Römer, "The Formation of the Book of Jeremiah as a Supplement to the So-Called Deuteronomistic History," in *The Production of Prophecy: Constructing Prophecy and Prophets in Yehud*, ed. D. V. Edelman and E. Ben Zvi (London: Equinox, 2009), 168–83, though he dates both in the Persian period.

28. K. M. O'Connor, "Surviving Disaster in the Book of Jeremiah," *WW* 22 (2002): 369–70.

29. K. M. O'Connor, "How Trauma Studies Can Contribute to Old Testament Studies," in *Trauma and Traumatization in Individual and Collective Dimensions: Insights from Bibli-*

B. THE COMPOSITION OF JEREMIAH AND THE COMPOSITION OF THE GOSPELS

A process of development generated the composition of the scroll that we have. But intensive study over more than a century has generated no consensus concerning this process or the process whereby individual chapters developed. As is the case with attempts to date messages of Jeremiah in specific contexts and to distinguish between more factual and more fictional in narratives, I therefore do not attempt to adjudicate over theories concerning the process whereby different chapters in the scroll developed or to formulate more theories about it. I do not object to people studying "textual genetics rather than poetics,"[30] but I focus on the latter, on what the curators who generated the documents present to us in each chapter and on the understanding of Jeremiah that they set forward. I take their understanding as an "authentic" one. While I include footnote references to some work on the possible development of material in the scroll so that readers may follow it up, in the commentary I focus on the text we have rather than seeking to uncover the compositional process whereby it may have developed.

I do have a mental picture of the general compositional process, partly imagined on the basis of the possibility that the New Testament Gospels provide a plausible model (or plausible models) for thinking about the composition of the Jeremiah scroll and about its relationship to events.[31] Like the Jeremiah scroll, the Gospels combine messages and stories, though they make the story the framework for the messages whereas the Jeremiah scroll makes the messages the framework for the stories. Like the Jeremiah scroll, the Gospels tell a story about what God was doing and saying historically

---

cal Studies and Beyond, ed. E.-M. Becker, J. Dochhorn, and E. K. Holt, Studia Aarhusiana Neotestamentica 2 (Göttingen: Vandenhoeck & Ruprecht, 2014), 210; *Jeremiah: Pain and Promise* (Minneapolis: Fortress, 2011).

30. A. R. P. Diamond and L. Stulman, "Analytical Introduction," in *Jeremiah (Dis)placed*, ed. A. R. P. Diamond and L. Stulman, LHBOTS 529 (London: T&T Clark, 2011), 3. The authors of this quotation do rather object, and H.-J. Stipp responds to them in "'But into the Water You Must Not Dip It,'" in *Thinking of Water in the Early Second Temple Period*, ed. E. Ben Zvi and C. Levin, BZAW 461 (Berlin: de Gruyter, 2014), 167–95; he says in effect that even if we are never going to agree on the nature of the redactional process in Jeremiah, he is going to do it anyway (170). For that decision, see also, e.g., R. P. Carroll, "Synchronic Deconstructions of Jeremiah," in *Synchronic or Diachronic: A Debate on Method in Old Testament Exegesis*, ed. J. C. de Moor, OTS 34 (Leiden: Brill, 1995), 39–51.

31. D. K. Jobling notes analogies between Jeremiah research and Jesus research in "The Quest of the Historical Jeremiah," *Union Seminary Quarterly Review* 34 (1978): 3–12; cf. R. P. Carroll, *Jeremiah: A Commentary*, OTL (London: SCM, 1986), 63. Oddly, Carroll refers specifically to the synoptic Gospels even though John provides a closer model for his understanding of Jeremiah.

but do so in a way that brings home its significance for the people of their day. In both respects, their telling corresponds to what one can envisage God wanting and inspiring.

Oddly enough, the time span between the first and the last events that the scroll relates (626 and 562) is not so different from the time span from Jesus's birth to the writing of the Four Gospels—or at least of the first three. A difference between Jeremiah and Jesus is that the Jeremiah scroll tells of the prophet having his message written down whereas the Gospels do not say that Jesus did so. In other respects, there are partial analogies between the processes of their composition. During Jeremiah's working life and over succeeding decades, some people held onto his messages while also adapting them so that they spoke in new ways. In addition, they told stories about him that also spoke to their contemporaries, doing so in a way that stayed narratively within the framework of his own life and work. In principle, one can therefore ask about the difference between their version of events and of his teaching on one hand and the actual events and his actual teaching on the other, though opinions differ on the results of such investigation, as in the case of the Gospels.

Again oddly enough, we have more than one version of the Jeremiah scroll, as we do of the Jesus story—a Hebrew version preserved in the Masoretic Text and a shorter Greek version preserved in the LXX (see "The Hebrew Text," pp. 43–46). Among the Gospels, Mark is the version nearest to actual history (while still being an interpretation of Jesus's story). Matthew pays more attention to working out the story's significance for its readers, who were Jews who believe in Jesus. Luke-Acts explicitly takes the story beyond Jesus's own day. And from Matthew and Luke one may be able to work back to another collection of Jesus's teaching that they both knew (Q). John is a version that takes a more creative and imaginative approach to narrating Jesus's significance. Accounts of the feeding of the five thousand (Mark 6; Matt 14; Luke 9; John 6) provide an illustration. Perhaps Jeremiah and Baruch's 604 scroll is a bit like Mark, LXX Jeremiah is a bit like Matthew, and MT Jeremiah is a bit like Luke. (It is another nice coincidence that Mark wrote before the fall of Jerusalem, Matthew and Luke after it.)

This comparison with the Gospels suggests several reflections in connection with Jeremiah.

- Our having multiple versions of the Jesus story establishes a richer but also more complicated baseline for thinking about the relationship between Jesus and the way people told his story, whereas we have only the two versions of the Jeremiah scroll.
- A way of formulating the question about the relationship between Jeremiah and the Jeremiah scroll is to ask whether the scroll is more

13

like Mark, more like Matthew or Luke, or more like John. And a way of categorizing scholarly work on Jeremiah is to classify it according to its answer to that question. But one's answer to that question is as much the hypothesis from which one starts as the conclusion that one reaches.

- The presence of all four Gospels in the Scriptures reflects an assumption that God likes all four ways of telling the Jesus story. The place of the Jeremiah scroll among the Scriptures then does not imply that in its relationship to Jeremiah himself it is more like Mark than like John. Either way, it is "authentic."

- If MT Jeremiah is an expanded edition of the version lying behind LXX Jeremiah, it is not therefore inferior any more than Matthew is inferior to Mark. Nor is it a basis for emending MT's text—or for that matter vice versa. Both MT Jeremiah and LXX Jeremiah need to be understood in their own right, like Matthew, Mark, and Luke, though a comparison of the versions may draw attention to significant features.

- A focus on getting behind the Jeremiah scroll and tracing the process whereby it came into being risks ceasing to pay attention to the scroll itself—as is the case with a focus on getting behind Mark or John. Tracing that process may be interesting and worthwhile, but it is a different enterprise from interpreting the scroll.

- If getting behind the Gospels to the Jesus of history is complicated (!), then tracing the process whereby the Jeremiah scroll developed is at least as complicated, as is reflected in the scholarly study of the past century or so.

- Christians may read the Gospels to listen to the message the Gospel writers brought as they reflected on Jesus's life and ministry with the assumption that in this way we may imagine our way into Jesus's life and ministry and learn from it. Thus, alongside "suspension of belief" in the "historical Jeremiah" in order to "read the text as if that character were the product of the tradition itself"[32] (that is, to read, interpret, and believe the received text as if the Jeremiah in it were the "real" Jeremiah), one might put suspension of belief in a redactional process that we cannot trace in order to read the text that issued from that process (that is, to read, interpret, and believe the received text without wondering if it is the "real" text).

- A chapter such as Jer 32 is instructive in this connection. It anticipates the form of some chapters in John's Gospel that open with a

32. R. P. Carroll, "Arguing about Jeremiah," 229.

14

symbolic act by Jesus that is the lead-in to a theme relating to the symbolic act. In those chapters, over a period of fifty years or so after Jesus's death and resurrection, the Holy Spirit inspired John to take events from Jesus's life and his actual words and make them the basis for a reflection on his significance, which John presents as Jesus's own words. The Christian community came to recognize the authenticity of that reflection in this connection. It may be anachronistic to imagine the community thinking about this process in a way that made the distinction that I might presuppose between what Jesus said and what John might infer from it,[33] but given that I cannot help making that distinction, then the way I express it involves affirming my trust that the Christian community did the right thing when it recognized that John had truly articulated the significance of Jesus and, for that matter, my assumption that Jesus himself would have liked the way John has put things on his lips that he did not say.

In light of this analogy with the Gospels, I picture the composition of the scroll along the following lines. The picture is shrouded in the word *possibly*, though I do not keep repeating that word below.

- Between 626 and 604, Yahweh was giving Jeremiah messages that he delivered in the temple courtyards and elsewhere. These messages appear within Jer 2–6. Jeremiah critiqued the Judahite religion that Josiah tried to reform and supported his reformation, but he opposed Josiah's political and military policies. He opposed the reversion to pre-reformation religious practices after Josiah's death.
- In 604, Yahweh told Jeremiah to write up all his messages. Jehoiakim destroyed the resulting document, but Jeremiah rewrote it, and Jer 2–6 is the rewritten version—perhaps annotated after 587. We cannot date most of the messages within Jer 2–6 to particular moments between 626 and 604.
- Through the reigns of Jehoiakim, Jehoiachin, and Zedekiah, Yahweh continued to give Jeremiah messages to deliver in the temple courtyard and in the palace. They provoked controversy and opposition. In the last years before 587 and the aftermath, Yahweh continued to give Jeremiah messages for Judah, some more promissory as the

33. See H. W. Frei's exploration of the development of thinking about biblical narrative during the eighteenth and nineteenth centuries in *The Eclipse of Biblical Narrative* (New Haven: Yale University Press, 1974).

catastrophe approached and after it happened. Before the city's fall, he continued to deliver these messages in the temple courtyard and in the palace; afterward, he delivered them in Mizpah.

- In Mizpah or in Egypt, Jeremiah got Baruch to write down the further messages that he had received during the reigns of Jehoiakim, Jehoiachin, and Zedekiah, which appear within Jer 7–36 and 46–51. They are or include the "many similar words" of 36:32. There is no reason to set verse and prose sharply apart within these chapters as Jeremiah's method of communication, but prose may more often indicate that curators are summarizing Jeremiah's message as they understand it.

- Storytellers in Mizpah or Egypt wrote the stories about Jeremiah up until his move to Egypt and its aftermath, beginning with 1:4–19 but mostly within Jer 26–45. They include messages by Jeremiah in prose whose wording the curators sometimes formulated, based on what they knew Jeremiah had said or on the implications of his message.

- Curators compiled the complexes of messages and stories that we can discern within the scroll (e.g., 39:1–44:30; 46:1–51:64) and placed the complexes end to end (as happened with the book of Psalms) in bringing together the material in 1:1–52:30 in an organized form. They added 52:31–34 in about 560.

- The scroll refers to the Medes as a serious power and potential threat for Babylon and to three peoples within the Median Empire; it shows no awareness of the Persians, who took over the Median Empire and turned out to be the actual threat to Babylon; it refers to the release of Jehoiachin as if that were a sign of hope but shows no awareness of the accession of Cyrus to which Ezra 1 can refer as a more telling sign of hope and the fulfillment of Jeremiah's promises; it speaks much of the fall of Babylon but shows no awareness of how Babylon actually fell and gives no indication that imperial power has passed from Babylon to Persia, that many Judahites have returned to Jerusalem, or that the temple has been rebuilt. By the 550s or 540s, then, the scroll reached something close to the version we have.

- Copies reached Judah and Babylon, and curators in Egypt, Judah, or Babylon produced the further versions that approximate to the Hebrew text that we have and to the Hebrew text lying behind the LXX version (the LXX *Vorlage*, or LXXV).

- Both scrolls may have been glossed later. MT Jeremiah includes a distinctive number of small variations between the *ketiv* and the *qere*, which may reflect this process.

C. THE PERSIAN PERIOD: A FOURTH HORIZON?

In the unresolved scholarly debate on the origin of the scroll, views focus more on the Persian and Greek periods than on the decades that more immediately followed the time of Jeremiah's own activity. In placing the scroll's finalizing in the Babylonian period, I take the minority opinion.[34] Much scholarship in the late twentieth and early twenty-first century has seen the Persian period as the key context in which First Testament scrolls in general came into existence. The illumination that emerges from postcolonial perspectives[35] and considerations of ideology[36] has especially encouraged the making of this connection, not least for Jeremiah.

Ezra 1–6 relates that Yahweh fulfilled one of Jeremiah's declarations when Judahites in Babylon returned to Jerusalem to rebuild the temple. They refused to let people whose ancestors had long ago been forced migrants into Samaria join in the project, and "the people of the country weakened the hands of the people of Judah" in connection with it (Ezra 4:4). They sought to get the Persian authorities to stop this work and the subsequent rebuilding of Jerusalem itself. On the other hand, people who had joined the returned exiles in the building project on the basis of separating themselves from the defilement of "the nations of the country" in order to have recourse to Yahweh did in due course join in the celebration of the temple rebuilding (Ezra 6:21–22). Identifying these groups is difficult, but it is enough to establish that there were tensions and conflicts between different groups in Judah, specifically between people who had returned from Babylon and people who had not gone into exile.

One could call them different interest groups. And just as different Christian groups see themselves as the heirs of the New Testament or parts of it, one can imagine different groups in Judah claiming to be the heirs of Jeremiah's message. One can further ask of the Jeremiah scroll itself the modern and postmodern question, "Whose interests does it serve?"[37] If "the political

---

34. But cf., e.g., J. R. Lundbom, *Jeremiah 1–20: A New Translation with Introduction and Commentary*, AB 21A (New York: Doubleday, 1999), 100–101; M. Leuchter, *The Polemics of Exile in Jeremiah 26–45* (Cambridge: Cambridge University Press, 2008), 1–17; for the opposite view, see, e.g., essays in Edelman and Ben Zvi, *Production of Prophecy*; J. Hill, "The Book of Jeremiah (MT) and Its Early Second Temple Background," in Goldingay, *Uprooting and Planting*, 153–71.

35. See, e.g., S. V. Davidson, *Empire and Exile: Postcolonial Readings of the Book of Jeremiah*, LHBOTS 542 (London: T&T Clark, 2011).

36. See, e.g., R. P. Carroll, "Jeremiah, Intertextuality and Ideologiekritik," *JNSL* 22 (1996): 15–34.

37. This question may be posed in connection with the question of gender, on which the

is primary,"[38] and if the scroll came into being in the Persian period, then it would not be surprising if these groups' claims were expressed in the scroll itself. If, for instance, its curators were people who had come back from Babylon or were their descendants, one can ask how they wrote their claims into their work.[39]

Several issues need distinguishing and evaluating here.

- The scroll may reflect conflicts and different interests among the Judahite communities over the relative status of the community in Judah, in Babylon, and in Egypt or over the status of Jehoiachin or over attitudes toward the Babylonian Empire itself. But the fact of such conflicts does not imply that they needed a century to emerge or find expression.[40]
- Reference to the tensions and conflicts of which Ezra 1–6 speaks has to be read into the Jeremiah text. While Jer 24 and 29 can be connected with them, they do not require such a connection or point directly to these tensions and conflicts (see the commentary on Jer 24 and 29).
- The connections can be made on the basis of redaction-critical study of the text. But the redaction-critical study emerges from the theory as much as the other way around.
- If one explains the scroll's capacity to combine two contrasting views (e.g., in its attitude toward Jehoiachin or in describing Nebuchadrezzar as Yahweh's servant and declaring that Yahweh's wrath is coming on Babylon) as reflecting the view of pro-Babylonian and anti-Babylonian groups, that "explanation" only pushes the question back a stage: if the two attitudes could not be taken by one group, how did both attitudes gain access to the same scroll? (On theological tensions in the scroll, see "Main Themes and Their Implications," pp. 59–60.)
- "Why would each of these groups," who all named the name of the one God, "have chosen to re-establish their identities in such ex-

Jeremiah scroll works with the gender assumptions of its culture while also deconstructing, harnessing, or subverting them (see, e.g., 3:7 and the comment), and one may interweave the two questions: see C. M. Maier and C. J. Sharp, eds., *Prophecy and Power: Jeremiah in Feminist and Postcolonial Perspective*, LHBOTS 577 (London: T&T Clark, 2013); M. E. Mills, *Jeremiah: An Introduction and Study Guide; Prophecy in a Time of Crisis* (London: T&T Clark, 2015), 70–82.

38. R. P. Carroll, *Jeremiah*, Old Testament Guides (Sheffield: JSOT, 1989), 98.

39. See, e.g., R. P. Carroll: *Jeremiah: A Commentary*, 65–82.

40. D. Rom-Shiloni, "Group Identities in Jeremiah," in *A Palimpsest: Rhetoric, Ideology, Stylistics and Language Relating to Persian Israel*, ed. E. Ben Zvi, D. Edelman, and F. Polak (Piscataway, NJ: Gorgias, 2009), 11–46.

clusivist ways?" Was it an inevitable aspect of the need to reformulate the faith? Does the reaction seem odd because of our modern, liberal, inclusive tendencies?[41] Or might we turn this question on its head? Whereas "Whose interests does it serve?" has become a familiar question in the West in the context of conflicts over the past century, perhaps we are imposing it on Ezra and Jeremiah, and people were less preoccupied by power than modern Western people or could disagree without being in conflict.

Further, the following considerations raise difficulties for the idea that the scroll reflects the Persian period.

- It makes no reference to anything we know about in the Persian period. It never refers to the Persians themselves or to the issues that surface in Ezra 7–Nehemiah 13. The First Testament does include material with a background in the Second Temple period (e.g., in Chronicles, Ezra, Nehemiah, Esther, Ecclesiastes, Daniel, Haggai, and Zechariah), which explicitly refers to this background and includes Persian words and represents features of Late Biblical Hebrew. Jeremiah does not have these characteristics.[42] (It also gives no concrete indication of links with the Greek period, such as Greek words or historical references; the question of development of ideas—specifically eschatological/apocalyptic ideas—involves arguing in a circle.[43])
- "There is thus some effort of the imagination involved in locating the scroll in this context" in that "passages are explained against a variety of proposed backgrounds of which we have little in the way of real knowledge."[44] To elaborate the point,

---

41. D. Rom-Shiloni, "*Exclusive Inclusivity*, the Transparent and the Invisible," *JHS* 18/1 (2018): 76–77.

42. See, e.g., A. Hornkohl, *Ancient Hebrew Periodization and the Language of the Book of Jeremiah: The Case for a Sixth-Century Date of Composition*, Studies in Semitic Languages and Linguistics 74 (Leiden: Brill, 2014); R. Hendel and J. Joosten, *How Old Is the Hebrew Bible?* (New Haven: Yale University, 2018); M. Tafferner, "The Linguistic Date of the Masoretic Extensions in the Book of Jeremiah" (paper presented at the Annual Meeting of the Evangelical Theological Society, San Antonio, TX, 15 November 2016); for the contrary view, see R. Rezetko, "The (Dis)Connection between Textual and Linguistic Developments in the Book of Jeremiah," in *Empirical Models Challenging Biblical Criticism*, ed. R. F. Person and R. Rezetko, AIIL 25 (Atlanta: Society of Biblical Literature, 2016), 239–69.

43. Cf. L.-S. Tiemeyer, "Will the Prophetic Texts from the Hellenistic Period Stand Up, Please?" in *Judah Between East and West: The Transition from Persian to Greek Rule (ca. 400–200 BCE)*, ed. O. Lipschits and L. L. Grabbe, The Library of Second Temple Studies 75 (London: T&T Clark, 2012), 255–79.

44. J. G. McConville, "Jeremiah: Prophet and Book," *TynB* 42 (1991): 85.

- "Few periods of biblical history have attracted as much attention in recent years as the Persian era. . . . As a result of this scholarly interest, many Old Testament texts and the most important processes in the development of the YHWH faith have been (re-)dated to this era. . . . [But] many of these processes (e.g. the emergence of the Torah in the Persian period) have merely been deduced and therefore remain hypothetical and speculative. . . . Primary and secondary sources for the approximately 200-year Persian supremacy in the ancient Near East are incredibly sparse, much more so than for the 100-years of Assyrian hegemony. . . . The scarcer and more problematic the sources, the greater the conjecture and speculation."[45]

- "The tough circumstance of the community in Judah in the Persian period indeed required Judahite intellectuals to be interacting with Israel's traditions: "Total abandonment of cultural heritage and identity must have seemed unthinkable."[46] And one can see scrolls such as Chronicles and Ecclesiastes as engaged in such reflection. The problem with suggesting that the Jeremiah scroll's development was an aspect of this reflection is the wide gap between its contents and the purpose that according to this hypothesis it was designed to fulfill. The content of those works looks quite different from that of the Jeremiah scroll.

- The quotations from Jeremiah within the First Testament take up the promises rather than the warnings, and the Ezekiel scroll includes much more by way of promise than the Jeremiah scroll. It's been said that "the prophetic books are about hope"[47] and that "predominantly . . . Jeremiah's book contains a message of hope."[48] Actually, the Jeremiah scroll is closer to being dominated by threat. *B. Baba Batra* 14b exaggerates only slightly in saying that "it is all of it the destruction" (see "The Jeremiah Scroll in the Canons of Judaism and of the Church," pp. 42–43). It is at least a "predominantly dystopian text,"[49] not the kind of text one would expect to develop to meet the needs of the Persian period.

45. O. Keel, *Jerusalem and the One God: A Religious History* (Minneapolis: Fortress, 2017), 135–36.

46. Diamond, "Jeremiah," 572.

47. E. Ben Zvi, "The Concept of Prophetic Books and Its Historical Setting," in Edelman and Ben Zvi, *Production of Prophecy*, 75.

48. R. E. Clements, *Jeremiah*, Interpretation: A Bible Commentary for Teaching and Preaching (Atlanta: John Knox, 1988), 3.

49. M. Brummitt, "Troubling Utopias: Possible Worlds and Possible Voices in the Book of Jeremiah," in Diamond and Stulman, *Jeremiah (Dis)placed*, 186.

D. DISUNITY OF COMPOSITION (A FIFTH HORIZON)

The suggestion that the Jeremiah scroll relates to the Persian period is an interpretation that arises from a Western scholarly context and reads the text in light of concerns that come from the time of the readers. To put it in anthropological terms, it is etic rather than emic.[50] It is an "in front of the text" reading rather than an "in the text" reading. Paradoxically, as an "in front of the text" reading, it becomes another "behind the text" reading of the kind that were common in connection with Jeremiah in the twentieth century. There is some irony about Jeremiah study's moving from a quest for the historical Jeremiah of the First Temple period to a quest for the historical Jeremianic authors and communities of the Second Temple period; the latter quest is another version of the former and is just as doomed. There is a further parallel with study of the Gospels, which moved from a quest for the historical Jesus to a quest for the communities that the Gospels addressed; this also did not work out very well and could thus lead back to asking questions about "the Gospels for all Christians."[51]

There is nothing wrong in principle with "in front of the text" readings just as there is nothing wrong with "behind the text" readings. Indeed, there is a sense in which any reading is an "in front of the text" one because, by definition, interpreters all live in front of the text as (e.g.) Western academics sympathetic to postmodern and postcolonial thinking in the twenty-first century. But the image of horizons presupposes that we seek to allow our horizon to merge with that of the text—at least to understand it, even if not necessarily to agree with it. The problem with the "in front of the text" Persian-period understanding of the Jeremiah scroll resembles the problem with an understanding of the Song of Songs as concerned with God's relationship with Israel or Jesus's relationship with a believer. It may illumine that relationship, but it loses the thrust of the text itself. And it ends up critiquing the text for fulfilling a different aim from the one that was its concern. The promise and the drawback of "in front of the text" approaches lie in their reading Jeremiah in light of Western insights, experiences, and culture. As they engage in ideological criticism of the scroll and look for ideological considerations that are reflected in the text, they do so in light of their own ideological convictions. Thus, paradoxically, postcolonial interpretation takes an imperial stance in relation to the text. Beginning from a position of power over the text, in the

---

50. P. R. Raabe, "What Is Israel's God Up To among the Nations?" in *The Book of Jeremiah: Composition, Reception, and Interpretation*, ed. J. Lundbom, C. A. Evans, and B. A. Anderson, VTSup 178 (Leiden: Brill, 2018), 234.

51. See R. Bauckham, ed., *The Gospels for All Christians* (Grand Rapids: Eerdmans, 1997).

name of marginalized people it marginalizes the text and advances its own ideological concerns.

If the curators of the Jeremiah scroll did live in the Second Temple period, they avoided drawing direct attention to themselves or their context and invited their readers to read the scroll in the context of the period from Josiah to the aftermath of 587. Readers are free to decide for themselves whether they will do so, but in this commentary, I have accepted the invitation.

To do so is not to imply that one abjures "in front of the text" readings, which one could call a fifth horizon. Such readings informed by post-structuralism, feminism, deconstruction, and intertextuality have flourished in the late twentieth and early twenty-first centuries.[52] In the commentary, I will refer to some exercises in interpretation that reflect the fourth and fifth horizons, but my focus will be on the first three.

E. THE TORAH, THE PROPHETS, AND THE PSALMS

Jeremiah has a background in the Torah, the Prophets, and the Psalms,[53] though none of these scrolls existed in his day in the form in which we know them. Not surprisingly, the length of the Jeremiah scroll means it has room for allusions to the key moments in the story that appears in the First Testament as we know it: God's act of creation, his promise to Israel's ancestors, his destruction of Sodom and Gomorrah, his getting Israel out of Egypt, his leading them through the wilderness, his making a pledge with them, his giving Moses his Ten Words, his listening to Moses and Samuel as intercessors, and his destroying Shiloh. These last references to an Ephraimite person and place remind us that the background information at the beginning of the scroll designates Jeremiah as someone from Anathoth in Benjamin, which could count as Ephraim rather than Judah (see the commentary on 1:1). There could then be some ambiguity about Jeremiah's position—living in Jerusalem but not quite belonging there. But it would be nice to think that his origin in a priestly family contributed to his wide knowledge of Israel's story and of the sacred traditions that we know from the Torah, the Prophets, and the Psalms, including priestly material.[54]

---

52. See, e.g., C. E. Carroll, "Another Dodecade: A Dialectic Model of the Decentred Universe of Jeremiah Studies 1996–2008," *CurBR* 8 (2010): 162–82.

53. See Holladay, *Commentary on Jeremiah*, 2:35–70.

54. See D. Rom-Shiloni, "The Forest and the Trees: The Place of Pentateuchal Materials in Prophecy of the Late Seventh/Early Sixth Centuries BCE," in *Congress Volume Stellenbosch 2016*, ed. L. C. Jonker, G. Kotzé, and C. M. Maier, VTSup 177 (Leiden: Brill, 2017), 56–92.

The most explicit single allusion to them appears in 26:18–19, which refers to Micah and to the story of Hezekiah and associates Micah with the kind of warning about disaster coming to Judah that Jeremiah also uttered. But it is not Jeremiah himself who refers to Micah in the text, but the elders of Judah. Jeremiah's own way of speaking about Yahweh's relationship with Israel as like that of a husband with his wife—a relationship that laid on the wife an expectation of submission to her husband that Israel failed to fulfill—recalls the message of the Ephraimite prophet Hosea. It is a plausible assumption that a scroll with Hosea's teaching was compiled in Jerusalem or taken there before or after the fall of Samaria in 722, which could provide means whereby Jeremiah got to know Hosea's message.[55] Further, Jer 48–49 indicates concrete acquaintance with Isaiah and Obadiah (unless the acquaintance is the other way around), and Jer 48 reflects Num 21. The scroll incorporates many further lines and images that may count as allusions to the messages of other prophets.

In his comments on that quasi-marital relationship, Jeremiah also takes up teaching from the Torah that appears in Deut 24, to which Jer 3:1 constitutes a more or less explicit reference. We have noted that Josiah's reformation was fueled by the emergence of a Torah scroll that seems to have corresponded with something like Deuteronomy as we know it, and there are various points at which Jeremiah seems to presuppose people's acquaintance with Deuteronomy. The question of acquaintance and allusion is complicated by the apparent fact that Deuteronomy as a whole as we know it came into existence during or after the time Jeremiah was active, while the Torah as a whole as we know it comes from after Jeremiah's day. I think of Ezra bringing it to Jerusalem in 458 (see Ezra 7) as the moment when it was propagated in Jerusalem. So Jeremiah's message may be background to Deuteronomy as well as Deuteronomy being background to Jeremiah. There are particularly close links between Jeremiah and Deut 32, and the influence might go either way.

Deuteronomy appears in the First Testament as a lead-in to Joshua through Kings, an account of Israel's story from Moses to the fall of Jerusalem. The telling of that story reflects the same ways of thinking as Deuteronomy, which provides key clues to understanding why Israel's story unfolded in the way it did. There is again a close relationship between the narrative in 2 Kgs 17–25 and the Jeremiah scroll. Much of Jer 39 and 52 are virtually identical with 2 Kgs 25, as, for example, Matt 4:1–11 is virtually identical with Luke 4:1–13. More subtly, the story of Josiah's coming to know that Torah scroll and his reaction to it (2 Kgs 22–23) provides a pattern for the story of

---

55. See H. Lalleman-de Winkel, *Jeremiah in Prophetic Tradition*, Contributions to Biblical Exegesis and Theology 26 (Leeuven: Peeters, 2000), 85–144.

Jehoiakim's coming to know the scroll of Jeremiah's message and his reaction to it (Jer 36)—a pattern with which the Jehoiakim story constitutes a chilling contrast. The teaching and stories in the Jeremiah scroll are related in ways that indicate more generally the influence of the thinking of Deuteronomy and of those succeeding books.

The praises and protest prayers in Jeremiah compare with their equivalents in the Psalms, against whose background Jeremiah praises and prays. Specific links may indicate that he picks up their phrases or may indicate that he influences them. He also has themes and language in common with Isa 40–55 and with Ezekiel that might indicate influence either way.[56]

F. WAS JEREMIAH A HISTORICAL FIGURE?

The contents of the Jeremiah scroll fit against a historical background in events in Judah in the late Assyrian and Babylonian period, the period to which the scroll's introduction refers. But the plausibility of this background does not determine how historical the Jeremiah story is. Fictional works are often set against a credible historical background, so having a plausible historical background and being history-like say nothing about whether a work presents itself as historical or succeeds in being historical, if it has that aim. And it has sometimes been argued that Jeremiah is more or less a fictional character. In the LXX, the Jeremiah scroll is followed by Baruch, a work in which Jeremiah's scribe delivers a message to the Judahites in Babylon, and then (after Lamentations) by a Letter of Jeremiah sent to the Judahites in Babylon. But these writings have no actual connection with a historical Jeremiah or Baruch and they never had a place in the Torah, the Prophets, and the Writings. Is Jeremiah comparable to them[57]—essentially a literary creation?[58] Or is the Jeremiah scroll more like the closing chapters of 2 Kings

---

56. See, e.g., B. D. Sommer, *A Prophet Reads Scripture: Allusion in Isaiah 40–66*, Contraversions: Jews and Other Differences (Stanford: Stanford University Press, 1998); H. Leene, "Blowing the Same Shofar: An Intertextual Comparison of Representations of the Prophetic Role in Jeremiah and Ezekiel," in *The Elusive Prophet: The Prophet as a Historical Person, Literary Character and Anonymous Artist*, ed. J. C. de Moor, OTS 45 (Leiden: Brill, 2001), 175–98; L. Boadt, "Do Jeremiah and Ezekiel Share a Common View of the Exile?" in Goldingay, *Uprooting and Planting*, 14–31.

57. See R. G. Kratz, "Why Jeremiah? The Invention of a Prophetic Figure," in Najman and Schmid, *Jeremiah's Scriptures*, 197–212.

58. T. Collins, *The Mantle of Elijah: The Redaction Criticism of the Prophetical Books*, The Biblical Seminar 20 (Sheffield: JSOT, 1993), 120; cf. R. P. Carroll, *From Chaos to Covenant: Uses of Prophecy in the Book of Jeremiah* (London: SCM, 1981), 5–30.

that give a basically factual account of the decades to which the Jeremiah scroll also relates?

The fact that the Jeremiah scroll is Yahweh's message, Yahweh's word, does not in itself indicate that it must be presenting itself as historical. Yahweh likes history, but he also likes works of the imagination; they can be a good way of conveying insight. Jonah is such a story about a prophet, and Ecclesiastes is a collection of testimonies and observations that half-invites readers to think they come from Solomon ("half-invites" in that it does not name him). Each of those works takes a historical person as its launching point but then constructs a work of imagination. It is inspired imagination; designating these scrolls in this way does not imply they are untrue. They are like Jesus's parables. They tell people the truth about Yahweh and about themselves, but they do so in a different way from historical works. "Counterfactual histories" can make it possible to think creatively about a better present.[59]

But a number of considerations suggest that the Jeremiah scroll is more like the closing chapters of 2 Kings in its relation to history than like Jonah or Ecclesiastes.

- Jonah is clearly structured in its literary nature and in its thinking. The Jeremiah scroll has some structure, but its material is much more diverse and variegated.[60] It has been called "a complicated, untidy accumulation," a "rolling *corpus*."[61]
- Ecclesiastes implicitly attributes its contents to someone whom everyone knew to be important, and even Jonah is a paradoxically appropriate subject for the message conveyed by the story about him. Likewise, by the time Baruch and the Letter of Jeremiah were written, Baruch and Jeremiah were well-known and respected. But in the case of the Jeremiah scroll itself, in the words of Overholt, "what puzzles me is why someone would collect material and then assign it to a 'fictional' character" if that is what Jeremiah is.[62]
- Jonah and Ecclesiastes no doubt reflect and interact with concrete historical contexts, but they do not directly refer to these contexts.

59. E. Ben Zvi, "The Voice and Role of a Counterfactual Memory in the Construction of Exile and Return," in *The Concept of Exile in Ancient Israel and Its Historical Contexts*, ed. E. Ben Zvi and C. Levin, BZAW 404 (Berlin: de Gruyter, 2010), 169.

60. B. M. Levinson, "Was Jeremiah Invented? The Relation of an Author to a Literary Tradition; A Response to Reinhard G. Kratz," in Najman and Schmid, *Jeremiah's Scriptures*, 217.

61. W. McKane, *A Critical and Exegetical Commentary on Jeremiah*, 2 vols., ICC (repr., London: T & T Clark, 2014), 1:l. McKane adds, "Small pieces of pre-existing text trigger exegesis or commentary" (lxxxiii).

62. T. W. Overholt, "'It Is Difficult to Read,'" *JSOT* 48 (1990): 52.

The material in the Jeremiah scroll interacts explicitly and concretely with Judah in the time from the 620s to the 560s.

- Jonah and Ecclesiastes do not seek to "explain the People of Israel's past against the background of God's presence, and in this way to interpret the present experience of God's people in order to shape its future" like the bulk of the First Testament.[63] The Jeremiah scroll does work in this way, and there is some tension between the idea of making the past the basis for looking to the future and the idea that the past in question is not at all a real past.
- More specifically, the story and message in the Jeremiah scroll concern Yahweh's involvement with the events of which it speaks, like Exodus, Joshua, and the Gospels. If the message and the narratives are simply fictional, the message deconstructs. It falls apart. Jeremiah's way of working suggests that the historical and the literary need to be held together.[64]
- Jeremiah, like Exodus, manifests points of connection with otherwise-known facts from Israel's world. References in the scroll to events and a comparison of names in the scroll with names known from seals at least suggest that a number of passages must have been written close to the time of the events described and written by people involved in those events.[65]

These considerations suggest that the Jeremiah scroll is more likely to be based on fact and to relate to an actual prophet called Jeremiah than to be purely a work of the imagination. But we may also note a paradoxical parallel with Jonah and Ecclesiastes. While one's view on whether these scrolls are fact or fiction makes a difference to an understanding of their significance for Judahite history, it may not make so much difference to interpreting the meaning of the scrolls in themselves or the message from God that they bring.

63. A. Berlejung, "Sources," in *T&T Clark Handbook of the Old Testament*, ed. J. C. Gertz et al. (London: T&T Clark, 2012), 3; cf. Z. T. Mohammad, "Jeremiah: The Prophet and the Concept; A Response to Reinhard G. Kratz," in Najman and Schmid, *Jeremiah's Scriptures*, 226.

64. R. R. Wilson, "Historicizing the Prophets: History and Literature in the Book of Jeremiah," in *On the Way to Nineveh: Studies in Honor of George M. Landes*, ed. S. L. Cook and S. C. Winter, American Schools of Oriental Research Books 4 (Atlanta: Scholars, 1999), 136–54.

65. L. L. Grabbe, "'The Lying Pen of the Scribes'?" in *Essays on Ancient Israel in Its Near Eastern Context: A Tribute to Nadav Na'aman*, ed. Y. Amit et al. (Winona Lake, IN: Eisenbrauns, 2006), 189–204; D. A. Glatt-Gilad, "The Personal Names in Jeremiah as a Source for the History of the Period," *Hebrew Studies* 41 (2000): 31–45; J. A. Dearman, "My Servants the Scribes," *JBL* 109 (1990): 403–21; Keel, *Jerusalem and the One God*, 119.

III. AUTHORSHIP AND DATE

In a literal, down-to-earth sense, the authors of the Jeremiah scroll are the curators who did their work in the period that came to an end in the 550s or 540s. But they would not have seen themselves as the scroll's authors. Their aim was to transmit the message of the real author, the prophet Jeremiah—poet, preacher, crusader, persuader.

A. JEREMIAH AS POET

The first half of the Jeremiah scroll is dominated by messages in poetic form. It suggests an image of Jeremiah chanting poetic messages as he stands in the temple courtyard, as perhaps did rival prophets. It was a natural way to preach. "The prophets were poets,"[66] and with prophets such as Jeremiah, "prophetic poets are most unpleasant people to have in the midst of any society."[67]

Formally, a distinctive feature of poetry in the First Testament is that it comprises sentences averaging four to eight words, divided into two parts. The second half usually complements the first half; the traditional but misleading term for this pattern is parallelism. I call the two parts cola; a sentence or line is then a bicolon, with two, three, or four words in each half. A Hebrew word has one stressed syllable (whereas in English, a word such as "individual" has two stressed syllables), so the number of words establishes the line's rhythm. In English translation, the lines are longer because Hebrew compounds words in a way that English does not. Hebrew can also hyphenate words, like English, so that two words count as one, and this convention increases the number of Hebrew words in a line but not the number of stresses.

A sequence of lines with a short second colon can convey shock or protest; the lines bring the listener up short (see, e.g., 13:18–20). Occasionally, other lines may not fit the pattern of two, three, or four stresses in each colon, and the Jeremiah scroll includes lines that are, for example, 4-1 (16:16), 5-2 (3:3; 4:17; 18:6), 5-3 (15:18), 5-4 (2:8; 16:18; 22:15), or 5-5 (10:11). Such exceptionally short or exceptionally long lines draw attention to themselves. In general, rhythm in prophets such as Jeremiah is looser than it is in the Psalms, Proverbs, and Job, where perhaps liturgical, pedagogical, and poetic/literary considerations generate a greater evenness. Perhaps prophets are more improvisational and less deliberate. I assume that they would chant their

---

66. R. P. Carroll, *From Chaos to Covenant*, 60.

67. J. Pixley, *Jeremiah*, Chalice Commentaries for Today (St. Louis, MO: Chalice, 2004), 49.

messages like rap artists, and the feasibility of such performance depends only on keeping the rhythm going, no matter how many words one uses.

Jeremiah is also fond of three-part lines (tricola), which draw attention to themselves by the unexpected third colon that brings a surprise. Tricola often begin or end a poem or a section of a poem. Further, Hebrew like English has conventions about word order. In English, the subject comes before the verb, whereas in Hebrew, the verb comes first; but Jeremiah likes varying the word order to make a point. Yet further, many of Jeremiah's lines are not self-contained—one will run into the next, and maybe into the next, by enjambment:

> I have been mindful about you, of your youthful commitment,
>   of your bridal love,
> Of your going after me in the wilderness,
>   in a country not sown. (2:2)

The rhythm of those two lines is 4-2 and 3-3 (or one could read the first as a 2-2-2 tricolon). They also illustrate a key feature of the substance of poetry: that it uses imagery to articulate what it has to say in a profound and communicative fashion (see "Theology Imaged," pp. 57–58). There are verses in the scroll that are rhythmic or pithy but lack imagery; it then becomes a judgment call whether one designates them as prosaic poetry or poetic prose (see e.g., 5:18–19; 9:23–26[22–25]; 10:11, 18; 11:17; 18:18; 25:33). If I err, it is on the side of being generous in designating verses as poetry.

In general, Jeremiah's poetic style is characterized by "staccato exclamations, rapid changes of scene and vantage point, frequent shifts of voice and discourse, use of invocation, plural command, and rhetorical question, a propensity for assonance and wordplay, a rich array of metaphors and similes from the natural landscapes and from human crafts and trades, and precision of metonymy and synecdoche."[68] It is succinct and terse; it is inclined to omit the little words that aid communication, such as the object marker and prepositions. It uses other forms of ellipsis that can produce jerkiness: it omits (say) a verb and expects the listeners to work out what the line means (see, e.g., 4:6; 12:9). Jeremiah's poetry is also fond of hyperbole (e.g., 5:1–6; 7:21–23; 20:8); while one needs to be wary of imposing figurative interpretation on extreme statements that are meant literally, indisputable examples of hyperbole (e.g., 40:11–12) are a reminder not to treat Jeremiah or his curators as if they are being extreme when they are not.

68. A. J. Rosenberg, "Jeremiah and Ezekiel," in *The Literary Guide to the Bible*, ed. R. Alter and F. Kermode (London: Collins, 1987), 185.

One verse in Jeremiah sometimes corresponds to one poetic line; 4:21 is an example. More often, a verse covers more lines: 4:20 comprises two, but 4:19 has three. Where necessary, I refer to a single line as, for example, 4:20a or 4:20b. If I need to refer to individual cola within those lines, I use Greek letters: I would refer to 4:20aα and 4:20aβ, then to 4:20bα and 4:20bβ. In a verse such as 4:19, with three bicola, I would refer to 4:19aα and 4:19aβ, then to 4:19bα and 4:19bβ, and finally to 40:19cα, and 4:19cβ.

B. JEREMIAH AS PREACHER

As Jeremiah was a priest, he could naturally be a teacher and preacher. Interwoven with his messages in poetry are messages in prose, and one can see why it should be so. Poetry communicates figuratively, indirectly, elliptically, obliquely, allegorically. It makes people scratch their heads. They have to work at understanding it. Prose is straightforward, direct, literal, prosaic, intelligible. It hits people between the eyes. They can hardly avoid understanding it.[69] Thus poetry and prose complement each other, like Jesus's parables and his ordinary teaching. Whereas the verse in the Jeremiah scroll is economical, the prose is prolix. Repetition is a natural feature of prose that is designed to persuade an audience, so that repetition in the written version of a sermon is as likely to indicate that an author is imitating oral style or incorporating a transcript of the preacher's actual address as it is to indicate that the text has been expanded and should be abbreviated.

Thus, the question whether Jeremiah himself could have communicated both in poetry and in prose is answered as soon as asked; if he wanted to communicate, he would naturally have used both. In wording and in substance, the poetry and the prose overlap, though in wording and in substance, they have distinctive features. In Jer 7, the slogan "Yahweh's palace/ temple" is a novelty, as is the warning about learning the lessons from the fate of Shiloh that recurs in the further prose story in Jer 26 and as are the references to the old "covenant" in Jer 11. There are further instructive features of Jer 11: it refers to a curse and to the response to the curse declaration, to being got out of the iron smelter, to the promise that Yahweh swore to the ancestors, and to "this very day" (11:2–5). These parallels distinguish the passage from other passages in Jeremiah, and in wording and substance such prose messages overlap with Moses's sermon-like address to Israel in Deu-

---

69. Cf. R. R. Wilson, "Poetry and Prose in the Book of Jeremiah," in *Ki Baruch Hu: Ancient Near Eastern, Biblical, and Judaic Studies in Honor of Baruch A. Levine*, ed. R. Chazan, William W. Hallo, and L. H. Schiffman (Winona Lake, IN: Eisenbrauns, 1999), 413–27.

teronomy, with other sermon-like addresses in Joshua through 2 Kings, and with further passages in 1 and 2 Kings. I like the observation that "Jeremiah was a self-proclaimed Deuteronomist."[70]

In Jeremiah, many poetic messages carry introductions such as "Yahweh's word came to me" (2:1), and some prose messages carry introductions such as "the message that came to Jeremiah from Yahweh" (7:1; 11:1). The former invite the hearers to take what follows as something Jeremiah is dictating— the result of the kind of process described in Jer 36. The latter invite the hearers to take what follows as mediated by a curator. The repetitiveness of 27:1–2, 4 ("This word came to Jeremiah from Yahweh. Yahweh said this to me. . . . Give them this order for their lords. Yahweh of Armies, the God of Israel, has said this: You will say this to your lords.") indicates that the curators are keen for us to receive their account as authentic to Jeremiah and authentic to Yahweh.

The difference in presentation and the comparison of prose with poetry and with Deuteronomy and 1 and 2 Kings again suggest something comparable to the nature of the Gospels. Their authors sometimes tell us exactly what Jesus said (translated into Greek). They sometimes tweak it to communicate his significance for their readers (some differences between Matthew, Mark, and Luke indicate examples). They sometimes put substantial presentations on Jesus's lips that they have devised on the basis of starting points in things he said and that expound the significance of what he said for their readers. I take it that something similar is true of the prose messages in Jeremiah. Sometimes the curators interpret by arranging: the five sections in 7:1–8:3 are of separate origin, but the curators have brought them together as Matthew and Luke bring together things Jesus said on different occasions to produce "the Sermon on the Mount" and "the Sermon on the Plain." Sometimes the curators may provide something close to a transcript or paraphrase or summary of what Jeremiah said. Sometimes they may tweak or develop it or translate it into other terminology. Sometimes they may turn a saying into a sermon. Sometimes they may start from their awareness of an aspect of Jeremiah's significance that he never articulated. One might attempt to put each prose message into the right category, though it would be speculative. I will go with the curators' account of their master.

---

70. M. Leuchter, *Josiah's Reform and Jeremiah's Scroll: Historical Calamity and Prophetic Response*, Hebrew Bible Monographs 6 (Sheffield: Sheffield Phoenix, 2006), 168; see further M. Leuchter, "The Medium and the Message," *ZAW* 126 (2014): 208–27. H. Weippert (*Die Prosareden des Jeremiabuches*, BZAW 132 [Berlin: de Gruyter, 1973]) argues that the "Deuteronomistic" prose could be Jeremianic. C. M. Maier (*Jeremia als Lehrer der Tora: Soziale Gebote des Deuteronomiums in Fortschreibungen des Jeremiabuches*, FRLANT 196 [Göttingen: Vandenhoeck & Ruprecht, 2002]) argues that in passages such as Jer 7; 11; 26, we have a portrait of Jeremiah that derives from the exilic or Persian period.

C. JEREMIAH AS CRUSADER

Modern readers may assume that prophets such as Jeremiah have one of two functions: either to promise the coming of the Messiah or to challenge people to put things right in their society. While Jeremiah does a little of each of these things, they do not describe more than five percent of his activity. His main focus lies on challenging people to be faithful to Yahweh and not to serve other deities and on declaring the consequences that will follow if they fail to do as he says. "The constant thread throughout the book is the apostasy of Judah."[71] The point is clear from the beginning of the scroll (see 1:4–19 and 2:1–37). The scroll is not organized chronologically or topically, and reading it can be confusing or wearying because it keeps coming back to the same issue, to a confrontation of Judah in connection with the way it relates to Yahweh, the way it worships, the way it prays, and the way its people relate to one another—which are all interconnected. The burden of the critique might vary in different decades—for instance, before Josiah's reformation and during the reigns of later kings. It might vary according to whether Jeremiah is speaking about the Jerusalem temple or other shrines and whether he is addressing official religion or family religion. But critique dominates.

One central critique is that Judahites serve other gods as well as Yahweh, making offerings to them and seeking their blessing. These other gods include the traditional gods of the region, the *bəʿālîm* ("Masters"), who are believed to facilitate the natural processes whereby crops grow and women have children. Judahites also consult the deities whose beings lie behind the planets—gods acknowledged by Assyria and Babylon as entities that decide earthly events in political and family life. In eighth-century Israel, the First Testament associates the worship of a variety of deities with Ephraim more than Judah, but in the seventh century, in Manasseh's day, it associates it also with Judah. Although turning to Yahweh and to no one else was basic to Yahweh's relation to Israel from the time of the exodus, both the First Testament and archaeological discoveries suggest that most Judahites did not realize it, much as vast numbers of people in "Christian" countries have no clue about Christian faith.

People can also be engaged in turning to Yahweh himself in ways that clash with who Yahweh is. The most horrific example is their willingness to sacrifice children to Yahweh. A more characteristic feature of their spirituality is their finding it helpful to make images of Yahweh as aids to worship. People's worship that is formally offered to a deity called Yahweh may thus imply such a distorted understanding of Yahweh that it is tantamount to worshiping a different deity. This ambiguity can make it difficult to be sure about the object

---

71. P. A. Viviano, "Characterizing Jeremiah," *WW* 22 (2002): 365.

of Jeremiah's critique—whether he refers to people's conscious recourse to other deities or to worship that they thought they were offering to Yahweh.

Josiah's reformation cleaned up aspects of Judahite religion, but Judah reverted to pre-Josianic practice after his death, which hints that not everyone agreed with his reforming activity—including members of his family, to judge from the Jeremiah scroll's comments about the policies of his sons Jehoiakim and Zedekiah. Taken literalistically, Jeremiah implies that they returned completely to Manassite practices. But 2 Kings does not report a reversion to overt worship of other deities, so Jeremiah's polemic may indeed presuppose that Judahites thought they were turning to Yahweh but were deceiving themselves.

A further aspect to Jeremiah's crusading is that people can be engaging in worship and prayer that recognizes Yahweh but be conducting their national and communal life in a way that clashes not only with who Yahweh is but also with his expectations of that communal life. So worship has its proper place in their spirituality, but outside worship they live with false attitudes toward property, sex, truthfulness, and so on. Their political policies may presuppose that they must take responsibility for their future by making alliances with other countries, whereas a prophet such as Jeremiah thinks that trust in Yahweh is key to political policies.

Jeremiah's crusade has the demanding and challenging aim of getting the community to turn from the various aspects of this failure to live an authentic life with Yahweh.

D. JEREMIAH AS PERSUADER

One could get the impression from the scroll's opening message in 2:1–37 (and other chapters) that Jeremiah simply declares that the pouring out of Yahweh's wrath is inevitable because of Judah's ingrained waywardness, but in 3:1–4:4 (and other chapters), Jeremiah raises the question whether Judah is going to turn back to Yahweh, with the implication that it would make a difference to Judah's fate. And what is the point of prophesying if it cannot? Is it simply to leave people without excuse, and encourage the small number of the faithful?[72] Is it to enable people after 587 to understand why the city's fall had to happen and to urge them not to make the mistake that the previous generation made (see "Unity of Composition," pp. 10–11)? The directness of Jeremiah's challenge to his contemporaries suggests that those functions of his preaching did not come first. Even when he is declaring that they are incorrigible and that calamity is inevitable, he is aiming to get them to prove

72. Calvin, *Jeremiah*, 1:454.

him wrong. He knows that Yahweh is still committed to his people; there is little difference between Jeremiah's and Paul's convictions about Yahweh's commitment to Israel.[73] Jeremiah is involved in persuasion.

Metaphor is essential to Jeremiah's work as a theologian who wants to articulate for himself the nature of Yahweh and his relationship with his people. Imagery makes it possible to think and say things that we could not otherwise think or say. But the pragmatic function of imagery is at least as important for Jeremiah as the theological one: "A problem which Jeremiah shared with all the prophets was that of attracting the audience's attention."[74] Talking in terms that come from the human experience of marriage, family, work, and politics makes it possible to bring home the nature of the relationship between Yahweh and Judah, of what Yahweh has done, of what Judah needs to do, and of the danger it risks by not doing it. Yahweh has married two sisters, Jeremiah suggests, and both are unfaithful (Jer 3). It is an aspect of "the prophets' rhetoric of horror designed to terrify their audience into reform."[75] Poetic form and the use of imagery are aspects of Jeremiah's rhetoric, and "biblical prophets are masters of rhetoric. They craft their message to persuade their audience of its truth and to inspire them to reform their behavior."[76] To this end, Jeremiah is forceful and unrelenting, shocking and incendiary.[77]

Like "ideology," "rhetoric" can be a pejorative word. It can suggest high-flown language to make a case that would not be compelling if put in plain terms, or it can suggest reference to Aristotelian rhetorical theory.[78] But regarding 14:21, Calvin says, "The Prophet joined together two verbs, not so much for the sake of ornament as rhetoricians do, as for the purpose of expressing the intenseness of his concern and anxiety."[79] In a broader sense of rhetoric, expressing his concern in this way is an aspect of his using language to bring home the truth of his case and to persuade people to make the response that the truth deserves.

Jeremiah does use classical rhetorical devices such as metonymy and synecdoche: people's houses are full of duplicity—that is, of the fruits of duplicity (5:27); their gateways are fading away—that is, their houses are fading away

---

73. Contrast M. Reasoner, "The Redemptive Inversions of Jeremiah in Romans 9–11," *Bib* 95 (2014): 388–404.

74. J. L. Berquist, "Prophetic Legitimation in Jeremiah," *VT* 39 (1989): 129.

75. A. Kalmanofsky, "The Dangerous Sisters of Jeremiah and Ezekiel," *JBL* 130 (2011): 300.

76. A. Kalmanofsky, *Terror All Around: The Rhetoric of Horror in the Book of Jeremiah*, LHBOTS 390 (London: T&T Clark, 2008), 1.

77. Viviano, "Characterizing Jeremiah," 366.

78. So S. J. Choi, "A New Heart to Know the Lord: Rhetorical Analysis of Jeremiah 21–24" (PhD diss., University of Gloucestershire, 2001).

79. Calvin, *Jeremiah*, 2:253.

(14:2). He uses catachresis or transferred epithets: a quiver is like a grave opened up—that is, its arrows bring death (5:16). He uses anaphora, purposeful repetition; an example is the repetition of the word duplicity (9:6[5]). He uses paronomasia (that is, "wordplay," but his wordplay is deadly serious), juxtaposing similar words or suggesting relationships between homonyms and thus making connections or underlining them (e.g., 1:10, 12). A related phenomenon is the use of a word such as *rā'â* that can refer both to the bad things that people do and to the bad things that happen to them. English translations use words such as "wicked" and words such as "trouble," but Jeremiah suggests the common (though not invariable) link between the two whereby bad actions can lead to bad consequences. I translate by expressions such as "dire action" and "dire experience."

The entirety of the Jeremiah scroll is rhetoric—not in a bad way, in order to manipulate, but in order to move. Jeremiah's rhetoric is not a way of getting people to avoid thinking but a way of getting them to think.

E. JEREMIAH AND HIS CURATORS AS ANTHOLOGISTS

Jeremiah's poetic messages are typically bite-sized, occupying a couple or a dozen or a score of lines. It is perhaps no coincidence that prophets in the present day, in my experience, bring bite-sized messages. If they are wise, they shut up after their soundbite; the more they go on, the more their message gets diluted and the more one senses their words come from them rather than God. Maybe this phenomenon provokes reflection on the relationship between poetry and prose in Jeremiah, though if so, one would need to add that continuing in one's own prose words need not exclude the possibility that God affirms the prose development as well as the poetic nucleus.

But Jeremiah and his curators have handed down his poetic messages linked to one another in chains. A chain may comprise a series of messages on the same subject, possibly announced by a heading such as "Regarding the household of the king of Judah" or "Regarding the prophets" or "Regarding Egypt" (21:11; 23:9; 46:2). Or the scroll may leave the readers to work out the link between different poems.

A chapter in a modern Bible will typically contain four to six poetic messages. The obvious indicators that we are moving to a different message are phrases such as "listen to Yahweh's word" or "Yahweh has said this" or "Yahweh's affirmation," which can mark a beginning or end. These phrases sometimes provided clues to the scribes who placed section markers in the Hebrew text and to the medieval scholars who added the chapter divisions in printed Bibles. But one needs to keep in mind that Jeremiah also uses these phrases resumptively in the middle of messages and uses them as attention-getters to emphasize a point. He can begin or end a message with no opening or closing phrase. One therefore also looks for changes of addressee, focus, and imagery that may mark a transition to a new message. The first and last sections of poetry in Jeremiah (Jer 2 and 50–51) provide spectacular examples of the scroll's combining messages to generate a comprehensive whole,[80] while they also provoke questions about the chapters' structure and components and compel interpreters to recognize the ambiguity of the indicators that they offer. Jeremiah 2 thus illustrates the use of the markers we have just referred to, which can indicate transition points within the chapter or points of emphasis:

- "Yahweh's message came to me" does mark the beginning of the whole chapter.
- "Yahweh has said this" suggests the beginning of a message.
- "Yahweh's affirmation," emphasizing the importance of what precedes, can mark the end of a message, but it can also have resumptive significance within one.
- "Listen to Yahweh's message" can introduce a section, but it can also be a resumptive exhortation.
- *Lākēn* commonly means "therefore" and suggests the approaching end of a section, but it can mean "that's why" or "thus" and have resumptive significance.
- *Kî* usually means "because" and thus suggests continuity with what precedes, but it can be asseverative, meaning "indeed," and open a section.
- "So now" or "now" (*wə'attâ* or *'attâ*) suggests the beginning or conclusion of a section.
- A tricolon commonly conveys emphasis and can mark the beginning or end of a section but can also convey emphasis within one (there are four tricola in four verses in vv. 19–22).
- The recurrence of words or of similar words can indicate continuity within a section or linkage between separate sections.
- A change in the gender or number of addressees (masculine/feminine, singular/plural) can indicate transitions between sections.
- MT itself provides section markers after 2:3, 28; 3:5.

The way themes and arguments develop in the chapter has to be set alongside the presence of such markers in identifying how the chapter may divide, and analysis of structure may turn out to be less objective than one might

---

80. In his study of Jer 2, H. L. Ellison also compares Isa 1 ("The Prophecy of Jeremiah," *EvQ* 32 [1960]: 4).

hope. Interpreters may thus analyze a chapter in varying but complementary ways—as interpreters of a landscape or portrait or musical composition may offer varying but complementary analyses of it.

IV. PLACE OF ORIGIN, OCCASION, AND DESTINATION

After the fall of Jerusalem, Jeremiah found his way to Mizpah and in due course to northern Egypt (40:1–43:13). There is no mystery about the scroll's not recording his death; the First Testament records the killing of various prophets, which issues from their work or is a sign of their killers' attitude to Yahweh's message, but it does not record the natural death of any prophets. When Jeremiah reached Egypt, he would have been about sixty, and we may infer that he died a natural death there. Were his message and story preserved there or somewhere else? Where did they become the Jeremiah scroll?

It makes sense to think of the two versions of the scroll, MT and LXX, as originating in different places. The scroll refers to Judahite communities in Babylon and Egypt and also to Judahites who took temporary refuge in places such as Ammon and among people in Samaria who identified themselves with Judahite faith. Oddly, the scroll implies that all the Judahite communities— in Babylon, Egypt, and Judah itself—were small, which might make them all seem unlikely locations for generating the scroll. It gives small numbers regarding the people forced to migrate to Babylon (52:28–30), it suggests hyperbolically that there was no one left in Judah, and it declares a death knell for the community in Egypt. Yet we know that the community in Babylon included as much of the Judahite leadership as the Babylonians could round up (in 597 and 587) and that much of the energy that issued in the rebuilding of the community in Jerusalem came from there (see Ezra, Haggai, Zechariah). Archaeological investigations suggest that Judah was not "an empty land" after the deportations—no doubt partly because refugees drifted back from places such as Ammon—and the composition of the poems in Lamentations suggests religious and theological life there. Whereas Jeremiah's writing off the communities in Egypt as well as Judah has been taken as an indication that "Jeremiah was *more frequently wrong than right*,"[81] the existence of the story and messages in 40:1–44:30 suggests that we should not be literalistic in interpreting Jeremiah's warnings in those chapters any more than in others; certainly the Judahite community in Egypt subsequently flourished.[82]

---

81. R. P. Carroll, "Century's End: Jeremiah Studies at the Beginning of the Third Millennium," *Currents in Research: Biblical Studies* 8 (2000): 22, his emphasis.
82. On the mythical nature of the empty land, see, e.g., D. Rom-Shiloni, "What Is 'Persian' in Late Sixth Century B. C. E. Prophetic Literature? Case Studies and Criteria," in

A promise such as the one in 7:7 implicitly favors people living in Judah,[83] but it need not have arisen or been preserved there. Conversely, when Jer 24 describes the people in Jerusalem who escaped the 597 exile as the bad figs (the figs with no future) and the 597 exiles as the good figs (the figs with a future), it would again be unwise to be literalistic in interpreting a comment that was devised to give a jolt to the people in Judah. In 587, the people who were the objects of that threat (the confident, prominent Jerusalemites) did have their comeuppance, and "while 24:8–10 promotes a perspective that the people left in the land are not the recipient of God's promises, this visionary word was related to the first deportation in 597 BC and times can change things."[84] Ezekiel 8 likewise attacks the Jerusalem community between 597 and 587 but hardly in itself provides a basis for inferring the "disenfranchisement" of people who remained in Judah after 587, though no doubt it could be used that way.[85] Like Jer 24, Ezek 8 had a function in its context: to warn the 597 exiles against thinking that Yahweh's action against Jerusalem was finished and they would soon be going home. The prayers in Lamentations suggest a different theology and spirituality in Judah after 587 from the one that Jeremiah and Ezekiel attack before 587. Conversely, Jeremiah also attacks the 597 exiles in Jer 29. Yahweh's treating Babylon and its king as his servant does not mean Jeremiah is pro-Babylonian or favors the Judahites who have been exiled to Babylon.[86]

The observation that "MT [of Jeremiah] is repeatedly oriented toward the Babylonian experience"[87] does not emerge from the text. It is hard to find significant evidence that a recension of the Jeremiah scroll aimed to make the exiles in Babylon "the sole standard-bearer of Yahweh's community in the future and to write off any participation in it by Judaeans who had emigrated to Egypt." Such an aim is a "hidden exegetical content which has to be excavated; it is not given by the text and there is nothing explicit in the text which would lead us to conclude that the interests and claims of the

---

Discerning Criteria for Dating Persian Period Texts, ed. R. J. Bautch and M. Lackowski, FAT 2/101 (Tübingen: Mohr Siebeck, 2019), 32–41.

83. M. Leuchter, "Jeremiah," in *The Oxford Handbook of the Prophets*, ed. C. J. Sharp (Oxford: Oxford University Press, 2016), 179.

84. T. E. Fretheim, *Jeremiah*, Smith and Helwys Bible Commentary (Macon, GA: Smith and Helwys, 2002), 540.

85. So G. L. Keown, P. J. Scalise, and T. G. Smothers, *Jeremiah 26–52*, WBC 27 (Dallas: Word, 1995), 263.

86. See, e.g., L. Stulman, "Insiders and Outsiders in the Book of Jeremiah," *JSOT* 66 (1995): 71–72.

87. M. Leuchter, "Remembering Jeremiah in the Persian Period," in *Remembering Biblical Figures in the Late Persian and Early Hellenistic Periods: Social Memory and Imagination*, ed. D. V. Edelman and E. Ben Zvi (Oxford: Oxford University Press, 2013), 394.

Babylonian *Gôlāh* [exile community] are served by it."[88] The text does not provide a basis for seeing the Babylonian community as the dynamic context in which the message and story of Jeremiah were preserved, developed, and curated.[89] While it is possible to imagine someone taking the raw material for the Jeremiah scroll to Babylon and its being developed there, even without that assumption about the aim of the work, this understanding seems unnecessarily complicated. The more obvious view is that Egypt was one location of the process and Judah the other. And if the older version is the one translated into Greek (the more common scholarly view), it would follow that this version had its origin in Egypt—the home of the LXX, where as far as we know Jeremiah and Baruch ended up—while the background of the MT version was Judah.[90] But all such possibilities are simply possibilities.

V. CANONICITY

Jeremiah claimed to speak a message from Yahweh and challenged people to respond to it as such. Few people before 587 did so; I have speculated that after the fall of Jerusalem, more did. The eventual wider recognition that he brought such a message and that it had purchase for a time long after his day made it influential on an ongoing basis for the community. The authority and canonicity of the Jeremiah scroll follow from the recognition that it records a message from Yahweh that lays down permanent expectations and offers long-standing insights.

A. THE SCROLL AS MESSAGE FROM YAHWEH

The word "message" points to a classic model for understanding a prophet's position, role, and authority. Prophets commonly introduce their words by saying, "Yahweh has said this," which corresponds to the way a messenger might introduce a message from a king (e.g., Isa 36:4, 14, 16). The prophet is Yahweh's messenger bringing a word from the great King. The word has

---

88. McKane, *Jeremiah*, 2:1091–92.

89. For the argument that an important level of tradition in the scroll is a redaction in Babylon, see, e.g., K.-F. Pohlmann, *Studien zum Jeremiabuch: Ein Beitrag zur Frage nach der Entstehung des Jeremiabuches*, FRLANT 118 (Göttingen: Vandenhoeck & Ruprecht, 1978); C. R. Seitz, *Theology in Conflict: Reactions to the Exile in the Book of Jeremiah*, BZAW 176 (Berlin: de Gruyter, 1989).

90. On various possibilities, see, e.g., H.-J. Stipp, *Studien zum Jeremiabuch: Text und Redaktion*, FAT 96 (Tübingen: Mohr Siebeck, 2015), 325–47. Stipp suggests that the first half was composed in Judah, the second half in Babylon.

to be received as such. A messenger represents the king in a strong sense, speaking in his master's name, using the king's "I" as if he is the king, though he can switch between this form of speech and a more literal reference to his master as "he" (e.g., 2 Kgs 18:20, 23). Likewise, Jeremiah can move between "I, Yahweh" and "he, Yahweh" or "Yahweh's affirmation" (e.g., 2:1–3). He can also move between addressing Judah or Jerusalem as "you" and speaking of them as "they" or "it." His model for understanding his position can be himself as a human being talking with Yahweh (in which case Judah and Jerusalem are "they" or "it") or it can be him speaking to them "as" Yahweh (in which case Judah and Jerusalem are "you"). The rhetorical effect of the two ways of speaking (the way they have an effect on Judah and Jerusalem) will then vary, but the claim is the same.

Sometimes one may not be able to tell the difference between Jeremiah speaking and Yahweh speaking. As Jer 5 unfolds, at some points the material makes a move from Jeremiah speaking to Yahweh speaking, but sometimes Jeremiah does not make the point of transition clear. One is tempted to try to identify the speaker each time, but Jeremiah's failure to mark the transitions is not simply a mistake; whether Yahweh or Jeremiah is speaking doesn't make any difference. It is always Jeremiah speaking, even when he speaks as Yahweh, and it is always Yahweh's message, even when Jeremiah speaks in his own name. Like other prophets, Jeremiah is also sometimes not specific about who is addressed or about other transitions in accounts of things people say. It may be because he is not sure or because it keeps the audience on their toes or because the content is the important thing.

The scroll's introduction sets Jeremiah as Yahweh's messenger in the context of a tumultuous half-century in the life of Judah. But its opening words ("the words of Jeremiah") raise further questions in connection with what directly follows, which indicates that the scroll comprises more than Jeremiah's words. It tells the story of Yahweh's commissioning him, which includes his answering Yahweh back. So the phrase "the words of Jeremiah" needs interpreting loosely. A further distinctive feature of the scroll is the number of stories about Jeremiah that it tells. Jeremiah's delivering his message was integral to the message itself. He embodied the straightness and care of Yahweh that were expressed in his words.

Even when Jeremiah speaks most explicitly in his own name and about himself, he is not sharing entries from a spiritual journal that is written for his own sake. The Jeremiah scroll is an account of his message (1:1–3), not a diary of his experiences or personal reflections that he formulates to help him understand what is going on. If he kept such a journal and includes excerpts from it in the scroll, he does so because they form part of Yahweh's message to Judah and Jerusalem. His protests, too, are part of a scroll designed to convey a message for his people, not simply to record his personal agonizing. Nor is there any indication that Jeremiah might have received a divine rebuke for his protests (cf. Isa 45:9; Rom 9:20–21).[91] Readers of the prayers and the protests in the scroll have to ask, how is this account of something from Jeremiah's experience designed to function as Yahweh's message? In 3:6–10, he reports a prose conversation in which Yahweh shares a reflection, which communicates with the audience in yet another way.

B. THE SCROLL AND THE SCRIPTURES

In due course, different Jewish communities came to recognize the importance of the collection of Jeremiah's messages and the stories about him and to pay serious attention to it. The fall of Babylon in 539, the ascendancy of the Persians, the freedom of Judahites to go home to rebuild the temple, the arrival of the Greeks, and the troubles of the second century are beyond the scroll's narrative horizon. But we know that people paid attention to the Jeremiah scroll during the Second Temple period.[92] Second Chronicles ends with a quotation from Jeremiah, and Ezra begins with the same quotation, witnessing to creative interest in the scroll's significance for events in the life of the Judahite community. Daniel 9 refers back to Jeremiah, engaging in greater hermeneutical creativity. While there are many cross allusions and virtual quotations within the Law, the Prophets, and the Writings—the Torah, Neviim, and Ketuvim; hence Tanak—the Jeremiah scroll is the only work within the Tanak that is explicitly quoted within the Tanak itself. In due course, anonymous Jews translated Jeremiah into Greek, revising it slightly or considerably, and created the letters of Baruch and Jeremiah preserved in the LXX. Qumran scribes copied it and created more "Jeremianic" writings.[93]

91. J. A. Thompson, *Jeremiah*, 222.

92. See, e.g., C. Wolff, *Jeremia in Frühjudentum und Urchristentum*, Texte und Untersuchungen zur Geschichte der altchristlichen Literatur 118 (Berlin: Akademie, 1976); A. H. W. Curtis and T. Römer, eds., *The Book of Jeremiah and Its Reception*, BETL 128 (Leuven: Peeters, 1997); J. Barton, "Jeremiah in the Apocrypha and Pseudepigrapha," in *Troubling Jeremiah*, ed. A. R. P. Diamond, K. M. O'Connor, and L. Stulman, JSOTSup 260 (Sheffield: Sheffield Academic, 1999), 306–17; Leuchter, "Remembering Jeremiah"; L. G. Perdue, "Baruch among the Sages," in Goldingay, *Uprooting and Planting*, 260–90; S. A. Adams, "Jeremiah in the Old Testament Apocrypha and Pseudepigrapha," in Lundbom, Evans, and B. A. Anderson, *Jeremiah*, 359–78; J. H. Newman, *Before the Bible: The Liturgical Body and the Formation of Scriptures in Early Judaism* (Oxford: Oxford University Press, 2018), 53–74; Najman and Schmid, *Jeremiah's Scriptures*.

93. See, e.g., E. Tov, "The Jeremiah Scrolls from Qumran," *Revue de Qumran* 14 (1989): 189–206; G. J. Brooke, "The Book of Jeremiah and Its Reception in the Qumran Scrolls," in Curtis and Römer, *Jeremiah and Its Reception*, 183–206; M. S. Moore, "The Laments in Jeremiah and 1QH," in Goldingay, *Uprooting and Planting*, 228–52; R. Goldstein, "Jeremiah between Destruction and Exile," *Dead Sea Discoveries* 20 (2013): 433–51; K. Davis,

Jesus and his contemporaries read it (Mark 11:17; Matt 16:14), Paul quoted from it (1 Cor 1:31; 2 Cor 10:17; perhaps 1 Cor 2:9; 2 Cor 6:17), Matthew read it (Matt 2:17), Luke takes up the theme of the persecuted prophet, and Hebrews quotes it (8:8–12; 10:16–17).[94]

One could say that recognizing the Jeremiah scroll in this way indicates that it has canonical status, though the word "canon" means different things in different contexts. The Greek word *kanōn* means a rule—something by which to measure things and thus to resolve disagreements. When the church came to apply this word to the Scriptures, it referred to a defined list of works, though not necessarily a closed or unalterable one. To ask whether the scroll is part of such a canon in the Second Temple period is anachronistic. We know virtually nothing about the process whereby a defined canon of Scriptures came into being or about anybody who decided which documents were in and which were out.[95] Once there is a canon, Jeremiah is part of it, but we don't know anything of how the scroll came to be recognized in this way. It was presumably among the Prophets to whom Jesus Ben Sira refers about 200 BC when he mentions "the Prophets" in the prologue to his teaching about "Wisdom."

In MT manuscripts, Jeremiah follows Isaiah, though *B. Baba Batra* 14b notes the logic of the order Jeremiah, Ezekiel, Isaiah:

> The Scholars taught: The order of the Prophets is Joshua and Judges, Samuel and Kings, Jeremiah and Ezekiel, and Isaiah and the Twelve. . . . Now: Isaiah was before Jeremiah and Ezekiel; Isaiah should come first. But Kings ends with the destruction, and Jeremiah is all of it the destruction, and Ezekiel begins with the destruction but ends with the comfort, and Isaiah is all of it the comfort. We join the destruction to the destruction and the comfort to the comfort.

The Cave 4 Apocryphon of Jeremiah and the Qumran Jeremianic Traditions, STDJ 111 (Leiden: Brill, 2014); A. Lange, "Texts of Jeremiah in the Qumran Library," in Lundbom, Evans, and B. A. Anderson, *Jeremiah*, 280–302.

94. See, e.g., C. A. Evans, "Jeremiah in Jesus and the New Testament," in Lundbom, Evans, and B. A. Anderson, *Jeremiah*, 303–19 (this volume also includes studies of the Tg, the Latin translations, and the Peshitta); J. Frey, "The Reception of Jeremiah and the Impact of Jeremianic Traditions in the New Testament," in Najman and Schmid, *Jeremiah's Scriptures*, 499–522; J. D. Hays, "The Persecuted Prophet and Judgment on Jerusalem: The Use of LXX Jeremiah in the Gospel of Luke," *BBR* 25 (2015): 453–73; M. Knowles, *Jeremiah in Matthew's Gospel: The Rejected Prophet Motif in Matthean Redaction*, JSNTSup 68 (Sheffield JSOT Press, 1993); J. W. Mazurel, "Citations from the Book of Jeremiah in the New Testament," in Kessler, *Reading Jeremiah*, 181–89; A. Rakotoharintsifa, "Jérémieh en action à Corinthe," in Curtis and Römer, *Jeremiah and Its Reception*, 207–16; M. F. Whitters, "Jesus in the Footsteps of Jeremiah," *CBQ* 68 (2006): 229–47.

95. For a review of the evidence, see, e.g., T. H. Lim, *The Formation of the Jewish Canon* (New Haven: Yale University Press, 2013).

C. THE JEREMIAH SCROLL IN THE CANONS OF JUDAISM AND OF THE CHURCH

The communities of people who came to believe in Jesus accepted the Tanak as one aspect of their being in origin part of Judaism or an offshoot of Judaism, though that statement conceals both some looseness and some greater precision.

One aspect of the looseness is that while the Scriptures to which the New Testament refers were at least roughly the same as the works that comprise the Tanak, we do not have evidence that the edges of those Scriptures were set in New Testament times. We do know that Jeremiah would have counted among them; it is quoted in Matt 2:17-18 in a way analogous to the quotations in Chronicles, Ezra, and Daniel. Another aspect of the looseness is that Christian congregations came to work with a broader collection of writings than the Tanak—one that included other works such as Wisdom and Tobit. More significantly for our present concern, its Jeremianic materials were both shorter and longer than the Jeremiah scroll in the Tanak. They were shorter in that this longer canon comprised works as they had been translated into Greek or had been written in Greek, and Greek Jeremiah is shorter than Hebrew Jeremiah (see "The Hebrew Text," pp. 43-46). They were longer in that they included Baruch and the Letter of Jeremiah.

The greater precision relates to these differences. Many later Christian communities were careful to define the contents of the canon of Scripture. Thus the Anglican Thirty-Nine Articles lists the books that comprise the Tanak (but in the LXX's order) then lists the "other books" such as Baruch (implicitly including the Letter of Jeremiah) as works read for edification but not to establish doctrine.

Readings in synagogue worship include one from the Torah (they cover the whole over a year) and one from the Prophets, including Jeremiah (from which they include selections over a year). The Tanak is among a variety of canonical works in Judaism, along with the Mishnah, the Talmud, and the teaching of certain rabbis.

Paradoxically, this precision coexisted with another form of looseness. As Jewish communities set the Tanak in the context of the Mishnah, the Talmud, and other works, Christian communities set "the Old Testament" (as they eventually came to call it) in the context of explicitly Christian writings, "the New Testament." Christian communities read only tiny sections of a scroll such as Jeremiah in worship and hear few sermons on Jeremiah, and it has little influence on Christian theology, ethics, or spirituality. Occasionally, Christians implicitly deny Jeremiah's canonical status—for instance, by questioning its portrayal of God or of prayer or of women or of attitudes to other nations. More often, they simply ignore Jeremiah and deny its canonical status in that way. This fact is especially regrettable in a context where the declining church in the United States is in a similar position to Judah in the late 600s and the declined church in Europe and elsewhere in the West is in a similar position to Judah after 587, while the growing church in Asia, Africa, and Latin America might be wise to see whether it can avoid going the way of these two. While Second Temple Judaism, the Qumran community, the New Testament, and the church fathers were not as interested in Jeremiah as they were in Isaiah or Daniel, the scroll's finding a place in the Torah, the Prophets, and the Writings implies that it presents testimonies, messages, and stories that are God-breathed (2 Tim 3:16) in the sense that they are full of illumination for people living way after the time and the context in which they came into being. But we miss the fact that in various senses, Jeremiah is "a spokesman 'out of time.'"[96]

VI. THE HEBREW TEXT

The commentary in this volume follows the version of Jeremiah in the Leningrad (St. Petersburg) Codex of the MT, to which I refer as MT[L]. It is this text that appears in *BHS* and NJPS. It dates from about AD 1009. Its copyist was Samuel ben Jacob; he writes in one of its colophons, "With all my heart I did my work; my heart rejoices in my lot."[97] Also from the ninth to eleventh centuries but less complete are the Aleppo Codex (which includes nearly all of Jeremiah and appears in HUBP), the Cairo Codex of the Prophets, the Petropolitan Codex of the Latter Prophets, and Sassoon Codex 1053.[98] Our oldest copies of MT thus come from fifteen hundred years after Jeremiah's day, and as is the case with any ancient document, our oldest copies of the Jeremiah scroll can hardly represent the original form of it. In order to get closer to that original form, one investigates other versions than MT.

A. THE TWO VERSIONS

Of the two major versions of the scroll, one in Hebrew preserved in MT and one translated into Greek and preserved in LXX, the Greek version is more

---

96. W. L. Holladay, *Jeremiah: Spokesman out of Time* (Philadelphia: United Church Press, 1974), 140.

97. See the Leningrad Codex at the Internet Archive, https://archive.org/details/Leningrad_Codex.

98. See E. Würthwein, *The Text of the Old Testament*, 3rd ed. (Grand Rapids: Eerdmans, 2014), 39–43. I have not had access to the Sassoon Codex 1053. The Cairo Codex of the Prophets is reproduced in D. S. Lowinger, *Cairo Codex of the Bible* (Jerusalem: Makor, 1971).

than 10 percent shorter than the Hebrew version, though the continuation of the LXX Jeremianic material in Baruch and the Letter of Jeremiah (not to say Lamentations) makes up for that shortfall. There is a series of possible ways of understanding the relationship between the two versions, and all have their advocates: that MT is an expanded edition of the Hebrew underlying LXX (the most common view), that LXX represents an abbreviated edition of the Hebrew underlying MT,[99] that LXX is sometimes older but sometimes represents abbreviation, or that both are independent recensions of an earlier text that we no longer have—which is my own working assumption.[100] Apart from length, the most substantial difference between MT and LXX is that

99. Jerome has a nice comment on what he sees as a well-intentioned LXX omission: "But what about the Hebrew truth?" (Jerome, *Commentary on Jeremiah*, trans. Michael Graves, Ancient Christian Texts [Downers Grove, IL: InterVarsity, 2011], 173). He has another comment on 17:1–4: "I do not know why the LXX translators omitted this passage, unless perhaps they were sparing their people. . . . And there are many other passages of this kind, but to discuss all of them would require not just a book but books" (*Jeremiah*, 104; I write with admiration and gratitude for the work of Jerome—Hebraist, translator, and commentator—who died in Bethlehem while writing his commentary). Augustine has a neat answer to Jerome's implicit question, at a different level: "If anything is in the Hebrew text but not in that of the seventy translators, it is something that the Spirit of God did not choose to say through the latter"—and the converse (*City of God* 18.43).

100. The classic studies are J. G. Janzen, *Studies in the Text of Jeremiah*, HSM 6 (Cambridge, MA: Harvard University Press, 1973) and such works of E. Tov as "Some Aspects of the Textual and Literary History of the Book of Jeremiah," in *Le livre de Jérémie: Le prophète et son milieu. Les oracles et leur transmission*, ed. P.-M. Bogaert, 2nd ed., BETL 54 (Leuven: Peeters, 1997), 145–67, 430; "The Literary History of the Book of Jeremiah in the Light of Its Textual History," in *Empirical Models for Biblical Criticism*, ed. J. H. Tigay (Philadelphia: University of Pennsylvania Press, 1985), 211–37. More recent studies and surveys of the question include R. P. Carroll, "Surplus Meaning and the Conflict of Interpretations: A Dodecade of Jeremiah Studies (1984–1995)," *Currents in Research: Biblical Studies* 4 (1996): 124–25; R. P. Carroll, *Jeremiah*, OTL, 50–55; G. Fischer, "Mysteries of the Book of Jeremiah," in Najman and Schmid, *Jeremiah's Scriptures*, 166–78; Y. Goldman, *Prophétie et royauté au retour de l'exil: Les origines littéraires de la forme massoretique du livre de Jérémie*, OBO 118 (Göttingen: Vandenhoeck & Ruprecht, 1992); J. R. Lundbom, "Haplography in the Hebrew *Vorlage* of LXX Jeremiah," *Hebrew Studies* 46 (2005): 301–20; Lundbom, *Jeremiah 1–20*, 57–62; McKane, *Jeremiah*, 1:xv–xxxi; R. F. Person, "A Rolling Corpus and Oral Tradition: A Not-So-Literate Solution to a Highly Literate Problem," in Diamond, K. M O'Connor, and Stulman, *Troubling Jeremiah*, 263–71; C. J. Sharp, "'Take Another Scroll and Write': A Study of the LXX and the MT of Jeremiah's Oracles against Egypt and Babylon," *VT* 47 (1997): 487–516; A. G. Shead, "The Text of Jeremiah," in Lundbom, Evans, and B. A. Anderson, *Book of Jeremiah*, 255–79; H.-J. Stipp, *Das masoretische und alexandrinische Sondergut des Jeremiabuches*, OBO 136 (Göttingen: Vandenhoeck & Ruprecht, 1994); L. Stulman, "Some Theological and Lexical Differences between the Old Greek and the MT of the Jeremiah Prose Discourses," *Hebrew Studies* 25 (1984): 18–23; M. A. Sweeney, *Form and Intertextuality in Prophetic and Apocalyptic Literature*, FAT 45 (Tübingen: Mohr Siebeck, 2005), 65–77;

MT has the block of messages about foreign nations near the end of the scroll, immediately before the final chapter, whereas LXX locates it in the middle of the scroll, following ch. 25. Both locations make sense in different ways. The order of the messages within the block also varies between MT and LXX.

In the translation notes, I draw attention to many of the detailed differences between MT and LXX, which usually consist in words that MT has but LXX lacks. MT keeps reminding us that we are reading something that is "Yahweh's affirmation," that Jeremiah is a "prophet" (in the context of Jeremiah's own work in Judah, "prophet" was not necessarily a compliment), and that the God of whom the text speaks is "Yahweh of Armies." MT sometimes repeats a message or part of a message, implying that it is significant in more than one context, whereas LXX lacks such repetitions.[101] Sometimes the longer MT text may be seeking to clarify things and make explicit things that are implicit. It sometimes underlines the deserved nature of Yahweh's action against Judah, and it introduces the designation of Nebuchadrezzar as "my servant" (see the commentary on 27:6). The significance of some other differences is harder to see, such as an inclination frequently to specify that the king of Babylon is Nebuchadrezzar, that Jeconiah is "ben Jehoiakim King of Judah," or that Hananiah is also "a prophet." MT often seems simply to like things to be filled out; LXX likes things more succinct. LXX may deliberately make things more concise, or it may be omitting things accidentally.[102]

Whatever the right answer to the question of the two texts' interrelationship, it is possible to study either in its own right.[103] But comparing them helps to draw attention to special features of each. If LXX is based on an earlier version of the scroll than MT, a desire to get back to its earliest version generates special focus on LXX; an interest in a version that was further developed to articulate the scroll's significance for people generates a focus on the Hebrew version that gained a place in the Tanak.[104] It might be too

---

R. D. Weis, "Textual History of Jeremiah," in *Textual History of the Bible*, ed. A. Lange and E. Tov, vol. 1B (Leiden: Brill, 2016), §7.1.

101. G. H. Parke-Taylor (*The Formation of the Book of Jeremiah* [Atlanta: Society of Biblical Literature, 2000]) systematically studies the doublets in the scroll and the verses that recur in and from other parts of the First Testament in order to see how they suggest insight into the formation of the scroll.

102. See J. R. Lundbom, *Jeremiah 37–52: A New Translation with Introduction and Commentary*, AB 21C (New York: Doubleday, 2004), 549–63.

103. For LXX in its own right, see esp. G. A. Walser, *Jeremiah: A Commentary Based on Ieremias in Codex Vaticanus*, Septuagint Commentary Series (Leiden: Brill, 2012). K. Finsterbusch and N. Jacoby lay out the two texts synoptically in German in *MT-Jeremia und LXX-Jeremia 1–24* (Neukirchen: Neukirchener, 2016) and *MT-Jeremia und LXX-Jeremia 25–52* (Neukirchen: Neukirchener, 2017).

104. B. S. Childs, *Introduction to the Old Testament as Scripture* (Philadelphia: Fortress, 1979), 352–53.

much to say that "the duty of a commentator on the Hebrew text is to maintain the final form of the text in MT,"[105] but it is a defensible stance. In this commentary I note ways in which LXX differs from MT but focus on MT.

B. BEHIND THE MASORETIC TEXT

Either the Greek or the Hebrew text may thus properly be studied in its own right, and greater appreciation of the integrity and distinctiveness of each version changes the focus of study. But for much of the twentieth century, a main focus in the study of LXX Jeremiah was the aim of getting behind MT to something nearer the original form of the scroll. Yet it is actually hard to define what we would mean by the original or most authentic form of a scriptural scroll, as can also be the case with modern works in the age of the word processor and the internet. You would hardly be interested in an earlier version of this commentary rather than the one you are reading. But difficulties in understanding MT and the existence of other versions of the text still encourage the study of the other versions with a view to getting behind it.

While there are many other copies of MT as well as the ones noted above, to which commentaries and the notes in *BHS* refer, they come from later in the medieval period, and it is unlikely that they preserve independent older versions of the text. I occasionally refer to them as "medieval manuscripts." On the other hand, there are a number of earlier fragments of Jeremiah from the Cairo Geniza (they are to be distinguished from the Cairo Codex, which was named after Cairo because it was long kept there).[106] And there are some fragments from Qumran, known as 2QJer and 4QJer, which as such are a millennium older than MT. Their text sometimes corresponds to MT and sometimes to a Hebrew text that one might see as lying behind LXX, which suggests that the Qumran community was acquainted with both versions of the scroll but also that MT does preserve a form of the text that is a millennium older than the actual MT manuscripts.

To gain access to older forms of the text than MT, we also have Greek translations later than LXX by Aquila, Symmachus, and Theodotion, as well as Jerome's Latin translation known as the Vulgate, the Syriac translation known as the Peshitta, and the Aramaic translation known as Targum Jonathan (the words Vulgate and Peshitta both designate their translation as "the people's"). On the assumption that we can work out from them what was the Hebrew text they were translating, those other textual traditions may put us on the

---

105. McKane, *Jeremiah*, 1:623. See further D. L. Christensen, "In Quest of the Autograph of the Book of Jeremiah," *JETS* 33 (1990): 145–53.

106. *BHS* refers to the codex by means of an ordinary capital C and to the geniza fragments by an ornate Gothic C.

track of a more intelligible text when MT Jeremiah is difficult to understand. And even when it is quite intelligible, they may put us on the track of an older text—though the various considerations I have noted about the relative independence of MT and LXX underline the care needed in connection with such extrapolation.[107] As with LXX, these translations also enable us to see how they were interpreting the text, which can help us with our own interpretation.

Four centuries ago, European scholars began making their own suggestions about ways in which the text might be restored to a more original form. Many of these suggestions appear in the notes to *BHS*, and some of the possibilities raised by those other versions of the text and by modern scholars may indeed lead us to an earlier form of the text. On the other hand, some of the apparent difficulties likely reflect the fact that the scroll expresses itself elliptically or uses unusual words. It is impossible to have great conviction about where the text has become mistakenly changed and what suggestions one should accept for its restoration. If I were to base my reading of Jeremiah on my version of a restored form of the scroll, I would probably be right at some points but wrong at others, and there is no assurance that my version of the text overall would be better than MT[L]. More or less invariably in this commentary, then, I follow MT[L] and try to make sense of it as it stands, though in the notes I draw attention to alternative versions of the text—especially readings that can be inferred from the old translations.[108]

In following MT, I also generally work with MT's punctuation and thus follow MT where it hyphenates words and they have only one stress. Although it is frequently tempting to rework the punctuation to produce a more consistent rhythm, I resist this temptation on the same assumption as I make regarding questions about the consonantal text and the vocalization: that it is unlikely that on the whole I will end up with a better text than the Masoretes have preserved. But in the notes, I sometimes draw attention to ways in which one could change the punctuation and thus make the rhythm more conventional. On the other hand, from time to time I feel free to rework MT's divisions of verses and cola where a recognition that the verses are poetic lines suggests such changes.

I use the term "units" to refer to the divisions within the text, as I identify them, whose size roughly corresponds to that of the medieval chapter divisions in printed Bibles. I use the term "sections" to refer to semicomplete sections within these units. Units and sections thus also roughly correspond to *petuhot* and *setumot* in the Qumran and MT Hebrew man-

---

107. See, e.g., Crouch, *Introduction*, 31–37.
108. W. L. Holladay argues the opposite way in "Text Criticism and Beyond: The Case for Jeremiah," *Textus* 23 (2007): 173–210, and illustrates his conviction in his commentary—as do most commentators.

uscripts. There, a *petuhah* is an "open" unit; at the end of a *petuhah*, the line is left empty and the next *petuhah* begins on a new line. A *setumah* is a "closed" section; at the end of a *setumah* there is a space in the line, but the next *setumah* may then continue on the same line or put the space at the beginning of the next line. *BHS* and *NJPS* print a *pe* or a *samek* where in MT^L or MT^A there is a new line or a space.[109] When I refer to a "unit marker" or "section marker," I imply that MT^L and MT^A agree on its location; where they disagree about which kind of break occurs, I use the unqualified ambiguous expression "marker." At Jer 8–9 and occasionally elsewhere, printed English Bibles and printed Hebrew Bibles vary in their chapter divisions: 8:1–23 in the Hebrew is 8:1–9:1 in the English. These differences are variant forms of the medieval chapter system; they do not denote differences between MT's Hebrew text and the English translations (MT has no marker after 8:22 or after 9:1 [8:23]). Where necessary, I give the English reference followed by the Hebrew, as in the reference at the end of the previous sentence.

VII. THEOLOGY

The Jeremiah scroll has almost as broad and wide-ranging a set of theological assumptions and implications as the Torah, the Prophets, and the Writings as a whole. It offers its own take on the nature of God, on the theological significance of Israel, on God's attitude to the nations, and on how to look at past, present, and future.

A. THE GOD OF ISRAEL

The God of the Jeremiah scroll is Yahweh, the God of Israel and the creator of the world, who claims sovereignty over both. Jeremiah offers no reason why he chose to be the God of a particular people or of this particular people. He might be quite happy with the nonanswer to this question in Deut 7, where Moses first affirms that it was not because Israel was so impressive that he chose it; he just did. He made a commitment to Israel's ancestors and then he couldn't get out of it if he wanted to. This "explanation" simply pushes the question back: why did he make such a commitment to Israel's ancestors?

109. For divisions in the LXX, see C. Amphoux and A. Serandour, "La composition de Jérémie LXX d'après les divisions du Codex Vaticanus (B)," in *XIII Congress of the International Organization for the Septuagint and Cognate Studies*, ed. M. K. H. Peters, SCS 55 (Atlanta: Society of Biblical Literature, 2008), 3–21.

Moses does not even go through the motions of answering that question. Jeremiah, too, goes behind Yahweh's commitment to Israel to his commitment to its ancestors without purporting to explain it. Like Moses, Jeremiah focuses on the results of making it. It was because he made that commitment that he got the Israelites out of Egypt, looked after them in the wilderness, and gave them their land. Jeremiah does not consider the question whether he was being fair to the Canaanites any more than considering the basis for giving the land to the Israelites.

The God of the Jeremiah scroll is faithful, committed, caring, and compassionate. He is also angry, wrathful, and raging. He has those characteristics because—well, because he has those characteristics. In other words, when he acts in those ways, he is being himself, and he can hardly not be himself.[110] His faithfulness (*ṣədāqâ*) means he acts in the right way in relation to people who belong to him and to whom he belongs. He fulfills his promises. He protects. His commitment (*ḥesed*) goes beyond his faithfulness. It means that when his people have been unfaithful, he stays faithful. His caring (*'ahăbâ*) means that he is love, not merely in the sense of an emotional response but in a self-giving sense. His compassion (*raḥămîm*) means he has the feelings of a mother for the children of her womb (*reḥem*).

He is also characterized by anger, wrath, and rage. Jeremiah does not assume that there is anything inherently wrong with anger. The question is who exercises it and to what ends. Whereas the First Testament elsewhere suggests that anger is a subordinate or more marginal aspect of Yahweh's character (e.g., Lam 3:33), Jeremiah offers no pointers in this direction. He rather emphasizes the monumental threat that Yahweh's wrath constitutes for Judah. Yet he incidentally and unconsciously indicates that Yahweh's bark is worse than his bite. Yahweh talks a lot about anger, but his actions fall far short of what the talk would make one expect.

The God of the Jeremiah scroll is insightful, sovereign, and powerful, while also interactive and resistible. He can make plans for events in the world and implement them, and when other people (such as Judah or Edom) think they can formulate policies and implement them, he can expose their pretentiousness. He can do as he likes in the world. Human "kings" exercise an authority and power that falls far short of the authority and power of the King. He is Yahweh of Armies, "a doxology in miniature that acclaims God as Divine Warrior leading the heavenly armies into battle."[111] The greatest human king that people know he can treat as his servant, his agent in implementing his

---

110. T. E. Fretheim, *What Kind of God? Collected Essays of Terence E. Fretheim*, Siphrut 14 (Winona Lake, IN: Eisenbrauns, 2015), 300.

111. C. J. Sharp, "Jeremiah," in *Theological Bible Commentary*, ed. D. L. Petersen and G. R. O'Day (Louisville: Westminster John Knox, 2009), 231.

will in the world. Yet Jeremiah does not imply that everything that happens in the world issues from Yahweh's will. Israel rather consistently ignores his wishes. His sovereignty is more theoretical than practical and more occasional than consistent. He works via human decision-making; Jeremiah speaks of no divine acts that do not work via human decision-making.

Yahweh is the one who made the heavens and the earth by his insight and power. He is the only God. Like the rest of the First Testament, Jeremiah is not interested in monotheism in itself but in mono-Yahwism. He insists not that there is only one God but that Yahweh alone is God. Monotheism follows, but it is not the important issue. The important question is Yahweh's own status, significance, and power over against other beings who are called gods. Jeremiah does not deny the existence of other gods; he rather declares that they are insignificant compared with Yahweh. They cannot do anything. Whereas other peoples believe it is possible to make images of their gods, Yahweh forbids the making of images of him. Jeremiah does not say it is impossible, nor does he give reasons for the ban, as Deuteronomy does, though he implies that the weakness of images is their being human-made.

Jeremiah's account of God raises for the church whether it takes seriously that he is a wrathful God and one active in world events, both of which convictions are accepted by the New Testament but not obvious in the church's thinking and talk.

B. THE ISRAEL OF GOD

In the expression "the God of Israel," the word "of" is systematically ambiguous. Jeremiah does not describe Yahweh as the God of Assyria, Egypt, Babylon, Moab, or Elam, and he does not describe God as creating or providing for or revealing himself to these peoples. He does describe Yahweh as acting in their national lives, mostly by bringing calamity but also by restoring them to fullness of life. And they are ultimately destined to recognize Yahweh—more for his sake or for the sake of the truth than for their own sake. They are inclined to be reliant on their own resources and capacities and need to be disabused of such stupidity, though it is a stupidity no worse and no better than Israel's. Not possessing the Torah or the words of prophets evidently does not leave them ignorant of what they ought to know in this connection.

But Israel is "my people." The prominence of the word "people" (*'am*) in Jeremiah points to the fact that Yahweh's primary relationship is with the people as a body as opposed to the individual. The name "Israel" then points to the fact that "people" suggests the community belonging together as a family—they have a shared genealogy as the descendants of Jacob/Israel. They are also a "nation" (*gôy*), which is a less warm word, but suggests something more numerous than a family. It designates Israel as a political entity, an important aspect of Israel in Jeremiah's day. They are Yahweh's "domain" (*naḥălâ*), his particular and inalienable possession, like the domain of land that belongs to a family.

Such is the good news. The bad news is that occurrences of the phrase "my people" usually come in troublesome contexts—contexts that refer to their not behaving as "my people" and to Yahweh's not treating them as "my people." Although Yahweh is Israel's God and Israel is Yahweh's people (lit. "God for you" and "a people for me"), that formulation represents Yahweh's original intention and his intention for the future (7:23; 11:4; 24:7; 30:22; 31:1, 33; 32:38) but not the present reality.

The formulation does draw attention to the mutuality of relationship between Yahweh and Israel, though the two are not partners—or if they are, Israel is the junior partner. Rather, Israel is Yahweh's servant (30:10; 46:27–28), though neatly, Jeremiah uses that word to suggest Israel's security as Yahweh's servant rather than its responsibility. With its worship, Israel is to serve him rather than serving other deities, which is its inclination (8:2; 16:11; 30:9).

Being Yahweh's servant means both security and vulnerability. This master will not ultimately cast off his servant, but he will feel free to discipline him in quite severe ways. In Jeremiah, Israel is indeed threatened with drastic discipline, discipline that amounts to being wiped out. It is cut down and cut down and threatened with being cut down again. In the background is the cutting down that happened a century previously, when Israel was virtually reduced to the rump state of Judah. One might have thought that this decimation could never be reversed. But Jeremiah affirms that Yahweh will restore Ephraim as well as Judah. The master cannot get out of it, because of who he is. Yahweh thus lives with a tension over the word "remainder" or "remnant." He threatens to cut Israel down even further, and does so, but he cannot actually eliminate it and promises to turn it into a numerous people again.

A family does not require kings or priests, perhaps not even prophets or experts. A nation does require them, and Israel has them. Their responsibility is to rule the nation in Yahweh's way, to pass on his teaching, to bring his messages, to mediate his insight, and to facilitate its worship and service. Israel's leaders comprehensively fail in these respects. Instead of enabling Israel to function as his servant, they hinder it. Yahweh's response is not to abolish monarchy, priesthood, prophecy, and expertise. Part of the background is that here, too, he is bound by commitments he has made in the past, as is the case with his relationship to Israel. He made commitments to Levi and to David. As with Israel, then, he may take severe disciplinary action against the current holders of Levitical and Davidic office, but he does not cast off the line.

Jesus and Paul give a similar account of Israel to Jeremiah's, which raises for the church whether it takes seriously the status of the Jewish people for

God. Jeremiah's critique of Israel also raises the question whether he would address the church in the twenty-first century in a similar way.[112]

C. THE NATIONS

Jeremiah's commission is to be a prophet regarding the nations. The scroll uses several prepositions that can be translated "regarding" (*lə, ʿal, ʾel*), which could denote "to," "for," "about," or "against."

There is no record of Jeremiah ever prophesying *to* foreign nations. In Jer 27, Yahweh commissions him to do so, but the story does not say that he does, which confirms that it is actually about his prophesying to Judah about the nations. The point is that the nations are important to Judah, and Yahweh's dealings with them are important to Judah. Judah needs to understand what Yahweh is doing with the nations because of the significance of Yahweh's actions for Judah's relationship with Yahweh.

Another apparent exception that proves the rule is that Jeremiah commissions Seraiah to read out his prophecies in Babylon (51:59–64). Again, there is no record of Seraiah's doing so, and again the story appears in the scroll because of its importance to Judah. Further, Jeremiah does not say that the reading is to be done in Babylon's hearing. It is to be done in Yahweh's hearing. The story thus illustrates how Jeremiah prophesies *against* the nations. The purpose of reading out the prophecies is to get Yahweh to do as he has said in his pronouncements about Babylon. It will work because Yahweh answers such prayers and because Seraiah will perform a sign-act that will contribute to the implementing of the pronouncements. And Babylon does fall, though in nothing like the way Yahweh has said.

Jeremiah prophesies *for* as well as against the nations in the sense that he promises that Yahweh will restore them. He will no more eliminate them than he will eliminate Judah. Admittedly, he does not issue that promise about Babylon as he does about some other nations. But he does have mercy on Babylon in the sense that it does not get destroyed—even though it does lose its position as the center of an empire.

Jeremiah prophesies *about* the nations in connection with the fact that they serve him, though they do not realize it. The point is explicit in connection with the great empire itself: Nebuchadrezzar is Yahweh's servant. It is unfortunate for Judah, because he will serve Yahweh by bringing catastrophe to Judah for rebelling against Yahweh and rebelling against Babylon. In

---

112. See J. Goldingay, "As a Commentator, One Might Ask, 'What Would Jeremiah or John Say?'" in *The Genre of Biblical Commentary: Essays in Honor of John E. Hartley on the Occasion of His 75th Birthday*, ed. T. D. Finlay and W. Yarchin (Eugene, OR: Pickwick, 2015), 234–40.

fulfillment of declarations by Jeremiah, 2 Chr 36 will describe a successor of his as in effect Yahweh's servant in a way that is fortunate for Judah, because Cyrus will serve Yahweh by commissioning Judahites to go home to rebuild the temple.

The converse of Nebuchadrezzar's being Yahweh's servant is that Yahweh is Nebuchadrezzar's master. He is Lord in relation to the nations. He has authority over them, and he has power over them. He is both for the nations as his servants and against them. He will demonstrate it by implementing the kind of proclamations that he issues in Jer 46–51, which contain promises as well as threats. A significant feature of those threats is the range of nations they concern:

- Egypt, the old oppressor but also current threat or potential resource
- Philistia, Moab, Ammon, and Edom, the neighbors that might also be threats or temptations
- Kedar, Hazor, and Elam, far-off peoples that are irrelevant to Judah but are within Yahweh's purview
- Babylon itself, the imperial power that rivals Yahweh and has brought such suffering to other peoples and such devastation to Zion

Jeremiah thus also prophesies about the nations because Yahweh wants Judah to look at them in the right way. Jeremiah implicitly agrees with Isaiah that Judah is neither to look to other nations as resources nor to be afraid of other nations as if they could bring Judah trouble—unless Yahweh wants them to do so, in which case Judah's problem is Yahweh, not the nations.

The New Testament picks up Jeremiah's theology of empire and thus raises questions for churches that are part of imperial nations while suggesting good news for churches within subaltern nations.

D. THE PRESENT, THE PAST, AND THE FUTURE

Although Jeremiah is not an exercise in narrative theology in the way that 2 Kings is, it is implicitly a narrative theology (the Gospels will take up the approach of 2 Kings, and Paul will take up the approach of Jeremiah). Its theology focuses on what Yahweh has done, is doing, and will do; it looks at the present in light of the past and the future and urges its readers to live their lives on that basis.

In the present, Judah looks to Yahweh to encourage the crops to grow and to help its women have children, but it does so in a way that pictures Yahweh rather like the *bə'ālîm*—the Masters. It may also consciously look to the Masters or other deities. And it looks to Egypt or other nations as resources in connection with its foreign policy.

In the present, it is thus ignoring the past. Its present is designed to be lived in light of the way Yahweh looked after it in the wilderness, the way it responded at that time, and the pledge that Yahweh made with it at that time. These events were designed to shape its theology, but "Jeremiah has to practice his ministry and his faith in a community alienated from and cut off from its founding, authorizing memory." In addition, "the prophet is rooted in a powerful vision of an alternative future" that he needs to get it to heed.[113]

Jeremiah's vision of the future is dominated by two great events: the day of Yahweh (though he uses that actual phrase only in 46:10) and the time when Yahweh will "bring about the restoration of Israel." One might think of the second as a subset of the first; Israel was used to seeing Yahweh's day as the time when his great positive purposes for Israel would be fulfilled in blessing and fruitfulness. Amos 5:18–20 presupposes that understanding, but Yahweh turns its implications upside-down. In line with Amos, Jeremiah thus speaks often of "that day" as a grave day, a day of dire trouble, a day of disaster, a day of distress (17:16–18; 18:17; 30:7). But "that day" can become the day of restoration (30:8). Indeed, on the one occasion when he uses the actual expression "the day of Yahweh," it has regained the positive significance it had for Amos's contemporaries and become the day when Yahweh takes action against Egypt. On the other hand, if Judah was trusting Egypt as its ally . . .

"That day" and the day of restoration are not eschatological events in the sense of belonging in a far-off time or a different epoch or bringing history to an end. If they are, they nevertheless find embodiment in the meantime during current history, during this epoch, and during a time that is near. The fall of Jerusalem will be that day (Lam 1:12; 2:1, 21–22). Yahweh will make its grim reality become actual within Israel's life; he will make the future become the present.

But Yahweh will not let that negative action be his last one. People had not wholly misunderstood him when they looked forward to a great day of blessing. Now it will need to be the day when Yahweh brings about his people's restoration. Yahweh announces it in 30:3, and the picture of the future that Jer 30–33 paints is implicitly a working out of the phrase's implications. It will mean building and planting instead of demolishing and uprooting. It includes bringing Ephraim and Judah back to the country he gave to their ancestors and having them serve David (past and future come together). It includes liberation from the service of strangers, the healing of wounds, the

---

113. W. Brueggemann, *Like Fire in the Bones: Listening for the Prophetic Word in Jeremiah* (Minneapolis: Fortress, 2006), 144, 151.

rebuilding of Jerusalem, the planting of vineyards in Samaria and its people making pilgrimage to Zion, the realization of that vision that they should be a people for him and he should be God for them, and the making of a new pledge that includes the writing of the Torah into their minds. It includes forgiving and forgetting. Like the vision of Yahweh's day, it is not eschatological in the sense of belonging in a far-off time or different epoch or in the sense of bringing history to an end. And as the threat of Yahweh's day found an embodiment in the lives of the people to whom it was issued (or in the lives of their children and grandchildren), so the promise of restoration found an embodiment in the lives of the people to whom it was issued (or in the lives of their children and grandchildren).

The New Testament presupposes a "now but not yet" theology like Jeremiah's that urges churches to live in light of both "now" and "not yet."

VIII. MAIN THEMES AND THEIR IMPLICATIONS

Broadly, the theology of the scroll as we have outlined it fits into that of the First Testament as a whole, and particularly the Latter Prophets.[114] What of ways in which the scroll stands out? The scroll's most distinctive theme is its focus on the prophet himself; the way people relate to him is an expression of their relationship to God. A second distinctive feature is the way he uses a range of images to describe God. That feature links with a third: that the scroll sees two sides to complex questions. One of its implications is thus that it equips readers to formulate a theology that is both inclusive and timely.

A. THEOLOGY EMBODIED: JEREMIAH AS SUBJECT

In Jeremiah, the message—the word (*haddābār*)—became flesh and dwelt among us, full of grace and truth. Some of the stories about Jeremiah that appear in the scroll are what have been called type scenes. Type scenes are stories about events that recur in human experience, so that the stories about them get told in similar ways. The kind of events are an annunciation, a birth, a betrothal, a wedding, a meal, a banquet, an appearing of God or another supernatural being, a dream, a death, a funeral, a coronation, an ordination, a cabinet meeting. A type scene gives an author the scaffolding for a story but also makes possible the construction of something with its own distinc-

114. W. Brueggemann considers Jeremiah's relationship with other First Testament books in *The Theology of the Book of Jeremiah*, Old Testament Theology (Cambridge: Cambridge University Press, 2007), 134–86.

tive nature. The scroll begins with a notable example of a type scene: the commissioning of a prophet. Sometimes one can see a story in Jeremiah as a play with several acts and scenes and as raising questions that it then goes on to answer—or sometimes does not. Jeremiah 26 is an example; Jer 28 is a more spectacular one, with its plot relating how a prophet with an encouraging message drops dead—a story characterized by unpredictable and shocking drama, all within seventeen verses. These stories illustrate the key role played by dialogue in Hebrew narrative, and they are often vivid and full of circumstantial detail (such as people's names). While their concreteness does not make it more likely that they are historical, any more than is the case with Jesus's parables, it does reflect how the author is an engaging storyteller. A number of the stories about Jeremiah relate how he undertakes symbolic actions (Jer 13; 18; 19–20). Here, too, there is both scaffolding for the stories and variation. Each enables the communication and interpretation of the story.

The message of grace finds expression in Yahweh's insistence on using Jeremiah to address Judah about its faithlessness, warn it about the catastrophe he intended to bring, and urge it to turn back to him in order that he need not do as he threatened. Its being a message of grace finds further expression in the way Jeremiah persists in doing so. Its being a message of truth finds expression in Jeremiah's insistence on speaking with truthfulness and on living out the opposite of deceit or falseness. All these characteristics are embodied in Jeremiah's person and life as well as in his words; he mediates the revelation of God through his person and his life. He also embodies what it means to respond to God. "The figure of Jeremiah assumes a paradigmatic value for his disciples." He is not merely a hero to admire but a model of accepting the word of God in a time of crisis.[115] Thus "the Book of Jeremiah does not so much teach religious truths as present a religious personality. Prophecy had already taught its truths, its last effort was to reveal itself in a life."[116] Jeremiah's life is crucial to his work and message.

Jeremiah may be the most embodied of the biblical prophets. His prophetic role clearly impacts his body. Once God's words enter Jeremiah's body, they burn within him (Jer 5:14), at times causing him delight (15:16), at times causing him physical distress (20:9). God commands Jeremiah not to marry and have children, thereby curtailing bodily pleasures and functions (16:2–3). Like other prophets, Jeremiah uses his body to communicate and engages in sign-acts. He wears and then buries linen un-

115. G. Barbiero, *"Tu mi hai sedotto, Signore": Le confessioni di Geremia alla luce della sua vocazione profetica,* Analecta Biblica Studia (Rome: Gregorian, 2013), 12.
116. A. B. Davidson, "Jeremiah the Prophet," in *A Dictionary of the Bible,* ed. J. Hastings, vol. 2 (Edinburgh: T&T Clark, 1899), 576.

derwear, smashes clay pots, and places a yoke around his neck (chs. 13, 18, 19, 27, 28). He also relies heavily on disturbing corporeal rhetoric such as the frequently evoked image of birds and beasts that consume Israel's unburied dead (7:33, 16:4, 19:7, 22:19, 34:20). Another prominent feature of Jeremiah's corporeal rhetoric is the image of the incurable sore.[117]

Jeremiah's reports of his protests and his interactions with Yahweh are an aspect of the way his life is part of his message. "He is a metaphor for God's word. Through him we see into God's pathos and purpose and into the plight and destiny of the people."[118] He is not the only figure in the scroll who is significant in this way: Baruch, Ebed-melech, and Uriah accompany him as people whose commitment risks their lives or costs their lives. The scroll thus reports the initiation of the way "the goodly fellowship of the prophets praise thee" and "the noble army of martyrs praise thee," as the ancient Christian hymn *Te Deum* puts it.

B. THEOLOGY IMAGED

Prophets do much of their thinking in imagery. It is necessarily so. There are few things one can say literally about God and his relationship with us; we are bound to use metaphor in this connection. It is imagery that makes ideas possible. It enables us to think and see things and then to communicate them. Metaphor makes it possible to speak about things that we could not otherwise speak of; it also makes it possible to say more about things that we can speak of because we can speak of one thing we know in terms of another thing that we know. Jeremiah is comparable to Hosea in the extravagant profusion of his metaphorical thinking and language.[119]

- God is king, and in different ways both the world and Israel are the people he governs. People must bow down before him. He has a cabinet. He sends messengers. He is commander-in-chief and sends his (heavenly and earthly) armies to bring trouble to rebels. He exercises authority. He makes pledges. He may listen to intercession.
- God is guide. He points out the path for people to walk. They must go after him rather than go after other guides (gods).

117. A. Kalmanofsky, "Israel's Open Sore in the Book of Jeremiah," *JBL* 135 (2016): 248.

118. T. Polk, *The Prophetic Persona: Jeremiah and the Language of the Self*, JSOTSup 32 (Sheffield: JSOT, 1984), 170–71.

119. See D. Bourguet, *Des Métaphores de Jérémie*, Études Bibliques 9 (Paris: Gabalda, 1987); J. Y. Jindo, *Biblical Metaphor Reconsidered: A Cognitive Approach to Poetic Prophecy in Jeremiah 1–24*, HSM 64 (Winona Lake, IN: Eisenbrauns, 2010).

- God is master. People must serve him and not serve other masters.
- God is builder, but also destroyer.
- God is shepherd. He provides.
- God is father. He begets children. He adopts children. Israel belongs to his household. He passes on a domain.
- God is husband. He marries a wife. He commits himself to faithfulness and expects faithfulness. He is lord. He is jealous, and he objects to his wife whoring and committing adultery. He divorces.
- God is teacher. He expects attentiveness and obedience.
- God is farmer. He plants vines, olives, and figs. He expects fruit. He plants trees and fells them. He irrigates or withholds irrigation. He controls access to his garden and resents its invasion and attack. But he can devastate it if it fails to produce fruit. He has a farmhand.

Jeremiah's view of God is characterized by a "robustness" to which his use of imagery contributes.[120] Yahweh is "an abandoned bridegroom, a water fountain, a betrayed father, a lion, a wolf, a leopard, a potter. . . ."[121] Jeremiah's use of imagery thus contributes to another feature of the scroll: its resistance to speaking univocally. There are subjects on which it is unequivocal: Israel must serve Yahweh alone and must exercise authority with faithfulness. But on some other matters, it speaks with considerable diversity. Ironically, the moment of the postmodern turn at the end of the twentieth century was also a moment when some scholarly study of Jeremiah became puzzled by the complexity of the attitudes that the scroll takes to a number of questions. It was an irony because this complexity makes Jeremiah more of a postmodern book. It does not offer simple answers to simple questions or simple answers to complex questions. "The claim of theological incoherence in Jeremiah is often due to the theology of interpreters; something does not make sense from within their own theological framework."[122] The scroll may speak in terms that are in tension with one another, and as readers we may prefer one to the other. Readers assess Jeremiah's ideology in light of their own ideology.[123] "Its combustible mix of politics and prophecy points to a Word of God that is dynamic, contextually responsive, and stubbornly resistant to commodification by any one group or ideology."[124]

---

120. W. Brueggemann, *Hopeful Imagination: Prophetic Voices in Exile* (Philadelphia: Fortress, 1986), 14.

121. Brueggemann, *Hopeful Imagination*, 14–15.

122. Fretheim, *What Kind of God?*, 296.

123. See, e.g., J. H. le Roux, "In Search of Carroll's Jeremiah," *OTE* 7 (1994): 7–20.

124. Sharp, "Jeremiah," 234.

C. THEOLOGY OF A BOTH-AND CHARACTER

The robustness and diversity of Jeremiah's portrait of God link with the both-and character of his proclamation as it emerges in connection with a series of questions raised by the scroll.

- Is Yahweh chiefly characterized by anger or by love? I have suggested the answer to this question in considering "The God of Israel" (see p. 49). Love and faithfulness are key to Yahweh's character, but he is capable of acting in wrath, and in Jeremiah's day that capacity finds strong expression. While the idea that Yahweh punishes people can have a destructive effect on people who are traumatized by horrific experiences,[125] the idea that Yahweh does not punish people might also have a destructive effect on them (so Heb 12). But maybe it is therefore significant that Jeremiah does not use the actual language of punishment or judgment (and hence I use words such as "catastrophe" and "calamity" rather than "judgment"). The scroll does not look at the relationship between God and humanity in the quasi-legal framework that has been common in Christian thinking since the medieval period. Its thinking is hierarchical but relational.
- Is catastrophe inevitable or can Judah avert it by turning to Yahweh?[126] Jeremiah gives both impressions in different contexts. Catastrophe is inevitable (if Judah carries on as it is). Judah must turn (catastrophe can then be avoided). There is no indication that either Jeremiah or Yahweh changes his mind about these possibilities at some point (e.g., when it becomes clear that Judah is not going to turn). It's never over until it's over. Jeremiah 36:3 makes explicit Yahweh's aim in issuing his threats, and 18:1–11 provides a clue to interrelating the two possibilities.
- Will the catastrophe mean the destruction of Israel or simply its decimation? Whereas the scroll explicitly provides a way to look at the alternatives of inevitability or turning, it simply proclaims the possibility both of total annihilation and of decimation that leaves something. "I am going to make an end of them" (*kālâ piel*, 14:12); "I will not make an end of you" (the noun *kālâ*, 5:18). It seems unlikely that Jeremiah simply juxtaposed the two kinds of statements within the main years of his proclamation (see, e.g., 4:27) because

125. C. G. Frechette, "The Old Testament as Controlled Substance: How Insights from Trauma Studies Reveal Healing Capacities in Potentially Harmful Texts," *Int* 69 (2014): 20–34.
126. See J. Skinner, *Prophecy and Religion: Studies in the Life of Jeremiah* (Cambridge: Cambridge University Press, 1922), 77–79.

the second undermines the force of the first. Perhaps the juxtaposition is an example of the development of the messages when the catastrophe had happened and people needed to be and could be reassured that Yahweh did not intend to bring about complete destruction—and did not do so. Perhaps Yahweh changed his mind about obliterating Israel. Perhaps he never intended to do so, and the first kind of statement involved a hyperbole. These possibilities interweave with questions raised by Jesus's statements (e.g., Matt 21:43) and discussed in Rom 9–11.

- Does Yahweh intend simply to put down the Davidic monarchy, or will it be restored? Again the scroll simply juxtaposes these possibilities, but they can be part of a bigger picture: in the long term, Yahweh must be faithful to his promise to David, but that fact does not give any individual king a basis for assuming he can do as he likes and get away with it.
- Does Yahweh simply despise Israel's worship, or can it be redeemed? Likewise, the scroll implies that the temple and its worship are part of the ongoing life of Israel, but Yahweh can be dismissive of the worship offered by a particular generation.
- Are other nations simply doomed, or is there hope for them? As I have already noted, in a number of cases the scroll makes clear that their prospects are the same as Israel's.

One implication of the scroll, then, is that it pushes readers to develop a theology that is both inclusive and timely. It recognizes that truth is complex and that theology needs to incorporate both-ands; it also pushes readers to perceive which of the both-ands needs bringing out now. A prophet is someone who "knows what time it is,"[127] someone who can "distinguish whether a historical hour stands under the wrath or the love of God."[128]

IX. ANALYSIS OF CONTENTS

When Western readers start to read through books such as Isaiah or Jeremiah, they can be bemused. Without obvious logic, these prophetic scrolls switch between subjects, between prose and poetry, between God speaking and a prophet speaking, between addressing Israel and addressing God, between narrative and direct address, between threatening and promising,

127. A. J. Heschel, *The Prophets* (New York: Harper, 1962), 106; cf. E. A. Martens, "Jeremiah," *Direction* 15 (1986): 3.
128. E. Osswald, *Falsche Prophetie im Alten Testament* (Tübingen: Mohr Siebeck, 1962), 22; cf. J. A. Sanders, *From Sacred Story to Sacred Text* (Philadelphia: Fortress, 1987), 84.

between foretelling and forthtelling, between what is imminent and what is far off. As a consequence, the prophetic scrolls can seem "virtually incomprehensible as *books*."[129] The Jeremiah scroll is the longest of the prophetic scrolls, and it is all the more difficult to find one's way around because its organization is less clear than that of the other prophetic scrolls. Indeed, one might infer that *"the Book of Jeremiah is not a work made from whole cloth. The book is not only without any discernible organization, on the contrary, there rules it a conspicuous lack of plan."*[130] Now premodern readers such as Jerome, Rashi, and Calvin apparently did not find Jeremiah unreadable, though it is not surprising that modern readers should find it difficult. It is more surprising if postmodern readers have this difficulty (as with the equivocal nature of its contents), because so much contemporary writing abjures logic and structure.

"The book of Jeremiah is an elaborate tapestry of meaning-making that honors complexity, delights in ambiguity, and relishes *heteroglossia* (Bakhtin's term)." But "while this meaning-making map is wild and unwieldy, it is not formless."[131] The scroll is bookended by a chapter relating how Jeremiah came to be a prophet and summarizing the nature of his message and a chapter telling of the fate of the Jerusalem to which he addressed that message. It then divides into two halves, with the first half dominated by messages and the second by stories. Jeremiah 25 both concludes the first half and opens the second.[132]

A. JEREMIAH 1–25

One difficulty that readers may feel when they work through the Jeremiah scroll is that "in the entire book the same argument keeps repeating."[133] In response to the repetitiveness, commentators "tend perhaps to consider themselves not so much servants of the word as its sedulous critics, even its improvers."[134] Over and over, Jeremiah declares that Judah is unfaithful to Yahweh and Yahweh intends to bring calamity upon it. One recalls the

---

129. R. P. Carroll, *Jeremiah*, OTL, 38.

130. Mowinckel, *Komposition*, 5, his italics.

131. L. Stulman, "Jeremiah as a Messenger of Hope in Crisis," *Int* 62 (2008): 13, 7.

132. For similar analyses to the one that follows, see A. Rofé, "The Arrangement of the Book of Jeremiah," *ZAW* 101 (1989): 390–98; S. J. Murphy, "The Quest for the Structure of the Book of Jeremiah," *BSac* 166 (2009): 306–18; R. D. Patterson, "Of Bookends, Hinges, and Hooks: Literary Clues to the Arrangement of Jeremiah's Prophecies," *WTJ* 51 (1989): 109–131; L. Stulman, *Order amid Chaos: Jeremiah as Symbolic Tapestry*, The Biblical Seminar 57 (Sheffield: Sheffield Academic, 1998), 23–55.

133. J. Oecolampadius, *In Hieremiam prophetam* (Strasbourg: Apiarius, 1533), 39.

134. D. Berrigan, *Jeremiah: The World, the Wound of God* (Minneapolis: Fortress, 1999), 141.

preacher who was asked why he kept repeating the same sermon: "When they listen to that one, I'll preach another." Jeremiah's messages are variants on one theme. But the written collection of these messages does divide into a series of major sections, signaled by the opening phrase "The word that came to Jeremiah from Yahweh" or a variant on it:

Prologue	1:1–19	
Part 1	2:1–6:36	Confrontation, Exhortation, Warning
Part 2a	7:1–10:25	Exhortations and Exchanges
Part 2b	11:1–13:22	Jeremiah's Arguments
Part 2c	14:1–17:27	Drought, Hunger, Sword
Part 2d	18:1–20:18	Concerning Plans and Counsels
Part 2e	21:1–24:10	On Kings and Prophets
Conclusion	25:1–38	

At a formal level, this framework provides Jer 1–25 with some structuring. One way or another, each of the major sections opens with a prose account of a message for Jeremiah to deliver to Judah; each section then comprises mostly messages in poetry. The themes of the prose and the poetry are similar, and the same message indeed recurs through the different sections as Jeremiah tries different ways of getting his message home. The logic of Jer 1–25 corresponds to the perspective on Ephraim expounded in 2 Kgs 17:7–23:

- Ephraim has served other gods.
- In doing so, it has ignored the prophets.
- Judah has acted in the same way.
- Its kings are especially to blame for Ephraim's downfall.[135]

The sections combine their repetitiveness with a subverting of the Judahites' possible or actual assumptions, whereby they avoid the thrust of Jeremiah's repeated message:

Part 1	begins by undermining assumptions about the exodus.
Part 2a	begins by undermining assumptions about the temple.
Part 2b	begins by undermining assumptions about Sinai.
Part 2c	begins by undermining assumptions about prayer.
Part 2d	begins by undermining assumptions about divine sovereignty.
Part 2e	begins by undermining assumptions about David.

135. R. E. Clements, "Jeremiah 1–25 and the Deuteronomistic History."

B. JEREMIAH 25–52

Whereas the first half of the scroll incorporates few dates, the second half is dominated by stories with dates that make clear that the stories cluster around 604, 597, and 587. The difficulty modern readers may then feel is that the chapters do not come in chronological order.[136] "Dischrononologization represents a significant tactic of time management from chs. 21 to 51."[137] It is again surprising if postmodern readers have difficulty with the chapters' order, because we watch movies and television series that work in dramatic sequence rather than chronological sequence ("three weeks earlier," "two years later"). The Jeremiah text points both to a reading as history and to a reading as drama.[138] A dramatic order rather than a chronological order can both entertain and make the audience think, and it can make connections that would not otherwise be apparent.

Like the first half of the scroll, the second half divides into major sections. On a broad canvas, the sequences are clear, though there is room for disagreement about some of the details:

Introduction	25:1–38	
Part 3	The Die Cast and the Possibility of Restoration	
a	26:1–29:32	Stories about Prophets
b	30:1–33:26	At Last, a Focus on Hope
c	34:1–36:32	Stories Implying a Reversion to Reality
Part 4	The Calamity and the Aftermath	
a	37:1–39:18	Last Chances, Calamity, and a Footnote for Ebed-melech
b	40:1–45:5	Aftermath, Missed Chances, and a Footnote for Baruch
Part 5	Messages about Other Nations	
a	46:1–28	Egypt
b	47:1–49:39	Neighbors and Distant Peoples
c	50:1–51:64	Babylon
Epilogue	52:1–34	

136. Commentators such as B. Blayney (*Jeremiah and Lamentations*, 2nd ed. [Edinburgh: Oliphant, 1810]) and J. Bright (*Jeremiah: Introduction, Translation, and Notes*, AB 21 [Garden City, NY: Doubleday, 1965]) thus rearrange them in order to comment on them.

137. Diamond, "Jeremiah," 546.

138. Cf. M. C. Calloway's study of Jer 37–38, "Black Fire on White Fire: Historical Context and Literary Subtext in Jeremiah 37–38," in Diamond, K. M O'Connor, and Stulman, *Troubling Jeremiah*, 173–74.

One feature of the scroll's second half is a series of false endings: Jer 33 might seem like an end, so might Jer 36, so might Jer 39, so might Jer 45, and so might Jer 51.[139] The placing of Jer 30–33 shows that one cannot suggest that "the book of Jeremiah moves along a plot trajectory from judgment to restoration." Indeed, actually "it would be difficult to argue convincingly for a large-scale plot unfolding from judgment to salvation in the book. The prophetic diction of chaos, terror, divine fury, and grievous loss controls the tenor of the book from beginning to end."[140] At the same time, Jer 30–33 does qualify the gloom, and the second half of the scroll does manifest a suggestive sequence of doom on Judah (chs. 26–45), on other nations (chs. 46–49), and on Babylon (chs. 50–51).[141] And the closing chapter has notes of hope that do not quite count as a Hollywood ending but do mitigate the gloom that would obtain if the scroll ended with the fall of Jerusalem or the killing of Gedaliah and its aftermath.

139. Indeed, Newman (*Before the Bible*, 53–74) notes that some people did not think it should end after Jer 52: they added Baruch and other "Jeremianic" works.

140. Sharp, "Jeremiah," 231.

141. H.-J. Stipp, "Legenden der Jeremia-Exegese (I)," *VT* 64 (2014): 500–501.

The Book of
JEREMIAH

Text and Commentary

PROLOGUE: AN INTRODUCTION TO THE SCROLL (1:1–19)

Like Isaiah, Ezekiel, and Hosea, the Jeremiah scroll begins with a long introduction (a chapter in Jeremiah's case; more than a chapter in the other cases). Like those other examples, it opens with a brief factual and chronological preface and then goes on to something more substantial and more distinctive in form as well as in content. As is the case in Hosea, this more substantial introduction takes the form of a narrative account of Yahweh's commission that anticipates the scroll's contents as a whole in terms of threat and promise. As is the case in Ezekiel, however, the narrative introducing Jeremiah takes first-person form, talks about the prophet's own reaction to Yahweh's commission, and homes in on the provision of words to speak. And as is the case in Isaiah, the introduction incorporates material from much later than the time of the commission in order to give a balanced account of where the commission led.

The chapter comprises a four-part introduction to the scroll:

vv. 1–3   A preface introducing Jeremiah and his times
vv. 4–10   Jeremiah's self-introduction describing his commission, with its challenge to speak boldly and its promise of protection
vv. 11–12 Jeremiah's report of a message from Yahweh about the coming implementation of his message
vv. 13–19 Jeremiah's report of a second (double) message from Yahweh:
　　vv. 13–16   Yahweh's intention to bring disaster on Judah by mean of enemy invasion

vv. 17–19   Yahweh's renewed commission to Jeremiah with
its challenge to speak boldly and its promise
of protection

This analysis broadly corresponds to the divisions in MT, which has section markers after vv. 3, 6, 10, 12, and 19. Jeremiah 1 thus forms a coherent section to introduce the scroll. It does so by bringing together some originally separate elements. Verses 1–3 is a third-person preface that corresponds to the prefaces in many prophetic scrolls. In substance, though not in form or structure, the first-person account in vv. 4–19 then follows an a-b-b'-a' order. Verses 4–10 tell of a commission. Verses 11–16 relate two occasions when Yahweh enabled the prophet to "see" something by looking at something ordinary—they might be two separate experiences, though they have become the subject of a linked testimony. Verses 17–19 continue this second report, but their content reverts to the theme and focus of vv. 4–10.

A. PREFACE (1:1–3)

¹*The words of*ᵃ *Jeremiah*ᵇ *ben Hilkiah, one of the priests who were in Anathoth in the territory of Benjamin,* ²*to whom Yahweh's message came*ᶜ *in the time of Josiah ben Amon King of Judah, in the thirteenth year of his reign,* ³*and came*ᵈ *in the time of Jehoiakim ben Josiah King of Judah, until the ending of*ᵉ *the eleventh year of Zedekiah ben Josiah King of Judah, until the exile of Jerusalem*ᶠ *in the fifth month.*ᵍ

a. LXX has "the word of God that came to," a formulation more like the one in Hosea, Joel, Micah, Jonah, and Zephaniah ("God" rather than "the Lord" is unique, though it corresponds to v. 2 here), whereas MT's formulation compares with that in Amos. In 1–2 Kings, *dibrê* denotes the deeds (of a king), and in Amos and Jeremiah it might imply both words and deeds (cf. Neh 1:1). At the beginning of a prophetic scroll, however, it likely suggests words (cf. Vg).

b. On the name, see J. J. Stamm, "Der Name Jeremia," *ZAW* 100 (1988): 100–106. He concludes it means "Yahweh gives life."

c. The formulation recurs in the introduction to messages in 14:1; 46:1; 47:1; 49:34, with the meaning "what came/happened" (*hāyâ*). Here the *'ăšer* has an antecedent, as in 1 Kgs 18:31, and the clause is a regular relative clause with a resumptive pronominal suffix on *'ēlāyw* (W. Rudolph, *Jeremia*, 3rd ed., Handbuch zum Alten Testament 12 [Tübingen: Mohr Siebeck, 1968], 2). Cf. also 25:2 with a different antecedent.

d. Lit. "happened," as in v. 2 (cf. vv. 11, 13). Verses 1–2 could have led directly into v. 4, and v. 3 might have been added to adapt the preface as part of the introduction to the entire scroll.

e. LXX lacks *the ending of*, perhaps omitting it because of the tension with the subsequent reference to the fifth month; or perhaps it is an MT expansion of the shorter text represented by LXX.

f. The expression involves a metonymy: it is the people of Jerusalem who are taken into exile.

g. MT has a marker here.

This conventional preface answers three questions that its author evidently thought were important to anyone reading the scroll.

- Who was Jeremiah?
- Where did his message come from?
- What was it about?

People need to know about the person, know his times, and recognize who gave him the message. The answers in vv. 1–3 are preliminary ones that raise as many questions as they resolve; vv. 4–19 will elaborate on them, and the scroll as a whole will fill them out. The preface simply offers preliminary pointers to guide the scroll's readers. It functions to "impose order on chaos"—on "the messy and terrible events of history" as these unfolded in the period it covers—and it hints at the replacement of defunct priestly and kingly lines by a prophetic line.[1] It also suggests a framework of order for the messy scroll that it introduces.

The prefaces to Jeremiah and Ezekiel are the longest prophetic prefaces. Jeremiah's also compares particularly with Hosea's and Amos's in giving the prophet's name and family background, the time of his commissioning, and the names of the kings during his time. The preface is presumably the work of the theologian-curators who compiled the Jeremiah scroll, who wanted to offer guidance to people reading it (the conventional scholarly term for them is the Deuteronomists; see "Jeremiah and His Curators," pp. 34–36). The third-person form underscores the objective, factual nature of the preface's contents.

On the kings and their dates, see "Background" (pp. 2–3).

1 In answer to the first question, the preface gives Jeremiah's name and family background. Anathoth can presumably be linked with the modern village of Anata, three miles north of Jerusalem.[2] It is thus across the boundary between Judah and Benjamin so that technically Jeremiah is a Benjaminite and a northern Israelite in Jerusalem.[3] The reference to Anathoth makes clear

1. Y. Raz, "Jeremiah 'Before the Womb': On Fathers, Sons, and the Telos of Redaction in Jeremiah 1," in Maier and Sharp, *Prophecy and Power*, 91, 93.

2. Lundbom (*Jeremiah 1–20*, 223–24) discusses possible locations.

3. On whether Jeremiah is really an Ephraimite or a Judahite, see H. B. Huffmon, "Jeremiah of Anathoth," in Chazan, Hallo, and Schiffman, *Ki Baruch Hu*, 261–72.

that Jeremiah's father was not the Jerusalem Hilkiah, senior priest in his time (2 Kgs 22–23), who would hardly be described simply as one of the priests who were in Anathoth; the name is common.[4] The expression "Jeremiah of Anathoth" (29:27) would similarly serve to distinguish the prophet from other Jeremiahs. It is tempting to infer that a priestly family in Anathoth comprised descendants of Abiathar, the senior priest in David's day who was banished to Anathoth after backing Adonijah rather than Solomon as David's successor, Anathoth being one of the towns where priestly families lived (Josh 21:13–19; 1 Kgs 2:26–27).[5] Ironically, then, from the place to which Solomon banished Abiathar comes a man who will speak the word against Solomon's edifice.[6] It would not be surprising if Abiathar's family had continued to act as priests at a shrine at Anathoth; if their shrine was one that was closed down by Josiah (2 Kgs 23), there might well have been animosity in Anathoth toward the Jerusalem authorities as well as animosity in Jerusalem toward someone who could be called "Jeremiah of Anathoth." Perhaps Jeremiah got caught in the crossfire between the two priesthoods by not being obviously loyal to either (see Jer 11–12). On the other hand, neither would it be surprising if the Anathoth priesthood kept alive an awareness of Israelite faith going back to Eli and behind Abiathar to Moses, the faith that then shaped Jeremiah and made him the man he was. There's no hint that Jeremiah functioned as a priest in Anathoth, though his priestly connections might lie behind the liberty with which he relates to the temple (e.g., 19:1; 35:1–4; see the commentary on v. 5).

2 The answer to the second question is: Yahweh spoke to him, in Josiah's time and subsequently. *The words of Jeremiah* (v. 1) were thus also *Yahweh's message* (word). Verses 7 and 9 will expand on the interrelationship of the expressions. *Came* or "happened" (hāyâ; cf. vv. 3, 4, etc.) suggests the objective factuality of this message. It did not issue from Jeremiah's wise reflection but from elsewhere. "The incongruence between the word of a human being and the word of Yahweh is abolished."[7] The expression *Yahweh's message came* suggests a "word event"[8] that represents "the incursion of potent, sovereign word

---

4. Duhm, *Jeremia*, 2. But see A. P. Jassen, "The Rabbinic Construction of Jeremiah's Lineage," in *Texts and Contexts of Jeremiah*, ed. K. Finsterbusch and A. Lange (Leuven: Peeters, 2016), 3–20.

5. See further S. D. McBride, "Jeremiah and the Levitical Priests of Anathoth," in *Thus Says the Lord: Essays on the Former and Latter Prophets in Honor of Robert R. Wilson*, ed. J. J. Ahn and S. L. Cook, LHBOTS 502 (London: T&T Clark, 2009), 179–196.

6. R. P. Carroll, *Jeremiah*, OTL, 90–91.

7. S. Herrmann, *Jeremia*, 2 fascicles, Biblischer Kommentar: Altes Testament (Neukirchen: Neukirchener, 1986, 1990), 1:11.

8. G. Fischer, *Jeremia*, 2 vols., Herders Theologischer Kommentar zum Alten Testament (Freiburg: Herder, 2005), 1:133.

into the life of prophet and nation."[9] This coming of Yahweh's word initially happened on the occasion of Jeremiah's commission in the thirteenth year of Josiah's reign, 626 BC (see v. 7). On the reckoning in 1 Kgs 22–23, it was five years before Josiah's reformation, though according to 2 Chr 34, the reformation had already been initiated, and Jeremiah's commission would come between two stages in the reformation. Given that Jer 1 and Jer 25 constitute the beginning and midpoint of the scroll, the date will turn out to make a link with 25:3.[10]

3 Whereas the initial reference to a message coming suggested a one-time event (the event on which vv. 4–19 will say more), v. 3 refers to a recurring series of events over subsequent decades: compare the plural *words* in v. 9. The preface thus provides information on the chronological/political background of the time. The other two kings listed reigned for nearly the entire period between their father Josiah and the fall of Jerusalem. The preface omits reference to Jehoahaz, who was also a son of Josiah and immediately succeeded him but reigned for only three months, to Jehoiakim's son Jehoiachin, who also reigned for only three months between Jehoiakim and Zedekiah, and to events after the fall of Jerusalem that Jer 40–44 relate. Zedekiah did not see his year eleven to its end; the *ending* of his eleventh year likely denotes the termination of his reign, which came during his eleventh year (for which, see 39:2; 52:5–6). The fifth month of a year reckoned to begin at Passover will refer to July/August (see 52:1–16). The preface's omitting mention of Zedekiah's ousting and death is not remarkable in light of its leaving out equivalent information about the other two kings, though it might still be a telling omission. The scroll will name Zedekiah more often than the rest of the Judahite kings put together and will portray Jeremiah involved in ongoing conflict with him.

The list as a whole and the place where v. 3 ends indicate that they are tough times. Josiah lost his life in battle. Jehoahaz was deposed by the Egyptians. Jehoiakim experienced invasion and attack from the Babylonians and other local peoples. His son Jehoiachin was deposed and taken off to Babylon (though in 52:31–34 he is implicitly a symbol of hope). Zedekiah was maimed in the aftermath of the fall of Jerusalem. In addition, with varying degrees of specificity, 2 Kings sees all these kings as going back on Josiah's reformation, as thus bringing trouble on their people, and as thereby earning the trouble that came to them.

Nevertheless, the event that counts in 587 is not the humiliating and horrifying end of Zedekiah's reign, nor his exile, imprisonment, and death

---

9. J. I. Lawler, "Word Event in Jeremiah," in *Inspired Speech: Prophecy in the Ancient Near East; Essays in Honor of Herbert B. Huffmon*, ed. J. Kaltner and L. Stulman, JSOTSup 378 (London: T&T Clark, 2004), 242.

10. Fischer, *Jeremia*, 1:127.

(52:1–11). It is the city's exile. Verse 3 thus concerns not merely the chronology of Jeremiah's time but the content of his message. While other prophetic prefaces often mention kings, they do not mention historical events, as Jeremiah's does. Further, this event is key to buttressing the idea that he was a true prophet. This closing reference to the exile in 1:1–3 pairs with the account of the city's fall and the exile that concludes the scroll as a whole in 52:1–34. The two—especially in combination—imply a point about the fulfillment of Jeremiah's message. The scroll as a whole will refer to events that followed on the fall of Jerusalem (see Jer 40–44), as it will refer to Jehoiachin. But v. 3, by stopping where it does, draws attention to the event that constituted the fulfillment of the warnings on which Jeremiah had been long focusing. Its stopping point is hardly a basis for hypothesizing that the preface originally introduced an earlier version of the scroll that did not include the account of events after the city's fall. Ending where it does, the preface makes a theological point. The fact of the exile hangs over the scroll; "the book of Jeremiah holds the record for the variety of *verbal phrases* used to denote exile."[11] Whether the city will fall is an open question through most of the scroll, but the preface knows that it will. And the scroll is written for people who know that the exile has happened, who need to understand it, and who need to know how to look to the future.

> The patient God was offering a respite even, so to speak, down to the day before the Captivity, urging hearers to repent so that he may prevent the misfortune of the captivity. Hence it is written, Jeremiah prophesied until the captivity of Jerusalem, until the fifth month. The Captivity begins, and still he prophesied, saying something like this: "Become captives, provided in such circumstances you can repent! For when you repent, the misfortunes of the captivity will not transpire, but God's mercy will be realized for you."[12]

Over against the fact that Jehoiakim and Zedekiah are the prominent kings in the scroll, events in the reign of Josiah, with its great reformation, are less prominent than one might have expected. Admittedly, any prophetic scroll is selective. There is no reason to think that the "Minor Prophets" (i.e., the Shorter Prophets) said less than the "Major Prophets" in the course of their ministries, but for one reason or another, fewer of their prophecies were preserved. Perhaps a related dynamic gave the Jeremiah scroll the length

---

11. D. Rom-Shiloni, *Exclusive Inclusivity: Identity Conflicts Between the Exiles and the People Who Remained (6th–5th Centuries BCE)*, LHBOTS 543 (London: T&T Clark, 2013), 212.

12. Origen of Alexandria, *Homilies on Jeremiah and 1 Kings 28*, trans. John Clark Smith, The Fathers of the Church 97 (Washington: Catholic University of America, 1998), 4–5.

and the balance it manifests. The disastrous early death of Josiah and the religious and moral reversion that followed meant that his reformation failed to generate the escape from calamity that one might have hoped for and that Jeremiah might have envisaged. As the Jeremiah scroll sought to bring its challenging and encouraging message to the next generation or three, the failure of Josiah's reformation was hardly a dynamic to draw attention to.[13]

B. JEREMIAH GIVES AN ACCOUNT OF HIS COMMISSION (1:4–10)

[4]*Yahweh's message came to me:*[a]

[5]*Before I formed you*[b] *in [someone's] insides, I acknowledged*[c] *you;*
   before you went out from a womb, I sanctified you;
   the nations' prophet[d] *I am making you.*[e]

[6]*I said, "Oh no, Lord Yahweh! There, I don't know how to speak, because I'm a kid."*[f] [7]*But Yahweh said to me,*

Don't say "I'm a kid,"
   because to everyone[g] *that I send you to, you are to go,*
   and everything that I order you, you are to speak.
[8]*Don't be afraid before them,*
   because I am with you to snatch you away (Yahweh's affirmation).[h]

[9]*Yahweh extended his hand and made it touch*[i] *my mouth. And Yahweh said to me,*

There, I'm putting my words in your mouth;
   [10]*see, I'm appointing you this day*
   over the nations, yes,[j] *over the kingdoms,*
To pull up[k] *and to pull down*
   and to wipe out and to smash;
   to build[l] *and to plant.*[m]

a. Here and commonly elsewhere, the text includes the word *lēʾmōr* (lit. "[by] saying"), which functions like a colon in English introducing a quotation. Some LXX MSS have "to him," not "to me."

13. See further H.-J. Stipp, "Die joschijanische Reform im Jeremiabuch," in *"Ich werde meinen Bund mit euch niemals brechen!" (Ri 2, 1): Festschrift für Walter Gross zum 70. Geburtstag*, ed. E. Gass and H.-J. Stipp, Herders Biblische Studien 62 (Freiburg: Herder, 2011), 101–29.

b. The *qere* has *'eṣṣorkā* from *yāṣar*; the *ketiv* implies *'eṣṣûrkā* from the byform *ṣûr*.

c. The common verb *yādaʿ*, meaning "know," is frequently used with the connotation of "acknowledge" (e.g., 2:8; 5:4–5) and then with the more precise sense of "choose" (cf. Gen 8:19; Exod 33:12; Amos 3:2): "a knowledge not intuitive only, but also approbative" (J. A. Trapp, *Commentary or Exposition upon These Following Books of Holy Scripture: Proverbs of Solomon, Ecclesiastes, the Song of Songs, Isaiah, Jeremiah, Lamentations, Ezekiel & Daniel* [Kidderminster: Simmons, 1660], 221).

d. While Vg translates, "I gave you to the nations as a prophet," Tg takes *laggôyim* to imply "against the nations" and has Jeremiah commissioned to make them drink the chalice to which 25:15 will refer; it then takes the negative verbs in v. 10 to refer to the nations. Syr and some LXX MSS have "to the nation" (cf. 18:7, 9; HUBP).

e. This third *qatal* verb is declarative/performative, denoting what Yahweh is doing at this moment, not what he did before Jeremiah was born; cf. the verbs in vv. 9, 10, and 18 (see the commentary there).

f. MT has an intriguing marker here.

g. Vg has "to all things"; Tg has "to every place" (implying that he will go to the nations).

h. This extrametrical phrase recurs through the scroll, more often in MT than in LXX; McKane (*Jeremiah*, 1:6) nicely paraphrases "you have my word." The entirety of v. 8 reappears in 42:11 as the promise that Jeremiah passes on to the rebels after the fall of Jerusalem.

i. The verb *wayyaggaʿ* is *hiphil*, from *nāgaʿ*, as in Isa 6:7; LXX, Vg "touched" implies *qal wayyiggaʿ*.

j. The *wə* is explicative.

k. Vg translates all six verbs "so that you may . . ."

l. LXX, Vg, Syr prefix the verb with "and"; MT's omission of "and" marks the switch from the negative infinitives to the positive ones.

m. MT has a unit marker here. "Plant" is *nāṭaʿ*, which makes for further assonance with the first pair of verbs, though the similarity has a paradoxical significance: it belies the contrast in the words' meaning.

Verses 4–10 and 11–19 form further elements in a prologue to the Jeremiah scroll as a whole. They provide more detailed answers to the three questions noted in connection with vv. 1–3, opening up themes and introducing key motifs:

- The person of Jeremiah himself is important to the scroll.
- Jeremiah is to be a prophet who has to speak about the nations.
- Yahweh is committed to implementing his threats and promises when it doesn't look as if he is.
- Disaster from the north is a central focus of Jeremiah's message.
- The background to the disaster is Israel's unfaithfulness to Yahweh.
- The restoration of Israel is also a motif in Jeremiah's message.
- People will oppose him.
- He must live in ongoing obedience to Yahweh's commission.
- Yahweh will protect him as he meets with opposition.

- He will need to be resolute in the fulfillment of his commission.
- Yahweh will be committed to enabling him to be resolute and unstoppable.

Verses 1–3 and 4–19 thus comprise parallel introductions to the entire scroll—vv. 1–3 in the third person with more stress on concrete chronology, vv. 4–19 in the first person with more stress on Jeremiah's commission and on the scroll's themes.

Verses 4–10 and their continuation in vv. 11–19 parallel other accounts of a prophet's commission and the accounts of the commissions of Moses and Gideon.[14] As is the case with the giving of testimonies in some churches or the formulation of prayers, the existence of a familiar way of giving such an account facilitates an individual's articulating their experience and also enables the listeners to recognize that the experience is real and that the prophet is the real thing; it constitutes his "credentials."[15] A comparison with other commissions helps highlight the significance of typical features while also drawing attention to this account's distinctive significance.

- Jeremiah's account comes near the beginning of the scroll, like Ezekiel's and Hosea's but unlike Isaiah's and Amos's. It forms part of the scroll's framework.
- Like the preface, it summarizes the agenda of the scroll as a whole—like the preface to Hosea but unlike that to Ezekiel (which refers only to the equivalent of pulling up and pulling down). It thus seems likely to have been composed to introduce a collection of Jeremiah's messages as a whole.
- It specifies that this message relates to "the nations."
- It takes first-person form, like Ezekiel's and Isaiah's but unlike Amos's and Hosea's. It thereby draws attention to the extent to which Jeremiah personally participates in his commission; he is not simply an uninvolved messenger.
- It emphasizes Yahweh's initiative in issuing the commission, as is the case with Amos. It is an initiative that antedates Jeremiah's birth; it does not suggest that Jeremiah was seeking to discover what his vocation might be, had a sense of vocation, or thought in any way

14. See D. Vieweger, *Die Spezifik der Berufungsberichte Jeremias und Ezechiels im Umfeld ähnlicher Einheiten des Alten Testaments*, Beiträge zur Erforschung des Alten Testaents und des antike Judentums 6 (Frankfurt: Lang, 1986).

15. P. D. Miller, "Jeremiah," in *The New Interpreter's Bible*, ed. L. E. Keck, vol. 6 (Nashville: Abingdon, 2001). See further G. Wanke, "Jeremias Berufung (Jer 1,4–10)," in *Alttestamentlicher Glaube und Biblische Theologie: Festschrift für Horst Dietrich Preuss zum 65. Geburtstag*, ed. J. Hausmann and H.-J. Zobel (Stuttgart: Kohlhammer, 1992), 132–44.

along these lines (and I avoid the word "call," which carries considerable baggage). Jeremiah is not a volunteer like Isaiah, and there is no suggestion that Yahweh chooses him because he has the right gifts. If vocation is "the place where your deep gladness and the world's deep hunger meet," Jeremiah has no vocation, or his vocation is "a call to dissent."[16]

- It comprises a report by Jeremiah of dialogue between Yahweh and Jeremiah, but it is not a Bakhtinian dialogue; Jeremiah contributes only an objection that Yahweh overrules and a pair of observations that Yahweh then interprets. The vast bulk of the "dialogue" is Yahweh's words.

- Like the preface, it underlines the factual or objective nature of what happens, as is the case with Ezekiel: "I am putting my words in your mouth." Another significance of its dialogic form is to point to the reality of the event, as is the case with the commissions of Isaiah and Ezekiel.[17]

- It relates how Jeremiah resists his commission, like Jonah (and Moses and Gideon) but unlike Isaiah, Ezekiel, and Hosea. It thereby underscores the implication that Jeremiah really is fulfilling Yahweh's commission. He is not doing what he wants to do.

- It incorporates a reassurance of Yahweh's presence and a sign, like Moses's and Gideon's.

- It emphasizes the opposition Jeremiah will receive.

- Like the other accounts, it makes no direct reference to Jeremiah's final response to Yahweh's commission. The focus lies on Yahweh's commission; implicitly, the rest of the scroll relates Jeremiah's response.[18]

Unlike Isaiah and Ezekiel, Jeremiah does not speak in terms of a vision,[19] nor does he speak of hearing the sound of Yahweh's voice like Samuel. I have myself had the experience of seeing God's hand pointing at something, of sensing God's embrace, and of having a conversation with God in which

16. P. E. Thompson, "Jeremiah 1:1–10," *Int* 62 (2008): 66, 67, quoting F. Buechner, *Wishful Thinking* (New York: Harper, 1973), 118.

17. E. Davis Lewin, "Arguing for Authority: A Rhetorical Study of Jeremiah 1.4–19 and 20.7–18," *JSOT* 32 (1985): 107.

18. P. C. Craigie, P. H. Kelley, and J. F. Drinkard, *Jeremiah 1–25*, WBC 26 (Dallas: Word, 1991), 11–12.

19. See E. R. Hayes, "The Role of Visionary Experiences for Establishing Prophetic Authority in Isaiah, Jeremiah and Ezekiel," in *"I Lifted My Eyes and Saw": Reading Dream and Vision Reports in the Hebrew Bible*, ed. E. R. Hayes and L.-S. Tiemeyer, LHBOTS 584 (London: T&T Clark, 2014), 59–70.

sometimes I might take an initiative and sometimes God might—though either way, God's words were not an articulation of something that I was thinking anyway. And I am able to distinguish these experiences from the sense that an idea has come to me and from a conviction that God has been present with me that is based on things that have happened. Whereas it is proper to be concerned about literalism in interpreting accounts of a prophet's experience, reductionism is a greater danger in the context of modernity, of the familiarity of Buddhism, and of new age thinking, and Jeremiah's account invites readers to infer that "'God' is not a device for objectifying inner convictions."[20]

How did vv. 4–19 come into being? There are subsets to this question.

- What were the roles of Jeremiah and his disciples? An obvious assumption is that a disciple wrote vv. 1–3 and Jeremiah dictated vv. 4–19. But a creative writer can write about someone else in the first person, and someone can write about him or herself in the third person.
- Are vv. 4–19 a transcript of what happened when Yahweh commissioned Jeremiah, are they a dramatization of the event as Gen 1 is a dramatization of creation, or are they something in between—an adaptation based on fact?
- Were they composed at the time of the event that they describe, in about 626 BC, were they composed from scratch as a dedicated introduction to the scroll sometime after the last events it relates, or do they represent a reworking of an account with a prehistory going back to that time?

These questions open up many possibilities, which themselves embrace further alternatives (e.g., did the final work on the scroll and therefore on this introduction happen in the Babylonian period or in the Persian period?). The attempt to answer these questions and to interpret Jer 1 as a whole may profit from comparing and contrasting the chapter with Hos 1:1–2:1 (1:1–2:3).

- The Hosea scroll, too, begins with a third-person preface.
- That preface leads into a narrative account of the beginning of Hosea's activity as a prophet.
- That account derives from a period later than his original commission (Hosea has had time to marry and have several children).

---

20. McKane, *Jeremiah*, 1:9, summarizing Rudolph, *Jeremia*, 9–10 (who says it's as real as Paul on the Damascus road), and Weiser, about whose views McKane is hesitant (A. Weiser, *Das Buch des Propheten Jeremia*, 2 vols, Das Alte Testament Deutsch [Göttingen: Vandenhoeck & Ruprecht, 1952]).

- It incorporates a number of statements by Yahweh presented as his actual words.
- It offers a perspective on the message of the scroll as a whole.
- It emphasizes threats but incorporates promises.
- It presupposes the downfall of the nation, which fulfills the threats.
- It presupposes a time when the promises have not yet been fulfilled.

The major difference is that Hos 1:1–2:1 (1:1–2:3) takes third-person form while Jer 1:4–19 takes first-person form. As is the case in connection with Jer 1:1–3, one cannot simply infer that Hoseanic theologians composed the third-person Hosea narrative while Jeremiah himself composed the first-person Jeremiah narrative, but my best guess is that this assumption is actually correct. The most plausible scenario is that a theologian wrote Jer 1:1–3, that Jeremiah dictated vv. 4–19, that in doing so he adapted the facts and his memory of his commission so that the account could function as an introduction to the deposit of his work, and that he did so in the 580s or 570s. Verses 4–19 are then "a mature reflection on a youthful experience."[21] That view is just one possible one.[22] I have more confidence in the conviction that whoever were the authors of vv. 4–19, they were inspired by the Holy Spirit to portray Jeremiah having the experience it describes in light of the actual process whereby he came to be a prophet and of his activity as a prophet so that the scroll's readers might take it as an introduction to the scroll that would help them understand it and respond to it.

Verses 4–10 are mostly Yahweh's words. Most of them manifest rhythm and parallelism that suggests they are poetic lines, which enhances their importance and eminence. Even the lines that lack parallelism are sufficiently rhythmic to make it feasible to lay out the entirety of Yahweh's words as poetry, albeit prosaic poetry. They comprise four tricola with one bicolon at the center (4-4-3, 3-4-4, 2-3, 4-4-2, 2-2-2). In the first tricolon, the opening two cola are closely parallel; in the second tricolon, the closing two cola are closely parallel; in the third tricolon, the opening two cola are broadly paral-

---

21. Pixley, *Jeremiah*, 11.

22. For theories regarding the development of Jer 1, see, e.g., J. Schreiner, "Jeremias Berufung (Jer 1,4–19): Eine Textanalyse," in *Homenaje a Juan Prado*, ed. L. Alvarez Verdes and E. J. Alonso Hernández (Madrid: CSIC, 1975), 131–45; B. Renaud, "Jér 1: Structure et Théologie de la Redaction," in Bogaert, *Livre de Jérémie*, 177–196; W. Thiel, "'Vom Norden her wird das Unheil eröffnet': Zu Jeremia 1,11–16," in *Prophet und Prophetenbuch: Festschrift für Otto Kaiser zum 65. Geburtstag*, ed. V. Fritz, K.-F. Pohlmann, and H.-C. Schmitt, BZAW 185 (Berlin: de Gruyter, 1989), 231–45; J. R. Lundbom, "Rhetorical Structures in Jeremiah 1," *ZAW* 93 (1991): 193–210; C. J. Sharp, "The Call of Jeremiah and Diaspora Politics," *JBL* 119 (2000): 421–38.

lel; in the final tricolon, all three cola are parallel, and they incorporate metaphor and paronomasia. In substance, vv. 4–10 follow an a-b-b'-a' order:

vv. 4–5   Yahweh speaks, recalling his past preparation of Jeremiah
          as a prophet to the nations
v. 6   Jeremiah objects
vv. 7–8   Yahweh responds
vv. 9–10 Yahweh acts, implementing his preparation of Jeremiah as a
          prophet to the nations

The formal parallels with other accounts of commissioning, such as those of Moses, Gideon, Samuel, Isaiah, and Ezekiel, are clear:

v. 4   A revelation from Yahweh
v. 5   A commission from Yahweh
v. 6   An objection
v. 7   A reply and a restated commission
v. 8   A reassurance
v. 9   A sign
v. 10   A restated commission

Comparison with these other accounts indicates that here the revelation is brief (esp. compared with those to Samuel and Ezekiel) and the objection is brief (esp. compared with that of Moses). The objection mainly becomes the opportunity for a twice-restated elaboration on the commission, which is put briefly in v. 5, slightly more fully in v. 7, and most elaborately in v. 10. In the focus on the content of the commission, Jeremiah compares with Samuel and Isaiah.

4 Jeremiah's opening formulation picks up the words of v. 2a: this is the message that came to him in the thirteenth year of Josiah's reign.

5a Forming or shaping like a potter (see Jer 18) is an image for God's original creation of the human and animal world (Gen 2:7–8; Ps 95:5; Isa 45:18) but also for his bringing each person into being (Pss 33:15; 94:9; 45:7; see Jer 10:16). In particular, it is an image for bringing into being someone with a specific role to play in his service (Isa 49:5) and an image for bringing Israel into being (Isa 44:2).[23] More than one of these ideas might apply here. Yahweh

---

23. J. M. Berridge, *Prophet, People, and the Word of Yahweh: An Examination of Form and Content in the Proclamation of the Prophet Jeremiah*, Basel Studies of Theology 4 (Zurich: EVZ, 1970), 41.

shaped Jeremiah as he shapes everyone. But here (paradoxically), he first *acknowledged*—or chose or destined—Jeremiah for a particular role and then shaped him accordingly. Yahweh could have used the verb "chose," which the First Testament applies to Abraham (Neh 9:7), Levi (Deut 18:5), Aaron (Ps 105:26), Saul (1 Sam 10:24), and David and Solomon (1 Chr 28:4–5). But "choice" simply implies taking responsibility, whereas "acknowledgment" implies making a commitment, as Jeremiah's frequent use of the verb will reflect (e.g., 2:8; 4:22; 5:4–5). Yahweh made a commitment to Jeremiah before Jeremiah existed. To judge from the scroll, he shaped him as someone with a commitment to Yahweh, with imagination, and with sensitivity. Yahweh's designation did not take place *in* the womb but before Jeremiah was even conceived. It is a unique designation in the First Testament, though paralleled by the designation of Jesus in Luke 1:26–38. Paul generalizes its point in Rom 8:29,[24] and Jeremiah may help one understand Paul's point: God foreknew people in the sense of acknowledging them ahead of time as people he intended to make part of his people because of something he wanted to achieve through them. In themselves, Yahweh's words do not indicate whether he formed Jeremiah in a way that he did not form other people. The First Testament elsewhere assumes that Yahweh forms everyone in the womb. But it can also speak in general terms about "opening the womb" while elsewhere applying that expression to particularly significant births. Yahweh may have in mind a forming that applies to Jeremiah in a distinctive way because of the role he intends for him. But it's the aim rather than the process that's different.

The second colon forms a perfect complement to the first:

| Before | I formed you | in [someone's] insides, | I acknowledged you; |
| before | you went out | from a womb, | I sanctified you. |

The temporal expression repeats; the verb adds Jeremiah's action (he had to come out) to Yahweh's action; the second prepositional expression makes the first more precise; and the final verb rephrases the parallel one. The most significant new note in the second colon is that Yahweh has *sanctified* Jeremiah—that is, made him holy or sacred, dedicated him, or set him apart for his service (*qādaš hiphil*). "Sanctifying" implies choosing someone in order to do what you wish with them, which is the regular connotation of the notion of choosing in the Scriptures. Sacredness is not a common theme in the Prophets except in Ezekiel, who is especially the priestly prophet; this difference illustrates how Jeremiah's priestly background does not mean he thinks

24. Rudolph, *Jeremia*, 5.

like a priest. Yahweh's sanctifying Jeremiah is not equivalent to his cleansing Isaiah (Isa 6:5–7) or to his choosing kings and having them anointed (e.g., 1 Sam 9; 16), where the language of sacredness does not occur, or to his separating Israel from the worship commitments of the Canaanites (Deut 7:6). The focus on Jeremiah's birth makes it closer to the sanctifying of firstborn (e.g., Num 3:13; 8:17), which is also the only context in the First Testament for the use of this (*hiphil*) verb with a human object. Jeremiah is especially claimed by God, like the firstborn of human beings and animals. Within the Jeremiah scroll, its nearest parallel is the sanctifying of warriors (the *piel* verb; e.g., 22:7; 51:27–28, where sanctifying is associated with appointing). As sanctifying suggests dedicating Jeremiah for a special task that relates to Yahweh's purpose, the aggressive nature of the vocation that Yahweh is giving Jeremiah (v. 10; also vv. 17–19) fits with this parallel.[25] But the people who are most often the object of the *piel* verb in the First Testament are priests (e.g., Exod 28–29), so the verb does deserve reading in light of v. 1. Jeremiah is like Ezekiel after all. Both prophets had priestly lineage; neither prophet could function as a priest in the temple; both are appointed as prophets by an act of consecration—explicitly so appointed in Jeremiah's case. In Israel and its royal court, there was such a thing as a prophetic office; people such as Nathan occupied it (e.g., 2 Sam 7; 1 Kgs 1). Jeremiah does not occupy this position, and in this sense it is misleading to speak of his being appointed to it.[26] On the other hand, there is a prophetic office in Yahweh's court that one could see Jeremiah as occupying (see Jer 23:21–22), and one could say that he is here reporting his appointment to that office (see v. 10).

5b Given that the 4–4 bicolon was neatly complete, a third colon is a surprise at one level—though at another level it is not. One of the ways in which parallelism functions is by the first colon leaving open a question that the second resolves, and v. 5 as a whole functions this way. But in substance, the opening two cola are incomplete in the sense that they raise a question they do not answer. What did Yahweh shape Jeremiah for? What did he come out to do? The third colon answers the question. To put it another way, the middle colon functioned only to raise suspense, which the third colon resolves in the manner of the second colon in a bicolon. *The nations' prophet I am making you.* This is a speech act, equivalent to "I hereby make you." The word order, with the description of Jeremiah as a prophet coming before the verb, underscores the significance of the designation. Admittedly, *prophet* (*nābî'*) could have various resonances, like "minister" in English. In

---

25. E. H. Roshwalb, "Jeremiah 1:4–10: 'Lost and Found' in Translation and a New Interpretation," *JSOT* 34 (2010): 351–76.

26. Berridge, *Prophet, People, and the Word*, 29; contrast H. G. Reventlow, *Liturgie und prophetisches Ich bei Jeremia* (Gütersloh: Mohn, 1963), 70.

Israel, there were many prophets linked with sanctuaries or functioning on the king's staff, offering advice to ordinary people and to the administration. Some would be committed to the faith in Yahweh that the First Testament affirms; some would be more open-minded. Some would be identified with the administration; some would find it easier to be more independent. To call Jeremiah a prophet is not an unequivocal compliment nor an unequivocal encouragement.[27] Yet here, the designation is free of polemical undertones,[28] despite the narratives that will follow in Jer 27–29 and in contrast to Amos 7:10–17, where Amos questions it.

What does it mean to be *the nations' prophet* (*nābî' laggôyim*; more literally "a prophet for the nations")? "This is a very strange designation of a prophet."[29] While v. 5b clarifies, it thus also tantalizes. Who are these nations? Ephraim and Judah (so that the nations are not set over against Israel—Israel is one of the nations)?[30] The regional and imperial powers Egypt, Assyria, and Babylon? Neighbors such as Philistia, Moab, and Ammon? While most prophets have to say things that relate to other nations, for Jeremiah this role will be more central—a fact that will emerge as the scroll unrolls. In v. 10, Yahweh will speak of Jeremiah being appointed about or against (*'al*) the nations; in 25:9, that formulation recurs, and *'al* unequivocally means "against." Jeremiah 25–28 expands on this theme. The description recurs again in 46:1, in the introduction to the messages about different nations in Jer 46–51. In the shorter term within the scroll, Jeremiah will speak of the nations coming to acknowledge Yahweh (3:17; 16:19), of their seeking blessing like Israel's (4:2), of Yahweh attending to them (9:25–26[24–25]), of Yahweh's pouring out his wrath on them (10:25), and of them witnessing to what Yahweh does and to who Israel is (4:16; 6:18; 18:13). As far as we know, none of this speaking will be actually addressed to the nations themselves (unless in Jer 27). It will be addressed to Judah's kings and their cabinets, to its priests and people (see v. 18), pointing out implications for foreign policy and religious policy and thus for what they need to decide to do. The Jeremiah scroll as a whole will suggest developing the idea of *the nations' prophet* in at least two directions:

27. See M. J. de Jong, "Why Jeremiah Is Not among the Prophets: An Analysis of the Terms *nby'* and *nb'ym* in the Book of Jeremiah," *JSOT* 35 (2011): 483–510; more broadly, see A. G. Auld, "Prophets through the Looking Glass: Between Writings and Moses," *JSOT* 27 (1983): 3–23; "Prophets and Prophecy in Jeremiah and Kings," ZAW 96 (1984): 66–82; cf., in response, T. W. Overholt, "Prophecy in History: The Social Reality of Intermediation," *JSOT* 48 (1990): 3–29.

28. Herrmann, *Jeremia*, 1:58.

29. R. P. Carroll, *From Chaos to Covenant*, 53.

30. H. Michaud, "La vocation du 'prophète des nations,'" in *Maqqel shaqedh: Hommage à Wilhelm Vischer* (Montpelier: Castelnau, 1960), 161.

It means Yahweh's judgment is coming against the entire world of nations. It also means that they may turn to Yahweh and thus be built and planted.[31]

Jeremiah's account prompts reflection on divine sovereignty, election, determination, and freewill,[32] invites (as often happens) a rethinking of modern categories if we are to understand, and offers an alternative way of thinking about the issues in question. Did Jeremiah have a choice about being who he was and about being a prophet? It's a logically odd question. Can I choose to be someone other than the person I am? Can I choose not to be myself? Sure! Will God let me make that choice? Maybe, maybe not. A vineyard owner (who stands for God) told his son to go and work in the vineyard, but he didn't go (Matt 21:28–32). On the other hand, there are stories about people who try to decline God's commission but fail (Moses, Saul, Jonah) and none about people who succeed in declining. Was Saul of Tarsus free to decline God's "choice" (Acts 9:15) after Jesus knocked him off his horse? Was Jonah free to decline Yahweh's commission after emerging from the fish? Sure! The dynamics of election are the dynamics of a personal interaction, and personal interactions don't follow systematic rules. Jeremiah is about to join the company of people who try to resist God's commission (people who decline to be themselves), and he is about to discover how Yahweh deals with his attempt as part of his relationship with him.

6 "What different answers God's chosen ones give to his voice!" (consider Amos, Isaiah, Moses).[33] Whereas Yahweh's words were poetically and vividly symmetrical and rhythmic, Jeremiah's response is unpoetic and unrhythmic, suggesting his confusion and sense of panic. This feature forms part of the passage's rhetoric; it helps establish that it was not because of his own inclination that Jeremiah delivered his message about Yahweh acting in wrath.[34] *Oh no* is *'āhâ*; the traditional translation "alas" is not far off. Jeremiah addresses the *Lord Yahweh*, but there is something illogical about his response given that he is not responding to Yahweh as if Yahweh is a Lord. With further irony, he picks up one of Yahweh's verbs: *yāda'*. Yahweh knew/acknowledged Jeremiah; Jeremiah doesn't know/acknowledge speaking. How can

31. C. J. Sharp, "Call of Jeremiah," 421–38. Sharp sees them as reflecting two different political agendas.

32. D. O. Idowu, "The Sovereignty of God in Jeremiah 1:4–10 and the Belief in Destiny among Yoruba People of Nigeria," *Practical Theology (Baptist College of Theology, Lagos)* 9 (2016): 146–170.

33. P. Volz, *Der Prophet Jeremia*, Kommentar zum Alten Testament, 2nd ed., vol. 10 (Leipzig: Deicher, 1928), 5.

34. Y. Gitay, "The Projection of the Prophet: A Rhetorical Presentation of the Prophet Jeremiah (according to Jer 1:1–19)," in *Prophecy and Prophets: The Diversity of Contemporary Issues in Scholarship*, ed. Y. Gitay, Semeia Studies 32 (Atlanta: Scholars, 1997), 45–46.

he address nations or take part in cabinet debates? He's a just a *kid* (*naʿar*). As a term denoting youth, the word might cover anything from a child to a young adult; David describes Absalom as a kid (2 Sam 18:5, 12), and King Solomon describes himself in the same terms—indeed, as a little kid (1 Kgs 3:7). While not much more than half of the First Testament occurrences of "kid" refer to someone of youthful years,[35] nearly half refer to someone who is (for instance) a servant (the first "kids" in the Scriptures are men capable of marching many miles to take part in a battle: Gen 14:24) or an apprentice, which is the nuance suggested by Jeremiah's reference to knowing *how to speak*. While he may not be very old, and "understanding is gray hair for men" (Wisdom 4:9),[36] his point concerns not his youthfulness but his lack of expertise, training, or gifting. His objection is not so different from that of Moses in Exod 4:10–17. After v. 5, his response is and is not a surprise. He speaks like someone praying in the manner of a psalm of protest or lament;[37] it is significant that his first words should be of this kind.[38]

7 "God's only answer was to make His instructions clearer."[39] Like Moses, Jeremiah subsequently shows a magnificent capacity to speak. It seems unlikely that God simply grafted on that capacity. It must be that Jeremiah didn't know he had it, he had never tried to exercise it, or he means he doesn't know what he would say. It is the last possibility that leads best into Yahweh's answer here. Yahweh does not simply ignore Jeremiah's objection but answers it, though the point is not immediately explicit. Again, Yahweh speaks in a tricolon, though here it is the second and third cola that are neatly complementary, once more comprising 4–4 cola through MT's judicious use of hyphens:

| Because | to everyone that | I send | you, you are to go, |
| and | everything that | I order | you, you are to speak. |

Jeremiah must go wherever he is told. Who is the *everyone* or where is the implicit everywhere? The nations are the antecedent of the statement, and 25:15 will have Jeremiah rhetorically sent to them.[40] So this command does nothing to solve the problem Jeremiah raised, though the parallel colon will provide an answer as it covers the action that will follow on fulfilling the command in the first. But the first colon ignores the problem. First there is

35. See BDB.

36. Jerome, *Jeremiah*, 4.

37. B. A. Strawn, "Jeremiah's In/effective Plea: Another Look at *nʿr* in Jeremiah i 6," *VT* 65 (2005): 366–77.

38. Fischer, *Jeremia*, 1:134–35.

39. H. L. Ellison, "The Prophecy of Jeremiah," *EvQ* 31 (1959): 214.

40. See H. P. Nasuti, "A Prophet to the Nations: Diachronic and Synchronic Readings of Jeremiah 1," *Hebrew Annual Review* 10 (1986): 253–54.

sending, and therefore there is a place (everywhere!), which makes things worse, and then there is to be the obedient going. Sending raises the question "To do what?" People are sent to do things, to discover things, to say things. But the designating of Jeremiah as a prophet makes the specification unsurprising: Jeremiah is sent *to speak*, sent as a kind of messenger. In connection with the fulfillment of the first instruction, there is the ordering, therefore the content of the order (everything!), and therefore the obedient speaking, which solves the problem of Jeremiah's correct apprehension that there is no way he can fulfill Yahweh's commission on his own. This complementary colon corresponds to Yahweh's promise concerning a prophet like Moses: "He will speak . . . everything that I order him" (Deut 18:18). We do not know whether Deut 18 antedates or postdates Jer 1, though in isolation from the broader considerations, it makes better sense to see Jer 1 portraying Jeremiah as a prophet like Moses than to see Deut 18 as promising someone like Jeremiah.[41] Jeremiah fulfills Moses's criteria for identification as a true prophet, though he needs not to be limited to reiterating what Moses said.[42] The audience is implicitly challenged to respond to Jeremiah in a way that recognizes his identity in this connection.[43]

8 Yahweh does now offer reassurance in a way appropriate to a lament-like protest such as Jeremiah has uttered,[44] but it relates to a different problem, which Jeremiah hasn't raised and apparently hasn't thought of. Yahweh's words are parallel with his response to that earlier problem:

> v. 7   Don't say . . .   because . . .
> v. 8   Don't be afraid . . .   because . . .

Literally, Yahweh bids Jeremiah not to be afraid of people's faces—an unusual expression. It wouldn't be surprising if he were afraid of the presence of the king and his cabinet or of other prophets (cf. vv. 17–19). But on the other occasions where Jeremiah uses the expression, it relates to the Babylonians (41:18; 42:11), and here the antecedent of *them* is the nations (v. 5). Within v. 8, the first colon thereby raises a question (How can Jeremiah not be afraid?), which the second colon answers. *I am with you* is then a key promise (cf.

---

41. See, e.g., C. M. Maier, "Jeremia am Ende: Prophetie als Schriftgelehrsamkeit," *EvT* 77 (2017), 51–53; G. Fischer also notes the differences between Jeremiah and Moses, in "Jeremiah—'The Prophet Like Moses'?," in Lundbom, Evans, and B. A. Anderson, *Jeremiah*, 45–66.

42. Mastnjak, *Deuteronomy*, 40–92.

43. See, e.g., G. E. Yates, "Intertextuality and the Portrayal of Jeremiah the Prophet," *BSac* 170 (2013): 288–93.

44. W. H. Schmidt, *Das Buch Jeremia*, 2 vols., Das Alte Testament Deutsch (Göttingen: Vandenhoeck & Ruprecht, 2008, 2013), 1:49.

Exod 3:12; Judg 6:16; Isa 41:10; 43:5),[45] as is the undertaking *to snatch you away*—more prosaically "to rescue you"—with the backing *Yahweh's affirmation* that Jeremiah himself will attach to words from Yahweh to the people on countless occasions.

9 Yahweh adds action to his words. So far, the commission has involved only a conversation. Jeremiah has simply had an awareness of Yahweh saying something, of responding, and of Yahweh replying. Although Jeremiah has indicated the objective nature of Yahweh's speaking in the form of his words in v. 4, there need have been no divine words that anyone else heard and no words that Jeremiah outwardly articulated. But Yahweh now adds an action with an even more explicitly objective nature. Although, again, maybe no one else would have been able to sense it, simply to call it a vision might be misleading. Touching (*nāgaʿ hiphil*) recalls Isa 6:7 (also 1 Kgs 19:5, 7, and passages in Daniel, though there the verb is *qal*). For both Isaiah and Jeremiah, there is a touching that deals with a problem they raise in connection with their commission, though the problems are different, and so is the significance of the touching. In Isa 6, a seraph applies a coal from the altar as a sacramental rite of cleansing. Here Yahweh's touch overlaps in significance with Ezekiel's eating a scroll that Yahweh gives him (Ezek 3): they are two ways by which Yahweh ensures that the prophet will speak Yahweh's words. The action in Ezekiel suggests that Yahweh causes Ezekiel to internalize his perspective. The action in Jeremiah suggests that Yahweh causes Jeremiah to externalize his perspective. It is a performative action. Putting words in someone's mouth means giving them a message that they will restate (Exod 4:15; 2 Sam 14:19; Ezra 8:17). Yahweh is here doing so in a once-for-all way for Jeremiah, opening his eyes (to use a different image) so that he sees how Yahweh views his people and grasps the message that has to be brought home to it. Yahweh thus continues the verbal performative action to which he referred in v. 5b, as he implements the plan formulated before Jeremiah's birth: *I'm putting* is the same verb (*nātan*) as *I am making* in v. 5, and Yahweh's *there* (*hinnēh*) corresponds to and confronts Jeremiah's *there* in v. 6. At the same time, Yahweh's words correspond further to his words concerning a prophet like Moses (Deut 18:18, except that there the verb is *śîm*). The correspondence again marks Jeremiah as a fulfillment of that promise. These words "will tear down much that his audience believes."[46]

10 The performative action and the implementing again continue. *The nations' prophet I am making you* (v. 5) becomes *I'm appointing you . . . / over the*

45. F. García López ("Élection-vocation d'Israël et de Jérémie," *VT* 35 [1985]: 1–12) also compares the account of Israel's election.

46. J. A. Dearman, *Jeremiah and Lamentations*, The NIV Application Commentary (Grand Rapids: Zondervan, 2002), on the passage.

nations, yes, over the kingdoms. If there was a touch of ambiguity in v. 5, which one could translate as "I am giving you to the nations," it is removed; Jeremiah is not a nice gift that Yahweh is "giving" the nations. He is appointing Jeremiah over them, as (ironically) Nebuchadrezzar will "appoint" Gedaliah "over" Judah (40:11). Yahweh adds reference to these nations being kingdoms, making more explicit that it will be kings such as Nebuchadrezzar, Pharaoh Neco, and the Median kings (e.g., 46:2; 51:11) over whom Jeremiah will be exercising authority—though in the immediate context the reference to kingdoms will be taken up in v. 15. Jeremiah is to be in charge of them. The implications are not yet made clear. Are the nations to be the victims of calamity from Yahweh? Are they to be Yahweh's agents? Verses 14–15 will suggest that the answer to both questions is "yes."

Yahweh has said nothing yet about Jeremiah being a prophet in relation to Israel, and one would initially assume that the six infinitives that now follow refer to action against these nations and their kings. Jeremiah will indeed involve himself with the potential fall of Babylon, and with the uprooting and wiping out of Judah's neighbors—and their reestablishing (12:14–17). But he focuses more on the fall and recovery of Israel itself, and it is in this connection that these verbs recur in 18:1–12; 24:6; 31:27–28, 40; 42:10; 45:4. The six infinitives thus raise a question that will be clarified only as the scroll unrolls. Nor does Yahweh indicate the verbs' subject. Is it Jeremiah? Is it the nations and kingdoms? Is it Yahweh himself? It will be Yahweh in the other passages that use these terms.

The balance between the six verbs is simultaneously solemn and encouraging. On one hand, four have negative implications; on the other, at least Yahweh does not stop there. The balance between negative and positive is more favorable than it is in the eighth-century prophets, though less so than it is in Ezekiel (their respective chronological locations make a difference). John Cassian reports that Abba Nestoros says, with a reference to this verse, that it is twice as hard to drive out vice as to acquire virtue.[47] But Jeremiah is talking about material as well as inward building and planting, not just salvation in an abstract sense.[48] The balance is also more favorable than the one in Jeremiah's actual messages. The difference would be encouraging for people reading the scroll in a context after the pulling up, pulling down, wiping out, and smashing have happened and hope is needed. At its very outset,

47. John Cassian, *Conferences* 14.3 (NPNF II, 11:436); cf. D. O. Wenthe, *Jeremiah, Lamentations*, Ancient Christian Commentary on Scripture: Old Testament 12 (Downers Grove, IL: InterVarsity, 2009), 8.

48. See G. H Wittenberg, "'To Build and to Plant' (Jer. 1:10): The Message of Jeremiah as a Source of Hope for the Exilic Community and Its Relevance for Community Building in South Africa," *Journal of Theology for Southern Africa* 112 (2002): 57–67.

the Jeremiah scroll, "which is so preoccupied with 'exile' . . . can anticipate the destruction of Babylon and the restoration of Jerusalem in the word pair 'plant and build.'" The scroll is "designed to walk Jews into, through, and beyond the reality of destruction and exile."[49] Perhaps the wording reflects the formulation of vv. 4–10 in that later context.

Pull up presupposes the image of a people as a plant such as a vine or an olive, apparently securely planted in its land but actually destined to be dug up. The image can apply to other peoples (12:14–17; 18:7) but it commonly applies to Israel in particular as a people planted in Canaan but in danger of being thrown out from that country (1 Kgs 14:15; 2 Chr 7:20; Pss 44:2[3]; 80:8[9]). It can also be a general metaphor to describe a people thriving like a plant or being uprooted from its land (Jer 31:40; 45:4; 2 Sam 7:10; 1 Chr 17:9; Ps 80:15[16]; Dan 11:4). While uprooting and planting is thus a familiar metaphor, *pull down* otherwise generally refers to the literal demolition of a structure (e.g., Jer 33:4; 39:8). The verbs for *pull up* and *pull down* are similar (*nātaš, nātaṣ*), which adds to the force of the double expression. *Wipe out* is a slightly less concrete term for terminating the life of something; *smash* has similar concrete implications to *pull down*. The language is the language of war—of siege and deportation.[50] But the four negative verbs do lead into two positive ones taking up the same imagery in a-b-b'-a' order: *pull down* will give way to *build*, and *pull up* to *plant*. The building metaphor is, again, more innovative, whereas the planting metaphor is familiar as a term for placing a people (back) on its land or causing it to flourish there (cf. 2:21; 11:17; 32:41; 42:10; Amos 9:15).

Typically, Yahweh's words leave open whether demolition/uprooting and building/planting are alternatives between which Judah must choose (which is the situation up until 587), experiences that will follow one another if Judah does not respond to the prophet (which is how things work out), or alternatives between which the recalcitrant and the repentant will *de facto* choose. Whereas in v. 3, with hindsight, the future was closed, here it is open. "The choice before us," Jeremiah would urge, is "repentance or ruin."[51] And if or when God decides to demolish, demolition will happen. But when God decides to plant, planting will take place. Jeremiah's audience might hope that the four negative verbs indicate Yahweh's intention for the nations, which facilitates the action on Israel's behalf indicated by the positive verbs.[52] If

49. W. Brueggemann, "Meditation Upon the Abyss: The Book of Jeremiah," *WW* 22 (2002): 347.
50. M. Fox, "Closer Look at Jeremiah 1:10 with Implications for (Re)Reading Jeremiah 1," *Didaskalia* 22 (2011): 61–84.
51. Berrigan, *Jeremiah*, 2.
52. Cf. H. Bardtke, "Jeremia der Fremdvölkerprophet," *ZAW* 53 (1935): 215.

anything, the opposite is the case.[53] But subsequent chapters of the scroll will imply that the two possibilities applying to Judah indeed also apply to the nations.[54]

With a side look at the spiritual teachers and theologians of his day, Jesus comments that any plant that his Father has not planted will be pulled up. He also declares that structures built on sand, not rock (that is, not built on obedience to his teaching), will be demolished. Indeed, he will consume it with the breath of his mouth. So his servant's work had better take into account that the people of God is God's planting, God's building (Matt 7:25–27; 15:13; 2 Thess 2:8; 1 Cor 3:19).[55]

C. JEREMIAH REPORTS A MESSAGE FROM YAHWEH: HE IS GOING TO DO WHAT HE HAS SAID (1:11–12)

[11]*Yahweh's message came to me: "What are you looking at, Jeremiah?" I said, "A watcher cane is what I'm looking at."* [12]*Yahweh said to me, "You've done well in looking, because I'm keeping watch over*[a] *my message, to act on it."*[b]

a. Syr, Tg have "hastening."
b. MT has a marker here.

See the introduction to vv. 4–10 above. These verses simply add a confirmation that Yahweh is definitely going to do what he said there. As the poetry added weight to the message in vv. 4–10 (it will do so again in vv. 17–19), here the quasi-visionary form, the questioning of the prophet, and the eventual responsive message from Yahweh have the same effect. To put it another way, in this subsection, v. 12b alone contains Yahweh's message. In content, vv. 11–12a do nothing, but they make a significant contribution to the impact of the message. There is no indication that the report relates something that happened soon after the commission described in vv. 4–10; it would make sense somewhat later, when the question concerning Yahweh's fulfilling his threats became pressing.

11 Jeremiah sees something of an everyday kind: a *cane* that one might use while walking; it happens to come from an almond tree, whose Hebrew

---

53. W. Vischer, "The Vocation of the Prophet to the Nations: An Exegesis of Jeremiah 1:4–10," *Int* 9 (1955): 314.
54. See Sharp, "Call of Jeremiah."
55. Jerome, *Jeremiah*, 4–5.

name can also mean *watcher*. Perhaps Jeremiah sees it only in his imagination, though that idea complicates things unnecessarily.[56]

12 The almond tree blossoms in a way that heralds the approach of spring, and the Syriac version of the Story of Ahiqar (2:7) urges, "Be not in a hurry, like the almond tree, whose blossom is the first to appear, but whose fruit is the last to be eaten."[57] But it seems unlikely that the Hebrew name of the almond tree (*šāqēd*) actually means that it is watching (*šāqad*) for spring, which makes little sense. Anyway, Jeremiah does not see a blossoming branch but a stick. More likely, his point depends on a paronomasia: the tree's name happens to recall the word for *keeping watch*. In connection with the six verbs in v. 10, Jeremiah will later speak of Yahweh keeping watch over Judah (31:28), though in the short term that watchfulness or keeping an eye on Judah will not be a comfort (cf. 44:27; Dan 9:14; see also Isa 29:20). "Keep watch" is not a comforting verb (see 5:6). Here the expression involves a metonymy: Yahweh is keeping watch over his message, which means he is paying attention to it and intends to act on it. In the arrangement of vv. 4–12, *my message* suggests the intention indicated by v. 10, so the metonymy extends the lack of specificity concerning the object of the verbs there. In the broader context of vv. 1–3 and of the chapters that will follow, the message would be that there is terrible trouble on its way but then wondrous renewal. The first will seem never to arrive, though eventually it does. The second will seem hopelessly implausible, and Jeremiah will not see it arrive. But Yahweh will be watching over both aspects of the message. He does not declare the intention to act soon. Rather, he is promising definitely to act in due course. The promise is significant in the context of there being the long gap between his declarations and his actions, to which Jeremiah periodically refers.

It is tempting for the church to think that it is responsible to see to its future. Here, watching is God's responsibility, not Jeremiah's. "He does not have to worry and wonder about the success of the word . . . ; he is only to be faithful in speaking and embodying that word."[58]

> If God's people are selected for some special mission, if God's people speak God's word, and NOTHING HAPPENS, what then? What then? The answer that is preserved in this text . . . does not seem to answer the question. God's response is that his word is his word! The prophet is to speak all God directs him to speak. The prophet is not to set himself as judge to determine whether God is fulfilling his word.[59]

---

56. K. van der Toorn ("Did Jeremiah See Aaron's Staff?" *JSOT* 43 [1989]: 83–94) suggests that he saw Aaron's staff in the temple (Num 17:1–11[16–26]).

57. Holladay, *Commentary on Jeremiah*, 1:37.

58. Fretheim, *Jeremiah*, 52.

59. W. E. March, "Jeremiah 1: Commission and Assurance," *Austin Seminary Bulletin* 86 (1970): 29.

D. JEREMIAH REPORTS A SECOND MESSAGE FROM YAHWEH: HE INTENDS TO BRING DISASTER ON JUDAH, AND JEREMIAH MUST BE BOLD (1:13–19)

[13] *Yahweh's message came to me a second time: "What are you looking at?" I said, "A fanned[a] pot is what I'm looking at, its face facing from northward."[b]* [14] *Yahweh said to me, "From the north there will open out dire trouble on all the people who live in the country.[c]* [15] *Because here am I, calling to all the kin groups of the kingdoms to the north[d] (Yahweh's affirmation). They will come and put each one his throne[e] at the opening to Jerusalem's gateways, against all its walls all around, and against all Judah's towns.* [16] *I will speak out my authoritative decisions to them[f] because of all their dire action in that they have abandoned me and burned offerings[g] to other gods and bowed down to things their hands made.[h]*

[17] *So you—you are to belt around your hips,*
  and set to and speak to them
  everything that I myself will order you.
Don't break down[i] from before them,
  so that I don't break you down[j] before them.
[18] *But I: here,*
  I am making you today
A fortified town, an iron pillar,[k]
  bronze walls[l] over against the entire country,
For Judah's kings and for its officials,
  for its priests[m] and for the people of the country.[n]
[19] *They will battle against you, but they will not win over you,*
  because I will be with you (Yahweh's affirmation) to snatch you away."[o]

a. This expression involves another metonymy; it is the fire under the pot that is fanned.

b. Lit. "its face from before northward." While the expression is thus tortuous, its meaning is clear enough. In a word such as *ṣāpônâ*, the apparently locative ending need not be pressed: *mibbābelâ* (27:16) simply means "from Babylon," *bəriblātâ* (52:10) simply means "at Riblah" (GKC 90e); cf. v. 15.

c. In light of vv. 4–10, readers might assume that *hāʾāreṣ* means "the world" (cf. 25:29, 30), but in vv. 15–16, Jeremiah is making a transition to talk about disaster for Judah (cf. the same phrase in 6:12; 10:18).

d. The double phrase combines expressions that appear separately in 25:9 (and cf., e.g., 10:25; 25:26), and LXX omits *the kin groups of*. In MT, kin groups (*mišpāḥ*) appropriately arrive to deliver the authoritative decisions (*mišpāṭ*) in the next verse.

e. This sentence involves a further metonymy: it is the kings rather than the kingdoms that will set up their thrones.

f. MT has *ʾôtām*, a second object for the verb, as in 4:12; 12:1 (cf. DG 94 remark 4; *IBHS* 10.3.1c); some medieval mss imply *ʾittem* ("with them") as in 39:5; 52:9 (*BHS*).

g. The verb may refer specifically to burning food offerings; so D. Edelman, "The Meaning of *qiṭṭēr*," *VT* 35 (1985): 395–404.

h. For MT's plural *maʿăśê*, Vg implies singular *maʿăśeh*.

i. *Tēḥat* from *ḥātat* might be *qal* (BDB) or *niphal* (*HALOT*, *DCH*); if it is *niphal*, the meaning will be intransitive rather than passive.

j. Vg "don't be afraid . . . because I will not let you be fearful" is suggestive and profound, but "because" is not a plausible rendering of *pen*, and if one translates *pen* "lest," then "don't be afraid . . . lest I make you fearful" makes poor sense. LXX "nor be terrified before them" also raises difficulties with the verb and with *pen*.

k. LXX lacks *an iron pillar*.

l. Possibly intensive: "a great bronze wall" (Lundbom, *Jeremiah 1–20*, 245); LXX, Vg, Syr, Tg have singular as in 15:20.

m. Syr nicely adds prophets (cf. 2:26; 32:32) while LXX lacks *for its priests*.

n. *ʿAm hāʾāreṣ* (cf. 34:19; 37:2; 52:25) may denote the Judahites in general or may be a technical term for landowners (see E. Lipiński, "עַם *ʿam*," *TDOT*, 11:174–75).

o. MT has a unit marker here.

See the introduction to vv. 4–10 above. This further report of a message arising from something Jeremiah sees follows up the commission in vv. 4–10 and parallels vv. 11–12 in its question and answer form:

- Jeremiah introduces the fact that Yahweh is speaking.
- Yahweh asks Jeremiah what he is looking at.
- Jeremiah gives the answer.
- Yahweh tells Jeremiah what the sight signifies.

Here, however, the initial comment on what Jeremiah is looking at, in v. 14, leads into a much longer explanation of the implications of what he has seen, in vv. 15–19. The report fulfills a different function from the one in vv. 11–12. It does more than confirm that Yahweh will act as he said; indeed, it fulfills a number of different functions:

- It indicates the means by which Yahweh will do as he said in exercising his authority over kingdoms to bring about a catastrophe in Judah (v. 15).
- It explains why he intends to take this action (v. 16).
- It reasserts his command to Jeremiah to pass on his message (v. 17).
- It promises that Yahweh will protect him as he does so, when people attack him (vv. 18–19).

As happened in vv. 11–12, the initial report of the quasi-visionary experience reveals Yahweh's message only in its second part (v. 14), but the introduction (v. 13) contributes to the impact of the actual message. Like vv. 11–12,

vv. 13–14 use prose to report the event, and vv. 15–16 continue in prose to report Yahweh's expansion of his message. But his instructions and promises to Jeremiah himself (vv. 17–19) then take poetic form, as was the case in vv. 4–10. The poetry is even more prosaic than that in vv. 4–10, but the lines manifest rhythm, parallelism, and metaphor (see v. 18). After an opening tricolon, five bicola follow, the middle three being syntactically interdependent. Whereas Yahweh's declarations of intent concerning Judah are thus expressed straightforwardly and factually in vv. 13–16, his instructions and promises are once more enhanced in their importance and eminence by their mildly poetic form in vv. 17–19.

13 Jeremiah again spots something (perhaps only in his imagination) that Yahweh uses to trigger an awareness of a message. Jeremiah sees a seething cooking pot on a fire with its opening facing toward him; he is aware that he is south of it. The reference to its face may suggest it is tilted and thus about to boil over, though there is no need for that assumption; the quasi-vision again operates verbally at least as much as visually, working first with an assonance between *fanned* (*nāpûaḥ*) and *from northward* (*ṣāpônâ*).

14 In an extension of the assonance, Yahweh enables the pot to trigger an awareness that something is going to *open out* (*pātaḥ niphal*). Opening is what gates, windows, a mouth, ears, or a fountain does, which makes one anticipate something good.[60] But this pot is going to open out *dire trouble* that will overwhelm everyone. "Jeremiah threatens disaster, indeed only disaster."[61] The picture complements the one in vv. 11–12. That earlier image simply affirmed that something was going to happen without indicating whether it was good or bad; this image resolves the ambiguity. The calamity will pour out from the north, the direction from which invaders commonly come. Assyria is in the north in Zeph 2:13; Babylon is in the north in Jeremiah; Media is implicitly in the north for Babylon itself in 50:9; and Gog is the north in Ezek 38:15. The multiple applications of the motif suggest that it combines political with supra-political reference and geographical with supra-geographical reference; *ṣāpôn* can suggest the divine abode.[62] The northern threat for Judah will recur through Jer 1–13, though only in 20:4–6 will Babylon be named, and only in 25:9 will Babylon at last be identified as

---

60. Holladay, *Commentary on Jeremiah*, 1:40.

61. W. H. Schmidt, *Jeremia*, 1:60.

62. Cf. D. J. Reimer, "The 'Foe' and the 'North' in Jeremiah," *ZAW* 101 (1989): 223–32; D. S. Vanderhooft, *The Neo-Babylonian Empire and Babylon in the Latter Prophets*, Harvard Semitic Monographs 59 (Atlanta: Scholars, 1999), 136–49. E. H. Roshwalb argues that the figure from the north *is* God ("Build-Up and Climax in Jeremiah's Visions and Laments," in *Boundaries of the Ancient Near Eastern World: A Tribute to C. H. Gordon*, ed. M. Lubetski, JSOTSup 273 [Sheffield: Sheffield Academic, 1998], 111–35).

the invader from the north. But here, even now, "God testifies that the fire was already kindled in Chaldea and Assyria."[63] Meanwhile, "the absence of a historical referent for the 'boiling pot, tilted from the north,' at the beginning of the book strikes an ominous note and is all the more fearsome for its lack of specificity. The threat from the north is greater than any human enemy. Boiling, burning fluid, tipped over and uncontrolled, advances upon Judah and Jerusalem with unstoppable horror."[64]

15 Whereas vv. 11–12 incorporated only a one-line interpretation of the watcher cane, vv. 15–16 offer a more substantial amplification of the cooking pot. While the audience could assume even in vv. 13–14 that Jeremiah is talking about the nations as the victims of Yahweh's attack, now its objects become explicit. Jeremiah's rhetoric compares with that in Amos 1–2. First, open up the possibility of trouble coming for other people; then, when the Israelite audience is sitting pleased with itself, put the boot in.[65] The picture is hyperbolic or mythic,[66] though slightly reminiscent of the invasion by four northern kings in Gen 14; it imagines the arrival of an enhanced version of such a coalition. Prosaically speaking, a commander-in-chief sets down his royal seat outside a capital city that he intends to capture, and he has his officers take their places around the city's *walls* and around the other fortified *towns* in the country. *Jerusalem's gateways* could include the gateways of the temple courtyard (e.g., 7:2; 22:4), and the image of a pillar in v. 18 suggests the temple (e.g., 27:19; 52:17, 20–22). The commander-in-chief waits for the city to surrender when it runs out of food and water (if he has plenty of time) or orders an assault (if he wants to be able to move on to the next recalcitrant people) before walking in due course through the gates as the city's conqueror. A northern king will do this in Jerusalem in 597 and in 587 (39:1–3).

16a There is a further ambiguity to Jeremiah's report. The idea of nations gathering around Jerusalem and planning to assault it recurs in the First Testament: see Isa 28–32; 36–37; Pss 46–48; Joel 3(4). In each case, in varying ways, the scenario works out differently than they expect, giving Jerusalem reason for relief and rejoicing as it turns out that the nations have gathered to be overwhelmed, not to overwhelm.[67] Jeremiah's audience could hear

---

63. Calvin, *Jeremiah*, 1:50.

64. K. M. O'Connor, "Jeremiah," in *The Oxford Bible Commentary*, ed. J. Barton and J. Muddiman (Oxford: Oxford University Press, 2007), 490.

65. Cf. E. K. Holt's broader argument in "The Meaning of an *Inclusio*: A Theological Interpretation of the Book of Jeremiah MT," *SJOT* 17 (2013): 181–205.

66. Duhm (*Jeremia*, 12) calls it an "apocalyptic" motif associated with the expression of a "later dogmatic eschatology."

67. R. P. Carroll, *Jeremiah*, OTL, 106–8.

his vision report within one of these frameworks but then could be as mistaken as they imagine the nations being. The rhetoric again works against them. There is a further metaphorical aspect to the report. While a royal commander-in-chief may take a suitable seat on a campaign, a *throne* belongs in another context. It is where a king sits to exercise authority, to announce *authoritative decisions (mišpāṭ)*, to issue judgments. It is for this reason that the king will sit on his throne outside Jerusalem. He is there to issue Yahweh's judgment against the city, against *them*. Yahweh's bringing dire trouble (v. 14), in the sense of a horrifying and disastrous cataclysm, is a response to Judah's *dire action*—that is, their unfaithfulness, their wrongdoing. Jeremiah frequently uses the same word (*rāʿâ*) to denote both what is *dire* in the latter sense (the action) and what is *dire* in the former sense (the consequences), suggesting that the consequences issue "naturally" from the action or that Yahweh ensures that they do.

16b There are three overlapping charges against Judah. They *have abandoned me*: they owed Yahweh faithfulness, and they have not shown it. This charge will recur. They have *burned offerings to other gods*. The verb (*qāṭar piel*) comes from the word for incense (*qəṭōret*) and strictly suggests the offering up of a sacrifice in flames accompanied by the fragrance of incense, but it functions by synecdoche to denote the entire process of sacrifice. And they have *bowed down to things their hands made,* contravening a fundamental requirement of Israel's relationship with Yahweh (Exod 20:4–5); indeed, human religion is all humanly-made. All three charges have parallels in the critique Huldah issued to Hilkiah (2 Kgs 22:17), and all three will recur throughout the Jeremiah scroll (e.g., 2:13, 17, 19; 5:7, 19; 7:9; 8:2; 10:3, 9; 11:12, 13, 17; 13:10). "Idolatry" in the sense of "worship of false gods" is "fundamentally the most serious charge that any ancient Israelite could face."[68] Yahweh is thus commissioning Jeremiah to confront Judah in connection with its faithlessness toward him rather than the people's faithfulness toward one another; and the question with which the Jeremiah scroll faces the church is whether it is faithful toward God.

17a There is no break in Yahweh's words and no suggestion of a formal transition from one section to another, but the last three verses in Jeremiah's report lift their eyes to drive home the implications of the report for Jeremiah himself in a way that continues the theme of vv. 4–10. "To work," Yahweh says.[69] As a bidding addressed to Jeremiah, the words make a transition to poetry to underscore their importance for him. A prophet's words such as the ones in vv. 13–16 can always give the impression of declaring something

---

68. Sharp, "Jeremiah," 228.
69. Volz, *Jeremia*, 11.

that is inevitably going to happen, but Jeremiah makes more explicit than other prophets that their fulfillment depends for good and ill on the response they receive (see 18:1–11). Jeremiah's job is to declare Yahweh's intentions so as to elicit a response. So he is to secure his clothing around himself to keep it from getting in his way (compare the English phrase "roll up your sleeves") as he takes up the challenge Yahweh has put before him.

17b The first colon in Yahweh's prohibition restates an earlier one:

v. 8   Don't be afraid before them
v. 17   Don't break down before them

Earlier, the potential object of Jeremiah's fear was the nations whose prophet he was to be. Here, the fear relates to Judah, of which the immediately preceding verses have now explicitly spoken.[70] In v. 8, the exhortation included a promissory reassurance, which will recur in v. 19. In the meantime, if readers expect simple repetition, they get something different: a threatening warning. Like the English expression, *break down* (ḥātat, niphal then *hiphil*) can have both a physical and a psychological meaning. Yahweh works with both. If Jeremiah breaks down psychologically because of them (lit. "from their face/presence"), Yahweh will bring physical disaster on him through them ("to their face/presence").

18 But a promise backs up the exhortation. It takes the familiar form of a divine undertaking to protect and deliver,[71] which can address someone about to do battle, though here Jeremiah's battle is a verbal one. Yahweh again speaks performatively. In the very act of speaking with Jeremiah in this way, Yahweh is acting on him psychologically and physically. Following the sequence in the pronouns in vv. 6–8, comprising Jeremiah's "I," then Yahweh's "I" quoting Jeremiah, then Yahweh's own "I," a sequence recurs in Yahweh's "I" (v. 15) followed by his "you" (referring to Jeremiah, v. 17) and his further "I" here. There is something Yahweh must do and something Jeremiah must do.[72] Once again, Yahweh picks up the verb *I am making* (see v. 5). As well as making Jeremiah a prophet, he is necessarily making him invincible. Only here (and when Yahweh refers back to this moment in 6:27) is a *fortified town* a metaphor for a person. A fortified town (4:5; 5:17; 8:14; 34:7) is one with a wall that makes it hard to take, but it is not invincible, so perhaps that metaphor is insufficient. On the other hand, there is no such literal thing as *an iron pillar*. Wooden pillars held up the Gaza temple, but they

70. Nasuti, "A Prophet to the Nations," 259.
71. Holladay, *Commentary on Jeremiah*, 1:31
72. Lundbom, *Jeremiah 1–20*, 244–48.

didn't withstand Samson's pushing (Judg 16:25–30). An iron pillar might be a different matter.[73] There is also no such thing as *bronze walls*. Again, regular stone walls can be penetrated (39:8; 50:15; 51:44), but bronze walls might be a different matter. These metaphorical ones will be capable of withstanding *kings, officials, priests, and people*. Whereas the towns, pillars, and walls of Jerusalem and Judah will fall (v. 15), Jeremiah will not.[74] "In contrast to Jerusalem, Jeramiah is the true invincible city."[75]

19 He is called to wage a *battle* for his people's minds, and they will oppose him, but they will not overcome him.[76] Jesus makes a similar promise to Peter (Matt 16:18).[77] Jeremiah will be under attack from Judah as Judah will be under attack from Babylon. Their fighting against him will link with his being a kind of embodiment of Yahweh's word.[78] They will oppose him because they are opposing Yahweh. The implicit reference to this dynamic is an aspect of the way the account of Jeremiah's commission flags some central themes of the scroll.[79] Once again, the first colon raises a question that the second has to answer. Jeremiah will stand not because of strength in him but because Yahweh is with him to rescue him, *to snatch you away*. Yahweh exactly repeats v. 8b except for the order of words at the end, completing the repetition that was initiated in v. 17 but broken off in threatening fashion.

"There is no happier man . . . than the man who, having been called by God to be a spokesman for God, has been obedient to the heavenly vision and has answered the call with a resounding 'Here am I. Send me!' (Isa 6:8)."[80] Jeremiah does not claim that response here, but what follows speaks louder than the omission.

73. M. Görg, "Die 'ehernen Säulen' (1 Reg 7,15) und die 'eiserne Säule' (Jer 1,18)," in *Prophetie und geschichtliche Wirklichkeit im Alten Israel: Festschrift für Siegfried Herrmann zum 65. Geburtstag*, ed. R. Liwak and S. Wagner (Stuttgart: Kohlhammer, 1991), 134–54.

74. On the iconographic background to this imagery, see P. Riede, *Ich mache dich zur festen Stadt: Zum Prophetenbild von Jeremia 1,18f und 15,20*, Forschung zur Bibel 121 (Würzburg: Echter, 2009).

75. Diamond, "Jeremiah," 550.

76. See further C. M. Maier, "Jeremiah as Yhwh's Stronghold," *VT* 64 (2014): 640–53; R. C. Bailey, "Jeremiah: Fortified City, Bronze Walls, and Iron Pillar against the Whole Land," *Hebrew Studies* 57 (2016): 117–38.

77. See B. T. Dahlberg, "The Typological Use of Jeremiah 1:4–19 in Matthew 16:13–23," *JBL* 94 (1975): 73–80.

78. H. Mottu, "Aux sources de notre vocation: Jérémie 1, 4–19," *Revue de théologie et de philosophie* 32 (1982): 105.

79. Herrmann, *Jeremia*, 1:91.

80. R. Youngblood, "The Call of Jeremiah," *Criswell Theological Review* 5 (1990): 108.

I. PART ONE: CONFRONTATION, EXHORTATION, WARNING (2:1–6:30)

Jer 2–6 is a compilation of messages that confront Judah about refusing to follow Yahweh, warn it about trouble that will follow, urge it to turn back, and promise Yahweh's restoration.[1] While individual messages within the compilation may combine a number of these features, the compilation focuses on one or another of them at different times in a way that mostly corresponds to the medieval chapter divisions:

2:1–37	Mostly confrontation/critique
3:1–4:4	Mostly exhortation to turn and associated promises
4:5–31	Mostly warnings
5:1–31	Mostly confrontation/critique
6:1–30	Mostly warnings

Although the compilation thus includes only one section that comprises explicit exhortation (exhortation does resume in Jer 7, but it takes a different form), the object throughout is to get Judah to turn.

Jeremiah 36 tells a gripping story about Jeremiah putting into writing the messages Yahweh had given him over the two decades from the time of Josiah to that of Jehoiakim. If he did indeed dictate his messages from memory on that occasion, it would not be surprising if the resulting scroll included something like Jer 2 or if Jer 2–6 were a (perhaps expanded) version of that scroll. And heuristically, to think of Jer 2–6 in that way facilitates an imaginative interaction between the chapters and events in the time of Jehoiakim. The chapters make hardly any concrete historical references (3:6 is a general one, and 2:16 may be an exception), but they make clear that they presuppose a situation in which Judah has abandoned Yahweh, is following other deities, and has Egypt as political overlord and resource, and yet it does not see itself as in the wrong in relation to Yahweh. A scroll with this background would include elements of what Jeremiah had begun saying at the time of his commissioning, before Josiah's reformation, but we would not expect to be able to separate out particular messages so as to link them with such earlier contexts. The sayings "correctly communicate the earlier message of Jeremiah, but never assumed precisely this form until he dictated them to Baruch."[2] They have become part of a statement focusing on what needed to

---

1. E. R. Hayes, *The Pragmatics of Perception and Cognition in MT Jeremiah 1:1–6:30*, BZAW 380 (Berlin: de Gruyter, 2008), is a "cognitive linguistics" study of these chapters; in "Hearing Jeremiah: Perception and Cognition in Jeremiah 1:1–2:2," *Hebrew Studies* 45 (2004): 99–119, Hayes considers 1:1–2:2 as an introduction to what follows.

2. D. R. Jones, *Jeremiah*, 96–97.

be said in Jehoiakim's time, when Judah's life again manifested the dynamics that Josiah's reformation had aimed to eliminate and when Egypt was a key factor in Judah's life (2 Kings 23:31–24:7).[3]

A. MOSTLY CONFRONTATION (2:1–37)

Printed Bibles treat Jer 2 as one unit, and it does hang together. The chapter as a whole is not an established form of speech but a monologue of an abandoned God.[4] It confronts people about going back on their commitment to Yahweh (which they deny) by turning to other religious resources and other political resources, both of which are useless, and it warns them about disaster that will result. It attributes to Judah a sequence of claims, declarations of intent, denials, and pleas that suggest a confused lack of ability to think straight.[5] It does not tell them what to do about it; such exhortation will come in 3:1–4:4. It offers a kaleidoscope of images for understanding aspects of the story of Yahweh and Israel and of their relationship, allowing the images and aspects of the understanding to tumble over one another and interweave rather than expounding them systematically or aiming to generate an argument or structure for the whole. In this connection, it uses a variety of communicative devices to seek to get its message home and provoke a response. It uses rhetorical questions, and it puts series of statements on the lips of Israel and its leadership (vv. 6, 8, 20, 23, 25, 27 [3×], 31, 35 [2×]) that may sometimes indicate what people actually say but are often articulating the implications of their attitudes or parodying them, all as part of seeking to communicate with them.[6] The chapter moves between speaking "as" Yahweh and speaking "as" Jeremiah, and both Yahweh and Jeremiah speak in poetry. It also moves between speaking to and about Jerusalem as a city (in the feminine singular), Judah as a nation (in the masculine singular), and the people of city, nation, or household (in the plural).[7] Both forms of variation (who

3. C. Hardmeier ("Geschichte und Erfahrung in Jer 2–6," *EvT* 56 [1996]: 3–29) instead associates the chapters with the time of Zedekiah and Jerusalem's imminent fall. See further R. Liwak, *Der Prophet und die Geschichte: Eine literar-historische Untersuchung zum Jeremiabuch,* BWANT 121 (Stuttgart: Kohlhammer, 1987).

4. Fischer, *Jeremia,* 1:151.

5. Wright, *Jeremiah,* 72.

6. See T. W. Overholt, "Jeremiah 2 and the Problem of 'Audience Reaction,'" *CBQ* 41 (1979): 262–73; S. Hildebrandt, *Interpreting Quoted Speech in Prophetic Literature: A Study of Jeremiah 2.1–3.5,* VTSup 176 (Leiden: Brill, 2017).

7. D. Böhler links these changes with the way the passage speaks of Ephraim in relation to the land: see "Geschlechterdifferenz und Landbesitz: Stukturuntersuchungen zu Jer. 2,2–4,2," in *Jeremia und die "deuteronomistische Bewegung,"* ed. W. Gross, BBB 98 (Weinheim: Beltz, 1995), 91–127.

speaks and who is spoken to or about) have different communicative or rhetorical effects. Repetitions constitute a feature of the chapter's rhetoric, of the way it seeks to communicate and persuade ("go after," "dire," "household," "empty," "country," "could not be any use," "argue," "changed," "cisterns," "abandon," "path," "what do you have for a path . . . to drink the water").

The images that Jer 2 exploits express a theology. They are:

- Yahweh as Jerusalem's husband and Jerusalem as Yahweh's bride. In the personal relationship of love and mutual commitment between Yahweh and Israel, the bride was full of love and commitment at the beginning. But she looked to other lovers—nations and deities. She turned into a whore, an alien woman. She is promiscuous, looking in all directions religiously and politically. It's as if she has put out of mind her bridal finery.[8] Argument is a feature of the relationship: Yahweh argues with Israel, challenges it to listen, asks it questions.
- Israel as a good-quality vine. The trouble is that it has produced corrupt grapes.
- Yahweh as Israel's master and Israel as Yahweh's servant. Yahweh's being master means he is provider and protector. Israel's being servant in the relationship means it is expected to rely on him in this connection and to accept control and restraint. It prefers to be free, to make its own decisions. People want "religious freedom" and "the right to choose whatever deity they wish." As a result, the master will see to the servant's disciplining.
- Jerusalem as being on a path. Whom it follows or goes after is vital to walking on this path. The trouble is it is inclined to be wayward, to choose its own path, to follow other guides, to wander all over the place like a camel or a wild donkey.

The chapter also works with a series of contrasts that express a theology. The contrasts are:

- Wilderness and cultivable land. The world divides into wilderness and orchard. Wilderness is characterized by steppe and pit, emptiness and darkness. Cultivable land means the fruitfulness of garden or orchard. Related is the fact that water is a key to life. Yahweh is

---

8. A. R. P. Diamond and K. M. O'Connor see "the metaphor of the broken marriage . . . as a root or foundational metaphor" for Jer 2–3: see "Unfaithful Passions," in Diamond and K. M. O'Connor, *Troubling Jeremiah*, 127; cf. G. E. Yates, "Jeremiah's Message of Judgment and Hope for God's Unfaithful 'Wife,'" *BSac* 167 (2010): 144–65.

the source of such provision; other deities are not, and neither are other political powers.

- The ordinary and the sacred. There is nothing wrong with being ordinary (six days are ordinary), but Israel is sacred to Yahweh (like the Sabbath), and Yahweh's land is his domain and must be treated as such. It must not be defiled and made offensive by the importing of other deities. Israel itself has become stained through engaging in worship that purports to honor Yahweh but actually defiles.
- The real God and the so-called gods. The real God has acted in Israel's experience. The so-called gods are empty, useless, non-gods. There is nothing behind the image of wood and rock. Yahweh is the only deity who can do anything useful.
- Honor and shame. Israel's being Yahweh's servant is the source of its honor. Following other masters is Israel's shame. Self-deceit is a key feature in its waywardness. Its religious and political leadership is particularly at fault.

Further, the chapter works with an understanding of Israel's story that expresses a theology:

- Yahweh got Israel out of Egypt, made it his personal domain, and protected it.
- Yahweh brought Israel through the darkness and emptiness of the wilderness, and Israel followed him on that path.
- Yahweh brought Israel into the fertile land of Canaan, but there Israel turned to other religious and political resources and defiled the country, forgetting the story.
- Yahweh has engaged in some disciplining of Israel, designed to turn it back, but this discipline has not worked.
- Yahweh intends to impose such discipline in a more devastating way. Israel will then look to Yahweh, but he will look the other way. It will be shamed by its religious and political resources.

I outline the chapter as follows (see also "Jeremiah and His Curators as Anthologists," pp. 34–36):

vv. 1–8	A wistful remembering
vv. 9–13	An extension to the argument
vv. 14–20a	An explanation of Israel's becoming plunder
vv. 20b–25	The defilement
vv. 26–31a	The shameful community
vv. 31b–37	The shaming to come

1. A Wistful Remembering (2:1–8)

[1]*Yahweh's message came to me:* [2]*Go,*[a] *proclaim*[b] *in the ears of Jerusalem:*

Yahweh has said this:[c]

I have been mindful[d] *about you, of your*[e] *youthful commitment,*
  of your bridal love,[f]
Of your going after me in the wilderness,
  in a country not sown.[g]
[3]*Israel was something sacred to Yahweh,*
  the beginning of his yield.[h]
All who ate it would incur liability—
  dire trouble would come[i] *to them (Yahweh's affirmation).*[j]

[4]*Listen to Yahweh's message, household of Jacob,*
  all the kin groups of the household of Israel.

[5]*Yahweh has said this:*

What did your forebears find in me by way of fraud[k]
  that they went far away from me?
They went after something empty[l] *and became empty,*
  [6]*and they didn't say, "Where is Yahweh,*
The one who got us up from the country of Egypt,
  who enabled us to go through the wilderness,
Through a country of steppe and pit,
  through a country of desert and deathly darkness,[m]
Through a country that no one passed through,
  and where no human being lived?"
[7]*I enabled you to come to orchard country,*
  to eat its fruit and its good things.
But you came and defiled my country;
  my domain you made into something offensive.[n]
[8]*The priests—they have not said, "Where is Yahweh?";*
  the people controlling the instruction—they have not acknowledged me.
The shepherds—they have rebelled against me;
  the prophets—they have prophesied through the Master;[o]
  after things that[p] *could not be any use*[q] *they have gone.*

a. Yahweh uses the infinitive absolute rather than the imperative of *hālak*, a common Jeremianic usage (3:12; 13:1; 17:19; 19:1; 28:13; 34:2; 35:2, 13; 39:16; cf. 2 Sam 24:12; 2 Kgs

5:10; Isa 38:5) with a more peremptory or solemn effect (GKC 113bb, noting that here it is followed by a *waw*-consecutive).

b. Theod translates *qārā'* as "read"; see the commentary.

c. LXX and Vg, here and elsewhere, have "says this," but the verb is *qatal*: lit. "thus Yahweh has said." The expression "reflects the prophetic consciousness of having received a message" from Yahweh (DG 57d remark 3). LXX has a shorter introduction to vv. 1–8: simply, "And he said, These things the Lord says."

d. *Zākartî* is also *qatal*, but it refers to an action whose effect continues into the present (GKC 106g); one could call such a verb quasi-stative (Joüon 112a).

e. The suffixes in this line might be objective (Vg; also Jerome, *Jeremiah*, 8; Qara, in MG) or subjective (LXX; Tg; Rashi, in MG); see the commentary.

f. LXX has *agapē*—a word with New Testament resonances—but those overtones mean it is really more an equivalent to *ḥesed* (for which LXX has its regular equivalent *eleos*, "pity"; cf. Vg *miserans*).

g. For *after me in the wilderness, in a country not sown*, LXX has "after Israel's sacred one."

h. The *qere* has *təbû'ātô*. The *ketiv tbw'th* may imply "its [the country's] yield," though see GKC 7c, 91d.

i. The *yiqtol* verbs suggest that Jeremiah is making a general/logical statement; past imperfect does not fit as well.

j. MT has a unit marker here.

k. *Mah* is followed by an accusative of specification; see *IBHS* 18.1e, 18.3b; DG 8 remark 2; Joüon 144d.

l. *Hahebel* with the article, as in 2 Kgs 17:15, may be a pejorative substitute for *habba'al*, "the Master" (Bright, *Jeremiah*, 15).

m. *Ṣalmāwet* may be a repointing of *šalmût* (see BDB; *HALOT*), but it gained a life of its own; cf. Tg, Syr, Aq, Sym, Theod. Vg has a composite rendering: "deathly image." On LXX "fruitless," see Holladay, *Commentary on Jeremiah*, 1:49; HUBP.

n. The line follows an a-b-b'-a' pattern. It ends a sequence of five lines where the word *country* plays a key role and with a sequence of different forms of parallelism (cf. *CHP*, 281).

o. LXX gives "Baal" (*the Master*) a feminine article, here and elsewhere, which encourages an association between Baal and (fem.) *bōšet*: "shame" (see 3:24; 11:13).

p. An unmarked relative clause follows the construct (see DG 11–12; GKC 155n; *IBHS* 9.6c, 19.6b).

q. "Could [not] be any use" (*yô'ilû*) makes for paronomasia with "Master" (*ba'al*) and thus comments on it.

Each of the major parts of Jer 1–25 begins by undermining an aspect of the faith that Judah was committed to—not because the faith was wrong, but because it had gotten twisted in Judah's thinking (see "Analysis of Contents," pp. 61–62). Part 1 begins with the exodus, which Yahweh sees as the beginning of his marriage relationship with Israel. He reminds Israel of how great their relationship originally was and puzzles over why Israel left him.

This opening section thus comprises an innovative and thereby attention-drawing variant on a recurrent pattern. Typically, a prophet reminds Israel of how Yahweh dealt with it in the past, and thus of how things used to be, and confronts it with the anomalous nature of how things are and of its rebelliousness. Other examples are Isa 1:2–3; Amos 3:1–2; Mic 6:1–8; and the series of such unhappy recollections in Hos 9:10–13:16 (9:10–14:1).[9] *Die Geschichte ist das Gericht*: the history is the judgment.[10] Here Jeremiah places a distinctive emphasis on Israel's original commitment to Yahweh as opposed simply to an emphasis on Yahweh's commitment to Israel.

The section provides an example of the ambiguity attaching to possible section breaks. One could get the impression that vv. 1–3 are a section and that v. 4 makes a new start (MT treats vv. 1–3 as a complete unit). But in substance, vv. 1–3 don't make sense on their own: Yahweh recalls the past here, but to what end? What is his point? It is the confrontation that now follows, beginning in v. 4, that indicates the point.[11]

> vv. 1–2a   Introduction to 2:1–6:30
> vv. 2b–3
>   v. 2b   Introduction to vv. 2c–3
>   vv. 2c–3   Yahweh's positive memory (four bicola, the first two
>   linked by enjambment)
> vv. 4–8
>   v. 4–5a   Introduction to vv. 4–8
>   vv. 5b–8   Yahweh's negative memory (eight bicola, five linked by
>   enjambment, and a closing tricolon)

1–2aβ Jeremiah begins with a testimony that repeats the expression from 1:3, 4, 11, 13 (*Yahweh's message came to me*; see the translation notes on 1:2 and 3). It thus suggests that what follows corresponds to what was happening there. Yahweh's commissioning of proclamation in *Jerusalem* also continues the commissioning that began there; vv. 1–2aα introduces Jer 2–6 as a whole. As this chapter follows on Jer 1 and suggests the beginning of Jeremiah's prophetic activity, the command *go* might encourage the scroll's readers to imagine Jeremiah taking the hour's walk to make the move from Anathoth to Jerusalem. But *go, proclaim* recurs in 3:12 and *proclaim (qārā') in the ears of Jerusalem* is also the expression for "read out in the ears" of Judah in 36:6, 10, 13, 14. This link encourages the scroll's readers to take Jer 2–6 as the content of what Jeremiah read out on the occasion related in Jer 36, when he was long settled in the city. The relationship between Jer 2 and Jer 36 thus parallels that between Jer 7 (a message Jeremiah delivered in the temple) and Jer 26 (the story of that message's delivery). In effect, the scroll implies, if you wonder

9. See J. Goldingay, *Hosea to Micah* (Grand Rapids: Baker, 2021), 135.
10. Volz, *Jeremia*, 16.
11. Cf. H.-D. Neef, "Gottes Treue und Israels Untreue: Aufbau und Einheit von Jeremia 2,2–13," *ZAW* 99 (1987): 37–58 (though he treats vv. 1–13 as a unit).

what Jeremiah said in the story told in Jer 36, you will not go far wrong if you read Jer 2–6. And if you wonder what it was like when Jeremiah proclaimed Jer 2–6, you will not go far wrong if you read the story in Jer 36. Presumably, Yahweh generally expected Jeremiah to preach where the maximum number of Jerusalemites would hear, which would include the temple gateways and grounds and the other gateways in the city itself (e.g., 7:2; 17:19; 19:2, 14; 22:2; 26:2; 28:1; 36:10). *Yahweh has said this* (Jeremiah speaks as the King's messenger) leads into what immediately follows in vv. 2–3, or perhaps into Jer 2 as a whole.

2aγ–δ Like other towns, Jerusalem is grammatically feminine, which opens up the possibility of addressing it as a girl or woman through much of the chapter. Immediately, Yahweh addresses Jerusalem as his one-time bride. A metonymy is involved; it was the city's population whose forebears journeyed through the wilderness. Yahweh is being *mindful* of the past, and as commonly happens, Yahweh's "remembering" (the traditional translation of *zākar*) is not an accidental recalling but a deliberate action, an intentional mental act with practical implications. Near the beginning of the scroll, there comes this indication that for Yahweh, there are a past, a present, and a future.[12] Further, the remembering is not just a past act but one with "an abiding significance, with continuing effects."[13] Yahweh's remembering is usually good news (31:20; cf. Pss 98:3; 105:8, 42; 115:12), though not always (Jer 14:10; 44:21), and the audience will do well to keep both possibilities in mind. After all, the picture of the community as Yahweh's wife goes back to Hosea, where the background is the wife's unfaithfulness, and this is the yet-unspoken implication here. By picturing the idyllic early years of their relationship, Yahweh anticipatorily underlines the horrific nature of his bride's unfaithfulness. The early years were characterized by the formidable combination of *commitment* (*ḥesed*) and *love* (*'ahăbâ*), which ought to make for a wonderful marriage. The juxtaposition of *youthful commitment* and *bridal love* is subtle: love is a more general word than commitment, but bridal is a more concrete and precise word than youthful. *'Ahăbâ* is an even more all-purpose word than the English word "love." It covers romantic love, other forms of affection, friendship, and a liking for food, but it can additionally imply loyalty and submission, and it can operate in the political sphere as well as the interpersonal (cf. 1 Kgs 5:15).[14] *Ḥesed* also operates in both spheres. It

---

12. T. E. Fretheim, "Jeremiah's God Has a Past, a Present, and a Future," in Lundbom, Evans, and B. A. Anderson, *Jeremiah*, 459–61.

13. W. H. Schmidt, *Jeremia*, 1:71.

14. See, classically, W. L. Moran, "The Ancient Near Eastern Background of the Love of God in Deuteronomy," *CBQ* 25 (1963): 77–87, but with the critique in J. E. Lapsley, "Feeling Our Way: Love for God in Deuteronomy," *CBQ* 65 (2003): 350–69.

expresses itself in two related ways. It can denote a commitment that some-one undertakes when under no obligation to do so (so it overlaps with grace or favor); it can denote a commitment that someone maintains when the other party has forfeited any right to expect it (so it denotes a faithfulness or truthfulness that goes beyond what was required).

2b Elsewhere, Yahweh's remembering commonly concerns the way he himself has related to Israel (cf. 31:2–3 in a recollection of the wilderness years), and here one might initially understand him to be recalling his own loving commitment to Jerusalem when it was his young bride. But this paral-lel line in the double bicolon resolves any ambiguity and indicates that Yah-weh is recalling his bride's loving commitment.[15] *Your bridal love* expands on *your youthful commitment*, then *your going after me in the wilderness* expands on *your bridal love*, and then *in a country not sown* expands on *in the wilder-ness*. It is the only occasion when Jeremiah speaks of *going after* in a positive way.[16] The (patriarchal) marriage presupposes that the bride's love and com-mitment expresses itself in submission to her husband, which means she does not walk alongside him: he leads the way and she follows. If this assumption worries Western readers, one might add that Jeremiah implies no model for marriage; he is simply picking up the way marriage works in a traditional context in order to communicate something. But he does imply a model for our relationship with God. We are not equal partners in an egalitarian relationship. He is the boss. Hosea, however, had complained about the com-mitment that faded too quickly and the love that Israel showed in another direction (Hos 6:4; 2:5–13[5–15]), and Jeremiah is about to do the same. In substance, Yahweh is first recalling the commitment Israel made to the *bərît*, or "pledge," at Sinai after leaving Egypt (on the word "pledge," see the intro-duction to 11:1–17, p. 315). That word does not feature, but the idea is present in the background: Judah has indeed gone back on a relationship.[17] Jeremiah makes no reference to the exodus (though he will make one shortly), to Sinai, or to a pledge. While Hosea spoke of a pledge and of the exodus, he overlaid the exodus/pledge theme with the talk of a marriage relationship, and it is this theme that he links with talk of the wilderness (see esp. Hos 2:15[17]). Jeremiah takes up the marriage-wilderness theme without referring to exo-dus or pledge at this point. To put it another way, the pledge metaphor can operate within the framework of marriage, adoptive parenthood, or politics; Jeremiah focuses on politics.[18] Yahweh is simply the husband, and Jerusalem

15. See further M. de Roche, "Jeremiah 2:2–3 and Israel's Love for God during the Wil-derness Wanderings," *CBQ* 45 (1983): 364–76.

16. Barth, *CD* IV, 2:534.

17. Fischer, *Jeremia*, 1:177.

18. D. Rom-Shiloni, "The Covenant in the Book of Jeremiah," in *Covenant in the Persian*

is the wife; there is no reference to the relationship involving a "pledge." Jeremiah presupposes the love and commitment of husband to wife, though they are not mentioned. The point about characterizing the wilderness as a place where not much grows is that the husband looked after his wife there. Jeremiah is not giving expression to a wilderness ideal. "It is . . . a matter of history rather than of culture." When things went wrong, "the fault lay with Israel and not with Canaan."[19] Further, in Jeremiah, the marriage between Yahweh and Israel/Jerusalem is more a model (and here an incidental one) than a ruling metaphor as it is in Hosea.[20]

3 Jeremiah now speaks of *Yahweh* in the third person, though the closing *Yahweh's affirmation* inhibits the reader from making a sharp distinction. Jeremiah is still passing on Yahweh's message. The wilderness journey had a further characteristic: it was dangerous because of the attacks of peoples such as the Amalekites and Amorites (Exod 17:8–15; Num 21:1–3). A patriarchal husband is protector as well as provider. The commitment and love are indeed mutual. Yet Yahweh's point in v. 3 is a more self-regarding one: a patriarchal husband is entitled to feel proprietary in relation to his wife. To put it another way, Jeremiah's point is theocentric. Actually, Yahweh changes metaphors. It is almost as if the talk about a region where nothing grows reminds him of things growing and of harvest, which suggests another image. The harvest reference would have particular resonance if Jeremiah delivered his message at the Sukkot festival.[21] At harvest time, the firstfruits, *the beginning of his yield*, belong to Yahweh (e.g., Exod 23:19; 34:26). By rights, the whole harvest does; it is his produce. But he is willing to share if people keep off what he claims. It is the principle that operates in connection with Sabbath and tithes. And as he claims firstfruits, Sabbath, and tithes, so he claims Israel. If other people try to take over what he claims, they get into dire trouble, like people who eat the firstfruits. It happened to Amalek and to the Amorites of Arad (Exod 17:8–15; Num 21:1–3). The threat recalls the way disaster could come to an adulteress through the ritual described in Num 5:11–31.[22] In the preceding line, the second colon made something explicit in relation to the first, answering a question it might raise: why was Israel

---

Period: From Genesis to Chronicles, ed. R. J. Bautch and G. N. Knoppers (Winona Lake, IN: Eisenbrauns, 2015), 153–74. But Rom-Shiloni implies that Jeremiah does effectively speak in terms of a marital and adoptive pledge in Jer 2–3 without using the word.

19. McKane, *Jeremiah*, 1:28, 33. See further B. Bowman, "The Place of the Past: Spatial Construction in Jeremiah 1–24," in *Constructions of Space IV*, ed. M. K. George, LHBOTS 569 (London: T&T Clark, 2013), 94–102.

20. J. Jeremias, "The Hosea Tradition and the Book of Jeremiah," *OTE* 7 (1994): 31–35.

21. Holladay, *Commentary on Jeremiah*, 1:80.

22. A. Miglio, "Ordeal, Infidelity, and Prophetic Irony in Jeremiah 2,1–9," *SJOT* 24 (2010): 222–34; and see the possible link with this passage noted in the commentary on v. 23 below.

sacred to Yahweh? He claimed it as he claimed the firstfruits of the harvest. In the present line (v. 3b), the question might be: did it make any difference to anyone to *incur liability* (or could people break the rules and get away with it)? And the parallel colon responds: "You bet it did." As sacredness means Yahweh has claimed something, liability and guilt (the verb *’āšam/’āšēm*) imply that one must make recompense one way or another (the verb links theory and action, like the verbs for love, remembering, and knowing). The two lines thus have a similar interrelationship to that of the cola. Does the sacredness of Israel as the people Yahweh claims have any implications for people who ignore that claim? You bet it does.

4 We still have not discovered the point of that touching and encouraging recollection. In light of it, Yahweh has something to say to Jacob/Israel. His "wife" now becomes the huge family of which he is head. Jeremiah is speaking mostly to Judahites, who form the main surviving expression of the *household of Jacob* and the *kin groups of the household of Israel,* though among people living in Judah are people from Ephraim who had moved south before or after the fall of Samaria. Once again, delivering a declaration addressed to the entire community would be especially appropriate if the occasion were a pilgrimage festival such as Sukkot.[23] Recollecting the marvels of the relationship of Yahweh and Israel, which the festival celebrated, would fit such an occasion.

5a It now becomes clear that Yahweh's recollecting in vv. 2–3 is only the background to his going on the attack (cf. Amos 1–2). "The words are a set-up."[24] Jeremiah still allows for some suspense as he proceeds, as he moves from the wilderness generation to the *forebears* of the Israel of his day; he is not yet talking about people alive in the present. These forebears are not the wilderness generation, who were faithful. Admittedly, the wilderness generation had their own moments of going after something empty (Deut 32:21), so the memory is rose-tinted; but it is in our interest that God has a "selective memory."[25] Nor are the forebears Ephraim, who were not the Jerusalemites' forebears. Nor are they Manasseh's generation in Judah, since Yahweh is reflecting on a more distant abandonment. They are the generation that entered into Canaan and its successors; Judges relates how *they went far away from me.* "Don't be far away from me," Israel sometimes pleads, accusingly (e.g., Ps 22:11[12], 19[20]). This verse resembles one of the occasions when Yahweh expostulates, "What? *You* accuse *me* of going far away?" The possibility of their suggesting that there is *fraud* (*‘āwel*) in Yahweh seems

23. L. C. Allen, *Jeremiah: A Commentary*, OTL (Louisville: Westminster John Knox, 2008), 34, 40.

24. P. D. Miller, "Jeremiah," on the passage.

25. P. D. Miller, "Jeremiah," in a reflection on 2:1–4:4.

monstrous. Fraud is the opposite of truthfulness or faithfulness; it suggests being deviant, perverse, false, unreliable, faithless; it is the opposite of *ṣedeq/ ṣadāqâ* or *'ĕmet/'ĕmûnâ*. There is no fraud in Yahweh (Deut 32:4; also the antitheses in 25:15–16). Jeremiah "by his rhetorical question forces the listener to conceive the inconceivable," and Yahweh's willingness to raise the possibility suggests a kind of self-denying self-emptying, a *kenosis* (Phil 2:7).[26]

5b–6 The grievous truth is that instead of going after Yahweh (v. 2), they *went after* other deities. And the odd truth is that these entities whom they decided to follow constituted *something empty* (*hebel*), a favorite word in Jeremiah to describe gods other than Yahweh.[27] They are something as evanescent as breath. There is no substance to them. They are hollow. Going after them rather than Yahweh is illogical. And further, following them means you end up like them (cf. Ps 115:8). It is indeed what happened to Ephraim (2 Kgs 17:15). Equally illogical is the fact that the forebears didn't ask *Where is Yahweh . . . ?* While this question can be a disbelieving one (e.g., Ps 42:3[4], 10[11]), it can be the question people properly ask when they are in trouble (Job 35:10; cf. Ps 89:49[50]; Isa 63:11, 15). It is the way they seek God (e.g., Jer 29:13). It was furthermore illogical for them not to ask the question because they had that experience of Yahweh's provision in the wilderness of which vv. 2–3 speak. It's at this point that Yahweh goes behind Sinai to the exodus itself, an important theme in its own right in Jeremiah.[28] The following three lines involve an enjambment in which Yahweh describes the *wilderness* itself in scarier terms. In general, wilderness is not a bad word or place; although wilderness has insufficient rainfall to grow regular crops, it can provide pasturage. But *steppe* (*'ărābâ*) is the word for the rainless area around the Dead Sea, *the* Arabah. And a *pit* is something you fall into and may not be able to get out of; the word here suggests the deep clefts characterizing the area south and east of Judah proper, or the Jordan Rift itself. *Desert* is waterless wasteland where you can die of thirst. *Deathly darkness* (*ṣalmāwet*) suggests a region of extreme and unpredictable danger (cf. Ps 23:4). It is not surprising that no one *passed through*, still less *lived* there; in the middle and last of the three lines, the second colon goes beyond the first each time. The problem is that the people have forgotten about the way Yahweh brought them through those places. They stopped telling the right stories. In the words of B. Katho, it is a mistake associated with "the banalization of God";

26. Holladay, *Commentary on Jeremiah*, 1:85.

27. Rudolph, *Jeremia*, 15.

28. G. Fischer, "Zurück nach Ägypten: Exodusmotivik im Jeremiabuch," in *A Pillar of Cloud to Guide: Text-critical, Redactional, and Linguistic Perspectives on the Old Testament in Honour of Marc Vervenne*, ed. H. Ausloos and B. Lemmelijn, BETL 269 (Leuven: Peeters, 2014), 73–92.

and "wrong stories can lead to death."[29] (I wondered whether "banalization" was a typo for "ba'alization"; I assume not, but it makes for a paronomasia worthy of Jeremiah, linking neatly with his characterization of *ba'al* as *hebel*, which implies banal. Further, maybe the word *hebel* suggests that Cain and Abel [*hebel*] lie buried in this passage.)[30]

7 Yahweh has been exaggerating; the wilderness isn't that bad. But the exaggeration points up the contrast with the land flowing with milk and honey and underscores the horrific nature of what followed. Canaan was *my country* and *my domain*: the second term enhances the first and makes the description more specific. A family's *domain* or possession (*naḥălâ*, traditionally "inheritance") is its tract of land that in theory no one can take away. Canaan has that status for Yahweh. It's special to him, as Naboth's vineyard (part of his *naḥălâ*) was special to him (1 Kgs 21:3). But the forebears *defiled* it (*tāmē'*) and made it *something offensive* (*tô'ēbâ*). "A central contrast in Jeremiah 2:1–4:4 is that between a pure and a perverted land."[31] Through their recourse to other deities, the land moves from one extreme to another, from being something precious to being something disgusting. "Yahweh's action leaves the land fruitful and good. Israel's action leaves it defiled and abominable."[32] Actually Yahweh doesn't say *they* did it, but *you* did it. *I enabled you to come* and take possession of my country, and *you defiled* it. His audience stands in continuity with its forebears. He does not imply that they share in the guilt of their forebears even though they have not continued the same lifestyle,[33] thus implying that people may be punished for wrongdoing they did not undertake. His words do recognize that one generation's wrongdoing can have an effect on the next generation—and the one after and the one after as those succeeding generations yield to their forebears' influence. That dynamic has operated in Judah. It continues to operate, as Josiah did not succeed in rooting out Manasseh's wrongdoing, which will bear terrible fruit in 597 and 587.

8a Yahweh makes another seamless transition from talking about the failings of the forebears in general, in the distant past, to talking about the failings of the leaders of the community in the recent past and as they continue

29. B. Katho, "Idolatry and the Peril of the Nation: Reading Jeremiah 2 in an African Context," *Anglican Theological Review* 99 (2017): 722, 725.

30. So N. C. Lee, "Exposing a Buried Subtext in Jeremiah and Lamentations," in Diamond, K. M. O'Connor, and Stulman, *Troubling Jeremiah*, 87–122.

31. R. Abma, *Bonds of Love: Methodic Studies of Prophetic Texts with Marriage Imagery (Isaiah 50:1–3 and 54:1–10, Hosea 1–3, Jeremiah 2–3)*, SSN 40 (Assen: Van Gorcum, 1999), 242.

32. W. Brueggemann, "Israel's Sense of Place in Jeremiah," repr. in *The God of All Flesh and Other Essays* (Cambridge: Clarke, 2016), 46.

33. See Jerome, *Jeremiah*, 9, 10.

into the present. He begins by taking up the critique in v. 6 and applying it to *the priests*. This first reference to priests among the community's religious leaders shows that he is not anti-priest. He does not critique priesthood as such (he came from priestly stock himself), nor does he imply that the Jerusalem priesthood is intrinsically illegitimate.[34] On the contrary, he indicates that he recognizes their vocation. Specifically, one of their roles was to lead people in prayer when they brought their sacrifices and to call on Yahweh on people's behalf when they were in need, as Joel exhorts (Joel 2:17). Their particular responsibility was to ask *Where is Yahweh?* on people's behalf. But they are not doing so. The people *controlling*, holding, or wielding (*tāpaś*) *the instruction* (the *tôrâ*) might be the theologians or scribes, the experts who possess Yahweh's instruction, in 8:8–9.[35] They appear with priest and prophet in 18:18. But there, *instruction* is the business of priests, and here, the parallelism would work well if *the people controlling the instruction* is another way of describing the priests. They hold onto the *tôrâ*. Deuteronomy 9:17 uses this verb to describe Moses holding the stones inscribed with the Decalogue before smashing them, which might provide a metaphor for the people Jeremiah is describing. The verb "control" comes more frequently in the Jeremiah scroll than anywhere else, commonly to denote taking control of someone to stop them acting or speaking (26:8; 34:3; 37:13–14; 52:9), which is also metaphorically suggestive. If only they were holding the instruction in order to wield it in accordance with its design, like warriors with their weapons or farmers with their implements (46:9; 50:16). Whether they are priests or scribes, *they have not acknowledged me*, a horrifying comment on either group; it is another key verb in the Jeremiah scroll.[36] "To know YHWH is to recognize him as the Lord, as the center of life, and this recognition is binding. But the Judahites have a problem of knowledge . . . due to a crisis of memory."[37] If the problem is not that they don't name the name of Yahweh but that they have assimilated Yahweh to the Master,[38] then Jeremiah is making an acerbic comment about the significance of their prayer and their teaching. They do call on Yahweh by name, but only nominally. Jeremiah functions by means of the device of "antilanguage," of redefining what people mean by their words—because they have already redefined them. "He tars

---

34. C. Patton, "Layers of Meaning: Priesthood in Jeremiah MT," in *The Priests in the Prophets: The Portrayal of Priests, Prophets, and Other Religious Specialists in the Latter Prophets*, ed. A. O. Bellis and L. L. Grabbe, JSOTSup 408 (London: T&T Clark 2004), 150–56.

35. Qimchi, in MG.

36. B. Katho, "La Connaissance de YHWH selon Jérémie," *OTE* 21 (2008): 38–39.

37. B. Katho, "To Know and Not to Know Yhwh: Jeremiah's Understanding and Its Relevance for the Church in DR Congo" (PhD. diss., University of Natal, Pietermaritzburg, 2003), 232–33.

38. Rudolph, *Jeremia*, 16–17.

all the religious expressions of his contemporaries with the same brush." Even if they don't see themselves as serving the Master, he talks as if they are.[39] They resemble modern congregations that refer to Jesus but have so reconceptualized him that their acknowledgment is in name only. It is also a worrying comment for scholars.[40]

8b *Shepherds* is another favorite expression in Jeremiah (e.g., 3:15; 6:3; 12:10; 23:1–4) and here another metaphor whose referent is not identified. Tg simply translates "kings," but the First Testament does not take over the use elsewhere of "shepherd" as a description of the king. "Only very hesitantly . . . did the OT connect the shepherd concept with the leadership exercised by kings and by God. . . . There is no evidence that the term 'shepherd' ever served as a title for a reigning king," though shepherding can be a metaphor for leading or ruling (2 Sam 5:2; 7:7).[41] Maybe *shepherds* is a metaphor for leaders in general. What is explicit is the nature of their wrongdoing: *They have rebelled (pāšaʿ) against me*. If they are rulers, this is an ironic indictment, as rebelling denotes defying the authorities' expectations. These people would be against rebellion when they were its object, but they are for it when they are its subject. In 10:21, the problem with the shepherds is that they have not been inquiring of Yahweh, which is another way of picturing rebellion. And inquiring of Yahweh is a prophet's job (21:1–2), so shepherds as leaders might at least include prophets; here, *the prophets* in the next colon might then clarify who are the people Jeremiah has in mind. Like the prophets in 1 Kgs 17, these prophets *prophesied* with the help of *the Master* (baʿal). Tg translates "false prophets," which they are, but the trouble is that they are at the same time simply prophets (see the commentary on 1:5b), as priests are simply priests. "He calls the false prophets 'prophets' as he calls those who are not gods 'gods.'"[42] In another sense, one could say there is nothing false about them at all. They really are prophets. The trouble is they are prophets in the service of the Master. They are false prophets insofar as they serve false gods. They are deceptive prophets because they serve one who embodies deception. But the Master's help is empty (as Yahweh put it earlier). They cannot *be any use*. Yahweh closes with that terrible verb that describes how people *have gone after* them instead of going after Yahweh. It is the thing that defiles Yahweh's own country and makes it disgusting. The extra colon to make the line a tricolon forms an unexpected follow-up to the

39. W. R. Domeris, "When Metaphor Becomes Myth: A Socio-Linguistic Reading of Jeremiah," in Diamond, K. M. O'Connor, and Stulman, *Troubling Jeremiah*, 254.

40. G. Fischer, "*wtpšy htwrh lʾ ydʿwny*: The Relationship of the Book of Jeremiah to the Torah," in *The Formation of the Pentateuch: Bridging the Academic Cultures of Europe, Israel, and North America*, ed. J. C. Gertz et al., BZAW 415 (Tübingen: Mohr Siebeck, 2016), 911.

41. G. Wallis, "רָעָה, rāʿâ," TDOT 13:549–50.

42. Theodoret of Cyrus, *Ermeneia tēs prophēteias tou Ieremiou*, PG 81:505.

previous four similarly-structured cola and also closes off the section with its reversed word order and its reuse of the expression "go after," which was where we began (v. 2).

2. An Extension to the Argument (2:9–13)

⁹*That's why*[a] *I will argue with you some more (Yahweh's affirmation),*
    and with your grandchildren[b] *I will argue.*
¹⁰*Because cross over to the Kittites' shores,*[c] *and see,*
    and to Qedar—send.
Consider well, and see,[d]
    if something like this has happened.
¹¹*Has a nation changed*[e] *gods,*
    and those were non-gods?
But my people—it has changed its honor[f]
    for something that[g] *could not be any use.*
¹²*Be desolate,*[h] *heavens, at this;*
    shudder,[i] *be totally devastated*[j] *(Yahweh's affirmation).*
¹³*Because two dire things my people have done:*
    me they have abandoned,
    the fountain of living water,
To dig themselves cisterns,
    breakable[k] *cisterns,*
    ones that can't hold the water.

a. LXX, Vg have "therefore," the common meaning of *lākēn*, not least when a prophet announces consequences that will follow from wrongdoing (e.g., 6:21; 7:20); but Jeremiah does not announce a consequence here. And *lākēn* can also signify "that's why" in a looser sense, introducing "the development of what is implicit" in what precedes, as in v. 33 (BDB); cf. 15:19; 18:13; 32:28. It is thus the resumptive beginning of a new section.

b. For *bənê bənêkem*, Vg implies simply *bənêkem*, which might indicate dittography or haplography; see the commentary.

c. LXX, Vg have "islands," but *'iyyîm* more generally denotes places at which one arrives by sea.

d. The recurrence of *see* illustrates how repetition is a feature of Jeremiah's rhetoric in Jer 2; see the introduction to the chapter (p. 100).

e. *Hēmîr* looks like a form from *yāmar*, which would be a byform of *mûr* (see *HALOT*).

f. Another traditional reading is "my honor"; see McKane, *Jeremiah*, 1:34.

g. Cf. v. 8 and the note on it.

h. *Šōmmû* might be a parody of *šimʿû* in a passage such as Isa 1:2 (Holladay, *Commentary on Jeremiah*, 1:91); it leads nicely into *šāmayim*. Jeremiah is not merely asking the heavens to do something for which they are ill-equipped (they have no ears) but to be something that goes against what they are: it is the earth, not the heavens, that can be desolated or made a desolation (see v. 15; also, e.g., 4:7, 27; 6:8; 10:25; 12:10–11). Only here does the word apply to the heavens.

i. Etymologically, "let your hair stand on end."

j. The further catachresis involved in this closing verb underscores the paradoxical point made by the first verb. *Ḥārab/ḥārēb* can mean both "be devastated" and "be dried up" (BDB thinks of homonyms, *HALOT* of one verb; *DCH* seems ambivalent). Both meanings apply naturally to the earth, not the heavens (e.g., 7:34; 25:9, 11, 18; 26:9). LXX reflects *harbēh* ("make much"), rendering things more straightforward (it also has finite forms for the first two verbs: the heavens already are appalled).

k. LXX, Vg have "broken," but for this meaning, one would expect a *qal* passive, not *niphal* (Joüon 121q).

An indictment like the one in vv. 2–8 might be expected to lead into a "therefore" declaring the consequences of what precedes, and the word translated *that's why* (*lākēn*) can have that significance (e.g., 6:18, 21; 7:20, 32). But here it does not introduce such a declaration. It rather announces Yahweh's intention to take further the critique in vv. 2–8, and *that's why* marks the resumptive beginning of a section. So v. 9 faces both directions. In vv. 2–8, Yahweh berated the way Israel's ancestors forgot the story of Yahweh's relationship with it—the story of how Yahweh had related to it at the beginning, how it had related to Yahweh, and how Israel's leaders have failed to turn to Yahweh and to pay attention to the Torah. To that indictment, he now adds the scandalous and nonsensical fact of Israel's turning to other deities, to alternative resources offered by the surrounding culture that are about as useful as a leaky human-made water cistern.

Verses 9–12 comprise six bicola; v. 13 then comprises a double tricolon held together by enjambment:

v. 9   Yahweh announces his intention to extend the confrontation in vv. 2–8

v. 10   He challenges Israel to go and look at other peoples

v. 11a   In light of what he knows they will see, he asks a rhetorical question

v. 11b   Presupposing an answer, he indicts their outrageous and unintelligible action

v. 12   He urges the heavens to respond with horror

v. 13   He gives the reason, expanding at length on the two aspects of the indictment

9 So Yahweh will take up the confrontation and add to it *some more*; the declaration that this is *Yahweh's affirmation* functions resumptively and supports the opening declaration (rather than suggesting that v. 9 marks the end of a section). This section first takes the argument further by moving from a focus on *your forebears* (v. 5, lit. "your fathers") and *you* (v. 7) to a focus on *you* and *your grandchildren* (lit. "your children's children"). Yes, the wrongdoing of parents does have repercussions, and not only in the next generation, whom Jeremiah here skips (Are they the audience when Baruch reads the scroll, as described in Jer 36?), but in the third generation, the *grandchildren* who will read Jeremiah's scroll in the exilic period and will have to think about this comment.[43] In each colon in his declaration of intent, Yahweh uses the same verb form, with the verbs and indirect objects in an a-b-b'-a' pattern:

> I will argue with you,
>> and with your grandchildren I will argue.

As English can speak of "arguing a case" in court, so Jeremiah's verb (*rîb*) can denote a confrontation before the elders at the town gateway, where a person brings a claim against another member of the community (e.g., Isa 1:17; cf. the noun in Exod 23:1–3, 6). In Genesis, it can also refer to conflicts between different groups over matters such as pasturage and water supplies (13:7; 26:20–22; 31:36). So Yahweh is not the judge here (v. 12 may identify the metaphorical decision-makers) but more like a husband bringing a claim against his wife. Being prepared to argue with his people as if he were just another citizen looks like another expression of self-denial or kenosis (see the commentary on v. 5a).

10 *Because* (*kî*) is another indication that v. 9 was not the end of a section; even taken as simply asseverative, it would be a stark beginning to one. Kition was a town in Cyprus that provided the First Testament with its name for Cyprus as a whole. *Qedar* was a people in the northern Arabian Desert, to the east, beyond the area of settled peoples such as Moab and Ammon. The exhortation encourages the audience to imagine going a long way west and east, toward the extremes of the known world.[44] But it doesn't reveal the aim; the line thereby makes the audience wonder why. The second line gives half an answer, clarifying a little the object of the investigation. The two lines in v. 10 are mutually parallel, but by providing only half an answer, the second line also heightens suspense. People are to ask *if something like this has happened*, but what is the "this"? Like the first colon of a bicolon, the verse raises a question that it doesn't answer.

11 Paradoxically, the answer comes in the form of another question, a reformulating and sharpening of the accusation in vv. 5–8. It is this reformulation that constitutes the elaboration of the argument that v. 9 announced. Abandoning Yahweh and going after the Master becomes the comment that

43. Duhm, *Jeremia*, 20.
44. Isaac Abravanel, *Commentary on the Latter Prophets*.

the nation has *changed gods*. Ezekiel 27:21 describes Qedar as a trading people (they were Ishmaelites, after all; see Gen 25:13; 37:25), and the same connotation would obtain for Cypriots as people whose island sat in the Mediterranean. Both peoples were used to exchanging or trading things.[45] Would they ever trade gods? Nations did sometimes add new gods to their pantheon, though they did not throw out the old ones.[46] But the point lies not in the mere fact of change but in the trade's stupidity, which is asserted in the following colon: no one trades gods for *non-gods*. The Kittites and Qedar would never make such a trade. This corresponds to the point made in vv. 5 and 8. There is no parallelism within the lines in v. 11, but the second line parallels the first, as happened in v. 10. Here the verse follows the pattern a-b-a'-b': the two opening cola are parallel and the two subsequent cola are parallel. Within the second line, the first distinctive expression is that Yahweh is talking about *my people*; it is the first occurrence of this term, which carries some poignancy, sadness, resentment, and sense of outrage. What Yahweh observes is that Israel has surrendered *its honor* (*kābôd*)—the God who is honorable and splendid and the one Israel is committed to honoring (cf. Ps 3:3[4]). The following colon underlines the implausibility of the trade that the verse is recording by picking up the description of the non-gods as things that *could not be any use* (v. 8).

12 Like Isaiah (1:2), Jeremiah appeals to the *heavens* in connection with his argument (see the translation note). It fits the model of Yahweh taking the position of a plaintiff at the town gateway. A plaintiff asks the elders to register their outrage at the action of another member of the community toward him and to make a decision accordingly. Looking around for someone equivalent to the elders, Yahweh fixes on the heavens.

13 Jeremiah goes on to express once again the nature of Judah's wrongdoing. He now uses another metaphor. There are two sides to the *dire* action of *my people*: something dire in relation to Yahweh and something dire in relation to themselves. Jeremiah thus uses the word "dire" or "bad" (*ra'*) with both connotations and juxtaposes the two meanings of the word, hinting at the link between them that he has already suggested in 1:14, 16 (see "Jeremiah as Persuader," p. 116). Direly, the people have *abandoned* Yahweh (Jeremiah picks up the verb from 1:16), and they have thereby put themselves in a dire position. Water is a life or death matter in Canaan.[47] Fortunately, Jerusalem has a *fountain of living water* (running water), the Gihon spring on the east

---

45. Holladay, *Commentary on Jeremiah*, 1:90.
46. P. D. Miller, "Jeremiah," on the passage.
47. Cf. E. K. Holt, "The Fountain of Living Water and the Deceitful Brook: The Pool of Water Metaphors in the Book of Jeremiah (MT)," in *Metaphor in the Hebrew Bible*, ed. P. van Hecke, BETL 187 (Leuven: Peeters, 2005), 102. Holt notes that 15:18 and 17:13 contradict 2:13.

side of the hill on which the city is built. Towns are regularly built near such a water supply, but most springs dry up during the summer, so towns also have *cisterns* for collecting rain during the winter to keep them going through the summer until the rains come again—though running water is much nicer than rain water stored in a tank.[48] So the first weird thing about Yahweh's people is that they have abandoned their source of running water for water from a cistern. Second, a crucial thing about a cistern is that it is well-plastered and thus sealed and watertight, but the metaphorical cisterns Yahweh describes are insecure—they haven't been plastered, or the plaster isn't thick enough, or it has cracks. They are *breakable*. They *can't hold the water*. That's how useless they are. This is the second aspect of Israel's dire action. As well as doing wrong by Yahweh, they are doing wrong by themselves. To what does the metaphor refer? How have the cisterns failed? Again, Jeremiah works by raising suspense that the subsequent verses will resolve in the next section.[49] Meanwhile, this section comes to an end in this double tricolon. The first colon sums up the point (MT unusually but appropriately puts the midpoint marker after just this first colon). In the first unexpected third colon, *the fountain of living water* expands on *me* in expounding the nature of the first dire thing. *To dig themselves cisterns* then identifies the second of the dire things; *breakable cisterns* gives further detail on the direness; and in the further unexpected third colon, *ones that can't hold the water* identifies the consequence of the cisterns' fragility.

3. An Explanation of Israel's Becoming Plunder (2:14–20b)

[14]*Was Israel a servant,*
   or was he a house boy:
   why has he become plunder?[a]
[15]*Over him, cougars*[b] *roar;*
   they have given their voice.
They have made his country into a desolation—
   his towns have fallen in ruins[c] *so that there is no one living there.*[d]
[16]*Yes, the people of Memphis*[e] *and Tahpanhes*[f]—
   they shepherd you[g] *on the skull.*[h]
[17]*This is what it does to you, isn't it,*

---

48. See further H. Ghantous and D. V. Edelman, "Cisterns and Wells in Biblical Memory," in *Memory and the City in Ancient Israel*, ed. D. V. Edelman and E. Ben Zvi (Winona Lake, IN: Eisenbrauns, 2014), 177–96.

49. But M. DeRoche compares Prov 5:15–18 with Song 4:12, 15 and sees a further pointer to quasi-sexual unfaithfulness ("Israel's 'Two Evils' in Jeremiah ii 13," *VT* 31 [1982]: 369–72).

your abandoning Yahweh your God,
at the time he's enabling you to go on the path.[i]

[18] *So now what is there for you in the path to Egypt*[j]
to drink Sihor[k] *water?*
What is there for you in the path to Assyria
to drink River[l] *water?*
[19] *The direness in you*[m] *should restrain you;*
your turnings—they should rebuke you.[n]
So acknowledge and see[o] *how dire and bitter*
your abandoning Yahweh your God,
And there being no awe[p] *for me in you (an affirmation of the Lord Yahweh*
of Armies[q]*),*
[20a-b]*because*[r] *of old you broke*[s] *your yoke.*
You tore off your restraints[t]
and said, "I will not serve."[u]

a. While *bûz* means *plunder* and this meaning fits what follows, after v. 14a one might be reminded of the root *bāzâ*, which could suggest being treated with contempt (*CHP*, 159).

b. *Kəpîr* is a less common word for lion than *'aryēh* (v. 30; Jeremiah prefers this to *'ărî*); BDB, *HALOT*, *DCH*, and *TDOT* translate "young lion," but the distinction between the words is unclear; they function simply as poetic alternatives.

c. The *qere* has *niṣṣətû* from *yāṣat*; the *ketiv* implies *niṣṣətâ*, which could be the singular of the same verb or could be from *nāṣâ*. The verb *yāṣat* commonly appears accompanied by a phrase indicating "in fire" (e.g., 49:2; 51:58), which indicates that it means "burn." But it also occurs in contexts such as the present one, which points to ruin and desolation and makes no reference to fire (e.g., 9:10[9], 12[11]; 46:19), suggesting that the verb is here a byform of *nāṣâ* III (see 4:7; and cf. Tg, Sym). Here, the feminine singular subject in the *ketiv* would be *'arṣô* in the previous colon. The asyndetic clause with the subject before the verb is subordinate to the previous clause.

d. Lit. "from lack of one living" (see BDB, 115).

e. The name of the Egyptian city Men-nepher in Hebrew is here *nōp* (elsewhere *mōp*) and in Greek Memphis.

f. For *taḥpanḥēs*, the *ketiv* has an alternative spelling without the second *ḥ*.

g. *Yir'ûkā* from *rā'â* (cf. v. 8); Aq, Sym imply *yərō'ûk* from *rā'a'*, with the more straightforward meaning "break [your] skull." LXX presupposes a form from *yāda'*, implying the common confusion of *r* and *d*; and Vg "ravished" may also presuppose this reading (see *CTAT* 2:466). The address changes to feminine singular as in vv. 2–3, a move back from masculine plural in vv. 4–12, 13b and masculine singular in vv. 13a, 14–15.

h. LXX "and mocked at you" implies a form from Postbiblical Hebrew *qrqr*, again misreading *d* for *r* (HUBP).

i. LXX lacks this last colon (by haplography or because of MT dittography? cf. v. 18a) and has an extra "the Lord your God says" (anticipating the phrase at the end of v. 19).

j. Hebrew *miṣrayim*. English "Egypt" comes from Greek *Aigyptos*, which apparently goes back to another term for Memphis.

k. *Šiḥôr* is a Hebrew equivalent to a term meaning "pond of Horus" (Rudolph, *Jeremia*, 18; see also *HALOT*, 1477–78). On LXX *geōn*, see S. Olofsson, "The Translation of Jer 2,18 in the Septuagint," *SJOT* 2 (1988): 169–200.

l. The Euphrates is known as *pərāt* elsewhere in the First Testament but thought of as *the* river.

m. Lit. "your direness," which could denote dire action or a dire fate.

n. LXX, Vg take the verbs as *yiqtol*, but in light of the next line, they are more likely jussive (Volz, *Jeremia*, 14). The line follows an a-b-b'-a' pattern, with the verbs enclosing the nouns—a structure of which Jeremiah is fond (e.g., 4:7, 9).

o. On these imperatives following jussives, see GKC 110i.

p. LXX "I took no pleasure in you" implies a verb *pāhadtî* for MT's *hapax legomenon* (elsewhere *pahad*, not *pahdâ*); LXX has translated the verb in a more plausible way than "I was in awe of you" (HUBP). One could take the verb as an example of the archaic second-person feminine, which recurs in v. 20 (see n. s), but it is then necessary to emend "of you" to "of me" (*BHS*). Aq, Sym have "fear": *pahad/pahdâ/pāhad*, like *yir'â/yārēh*, covers both (negatively) being afraid (e.g., 30:5; 36:16) and (positively) being in awe (e.g., 33:9; 36:24). It is doubtful whether *pahad/pahdâ/pāhad* implies a stronger fear or awe than *yir'â/yārēh*.

q. On this translation of *yhwh ṣb'wt*, see J. A. Emerton, "New Light on Israelite Religion," *ZAW* 94 (1982): 2–20. This long formulation of the affirmation recurs in Jeremiah only in 49:5; 50:31, both times in the middle of a line as here. LXX lacks *of Armies*, as it usually does in Jeremiah, perhaps out of a desire not to encourage belief in lesser deities (A. Rofé, "The Name YHWH ṢĔBĀ'ÔT and the Shorter Recension of Jeremiah," in Liwak and Wagner, *Prophetie und geschichtliche Wirklichkeit*, 307–16).

r. Vg omits "because," perhaps taking *kî* as asseverative.

s. *Šābartî*, and *nittaqtî* in the parallel colon, are usually first-person forms; understood thus, they refer to Yahweh's graciousness to Israel (cf. Aq, Theod, Tg, Syr), and the third colon then describes Israel's response (B. A. Bozak, "Heeding the Received Text: Jer 2.20a, a Case in Point," *Bib* 77 [1996]: 524–37). But they are also archaic second-person forms (cf. LXX), which are frequent in Jeremiah (see GKC 44h). Jeremiah 5:5 uses these expressions with Israel as subject in an unambiguously negative way, 30:8 with Yahweh as subject in an unambiguously positive way.

t. Vg has "my yoke" and "my restraints." *Môsēr* apparently comes from *'āsar*, not *yāsar* (the verb in v. 19), which generates *mûsār* (v. 30), but Jeremiah's audience would likely associate the words in vv. 19, 20, and 30.

u. So the *ketiv 'bd*. The *qere* has *'e'ĕbôr*: "I will not pass [to other deities]/transgress [your instruction]" (cf. Tg). The two lines in vv. 19b–20 follow an a-b-b'-a' pattern: *there being no awe* and *said, "I will not serve"* are parallel; *you broke your yoke* and *you tore off your restraints* are also parallel.

Verses 2–13 have not spoken as if disaster has actually fallen on the people of God; they have focused more on its dire life than on its dire experience. This next section begins with the disaster before speaking more of the reasons. It describes the consequences for Israel of abandoning Yahweh by relying on political resources in Egypt as well as on other deities. Jeremiah speaks as if disaster has happened, but in the period before 604, we don't know of disasters that he could be referring to. More likely, he speaks of what he has seen in a vision of the future (which is past reality for people reading the scroll). If this section is indeed relating what will happen rather than what has happened, it would fit with the order of the sections—first the indictments in vv. 2–13, now the threat. The section is structured in three parts:

vv. 14–17   The questions raised by the arrival of disaster (an opening tricolon, three bicola, and another tricolon at a pausing point)

vv. 18–19a   Another question that therefore arises: issues for present and future policy (three bicola)

vv. 19b–20b   The challenge about what Judah needs to acknowledge (three bicola, the first two forming a linked pair by enjambment)

14 A jump in the imagery (*servant*/*house boy*), a jump in the rhetoric (a return to questions), a tricolon, and a jump in the substance (Israel has become plunder) mark the new section. The audience gets a question out of the blue whose subject bears no immediately obvious relationship to what preceded. There's been no concrete indication so far that Israel is in trouble, only that it deserves to be and risks being because it is relying on resources that will turn out to be unreliable. The tricolon begins with two parallel cola asking one question in two slightly different forms. The right answer to the first question might not be immediately obvious because the right answer could be "yes" in the sense that *Israel* is Yahweh's *servant* (30:10; 46:27–28). After all, Israel is sacred to Yahweh (v. 3).[50] But it will become clear that in this context, being a servant lacks those positive implications. Likewise, there is nothing wrong with being a *house boy* (*yəlîd bêt*)—someone born into a household as the child of a servant (see, e.g., Gen 14:14; 17:12–13). As a house boy, you are a member of the family; you can be a valued one, and you count as within Yahweh's people. But Israel is a servant more in the sense to which Jer 34 refers; no doubt Jer 34 also hints at how things really were for many house boys. The question additionally recalls how Israel was once a bunch of servants in Egypt—with negative connotations. *Servant* can have political connotations, too; a servant nation is the underling of an imperial power. That kind of servanthood can also be okay, but actually Israel as a people has *become plunder* as a family servant or house boy can be subject to abuse (see the translation note). It is what "his servants the prophets" had said would happen in the time of Josiah's grandfather (2 Kgs 21:10–14), and it is what did happen in 597 and 587 (Isa 42:22), as Jeremiah warned (20:5). To put it another way, Israel is the kind of servant whose servitude issues from having been captured in war.

50. Craigie, Kelley, and Drinkard, *Jeremiah 1–25*, 32.

15 Or it is as if Israel has become the victim of ravenous beasts that have made it their prey. The *cougars* are the victors who have turned Israel into serfs or slaves. The two lines repeat the sequence of v. 14: first a metaphor, then a literal description, which here becomes more concrete. Israel has been subject to invasion and destruction of the kind that makes it uninhabitable. Whom do the cougars stand for? Who are the *they* in v. 15b? What experience of *desolation* is Jeremiah referring to? A century before, Assyria wrought terrible devastation in Ephraim, but that event belonged to another place and time.[51] The Egyptians marched through Israel in 609 on the occasion when Josiah took them on and lost his life, but it was not an event that brought great devastation—Pharaoh was on his way somewhere else and was just brushing off a flea. More likely, then, this invasion is indeed one that Jeremiah has seen in his mind's eye, as was the case in 1:13–16; he is referring (though he doesn't know it) to the Babylonian invasions and destructions of 597 and 587.

16 He adds an even more specific picture, though also one heavy in metaphor. *Memphis*, near modern Cairo, was at one time the capital of Lower Egypt. *Tahpanhes* was closer to Egypt's northeastern border and was thus on the route between Egypt and Canaan (see Jer 43–44). Jeremiah's enigmatic comment reflects Judah's ambivalent relationship with Egypt, the major power in Judah's region between the decline of Assyria and the hegemony of Babylon. At different times, Judah regarded Egypt as a potential or actual senior ally or as an enemy, and Jeremiah's formulation captures this ambiguity. Second Kings 23:28–24:7 indicates something of the tortuous and changeable relations between Judah and Egypt between 609 and 597 (against the background of Babylon's rise as the regional power). In this context, v. 16 provides a collection of dots that can be connected in various ways with the aid of some creative imagination.[52] Egypt could *shepherd* Judah with its power both as authority and as protector. But in 609, it hit Judah *on the skull* only too literally. Maybe Jeremiah had originally (earlier in Josiah's day?) been speaking of the kind of thing that he knew would happen, which in this event became concrete reality.[53]

17 Jeremiah picks up the theme of *abandoning* (v. 13), which goes back to his commission (1:16), and the associated motif of going (after) (2:2, 5, 8). His verb is again *yiqtol*, so it could be translated as future or as present and

51. But J. M. Henderson urges that Jeremiah is talking about Ephraim's history in the chapter ("Jeremiah 2–10 as a Unified Literary Composition," in Goldingay, *Uprooting and Planting*, 141–44; cf. Henderson, *Jeremiah under the Shadow of Duhm*, 324–28).

52. See, e.g., W. Brueggemann, *1 & 2 Kings*, Smith and Helwys Bible Commentary (Macon, GA: Smith & Helwys, 2000); M. A. Sweeney, *I & II Kings*, OTL (Louisville: Westminster John Knox, 2007).

53. Lundbom, *Jeremiah 1–20*, 272.

could be describing something Jeremiah had known would happen and now
has happened. In restating his indictment, he adds another key motif: that of
path (*derek*). Israel's life is a path or journey on which Yahweh leads it. He is
enabling you to go on the path, as long as you go with him and don't go after
other deities. Yahweh had enabled Israel to go through the wilderness (v. 6),
but in the last colon, the present participle suggests that this enabling was not
confined to the past. Israel is on a journey now, and Yahweh is the one who
enables it. The tricolon thus brings vv. 14–17 to a stinging semi-conclusion:
This (what vv. 14–16 described) is *what it does to you*. What is the "it"? *Your
abandoning Yahweh your God*. To underline how shocking that action is, note
the circumstances under which it happens: it is when he is *enabling you to go
on the path*. The unexpected third colon encourages a moment's pause.

18a Introducing the reference to Egypt in v. 16 and the image of a path in v.
17 opens up the way to an aggressive question. Judah is supposedly committed
to a path on which it follows Yahweh. Jeremiah sets against that commitment
any journeying on a literal or metaphorical *path to Egypt* to get support and
resources from there. Is there anything for Israel to gain in taking such a path?
The answer to the rhetorical question was implicit in what Jeremiah just said
about the actual and potential cost of abandoning Yahweh when he is the one
who enables Israel to go on its path. Jeremiah thus simply dismisses political
policies and religious commitments that would have seemed reasonable and
responsible;[54] they were neither reasonable nor responsible. We have no information on such moves in Jeremiah's day, but it could be an angle on aspects
of what was going on in the late 600s according to 2 Kgs 23:28–24:7. Recourse
to Egypt had been policy in the past, and it could be a recurrent temptation
(cf. Isa 30:1–7; 31:1–3). Metaphorically, Judah would then be going to drink
from the Nile, of which the Sihor was a branch or lake on the Canaan side of
the country. So the reference to Egypt picks up the more concrete allusion to
Memphis, and the reference to the Sihor could recall the mention of Tahpanhes, which was also on the Canaan side of Egypt. There is an ironic contrast
between Egypt as attacker in v. 16 and Egypt as resource here. Can they not
see it? The imagery ought to help make the point. Once more, Jeremiah talks
about an alternative water source and invites Judah to think again about who
is the real source of running water.

18b The verse again comprises two lines that are parallel, with the two
opening cola parallel and the two closing cola parallel. While Assyria is still
a military and political player during the earlier part of Jeremiah's lifetime, it
is in terminal decline. Indeed, a presupposition of Josiah's reformation is that
Assyria is finished as an imperial power and that Josiah can take action that
signifies a claim to independence as well as a commitment to religious re-

---

54. R. P. Carroll, *Jeremiah*, OTL, 126, 128.

form. Nineveh fell to Babylon and Media in 612, though Jeremiah the prophet to the nations does not refer to this event.[55] But Assyria is not totally done even in 609; when he fought and killed Josiah, Pharaoh Neco was on his way to support Assyria against Babylon, whose ascendancy Neco wanted to oppose. Yet Assyria was hardly a potential resource for Judah any longer. In v. 18, therefore, Egypt and Assyria may simply be a conventional word pair (cf. Isa 52:4; Lam 5:6; Hos 11:11), and Jeremiah may speak of the path to Assyria purely as makeweight for the idea of the path to Egypt;[56] Hosea does the converse (Hos 11:5). Or maybe Jeremiah speaks sarcastically: "In Israelite experience, looking to Assyria hasn't worked very well, has it?" (cf. v. 36). Or maybe the unfeasible nature of recourse to Assyria supports the possibility of the recourse to Egypt being only a theoretical option, not one we have to fit into known historical events.

19a Recourse to Egypt or Assyria would have dire implications. In v. 13, *direness* characterizes both Judah's action and its consequent fate, and here the opening colon trades on this duality. It's possible to derive a lesson from your mistakes even before you pay the full price for them. In effect, Jeremiah is inviting Judah to learn from the direness of its action in order not to have to learn from the direness of the results. In parallelism with the reference to direness, he casually introduces another of his key themes in speaking of *turnings*: this noun will recur (for instance) in 3:6, 8, 11, 12, 22, and the verb "turn" in 3:1, 7, 10, 12, 14, 19, 22. It belongs to the same semantic field or controlling metaphor as "going after," "abandoning," and "path." Israel is inclined to turn away and needs to turn back. Turning to Egypt or Assyria is turning away from Yahweh as provider, protector, and lord. Turning to the Master has the same significance. The verbs *restrain* or "discipline" (*yāsar*) and *rebuke* (*yākaḥ*) suggest that Israel is a schoolboy. His teacher is life itself, but "Israel is like the incorrigible son or pupil who is incapable of submitting to parental or scholastic discipline, or of deferring to wisdom and experience."[57] Restraining or disciplining can be a matter of words (Isa 8:11; 28:26), but words tend not to be enough (Prov 29:19), and they certainly haven't been enough for Judah. So the idea that direness and turning should be a restraint and rebuke can involve another metonymy; it is the dire consequences of the turning that will need to function as rebuke and to teach restraint. The implicit good news is that even when Yahweh makes dire things happen to his people, it is not so much judicial punishment as educative chastisement, which can teach them.[58] Indeed, Yahweh does not claim to have brought

55. J. R. Lundbom, *Jeremiah: Prophet Like Moses* (Eugene: Cascade, 2015), 132.

56. R. P. Carroll, *Jeremiah*, OTL, 129–30.

57. McKane, *Jeremiah*, 1:39.

58. A. Weiser, *Das Buch des Propheten Jeremia*, 2 vols., Das Alte Testament Deutsch (Göttingen: Vandenhoeck & Ruprecht, 1952), 1:23–24.

about the political and military disasters to which this section refers. Perhaps the implication is that they just happened as a "natural" consequence of Judah's political stupidity, which issued from its religious stupidity. History can work that way. They can still be experiences to learn from.

19b–20a But will Judah ever learn? It has not done so yet. It needs to *acknowledge* the facts. Things being *bitter* denotes their being tough and unpleasant; direness now refers unequivocally to the *dire* consequences of dire actions. In the complex double line, the middle cola redefine *abandoning Yahweh* as lacking reverence or *awe* for Yahweh, lacking the worshipful trembling that is appropriate before God.[59] Twice, Yahweh has used the poignant but aggrieved expression "my people" (vv. 11, 13); twice he has now used the poignant but aggrieved expression *your God* (vv. 17, 19).[60] The double line comes to an end by revisiting the idea of serving, with which the section began. In this connection, it implicitly adds the image of Israel as an ox, which needs a *yoke* for the farmer to direct it. In itself, there's nothing negative about wearing a yoke and working as an ox, as is the case with being a servant. "The question . . . is not the presence or absence of yoke, but which yoke is to be present,"[61] though admittedly an ox may prefer to wander free or just lie about, like a human being who would rather have an "unyoked life."[62] *Of old* (*mēʿôlām*, practically "from eternity") makes one think of the ancestors of v. 5, whose example their descendants follow.

20b Literal *restraints* (*môsēr*, 2:20; 5:5; 27:2; 30:8—Jeremiah uses this noun more than any other book) are the ropes tying the wooden part of a yoke around the ox, which a wise farmer will make sure fits well. The word recalls the verb for the "restraining" undertaken by a teacher (*yāsar*, v. 19; cf. 6:8; 10:24; 30:11; 31:18; 46:28—more than any book except Psalms; see the translation note). *Serve* is taken up from v. 14. A yoke is commonly a political image, like the image of being a servant (e.g., 27:8–12), and in that context it can have negative connotations. But the city's throwing off its servanthood and its restraints in the past is what now necessitates its letting its dire actions and their consequences "teach it a lesson." It was unwilling to serve, so it has found itself serving in a dire way. This closing colon is the first example of Jeremiah's stratagem of quoting statements by Israel that it hasn't made but has implied or should have made or could have made; more examples will follow (see the introduction to this chapter, p. 99). Israel hasn't said *I will not serve*, but its behavior has implied this refusal. Jeremiah's rhetoric points

---

59. H. F. Fuhs ("יָרֵא, *yārēʾ*," *TDOT* 6:293) and H. P. Müller ("פָּחַד, *pāḥad*," *TDOT* 11:517–23) suggest that *paḥad/paḥdâ/pāḥad* connotes trembling.

60. Fretheim, *Jeremiah*, 67.

61. Holladay, *Commentary on Jeremiah*, 1:97.

62. E. R. Achtemeier, *Jeremiah*, Knox Preaching Guides (Atlanta: John Knox, 1987), 22.

to the mysterious ease with which human beings hide the real truth from themselves, which may be more of a problem with the people of God because we cannot afford to recognize the truth about ourselves (or we think we cannot). The pseudo-quotation in v. 20b compares with Paul's in Rom 6:1.[63] He imagines people asking, "Shall we sin in order that grace may abound?" If you ask that question, you show you've fundamentally misunderstood the relationship between God and his people and the reason why he's been involved in its story. Thinking you could belong to God but not serve God betrays the same misunderstanding.

4. The Defilement (2:20c–25)

[20c]*Because on every high hill*
  and under every verdant tree
    you're bending over as a whore.
[21]*Whereas I—I planted you as a red vine,*[a]
  all of it true seed,
How you transformed yourself in relation to me,
  as people corrupted[b] *vis-à-vis the vine*[c]*—an alien woman!*[d]
[22]*Even if you launder*[e] *with soda*[f]
  and use much cleanser[g] *for yourself,*
    your waywardness will be staining[h] *before me (an affirmation of the*
      Lord Yahweh).
[23]*How could you say, "I have not defiled myself;*[i]
  the Masters[j]*—I have not gone after them"?*
Look at your path into the Ravine,
  acknowledge what you have done.
A light-footed she-camel criss-crossing her paths,
  [24]*a wild donkey taught about the wilderness,*
In her consuming desire,[k] *she has panted after wind;*
  her season[l]*—who can turn her?*
Any who seek her will not get weary—
  in her month they will find her.[m]
[25]*Hold back your foot from being bare,*
  and your throat[n] *from thirst.*

But you say, "Futile,[o] *no,*
  because I love foreigners,
    and it is after them that I will go."

63. Calvin, *Jeremiah*, 1:109.

a. A *śōrēq* (cf. Isa 5:2) as opposed to a common or garden *gepen*. LXX, Vg take the term to mean a high-quality vine, which is doubtless right; etymologically, *śōrēq* specifically suggests a red one.

b. LXX and Vg paraphrase the obscurely-constructed colon; according to *CTAT* 2:470, J. D. Michaelis in his *Orientalische und exegetische Bibliothek* described it as "grammatically deformed" (*vicieuse*). But LXX and Vg incorporate words for bitterness/corruption, which supports the suggestion that the passive participle *sûrê* comes from a *sûr* that is a byform of the verb *sārâ* in Aramaic, meaning "decay/stink" (see *DCH*; *DTT*, 1026).

c. The puzzling construct is epexegetical (see *IBHS* 9.5.3c).

d. LXX, Vg assume that *alien* describes *the vine*, which the lack of the article makes difficult; rather it describes *you*, Jerusalem as whore.

e. *Kābas* (*piel*) usually denotes washing clothes, not washing the person (for which the verb is *rāḥaṣ*); the *piel* suggests something intensive (J. A. Thompson, *Jeremiah*, 176).

f. Strictly speaking, natron, a sodium compound used for cleaning.

g. This parallel term, *bōrît*, suggests a plant-based cleanser; see McKane, *Jeremiah*, 1:42.

h. *Kātam* ("stain"; here a *niphal* participle and thus suggesting odious or offensive) comes only here in the First Testament, but it is well-known in Postbiblical Hebrew.

i. LXX has a passive verb, but the verb is again *niphal*.

j. LXX has singular and, as usual, gives "Baal" a feminine article (see the translation note on v. 8).

k. "The desire of her being" (*nepeš*). The *qere* has a feminine suffix, which fits what follows; the *ketiv npšw* implies masculine, which fits the preceding reference to the masculine donkey.

l. The noun comes only here in this "exclamation" (Allen, *Jeremiah*, 44). Vg "love" perhaps infers its meaning from the parallelism with the preceding colon (but see BDB, 58); *season* rather implies an anticipatory parallelism with *month*.

m. The asyndetic clause with the prepositional expression before the verb is subordinate to the previous clause.

n. The *qere* has the expected spelling *gārôn*; the *ketiv gwrn* is "presumably a slip of the pen influenced by *gôrān* 'threshing-floor'" (Holladay, *Commentary on Jeremiah*, 1:53).

o. More literally, "It's desperate" (cf. Vg); see BDB, 384.

This fourth section continues the indictment but again changes metaphors. Instead of speaking in terms of an ox or a servant, Jeremiah speaks in terms of a wife, reverting to the image with which the chapter began—except that Yahweh's wife is a whore, an alien woman, indeed a donkey in heat that is interested in only one thing. The section is structured in three parts:

vv. 20c–22	Yahweh's critique (a tricolon, two linked bicola, and another tricolon at a pausing point)
vv. 23–25a	Yahweh's response to denials (six bicola, the middle two linked as the first again cannot stand alone)
v. 25b	Judah's refusal (a single tricolon closing off the section)

20c Like the *That's why* that introduced vv. 9–13, the *because* that opens vv. 20c–25 suggests continuity with what precedes but also introduces a new stage in the argument. Here, another tricolon leads into a re-expression of the point by means of another image for Judah's abandoning of Yahweh— indeed, a series of images: a whore, a vine, a washerwoman, a camel, a donkey. All are based on everyday life but also reflect the influence of Jeremiah's prophetic predecessors.[64] The first two cola are exactly parallel:

because	on	every	high	hill
and	under	every	verdant	tree

The cola lack verbs, so they raise suspense, though in general terms their implication is obvious enough. In 1 Kgs 14:23, the same phrases describe Judahite worship practices (see similar phrases in 2 Kgs 16:4; Ezek 6:13), and in 2 Kgs 17:10, they describe Ephraimite worship practices (similar phrases in Jer 3:6). Yet one waits to discover the explicit accusation, aware that Jeremiah might be playing yet another trick on his listeners. In Judah, these phrases could imply practices involved in the worship of Yahweh, not of other gods. Judahites could indeed say they didn't serve other gods like those renegade Ephraimites, did they? But Jeremiah has already indicated that he doesn't see it this way; actually, they have abandoned Yahweh and gone after other deities. Here, the third colon makes the point in a dreadful insult. They are not simply worshiping Yahweh in an innovative fashion. They are behaving as a *whore*, like the Ephraimites (e.g., Hos 1:2; 2:2[4], 5[7]; 4:10, 12, 13, 14, 15, 18). In Jeremiah, as in Hosea, whoring (*zānâ*) need not imply engaging in sex for money. It rather denotes engaging in any sexual activity outside the framework accepted as proper by the community, so it is closer to the idea of sexual immorality; it includes promiscuity and adultery. The colloquial use of "whore" in English fits. Jeremiah adds a graphic extra verb to describe a whore making herself available: *bending over*. There is little evidence that traditional (Canaanite) worship involved sexual rites and little reason to see Jeremiah as implying that sexual rites are part of Judah's worship. Sexual promiscuity is a metaphor for religious and political promiscuity, of which Jeremiah does accuse Judah, whereas Jerusalem doesn't see its religious or political practice as promiscuous.[65]

21 Yahweh adds another metaphor, reverting to one he used in commissioning Jeremiah (1:10; see the commentary there). There, he promised eventual replanting; here, he recalls how Yahweh had originally *planted* the people in the land as not merely an ordinary vine but a *red vine*—one that produces red grapes or red wine or has red leaves, which were valued for

---

64. Rudolph, *Jeremia*, 19–20.
65. S. Van Den Eynde, "Taking Broken Cisterns for the Fountain of Living Water," *Biblische Notizen* 110 (2001): 86–96.

their medicinal qualities. The parallel colon reinforces his statement. Its *seed* was *true*, or reliable—*all of it*. There was no reason why it should not produce good grapes. In convoluted language that matches the convoluted nature of the event, Jeremiah declares that Jerusalem the *vine* has become *corrupted* and produced rotten grapes (cf. Isa 5:4). To revert to the earlier image, Jerusalem has turned into *an alien woman*. It's another way of calling her a whore: "A whore is a deep pit; an alien woman is a narrow cistern" (Prov 23:27).[66]

22 For a moment, Jeremiah changes images once again. The tricolon works like the one in v. 20b. The first two cola suggest complementary possibilities about getting clean. Jeremiah might be referring to removing a stain of guilt (so Tg), whose reality the people deny (cf. Matt 27:24) or acknowledge (like Lady Macbeth when she tried to wash the blood off her hands in Shakespeare's play). But he may simply be starting from an aspect of everyday life. Jerusalemites no doubt like their clothes clean and like being clean, especially on special occasions. They *launder* and wash themselves thoroughly, with *much cleanser*. Why does Jeremiah mention this fact? The third colon provides the answer. Such washing can cleanse the body in a superficial sense, but it doesn't remove the body's more serious *stain,* and Yahweh will still be able to see it (Jeremiah continues to have the body in mind: he is not contrasting outward and inward). The stain is the one that results from the city's *waywardness* ('āwōn): Jeremiah introduces another key term. In 3:21, he will use the verb lying behind this noun ('āwâ) in a way that links with the noun's etymology. Verb and noun suggest going astray by choosing the wrong path. The noun links with the image of a path and of going after the right person or the wrong person.

23a–b Wherein do the waywardness and thus the stain lie? Jerusalem has been stained with blood (Isa 1:15), and the verb in v. 22 commonly suggests bloodstain (again, compare Lady Macbeth). But here, the denial parallel with

66. On feminist disquiet or hostility regarding the way this passage speaks of women (concerning which see also the commentary on 3:7), see, e.g., J. C. Exum, "The Ethics of Biblical Violence against Women," in *The Bible in Ethics: The Second Sheffield Symposium*, ed. J. W. Rogerson, JSOTSup 207 (Sheffield: JSOT, 1995), 248–71; A. Brenner, "On Jeremiah and the Poetic of (Prophetic?) Pornography," in *On Gendering Texts: Female and Male Voices in the Hebrew Bible*, ed. A. Brenner and F. van Dijk Hemmes, BibInt 1 (Leiden: Brill, 1993), 177–93; cf. A. Brenner, "On Prophetic Propaganda and the Politics of 'Love,'" in *A Feminist Companion to the Latter Prophets*, ed. A. Brenner, A Feminist Companion to the Bible (Sheffield: Sheffield Academic, 1995), 256–74; R. P. Carroll, "Desire under the Terebinths," in Brenner, *Feminist Companion to the Latter Prophets*, 275–307; A. Bauer, *Gender in the Book of Jeremiah: A Feminist-Literary Reading*, StBibLit 5 (New York: Lang, 1999); E. K. Holt, "'The Stain of Your Guilt Is Still before Me,'" in Maier and Sharp, *Prophecy and Power*, 101–16; S. Macwilliam, "Queering Jeremiah," *BibInt* 10 (2002): 384–404; M. E. Shields, "Impasse or Opportunity or . . . ?," in Diamond and Stulman, *Jeremiah (Dis)placed*, 290–302; A. Brenner, "Response to Mary E. Shields," in Diamond and Stulman, *Jeremiah (Dis)placed*, 303–6.

the expression *defiled myself* moves to the more common religious language used in v. 7. "I'm not like the adulterous woman in Num 5:11–31."[67] Actually, the holy city has indeed incurred defilement, because it has *gone after the Masters* instead of Yahweh or as well as Yahweh. Jeremiah again takes up the motifs of going after and of the path and repeats the charge that dominates the chapter. The Masters are here plural, which may reflect the assumption that the Master had different names and identities in keeping with the different places he had supposedly made himself known, as, for example, Master of Hazor and Master of Peor (2 Sam 13:23; Hos 9:10)—a little like "Our Lady of . . ." or "Jesus of . . . ." Jerusalem denies the defilement, and Jeremiah therefore draws attention to the evidence. *The Ravine* can refer to a number of places, including Beth-pe'or (Deut 3:29), which would be relevant in this context (cf. Tg). But it most commonly denotes (Ben-/Bene-)Hinnom, the valley to the west and south of Jerusalem. LXX here calls it the cemetery, and 19:1–15 links burial with the Hinnom Ravine (where people burned children; see 7:31–32), while 2 Kgs 23:6 locates a common burial ground in the adjacent Kidron Wadi. It would be a natural location for making offerings in connection with burials and with maintaining relationships with family members who had passed.[68] Josiah put an end to these practices for a while, but 2 Kgs 23–24 and Ezekiel imply that they revived. While some people engaging in them might be consciously worshiping other deities, others could see themselves as worshiping Yahweh while using those traditional forms and means of worship, and they could therefore issue the denial that Jeremiah quotes. Jeremiah doesn't imply that they are insincere in their faith; they may be quite sincere. But worship that takes such forms cannot really serve Yahweh. It implies serving the Masters, even if people don't *acknowledge* it. It's time they did instead of claiming they are not defiled because they haven't gone after the Masters.

23c–24 In light of the reality he has portrayed, Jeremiah has two insulting comparisons for Jerusalem: the city is a camel and a donkey. These comparisons would not in themselves be insults; camels and donkeys were valuable and appreciated creatures without which human life would be much harder. But on her own a *light-footed she-camel* would run about in an aimless way. Jeremiah further reworks the *paths* image from earlier in v. 23, as he did in vv. 17–18; see also v. 36. Jerusalem could think that its missions to Egypt were very purposeful, but they were not so at all. Something similar can be said of

67. D. Rom-Shiloni notes that most occurrences of this verb in the *niphal* come in that passage: see "'How Can You Say, "I Am Not Defiled . . ."?' (Jer 2:20–25): Allusions to Priestly Legal Traditions in the Poetry of Jeremiah," *JBL* 133 (2014): 757–75.

68. See Isa 57:3–10 and J. Goldingay, *A Critical and Exegetical Commentary on Isaiah 56–66*, ICC (London: T&T Clark, 2014), 94–130.

the *wild donkey* that knows the *wilderness* well and wanders about in it but does so in an apparently directionless and purposeless way (now if only it were a domesticated donkey . . .). The donkey in the first colon of v. 24 seems to be male, but then it becomes female; perhaps the switch is influenced by the addressing of Jerusalem as feminine in previous lines. She is a donkey keen to find a mate when she is in heat. The bicolon in v. 24b works a-b-a'-b': *her consuming desire* occupies her when it is *her season*. It means she has *panted after wind* and caught the whiff of a male, and so no one will be able to *turn her* back from seeking him out. There's no stopping her. The subsequent bicolon in v. 24c extends the point: it's easy for *any* male donkeys to locate her: *in her month*, her time in heat, she'll be looking for them. If it's not too allegorical, we can infer that Jeremiah's point is that anyone who wants to find the Jerusalemites seeking the Masters will easily find them. They are full of enthusiasm, and they don't hide.

25a Yahweh has one more thing to say about Jerusalem's path before changing the subject. He first picks up two ways in which a journey along a lengthy path (in a climate like Israel's or in the wilderness) may take a toll on you:

Hold back	your	foot	from	[being] bare
and	your	throat	from	thirst.

The opening colon thus has a verb applying to both cola, a feminine noun, then an adjective at the end; the parallel colon has a masculine noun and then a noun at the end. Boots may wear out and you may die of dehydration, Yahweh says. Don't do it. He's not talking about an ordinary hike but about the costly nature of the journey that the Jerusalemites are engaged in. It's not the kind of path he imposed on them. In v. 20, he talked about a yoke; he did not impose a heavy yoke on them (see Matt 11:30). He didn't ask them to sacrifice their children in the Ravine in the demanding way of serving God that the traditional religion of Canaan expected (see v. 23). Nor does he want them to trudge through the wilderness to Egypt to do political deals, which was the context of the earlier yoke talk (Isa 30:1–7 implies a complementary argument).

25b The reference to *foreigners* in the closing tricolon could suggest both religious resources (3:13; Deut 32:16) and political resources (5:19; 30:8; 51:51). The former would link with vv. 20c–23a; the latter would link with the allusions to Egypt and Assyria earlier in this chapter. Religion and politics were interwoven. "If Israel does not embrace Yahweh, perforce she will embrace the political might of foreigners and their deities."[69] While it may

69. Holladay, *Commentary on Jeremiah,* 1:102.

confuse Western readers that Jeremiah declines to speak in a way that makes a clear distinction between religion and politics,[70] his declining to dissociate them is instructive. When Jerusalem says it's *futile* for Jeremiah to seek to wean it from its alien commitments, its reference to its love of foreigners could cover both religion and politics, given that the Hebrew word translated *love* can cover political commitments as well as religious and romantic ones (see v. 2 and the commentary on it). Jerusalem's response could imply either "I can't stop" or "I won't stop." Perhaps both are true. With regard to politics as well as religion, Judah need not see itself as serving masters other than Yahweh. It could take the view that responsible political policies (as it saw them to be) were part of serving Yahweh.[71]

5. *The Shameful Community (2:26–31a)*

[26]*Like a thief's shame when he's found out,*
  so have Israel's household acted shamefully[a]—
They, their kings, their officials,
  and their priests and their prophets,[b]
[27]*Saying*[c] *to wood, "You're my father,"*
  and to rock, "You're the one who gave birth to us."[d]
Because they have faced me with the back of their neck,[e]
  not their face.

At the time of their dire trouble, they will say to me,
  "Set to and deliver us."[f]
[28]*But where will be your gods,*
  the ones that you made for yourself?
They should set to, if they can deliver you,
  at the time of your dire trouble.

Because the number of your towns—
  so your gods have become, Judah.[g]
[29]*Why would you argue with me?—*
  all of you have rebelled against me[h] *(Yahweh's affirmation).*
[30]*To no effect did I strike down your children—*
  they did not accept restraint.

---

70. R. P. Carroll, *Jeremiah*, OTL, 142.
71. See the imaginary argument between prophet and politician in J. Goldingay, "Proverbs and Isaiah 1–39," in *Reading Proverbs Intertextually*, ed. K. Dell and W. Kynes, LHBOTS 629 (London: T&T Clark, 2018), 49–64.

Your sword devoured your prophets
like a devastating lion:
³¹ᵃ*you are the generation.*ⁱ

a. *Hōbîšû* is an inwardly transitive *hiphil* (GKC 53d). LXX has a future verb, a not inappropriate piece of interpretation (see the commentary).

b. The enjambment could make one ask whether alternatively *hōbîšû* is transitive with *household* as its object: So have they shamed Israel's household— / Their kings, their officials, / and their priests and their prophets.

c. The participle suggests an ongoing practice.

d. The *qere yəlidtānû* ("us") makes for variation over against the parallel colon; the *ketiv*, LXX, Vg have *yəlidtānî* ("me").

e. For this translation, see Lundbom, *Jeremiah 1–20*, 283.

f. *Deliver us* is *hôšî'ēnû*, one of the common forms of that imperative; another of them, *hôšî'â nā'* (Ps 118:25), becomes "Hosanna" (e.g., Mark 11:9).

g. MT has a marker here. LXX has an extra line equivalent to 11:13b.

h. The asyndetic clause with the subject before the verb is subordinate to the previous clause; cf. v. 30αβ, with the object before the verb.

i. Jerome (*Jeremiah*, 17) thus links v. 31a with v. 30; cf. A. J. O. van der Wal, "Jeremiah ii 31: A Proposal," *VT* 41 (1991): 360–63.

Once again, Jeremiah changes the subject of his indictment; he now critiques the making and using of divine images. Israel has acted shamefully by manufacturing them and bowing down to them and thus turning away from Yahweh. It will mean that when trouble comes, these "gods" will be exposed and the people will be shamed. Yahweh then recalls his acts of chastisement, which made no difference to their inclination to multiply gods and to kill prophets who opposed the practice, leaving them without defense to his indictment. A final colon apparently brings home the point to the later generation—perhaps the 604 generation, perhaps people who have seen the threats fulfilled in 597 or 587. The section is structured in three parts:

vv. 26–27b   Judah's turning away (the first version of the indictment) (a three-line enjambment and an additional bicolon)

vv. 27c–28b   Judah's coming predicament (three self-contained bicola)

vv. 28c–31a   Judah's turning away (the second version of the indictment) (three self-contained bicola and a tricolon to close)

26 Jeremiah introduces another of his recurrent motifs. Whereas *honor* means acting in a way society recognizes and praises, *shame* means acting in a way society critiques as unworthy. It means public disgrace, not merely feeling chagrined[72]—an awareness of exposure and humiliation, the opposite of (proper) pride. It is an oversimplification to say that Western cultures are guilt-focused and traditional cultures are shame-focused. The Western notions of identity, self-worth, and especially dignity overlap with the notion of shame; and if reviewers accuse this commentary of bad judgment, ignorance, or plagiarism, I will be shamed and ashamed. But shame is indeed a significant issue in traditional cultures. Admittedly *a thief's shame* is the least of his problems (see, e.g., Exod 22:1–8 [21:37–22:7]). But Rachel would have been shamed if she had been *found out*, and Achan was shamed when he was found out (Gen 31; Josh 7). In his deceit and unfaithfulness, Achan behaved shamefully, and he was shamed by the exposure of his deceit and unfaithfulness. Shame is both an individual reality and a community reality, and similar dynamics apply to Israel, though there is some pregnancy in Jeremiah's formulation. The shameful action is actual; the shaming is still future. The shamefulness that Jeremiah sees and the shaming that he foretells affect the entire community and all its strata of leadership (cf. 1:18). What is its cause? Verse 26 sets up the question. The following lines will answer it.

27a–b Jeremiah begins with another quotation of something that people don't quite say—the people being the ones he is actually addressing. It is part of trying to shake them to their senses. Revering images implies that the images are deities, and the shamefulness lies in being people who implicitly hold that assumption. Another line combines parallelism with variation:

saying	to wood	father of me	you [masc.]
and	to rock	you're the one who [fem.]	gave birth to us

The opening participle applies to both cola: rock complements wood, feminine complements masculine, verbal predicate complements noun predicate, "us" complements "me." In the opening colon, the subject follows the predicate (the way Hebrew usually works) while in the complementary colon the subject precedes the predicate (because the predicate is a verb, the "you're" was unnecessary, but its inclusion helps further the parallelism as well as adding emphasis). Wood is the main thing an image was made of; Jeremiah ignores the gold or silver overlay to underline the stupidity of the statement that people make to the image (compare and contrast 10:1–16). Rock appears rarely in this connection and might be a makeweight (cf. Deut 4:28; but cf. 3:9). Literally, it would refer to stone obelisks (43:13), and there could be variation in whether people regarded them as images of a god.[73] Whereas images were always forbidden, obelisks were fine in Genesis (e.g., 28:18, 22),

---

72. McKane, *Jeremiah*, 1:48.
73. See E. Bloch-Smith, "Massebot Standing for Yhwh," in *Worship, Women, and War:*

but they were banned when they came to be associated with the Master. Both wood and rock might refer to totem poles that could be understood as standing for Asherah and pillars that stood for Yahweh himself (Deut 12:3; 2 Kgs 23:14)—in which case, Jeremiah speaks sarcastically, since the totem pole would represent a mother figure and the pillar a father figure. People would not actually think that the wood and stone were father and mother, but Jeremiah presupposes a kind of syllogism. Yahweh was Israel's father and mother (e.g., Deut 32:18). Yahweh cannot be imaged with something material. People pray to something material. Therefore, they are not praying to Yahweh, even if they think they are. But perhaps they did think they were praying to Asherah.[74] Corporately, Israel may have come into the country as outsiders who experienced Yahweh revealing himself to them, rescuing them, and bringing them there. But ask the average Israelite about his or her background, and it was not so different from that of the average Canaanite.[75] Whatever they think they are doing, they are turning their back on Yahweh, which is to say ignoring him. "How can Yahweh carry on a relationship with the back of a neck?"[76] In contrast, turning one's face means "looking to" him, as we say in English.

27c–28b Yahweh jumps a stage in his argument and returns to a picture of Israel having to handle disaster, making his point in an a-b-c-c'-b'-a' pattern:

> At the time of their dire trouble, they will say to me,
>> "Set to and deliver us."
>>> But where will be your gods,
>>> the ones that you made for yourself?
>> They should set to, if they can deliver you,
> at the time of your dire trouble.

Jeremiah again speaks in anticipation of *dire trouble* he knows is coming, as it will in 597 and more finally in 587. People may then come before their images and plead for help, but they will not get any help from these *Ersatzgöttern*.[77] He pictures them realizing their stupidity and turning to the real Yahweh as people do in temple worship: their plea, *Set to and deliver us*, comes in 1 Chr 16:35; Ps 106:47 ("set to and deliver me" comes in Jer 17:14 and Ps 3:7[8]).[78]

Essays in Honor of Susan Niditch, ed. J. J. Collins, T. M. Lemos, and S. M. Olyan, Brown Judaic Studies 357 (Providence, RI: Brown University Press, 2015), 99–115.

74. S. M. Olyan, "The Cultic Confessions of Jer 2,27a," *ZAW* 99 (1987): 254–59.

75. See, e.g., W. R. Domeris, "Jeremiah and the Religion of Canaan," *OTE* 7 (1994): 7–20.

76. Holladay, *Commentary on Jeremiah*, 1:104.

77. Fischer, *Jeremia*, 1:171.

78. Weiser, *Jeremia*, 1:27.

But Yahweh will give them a dusty response. "You have your gods you made. Where are they now?" The acerbic question nicely reverses the one Yahweh sometimes had to listen to (Pss 42:3[4], 10[11]; 79:10; 115:2), but it also recalls the comment about people's failure to ask, "Where is Yahweh, the one who got us up from the country of Egypt" (v. 6). Both questions bring to mind Jeroboam's declaration, "Here are your gods who brought you up from the country of Egypt" (1 Kgs 12:28)—the declaration by which Ephraim lived.[79] In asking his question, Yahweh moves to addressing the people directly; here he does so in the masculine singular, implicitly speaking to Judah. Don't turn to me then, says Yahweh. He speaks rhetorically, like a mother who threatens to divorce her kids out of a sense of offense or pain, and his confrontational language is designed to shake them to their senses. Yet he indeed did let the city fall in 597 and 587. In his mind's eye, Jeremiah has seen it and has already seen Israel shamed.

28c–29 After all, they have lots of gods, don't they? Any town would have a shrine (a "high place"), and each shrine might have an image. People could see it as an image of Yahweh, but it cannot be (because by definition there is no such thing). It is therefore really an image of another deity. Yahweh now reverts to addressing people in the plural. Back in v. 9, he declared his intention to argue with them. He knows he has a case. He does not grant that they have one. The *why* implies that their attempting to *argue* with him would be pointless. Again, he jumps a stage in his argument. Bringing a case would involve them challenging him as people do in the Psalms, urging him to act on their behalf on the basis of being people committed to him to whom he therefore has an obligation but whom he has let down or is ignoring. Yet the fact that they have *rebelled* makes their case collapse. They can't argue that way.

30–31a What letdown could they be protesting? Their charge is that he has struck them down as if they were the Egyptians or the Canaanites (cf. 14:19; also 5:3). The image of the lion, and the verb *devastate* (*šāḥat*), are important through the Jeremiah scroll.[80] Yahweh apparently imagines them looking back on the history of *your children* in the sense of the "children of Israel," who are part of the *all of you*. On a gloomy day, they could see their history as dominated by invasions and defeats. Sure, I struck them down, Yahweh says, reintroducing from vv. 19–20 the motif of restraint or discipline (*mûsār*; cf. 5:3; 7:28; 17:23; 32:33; 34:13; only Proverbs uses the word more; see the translation note and the commentary on 2:19–20). Maybe his point is that he hit them because they rebelled and did not *accept restraint*, so they deserved it; or maybe it's that striking them down was designed to achieve something positive by way of restraint or discipline,

79. J. S. Burnett, "Changing Gods: An Exposition of Jeremiah 2," *RevExp* 101 (2004): 289–99.
80. Bourguět, *Métaphores*, 199–334.

but alas, it failed. Slaughtering *prophets* (cf. 26:7–24; 1 Kgs 19:10, 14) will have been a horrific expression of that rebellion and resistance to restraint and a concrete indication that they have no *case* to bring. But *your children* also recalls v. 9, where "the children of your children" feature in Yahweh's argument. This link might suggest that Yahweh is again anticipating the time after 597 and 587. For the audience in 604, *your children* are then the coming generation. Either way, the confrontation in v. 31aα would point out to subsequent audiences that they *are the generation* that needs to apply Jeremiah's message to themselves. This direct challenge brings the tricolon and the section to a close.

6. *The Shaming to Come (2:31b–37)*

31b-d*Look at Yahweh's message:*

A wilderness—is that what I have been to Israel,
    *or a country of supernatural gloom?*a
*Why have my people said, "We have wandered about*b—
    we will not come to you anymore"?
32*Can a young girl*c *put her adornment out of mind,*
    *a bride her bows?*d
But my people—they have put me out of mind
    days without number.
33*How good you make your path*
    for seeking love!
Thus, yes, dire things—
    *you have taught them to your paths.*e
34*Yes, on your sleeves*f *is to be found*
    *the life blood*g *of the needy,*h *people who are free of guilt;*i
    *it was not in breaking in that you found them.*j

Because for all these things:

35*You have said, "Indeed I am free of guilt;*
    in truth, his anger has turned from me."
Here am I, entering into the exercise of authority with you
    *for your saying*k *"I haven't done wrong."*
36*How very casually you go about*l
    in changing your path!
Yes, through Egypt you will be shamed,
    as you were shamed through Assyria.

³⁷ *Yes, from this you will go out,*
  your hands on your head.
Because Yahweh has rejected the people on whom you rely
  and you will not succeed through them.

a. *Ma'pēlyâ*, which comes only here, is a lengthened version of words such as *'ōpel*. It parallels *šalhebetyâ* (Song 8:6) and could thus make people think of "Yahweh's darkness" (Qimchi, in MG), which would fit in this context.

b. LXX "we will not be ruled," with "free add[ition]" of a negative (HUBP)(!) apparently derives *radnû* from *rādâ* (Craigie, Kelley, and Drinkard, *Jeremiah 1–25, 39, 40*) rather than *rûd*. Syr "we have gone down" implies a form from *yārad*; Vg, Aq, Sym "we have gone back" might imply *rûd* or *yārad*.

c. See the translation note on 18:13.

d. *Qiššureyhā*, from a verb meaning "tie" or "bind," perhaps suggests elements in her outfit that are tied on or tied together.

e. *Lāmad piel* can take two objects, and thus, e.g., NRSV takes the line to signify teaching your paths to bad women, but the adjective *ra'* is set against the opening verb *yāṭab*, so the context and the parallel in 3:5 suggest that *hārā'ôt* denotes bad things, not bad women, and the line signifies teaching bad things to your paths.

f. Lit. "your wings/edges." For *bikǝnāpayik*, LXX and Syr imply *bǝkappayik* ("on your palms").

g. Lit. "blood of lives."

h. LXX lacks *'ebyônîm*, perhaps a later elaboration in MT, making Jeremiah's point more general; see the commentary.

i. Vg *innocens* for *nāqî* generates the English translation "innocent," which is not exactly wrong but changes the emphasis. *Nāqî* means free of liability in various senses: free of obligation, free of guilt, free from punishment, in the clear.

j. LXX, Vg have "I found them."

k. Rashi (in MG) infers "saying in your heart."

l. I take *tēzǝlî* as a composite form with consonants from *zālal* "make light of" (cf. LXX, Vg, Syr) and pointing from *'āzal* "go about" (BDB).

The chapter's final section of indictment and threat incorporates a series of word pictures (vv. 31, 32, 34, 37), more questions (vv. 31c, 31d, 32), more pseudo-quotations (vv. 31d, 35a, 35b), more confrontational exclamations (vv. 33, 34, 36), and some final threats (vv. 35–37). Once again, Yahweh protests at his bride's turning her back on him, at her going after other lovers, at the slaying of the innocent, at the people's self-deceit, and at their wayward and stupid political policies. In other words, this final section brings together almost everything from the entire chapter.

      vv. 31b–34a
          v. 31b   Introduction to vv. 31c–34a
          vv. 31c–34a   Yahweh's indictment (six bicola and a tricolon before
                           the pause)

vv. 34b–37
    v. 34b   Introduction to vv. 35–37
    vv. 35–37   Yahweh's threat (six bicola)

31b–d A bidding to pay attention opens the chapter's final section. Regarding the catachresis[81] *look at Yahweh's message* (one doesn't look at a message!), compare 23:18 and Amos 1:1; Qoheleth comments that he has "seen" much wisdom and knowledge (Eccl 1:16).[82] Maybe it is significant that Yahweh now paints a number of further word pictures. His challenge again suggests a response to protests Israel has voiced. While *wilderness* is not too bad a place if you are a shepherd, Jerusalemites would find the city preferable, as vv. 2, 6–7 have presupposed. *A country of supernatural gloom* complements the expressions there. Someone from Anathoth, from where the land falls straight down into the desert of the Rift Valley and the Dead Sea, might be even more aware of the nature of wilderness.[83] The further pseudo-quotation that follows carries some irony. Yahweh pictures the people seeing themselves to be wandering about (as if in some trackless wilderness) but not actually protesting to him—implicitly because they see Yahweh himself as a wilderness and a country of supernatural gloom. They see no point in consulting him about their policies.

32 In response to that declaration, Yahweh segues to a second picture, returning to the marital imagery of v. 2, though it is a moment before the point is explicit. First, he invites us to imagine a pretty girl. The line is neatly parallel:

Can put out of mind   a young girl   her   adornment,
                           a bride   her   bows?

In the parallelism, *bride* makes explicit what kind of *young girl* we are talking about, and *bows* makes explicit what kind of *adornment*. The next line then makes a double comment. Israel has been able to do the impossible thing; indeed, *put me out of mind* is no recent phenomenon. Isaiah 49:14–18 will turn Jeremiah's point upside-down.[84]

33 Following the reference to a bride, Yahweh naturally reverts to second-person feminine singular address. The corollary of putting out of mind is *seeking love* elsewhere. Yahweh again picks up the path image. Having put

81. Blayney, *Jeremiah*, 234.
82. Qimchi, in MG.
83. Craigie, Kelley, and Drinkard, *Jeremiah 1–25*, 3.
84. Sommer, *Prophet Reads Scripture*, 37.

Yahweh out of mind, how good Jerusalem has been at finding other lovers: other deities to follow instead of Yahweh[85] and other political allies.[86] Jerusalem has thus been able to teach *dire things* to its *paths*. Yahweh compliments Jerusalem on how good it is at doing what is bad.[87]

34a What are the dire things? So far, dire behavior has been unfaithfulness to Yahweh expressed in alien worship forms, alien political policies, and the killing of prophets. In the section's third picture, Jerusalem walks around in a flowing robe on whose hems or sleeves one can see the blood of *people who are free of guilt*. The blood noted in 2 Kgs 24:4 still sits on them. It would initially be the blood of the prophets—people it put to death when they had done nothing to deserve it. It is in connection with such a threat to him that 26:15 warns Jerusalem about shedding "innocent blood." The flowing outfits worn by people in leadership might have blood on them both because they were actively engaged in action like that taken against Jeremiah and Uriah (Jer 26) and Naboth (1 Kgs 21) and because they simply failed to exercise their authority in a way that protected the innocent. Jeremiah cares about innocent blood more generally (e.g., 22:3, 17) and about *the needy* (5:28; 22:16). Thus, his message now incorporates talk of unfaithfulness within the community. There can be excuses for shedding blood; if you tackle someone whom *you found* was *breaking in* to your house and you killed him, it was not murder (Exod 22:2–3[1–2]). But Jerusalem does not have this kind of excuse.

34b The final colon in v. 34 forms an introduction to the chapter's conclusion and thus to Jeremiah's challenge: *for* (*'al*) might imply "because of" or "despite." The situation is made worse by people's living in denial. They killed the prophets and needy or colluded in their killings on the basis that they were false prophets and dishonest people. Ironically, those people were innocent but were treated as guilty, whereas Jerusalem is guilty but assumes innocence. According to the further convictions that Yahweh puts on its lips, it knows that Yahweh's wrath hung over it (2 Kgs 22) but that Josiah cleaned it up. It therefore believes that Yahweh's *anger has turned* from it and thus that it can turn to Yahweh in the way the Psalms do on the basis of being right with Yahweh. But its worship and life indicate that it has not actually turned back, and with later hindsight 2 Kgs 23:26 affirms that Yahweh's anger has not turned back either. The reformation did not reach far enough, or did not do so in a way that prevented Jehoiakim and Zedekiah from reversing it. So Yahweh is going to argue things out with Jerusalem. In v. 9, he spoke of arguing a case (*rîb*) with them and against them, which implicitly described what he had

85. Rashi, in MG.
86. Tg; Qimchi, in MG.
87. Allen, *Jeremiah*, 50.

139

already been doing in vv. 1–8. Here, the expression *entering into the exercise of authority with you* (*šāpaṭ niphal*) implies some mutuality of argument, but the implication is ironic (cf. 25:31). There's no doubt that the city is guilty, even though (or especially because) it claims otherwise, and no doubt that Yahweh is going to exercise his authority. Verse 35 has an a-b-b'-a' structure:

> you have said "Indeed I am free of guilt
> > in truth his anger has turned from me"
> > here am I exercising authority with you,
> for your saying "I haven't done wrong"

36 Jeremiah once again confronts the city about its path and begins as he did in v. 33 with a *how . . . your path* and another twofold *yes* (*gam*). Yahweh has a path he wants Jerusalem to take, but it has made its unilateral declaration of independence in *changing* its path so that it could wander about. This time, Jeremiah doesn't refer to love, but he does refer to *Egypt* and *Assyria*, who have long been the city's traditional political love objects. Assyria had that position in the past, but it is a spent force by Jeremiah's day. Egypt belongs to the present. While we have no concrete references to Judah seeking alliance with Egypt in Jeremiah's time (contrast Isa 30–31), this policy option was flagged in vv. 13–19. In connection with such possibilities, Jeremiah returns to the theme of being *shamed*, with another a-b-b'-a' sequence:

yes		through	Egypt	you will be shamed
as	you were shamed	through	Assyria.	

If Judah trusted in Egypt in the decades before 587, 2 Kgs 23:29, 33–35; 24:7 vindicate Jeremiah's point.

37 His fourth word picture at the close of this section and of the chapter hints at Jerusalem's going out to exile. *Hands on head* would be a plausible image for the distraught shame that will be involved (2 Sam 13:19). Passages such as Isa 30:12–15 from the context of Judah's Egyptian adventures in Hezekiah's day remind Judah about the disastrous consequences that follow when people *rely* on the wrong support and protection. They will *not succeed* in saving the nation that way. "All the addresses of the prophets" aim "to make the people to rest contented under the protection of God."[88]

---

88. Calvin, *Jeremiah*, 1:122.

B. MOSTLY EXHORTATION: TURNING AND TURNING BACK (3:1–4:4)

The themes, motifs, and images of Jer 2 recur in 3:1–4:4, but they are now set in the context of an emphasis on turning (*šûb*).[89] Jeremiah 2 has hinted at the potential offered by this verb and its derivatives.

> Your turnings—they should rebuke you. (2:19)
> Her season—who can turn her? (2:24)
> "In truth, his anger has turned from me." (2:35)

Jeremiah 3:1–4:4 exploits the word's possibilities, particularly its capacity to denote both "turn away" and "turn back," as well as a physical return from exile. The medieval chapter division recognizes this change at 3:1 and thus makes it a beginning. While putting the end of the chapter at 3:25 corresponds to a section break in MT, the talk of turning continues in 4:1–2. The theme continues in 4:3–4, though those verses do not use the word, but they conclude this hortatory section of the scroll. So 3:1–4:4 makes a section.[90]

One could call 2:1–4:4 as a whole "a *teshuva* speech."[91] Jeremiah 2 was implicitly concerned with the need for Judah to turn back to Yahweh. It portrayed Judah's religion as characterized by degeneracy, sensuality, double-mindedness, and unreality.[92] The extent to which Israel was so characterized was masked by the fact that it continued to talk in terms of Yahweh, but it had come to picture Yahweh as if he were the Master. So Judah needed to turn, but the chapter did not make the point explicit. Even 3:1–4:4 comes at the point only indirectly: first it presupposes it and then it raises problems about it before it issues a straightforward exhortation to which it then adds some promises. The combination of confrontation, exhortation, and promises in 3:1–4:4 means that the section encompasses the main themes of the entire

---

89. See W. L. Holladay, *The Root šûbh in the Old Testament* (Leiden: Brill, 1958); and on the imprudence of translating the word "repent," see D. A. Lambert, *How Repentance Became Biblical: Judaism, Christianity, and the Interpretation of Scripture* (Oxford: Oxford University Press, 2016), 71–90.

90. So, e.g., Fischer, *Jeremia*, 1:183.

91. R. Abma, *Bonds of Love: Methodic Studies of Prophetic Texts with Marriage Imagery (Isaiah 50:1–3 and 54:1–10, Hosea 1–3, Jeremiah 2–3)*, SSN 40 (Assen: Van Gorcum, 1999), 243. Holladay (*Commentary on Jeremiah*, 1:47–131) likewise treats 2:1–4:4 as one section. On the possible process whereby the chapters might have developed, see M. E. Biddle, *A Redaction History of Jeremiah 2:1–4:2*, Abhandlungen zur Theologie des Alten und Neuen Testaments 77 (Zürich: Theologischer Verlag, 1990).

92. J. Skinner, *Prophecy and Religion*, 64.

scroll: "Nothing in the remainder of the book—save the judgment upon the nations—adds substantially to this."[93]

The section shifts between prose and poetry (though some of the prose is rhythmic enough to be laid out as poetry), with gender shifts roughly corresponding to this alternation.[94] But an argument develops through the section:

3:1   Prose: a problem about Israel's turning, from Yahweh's side (second person singular feminine addressee)

3:2–5   Poetry: a problem about Israel's turning, from Israel's side (second person singular feminine addressee)

3:6–10   Prose: a recollection concerning Ephraim's failure to turn and Judah's faulty turning (third person singular feminine subject)

3:11–18   Prose: a challenge to Ephraim to turn and promises to Ephraim and Judah (second person singular feminine then second person plural masculine addressees)

3:19–25   Poetry: an explicit exhortation to Israel to turn (second person singular feminine then second person plural masculine addressees)

4:1–4   Poetry: the need for the turning to be real (second person plural masculine addressees)

It broadly works to read 3:1–4:4 in connection with the scroll whose origin is described in Jer 36, as is the case with Jer 2, though a distinctive feature of this section is that its long prose paragraphs in 3:6–18 are also the only part of the entire Jeremiah scroll that carries a date in Josiah's time. But any transcription of Jeremiah's messages from Josiah's reign apparently happened in connection with the production of the 604 scroll, and any attempt to identify the original form of individual messages as Jeremiah preached them in (say) the 620s is made implausible by the process that turned them into the text we have. The immediate context for reading 3:1–4:4 as a whole is the reign of Jehoiakim. On the other hand, since 1:1–3 set the Jeremiah scroll as a whole

93. Lundbom, *Jeremiah 1–20*, 299.

94. M. E. Shields, *Circumscribing the Prostitute: The Rhetorics of Intertextuality, Metaphor and Gender in Jeremiah 3.1–4.4*, JSOTSup 387 (London: T&T Clark, 2004), 17; Shields systematically considers the gender movements in the section. See, earlier, M. E. Shields, "Circumcision of the Prostitute: Gender, Sexuality, and the Call to Repentance to Jeremiah 3.1–4.4," *BibInt* 3 (1995): 61–74; and later, C. M. Maier, "Reading Back and Forth," in *Interested Readers: Essays on the Hebrew Bible in Honor of David J. A. Clines*, ed. J. K. Aitken, J. M. S. Clines, and C. M. Maier (Atlanta: Society of Biblical Literature, 2013), 137–50.

in the context of the time of Josiah, Jehoiakim, Zedekiah, and the period after 587, the section can profitably be read imaginatively against all those contexts. And its message might have been further elaborated as those later contexts unfolded. In particular, the promises in 3:16–20 seem to presuppose the presumed destruction of the "ark of the covenant" in 587, and they bring good news to people in that context.

1. The Impossible Possibility? (3:1)

[1]*Saying:*[a] *If a man sends off his wife, she goes from being with him, and she comes to belong to another man, can he turn back to her again?*[b] *That country would be polluted, polluted,*[c] *wouldn't it. But you—you have whored with many partners,*[d] *turning back to me. . . .*[e] *(Yahweh's affirmation).*

a. The terse introduction might be a way of introducing a question that seeks a ruling (cf. Hag 2:11) or of introducing a ruling that needs to be applied to a question. M. I. Gruber compares this with the "it has been said" formula in Matt 5:21 ("Jeremiah 3:1–4:2 between Deuteronomy 24 and Matthew 5," in *Birkat Shalom: Studies in the Bible, Ancient Near Eastern Literature, and Postbiblical Judaism Presented to Shalom M. Paul on the Occasion of His Seventieth Birthday*, ed. C. Cohen et al. [Winona Lake, IN: Eisenbrauns, 2008], 233–49).

b. LXX has a denial of *her* being able to return to *him*, which might fit Deut 24:1–4 and Jeremiah's allegory better.

c. An infinitive precedes the finite verb, underlining the fact. On this common usage in Jeremiah, see Y. Kim, "The Tautological Infinitive in the Book of Jeremiah," *Korean Journal of Christian Studies* 66 (2009): 23–38. LXX, Vg have the woman being polluted, which again fits Deut 24:1–4.

d. LXX, Syr "shepherds" implies *rōʿîm* (as in 2:8; 3:15) for *rēʿîm* (as in 29:23).

e. Vg, Syr, Tg take the infinitive absolute *šôb* as equivalent to an imperative (cf. 2:2; DG 103 remark 2). LXX may take the clause as an unmarked question: "Have you turned back to me?" (cf. *NETS*; Joüon 123w; GKC 113q, ee).

This question in prose[95] takes up the rule in Deut 24:1–4, though it is shorter than that rule.[96] In Deut 24:1, the man discovers "the nakedness of a thing" in his wife, which likely refers to sexual misconduct. Jeremiah does not include any reference to the reasons why the man *sends off his wife* (the usual term for divorce), notwithstanding the fact that such background would have been

95. But, e.g., W. H. Schmidt (*Jeremia*, 1:100, 102) lays out the verse as poetry.

96. M. A. Fishbane has a detailed comparison in *Biblical Interpretation in Ancient Israel* (Oxford: Oxford University Press, 1984), 307–11. See, more recently, D. Rom-Shiloni, "Actualization of Pentateuchal Legal Traditions in Jeremiah," *ZABR* 15 (2009): 254–81; "Priestly and Deuteronomic References in the Book of Jeremiah," in Gertz et al., *Formation of the Pentateuch*, 913–41.

quite apposite, nor any reference to her second husband divorcing her. The focus lies on the ban regarding the husband's marrying her again, as Deut 24 puts it, or turning back to her; the verb in Jer 3 is *šûb*, which will be key to the chapter. Deuteronomy 24 is thus concerned with a rule for the man, not a rule for the woman, but Jer 3 is concerned with whether *she* may go back to *him*. Everybody would know the answer to the question. As is the case with the questioning in Hag 2:10–14, there's nothing controversial here.

Deuteronomy 24 does use the verb *šûb*, but not with the meaning "turn back." It is only a quasi-auxiliary verb signifying the repetition of an action. In addition, Deut 24 refers to defilement, but only to the woman's defilement through her first marriage rather than to the country's defilement, and it uses the verb *ṭāmē'* ("be defiled/unclean") rather than Jeremiah's stronger verb *ḥānap* ("pollute"). On the other hand, Deut 24 does go on to say that the remarriage would put the country in the wrong and in need of purification (*ḥāṭā' hiphil*). Deuteronomy is not banning every second marriage after divorce, only a woman's remarriage to her first husband. It is solely in relation to him that she is defiled. It does not explain why she is defiled nor why Israel needed a rule to cover this exceptional circumstance; fortunately, we don't need to know the answers to the questions raised by Deut 24 in order to understand Jeremiah's argument. Given that a remarriage would cause defilement, the husband's ignoring this consideration would inevitably put the country in the wrong or bring pollution on it—like the ignoring of any rule about defilement. Becoming defiled does not imply having sinned; it can be just something tied up with life. It happens through contact with a corpse, for instance, which is inevitable if you need to bury a family member. You then simply have to follow the appropriate observance, like Mary when she has given birth to Jesus (Luke 2:22–24). But becoming *polluted* implies desecration, a deliberate profaning, "an act or attitude through which a state of sacral relation to the Godhead is intentionally set aside."[97]

While Jeremiah's audience would have no problem nodding their heads at his opening question, by doing so they have skewered themselves. They are like David, who was skewered by Nathan's story. In effect, Jeremiah says, "You are the man" (2 Sam 12:7).[98] Except that he says, "You are the woman," and he is speaking to an audience that would likely be mostly men, especially among Jehoiakim's cabinet. His confrontation is aided by the fact that he is addressing the city of Jerusalem, which is thought of as a woman. He asks: A man could not *turn back* to a woman who has been with a number of men, could he? *A fortiori*, *turning back* to Yahweh is not a possibility for Jerusalem

97. F. Horst, *Hiob*, Biblischer Kommentar: Altes Testament (Neukirchen: Neukirchener, 1968), 1:132, as quoted by K. Seybold, "חָנֵף, *ḥānēp*," *TDOT* 5:37.
98. Shields, *Circumscribing the Prostitute*, 56.

when she has been with a number of *partners*. Could she turn back? Could he agree to it? The message ends in mid-air, or mid-sentence, with a deliciously ambiguous verb (see the translation note). It could be translated, "But turn back to me"; that is, I don't have to be bound by that rule—it needn't apply to you and me. "I am above law, saith God, and will deal with thee, not according to mine ordinary rule, but according to my prerogative."[99] Or it could be a question: "So would you turn back to me?" That is, could I accept you without polluting myself? In light of the ambiguity, the closing *Yahweh's affirmation* is ironic. Surely it's always possible for people to return to Yahweh? Isn't it? One can imagine that the verse was designed to raise questions for Judah in Josiah's day, in Jehoiakim's day as part of the 604 scroll, during the years leading up to 587, or in the context of the exilic period. The rest of the section will explore possibilities with regard to whether Yahweh can or will have Judah back.

2. The Implausibility (3:2–5)

²*Raise your eyes to the bare heights*[a] *and look;*
  where have you not been laid?[b]
By the paths you have sat for them,
  like a Bedouin[c] *in the wilderness.*
You have polluted the country
  with your whorings, your dire behavior.[d]
³*Downpours*[e] *have held back,*
  late rain—it hasn't happened.
But in that you have had the forehead of a whorish woman,[f]
  you have refused to feel disgrace.
⁴*Just now you called*[g] *to me, didn't you,*
  "Father, you are the guide[h] *of my youth.*
⁵*Does he hold onto things for all time,*
  or does he keep things perpetually?"
There, you have spoken,
  but you did dire things, as much as you could.[i]

a. LXX, Vg "straight ahead" reflects uncertainty about the meaning of *šəpayim* (most of whose occurrences come in Jeremiah). Here it apparently denotes places that people look up to; they are or can be locations where people gather and pray (3:21; 7:29; 12:12; 14:6); they are or can be in the wilderness (4:11), where wild donkeys stand (14:6). But as bare heights, maybe they are simply "open plains in contradistinction to woodland" (Blayney, *Jeremiah*, 243–44).

99. Trapp, *Commentary*, 230.

b. For the *qere šukkabt* (cf. Aq, Sym), the *ketiv* implies *šuggalt*, the equivalent of the F-word (R. P. Carroll, *Jeremiah*, OTL 141), which is therefore regularly replaced by something a bit more delicate.

c. *'Ărābî*; Tg has the gloss "who dwell in tents"; Vg has "bandit." LXX has "raven," implying *'ōrēb*.

d. Lit. "your whoring and . . .": a hendiadys.

e. Vg "drops of rain" suggests that *rabibîm* were just showers, but etymology suggests that they were a more copious provision (BDB; Qimchi, in MG), as LXX implies (see McKane, *Jeremiah*, 1:60; he also notes that for MT's *malqôš*, late rain, LXX's "snare" implies *môqēš*).

f. The word order (object preceding verb) and the asyndesis suggest that this clause is subordinate to what follows.

g. Vg has an imperative, as in v. 1 (cf. Tg).

h. LXX, Vg; *'allûp* hardly means "companion/friend" (BDB, *HALOT*, *DCH*) in this context, following directly on the invocation as father.

i. Lit. "and you could." MT has a marker here rather than after 2:37, making 3:1-5 simply a continuation of ch. 2's confrontation.

This confrontation links with 3:1, taking up the references to the country being polluted, to whoring, and to the nation having many sexual partners, but it does not refer to turning, and poetically and thematically it stands in more obvious continuity with what preceded in Jer 2. The imagery continues that of Jer 2 except for the new simile in v. 2bβ. If 3:1 had not intervened, 3:2-5 would simply be a continuation of Jer 2 (see the translation note on v. 5). Yahweh thus continues to berate his people in unsavory terms for their promiscuity in going after other deities and their self-deception in thinking that their relationship with Yahweh is in good order; if anything, he does so in even more forceful terms. He also speaks of the dire consequences of their unfaithfulness, though now in terms of nature rather than politics and war.

Thus 3:1-5 as a whole binds together the confrontation of 2:1-37 and the comments on turning back in 3:6-4:4, in that 3:1 links forward and 3:2-5 links backward. The binding is a small-scale version of the binding of Isa 34-39 to Isa 1-33 and 40-66 (where Isa 34-35 links forward with Isa 40-66 and Isa 36-39 links backward with Isa 1-33). Because of this overlap, the two sections (2:1-37 and 3:1-4:4) cannot be pried apart (see the introduction to 3:1-4:4, p. 141).

Verses 2-5 comprise eight straightforward bicola, except that v. 3b is one of Jeremiah's signature 5-2 lines. The discipline of this structure is matched by a prosaic style of expression. Only two of the lines are characterized by classic complementary parallelism (vv. 3a, 5a); in most lines, the second colon simply completes the line to form a prosaic sentence, with no enjambment. As in Jer 2, Yahweh indicts, asks rhetorical questions, and puts things on the people's lips as he seeks to get through to them.

2 Jeremiah continues to use the second-person feminine and continues to expound his theme from Jer 2: the quasi-sexual unfaithfulness of Jerusalem and its people. The exhortation to *raise your eyes* suggests a deliberate action; it's a call to look facts in the face and own them. To judge from the second colon, the *bare heights* to which people are urged to look are the places where traditional shrines were located in the area around Jerusalem (and no doubt further afield), the "high places," where people went to pray (cf. v. 21). The city is urged to think about what happens at those places of worship. People fool themselves that that they are honoring Yahweh there (see v. 4), but they need to face the truth. They go there for multiple worship events in honor of a variety of deities (v. 13), and they need to acknowledge the nature of these events. Bedouin sat *by the paths* along which people traveled *in the wilderness* with wares for sale such as metalwork objects, and Jerusalem sits there like Tamar (Gen 38:14–16; cf. Prov 7:12) waiting for "companions" (v. 1). It has *polluted* the country (*ḥānēp hiphil*: cf. v. 1) by its involvement with other deities—like the hypothetical man or woman of v. 1, though in a different way.

3 Dire consequences have followed the city's *dire behavior* (v. 2; cf. 2:13, 19). Maybe there is a link between the references to bare heights and the wilderness and the reference to the rain having failed—more than one link. While the shrines would be places where people prayed, their very treeless nature could testify to the prayers' failure. The pollution has caused the drought, and "the connection between harlotry and drought is ironic," since the practices of traditional religion that Judah had observed "were designed to guarantee the cycle of nature."[100] While the failure of the rains might be something Jeremiah has seen in his imagination, like the political and military disasters to which Jer 2 referred, the picture here is perhaps more matter-of-fact, and drought was a recurrent reality. It was such a drought that prompted Jehoiakim's fast and thus Baruch's reading of Jeremiah's original scroll (36:9).[101] If a focus of people's worship at the shrines was prayer for rain (cf. Jer 14), it was counterproductive. The parallel cola in v. 3a talk in general terms about *downpours* and then about the *late rains* in about April, which help bring the crops to maturity. The cola describe how the rains *have held back* (*māna' niphal*) as if they had a mind of their own. They further describe how the spring rains simply *haven't happened*. Yahweh doesn't say that he prevented them. He rather implies that "moral order affects cosmic order."[102] He thus speaks in a similar way to his earlier comments on the (threatened) arrival of political and military disaster (2:14–20b). One can imagine farmers anxiously looking to the sky through the fall and early winter and then through the late winter and spring and inviting people to pray some more and sacrifice some more. But people didn't get it—didn't get that they were

---

100. R. P. Carroll, *Jeremiah*, OTL, 143.
101. Holladay, *Commentary on Jeremiah*, 1:66.
102. Fretheim, *Jeremiah*, 76.

thereby making matters worse. Perhaps some wrongdoers were ashamed of their behavior, but a whore needs to be brazen, and this whore was. She could look the world straight in the eye. She *refused to feel disgrace* (*kālam niphal* and the noun *kəlimmâ*, v. 25, are alternatives to the words translated "shame," *bôš* and *bōšet*; see 2:26, 36). The two neat, brisk, brief parallel cola of the first line, describing the toughness of the situation all too succinctly, lead into a second line with a first colon whose length breaks all bounds, matching the scandalous disorderliness of what it refers to.

4 Jerusalem didn't think she was doing anything wrong (cf. 2:35). She *called to me* in worship and prayer—for example, for rain. She addressed God as *Father* with the confidence in God's fatherly care and love that the First Testament characteristically shows—no negative fear of God here. She addressed God as *the guide of my youth*. With irony, the phrase recalls 2:2, and with further irony it recalls 2:19, its reference to learning, and its implication that Yahweh is the people's teacher, like the father in Proverbs.[103]

5 But the rains' consistent failure suggests that God is carefully preserving and stoking his attitude. The people move from speaking to Yahweh to asking themselves a question about him. The trouble is that their question is rhetorical and is articulated about him rather than addressed to him. The exactly parallel cola underline the question that (they think) Yahweh himself needs to face.

| Does (*hă*) | he hold onto | [things] | for all time, |
| or does (*'im*) | he keep | [things] | perpetually? |

What has happened to Yahweh's famous long-temperedness? In effect, they are claiming the theology of Exod 34:6–7[104] (see also Pss 30:5; 79:5). They cannily appeal to the reflection of its wording and theology in Ps 103:8–9, 13, with its reference to God being like a father (cf. v. 4) and to his not "holding onto" his anger (the verb *nāṭar* comes only six times in the First Testament outside Ps 103 and Jer 3). But the trouble with rhetorical questions is that someone may reply to them, and Jeremiah gives the obvious response. People who *have spoken* as Jerusalem has in v. 5a need to ask whether they have deliberately done the kind of *dire things* that make it impossible to complain about Yahweh's keeping his anger going. There's an incoherence about Jerusalem's attitude that implies not only self-deception but a naivety in its assumptions about how ingenuous Yahweh himself is. It talks about him as father-teacher, but in its life, it takes no notice of his teaching, which is moral and religious as well as pragmatic.

103. Volz, *Jeremia*, 38.
104. Weiser, *Jeremia*, 1:33.

3. Judah's Faulty Turning (3:6–10)

⁶*Yahweh said to me in the time of Josiah the king:*

*Have you seen what Turning*ᵃ *Israel did when she was going onto every high mountain and under every verdant tree and whoring*ᵇ *there?* ⁷*I said, "After she has done all these things, to me she will turn back."*ᶜ *But she didn't turn back; and False, her sister Judah, saw.*ᵈ ⁸*I saw*ᵉ *that for all the occasions when Turning Israel committed adultery, I sent her off, and gave her the cutting off document, but False,*ᶠ *her sister Judah, wasn't in awe.*ᵍ *She went and whored, she too,* ⁹*and*ʰ *through the lightness of her whoring she was polluted, with the country.*ⁱ *She committed adultery with rock and with wood.* ¹⁰*Even through all this, False, her sister Judah, didn't turn back to me with her entire heart but with deception (Yahweh's affirmation).*ʲ

a. LXX *katoikia* ("settlement") derives *məšûbâ* from *yāšab* rather than from *šûb* (cf. Syr).

b. The finite verb continues the participial construction, though its form is anomalous (GKC 75ii).

c. LXX, Vg, Syr translate *tāšûb* as imperative.

d. For the *qere wattēre'*, the *ketiv* implies the alternative spelling *wattir'eh*.

e. Syr (also some LXX MSS) "she saw," implying *wattēre'* for MT *wā'ēreh*, assimilates to the preceding verb.

f. Whereas vv. 7 and 10 have the adjective *bāgôdâ*, vv. 8 and 11 have the participle *bōgēdâ*—without an apparent difference.

g. In the context, "being in awe" works better than "being afraid" (cf. 5:22, 24). Either way, there ought to be a link between looking (*rā'â*; v. 7) and being in awe/being afraid (*yārē'*), but there isn't.

h. The verse begins *wəhāyâ* ("and it happened") when one would have expected *wayyəhî*; this oddity recurs in 37:11; 38:28; 40:3.

i. LXX lacks the phrase, which may be an expansion in MT (*CTAT* 2:481–82). Vg, Aq, Theod "she polluted the country" implies *wattaḥănēp* (*hiphil*) instead of *watteḥĕnap* (*qal*) (cf. v. 1).

j. MT has a unit marker here.

Jeremiah and Yahweh here try another way of getting through to Judah to persuade it to face the facts about itself. The new section picks up the talk of whoring and polluting the country from vv. 2–5 and the talk of turning back and sending off from v. 1; like vv. 1–5, it also picks up motifs from Jer 2 (see the commentary on vv. 6, 9). One could call it a midrash[105] on vv. 1–5 or "a narrative reinterpretation" of those verses,[106] though it takes the form of a

105. Holladay, *Commentary on Jeremiah*, 1:116.
106. Shields, *Circumscribing the Prostitute*, 71 (referring to vv. 6–11).

testimony to Yahweh's addressing Jeremiah. Maybe Jeremiah wrote his own midrash, or maybe a curator created it later in his name.

Jeremiah reports a conversation between Yahweh and himself, which Judah "overhears" through Jeremiah's report; overhearing something said about oneself can be more influential than being directly addressed. Indeed, the conversation is not just about Judah but about Ephraim. (For the Northern Kingdom, Jeremiah here uses the name Israel, which the Northern Kingdom had inherited as the bigger of the two nations into which the Israel of David and Solomon split, but for clarity I will refer to it as Ephraim in my own comments, as Jeremiah occasionally does and as Hosea often does.) So Judah overhears what Yahweh is saying about Ephraim, too, which might be influential in a further way. It wouldn't be surprising if Judah took a superior stance in relation to Ephraim. Judah had not met with the disaster that came upon Ephraim in 722 as a result of Ephraim's going after other gods; indeed, Judah had experienced the great act of deliverance related in Isa 36–37. And even if Judah had served other gods in Manasseh's day, it hadn't been doing so since Josiah's reformation (as it saw things). Like Amos 1:3–2:16, Jeremiah thus combines the rhetorical device of overhearing with the rhetorical device of talking about other people in order to give one's actual audience a false sense of security and then strike them a blow designed to devastate. If Judah thought in terms of a contrast between itself and Ephraim, Jeremiah first turns the contrast into a comparison, then makes the contrast work the other way. Jeremiah shares the imagery of marriage and whoring with the Hosea scroll, which also periodically digs Judah in the ribs with an exhortation to learn from Ephraim's mistakes, and Jeremiah may derive these motifs from there (see "The Torah, the Prophets, and the Psalms," p. 23). Certainly Jeremiah aims to get Judah to learn from Ephraim as Hosea does—or rather, at the moment at least, mourns over its resistance to doing so.

6 The scroll invites readers to imagine themselves *in the time of Josiah the king*, a time when people did turn back to Yahweh, but not in a lasting way. In the context of the production of the 604 scroll, this section would make sense as a recollection, in Jehoiakim's day, of dynamics that Jeremiah had come to recognize later in Josiah's reign, in the 610s. He reports a conversation that Yahweh initiated, as happened in 1:11–14, though in this case he simply reports something that *Yahweh said to me*; no response from Jeremiah is required. Yahweh begins by immediately playing with the motif of turning. He asks Jeremiah a rhetorical question in order to draw his attention to something and to give him a message to transmit in dramatic form to Judah. He could have given Jeremiah some poetry like that in vv. 2–5, but the report of a prose conversation in which Yahweh shares a reflection communicates in a different way. The title *Turning Israel* is the first time the name *Israel* has referred to the Northern Kingdom rather than to the people of Yahweh of which Judah (with some surviving northerners) is now the embodiment. "Israel," denoting Ephraim, will be a recurrent usage from now on in the Jeremiah scroll, though sometimes it will be less clear what "Israel" refers to. The noun *Turning* is an appellative (a noun qualifying the name of a person) only in this passage. Even as a common noun, it is mostly a Jeremianic usage (e.g., 8:5), though Jeremiah maybe got it from Hosea (see 11:7; 14:4[5]; it otherwise comes only in Prov 1:32). It always denotes a negative turning. *Onto every high mountain and under every verdant tree* and *rock and wood* pick up from 2:20, with variation.

7 Yahweh had hoped that Ephraim would *turn back* (more literally, simply "turn"), but his hope was disappointed. It is a characteristic divine experience. Yahweh had hopes for the world when he created it and for Israel when he married her and for the church when he brought it into being, but his hopes tend not to find fulfillment. Yet he doesn't give up (as this message shows). Unlike Hosea, who envisages the restoration of Yahweh's wives, Jeremiah makes no such reference.[107] His aim is to win Judah back, not to throw her out (and then restore her). While there is some sense in which Yahweh knows everything before it happens, at some other level he lives in narrative sequence with the world and with his people and thus lives with hope, anticipation, and uncertainty, waiting to see how people will react and how things will turn out. The notion of being *False* is another that will recur in Jeremiah (e.g., 3:20; 5:11). It suggests making promises and commitments (e.g., in marriage) and not keeping them. It connotes deception, betrayal, letdown, and disappointment, habits to which Samaria had been inclined and that led to Samaria's fall in 722. Although Yahweh could have called Judah *False* on the basis of its behavior before and after that time, the following verses suggest that he has in mind its more recent failure—or perhaps has in mind the inner nature that finds expression in those failures. Yahweh also notes that Judah and Ephraim are sisters; Yahweh married two sisters, and both are unfaithful. It's another aspect of "the prophets' rhetoric of horror designed to terrify their audience into reform" in the way it talks about women.[108]

8–9 Jeremiah adds explicit reference to Ephraim's having *committed adultery* (he has not used this expression so far, though he has implied this judgment) and adds that it was not just a one-time mistake. Yahweh therefore *sent her off* (cf. v. 1) and confirmed the process by giving her a *cutting off document*—divorce papers that put her status in writing and thus established

---

107. Diamond, "Jeremiah," 554–55 (though he draws a different inference).

108. A. Kalmanofsky, "Dangerous Sisters," 299; cf. R. J. Weems, *Battered Love: Marriage, Sex and Violence in the Hebrew Prophets*, Overtures to Biblical Theology (Minneapolis: Fortress, 1995), 52–58; see further the commentary on 2:21.

that someone who has a relationship with her is not committing adultery with her as a married woman (another link with Deut 24:1–4). Noting that he metaphorically fulfilled this part of the process confirms that he really did cast Ephraim off; actually, what he did was let Assyria eradicate her as a people. There was no literal divorce document, but "the downfall and mass deportation of Israel was evidence of divorce, God's final break in the covenant relationship."[109] Of course, it wasn't a final break, as this section will make clear. Isaiah 50:1 takes up the divorce image in a way appropriate to its context that may indeed imply that Yahweh did not divorce Israel at all[110] and thus in a way that can worry readers who do not keep in mind that Jer 3 and Isa 40–55 are using a metaphor and doing so in different ways in their different contexts. But such readers may also be on the verge of recognizing a theological conundrum that can hardly be resolved. Can God finally cast off his people? Well, yes, if they persist in their turning away! Well, no, if he is faithful! One might have hoped that Judah would learn from what happened to her sister, but she *wasn't in awe* and *she went and whored, she too.* Given the chronological sequence, Jeremiah might be referring to Hezekiah's Egyptian ventures (which Jer 2 would implicitly regard as whoring), but what follows will suggest he is especially referring to the religious innovations of Manasseh's reign. Judah was quite casual and unthinking about the way she followed Ephraim's example instead of learning from it. She operated with a *lightness* that matched that of the she-camel in 2:23. It was casual sex.[111] So she *polluted* the country (cf. v. 1) with her *adultery* (cf. v. 8) *with rock and with wood* (as 2:27 said).

10 Jeremiah makes a jump. He implies that Judah did *turn back* (through Josiah's reformation), as Ephraim did not, but not *with her entire heart,* or mind, as the Torah scroll urges (see Deut 6:5; 4:29; 10:12; 11:13; 13:3[4]; 26:16; 30:2, 6, 10)[112] and as Josiah challenged (2 Kgs 23:3). Images could be destroyed and the Shameful Fireplace could be defiled and obelisks could be shattered (2 Kgs 23), but such means of worship met needs that people felt, and the reformation did not change those felt needs. The next generation could reverse the reformation, and it did. It happened after Hezekiah's reformation, and it happened after Josiah's. Judah's turning thus involved *deception* (*šeqer*)—yet another key Jeremianic word; it comes more in Jeremiah than anywhere else (e.g., 3:23; 5:2, 31; 6:13; 7:4, 8, 9). Whereas

109. Allen, *Jeremiah*, 56.
110. See the discussion of the passage in J. Goldingay and D. Payne, *A Critical and Exegetical Commentary on Isaiah 40–55*, ICC (London: T&T Clark, 2005), 2:200–201.
111. Lundbom, *Jeremiah 1–20*, 308.
112. Though Deuteronomy consistently uses *lēbāb*, whereas Jeremiah has *lēb*.

falsehood suggests words you say but then don't live by, deception suggests words you say but never meant or words that have no correspondence in reality. It links with the notion of emptiness in 2:5; both words apply to the nature of the non-gods that people inexplicably serve. In reality, "Judah has learned nothing from the fall of Israel to the Assyrians."[113] It is easy to follow Judah's example:

> When he speaks first that I sent away Israel due to her sins and I sent her into exile, but Judah did not turn back when she heard about what happened to Israel, he speaks about our sins. When the events which refer to Israel and the mistakes of that people are known, we should be fearful and say: "If he did not spare the natural branches, how much more will he not spare us. . . ." For note the kindness and severity of God. For he is not kind without being severe nor severe without being kind. . . . We men who repent need his kindness, but those of us who persist in sins need his severity.[114]

4. The Implausible Model (3:11–18)

[11]*Yahweh said to me:*
Turning Israel has made herself[a] more faithful than False Judah. [12]*Go[b] and call out these words northward, and say,[c] "Do turn back,[d] Turning Israel (Yahweh's affirmation). I will not make my face fall against you, because I am committed (Yahweh's affirmation). I don't hold onto things for all time.* [13]*Only acknowledge your waywardness. Because against Yahweh your God you have rebelled and scattered your paths to foreigners under every verdant tree, and to my voice you have not listened (Yahweh's affirmation).* [14]*Turn back, turning children (Yahweh's affirmation), because I am the one who was husband to you.[e] I will get you, one from a town and two from a kin group, and enable you to come to Zion.* [15]*I will give you shepherds in accordance with my thinking,[f] and they will shepherd you with acknowledgment and understanding.* [16]*And when you become many and become fruitful in the country:*
In those days (Yahweh's affirmation), people will no more say, "Yahweh's pledge[g] chest."[h] It will not come up into their thinking, they will not be mindful of it, they will not attend to it, and it will not be made again.

113. Dearman, *Jeremiah*, on the passage.
114. Origen, *Jeremiah*, 35, quoting from Rom 11:18, 21–24.

¹⁷*At that time, people will call Jerusalem "Yahweh's throne," and all the nations will gather to it, to Yahweh's name, to Jerusalem. People[i] will no more go after the determination of their dire thinking.*[j]
¹⁸*In those days, the household of Judah will go, along with the household of Israel, and they will come together from the northern country*[k] *to the country that I gave by way of domain to your ancestors.*

a. *Made herself* in the sense of declaring herself—the declarative or linguistic factitive *piel*; see *IBHS* 24.2f. Duhm (*Jeremia*, 38) compares Luke 18:14.
b. The infinitive absolute is used as an imperative (cf. 2:2 and the translation note on it).
c. The two *waw*-consecutives continue the quasi-imperative.
d. Yahweh uses the form of the imperative with an additional suffformative, *šûbâ*, which might suggest emphasis or be honorific (Joüon 48d).
e. LXX "I will be Lord over you" takes the verb as an anticipatory *qatal* (see the introduction to 13:18–22, pp. 354–55).
f. Lit. "heart" or "mind"; cf. vv. 16, 17.
g. For this translation of *barît*, see the commentary on 11:1–17.
h. The English word "ark" for *'ărôn* derives from Vg *arca*, but that Latin word is not a technical term; it means a chest, as does *'ărôn*. It can also denote an offerings box in the temple or a coffin.
i. Lit. "they"; the verb's subject is impersonal, like that of the other verbs in vv. 16–17. The antecedent is not *the nations*, since dire determination is Israel's problem (e.g., 7:24; 9:14[13]); *no more* has the same implication (Allen, *Jeremiah*, 53).
j. MT has a section marker here.
k. LXX adds "and from all the countries."

Jeremiah continues to report what Yahweh has to say about Ephraim in order to get his message home to Judah as it overhears what Yahweh has said to him. Yahweh takes further the comparison between Turning Ephraim and False Judah. Not only was Judah just as bad as Ephraim and not only did Judah fail to learn the lesson from Ephraim's fate, but the fact that Judah had Ephraim's fate to profit from meant that Judah was actually more negligently false than Ephraim, and Ephraim was less guilty than Judah! So in his mercy, Yahweh commissions Jeremiah to go and urge the Ephraimites to return and promises to be merciful to them. Maybe Yahweh literally did send Jeremiah to preach to Ephraim,[115] but in the context, the point is to communicate to Judah itself by means of a kind of parable. The content of vv. 11–13 is a surprise, and the following verses offer more surprises.
Verse 12 picks up the language of turning back from v. 1, of maintaining for all time from v. 5, of things happening under every verdant tree from v. 6 and

115. So Holladay, *Commentary on Jeremiah*, 1:62–73. M. A. Sweeney (*Form and Intertextuality*, 94–108) sees Jer 2–6 as a whole ultimately going back to Jeremiah's preaching in Ephraim in Josiah's day.

2:20, of foreigners from 2:20, and of shepherds from 2:8. Yahweh speaks of Israel as feminine in v. 11, addresses it as masculine singular then as masculine plural in v. 12, and addresses it as feminine and then masculine plural in vv. 13–18. As is the case with v. 1, there is a rhythmic aspect to Yahweh's words in vv. 12–15 but little imagery or other poetic language and little parallelism; the section is rhythmic prose rather than poetry.

v. 11a   Jeremiah's resumptive introduction (one could treat
          vv. 6–18 as one section)
v. 11b   Yahweh's assessment of Ephraim
vv. 12–18 Yahweh's commission to Jeremiah regarding Ephraim
    v. 12a   Introduction
    v. 12b   A challenge to turn, with an encouragement
    v. 13   A challenge to acknowledge waywardness
    v. 14a   A challenge to return, with a reminder
    v. 14b   A promise about a return
    v. 15   A promise about shepherds
    v. 16   A promise about increase and about the pledge chest
    v. 17   A promise about Jerusalem and about the nations
    v. 18   A promise about Judah and Ephraim returning
              together

11 Yahweh's words intriguingly compare with the ancestor Judah's words in Gen 38:26. But Yahweh here speaks hyperbolically for the sake of making a contrast. *Turning Israel* has not truly *made herself faithful*, shown that she is in the right, or even counted herself in the right (*ṣādaq hiphil*; this key First Testament root is not very common in Jeremiah). But you could say that she was less guilty than *False Judah*, who had her example to learn from— or better, not to learn from.[116] Judah got the warning by example and still didn't turn.[117]

12 But the hyperbole opens up the possibility of painting the imaginative picture that follows. While I assume Yahweh did inspire Jeremiah to relate this conversation, I don't imagine he really meant Jeremiah to *go and call out these words northward* and issue this exhortation and invitation to Ephraim to *turn back* any more than he literally intends Jeremiah to do as he says in 25:15 or to give the message he specifies in 25:27 or 30, or in 46:14 or 50:2. He is giving Jeremiah a piece of rhetoric to use on Judah, as he is in those other passages. There is, in any case, no corporate Ephraim to address; there are only Ephraimites scattered where Assyria has transported them,

---

116. Rashi, in MG.
117. Jerome, *Jeremiah*, 22.

living as refugees elsewhere, living a discretely anonymous life in the old country (having escaped deportation), or living in Judah. Jeremiah cannot go and address Ephraim as he can go to Jerusalem and more or less address Judah in the temple courtyards or address the king and his cabinet in the palace. Making his face fall against them would be the opposite of lifting his face, making it shine—blessing, keeping, and making life work out well (Num 6:24–26). Only here and in Ps 145:17 is Yahweh described as *committed* (*ḥāsîd*), though there are many ascriptions of commitment (*ḥesed*) to him. Some irony attaches to his declaring that he has this human quality given that some people couldn't make that claim (see 2:2). *I don't hold onto things for all time* responds to the anxious question that Judah articulated in v. 5. "There is nothing that a man is more ready to keep than his wrath."[118] Fortunately Yahweh is not human-like in this respect.

13 You just have to *acknowledge your waywardness.* But acknowledgment is more demanding than it sounds, given that it means doing something about it (see 1:5; 2:8, 19, 23). The image of waywardness works with the image of turning back: they have gone astray and chosen the wrong path, and they need to change their path. In case the image of waywardness is too mild (poor them, they lost their way, they missed the path), Yahweh adds that they lost their way only because they *rebelled* against going his way. To put it in a more original and vivid fashion, *You . . . scattered your paths.* The reference to *every verdant tree* (see 2:20; 3:6) helps to interpret the image. Instead of making their way to the one Yahweh, they had lots of shrines, and all had their own god, as Jeremiah sees it with deliberate misunderstanding when he speaks of Judah this way (2:28). Scattering may also be an image for sexual promiscuity.[119] And these gods were *foreigners* (2:25), which in this context means alien religious resources. There is further irony in this term because these objects and forms of worship were native to the land, but they were foreign to what Israel was supposed to be. *And to my voice you have not listened,* Yahweh adds. Listening, like acknowledging, means doing something (thus *šāmaʿ* is often translated "obey").

14a *Turn back* restates the exhortation in v. 13 but resumes terms from v. 12, and the verb is now plural, like *you* in v. 12 and *you have not listened* in v. 13; Yahweh keeps switching between singular and plural. *Turning children* corresponds to *Turning Israel,* and Yahweh keeps utilizing the two meanings of *šûb.* It's surprising that Yahweh says he is *the one who was husband to* the Ephraimites, who are his *children.* The metaphors clash, but the oddity arises through his combining the reference to Deut 24:1 (which has the verb "be husband to") with references to his people as his "children" (Jer 2:9, 30;

118. Trapp, *Commentary,* 232.
119. Rashi, in MG.

3:19, 21, 22). On one hand, the reminder of Deut 24:1 makes for a more pro-found surprise, as is hinted by the fourth *Yahweh's affirmation* in these three verses that say what might be especially unbelievable. Yahweh is ignoring the implications of the Deuteronomic rule, showing he is not bound by his own laws[120] or that he presupposes Deut 24 to be his rule for human beings only, whereas "Yahweh is God, not 'man'" (Hos 11:8–9).[121] It doesn't resolve all the ambiguity about the infinitival *turning back* in v. 1, but it rules out one discouraging way of understanding its implications. On the other hand, Yahweh's calling the Ephraimites points to his authority over them, which suggests another significance of the way he speaks in terms of marriage. *Was husband* is the patriarchal term (as in Deut 24:1), which rarely appears in the First Testament. It is the verb *bāʿal* with its multiple resonances. It's not "the Master" (*baʿal*) who is their master; and Yahweh is indeed their master, not their buddy or daddy. The verb recurs once in Jeremiah, in 31:31–34, of which the present passage is a kind of anticipation and an anticipatory widening, as v. 17 also goes on to embrace the nations.[122]

14b Perhaps even more astonishing is the following promise to *get you, one from a town and two from a kin group, and enable you to come to Zion.* Something of this kind had happened after the fall of Samaria in 722 and again as an aspect of Josiah's reform program, providing an image for the promise to Ephraim. A hundred Ephraimites were transported to Assyria for every Ephraimite who made it to Judah. Yahweh promises that at least some will come back—not back to Ephraim, but back to Zion, where that Ephraimite remnant is, and where Ephraim should be as it gives up its deviant attach-ment to Dan and Bethel. If that remnant includes people who are still living discretely in the old Northern Kingdom, well and good. In the context, *one* and *two* need not imply only a small number; the emphasis lies rather on there being representatives from every town and every extended family or clan. If Jeremiah had profound unease about Judahite attachment to Zion, as if it guaranteed Yahweh's presence with them, evidently this unease did not mean he had turned his back on the importance of Zion.[123] Further, while Jeremiah has given no indication that Yahweh has moved away from (rhetor-ically) addressing Ephraimites, it was always a way of indirectly addressing Judah, and after 597 and 587, the talk of children and of returning individuals

120. Calvin, *Jeremiah*, 1:157; Calvin notes there were good reasons the law applying to humanity need not apply to God.

121. W. Brueggemann, *Jeremiah 1–25*, International Theological Commentary (Grand Rapids: Eerdmans, 1988), 41.

122. B. Gosse, "L'ouverture de la nouvelle alliance aux nations en Jérémie iii 14–18," *VT* 39 (1989): 385–92.

123. W. J. Wessels, "Zion, Beautiful City of God—Zion Theology in the Book of Jere-miah," *Verbum et Ecclesia* 27 (2006): 743–44.

from towns and families would surely make survivors in Judah as well as refugees and exiles think about their own people returning to Zion; it could contribute to their recovering from their own trauma.[124]

15 Likewise, the talk of *shepherds* would ring bells for Judahites, as it counters 2:8.[125] Now Judah and Ephraim will have shepherds (leaders in general) *in accordance with my thinking*, people who think Yahweh's way and shepherd in the way he has in mind, unlike Ephraim's past shepherds or Judah's present shepherds. *They will shepherd you with acknowledgment* (see v. 13) *and understanding* (which is also a moral and religious as well as an intellectual capacity). The three main connotations of shepherding are feeding, protecting, and leading; the third is the one in focus here.[126]

16 *Become many* and *become fruitful* recur (in the opposite order) as God's commissions and promises in Genesis (1:22, 28; 8:17; 9:1, 7; 17:20; 28:3; 35:11). So Yahweh is now presupposing that for Ephraim (and by implication for Judah), his longstanding promise will find fulfillment—if they do turn. *Say, "Yahweh's pledge chest"* compares with "say, 'Yahweh lives,'" an expression people use in taking an oath (4:2; 5:2), or "say, 'Yahweh's palace'" (7:4), which could belong in the same context (Matt 23:16–22). Yahweh's pledge chest (more traditionally, "the Ark of the Covenant") was a symbol of the relationship between Yahweh and Israel. Inside it were the rocks inscribed with the basic terms of the pledge. In the absence of images of Yahweh, it could also symbolize Yahweh's presence. It could be thought of as the base or footstool of the invisible Yahweh's throne as he sat enthroned above it (cf. 1 Sam 4:4; 2 Sam 6:2; 2 Kgs 19:15; Ps 80:1[2]). Even Ephraimites might miss it (Jeroboam oddly did not seek to replace it in Bethel or Dan). But now *it will not come up into their thinking, they will not be mindful of it, they will not attend to it, and it will not be made again.* People might naturally think about it and think about making a new one, like twenty-first-century people making plans to build the Third Temple. But the Ephraimites (and the Judahites) will not think about it anymore. Along with 2 Chr 35:3 in connection with Josiah's reformation, this verse is the last reference to the pledge chest in the First Testament. Perhaps it had already disappeared,[127] or perhaps it

124. See K. M. O'Connor, "A Family Comes Undone (Jeremiah 2:1–4:2)," *RevExp* 105 (2008): 208; cf. K. M. O'Connor, "Reclaiming Jeremiah's Violence," in *The Aesthetics of Violence in the Prophets*, ed. J. M. O'Brien and C. Franke, LHBOTS 517 (London: T&T Clark, 2010), 37–49; Mills, *Jeremiah*, 60–69.

125. Allen, *Jeremiah*, 57.

126. B. A. Foreman, *Animal Metaphors and the People of Israel in the Book of Jeremiah*, FRLANT 238 (Göttingen: Vandenhoeck & Ruprecht, 2011), 93–102.

127. M. Haran, "The Disappearance of the Ark," *Israel Exploration Journal* 13 (1963): 46–58; *Temples and Temple Service in Ancient Israel* (repr., Winona Lake, IN: Eisenbrauns,

was still in the temple in 604 and it then disappeared or was destroyed in 587 and never seen again. This reference might reflect a post-587 origin of this verse and of more of vv. 11–18. The phrase *in those days* (cf. vv. 17, 18) shares in this ambiguity, though there is nothing inherently "eschatological" about such expressions.[128] They can simply refer back to a time just mentioned or denote a time of awesome fulfillment that will certainly come (without any implication that it is far off or refers to a new world order); vv. 14–16 suggest they have the latter significance here.

17 How will it be possible not to miss the chest? It will be on the basis of seeing *Jerusalem* and not just the chest as *Yahweh's throne*, the place to which *all the nations will gather* in order to acknowledge Yahweh enthroned there (cf. Isa 2:2–4; Mic 4:1–3; Rev 21:22–25).[129] *En passant*, Jeremiah thus notes that Israel's turning back serves God's mission in relation to the world as a whole.[130] "In this expectation a revolution in the history of the faith comes about."[131] For people who know Yahweh, *Yahweh's name* suggests the reality of Yahweh in the fullness of what the name means and refers to, as the name Jeremiah suggests all that the name denotes for people who know him. If Yahweh's name is there, Yahweh is there (cf. 7:12). And people like the Ephraimites will acknowledge Yahweh enthroned in Jerusalem not just nominally but really, because they will give up the *determination of their dire thinking*. Jeremiah introduces yet another distinctive expression (e.g., 7:24; 11:8). Etymologically, *determination* (*šərirût*) should not have negative connotations, but in the First Testament its implications are always negative; it suggests stubbornness.

18 There has been some ambiguity about the addressees in this section, and about the chronological context of vv. 14–17. Rhetorically, the addressees are the Ephraimites in the time of Josiah or Jehoiakim, but indirectly Jeremiah speaks to the Judahites, and the verses hint at a context after 587. Verse 18 sidesteps or resolves one aspect of the ambiguity by talking directly about both *the household of Judah* and *the household of Israel* in the third person. It more directly implies that later chronological context in presupposing that both peoples need to be brought back from *the northern country*, which for Ephraim means especially Assyria, where they already are in 604, but for Judah will mean Babylon after 597 and 587. The talk of the two households undermines any gloomy interpretation of *one* or *two* in v. 14, as does the word

---

1985), 276–88; see further J. A. Soggin, "The Ark of the Covenant," in Bogaert, *Livre de Jérémie*, 215–21.

128. E.g., Volz, *Jeremia*, 48.

129. Allen, *Jeremiah*, 58.

130. J. Hwang, "The *Missio Dei* as an Integrative Motif in the Book of Jeremiah," *BBR* 23 (2013): 489–90.

131. W. H. Schmidt, *Jeremia*, 1:112.

together (*yaḥdāw*), which suggests both abundance and togetherness; Ezek 37:15–28 develops the togetherness motif. In speaking of the country that he *gave by way of domain* (*nāḥal hiphil*) *to your ancestors*, Yahweh again looks back, though not to promises in Genesis but to later promises in the Torah (e.g., Deut 12:10; 19:3; 32:8).

5. *The Explicit Urging (3:19–25)*

¹⁹*I for my part said*
   how I would put you among the children.
*I would give*ᵃ *you a desirable country,*
   the most beautiful domain of the nations,
   *the beautiful domain of the armies of the nations.*ᵇ
*I said: You*ᶜ *will call me "Father,"*
   *and not turn from going after me.*ᵈ
²⁰*Actually, a woman being false because of her partner—*
   *so*ᵉ *you have been false with me,*
   household of Israel (Yahweh's affirmation).

²¹*A voice on the bare heights is making itself heard,*
   a crying that pleads for grace by the Israelites.
Because they have made their path wayward,
   they have put Yahweh their God out of mind.
²²*Turn back, turning children,*
   so I may heal your turnings.

Here we are, we have come to you,
   *because you, Yahweh, are our God.*ᶠ
²³*Actually, [what comes] from the hills belongs to deception,*
   *[from] the mountains—[to] noise.*ᵍ
Indeed, in Yahweh our God
   is Israel's deliverance.
²⁴*But the Shame—it consumed*
   the earnings of our ancestors from our youth,
Their flock and their herd,
   their sons and their daughters.
²⁵*We must lie down*ʰ *in our shame so that our disgrace may cover us,*ⁱ
   because by Yahweh our God we have done wrong,
We and our ancestors,
   from our youth and until this day.
We have not listened
   *to the voice of Yahweh our God.*ʲ

a. The simple *waw* plus *yiqtol* suggests that this verb is coordinate with the verb in v. 19a.

b. MT combines two versions of this colon: *ṣib'ôt* has the consonants of the word for armies and the vowels of the word for beauties. The first version corresponds to the *qere*: lit. "the domain of the beauty of beauties," which incorporates a regular way of expressing a superlative. But the *ketiv* implies *ṣābā'ôt* ("armies"; cf. LXX, Vg).

c. In both cola, the *ketiv*, LXX, Syr have plural; the *qere*, Vg, Tg have singular.

d. The line might state what Yahweh requires Israel to do or what he expects Israel will actually do. LXX and Vg keep the ambiguity, but Tg resolves it, making clear that these are Yahweh's requirements. But v. 7 unambiguously referred to assumptions by Yahweh that were disappointed, and v. 20 likely reiterates this.

e. One would have expected an "as" to lead into this "so," but Hebrew comparisons sometimes lack it (GKC 161b).

f. In the context, this understanding of the noun clause is more likely than LXX and Vg's "You are Yahweh our God."

g. The two prepositions carry over from the parallel colon. LXX, Vg, Syr imply *hămôn* ("the noise of the mountains") for MT *hāmôn*—for which *CTAT* 2:485 suggests "brouhaha."

h. *Niškəbâ* is cohortative.

i. LXX has past tenses for this colon.

j. MT has a section marker here.

The theme of v. 18, with its reference to the gift of the land, continues in v. 19; the references to children and father also link back to vv. 4 and 14. But the section goes on to advance the motifs of turning and falsehood, moving away from promises back to confrontation and issuing a more direct challenge to turn back. Initially, it uses the feminine singular instead of the masculine plural. It becomes more rhythmic, and it manifests parallelism and imagery, indicating a switch to poetry that lasts through the section.

> vv. 19–20   Yahweh's recollection, hope, and disappointment (three bicola and a tricolon signaling the pause point)
>
> vv. 21–22a   Israel's prayer for grace and Yahweh's responsive exhortation to turn (three bicola)
>
> vv. 22b–25   The prayer Yahweh wishes Israel would actually pray (eight bicola, two linked by enjambment)

19a–b Yahweh resumes speaking to his bride in the feminine singular, combining that move with talk of *how I would put you among the children*; the mixed metaphor is taken up from v. 14 and fits with the implication that Yahweh continues to address Ephraim rhetorically. Here, Deut 32:8–9 suggests an aspect of the background thinking:

> When the One On High gave domains to nations,
>   when he divided the children of humanity,
> He set the boundaries of peoples
>   in relation to the number of the children of Israel.

Deut 32 goes on to describe what a wonderful allocation of land he gave Israel, though they were then unfaithful and incensed him with foreigners. Jeremiah 2–3 has other general and particular links with Deut 32 on the way to 3:18 (see specifically 2:5, 25, 27). So Yahweh is "a loving father, yearning to give the best to his daughter"[132] and treating her the way a father treats his sons by giving her an inheritance. In a neat heightening parallelism, he describes Canaan not only as *a desirable country* (*ḥemdâ*, from the verb *ḥā-mad*; see Exod 20:17) but as an extraordinarily *beautiful domain* among the domains of *the nations*.

19c–20 Yahweh goes on with a reference back to v. 7 in his recollection of what *I said* in connection with the question whether she would turn back, though here he speaks of whether she will *turn from going after me* (taken up from Jer 2). In the recollection of how *I said: You will call me "Father,"* the parallel lies with v. 4. But, *actually*, how wrong Yahweh was again. "Yahweh seems shaken by the former infidelities."[133] Jeremiah picks up the word *partner* from v. 1, though with irony, and once more takes up the reference to being *false* from v. 14. The tricolon and the reminder that these words are *Yahweh's affirmation* prepare us for a pause and a jump. The *household of Israel* is Ephraim, as in v. 18.

21–22a Suddenly *a voice . . . is making itself heard*. It is *on the bare heights*, which reappear from v. 2, where Israel sits looking for lovers; it is presumably not addressing Yahweh. The plea people utter as they pour out their tears is a supplicatory cry, one that *pleads for grace* (*taḥănûnîm*, from the word for grace, *ḥēn*). They need to pray because *they have made their path wayward*, as Jer 2 has said; that is, in the parallel, *they have put Yahweh their God out of mind*. Perhaps they are praying for rain, in the context of drought (cf. v. 3). The second line implies that the crying and praying do not mean they have turned back to Yahweh, even if they think they have (as vv. 4–5 may imply). Does the verse contain a note of mockery?[134] Perhaps this is a crying that makes matters worse, that actually expresses waywardness as well as being necessitated by it. There needs to be a proper turning back (compare the words in v. 14): to Yahweh. Then Yahweh may *heal*. He is now the prodigal father of Luke 15:11–32.[135] When Jeremiah speaks of healing, it normally relates to the wounds that have issued from the people's wrongdoing (30:17; 33:6), so Yahweh will here be referring to trouble that has come as a result of their turning, the trouble they were lamenting in v. 21. If they do turn from their waywardness, Yahweh will do something about their trouble. The colloca-

132. Shields, *Circumscribing the Prostitute*, 116.
133. Berrigan, *Jeremiah*, 18.
134. H. L. Ellison, "The Prophecy of Jeremiah," *EvQ* 32 (1960): 215.
135. Jerome, *Jeremiah*, 25.

tion of healing with shame (vv. 24–25) will recur in 6:14–15; 8:11–12. Healing suggests a deep restoration of the deeply and publicly wounded person.[136]

22b–23 There follows a prayer that would constitute turning if Israel prayed it. (Perhaps Jeremiah prays it on their behalf.[137]) When we respond to God's invitation "and say, *We will be yours*, let us remember that we submitted ourselves to God" and remember that "we belong to no other."[138] If only they would pray along these lines: *We have come to you, because you, Yahweh, are our God.* If only they would recognize the deception of what they trust in ("The hills are a swindle"[139]), which their deception (v. 10) mirrors (*They went after something empty and became empty*, 2:5). Yes, they were praying *to deception*. If only they would recognize that the worship they offer at the shrines on the *hills* and the *mountains* (see 2:20; 3:6) was just noise, as it was addressed *to noise*. If only they would recognize that *in Yahweh our God is Israel's deliverance* (see 2:27–28). The proposed prayer is part of a "liturgy of repentance";[140] it is also an appeal to the imagination.

24 They need to recognize that the Master was actually *the Shame*, "the Shamefulness," or "the Shaming." In names such as Ishbosheth, the name of the Master, *ba'al*, has been replaced by the word for shame. Here, Jeremiah replaces *habba'al* ("the Master") with *habbōšet* (*the Shame*). The substitution suggests what a disgrace it was, what a deeply offensive and degrading thing, that Israel worshiped the Master. So Jeremiah gives them a prayer to pray that owns the fact. They acknowledge that not only have they gained nothing from serving the Master—they have lost everything. They have given him *their flock and their herd, their sons and their daughters.* It was what Israelites were expected to do in relation to Yahweh, too, but not in the same devastating sense, and not in order simply to lose out. The way they lost out may have involved politics and economics as well as religion and nature, insofar as the state identified with the Shame/the Master and took advantage of people's commitment to it.[141]

25 Ideally, people need to go in for serious turning because it's right and not because of what they get out of it (see the story of Achan in Josh 7). The turning Jeremiah would like to see is not undertaken because people

136. Fretheim, *Jeremiah*, 77.
137. A. F. Wilke finds the beginning of prayer in the Prophets in Jer 1–10, in passages such as this one: see *Die Gebete der Propheten: Anrufungen Gottes im "Corpus propheticum" der Hebräischen Bibel,* BZAW 451 (Berlin: de Gruyter, 2014), 12–16.
138. Origen, *Jeremiah*, 43.
139. Bright's translation (*Jeremiah*, 20).
140. Weiser, *Jeremia*, 1:38. Isaac Abravanel (*Commentary on the Latter Prophets*, as paraphased by A. J. Rosenberg, *Jeremiah*, 2 vols. [New York: Judaica, 1985], 1:33) pictures Jeremiah portraying Israel praying the prayer and God replying.
141. See D. Buchner, "*Boshet* in Jeremiah 3:24," *JTS* 59 (2008): 478–99. Buchner sees Boshet as a goddess, not as the Master.

think they will thereby escape the consequences of their waywardness. He pictures them accepting their *shame* and *disgrace* (*kəlimmâ*; to the recurring word *shame*, Jeremiah adds this synonym whose related verb he used in v. 2). Perhaps the implication is that they would *lie down* in sack like Ahab (1 Kgs 21:27; cf. Isa 58:5) or lie down as in bed with disgrace as their blanket (or does Jeremiah have in mind lying down and going to sleep as an escape, like Jonah?).[142] They need to acknowledge that they *have done wrong* by *Yahweh* through the nation's life, even from the time of *our ancestors* and thus *from our youth*—as 2:5–8 said (cf. 3:24). "The sins of the individual and the sins of the generation that is addressed" are part of a long history of defiance of Yahweh, "part of Old Testament 'church'-history as a whole."[143] No, *we have not listened to the voice of Yahweh our God* in the sense noted in connection with v. 13. So Jeremiah brings to an end the litany he wants to put on their lips. But it's "a litany that hasn't been used."[144]

6. *Make It Genuine (4:1–4)*

[1]*If you turn back, Israel (Yahweh's affirmation),*
  [if] to me you turn back,[a]
If you remove your detestable things[b] *from before me,*[c]
  and don't quiver,[d]
[2]*And swear "Yahweh is alive,"*[e] *with truthfulness—*
  with authority exercised with faithfulness—[f]
Then nations will pray for blessing by him,
  and by him give praise.[g]

[3]*Because Yahweh has said this to the individual in Judah and to Jerusalem:*

Till the tillage for yourselves,
  but don't sow into the thorns.
[4]*Circumcise yourselves in relation to Yahweh,*[h]
  remove the foreskins from your mind (individual in Judah and people
    who live in Jerusalem),
So that my fury does not go out like fire,
  and burn—and no one is going to put it out—
  in the face of the dire nature of your practices.[i]

142. Qimchi, in MG.
143. R. Mosis, "Umkehr und Vergebung: Eine Auslegung von Jer 3,21–4,2," *Trierer Theologische Zeitschrift* 98 (1989): 55.
144. C. J. H. Wright, *The Message of Jeremiah*, The Bible Speaks Today (Nottingham: InterVarsity, 2014), 85.

a. The force of the "if" in the first colon carries over into the second. Vg has "[Then] to me you are to turn back" (cf. LXX); but the fronted position of "to me" would then imply that there was some question of turning back to someone else, which is surely not so, notwithstanding 3:21.

b. LXX nicely adds "from his mouth" (the whole LXX passage is third person).

c. For *mippānay*, the Cairo Codex of the Prophets has *mippāneykā* ("from before your face").

d. Again, Vg understands "then you will not quiver/wander" and takes v. 2 as continuing this promise.

e. *HALOT* takes *ḥy yhwh* to mean "[by] the life of Yahweh," but this understanding does not work with phrases such as *ḥay ʾānî* ("[as] I am alive"; cf. the long list in *DCH*). More likely, *ḥay* is always an adjective in such expressions (cf. LXX, Vg, Tg).

f. Lit. "with authority and with faithfulness"; these two are thus held together as a hendiadys (see the commentary).

g. MT has a section marker here, but the exhortation continues in vv. 3–4; see the introduction to 3:1–4:4 (p. 141).

h. The imperative makes it less likely that Yahweh is saying "be circumcised by Yahweh" (R. Althann, "*mwl*, 'Circumcise' with the *Lamedh* of Agency," *Bib* 62 [1981]: 239–40).

i. The noun *rōaʿ* (rather than the adjective *raʿ*) followed by *maʿalalêkem* forms a recurrent construct phrase in Jeremiah (e.g., 21:12; 23:2, 22), suggesting "your active/practical direness."

Judah "didn't turn back to me with her entire heart but with deception" (3:10). The section on turning in 3:1–4:4 comes to a conclusion with an exhortation about what is needed to put that situation right. As would happen in a worship liturgy when the community articulated its prayer, there here follows Yahweh's response to the (proposed) confession in 3:22b–25. The response is equivocal.[145] Yahweh answers the people's (proposed) self-abasement with a challenge to turn in truth.[146] It comprises two short messages that express themselves in different ways but reinforce each other.

vv. 1–2   An implicit exhortation by way of conditional clauses, but leading into a promise (four bicola, all linked by enjambment)

vv. 3–4   An introduction, then an explicit exhortation and a warning (two bicola and a tricolon of warning closing off the section and the unit)

1 Initially, the exhortation takes a conditional form, and it's possible to slide over it. The second line safeguards against that possibility by spelling out negatively what turning back looks like. *Detestable things* (*šiqqûṣîm*) is another term for what 2:7 called things that are offensive (*tôʿēbâ*). They are

145. Rudolph, *Jeremia*, 31.
146. Duhm, *Jeremia*, 45.

the images of wood and rock that people use in worship, which Jer 2 has attacked and which pollute Yahweh's country. They are *before me*: which likely implies they are present in the temple, but whether they are there or elsewhere in some other shrines or in people's homes, they sit there insulting Yahweh, and he cannot ignore them (cf. Exod 20:3, though the expression is not quite the same). The parallel colon, with its condition that you *don't quiver* (*nûd*), underlines the point and reflects the realities of what happened in Jeremiah's day. Judah had removed its detestable things in the course of Josiah's reformation (2 Kgs 23:13, 24) but then surreptitiously (or not) put them back, as if it thought he wasn't looking. Quivering might suggest being aimless and willful like the camel in 2:23 or like Cain as he is condemned to settle in the land called Nôd (Gen 4:14, 16). It's also Jeremiah's word for shaking in grief or sadness or horror (15:5; 16:5; 18:16; 22:10; 31:18; 48:17). So Yahweh is saying, get rid of those things, and don't regret it, and don't look at them wistfully, and don't think about bringing them back. Only Ezekiel complains about *detestable things* more often than Jeremiah, which implies that Judah did not meet this challenge.

2a Put positively, the condition is that Israel starts operating with sincerity in the way it refers to Yahweh. [*As*] *Yahweh is alive* is a declaration you might make to add credibility to a statement or an undertaking (e.g., 5:1–2; 38:16). It is an alternative to "as the Master is alive" (see 12:16). The temptation is to take Yahweh's name thus but to attach your statement to something empty (Exod 20:7). You might do so in worship or in giving evidence or in making a promise to someone. Yahweh says to do it *with truthfulness* (*'ĕmet*), a characteristic of Yahweh himself (10:10; 42:5) and thus a characteristic of Yahweh's involvement with Israel (2:2). And do it *with authority* (*mišpāṭ*) *exercised with faithfulness* (*ṣədāqâ*); Jeremiah thus introduces a recurrent First Testament word pair (cf. 22:3; 23:5; 33:15).[147] The conventional translation, "justice and righteousness," is misleading. Authority suggests legitimate power and the capacity to make decisions; faithfulness suggests doing so in the right way—in a way that recognizes a responsibility to do the right thing by the people with whom one lives in community. In the account of Josiah's reformation in 2 Kgs 22–23, there is no reference to action on behalf of truthfulness or the faithful exercise of authority in the life of the community, and Jeremiah has a nose for such falsehood or "ideology,"[148] though he does later commend Josiah in these terms (22:15).

2b At last, we reach what the three-line *if*-clause leads into, and it is a surprise, though it links neatly with 3:16–17. The move from *if*-clauses to *then*-clauses also brings a move from second person to third person. Israel's action will have implications for other people; they stand at the center of the line:

147. Cf. J. M. Bracke, "Justice in the Book of Jeremiah," *WW* 22 (2002): 387–95.
148. Pixley, *Jeremiah*, 19.

they will pray for blessing
>by him
>>nations
>>and by him
>they will give praise

Perhaps there is also an implication that the nations will flock to Jerusalem (as 3:17 envisaged) to pray thus because Yahweh causes Israel to become many and fruitful. There is such a link in Genesis; the expression *pray for blessing by* (*bārak* [hithpael] *bə*) comes otherwise only in Gen 22:18; 26:4 with reference to Abraham's people, in Ps 72:17 with reference to the king, and in Isa 65:16 with reference to Yahweh. *By him* (or "by his name") *give praise* (*hālal* [hithpael] *bə*)—on account of him and on account of his name (Isa 41:16; 45:25; Pss 34:2[3]; 105:3)—contrasts with giving praise by or on account of godlets (Ps 97:7), as Ephraim and Judah have been doing. By implication, at present, "God's mission to the nations is being hindered because of Israel's continuing spiritual and ethical failure."[149]

3 The final lines of 3:1–4:4 begin by dramatically re-expressing the point of the entire section in two new ways. These lines could originally have stood on their own, and Jeremiah might or might not have included them at this point in the 604 scroll. But the heading *because Yahweh has said this to the individual in Judah and to Jerusalem* now attaches them firmly to the "turning and turning back" material so that they offer two new images of what genuine turning back looks like—new in Jeremiah, though not novel in the First Testament. Both relate to the negatively constructed description of turning in v. 1.

First, there is a farming image. *Tillage* is new land or fallow land that one needs to plow or *till*. The phrase exactly repeats one in Hos 10:12; they are the only occurrences of the verb in the First Testament. While the phrase might be an aphorism, "the influence of Hosea (never far away from 3:12–25)" may be present here.[150] The parallel colon makes the complementary point that the sensible farmer will *sow* only after removing *the thorns*, which will otherwise choke the growing crop. Judah and Jerusalem need to do some removing. "Repentance in the biblical sense is not just the repairing of some damage but a new beginning from the ground up."[151]

4 *Circumcise yourselves for Yahweh* makes the same point in a different way. As appendages, *foreskins* are only a nuisance. They get in the way; they encourage infection. Minds also have foreskins. So remove them, too—

---

149. C. J. H. Wright, "'Prophet to the Nations': Missional Reflections on the Book of Jeremiah," in *A God of Faithfulness: Essays in Honour of* J. Gordon McConville *on His 60th Birthday*, ed. J. A. Grant et al., LHBOTS 538 (London: T&T Clark, 2011), 123–24.

150. R. P. Carroll, *Jeremiah*, OTL, 157.

151. Weiser, *Jeremia*, 1:41.

though be aware that circumcision "is a cutting that makes for blood and pain."[152] The negative male image complements the negative female one of the whore.[153] It is at least as radical in its implications. "To depict Israel as an uncircumcised male" is to say that "Israel no longer belongs to the covenant community simply on the basis of an external cutting."[154] Whereas the first image recalls Hosea, the second image recalls Deut 30:6 (where Yahweh acts) and 10:16 (where it is people's responsibility, as here).[155] The image reappears in Rom 2:29,[156] and Jesus reaffirms the reality to which it refers when he says that anyone who wants to "go after me" (the key image in Jer 2–3) has to prepare for crucifixion (Mark 8:34).[157]

Carrying out the negative action symbolized by the two images is vital; otherwise terrible consequences will follow. In the closing tricolon, the first two cola both portray divine wrath as the agent of destruction, which contrasts with or complements the idea that Yahweh himself is simply the agent (as is the case especially in Ezekiel) or that wrongdoing issues in trouble by a kind of natural process (as 2:14–19; 3:3 suggested).[158] While these cola are thus parallel, the second takes the first for granted and goes beyond it in a frightening way:

> So that there does not go out   like fire   my fury
> and burn   and no one is going to put it out.

The unexpected third colon (*in the face of the dire nature of your practices*) then restates one of the key motifs in this section (3:2, 5, 17) and the previous one (2:13, 19, 33) and brings the section to a close. Chillingly, the answer to the question in 3:5 (*Does he hold onto things for all time?*) can be yes (cf. Mark 9:42–48). Jeremiah's readers might be wise to pray with Calvin:

> Grant, Almighty God, that since thou hast been pleased that the prophetic writings should be preserved for our use, that they may continually excite us to repentance, and that since thou stiffest up daily those who urge us by their exhortations, and draw us, as it were by force, to repent,—O grant, that . . . we may render ourselves teachable.[159]

---

152. Fretheim, *Jeremiah*, 88.
153. R. P. Carroll, *Jeremiah*, OTL, 158.
154. Fretheim, *Jeremiah*, 88.
155. Shields, *Circumscribing the Prostitute*, 145.
156. Calvin, *Jeremiah*, 1:214–15.
157. P. D. Miller, "Jeremiah," in his reflection on 2:1–4:4.
158. See S. Joo, "'Dynamistic Thought' in Context: The Theology of Divine Wrath in the Books of Ezekiel and Jeremiah," *Korean Journal of Christian Studies* 84 (2012): 49–67.
159. Calvin, *Jeremiah*, 1:494.

C. MOSTLY WARNING: THE WHOLE COUNTRY DESOLATE (4:5-31)

If Judah does not take seriously Yahweh's confrontation (2:1-37) and heed Jeremiah's exhortations (3:1-4:4), Yahweh's fury will blaze out (4:4). What will happen then? Jeremiah 4:5-31 begins to provide the answer, spelling out the danger in a sequence of vivid warnings.[160] In the first half of the section (vv. 5-18), the portrayal mostly comprises literal (though imaginary) descriptions of what invasion will be like, though it also incorporates one or two images (the lion, the wind). In the second half (vv. 19-31), this balance is the opposite: mostly a figurative presentation, though also incorporating one or two elements of literal portrayal.

While warnings of trouble were a motif in 2:1-4:4, there they were less prominent than critique of Judah's unfaithfulness and exhortation to turn back. Here, the balance is the reverse. There is still critique (v. 22) and still indication that turning is possible (v. 14). To describe wrath does not mean it is inevitable. The section incorporates reasons why Yahweh must act, but its emphasis lies on warning about the action itself. The balance of warning with critique and exhortation will reverse again in 5:1-31.

Like 2:1-4:4, the section brings together messages that were separate in origin but have been assembled into sequences. They thus become mutually reinforcing and illuminating, though without taking the form of a systematic, structured argument. One could again think of the section going back to Jeremiah's dictating, in 604, an anthology of messages that he had delivered over the preceding two decades, which was then enlarged by him, by Baruch, or by later curators. But the individual messages make no specific reference to contexts or people, and they might have their origin any time in the period referred to in 1:1-3. "The undefined character of the threat invites the hearer to focus less on historical and political identities and facts than on the real danger and the reasons for it. The oracles of Jeremiah are more interested in the specifics of the reasons than the specifics of the danger."[161] If Jeremiah knew during those earlier decades that the invader from the north would be Babylon, he apparently kept quiet about it, and he does not even refer to it in his 604 version of the messages. "The fundamental cause of the coming calamity is the Holy One's intention not to let such evil go unpunished."[162] Babylon will be merely his means of acting.[163]

---

160. Bright, *Jeremiah*, 33.

161. P. D. Miller, "Jeremiah," on 4:11-18.

162. Pixley, *Jeremiah*, 20.

163. K. Finsterbusch suggests a similar perspective on the basis of a pre-587 and post-587 reading ("Violence against Judah and Jerusalem: The Rhetoric of Destruction within

1. *It's War*[164] *(4:5–18)*

[5]*Announce in Judah,*
    in Jerusalem make it heard.[a]
Say, "Blast[b] *a horn in the country,*
    call out, do it fully."[c]
Say, "Gather together,
    we must come to the fortified towns!
[6]*Lift up a flag,*[d] *to Zion,*
    make safe,[e] *don't stand around."*
Because I am making dire trouble come from the north,
    a great shattering.
[7]*A lion has gone up from its thicket,*
    a devastator of nations—he has made his move.[f]
He has gone out from his place
    to make your country into a desolation.
Your towns will fall into ruins,
    so that there is no one living there.
[8]*Because of this put on sack,*
    lament and wail,
Because it has not turned back—
    Yahweh's angry blazing—from us.[g]

[9]*And on that day (Yahweh's affirmation):*

The king's mind and the officials' mind will give up the ghost,
    the priests will be desolate, the prophets—they will be bewildered.[h]

[10]*I said,*[i] *"Ah, Lord Yahweh, therefore you have deluded, deluded*[j] *this people and Jerusalem, saying, 'It will be well with you,' and the sword has reached*[k] *right to the throat!'"*[l]

[11]*At that time, it will be said of this people and of Jerusalem:*

A scorching wind[m] *on the bare heights in the wilderness,*
    the path of my dear people![n]
Not to winnow,
    not to sift![o]

Jeremiah 1–6," in *Encountering Violence in the Bible*, ed. M. Zehnder and H. Hagelia, Bible in the Modern World 55 [Sheffield: Sheffield Phoenix, 2013], 79–93).
    164. "Es gibt Krieg!" (Rudolph, *Jeremia*, 32).

¹²*A wind too full for these^p—it comes for me;*
  now I too will speak out authoritative decisions to them.

¹³*There, like clouds he goes up,*
  like a tornado his chariots.
His horses are lighter than eagles,
  alas for us, because we are destroyed!

¹⁴*Wash your mind of dire behavior, Jerusalem,*
  in order that you may find deliverance.
How long will it lodge within you,^q
  your baneful^r plans?
¹⁵*Because a voice is announcing^s from Dan,*
  it is making something baneful^t heard from the highland of Ephraim.
¹⁶*"Make the nations mindful, 'There,'*
  make it heard, 'Against Jerusalem!'"
Watchers^u are coming from a country far away,
  they are giving^v their voice against the towns of Judah!
¹⁷*Like people keeping guard of the open country, they have come against*
    her all around,
  because she has rebelled against me (Yahweh's affirmation).
¹⁸*Your path and your practices—*
  they have done^w these things for you.
This is your direness, because it's something bitter,^x
  because it has reached right to your inner being.^y

a. The a-b-b'-a' order of the line, with the verbs enclosing the noun phrases, makes for a strong beginning.

b. The *ketiv* prefixes the verb with *wə* (cf. Vg; haplography in the *qere* or dittography in the *ketiv*). The prospective announcers through v. 5 are then lookouts addressing Judah and Jerusalem rather than supernatural aides told to commission the lookouts.

c. The use of *mālē' piel* is unique; the nearest parallel is the *hithpael* meaning "mass together" (cf. the noun *məlō'*; Rashi, in MG). Following *qārā'* asyndetically, it looks like an auxiliary verb, though such verbs usually precede the main verb (GKC 120h; Joüon 177g).

d. LXX has "flee"; see the translation note on v. 21.

e. Whereas LXX, Vg imply an intransitive *qal* meaning "take refuge, be safe," *hā'îzû* is *hiphil* (see BDB), suggesting "get people to safety"; *make safe* can be understood either way.

f. Like the verbs in vv. 5a and 9b, the verbs enclose this broadly a-b-b'-a' line.

g. LXX has "from you." MT has a unit marker here.

h. The verbs again enclose the a-b-b'-a' cola in v. 9b, hold the parallel cola tightly together, and add to the force of the 4-4 line in bringing vv. 5–9 to a close. MT^A has a section marker here.

i. The Alexandrian MS of LXX has "they said," which enables v. 10 to read as the response of the leadership to whom v. 9 referred.

j. The infinitive precedes the finite verb, underlining the factuality of the action. Tg re-works the text so that it is the false prophets who have deluded, Syr so that it is Jeremiah who has done so.

k. DG 84 sees the verb with simple *waw* as referring to the same time as the previous verb but expressing contrast, though it does not really have this relationship with *hiššē'tā*; perhaps it continues the infinitive *lē'mōr* with overlapping implications.

l. LXX, Vg have "the life"; see *HALOT* for this concrete meaning of *nepeš*.

m. Perhaps lit. "a wind of scorching" (Rudolph, *Jeremia*, 34).

n. *Bat-'ammî* is a defining genitive like "city of Jerusalem"; but "daughter of my people" gives the wrong impression.

o. *Bārar* means "purify," but it gains its nuance here from the fact that *bar* denotes grain (cf. 23:28).

p. The paronomasia *mālē' mē'ēlleh* generates some ambiguity. Vg has "a spirit full from these"—meaning from the bare heights? Vg thus takes *rûaḥ* to denote wind in v. 11, spirit in v. 12. Tg, having understood v. 10 to refer to false prophets, takes the wind to refer to the (false) spirit of prophecy. LXX has spirit both times. LXX and Vg thus imply that the "I" in vv. 11–12 is Jeremiah, as in v. 10. While it is difficult to envisage Jeremiah as the one who dis-penses "authoritative decisions," the verses do illustrate how it can be difficult to distinguish the "I" of Yahweh and the "I" of Jeremiah.

q. LXX, Vg, Tg thus take *tālîn* as third-person feminine singular *qal* (even though the subject is plural) rather than second-person singular masculine *hiphil*, meaning "you allow to lodge" (despite the feminine subject).

r. LXX, Aq, Vg take *'āwen* to denote trouble experienced, Sym to denote wickedness.

s. LXX, Vg have "a voice of one announcing."

t. Vg assumes that *'āwen* refers to idolatry.

u. *Nāṣar* is used with the connotation of *ṣûr* ("besiege") or *ṣārar* ("attack").

v. The finite verb continues the participial construction.

w. For *'āśô*, infinitive absolute, the Cairo Codex of the Prophets has the expected *qatal*, *'āśû*.

x. Rebelling (*mārâ*, v. 17) appropriately issues in bitterness (*mār*) (Allen, *Jeremiah*, 66); the masculine gender of *mār* suggests that the word is being treated as a noun rather than as an adjective qualifying *rā'ātēk*.

y. MT has a marker here.

Here, "God declares war on his people. . . . There had never been war poetry quite like this in the Israelite tradition."[165]

vv. 5–7   Yahweh commissions his aides to warn Judah of an invasion (eight bicola)
v. 8   Jeremiah urges Judah to mourn in light of this event (two bicola)

---

165. Holladay, *Spokesman out of Time*, 47, 59.

v. 9   Yahweh warns how Judah's leadership will be confounded
          by it (a resumptive introduction followed by a tricolon
          concluding vv. 5–9)
v. 10   Jeremiah responds in horrified protest (prose)
vv. 11–12 Yahweh warns of a scorching wind coming (an introduction
          followed by three bicola)
v. 13   The people react with horror (two bicola)
vv. 14–18 Yahweh urges a response that can forestall the horror
          (eight bicola)

5–6a Without announcement or introduction, Jeremiah plunges into a series of commands. It is one of the occasions when he does not specify who is speaking or who is addressed—because he is not sure, because it keeps the audience on their toes, or because the content is more important than the speakers. By implication, Yahweh speaks to his supernatural aides, as happens in Isa 40:1 with a message the reverse of the one here;[166] Jeremiah has perhaps overheard Yahweh giving the commission in the divine cabinet to which he refers in 23:22. The implication is not that the invasion is happening but that Yahweh has decided to make it happen and has begun implementing the decision. Jeremiah's audience is therefore to picture it and to understand that they need to do as the lookouts urge and as Jeremiah will urge in v. 8 to forestall the implementing of the decision (cf. v. 14). The commission to *blast a horn . . . ; call out, do it fully* is the message the aides are to give to lookout-type figures in *Jerusalem* and *Judah*. The imperatives are all plural; Yahweh is not commissioning Jeremiah himself here. The lookouts are to urge Judah to get ready for the invasion by taking refuge where things may be safer. During an invasion, people who lived outside of towns might move inside them, hoping to sit out any siege. Sounding a horn is the way lookouts herald the approach of unexpected visitors, who are possibly hostile (Ezek 33:1–6; Joel 2:1; Amos 3:6), or announce some other imminent event. *Do it fully* implies doing it throughout Judah. Jeremiah is not talking about a little local difficulty. The sequence in the order to the lookouts is hurried and elliptical, reflecting its urgency. "Lift up a flag under which people can gather, get them to Zion, take them to refuge there, and do it now." The *flag* (*nēs*) will mark the point where people are to *gather together*; the noun is uncomfortably close to the verb for "flee" (*nûs*). Referring to their goal as Zion rather than Jerusalem when they seek to *make safe* designates the place as the one to which Yahweh has made a special commitment; it is not just

---

166. McKane, *Jeremiah*, 1:114–15.

the capital city, the place with the best fortifications, or the natural center of resistance.[167] Yahweh will surely protect them on Zion.

6b–7 An irony emerges: the one from whom they ultimately need protection is Yahweh himself. *Dire trouble* is what Jeremiah has been warning about (2:19, 27–28), and talk of *dire trouble from the north* goes back to 1:14, so it is appropriate that it should feature at the beginning of this section of warning. The country is going to be shattered like a pot or yoke or neck or leg or arm—or broken down like a wall. Human beings can shatter things; but this *great shattering* will be effected by someone who is more like a *lion*. Is this a ferocious human commander (cf. 2:30, ironically, since there the people themselves are the lion)? Or is it Yahweh himself (cf. 49:19; 50:44; Hos 11:10; Amos 3:8)? Either way, at one level the problem is an advancing army, at another level it is Yahweh. Already (in Jeremiah's imagination and in Yahweh's decision-making) the *lion has gone up from its thicket*. To go back to literal language, already (in Jeremiah's vision) *a devastator of nations is on the move* to assert or extend its authority over its empire, as great powers like Assyria, Babylon, or Persia do. Perhaps the implication is that the reason he is coming *to make your country into a desolation* is that it has rebelled against his authority (as Judah did more than once not long after 604); otherwise, destruction is hardly in his interests. But anyway, Yahweh is talking about an invasion of mindless ferocity. The warning that *your towns will fall into ruins, so that there is no one living there* constitutes another irony in light of the fact that the only other occurrence of the verb for *fall into ruins* comes in Isaiah's promise about Assyria's destiny (Isa 37:26). In v. 5, Yahweh had bidden them take refuge in the towns, but now he indicates that his advice will be useless.

8 Without any indication of transition, Jeremiah now speaks to commission a further appropriate reaction to the message he has overheard and passed on. *Sack* is the coarse cloth out of which working clothes would be made. You would not wear it in public, but it is the appropriate clothing if you are going to *lament and wail*. Lamenting (*sāpad*) commonly implies mourning a death, but it can denote a reaction to other calamities and a grieving over one's wrongdoing, while wailing or howling can be a reaction to any distress. Jeremiah doesn't make clear which significance attaches to this lamenting or what it might be designed to achieve. Maybe Yahweh can be prevailed on to have pity on the people? Maybe the divine decision can be revoked, the invader diverted? But the point about mentioning it is that it constitutes another indication of how horrific the coming catastrophe will be and thus another note designed to affect Jeremiah's listeners. He has reported the people's conviction that Yahweh's anger had *turned back* from the people

---

167. McKane, *Jeremiah*, 1:92.

(2:35), perhaps because of Josiah's work. They need to face the fact that it hasn't, as 2 Kgs 23:26 says. Indeed, it's not just anger but *angry blazing* (or "blazing of anger"), the phrase in 2 Kgs 23:26.

9 If this strong 4-4 line was originally a separate entity, its attachment to vv. 5–8 is apposite, and if in some other context *that day* was the day of Yahweh, then here it simply refers back to the day of which vv. 5–8 spoke[168] (which could indeed be thought of as at least *a* day of Yahweh). When trouble threatens, leaders may not see it or may be paralyzed because they have to accept responsibility for its having happened or because they don't know what to do about it. It's not an unfair description of the response the leadership gave in 604 as Jer 36 describes it. Here, Jeremiah may imply that the leadership will fail to make or to encourage the response that v. 8 prescribed. It is as if their *mind* stops functioning (lit. "perishes"; see KJV) or their courage fails (Jeremiah actually refers to their heart, and either mind or courage would be possible implications of the reference). *The priests* will be as *desolate* as the country is destined to be (v. 7). *The prophets* who are supposed to be a resource of guidance will instead *be bewildered* like everyone else. It is almost as if Jeremiah feels some sympathy for the leaders. Who could blame them in light of the advice they've been given by those prophets? Yet they ought to have expected it—for moral and religious reasons and because they ought to have paid heed to Jeremiah.

10 Jeremiah's own response follows on that strong line in a verse of powerful prose that adds to the hint that Jeremiah feels some sympathy for Judah's leaders. Is it a protest that bursts the bounds of verse? It might be another originally separate element, but it works as a footnote to vv. 5–9, and the parallelism of v. 18 with the end of v. 10 is clever. It is the first of the many confrontational responses Jeremiah makes to Yahweh. Amusingly, he is inclined to call God *Lord* when he's being rebellious (cf. 1:6). Like v. 7, the rare verb *deluded* (*nāšā'*) resonates with the Hezekiah-Sennacherib story, which includes a warning about not letting Yahweh delude you (Isa 36:14; 37:10). It also resonates tellingly with 29:8, where Yahweh warns exiles in Babylon about being deluded by prophets whom Yahweh did not send, who did tell people, *It will be well with you* and that they would have "shalom" (e.g., 6:14; 8:11; 23:17; 28:9). On the contrary, Jeremiah notes, the city is like an individual who has been attacked by an enemy in such a way *that the sword has reached right to the throat* and is about to take his life. The proclamation of *šālôm* would be at home in the worship of Jerusalem (see Pss 122; 147). People would pray for Jerusalem's *šālôm*. Jerusalem is the source of *šālôm*;[169] its name says it. One consideration that might lie behind Jeremiah's protest is

168. Rudolph, *Jeremia*, 34.
169. McKane, *Jeremiah* 1:94–95.

175

that Yahweh had indeed promised his people that things would be well with them; he did it quite regularly (e.g., Num 6:26; Pss 29:11; 85:8[9], 10[11]). The more subtle consideration is that (paradoxically) Yahweh sometimes accepts responsibility for the prophets whom he did not send. Sending (false) prophets can be an act of judgment (cf. 1 Kgs 22:19–23; Ezek 14:1–11), without it taking away their responsibility for delivering a deceptive message (just as Sennacherib and Nebuchadrezzar did not escape responsibility for their military violence even though they were acting as Yahweh's agents). But why does the scroll include this protest as part of the message for people? Is Jeremiah speaking sarcastically, deriding the bewildered prophets just referred to, who had promised that things would be well?[170] They are people commissioned by Yahweh, as they said—but they are commissioned as deceivers. People reading the scroll needed to think about this aspect of the picture.

11a–b Yahweh does not directly react to Jeremiah's accusation with answer or rebuke; there is a parallel with the many protest psalms that end without response or resolution. The verses that follow look like an originally separate message, but the phrase *at that time* now makes a link with vv. 5–10, and once more they make an apposite follow-up to what precedes them. Eventually they will imply some explanation of why Yahweh could have failed to make things go well for Jerusalem or could have sent those false prophets. In the meantime, the possibility of some explanation is hinted by the phrase *this people*, which can be a dismissive, contemptuous expression (see 5:23). The beginning of the actual message comprises a sequence of noun phrases whose connections the audience has to make. The *scorching wind* (the khamsin or sirocco) from the east, which often afflicts the Middle East in spring and fall, blows over *the bare heights in the wilderness* and onto *the path of my dear people*—more literally, of "the daughter [who is] my people"; that is, my people who are like my daughter. The *my* makes it a term of endearment; it recurs in Jeremiah. *This people* is also *my dear people*. It would be grammatically simpler to infer that Israel's path *is* the scorching wind on the bare heights, the place of their whoring; once more, the direness of Israel's life is finding fulfillment in the dire trouble it brings on itself (see v. 18).

11c–12 Either way, whereas wind is useful in fall for separating chaff from wheat and thus purifying it so that only grain remains, this wind is too strong for that purpose; it will blow everything away. Like the lion and the destroyer who are doing what lions and destroyers do yet are fulfilling Yahweh's purpose, the wind is doing what wind does. It isn't commissioned by Yahweh, but he says that nevertheless *it comes for me*. In following up that statement, Yahweh gets closer to answering the question raised by v. 10. Having *šālôm* fail and sending false prophets are ways that Yahweh is announcing

---

170. Calvin, *Jeremiah*, 1:224.

judgment. *I too*—I as well as the wind, which makes its own decisions—*will speak out authoritative decisions to them.* Once more, the language goes back to Jeremiah's account of his original commission (1:16; see the translation note there).

13 Again, Jeremiah speaks on the people's behalf and returns from metaphor to more direct description of the destroyer to portray the speed of his advance with his army (though still portraying it in similes) and the frightening implications *for us* of the destruction he pictures. He presents three similes in staircase parallelism.[171]

there,	like	clouds	he goes up
	like	a tornado	his chariots
lighter	than	eagles	his horses

The army could make people think of clouds racing across the sky, of the overwhelming velocity of a tornado, or of the lightning-fast swoop of an eagle. Jeremiah invites them then to imagine their response to what he presents.

14 Yet all is not lost, notwithstanding the picture of authoritative decisions being implemented in the destroyer's being already on his way. There is a justification for those decisions and thus for Yahweh's failure to make things go well for Jerusalem. But the fact that Yahweh has formulated a plan to bring trouble and has even commissioned its implementation doesn't mean everything is fixed (see 18:1-11). "Jeremiah never thought an appeal to repent was too late."[172] Indeed, why bother with all these messages if there was no prospect of their threat being withdrawn? Yahweh is the one who is planning to bring trouble, but Yahweh is also the one who is giving warnings. There is no need to think that v. 14 must be a later addition to Jeremiah's message.[173] Indeed one might see it as the center of the section.[174] There is still the possibility of *deliverance*. Various forms of washing can apply to various forms of stain, some more useful than others. Cleansing can be an image for removing defilement through a physical rite (e.g., Lev 14–15)[175] or for something God does in response to people's turning (Ps 51:7[9]). But trying to remove the stain that comes from wrongdoing when you're continuing in the wrongdoing—it gets you nowhere. The kind of washing Jeremiah described in 2:22 doesn't solve anything in this connection. But to *wash your*

171. Lundbom, *Jeremiah 1–20*, 345.
172. J. A. Thompson, *Jeremiah*, 225.
173. Duhm, *Jeremia*, 51.
174. Fischer, *Jeremia*, 1:230.
175. Rom-Shiloni ("Forest and the Trees," 79–83) cites this passage as a noteworthy example of the influence of the thinking of Leviticus (of the Priestly and Holiness Codes) on Jeremiah.

mind of dire behavior is a different matter. It's a parallel image to that of circumcising your mind. Yahweh follows up mention of Jerusalem's mind with reference to *your baneful plans*. These plans that occupy your mind must not be allowed to *lodge within you* like an overnight guest to whom you properly offer hospitality. They must be thrown out. In the more conventional terms of 3:1–4:4, people need to turn back.

15–16 *Baneful plans* will issue in *baneful* news: "bane" (*'āwen*) is another word suggesting a link between bad things that people do and bad consequences that follow (these two are the only occurrences of *'āwen* in Jeremiah). The line works with neat double-duty parallelism:

because a voice	is announcing		from Dan
	is making heard	something baneful	from the highland of Ephraim

Yahweh reverts to portraying the advance of an army from the north, now described as the report of an imaginary anonymous voice, the voice of the army's commander-in-chief. It is first speaking from *Dan*, which is on the far northern border of Israel and thus of old Ephraim but has long been part of the Assyrian Empire. It is then speaking *from the highland of Ephraim*, the main body of the mountain range to the north of Judah, worryingly nearer. *The nations* are peoples such as Ammon and Moab. While they might need to know because they are also in danger, *against Jerusalem* rather suggests that the commandant is bidding his aides give them a summons to join in the attack—as they indeed did in 597 and 587. The *watchers* are the troops who will be keeping watch on the city and on *the towns of Judah* as they besiege them.

17–18 In one of Jeremiah's distinctive 5-2 lines, Yahweh compares the watchers to *people keeping guard of the open country,* keeping watch on the maturing crops in the fields to guard them from thieves or animals—except that these guards are *all around* as attackers, not allies. And it's *because she has rebelled against me* that Yahweh has deprived her of her *šālôm* (v. 10). The way she has walked her *path* and the *direness* of her practices (cf. v. 4) explain what is happening to her path (v. 11). The direness of her fate (cf. v. 6) issues from the direness of her behavior or her nature (v. 14). That direness is thus *bitter* in its results and bitter because *it has reached as far as your inner being* or mind (this formulation parallels the one in v. 10). It "threatens the very core of her being."[176] Yet the challenge of v. 14 to *wash your mind* stands.

---

176. Holladay, *Commentary on Jeremiah,* 1:160.

Yahweh's words are elliptical as he plays on the link between dire behavior or nature and dire trouble—perhaps because he treats direness as one thing and moves between behavior and fate as aspects of the one thing. It would be less confusing for Western readers to think of the dire trouble as being bitter and of the dire behavior or nature as reaching as far as the inner being, but Jeremiah does not encourage this distinction. Jerusalem's nature and life has found its organic outworking in the calamity that has come to it. Actions issue in consequences, which are aspects of the same reality.

2. *Formless and Empty (4:19–31)*

¹⁹My insides, my insides, I writhe,^a
  the walls of my heart!
My heart moans for me,
  I cannot be quiet.
Because the sound of a horn you have heard,^b *my spirit,*
  the blast for battle.
²⁰Shattering upon shattering has been proclaimed,^c
  because the entire country has been destroyed.
Suddenly my tents have been destroyed,
  in a moment, my tent walls.
²¹How long am I to look at a flag,^d
  am I to listen^e *to the sound of a horn?*^f

²²Because my people is stupid,
  me it does not acknowledge.
They are foolish children,
  they are not insightful.^g
They are smart at doing dire things,
  but they don't know how to do good.

²³I looked at the earth, and there, it was void and empty,^h
  and to the heavens, and there was no light in them.
²⁴I looked at the mountains, and there, they were quaking,
  *and all the hills, they were light-footed.*ⁱ
²⁵I looked, and there, no human being,
  and all the birds in the heavens—they had fled.
²⁶I looked, and there, the orchard was wilderness,
  and all the towns, they were demolished,^j
From before Yahweh,

from before his angry blazing.[k]

[27]*Because Yahweh has said this:*

Desolation is what the entire country will become
  (but I will not make an end).
[28]*Because of this the country will mourn,*
  the heavens will be dark above.
Because I have spoken—I have schemed,
  and I have not relented, I will not turn back from it.[l]

[29]*At the voice of cavalryman and archer,*
  every town[m] *is fleeing.*
People have come into scrublands,[n]
  onto rocks they have gone up.
Every town is abandoned,
  so that there is no one living in them, not one.

[30]*So you, one about to be destroyed,*[o]
  what do you do when you wear scarlet,
When you adorn yourself in gold adornment,
  when you enlarge your eyes with mascara?
To no end will you make yourself beautiful—
  your paramours despise you, they will seek your life.
[31]*Because a voice like a woman writhing*[p] *I have heard,*
  distress like a woman having her first baby,
The voice of Miss Zion[q]—
  she pants,[r] *she stretches out the palms of her hands:*
"Alas for me, please, me,
  because my life is faint with the killers."[s]

a. Following the *ketiv*, which implies *'āḥûlâ*; the *qere 'ôḥîlâ* should mean "I intend to wait"—perhaps "a mitigating reading" (Holladay, *Commentary on Jeremiah*, 1:142). The cohortative verb might imply "I must writhe" but may be cohortative only in form—a pseudo-cohortative (GKC 108g; *TTH* 53; Joüon 114c).

b. The *ketiv* has the archaic second-person feminine form; see the translation notes on 2:19 and 20.

c. Cf. LXX, Aq, Sym, Vg, deriving the verb from *qārā'* I. Tg, Syr "have happened" derives it from *qārā'* II.

d. *Nēs* as in v. 6; LXX, Vg, Syr "fugitives/a fugitive" suggests a different vocalization (HUBP), deriving it from *nûs*—a paronomasia that listeners might pick up.

e. Perhaps another pseudo-cohortative (see note a).

f. MT has a marker here.

g. The children (*bānîm*) are not insightful (*nəbônîm*). It is not surprising, even though the words are similar; after all, they are only children.

h. LXX has simply "nothing" for the two Hebrew words, which might indicate that its Hebrew text had only *tōhû* (K. M. Hayes, "Jeremiah iv 23: *tōhû* without *bōhû*," *VT* 47 [1997]: 247–49).

i. *Hitqalqālû* from *qālal* (related words in 2:23; 3:9).

j. *Nittəṣû*, from *nātaṣ* (cf. 1:10); LXX implies *niṣṣətû* ("are burned"), from *yāṣat* (cf. 2:15).

k. MT has a section marker here.

l. LXX has a tidier version: "I spoke and I will not relent; I have initiated and I will not turn back from it."

m. Vg's "the entire town" could make sense, but the phrase recurs in v. 29b followed by "in them" and thus has to denote "every town" there; the same meaning is likely here.

n. For *bā'û be'ābîm*, LXX suggests something like *bā'û bammə'ārôt nehbə'û be'ābîm* ("they have come into caves, hidden in scrublands"), implying homoioteleuton in MT; *CTAT* 2:491 thinks it would be "astonishing" if Jeremiah had omitted reference to taking refuge in caves.

o. Whereas *you* is suddenly feminine, and the feminine is picked up and developed in the rest of the verse, the passive participle *šādûd* referring to what is about to happen is oddly masculine (hence *one*); it is omitted in LXX.

p. The participle presumably comes from *hûl* (cf. v. 19), though it looks like a form from *hālâ*, which would mean "weak"; see GKC 72p.

q. Lit. "Daughter [of] Zion" (see the translation note on v. 11), which almost has the overtones of "Little Girl Zion."

r. *Tityappî* (*you make yourself beautiful*, v. 30) becomes *tityappēaḥ* (perhaps a *hapax legomenon* chosen or invented as an alternative to a form from *nāpaḥ* or *pûaḥ*, for the sake of the paronomasia?).

s. MT has a unit marker here.

Verses 19–31 continue the warning about the approach of the destroyer, but they bring home this warning by means of a series of poetic tropes:

- personal horror (vv. 19–21)
- teacherly disenchantment (v. 22)
- cosmic dissolution (vv. 23–26a)
- divine fury (v. 26b)
- divine mercy (v. 27)
- ecological mourning (v. 28a)
- divine determination (v. 28b)
- urban flight (v. 29)
- fanciful denial (v. 30)
- parturient despair (v. 31)

The section is structured in six parts:

vv. 19–21	Jeremiah utters a lament reacting to the imagined catastrophe (six bicola)
v. 22	Yahweh explains the catastrophe (three bicola)
vv. 23–26	Jeremiah relates a vision of a disaster in nature as having happened (five bicola, the last two linked by enjambment)
vv. 27–28	Yahweh makes an announcement of such a disaster as coming (an introduction followed by three bicola)
v. 29	Jeremiah portrays the disaster as a military invasion (three bicola)
vv. 30–31	Jeremiah says Miss Zion is to face the facts rather than hide from them (six bicola, the first two linked and the last three linked)

The scroll brings together at least three messages in vv. 19–31. In each of them, the second item might also be of separate origin, but if so, in each case it has been given a link with what it now follows (*because*, v. 22; *because*, v. 27; *so*, v. 30).

19 As often happens, Jeremiah starts in the middle of things and raises suspense. He is physically and emotionally overwhelmed by something. But what? He is again conveying his response to an anticipatory experience of the coming disaster. *I writhe* and *my heart moans for me; I cannot be quiet.* Maybe he feels this way because of what he has already experienced in a vision, or maybe he imagines what it will be like for him and for everyone else when people hear *the sound of a horn* as it gives *the blast for battle.*[177] Either way, his reason for describing this reaction is again to get people to see what the catastrophe will be like for him and for everyone else. He is inviting his audience into an act of imagination as he was in vv. 5–18, but a different kind of act of imagination. "Conjure up what you will feel during the city's siege and fall and the devastation of Judah's towns. Your heart will pound and throb."[178] The poetry is not a lament of the prophet as opposed to a lament of the people,[179] though it illustrates how "Jeremiah and all real historymakers have a profound sense of anguish, pathos, and incongruity that touches the

177. N. C. Lee sees a different voice, the voice of a lament-singer, in such passages in Jeremiah ("Prophet and Singer in the Fray: The Book of Jeremiah," in Goldingay, *Uprooting and Planting*, 190–209).

178. Calvin, *Jeremiah*, 1:239–40.

179. Weiser, *Jeremia*, 45. But S. Köhler makes it the first of her comparisons with an Old Babylonian kalu priest (*Jeremia—Fürbitter oder Kläger: Eine religionsgeschichtliche Studie zur Fürbitte und Klage im Jeremiabuch*, BZAW 506 [Berlin: de Gruyter, 2017]).

historymaker quite personally."[180] Nor is Jeremiah embodying God's suffering (at least, such an understanding does not emerge from this text). He voices the coming lament of people and prophet.[181] "This anguish is not a means of gaining insight into his soul; it is itself prophecy."[182]

20–21 So imagine that the invasion and destruction have happened—*shattering upon shattering*—and the awful news *has been proclaimed* to you, as a similar anonymous voice not so long ago reported forces advancing past Dan and through Ephraim (v. 15). Perhaps an actual vision comes to Jeremiah, but as an act of communication, the description is an appeal to the audience's mind's eye and mind's ear; the word for "voice" or *sound* (*qôl*) comes more often in Jeremiah than in any other First Testament book (including Psalms),[183] and vv. 19–21 are dense with references to sound. In the imagination, as in a dream, a siege and the destruction that in reality take some time can seem to happen *suddenly* and *in a moment*. Picture your home precipitously *destroyed*; it's possible to speak figuratively of people's ordinary homes as their *tents* (e.g., 1 Kgs 8:66). Imagine longing for it to be all over. *How long*, you ask, as when you pray a prayer of protest from the Psalms (e.g., 6:3[4]; 12:1–3; 78:5; 79:5–6). How long will the *flag* need to be there to lead people to some possible escape? How long will I have to *listen to the sound of a horn*? These motifs reappear from the very beginning of the section (vv. 5–6) as if to say that this invasion and siege go on forever—as it will seem they do (see 52:4–5).

22 As was the case in vv. 11–18, there follows Yahweh's explanation of why it had to happen. In the arrangement of the section, it offers further response to Jeremiah's protest in v. 10 as well as a response to his rhetorical questions in v. 21. "Prophetic anguish" gives way to "divine frustration" at the people's wickedness and moral obtuseness.[184] A "stunning" contrast of mood comes about between vv. 19–21 and 22: Yahweh now speaks "as a schoolmaster would, marking his students," and setting his *my people* (*'ammî*) over against Jeremiah's *my insides* (*mē'î*).[185] The city's suffering comes about because it is *stupid* and *foolish* as opposed to *insightful*. The Judahites are smart all right— *smart at doing dire things*.[186] They are "God's uniquely dumb people."[187] They are unwilling to *acknowledge* Yahweh. Jeremiah again assumes the link be-

---

180. Brueggemann, *Like Fire*, 192.

181. M. C. A. Korpel discusses possibilities in "Who Is Speaking in Jeremiah 4:19–22?" *VT* 59 (2009): 88–98.

182. D. R. Jones, *Jeremiah*, 115.

183. See R. Graybill, "'Hear and Give Ear!' The Soundscape of Jeremiah," *JSOT* 40 (2016): 467–90.

184. P. D. Miller, "Jeremiah," on the passage.

185. Holladay, *Commentary on Jeremiah*, 1:147–48.

186. Lundbom, *Jeremiah 1–20*, 355.

187. Fischer, *Jeremia*, 1:223.

tween *acknowledge* and *know* (*yāda*ʿ). Yahweh's explanations hold together insight, religion, and ethics in a way that parallels the aim of Proverbs, to enable people

> To know smartness and discipline,
>> to understand words that express understanding,
> To get discipline so as to act with insight,
>> faithfulness, the exercise of authority, and uprightness,
> To give shrewdness to the naïve,
>> knowledge and strategy to the youth,
> So that the smart person may listen and increase in his grasp,
>> the understanding may acquire skill,
> So as to understand an aphorism and a parable,
>> the words of the smart and their conundrums:
> The first principle of knowledge is awe for Yahweh;
>> dense people despise smartness and discipline. (Prov 1:2–7)

Insight, religion, and ethics are part of the same reality, though the Western instinct is to separate them.[188]

23 There follows another report of imaginative awareness, another visionary testimony,[189] which presumably had a separate origin from what precedes. Jeremiah imagines the country as a small-scale version of the world as a whole in its pre-creation state, its Gen 1:2 state, *void and empty*. The words say it: the world is *tōhû wābōhû*. It's like the wilderness. It's not chaotic or disorderly; it's simply shapeless and unstructured. LXX captures the picture: "I looked at the earth and behold, nothing"; the Vg has: "And behold, it was empty and nothing." The horror lies not in what it is but in the contrast with a creation that has been made into something shapely and beautiful. It's as if God has not yet said, "Light!" Darkness is all there is. All you can see is gloom, which, again, is not evil. It's just—well, gloomy. But it speaks of the absence of God, who has not come to it with his order and beauty. "According to this phrase, the situation in which the earth finds itself is the very opposite of promising. It is quite hopeless." The earth as *tōhû wābōhû* is "the earth which is nothing as such, which mocks its Creator and which

---

188. See further S. Balentine, "Sagacious Divine Judgment: Jeremiah's Use of Proverbs to Construct an Ethos and Ethics of Divine Epistemology in the Book of Jeremiah," in Lundbom, Evans, and B. A. Anderson, *Jeremiah*, 113–25.

189. W. Zimmerli discusses it as one of Jeremiah's three actual visions, along with 1:11–16 and (perhaps) 24:1–10 ("Visionary Experience in Jeremiah," in *Israel's Prophetic Tradition: Essays in Honour of Peter R. Ackroyd*, ed. R. J. Coggins, A. Phillips, and M. Knibb [Cambridge: Cambridge University Press, 1982], 99–104).

can only be an offence to the heaven above it, threatening it with the same nothingness."[190]

24 After making us think of Gen 1,[191] Jeremiah makes us think of the Prophets and the Psalms, and here the word "chaos" might be more apposite. *Mountains* and *hills* stand for stability, but in Jeremiah's picture they are *quaking* and *light-footed*, agile, able to jump up and down—not what you want of your hills and mountains. This picture, too, speaks of the absence of God, whose stability and steadiness form a reassuring contrast over against mountains quaking (Ps 46:3[4]). It speaks of the disorder and chaos brought into the political and historical events of which Jeremiah is warning (cf. Isa 13:13). It speaks of Yahweh's wrath, which makes the earth quake (Jer 10:10).

25 Or it's as if he has not yet created the living beings. *No human being* is part of the description in Gen 2:5, except that the two words *no* and *human being* come in the opposite order. There were no *birds in the heavens*: it is not that creation has not reached this point but rather that they have *fled*. So there is a similar movement within v. 25 to the movement from v. 23 to v. 24; at first it seems like a mere "not yet," but then it becomes explicit that creation has been undone. There were no birds to be seen at Birkenau; "they had fled the skies above all the death-camps."[192]

26a The dynamic recurs. It's as if Yahweh has not yet planted the *orchard* and the land remains a *wilderness*; to extend the link with Gen 2, there is not yet a human being to serve the garden and look after it. The second colon suggests that the problem is rather that the orchard has gone back to being wilderness, as the towns have become nothing but those remains of towns that characterize archaeological tells in Israel, mute witnesses to there once having been a town there. Here too, the world bears the marks of a creation that has returned to being formless and empty rather than one that has not yet been formed and filled.[193] Whereas Yahweh brought Israel from the wilderness into the orchard (2:6–7), now the orchard has become a wilderness. The use of the two words together "evokes the whole history

190. Barth, *CD* III, 1:104, 105.

191. On which relationship, see, e.g., J. T. A. G. M. van Ruiten, "Back to Chaos: The Relationship between Jeremiah 4:23–26 and Genesis 1," in *The Creation of Heaven and Earth: Re-interpretations of Genesis I in the Context of Judaism, Ancient Philosophy, Christianity, and Modern Physics*, ed. G. H. van Kooten, Themes in Biblical Narrative 8 (Leiden: Brill, 2005), 21–30; B. Janowski, "Eine Welt ohne Licht: Zur Chaostopik von Jer 4, 23–28 und verwandten Texten," in *Disaster and Relief Management—Katastrophen und ihre Bewältigung,* ed. A. Berlejung, FAT 81 (Tübingen: Mohr Siebeck, 2013), 119–41.

192. E. Wiesel, *Five Biblical Portraits* (Notre Dame: University of Notre Dame, 1981), 126 (cf. R. P. Carroll, *Jeremiah*, OTL, 170).

193. H. C. P. Kim makes a link with the story of the flood as an act of uncreation: see "Tsunami, Hurricane, and Jeremiah 4:23–28," *BTB* 37 (2007): 54–61.

of the Israelites."[194] The end is the same as the beginning, *Endzeit* the same as *Urzeit*.[195] "War is . . . regarded here as the end of the world."[196] The implication is not that Jeremiah's vision is apocalyptic[197] or eschatological in the sense that it portrays an End that is far off or unrelated to this world or this time.[198] Creation and uncreation find concrete expression in the experience of the people of God.

26b In vv. 23–26, each line is shorter than the last: "The progressively shorter lines simulate the undoing of creation, heightening the sense of loss and leaving the audience to experience an eerie silence at the end."[199] Except that it leaves them not with silence but with the judgment in v. 26b. The country is in a state of devastation that has come *from before Yahweh, from before his angry blazing*. At the end of his creating, God said his creation was very good and then rested. The end of this vision differs. "This poem is almost more than we dare to utter. . . . Its substance is too ominous. The poet, one element at a time, plucks up and tears down the whole of the created order."[200] And

> although there might have been a time when such harsh images of death and destruction could have been ignored, those days are forever gone. . . . Death and destruction now shroud our own immediate vision of reality. . . . The prophet's vision of a cohesive and orderly world reverting to chaos and formlessness clearly transcends his own time and space.[201]

27 Following on what Jeremiah has spoken of as actual, as already having happened, Yahweh adds a footnote to confirm that it indeed will happen,

194. K. M. Hayes, *"The Earth Mourns": Prophetic Metaphor and Oral Aesthetic*, Academia Biblica 8 (Atlanta: Society of Biblical Literature, 2002), 75.

195. Cf. H. Gunkel, *Schöpfung und Chaos in Urzeit und Endzeit* (Göttingen: Vandenhoeck & Ruprecht, 1895), a study of Gen 1 and Rev 12.

196. Berrigan, *Jeremiah*, 23.

197. Cf. Á. Borges de Sousa, "Jer 4,23–26 als P-orientierter Abschnitt," *ZAW* 105 (1993): 419–28. D. C. Olson sees the passage as dependent on Enochic materials: see "Jeremiah 4.5–31 and Apocalyptic Myth," *JSOT* 73 (1997): 81–107.

198. It is one of the few passages that Y. Hoffman is prepared to call possibly eschatological in his study of "Eschatology in the Book of Jeremiah," in *Eschatology in the Bible and in Jewish and Christian Tradition*, ed. H. G. Reventlow, JSOTSup 243 (Sheffield: Sheffield Academic, 1997), 75–97. Contrast M. A. Sweeney's happiness with the word in his "Eschatology in the Book of Jeremiah," in *Marbeh Ḥokmah: Studies in the Bible and the Ancient Near East in Loving Memory of Victor Avigdor Hurowitz*, ed. S. Yona (Winona Lake, IN: Eisenbrauns, 2015), 525–39.

199. Lundbom, *Jeremiah 1–20*, 358.

200. W. Brueggemann, *Texts Under Negotiation* (Minneapolis: Fortress, 1993), 84.

201. Stulman, *Order amid Chaos*, 11–12.

because he has determined on it. Whereas *hā'āreṣ* was the earth in v. 23, here it is presumably *the country*; the reference to the towns in v. 26 facilitates this transition, and it reminds us that Jeremiah's description of uncreation in vv. 23–26 is itself really a description of the imminent fate of the country. Viewed either way, the vision in vv. 23–26 is a vision of *desolation*, and it will have a desolating effect. In a sidebar, Jeremiah therefore includes a reassurance that Yahweh's intention is not as final as that account sounds. Yahweh does not actually intend to bring creation or country to an *end*. The dynamics of vv. 19–31 parallel the dynamics of vv. 5–18. As Yahweh's intention to bring calamity raised a question about the way he has encouraged people to understand him as a God who makes things work out well for them (v. 10), so his intention of total devastation raises a question about his ultimate commitment to his people and to his world. Once again, it may be that this verse (or simply the last colon) has a different origin from the material on either side, but it deals with a question that one can imagine arising for Jeremiah's audience and for the readers of his scroll—as it does for Paul in Rom 9–11. It's a question that God has to live with. One of the ways in which the Jeremiah scroll can seem unreadable is its conflicting statements about whether the actual end has come or is coming.[202] One could say that God is here indicating his ambiguity about bringing what looks like final devastation.[203] Yet there is nothing novel about the reassurance that appears here, which will recur in 5:10, 18. "The idea of a remnant . . . was actually settled in passages such as Exod 32:9–14 and Deut 32:26–27"[204] and Lev 26:44.[205]

28 The desolation will nevertheless mean that everything is dark in the *country*, as if it *will mourn*, and the gloom will indeed be as if the *heavens above* have not heard God say, "Light!" Once again, cosmos and country mirror each other: "The whole world comes unglued when Israel is disobedient long enough,"[206] and, "In a way the whole cosmos is in mourning for itself."[207] It is doing so because Yahweh has formulated an intention that he intends to implement. The word rendered *schemed* (*zāmam*) is usually a bad word, like that English equivalent, and maybe it hints at people's accusations: "You accuse me of formulating bad intentions toward you? You bet I have!" And Yahweh does not intend to go back on them. Three times he speaks in the past tense: *I have spoken . . . schemed . . . not relented.* It is the basis for saying, so *I will not turn back.* Jeremiah thus juxtaposes the First Testament's two

---

202. See W. Brueggemann, "An Ending That Does Not End: The Book of Jeremiah," in *Postmodern Interpretations of the Bible*, ed. A. K. M. Adam (St. Louis: Chalice, 2001), 117–28.

203. Brueggemann, *Jeremiah 1–25*, 57.

204. Lundbom, *Jeremiah 1–20*, 362.

205. Qimchi, in MG.

206. Brueggemann, *Jeremiah 1–25*, 56.

207. Holladay, *Commentary on Jeremiah*, 1:168. See my commentary on 12:4.

words for repentance. *Relented* (*nāḥam niphal*) can suggest the feelings that someone has in relation to the past, but it more consistently suggests making a decision to behave in a different way compared with the past.[208] *Turn back* (*šûb*) is an action word explicitly referring to the future. One almost expects another sidebar to deal with the question of whether Yahweh doesn't sometimes turn back, but the scroll forbears. Yet what Yahweh says here is not his final statement on the matter (see, e.g., 12:15; 18:1–10), and 3:1–4:4 has already implied that everything depends on Jerusalem's own stance, on its turning.

29 The scroll adds yet another imaginative portrait, again based on what actually happens in war. While one way of coping with invasion is for everyone to come into the fortified towns and sit out the siege, another way is to run for it, knowing you can come back later when the enemy is gone. So, when *cavalryman and archer* arrive (like bank robbers, they work in pairs: one to drive, one to shoot), they don't need to fire an arrow or charge. As they approach, the town's inhabitants hear their *voice* (their shout or the noise), and they are *fleeing* to hide among the bushes in the *scrublands* or to climb *rocks* and look for caves. It's a wise strategy. It means *every town* is eerily empty when the foe arrives.

30 The scroll appends another pointed message of Jeremiah's, in which he addresses Jerusalem itself. While the wise inhabitants of an unwalled town are fleeing, what about Jerusalem? Its position and its walls make it less vulnerable, and it has sat out sieges before, as it did when Sennacherib came (see Isa 36–37). Is that what you think you will do, Miss Jerusalem? And are you tarting yourself up instead of fleeing? We see the woman/city taking care of her appearance, putting on clothing, jewelry, and makeup, as if getting ready to go out and enjoy herself.[209] The city's *paramours* are the allies who she might think will be her deliverance (see Jer 2). Whom are you thinking of, Jerusalem? The Egyptians? Your cousins the Moabites, the Ammonites, and the Edomites? You are in for a rude awakening. At best they *despise you*. Actually, they will join in with the Babylonians when the day comes. They *will seek your life*.

31 Jerusalem is trying to anticipate the future and make it work her way. Jeremiah has heard the future. In his message, contempt moves to compassion,[210] but rhetorically the aim does not change. Everything is designed to get Jerusalem to come to its senses. He draws attention to a different woman, but it will turn out to be the same woman. It is *Miss Zion* whose *voice* he has *heard*, but *like a woman writhing* in labor instead of like a whore prettying

---

208. See H.-J. Fabry, "נחם, nḥm," *TDOT* 9:342.

209. A. Bauer, "Dressed to Be Killed: Jeremiah 4.29–31 as an Example for the Functions of Female Imagery in Jeremiah," in Diamond, K. M. O'Connor, and Stulman, *Troubling Jeremiah*, 295.

210. Holladay, *Commentary on Jeremiah*, 1:149.

herself up. This woman in *distress* is *having her first baby*. It is commonly a tougher experience than subsequent births, even apart from examples like Rachel's (Gen 35:16–20), and there are no epidurals in seventh-century Judah. She is exhausted. All she can do is appeal incoherently for help: *Alas for me, please*. "In the spreading of the hands and the *nāʾ* ['please'] lies the desperate plea: do help me!"[211] She is in danger of losing her life like Rachel, but unlike Rachel her death will not be life-giving but simply death-dealing. Although Miss Zion is *like* a woman giving birth in the way she is crying out, it is not actually a description of Miss Zion giving birth. Miss Zion is experiencing the fate that often comes to the victims of invasion (e.g., Hos 13:16 [14:1]; Amos 1:13). Her cry is not the cry of a woman in labor but the cry of a woman being raped and killed. If "war-related aggression against women is 'one of history's great silences,'"[212] Jeremiah is not wholly silent about it (see 5:17; 13:22; 51:35). Jeremiah 4:5–31 began with Zion as refuge, and we may be able to hear a woman's voice through much of this section.[213] It ends with Zion pleading for mercy from her killers. "Why such furious poetic descriptions of such terrible themes? . . . Many people had no sense of the impending calamity. The prophet must shock them into facing reality."[214] If these verses were part of the 604 scroll, "one understands more and more the terror of Jehoiakim's ministers."[215]

D. MOSTLY CONFRONTATION (5:1–31)

Chapter 5 makes for a new start as the scroll reverts to a focus on attacking Jerusalem and Judah concerning its life and its unfaithful relationship with Yahweh, which make it necessary for Yahweh to act. It confronts a people in denial.[216]

- They are faithless in their relationships with one another.
- They are resistant to facing the implications of Yahweh's discipline.

---

211. Duhm, *Jeremia*, 55.

212. F. R. Ames, "The Cascading Effects of Exile: From Diminished Resources to New Identities," in *Interpreting Exile: Displacement and Deportation in Biblical and Modern Contexts*, ed. B. E. Kelle, F. R. Ames, and J. L. Wright, AIIL 10 (Atlanta: Society of Biblical Literature, 2011), 176, quoting E. Rehn and E. Johnson-Sirleaf, *Women, War, Peace* (New York: United Nations Development Fund for Women, 2002), 19.

213. See B. B. Kaiser, "Poet as 'Female Impersonator': The Image of Daughter Zion as Speaker in Biblical Poems of Suffering," *Journal of Religion* 67 (1987): 166–74.

214. Pixley, *Jeremiah*, 20–21.

215. D. R. Jones, *Jeremiah*, 119.

216. Fischer, *Jeremia*, 1:254.

- They are faithless in their relationship with Yahweh.
- They are resistant to heeding his warnings.
- They accumulate stuff by deceit and by denying needy people their rights.
- Prophets, priests, and people collude in following this lifestyle.

Yahweh therefore threatens them with invasion and devastation, though he will not wipe them out.

Strings of imperatives appear in vv. 1, 10, and 20, and I have yielded to the temptation to treat these as the beginnings of sections. They thus initiate three sections of similar length, vv. 1–9, 10–19, and 20–31. Another set of imperatives begins in 6:1, marking the beginning of another unit; they constitute more warnings than confrontations. Designating the imperatives in 5:1, 10, and 20 as beginnings does not carry the implication that the entirety of what follows originally belonged with them. In each case, some verses introduced by imperatives are supplemented by further material. The bulk of the chapter can again be read against the background of the story in Jer 36, but once more it will be a reformulation by Jeremiah of messages given over the previous twenty years, so one cannot try to relate it to particular times within that period. Further, some of it could have been added over the subsequent twenty years or more. In the context of the exile, it could function to justify Yahweh's action in letting Jerusalem fall,[217] but it is not expressed as if originally designed to fulfill this function. It indicates that Yahweh has taken action against Jerusalem, but not in a final way, and it focuses on action Yahweh will yet take.

Throughout ch. 5, the material is formulated by Jeremiah or someone who speaks in his name, and throughout it addresses the people of Judah and Jerusalem. But in form, it works in many ways. Yahweh speaks in v. 1 and addresses some aides, but it is Jeremiah who is informing us of that fact. In vv. 2–3, Jeremiah himself speaks to Yahweh but leaves us to work this fact out, and readers would not know that Jeremiah speaks in v. 2 until they read v. 3. As the chapter unfolds, it continues to move between Jeremiah and Yahweh speaking, and it is neither possible nor necessary to identify the speaker at every point. It is always Jeremiah speaking, even when he speaks as Yahweh,

217. See R. P. Carroll, "Theodicy and the Community: The Text and Subtext of Jeremiah V 1–6," in *Prophets, Worship and Theodicy: Studies in Prophetism, Biblical Theology and Structural and Rhetorical Analysis and on the Place of Music in Worship*, ed. A. S. van der Woude, OTS 23 (Leiden: Brill, 1984): 19–38. It is the first passage C. Bultmann discusses in arguing that theodicy is the central question in Jeremiah ("Grausamkeit: Kriterien religiöser Vorstellungen im Jeremiabuch," in *Ein Herz so weit wie der Sand am Ufer des Meeres. Festschrift für Georg Hentschel*, ed. S. Gillmayr-Bucher, A. Giercke, and C. Niessen, Erfurter Theologische Studien 90 [Würzburg: Echter, 2006], 273–98).

and it is Yahweh's message even when Jeremiah speaks in his own name. Readers of the scroll have to ask, how does this account of something that Jeremiah experienced function as Yahweh's message?

1. The Universal Deceptiveness (5:1–9)

[1]*Go about through the streets of Jerusalem,*
  look, please, and get to know.
Seek in its squares,
  if you can find an individual,
If there is someone exercising authority,
  seeking truthfulness, so that I may pardon it.[a]

[2]*Even if they say, "Yahweh is alive,"*[b]
  then they swear to deception,
[3]*Whereas Yahweh, your eyes—*
  they are to truthfulness, aren't they.[c]
When you struck them down, they didn't writhe,[d]
  when you made an end of them, they refused to accept restraint.
They made their faces stronger than rock—
  they refused to turn back.

[4]*But I—I said,*
  those are only poor people who show themselves stupid,
Because they do not acknowledge Yahweh's way,
  the authority of their God.
[5]*I'll get myself off*[e] *to the big people,*
  and I'll speak to them,
Because those people—they acknowledge Yahweh's way,
  the authority of their God.
Actually, those people, altogether, had broken the yoke,
  torn off the restraints.
[6]*That's why a lion from the forest has struck them down;*
  a wolf from the steppes—it destroys them.[f]
A leopard is watching over their towns—
  anyone going out from them gets mauled.
Because their rebellions are many,
  their turnings are numerous.

[7]*How for this could I pardon you—*
  your children have abandoned me,

and sworn by non-gods.
I filled[g] them, and they have committed adultery,
   and to the whorehouse they troop off.[h]
[8]*Well-fed, sex-mad,[i] big-balled[j] horses they were—*
   they neigh, each at his fellow's wife.
[9]*To these people[k] I should attend, shouldn't I (Yahweh's affirmation),*
   and on a nation that's like this
   my spirit should take redress, shouldn't it?[l]

a. LXX implies "(Yahweh's affirmation)" here.

b. See the translation note and commentary on 4:2.

c. The asyndetic sequence whereby v. 3a follows v. 2 and the word order suggest that v. 3 is subordinate to what precedes it.

d. The accent on the first syllable implies a form from *ḥûl*; Syr "were sick" implies an accent on the second syllable and a form from *ḥālâ* (Rashi, in MG; contrast Qimchi in MG).

e. *'Ălăkâ-lî*, the cohortative of *hālak* followed by a dative of advantage.

f. The verbs at either end (with complementary tenses) hold the parallel a-b-b'-a' bicolon together.

g. *Sworn* is *šābaʿ*; *filled* is *śābaʿ*: the words' similarity belies the contrast between human swearing and divine filling.

h. For *yitgōdādû*, LXX implies *yitgōrārû* (confusing *d* and *r*) from *gûr* ("lodge"); Vg, Syr assume HALOT's *gādad* I ("cut [themselves]") rather than *gādad* II ("band together").

i. I include both the *ketiv*, which implies *mûzānîm* from *zûn* (see BDB), and the *qere məyuzzānîm*, a *hapax legomenon* understood in light of LXX, Vg, Tg.

j. Explaining *maškîm* by *'ešek* ("testicle"; see Duhm, *Jeremia*, 59; BHS suggests *maʾăšikîm*). Cf. Vg "stud." Aq, Theod, Sym "dragging" implies *mōšəkîm*, a participle from *māšak* (HUBP). LXX omits.

k. Rather than "things"; see Holladay, *Commentary on Jeremiah*, 1:182.

l. MT has a section marker here.

Yahweh (by implication) commissions agents to investigate whether there are any faithful people in Jerusalem. There are none among the ordinary people, so Jeremiah goes off to investigate the important people and also finds none among them. That discovery explains the necessity for Yahweh to strike them down rather than pardon them. Jeremiah speaks as if one stage of striking down has happened but further action must follow.

v. 1	The commission (three bicola, the second and third linked by enjambment)
vv. 2–3	Jeremiah's initial response (four bicola, the first two linked by enjambment)
vv. 4–6	Jeremiah's report of his further discovery and reflection (eight bicola, the first four forming parallel linked pairs)
vv. 7–9	Yahweh's conclusion (two tricola framing two bicola)

1 Yahweh once again issues a commission to unidentified agents (cf. 4:5). To ask who they are may be a bit like asking where Cain got his wife from. But if we should seek to identify them, they will be his heavenly aides, like the two in Gen 18 who go to check things out in Sodom. There are overlaps between this section and that story; it might also remind listeners of Isa 1, which told Jerusalem it was only too like Sodom and also spoke in terms of acknowledging, authority, being truthful, rebellion, children, whoring, abandoning, moving away, aliens, consuming, striking down, and redress. The uncommon verb *go about* (*šûṭ*, here *polel*) fits a task like that of those other aides; it usually denotes a purposeful trek designed to find something or discover something (e.g, 2 Sam 24:2, 8; Job 1:7; 2:2).

Exercising authority and *seeking truthfulness* are the particular vocation of people with responsibility for justice in the city. In a village or an ordinary town, they would be the elders gathered at the gateway who sort matters out for the community, though in the big city it would be different. But the commission to look through the streets and in the squares implies that there are other levels at which authority is exercised and power is employed and thus where truthfulness matters. Heads of households exercise authority in families. Whereas 4:2 spoke of authority and faithfulness, Yahweh here speaks of authority and truthfulness, but it comes to the same thing. Nowhere in the city do the people with power operate in a way that respects truth. To understand this message as picturing Jeremiah as the naïve country boy who doesn't realize that things are as bad in Jerusalem as they are[218] is to allegorize it. The message is not about Jeremiah discovering something or engaging in reflection. It's a story to appeal to his people's imagination. It's not a story that anticipates the modern Western preoccupation with theodicy. Insofar as it is, it works with a different framework for approaching that question. While its implications overlap with Gen 18:22–33, it starts from a different assumption. When Yahweh has to reconcile the importance of taking waywardness seriously and of taking seriously his own commitment to the community and to his own purpose, then one way of doing so is to allow a remnant to survive, another is to let the entire community survive on the basis of the faithfulness of the few, but another is to let the entire community survive on the basis of the presence of just one person exercising authority with truthfulness. Yahweh is then not looking for just an ordinary individual but for someone like Moses, Aaron, Phinehas, or Samuel[219]—someone who is pushing the city to live in a way that matches his concern for faithfulness. If there is such a

218. Duhm, *Jeremia*, 57.
219. J. Mayer, *A Commentary upon All the Prophets Both Great and Small* (London: Millar and Cotes, 1652), 350.

person, then all is not lost. It opens up the possibility of *pardon*. Pardoning (*sālaḥ*) differs from forgiving (*nāśā'*). Forgiving means a person who has been wronged "carries" the consequences of the wrong action, declining to make the wrongdoer "carry" them. Pardoning means a person with authority stops treating a rebel or transgressor as a rebel or transgressor.

2–3a Because of the rhetorical nature of the commission, Jeremiah does not have to wait for the return of the investigatory body before pronouncing on the results of its research, like David in 2 Sam 24 or Yahweh in Job 1–2. A key factor in the maintaining of community life and the administration of justice is the people's honesty. It's not the whole of truthfulness, but it is an aspect of it. But community life, home life, trade, and decision-making processes are utterly screwed up by the willingness of people to lie and to take Yahweh's name in vain as they do so. They swear not merely with or by deception (e.g., 3:10; 5:31) but *to deception* (e.g., 3:23; 7:9). Foreigners may come to swear allegiance "to Yahweh" (e.g., Isa 19:18; 45:23); the Jerusalemites are people who have moved their allegiance in the opposite direction even though they go through the motions of swearing by Yahweh's name. "The people mouth proper confessional statements . . . but this God-language is full of pretense."[220] It's really addressed to non-gods. Jeremiah knows that what he has seen is gravely offensive to Yahweh; his eyes look for a commitment to *truthfulness*, for statements that correspond with reality and to the God whose being corresponds with reality (the antonyms of *deception* are words such as "truth," "truthfulness," and "faithfulness").[221]

3b–c Jeremiah's awareness of the investigation generates a further revelation (or the awareness expressed in his parable has another facet). There's nothing new about the facts that he has described, and Yahweh knows all about them. He has already acted in light of them. The city has experienced the results. Yahweh has *struck them down* (cf. 2:30). In light of the movement between past tenses and explicit statements of future intent in this chapter, I take these past tense verbs to refer to something that has actually happened, not to something Jeremiah has simply seen in a vision. If one should look for a historical event not long before 604 to which Jeremiah might be referring, then the defeat by Egypt that brought Josiah's death in 609 would qualify. Yahweh has *made an end of them*, notwithstanding 4:27; this reference to an end indicates particularly clearly that Jeremiah speaks hyperbolically (making an end of them is still a threat in 9:16[15]). But they *refused to accept restraint*, like an ox throwing off the reins that held it to the yoke (2:19–20, 30; see the translation notes and commentary there). They were quite prepared to tough it out. They *refused* (cf. 3:3) *to turn back*. That comment also makes

220. Fretheim, *Jeremiah*, 109.
221. *DCH*, 8:559.

the hyperbole clear;[222] if he had brought the community to an actual end, the question would not arise, and Jeremiah would not be preaching this sermon. (Amos 4:6–11 is a more detailed hyperbolic comment on chastisement failing to make people "turn back.")

4 The people whom the investigatory commission would have found in the city's streets and squares would be the ordinary people, "merchants, craftsmen, porters, and so on,"[223] and the people patronizing them. In their everyday life, they operate in a way that nominally recognizes Yahweh but in reality leaves Yahweh out of account. They *show themselves stupid* and *they do not acknowledge Yahweh's way, the authority of their God*, perhaps both in the way they conduct their lives and in the way they don't recognize what Yahweh is doing with them. In his comment, Jeremiah risks looking elitist, but he is operating rhetorically (see the commentary on 1:15). He'll let the more important people nod at the feckless proletariat, then he'll put the boot in. He is speaking dramatically, and he is on his way to the indictment that follows.

5 Whichever form of stupidity he means, he himself will go to do his own investigation of *the big people*, not just the little people. *They acknowledge Yahweh's way*, don't they? Actually, they too have *broken the yoke, snapped the restraints*—Jeremiah more systematically reuses the terminology of 2:19–20, 30 (see the translation notes and commentary there). If anything, "the teachers were worse than the students."[224]

6 So it is their fecklessness that explains the chastisements v. 3 refers to, which Jeremiah now describes more vividly and metaphorically—and with further hyperbole. Ethics are intrinsic to leadership, and ethical failure on the part of leaders means disaster.[225] Jeremiah combines *qatal*, *yiqtol*, and participle, which fits with the implication in v. 3 that some assaults have already come but forbids any hope that they are now over. In light of later developments in visions such as Daniel's—developments that have a background in schemes not so distant chronologically from Jeremiah—the lion, the wolf, and the leopard come to signify Babylon, Persia, and Greece.[226] People think the towns are safe, but Jeremiah again reminds them that things will not work out that way (cf. 4:5–7, 16). The verse closes with a final twist on "turning." Jerusalemites will not turn back (v. 3); they are too set on their *turnings*—the word earlier used to describe "Turning Israel" (3:6, 8, 11, 12).

---

222. McKane, *Jeremiah*, 1:116.

223. Rudolph, *Jeremia*, 37.

224. Jerome, *Jeremiah*, 34.

225. See W. J. Wessels, "Calling Leaders to Account: A Dialogue with Jeremiah 5:1–9," *OTE* 8 (2015): 874–93.

226. E.g., Rashi, in MG; Tg takes them as king, nation, and officer.

7 Jeremiah moves on from "can Yahweh pardon?" (v. 1) to "why should he pardon?"[227] The *this* refers to the indictment that will follow in vv. 7–8, and the address in the feminine singular is a reminder that Yahweh has really been speaking to the city of Jerusalem all along. In addressing her, he excludes the possibility of *pardon*. Here, the basis for that judgment is expressed in the more familiar terms: that her *children* (cf. 2:30) *have abandoned* Yahweh (1:16; 2:13, 17) and *sworn by non-gods* (2:11), which is what v. 2 implied. Yahweh provided them with all the food they needed and more—he *filled them*. Their response: *they have committed adultery* in going after those other so-called gods (3:8–9). It was odd as well as ungrateful, given that Yahweh had shown that he was the one who could fill them. But *to the whorehouse they troop off.*

8 Jeremiah develops the metaphor in more systematically explicit fashion than in 2:20. While he will (probably) refer later to literal adultery (7:9), the context here indicates that his graphic account refers allegorically to people's (specifically, men's) unfaithfulness to Yahweh; he focuses on "theological prostitution not on prostitution *per se*."[228] He can picture infidelity in female or in male terms.[229] Perhaps the men are upstanding members of the community, not people who would think of being unfaithful to their wives or visiting the whorehouse or who would like being compared to horses. Their being *well-fed* would make a link with v. 7b and add to the critique. If the audience knew that (apparently) horses have a strong sex-drive and reproductive instinct but are quite loyal, it would add to the effectiveness of the metaphor.[230]

9 *These people* and *this* tie off vv. 7–9 as *this* opened these four lines, and the questions form the converse of the opening question in v. 7.[231] The tricolon brings the section to a close; the second and third cola together expand on the first:

To	these people	I should attend,	shouldn't I?
On	a nation that's like this	my spirit should take redress,	shouldn't it?

Attend to (*pāqad*) is a suggestive First Testament verb whose negative or positive connotations emerge from its context. Here in the parallelism, *take redress* (*nāqam hithpael*) spells out its implications. Translations of this second verb such as "take revenge" give a misleading impression of emotional

---

227. Cf. Weiser, *Jeremia*, 1:50, 52.
228. Holladay, *Commentary on Jeremiah*, 1:180.
229. Fretheim, *Jeremiah*, 110.
230. Foreman, *Animal Metaphors*, 119.
231. Brueggemann, *Jeremiah 1–25*, 61.

overreaction, while translations such as "punish" give a misleading impression of cool objectiveness. *Redress* suggests an appropriate recompense that recognizes wrongdoing, yet one that is enacted by the person who has been wronged. Including the word *spirit* (*nepeš*) and using the *hithpael* underlines the involvement of Yahweh's emotions in taking action against his own people, who have been unfaithful. "The LORD can . . . breathe easily when justice has been achieved."[232] He chastises for the people's sake (v. 3) and for his own sake. He indeed declares that "vengeance is mine, I myself will repay" (Rom 12:19; cf. Deut 32:35). He is not a God who is simply a cool detached observer in accordance with the ideal we might have for a judge. He is more like a father whose position and relationship with his children require him to combine fairness with relationship and justice with commitment and to work with the tension between the two.

2. *The Foreign Service (5:10–19)*

[10]*Go up among her terraces*[a] *and devastate,*
  but do not make an end.
Remove her tendrils,
  because they do not belong to Yahweh.
[11]*Because they have been false, been false*[b] *to me,*
  the household of Israel and the household of Judah (Yahweh's
        affirmation).
[12]*They have duped Yahweh,*
  but they have said, "Not him!—
Dire trouble will not come upon us,
  sword and hunger we will not see.
[13]*The prophets—they will become wind,*
  what has been spoken[c]*—it's not in them;*
  this is what will be done to them."[d]

[14]*Therefore, Yahweh, the God of Armies, has said this (because you*[e] *have spoken this thing):*

Here am I, putting my words in your[f] *mouth as fire;*
  this people are trees, and it will consume them.
[15]*Here am I, causing a nation from far away to come against you,*[g]
  Israel's household (Yahweh's affirmation).
It's an enduring nation,

---

232. D. R. Jones, *Jeremiah*, 122.

it's a nation from of old,
A nation whose language you won't know,
*   so you won't hear what it speaks.*
[16] *Its quiver is like a grave opened up;*
*   all of them are strong men.*
[17] *It will consume your harvest and your bread,*
*   they will consume your sons and your daughters.*
It will consume your flock and your herd,
*   it will consume your vine and your fig.*
It will pulverize your fortified towns,
*   on which you are reliant, with the sword.*
[18] *But even in those days (Yahweh's affirmation),*
*   I will not make an end of you.*

[19] *And when you say, "On what account did Yahweh our God do all these things to us":*

You[h] will say to them,

"As you abandoned me,
*   and served alien gods in your country,*
So you will serve foreigners
*   in a country that is not yours."[i]*

a. *Šārâ* comes only here, though it resembles and overlaps in meaning with words such as *šûr* and *šûrâ*; see *HALOT*, 1453–54, 1653.

b. The infinitive precedes the finite verb, underlining the factuality of the action.

c. The noun *dibbēr*, which comes only here in the First Testament, denotes the word of God in Postbiblical Hebrew (R. C. Steiner, "A Colloquialism in Jer. 5:13," *JSS* 37 [1992]: 11–26).

d. Lit. "thus it will be done to them." MT has a section marker here.

e. This *you* is plural.

f. This *your* is singular.

g. This *you* is plural.

h. This *you* is singular.

i. MT has a marker here.

The section again begins with a command to take disciplinary action in light of the falsehood of Ephraim and Judah, continues with words to Jeremiah that spell out the implications of the action, reassures the listeners that it will not be the end, and adds a rationale implying that the punishment will fit the crime. Once again, the section juxtaposes several subsections that might well be of separate origin.

vv. 10–13 A commission (by implication Yahweh's) of some hard
pruning (three bicola, two linked bicola, and a tricolon
closing the subsection)

vv. 14–18 Yahweh's announcement that he is putting devastating
words in Jeremiah's mouth (an introduction and nine bicola, two linked)

v. 19 An explanation (a double introduction and two linked
bicola)

10 Yahweh gives another commission, paralleling the one in v. 1. He is again
not speaking to Jeremiah but (if it is proper to attempt to identify them) to
unspecified aides, who now have a destructive job to do (cf. Ezek 9): *Go up
among her terraces and devastate*. While in origin the message that begins
here may have been independent of what precedes, it has been appended
to vv. 1–9 in a way that makes this commission the working out of Yahweh's
determination expressed in v. 9; the antecedent to *her* is the Jerusalem of vv.
1–9. Yahweh speaks of Jerusalem as if it were a vineyard whose vines have
trailing tendrils. One should not ask what the tendrils specifically represent;
it's not an allegory. Isaiah 5:1–7 speaks of Israel as a vineyard that Yahweh intends to destroy, though Isaiah's statements on other occasions warn against
taking that threat too literally. But sometimes, for one reason or another,
vines do have to be uprooted and the vinedresser has to start again (cf. 1:10),
and here, *devastate* might make one think in such terms. Yet immediately
there follows the proviso that came in 4:27: *But do not make an end*. Although
the proviso might have been added to a more radical commission to qualify it
and make it less devastating (v. 10 would then work as a tricolon), the further
instruction to *remove her tendrils* likely has the same implications as the proviso; the aides are not told to uproot the vine. One might compare Paul's talk
of the savage lopping of a vine in Rom 9–11. The reason for the devastation
is that these tendrils *do not belong to Yahweh*. That is, he disowns them.

11 The further reason is that Ephraim and Judah *have been false* to Yahweh in the way Jer 3 has expounded. The order of words, with the subjects
held back until the second colon, corresponds to the regular Hebrew order
whereby the subject follows the verb, yet it is an extreme example of this
order, and it raises a little suspense, especially for Judahites who may think
they will be let off the hook in disfavor of those pesky northerners but who
then find themselves appearing at the end of the line, followed by a *Yahweh's
affirmation* in case there was any doubt. It's happened to Ephraim and it will
happen to Judah.[233]

---

233. Weiser, *Jeremia*, 47.

12 In being totally false, they have *duped* Yahweh or disappointed him (*kāḥaš*), as a vine or an olive tree may disappoint its owner when it produces no fruit—a connotation that fits because v. 12 follows on v. 10. They are also duping themselves in that they are saying, "He wouldn't do that kind of thing." *Not him* thus refers back to the commission in v. 10, but its connotations are spelled out in the second line—the standard piece of self-delusion and false self-reassurance that Jeremiah is continually having to deal with. "People say, 'Yah doesn't look, the God of Jacob doesn't pay attention" (Ps 94:7).[234] It is expressed in neat parallelism and paronomasia:

will not come	upon us		dire trouble (*rā'â*)
	sword and hunger (*ḥereb, rā'āb*)		we will not see (*nir'eh*)

Dire trouble and *sword and hunger* thus link, as do *dire trouble* and *see*, while the verbs hold the entire line together. The people's words unconsciously convey the integral and inescapable unity of what they try to deny. The first colon exactly corresponds to Mic 3:11, where Micah quotes the other prophets in a verse that immediately precedes the declaration that will be taken up in Jer 26:18. *Sword and hunger* give specificity to *dire trouble* in a way characteristic of Jeremiah (e.g., 14:13, 15, 16; 16:4) and also of Ezekiel. Both prophets often add epidemic (e.g., Jer 14:12; 21:7). It is a horribly realistic analysis, as sword, hunger, and epidemic are the great killers in warfare.

13 The self-delusion depends upon dismissing warnings they are given. Plural *prophets* commonly refers to prophets who tell people things will be fine (cf. 4:9; 5:31). Here more likely Jeremiah continues to quote the people, who are therefore referring to prophets such as Jeremiah (cf. 2:30; 7:25); he is maybe less isolated than we may sometimes infer. This understanding will also be implied by v. 14 when it refers back to vv. 12–13. The Jerusalemites dismiss such prophets as mere *wind*: they may have claimed to be people possessed by *rûaḥ*, but the ambiguity of that word can be used against them. There's nothing in *what has been spoken*, no real message from Yahweh *in them*. The warnings they issue when they declare, "Yahweh has said this"—threats such as are mentioned in vv. 10 and 12—are what *will be done to them*. It's the sort of thing Jeremiah says about the false prophets, which we now hear is what people are saying about prophets like him. The implication is that the people will pay a price. The third colon in the tricolon closes off their words and closes off what may have originally been a self-contained message.

14 Once more, vv. 14–17 or 14–18 may be an originally separate message, but by means of the *because* clause the introduction now links it with what

---

234. Blayney, *Jeremiah*, 249.

precedes: *this thing* is what was said in vv. 12–13, and the plural *you* is the people
as they were speaking then. But in speaking of *your mouth*, Yahweh addresses
Jeremiah in a way that recalls his commission (1:9). There, it was a speech act;
one could have translated Yahweh's words, "I hereby put . . ." Here, it is a declaration of intent; one could translate Yahweh's words as, "I'm going to put."
More chillingly, Yahweh adds to the earlier formulation an indication of what
the *words* are going to do, which is in keeping with the commission (to pull
up, pull down, wipe out, smash) but more specific. *Fire* is a standard image for
God-implemented disaster in the Prophets (e.g., 4:4; 17:4); archaeological investigations reveal how fire was commonly the destroyer of towns, whether by
accident or through enemy action (cf. 17:27). But only Jeremiah speaks of his
own words as the means of igniting Yahweh's destructive fire (cf. 20:9; 23:29).
They are themselves a speech act. God said "Light!" and there was light (Gen
1:3). Jeremiah will say "Fire!" and there will be fire. The fuel is *this people*, who
are thus *trees* (it's a forest fire), and *it will consume them.*

15 Yahweh goes on to interpret his allegory. When he originally put his
words in Jeremiah's mouth, they concerned nations and kingdoms, and one
could ask whether the agents that were given a charge just now in v. 10 are
the human armies that will do the job. Here, Jeremiah is to be the means
of summoning *a nation from far away to come against you. You* is now again
Israel's household (which in this context means Judah). This is no fly-by-night
nation, like some that Yahweh could mention; *enduring* is the word to describe a stream or river that flows reliably all year as opposed to a wadi that
flows only from time to time, when it rains somewhere else. This nation
is also *from of old,*[235] not some Johnny-come-lately entity that may fade as
quickly as it arises; Israel can't say, "Don't worry, it will soon disappear." In
keeping with its coming from far away, it is *a nation whose language you won't
know, so you won't hear what it speaks.* When an overlord gives you orders
and you can't understand them, what are you to do (see Deut 28:49–53)? It
will be worse than it was with Assyria (see Isa 37:11).

16 Nor is that fact the most disturbing thing about this nation. It has an
insatiable appetite for killing, and its men are capable of doing their job. The
simile of the quiver involves a transferred epithet or catachresis: it is the
arrows in the quiver that bring death.

17 When an ancient army goes on an expedition, it doesn't worry too
much about supply lines. It just eats what has been grown, bred, and nur-

---

235. The two expressions *enduring* and *from of old* recur in Bernadino de Sahagún's description of the fate of Latin American peoples at the hands of the conquistadores (see
Y. Sherwood, "Prophetic 'Postcolonialism': Performing the Disaster of the Spanish Conquest on the Stage of Jeremiah," in *Congress Volume Munich 2013*, ed. C. M. Maier, VTSup
163 (Leiden: Brill, 2014), 327.

tured by the people it invades. The army also kills the boys who fight and rapes the girls who don't. It's not put off by *the fortified towns on which you are reliant*, where Yahweh himself ironically told the people to take refuge (4:5). After *consume . . . consume . . . consume . . . consume*, the ordinary word for "eat" here used both literally and metaphorically and suggesting that "the enemy will eat without stopping,"[236] Yahweh brings his threat to a climax with an unordinary word: *pulverize* (*rāšaš*—it otherwise comes only in Mal 1:4). He finally underscores the awfulness by means of the last word in the three lines, *with the sword*, which reaffirms that he is not talking merely about the demolition of buildings but about the slaughtering of people—the people who are listening to Jeremiah's message. (Tg expands on Jeremiah's word by speaking of "the fortified cities of your land on which you rely to be saved from before those who kill with the sword.")

18 In isolation, that message would raise familiar questions. First, "What is this nation?" As usual, it is not a question Yahweh is interested in clarifying, though in the light of subsequent events, there is no doubt it is Babylon. Maybe it was obvious to Jeremiah and his audience, as it was certainly obvious by the time any version of the scroll came into being. Second, "Is he talking about total annihilation?" Again, in the light of subsequent events, the answer would be obvious, and the incorporation of *I will not make an end of you* would affirm the nature of Yahweh's intention from the beginning. At the same time, it would not be surprising if Yahweh wanted to reassure Jeremiah and people like Baruch about the nature of that intention and thus that these words of reassurance go back to them. In this chapter, the promise not to make an end of them (the noun *kālâ*) is set in the context of the claim already to have done so (the verb *kālâ piel*, v. 3). Indeed, if this line is a later addition to the message in vv. 10–17,[237] it functions to complete a neat frame, with v. 10, around the section. Either way, "no shadow of ambivalence or uncertainty betrays the Lord's fierce ability to do both things at once: passionately to rage against this way of life that must come to an end and in the same instant passionately to refuse to allow the story to come to this sort of an ending."[238]

19 The third familiar question is, "Why?" As was the case in v. 14, the movement between *you* plural, *you* singular, and *they* is confusing, especially in English where we cannot distinguish between *you* plural and *you* singular. Here, the imagined perspective is explicitly that of people living on the other side of the disaster. In the context rhetorically implied by the chapter, the message presses Jeremiah's hearers in (say) 604 to think of themselves in that

236. Lundbom, *Jeremiah 1–20*, 394.
237. E.g., Volz, *Jeremia*, 65.
238. P. J. Willson, "Jeremiah 5:20–29," *Int* 62 (2008): 72.

later situation asking the question to which they need to hear the answer now in their 604 context and respond to it, to obviate the necessity to ask it and hear it in the future. The answer to the question ought to be obvious, but the need to articulate it never disappears, and Jeremiah articulates it in a way that incorporates a new element. The initial explanation lies in *you abandoned me*, the declaration that again goes back to Jeremiah's commission (1:16; cf. 2:13, 17, 19; 5:7). Here, Yahweh accompanies it with the reminder that *you . . . served alien gods in your country*; it is the scroll's first reference to "serving" other gods. In 3:13, they were "foreigners" (*zârîm*); Jerusalem herself had then become an "alien" woman (*nokriyyâ*) in 2:21. Yahweh now adds that the punishment will suit the crime. *You will serve foreigners in a country that is not yours.* Foreigners were gods in 3:13, will be people in 30:8, and in 2:25 could be either, so they could be either here.[239] It's also the scroll's first reference to exile (at least since 1:3). The theme will grow in prominence as the scroll unrolls and as time goes by (e.g., 7:15; 9:16[15]; 15:2, 14; 16:13; 17:4).

3. *The Way People Became Big and Wealthy (5:20–31)*

20Announce this in Jacob's household;
   make it heard in Judah:
21Hear this, please, foolish people
   that has no mind,
Who have eyes but don't look,
   who have ears but don't listen.
22Of me are you not in awe (Yahweh's affirmation),
   or before me do you not writhe,
I who set sand as the sea's boundary,
   a decree for all time, that it cannot cross over?
They heave but they cannot win—
   its heaps roar, but they cannot cross over it.
23But this people—
   it had a determined and rebellious mind;
   they were defiant^a and they went.

24So they did not say in their mind,
   "Let us please be in awe of Yahweh our God,
Who gives rain, early rain^b and late rain in its time,

---

239. Isaac Abravanel (*Commentary on the Latter Prophets*) nicely comments that serving foreign gods is, after all, entirely appropriate in a foreign country whereas it is horribly inappropriate in the holy land.

while the weeks decreed for harvest[c] he keeps for us."
[25]*Your wayward acts—they have diverted these things,*
your wrongdoings—they have withheld what is good from you.
[26]*Because faithless people were to be found within my people;*
one watches, like bird catchers crouching.[d]
They have set up a devastator,[e]
so they may catch—human beings.[f]
[27]*Like a cage full of birds,*
thus their houses are full of duplicity.[g]
That is how they've become big and wealthy—
[28]*they've become fat, become stout.*[h]
Yes, they have passed over[i] *dire actions—*
they have not decided a case,
The case of a fatherless person—so they might make it succeed,[j]
and for the case of the needy they have not made decisions.
[29]*To these people I should attend, shouldn't I (Yahweh's affirmation),*
and on a nation that's like this
my spirit should take redress, shouldn't it?[k]

[30]*A desolating, horrific thing*[l]*—*
it has happened in the country.
[31]*The prophets—they have prophesied by deception,*[m]
the priests—they rule in accordance with their direction.[n]
And my people—they love it so;
but what will you do at the end of it?

a. *Determined* in the previous colon was *sôrēr*, and *were defiant* is *sārû*: the words' similarity matches the link in what they refer to (Allen, *Jeremiah*, 80–81).

b. For the *qere yôreh*, the *ketiv* implies *wəyōreh*, with the *waw* presumably meaning "both" (the line hardly distinguishes three forms of rain).

c. Lit. "weeks of decrees of harvest."

d. Lit. "like the crouching of bird catchers," though it is the only occurrence with this meaning of the rare verb *śākak* (see BDB; *DCH*). Syr suggests a word from *śākak/sākak*, which could mean a screen, a thicket, or a covert (HUBP).

e. Vg has "trap," but there are no parallels for this more concrete meaning; LXX has the verb *diaphtheirai* ("devastate").

f. The asyndetic verb (with the object before the verb), subordinate to the one that precedes it, suggests a purpose clause.

g. A metonymy for the fruits of duplicity.

h. For the *hapax legomenon* '*āšat*, BDB notes possible links with '*ešet* or '*āšût*; on the basis of the context, Rashi (MG) goes in the first direction (cf. Rudolph, *Jeremia*, 40); Qimchi (MG) rather takes it to mean "sleek" (cf. *DCH*, 6:623–24).

i. For this meaning of '*ābar*, see BDB, 717.

j. I treat *dîn yātôm* as an extraposed phrase followed by the simple *waw* on *wəyaṣlîḥû*, suggesting purpose; see Craigie, Kelley, and Drinkard, *Jeremiah 1–25*, 94–95.

k. MT has a section marker here.
l. Lit. "a desolation and a horror."
m. I.e., by the Master (Rudolph, *Jeremia*, 32).
n. Lit. "on their hands"; cf. 1 Chr 25:2, 3, 6.

The chapter's third section once more comprises two or three subsections that might be of independent origin. It, too, begins with an imperative, here aiming to urge Israel to start taking notice of Yahweh. It implicitly details the background to that need: Israel will not learn the lesson from hurts it has experienced. The background again lies in the lack of faithful exercise of authority in the community, which facilitates the well-off becoming more well-off. Jeremiah adds the critique that spiritual leaders and people are in collusion in this connection.

vv. 20–23   A charge (by implication Yahweh's) of agents to confront Israel about its heedlessness (six bicola, with the middle four in linked pairs, and a tricolon suggesting a pause)

vv. 24–29   Yahweh's reflection on the people's failure in love for God and for neighbor (two pairs of bicola enclosing five bicola, followed by a closing tricolon)

vv. 30–31   Yahweh's further horrified reflection on prophets, priests, and people (three bicola)

20 Once more, Yahweh starts with a (plural) commission and a message that warns of redress but focuses on wrongdoing. Perhaps one should once more assume that the notional addressees are Yahweh's aides, though it is obvious here that, rhetorically, Jeremiah's point is that his audience needs to see itself on the receiving end of a message that has been commissioned. *Jacob's household* is now *Judah*.

21 The anonymous proclaimers are thus to address this audience with a "lecture of Yahweh the schoolmaster to his refractory people."[240] The audience is still spoken of in the third person; they are "overhearing" the message that the proclaimers are commissioned to give them. It is a snide message, with its *please* combined with its imperative *hear*: "hear this, please" is usually hostile and threatening.[241] The cutting tone continues in its characterization of this people as one *that has no sense* (no mind, *lēb*) and in its vocative *foolish people*, which combines nicely with "stupid" in v. 4 (both words came together in 4:22). They are supposed to be rational, but they are irrational, he might have added.[242] Yahweh maintains the same tone in the description

240. Holladay, *Commentary on Jeremiah*, 1:195.
241. Holladay, *Commentary on Jeremiah*, 1:195.
242. Theodoret, *Ermeneia*, PG 81:540.

that continues: they *have eyes but don't look, have ears but don't listen.* The expression reappears in other prophets (Isa 43:8; Ezek 12:2), and elsewhere it is tellingly applied to the gods that attract the Judahites. The wording is the same or almost the same in Pss 115:5b–6a; 135:16b–17a. Jeremiah might also say that the people he confronts embody a fulfillment of the two psalms' further comment that people who revere the images that have these qualities become like them.[243] The seeing and hearing may have as their object the news about international political developments that were pointing in only one possible direction in 604, or Jeremiah may be referring to the things people can see and hear in the city, of which he will say more in vv. 26–31.

22 What follows makes that second understanding more likely, though a little inference is required. People who did not perceive the city's religious and societal waywardness showed they were *not in awe* of Yahweh. That verb is quite a usual one for a proper submission to Yahweh, but here Yahweh distinctively adds that they do *not writhe* (ḥûl, tellingly the verb in 4:19, 31; 5:3). In the parallelism:

| Are you | of me | not | in awe? | (Yahweh's affirmation.) |
| Or do you | before me | not | writhe? | |

They ought to be squirming or torturing themselves in light of who Yahweh is: the one who keeps the potential disorderly forces of creation under control. Notwithstanding their lack of great proximity to the sea, the Israelites were keen on the idea that Yahweh had set a *boundary* to it by his *decree* (ḥōq) so that it could not overwhelm the earth (Ps 104:9; Prov 8:29). Its waves can *heave* and *roar*, but *they cannot cross over* the bound God set for them, the bound here defined by the *sand* at the water's edge. Nearly all the First Testament references to sand make it an image for great numbers or quantities. Only here is it a barrier for the sea, but it makes for a paronomasia, since there is a link between not writhing (ḥûl) and not recognizing the blessing that the sand is (ḥôl).

23 The one who set bounds for *the sea* (yam) that it may not *cross over* also set bounds for *this people* ('am) that they may not cross over—but they have.[244] Yahweh repeats some standard charges (cf. vv. 11, 14). The people is *determined* in its *mind* (3:17) and *rebellious* (4:17). It is the description of a son who deserves death in Deut 21:18–20: so what does a people with a determined and rebellious mind deserve?[245] Further, individually *they were defiant* (sûr; more literally, "they moved away") and *they went* (after other deities). It is an abrupt, curt close to the tricolon.

---

243. Calvin, *Jeremiah*, 1:310–11.
244. N. R. Bowen, "Out of Bounds," *Brethren Life and Thought* 57 (2012): 17–18.
245. Holladay, *Commentary on Jeremiah*, 1:197.

24 Yahweh takes the comment on the people's *mind* further—now not on what characterized it (determination and rebelliousness) but on what they *did not say* within it, within themselves. The cutting divine "please" of v. 21 is not matched by a *please* of their own that might take them into the *awe* of which v. 22 spoke, which is here linked with a different aspect of divine provision. The importance of rain is underscored by the three words Jeremiah has the people using, only the last of which corresponds to the "rains and late rain" of 3:3. Here there is reference to *rain* in general, then to the *early rain* and the *late rain*. It is also important that rain comes *in its time* and thus ensures that *the weeks decreed for harvest* unfold. As there is a decree applying to the sea that keeps it under control (v. 22), there are decrees (*ḥuqqôt*) applying to the seasons, particularly in connection with the growth of crops, that ensure that the seasons work out according to schedule—for example, during the seven weeks that take the wheat crop to maturity between Pesach (Passover) and Shavuot (Pentecost). The tricolon encourages a moment's pause.

25 But the message belongs to one of the years when things have not worked out this way (cf. 36:9; again see 3:3). Once more, Yahweh repeats a standard charge and gives a standard explanation expressed in a neat parallelism that corresponds to the straightforward reasoning and puts the key words up front:

your	wayward acts	have diverted	these things	
your	wrongdoings	have withheld	what is good	from you

There is an extra kick in the supernumerary *from you* at the end.

26 Jeremiah goes on to spell out what the waywardness and wrongdoing consist in. Usually, he focuses on wrongdoing in relation to Yahweh, in religion and politics; here he talks about abuse within the community, as he did in vv. 1–2. Different prophets focus on different things; it's impossible to know why they should, but it is noteworthy that the Prophets (like the Torah) do show a concern with both questions about religion and questions about society. Readers of the Scriptures can thus be confronted by things that they are not inclined to focus on. Once more, the difference in the form of expression in these verses may indicate that they belong to an element of separate origin, with a *because* added now to make the link. The verses provide a neat instance of its being hard to say who is the speaker or who is the addressee, though it's clear that the Judahites are the subject. One might think that Jeremiah speaks; but by v. 29 it is Yahweh, so the addressee might be Jeremiah. It matters little, given that at another level the words are both Yahweh's and Jeremiah's, and the addressees are—the Judahites. *Faithless people* (*rəšāʿîm*) are the opposite of faithful people (*ṣaddîqîm*); they are people who ignore the obligations of community and the commitment they owe God and one another. They are *to be found* within the community, whereas an individual exercising authority and seeking truthfulness could not be found (v. 1). The nature of their faithlessness is spelled out in the rest of vv. 26–28 as the passage moves from metaphor to literal description. Jeremiah's opening comment is that the people itself simply *watches* what is going on. For a straightforward, literal understanding of what follows, one might read vv. 26–28 in reverse order, but Jeremiah's rhetoric presupposes that people know the literal; what they need is metaphors to help them understand what they are doing and to recognize its enormity. So first, he invites them to think about *bird catchers crouching* to go about capturing their victims. One of them *watches*, being *set up* as *a devastator* who will ultimately be the death of his prey. The company set that trapper to *catch human beings*.[246]

27–28a Then imagine *a cage full of birds*, whom the bird catcher has caught and is keeping until he sells them or until he has fattened them up (Tg), until the moment for killing and eating arrives. Set alongside that picture the image of the bird catchers' *houses*, which are also full—of things that they possess through the *duplicity* that hunters necessarily practice in order to catch birds. It has enabled them to become the *big* and *wealthy* people they are in the community, *fat* and *stout*.

28b–29 How did the catching of men and the accumulation of things happen? The faithless people had *passed over*, turned a blind eye to, *dire actions* or dire words when a case came for consideration by the body that decides things—the elders in the village, or whatever was the more structured arrangement in Jerusalem. *They have not decided a case* in the proper way. A loser in a case of this kind might be someone whose father, the head of the household, has died and who is trying to get possession of the family estate but is being denied it by shady legal means. It would be the responsibility of the big people, the people with power and influence, to see that *the case of the fatherless* gets decided in his favor, that the case can thus *succeed*. But they don't. More generally, *for the case of the needy they have not made decisions*. The needy might be people who have gotten into economic difficulty and had to use their property as collateral; their creditor now insists on taking possession of it. Fatherless and needy are people that the big and the powerful have been able to "catch" so as to find ways of filling their own houses with their possessions. The problem is equivalent to the Western one whereby "it is much easier for prosperous people to acquire the best legal representation, something the poor and the orphaned cannot afford."[247] Yahweh's closing rhetorical question (repeated from v. 9) requires no answer.

246. On bird hunting and catching, see Foreman, *Animal Metaphors*, 202–11.
247. W. J. Wessels, "Prophet, Poetry and Ethics: A Study of Jeremiah 5:26–29," *OTE* 21 (2008): 741.

30 Once again, there is a transition of agenda in another subsection that may have been separate originally, though once more it reformulates a familiar agenda. Something *desolating . . . has happened in the country.* One would initially assume that Jeremiah is talking again about the desolation he has seen in his mind's eye (2:15; 4:7). But the only other reference to a *horrific thing* (*ša'ărûr*) relates to the behavior of the prophets (23:14), though Judah itself is also called *ša'ărûrî* in 18:13, and the rotten figs are called *šō'ār* in 29:17.[248] The *horrific thing* is the thing he is about to describe.

31 *The prophets—they have prophesied by deception.* They are not consciously trying to deceive people. They are entirely sincere. But there is no correspondence between what they say and what Yahweh thinks and intends, because of the direction in which they are looking for their guidance. Whether they are conscious of looking in that direction or not, they are relying on deities that by their nature can only deceive. Then there are *the priests.* Usually, Jeremiah simply lumps prophets and priests together as equally reprehensible (e.g., 6:13–15; 26:7–11), but here he makes a distinctive comment on their interrelationship. The priest's job is to *rule* when someone comes to ask for guidance (e.g., Does this symptom count as skin disease [leprosy]? I did this wrong thing; can I still come to worship?). Jeremiah says the priests are following the alleged divine revelations of prophets (e.g., 27:16; 29:24–32).[249] They are giving rulings on the wrong basis—following the direction of those misguided prophets (instead of giving a lead as guardians of the Torah?). The priests going astray "ought to be carefully noticed, that we may not at this day be too much disturbed when we see the pastoral office assumed by ignorant asses."[250] *And my people—they love it so.* In the usual fashion, there is collusion between congregation and pastor. The pastor says things people want to hear; the people pay his salary. But it works only in the short term, only until there is a crisis. So *what will you do at the end of it?* The last colon indicates that the people are being indirectly addressed and accused in the previous four.[251]

E. MOSTLY (FINAL) WARNING (6:1–30)

The question "What will you do at the end of it?" (5:31) could have served nicely as a conclusion to the 604 scroll, but it is Jer 6 that brings the Jeremiah scroll's opening chapters to a climax. They look back over where we have been, tighten the screw further on the argument, and conclude the night-

---

248. R. P. Carroll, *Jeremiah*, OTL, 190.
249. Lundbom, *Jeremiah 1–20*, 410.
250. Calvin, *Jeremiah*, 3:402.
251. Holladay, *Commentary on Jeremiah*, 1:200.

mare vision in the collection of messages with a "massive announcement of disaster."[252] It is a paradigm "horror text."[253]

vv. 1–8	In a frightening ironic revisiting of 4:5–9, Yahweh declares that fleeing to Jerusalem will not work: it is necessary to flee *from* Jerusalem
vv. 9–15	Yahweh commissions the stripping even of the remains of the vine; his wrath will pour out indiscriminately
vv. 16–21	Yahweh declares that the people's worship is unacceptable and that he will trip them up
vv. 22–26	Yahweh pictures the coming of the northern invader as a horrifying reality
vv. 27–30	Yahweh engages in a chilling retrospective on the fulfilling of Jeremiah's commission in 1:18

After the first section, each section begins with a form of the declaration "Yahweh has said this." Each section majors on announcing the disaster but also includes some account of the reasons for it and a little explicit or implicit exhortation to respond. I follow MT's section divisions except for seeing v. 27 as making an additional new start, notwithstanding the lack of any such declaration there.

1. Sanctify a Battle (6:1–8)

[1]*Make safe,*[a] *Benjaminites,*[b]
   from inside[c] *Jerusalem!*
In Tekoa blast the horn,[d]
   over Beth Hakkerem raise a beacon!
Because dire trouble—it has peered out from the north,
   a great shattering.
[2]*The lovely pasture,*[e] *the daintily bred:*
   I am quashing[f] *Miss Zion.*[g]
[3]*To her come shepherds and their flocks—*
   they have pitched[h] *tents against her all around—*
   they have shepherded each one his hand.[i]

[4]*"Sanctify*[j] *battle against her,*
   set to, let's go up at noon."

252. Allen, *Jeremiah*, 84.
253. Kalmanofsky, *Terror All Around*, 104.

"Alas for us, because the day has turned,
because the evening shadows decline."
5*"Set to, let's go up in the night,*
and devastate her citadels!"[k]

6*Because Yahweh of Armies has said this:*

Cut her wood,[l]
pour a ramp against Jerusalem!
She is the city all of which has been handed over[m]*—*
fraud is in her midst.
7*Like a well*[n] *keeping its water cool,*[o]
so it keeps its dire behavior cool.
Violence and destruction[p] *makes itself heard in her—*
before my face continually are sickness and wound.[q]

8*Accept restraint, Jerusalem,*
so that my spirit does not recoil[r] *from you,*
So that I do not make you a desolation,
a country not lived in.[s]

a. LXX, Vg derive *hāʿizû* from *ʿāzaz* ("be strong") rather than from *ʿûz* ("take refuge") and give the verb a *qal* rather than a *hiphil* meaning (see the translation note on 4:6).

b. Given the paronomasia in the coming reference to Tekoa, one might note that *Benjaminites* are *bənê binyāmin* ("sons of the son of the right hand/south"); see the commentary.

c. Vg has simply "inside."

d. *Tekoa* comes from the word for blast, and one could even translate, "With a blast, blast the horn"; the paronomasia might be the reason for mentioning Tekoa in particular.

e. While *nāʾwâ* is usually the word for "lovely" and *nāwâ* means pasture, here the pairing of *nāwâ* with the word for *daintily bred* suggests that it carries both connotations, so I give a double translation for the word.

f. The *qatal* is declarative/performative (see the commentary on 1:5). There are several verbs *dāmâ* and *dāmam* with the overlapping meanings "be silent/cease/destroy" (see *DCH*); *quash* is an attempt to preserve the overlap. There is also a *dāmâ* meaning "resemble," and Syr takes *dāmîtî* here as an archaic second-person feminine (see the translation notes on 2:19 and 20) from this *dāmâ*; Vg "liken" also derives *dāmîtî* from this *dāmâ*. Actually, the *piel* would be required for this meaning, yet the two understandings might suggest a paronomasia and a conflict within Yahweh, who is both destroying and comparing/imagining (Jindo, *Biblical Metaphor Reconsidered*, 129–30).

g. See the translation note on 4:31.

h. *Pitched* is *tāqaʿ*, which meant "blast" in v. 1, where it accompanied the place name *təqōaʿ* (*Tekoa*).

i. Vg, plausibly, "those who are under his hand."

j. LXX "prepare."

k. MT has a marker here.

l. MT's *'ēṣâ* is a *hapax legomenon*; a substantial tradition reads *'ēṣāh* (*BHS*).

m. Tg takes *hopqad* (which follows the feminine *hā'îr*) as an unmarked relative clause, and Allen (*Jeremiah*, 82–83) renders "handed over"; I have taken *kullāh* as the subject. "To be visited" (Vg) does not fit the *hiphil/hophal*.

n. The *qere* has the odd form *bayir*, which might be equivalent to *bə'ēr*; the *ketiv* implies *bôr*, which should denote a cistern, and a cistern can hardly act as this colon says (see 2:13).

o. R. S. Hess ("Hiphil Forms of *qwr* in Jeremiah vi 7," *VT* 41 [1991]: 347–50) derives *hāqîr* from *qûr* rather than *qārar* (BDB).

p. The words form a hendiadys: "violent destruction" or "destructive violence." A singular verb follows.

q. Another hendiadys (Blayney, *Jeremiah*, 253). LXX links "sickness and wound" with v. 8.

r. The form *tēqa'* makes a link with *təqōa'* and *tiq'û* in v. 1 so that these words hold vv. 1–8 together.

s. MT has a unit marker here; further, this verse marks the center of the Hebrew Bible (Fischer, *Jeremia*, 1:265).

Rhetorically, Yahweh urges Judah to seek protection in light of what he is doing and of what his initiative will issue in. The first section goes on to relate the words of the city's attackers and defenders. A further subsection goes back to Yahweh's commissioning of the attackers and the rationale for it before the section closes with a challenge to the city to heed his warning so that the devastation may not actually happen. In origin, the section may bring together two or three or four elements of separate origin.

vv. 1–3	Yahweh urges Judah to protect itself in light of the action he is commissioning (four bicola and a tricolon marking a pause)
vv. 4–5	The attackers and the defenders speak (three bicola)
vv. 6–7	Yahweh urges the attack and recollects the reasons but notes the coming suffering (an introduction and four bicola)
v. 8	In light of v. 7b, Yahweh urges Jerusalem to take action to protect itself (two linked bicola)

1 Yet again an unnamed speaker issues a commission; v. 2 will suggest it is Yahweh. Yet again Jeremiah invites people to imagine that invasion and attack is imminent. First he urges *Benjaminites* to *make safe* by getting themselves or their people out of *Jerusalem*, with irony since many would have taken refuge there because they thought it was safe and because 4:6 had issued a commission to get people to take refuge in Zion (with further irony, Jeremiah is himself a Benjaminite). No, even Jerusalem is not safe; actually, it is especially not safe, because it's the capital. Since the city straddled the Judah-Benjamin

border and could indeed be thought of as within Benjamin (e.g., Josh 15:8, 63; 18:16, 28; Judg 1:21), one might speak of Jerusalemites as Benjaminites, especially if one wanted to distinguish them from Judahites in general. Given that the invaders are coming from the north, it would be logical to go south; and Benjamin means "son of the right hand"—that is, "son of the south." Fortunately, Yahweh created both north and south (Ps 89:12[13]). But even *Tekoa*, a town ten miles or so south that might make a refuge, is not safe; there, too, people will need to *blast the horn* to give warning. An attractive candidate for identification as *Beth Hakkerem*, presumably another place south of Jerusalem, is Ramat Rahel near Bethlehem, a strategic site where a new royal citadel and fortification were being built in Jeremiah's day.[254] A *beacon* (*maś'ēt*) is something that people *raise* (*nāśā'*), which perhaps implies a fire or smoke signal whose smoke goes up. It's all because *dire trouble* is coming *from the north*. Its arrival will mean *a great shattering*, as we know, because these words repeat from 4:6, where Zion was commended as a refuge. The complementary difference in the formulation over against 4:6 is that there Yahweh said he was making the dire trouble come, whereas here the dire trouble is the subject of the verb. It has itself *peered out* on Jerusalem (*šāqap*), like someone leaning out of a window to see what is going on in order then to take some action. It is hanging over the city. The past tense verb expresses the certainty of what is about to happen. In Jeremiah's imagination and in Yahweh's intention it has already happened. Yes, the listeners really are in trouble.

2–3 So *Miss Zion* is doomed. Yahweh first describes the city with some touching expressions that correspond to its associations for its people (Pss 48:1; 50:2; Song 6:4; Isa 33:20). Then he strikes. Having held back in v. 1 from taking responsibility for the imminent trouble, so that one might read the exhortation as a friendly warning by someone who cares, here Yahweh asserts ownership of events with a strong verb: *I am* [hereby] *quashing*. He then takes up the pasturing image and reverses its implications. *Shepherds* come to this pasture bringing *their flocks*, but they are hostile shepherds; in the background is the use of the word "shepherds" for rulers or leaders and the verbal link between being a shepherd (*rō'ēh*) and bringing dire trouble (*rā'â*), not to say being a friend or lover (see 2:8 and the commentary on it).[255] The shepherds and flocks are kings and their armies; further, *come to her* is a term for having sex (e.g., Gen 16:2). The girl is going to be invaded, penetrated. While it's natural enough that the shepherds *have pitched their tents*, they

254. See O. Lipschits et al., "Palace and Village, Paradise and Oblivion: Unraveling the Riddles of Ramat Rahel," *Near Eastern Archaeology* 74 (2011): 1–49.

255. Jerome, *Jeremiah*, 41; cf. J. Barr, *Comparative Philology and the Text of the Old Testament* (Oxford: Clarendon, 1968), 212.

have done so *against her* and *all round*. "Sheep may *not* graze safely here."[256] The shepherds are careful and systematic: each has his allocated area.

4–5 More anonymous imperatives follow. It becomes clear that they are not Yahweh's words again but the words of the shepherds urging one another to *sanctify battle*. The assumption is that war-making in itself is not holy or sacred (the Scriptures never use the expression "holy war"), though neither is it unclean or impure. It is neutral, like work or food or time. But one can sanctify it, dedicate it to God's service, and seek God's aid and protection in the midst of it (cf. Joel 3:9 [4:9]; Mic 3:5); one might thus pray and offer sacrifice before a battle (1 Sam 7:7–9).[257] Jeremiah imagines the attackers aware that they are serving God in undertaking this "just war," in which they are the means of God's proper judgment being implemented on Jerusalem. If Israel did have the idea of a war being holy, it is turned back on them.[258] Jeremiah imagines a dialogue that goes on as the day passes; it's as if we are right there.[259] The twofold *set to, let's go up* is the attackers' battle resolve. One might expect them to initiate their action in the early morning, when there's a whole day ahead (and when it's not too hot yet?); cf. Josh 10:12–14. Actually, they are going to attack *at noon*, and then they are quite prepared to make another assault *in the night*. Maybe implementing their resolve at these unlikely hours shows their confidence. Whatever the time, they will *devastate her citadels*, the fortresses and palaces at the highest, most heavily defended points in the city. In between the two accounts of their resolve, the anxious *alas for us* expresses Jerusalem's converse awareness and fear. Even if morning passes without attack, there is no time that is safe, neither midday nor evening.[260] As *the evening shadows decline* and the day is wearing on and they have perhaps been fighting all day, "the people sense that their time is running out."[261] In contrast, the attackers are full of get up and go as the evening comes, and they prepare to attack again.

6 Jeremiah now provides some background. The siege of a walled city requires attackers to *cut down* the city's own *trees* to construct scaffolding-like structures that they push against the walls and onto which they can climb, the battering ram they will use, or the inner reinforcement of the *ramp* up which they will push the battering ram, for which they will also need to *pour* large quantities of earth (see 52:4; Ezek 4:1–2; 26:8–9). Yahweh commissions

---

256. R. P. Carroll, *Jeremiah*, OTL, 191, alluding to words by Salomon Franck set to music by J. S. Bach.

257. See Weiser, *Jeremia*, 1:59–60.

258. J. A. Soggin, "Der Prophetische Gedanke über den Heiligen Krieg, als Gericht Gegen Israel," *VT* 10 (1960): 79–83.

259. Volz, *Jeremia*, 72.

260. Jerome, *Jeremiah*, 41–42.

261. Miller, "Jeremiah," on the passage.

the attackers to do the work he needs them to do. A further account of Yahweh's reasoning follows. *The city* is to be totally *handed over*, a form of an unassuming key verb (*pāqad*) that Yahweh has used before (cf. 5:9, 29). It is because of her *fraud* (*'ōšeq*), the activity or neglect described in 5:26–28, the oppression exercised by powerful people using dishonest means to deprive powerless people of what belongs to them or what they have a right to. The scroll is resolute in looking at the "dark side" of the community.[262]

7 Yahweh adds a new, clever, sharp, acerbic simile. A lovely thing about a *well* is that *its water* stays *cool* deep in the ground for when you want a drink. Jerusalem has the capacity to keep its *dire behavior* ever *cool*. "Israel digs deep into their imaginations to devise ever new and fresh ways to pursue their wickedness, just like ever fresh water bubbles up from deep within a well. Israel's well for generating such behaviors is bottomless."[263] And Jeremiah digs deep into his imagination for ever new and fresh ways to communicate Yahweh's message. Then he reverts to more abstract description. *Fraud* can be committed discretely and quietly. Even *violence* (*ḥāmās*) can be quiet when it means the violation of the norms Yahweh has given his people. But violence is often accompanied by *destruction* (*šōd*) (cf. 20:8; Ezek 45:9; Amos 3:10; Hab 1:3), and any uncertainty disappears. Destructive violence *makes itself heard in her* all right. But there is another ambiguity here. Yahweh is the one who commissions destroyers, while at the same time destruction or destroyers have an energy or force of their own (cf. 4:6–7). So the violence and destruction might be what he is commissioning. More certainly, when Yahweh moves to talking about *sickness and wound*, he is returning to speak of suffering imposed on the city rather than suffering its people impose on one another (Tg; see 10:19; 14:17; and the vivid description in Isa 1:5–6). In his mind's eye, this suffering is before his face continually as the trouble he intends to bring about, just as he can see the felling of the trees and the shaping of the ramp. He can see the metaphorical sickness and wounding that will come to the city and the literal sickness and wounding that its siege and fall will bring to its people, and he grieves over them while also being determined to impose them. Covenant makes violence necessary.[264] "Those who make use of violent means will eventually suffer violence themselves brought about by Yahweh."[265]

262. G. Fischer, "Is there *Shalom*, or Not? Jeremiah, a Prophet for South Africa," *OTE* 28 (2015): 352.

263. Fretheim, *Jeremiah*, 121.

264. E. A. Martens, "Toward an End to Violence: Hearing Jeremiah," in *Wrestling with the Violence of God: Soundings in the Old Testament*, ed. M. D. Carroll R. and J. B. Wilgus, BBRSup 10 (Winona Lake, IN: Eisenbrauns, 2015), 134–38.

265. S. D. Snyman, "A Structural-Historical Investigation of *ḥms wśd* in Jeremiah 6:1–8," *HTS* 58 (2002): 1602.

8 So he begs *Jerusalem* to *accept restraint* from him, to let herself be disciplined by him (see 2:19–20, 30 and the translation note and commentary on it). The rare but vivid verb *recoil* (*yāqaʿ*) is most familiar from the description of what happened to Jacob's groin to terminate his wrestling (Gen 32:26). *So that I do not make you a desolation* expresses the implications in more familiar, down-to-earth terms (4:27). The two middle cola are parallel "so that . . . not" (*pen*) clauses, and the section could easily close with them, but the extra colon adds additional bite. *A country not lived in* (*yāšab niphal*) makes another familiar point (2:15; 4:7, 29) in a slightly unfamiliar way. Jesus will take up Yahweh's holding together a commitment to the necessity of judgment, a regret at its necessity, and a wish to draw Jerusalem to the kind of change that will make it unnecessary (Luke 19:41–48).[266]

2. Strip the Vine (6:9–15)

[9] *Yahweh of Armies has said this:*

They are to garner, garner,[a]
   like a vine, the remainder of Israel!
Turn back your hand,[b]
   like a grape-picker, over the tendrils!

[10] *To whom am I to speak,*[c]
   so that I may testify and they may listen?
There, their ear is foreskinned,
   they can't pay heed.
There, Yahweh's message has become for them
   an object of reviling that they are not partial to.
[11] *But Yahweh's fury: I am full of it—*
   I am weary of holding it.

Pour it[d] *on the baby in the street*
   and on the group of young people, together.
Because man with woman, they are to be captured,
   the old person with the one who is full of years.[e]
[12] *Their houses will pass to other people,*[f]
   fields and wives, together.
Because I will stretch out my hand
   over the people who live in the country (Yahweh's affirmation).

266. Rudolph, *Jeremia*, 44.

¹³*Because from the smallest of them to the biggest of them,*
*everyone*ᵍ *is grabbing what can be grabbed.*
*And from prophet*ʰ *to priest,*
everyone is practicing deception.
¹⁴*They have healed my people's shattering*ⁱ *lightly,*ʲ
*saying, "Things are perfectly well,"*ᵏ
when things are not well.
¹⁵*They have acted shamefully, because it is something offensive that they*
have done—
*they neither feel shame at all*ˡ
*nor do they know how to show that they feel disgrace.*ᵐ
Therefore, they will fall among those who fall;
*at the time I am attending to them,*ⁿ *they will collapse (Yahweh*
*has said).*ᵒ

a. The infinitive precedes the finite verb, underlining the factuality of the action.

b. The verb and the pronoun are singular.

c. The verb is cohortative.

d. For MT *šəpōk*, LXX implies first-person *'espōk*, assimilating to the context.

e. Lit. "days."

f. Verses 12–15 appear in a slightly variant form as 8:10–12.

g. Lit. "all of it," but there is no antecedent for the suffix on *kullô*, which recurs in v. 13b (and cf. *kullōh* in 8:10; 15:10; 20:7). BDB (481–82) calls it an idiomatic usage; Joüon 146j compares it with the "vague" suffix on *yaḥdāw* (*together*), which came in vv. 11 and 12.

h. For the first time, LXX translates "false prophet"; see the commentary. See also the commentary on 2:8.

i. The *šeqer* ("deception," v. 13) consists in failing to minister properly to the potential *šeber* ("shattering").

j. The *niphal* feminine participle has apparently become a quasi-noun, so the phrase means literally "upon a light thing" or "with lightness" (Joüon 134n).

k. *Šālôm*, *šālôm* is a kind of superlative (GKC 133l).

l. The infinitive preceding the finite verb underscores the verb, especially its being negated (DG 101b).

m. An inwardly transitive *hiphil* (see GKC 53de).

n. The (anticipatory) *qatal* verb (see the introduction to 13:18–22, pp. 354–55) depends on the construct noun (GKC 130d).

o. MT has a section marker here.

This second section essentially repeats the message of the first, but it does so by means of different imagery and rhetoric. First, there is the image of the vinedresser. Second, there is Jeremiah speaking of himself as consumed to overflowing with Yahweh's wrath and needing to express it, to which Yahweh agrees. Third, using the image of the medic binding up wounds, there is another account of the necessity of Yahweh's action because of the people's acquisitiveness and their leaders' collusion.

v. 9	Yahweh commissions Jeremiah to set about stripping the vine (an introduction and two bicola)
vv. 10–11a	Jeremiah raises questions: To whom and how can he speak? But how can he not? (four bicola)
vv. 11b–12	Yahweh answers with another version of the commission (four bicola)
vv. 13–15	Yahweh explains the need to act given who people, prophets, and priests are (three bicola with two tricola in their midst)

9 The new section resumes the theme from v. 8 but makes its point in a new way. For once, it is explicit that Yahweh speaks, though not whom he addresses or who *they* are. In effect *they* are the attackers, and the implicit indirect audience is, as usual, the people of Judah, while the second bicolon will imply that the more direct addressee is Jeremiah himself. The jussive in the first bicolon conveys an un-Israelite bidding. Harvesters in Israel are not supposed to *garner* and *garner*, and specifically not to garner *a vine* over again (Lev 19:10; Deut 24:21), which is the implication of *turn back your hand over the tendrils*. These metaphorical harvesters are to do what a literal *grape-picker* was not supposed to do: the fact is underscored by the declaration that they are to garner *the remainder of Israel*, because remainder (*šəʾērît*, traditionally "remnant") is a term for the portion of Israel that Yahweh has intended to keep in being so that there should continue to be an Israel (e.g., Isa 37:32). Nearly half the First Testament occurrences of this word for *remainder* come in Jeremiah, though it does not usually have a technical meaning. There is a tension between the talk here of eliminating the remainder and the scroll's talk elsewhere of not bringing an end to Judah (4:27; 5:10, 18). Yahweh has indeed kept in being a remainder of Israel, even though he got Assyria to put an end to Ephraim and allowed it to devastate Judah. Now he intends "harvesters" (the same people as the shepherds of vv. 1–8) to eliminate that remainder. In the command to *turn back*, Yahweh apparently indeed speaks to Jeremiah, the agent of the elimination through his prophecy,[267] as v. 10 will presuppose.

10 Jerusalem needs to hear Yahweh issuing this commission to its attackers, paradoxically so that the commission need not be implemented, and it is Jeremiah's job to bring about that hearing. While he is metaphorically involved in the garnering, his more literal job is to *testify*. He is like a witness in a case being discussed by the elders; if he has seen or heard something that relates to the case, he must say so. Otherwise he is in deep trouble (Lev 5:1).

---

267. Craigie, Kelley, and Drinkard, *Jeremiah 1–25*, 103. Calvin (*Jeremiah*, 1:345) neatly thinks of one harvester speaking to another, but this understanding involves considerable inference.

Jeremiah has heard and seen because he has been sitting in Yahweh's cabinet meeting. He must testify. But how can he? No one will *listen*. They seem to be unable to. Their *ear* is (as it were) *foreskinned*, uncircumcised, which is much worse than being full of wax. While 4:4 referred to circumcision or non-circumcision of heart or mind (cf. Deut 10:16; 30:6; Ezek 44:7, 9), within the First Testament only this passage refers to circumcision of hearing; the image is taken up in 1QH^a 10:7; Acts 7:51; and Barn. 10.12.[268] There is little difference between the two images: the heart or mind is where one thinks and makes decisions, the ear is where one listens and responds (mind and ear come together in 7:24). The state of the Judahites' ears means *they can't pay heed*. Apparently, it doesn't relieve them of responsibility, perhaps because they have blocked their own ears since *Yahweh's message has become for them an object of reviling*. Elsewhere, possessing a foreskin conveys reviling or scorn (Gen 34:14; Josh 5:8–9); here it issues in or issues from reviling or scorn. People feel free to taunt or rebuke Jeremiah over Yahweh's message. Yahweh cannot intend to take action against them. He is a God of love and faithfulness. A message implying the opposite is ridiculous. It is also, of course, something *that they are not partial to*. When Jeremiah or anyone else speaks the truth to them in Yahweh's name, they don't like it. The warnings in Isa 6:9–10 seem to have been fulfilled.

11a That dynamic makes Jeremiah's position seem impossible. The message about the grape-gatherers is a message about *Yahweh's fury*, and people will not take it seriously. The trouble is that Yahweh has given it to him and he is *full of it*. It's not surprising that he is *weary of holding it*. He's like a full skin of wine—or a man who needs to vomit. He is supposed to pass on the message Yahweh has given him, but people respond with scorn and opposition. He therefore tries to hold it in, but he can't (20:7–10 expands on the dynamics of this experience). Even here, "the personal thrust in this oracle serves to draw attention, not to the emotional involvement of Jeremiah, but to the horror of the content of the message with which he is entrusted. He is himself a signal of the divine judgment."[269] His weariness matches Yahweh's in Isa 1:14.[270] "I am full of prophecy," Tg paraphrases him, and

> the most basic dimension of that God-given word is wrath. To be full of wrath means that there is no room in him for any other kind of word from God (as in 15:17; see the image of fire in 20:9; 5:14). He has held back from

---

268. See B. A. Thomason, "The Circumcision of the Ear: The Multiple Meanings of a Metaphor in Its Context in Second Temple and Early Christian Texts" (PhD diss., Durham University, 2016).

269. D. R. Jones, *Jeremiah*, 135.

270. Fischer, *Jeremia*, 1:268.

proclaiming this hard word; he has not wanted to speak it. But he has become weary in holding it back and can no longer do so (as in 20:9). He must get that word out. In this regard he has become conformed to God's own situation (15:6); just as God has become weary of holding back, so also has God's prophet. Weariness is characteristic of both prophet and God, and so is wrath. This should not be interpreted in terms of a clinical compulsion, but of a sense of call that must be fulfilled.[271]

11b Yahweh's response is designed to horrify Jeremiah's listeners—again we have to recall that this section, like others, is created as a piece of communication with his Judahite contemporaries rather than as an account of Jeremiah's struggles. He has been seeking to confront them with Yahweh's threat to annihilate them, with their own unwillingness to listen to him, and with the fact that Yahweh's wrath hangs over them. There is hardly anything that would devastate a parent more than the death of a child, especially a baby. So in his determined commitment to get through to them, Yahweh starts here with the affect that Jeremiah's delivering his message will have on a *baby* hanging onto its mother *in the street*, then on a *group of young people*, a gang of teenagers laughing and joking, then on everyone, *man with woman*, and then on the *old person* (maybe those in their fifties and sixties) *with the one who is full of years* (people in their seventies and eighties). Jeremiah is not to protect the children from hearing the bad news, nor the women, nor the old people. Once more, this is a piece of rhetoric designed to reach Jeremiah's actual hearers, to whom he must testify in a shocking way that might get home to them. Here, the Jerusalemites' fate is not to die but *to be captured* like the man caught in a snare in the manner of an animal, of which Jeremiah spoke just now (5:26). It will be poetic justice. Jeremiah is to pour out on the people the entirety of his message about Yahweh's wrath. He is not to try to hold it in. They need to hear it. "The rhetoric of wrath is filled with passion and a lack of restraint."[272]

> Mine eyes have seen the glory of the coming of the Lord;
> he is trampling out the vintage where the grapes of wrath are
>   stored;
> he has loosed the fateful lightning of his terrible swift sword.

12 To judge from what happened when Samaria fell, the people who live in Jerusalem will be displaced and will lose their *houses*, which will *pass to other*

---

271. Fretheim, *Jeremiah*, 122.

272. Brueggemann, *Jeremiah 1–25*, 68. Brueggemann goes on to quote the following words from Julia Ward Howe's "Battle Hymn of the Republic," composed during the America Civil War as an encouragement to northern soldiers.

people—people from elsewhere whom the conqueror will import, or members of the conquering people, or neighbors like the Edomites who will be able to profit from what happens. It will not just be the houses but the *fields*, the land, as again the Edomite takeover of Judahite land will illustrate and as the apparent insanity of Jeremiah's investing in real estate (Jer 32) will imply. It will include the *wives*, who commonly pay a terrible price at the hands of invaders when a country is conquered because it is one way conquerors assert themselves over the men (who are implicitly Jeremiah's immediate audience?).

13a The declaration of wrath that Jeremiah must pour out is necessitated by the total social collapse in Jerusalem. Jeremiah 5 pictured Yahweh undertaking a social and moral inventory of the city, in which he started with the ordinary people and then went on to the big people; here he reprises the result. It is not just the wealthy and powerful who are prepared to cheat and deprive other people of their rights in order to fill their homes with good things. *From the smallest of them to the biggest of them*, the entire city is *grabbing what can be grabbed* (*bôṣēaʿ beṣaʿ*) in a way that takes no notice of right and wrong. LXX translates "lawlessness" and Vg translates "greed," both of which are appropriate if less vivid than Jeremiah's words. A spirit of Mammon possesses the entire community.[273] It is hardly surprising that ordinary people also want their share of stuff—people like Joseph's brothers, who use that expression (Gen 37:26). But the wealthy and powerful people involved in the grabbing include Jehoiakim, to whom this description applies in 22:17 and who is in the audience if these words are part of the 604 scroll (cf. also 1 Sam 8:3; Ezek 22:27).

13b–14 As he did in 5:31, Jeremiah moves straight from the perverting of judicial procedures to a condemnation of *prophet* and *priest*. Either they are involved in the wrongdoing (it is not surprising if religious leaders also want nice houses) or they are colluding with it—or both. They are *practicing deception*—that word again recurs from 5:31. What is the nature of the deception? All is not well in Judah. If we think in terms of the 604 context, the Egyptians had defeated and killed Josiah, deposed Jehoahaz, and imposed tribute, and there was reason to declare a fast, perhaps linked to a drought (cf. 5:3 and see the commentary on it). People are suffering. But a much worse breaking in is on its way (4:6, 20; 6:1). The question is, "Do prophet and priest see the state of the community, its 'breaking,' as deeply as Jeremiah?"[274] They do not acknowledge it. While the problem with the people whom Tg calls false prophets at 2:8 is that they were prophesying in the name of the Master, the problem with the people LXX calls false prophets here is the nature of the message they bring in Yahweh's name (Tg calls them "scribes" here, and often elsewhere). They are encouraging, positive prophets, unlike Jeremiah.

---

273. Rudolph, *Jeremia*, 45.
274. W. H. Schmidt, *Jeremia*, 1:163.

It is unlikely that the false prophets were shameless charlatans. They were presumably sincere patriots, ardent lovers of the people and zealous in their devotion to state and sanctuary. They as well as the leaders of the state, who had the interest of the country at heart, resented the invectives and exaggerated accusations of Jeremiah and entertained a profound trust in God's attachment to Israel.[275]

But they *have healed my people's shattering lightly* by *saying, "Things are perfectly well"* (*šālôm, šālôm*), that Yahweh loves his people and will keep them safe and restore them. Actually, *things are not well* at all. A better term for "false prophets" would be *šālôm* prophets.[276] In reality, there is no *šālôm*. "A prophet is made 'false' and known to be so on the basis of his message alone," and the terrible thing about the prophets' false message is that "it is positively destructive, since by glossing over the real seriousness of the situation, it prevents the only action on the part of the people which could possibly forestall the coming destructive judgment."[277] In Theses 92 and 93, Martin Luther declares, "Away with all those prophets who say to Christ's people, 'Peace, peace,' and there is no peace," but "May it go well for all of those prophets who say to Christ's people, 'Cross, cross,' and there is no cross!" Contrary to the view of false prophets, "the Christian life goes *through* the cross to peace not around the cross."[278]

15 While shame attaches to the entire community (2:26, 36; 3:3, 24–25), in this context the people who *have acted shamefully* continue to be the prophets and priests. Their action counts as something *offensive* and disgusting, the very antithesis of what meets with acceptance by Yahweh, the kind of thing that reeks of adherence to the Master rather than adherence to Yahweh (2:7; 7:10; 16:18). The words reformulate the declaration that the prophets practice deception. Yet they do not *feel shame at all*. The recurrence of the word *shame* puts together the relationship (or lack of relationship) between objective and subjective shamefulness, shame as a fact and shame as a feeling. To make the same point in other words, *they do not know how to show that they feel disgrace*. They do not feel disgrace and therefore they do not know how to show it. Jeremiah's putting healing (v. 14) and shame next to each other also prompts reflection on how Yahweh's healing needs to involve restoring the inner being as well as the outward wounding. Unless Yahweh does so, *they*

---

275. Heschel, *Prophets*, 482; cf. Fretheim, *Jeremiah*, 123; see the commentary on 5:31.

276. P. D. Miller, "Jeremiah," in an introductory comment on 23:9–40.

277. T. W. Overholt, *The Threat of Falsehood: A Study in the Theology of the Book of Jeremiah*, SBT 2/16 (London: SCM, 1970), 85.

278. T. J. Wengert, "The *95 Theses* as Luther's Template for Reading Scripture," *Lutheran Quarterly* 31 (2017): 257–58.

will fall among those who fall: the community will meet with defeat, loss, and death, and prophet and priest will be among them. When Yahweh attends to the rest of the community who fall, they will also *collapse*.

Therefore, they will fall   among (*bə*) those who fall;
                      at (*bə*)   the time I am attending to
                                   them, they will collapse.

The section thus ends with another line combining parallelism with an a-b-b'-a' structure in which the verbs enclose the whole and tie it together.

3. *Put Things in Place to Trip People (6:16–21)*

[16]*Yahweh has said this:*

Stand by the paths and look;
    ask about the age-long routes,
    where actually is the path to what is good.[a]
Then go on it, and find repose for yourselves;
    but they said, "We won't."
[17]*I would set up lookouts for you:*
    "Pay heed to the sound of the horn!"
    But they said,[b] *"We won't."*

[18]*Therefore listen, nations,*
    acknowledge, assembly,[c] *what is in them,*[d]
      [19]*listen, earth.*
Here am I,
    causing dire trouble to come on this people,
    the fruit of their plans.
Because to my words they have not paid heed;
    my instruction: they have rejected it.[e]

[20]*What use actually*[f] *is frankincense to me*
    though it comes[g] *from Sheba,*
Or cane, the good kind,[h]
    from a far-off country?
Your whole offerings are not acceptable,
    your fellowship sacrifices don't seem sweet to me.[i]

[21]*Therefore, Yahweh has said this:*

Here am I, giving to^j this people things to make them collapse,
  and they will collapse on them,
Parents and children together,
  a neighbor and his fellow, and they will perish.^{k}

a. For *derek haṭṭôb*, LXX, Vg have "the good path"; while anarthrous *derek* can be used thus with a definite adjective (*IBHS* 14.3.1d; DG 42 remark 2), the more predictable expression would be *hadderek haṭṭôbâ* (1 Kgs 8:36), and *haṭṭôb* was a noun in 5:25.

b. The *wǝqatal* is followed by *wayyiqtol*, perhaps because the frequentative nature of the events has been sufficiently indicated and Jeremiah can revert to the ordinary usage in prose narrative (*TTH* 114, 120).

c. Aq takes this to be the *ʿēdâ* meaning testimony (from *ʿûd*; see v. 10) rather than the *ʿēdâ* meaning assembly (from *yāʿad*; see 30:20).

d. Vg "what I will do to them."

e. *Wayyim'ăsû-bāh* follows an extraposed subject (GKC 143d).

f. On *zeh*, see BDB, 261.

g. The asyndesis and the postponed placing of the verb suggest that this colon is subordinate to the previous one. For *tābô'*, LXX, Vg, Syr imply *tābî'* ("you bring").

h. Anarthrous absolute *qāneh* followed anomalously by definite *haṭṭôb* corresponds to *derek haṭṭôb* in v. 16, but the noun does not belong to a category that can be used as if this phrase were a regular noun and adjective expression (*IBHS* 14.3.1d; DG 42 remark 2).

i. MT^L has a section marker here.

j. Modern translations (e.g., NRSV, NJPS, NIV) have something like "put before," but *DCH* (5:806) gives no other example of *nātan 'el* with this meaning.

k. For the *qere*'s *wǝ'ābādû*, the *ketiv* implies the more expected *yō'bēdû*. MT has a unit marker here.

The section divides into two sets of two, with each of the pairs beginning with an implicit or explicit rebuke. The first issues an exhortation to return to the proper Israelite ways of the past but recognizes that it's not going to happen. The second repudiates the costly worship that the people offer. Each rebuke leads into a "therefore" stating the consequences that Yahweh will ensure follow. The two pairs of subsections are different in focus and theme and are likely of separate origin.

vv. 16–17   Yahweh issues a bidding, but people resist it in accordance with past practice (an introduction, an opening tricolon, a bicolon, and a tricolon before the pause)

vv. 18–19   "Therefore": Yahweh bids the world to note what will follow (two tricola and a bicolon)

v. 20   Yahweh issues a more explicit rebuke (two linked bicola and a single bicolon)

v. 21   "Therefore": Yahweh gives a warning about what will follow (an introduction and two linked bicola)

16 Jeremiah's new introduction to Yahweh's words and Yahweh's new bidding open the sixth consecutive section to begin with an imperative. It is in the last colon that the identity of the addressees becomes indisputably clear: it is the Judahite community that is urged to *stand by the paths and look* and to *ask about the age-long routes*. So far, Jeremiah has made only negative reference to the paths that the people have followed (see esp. 2:33; 3:13; cf. 7:3, 5), and *routes* will otherwise feature only negatively (18:15). In the first colon, it is not immediately obvious what paths Yahweh wants people to examine (is he being ironic?), but *age-long* (ʿôlām) at the end of the parallel colon qualifies "paths" as well as "routes" and points to the answer. They are paths such as the ones Deuteronomy lays before Israel (Deut 8:6; 10:12; 11:22; 19:9; 26:17; 28:9; 30:16; 32:4). There could be people who questioned whether the paths laid out by Deuteronomy and by Jeremiah are really the age-old paths; compared with the traditional religion of the land, they might seem rather innovative. Reformers like Josiah and prophets like Jeremiah often claim to be restoring the old rather than introducing the new (they claim that they are reformers, not revolutionaries). But Jeremiah and Deuteronomy know that the paths in question correspond to the nature and priorities of the age-old God. Deuteronomy further promised that these paths, which are also *the path* (singular), lead *to what is good* (e.g., Deut 8:6–7)—another way of referring to šālôm (v. 14; cf. the parallelism in 8:15). At the moment, the people's wrongdoings hold back "what is good" from them (5:25). Walking on the path Yahweh maps out is the key to what is good or to šālôm. It's the way to *repose*, or "rest" or "relaxation" (margôaʿ). That word comes only here; perhaps it suggests the opposite of the disturbance and turmoil that Jeremiah is otherwise predicting for people. At the moment, they have every reason to be concerned about what is going to happen and to be working feverishly in order to safeguard their future. If they would just follow the way Yahweh maps out . . . *But they said, "We won't."*

17 "Lookout" is Yahweh's description of Ezekiel's role as a prophet (Ezek 3:17; 33:7), and here the *lookouts* whom Yahweh has *set up for you* are prophets such as Jeremiah. Metaphorically, these prophets sound the horn that tells people of danger coming (4:5–6a; see the commentary there). But again, when the Judahites played their part in this "mock liturgy,"[279] *they said, "We won't."*

18–19 Formally, Yahweh turns from speaking to Judah and addresses himself elsewhere, but Jeremiah's actual audience is still the Judahites. Rhetorically, he summons the *nations* as witnesses to his people's intransigence. He pictures them gathered as an *assembly* like the "assembly of the peoples" gathered around him in Ps 7:7(8) to *listen* to him giving account and

---

279. Craigie, Kelley, and Drinkard, *Jeremiah 1–25*, 106.

to *acknowledge what is in them* (that is, in this people) to acknowledge "the direness that is in their hand."[280] To put it another way, he summons *earth* to *listen* to what he has determined to do in response to that intransigence: *Here am I, causing dire trouble* (that expression familiar since 1:14) *to come on this people* (that slightly dismissive description; see, e.g., 5:23) as *the fruit of their plans*, which are thus indeed their "baneful plans" (4:14). The plans produce fruit by their inherent nature (direness issues in direness), though it happens also by divine resolve (I am *causing*): Jeremiah combines both ways of thinking about cause and effect. It happens because *they have not paid heed* to *my words*; paying heed is something one does by listening (cf. vv. 10, 17), so the reference is to the words of prophets, of the lookouts. Further, *my instruction* (*tôrâ*): *they have rejected it*; instruction is the business of priests (e.g., Deut 33:10; 2 Chr 15:3). While Jeremiah often talks about prophets and priests as if they are all bad guys, he also makes clear from time to time that this interpretation of his words would be mistaken. The priests' instruction as embodied in Deuteronomy or Leviticus says the same thing Jeremiah does about commitment to Yahweh, about social and moral life, and so on. But people ignore such priestly instruction as they ignore his prophetic word. And if you ignore how they point you to the way that leads to something good, then dire trouble is what you find instead. The good (*tôb*) and the dire (*ra'*; conventionally "bad" or "evil") are antonyms. You either follow one and experience it or you follow the other and experience it.

20 The juxtaposition of two elements that may be of separate origin suggests that instead of paying heed to what prophets said and following what priests wrote or read, people have focused on worship. The resin *frankincense* was an element in the incense used in worship. It had an aroma that delighted both worshipers and deity; its ascent symbolized the ascent of prayers to God. *Sheba* in Arabia was a major source of spices; the distance that frankincense had to travel made it expensive. Fragrant *cane* or grasses (Tg has "calamus") was an element in the oil for anointing; it also came from a distance at great expense. There was nothing specific to Israel about these components of its worship. Vergil comments about Venus,

> Her temple and its hundred altars
> steam with Sabean incense, fragrant with fresh garlands.[281]

Similarly, *whole offerings* and *fellowship sacrifices* were Israelite versions of forms of worship known in many cultures. While Deuteronomy doesn't talk about frankincense or cane, it does talk about whole offerings and fellowship sacrifices. Jeremiah sets these two forms of animal sacrifice over against

---

280. Rashi, in MG.
281. Vergil, *Aeneid* 1:416–17; see Rudolph, *Jeremia*, 47.

those more exotic elements. Altogether, the four terms cover a wide range of forms of worship. Whole offerings or burnt offerings meant giving something to God in its entirety. Fellowship sacrifices were occasions where God and people shared the offering. But both kinds of offering *are not acceptable*, a technical term in the Torah in connection with the proper observance of the order of worship (see esp. Lev 22:17–30).[282] To Yahweh, they don't actually *seem sweet,* a more poetic word, applicable to the voice of one's beloved (Song 2:14). Jeremiah doesn't hint that people were insincere in their worship; their hallelujahs came from the heart. And he and other prophets make clear in other contexts that they themselves can enthuse over frankincense, for example (Jer 17:26; Isa 60:6). But in this context, none of it means anything to Yahweh. Self-sacrificial worship is valueless if it is not matched by a self-sacrificial life outside worship. Although MT will have a unit break in only one verse's time, MT[L] also puts a section break here, perhaps because the next verse has its own resumptive introduction from Yahweh. Its effect would also be to encourage people to think for a moment about what Yahweh has just said.

21 Yahweh has a further solemn thing to say before the end of this section. It constitutes a restatement of what the dire trouble of v. 19 will look like. People will be walking along the path they have chosen, there will be something there that they don't see, and they will tumble to their deaths. Again, Jeremiah declares that everyone will be affected: within the family, both *parents* and their *children*; within the community, both *neighbor* and other *fellow* members.

4. All Around Is Terror (6:22–26)

²²*Yahweh has said this:*

There, a people is coming from a northern country,[a]
a big nation—it stirs itself[b] *from the furthest parts of the earth.*
²³*Bow and sabre*[c] *they grasp hold of,*
it's fierce, and they have no compassion.
The sound of them—it's like the sea that roars,
and on horses they ride.
Drawn up like an individual[d] *for battle,*
against you, Miss Zion.[e]

---

282. D. Rom-Shiloni ("The Forest and the Trees," 71–76) thus cites this passage as another noteworthy example (alongside 4:13–18) of the influence of the thinking of Leviticus (of the Priestly and Holiness Codes) on Jeremiah.

²⁴*We have heard the news of it—*
  our hands have drooped.
Distress has grasped hold of us,
  writhing like a woman giving birth.
²⁵*Don't go out into the open country,*
  *on the path—don't go,*ᶠ
Because the enemy has a sword,
  all around is terror.

²⁶*My dear people, put on sack,*
  *roll yourself in*ᵍ *ash.*
*Make the mourning for an only*ʰ *child for yourself,*
  *most bitter lamenting.*ⁱ
Because suddenly
  the destroyer will come upon us.

a. Verses 22b–24 appear in a slightly variant form as 50:41–43.

b. The *yiqtol* verb continues the participial construction; with LXX, Vg, and Tg, I take the *niphal* as intransitive rather than passive.

c. Strictly, a short sword, two feet long (Lundbom, *Jeremiah 1–20*, 443).

d. The passive participle is singular; its number is attracted to that of *'iš*, and the colon is compressed. In effect, it means they are drawn up with a kind of denseness and discipline that it is as if they are one man (cf. Lundbom, *Jeremiah 1–20*, 444). For MT *'iš*, LXX "fire" implies *'ēš*.

e. *Miss Zion* and *my dear people* in v. 6 both begin *bat* (lit. "daughter"); see the translation notes on 4:11, 31.

f. In each colon, the imperative is masculine plural in the *qere*, feminine singular in the *ketiv*. The line works a-b-b'-a', the order binding it tightly and underscoring the negative.

g. Not just "sprinkle yourself with" (LXX, Vg).

h. LXX "beloved" brings out a connotation.

i. Lit. "lamenting of bitternesses."

Once again, Yahweh warns Jerusalem, this time in more literal terms, of the peril from the north that is coming. Jeremiah imagines the city's panicked response and urges people to lament as if they are mourning a bereavement. The three subsections may belong together in origin or may have been brought together in the context of the scroll.

vv. 22–23	Yahweh's warning of what is coming (an introduction followed by four bicola)
vv. 24–25	The people's anxious response (two bicola, then a linked pair of bicola)
v. 26	Jeremiah's bidding concerning a response (three bicola)

22-23 The new section again follows on what precedes; it makes explicit the means whereby the community is destined to tumble on its path. The portrait begins with two precisely parallel cola:

there	a people	is coming	from a country	of the north
and	a big nation	stirs	from the furthest parts	of the earth

The tumbling will thus come about through the arrival of the army coming from *a northern country* (1:13–16; 4:6; 6:1), the army of a nation characterized as in 5:15, equipped with its threatening, death-dealing *bow* to wield from a distance and *sabre* to wield when close up and with its threatening personal qualities: *fierce* like a warrior and lacking the restraining motherly quality of *compassion*. They will be a huge force so that *the sound of them* is *like the sea that roars*, and they will possess the battle animals that Israelites do not have much to do with: *On horses they ride* (cf. 4:13; the taunt in Isa 36:8). Yes, it is *drawn up like an individual*, as if it were a single man, *for battle*, and it is coming *against you, Miss Zion*—who turns out to be the addressee. The content of vv. 22aβ–24 reappears in 50:41–43 applied to Babylon, which confirms that "these poems should not be understood as literal descriptions of the invading armies but as conventional proclamations."[283] As Jeremiah portrays the invaders setting out and gathering around Jerusalem, "the general impression . . . is similar to watching a sandcastle threatened by successive waves crashing onto a beach."[284] But there is no playfulness about the image, because ever since the exodus, the sea has stood for "the force of the human world which is hostile to Israel, and therefore opposes the interests and glory of Israel's God, but which is nevertheless ruled and guided and used by Him."[285]

24-25 Jeremiah imagines the Jerusalemites describing their reaction to the *news* that their literal lookouts were bringing them. Faced with invasion, their *hands* need to be grasping their own weapons, but instead they have *drooped*—they are paralyzed, and they are themselves *grasped* by *distress*. Jeremiah returns to the image of *writhing like a woman giving birth* (4:31). No one would be wise to leave the city for *the open country* (to do the necessary work in their fields or to get something to eat from there) or take *the path* that might lead to a place of refuge, because *the enemy has a sword* and

283. R. P. Carroll, *Jeremiah*, OTL, 202–3.

284. Henderson, "Jeremiah 2–10," 145; cf. Henderson, *Jeremiah under the Shadow of Duhm*, 329.

285. Barth, *CD* III, 1:148.

is surrounding the city. *All around is terror*: it became a phrase that summed up Jeremiah's message (20:3, 10; 46:5; 49:29).[286]

26 Jeremiah returns to his own voice and points out the implications for *my dear people* (contrast *this people* in v. 19; see the collocation of the two expressions in 4:11). If he is correct in his account of the northern invader and of the response that it will arouse from them, then they should start grieving about what is to happen as if it's actually happening. Maybe imagining this experience will bring about a change in them now. So start expressing grief. *Put on sack* (cf. 4:8). *Roll yourselves in ash*: never mind about sprinkling just a little of it on your head. *Make the mourning for an only child for yourself,* the kind of mourning that would indeed involve a *most bitter lamenting* (cf. 4:8). The death of one's only child is both a cause of deep personal pain and a reason for deep anxiety about the future of the family. The arrival of an invader *suddenly* is a cause of special fear so that this prospect adds to the reasons to begin mourning now—or rather, in light of that prospect, to turn back now.

5. Reject Silver (6:27–30)

[27]*An examiner I made you among my people,*
   a fortress, so you may acknowledge and examine their path.
[28]*All of them are the most defiant of determined people,*[a]
   people who live as liars.
Bronze and iron,
   they are all of them devastators.
[29]*Bellows have puffed,*[b]
   so from the fire lead has come to an end.[c]
In vain someone has smelted and smelted,[d]
   but dire ones—they have not poured out.
[30]*Reject silver, people would have called*[e] *them,*
   because Yahweh has rejected them.[f]

a. While one could take both *sārê* and *sôrərîm* as from *sārar*, comparison with 5:23 suggests that the compound expression more likely again represents the collocation of forms from *sûr* and from *sārar*, though the combination of a construct participle and an absolute participle also suggests a superlative construction. Vg, Aq, Syr, Tg imply *sārê* ("officials") for *sārê* (LXX omits), which generates another link with Jer 1, but there and regularly elsewhere, "officials" appear only in the company of the king and others.

286. On the origin of the phrase, see A. H. W. Curtis, "Terror on Every Side,'" in Curtis and Römer, *Jeremiah and Its Reception*, 111–18.

b. Taking *nāḥar* as the citation form of that verb (*HALOT*), a *hapax legomenon*, rather than as *niphal* from *ḥārar* (BDB), which would also be a *hapax legomenon* in meaning (bellows are not supposed to burn).

c. The asyndesis and the verb's postponement suggest that the second clause is subordinate to the first. The *qere mē'ēš tam* (*from the fire has come to an end*) appears in the *ketiv* as the single word *m'štm*, which "cannot be read" (Lundbom, *Jeremiah 1–20*, 451).

d. Lit. "has smelted to smelt"; an infinitive following a finite verb can indicate continuance in doing something (GKC 113r).

e. The calling has not actually happened; I take the *qatal* verb as irreal (see GKC 104p; Vg has an imperative).

f. MT has a unit marker here.

In the closing section of the unit and of Jer 2–6, and thus perhaps of the rewritten 604 scroll, Yahweh recalls his commission of Jeremiah (v. 27), and Jeremiah reports his devastating conclusion (v. 30). While vv. 28–29 indicate no change of speaker and might indicate Yahweh's own provisional assessment (v. 28) and Jeremiah's blow by blow (!) account of his process, more likely the section's logic parallels that in 5:1–9, where Jeremiah's report of Yahweh's issuing a commission leads immediately into Jeremiah's conclusion. Like that passage, the section is a rhetorical piece designed to communicate to Judah.

v. 27	Yahweh's recollection of his commissioning Jeremiah (one bicolon)
vv. 28–30	Jeremiah's conclusion on the basis of fulfilling the commission (five bicola)

27 While there is no formal marker that a new section begins here, there is a marked change in the rhetoric. In revisiting his commission of Jeremiah, Yahweh uses terms that overlap with Jer 1. But here he speaks of making Jeremiah a metal worker, *an examiner among my people*, as another way of describing his role as prophet. In that vocation, Yahweh made him a *fortress* (cf. 1:18), someone invincible who would stand firm to *acknowledge and examine their path*.

28 Jeremiah's assessment on the basis of having fulfilled his commission over the years takes up the phraseology of 5:23, affirming again that the Judahites are quite *determined*, as tough as nails in their *defiant* behavior—more literally, in the way they move away (*sûr*) from Yahweh. The description applies to *all of them*. Here, too, as in 5:23, Jeremiah comments on how they *live* or "go about" (*hālak*) after making the move away. Here, he is more explicit: they live as *liars*. Falsifying the truth about people is the way they get the work done that 5:26–28 described. In that work, they are as strong as *bronze and iron*, which is what made it possible to be *devastators* (see 5:26). It is why 1:18 also indicated that Yahweh would ensure that Jeremiah had the same qualities.

29 In itself, examining simply means looking at something,[287] but discovering the truth about something may also involve testing it—putting it under pressure to see what happens. Further, testing is in turn a different process from refining, of acting to purify, filter, or hone. In practice, these two also overlap (Yahweh's testing of Job does more than reveal who he is), and in what follows here, Jeremiah is by implication Yahweh's smelter and refiner as well as examiner and tester, or is smelter and refiner through being tester, or is tester through being smelter and refiner. He moves on to describe the process and the results of his testing activity, which indeed involves action and not merely observation. His metaphor for testing is the process whereby a metalworker smelts and refines silver (rather than the earlier process whereby silver is initially extracted from lead ore).[288] It involves adding lead to the impure silver; when heated, lead has the capacity to absorb the impurities. As a smelter, he would have ensured that *the bellows have puffed* so that *the fire* got red hot and thus that all the *lead has come to an end*, smelted away. But on this occasion, the process failed; the impurities remained. It is *in vain* that *someone*—in the real-life example, Jeremiah—*has smelted*. The equivalent of the impurities in the real life example is the *dire ones*, and they *have not poured out* like the impurities in the smelting process. The refining and smelting has been unsuccessful. Truly "the way is broad that leads to destruction, and many find their way to it" (Matt 7:13).[289]

30 "Once you have tested them . . . and you have come to know the ways of my delinquent people, then you will understand that silver mixed with copper can in no way be purified."[290] Anyone who assesses the results of the smelting process would come to a negative assessment of its results. *Reject silver, people would have called them.* Such is the assessment that Yahweh has reached regarding Judah: *Yahweh has rejected them.* It is an appropriate response to their rejection of Yahweh's instruction (v. 19).[291] That last comment implicitly identifies Yahweh as the tester/refiner/smelter behind Jeremiah. With regard to the community as a whole, 5:1–9 involved some hyperbole, and one cannot infer from this passage that there was not a single

287. See M. Tsevat, "בחן, *bḥn*," *TDOT* 2:69–72.
288. See further Holladay, *Commentary on Jeremiah*, 1:230–32.
289. Dearman, *Jeremiah*, on the passage.
290. Jerome, *Jeremiah*, 48.
291. Y. Hoffman, "'Isn't the Bride Too Beautiful?' The Case of Jeremiah 6.16-21," *JSOT* 64 (1994): 113. Hoffman sees it as an example of how 6:16–21 was composed to dovetail into this context.

good person in Judah. What Jeremiah's commission has revealed is that the community as a whole cannot be saved. It is a horrifying ending to Jer 2–6 and perhaps to the scroll that Baruch read out on the occasion of fasting that Jer 36 describes. For people hearing Jeremiah in 604 or afterward, the conclusion remains one that they are challenged to disprove, like people who heard Isaiah recount his equivalent testimony in Isa 6:9–10. For people reading the scroll some decades later, it helps explain how things actually turned out. For them, too, "the mention of God's rejection of Israel at the close of Jer 6 is an apt conclusion to a horrific passage designed to scare and shame its audience into transforming its behavior."[292]

292. Kalmanofsky, *Terror All Around*, 129.

II. PART TWO: TWENTY MORE YEARS (7:1–24:10)

As Jer 2–6 began *Yahweh's message came to me*, a similar phrase in the third person occurs in 7:1 and will recur in 11:1; 14:1; 18:1; 21:1. For the scroll's readers, these introductions provide useful divisions of the material through Jer 7–24, the whole of which I call Part Two of the scroll. Whereas the first-person form in 2:1 makes sense if Jer 2–6 is basically the 604 scroll, this use of the third-person form makes sense if what follows issues from the collating work of Jeremiah's curators, presumably after 587.

A. PART 2A: EXHORTATIONS AND EXCHANGES (7:1–10:25)

While Jer 7:1–15 links chronologically with the period just before 604 (see the comment), 10:1–25 suggests a time after 597. This first compilation of part 2 outlines as follows:

7:1–8:3	Five exhortations, confrontations, and warnings about worship
8:4–9:26(25)	Three exchanges between Yahweh, Judah, and Jeremiah
10:1–25	Another exhortation and another exchange

1. Five Exhortations, Confrontations, and Warnings about Worship (7:1–8:3)

Within Jer 7–10 as a whole, 7:1–8:3 comprises a series of five originally inde-pendent messages in prose (with one two-line poetic component). The first, 7:1–15, is much longer than the others (one might see vv. 3–7, 8–11, and 12–15 as originally separate). All relate to worship,[1] but within that topic they cover different subjects. Whereas part 1 began by raising questions concerning Judah's attitude to the exodus, part 2 begins by raising questions concerning Judah's attitude to the temple. All five sections concern unacceptable wor-ship that earns Yahweh's wrath and leads to banishment:

7:1–15	Worship not accompanied by truthfulness in the community
7:16–20	Worship of the Queen of the Heavens

---

1. C. D. Isbell and M. Jackson, "Rhetorical Criticism and Jeremiath vii 1–viii 3," *VT* 30 (1980): 26.

While the specific subject changes for each section, only the first and third have introductions declaring that what follows is what *Yahweh of Armies, Israel's God, has said*. These headings bind together the first two messages and then the last three so that the whole divides into two approximately equal halves. Each half begins with worship of Yahweh that is accompanied by wayward attitudes and moves on to worship that is itself wayward in how or to whom it is offered.[3] In content, the messages overlap with Jer 2–6. Like those poetic sections, they challenge people with confrontations about their worship and their community life, exhortations to change, and warnings about the consequences of not changing. They reinforce the implications of what has preceded in Jer 2–6.[4]

a. About the Temple (7:1–15)

[1]*The message that came to Jeremiah from Yahweh.*[a]

[2]*Stand in a gateway of Yahweh's house and proclaim*[b] *there this message. Say: Listen to Yahweh's message, all Judah who come through these gateways to bow down to Yahweh.*[c]
[3]*Yahweh of Armies, Israel's God, has said this: Make your paths and your practices good so that I may have you dwell*[d] *in this place.* [4]*Do not rely for yourselves on words of deception, "Those*[e] *are Yahweh's palace, Yahweh's palace, Yahweh's palace."* [5]*Because if you really make your paths and your practices good,*[f] *if you really exercise authority between an individual and his fellow,* [6][*if*] *resident alien, fatherless, and widow you do not defraud (and the blood of the person who is free of guilt*[g] *you are not to pour out in this place),*[h] *and after other gods you do not go with dire results for you,* [7]*then I will have you dwell in this place, in the country that I gave to your ancestors, from all time and for all time.*

---

2. Cf. T. Seidl, "Jeremias Tempelrede: Polemik gegen die joschijanische Reform?" in Gross, *Jeremia und die "deuteronomistische Bewegung,"* 141–79, though he sees the section as entirely Deuteronomistic; cf. J. P. Floss, "Methodologische Aspekte exegetischer Hypothesen am Beispiel von Theo Seidls Beitrag zur 'Tempelrede,'" in Gross, *Jeremia und die "deuteronomistische Bewegung,"* 181–85.

3. Allen (*Jeremiah*, 93, 94, 100–101) works out the comparison in detail.

4. Fretheim, *Jeremiah*, 131.

⁸ *There, you are reliant for yourselves on words of deception that could not be any use.* ⁹ *Is there theft—murder—and adultery—and swearing to deception—and burning offerings to the Master*ⁱ*—and going after other gods that you had not acknowledged,*ʲ ¹⁰*then you come and stand before me in this house over which*ᵏ *my name has been proclaimed and say, "We have been rescued in order to do all these offensive things"?*ˡ ¹¹*A robbers' cave—is that what this house over which my name has been proclaimed has become in your eyes? Yes, I—there, I have looked (Yahweh's affirmation).*ᵐ

¹²*Because go, please, to my place that was at Shiloh, where I had my name dwell*ⁿ *at the first, and look at what I did to it in the face of my people Israel's direness.* ¹³*So now, because of your doing all these things (Yahweh's affirmation), and I have spoken*ᵒ *to you, speaking assiduously,*ᵖ *and you have not listened, and I have called to you and you have not answered,* ¹⁴*I will do to the house over which my name has been proclaimed and on which you are reliant and to the place that I have given to you and to your ancestors as I did to Shiloh.* ¹⁵*And I will throw you out from before my face as I threw out all your brothers, Ephraim's entire offspring.*ᵠ

a. LXX lacks v. 1 and has a briefer form of vv. 2–4. MT makes more explicit the link with the story in Jer 26.

b. This finite verb and the next one continue the imperative.

c. MT has a section marker here.

d. Vg, Aq "I will dwell with you"; cf. v. 7. *CTAT* 2:515 sees this reading as reflecting a theology of the Shekinah.

e. That is, the multiplex of temple buildings (cf. Ps 84:1[2]; 2 Chr 8:11).

f. The infinitive preceding the finite verb underscores the requirement; so again in the next clause.

g. On *nāqî*, see the translation note on 2:34.

h. Taking the jussive clause as parenthetical (*TTH* 57).

i. As usual, LXX gives "Baal" a feminine article (see the translation note on 2:8).

j. In vv. 8–9, a sequence of bare infinitives articulate "indignant questions" (*IBHS* 35.52a).

k. Vg "in which," here and later, makes an appropriate but different point.

l. MT's accentuation implies "and say, 'We have been rescued,' in order to do all these offensive things" (Holladay, *Commentary on Jeremiah*, 1:246). But Jeremiah quite likely implies the greater irony of making the people themselves say, *"We have been rescued in order to do all these offensive things"* (Calvin, *Jeremiah* 1:398).

m. MTᴸ has a section marker here.

n. For *šikkantî šamî*, Vg has "where my name dwelt"; cf. Vg at, e.g., Deut 16:2, 6, 11.

o. The finite verbs through v. 13 continue the infinitival construction.

p. Lit. "spoken to you, being assiduous and speaking"; the finite verb is followed by two infinitives.

q. MT has a section marker here.

The message of vv. 1–15 matches that of Jer 2–6 in speaking of bowing down in worship, burning offerings, going after other gods (and specifically the Master), offensive things, what is good and what is dire, paths to walk, deception, authoritative decisions, not cheating a person whose father has died, the blood of the person who is free of guilt, things on which Judah unwisely relies, and Ephraim's fate being a warning to Judah. It is distinctive in speaking of the Judahites dwelling in Yahweh's place, reliance on Yahweh's palace, its being the house over which Yahweh's name was proclaimed or where his name dwells, the resident alien and widow, pouring out blood, theft, murder, and adultery, Shiloh, Yahweh acting assiduously, his throwing the Judahites out of the country, and the Ephraimites as the Judahites' brothers. The references to Yahweh having his name dwell in this place correspond to the language of Deut 12; 14; 16, but in other respects the language has little by way of distinctive links with the rest of Jeremiah or with other material within the First Testament.[5]

"Jeremiah—book and prophet—foregrounds 'place' as locus of encounter between God and people, and as the scene of living rightly with all that implies for the relationship of this people, this place, and this God."[6] But these verses make a link between Yahweh's destruction of the Shiloh place and the threatened destruction of the Jerusalem place. Jeremiah 26 relates how Jeremiah delivered such a message, or rather how people responded to it and what followed. Jeremiah 7:2–15 is thus a report of that message. Jeremiah 26 sets its story in "the beginning of the reign of king Jehoiakim," about 609 or 608 and some four years before the writing of the 604 scroll. If Jer 2–6 more or less comprises that scroll, either the command that the scroll contain "all the words that I have spoken to you" (36:2) need not be taken too literally, or Jer 7 and 26 are more like imaginative creations by the curators than historical accounts. In the context of 609 and the next decades, the sermon would urge people toward a change of community life that would forestall the temple destruction, as 26:1–3 suggests. After 587, it would explain that event. After 516, its message about community life and not trusting in possession of the temple would again become important.[7]

vv. 1–3a   A multiple introduction
v. 3b   An initial positive challenge and promise

5. D. R. Jones (*Jeremiah*, 143–46) surveys in detail how the thinking and language of 7:1–15 overlaps with that of Deuteronomy and of Joshua–Kings but also compares with the messages in Jer 1–6.

6. D. J. Reimer, "God and Place in Jeremiah," in Lundbom, Evans, and B. A. Anderson, *Jeremiah*, 485.

7. E. Scheffler, "The Holistic Historical Background against Which Jeremiah 7:1–15 Makes Sense," *OTE* 7 (1994): 381–95.

vv. 4–7	A developed negative and positive challenge and promise
vv. 8–11	A confrontation
vv. 12–15	A warning

1 The opening verse introduces 7:1–10:25, and specifically 7:1–8:3. The third-person formulation suggests that these words are an introduction by Jeremiah's curators to what follows. It implies a conviction that the message's content came from Yahweh, but the formulation might be the prophet's or the curators' creative articulation.

2 The temple area had a number of *gateways*, so Jeremiah is simply to *stand* at one where lots of people would hear. Jeremiah 26:2 has Yahweh bidding him stand in the temple courtyard; one might picture this gateway as the one between the outer and inner courtyard.[8] It would be logical for Jeremiah to *proclaim there this message* on an occasion when as much of *Judah* as possible came to *Yahweh's house*, an occasion such as a festival, and his doing so fits with the stir the message causes (see Jer 26).[9] There people *bow down*, a standard First Testament term for worship, denoting the physical expression of giving honor; people are bowing before the King in his palace. It was the job of priests to communicate the qualifications people need in order to come to worship: they need to be clear of any impurity and be in a proper moral state (see Pss 15; 24). The temple gateways might be the places where priests did so.[10] In effect, Jeremiah is to intervene to tell people that, actually, they don't meet the criteria.[11] There are thus some ironic implications in calling 7:1–8:3 "a gathering chapter":[12] some liturgical traditions begin worship with "a gathering prayer," and Jeremiah is about to subvert such prayers and proclaim that people must not think "that with your coming here to prostrate yourselves your sins will be forgiven, for it is not so."[13]

3 *Yahweh of Armies* is a familiar expression from Jer 1–6 (see 2:19). *Israel's God* is not. The two phrases point to two aspects of this God's identity—his power in having all war-making capacities at his disposal and his involvement with Israel in particular. The combination is good news and also a challenge, as the message will indicate. *This place* (*māqôm*) can be a worship place, a site (so in vv. 12, 14); to *make your paths and your practices good* is then necessary to gain access to it. But more often, *this place* refers to the land of Judah or the

---

8. Weiser, *Jeremia*, 1:67–68.
9. P. D. Miller, "Jeremiah," on the passage.
10. McKane, *Jeremiah*, 1:159.
11. P. D. Miller, "Jeremiah," on the passage.
12. Fretheim, *Jeremiah*, 131.
13. Isaac Abravanel, *Commentary on the Latter Prophets*, as paraphrased by Rosenberg (*Jeremiah* 1:64).

city of Jerusalem (cf. vv. 6, 20), which fits here when Yahweh talks of having the people *dwell* there (*šākan*). A neighbor (*šākēn*) dwells with you or near you, and dwelling as opposed to living implies settled-ness and security, spelled out in 23:6; 33:16.[14] The possible ambiguity of the reference to *this place* links with a difference between Jer 7 and 26. Whereas Jer 26 talks about city and temple, Jer 7 does not refer to the city, and the initial reference to a place prepares the way for the focus on the temple in vv. 2–15. Yet in the context of Josiah's reformation, "this place" denotes city as well as temple (2 Kgs 22:16–20), both being "the place" that Yahweh chose (e.g., Deut 12), and one aspect of Jeremiah's message is that the "place" with which Yahweh is involved is the country as a whole.[15] In Jer 7, *place* "carries the weight of ambivalence."[16]

4 Jeremiah has already noted stupidities in what the people *rely on* (2:37; 5:17). There is a more subtle stupidity. After Josiah's death and Jehoahaz's deposing, a key question for Judah is what gives protection. People can always be tempted to make assumptions about where security lies. Here their answer is the temple.[17] They can point and say, *those* are a splendid collection of buildings. They can go on and on about *Yahweh's palace, Yahweh's palace, Yahweh's palace*. English translations have "temple," but the word is *hêkāl*, equivalent to the word for a king's residence. The "temple" is Yahweh's house, the place where he dwells (vv. 2, 10, 11, 14), and it is his palace, his house fit for a king. *Palace* comes otherwise in Jeremiah only in 24:1; 50:28; 51:11, each time in connection with Nebuchadrezzar, his conquest of Jerusalem, his exiling of its people, and his destruction of the temple. "This is the house of the real King. The fact that the real King has his palace here means we do not have to fear the king of Babylon." But the repetition almost sounds like a lucky charm phrase or an incantation.[18] The people's assumption about security is fallacious. Their words are *words of deception*, deceptive words. Whereas Jeremiah has previously associated deception with the Master, the great deceiver or the great vehicle whereby Judah engaged in self-deception, here the means of Judah's self-deception lies elsewhere. Like much self-deception, the people's declaration is subtly and simultaneously a slight but

---

14. See M. Görg, "שָׁכַן, *šākan*," *TDOT* 14:691–702.

15. M. Leuchter, "The Temple Sermon and the Term *mqwm* in the Jeremianic Corpus," *JSOT* 30 (2005): 93–109; *Josiah's Reform*, 111–25.

16. S. V. Davidson, "Ambivalence and Temple Destruction: Reading the Book of Jeremiah with Homi Bhabha," in Diamond and Stulman, *Jeremiah (Dis)placed*, 165.

17. Volz, *Jeremia*, 89.

18. See Lundbom, *Jeremiah 1–20*, 462, for examples of threefold repetitions, including Jeremiah's own in 22:29; also see D. J. Reimer, "On Triplets in a Trio of Prophets," in *Let Us Go Up to Zion: Essays in Honour of H. G. M. Williamson on the Occasion of His Sixty-Fifth Birthday*, ed. I. Provan and M. J. Boda, VTSup 153 (Leiden: Brill, 2012), 211–13.

monumental distance from the truth. There is nothing wrong with their conviction that the temple is Yahweh's palace. He is indeed the great King, and he does live there. But they need to consider some implications of that fact to see that you cannot come into his palace unless you *make your paths and your practices good*. Yahweh is prepared to let his palace be destroyed rather than have them think that in itself it guarantees their security.[19]

"Jeremiah gives no details about the temple" and "gives no details here of the land and very little elsewhere. In fact, he shows little interest in the physical demarcation of space." He contrasts with Ezekiel, who "pays great attention to space and its boundaries, especially the protection of sacred space," and later gives "careful descriptions of land division" (chs. 45, 48).[20] Jeremiah's omission of such details perhaps facilitates the adapting of his words to a Christian context:

> Do not put your hopes in deceptive words that say, "Here is the temple of the Lord," that imply you are his temple. They are only trying to assure that you will never be left by God as though God would decide to preserve his blessed temple. . . . If you have not corrected what you are doing, then you are no temple of God, and God will not save you on account of the sacredness of his temple that is desecrated by you. His soul is disgusted by the multitude of your sacrifices that you offer in your wickedness.[21]

5–7 Like a preacher, Jeremiah now restates his opening point but expands and intensifies it, "raising the rhetorical level a notch or two"[22] as he fulfills his vocation to "speak the truth in the place of untruth."[23] *Make your path and your practices good* first means *exercise authority between an individual and his fellow* (see 4:2; 5:1). Second, it means refusing to *defraud* the *resident alien, fatherless, and widow*. In 5:25–28, Yahweh mentioned the fatherless as one instance of "the needy." Here he adds resident alien and widow. The resultant threefold reference matches Exod 22:21–22(20–21) and Deut 24:17–22 (other passages such as Deut 16:11, 14 also include servants and Levites). All are people who one way or another do not have land and therefore a secure place to live and to grow something to eat. *Widow* goes along with *fatherless* as designating a person vulnerable to being swindled or tricked out of the family estate when the head of the household has passed (see Luke 18:1–8).

19. E. K. Holt, "Jeremiah's Temple Sermon and the Deuteronomists," *JSOT* 36 (1986): 75.

20. K. M. Rochester, "Prophetic Ministry in Jeremiah and Ezekiel" (PhD diss., Durham University, 2009), 172.

21. Ephrem the Syrian, *Commentary on Jeremiah*, quoted in Wenthe, *Jeremiah*, 64.

22. P. D. Miller, "Jeremiah," 2:113.

23. Berrigan, *Jeremiah*, 40.

Jeremiah is not talking about empathy for people who feel vulnerable or about weeping with those who weep but about the administration of the law, and he is being quite hard-headed. Further implications of making your path and your practices good are refusing to *pour out* the *blood of the person who is free of guilt* in the city or country (see 2:34) or to *go after other gods* (see, e.g., 2:5). In effect, vv. 5 and 6 are talking about fulfilling the two great commands, about loving one's neighbor and loving Yahweh. And Jeremiah is functioning as a teacher of Torah.[24] Ignoring such imperatives will mean that dire paths lead to *dire results* (see, e.g., 1:14–16). Yahweh uses a distinctive expression (more literally, "to a dire thing for you"—otherwise only in Eccl 8:9) that suggests bringing trouble on themselves (cf. 25:7). Good paths and practices lead to good results: Yahweh repeats the promise from v. 3, adding the reminder that this is *the country that I gave to your ancestors* (see 3:18), *from all time and for all time* (more literally, "from age to age" or "from ever to ever"). This "startling" phrase applies elsewhere to Yahweh and his commitment (Pss 90:2; 103:17),[25] though giving the country as a domain (3:18) has the same implication. It has belonged to you since way back, and it is impossible to think of it ever not belonging to you. People do have a basis of security, but it doesn't lie simply in the presence of the Great King's palace; it lies in their commitment to walking his ways.

8–10 There might have been nothing surprising about vv. 3–7, especially if, for example, priests declaimed such expectations in the gateways or if the occasion was Sukkot and the Decalogue was proclaimed.[26] But there is more for the community to face, a second facet to the *words of deception* on which *you are reliant for yourselves* and which *could not be any use*. The problem does not lie in people's confidence in the Great King's dwelling among them in his palace. It lies in their assumption that they can maintain that confidence when they are engaged in practices that contrast with the expectations in vv. 5–6: *theft—murder—and adultery—and swearing to deception* (see 5:2)—*and burning offerings to the Master—and going after other gods that you had not acknowledged* (see 1:16; 2:5, 23; 3:24). People behave in such ways and then *come and stand before me in this house over which my name has been proclaimed*. Proclaiming a name over something—of the people (14:9), of the prophet (15:16), of the city (25:29)—signifies ownership and mutual commitment. This house belongs to Yahweh as king, and bowing down before a king is an expression of submission and dependence,

---

24. See C. M. Maier, "Jeremiah as Teacher of Torah," *Int* 62 (2008): 22–32; and further C. M. Maier, *Jeremia als Lehrer der Tora: Soziale Gebote des Deuteronomiums in Fortschreibungen des Jeremiabuches*, FRLANT 196 (Göttingen: Vandenhoeck & Ruprecht, 2002).

25. Holladay, *Commentary on Jeremiah*, 1:243.

26. Craigie, Kelley, and Drinkard, *Jeremiah 1–25*, 123.

while standing before a king signifies adopting the position of a servant in attendance, ready to do as the king says. But people deny that commitment by ignoring the king's expectations, even though they acknowledge that he has signified his ownership of and commitment to them. The concrete references to theft, murder, and adultery make v. 9 as a whole redolent of the Decalogue, though reversing the order of its two main parts that focus on obligations to other people and to Yahweh. (Perhaps there was no more theft, murder, and adultery in seventh-century Jerusalem than in twenty-first century Jerusalem, Los Angeles, or Oxford, in which case Jeremiah's confrontation shows that the incidence and the tolerance of such wrongdoing pollute the whole community.) *They say* (in the course of their worship in this temple), *"We have been rescued."* The verb (*nāṣal niphal*) can apply to the exodus (Exod 3:8; 18:8–11, *hiphil*) and to the deliverance from Sennacherib (2 Kgs 18:29–35; 19:11–12, *niphal* and *hiphil*), and reference to either rescue would be relevant here; their words might also be a statement of faith about what Yahweh is going to do. The trouble is their implicit perception of the aim of their rescue, however understood. "The long question, begun in v. 9" comes to a "provocative conclusion with the final clause": *in order to do all these offensive things.*[27]

11 Their behavior therefore makes them no different from a band of robbers hiding up in a cave. But they are actually visible to Yahweh. "I'm not blind,"[28] Yahweh reminds them. There is a sense of "outrage"[29] in what he says about people coming to the temple who are dishonest and faithless in their everyday lives, like robbers, and are then trying to use the temple as a refuge. It won't work. Jesus picks up Jeremiah's words and takes them in a different direction (Mark 11:15–17);[30] people are bringing trade into the temple. In the twenty-first century, the collocation of these two themes suggests questions about the dominance of the market in world economics in the context of globalization and about the way Christians in business relate to economic thinking and practice.[31]

12 Dire results will follow from people's wayward attitude to Yahweh and wayward community life. There was nothing wrong with their conviction that the temple was Yahweh's dwelling place, but there was something wrong with their assumptions about what followed. Yahweh has implied that he will not continue to have them dwelling in the country and he will not continue

---

27. Fischer, *Jeremia*, 1:301.

28. Volz, *Jeremia*, 92.

29. R. P. Carroll, *Jeremiah*, OTL, 208.

30. R. S. Snow sees Jer 7 also behind Mark 13:14: see "Let the Reader Understand: Mark's Use of Jeremiah 7 In Mark 13:14," *BBR* 21 (2011): 467–77.

31. See J. W. McClendon, *The Collected Works*, ed. R. A. Newson and A. C. Wright (Waco: Baylor University Press, 2014), 2:313–37.

to live in his palace there. Implication now becomes statement. *Go, please, to my place that was at Shiloh.* "Place" now has an explicitly narrower reference, to "the place where I live, my sanctuary." Shiloh, midway between Bethel and Shechem, had once been the location of Israel's central sanctuary and of the pledge chest (see, e.g., 1 Sam 1–4), but it had been destroyed—we don't know when or how. Yahweh here claims responsibility for the destruction as an act of retribution *in the face of my people Israel's direness.* It had been *where I had my name dwell at the first*: Yahweh rings changes on the way he speaks about his name and about dwelling, now using a form of words used in Deut 12:11; 14:23; 16:2, 6, 11; 26:2. As well as being proclaimed over the sanctuary, his name was proclaimed within it. It meant he was really there, because the name embodies the person (see 3:17 and the commentary on it). Shiloh would have been the original place to which Deuteronomy's words applied (they are otherwise used only in Neh 1:9).

13–14 If Yahweh was prepared to act in that way to the place where he had previously had his name dwell, he will be prepared to take such action again. To forestall doing so, *I have spoken to you, speaking assiduously*: Jeremiah introduces another of his signature expressions to denote Yahweh's going out of his way to act tirelessly (*šākam hiphil*)[32] in doing something that shows his commitment to it (cf. v. 25), like Abraham when he gets up early to check out what has happened to Sodom, or to send off Hagar, or to sacrifice Isaac (Gen 19:27; 21:14; 22:3). But *you have not listened.* Further, *I have called to you*, as a master does to a servant, *and you have not answered.* Whereas in vv. 3–10, the basis for critique was people's ignoring the teaching of priests based on established Torah, here the basis for critique is people's not listening to the message of prophets (cf. 6:19). So, says Yahweh, I am prepared to treat my Jerusalem palace as I treated my place at Shiloh. Yahweh's references to Shiloh and Jerusalem make for a suggestive and ironic contrast with Ps 78,[33] which tells of Yahweh's abandoning Shiloh and choosing Zion, where he built his sanctuary (and of Yahweh's choice of David, who gets no reference here).[34] That story could function as a "self-serving Jerusalem ideology."[35] Yahweh turns that possibility on its head. The logic will be taken up by Paul in Rom 9–11, which warns the church not to think that it has replaced Israel in God's

32. See R. Bartelmus, "שכם, *škm*," *TDOT* 14:681–88. Syr thus nicely paraphrases "early and late," though Vg has simply "getting up early." Hugh of St. Cher opposes the inference that there should therefore be no preaching after breakfast ("Liber Jeremiae," in *Praedicatorum Tomus Quartus* [Venice: Pezanna, 1703], 197, quoted in J. A. Schroeder, *The Book of Jeremiah*, The Bible in Medieval Tradition [Grand Rapids: Eerdmans, 2017], 125).

33. F. E. Deist, "The Implied Message of the Reference to Shiloh in Jeremiah 7:12," *Journal for Semitics* 5 (1993): 57–67.

34. M. Avioz, "A Rhetorical Analysis of Jeremiah 7:1–15," *TynB* 57 (2006): 188.

35. Brueggemann, *Jeremiah 1–25*, 77.

purpose. "As the destruction of Shiloh is an example of the destruction of Jerusalem or the temple, so the destruction of the temple is an example of the destruction of the church. Romans 11:21: 'If God did not spare the natural branches, we should be afraid, lest God spare us even less.'"[36] When Yahweh entered into a relationship with Israel, it was not because Israel satisfied certain conditions; they did not do so. His love for them was not conditioned or conditional. But once they belonged to him, their relationship with him required their living faithfully with him and with one another, and unfaithfulness imperiled the relationship. Maybe one should therefore say that his originally unconditional relationship with them becomes conditional. To his disciples, Jesus indicates that God's love for them works in this way: "If you forgive other people their trespasses, your heavenly Father will forgive you; but if you do not forgive other people, neither will your Father forgive you" (Matt 6:14–15).[37] Indeed, love without conditions may not be real love if it leaves people free to continue as they are.[38]

15 As well as destroying the temple, *I will throw you out from before my face*—not merely out of the temple but out of Canaan. And if they wonder whether he would do such a thing, they should remember the way *I threw out all your brothers, Ephraim's entire offspring*, whose example featured prominently as a warning in Jer 2.

b. About Whether It's Possible to Pray (7:16–20)

[16]*And you: do not plead on account of this people, do not lift up on their account a chant by way of plea,*[a] *do not press me, because I'm not going to listen to you.* [17]*You see what they are doing in Judah's towns and in Jerusalem's streets, don't you.* [18]*The children are gathering pieces of wood, the fathers are kindling the fire, and the women are kneading dough to make loaves for the Queen*[b] *of the Heavens—and pouring*[c] *libations to other gods for the sake of irking me.* [19]*Is it me that they are irking? (Yahweh's affirmation.) It's themselves, isn't it, for the sake of their visible shame.*[d] [20]*Therefore the Lord*[e] *Yahweh has said this: There, my furious anger*[f] *is going to pour*[g] *on this place, onto the human being, onto the animal, onto the tree in the open country, and onto the fruit of the ground. It will burn and not go out.*[h]

---

36. Hugh of St. Cher, "Liber Jeremiae," 197, quoted in Schroeder, *Jeremiah*, 124; cf. the quotation from Ephrem above in connection with v. 4.

37. See further J. Goldingay, *Biblical Theology* (Downers Grove, IL: InterVarsity, 2016), 112–19.

38. S. G. Post, "Conditional and Unconditional Love," *Modern Theology* 7 (1991): 435–46.

a. A hendiadys; lit. "a chant and a plea."

b. MT's spelling *mǝleket*, rather than *malkat*, suggests seeing the word as a variant on *mǝle'ket*, the reading in some medieval manuscripts (cf. Syr), which compares with LXX "army," and seeing people as worshiping the handiwork/army of the heavens (as in 8:2; Qimchi, in MG) rather than *the Queen of the Heavens* (Aq, Sym, Theod, Vg). Tg has "the star of the heavens." LXX has "Queen" at 44:17–25 (LXX 51:17–25). See BDB, *BHS*.

c. This last verb is an infinitive; see the translation note on vv. 8–9.

d. Lit. "the shame of their face." MT^L has a section marker here.

e. Not in LXX; see the commentary.

f. Another hendiadys; lit. "my anger and my fury" (the verb that follows is singular).

g. For *nātak niphal*, Aq, Sym have "trickle" (*stazō*) instead of LXX's "pour out" (*cheō*), which is beautiful (Jerome, *Jeremiah*, 52) but unfortunately not what Yahweh says.

h. MT has a section marker here.

"Suddenly Jeremiah no longer stands in the temple court before 'all Judah' but somewhere else before Yahweh."[39] Initially, one might nevertheless see this instruction to Jeremiah as continuing the first message, but what follows indicates that there are other reasons for it. In a further attempt to get Judah to see the peril of its situation and to respond to it, Jeremiah reports that Yahweh isn't going to be listening to any prayers from him on their behalf because of the way they have compromised their loyalty to Yahweh.

v. 16a	Don't pray for this people
v. 16b	The reason
vv. 17–19	The rationale: what they are doing
v. 20	The rationale: what Yahweh intends to do

16 The opening *and you* (with the singular pronoun expressed) signals a transition in the form of the section. People may *plead* (*pālal hithpalel*) for themselves in connection with some need or desire, but kings, prophets, and priests also do it for their people (e.g., 1 Kgs 8; 1 Sam 12:23; Ezra 10:1), and the scroll refers elsewhere to Jeremiah praying on the people's behalf (18:20; 21:2; 37:3; 42:1–6). Behind the language may be the model of someone of status being able to intervene with another powerful person on one's behalf; a prophet can do so through taking part in meetings of Yahweh's cabinet. A plea for someone else is an act of intervention on their behalf. But the verb does become simply a general word for prayer.[40] *A chant by way of plea* would imply being prepared to make quite a noise in doing so. It is a sign that one really means the plea and knows that one needs to get the attention of the

39. Duhm, *Jeremia*, 78.

40. See J. F. A. Sawyer, "Types of Prayer in the Hebrew Bible," in *Sacred Texts and Sacred Meanings: Studies in Biblical Language and Literature*, J. F. A. Sawyer, Hebrew Bible Monographs 28 (Sheffield: Sheffield Phoenix, 2011), 281–87.

object of the plea, who doubtless has other things to think about. Yahweh reformulates the point when he talks of it as an act whereby one might *press* someone on another person's behalf (*pāgaʿ*). The word commonly means "reach," so intercession means reaching out to someone on another person's behalf and making contact with them. It also commonly means "fall on" in a hostile fashion, so it could suggest putting pressure or "lobbying."[41] Interceding is to "elbow someone in the ribs."[42] It is a powerful activity. It can make things happen. Not praying therefore means that things may not happen. While in principle "the prayers of the saints are able to check the anger of God,"[43] there is such a thing as the sin against the Holy Spirit (Matt 12:31–32; 1 John 5:16).[44] And at this moment, praying on Judah's behalf is forbidden and pointless *because I am not going to listen to you.* Yet for all their sins, Jeremiah loves his people,[45] and telling them about this prohibition is actually an expression of his love and of Yahweh's love. Yahweh's issuing the prohibition and Jeremiah's reporting it are yet another attempt to get through to people. As usual, Jeremiah thus relates what is going on between himself and Yahweh because it contains a message for people. Declaring that he cannot fulfill his intercessory role as a prophet is a terrible threat. They need to imagine Yahweh implementing such a threat and to repent while they have the chance. If the prohibition and Jeremiah's reporting of it are thus part of an attempt to get through to the people, there need be no implication that Jeremiah is being actually or permanently forbidden to pray. Certainly Jer 37 and 42 imply that he didn't take the prohibition literally, or that he didn't do so permanently; the subsequent repetition of the injunction (11:14; 14:11) may imply that he never stopped praying.[46] Indeed, perhaps the "dire command" that Jeremiah should not pray is "all the while implying its opposite. . . . Is not a plea implied in the command to cease and desist? In effect: Do not give up on this people!"[47] But anyway, the reporting of the command is an element within Jeremiah's preaching, and its repetition underlines how terrible a message was the reporting of this injunction to the people and how powerfully it was thus hoped to move them.

17–18 The reason for the prohibition does not lie in what people are doing in the temple, which may be quite orthodox. Nor does it lie in what they are doing in mutual relationships in the community (as in vv. 2–15). But it is a variant on going after other deities, to which that first message

---

41. McKane, *Jeremiah*, 1:169.
42. P. Maiberger, "פָּגַע, *pāgaʿ*," *TDOT* 11:473.
43. Jerome, *Jeremiah*, 51.
44. Hugh of St. Cher, "Liber Jeremiae," 197, quoted in Schroeder, *Jeremiah*, 127–28.
45. Rudolph, *Jeremia*, 55.
46. Bright, *Jeremiah*, 56.
47. Berrigan, *Jeremiah*, 42.

referred. It lies in *what they are doing in Judah's towns and in Jerusalem's streets.* Jeremiah is contrasting what happens in the temple in public worship and what happens elsewhere and suggesting that the practices in question took place throughout city and country. *The children* and *the fathers* are involved in making the fire ready for baking, as *the women are kneading dough to make loaves for the Queen of the Heavens,* ready for a family celebration. "He mentions the various household members, the 'children,' the 'fathers' and the 'mothers' (or 'wives'), in order to show that there was no age group that was dissenting from this impiety"[48] and that it involved people of both sexes. Understood positively, this worship was a homely, family affair that gave women a role that they didn't have in temple worship. Is Yahweh being snide toward the men in implying that they've been sucked into involvement in family celebrations centered on women and children when they ought to have been exercising some authority as the heads of households?[49] "Queen of the Heavens" is an all-purpose title like "Lord"; it could be applied to a chief goddess in a number of different religious systems.[50] Jeremiah doesn't indicate what name she would have had, so his condemnation could cover any goddess who might be conceptualized in these terms.[51] In the context of Josiah's reformation, 2 Kgs 23:13 mentions Ashtoreth,[52] so either Josiah's reformation didn't reach family spirituality or the message reflects the revival of practices that Josiah terminated. Certainly the Queen of the Heavens continued to figure in popular spirituality (44:15–25). The loaves or cakes would incorporate a symbol of her (cf. 44:19)[53] or might be figurines,[54] and they might be presented to her in some way, as *pouring libations to other gods* was another aspect of this family worship. Yahweh says it's as if people are deliberately engaged in these observances *for the sake of irking me,* to exasperate me, make me gnash my teeth (Ps 112:10), provoke me to anger, and drive me to take action in light of them.[55]

---

48. Jerome, *Jeremiah*, 52.

49. Volz, *Jeremia*, 100.

50. See C. Houtman, "Queen of Heaven," *DDD*, 678–81.

51. M. Leuchter, "Cult of Personality: The Eclipse of Pre-Exilic Judahite Cultic Structures in the Book of Jeremiah," in *Constructs of Prophecy in the Former and Latter Prophets and Other Texts*, ed. L. L. Grabbe and M. Nissinen, Ancient Near East Monographs 4 (Atlanta: Society of Biblical Literature, 2011), 106.

52. See N. Wyatt, "Astarte," *DDD*, 109–14.

53. See W. E. Rast, "Cakes for the Queen of Heaven," in *Scripture in History and Theology: Essays in Honor of J. Coert Rylaarsdam*, ed. A. L. Merrill and T. W. Overholt (Pittsburgh: Pickwick, 1977), 167–80.

54. K. J. H. Vriezen, "Cakes and Figurines: Related Women's Cultic Offerings in Ancient Israel?" in *On Reading Prophetic Texts: Gender Specific and Related Studies in Memory of Fokkelien van Dijk-Hemmes*, ed. B. Becking and M. Dijkstra, BibInt 18 (Leiden: Brill, 1996), 251–63.

55. On the verb *kāʿas hiphil* in Jeremiah, see S. Joo, *Provocation and Punishment: The*

19–20 Yahweh oversimplifies when he asks, *is it me that they are irking* or is it really *themselves*; his point is that they are going to end up as exasperated as he is. It's as if they are deliberately acting *for the sake of their visible shame*; they are going to end up shamed and ashamed when Yahweh responds (see 2:26). How much Yahweh has oversimplified becomes explicit when he describes how *my furious anger is going to pour on this place*, on *human being* and also on *animal, tree, and fruit*—because humanity depends on them. "There is no talk here of sparing innocent civilians, women and children, animals, or the rest of Yahweh's good creation."[56] Humanity and the animal world were created on the same day; they were given the same blessing. They are also burdened with the same curse (cf. 12:4). Animals share in the confusion of humanity's existence, but they will also share in its deliverance from bondage into liberty.[57] In the meantime, Yahweh's wrath *will burn and not go out*. The people are storing up wrath for themselves on the day of wrath (Rom 2:5).[58] It is *the Lord Yahweh* who says so, which aptly affirms the sovereign status of Yahweh over against the Queen of the Heavens, as Isa 6:1 affirms Yahweh's sovereign status over against the earthly king.[59] The long declaration of Yahweh's intent in v. 20, which occupies nearly one-third of the section, is a clue to the fact that the indirect audience of this message to Jeremiah is still the Judahite people. They need to know what Yahweh has said to Jeremiah. It is a terrible threat to talk of lighting such an unquenchable fire, and they need to imagine Yahweh implementing such a threat and repent while they have the chance.

c. About Yahweh's Priorities (7:21–28)

[21]*Yahweh of Armies, Israel's God, has said this: Your whole offerings—add them*[a] *to your fellowship sacrifices and eat meat.* [22]*Because I didn't speak with your ancestors and I didn't order them, at the time of my getting them out*[b] *of the country of Egypt, on matters of whole offering or fellowship sacrifice.* [23]*Rather, this thing I ordered them: Listen to my voice, and I will become God for you and you will become a people for me, and go by the entire path that I order you, so that it may be good for you.* [24]*But they didn't listen, they didn't bend their ear, but went by plans, by the determination*[c] *of their dire thinking. They became backward, not forward,* [25]*from the day when your*[d] *ancestors got out*

Anger of God in the Book of Jeremiah and Deuteronomistic Theology, BZAW 361 (Berlin: de Gruyter, 2006), 155–223.

56. Lundbom, *Jeremiah 1–20,* 479.
57. Barth, *CD* III, 1:180–81.
58. Hugh of St. Cher, "Liber Jeremiae," 197, quoted in Schroeder, *Jeremiah,* 129.
59. Allen, *Jeremiah,* 99.

of the country of Egypt until this day. I sent to you all my servants the prophets, by day,[e] *sending assiduously.*[f] [26]*But they didn't listen to me, they didn't bend their ear, but stiffened their neck—they acted more direly than their ancestors.*

[27]*You will speak to them all these things, but they won't listen to you. You will call to them but they won't answer you.* [28]*And you will say to them:*[g] *This is the nation that didn't listen to the voice of Yahweh its God and didn't accept restraint—truthfulness has perished and cut itself off from their mouth.*[h]

a. Cf. LXX, Vg, Tg, though *səpû* is also the imperative from *sāpâ* ("sweep away"), and Jeremiah might have no objection if his audience picked up this nuance.

b. The *qere* has *hôṣî'î*; the *ketiv* implies simply *hôṣî'*.

c. The combination of *by plans* and *by the determination of their . . . thinking* corresponds to the parallelism in Ps 81:12(13), but the combination may result from the texts being conflated.

d. LXX, Vg have "their."

e. Vg has *per diem* ("day after day" or "day by day"), which makes good sense, but there are no other instances of *yôm* having this meaning (see *DCH*, 4:182); Syr does imply *yôm yôm*.

f. See the translation note and commentary on v. 13.

g. LXX has a much shorter version of vv. 26–28, lacking the whole of v. 27.

h. MT has a section marker here.

This time, a new introduction marks a new message. Whereas people offer proper worship, Yahweh returns to the problem on which vv. 1–15 focused: outside worship there is no discipline or truthfulness about their life. The argument here is that the scriptural story shows that God sees truthfulness as the first priority; without it, worship means nothing.

v. 21a	Introduction
v. 21b	Yahweh's bidding to the people
vv. 22–26	The rationale
vv. 22–23	What Yahweh did not and did say
vv. 24–25a	How people responded
v. 25b	What Yahweh further did
v. 26	How people further responded
v. 27	Yahweh's double bidding to Jeremiah and the response they will give
v. 28	Yahweh's further bidding to Jeremiah—what he is to say to them

21 Yahweh's instructions recall the instructions a priest might give to potential worshipers, as in vv. 3–11, though here they are more like a "parody."[60] The one who speaks is again *Yahweh of Armies, Israel's God* (see

60. Holladay, *Commentary on Jeremiah*, 1:259.

v. 3), with the implications of that double description. He is again being dismissive of *whole offerings* and *fellowship sacrifices* (see 6:20), though here he neatly nuances the point. God and people share fellowship sacrifices, whereas people give the entirety of whole offerings to God. You can keep both of them, Yahweh says. *Eat meat.* It's just a meal. Enjoy your steak, kiddo. There's nothing religious or sacred about it. "Eat, then, and stuff your stomachs."[61] Elsewhere in Jeremiah, Yahweh speaks positively about whole offerings and fellowship sacrifices (17:26), about priests enjoying their share of the sacrifices (31:14), about the people bringing thanksgiving sacrifices in the rebuilt temple (33:11), and about priests there overseeing whole offering and fellowship sacrifice (33:18). Even in this chapter, his reference to his name being proclaimed in the temple, its dwelling in the sanctuary at Shiloh, and his outrage at the temple being turned into a robbers' den indicate that he is not in principle dismissive of its worship.[62] But those facts don't hinder him from being scornful here for the reasons that will follow.

22–23 Neither do they hinder him from offering a selective account of his relationship with Israel. Whereas people think he views sacrifices as important, history should remind them of the relatively low place they have in his interests. *I didn't speak with your ancestors* about them, *and I didn't order them, at the time of my getting them out of the country of Egypt.* Recall the story, will you. Yahweh again speaks hyperbolically. The ordinances in Exod 20:22–23:33 begin with an altar for whole offerings and fellowship sacrifices, and maybe these ordinances shaped people's thinking.[63] Indeed, before the exodus, Moses spoke about such offerings (Exod 10:25). But it was way earlier that Yahweh had said, "I shall take you for myself as a people, and I shall become God for you" (Exod 6:7), and the first thing he said to Israel at Sinai was, "If you really listen to my voice and keep my pledge, you'll be for me personal treasure from among all the peoples" (Exod 19:5). Possibly, Yahweh here refers to individuals bringing whole offerings and fellowship sacrifices rather than to the regular order of sanctuary worship.[64] But his first requirements of individuals that Exodus reports, in the Decalogue, make no mention of offerings; at Sinai he mentioned individual offerings only later (e.g., Lev 1–3). *To go in the entire path that I order you* does not have its focus on sacrifices; what Yahweh wants is that they should *listen.* The synagogue lectionary nicely sets this Jeremiah passage alongside a reading from Levit-

---

61. Calvin, *Jeremiah* 1:419.
62. R. P. Carroll, *Jeremiah*, OTL, 209.
63. Holladay, *Commentary on Jeremiah*, 1:261.
64. J. Milgrom, "Concerning Jeremiah's Repudiation of Sacrifice," *ZAW* 89 (1977): 273–75.

icus about offering sacrifices; it would have been a comfort once sacrifices became impossible after AD 70,[65] and it might have already been a comfort after 587. Anyway, Yahweh's hyperbole should not be taken simplistically any more than his saying that he didn't make the pledge with the exodus generation but with the next generation (Deut 5:3) and spoke more unequivocally than he meant (cf. Mark 9:37; John 12:44; Acts 5:4; 1 Cor 1:17).[66]

24 *But they didn't listen*: he will repeat this in v. 26 and v. 27 and v. 28. *They didn't bend their ear*: more literally, they didn't turn their ear (*nāṭâ hiphil*) in the right direction in order to hear what was being said to them. It is another distinctively Jeremianic expression (cf. v. 26), which otherwise comes mostly in the Psalms in appeals to Yahweh to turn his ear and in Proverbs in comments on the wisdom of turning one's ear to good teaching. The Israelites weren't prepared to pay God the compliment of doing to him as they asked him to do to them, and they were like the fool rather than the wise person in their openness to learning. It's as if they didn't have ears (5:21) or as if their ears had flaps over them (6:10). Instead of bending them, people made up their own minds about how to live. They *went by plans, by the determination of their dire thinking* (see 3:17). They went *backward*, away from the direction Yahweh pointed (cf. Isa 1:4), *not forward* in the direction he did point—like oxen "which, when put to the yoke, pull back their necks, and will not draw as they are directed."[67]

25–26 When Yahweh thinks back, less happily than he did in 2:2, to *the day when your ancestors got out of the country of Egypt*, he recalls that they were doing so from the beginning; the memory is less rose-tinted here.[68] And they have been behaving that way *until this day*. He has been trying to get through to them all this time: *I sent to you* (here the present generation whom Jeremiah identifies with their ancestors poke through the rhetoric) *all my servants* (sending servants is what a king does) *the prophets*, *by day* (maybe implying "daily," another hyperbole; see the translation note), *sending assiduously*. He thus reformulates the words in v. 13, making explicit that his prophets were his means of speaking (see 2:30; 5:13; 6:17). And he reformulates the image of turning their ears so as to listen: instead, they stiffened their neck, so that their head would not turn and listen. To put the rose-tinted glasses back on, they have been worse than their ancestors in this respect. *My servants the prophets* is a distinctively Jeremianic phrase

---

65. M. A. Fishbane, *Haftarot*, The JPS Bible Commentary (Philadelphia: Jewish Publication Society, 2002), 161.

66. Lundbom, *Jeremiah 1–20*, 488–89.

67. Blayney, *Jeremiah*, 261.

68. Rudolph, *Jeremia*, 59.

(25:4; 26:5; 29:19; 35:15; 44:4) and consistently "characterizes the Israelites as stubbornly rebellious throughout their history," though it is introduced to make different points in the different passages.[69]

27 So don't expect people to listen, Yahweh bids Jeremiah. You will have the same experience as I have had (v. 13), he says encouragingly. Perhaps he gives Jeremiah this bidding so that he's not surprised or put off by the results of his work or inclined to blame himself as a failure. But the words are again meant for the Judahites to hear, to push Jeremiah's audience to a reaction that disproves them. They also function as a strange reassurance for people reading them the other side of 587. "The threat of God's failure and the failure of prophecy is the great mythic terror haunting . . . [the book called] 'Jeremiah.'"[70] Yahweh's words affirm that the people's resistance didn't catch Yahweh (or Jeremiah) out.

28 These functions fit with the rhetorically strange nature of what follows. Perhaps this third-person description of the Judahites may encourage them to look at themselves from the outside and encourage people living decades later to think of them this way and to be warned by their example. Calvin thus prays: "Grant, Almighty God, that since we have been abundantly taught by ancient examples how insane they are who bend not under thy threatenings, and repent not in due time while thou invitest them to repentance,—O grant, that we may wholly give up ourselves to be disciplined by thee."[71] But they *didn't accept restraint*—constraint or discipline or instruction (see 2:19–20, 30; 5:3, 5; 6:8). They were an embodiment of stupidity. *Truthfulness* (see 5:1, 3) has disappeared from the community. It has *cut itself off from their mouth*. The way they are acting is not just a temporary aberration (see 5:1–5). Truthfulness *has perished*. It has died.

The closing verses manifest rhythm and parallelism, and one could read them as poetic lines:[72]

> I sent to you all my servants the prophets,
>> by day, sending assiduously.
> But they didn't listen to me,
>> they didn't bend their ear.
> They stiffened their neck—
>> they acted more direly than their ancestors.

69. Sharp, *Prophecy and Ideology in Jeremiah*, 43; Sharp goes on to suggest how the chapter developed redactionally.
70. Diamond, "Jeremiah," 549.
71. Calvin, *Jeremiah*, 1:481.
72. For v. 28, see Duhm, *Jeremia*, 74.

You will speak to them all these things,
    but they won't listen to you.
You will call to them,
    but they won't answer you.

You will say to them: This is the nation that

Didn't listen to the voice of Yahweh its God
    and didn't accept restraint.
Truthfulness has perished,
    and cut itself off from their mouth.

A transition to poetry (albeit prosaic poetry) as Yahweh moves from speaking about Judah to addressing Jeremiah himself would correspond to this move at 1:17. More certainly, the verse that follows comprises two poetic lines.

d. About an Ultimate Sacrifice (7:29–34)

[29] *Shave your consecration*[a] *and throw it away,*
    raise a mourning song on the bare heights.
Because Yahweh has rejected,
    deserted the generation with which he is furious.[b]

[30] *Because the Judahites have done what is dire in my eyes (Yahweh's affirmation)—they have put their detestable things in the house over which my name has been proclaimed, to defile it.* [31] *They have kept building*[c] *shrines*[d] *at the Shameful Fireplace,*[e] *which is in the Ben-Hinnom Ravine, to consume their sons and their daughters in fire, which I did not order; it did not arise in my mind.*[f] [32] *Therefore, there, days are coming (Yahweh's affirmation) when "the Shameful Fireplace" and "Ben-Hinnom Ravine" will no more be said, but rather "Slaughter Ravine." They will bury in "a shameful fireplace" because there is no room.* [33] *This people's corpse*[g] *will be for food for the bird in the heavens and for the animal in the earth, with there being no one disturbing them.*[h] [34] *I will stop from Judah's towns and from Jerusalem's streets the voice of joy and the voice of rejoicing, the voice of bridegroom and the voice of bride, because the country will become a waste.*

a. Sym appositely renders *nēzer* "the sacred hair of your Naziriteship."
b. Lit. "the generation of his fury."
c. The *wǝqatal* perhaps refers to the building and then rebuilding after Josiah's reformation or links with the plural "shrines" that follows.

253

d. LXX, Tg have singular "a shrine."

e. Etymologically, *tōpet* suggests a hearth (see *HALOT*), which fits the role it fulfills, but the spelling make a connection with the *bōšet* ("shame"; LXX has *tapheth*).

f. MT has a section marker here.

g. *Nəbēlâ* is both numerical singular and collective singular—here the latter; thus LXX, Tg have plural "corpses," though Vg has singular.

h. Verses 30–31 appear in an alternative form as 32:34–35, and vv. 31–33 as 19:5–7.

In 7:29–8:3, Jeremiah brings this section's accusations to a horrifying double climax. First, the people are involved in forms of worship to other deities that involve sacrificing their children. Death will follow. As Jer 26 gives the narrative context for 7:1–15, Jer 19:1–13 provides a narrative context for 7:29–34 (see esp. 19:5–7). The message again suggests the revival of practices such as Ezekiel documents, which Josiah terminated (see 2 Kgs 23:10; cf. vv. 17–18 and the commentary on them).

7:29	A summary declaration of punishment in two bicola
7:30–31	The background: a confrontation
7:32–34	The foreground: a series of warnings

29 *Your* is feminine singular, so Jeremiah reverts to addressing Jerusalem, now with an isolated poetic declaration that will be explained by the horrors of vv. 30–34. As the object of *shave*, the noun *your consecration* (*nēzer*) refers to the hair as a sign of the consecration involved in a Nazirite vow (see Num 6). Jerusalem is like a woman who has undertaken such a vow of dedication to Yahweh. At the completion of the consecration period, one would cut one's hair and make it part of an offering. Here, Yahweh dismisses this offering as he dismissed people's sacrifices when he told them to treat them as a steak dinner. Don't think of offering your cut hair. Just *throw it away*. And *raise a mourning song on the bare heights*—not in the temple, and perhaps not even in some shrine on those heights (but see 3:2, 21 and Lamentations for such expressions of grief that could be offered in the ruins of the temple after the fall of Jerusalem). The relationship of dedication presupposed by the vow is over. "Life has taken a cruel turn; lamentation is the only adequate response."[73] *Because Yahweh has rejected* not just people like Egypt and Assyria on whom Judah relied (2:37) but Judah itself (6:30).

30 Why has he taken that drastic action? The readers know the answer if they are reading the Jeremiah scroll sequentially, or even if they are reading the messages in this section sequentially. But Yahweh has more horrendous things to say that explain Yahweh's walking out on *the Judahites* because

73. Berrigan, *Jeremiah*, 44.

they *have done what is dire in my eyes*. In 4:1, it wasn't quite explicit whether they had *put their detestable things* (presumably divine images) *in the house over which my name has been proclaimed* or whether the images were just in other shrines or in people's homes, but now it is explicit. On the other hand, Yahweh doesn't quite say here that they have done so "in order to defile it" (contrast v. 10). But the effect of their action is *to defile it* as their ancestors defiled the country (2:7). To say that the temple is defiled is a horrifying statement. The Day of Atonement cleansed it of defilement because the accumulation of defilement would make it impossible for Yahweh to be present; one doesn't want to go into one's own house if someone has defiled it. The Judahites have turned the temple into a place that Yahweh is bound to abandon.

31 By no means is that all. They have also defiled themselves by their activities in the *Ben-Hinnom Ravine* (2:23), where *they have kept building shrines at the Shameful Fireplace*. A shrine is a *bāmâ*, conventionally a "high place." But this reference to shrines in a canyon indicates that there is no need for these places to be on high. They are simply worship places. The Shameful Fireplace appears only in 7:31–32; 19:1–15; 2 Kgs 23:10 (cf. also Isa 30:33). When 2 Kgs 23:10 refers only to passing one's children through fire (so also, e.g., Jer 32:35), it may imply only a dedication ceremony that does not involve their death; they would come out the other side of the fire after a rite that was perhaps something like an ordeal by fire. Here the rite involves parents offering children in sacrifice. Yahweh implies that they thought they were offering them to Yahweh, but 19:5 sees them as offered to the Master, and 32:35 nuances the point by speaking of them as offered to Molek (see the commentary on Jer 32:35). Second Kings 23:10–13 mentions Molek in the same context as Ashtoreth (see the commentary on v. 18). Parents would first slaughter them, then *incinerate their sons and their daughters in the fire*, as happened with a sacrificial animal in the temple (cf. Ezek 16:21). Jeremiah uses a distinctively everyday word for burning (*šārap*), a term you would use for disposing of the remains of an offering, not the term for the proper burning of a sacrifice (*qāṭar piel*; 33:18), which Jeremiah uses even for the less horrifying offerings to other deities (v. 9). To sacrifice your child is an ultimate sacrifice that parents were prepared to make when they were under pressure (see 2 Kgs 3:27).[74] But while Yahweh did "claim" firstborn sons, whose parents bought them back by providing an animal as a substitute, actually sacrificing sons or daughters was something *which I did not order; it did not arise in my mind*. The comment (repeated in 19:5; 32:35) suggests

---

74. For child sacrifice in the ancient world, see, e.g., Lundbom, *Jeremiah 1–20*, 496–97.

that people thought he had done so, but Deut 12:31 makes explicit that people were not to make this kind of offering to Yahweh.

32–33 Yahweh will definitely take action in relation to this practice in due course. *Days are coming* is another characteristically and distinctively Jeremianic phrase; it comes fifteen times in Jeremiah and only six times elsewhere.[75] It refers to an event that will be of huge importance, will make a big difference, may be bad news or good news, is quite certain, but may not happen tomorrow (e.g., 23:5, 7). Yahweh will then take action as a result of which the names *"the Shameful Fireplace" and "Ben-Hinnom Ravine" will no more be said, but rather "Slaughter Ravine."* In Yahweh's assessment of the sacrifices people offer there, *slaughter ravine* is what it is already. It's just a place where people kill their children. The name will become appropriate for another reason. People *will bury in "a shameful fireplace" because there is no room* anywhere else in Jerusalem when Yahweh lets loose his fury on the city. To tweak the image again, that event will mean the death of the city or the people itself, and it then will be as if this people's corpse will be for food for the bird in the heavens and for the animal on the earth. There will be no one to stop these creatures enjoying their feast, *no one disturbing them*, as Deut 28:26 says. There will be no Rizpah guarding this corpse (2 Sam 21:10).

34 Yahweh adds that he *will stop from Judah's towns and from Jerusalem's streets the voice of joy and the voice of rejoicing, the voice of bridegroom and the voice of bride.* It is to add another image for the death of the city and the people.[76] Logically, child sacrifice leads to an end to childbearing.[77] More broadly, marrying and being willing to have children is a statement of hope for the future. In Jerusalem, there will be no marriage, no children, and no future, *because the country will become a waste* and will stay that way.[78] "Instead of a wedding there will be a funeral, or rather a non-funeral. Since a funeral would be more than Israel deserves, according to God, her dead body will instead be left uncared for and unburied on the earth, exposed to the elements, food for birds of prey and wild animals."[79]

---

75. M. Weinfeld, "Jeremiah and the Spiritual Metamorphosis of Israel," *ZAW* 88 (1976): 18.

76. Calvin, *Jeremiah*, 1:446.

77. Lundbom, *Jeremiah 1–20*, 500.

78. McKane, *Jeremiah*, 1:180.

79. D. Lipton, "Food for the Birds of Heaven: Staged Death and Intercession in Jeremiah in Light of Shakespeare's Cymbeline," in *Leshon Limmudim: Essays on the Language and Literature of the Hebrew Bible in Honour of A. A. Macintosh*, ed. D. A. Baer and R. P. Gordon, LHBOTS 593 (London: T&T Clark, 2013), 127.

e. About Looking to the Sun, the Moon, and the Stars (8:1–3)

¹*At that time (Yahweh's affirmation) people will get*ᵃ *the bones of the kings of Judah, the bones of his officials, the bones of the priests, the bones of the prophets, and the bones of the people who live in Jerusalem out of their graves.* ²*They will spread them out to the sun, to the moon, and to the entire heavenly army that they loved, that they served, that they went after, that they had inquired of, and that they bowed down to—they will not be gathered and they will not be buried; manure on the face of the ground they will become.* ³*And death will be chosen rather than life by the entire remainder of the people who remain from this dire kin group in all the places of the people who remain where I have driven them away (an affirmation of Yahweh of Armies).*ᵇ

> a. For the *qere yôṣî'û*, the *ketiv* implies *wəyōṣî'û* (simple *waw* plus *yiqtol*) following the extraposed phrases (*TTH* 125).
> b. MT has a marker here.

The chapter division in printed Bibles is odd; MT continues without even a section break. These three verses do move to a different offense of seeking the help of the gods that lie behind sun, moon, and stars. For this offense, too, there will be redress.

> vv. 1–2   What will happen to Jerusalemites
> v. 3   How the survivors will react

1 There is thus another grisly scene to portray, though the gruesomeness lies in the punishment rather than in the offense. *That time* is apparently the time when the outpouring of Yahweh's fury (7:29) has happened and people have come to recognize what earned it. In their anger and resentment, they *will get the bones of the kings of Judah . . . his officials . . . the priests . . . the prophets, and . . . the people who live in Jerusalem out of their graves,* a terrible act of redress. The list covers everyone, in keeping with the critique's covering everyone (e.g., 5:1–9); it would be literalistic to ask who is left to do the exhuming. When one's loved ones die, one buries them carefully so that they are "at rest"; their body's resting is the outward equivalent of their spirit's resting in Sheol. But if their body is not thus at rest, their spirit cannot be, because they are the two aspects of the person. And it will be impossible for the living to relate to them anymore, for instance by going to their tomb: "The living and the deceased individual [are] permanently estranged."[80]

> 80. F. Stavrakopoulou, *Land of Our Fathers: The Roles of Ancestor Veneration in Biblical Land Claims*, LHBOTS 473 (London: T&T Clark, 2010), 109.

2 There will thus be some poetic justice about what people do with these bones. They will *spread them out to the sun, to the moon, and to the entire heavenly army.* The observance of celestial phenomena was basic to Assyrian and Babylonian thinking, policy-making, and religion. It generated clever and sophisticated algorithms, and the Judahites had been accustomed to turn to the gods represented by the planets. The reference here is thus to a more public and officially-sponsored form of worship (cf. 2 Kgs 21:3; 23:5; Ezek 8:16) than the family worship of 7:29–34.[81] "The judgment takes on an ironic twist"; it was Judah's worship of these deities that had led to the judgment.[82] A terrible list of the aspects of that worship follows. These are the deities *that they loved, served, went after, had inquired of,* and *bowed down to.* All but the fourth verb have come already in this scroll (the fourth will come in 10:21). They could sum up a relationship with Yahweh. But in these people's spirituality, they have other objects. So let them lie before these other entities that they once honored. The spreading will be their final fate. While grave robbing is one reason for such action,[83] it's also simply a dishonoring, disturbing, and defiling (cf. 2 Kgs 23:16). *They will not be gathered and they will not be buried; manure on the face of the ground they will become.* They will never have any rest.

3 People who escape death in the city (perhaps they are the people who take the action just described) might congratulate themselves on being *the remainder . . . who remain . . . the people who remain.* The excessive repetition underlines the idea of their being the remnant—what Jer 24 will later call the good figs. But perhaps their being *in all the places . . . where I have driven them* (another Jeremianic phrase) should have given them a hint that they are not destined for much of a life there. "Shall they be called 'the living'? They are no more alive . . . than stalking corpses."[84] They will end up wishing they hadn't escaped death in Jerusalem. Their life will be so horrible that *death will be chosen rather than life* by them, if they had the choice. Fortunately, it's not the last thing Yahweh has to say about them (see, e.g., 23:1–8). Meanwhile, in view of the possibility of being reduced because of their dire behavior so that they remain as only a tiny number and are thrown out of the country that Yahweh is giving them, Deut 30:19–20 urges people to choose life rather than death by loving Yahweh, listening to Yahweh, and holding onto Yahweh.

---

81. P. A. Viviano makes broader comparisons between this section and 2 Kgs 21 ("Exhortation and Admonition in Deuteronomistic Terms: A Comparison of Second Kings 17:7–18, 34–41, Second Kings 21:2–16, and Jeremiah 7:1–8:3," *Biblical Research* 56 [2001]: 35–54).

82. Craigie, Kelley, and Drinkard, *Jeremiah 1–25,* 127.

83. Blayney, *Jeremiah,* 263.

84. Berrigan, *Jeremiah,* 46.

2. Three Exchanges (8:4–9:26[25])

Within part 2a, we move to a new compilation of messages in poetry running from 8:4 to 9:26(25), after which 10:1 marks another new start; for convenience I will refer to this unit as Jer 8–9. It compares with Jer 2–6 in constituting a compilation of short poetic messages that interweave confrontation concerning the life of Judah, warning about trouble that will follow, and exhortation to turn back, and thus it might form part of the "many words like them" that were added to the original 604 scroll. But compared with Jer 2–6, it includes much more by way of comments and reactions by Jeremiah and Judah. Indeed, its central, dominant, and distinctive feature is a series of spirited exchanges between Yahweh and Judah, Yahweh and Jeremiah, and Jeremiah and Judah. We hear the voice of Judah and the voice of Jeremiah himself as well as the voice of Yahweh interacting with these two voices. The chapters bring into focus the "polyphonic" nature of the scroll[85] and suggest a move away from simply assertive discourse.[86] They thus constitute the first of a number of sections in Jer 7–20 that represent "voices in dialogue,"[87] though all three voices are as Jeremiah articulates them, and the voices are not so much in conversation as talking past each other or interrupting each other.[88] Thus, "the interweaving of speakers gives the text a certain liturgical character, but it may be more accurate to say that we hear a *cacophony* of mourning at Israel's destruction."[89] It points to the fact that the scroll reflects a situation of conflict.[90] It commonly moves without announcement between words of Yahweh, words of Jeremiah, and words of Judah—sometimes in ways that are clear (e.g., at 8:14, 17, 19b, 20), sometimes in ways that are more ambiguous (e.g., at 8:18, 21, 22; 9:1 [8:23]; 9:2[1]). The unannounced shifts also suggest "the chaos . . . of traumatic contemplation."[91] The alternating is marked in MT by a much-increased frequency of section markers. In the translation, I have sometimes added quotation marks to make transitions in the exchanges more visible.

---

85. Cf. R. P. Carroll, "The Polyphonic Jeremiah: A Reading of the Book of Jeremiah," in Kessler, *Reading Jeremiah*, 77–85.

86. J. R. Lundbom, "Jeremiah and the Break-Away from Authority Preaching," *Svensk Exegetisk Årsbok* 56 (1991): 7–28.

87. M. E. Biddle, *Polyphony and Symphony in Prophetic Literature: Rereading Jeremiah 7–20*, Studies in Old Testament Interpretation 2 (Macon, GA: Mercer University, 1996), 17.

88. Cf. K. Finsterbusch, "Unterbrochene JHWH-Rede: Anmerkungen zu einem rhetorischen Phänomen im Buch Jeremia," *BZ* 60 (2016): 1–13.

89. Fretheim, *Jeremiah*, 148.

90. Seitz, *Theology in Conflict*, 3.

91. E. K. Holt, "Daughter Zion: Trauma, Cultural Memory and Gender in OT Poetics," in Becker, Dochhorn, and Holt, *Trauma and Traumatization*, 173.

a. The Opening Challenge and Exchanges between Yahweh and Judah (8:4–20)

⁴*And you will say to them:*ᵃ

Yahweh has said this:

Do people fall and not get up,
  or does someone turn and not turn?
⁵*Why is this people one that turns,*ᵇ
  *Jerusalem a turner,*ᶜ *perpetually?*ᵈ
They have grasped hold of duplicity—
  they have refused to turn.
⁶*I have paid heed and listened*ᵉ*—*
  *they do not speak thus.*ᶠ
There is no one relenting of his dire action,
  saying, "What have I done?"
*Everyone*ᵍ *has turned, running,*ʰ
  *like horse*ⁱ *flooding into the battle.*
⁷*Even a stork in the heavens—*
  she acknowledges her seasons.
*And pigeon, swift,*ʲ *and swallow—*
  they keep the time for their coming.
But my people—they do not acknowledge
  Yahweh's authoritative decision.

⁸*How can you say, "We are smart,*
  and Yahweh's instruction is with us"?
Actually, there, it is for deception
  that the scribes' pen of deception acts.
⁹*Smart people act shamefully—*
  *they break down*ᵏ *and get caught.*ˡ
There, Yahweh's message they reject;

smartness in what do they have?[m]

[10]Therefore I will give their women to others,
  their fields to dispossessors.
Because from small to big,
  everyone[n] is grabbing what can be grabbed.
From prophet to priest,
  everyone is practicing deception.
[11]They have healed my dear people's[o] shattering lightly,
  saying, "Things are perfectly well."
But things are not well—
    [12]they have acted shamefully, because it is something offensive that they
      have done.
Moreover they do not feel any shame at all,
  they do not know how to feel disgrace.
Therefore they will fall among the people who fall;
  at the time of their being attended to, they will collapse (Yahweh has
    said).[p]
[13]I will gather and finish them off[q] (Yahweh's affirmation),
  no grapes on the vine,
  no figs on the fig tree.
The foliage withers,
  and what I have given them[r] will pass away for them.[s]

[14]For what reason are we sitting?—
  gather, so we can come to the fortified town.
We can perish there,[t]
  because Yahweh our God has doomed us to perish.[u]
He has made us drink polluted water,[v]
  because we did wrong by Yahweh.
[15]Hoping[w] for things to be well, but no good,
  for a time of healing, but there, terror.
[16]From Dan has made itself heard[x]
  his horses' snorting.
From the sound of his sturdy ones' neighing
  the entire country has quaked.
They have come and consumed the country and what fills it,
  the city and the people who live in it.[y]

[17]"Because here am I,
  sending off snakes[z] against you,
Adders for which there is no charming,
  and they will bite you (Yahweh's affirmation)."[aa]

261

¹⁸*My cheerfulness*^{bb} *in sorrow—*
  in me my heart is sick.
¹⁹*There, the sound of my dear people's cry for help,*
  from the country far off.
Isn't Yahweh in Zion,
  or her King, isn't he in her?

"Why have they irked me with their images,
  with alien, empty things?"

²⁰*Harvest has passed, summer is gone,*
  and we—we haven't found deliverance.

a. LXX has a tighter link with what precedes: "Because the Lord says these things."

b. LXX, Vg take feminine *šôbəbâ* as a verb, but its subject, "this people," is masculine. Taking it as a noun (Volz, *Jeremia*, 107) is less harsh; it then anticipates feminine "Jerusalem" (which LXX lacks).

c. LXX, Vg give *məšubâ* its common abstract meaning, "turning" (cf. 2:19; 3:22; 5:6; 14:7—all plural), but the concrete meaning (cf. 3:6, 9, 11, 12—all singular) fits here; it then stands in apposition to *šôbəbâ* as a variant way of saying the same thing.

d. *Niṣṣaḥat* (*niphal* participle), lit."being perpetual"; at the end of the line it qualifies both *šôbəbâ* and *məšubâ*.

e. LXX has imperatives (Aq, Sym have first person).

f. Cf. LXX for *kēn* meaning *thus* (BDB, 485–87) rather than "what is right" (Vg; BDB, 467).

g. Lit. "all of it"; see the translation note on 6:13.

h. Lit. "in their running" (cf. 23:10). A homonym *mərusâ*, from *rāṣaṣ*, means "crushing, oppression" (22:17), and Jeremiah's hearers might pick up its overtones in this context (cf. 23:9 and the commentary on it). Tg, Syr derive the word from *rāṣâ* ("be pleased with/determined") rather than *rûs* ("run"), and the *ketiv*'s plural *mərusôtām* for the *qere*'s singular *mərusātām* might imply this understanding (cf. Syr).

i. Like other terms for animals, *sûs* can be collective (cf. 51:27; Volz, *Jeremia*, 107); a single horse cannot really flood (*šāṭap*).

j. The *ketiv* has *sûs*, a homonym for the word for "horse"; the *qere* has *sîs*, perhaps to distinguish it from that other *sûs* (BDB). There is some uncertainty about the identity of this bird and the third, *'āgûr*.

k. LXX and Vg imply a metaphorical meaning, Tg and Syr a literal shattering.

l. The verbs in vv. 8b–9 are *qatal* and *wayyiqtol*; LXX, Vg thus translate as past. But the two in this colon (at least) must refer to a future event; for consistency I have translated all the verbs in vv. 8b–9 by a "timeless" English present. See the introduction to 13:18–22 (pp. 354–55).

m. MT^L has a section marker here.

n. See v. 6 and note g; cf. v. 10b.

o. Lit. "my daughter-people's"; cf. vv. 21, 22; 9:1 (8:23); 9:7(6).

p. MT has a marker here. Verses 10–12 are a variant on 6:12–15 (see the translation notes there). LXX lacks vv. 10b–12.

q. Lit. "in gathering I will finish them off": infinitive of *'āsap* and *hiphil* of *sûp*. Jer 5:23; 6:28 similarly combine forms from *sûr* and *sārar* (23:39; 48:9 are further examples of paronomasia involving an infinitive and a finite verb; see DG 101 remark 1). Aq derives both verbs from *sûp*, which would be more common.

r. With the unmarked relative clause in this elliptical colon, cf. 2:8; cf. Vg's understanding of the second clause. McKane (*Jeremiah*, 1:189) comments, "Since [the words'] sense is so suspect, they should be deleted." LXX lacks the colon, perhaps because it didn't understand it (*CTAT* 2:528).

s. Dative of disadvantage (Holladay, *Commentary on Jeremiah*, 1:286).

t. A single-stress colon in MT, which hyphenates *wǝnidmâ-šām*.

u. On this verb, see the translation note on 6:2. Vg, Aq, Sym, Syr take the verb each time as *DCH*'s *dāmam* I ("be silent"). *DCH* itself links it with its *dāmam* II ("weep"). On LXX "throw out," see D. Weissert, "*APORRIPTEIN* 'To Pass Over in Silence,'" *Textus* 22 (2005): 77–86.

v. See the commentary on 9:15(14).

w. The infinitive absolute takes the place of a finite verb and perhaps makes for some vividness (DG 103b; GKC 113ff).

x. LXX parses *nišmaʿ* as a first-person plural *qal yiqtol* (cf. 35:8, 10; 42:6, 14) rather than a third-person singular *niphal qatal* (cf. 3:21; 9:19[18]; 31:15; 38:27; 49:21; 50:46; the context of the last two occurrences parallels the context here).

y. MT has a marker here.

z. Tg makes explicit that the snakes stand for armies.

aa. MT's section marker here corresponds with v. 18's being the start of Jeremiah's expressing his own anguish; but see the introduction to 8:21–9:16(15) (p. 274).

bb. *Mablîgîtî* is a *hapax legomenon* from the rare verb *bālag* (cf. Aq). Vg "my sorrow" might imply "my grimace" (Allen, *Jeremiah*, 107, 108). The accents in the Cairo Codex of the Prophets imply a division of the word into two (cf. LXX): *mibbǝlî* followed by a form from *gāhâ* such as *gēhâ* (*HALOT*, 542), suggesting "from want of curing."

The opening section in 8:4–20 introduces and then records the first set of exchanges, between Yahweh and Judah, perhaps bringing together some originally separate units (e.g., vv. 4–7, 8–13, 14–17, 18–20).

vv. 4–7	Yahweh issues an opening challenge about turning and acknowledging (a double introduction, then nine bicola)
vv. 8–13	Yahweh raises a question with Judah and declares an intent (eleven bicola, then a tricolon and a bicolon)
vv. 14–16	Judah expresses a sense of panic (seven bicola)
v. 17	Yahweh comments on the panic (two linked bicola)
vv. 18–19b	On Judah's behalf, Jeremiah laments its situation (three bicola)
v. 19c	Yahweh comments on the lament (one bicolon)
v. 20	Judah expresses its anguish (one bicolon)

4a–b *And you will say to them* makes a link with what precedes, though not simply with what immediately precedes in 8:1–3 (contrast "and you will say" in 3:12; 5:19; 7:28) but rather with 7:2–8:3 as a whole. It thus picks up from 7:2, the introduction to 7:2–8:3 as a unit within Jer 7–10, and in a parallel way introduces 8:4–9:26(25), the second unit within Jer 7–10. *Yahweh has said this* then introduces v. 4c–7 in particular.

4c The words that follow are an implicit exhortation to Judah to turn back to Yahweh. Admittedly, everything in the Jeremiah scroll is an implicit exhortation of one kind or another. Here, the description in vv. 4–7 suggests a comparison and contrast with the exhortation in 3:1–4:4. There, Yahweh explicitly urged Judah to turn (e.g., 3:12, 14). Here, he talks about turning, but it is only by implication that he urges Judah to turn. Yet in a strange way, something left implicit can have a distinctive force if it succeeds in driving the audience to think, and vv. 4–7 has even been called "an emphatic call for repentance."[92] In form, it has some analogy with Amos 3:3–8 in starting from realities of everyday life and appealing to aspects of nature[93] and in seeking to get people's attention with a rhetorical question and a metaphor. If *people fall*, they *get up*, don't they? They don't just lie there if they can help it. But people who fall often can't get up again; 6:15 might be worrying background, though there is even more worrying background elsewhere (Amos 5:2; 8:14).[94] Similarly, however, *does someone turn and not turn?* Jeremiah again works with the two sides to the idea of turning (*šûb*). If people turn off the right road, they eventually realize it and turn back, don't they? Let's take the risk of saying yes. What's your point, Jeremiah?

5 In the context of the scroll, we know the answer, and people who had listened to Jeremiah before would know the answer. *Turn* and related words have been prominent, especially in Jer 3. Whatever was the right response to the questions in v. 4, there is a mystery about *this people* as *one that turns*, a mystery about *Jerusalem* as *a turner*. It has turned *perpetually*. With his talk of permanency, Jeremiah nicely flips back on Judah its question in 3:5. The Judahites *have grasped hold of duplicity* (*tarmît*) too (he has also previously talked about grasping hold of weapons and being grasped by distress in 6:23–24). Duplicity is the quality that enables them to fill their houses with stuff (see 5:27; there *mirmâ*). So *they have refused to turn*.

6 Either Jeremiah (cf. 5:1–7) or Yahweh (cf. 7:11) says, *I have paid heed and listened*. God or prophet has heard what *they speak*, and they don't speak about turning. Verse 6b restates the point about refusing to turn: *there is no one relenting* and facing the question *"What have I done?"* The verb *relenting*

92. Lundbom, *Jeremiah 1–20*, 515.
93. Weiser, *Jeremia*, 1:76–77.
94. Holladay, *Commentary on Jeremiah*, 1:278.

has a hint of feeling regret but is more focused on deciding to act differently (see the commentary on 4:28). But the people's turning is all of the turning away variety. Here, Jeremiah nuances the accusation. They have *turned* all right, and they are *running* "at full speed,"[95] *like horse flooding into the battle.* They manifest flooding water's "powerful impetuousness."[96] In effect, Jeremiah is talking about "the demonic power of sin" as Paul will analyze it in Rom 7.[97]

7 Yahweh offers another puzzled metaphor. The Jordan Valley is a major migration route for birds. Storks, pigeons, swifts, and swallows migrate from Europe and Asia to Africa in autumn via the Rift Valley and return in spring.[98] A bird thus *acknowledges* the time for migrating, acknowledges the *seasons*— etymologically, the appointed times. The two lines are neatly parallel:

| Even | a stork in the heavens— | she acknowledges | her seasons. |
| And | pigeon, swift, and swallow— | they keep | the time for their coming. |

So why is it that *my people . . . do not acknowledge Yahweh's authoritative decision* about the course of their life? They don't acknowledge the way Yahweh exercises authority, which they are supposed to follow (4:2; 5:1, 4, 5, 28; 7:5) or the decision about them that Yahweh has made (1:16; 4:12). It would be smart to let such acknowledgment drive them to turn back. Like Proverbs, Jeremiah appeals to common sense.[99] But Judah lacks the smartness that ordinary creatures show (cf. Isa 1:3;[100] Job 12:7–8[101]). "Every creature is wiser than fickle Israel."[102] Like v. 5, this contrast with the animate creation suggests that there is something profoundly unnatural about Judah's behavior. Regular human life and experience show it; the world of nature shows it.

8a The implicit exhortation and confrontation becomes explicit. The *you* Jeremiah now directly addresses are the people Yahweh was indirectly addressing in vv. 4–7. Despite what the Judahites *say*, their unwillingness to acknowledge Yahweh's authoritative decision shows that being *smart* is not their strong suit—or as Jeremiah said earlier, they are smart only at doing

95. Blayney, *Jeremiah*, 264.
96. Rudolph, *Jeremia*, 58.
97. Weiser, *Jeremia*, 1:77.
98. See Lundbom, *Jeremiah 1–20*, 510–13; Foreman, *Animal Metaphors*, 211–21.
99. D. R. Jones, *Jeremiah*, 158–59.
100. Qimchi, in MG.
101. Hugh of St. Cher, "Liber Jeremiae," 199, quoted in Schroeder, *Jeremiah*, 149.
102. Brueggemann, *Jeremiah 1–25*, 83.

dire things (4:22). Here, they associate their claim to smartness with their (purported) possession of *Yahweh's instruction* (*tôrâ*). Within Jeremiah's lifetime, an instruction scroll turned up in the temple and was part of the basis for Josiah's reformation (2 Kgs 22:8, 11; 23:24); the usual scholarly view has been that this scroll was some form of Deuteronomy. While Josiah had implemented some basic requirements of the scroll, the account of his reformation refers only to religious changes, not to changes in community life, and both 2 Kings and Jeremiah make clear that even the religious changes were short-lived. Whereas Jer 7 focused more on religious issues, Jer 8–9 focuses as much on community issues. It's always easy for the people of God to slip into thinking that possessing something like an instruction scroll—a set of Scriptures—is a sign that they are people who acknowledge God, and this dynamic operates in Judah. In theory people acknowledge the authority of Yahweh's instruction, but in practice they ignore it or acknowledge it only selectively (cf. 6:19), which could be a reason for Jeremiah raising the question he does.

8b His subsequent comment suggests he has another issue in mind. It was the priests' business to teach about Yahweh's instruction (2:8), and if any of that instruction needed to be put into writing, *scribes* were presumably the people who did that work. A priest could also be a scribe, as Ezra later was, and doubtless a prophet could be too. Here, the scribes' *pen* was a means of *deception*. It would have been scribes who put the instruction scroll itself into writing, but in his reference to a pen used deceptively, Jeremiah can hardly be talking about that scroll.[103] His concern for exclusive faithfulness to Yahweh and faithful living in community corresponds to the concerns of Deuteronomy and of the rest of the Torah. Elsewhere, he indicates that he is not negative about the Torah in itself (e.g., 2:8; 6:19; 9:13[12]). But the scribes were presumably also the people who put into writing the words of prophets (as Baruch did for Jeremiah) as well as the teaching in Proverbs; they will have been teachers in the community as well as writers. They might also have put into writing the messages of prophets such as Hananiah, priestly teaching that Jeremiah opposed, or more radical alternative instructions about worship—for instance, instructions about making offerings to the Master, to the Queen of the Heavens, to the gods to whom people sacrificed children, and to the sun, the moon, and the heavenly army. The double reference to deception (*šeqer*) supports these latter possibilities (see references to deception such as 3:23; 5:31; 7:9; 9:3[2]). The situation is not one in which written Torah and spoken message stand in opposition; in their basic thrust, the written Torah in Deuteronomy and the preaching

---

103. So Duhm, who in this connection calls vv. 8–13 "one of the most important [poems] in the Book of Jeremiah" (*Jeremia*, 88).

of Jeremiah were similar (not least in their rejection of the sacrifice of chil-dren).[104] Conversely, the people whose instruction Jeremiah opposes would associate themselves with prophets whose message Jeremiah also opposes. While a conflict between Jeremiah and these scribes may link with broader questions concerning the relationship between written text and spoken word (the period is one in which written text is coming to be significant),[105] here Jeremiah refers to a conflict between rival groups, each with its own Torah[106] and its own prophetic message. Jeremiah's point is not that people are ex-cessively or exclusively attached to something in writing that presents itself as Yahweh's instruction. It's that the thing they are attached to is not really Yahweh's instruction at all. It's a "lying Torah."[107] But exactly how it performs its deception is hard to be sure of. "In the end, such a slim verse resists exact historical placement."[108]

9 Whatever this instruction scroll was, it encouraged these allegedly *smart people* to *act shamefully*, actually (cf. 2:26). Here, in the parallel colon, *they break down*, then *they get caught* (cf. Isa 8:15), which suggests reference not merely to the objective shame of their conduct but also to the disgrace they will experience when the untruth of their work is exposed. The inevita-bility of that exposure lies in the simple fact that *they reject Yahweh's message*. In propagating the teaching they have given or in following that teaching, they have gone against the message Yahweh gives through Jeremiah. So *smartness in what*—smartness of what kind—*do they have?* The references to *Yahweh's message* and to *smartness* neatly close off vv. 8–9 as they pair (a-b-b'-a') with the opening references to people claiming they are *smart* and to *Yahweh's instruction*.[109]

10–12 *Therefore* indicates that the critique in vv. 8–9 is the rationale for the announcement that now follows, a reworking of 6:12–15. To the people who compliment themselves on their smartness, it applies the warning that was articulated there more generally. In this version, Yahweh takes more responsibility for what will happen: *I will give their women to others*. Both the men and the women are wayward, and both the men and the women

---

104. Cf. B. Halpern, *From Gods to God: The Dynamics of Iron Age Cosmologies*, FAT 63 (Tübingen: Mohr Siebeck, 2009), 132–41.

105. See W. M. Schniedewind, "The Textualization of Torah in Jeremiah 8:8," in *Was ist ein Text? Alttestamentliche, ägyptologische und altorientalistische Perspektiven*, ed. L. Morenz and S. Schorch, BZAW 362 (Berlin: de Gruyter, 2007), 93–107; *How the Bible Became a Book: The Textualization of Ancient Israel* (Cambridge: Cambridge University Press, 2004), 114–17.

106. R. P. Carroll, *Jeremiah*, OTL, 229.

107. Rudolph, *Jeremia*, 61.

108. C. L. Eggleston, *"See and Read All These Words": The Concept of the Written in the Book of Jeremiah* (Winona Lake, IN: Eisenbrauns, 2016), 64.

109. *CHP*, 205.

will suffer; this comment starts from the angle of the men as Jeremiah's immediate hearers (it thus contrasts with Amos 4:1). This version also introduces the word *dispossessors* (*yāraš*), a telling verb that occurs mostly as a description of what Israel will do to the Canaanites—more than fifty times in Deuteronomy alone (this participial form comes in Deut 12:2; 18:14). The God who could dispossess Canaanites for their enormities can dispossess Israelites for theirs. Further, the extra prominence Jeremiah thus gives to *their fields* hints more strongly at a link with the theme of accumulation of fields in Isa 5:8.[110] Yet another aspect of the repetition's significance is that Jeremiah incorporates two more references to *shame* (*bûš*). The audience might notice that the three references follow up the six references to turning (*šûb*) in vv. 4–7 and that the opposite spelling of the two words corresponds to their opposite meanings.[111]

13 Yahweh adds a further vivid image, familiar but distinctively expressed, to underscore the implications of the repeated lines. Lack of fruit can be a critique of Israel the vine (e.g., Isa 5:1–7), but it here results from Yahweh's action. Harvesting is uncomfortable for grain and fruit. It can thus be a negative image (cf. 6:9): *I will gather and finish them off.* The declaration about *grapes* and *figs* is not all. If there is no fruit, well, maybe next year it will be back. But if *the foliage withers*, it suggests the tree is dying.[112] Nothing will be left of Judah when Yahweh is done. Yahweh again affirms that it will be his own action. The attackers will seize the things that can be eaten, but it is Yahweh who will wither the foliage, reversing his usual involvement in making nature work.[113] *What I have given them*—the fruit, the land, the people—will be taken back. It will *pass away for them.*

14 Suddenly, there is a more marked transition than the one between vv. 4–7 and vv. 8–13, though this subsection, with its exhortation to *gather*, makes a link with the talk of gathering in v. 13. In Jeremiah's imagination, the situation has jumped forward and the calamity is actually unfolding. The invasion has begun. Residents of villages in Judah speak; we could think of them as responding to the bidding in 4:5. Their question (*For what reason are we sitting* here?) recalls the exhortation to *come to the fortified towns* in 4:6. But the despairing non-rationale for the exhortation (*We can perish there, because Yahweh our God has doomed us to perish*) presupposes the perspective suggested by the additional comment on fortified towns in 5:17: there's nothing to be gained by taking refuge. The people are in an understandable

110. P. D. Miller, "Jeremiah," on the passage.
111. Allen, *Jeremiah*, 110.
112. Lundbom, *Jeremiah 1–20*, 524.
113. Holladay, *Commentary on Jeremiah*, 1:285; see further M. DeRoche, "Contra Creation, Covenant and Conquest (Jer. viii 13)," *VT* 30 (1980): 280–90.

state of panic, but the action they intend has no logic; human beings often react thus in a crisis. In the context, the comment that Yahweh *has made us drink polluted water* is likely a metaphor, though people would sometimes have this literal experience. The language recalls the image of a chalice that's been spiked (e.g., Isa 51:17–22). As the invasion begins to happen, Judahites are having to drink that water. They recognize that it is *because we did wrong by Yahweh*. There is a poignancy or sadness about the acknowledgment. It implies either, "We have somehow got on the wrong side of Yahweh, but we don't know how," or, "We have done wrong and there's nothing that can be done about it." It's more like a continuation of the cry of despair than a proper confession or act of repentance. Either way, they are uttering it only in Jeremiah's imagination.

15 The continuing poignancy or sadness suggests the other side to the critique of Judah's leadership that was just repeated in v. 11. People believed their priests and prophets, but now (in Jeremiah's imagination) they recognize how they were betrayed. Jeremiah puts the point in two neatly parallel cola.

Hoping	for things to be well,	but	no	good,
	for a time of healing,	but	there,	terror.

16 They continue to give their report, which is the other side to those biddings in Jer 4 (esp. 4:13, 15), as the invader from the north makes his way toward Judah. They haven't actually heard the horses' snorting from a hundred miles away, but they speak as people who know that the invasion has begun and can imagine it unfolding. Are *his horses* the invader's horses? Or are they Yahweh's, as Yahweh is the only antecedent for the *his*?[114] Does the country quake because of the thundering of their hooves or because thundering happens when Yahweh advances? In Jeremiah's imagination projected onto the Judahites' imagination and exercised for the benefit of the Judahites to whom Jeremiah speaks, the invading horde has advanced in a flash across the hundred miles, has consumed (literally) everything in its path, and has already entered the city where a moment ago the villagers were thinking of taking refuge.

17 Once more, there is an unannounced but clear shift as Yahweh now speaks in a tough response to the poignancy and apprehension of vv. 14–16. The response presupposes that the comment about having done wrong by Yahweh indeed fell short of a serious acknowledgment of waywardness and a seeking of restoration. It amounts to, "Too right! Indeed I did make you drink contaminated water. To tweak the metaphor, the attackers riding those horses and steeds: you may picture them as *snakes*, specifically as *adders* whose

---

114. Calvin, *Jeremiah*, 1:477.

venom is especially lethal, and you may be sure that they are the kind of snakes *for which there is no charming.* They are not going to be stopped from biting. And *here am I;* I am indeed the one who is *sending* them *against you.*"

18 Another unannounced shift follows. While it is a popular and important insight that God suffers with his people,[115] the transition and contrast between wrath and sorrow suggests that here it is Jeremiah who grieves with his people as they are on the receiving end of that wrath—even though he also accepts that this wrath must be exercised. Imagining the catastrophe is therefore no encouragement to Jeremiah, who identifies with his people as well as with Yahweh. The enigmatic phrase *my cheerfulness in sorrow* perhaps suggests that Yahweh is supposed to be or frequently is the one who enables him to be in good spirits even in a context like the one he has been envisaging, as some psalms testify. But it is not working in this situation: *in me my heart is sick*—more literally, "upon me my heart is sick." The idiomatic use of the proposition in each colon functions "to give pathos to the expression of an emotion, by emphasizing the person who is its subject, and who, as it were, feels it acting *upon* him."[116]

19a–b In the background, then, lies *my dear people's* anguish, its *cry for help* coming from all over *the country*, from the villages that have just been talking about taking refuge in the fortified towns (or perhaps from the people in a country that is itself far off, to which they have been exiled). Jeremiah grieves over their fear, but he also grieves about the lack of insight that it shows, which was implied by the idea that the fortified towns could be a safe refuge. There is only one safe refuge, and that refuge is a person. *Isn't Yahweh in Zion, or her King, isn't he in her?* It's the affirmation that people make in their worship (e.g., Pss 46; 48; 99) and that Jeremiah's contemporary Zephaniah was fond of (e.g., Zeph 3:15, 17), though Jeremiah isn't fond of it except in relation to other nations and their gods.[117] Actually, the answer might be

115. For this understanding of Jeremiah, see, e.g., J. J. M. Roberts, "The Motif of the Weeping God in Jeremiah and Its Background in the Lament Tradition of the Ancient Near East," *OTE* 5 (1992): 361–74; A. C. Pilarski, "A Study of the References to *bt-'my* in Jeremiah 8:18–9:2(3)," in *Why? . . . How Long? Studies on Voices of Lamentation Rooted in Biblical Hebrew Poetry*, ed. L. S. Flesher, C. J. Dempsey, M. J. Boda, LHBOTS 552 (London: T&T Clark, 2014), 20–35. While resistance to the idea that it is Yahweh who weeps in Jer 8–9 may have an ideological basis (e.g., K. M. O'Connor, "The Tears of God and Divine Character in Jeremiah 2–9," in Diamond, K. M O'Connor, and Stulman, *Troubling Jeremiah*, 400), the same is true of advocacy of that idea, given that we like the idea of the suffering God. See further M. R. Schlimm, "Different Perspectives on Divine Pathos: An Examination of Hermeneutics in Biblical Theology," *CBQ* 69 (2007): 673–94.

116. BDB, 753.

117. Fretheim, *What Kind of God?*, 298–99; Fretheim adds that if Yahweh behaved more like a king, he might have less of a problem.

that he is not in Zion, precisely because of lack of insight and unwillingness to acknowledge Yahweh or to turn to him in a meaningful way.

19c Again, Jeremiah hears Yahweh's retort. "God is indeed present, but present in wrath."[118] Jeremiah "inverts the problem of theodicy. Instead of attempting to justify the ways of God to humans, Jeremiah poses the question in reverse order: how can you justify the ways of humans to God?"[119] If they are asking questions about the crisis overwhelming them, how about answering this question: *Why have they irked me with their images,* which as such constitute a contravention of the basic terms of the relationship between Yahweh and Israel? What about the *alien* nature of these images (cf. 2:21; 5:19)? Even if it they are indigenous to Canaan, they are alien to what it means to be Israel. And what about the fact that they are *empty things*? (2:5). They are solid, but in a more profound sense they are hollow.

20 Yet again there is an abrupt shift. The people, or Jeremiah speaking on their behalf, perhaps quote a saying.[120] *Harvest* refers to the barley and grain maturing in April, May, and June. *Summer* then denotes the period when olives, grapes, and other fruits ripen and are gathered, through July, August, and September. Each year, the entire period would be a time of anticipation and anxiety. The ripening of the produce over these months decides whether there will be something to eat (and seed to sow) over the next year. The second colon jumps from the metaphor of harvest to the literal reality. What if these seasons metaphorically pass and there is no *deliverance*? The people are portrayed as going through the political and military equivalent of a failure of the harvest, on which Jeremiah imagines them reflecting in anguish. If only the actual Judahites to whom he speaks would themselves imagine that experience and therefore turn back to forestall these horrors!

b. Exchanges between Yahweh and Jeremiah (8:21–9:16[15])

²¹*By the shattering of my dear people I have been shattered—*
    I am in darkness, desolation has grasped hold of me.
²²*Is there no ointment in Gilead,*
    or is there no healer there?
Because why has it not gone up—
    *my dear people's recovery?*ᵃ
⁹:¹ ⁽⁸:²³⁾*I wish I had*ᵇ *my head made of water,*
    my eye a fountain of tears,

---

118. Fretheim, *Jeremiah*, 152.
119. R. J. Gench, "Jeremiah 8:18–9:3," *Int* 62 (2008): 74.
120. J. A. Thompson, *Jeremiah*, 306.

So I could cry day and night
   for those who have been run through from my dear people.^c

²⁽¹⁾I wish I had in the wilderness
   a travelers' lodging
So I could abandon my people,
   go from being with them.
Because all of them are adulterers,
   a convocation of false people.
³⁽²⁾They have directed^d their tongue, deception their bow;
   not for truthfulness have they been strong^e in the country.
Because from dire action to dire action they have gone out,
   and me they have not acknowledged (Yahweh's affirmation).^f
⁴⁽³⁾They should be wary, each individual of his fellow;
   on every brother do not rely.
Because every brother swindles, swindles,^g
   and every fellow lives as a liar.
⁵⁽⁴⁾They trick, an individual his fellow,
   and truth they do not speak.
They have taught their tongue to speak deception—
   they have gotten weary in going astray.^h
⁶⁽⁵⁾Your living is in the midst of duplicity;
   in duplicityⁱ they have refused to acknowledge me (Yahweh's
      affirmation).^j

⁷⁽⁶⁾Therefore Yahweh of Armies has said this:

Here am I, smelting them and examining them,
   because how can I act^k in the face of^l my dear people?
⁸⁽⁷⁾Their tongue is a hammered^m arrow,
   which has spoken duplicity.
With his mouth someone speaks of peace with his fellow,
   but inside him he sets an ambush for him.
⁹⁽⁸⁾For these thingsⁿ I should attend to them, shouldn't I (Yahweh's
      affirmation),
   and on a nation that is like this
   my spirit should take redress, shouldn't it?^o
¹⁰⁽⁹⁾Over the mountains I will lift up^p crying and wailing,
   over the wilderness pastures a mourning song.
Because they are laid waste^q so that no one passes through,
   and people have not heard the sound of cattle.
From bird of the heavens to animal,
   they have fled and gone.

$^{11(10)}$*I will make Jerusalem into heaps,*
a home for jackals.
The towns of Judah I will make a desolation
with no one living there.^{r}

$^{12(11)}$*Who is the person who is smart*^{s}
so he reflects on^t *this,*
and to whom has Yahweh's mouth spoken so that he can tell it?
For what reason has the country perished,
become waste^u *like the wilderness,*
with no one passing through?^{v}

$^{13(12)}$*Yahweh said:*

Because of their abandoning my instruction,
which I put before them.
They didn't listen to my voice,
and they didn't go by it.
$^{14(13)}$*They went after the determination of their mind*
and after the Masters,
which their ancestors taught them.^{w}

$^{15(14)}$*Therefore Yahweh of Armies, Israel's God, has said this:*

Here am I, making them, this people, eat wormwood^x
and making them drink poisoned water.
$^{16(15)}$*I will scatter them among the nations*
that they and their ancestors have not acknowledged.
And I will send off the sword after them
until I have made an end of them.^{y}

a. MT^A has a section marker here.
b. Lit. "who will grant/make"; see, e.g., *DCH*, 5:800–801. The idiom recurs in the next verse.
c. MT^A has a section marker here.
d. The obvious meaning of *dārak* is "show the way" (*derek*), but the subsequent reference to a bow adds a different nuance (see 46:9 and the translation note on it).
e. LXX "it has grown strong" implies *gābərâ* for MT *gābərû*.
f. MT^L has a section marker here.
g. The infinitive preceding the finite verb underscores the reality of the action. LXX, Vg "trip up" correspond to the etymology of *'āqab*.
h. The asyndeton combined with the reversal of the expected word order suggests that the second clause is subordinate to the first.
i. The second occurrence of *mirmâ* is preceded by a preposition; the repetition is another

instance of anaphora rather than denoting emphasis or indicating the superlative (contrast 6:14; 7:4).

j. MT has a section marker here.

k. Vg has "what else can I do?"

l. LXX, Tg add "the direness of."

m. For the *qere šāḥuṭ* (cf. Syr, Tg), the *ketiv* implies the active participle *šôḥēṭ* (cf. LXX, Vg).

n. The inclusion of *to them* (with *b*) later in the colon suggests that *ʿal-ʾelleh* means *for these things* rather than "to these people" (contrast 5:9), which is confirmed by the parallel expression "on a nation" (*b* again).

o. MT has a section marker here.

p. For MT *ʾeśśāʾ*, LXX implies *śaʾû* ("lift up"), which avoids the impression that Yahweh is lifting up the cry.

q. Vg derives *niṣṣatû* from *yāṣat* ("burn"), suggesting a "scorched earth policy" (McKane, *Jeremiah*, 1:204); but see the translation note on 2:15.

r. MT has a section marker here.

s. Verses 12–16(11–15) are more pedestrian in expression and use some prose forms (the accusative marker, the relative conjunction), but they manifest rhythm and parallelism, and their words and imagery were characteristic of the poetry in Jer 1–6, so I treat them as prosaic verse.

t. LXX, Vg take the ambiguous *wəyābēn* as *qal* (cf. v. 17[16]), but the parallelism with the next colon suggests *hiphil* (Rudolph, *Jeremia*, 66); maybe it needs to be taken both ways.

u. See note q.

v. MT has a marker here.

w. MT has a marker here.

x. Vg has "absinth," which Aq has in the second colon, but this translation is misleading in a modern Western context.

y. MT has a unit marker here.

In 8:18–20, Jeremiah began to interweave his talk about Judah's anguish and Yahweh's exchanges in relation to Judah with talk about his own anguish. "Jeremiah stays close to Yhwh in his articulation of pained, anguished, overwhelming despair."[121] In 8:21–9:16(15), his laments and Yahweh's responses to him come into focus.[122]

8:21–9:1 (8:21–23)	Jeremiah's lament at the suffering of Judah (five bicola, the last pair linked)
9:2–9(1–8)	Yahweh's response, reminding Jeremiah of the need for his action (a linked pair of bicola and eight self-contained bicola; then a resumptive introduction, three bicola, and a closing tricolon)

121. Brueggemann, *Like Fire*, 184.

122. J. T. Willis includes 8:18–23 as one example of "Dialogue Between Prophet and Audience as a Rhetorical Device in the Book of Jeremiah," *JSOT* 33 (1985): 70–71.

| 9:10(9) | Jeremiah's further lament at the suffering of Judah (three bicola) |
| 9:11–16(10–15) | Yahweh's further response, affirming the need for his action (two bicola and two tricola a resumptive introduction, two bicola, a tricolon, another resumptive introduction, and three bicola) |

Once again the exchange may bring together messages of separate origin; for example, 9:2–9(1–8) and 11–16(10–15) could have stood on their own, while the multiple introductions and tricola within 9:11–16 may indicate that it is itself a compilation. The medieval chapter division happens one verse earlier in English Bibles than in Hebrew Bibles; thus the English 9:1 is 8:23 in Hebrew. The Aleppo Codex has a section marker at both points, and in general the MT manuscripts have a bewildering variety of markers in Jer 8–9, reflecting the uncertainty of the structure of the chapters.

21 For all his accepting the propriety of Yahweh's action, Jeremiah is distraught about it. After all, they are *my dear people*. Jeremiah's connectedness to his people is key to his work; the rhetoric conveys the prophet's passion for the wounded and broken Judahites.[123] Once again, Jeremiah speaks of the *shattering* that he knows is coming to them (4:6, 20; 6:1, 14; 8:11): it will be like the breaking of a leg or neck or back, for which there can be no healing. The prospect of their breaking already means *I have been shattered*. He cannot but be implicated in what happens. He shares in their fate in more than one sense—if in Hebrew as in English the image of shattering can picture what happens to people's spirits as well as to their bodies and their towns. When he speaks of being *in darkness* (*qādar*; the verb often links with mourning, as in 4:28; 14:2) and of *desolation*, he might then be rephrasing what he said in v. 18, but the parallelism may reflect his awareness that he will share in their experience of attack and conquest. When darkness overwhelms them, it falls for him. When desolation overwhelms them (2:15; 4:7, 27; 6:8; 9:11[10]; 10:22), it falls on him as a member of the community. Being a prophet does not mean he is exempted from what happens any more than being his scribe does (45:1–5).

22 If Judah is injured, is there not at least some *ointment*, some balm, some dressing to put on the wound? We have no evidence that *Gilead*, the area east of the Jordan that had once belonged to Reuben, Gad, and Manasseh, was known for a healing resin that its trees could produce (LXX and Vg have words for resin); more likely Gilead features because it is on the

---

123. W. J. Wessels, "Connected Leadership: Jeremiah 8:18–9:3," *Koers* 75 (2010): 483–501.

trade routes from which such foreign resources would arrive (cf. Gen 37:25)[124] and therefore a natural direction for a *healer* to look for resources. So why has no one acted to encourage the *recovery* or repairing of the flesh *of my dear people* so that the wound heals? Jeremiah's question is rhetorical. He knows the answer, and he wishes they would work it out and turn to Yahweh so that something could be done about it, so the shattering need not happen. (Whereas the implication of the opening question is that there is indeed balm in Gilead but that it will be of no use to facilitate the healing Judah will need, the song "There's a Balm in Gilead" ironically takes the image in a positive direction; Edgar Allen Poe does something gloomier with it.)[125]

9:1(8:23) Jeremiah continues his lament (the English Bibles' chapter division is odd). He is living with a vision of what he knows is inevitable unless the Judahites turn. He can see the bodies of *those who have been run through from my dear people*, the victims of slaughter during invasion, siege, and conquest. No doubt he continues to speak of his actual distraught feelings, but the point about articulating them is to confront people with the facts that the feelings respond to. Actually, a gargantuan amount of mourning will be required when the disaster comes. There will be so much need to *cry* that one would need to observe the rituals of mourning *day and night*. One would need one's *head* to be *made of water* and one's *eyes* to be *a fountain of tears* that keeps refilling itself like a spring in order to do justice to the catastrophe. He speaks in the manner of a lament psalm or protest psalm;[126] such psalms can function not merely to articulate one's own protest but to articulate a protest on behalf of people with whom one identifies. It is in this connection that he wishes to be "the weeping prophet." Yet nobody actually weeps in this poem.[127] It's as if in the trauma, they can only talk about weeping.

2a–b(1a–b) The printed Hebrew Bibles in their version of the medieval chapter divisions more appropriately locate the chapter break here, as Jeremiah moves from speaking for himself to speaking for Yahweh. The transition from Jeremiah's lament or protest to Yahweh's lament or protest might be seen as marking Yahweh's response to Jeremiah's but it also constitutes indirect confrontation of Judah.[128] By linking this verse to the preceding one, the

124. Keown, Scalise, and Smothers, *Jeremiah 26–52*, 292.

125. R. P. Carroll, "The Discombobulations of Time and the Diversities of Text: Notes on the Rezeptionsgeschichte of the Bible," in *Text as Pretext: Essays in Honour of Robert Davidson*, ed. R. P. Carroll, JSOTSup 138 (Sheffield: Sheffield Academic, 1992), 78–80.

126. C. J. Sharp nicely defines "lament" as "sociopolitical protest that names woundedness and loss" ("Buying Land in the Text of Jeremiah," in *Prophecy and Power: Jeremiah in Feminist and Postcolonial Perspective*, ed. C. M. Maier and C. J. Sharp, LHBOTS 577 [London: T&T Clark, 2013], 155).

127. K. M. O'Connor, *Jeremiah*, 64.

128. See J. M. Henderson, "Who Weeps in Jeremiah viii 23 [ix 1]?," *VT* 52 (2002): 191–206.

English chapter division does draw attention to the parallel in their openings. Jeremiah has said, *I wish I had . . .* Now Yahweh counters with his own *I wish I had . . .* Yahweh is also both like and unlike Elijah in 1 Kgs 19.[129] There will be a parallel in Jesus's story (see Mark 9:19).[130] Jeremiah's desire is a reaction to his people's threatened calamity. Yahweh's desire is a reaction to what makes the calamity necessary. It is his response to the questions in 8:19, 22.[131] But the link is thus a "cosmetic hinge" underscoring the transition from sympathy to disgust.[132] A little way from Jerusalem, there are khans like the Inn of the Good Samaritan, conveniently located *in the wilderness* halfway to Jericho. But Yahweh is not looking for company in an inn; he is not referring to a place where people offer hospitality (for a fee), but simply to a place on the road where a traveler might stop (cf. Gen 28:11).[133] The only people in such a *travelers' lodging* are people who stay for the night and then move on. There *I could abandon my people, go from being with them.* Jeremiah has used both expressions to describe Israel's leaving Yahweh (e.g., 1:16; 3:1).

2c(1c) Whereas Jeremiah identifies with his people and shares in their pain, Yahweh wants to get away from them *because all of them are adulterers*, indeed, *a convocation of false people.* A convocation (*'ǎṣeret*, sometimes *'ǎṣārâ*) is a worship gathering (the traditional translation is "solemn assembly"); they gather for great worship occasions, but they are a congregation of people who are *false.* While Yahweh was not the one lamenting in 9:1 (8:23), he does not view their adultery and falsehood, the theme expounded in Jer 3 (see also 4:7; 5:11), "with a kind of detached objectivity."[134] It would not be unreasonable for the cuckolded husband to wish to walk out on his wife. But Yahweh will go on in vv. 3–6(2–5) to other aspects of their community life, which may suggest that he is referring to adultery and falsehood within the community (cf. 7:9) as well as in relation to him.

3(2) The two aspects to their waywardness may again feature: *they have directed their tongue* in their worship with *deception* and *not for truthfulness.* Deception featured alongside falsehood in 3:10. But truthfulness has so far referred to community relationships (5:1, 3; 7:28), and here Yahweh speaks about people directing their tongue in the way they direct *their bow*, with its arrows pointed at other people whom they cheat of their rights. Thus "speech is not a cement or a therapy; it does not promote understanding, tolerance and social health. . . . Mistrust has become part of the ordinary

129. Weiser, *Jeremia*, 1:85.
130. Jerome, *Jeremiah*, 60.
131. W. H. Schmidt, *Jeremia*, 1:204.
132. Allen, *Jeremiah*, 115.
133. Blayney, *Genesis*, 268.
134. Fretheim, *Jeremiah*, 153.

life of the community and . . . every social encounter has to be regarded as a possible trap."[135] People *have been strong in the country* like warriors, in particular archers (see 5:20–31), as *from dire action to dire action they have gone out* to act in a way that pays them. The pressure of invasion might put even more pressure on community relationships:[136] while danger and adversity can drive people together, they can also drive them apart. Yahweh finally reverts to the way *they have not acknowledged* him—the word *me* opens the colon. The duplicity of their worship and the duplicity of the rest of their lives are two sides of a coin of unacknowledgment.

4(3) Some logical though sad advice follows. *Each individual* needs to *be wary of his fellow* and not trust him. A fellow member of the community, your neighbor, is the person who most easily wrongs you. He *lives as a liar* (cf. 6:28), which implies not harmless gossip but falsehood that is the means of robbing you. No wonder the exhortation not to live as a liar is the context in which the Torah tells people to love their neighbor (Lev 19:16–18); and no wonder that loving your enemy is another way to describe loving your neighbor (Matt 5:44). Yahweh's warning applies regarding *every brother*, on whom you should also *not rely* as a speaker of truth. To Western ears, this statement about brothers sounds harsher than it is, because "brothers" means other members of the community—they are the same people as your neighbors. The First Testament invites the community to see itself as the family writ large; your neighbors are part of your big extended family. Cheating members of the community is therefore an intra-family wrong. Yahweh underlines the point by his emphatic use of the verb *swindle* (*'āqab*), which is linked with Jacob's name and is used in Genesis in connection with his relationship with his brother; so perhaps Jeremiah implies that *brother* may need to be taken in the narrow sense. The only other sure occurrence of the verb outside Genesis comes in a reference to Jacob in Hos 12:3(4) (though see also Jer 17:9). Jacob's name suggests he was a crook; being a liar was a means of being a cheat. In an example of hyperbole like that in 5:1–9, Yahweh declares that everyone in Judah is a Jacob (*every . . . every . . . every*).

5(4) Thus *an individual tricks his fellow*: Yahweh goes on to use the verb that (ironically) Jacob used when accusing his uncle (who counted in that broad sense as his brother) of cheating him (Gen 31:7). *Truth* is not what people's fellows *speak; they have taught their tongue to speak deception*. It is the way they *have directed their tongue,* with *deception* as *their bow* (v. 3[2]). The move to talk of *going astray* indicates a transition back to talk about relationships with Yahweh as well as relationships in the community; the verb (*'āwâ*, cf. 3:21) is etymologically related to "waywardness" (*'āwôn*; cf. 2:22;

---

135. McKane, *Jeremiah*, 1:200.
136. Fretheim, *Jeremiah*, 158.

3:13; 5:25). Ironically, people have put so much effort into *going astray* that *they have gotten weary*, but the irony is itself ironic, because the weariness has not made them reach the point where they would stop. Will they please think about this irony?

6(5) Presumably Yahweh is now speaking to Jeremiah (as an individual in Judah who is the exception to the rule) when he points out that *your living is in the midst of duplicity*. "As if he didn't know"![137] Again, it's rhetoric: the people who hear this message from his scroll are the people characterized by such duplicity, from which Jeremiah longs to wean them. This noun (*mirmâ*) is also used to characterize Jacob (Gen 27:35). The reminder that Yahweh is talking about relationships with him as well as relationships within the community is underlined when he comes to an end in his indictment by repeating the verb from v. 3b: *in duplicity they have refused to acknowledge me*. So people should beware of their fellows/brothers. But they need to see this necessity as part of the explanation for Yahweh's desire to get away from them and for the inevitability of the catastrophe he intends to bring on them, unless . . .

7(6) Such a *therefore* commonly heralds a transition to declaring the action that Yahweh will take; here it does so indirectly. Yahweh is *smelting them and examining them;* the pronouncement overlaps with 6:27–30 (and compare Pss 7:9[10]; 26:2).[138] While such participles often describe something Yahweh is about to do, here they describe what Yahweh is already engaged in through Jeremiah. It is his means of testing Judah, of discovering what it is made of, a means of smelting it, because getting Jeremiah to declare Yahweh's word is also Yahweh's means of taking action. Jeremiah 6:27–30 did not quite put it that way, but it more or less implied it. Here, there is a little ellipsis between the pronouncement and the question. Yahweh's point is, what is he to do with Judah in light of what he has affirmed in vv. 2–6(1–5)? They are still *my dear people*. And his answer is that he needs to smelt and test them in order to reveal whether there really is any silver there—to clarify whether his earlier statements were hyperbole.

8–9(7–8) The parallel with 6:27–30 suggests that Yahweh now describes the result of the smelting and testing, which confirms the judgment in vv. 2–6(1–5). Again, Yahweh speaks about a *fellow*, a *tongue*, and *duplicity*. By implication, he also speaks about a bow in that he refers to an *arrow*, but the arrow is now *hammered* into a sharp and efficient profile. And Yahweh sharpens the "point" of his own barbed response.[139] Yahweh reformulates the

---

137. Lundbom, *Jeremiah 1–20*, 545.

138. B. Gosse, "Le prophète Jérémie selon le Psautier et selon le livre d'Ézéchiel," *RB* 112 (2005): 511–20.

139. But see the translation note; the equivalent comment on the basis of the *ketiv* would be that Yahweh's point is going to hammer away.

comment by speaking about a *mouth* and about *peace* (*šālôm* here having its narrower meaning) and about the contrast with what is *inside* the plotter—in his thinking and intentions. *He sets an ambush,* planning to trap his fellow and cheat him in a meeting of the elders (see 5:26–28). Yahweh's language continues to parallel that of the Psalms (e.g., 11:2; 37:14; 64:2–5[3–6]); it would encourage people who are praying such psalms for themselves or for others that he listens to such prayers and does smelt and test, and it would continue to warn the duplicitous of that fact. The results of the smelting and testing determine what the action must be. Jeremiah slightly reworks 5:9; calling Judah a *nation* can be pejorative (cf. 5:29; 7:28).[140]

10(9) Jeremiah once more responds to Yahweh's protest with his own lament for "his ravaged land, the country where he has grown up and which he knows so well,"[141] as he imagines Yahweh having begun to implement his threat.[142] The terms for lament become more worryingly specific. *Crying* (*bəkî*) is what many people do in tough contexts. *Wailing* (*nehî*) is what they do in more desperate situations. *Mourning* (*qînâ*) implies that someone has died.[143] In 8:14, the threat of invasion made people in the open country determine to take refuge in the fortified towns; in this lament, in Jeremiah's imagination the invasion has begun. *The mountains* of Judah, which implies *the wilderness pastures* that are a key feature of them, *are laid waste* so that *no one passes through.* In 6:25, no one would be passing through because they are not taking any risks. Here it links with there being no *sound of cattle* to be heard:[144] either they have been killed or captured by the invaders or their herdsmen have secreted them away somewhere. *Bird* and *animal* of the wild have disappeared (cf. 4:25). The world is eerily empty.

11(10) And I am not finished, Yahweh responds as he takes up his side to the exchange. People think Jerusalem or the fortified towns are a place of refuge (4:5–6)? Think again (cf. 8:14). Each of the two lines has a short second colon in keeping with a pattern that often applies to solemn lines in a prayer. Here, each second colon parallels the first by giving a further description of the verb's object, and the two lines as wholes are thereby parallel (a-b-c-d-b'-a'-c'-d'):

I will make	Jerusalem	into heaps,	a home for jackals.
The towns of Judah	I will make	a desolation	with no one living there.

---

140. J. A. Thompson, *Jeremiah*, 310.

141. Lundbom, *Jeremiah 1–20*, 550.

142. D. A. Bosworth sees v. 9 as a particularly clear case of Yahweh weeping in "The Tears of God in the Book of Jeremiah," *Bib* 94 (2013): 30–31; cf. M. S. Smith, "Jeremiah ix 9," *VT* 37 (1987): 97–99.

143. See further G. Fleischer, "קיא, *qî'*," *TDOT* 13:17–23.

144. Qimchi, in MG.

Heaps was a description of Assyrian towns to be devastated in Isa 37:26, and the term will be reapplied to Babylon in Jer 51:37. There too it is nuanced with the image of a den for jackals, and it is an equivalent (in slightly varying words) to *a desolation with no one living there*. Here, it is part of a declaration about Judah itself. Yahweh plans no mercy. Verses 2–9(1–8) have established the necessity of this.

12a(11a) The dialogue we have been reading has been designed to open people's minds. "Have you got it yet?" You don't have to be very intelligent. Jeremiah and Yahweh have been making it quite clear.[145] But have people understood? Teachers often teach by asking questions; Proverbs operates this way. Teachers also ask questions as a way of discovering whether people have understood. There follow two tricola asking questions and two tricola giving answers. Their rhetoric is more subtle than their simple structure.

> v. 12   a question that incorporates another question and then another
> vv. 13–14   an answer to the second question that leaves the first question hanging

Jeremiah begins by asking a question about understanding. One could almost call it an epistemological question. It recalls Agur's questions in Prov 30:1–4 or the questions in Ecclesiastes. *Who is the person who is smart* enough to *understand* and answer the question that the teacher is about to ask? The unexpected third colon in the verse suggests that the answer will not come from someone with ordinary human insight or even extraordinary human insight. Yet this implicit confession is not a reason for despair such as that of Agur or Ecclesiastes, because the colon actually asks another question that opens the way toward an answer. Although *to whom has Yahweh's mouth spoken so that he can tell it* is articulated as another question, by its nature it hints that there is an answer. Paul's form of argument in Rom 9–11 will work like Jeremiah's as it asks a question that looks like one to which the questioner does not have the answer (like Agur and Ecclesiastes indeed) but to which the questioner actually knows the answer.

12b(11b) That first tricolon thus raised a question but did not tell us what the question was—it did not indicate what *this* refers to. As well as overtly asking a question (actually a double one), it indirectly raises another, which the second tricolon answers. The question concerns *for what reason the country has perished*. The question thus turns out to be the one raised by vv. 10–11(9–10). But a look back at those verses (and at the entire scroll) would make clear that this question has been copiously answered; even someone listening to this little exchange in isolation from its present

---

145. Brueggemann, *Jeremiah 1–25*, 93.

context would have heard the answer. To whom has Yahweh's mouth spoken? To Jeremiah, of course, and he has been making clear *ad nauseam* what the answer is.

13–14(12–13) It's *because of their abandoning my instruction, which I put before them. They didn't listen to my voice, and they didn't go by it*. It's not just Jeremiah's speaking voice; it's the Torah's written instruction (or perhaps it's Moses's voice).[146] After all, "*there is no free person* other than one who occupies himself with the study of Torah,"[147] and they have given up that freedom. The following tricolon still doesn't explicitly answer that question about the person to whom Yahweh's mouth has spoken—it leaves it implicit. It's more interested in the question within the questions, the question in v. 12b(11b). In case you haven't got it, here is the answer again: Yahweh once more sums up the message of the scroll so far. Everything he says he has said before, though the final phrase, *which their ancestors taught them*, articulates that point more explicitly. "Jeremiah's Yahweh is a great one for uttering a shattering insight" as a kind of "afterthought"—here about the way "idolatry is passed on, parent to child, and on and on." It is how original sin works. "No new start. . . . Practice makes perfect."[148] But there is a further aspect to v. 12a(11a) that Jeremiah has left hanging. The question "to whom has Yahweh's mouth spoken" is "Jeremiah." But the question "who is the person who is smart, so that he can understand this" is a broader one. Smartness is not confined to prophets, scribes, politicians, and priests. The assumption in 8:8 was that people in general could claim this quality. Indeed, Jeremiah has sardonically commented, it is a quality shown by the people in general, though in a bad way (4:22). They should be smart in a good way, which means recognizing the truth in what vv. 13–14(12–13) say. So the question in v. 12a, *who is the person who is smart, so that he reflects on this*, addresses people who should be smart and who claim to be smart and challenges them to recognize the smartness in what vv. 13–14 say and respond accordingly. In speaking like Agur or Ecclesiastes, Jeremiah is as usual engaged in rhetoric or persuasion. Once more he seeks to draw his audience into imagining what the catastrophe will be like and into acknowledging at last what made it necessary. His aim is that by seeing it now they may forestall it, because that is what they will do if they are smart. In a context after the catastrophe, when they had failed to do so, it could perhaps help to drive people who had survived it to see the point. But in the context of 604 or the years that followed up to 587, he would be saying, "Don't wait till then. Be smart now."

---

146. See H. Marlow, "Law and the Ruining of the Land," *Political Theology* 14 (2013): 655–56.
147. Joshua ben Levi, *Pirkei Avot* 6:2.
148. Berrigan, *Jeremiah*, 50.

This implicit exhortation reflects the importance of the emphasis on smartness or wisdom in Jer 7–10.[149]

15–16(14–15) Jeremiah has three images for the redress that Yahweh will otherwise take—images from earlier chapters that he now develops. In the first (cf. 8:14), *wormwood* is a plant with a strong smell and bitter taste that can be used medicinally but has a reputation for toxicity. The *water* in the parallel colon may have the same ambiguous implications, insofar as *poisoned* (*rōʾš*) actually refers to an (unidentified) plant. LXX and Vg have words for gall or bile, implying bitterness. The two words for plants come together in 23:15 as well as Deut 29:18 and Lam 3:19. The second image is to *scatter them among the nations*. While Yahweh has spoken more about devastating Judah's country, he has also threatened to throw Judah out from it (e.g., 5:19; 7:15). If the entities *that they and their ancestors have not acknowledged* were alien gods (7:8–10), they are now the nations themselves. Third, the image of the *sword* picks up from 4:10; 5:12, 17; 6:25; *sending off* the sword is a more literal version of sending off snakes (8:17). When Jeremiah earlier noted that Yahweh had *made an end of them* (5:3), he was exaggerating. He looks as if he is not overtly exaggerating here, though in the event his action will be less harsh than his threat, as usual (Ezek 12:15–16 makes the point explicit).[150]

c. Exchanges between Yahweh and Judah and the Closing Challenge (9:17–26[16–25])

17(16) *Yahweh of Armies has said this:*

Reflect, and call for the mourning women so that they come,
*   for the smart women, send off so that they come,*[a]
18(17) *And so that they hurry and lift up a wailing over us,*
*   so that our eyes may run down with tears,*
*   and our eyelids, so they may flow with water.*[b]

19(18) *Because the sound of wailing,*
*   it has made itself heard from Zion.*
How we have been destroyed—
*   we have been deeply shamed.*

149. L. C. Allen, "The Structural Role of Wisdom in Jeremiah," in *Riddles and Revelations: Explorations into the Relationship between Wisdom and Prophecy in the Hebrew Bible*, ed. M. J. Boda, R. L. Meek, and W. R. Osborne, LHBOTS 634 (London: T&T Clark, 2018), 95–108.

150. D. Rom-Shiloni, "Ezekiel and Jeremiah: What Might Stand behind the Silence?" *Hebrew Bible and Ancient Israel* 1 (2012): 221.

Because we have abandoned the country,
    because they have thrown down our dwellings. c
20(19) *Because listen, women, to Yahweh's message;*
    your ear is to accept the message from his mouth.
Teach your daughters wailing,
    one woman her neighbor mourning.
21(20) *Because death has gone up through our windows—*
    it has come into our citadels,
To cut off babies from the street,
    young men from the squares.

22(21) *Speak like this (Yahweh's affirmation):*

So the corpse d *of humanity will fall*
    like manure on the face of the open country,
Like a swath behind the harvester,
    with no one to gather. e

23(22) *Yahweh has said this:* f

A smart person is not to exult in his smartness,
    a strong person is not to exult in his strength,
    a wealthy person is not to exult in his wealth.
24(23) *Rather, in this someone who exults is to exult:*
    understanding and acknowledging me.
Because g *I am Yahweh,* h
    acting with commitment,
With authority and faithfulness i *in the country,*
    because in these I delight (Yahweh's affirmation). j

25(24) *There, days are coming (Yahweh's affirmation)*
    when I will attend to everyone circumcised in the foreskin,
26(25) *To Egypt and to Judah and to Edom,*
    to the Ammonites, to Moab,
To all the people who are clipped at the forehead,
    who live in the wilderness.
Because all the nations are foreskinned,
    and the entire household of Israel is foreskinned in mind. k

a. By anaphora, the verb recurs at the end of successive cola, with different pointing because of the pausal position of the first occurrence, though Rudolph (*Jeremia*, 68) compares Ezek 16:55.

b. LXX has "you . . . your . . . your," an easier reading (but *NETS* has "us . . . our . . . our").

c. MT has a section marker here. Vg, taking the third plural as impersonal, translates with a passive; LXX has "we have thrown down."

d. See the translation note on 7:33.

e. MT has a marker here.

f. Like vv. 12–16(11–15), vv. 23–26(22–25) are more pedestrian, but they manifest rhythm and parallelism, and I treat them as prosaic verse.

g. LXX, having omitted *me*, implies "that."

h. Cf. LXX, Vg. MT's accents imply "I, Yahweh, act . . ."

i. A hendiadys; there is no "and" after "commitment," but there is an "and" linking these two words (cf. 4:2).

j. The two lines comprising v. 24b(23b) and 24c(23c) have an a-b-b'-a' structure, closing off vv. 23–24. MT has a marker at the end.

k. MT has a marker here.

MT starts a new unit as the scroll again moves away from recording an exchange between Yahweh and Jeremiah. Verse 17(16) makes one expect that Yahweh will simply be addressing Judah, but what ensues looks more like Judah's self-exhortation voiced by Jeremiah. A similar dynamic recurs in vv. 20–21(19–20) and perhaps in v. 22(21). Even more than before, then, these are "exchanges" in which the statements of the participants are more like soliloquies; the participants are not listening to each other. They are not in real dialogue. Both parties speak about death; Yahweh speaks about proper exultation and true circumcision.

vv. 17–21		
	v. 17a	An introduction to Yahweh's message
	vv. 17b–21	Jeremiah's bid to summon mourners (a bicolon linked to a tricolon at a pause point, then seven bicola)
v. 22		
	v. 22a	An introduction to Yahweh's instruction to Jeremiah
	v. 22b–c	Jeremiah's message about people dying (two linked bicola)
vv. 23–24		
	v. 23a	An introduction to Yahweh's message
	vv. 23b–24	A message about exulting (an opening tricolon, a bicolon, and two linked bicola)
	vv. 25–26	A message about circumcision (four bicola, the first three linked)

The four subsections look as if they were of separate origin; the opening verb *reflect* (*bîn*) might have encouraged the placing of vv. 17–22(16–21) after vv. 12–16(11–15).

17(16) The new introduction need not imply a separate message, but the subsequent imagery confirms that the message is separate. It starts *in medias res*: who is to *reflect* on what and why? In light of what we have heard Jeremiah say before, it is not hard to guess, but it will be a while before he makes it explicit. In the meantime, he heightens suspense by spelling out the result of the reflection. "Death stalks the land, and the only appropriate response is to evoke the dirges that are regularly sung over the dead."[151] His addressees will need to *call for the mourning women*, the women who are expert at chanting funeral songs to aid mourners in their expression of grief.[152] Like Western culture, Judah professionalized some aspects of dealing with death. While a family would do its own caring for the body of someone who had died, it would commission expert mourners, as Western mourners may value the support and assistance of the church choir and the organist. Whose death do people need to mourn? Jeremiah indeed raises suspense.

18(17) He does so further when he goes on to insist that they must *hurry*. It's urgent. When it's time for *wailing*, you need to wail now. The movement within the verse indicates that the mourning women help people who need to cry to do their crying, and a lot of crying needs doing: *eyes* need to *run down with tears* and *eyelids* need to *flow with water*. In effect, Jeremiah has now repeated the three expressions from v. 10(9)—crying, wailing, and mourning—though in reverse order. There he spoke of the lamenting he was going to do. Here, it is the community's lamenting that it needs help with. Of course, when the catastrophe happens, there will be no need to commission the mourners. Jeremiah is again using his imagination and appealing to that of his people. The passage assumes "the power of the call to lament as prophecy."[153] The surprising note here is the *us ... our ... our* since we had the impression that Yahweh was speaking. Simply deleting v. 17a(16a) as a mistake[154] seems too easy. Is Yahweh identifying with the community?[155] It might work for this verse, but not for the next. Perhaps the introduction is an anticipation of the introduction in v. 20a(19a) or an introduction to the entire passage designating it as Yahweh's message.[156] Perhaps we need to assume an ellipsis: the opening words introduce what follows as the instruction Jeremiah is to give to the women; the pronouns do suggest that "there is no distance possible when death and destruction descend."[157] One way or another, however, Yahweh is bidding Judah to get ready to mourn.

151. P. D. Miller, "Jeremiah," on the passage.
152. See Lundbom, *Jeremiah 1–20*, 559–60.
153. D. R. Jones, *Jeremiah*, 166.
154. E.g., Volz, *Jeremia*, 117.
155. Fretheim, *Jeremiah*, 162.
156. R. P. Carroll, *Jeremiah*, OTL, 245.
157. A. Bauer, "Death, Grief, Agony, and a New Creation: Re-Reading Gender in Jeremiah after September 11," *WW* 22 (2002): 382.

19(18) It would further be wooden to ask why Jeremiah wants women summoned to lead wailing if *wailing* is already sounding out. The picture of actual wailing complements the image of summoning the wailers. When Jeremiah goes on to articulate the grief that the people are themselves expressing, the further significance of his words is that they answer the question raised by vv. 17–18(16–17). It is of course the devastation of Zion that the mourners need to bewail. Jeremiah again asks people to project themselves into the situation when Jerusalem has been taken. Again he speaks of the people being *destroyed* (cf. 4:13, 20, 30; 6:26). And *how* terrible is this destruction. It means they have been *shamed* (cf. 2:36), though maybe not yet in the sense Jeremiah wants (2:26; 3:25; 6:15; 7:19; 8:12). At the moment, their shame relates to what has happened rather than to why it happened. Jeremiah imagines them describing the reason for their sense of shame in a neatly parallel line:

> Because we have abandoned [our] country,
> because they have thrown down our dwellings.

The third-person verb complements the first-person verb, the plural *dwellings* complements the singular *country*, and the suffix *our* can be applied respectively to that word *country*. The mourning presupposes both the destruction of the *dwellings* in the land and the need to *abandon* the land itself as people are forced into exile (cf. v. 16[15]). But *abandon* and the word order (leaving then destruction) might also suggest the decision to flee as refugees before the invading army arrives to wreak death and destruction.

20(19) Once more, Jeremiah's words don't follow logically from what precedes; they paint another parallel picture. He passes on an unusual instruction from Yahweh. Yahweh bids the Jerusalem women to *teach* their *daughters wailing* and each one to teach *her neighbor mourning*; mourning women who are experts in these skills are not part of the picture. Perhaps the implication is that more women need to learn this expertise because there is going to be a lot of need for it.[158]

21(20) The preceding verses never quite articulated why mourning was necessary. Now Jeremiah does so. Joel 2:9 describes the extraordinary ability of locusts that have *gone up through our windows* like a thief, or like the attackers of a town who have to scale its walls. *Death* assails the windows and thus the homes of Jerusalem like a thief or like locusts or like an invading army; in this context it is an invading army that brings death through the city's literal and metaphorical windows.[159] It *has come into our citadels*, where the palace is, where the toughest fortifications are. Jeremiah imagines the

---

158. Rudolph, *Jeremia*, 68.
159. There may also be an allusion to the motif of death coming in through the windows

attackers having fulfilled the resolve of 6:5. If death thus invades ordinary people's homes and the king's palace, it will indeed *cut off babies from the street* and *young men from the squares.* There is no doubt of the truth in Yahweh's advice that the women (these babies' mothers and these young men's sisters) will need to wail and mourn. "The expert mourning women were to become tradents of the prophetic word."[160] And they are to encourage the "remembrance" that "is crucial in the face of death."[161]

22(21) In a more distinctive exchange, Yahweh adds a further horrifying nuance to that picture of death's invasion. Initially, one might think of a single human *corpse* that is to *fall* in the fields, *on the face of the open country.* But the comparison *like manure* indicates that Jeremiah is thinking of something more like the army of corpses on the killing fields of the Civil War or the First World War (cf. Ezek 37:1-2). To complement that picture, then, is the image of a *swath* of grain, a cluster scattered over the field as the *harvester* cuts and gathers the grain but leaves the leftovers for the birds, as there is *no one to gather.*

23(22) As the end of Jer 8–9 draws near, Jeremiah comes back to smartness and to acknowledging, which makes a link with where the section began (8:7-9). The scroll now presents a collocation of the possibility of being *smart*, being *strong*, and being *wealthy.* Ecclesiastes 2 covers smartness and wealth in this connection. Though it doesn't mention strength, its talk of achievements and of the king's power is not so different. These things would come near the top of any list of what gives people something to exult in (*hālal hithpael*). But none is worth saying one's ultimate hallelujah about.

24(23) When these lines begin to spell out the positive, they rather suggest that it was not by chance that this little message began with the smart person. One might see the smart people (as opposed to the prophets and priests) and their perspective and questions as Jeremiah's problem in his own person.[162] In effect, this little message is simply about the nature of real smartness. It lies in *understanding and acknowledging me.* It is in the knowledge of Yahweh that "true glorification" lies.[163] Thus "the person who exults should exult in the Lord" (1 Cor 1:31 and 2 Cor 10:17; James 1:9-11 and Philo also reflect the influence of this saying).[164] It is deceptively simple but profoundly decisive when set against the alternatives. Judahites may think the Master and other

in Mesopotamian and Ugaritic myth; see M. S. Smith, "Death in Jeremiah, ix, 20," *Ugarit-Forschungen* 19 (1987): 289-93.

160. P. J. Scalise, "The Way of Weeping: Reading the Path of Grief in Jeremiah," *WW* 22 (2002): 417.

161. Bauer, "Death, Grief, Agony, and a New Creation," 382.

162. So M. S. Moore, "Jeremiah's Progressive Paradox," *RB* 93 (1986): 386-414.

163. Katho, "To Know and Not to Know Yhwh," 237-88.

164. See G. O'Day, "Jeremiah 9:22-23 and 1 Corinthians 1:26-31," *JBL* 109 (1990): 259-67; H. H. D. Williams III, "Of Rags and Riches: The Benefits of Hearing Jeremiah 9:23-24 within

deities matter; in reality they are empty, hollow nonentities, non-gods (see 8:19; 9:14[13]). Set over against them, *I am Yahweh* is a compressed way of saying "I am Yahweh, and Yahweh is the only deity who really deserves to be called God, because he is substantial, not hollow and empty." The facts about Yahweh are thus what smart people recognize: his acting with *commitment* (see 2:2) and with *authority and faithfulness* (see 4:2).

> When these two words are joined together, they denote perfect govern-
> ment; that is, that God defends his faithful people, aids the miserable,
> and delivers them when unjustly oppressed; and also that he restrains
> the wicked, and suffers them not to injure the innocent at their pleasure.
> These then are the things which the Scripture everywhere means by the
> two words, judgment and justice [the translation's equivalent to *authority*
> and *faithfulness* as renderings of *mišpāṭ* and *ṣədāqâ*]. The justice of God
> is not to be taken according to what is commonly understood by it; and
> they speak incorrectly who represent God's justice as in opposition to his
> mercy: hence the common proverb, "I appeal from justice to mercy." The
> Scripture speaks otherwise; for *justice* is to be taken for that faithful pro-
> tection of God, by which he defends and preserves his own people; and
> *judgment,* for the rigor which he exercises against the transgressors of his
> law. But, as I have already said, judgment and justice, when found together,
> are to be taken for that legitimate government, by which God so regulates
> the affairs of the world, that there is nothing but what is just and right.[165]

The triad in v. 24(23) stands in contrast to that in v. 23(22),[166] and "in these three graces the self-revelation of Yahweh is complete."[167] Jeremiah adds that these qualities are not simply random characteristics of Yahweh's acting. Be-hind his acting in these ways is his *delight* in them. So don't brag about those other things: "Brag about the things that please the God of Israel."[168] Recog-nizing these facts and glorying in them matters because it "excludes the false trust in escape."[169] It means one resists the temptation to assume that might is right or money talks or scholarship matters. Conversely, it means that one lives in hope; the hopelessness that Jeremiah might have engendered and that the fall of Jerusalem might in due course engender does not have the last

---

James 1:9–11," *TynB* 53 (2002): 273–82; A. Kovelman, "Jeremiah 9:22–23 in Philo and Paul," *Review of Rabbinic Judaism* 10 (2007): 162–75.

165. Calvin, *Jeremiah*, 1:538.

166. W. J. Wessels, "Social Implications of Knowing Yahweh: A Study of Jeremiah 9:22–23," *Verbum et Ecclesia* 30 (2009): 2.

167. Berrigan, *Jeremiah*, 54.

168. W. Brueggemann, "Bragging about the Right Stuff," *Journal for Preachers* 26 (2003): 31.

169. Thomas Aquinas, *Commentary on Jeremiah*, quoted in Schroeder, *Jeremiah*, 169.

word. For Yahweh to claim to act with commitment is especially dangerous, as commitment (*ḥesed*) is a quality that a person continues to maintain when the other party has forfeited any right to it (cf. the appeal or reassurance in Lam 3:22, 32), though one can never expect to claim that Yahweh must show such qualities unless one is pledged to them in one's own life. Recognizing these facts about Yahweh has to mean that one lives by them.

25–26(24–25) These closing verses also concern smartness and acknowledging Yahweh, though those words do not feature in it. Once again, Jeremiah takes his time about getting to his point; it is not at all clear from the beginning where he is going. *Days are coming* (see 7:32) when Yahweh is going to *attend to* the peoples who are circumcised (circumcision is not confined to Israel, though Yahweh gave it particular significance for Israel). Will his attending have negative implications (e.g., 5:9, 29; 6:15; 9:9) or positive ones (e.g., 15:15; 27:22)? And why this list of circumcised nations? The list comprises Judah and the surrounding peoples; the people *clipped at the forehead, who live in the wilderness* are the tribes in the desert east of Ammon and Moab. It thus overlaps with the list in Amos 1:3–2:5. Judah's being randomly listed as number two out of six compares with the list of nations in Isa 13–23, where Jerusalem appears randomly between Dumah and Tyre. Why is Yahweh treating Judah as just one nation among others, as in Isa 22 he treats Jerusalem as just one people among others? The answer emerges in the last line, especially its very last word. Being physically circumcised doesn't distinguish the nation of Judah, and in itself physical circumcision offers no protection from Yahweh's (negative) attentiveness. Notwithstanding their physical circumcision, the nations are still *foreskinned*. Excuse me? In the last colon Yahweh explains what he means as he moves from speaking of *all the nations* including Judah to speaking of a *household*, namely *Israel*, which is *foreskinned in mind*. Smartness will mean seeking circumcision of mind so that one acknowledges Yahweh.[170]

3. Another Exhortation and Another Exchange (10:1–25)

Part 2a of the scroll (Jer 7–10) concludes with another exhortation and another exchange. The material suggests a time between 597 and 587.

> 10:1   An introduction to the unit
> 10:2–16   An exhortation for the 597 exiles about images and the
>   deities they represent

---

170. Jeremiah may allude specifically to a less radical form of circumcision practiced by some other peoples, which made Judahites feel superior: see R. C. Steiner, "Incomplete Circumcision in Egypt and Edom," *JBL* 118 (1999): 497–526.

10:1–16 An Exhortation about Images

a. An Exhortation about Images (10:1–16)

¹*Listen to the message that Yahweh has spoken over*ª *you, household of Israel.*

²*Yahweh has said this:*

*In regard to the nations' path*ᵇ—*don't learn;*
   the heavens' signs—don't break down because of them.
Because the nations may break down because of those,
   ³*because the peoples' decrees are empty.*

Because a tree from the forest—someone cuts it,
   the work of a craftsman's hands, with a saw.
⁴*With silver and with gold they beautify it,*ᶜ
   with nails and with hammers they make them fast,
   so it can't wobble.
⁵*They're like a metalwork*ᵈ *pillar,*ᵉ
   so they can't speak.
*They are carried, carried,*ᶠ
   because they can't walk.
Don't be in awe of them,
   because they can't do anything dire;
   *doing good, too—it's not in them.*ᵍ

⁶*There is absolutely no one*ʰ *like you, Yahweh—*
   you are big and your name is big, with strength.
⁷*Who would not be in awe of you, king of the nations,*
   because to you it's fitting.
Because among all the nations' smart people and in all their dominion,
   *there is absolutely no one like you.*ⁱ

⁸*As one, they are stupid, they are foolish—*
   *the restraint that comes from empty things: it's wood*ʲ—
⁹*Beaten silver that's brought from Tarshish*
   *and gold from Uphaz,*ᵏ
The work of a craftsman
   and the hands of a smith,
Blue and purple their clothing,

the work of smart people, all of them.
[10]But Yahweh is God who is truth,[1]
  he is the living God, the eternal king.
At his rage the earth quakes;
  the nations cannot endure his condemnation.[m]

[11]In accordance with this you are to say to them:[n]

The gods who did not make the heavens and the earth—
  these will perish[o] from the earth[p] and from under the heavens.[q]

[12]Maker of earth by his energy,[r]
  establisher of the world by his smartness,
  who[s] by his insight stretched the heavens,
[13]With[t] the sound of his giving[u] a roar of water in the heavens,
  and his causing billows to go up[v] from the end of the[w] earth,
Lightnings with[x] the rain he makes,
  and he causes wind to go out from his stores.[y]

[14]Every human being shows himself stupid through his knowledge,
  every goldsmith is put to shame through his image.
Because his model is deception;
  there is no spirit in them.
[15]They are empty, a work for mockery—
  at the time of their being attended to, they will perish.

[16]Not like these is Jacob's share,
  because he is the shaper of everything.
And Israel is the clan that is his domain:[z]
  Yahweh of Armies is his name.[aa]

a. Cf. Vg; LXX has "to," but the preposition is 'al, not the usual 'el or lə (see DCH, 2:391–94).

b. The preposition 'el instead of the accusative marker 'et is odd (in contrast, 12:16 has the accusative marker); maybe it issues from the prophet's putting the object before the verb, as when, conversely, a feminine subject follows a masculine verb.

c. For MT yəyappēhû, Tg implies yəṣappēhû ("they cover it").

d. As Vg, Sym, Aq, Tg recognize, in this context miqšâ is not a cucumber patch but the more common homonym denoting hammered work (LXX also lacks the cucumber patch). Contrast Isa 1:8 and see the Deuterocanonical Letter of Jeremiah 69, whence the cucumber patch has been superimposed on Jer 10:5 in modern translations; see B. D. Thomas, "Re-evaluating the Influence of Jeremiah 10 upon the Apocryphal Epistle of Jeremiah," ZAW 120 (2008): 557.

e. In its only other occurrence (Judg 4:5), *tōmer* is an alternative to *tāmār* as a word for a palm tree (Vg, Aq, Theod here), while a *təmōrâ* is a decorative palm tree-like carving similar to a totem pole (cf. Sym, LXX here). The implication is that Jeremiah refers to a palm tree-like pillar. Letter of Jeremiah 69 has *probaskanion*, which usually denotes an amulet (to ward off spirits or thieves from the cucumber patch), but this seems less relevant here; for *probaskanion*, Vg has something like "scarecrow," and the pillar here became a scarecrow in modern translations. "It is a splendid taunt": the poet pictures people watching the great procession of images and "says to them, Look at the scarecrows! Aren't they a horrible sight?" (Volz, *Jeremia*, 125); how unfortunate that the interpretation is fanciful. See *HALOT*; also N. Mizrahi, *Witnessing a Prophetic Text in the Making: The Literary, Textual and Linguistic Development of Jeremiah 10:1–16*, BZAW 502 (Berlin: de Gruyter, 2017), 54–56.

f. The (*qal*) infinitive preceding the finite verb emphasizes the verb.

g. MT has a marker here. LXX, 4QJer[b] lack vv. 6–8 and 10.

h. For this translation of *mē'ên* (recurring in v. 7), see *CTAT* 2:466. Theod implies *mē'ayin* ("whence is there anyone").

i. The repeated noun clause forms a framework around the act of praise in vv. 6–7; see J. R. Lundbom, *Jeremiah: A Study in Ancient Hebrew Rhetoric*, 2nd ed. (Winona Lake, IN: Eisenbrauns, 1997), 60–61.

j. Distinguishing subject and object in a noun clause is tricky, and one could translate "wood is the restraint offered by empty things"; I here follow the principles formulated in *IBHS* 8.4.2.

k. Syr, Tg have the more familiar "Ophir."

l. The comparable expressions in the following parallel colon suggest that *'ĕmet* is in apposition to *'ĕlōhîm* rather than adverbial ("in truth"; see Joüon 131c).

m. MT has a marker here.

n. V. 11 is in Aramaic.

o. LXX, Vg take *yē'badû* as jussive, but the context suggests *yiqtol* (cf. Tg). The paronomasia with the preceding word (*'ābadû*) underlines the link and contrast between *not make* and *perish*.

p. *Earth* is spelled *'arqā'* the first time and *'ar'ā'* the second time, apparently just for variety; the two spellings coexisted (Allen, *Jeremiah*, 127).

q. MT has a section marker here.

r. Verses 12–16 reappear in a slightly variant form as 51:15–19, appropriately as part of a message about Babylon, and vv. 12–13 in a Qumran psalm (11QPs[a] 26:13–15; *DSS* 2:1178–79).

s. Lit. "and he," idiomatically continuing the participial sequence with a finite verb.

t. For *lə* meaning "(in connection) with," cf. v. 13b and 11:16.

u. Cf. Rashi, in MG. It is not "his giving of voice" (cf. Vg); the suffix in *ləqôl tittî* is on the "wrong" word, and the rest of the colon is then stranded. LXX lacks the phrase.

v. The finite verb continues the infinitival construction (cf. n. s).

w. The *ketiv* lacks *the*.

x. The unusual use of *lə* (LXX, Vg have "into," which makes poor sense) corresponds to that in v. 13a (see n. t).

y. "In some poetic texts, celebrating the greatness of God, the use of tenses, of qatal especially, is very peculiar. . . . These qatals have not been satisfactorily explained" (Joüon 113l). This comment refers to Jer 10:12–13, though v. 12 doesn't seem a problem because it refers to a past act; on the other hand, one could extend its reference to the *wayyiqtols* in v. 13. *IBHS* 33.3.5d sees that usage as gnomic (cf. DG 82a) but also notes that the troublesome verbs follow on the infinitive *titô* ("his giving"); and finite verbs picking up from infinitives and participles (see GKC 111v; and see n. s) can seem a bit random in tense.

z. LXX "he is his [Jacob's] inheritance" reverses the point, making it a restatement of the first colon; Tg conversely makes Jacob into God's share in the first colon.

aa. MT has a marker here.

After an introduction to the chapter in v. 1, vv. 2–16 constitute an exhortation to Judahites not to be impressed by—and thus follow—a religion that focuses on images. Four times it draws a contrast between images (and image-makers) and Yahweh. The passage is not unique in spelling out this contrast, but "it is unique in achieving this contrast by the technique of alternation."[171]

v. 2a	Introduction to vv. 2–16
vv. 2b–3a	The exhortation and its basic rationale (two bicola)
vv. 3b–7	First contrast
vv. 3b–5	How an image gets made, what the result is like, and the implications (a bicolon and a tricolon before the pause, then two bicola and a tricolon to make a snide comment before the next pause)
vv. 6–7	Yahweh with his contrasting and unique person: an act of confession (three bicola)
vv. 8–10	Second contrast
vv. 8–9	How an image gets made: a restatement of the grounds for the exhortation (four linked bicola in a substantial enjambment)
v. 10	Yahweh as the true, living God: a restatement of the confession (two bicola)
vv. 11–13	Third contrast
v. 11	The limitations of other gods: a further elaboration of the grounds (an introduction and a 5-5 bicolon)
vv. 12–13	Yahweh as the creator: a further restatement of the confession (an opening tricolon and two bicola with exposition and enjambment)
vv. 14–16	Fourth contrast
vv. 14–15	The stupidity of image-makers, their images, and the gods: a final dismissal (three bicola)
v. 16	Who Yahweh is and who Israel is: a contrasting final declaration (two bicola)

171. Holladay, *Commentary on Jeremiah*, 1:328; cf. E. R. Clendenen, "Discourse Strategies In Jeremiah 10:1-16," *JBL* 106 (1987): 401–8.

In terms of form criticism, the verses alternate between satire and hymn, and in terms of literary development, the hymnic elements have been seen as added to the satirical.[172] It is the first passage in the scroll where MT and LXX substantially differ; the Qumran manuscript of the Hebrew text corresponds to LXX. Opinions differ as to which is older.

While there is no tidy structuring of the content of the theological observations, a profile does emerge from them. On one hand, the nations' gods did not make the cosmos and there is no reason to be in awe of them, though the nations do thus have reason to be afraid of what the heavens portend. Their gods are represented by things that are outwardly impressive (clothed in economics and aesthetics) but humanly manufactured. They can't speak, move, or act; there is no spirit in them. The nations' religion is hollow, ineffective, and deserving of mockery. Their gods and their representatives are stupid, deceptive, and destined to be exposed as such and to perish. In contrast, Yahweh is impressive, strong, truthful, living, eternal, energetic, smart, insightful, and decisively wrathful. He created the cosmos and continues to make it work. He is Jacob's share and Israel is his domain. There is thus reason to be in awe of Yahweh and no need to fear what the heavens may portend. While only vv. 6–7 are formally expressed as praise, all four confession passages are hymnic; both second-person address and third-person description parallel the Psalms. "The idols are mocked in a kind of doggerel poetry, laughed to scorn; Yahweh is addressed and hymned in the solemn language of liturgy."[173]

Although Judah has a long history of involvement with the gods represented by the planets (see 8:1–3), the additional focus here on divine images of the kind that are attacked in Isa 40–48 suggests a link with the forced migration of Judahites to Babylon. Tg sees v. 11 (in Aramaic, the international language) as part of a letter Jeremiah wrote to the 597 exiles. If the passage comes from after 597, it is quite a message from and for "a defeated population lost among all the populations in the vast Babylonian Empire."[174] It "projects an implicit audience ideologically besieged and demoralized as a result of its colonization by more powerful cultural forces."[175] Jeremiah's aim is then "for his fellow-Judahites to overcome their fear of the gods."[176] He wants to emphasize that Yahweh alone is God and that humanly-made

---

172. See Mizrahi, *Witnessing a Prophetic Text*. For further possibilities regarding the text's development, see, e.g., P. M. Bogaert, "Les mécanismes rédactionnels en Jr 10,1–16 (LXX et TM)," in *Le livre de Jérémie*, 222–38, 433–34; J. Ben-Dov, "A Textual Problem and Its Form-Critical Solution: Jeremiah 10:1–16," *Textus* 20 (2000): 97–128.

173. Holladay, *Commentary on Jeremiah*, 1:336.

174. Holladay, *Commentary on Jeremiah*, 1:337.

175. Diamond, "Jeremiah," 563.

176. Volz, *Jeremia*, 124.

images are "just that and no more."[177] If he misunderstands divine images, as if people identified them with the gods they represented rather than simply finding them something helpful to focus on, it is a kind of willful misunderstanding. He may think that this theology is a little sophisticated for many people. More profoundly, he knows the idea that an image can represent a deity is vulnerable to deconstruction. Either the image is totally misleading or the deity is pathetic (cf. Deut 4).

The passage reflects how "monotheism" is not an especially helpful category to articulate the scriptural understanding of the nature of God. On one hand, there are many gods, though not all deserve the title God (it is useful that English has the convention of capitalizing the first letter of some words, which enables us to make that point visually). On the other, the key truth about God is not merely that there is only one of him but that Yahweh is the one God. To adapt the point to a modern context, "the critical faith issue is not atheism but idolatry."[178] Not that modernity is actually atheistic: our gods are growth, democracy, justice, trade, technology, security, diversity, sex, travel, power, conservation, independence, and education (among others), which (like Babylon's gods) are not powerless, nor are they evil except when we treat them as such. But they are not God. Another way of approaching the question of idolatry in the context of modernity would be to ask whether words have a place in European culture that is analogous to the place of manufactured images in traditional cultures. "Whatever we have said about idols can also be applied to all teachings that are contrary to the truth."[179]

1–2a Like 7:1–8:3 and 8:4–9:26(25), the unit begins with an introduction to the chapter as a whole (v. 1) then goes on to its dedicated introduction to vv. 2–16 (*Yahweh has said this*) before coming to the substance.

2b–3a *The nations* have featured so far in the scroll as people about whom Jeremiah would bring a message (1:5, 10), as gathering to acknowledge Yahweh (3:17), as blessing themselves by him (4:2), and as witnesses to Yahweh's action against Judah (6:18) but also as the place of Judah's scattering (9:16[15]). *In regard to the nations' path—don't learn* follows from that scattering. Judah's vocation is to walk on Yahweh's path, to follow the way of relating to him on which Yahweh directs his people and which corresponds to who he is. It may include a community and ethical aspect, but it suggests especially the way of worship and truthfulness in calling on his name (e.g., 2:23, 33, 36; 3:21; 4:18; 5:4, 5). Here, what will follow will have similar impli-

---

177. M. Lundberg, "The *Mis-Pi* Rituals and Incantations and Jeremiah 10:1–16," in Goldingay, *Uprooting and Planting*, 227.

178. Brueggemann, *Jeremiah 1–25*, 97.

179. Jerome, *Jeremiah*, 66.

cations as it speaks of the way the nations make their gods. There were many points at which proper First Testament faith broadly corresponded with the nations' forms of worship and prayer, but that faith was also characterized by some key theological differences. Yahweh's instruction raises related issues for the church. Its forms of worship commonly follow the ways of the culture, which raises the question whether the theology of the church's worship differs from that of the culture. After his opening exhortation, Jeremiah adds that people shouldn't *break down* because of *the heavens' signs*. While this reference to the heavens' signs does recall Judahite attentiveness to the sun, the moon, and the heavenly army to which 8:2 referred, this aspect of Babylonian religion and learning might seem newly impressive to Judahites taken off to Babylon. If celestial signs seemed to portend some disaster, they would tempt people to *break down*, to panic. Scriptures that relate to this context (Gen 1; Isa 40) therefore confront it. It isn't so unreasonable that *the nations may break down because of those*; they have nowhere else to turn. When the heavens' portents are sinister, *the peoples' decrees*, the revelations and prescriptions of their religion (in effect, *decrees* is another word for *path*), *are empty* (*hebel*), as empty as the gods who (allegedly) lay them down. The two lines in vv. 2aβ–3a thus form an a-b-b'-a' structure:

> In regard to the nations' path—don't learn
> > the heavens' signs—don't break down because of them.
> > Because the nations may break down because of those,
> because the peoples' decrees are empty.

3b–4 If vv. 3b–5 "are a *non sequitur*" after v. 2,[180] it is because Jeremiah segues into disdaining the aspect of Babylonian religion on which he will focus, the aspect that for Judahites is more distinctive in the context of Babylon itself. You only have to consider the nature of the Babylonians' gods—or at least that of their images—to be convinced that the nations' religion is empty. Jeremiah's straight but implicitly mocking description of the making of an image allows the description more or less to speak for itself, as happens in Isa 40–48. The image comes simply from *a tree from the forest*. A human being *cuts it* and *the work of a craftsman's hands* constructs it. The process involves working with *a saw*. There does follow the sacrifice of *silver and gold* with which the craftworkers *beautify it* so that people end up with something truly splendid, and no one who rejoices in the glory of a medieval cathedral can simply despise such religious artifacts. But then the craftworkers have to bring in *nails and hammers* so as to *make them fast*. The first two cola in v. 4 are neatly parallel:

180. McKane, *Jeremiah*, 1:219.

With	silver	and	with	gold	they	beautify it;
with	nails	and	with	hammers	they	make them fast.

Why do they need to make the images fast? Structurally, the extra colon that follows is all the more a surprise after that neat bicolon, but the bicolon raises a question that needs answering, and the short extra colon is the more forceful as it provides the answer. They have to secure the image *so it can't wobble* (cf. Isa 41:7). It's bad for morale if your god falls over or disintegrates.[181] The last colon in the tricolon is the first almost-explicit note of scorn in this initial account.

5 Jeremiah goes on to be more scathing. First, the images are *like a metalwork pillar* of a kind familiar to Judahites (see the translation note). The cherubim and candelabra in the wilderness sanctuary were metalwork (Exod 37:7, 17, 22), and the temple had decorated pillars and palm-tree-like carvings (e.g., 1 Kgs 6–7); they also resemble Assyrian sacred trees.[182] Such pillars are a nice decorative adjunct to worship, and the comparison between Israelite ones and the objects critiqued here confirms that one should not absolutize the dismissal of the nations' path and decrees.[183] But images *can't speak*, as any decent God (or rather the one decent God) can. Second, *they are carried*—actually *carried*—*because they can't walk.* The great processions in which gods were carried about were an impressive feature of Babylonian worship, but the Babylonians seem not to have noticed the implications of the need to carry the images everywhere every year (cf. Isa 46:1–4). Thus, third, they can't actually *do anything*—anything *dire* or anything *good* (cf. Isa 41:23). *It's not in them.* Israel derides gods that have all the right body parts but none of them work (e.g., Ps 115:4–7) and draws a contrast with Yahweh who has ears, eyes, a nose and so on that work—he can see, listen, and savor things. The gods "'can do you no harm'. . . . What assurance! Yahweh speaks from an ample sense of who he is—and who the idols are not."[184] Therefore, *don't be in awe of them.* In effect, the exhortation with its rationale restates the initial exhortations in vv. 2–3a with their rationales. In vv. 4–5b, three successive lines ended with a short and brisk negative closing colon about the images; the tricolon comprising v. 5b is an enhanced instantiation of that pattern.

6 Those negatives issue from some positives. It is Yahweh's impressiveness that makes the images lose their grandeur. *There is absolutely no one like you, Yahweh.* Whereas vv. 2–5 had the form of a message from Yahweh,

181. A possible alternative meaning for *yāpîq*; see *DCH*, 6:669.
182. See R. Eichler, "Jeremiah and the Assyrian Sacred Tree," *VT* 17 (2017): 1–11.
183. Pixley, *Jeremiah*, 34.
184. Berrigan, *Jeremiah*, 55.

the prophet now forgets himself and finds himself speaking to Yahweh—but doing so in a way that the Judahites can overhear, so he is still addressing them. What makes Yahweh distinctive is (as it were) size. Yahweh is a *big guy*, by analogy with the big guys and nations that Jeremiah has mentioned (5:5; 6:13, 22; 8:10). He is imposing and impressive. *And your name is big* (it is imposing and impressive) because the name speaks of the person, and when one thinks of the name *Yahweh*, one is intimidated—in a good way. One is overwhelmed. That name is big *with strength*: it's quite a statement about a deity whom the Babylonians would claim had suffered defeat by their god. Jeremiah knows that Yahweh is the sovereign who has been manipulating these very Babylonians with that strength.

7 So whereas no awe is due to the Babylonian deities whose images accurately embody their incapacity to do anything, *who would not be in awe of you* (actually, most of the Judahites, which shows how stupid they are), *king of the nations* (yes, the Babylonians are his unwitting servants). Jeremiah doesn't want his people to have a small and local view of God.[185] To Yahweh, awe is *fitting*. Because among all the deities that are served *among all the nations' smart people and in all their dominion, there is absolutely no one like you*.

8 Jeremiah gives up addressing Yahweh and restates both parts of his point so far: first the nature of images, then the nature of the real God. The supposedly smart people who worship by means of the images actually *are stupid, they are foolish*, as is clear when one reflects on the nature of the images' *restraint*, their discipline or instruction (*mûsār*: 2:30; 5:3; 7:28); in effect, it is another term for *path* or *decrees*.[186] The images are *empty things* (*hebel* pl.). Their basic constituent is *wood*. It can't direct you onto the right path or hold you back from the wrong one.

9 That consideration is hardly palliated by adding an impressive coating for the wood: *beaten silver that's brought from Tarshish and gold from Uphaz*. We can't identify either place, though the usual candidates are, respectively, west across the Mediterranean (maybe as far as Tartessus in Spain) and some way south in Arabia, in modern Yemen. How far the precious metals were brought! Again, Jeremiah notes that the images are simply items of human manufacture, *the work of a craftsman and the hands of a smith*—someone who works in (etymologically, "smelts") gold or silver. As well as the gold and silver plating, there are the images' glorious *blue and purple clothing*, also fine human craftwork—*the work of smart people, all of them*. But there is some irony in calling these people *smart*. "How can smart people engage in an insane thing like this?"[187] Craftworkers "'deck it with silver and gold

---

185. Theodoret, *Ermeneia*, PG 81:565.
186. Duhm, *Jeremia*, 98.
187. Altschuler, *Mesudat David*, in MG.

299

. . .' so that the simple may be deceived"—and not just the simple, but people who "are wise and at the same time foolish."[188]

10 In contrast, there is the nature of *Yahweh*, the real God. First, he is the *God who is truth* (*'ĕmet*), the real thing, as opposed to something false and empty, whose reality doesn't correspond to its appearance. Second, he is *the living God*, not only living as opposed to dead but living as opposed to lifeless, comatose, and motionless, like the images. Third, he is *king*, sovereign in world events (cf. v. 7). Fourth, he is *eternal*, the king of eternity in the sense of the king of the age, the king from the beginning of the age until the end of the age. And fifth, when he gets angry, you know about it. Any temptation to see the noun phrases in v. 10a as static descriptions "is dispelled by the violent verbal clauses that follow."[189] As king, he gets angry with things that offend him and go against his plans, and he doesn't then sit by. After 597, Judah should be more convinced that this is true, though all being well, they won't have to endure it again (but actually they will). On the other hand, there are the nations. They come at the end of vv. 8–10, as they came at the end of vv. 2–3a and 3b–7. "The idol-gods can only shake the earth by falling over, but they are prevented from falling over by being nailed down. The earth, however, shakes at the wrath of the Lord, and the nations shake at his anger."[190] While *condemnation* (*za'am*) suggests wrath, it relates to words for threat and curse; it suggests denunciation that issues in acts of judgment.[191]

11 While one might wonder whether this verse of Aramaic is a later addition to supplement Jeremiah's point, it is present in the shorter LXX text of this chapter and it is integral to the alternating structure of vv. 2–16. Like many people in the modern world outside of circles where English is people's first language, many Judahites could switch easily between their first language and an international language, as happens with the longer Aramaic sections in Ezra and Daniel. Jeremiah himself might make that switch for rhetorical effect as he talks about Babylonian religion, especially if he speaks for the benefit of Judahites living in a Babylonian context;[192] Tg sees *them* as the exiles. MT frames v. 11 as a separate section, of which the main part makes for a neat parallel line, juxtaposing the two verbs at the center and repeating the heavens and the earth in a-b-c-d-d'-c'-b'-a' order:

188. Jerome, *Jeremiah*, 66, 67 (but the editor's footnote suggests a slip of the pen in Jerome's neat remark).

189. Holladay, *Commentary on Jeremiah*, 1:334.

190. Craigie, Kelley, and Drinkard, *Jeremiah 1–25*, 159.

191. B. Wiklander, "זעם, *zā'am*," *TDOT* 4:106–11.

192. See G. Reid, "'Thus You Will Say to Them': A Cross-Cultural Confessional Polemic in Jeremiah 10.11," *JSOT* 31 (2006): 221–38.

> the gods
>> who the heavens
>>> and the earth
>>>> did not make
>>>> will perish
>>> from the earth
>> and from under the heavens
> these [gods]

So far Jeremiah hasn't talked about the gods themselves, only about the images. Now he speaks of the deities they represent, whose reality he grants (for the sake of argument at least) but who do not match up to Yahweh. His two comments about them relate to Yahweh's being God from the beginning of the age until the end of the age (v. 10). Retrospectively, they are *the gods who did not make the heavens and the earth.* Prospectively, *they will perish from the earth and from under the heavens.* Psalm 82:6–7 makes the same point in connection with a critique of these gods for their failure to oversee the implementing of faithful exercise of authority in the world. Perhaps they die for such a reason, though Jeremiah does not say so. His explicit point is rather that they are not eternal by nature as Yahweh is. They do not have life in themselves any more than humanity did when created.

12 The resumptive confession about Yahweh now expands on something that was presupposed by the Aramaic line, whose first colon was an anticipatory corollary of what now follows. Notwithstanding the participles, the acts here described are aspects of Yahweh's original act of creation. The characteristics that enabled Yahweh to be the creator were *his energy* or power, *his smartness* or expertise, and his *insight* or discernment.[193] They enabled him to be the *maker of earth* and (to take the point further in the parallelism) the *establisher of the* (habitable) *world*, so that it not only exists but has some security. The extra third colon necessarily affirms that he also brought the heavens into being. The sky is a great tent over the earth, protecting it; creation meant that Yahweh was pitching this tent. Jeremiah thus makes the point by means of a vivid metaphor of which the First Testament is fond when describing creation (e.g., Ps 104:2). The affirmation in the first two cola also uses psalmic language: Yahweh is "establisher of the mountains by his energy" (Ps 65:7[6]).

13 As often happens in portraits of Yahweh as creator (outside Genesis), Jeremiah goes on to Yahweh's continuing activity as sovereign in creation. He thereby completes a matching of the heavens-earth-earth-heavens sequence

---

193. On the link between creation and wisdom in this passage, see Dell, "Jeremiah, Creation and Wisdom," 375–90.

in v. 11 with an earth-heavens-heavens-earth sequence in vv. 12–13a. When there is "the sound of the roar of rain" approaching and bringing the end of a drought (1 Kgs 18:41), it is Yahweh who is causing the *sound* and *giving a roar of water in the heavens*. It is Yahweh who then generates the *billows* of cloud; etymologically, they are "things that rise"—the word comes only in the context of phrases like this one. He makes these clouds *go up from the end of the earth*, rising from the distant horizon to bring the rain (cf. 1 Kgs 18:44–45). Then there are the *lightnings* that he *makes* in connection with *the rain*, and the *wind* that *he causes to go out from his stores* (cf. 1 Kgs 18:45) to accompany the rain. So when things are still, it is because he is keeping shut the doors of his storehouses (which lie on the other side of the sky dome?), and it is when he opens those doors that a gale blows and rain falls. (The last three cola in v. 13 appear in a slightly different form as Ps 135:7, in a psalm that derides images in terms similar to those in Jer 10 and in 5:21.)

14a "What, then, is man with his graven images?"[194] Jeremiah moves back to the contrast with images—or rather, moves back first to the people who make images. He begins with a subtle neat parallelism in which the second colon systematically clarifies the first:

every human being	shows himself stupid	through [his] knowledge
every goldsmith	is put to shame	through [his] image

The eyebrow-raising declaration *every human being shows himself stupid* achieves its aim when it makes the audience listen up to find out what Jeremiah can possibly mean. The second colon then makes clear that *every human being* means *every goldsmith*. A further ambiguity in the first colon is the preposition (*min*) on the word *knowledge*: is it "apart from" or "without" or "despite" or something else? The second colon again clarifies the point. A goldsmith is someone who has considerable knowledge but who in another sense shows himself stupid *through* his knowledge because he uses his expertise to make images. And the verb in the second colon builds on the verb in the first. When his stupidity in this connection is exposed, he will find himself *put to shame through his image*. The reference to shame (cf. Gen 2:25) is the most specific indication that Jeremiah might be critiquing the pretension of the human craftworker to be creative like God.[195]

14b His image (*pesel*; etymologically, something cut into shape) is alternatively *his model* (etymologically, something poured out). Neither word is pejorative in itself; both gain their negative associations through the ways

---

194. Barth, *CD* III, 1:38.
195. See D. Rudman, "Creation and Fall in Jeremiah x 12–16," *VT* 48 (1998): 63–73.

they are used. And actually, the image/model *is deception*, that key word in Jeremiah (e.g., 5:31; 7:4; 8:8), which associates the figure with many false and lying realities or non-realities that are the opposite of anything to do with the real God. Jeremiah takes the point further with the extra comment, *there is no spirit in them*. His point is not merely that they have no breath, that they are not alive, though he would affirm that point. In this context, it is that they lack energy and dynamism. The word for spirit is the word for wind in v. 13 (*rûaḥ*; the only other place in Jeremiah where the word means something other than wind is 51:11).

15 Thus the images *are empty* (*hebel*; see vv. 3, 8; 2:5; 8:19), which contrasts with being *rûaḥ*.[196] All they are is breath in its thinness and evanescence. There is no substance to them. Consequently, they are *a work for mockery*, "a joke";[197] Jeremiah expresses this conviction by putting it into practice. Whether or not he would ever believe that one should think and speak of other people's faith with empathy and respect, this is not such a context. His fellow-Judahites need to be buttressed in their resistance to the attractiveness of images, and mockery is one way Jeremiah seeks to prop up their commitment. Yet the colon leaves open the question who will do the mocking, and the second colon may again clarify the first. There will come *the time of their being attended to*, "the Day of Yahweh," when "idols will pass away—indeed, men will throw them away," and "the host of heaven will also be punished" (Isa 2:18, 20; 24:21).[198] The one who will attend to them and maybe mock them then is Yahweh, the God who laughs (Pss 2:4; 37:13; 59:8[9]; Isa 37:22). Certainly then *they will perish*. This final verb draws attention to Jeremiah's way of moving nonchalantly between speaking of the images, of the gods they represent, and of the people who make them: the entities that will perish are not the images but either of the latter parties.

16 One final time, Jeremiah returns to describing the real God whose being contrasts with those images and what they represent. A series of important theological observations spreads over two lines where the parallelism between the lines rather than parallelism between the cola is significant; the lines have an a-b-a'-b' structure. The first observation is the novel one: Yahweh is *Jacob's share* (*ḥēleq*), as an Israelite family possesses a share of land that signifies its provision, security, and future. Only here is Yahweh called his people's share, though the metaphor is applied to individuals elsewhere (Pss 16:5; 73:26; 119:57; 142:5[6]; Lam 3:24). Conversely, *Israel is the clan that is his domain* (*naḥălâ*; see 2:7; 3:19–20). It is a two-way relationship. While Jeremiah could also have said that Israel is Yahweh's share (Deut 32:9),

---

196. Volz, *Jeremia*, 125.
197. Lundbom, *Jeremiah 1–20*, 598–99.
198. Lundbom, *Jeremiah 1–20*, 599.

instead he takes up this other term for a family's tract of land. Third, the one who is Jacob's share is *not like these*, the images and the gods they allegedly represent, because he is *the shaper of everything* (see 1:5). He is not a deity who is shaped by his worshipers. Fourth, could Jeremiah say anything more impressive about him than that he is *Yahweh of Armies*? The name Yahweh has not been uttered since v. 10, for all the statements that have been made about him, so this colon brings vv. 1–16 to a resounding climax; the dynamic corresponds to that in the ascriptions of praise to Yahweh as creator and present lord in Amos 4:13; 5:8; 9:6. The implication is that Israel would itself be stupid to think about turning away from Yahweh.

b. An Exchange between Yahweh and Judah (10:17–25)

[17] *Gather up from the land*[a] *your bundle,*[b]
  you who are living[c] *during the siege.*[d]

[18] *Because Yahweh has said this:*

Here am I, shooting out the people living in the land
  on this occasion.
I will bind them up[e]
  in order that they hit it.[f]

[19] *Alas for me, for my shattering,*
  my wound is sick.[g]
I myself have said,
  "Yes, this is my sickness,[h] *and I must carry it."*
[20] *My tent*[i]*—it's been destroyed,*
  and all my ropes—they've snapped;
My children—they've gone away from me, and there are none of them;
  there is no one anymore to stretch out my tent
  and put up my curtains.

[21] *Because the shepherds—they have shown themselves stupid;*
  Yahweh they have not inquired of.
That's why they have not shown understanding,[j]
  and their entire flock[k] *has scattered.*[l]
[22] *The sound of a report, there, it's coming,*
  a great quaking from the northern country,
To make the towns of Judah a desolation,
  a home for jackals.[m]

²³*I acknowledge, Yahweh,*
that his path does not belong to an individual.
It does not belong to a person as he goes
*and determines*ⁿ *his step.*^o
²⁴*Restrain me, Yahweh, yes, by exercise of authority*^p—
not in your anger, so that you don't make me small.^q
²⁵*Pour out your fury on the nations*
that have not acknowledged you
And on the kin groups
that have not called on your name.
Because they have consumed Jacob,
consumed him^r *and made an end of him,*^s
and his habitat they have laid desolate.^t

a. LXX takes "the land" to denote the country outside the city (Jerome, *Jeremiah*, 69), which makes good sense of this colon but is hard to fit with the parallel colon.

b. For the *hapax legomenon kin'â*, Sym, Tg have "merchandise," linking the word with *kəna'an* and related words meaning merchant. Vg, Syr have "humiliation"; the verb *kāna'* means "be humble." LXX has "dregs."

c. For the *qere yōšebet*, the *ketiv* implies *yōšabtî* (a variant participial pointing) or *yāšabtî* (the archaic second-person feminine *qatal*).

d. LXX implies *bəmibḥār* ("in the choice/chosen one") for MT *bammāṣôr*. MT has a section marker here.

e. As ammunition in a sling: for this meaning of *ṣārar*, cf. *DCH*, 7:166.

f. That is, the target; see *CTAT* 2:547. LXX, Vg suggest *yimmāṣē'û* ("be found") for MT *yimṣā'û*. Presupposing the usual meaning of *māṣā'*, Syr has "inquire of me and find me," suggesting a link with Deut 4:29, where Israel has been scattered for making images, has been reduced to serving human-made deities, and lives in distress (cf. the references in v. 21 to inquiring of and scattering). Verse 18 is integral to Jeremiah's poetic message in vv. 17–22, and notwithstanding its virtual lack of poetic features, it seems likely to be a pair of verse lines. MT has a section marker after v. 18.

g. LXX has this line addressing Jerusalem.

h. LXX, Vg, Tg, Syr, Aq, Sym "my sickness" suggests that *ḥŏlî* is a contraction for *ḥolyî* (GKC 126y); it makes for a closer paronomasia with the next colon.

i. *My sickness* was *ḥŏlî*; *my tent* is *'āhŏlî* (Brueggemann, *Jeremiah 1–25*, 102).

j. *Śākal hiphil* can suggest both attentiveness or understanding and the resultant success; its "meanings [are] hard to classify" (BDB, 968). Here, "succeed" would mediate well between "not inquired of" and "flock has scattered" (cf. BDB); but see the commentary.

k. Lit. "pasturage."

l. MT has a section marker here.

m. MT has a section marker here.

n. The infinitive continues the participial construction (cf. LXX, Vg).

o. The verse recurs in a variant form at Qumran in the Community Rule (1QS 11:10; *DSS* 1:98–99) and the Thanksgiving Psalms (1QHª 7:16; *DSS* 1:154–55).

p. Tg has "but with lenient judgment," and Rudolph calls this occurrence of *mišpāṭ* the earliest example where the word suggests moderation (*Jeremia*, 77; he refers to H. W.

Hertzberg, *Prophet und Gott* [Gütersloh: Bertelsmann, 1923], 175). But this understanding reflects a questionable inference from the parallelism. See further 30:11 and the translation note on it.

q. LXX has "us" for "me" both times in v. 24, an appropriate "exegetical rendering" (Allen, *Jeremiah*, 131).

r. The simple *waw* plus *qatal* reflects the fact that the verb repeats the previous one; it does not denote a subsequent event.

s. The effect of the colon is enhanced through the anaphora (repeating forms of the verb *'ākal*) and the paronomasia (adding a form of the verb *kālâ*).

t. In the tricolon that closes the section and part 2a of the scroll, the first two cola are parallel as the second takes further the verb in the first; the first and third cola are more systematically parallel, with verb and noun in a-b-b'-a' order and the final noun-verb sequence adding to the sense of closure.

A link with the events of 597 or 587 was implicit in vv. 1–16. Such a link now becomes more explicit. While the fall of Jerusalem has been in focus all through the scroll, here it becomes a vivid reality; it is in the midst of happening. One need not infer that in the real world things have moved on—they may have done so only in Jeremiah's imagination or may do so only in his rhetoric. In light of his way of speaking in Jer 8–9, it makes sense to think of him as the speaker mediating between Yahweh and Jerusalem through vv. 17–25.

> vv. 17–18 Jeremiah speaks to Jerusalem, bidding it to get going into exile (three bicola plus an intervening introductory phrase)
>
> vv. 19–20 Jeremiah speaks for Jerusalem in lament and protest at its destruction and emptying (three bicola and a closing tricolon)
>
> vv. 21–22 Jeremiah speaks to Jerusalem, explaining why the calamity has come (four bicola, the last two linked)
>
> vv. 23–25 Jeremiah speaks for Jerusalem, bowing to Yahweh but urging action on the assailants (three bicola, two linked bicola, and a closing tricolon)

17 After the hymn of praise to Yahweh's greatness and glory and the celebration of Israel's identity and security, what now follows is shocking and shattering.[199] Once again we are *in medias res*. The verbs are second-person feminine, so Jerusalem is the addressee. In reality or in imagination, the city is *living during the siege*, as happened in 597 and in 587. It will be hoping to last out the siege. Jeremiah wants it to face the fact that it will not. In his imagination and appealing to its imagination, he bids, *gather up from the*

---

199. Wright, *Jeremiah*, 137.

land your bundle. While he addresses the city corporately, each family will need to get together the things it can carry off the land and get ready to take them with it out of the country (Jeremiah utilizes two aspects of the range of meanings of the word for land/country, *'ereṣ*). Passengers can take only hand luggage on this flight.

18 In evaluating their prospects of lasting out a siege, people would be calculating the answers to practical questions (e.g., how much food and water do we have?), reflecting on theological questions, and praying for Yahweh to deliver them as he had before. Jeremiah's message from Yahweh makes the first sort of calculation irrelevant, the second unnecessary, and the third impossible. *Here am I* is always a solemn beginning to underline a commitment to what follows. Yahweh is *shooting out the people living in the land* (he picks up the verb and the word for land from v. 17). Only here does the First Testament use the word *shoot* (*qālaʿ*) in such a connection. Elsewhere it denotes what David did with his sling (cf. Tg). Such will be the sharp, violent, and final action Yahweh will take. *On this occasion* there will be no relenting and rescuing, as there has been on other occasions. Like David, *I will bind them up* in a sling and shoot them off and ensure that they *hit* the target in Babylon that I intend.

19 Jeremiah moves to expressing Jerusalem's distress in light of vv. 17–18, taking up the way he has spoken of the city's suffering in previous messages. Jerusalem again says *alas for me* (see 4:31). It laments its painful *shattering* (see 4:6, 20; 6:1, 14; 8:11, 21). Its *wound* (see 6:7) *is sick*. Picking up that last expression, Jerusalem acknowledges, *Yes, this is my sickness and I must carry it.* "There is no escape from this time of suffering and despair," so the city has to be committed to "a tragic acceptance of the inevitable."[200] Jeremiah speaks for Jerusalem yet continues to speak to her, especially if the events he portrays still lie in the future. Articulating what she will experience or how she should think is a way of getting through to her. The declaration about Jerusalem corresponds to the one about Nineveh in Nah 3:19. The fate of Nineveh will be the fate of Jerusalem.[201]

> We must then bear in mind that the Prophet speaks not here according to the feeling which the people had, for they were so stupified that they felt nothing; but that he speaks of what they ought to have felt, as though he had said,—"Were there in them a particle of wisdom, they would all most surely bewail their approaching calamity, before God begins to make his judgment to fall on their heads; but no one is moved: I shall therefore

200. McKane, *Jeremiah*, 1:231.
201. Fischer, *Jeremia*, 1:391.

weep alone, but it is on your account." There is yet no doubt but he intended to try in every way whether God's threatenings would penetrate into their hearts.[202]

20 On the city's behalf, he takes up another image from earlier in the scroll, where it also accompanied the image of breaking. I'm like a woman whose *tent* has *been destroyed* by a hurricane (4:20). Further, *my children have gone away from me, and there are none of them.* It's as if the city still exists even though its people have all gone into exile. Their departure means there's no one to rebuild it. The image of the tent is taken up in Lam 2:4, but the lament is nicely reversed in Isa 54:1–3.[203]

21 Whereas Jeremiah has been speaking on the city's behalf, he can segue into answering a question from them that might be raised by v. 20. Why have the children gone? Because another way to describe them is as a *flock* that *has scattered* (see 9:16[15]). So why have they scattered? Because their *shepherds* were incompetent: *they have shown themselves stupid* (see vv. 8, 14). How did they do so? The same way as the stupid makers of images: *Yahweh they have not inquired of.* We know whom they have inquired of (8:2). Their foolishness means they are not shepherds who *have shown understanding*, a basic requirement of shepherding (3:15), which is why the flock has scattered. To speak more literally, Jeremiah reasserts his awareness that the leadership of Judah (prophets, priests, scribes, kings) has failed to have the good sense to lead the community in turning to Yahweh. This foolishness is why the city is falling. There is an urgent need for the leadership and the people to turn now if they don't want to have to chant the lament Jeremiah has just been articulating.

22 Jeremiah underscores that urgent need by again imagining the invading army near the city gates. The two lines systematically recycle expressions from 4:5–31. Jeremiah hears *the sound* (*qôl*) *of a report* (*šəmûʿâ*) and hears about *a great quaking from the northern country*, the thundering of the hooves of the advancing cavalry or the ground reverberating because of the coming of Yahweh himself. He thus hears about events that will *make the towns of Judah a desolation.* His words directly recall the warnings in 4:5–31 about a voice (*qôl*) making news heard (*šāmaʿ*) from the north and about making the towns of Judah into a desolation and about mountains quaking. The only element that did not appear there is the picture of *a home for jackals*, the exact phrase that did come in 9:11(10).

23 One more time, Jeremiah reverts to speaking for Jerusalem; in speaking of herself as an "I," Jerusalem nevertheless speaks as a male "I" or speaks

202. Calvin, *Jeremiah*, 2:46.
203. Sommer, *Prophet Reads Scripture*, 38–39.

metaphorically as a male individual. Once again, the words are the response to Yahweh that Jeremiah wishes Judah would make or the one he makes on Judah's behalf rather than one it actually makes. If only Judah would indeed *acknowledge that his path does not belong to an individual*! Yahweh's problem with Judah has been that he wanted to shape its path, but it insisted on taking the path to Egypt and Assyria, the path into the Ravine, the path to seek love from other deities (2:17–18, 23, 36). It has long assumed that it could choose its path, follow whomever it wished, and wander all over the place—as the comments about Judah's path in Jer 2 asserted. Irony continues as Jerusalem speaks of *a person as he goes and determines his step*. Yahweh has continually raised questions about Judah's going after other deities. Jeremiah 2 again referred to Israel's going after Yahweh in the wilderness and Yahweh's enabling Israel to go through the wilderness and getting it to go on a certain path, but also Judah's going after the Masters, foreigners, and emptiness. Does Judah then have no freedom to make its decisions about its path? Both cola in v. 23 recall statements in Proverbs (16:9; 20:24; 21:29 *ketiv*) and might raise questions about divine sovereignty and human freedom,[204] but Jeremiah is not talking about freedom in a metaphysical sense; he is talking about freedom in a moral or religious or spiritual sense. Is Judah metaphysically free to make its own decision about the path it treads? It has been exercising that freedom. Is it religiously and morally free? It needs to acknowledge that it is Yahweh's servant; in this sense it is not free!

24 In Jeremiah's imagination, then, Judah has recognized that it needs Yahweh to *restrain* or correct or instruct it (*yāsar piel*): again, if only! (see 6:8; and the noun in 2:30; 5:3; 7:28; and the comment about images in v. 8). In Jeremiah's imagination, Judah submits to Yahweh's exercise of authority (contrast 8:7) in keeping with his declarations about its exercise (1:16; 4:12). It is as if it has recognized and yielded to Jeremiah's message. It can submit to Yahweh's exercise of authority with confidence in light of Yahweh's being one who acts with commitment and with authority and faithfulness. In 9:24(23), Yahweh's talk of authority locates it in between those other qualities. So on Judah's behalf, Jeremiah could express the hope that Yahweh will not exercise authority *in your anger*. It might seem a more-than-slightly far-fetched plea; Yahweh has spoken of anger in connection with exercising authority over Judah (2:35; see also 4:8, 26—and then there are the references to fury and wrath . . .). Yet casting oneself on God's mercy may open up the possibility of Yahweh abandoning his anger. So Jeremiah can lay this possibility before Judah in this prayer that they can overhear him putting on their lips. And given Yahweh's talk about not finishing them off (e.g., 4:27), Judah can add the aim that *you don't make me small*. In effect, Jeremiah invites Jerusalem to

204. Calvin, *Jeremiah*, 2:57–59.

believe in some theological statements that Ezekiel is making between 597 and 587 in Babylon (Ezek 18:23; 33:11).[205]

25 Furthermore, Jeremiah feels justified, or can imagine Judah feeling justified, in urging Yahweh to take action on the nations that are his agents in bringing catastrophe to Judah: *Pour out your fury on the nations* and *kin groups*. The idea that Jeremiah or Judah should pray that way is often unacceptable to Western Christians (wisely, because we are "the nations"), but it is in keeping with the Prophets, the Psalms, and the New Testament, and Yahweh in due course does as Jeremiah asks. This verse appears in an alternative form as Ps 79:6–7 as part of a much longer prayer that people might pray in the context of an event such as the fall of Jerusalem. While the preacher more often quotes the hymnbook than the hymnbook quotes the preacher, the language of the verse fits Jeremiah. Its background is the fact that the nations and kin groups *have consumed Jacob, consumed him and made an end of him, and his habitat they have laid desolate*. There is a useful ambiguity about the word *habitat* (*nāweh*), which can refer both to a sheepfold and to a human homestead. So here it can directly denote the place where Israel lives or metaphorically suggest the place where the Israelite flock dwells. Either way, these marauders were acting not because they were committed to being Yahweh's servants but because they wanted to extend their power and wealth. In other words, they *have not acknowledged you* or *called on your name*. And one of the theological assumptions or implications in the plea is that being Yahweh's agents does not mean the nations evade the consequences of actions that they undertake for their own benefit. But only a people that has itself turned from not acknowledging Yahweh (contrast, e.g., 9:3[2]) could pray this prayer (see, e.g., 2 Thess 1:5–10; Rev 6:9–11). Otherwise, the plea would rebound on the people praying (see 6:11). Indirectly, as usual, in inviting people to pray this way, Jeremiah is seeking to draw Judah to turn back to Yahweh.

B. PART 2B: JEREMIAH'S ARGUMENTS (11:1–13:27)

As part 1 began by raising questions about Judah's attitude to the exodus and part 2a began by raising questions about Judah's attitude to the temple, part 2b begins by raising questions about Judah's attitude to the pledged relationship between it and Yahweh—in shorthand, its attitude to Sinai. It opens with a prose account of Yahweh's giving Jeremiah a message for Judah that in this respect compares with 7:1–8:3, and like that earlier message, it will in due course incorporate a snippet of verse and a prohibition on Jeremiah's praying for Judah.

205. Weiser, *Jeremia*, 98.

11:1–17   A confrontation and warning about Yahweh's pledge
11:18–12:17 Three exchanges between Yahweh and Jeremiah
13:1–27   Five more warnings to Judah

The exchanges between Yahweh and Jeremiah introduce the motif of protests by Jeremiah concerning the task Yahweh imposes on him and Yahweh's responses. These exchanges run through Jer 11–20, which as a whole "portrays the course of Jeremiah's prophetic mission as a dialogue in which prophet, Yahweh, and nation are the participants."[206]

1. Another Confrontation and Warning, about the Pledge (11:1–17)

¹*The message that came to Jeremiah from Yahweh:* ²*Listen to the words in this pledge.*

*So you are to speak*ᵃ *them to the individuals in Judah, and over the people who live in Jerusalem,* ³*and say to them: Yahweh, the God of Israel, has said this. Cursed is the individual who does not listen to the words in this pledge,* ⁴*which I ordered your ancestors at the time of my getting them out of the country of Egypt, out of the iron smelter, saying, Listen to my voice and act on them in accordance with everything that I order you, and so become a people for me, and I for my part will become God for you,* ⁵*in order to implement the promise that I swore to your ancestors to give them a country flowing with milk and syrup*ᵇ *this very*ᶜ *day. I answered, Indeed, Yahweh.*ᵈ

⁶*Yahweh said to me, Proclaim all these words in the towns of Judah and in the streets of Jerusalem: Listen to the words in this pledge and act on them.* ⁷*Because I testified, testified*ᵉ *against your ancestors at the time of my enabling them to go up from the country of Egypt, and until this time, testifying assiduously:*ᶠ *Listen to my voice.* ⁸*But they didn't listen, they didn't bend their ear. They went, each one, by the determination of their dire mind. So I have let come upon them all the words in this pledge that I ordered them to act on but they didn't act on.*ᵍ

⁹*Yahweh said to me, A conspiracy is present among the individuals in Judah and among the people who live in Jerusalem.* ¹⁰*They've turned to the wayward acts of their ancestors of old, who refused to listen to my words. So those people, they've gone after other gods to serve them—the household of Israel and*

---

206. Cf. Diamond, *Confessions of Jeremiah*, 181–82, though I question his view that theodicy is the controlling principle in the composition; cf. Henderson, *Jeremiah under the Shadow of Duhm*, 283–317. For approaches to the arrangement of Jer 11–20, see C. S. W. So, "Structure in the Confessions of Jeremiah," in Lundbom, Evans, and B. A. Anderson, *Jeremiah*, 126–48.

the household of Judah have violated[h] my pledge that I solemnized[i] with their ancestors.[j]

[11]*Therefore Yahweh has said this: Here am I, bringing upon them dire trouble that they will not be able to get out of. They will cry out to me, but I will not listen to them.* [12]*The towns of Judah and the people who live in Jerusalem will go and cry out to the gods that they are burning offerings to, but they will certainly not deliver them in the time of their dire trouble.* [13]*Because the number of your towns—[so] your gods have become, Judah, and the number of [your] streets, Jerusalem—[so] you have set up altars for Shame,[k] altars for burning offerings to the Master.[l]*

[14]*And you, do not plead on account of this people. Do not lift up on their account a chant by way of plea, because I am not going to be listening at the time of their calling to me on account of[m] their dire trouble.[n]*

[15]*What [place] is there for my dear one[o] in my house[p]—*
    her acting on an intention (so many people)?[q]
The sacred flesh—they will make it pass away[r] from you
    because your dire trouble[s]—then you will exult!
[16]*Flourishing olive,*
    beautiful for its lovely fruit,
Yahweh named you[t]
    with the sound of a big tumult.[u]
He has lit a fire on her,[v]
    and its[w] branches will break.[x]
[17]*Yahweh of Armies, who planted you—*
    he has spoken over you of dire trouble[y]
On account of the dire action of Israel's household
    and Judah's household,
Which they performed for themselves
    to irk me by burning offerings to the Master.[z]

a. Whereas *listen* was plural and constituted the challenge Jeremiah is to give to the people, the *waw*-consecutive that continues the imperative is singular and is addressed just to Jeremiah; cf. the next *waw*-consecutive in v. 3. Vg has plural for *speak*, which is syntactically more logical but makes for poorer sense.

b. *Dəbaš* covers both bees' honey and a syrup made from fruit such as dates and figs, which was the main source of sweetness in Israel; the latter will apply in this context (cf. Altschuler, *Mesudat David* on 32:22, in MG).

c. LXX, Vg have "as at this day," but in such expressions, *kə* denotes the exact point of time rather than suggesting a comparison; see J. Goldingay, "*kayyôm hazzeh* 'On This Very Day,'" *VT* 43 (1993): 112–15.

d. MT has a marker here.

e. The infinitive precedes the finite verb, underlining the factuality of the action; this idiom recurs in v. 12.

f. See the translation note and commentary on 7:13.

g. MT has a section marker here. LXX lacks vv. 7–8 except for the last clause.

h. *Pārar* suggests contravening and thus making ineffectual (cf. Vg, Sym); LXX "scatter" may imply BDB's *pārar* II. Tg has "changed."

i. Lit. "cut"; see 34:18–19; Gen 15:7–21.

j. MT has a section marker here.

k. LXX omits "altars for Shame," perhaps simplifying the repetition deliberately or accidentally, or perhaps indicating that MT is a conflated text.

l. As usual, LXX gives "Baal" a feminine article here and in v. 17 (see the translation note on 2:8). MT has a section marker here.

m. For MT *bəʿad*, LXX, Vg, Syr imply *bəʿēt* ("at the time of").

n. MT has a section marker here.

o. The adjective is masculine, following on the masculine singular "this people," but feminine for Jerusalem (or Judah) reappears in the parallel colon, and the two genders mix throughout vv. 14–17, as do singular and plural number; there is considerable jerkiness and ellipsis in these lines.

p. LXX, Vg take "my dear one" as the explicit subject of the verb in the next colon, but the difference in the gender of noun and verb works against that understanding.

q. Lit. "the many." Vg, Aq take *məzimmātâ hārabbîm* to denote "many wrongful purposes," but *məzimmātâ* is anarthrous feminine singular, whereas *hārabbîm* is definite masculine plural. Rather, *hārabbîm* is in apposition to the subject of the infinitive (Rashi, in MG). LXX, Tg divide the line before *hārabbîm* and take it as (part of) the subject of the plural verb that follows, which is easier syntactically, but the colon becomes harder to make sense of. For *hārabbîm*, LXX perhaps implies *[hă]nədārîm* ("[would] vows"); but HUBP sees the influence of Deut 12:6) while OL implies *[hă]ḥălābîm* or *[hă]bəriyyîm* ("[would] fat things").

r. MT's *yēʿabərû* looks like a *qal* form, but GKC 53n sees it as hiphil; cf. LXX, Vg "make your dire behavior pass away"—though it implies seeing the subsequent *kî* ("because") as dittography.

s. *Rāʿātēkî* is an archaic form for *rāʿātəkā* (GKC 91e).

t. The suffix is again feminine singular, referring to Jerusalem.

u. MT's accents link this colon with what follows and thus give *hămullâ* a negative connotation (cf. Tg), but in its only other occurrence (Ezek 1:24) the word is not negative (cf. Vg "utterance"); *HALOT* has "tumultuous crowd," and A. Baumann ("הָמָה, *hāmāh*," *TDOT* 3:415) links the word with a worship gathering.

v. That is, on Jerusalem.

w. The masculine suffix refers to the tree.

x. *Rāʿû* from *râʿaʿ* II. LXX derives it from *râʿaʿ* I ("suffer dire trouble"), and at least a paronomasia with that root might occur to listeners in this context. Tg derives it from *râʿâ* ("befriend," referring to military allies). Vg "burn" implies *bāʿărû*.

y. *Rāʿâ* picks up from vv. 11, 15, but it is also from *râʿaʿ* (v. 16).

z. MT has a marker here.

Like 7:1–15 as the opening to part 2a, this first unit in part 2b functions to undermine an aspect of the people's assumptions about the nature of their relationship with Yahweh—here, their assumptions about Yahweh's pledged relationship with them. The symbolic role of the temple in the opening of part 2a is thus taken by the pledge that Yahweh had imposed on the people in part 2b. This first unit critiques the people for failure to act as Yahweh instructed them, warns them of calamity to come, and instructs Jeremiah not to pray for them, though it contains no account of Jeremiah's delivering the message; it simply comprises Yahweh's giving him the message.

The passage is choppy, with a sequence of starts and restarts as well as switches in the addressees' identities:

vv. 1–2a
   v. 1   An introduction to Yahweh's words to Jeremiah
   v. 2a   The challenge to listen that Jeremiah is to give the people

vv. 2b–5a
   vv. 2b–3a   Yahweh's bidding to Jeremiah to speak to the people
   vv. 3b–5a   The content of the message: a reminder about Yahweh's pledge

v. 5b   Jeremiah's response to Yahweh

vv. 6–8
   v. 6a   Yahweh's bidding to Jeremiah to proclaim the message to the people
   v. 6b–8   The challenge to listen to the pledge that he is to give them

vv. 9–10
   v. 9a   An introduction to Yahweh's words to Jeremiah
   vv. 9b–10   An accusation about them

vv. 11–13
   v. 11a   A resumptive introduction to Yahweh's words to Jeremiah
   vv. 11b–12 A declaration about calamity that will follow
   v. 13   A further accusation, addressed to the people, about other gods

v. 14   An instruction to Jeremiah not to pray for the people

vv. 15–17 Eight lines of bicola without much parallelism, with two of the lines running together in v. 16a–b and three running together in v. 17
   v. 15a   Critique
   v. 15b   Warning
   v. 16a–b   Background to the critique
   vv. 16c–17a Warning
   v. 17b–c   Critique

Where readers might have expected a report of Jeremiah's delivery of the message, they thus get an account of Yahweh's prohibition on his praying for them. This feature reflects the unit's nature as a literary entity designed to persuade. The passage is composed to have an effect on people hearing it as opposed to their simply hearing the message to which it refers when Jeremiah delivers that message. The substance of its confrontation is the same as preceding ones: Yahweh challenges Judah about going after other gods. Much of the language is the same—for example, reference to burning offerings to the Master, to dire behavior, and to dire trouble. The big difference lies in the focus on the *pledge* that Yahweh imposed on Judah's ancestors, which the people have contravened. This chapter is the first in the Jeremiah scroll to use the word *pledge* except for the reference to the pledge chest in 3:16.

Pledge is the word *bərît*. I avoid the traditional translation "covenant," which carries deceptive freight;[207] *pledge* has the advantage of not being a technical theological term. The English word "covenant" has been an important theological term with a meaning of its own and an important historical/ cultural term in the United States. In both contexts, the relational significance of the covenant idea has been important. It suggests mutual relationships between God and people and mutual relationships within the community. There are several contrasts between "covenant" and *bərît*. First, *bərît* parallels "covenant" in having a wide range of meanings, but it is a different range; for instance, *bərît* covers treaties as well as covenants. Second, *bərît* does not suggest mutuality. A *bərît* is a solemnly made commitment. While it can be made by two parties to one another, it can also be made by one party to another or required as an obligation by one party of another.[208] The word is particularly common in Genesis with a stress on Yahweh's making commitments and in Deuteronomy with more stress on a commitment Yahweh requires, but Hosea's five references to a *bərît* are also noteworthy in light of Hosea's brevity and the other indications of its influencing Jeremiah.

In this passage, the *bərît* is a solemn commitment or obligation that Yahweh imposed on Israel as a consequence of his getting the people out of Egypt. He ordered it (v. 4). The *bərît* is thus part of a mutual relationship in that Israel's living by this commitment will open up the possibility that it might become a people for Yahweh and he might become God for it. Elsewhere, Jeremiah uses the word *bərît* rarely (in 14:21; 22:9; 50:5; and a number of times in 31:31–34:22). Yet the relationship between Yahweh and Israel that he regularly presupposes is a solemnly committed mutual relationship

---

207. See M. Kartveit, "Reconsidering the 'New Covenant' in Jeremiah 31:31–34," in Lundbom, Evans, and B. A. Anderson, *Jeremiah*, 149–69.

208. See, e.g., M. Weinfeld, "בְּרִית, *bᵉrît*," *TDOT* 2:253–79. E. Kutsch especially stresses the element of obligation; see *TLOT*, 1:256–66.

between Yahweh and Israel. In that broad sense, he does think in terms of something like a marriage covenant or adoption covenant.[209]

Speaking in terms of a *bərît* here, when he does not usually do so, contributes to communicating with Judahites, because they were used to talking about a *bərît*. They were familiar with Deuteronomy, which speaks of Yahweh solemnizing a *bərît*, warns of Israel contravening a *bərît*, and refers to the words in "this *bərît*" (e.g., 4:23; 5:2, 3; 29:1 [28:69]; 31:16, 20). Deuteronomy also contains nearly half the First Testament occurrences of the word *cursed* and refers to Egypt as an *iron smelter* (see vv. 3–4 here). Further, 2 Kgs 23:2–3 describes the document that came to light in the temple as the "*bərît* scroll," refers to the words in the *bərît* scroll, and relates how Josiah led the people in solemnizing the *bərît* before Yahweh, which fits with other indications that the scroll was some form of Deuteronomy. The language also fits the likelihood that there was a relationship between Assyria (and subsequently Babylon) and Judah in which the imperial power imposed a *bərît* on Judah. For Deuteronomy, for 2 Kings 23, and for Jer 11:1–17, then, talk in terms of Yahweh's *bərît* could say to people, "You know Assyria laid a *bərît* on us? Well, so did Yahweh. And you know how dangerous it would have been to ignore the Assyrian *bərît*? How much more danger have we risked by ignoring Yahweh's *bərît*." So Jeremiah thinks of the relationship between Yahweh and Israel quite broadly but will think of the *bərît* relationship in particular politically.

The fact that this message is in prose (like 7:1–8:3) rather than poetry has no necessary implications regarding who composed it. It has many phrases characteristic of Deuteronomy as opposed to Jeremiah and many characteristics of Jeremiah as opposed to Deuteronomy.[210] Its distinctive formulation of Yahweh's relationship with Israel in terms of a *bərît* might be the work of Jeremiah, and one can imagine Jeremiah or his aide reading out this passage sometime in (say) Zedekiah's day, perhaps when Jeremiah was under confinement. Its aim would be the usual one of getting the people to turn. Or one can imagine a disciple of Jeremiah reading it out after the fall of Jerusalem; its aim might again be to get people to turn or to reassure them that there was a logic behind the disaster. Alternatively, the passage may parallel the way Jesus in John talks much about the life of the age to come ("eternal life"), whereas Jesus in the Synoptic Gospels hardly mentions it. As John reworks Jesus's way of speaking in order to communicate with his audience, so might the composer of the message in Jer 11:1–17.

209. See the commentary on 2:2b with the reference there to Rom-Shiloni, "Covenant in the Book of Jeremiah."
210. See Kelley, *Jeremiah*, 1:168–69; Holladay, *Commentary on Jeremiah*, 1:350–51.

1 As 10:17–25 constituted a sobering but thus plausible closure to Jer 7–10, so the phrase *the message that came to Jeremiah from Yahweh* constitutes a plausible and distinctive if low-key beginning to a new compilation. Briefer first-person introductions along the lines of *Yahweh said to me* will recur within the compilation in 11:6, 9; 13:1, 3, 6. The third-person formulation repeats that in 7:1 (see the commentary there).

2–3a The introduction goes on to summarize the message of vv. 1–17, that people are to *listen to the words in this pledge* (on the word *bərît*, see the introduction to vv. 1–17 above). In passages such as Deut 5:3; 29:9(8), 14(13); 2 Kgs 23:3, *this pledge* is the one expounded in Deuteronomy or the related one made by Josiah. But in such passages, the previous verses have already alluded to the pledge, and so *this pledge* is referring back to those allusions. Here, the phrase is the first of a number of intertextual links with Deuteronomy, but Jeremiah is characteristically giving the Deuteronomic expressions a new meaning. The word *this* must rather incite the audience to listen to what follows so as to discover what *this pledge* is, as when Jeremiah says *this* in 7:2 with reference to the message he is about to give.

3b–4a *Cursed* (*’ārûr*) is then a solemn beginning for the actual message. In Deuteronomy, curses come near the end of the scroll, but in Jeremiah's context it is the motif that needs emphasis. The word opens each of the curses in Deut 27:15–26. Indeed, "a plethora of linguistic markers tie Jer 11:1–14, and specifically vv. 1–5, to Deuteronomy 27."[211] Indirectly, Yahweh is indeed referring to the terms of the pledge in Deuteronomy. Here, the pledge is linked to the exodus event by the reference to an *iron smelter*. It is an especially frightening image, since smelting involves heating ore to dissolve slag and thus produce pure metal, and iron requires a furnace to be heated to a high temperature. The message reminds the hearers of the exodus and of the obligations Yahweh then imposed on Israel in a way parallel with Deuteronomy (see esp. 4:20), set in the later context of Israel's being on the edge of the promised land.

4b Jeremiah goes on to describe the pledge's significance. Yahweh's aim in laying his obligation on Israel at the beginning of its story, following on his getting Israel out of Egypt, was that there should be a relationship of mutual commitment between them and him. Here, being Yahweh's people is not the basis for obedience as it is in Deut 26:16–19 but the result of it.[212] "God does not belong to Israel, and Israel to God, because of the privilege of race, the wound of circumcision, or the leisure of Sabbath." Rather, the logic compares

---

211. D. Rom-Shiloni, "'On the Day I Took Them out of the Land of Egypt': A Non-Deuteronomic Phrase within Jeremiah's Conception of Covenant," *VT* 65 (2015): 627.
212. D. Rom-Shiloni, "On the Day," 631.

with the logic whereby "the Lord says to his disciples, 'You are my friends if you do what I order you.'"[213] *Become a people for me, and I for my part will become God for you* expresses the nature of the relationship between Yahweh and Israel, yet it does not define a *bərît* between Yahweh and Israel. There are one or two other places where the word *bərît* and that phrase come in close association, with an implication that they are linked, but in such contexts they come in association with other linked ideas such as the promise that Israel will enter the land and that the Torah will be inscribed into Israel's thinking; the *bərît* and the mutual relationship are not identical (see Exod 6:4–7; Jer 31:31–34; Ezek 36:26–27). But *become a people for me, and I for my part will become God for you* does give expression to a special relationship between Yahweh and Israel. On Israel's side, at least, it is an exclusive relationship, like that of a wife to a husband.[214] It might be misleading to call it an exclusive relationship on Yahweh's side in that Yahweh has other commitments. One could rather compare it with the relationship of a father and his child. For a child, only this man is father. For a father, this position means a total and unqualified commitment to this child, though it does not exclude being committed in the same way to other children. A father just has to solve the problem when commitments to more than one child stand in tension—as happens when Yahweh wants to give the land of Canaan to Abraham but cannot do so because it would not be fair to the Canaanites (Gen 15:16).

5a Historically, then, Yahweh speaks of the relationship between himself and Israel as having involved four stages: (1) I got Israel out of Egypt; (2) I challenged Israel to make a commitment to me; (3) supposing it does so (but Yahweh makes no reference to that stage), a mutual relationship comes into being; (4) I will then *implement my promise to your ancestors* to give them the country of Canaan. Jeremiah's language again follows Deuteronomy (see especially Deut 8:18).[215] That link means that the *ancestors* in v. 4 (the Sinai/Moab generations) now in v. 5 become the ancestors whose story is told in Genesis. The description of Canaan as *a country flowing with milk and syrup* goes back to the exodus (see, e.g., Exod 3:8, 17; 13:5; Lev 20:24; Num 13:27; Deut 6:3; 11:9; Josh 5:6). The country has good pasturage for the sheep who will produce milk, and it has flourishing fruit trees from which sweet syrup can be made. The description does not make for a contrast with Egypt (whose produce is if anything more spectacular) but it does make for a contrast with the desert. Yahweh made the promise on *this very day*, but that day

---

213. Jerome, *Jeremiah*, 72.

214. Cf. J. T. Willis, "'I Am Your God' and 'You Are My People' in Hosea and Jeremiah," *Restoration Quarterly* 36 (1994): 291–303.

215. Duhm, *Jeremia*, 109.

is not limited to a moment in the past. More literally, the phrase is "as at this day," and even if this translation is too literal, the phrase suggests an analogy between one day and another. Yahweh acted and spoke and promised back then; he has fulfilled his promise, and the Judahites are still the beneficiaries of its fulfillment *this very day*, today.

5b The ambiguity in the passage's connection with Deuteronomy suggests that the relationship is intertextual and that Jeremiah is making allusions but giving the language different significance from that in Deuteronomy. The ambiguity continues in Jeremiah's response to Yahweh. *Indeed, Yahweh* is the response Israel was to give to each of the curses in Deut 27; it turned a curse into a self-curse. Jeremiah's use of the expression does not have that significance. It does mean he presents himself as giving Yahweh the kind of response for which Yahweh looks from the entire people.

6 Yahweh goes on to a second formulation of the commission and the message. Is the author "totally and emphatically a preaching theologian and unable to approach history historically"?[216] Rather, he is totally and emphatically a preaching theologian who approaches history rhetorically. The commission to Jeremiah no more suggests a preaching tour than, say, 25:30 suggests a trip to Babylon. *In the towns of Judah and in the streets of Jerusalem* is in any case a stereotypical expression (e.g., 33:10; 44:6).[217] While Jeremiah could proclaim the message to the townspeople in Jerusalem for a festival,[218] the idea of Jeremiah going off to preach is an image within the message; the message is what people will hear. They will picture Jeremiah going on a preaching tour; it suggests the idea that everyone in Jerusalem and Judah needs to pay heed to this message that reminds the hearers that the obligations of the pledge rest on Judah now.

7 Once again Jeremiah picks up an expression in Deuteronomy, though it also comes elsewhere. After reaffirming the promise whose language reappeared in v. 5 to implement the pledge he made to Israel's ancestors, Yahweh recalls that he had *testified against* them that on the other hand they would perish if they went after other gods (Deut 8:19). Once more, Jeremiah adapts the language: he again refers to the exodus rather than to the point when Israel is on the edge of Canaan, and the testifying is not merely something in which Yahweh engaged then but something in which he has been repeatedly engaged over the years. Etymologically, *testify* (*'ûd hiphil*) suggests giving solemn testimony in court with an appeal to witnesses and a self-curse if you are lying, which tells us how seriously Yahweh is speaking.

---

216. Duhm, *Jeremia*, 110.
217. Bright, *Jeremiah*, 89.
218. Allen, *Jeremiah*, 138.

8 When did Yahweh *let come upon them all the words in this pledge that I ordered them to act on but they didn't act on?* The words recall Huldah's warning (2 Kgs 22:16).[219] In isolation, one might take Jeremiah to be referring to the fall of Jerusalem; the message would then belong after 587.[220] But in vv. 11–17, in what looks like the main point of the message, he will be threatening a disaster still to come, the threat that was fulfilled in 587. So this action is an earlier one. Yahweh acted in this way when he allowed Samaria to fall, and Jeremiah is indeed inclined to urge Judah to learn from Ephraim's story. But that disaster was a century ago, in another place at another time. More likely, the reference indicates that the message belongs in the reign of Zedekiah, after the fall of Jerusalem and the exile of 597.

9–10 Once more, Yahweh begins again. *Conspiracy* is a political image.[221] It was a conspiracy by Hoshea that drove Shalmanezer to invade Ephraim, capture Samaria, and exile its people (2 Kgs 17:4–6), and this link might support the idea that v. 8 refers to the fall of Samaria. It was a similar action, though 2 Kgs 24 calls it an act of rebellion, that led to Nebuchadrezzar's invasion in 597, and it would be another such rebellion that led to his invasion in 587. It had been a conspiracy that deposed Amon and put Josiah on the throne (2 Kgs 21:23–24). Verse 10 will suggest that the conspiracy has a religious aspect, but it is the only such First Testament passage, and the political connotations likely apply here too. Jeremiah will later also make clear that Judah is supposed to submit to Babylon as Yahweh's servant, so a conspiracy against Babylon is also a conspiracy against Yahweh. There are thus two aspects to Judah's *wayward acts* and its *conspiracy*. The combined reference to *the household of Israel and the household of Judah* again suggests a link with the political and religious realities of the eighth century. The two peoples *have violated my pledge that I solemnized with their ancestors.* Jerusalem and Judah are acting the same way as Ephraim, and they have at least imperiled the *bərît* imposed by Yahweh—and thus risked the sanctions attached to it, which fell on Ephraim. It is the "most massive indictment" of Ephraim and Judah's violation of that pledge that comes on Yahweh's lips in the First Testament.[222]

11–13 For a fourth time, Yahweh starts again, declaring that *dire trouble* will indeed follow. Once more, Jeremiah suggests a link between dire thinking, dire action, and dire trouble (cf. v. 8). Yahweh got them out of Egypt,

219. Fischer, *Jeremia*, 1:413.
220. Isaac Abravanel (*Commentary on the Latter Prophets*) takes the *qatal* as anticipatory (see the introduction to 13:18–22, pp. 354–55); it refers to what Yahweh is about to do (cf. v. 11).
221. Wright, *Jeremiah*, 144.
222. Fischer, *Jeremia*, 1:405.

the iron smelter (v. 4), but he won't get them out of this calamity, because he is the one who is causing it, and they themselves *will not be able to get out of* it. He will make sure of it. It will be no use for them to *cry out* to him for deliverance, because he *will not listen to them*. It's a hard saying because it clashes with what Yahweh elsewhere says to his people:

> They cry out, and Yahweh listens,
>> and from all their troubles he rescues them. (Ps 34:17[18])

The psalm fits with the exodus story to which Yahweh has been referring in this message—*cry out* and the associated noun come more often there than anywhere (e.g., Exod 3:7, 9). But in Ps 34, the implied subject is "the faithful" (Ps 34:15[16]), which is not the term that applies to the people Yahweh is addressing. They have not listened—and now he will not listen.[223] In this situation, he will become "the God of no answer."[224] Nor will it be any use their crying out to anyone else, though there are lots of entities to whom they might uselessly pray (cf. 2:28). And the fact that Yahweh envisages them envisaging this possibility suggests part of the background to his determination not to listen to them. They *are burning offerings* to these other deities. They cannot expect to combine turning to Yahweh with maintaining that allegiance. Of course, if they do turn to Yahweh and they abandon serving other deities, the situation could be different.

14 By the same logic, Jeremiah is not to pray for their deliverance: Yahweh repeats the instruction from 7:16. No, *I am not going to be listening at the time of their calling to me on account of their dire trouble.*

> Call me on the day of pressure;
>> I'll pull you out, then you will honor me. (Ps 50:15).[225]

Not this time. There are contexts in which you can pray for your brother or sister but also contexts in which you cannot (1 John 5:16). There are limits. But maybe you don't take any notice and pray anyway, as Paul does (Rom 9:1).[226] Who knows whether God will be unable to resist the temptation to respond?

15a The verses of poetry with which the section closes constitute another backing for vv. 11–14 and deal with the same issues. They parallel 7:29 within

---

223. Pixley, *Jeremiah*, 42.
224. Berrigan, *Jeremiah*, 59.
225. See Mayer, *Commentary*, 367.
226. Volz, *Jeremia*, 134.

that earlier section, imply the same context (festival, temple), and pursue the same argument about the relationship between election and obedience, though in different terms.[227] The move to a reference to *my house* also parallels 7:1–16; it is another indication that the subtext of 11:1–17 is not so different from that of 7:1–16. Once again, Yahweh declares that the people of Judah have no business coming to the temple. In the parallelism, the first colon raises a question (Why on earth should Yahweh be asking *what [place] is there for my dear one in my house?*) to which the second colon provides an answer (*so many people* among them are *acting on an intention*—and not a legitimate one). The people are guilty of conspiracy, you could say. The description of Jerusalem as *my dear one* (*yədîdî*) compares with the affectionate *Miss Zion* elsewhere (e.g., 4:31; 6:2) and, like that expression, carries some irony.

15b Yahweh goes on to address the dear one. The city thinks it should be able to come to the temple and take part in the sacrifices with *the sacral flesh*. But the result of its wrongful lifestyle will be that *they* (who are not identified, though in the event it will be the Babylonians) *will make it pass away from you*. In due course (when the temple is destroyed), there will be no more offerings. At the moment the city can exult over the temple and the offerings (cf. 7:4, 10, 21). The arrival of the *dire trouble* that will issue from its going after other gods (cf. 7:6) makes *then you will exult* purely ironic.

16 Only here is the *olive* a metaphor for Jerusalem; it is a simile in Hos 14:6(7) and Ps 52:8(10),[228] while Paul takes up the metaphor and runs with it in Rom 11. The heightening reference in the parallel colon to *lovely fruit* gives extra force to the allusion to the olive, with its multifaceted importance (you eat it, you spread its oil on your bread, you cook with it, you get light from it, etc.). It is an honorable name for Yahweh to give to Jerusalem. The second colon of the second line also heightens the first as once more Jeremiah alludes to the presence of the Jerusalem community in the temple *with the sound of a big tumult* (cf. Ps 42:4[5]) as it engages in worship. The trouble is that the lovely fruit of the olive contrasts with the actual "fruit" of the Jerusalem "olive"; hence the horrifying picture Jeremiah paints with his metaphor, in which Yahweh *has lit a fire on her*—on Jerusalem—which will mean that *its branches will break*. Romans 11:17 will invite us to picture such a breaking off as not meaning the total destruction of the tree, in keeping with Jeremiah's promises about Yahweh not making an end of the people (4:27; 5:10).

17 But one should not underestimate the magnitude of the disaster that Yahweh threatens. *Dire action* will indeed issue in *dire trouble*. And even if the two direnesses naturally interrelate, Yahweh is involved in the way one

227. Weiser, *Jeremia*, 1:104.
228. Holladay, *Commentary on Jeremiah*, 1:349.

issues in the other; *Yahweh of Armies, who planted you* has also *spoken over you*. Once again, Yahweh juxtaposes reference to *Israel's household* and *Judah's household*. It's as if they were deliberately seeking *to irk me by burning offerings to the Master*. Like 7:1–20 (and the continuation in 7:21–8:3), this message does not conclude with a challenge to turn back to Yahweh, though like that section, it has incorporated such challenges near the beginning (see vv. 3, 6). Once more, the absence of overt challenge or invitation need not mean that the time when Judah is being provoked to turn is over. Even if there is not an explicit challenge or invitation, the point of the message is to make an implicit one.

2. *Three Exchanges (Protests and Responses) (11:18–12:17)*

Within 11:1–13:22, this second unit consists of a block of material that is nearly all verse set between a message that's nearly all prose (11:1–17) and a story in prose (13:1–12a). It includes the first of what are commonly called Jeremiah's confessions, but that title is inappropriate, even if it is intended to recall Augustine's *Confessions*. Jeremiah does not do much confession of sin nor much confession of Yahweh's greatness, nor is he sharing his spiritual autobiography (a popular way of reading Augustine).[229] In the twentieth century, these "confessions" came to be treated as key to an understanding of the Jeremiah scroll; "the lamenting prophet" came to be understood in a way that appeals to "the modern self,"[230] and the reading of Jeremiah in church lectionaries came to focus more on his life than on his message.[231] But the section continues to have the aim of reaching out persuasively to Judah during the last decades of the Judahite monarchy and the decades that followed and of drawing Judah to turn back to Yahweh. The misnamed confessions are in fact prophecy or proclamation.[232] They are part of Jeremiah's rhetoric.[233] They "illustrate the people's rejection of God's word in the person of the prophet," and after 587 they would "justify the Fall of the nation."[234] Before that final event, they would summon it to turn.

229. Allen, *Jeremiah*, 144–45.
230. M. C. Calloway, "The Lamenting Prophet and the Modern Self," in Kaltner and Stulman, *Inspired Speech*, 48–62.
231. T. M. Raitt, "Jeremiah in the Lectionary," *Int* 37 (1983): 161.
232. D. R. Jones, *Jeremiah*, 188; Fretheim, *Jeremiah*, 189.
233. M. J. Boda, "'Uttering Precious Rather than Worthless Words': Divine Patience and Impatience with Lament in Isaiah and Jeremiah," in Flesher, Dempsey, Boda, *Why? . . . How Long?*, 83–99.
234. K. M. O'Connor, *The Confessions of Jeremiah: Their Interpretation and Role in Chapters 1–25*, SBLDS 94 (Atlanta: Scholars, 1988), 158.

This significance of the section appears from the links it has with what precedes in Jeremiah's activity and in his message. Its language takes us back to the beginning of the scroll in Jer 1,[235] to Anathoth, to Yahweh's acknowledging and Jeremiah's knowing, to Yahweh's sanctifying, to the speaking out of authoritative decisions, to pulling up, pulling down, building, and planting, and to people doing battle with Jeremiah. But the situation has moved on. "It might be said that [Jeremiah's] confessions to Yahweh are his response to Yahweh's call in the light of his living out that call."[236]

This point also emerges from the way the section takes up motifs from the intervening chapters, from Jer 2–10. While many expressions that recur (e.g., "path," "dire," "faithless," "wilderness," "desolate") are too common to count as significant points of connection, other links are more distinctive: reference to people's "practices" (4:4, 18; 7:3, 5); the word 'allûp, though with a different meaning (3:4); "plans" (4:14; 6:19); "tree" (esp. 5:14); "devastate" (5:10, of a tree); "we will destroy" (cohortative, 6:5); "cut down" (6:6; 9:21[20]); "examine" (6:27; 9:7[6]); "redress" (5:9, 29; 9:8[7]); seeking someone's life (4:30); "sword and hunger" (5:12); "sons and daughters" (3:24; 5:17; 7:31); "remainder" (6:9; 8:3); their being attended to (8:12; 10:15); "I will argue" (2:9); "succeed" (2:37); "false" (specifically the participle, 3:8, 11); "tear off" (2:20; 5:5); "slaughter" (7:32); "the country will mourn" (4:28); "end" (5:28); "weary" (6:11; 9:5[4]); that things are well (4:10; 6:14; 8:11, 15; 9:8[7]); "reliant" (5:17; 7:8, 14); "abandon" (9:2[1]); "my domain" (2:7; 3:19); "shepherds" (6:3); "share" (10:16); "desirable" (3:19); "bare heights" (3:2, 21; 4:11; 7:29); "destroyer" (6:26); "sow" and "thorns" (4:3); "be sick" (10:19). Yet the section stands in some contrast with 11:1–17, which affirmed that Yahweh makes life work out in a religiously and morally intelligible way. Jeremiah's protest now declares, "No, he doesn't."[237]

The section brings together at least four subsections of separate origin (11:18–23; 12:1–6, 7–13, 14–17), with the opening verse (11:18) making a link with what precedes.[238] In their assembled form, the four subsections comprise a threefold pattern of protest and response:

235. Thus G. Barbiero (*"Tu mi hai sedotto, Signore,"* 15–61) begins his study of Jeremiah's "confessions" with a substantial study of Jer 1.

236. Holladay, *Commentary on Jeremiah*, 1:358.

237. Cf. L. Stulman, "Jeremiah as a Polyphonic Response to Suffering," in Kaltner and Stulman, *Inspired Speech*, 308

238. For accounts of the possible process of development that generated the text as we have it, see, e.g., J. Vermeylen, "Essai de *Redaktionsgeschichte* des 'Confessions de Jérémie,'" in *Le livre de Jérémie: Le prophète et son milieu. Les oracles et leur transmission,*

11:18–20	protest	11:21–23	response
12:1–4	protest	12:5–6	response
12:7–13	protest	12:14–17	response

In form, the section recalls the prayers of protest that are a dominant feature of the Psalms.[239] Jeremiah uses their familiar form in order to talk to Yahweh and indirectly to his people about his experience as a prophet.[240] The sequence in 11:18–12:17 compares and contrasts with the psalms in a variety of ways:

- The protest feature is the clearest correspondence. It describes literally and figuratively the words and actions of the people who have acted wrongly toward Jeremiah and toward Yahweh. They are people who profess commitment to Yahweh but simultaneously deny that commitment, not least by their repudiating Jeremiah's message. The language of the protests does not especially correspond to that of the Psalms, though the questions "why" and "until when" recur there.
- Each protest leads into a demand regarding what needs to happen in light of it. The focus is on Yahweh bringing redress to people for their wrongdoing toward Jeremiah as Yahweh's representative and to the community and its leadership because of their devastation of Yahweh's own domain.
- The first two protests include a statement of trust in Yahweh. Most radically, the third protest is different because it is Yahweh's own.
- The expectation of a response is integral to the protest psalms, though actual responses occur in them only occasionally, as is to be expected in a prayer text; perhaps a prayer composer can prescribe how people might pray but not prescribe Yahweh's reply. These examples in Jeremiah illustrate this point; the divine response does not follow on the protest in the way one might anticipate.

---

ed. P.-M. Bogaert, 2nd ed., BETL 54 (Leuven: Peeters, 1997), 239–70; D. H. Bak, *Klagender Gott—klagende Menschen: Studien zur Klage im Jeremiabuch*, BZAW 193 (Berlin: de Gruyter, 1990); J. Kiss, *Die Klage Gottes und des Propheten: Ihre Rolle in der Komposition und Redaktion von Jer 11–12, 14–15 und 18*, WMANT 99 (Neukirchen: Neukirchener, 2003); H. Bezzel, *Die Konfessionen Jeremias: Eine redaktionsgeschichtliche Studie*, BZAW 378 (Berlin: de Gruyter, 2007).

239. Cf. W. Baumgartner, *Jeremiah's Poems of Lament* (Sheffield: Sheffield Academic, 1987).

240. Cf. K. M. O'Connor, *Confessions of Jeremiah*.

a. A Lamb Led to Slaughtering/I Will Attend to Them (11:18–23)

[18] *So Yahweh—he let me know, and I knew*[a]—
  at that time[b] *you let me see*[c] *their practices.*
[19] *But I was like a lamb,*
  an ox[d] *that is led to slaughtering.*
I didn't know that against me they formulated plans:
  We will devastate[e] *the tree*[f] *through someone doing battle with him.*[g]
We will cut him off from the country of the living people,
  and his name—it will not be kept in mind anymore.[h]
[20] *So Yahweh of Armies, one who exercises authority with faithfulness,*
  one who examines heart and mind:[i]
May I see[j] *your redress from them,*
  because to you I have rolled[k] *my argument.*[l]

[21] *Therefore Yahweh has said this over the people of Anathoth who are seeking your life, saying,*

You will not prophesy by Yahweh's name,
  then you will not die by our hand.[m]

[22] *Therefore Yahweh of Armies has said this:*[n]

Here am I, I am going to attend to them—
  the young men, they will die by the sword.
Their sons and their daughters, they will die by hunger,
  [23] *and remainder, they will have none.*
Because I will bring something dire to the people of Anathoth,
  the year of their being attended to.[o]

a. LXX takes the first verb as imperative and for the second implies simple *waw* ("so I may know") rather than *waw*-consecutive. Vg has "you let me know," which leads more smoothly than MT into what follows.

b. "Then" (LXX, Vg) could give the impression that the seeing is subsequent to the knowing, but the parallelism indicates that the second colon restates the first (see the commentary; see *DCH*, 1:167).

c. LXX's "and I saw" is perhaps translating loosely.

d. For *'allûp*, LXX has "innocent"; Vg, Aq, Theod, Sym have "tame," qualifying *lamb*, but there are no parallels for these meanings. Usually *'allûp* means something like "guide" (3:4). For *ox*, cf. Ps 144:14; Sir 38:25. Using this form of the word rather than the more common *'elep* makes for a verbal link with 3:4.

e. For *našḥîtâ*, LXX, Vg imply a verb such as *nāśîtâ* ("we will put").

f. Tg has "poison," also implied by LXX, Vg.

g. MT has *laḥmô* ("his bread"); for the idea of destroying trees along with the food they produce, cf. Deut 20:19–20 (*CTAT* 2:569). But in the context, it is hard to make sense of "his bread"; Holladay (*Commentary on Jeremiah*, 1:363) suggests *lōḥămô* (cf. Ps 35:1), which fits with 1:19.

h. The a-b-b'-a' order of verbs and nouns in the line contributes to signaling a sense of finality to their intention.

i. Literally and anatomically, "kidneys" (which can imply a wide range of emotions and inner workings; see D. Kellermann, "כְּלָיוֹת, *kelāyot*," *TDOT* 7:179–80) and "heart" (which most commonly implies thinking, forming attitudes, and making decisions).

j. *'Er'eh* is cohortative.

k. LXX, Vg "revealed" derive *gillîtî* from *gālâ*, but MT implies the verb *gālal* (see the commentary).

l. MT has a section marker here.

m. MT has a marker here.

n. LXX lacks this resumptive clause.

o. MT has a marker here.

The first section of protest reveals gradually and dramatically that Jeremiah is under attack and that it is the people of his own town who are making plans to get him unless he shuts up. He appeals for Yahweh to take redress from them, and Yahweh responds with a horrifying promise.

> vv. 18–19 A protest at how people are thinking of ways to get rid of Jeremiah (four bicola)
>
> v. 20 A plea for Yahweh to take redress from them (two linked bicola)
>
> vv. 21–23 A response relating how Yahweh intends to do so (an introduction and one bicolon with more background, then a further introduction and three bicola comprising the actual response)

18 Jeremiah speaks to Yahweh, though as usual the indirect audience is the Judahites. What did Yahweh *let me know*, and what was it that Jeremiah consequently *knew*? The section's subsequent links with Jer 1 make this colon's two references to knowing resonate with the two references there,[241] where Yahweh knew/acknowledged Jeremiah and Jeremiah talked about what he didn't know. Yahweh has gotten Jeremiah to acknowledge him, and Jeremiah now recognizes that he does know how to speak. But the opening *so* (*wa*) indicates that this new section of verse continues from what precedes and begins to

---

241. Cf. J. S. Runck, "A Pentecostal 'Hearing' of the Confessions of Jeremiah: The Literary Figure of the Prophet Jeremiah as Ideal Hearer of the Word" (PhD diss., University of South Africa, 2017), 136.

clarify what it is that *he let me know*. We have been made aware of what it was in 11:1–16 (not to say in Jer 1–10). The second colon confirms that implication: it parallels the first, with *you let me see* restating *he let me know* and with *their practices* providing the object for *see* and *know/knew*. Yes, Yahweh has made sure that Jeremiah knows the Judahites' *practices* (4:4, 18; 7:3, 5).

19 But there were other things that *I didn't know*. Perhaps it shouldn't be surprising that the Judahites' plans were similar to their practices. After all, Jeremiah has been implacably hostile to them. If they made plans that went against Yahweh (4:14; 6:19), it's not surprising that they *formulated plans against me*. What plans? The parallel colon provides the answer. Jeremiah knows that they had set up *a devastator* so as to *catch human beings* (5:26) and that actually *they are all of them devastators* (6:28). So he might almost have expected them to be saying of him, *We will devastate the tree*. This image for cutting down a person appears only here, though the comparison of a person's flourishing with a tree's flourishing is familiar (Ps 1), and Jeremiah's attackers are intent on proving that his version of that psalm's promise (17:5–8) doesn't work out. Nor is it surprising that Jeremiah should picture them resolving to take this action *through someone doing battle with him*, because it's what Yahweh had warned him of (1:19). If the language in the colon about the tree is a little elusive, the language in the next line is clear enough. Yes, they will cut the tree down—*cut him off from the country of the living people*. They will finish him off, now and for the future: *His name—it will not be kept in mind anymore*. A person's name stands for the person. The name on a gravestone or a commemorative park bench is a reminder of them. If the inscription on the gravestone is worn down and unreadable, they are forgotten. Jeremiah's name being put out of mind is a way of expressing emphatically how he himself is put out of the community's mind. He no longer exists. Maybe he should have suspected that intention of theirs, but he hasn't, and Yahweh hadn't previously enabled him to do so. He thought he was serving them by confronting them, but they of course didn't see it that way. So he has been *like a lamb*, or for that matter *an ox*. What is the point of the comparison? The parallelism provides the answer: he has been like such a creature *that is led to slaughtering*, not realizing where it is going. There's nothing sacrificial about the language. The animal is simply about to be butchered.

20a As the grievance expressed in v. 19 recalls the complaint of a protest psalm, so does the plea that follows. First, there is the double basis for the plea. On one hand, there is the character of Yahweh. He is, after all *Yahweh of Armies*, the God who has at his disposal all the forces in existence; and he is *one who exercises authority with faithfulness*, who implements his sovereign power in a way that does the right thing by people (see, e.g., 4:2; 9:24[23]). On the other hand, there is the character of the person who is praying, who needs to recognize that Yahweh is *one who examines heart and mind*. Some-

328

one who is the agent of testing (6:27) needs to be able to submit to testing and emerge vindicated, not caught out. Further, one who pleads with Yahweh for action against wrongdoers needs to take into account that Yahweh can examine motives and intentions (heart and mind) as well as actions. Is it the case that we can only pray for redress if our statements about our heart and mind are true? It is thus people like dead saints who can do so (Rev 6:9–11).

20b On that double basis, it is possible to plead, *May I see your redress from them.* As usual, a First Testament victim of attack does not expect to take redress but does expect God to do so, like those dead saints. Such prayers are one response to wrongful attack; Isa 53:8 is another.[242] As usual, too, the Scriptures do not give people just one answer to a question (such as "how should I react to attack?") but several answers to reflect on while also implying the exclusion of some answers (such as taking redress oneself). Jeremiah asks God to act as he has said he would (5:9, 29; 9:9). His way of affirming that he will not take redress himself is to note that *to you I have rolled my argument.* He is not even entering into an argument with them; he is committing it to God (for the verb "roll" in this connection, cf. Pss 22:9[8]; 37:5; Prov 16:3).[243] "Curses are the last resort of the weak."[244] The prayer is part of Jeremiah's personal relationship with Yahweh, but he includes it in this scroll because it expresses the conviction that God's messenger and representative will be vindicated and his opponents put down, that justice does work out, and that God does act as judge. It is an encouragement to the weak and a warning to the strong, not least the plotters, who would be wise to desist.

21 The introduction to Yahweh's response tells us something Jeremiah hasn't told us: the people of his own town are behind the threat to his life. Here, the section links with 1:1. What might underlie the hostility? Are the priests and people of Anathoth the kind of people who would be particularly engaged in worship of the Masters at the shrine there, or are they par-

---

242. On the link between Jeremiah and the servant of Isa 40–55, see, e.g., Sommer, *Prophet Reads Scripture,* 64–67; K. J. Dell, "The Suffering Servant of Deutero-Isaiah: Jeremiah Revisited," in *Genesis, Isaiah, and Psalms: A Festschrift to Honour Professor John Emerton for His Eightieth Birthday,* ed. K. J. Dell, G. Davies, and Y. Von Koh, VTSup 135 (Leiden: Brill, 2010), 119–34; U. Berges, "Servant and Suffering in Isaiah and Jeremiah," *OTE* 25 (2012): 247–59; G. Fischer, "Riddles of Reference: 'I' and 'We' in the Books of Isaiah and Jeremiah," *OTE* 24 (2012): 277–91; G. Fischer, "Jeremiah, God's Suffering Servant," in *Uomini e profeti: Scritti in onore di Horacio Simian Yofre SJ,* ed. E. M. Obara and G. P. D. Succu, AnBib 202 (Rome: Pontifico Instituto Biblico, 2013), 75–10 (Fischer suggests that Jeremiah has made use of Isa 40–55); K. M. O'Connor, "Figuration in Jeremiah's Confessions with Questions for Isaiah's Servant," in *Jeremiah Invented: Constructions and Deconstructions of Jeremiah,* ed. E. K. Holt and C. J. Sharp, LHBOTS 595 (London: T&T Clark, 2015), 63–73.

243. Duhm, *Jeremia,* 113.

244. M. Avioz, "The Call for Revenge in Jeremiah's Complaints," *VT* 55 (2005): 436.

ticularly offended that one of their own number has turned against them? Anyway, they want to shut him up, like Amaziah in Amos 7:10–17: *You will not prophesy by Yahweh's name.* Otherwise, they are the people who will take the action described in v. 19. They will treat him in light of Deut 13:1–5(2–6).[245] The neat a-b-c-a'-b'-c' parallelism makes the link between offense and consequences:

you will not	prophesy	by Yahweh's name
then you will not	die	by our hand

They hardly mean he can prophesy in someone else's name. They are forbidding the kind of prophesying in Yahweh's name that Jeremiah engages in; they would not mind Hananiah's kind of prophesying in Yahweh's name (Jer 27–28). They don't believe Jeremiah is a true prophet.

22–23 The substance of Yahweh's response takes fairly standard form; its language corresponds to terms that Jer 1–10 has made familiar. Structurally, it corresponds to the threat that Jeremiah reported in v. 19: one cola by way of a general expression of determination in v. 22bα, then three cola spelling out the implications in vv. 22bβ–23a. The punishment fits the crime. What is distinctive is that threats applying to the people as a whole in Jer 1–10, which there suggest the kind of destruction that came to Judah in 587, here apply specifically to the people of Anathoth. They do so because Jeremiah is not just an ordinary Judahite but one who brings Yahweh's message; attacking him implies resisting Yahweh. Yahweh ultimately did not implement the threats to annihilate Judah that he sometimes seems to be making, and neither did he annihilate the people of Anathoth; 128 men from Anathoth returned from Babylon (Ezra 2:23). It might mean they turned back to Yahweh,[246] or it might mean they experienced the compassion of Yahweh that anticipates such turning, of which 12:15–16 will speak.

b. Why Does the Path of Faithless People Succeed/How Will You Compete with Horses? (12:1–6)

¹*You will be faithful, Yahweh,*
when I argue with you.
Indeed of authoritative decisions
I will speak out to you. [a]
Why does the path of faithless people succeed,

245. Wright, *Jeremiah*, 147.
246. Qimchi, in MG.

[why] do they flourish, all the people who are so false?[b]
[2]*You have planted them, yes, they have rooted,*
they progress,[c] *yes, they have produced fruit.*
You are near in their mouth,
but far from their heart.[d]

[3]*Now you, Yahweh, you have acknowledged me;*
you see and you examine my mind with you.
Tear them off like sheep for slaughtering,[e]
sanctify them for the day of slaying![f]
[4]*Until when will the country mourn,*[g]
the grass in all the open country wither?[h]
Through the dire action of the people who live in it,[i]
cattle and bird have come to a finish.
Because they say,
"He will not see our end."[j]

[5]*When it is with people on foot that you have run and they have made you*
weary,
then how will you charge[k] *with horses?*
And when it is in a country where things are well that you are reliant,[l]
then how will you do in the Jordan swell?
[6]*Because your brothers and your father's household, too,*
they—they have been false to you, too,
they—they have called fully[m] *after you, too.*[n]
Don't trust them,
when they speak of good things to you.[o]

a. See the translation note on 1:16.

b. Lit. "people who are false in falsehood." After the *why*, which applies to both cola, the line has an a-b-b'-a' structure, with the verbs juxtaposed at the center—the opposite arrangement to the more usual a-b-b'-a' structure with the verbs at the flanks in v. 4.

c. LXX "they had children" suggests *yālǝdû* for MT *yēlǝkû*; Vg "they prosper" is perhaps a paraphrase. For the use of *hālak*, cf. Hos 14:6(7).

d. Lit. "kidneys," as in 11:20.

e. LXX lacks this colon.

f. MT has a section marker here.

g. I assume there is a single verb *'ābēl* meaning "mourn" (cf. BDB, *DCH*), but this line is one piece of evidence that there is a second verb *'ābēl* meaning "wither" (*HALOT*).

h. The line has an a-b-b'-a' structure, with the two words for the land at the center and the two verbs on either side.

i. This colon recurs in Ps 107:34.

j. For MT *'aḥărîtēnû*, LXX implies *'orḥôtēnû* ("our ways").

k. Lit. "burn," on the assumption that *tǝtaḥăreh* comes from *ḥārâ*; see BDB 354; *HALOT*

351b; *DCH*, 3:314a; J. M. Hutton and S. Marzouk, "The Morphology of the tG Stem in Hebrew and Tirgaltî in Hos 11:3," *JHS* 12/9 (2012).

l. *HALOT* derives the verb from its *bāṭaḥ* II ("fall flat") along with Prov 14:16 (cf. Lundbom, *Jeremiah 1–20*, 647), but *DCH* does not mention it.

m. *Mālē'* compares with the *piel* verb in 4:5. LXX, Vg assume the meaning "loudly," but the expression is more subtle, and "loudly" does not fit the picture of deception. Rashi (in MG) takes it as a noun meaning a group of men.

n. A tricolon before the end of the section is unexpected, but the parallelism between the three cola makes the interrelationship clear.

o. MT has a marker here.

The transition to a new chapter in printed Bibles reflects the lack of any link between the exchange in 11:18–23 and the exchange that now follows, though this one will manifest a parallel dynamic.

vv. 1–2   Jeremiah's protest, in which he asks why Yahweh lets faithless people do well (five bicola)

vv. 3–4   Jeremiah's plea for Yahweh to see to the death of the faithless (five bicola)

vv. 5–6   Yahweh's challenge to Jeremiah: things are going to get worse, not better (two bicola, a tricolon, and a final bicolon)

"The text is not so much concerned with the problem of innocent suffering, nor the persecution of the prophet, but rather the miscarriage of divine justice in perpetuating the life and well-being of Israel in the land in view of her apostasy." Yahweh's response is to persevere with his commission. "The prophetic mission is to be a mirror of the conflict between Yahweh and Israel."[247] These prayers of Jeremiah evidence "that the vocation of the prophet is a *conflicted way to live*." He is restless and homeless and in conflict with God as well as with his community.[248]

1a–b Jeremiah starts again, with a protest going over the same ground as 11:18–23, though without any reference to Anathoth. The opening pair of parallel lines take up the same motifs as 11:20. There is Yahweh's faithfulness, though here alone does Jeremiah use the adjective *ṣaddîq* of Yahweh. There is Jeremiah's intention to argue, though here he uses the verb *rîb* rather than the noun *rîb*: "I will speak with you like a person who argues with his friend," says Jeremiah.[249] And there is the term for exercising authority, though here instead of the participle Jeremiah uses the noun *authoritative decisions*, in

247. A. R. P. Diamond, *Confessions of Jeremiah*, 51.
248. W. Brueggemann, "The Book of Jeremiah," *Int* 37 (1983): 133, 134; see further 142–44.
249. Qimchi, in MG.

the plural as in 1:16; 4:12. In this last parallel, Jeremiah is thereby turning Yahweh's own point back on him. "You said you would speak out your authoritative decisions in relation to them. What about the application of this principle to me?" Perhaps the pair of lines as a whole is somewhat ironic.

1c The questions spell out Jeremiah's protest: the implementing of Yahweh's authoritative decisions is not happening. The first half of Ps 1 closes with a declaration that the faithful person "makes all that he does succeed"; the second half closes with a converse declaration that "the path of faithless people perishes." So why at the moment *does the path of faithless people succeed* while *all the people who are so false flourish*? The second colon heightens the first by using the rare synonymous verb *flourish* (*šālâ*), then by adding *all*, then by using the rarer root *be false* in a compound expression. At the same time, all the words in this line except *flourish* pick up from, for example, 5:4, 5, 11, 26, 28. Gerard Manley Hopkins makes v. 1 in Vg the epigraph to the opening of a sonnet:

> Thou art indeed just, Lord, if I contend
> With thee; but, sir, so what I plead is just.
> Why do sinners' ways prosper? and why must
> Disappointment all I endeavour end?[250]

Like Jeremiah, Hopkins is respectful but direct, tortured but still pleading. He writes the sonnet just before his death, when he is perhaps disappointed with his life and work, which suggests another parallel with Jeremiah. In both cases, their questions are personal ones. In a Western context, Jeremiah can seem to be raising the question of theodicy, but he is not starting from a general philosophical question; he's starting from a concrete, practical one.[251] He is concerned about his particular faithless community, the people of Anathoth.[252] Nor is it the case that before Jeremiah's day people had failed to notice that promises like the ones in Ps 1 did not always work out or that people in the Second Temple period stopped comforting themselves with the kind of reassurances that Ps 1 offers. As far as we can tell, comforting generalizations and urgent questioning have always coexisted,[253] and they always will, because both make important points.

---

250. See P. S. Hawkins, "Singing a New Song: The Poetic Afterlife of the Psalms," in *Psalms in Community: Jewish and Christian Textual, Liturgical, and Artistic Traditions*, ed. H. W. Attridge and M. E. Fassler, SBL Symposium Series 25 (Atlanta: Society of Biblical Literature, 2003), 384–86.

251. Rudolph, *Jeremia*, 85.

252. Mayer, *Commentary*, 370.

253. See, classically, J. L. Crenshaw, "Popular Questioning of the Justice of God in Ancient Israel," *ZAW* 82 (1970): 380–95.

2 Jeremiah continues to use the language of Ps 1 ("plant," "root," "fruit") with some irony, and also again picks up language from the account of his commission. Future planting was where Yahweh ended in 1:10. Here he begins with past planting: *You have planted them* (2:21; 11:17). And *they have rooted* and *produced fruit* as he intended (2:7; 7:20; 11:16), though apparently in a rather ironic sense (see 6:19). To say they have produced fruit is another way of saying that they have flourished—but not in a good sense. The problem is that *you are near in their mouth* in that they profess faithfulness to Yahweh, come to worship, make the right confessions, and sing the right hallelujahs. But you are *far from their heart*, from the inner seat of emotions. Jeremiah makes the point with neat syntactic parallelism that clashes with the contrast in what the line says:

	near	(qārôb)	are you	in	their	mouth
but	far	(rāḥôq)		from	their	heart

The rhyme and assonance of the words for *near* and *far* enhance the comparison and contrast. Even if they say, "Yahweh lives," then they swear to deception (5:2). "The people mouth proper confessional statements . . . but this God-language is full of pretense."[254] But the reference to the heart suggests that Jeremiah is not just making the conventional point about a mismatch between worship and life. Here he points rather to the idea that the distinction between faithful and faithless "exist[s] at a level *deeper* than orthodoxy; it exists at the level of *orthopathy*, rightly-ordered affections." In thus emphasizing the affective, the passage "is making an important affective claim upon the listener."[255]

3 Following the dynamic of 11:18–20, Jeremiah moves from his complaint to the further basis for a plea and to the plea itself. Yet again he recalls his commission: *Yahweh, you have acknowledged me* (cf. 1:5). The implication is that Jeremiah has a claim on Yahweh. Again, he notes, *you examine my mind with you* (cf. 11:20). Yahweh checks the inward attitude and the intention—a checking that Jeremiah knows the faithless will not survive. Only on the basis of his being able to survive such a check can he pray as he does. If we wonder whether "he blames his opponents and challenges Yahweh but does not seem to allow for the fact that he may not have gotten it completely right himself,"[256] then he implies, "I am open to Yahweh putting me right."

254. Fretheim, *Jeremiah*, 109.
255. Runck, *A Pentecostal "Hearing,"* 203, 207.
256. R. C. Culley, "The Confessions of Jeremiah and Traditional Discourse," in *"A Wise and Discerning Mind": Essays in Honor of B. O. Long*, ed. S. M. Olyan and R. C. Culley, Brown Judaic Studies 325 (Providence: Brown University Press, 2000), 81.

His logic is the same as that in Ps 139,[257] where the psalmist urges Yahweh to examine him in order to see that he can properly urge Yahweh to act against faithless people. There are further retrospective links in Jeremiah's language, though they are impish links. He had said that he was like a sheep on its way to slaughter. Now he wants them to be like *sheep for slaughtering*. He urges Yahweh to *sanctify them for the day of slaying*, as Yahweh had sanctified him for his task when acknowledging him (1:5) and as he imagined Judah's foes speak of sanctifying battle (6:4). He prays that on the same day, in different ways, battle will be sanctified and the faithless will be sanctified. His use of *sanctify* underlines the irony of his not speaking of sheep (or a lamb; see 11:19) for sacrifice but just for slaughter in order to be eaten.

4 "Why" (see v. 1) is one regular feature in protest prayers in the Psalms; "how long" is another. While the first kind of question naturally belongs in the actual protest, the second kind can be part of the plea, as an aspect of urging Yahweh to take action (Pss 6:3[4]; 80:4[5]; 90:13; 94:3). So it is here in this question that continues the plea and might even be its climax.[258] Verses 1–3 have indicated that there are people who are doing well and shouldn't be, and Yahweh ought to do something about it. But there are other facts about the current situation that need to be faced and about which Yahweh ought to take action. When is he going to do so? *Until when will the country mourn, the grass in all the open country wither?* The following lines imply that it is doing so in fulfillment of Yahweh's statement of intent and precisely because of the faithlessness and falsehood to which vv. 1–2 referred (see, e.g., 4:28). But Jeremiah grieves over it. Jeremiah 14 will explicate further the kind of situation he presupposes. It's as if the land is mourning.[259] Such statements can seem to involve a transferred epithet or catachresis: the land is not something alive that can mourn. But they recur in the First Testament (e.g., 4:28; 12:11; 23:10; Isa 24:4; 33:9; Hos 4:3; Joel 1:10; Amos 1:2), and they are accompanied by many correlate references to nature rejoicing in happier contexts, so they rather suggest the recognition that nature is alive even if not conscious in the human way. It can give praise to God and it can mourn. Thus, mourning is related to being devastated (*ḥārab/ḥārēb*, 2:12) which—like that English word—can suggest both being dried up and being confounded by that happening. Perhaps there is also an implication that in its withered state, the land looks like something mourning.[260] "For each of

257. Duhm, *Jeremia*, 115.

258. T. E. Fretheim, "The Earth Story in Jeremiah 12," in *Readings from the Perspective of Earth*, ed. N. C. Habel, The Earth Bible 1 (Sheffield: Sheffield Academic, 2000), 96–110.

259. See K. M. Hayes, *"The Earth Mourns,"* 94–97.

260. K. M. Hayes, "When None Repents, Earth Laments," in *The Origins of Penitential Prayer in Second Temple Judaism*, vol. 1 of *Seeking the Favor of God*, ed. M. J. Boda, D. K. Falk, and R. A. Werline, Early Judaism and Its Literature 21 (Atlanta: Society of Biblical Literature, 2006), 129.

us then the *earth* either *mourns* or rejoices. For either it *mourns* from the *evil of those who inhabit it* or it rejoices from the virtue *of those who inhabit it.*"[261] And "Jeremiah wants God to remove the faithless from the land not only for his sake" (actually he did not mention himself in vv. 1–3) "but also for the sake of the land." Only thus "can the land be saved."[262] He restates the rationale for the land's suffering in the two further lines. On one hand, it's *through the dire action of the people who live in it,* which explains why *cattle and bird have come to a finish* (cf. 8:13). And on the other, it's *because they say, "He will not see our end,"* the end of which 5:31 spoke. But it's dangerous to work out what God will not do (e.g., 5:12). Their words recall Deut 32:20, where Yahweh declares the intention to see what their end will be when he hides his face from them. By implication, they do not believe this declaration of intent.[263] That disbelief will undergird their continuing in their faithless lives. Jeremiah's words are another example of his putting on people's lips the implications of their attitude. They did not utter those words; v. 2 has pointed to their actual words. But it is the conviction they dare not articulate.

5 When people pray the protest prayers in the Psalms, the Psalter usually doesn't indicate the nature of Yahweh's response (Pss 12 and 60 are the exceptions, and even they test the rule); it cannot predict or lay down that response in the same way it can provide the words for the protest that people are free to pray. In Job and in Jeremiah, we get the responses, in which Yahweh is usually confrontational one way or another and declines to answer the questions that have been put to him.[264] Here, his response is neither a simple yes nor a simple no, but an expression of his distinctive perspective on the content of the protest. He brings the discouraging news that things are going to get worse before they get better, so Jeremiah needs to brace himself. He offers two images; he is perhaps quoting proverbial sayings.[265] First, whereas running to keep up with people on foot (e.g., infantrymen) is not so demanding, Jeremiah is going to be like someone who has to *compete with horses*, not just runners. In the parallel line, he is going to be like someone hiking through the *Jordan swell*, the thick bushes and trees that grow in abundance along the Jordan banks, nurtured by the swell when the Jordan rises high and providing cover for prowling lions (49:19; 50:44). It will not be like hiking through easy country like the mountain ridge where he lives. In this second line, literal reality pokes through. *A country where things are*

261. Origen, *Jeremiah*, 99–100.
262. Fretheim, *Jeremiah*, 193.
263. Holladay, *Commentary on Jeremiah*, 1:379.
264. Weiser, *Jeremia*, 1:110.
265. D. R. Jones, *Jeremiah*, 190. See further T. R. Hobbs, "Some Proverbial Reflections in the Book of Jeremiah," ZAW 91 (1979): 69–70.

well, a country of *šālôm*, is not the obvious way to describe a country where walking is not hard work, but v. 4 has indicated that neither is it the obvious way to describe the situation in Judah at present. If it seems characterized by problems, conflict, and insecurity, things are going to get much worse, for Jeremiah and for the community as a whole. So being *reliant* (*bāṭaḥ* participle) in or on such a country looks a questionable stance. One could be falling into the same trap as the Judahites, who are reliant on their fortified towns, their words of deception, or the temple (5:17; 7:8, 14). There is only one appropriate object for this verb (see, e.g., 17:5–8). In book 1 of G. K. Chesterton's epic *The Ballad of the White Horse* (the White Horse is a vale that happens to start a mile southwest of where I write), the Virgin Mary addresses King Alfred, about to do battle in the name of Christ:

> I tell you naught for your comfort,
> Yea, naught for your desire,
> Save that the sky grows darker yet
> And the sea rises higher.[266]

The first line of that stanza provided Trevor Huddleston with the title for his book about South Africa, *Naught for Your Comfort*.[267]

6 The interpretation of the imagery follows. Jeremiah knows very well that there are people in Anathoth who are against him, and such people might be called *your brothers and your father's household*; understood in that way, this revelation from Yahweh would explain his plea in 11:18–23.[268] But the order of the material in the scroll implies that this revelation followed on that prayer and thus that these terms do not simply refer to the Anathoth community. Within that community, he might have expected his own extended family to be on his side. But this revelation warns him that the opposite is the case. Perhaps it reflects their being most affected by attacks on local shrines such as the one where the family priesthood had operated. People who *have been false* commonly aim to maintain secrecy; Jeremiah's apparent ignorance of their falsehood suggests that his family has done so. The unexpected third colon in the line underlines the shocking point. *They have called fully after you* thus likely emphasizes the concerted nature of their plotting. If they *speak of good things to you*, promising their support, Jeremiah is not to *trust them*. He needs to keep in mind the advice he delivered in 9:4(3).

---

266. Cf. Berrigan, *Jeremiah*, 63.

267. Trevor Huddleston, *Naught for Your Comfort* (London: Collins, 1956).

268. Thus Volz (*Jeremia*, 136), for instance, suggests that part of the revelation in 12:1–6 originally preceded 11:18–23.

c. I Have Abandoned My House/I Will Again Have Compassion (12:7–17)

7 *I have abandoned my house,*
I have deserted my domain.
I have given my soul's delight
into her enemies' clutch.
8 *My domain became to me*
like a lion in the forest.
She gave her voice against me—
as a result I have repudiated[a] *her.*
9 *Is my domain a hyena's lair,*[b]
is there bird of prey[c] *all around, against her?*
Go, gather every living thing in the open country—
bring them to devour.
10 *Many shepherds have devastated my vineyard*[d]*—*
they have trampled my share.
They have given over my desirable share
to be a desolate wilderness.[e]
11 *He has made it*[f] *into a desolation—it has mourned,*[g]
because of me desolate.[h]

The entire country has become desolate
because there is no one laying it to heart.[i]
12 *Upon all the bare heights in the wilderness destroyers have come,*
because Yahweh's sword—it is consuming.
From one end of the country to the other end of the country,
for no flesh are things well.[j]
13 *They have sown wheat, but thorns are what they have reaped*[k]*—*
they got sick[l] *[through things that] could not be any use.*[m]
So be shamed[n] *because of your harvests,*
because of Yahweh's angry blazing.[o]

14 *Yahweh has said this.*

About all my[p] *dire neighbors who touch the domain that I gave to my people Israel:*

Here am I, pulling them up from upon their soil,
and the household of Judah I will pull up from among them.
15 *But after I have pulled them up,*
I will again[q] *have compassion on them.*

I will return them, each one to his domain,
   each one to his country.

[16]*And if they really learn my people's paths so as to swear by my name, "Yahweh is alive,"*[r] *as they taught my people to swear by the Master,*[s] *they will build themselves up among my people.* [17]*But if they do not listen, I will pull up that nation, pull it up and wipe it out*[t] *(Yahweh's affirmation).*[u]

a. LXX, Vg translate "hated," but *śānē'* is as much an action word as a feelings word (cf. Tg's *rəḥêqətāh*).

b. For *'ayiṭ ṣabûaʻ*, Vg implies "a colored bird of prey" (cf. BDB). But see *DCH* and J. A. Emerton, "Notes on Jeremiah 12 9," *ZAW* 81 (1969): 182–88, following G. R. Driver, "Birds in the Old Testament," *Palestine Exploration Quarterly* 87 (1955): 139. Driver in turn is following H. B. Tristram, *The Natural History of the Bible*, 7th ed. (London: SPCK, 1883), 107–9.

c. By paronomasia, *'ayiṭ* now has its more usual meaning (cf. McKane, *Jeremiah*, 1:271–72).

d. The position of the subject before the verb and the asyndeton suggest that this clause is subordinate to the following one.

e. More idiomatically, "They have made my desirable share into a desolate wilderness"; but ascribing to *nātan* its common meaning "give" makes the link with the other occurrences of the verb in vv. 7 and 8.

f. LXX takes the verb as impersonal and translates "it was made"; Vg has a plural verb. The suffixed singular verb *śāmāh* follows on *šəmāmâ* (*desolation*) and leads into three related words, followed by *śām* (*laying*)—a substantial paronomasia (J. A. Thompson, *Jeremiah*, 358).

g. See the translation note on v. 4.

h. The reversal of prepositional phrase and adjective is a marker of this colon being the end of a subsection comprising vv. 7–11a.

i. *Śâm* generates yet another paronomasia with the various forms of words for desolate/desolation and thus makes a link with the preceding subsection.

j. MT has a section marker here.

k. An a-b-b'-a' colon; LXX has imperative verbs.

l. LXX, Aq, Sym, Vg imply *nāḥālû* ("[what] they had as a domain") for MT *neḥlû* and suggests another paronomasia: it is their domain that has become something that made them sick.

m. The unmarked relative clause recurs from 2:8; here there is no preposition, as in 8:13. LXX sees the first clause as the relative clause; see the translation note on 8:13.

n. What precedes in v. 13a would make it natural to take *bōšû* as a third-person *qatal*, but the object that follows in this colon, with its second-person suffix, suggests it is imperative.

o. LXX has "because of your boasting, because of your reproach before the Lord"; HUBP suggests it is interpreting in light of Arabic. MT has a marker here.

p. LXX lacks the *my*.

q. LXX, Vg are aware of the use of *šûb* as a quasi-auxiliary verb denoting "do again," but they do not treat this verse as an example, and BDB does not list it; the importance of *šûb* in Jeremiah and the verb's recurrence in the next line suggest that at least the overtones of "I will return" are present here.

r. See the translation note and commentary on 4:2.

s. As usual, LXX gives "Baal" a feminine article (see the translation note on 2:8).

t. With the double infinitive construction, first repeating the finite verb, cf. 7:13; 11:7; but in this example, the first infinitive is the repeating one, and the construction suggests purpose (Joüon 123m; DG 102; *IBHS* 35.3.2d).

u. MT has a marker here.

In its context in 11:18–12:17, this third protest has a doubly subtle function. Each line in vv. 7–11a has the short, two-stress second colon characteristic of protests and mournful prayers. Shockingly, the mourner is Yahweh. He refers three times to *my domain* (*naḥălātî*) in vv. 7–9; it is the "key word."[269] "Give" (*nātan*), which overlaps with it in sound, also comes three times, but in vv. 10–11 it links with the term *desolate*, which then tolls, "bell-like."[270] Yahweh's words also function as a further response to Jeremiah's own protest;[271] in addition, they include an exhortation to the animals of the wild that one might see as the nearest thing to a plea. Verses 11b–13 give up the mournful rhythm and refer to Yahweh in the third person, with the implication that Jeremiah takes up the protest again; these verses close with their nearest thing to a plea, in v. 13b. After the double protest comes a response in vv. 14–17, so that vv. 7–17 in their own way follow the pattern of the previous two sections, with the irony that Yahweh has to respond to his own protests and pleas, and they incorporate the further surprise of his unheralded commitment to restoring his neighbors as well as Israel.

vv. 7–11a   Yahweh's protest (nine bicola with short second cola)

vv. 11b–13   Jeremiah's echoing protest and exhortation to the people (five bicola)

vv. 14–17   Yahweh's response (three bicola, followed by two verses in prose)

7 After the exhortation and the revelation about Jeremiah's family, there is a revelation about Yahweh himself. You protest, Yahweh says: How do you think I feel? Yahweh is as distressed at the state of things in Judah as Jeremiah. He had said he wanted to walk out on his people (9:2[1]). But doing so would be as grievous as a wife walking out on her husband or a mother walking out on her children. And *I have abandoned my house, I have deserted my domain.* Yahweh's domain was the country in 2:7 and the people in 10:16, and in principle *my house* could refer to either; v. 6 referred to Jeremiah's family

269. Lundbom, *Jeremiah 1–20*, 651.

270. Allen, *Jeremiah*, 153.

271. W. H. Schmidt, *Jeremia*, 1:243–44; cf. D. P. Melvin, "Why Does the Way of the Wicked Prosper? Human and Divine Suffering in Jeremiah 11:18–12:13 and the Problem of Evil," *EvQ* 83 (2011): 99–106.

house(hold). But elsewhere in Jeremiah, "Yahweh's house" always refers to the temple, which will be what Yahweh here refers to abandoning (see Tg). The following lines will suggest that *domain* refers to the people, as will *my soul's delight*, which *I have given into her enemies' clutch*. In an interim way, he abandoned them in 597 when he let Nebuchadrezzar invade the country and pillage the temple (2 Kgs 24:10–16). Then he left temple and people in 587 in a way that could look final. So the past tense verbs might be wholly anticipatory, might come from between 597 and 587 (cf. v. 9), or might come from after 587, the context in which people read the scroll.

8 His action was a response to his people's hostility: *My domain became to me like a lion in the forest* (not the Judah lion of Gen 49:9).[272] You think you are in trouble with people's hostility, Jeremiah? "Yahweh has become the prey of Israel the lion"![273] The accusation would puzzle people; they didn't think they were hostile to Yahweh. Once again, Jeremiah is articulating the implications of their attitude. Only here and in 44:4 does Jeremiah talk about repudiating something (*śānē'*); the verb is the antonym of "love" (*'āhēb*). Both words denote a commitment, negative or positive; repudiation was expressed in the action described in v. 7. What would it mean for the church if God hated us and repudiated us, and why might God do so?[274]

9 In one of his elliptical lines, Jeremiah declares that the punishment fits the crime. The hyena is the animal equivalent of the vulture as a bird of prey; it kills for food and feeds on carrion, and it would thus count as an unclean creature. So comparing *my domain* with *a hyena's lair* might be a way of declaring how unclean Yahweh's land has become. Or it might suggest that Yahweh's land has become the victim of a hyena's aggressiveness—the hyena would then be an alternative image to the lion of v. 8. It's been said that the hyena "is more feared than the lion," and one of the reasons for aversion toward it is "the hyena's practice of stripping the bones of the fallen in battle."[275] That understanding would fit the reference to a *bird of prey* in the parallel colon, which is later an image for Cyrus (Isa 46:11); the equivalent in the community's experience will have been Nebuchadrezzar. But *all around* may suggest that *bird of prey* is a collective singular and refers to an army or a collection of forces like the ones referred to in 2 Kgs 24:2. The questions in v. 9a lead into Yahweh's exhortation to gather hyenas and all other carnivores to come and behave in relation to his domain as hyena and bird of prey do and have already been doing—which might suggest that this section does

---

272. K. Seybold, "Der 'Löwe' von Jeremia xii 8," *VT* 36 (1986): 93–104, though he then emends the reference to a lion.

273. Foreman, *Animal Metaphors*, 173.

274. Achtemeier, *Jeremiah*, 68.

275. A. Alon, *The Natural History of the Land of the Bible* (London: Hamlyn, 1969), 252.

belong between 597 and 587. If we ask whom Yahweh addresses, it will be his supernatural aides. It is another answer to Jeremiah's protest, and a more direct answer to the question "how long."

10–11a Forces like the ones described in 2 Kgs 24:2 are led by *many shepherds,* many kings such as Babylonian, Aramean, Moabite, and Ammonite (cf. 6:3). They *have devastated my vineyard,* another term for his people or his country, an image used by Jeremiah only here and not common elsewhere. But Isaiah's vineyard song (Isa 5:1–7) brings home the importance of one's vineyard, as does the image of sitting in one's vineyard under one's vine (Mic 4:4). If a foreign army has devastated Yahweh's vineyard (by his own action!), there is no grape harvest and no place to sit. Yahweh then moves to another image: *They have trampled my share* (*ḥelqâ*). Compare 10:16, which juxtaposed domain and share (there *ḥēleq*). Yahweh underscores the point when he repeats the word: *They have given over my desirable share to be a desolate wilderness.* The country is my domain, my vineyard, my share, my desirable share—and look at what I have done to it! So *it has mourned,* and *because of me* it is *desolate,* Yahweh goes on, lamenting the earth's mourning like Jeremiah (v. 4). Mourning again presupposes the country's physical desolation but also suggests that its desolation is emotional as well. Yet what precedes and follows implies that there is limited value in this mourning. If people are grieving over what has happened, they haven't thought through where they need to go from there. Yahweh still speaks as "I," so the *he* who has *made it into a desolation* is presumably not Yahweh; historically, the obvious candidate is Nebuchadrezzar. Yet substantially the *he* is Yahweh (perhaps we should imagine v. 11aα as the people's words). The three occurrences of "desolate"/"desolation" in vv. 10–11a bring Yahweh's lament to a bleak close.

11b–12 The poetry now gives up the consistent mournful rhythm that characterized vv. 7–11a, and Yahweh is now "he" rather than "I." If Jeremiah takes up the protest, he also takes up the motif of desolation: *The entire country has become desolate.* It is *because there is no one laying it to heart.* The people who might not care could be the attackers, the Babylonians, Arameans, Moabites, and Ammonites. In other contexts, the words might suggest the conviction that Yahweh doesn't care, despite all their mourning before him; they groan, but their groan doesn't come up to God (cf. Exod 2:23). More likely, Jeremiah's point is that the Judahites themselves are not taking to heart what is happening—what Yahweh is doing and why. It is this failure that lies behind their desolation. Jeremiah continues to describe the desolation, brought about both by *destroyers* like those neighboring and far-off peoples and by *Yahweh's sword* which *is consuming.* While Yahweh's sword may become an eschatological motif,[276] it is also a recurrent way of seeing

276. Rudolph, *Jeremia,* 86.

Yahweh at work in the reversals he brings (e.g., 47:6; Amos 7:9). Here, the whole country has lost its well-being (contrast the message in 6:14; 8:11). *For no flesh are things well.*

13 To put it another way, *they got sick,* and the cause is the recurrent one: they are committed to *[things that] could not be any use* (2:8, 11; 7:8). The evidence for this gloomy statement and the further background to v. 12 is the devastating experience of the failure of the harvest. The droughts to which Jeremiah periodically refers would mean that *they have sown wheat, but thorns are what they have reaped* (it may be a popular saying).[277] It is therefore appropriate for them to *be shamed*—Jeremiah switches to direct address in the final line of the subsection as he articulates the exhortation that occupies the place of a plea. Paradoxically, the result of trusting in things that could not be of any use, in entities that are powerless, is to become the victims of one who has power that he will use to a painful end: the harvests fail *because of Yahweh's angry blazing.*

14 A protest deserves a response. If you are Yahweh, you have to provide your own response, though perhaps Jeremiah helps. In his response, Yahweh has two further things to say about those enemies/animals/shepherds/destroyers, one of them less surprising than the other. The less surprising one is that, as usual, their being Yahweh's agents in bringing calamity upon his people does not mean they get a free pass from the consequences of their own guilt for their aggression. The description of the attackers as *my neighbors* is doubly striking. On one hand, there is the *my*; it's his domain (the word is again a key one in these verses),[278] so the attackers are neighbors to him. It is "a bold anthropomorphism."[279] Here, at least, Yahweh is likely referring to people such as Ammon, Edom, and Moab, not Babylon (which gets covered elsewhere). On the other hand, they are his *neighbors.* Neighbors are people who are supposed to care for each other, not attack each other and take advantage of each other's weakness. This "neighbor" (*šākēn*) is not the word that comes in the commandments (that word is *rēaʿ*), but it still suggests someone living near you and sharing life with you in the community (see 6:21). But these are neighbors whose behavior is *dire,* like Judah's. They *touch the domain that I gave to my people Israel,* and not with a gentle *touch* (4:10, 18 are Jeremiah's other uses of *nāgaʿ qal*). Therefore, *here am I, pulling them up from upon their soil* as he will be pulling up Judah and taking Judah off into exile (cf. 1:10). Yet *the household of Judah I will pull up from among them* when I bring Judah back to its land. Jeremiah can imagine

---

277. Duhm, *Jeremia,* 118.

278. Volz, *Jeremia,* 147.

279. Lundbom, *Jeremiah 1–20,* 661; he also notes *pull up, among,* and *it will happen* as key expressions in vv. 14–17.

Judahites fleeing to places such as Moab, Ammon, and Egypt (perhaps by the time of this message some had already done so). They will not be stuck there forever. They will not take root there. For people taken off to Babylon in 597 or 587, this promise gives hope against the background of the earlier talk of divine abandonment.

15 In a way, it is not so surprising that the response to the protest has another, more striking facet given that in principle Yahweh's responses to protests are not predictable (e.g., vv. 5–6). In this response, the surprising declaration is that there is another parallel between Yahweh's intention for Judah and for its predatory neighbors. *After I have pulled them up, I will again have compassion on them.* And the compassion will have the same fruit for them as for Judah: *I will return them, each one to his domain, each one to his country.* One could compare this commitment by Yahweh with his comment in Amos to the effect that as well as getting the Israelites up from Egypt, he got the Philistines from Caphtor and the Arameans from Kir (Amos 9:7). His sovereign and generous involvement with them in giving them their domain in the first place will be matched by a correlative sovereign and generous involvement with them in restoring them to their domain. In Amos and in Jeremiah, Yahweh's focus is on Israel; but in a sidebar and in connection with getting Israel to see things his way, he makes sure that Israel realizes that he also has a positive purpose for other nations. Each of them, too, has its *domain.*

16–17 Nor will they merely get their land back; indeed, it is necessary that things should not stop there. Once again, there is a parallel with Yahweh's dealings in relation to Israel. It was necessary that Yahweh's giving Israel its domain (which was also his domain) should lead into Israel's living there in accordance with his expectations. The ex-predators, too, need to *learn my people's paths.* The form of words makes for an irony. Every reference to Israel's paths in Jeremiah is negative. Israel's paths are paths that need to change (e.g., 7:3, 5). Of course, what Yahweh has in mind is that the nations come to walk in *the entire path that I order you* (7:23), to "walk by all his paths" (Deut 10:12; 11:22). The idea of Yahweh's paths is a familiar one in Deuteronomy, but the idea of learning his paths comes only in this verse in Jeremiah (Ps 25:4 is the nearest parallel). The concrete expression of learning Israel's (supposed) ways will be *to swear by my name, "Yahweh is alive."* Again, there is irony, because Israel does swear thus, but only nominally; in reality, Israelites swear *to deception* (5:2). But Jeremiah has already envisaged Israel swearing "Yahweh is alive" *with truthfulness* and has associated this idea with the nations praying for blessing by Yahweh (4:2). He here takes these ideas further. The fact that their neighbors *taught my people to swear by the Master* (strictly, that would have to be the Canaanites, not those other neighbor nations) does not mean that Yahweh simply punishes these nations. It has the opposite implication for their sake, but even more for his sake—for the sake of the truth. They will thus *build themselves up*. It will be another aspect of Jeremiah's being engaged in seeing to the fulfillment of 1:10. He becomes a prophet to the nations in a new sense.[280] In effect, these neighbor nations will come to share in the same relationship with Yahweh that Israel has, with the same assumption that they will conform to Yahweh's expectations of their way of life and with the same sanction attached.[281] This aspect of his purpose is a subordinate motif in First Testament faith; Yahweh's revelation to Israel focuses on what he is doing with Israel. But it is nevertheless an integral aspect of First Testament faith. The vision compares with the one in Isa 19:19–25, though that vision focuses on imperial powers rather than Israel's neighbors. Jeremiah thereby illustrates how Yahweh has a positive purpose for the nations. His revealing his ways to Israel did not imply that Israel alone was to live by those ways. The nations were destined to do so. Thus, a further difference over against Isa 19:19–25 is that here "the future of the nations is conditioned by the torah."[282] This assumption does fit Isa 2:2–4, where nations come to Jerusalem for Yahweh to teach them his paths. For Israel's neighbors as for Israel, walking by Yahweh's paths will follow on the compassion and return; it is not a condition of it. But it must so follow for them as for Israel. *If they do not listen* to the teaching that instructs them in Yahweh's paths, *I will pull that nation up, pull it up and wipe it out*, as 1:10 also said.

3. Five More Warnings (13:1–27)

Jeremiah 13 begins afresh with a story conveying a warning; indeed, the chapter as a whole comprises five sections of warning:

vv. 1–12a	About name, praise, and splendor
vv. 12b–14	About ruin or devastation
vv. 15–17	About exaltedness
vv. 18–22	About the flock
vv. 23–27	About exposure

At the different points in the monarchic period to which the warnings might belong, the five sections would function to push people toward changing; the middle of the five makes that aim explicit. After the fall of Jerusalem, they would offer some rationale for the disaster. The sections are separate in

---

280. R. P. Carroll, *Jeremiah*, OTL, 292.
281. Cf. Rudolph, *Jeremia*, 90.
282. Brueggemann, *Jeremiah 1–25*, 120.

origin and varied in form, but they have verbal links. Verses 1–12a are about the *ruin* of the *exaltedness* of Judah and Jerusalem, which had been created for *splendor*. Verses 12b–14 take up the theme of *ruin* and vv. 15–17 the theme of *exaltedness*. Verses 15–17 speak of Yahweh's *flock*, and in vv. 18–22 Yahweh's *flock* and its *splendor* reappear. Verses 18–22 close with the exposure of Jerusalem's *skirts*, and vv. 23–27 take up that motif.

a. About Name, Praise, and Splendor (13:1–12a)

¹*Yahweh said this to me: Go*ᵃ *and get hold of linen shorts*ᵇ *for yourself and put them on your body,*ᶜ *but don't let them come into water.*ᵈ ²*So I got hold of the shorts in accordance with Yahweh's message and put them on my body.*ᵉ

³*Yahweh's message came to me a second time:* ⁴*Get the shorts that you got hold of, which are on your body, and set to, go to Perat.*ᶠ *Hide them there in a crevice in the cliff.* ⁵*So I went and hid them in Perat as Yahweh ordered me.* ⁶*At the end of a long time, Yahweh said to me: Set to, go to Perat and get the shorts from there, which I ordered you to hide there.* ⁷*So I went to Perat and dug out*ᵍ *the shorts and got them from the place where I'd hidden them. And there, the shorts had gone to ruin—they would be no use for anything.*ʰ

⁸*Yahweh's message came to me.* ⁹*Yahweh said this: In this way I will ruin the exaltedness of Judah and the exaltedness of Jerusalem, which is great.* ¹⁰*This dire people who refuse to listen to my words, who walk by their mind's determination and go*ⁱ *after other gods to serve them and bow down to them, it is to become*ʲ *like these shorts that would be no use for anything.*ᵏ ¹¹*Because as the shorts stick to a person's body, so I made the entire household of Israel and the entire household of Judah stick to me (Yahweh's affirmation), to become my people, for name, for praise, and for splendor. But they haven't listened.* ¹²*So you will say this message to them.*ˡ

a. The infinitive absolute is used as an imperative; cf. 2:2 and the translation note on it.

b. Hebrew *'ēzôr* is singular, like English "undergarment," and thus subsequent pronouns are singular; the word for linen is plural.

c. Lit. "on your thighs," here and subsequently.

d. *Into water* comes before the verb, putting emphasis on the phrase.

e. MT has a marker here.

f. LXX, Vg, Sym have "Euphrates"; Aq has "Pharan."

g. Presumably not "dug up," as if the shorts were buried in the ground; *ḥāpar* can denote searching things out more generally (e.g., Deut 1:22; Job 39:29).

h. MT has a unit marker here.

i. The clause with a *qatal* verb continues the participial construction.

j. *Wîhî* follows the extraposed clause; LXX and Vg translate the verb as future, implying it is an example of the jussive used as if it were an ordinary *yiqtol* (on which see GKC 109k; *TTH* 56–58; Joüon 114l).

k. MT[A] has a section marker here.

l. MT has a section marker here, associating v. 12a with what precedes. LXX has a short version of this clause and the next one.

Yahweh commissions Jeremiah to take some action that would count as an acted parable if there were people watching, but people are only to hear the story; they do not see the event. In this sense, Jeremiah's original hearers are in the same position as people reading the scroll later. The story is thus a cross between Jer 7 (the text of the temple sermon) and Jer 26 (the account of its delivery). The action's not having an audience reflects its being a performative act whereby Yahweh puts his intentions into effect; it implements the ruining that it portrays. As such, it needs no audience. But the fact that Jeremiah reports it implies (in the context of the monarchic period) that the ruin it symbolizes is not inevitable but that it is unstoppably on its way if the people do not turn back to Yahweh. After 587, it would explain how Yahweh's sovereign power had indeed been inexorably unleashed.

vv. 1–2	Yahweh bids Jeremiah get a pair of shorts, and he does so
vv. 3–5	Yahweh bids him go and deposit the shorts, and he does so
vv. 6–7	Yahweh bids him go and collect them; he does so and finds they have gone to ruin
vv. 8–11	Yahweh interprets the significance of the events
v. 12a	Yahweh bids Jeremiah give people the message expressed in what has happened[283]

1–2 Possibly Jeremiah had to buy the *linen shorts*, but as far as we know there were no clothing stores in Jerusalem, and the verb *got hold of* (*qānâ*) denotes acquisition more generally—like Eve's acquiring of Cain (*qayin*) or Yahweh's acquiring of Israel (e.g., Exod 15:16; Isa 11:11). To make explicit that an acquisition is a purchase, Jer 32 will specify that Jeremiah acquires a piece of land for silver. The garment might be more like a short skirt than shorts; most occurrences of the word (*'ēzôr*, from a verb meaning "put around") come in this story. *Linen shorts* does not suggest a humble, ordinary person's garment (Ezek 23:15). They would be especially appropriate to a priest (Ezek 44:17–18); maybe Jeremiah got them from a priestly supply. As a material, linen would be more impressive than sack, less so than leather, and less liable to generate and be affected by sweat than wool, as Ezek 44:17–18 notes. Yahweh gives Jeremiah a related

---

283. On the process whereby the section might have developed, see H.-J. Stipp, "Into the Water," 167–95.

instruction to avoid letting the garment touch water (by way of a prewash or after wearing). It needs to be in pristine condition, unaffected by damp, for the experiment that follows, though to judge from the way Jeremiah tells the story, he doesn't yet know about the experiment. It will transpire that unbeknown to himself, "the Prophet takes the place of God when the linen waistcloth is girded around his hips, as God is girded by the people. For I have caused to cling to myself, he said, this people. God speaks as if the waistcloth becomes the people of God."[284] It is "a picture of marvelous subtlety."[285]

3-5 *Yahweh's message came to me* is a conventional-looking introduction, though it has mostly occurred in connection with some visual or experiential event (1:4, 11, 13; cf. v. 8 here) so that the more literalistic translation "Yahweh's word happened to me" might thus be apposite. In 51:63 (in another report of an unwitnessed performative act) *Perat* denotes the Euphrates (cf. 46:2, 6, 10, which use the full expression *River Perat*), but Jeremiah doesn't give the impression that he traveled that far (just one return journey might take half a year), nor that he did so in a vision, nor that he enacted a symbolic representation of such a journey (like Ezekiel in Ezek 4).[286] Possibly *Perat* is an alternative version of the name Parah, a town three miles from Anathoth in the area of Benjamin, Jeremiah's clan (Josh 18:23), which presumably took its name from or gave its name to the Wadi Farah (Parah) running down to the Jordan Valley. The place is hardly a random one, and the similarity of names will be significant. While a journey to the Euphrates and back would constitute a plausible symbolic act in light of the Judahites' imminent exile there, the point that vv. 1-12a make is different. Even elsewhere, the Euphrates is not associated with talk of exile. It would more likely suggest the frightening power of imperial Mesopotamian forces (Isa 7:18-20; 8:7-8; this latter passage also includes the only other First Testament reference to crevices in cliffs, apart from Jer 16:16). So the name could suggest "the threat of the Euphrates to inundate Judah. . . . Parah represents the Euphrates on Judah's soil." It evokes the northern enemy, to be mentioned in v. 20.[287]

6-7 Yet the story makes no reference to a river. Indeed, Yahweh had told Jeremiah to keep the shorts dry, and the area is dry wilderness. There was no reason for the shorts to rot. So the discovery that they have gone to ruin is shocking and inexplicable.

---

284. Origen, *Jeremiah*, 107.

285. Volz, *Jeremia*, 149.

286. D. R. Jones, *Jeremiah*, 196.

287. Holladay, *Commentary on Jeremiah*, 1:398; cf. C. H. Southwood, "The Spoiling of Jeremiah's Girdle," *VT* 29 (1979): 231-37. D. Bourguet also proposes that the Euphrates suggests the home of magic; Yahweh is the real "magician" (*Des Métaphores de Jérémie*, Études bibliques 9 [Paris: Gabalda, 1987], 240-58; "La métaphore de la ceinture: Jérémie 13,1-11," *Etudes théologiques et religieuses* 62 [1987]: 165-84).

8–10 The ruin of Judah and Jerusalem will likewise be a shock. In 11:19 and 12:10, the agents of ruin or devastation (*šāḥat*) were Jeremiah's towns-people and foreign kings, but now it will be Yahweh himself who brings about the ruin that will come to Judah and Jerusalem, and it will come from the Euphrates. While *exaltedness* (*gā'ôn*) can have pejorative implications, it need not; it was neutral in significance in 12:5. Judah and Jerusalem could properly see themselves as important and impressive places in the context of Yahweh's purpose. But seeing yourself that way is inclined to segue into haughtiness, and what follows here points in that direction. Being import-ant generates a self-confidence that makes people *refuse to listen to my words* as spoken by Jeremiah and instead to *walk by their mind's determination*. They thus feel free to *go after other gods to serve them and bow down to them*. The expressions are familiar from earlier chapters in Jeremiah; what is new is the explanation in terms of exaltedness (the Hebrew words for *ruin* and *exaltedness* recur from 12:5, 10[288]) and the curious picture of the consequences that will follow. Judah will *become like these shorts that would be no use for anything*.

11 The further explanation involves pushing the imagery in a direction that is also somewhat curious, though telling. *Stick* (*dābaq*) is what Adam did to Eve, what Ruth did to Naomi, and what Israel was supposed to do to Yahweh (e.g., Deut 10:20; 11:22; 30:20). Jeremiah develops this image by noting that it was what Yahweh sought to make happen (only he uses the *hiphil* of *dābaq* in this connection) and adds the extra note that it was *for name, for praise, and for splendor* (as in Deut 26:19, though in a different or-der). It's another way of referring to the people's *exaltedness* and of spelling it out.[289] No, there had originally been nothing wrong with the exalted-ness. The shorts "represented the people of God, pure and untarnished at the time of their call" (2:2, 3).[290] But Yahweh's donning this garment didn't work. There were three stages to the story of the shorts: Jeremiah put them on, he walked, and they went to ruin. There are three stages in the story of Israel: Yahweh put it on, Israel walked, and it went to ruin.[291] The truth can only be told by a people characterized by "the accuracy of its careful listen-ing," so in order to be formed by Yahweh, "the waiting community must, necessarily, shut up so that it can hear (Deut 6:4–6)."[292] But this community hasn't done so.

288. There, I translated them *devastated* and *swell*.
289. K. A. D. Smelik, "The Girdle and the Cleft: The Parable of Jeremiah 13,1–11," *SJOT* 28 (2014): 127–29.
290. J. A. Thompson, *Jeremiah*, 365.
291. Cf. Allen, *Jeremiah*, 159.
292. E. Searcy, "'A People, a Name, a Praise, and a Glory': False and True Faith in Jere-miah," *WW* 22 (2002): 337.

12a Accounts of a symbolic or performative action by Jeremiah usually include instructions on making it known, but there is variety about the nature of the instruction and when it comes. The next two such accounts have it at the end (16:10; 18:11), which supports the implication in MT's section break (as opposed to its verse division) that this sentence constitutes such an instruction.

b. About Ruin or Devastation (13:12b–14)

[12b]*Yahweh, the God of Israel, has said this: Every pitcher—it will fill with wine. They will say to you, We know very well[a] that every pitcher will fill with wine, don't we.* [13]*And you will say to them, Yahweh has said this: Here am I, filling all the people who live in this country—the kings who sit for David on his throne and the priests, the prophets, and all the people who live in Jerusalem—with drunkenness.* [14]*And I will smash them,[b] each against his brother, both the parents and the children altogether (Yahweh's affirmation)—I will not pity, I will not spare, I will not have compassion, so as not to devastate.[c]*

a. The infinitive precedes the finite verb, underlining the factuality of the action.
b. LXX "I will scatter them" derives the verb from *nāpaṣ* II.
c. MT[L] has a section marker here.

Yahweh commissions Jeremiah to deliver another enigmatic message that comes to its conclusion with another reference to ruin or devastation.

12b–13 This further enigmatic message will ultimately take up the one about ruin and devastation, but (like the story about the shorts) it does not announce this destination at the beginning. *Every pitcher—it will fill with wine* looks like a popular saying, perhaps a phrase you might repeat when you knew the grape harvest was going really well[293] or one signifying the great time people are going to have at a festival or a wedding (cf. John 2:1–11).[294] Alternatively (to judge from v. 13), it might be the drinkers who are the metaphorical pitchers.[295] Or has Jeremiah adapted a popular saying that "every fool [*nābāl* as opposed to *nēbel*]—he will fill with wine"?[296] Even if people knew what the phrase meant, Jeremiah's declaiming it (especially as a message from Yahweh) would be a puzzle, but it will fulfill its function as an

293. D. R. Jones, *Jeremiah*, 197.
294. Lundbom, *Jeremiah 1–20*, 673.
295. Bright, *Jeremiah*, 94.
296. J. D. Michaelis, *Observationes philologicae et criticae in Jeremiae Vaticinia et Threnos* (Göttingen: Vandenhoeck & Ruprecht, 1793), 116; cf. Holladay, *Commentary on Jeremiah*, 1:402.

attention-getter. *They will say to you, We know very well that every pitcher will fill with wine, don't we.* What's your point, Jeremiah? The answer is that they are going to be filled with drunkenness (*šikkārôn*, from the noun for liquor, *šēkār*, and the verb for getting drunk, *šākar*). Plural *priests* and *prophets* is to be expected; plural *kings* might seem odder, as a nation normally has only one at a time, though between 609 and 597 Judah had five of them.

14 Jeremiah does not suggest a reference to drink that has been spiked (as may be the case in 25:15–29). People are just going to be mysteriously intoxicated so that they will collapse on each other in their drunken state. They will be smashed and they will get smashed.[297] Their falling on each other perhaps suggests a collapse of the society, a different sort of ruin or devastation from the one in v. 8. But Yahweh is the one who will make it happen—even if (like a Babylonian invasion) it comes about by means that are explicable in human terms. So Yahweh's threat ends with the familiar reference to devastation, but the frightening novelty in the closing sentence is the commitment that will mean he does not hold back from it. *I will not pity, I will not spare, I will not have compassion*: Jeremiah piles up semi-synonyms to underscore the painful point. In 21:7, it will be Nebuchadrezzar's sword that does not spare, pity, or have compassion for Zedekiah and his associates. Yes, Yahweh will work via human means, but he claims responsibility. He rules out any hope that there might be restraint in the act of judgment.[298]

c. About Exaltedness (13:15–17)

[15]*Listen and give ear, do not be superior,*
   because Yahweh has spoken.
[16]*Give Yahweh your God honor,*
   before he makes it dark,
Before your feet stumble
   on the twilight mountains,
And you hope for light but he makes it deathly darkness,[a]
   turns it[b] *into pitch black.*
[17]*So if you will not listen, in the hidden places inside,*[c]
   my[d] *whole being will cry in the face of [your] exaltedness.*[e]
It[f] *will weep and weep,*[g]
   my eye will run down with weeping,
because Yahweh's flock has gone into captivity.[h]

297. R. P. Carroll, *Jeremiah*, OTL, 298–99.
298. Fischer, *Jeremia*, 1:457.

a. See the translation note on 2:6.

b. The *ketiv yśyt* signifies "he turns"; the *qere wəśît* signifies "and turn" (infinitive absolute).

c. Rudolph (*Jeremia*, 92) thus links *bəmistārîm* with this colon (against MT), though he also emends the word; cf. also Aq as well as Vg, to judge from Jerome, *Jeremiah*, 84.

d. LXX has "your" here and in v. 17b.

e. The "your" is understood from the first colon.

f. My whole being, on the assumption that *napšî* is the antecedent, but my eye if *'ênî* is the delayed subject, as in 5:22.

g. The infinitive precedes the finite verb, underlining the factuality of the action.

h. LXX implies *nišbar* (shatter) rather than MT *nišbâ*. MT has a section marker here.

Jeremiah reverts to poetic form to challenge Judah, addressing imperatives to Judah for the first time since 11:1–8 and the only time in 13:1–27. Notwithstanding his recurrent warnings such as the ones in vv. 12b–14, Judah sees itself as superior and quite able to look after itself. The opening reference to being superior (*gābah*) hints at a link with the theme of exaltedness (*gā'ôn*) in vv. 1–12a; the link becomes explicit in v. 17. There, Jeremiah also refers to the people as Yahweh's flock, a motif taken up in the next section. The section comprises five bicola (the first and last linked by the references to listening and the theme of superiority/exaltedness; the middle three linked by enjambment), then a closing tricolon.

15 As is typical, the apparent declaration of inescapable disaster leads into a bidding that implies disaster is escapable after all. It's never over till it's over. Indeed, vv. 15–16 have been seen as the inner center of Jer 13.[299] The bidding to *listen* is the same as 11:2; *give ear* restates it with a verb that Jeremiah uses only here, then *do not be superior* restates it in more innovative fashion. Like *exaltedness* in v. 9, being superior need not indicate arrogance, but it is inclined to do so; it thus commonly implies having the confidence to rely on your own ideas about what to do and ignoring Yahweh and his orders. So it is here.

16 To *give Yahweh your God honor* thus implies the converse; the word order suggests giving honor to Yahweh rather than holding onto it for yourself or giving it to someone else (see v. 10). Jeremiah goes on to expound an image that is not new to him (see 2:6; 4:28; 8:21) but that he here develops over three lines. Yahweh brought Israel through dark places at the beginning of their relationship (2:6), but if it stops giving him honor (2:11), it risks losing the light when Yahweh *makes it dark*. First, as you are trying to find your way along a mountain track and the light begins to fail, you find that *your feet stumble on the twilight mountains*. You may *hope for light*, but there are

299. Fischer, *Jeremia*, 1:466.

no street lights, and as time goes on, *he makes it deathly darkness* and *turns it into pitch black*—into intense, thick gloom. The subsequent reference to a flock (v. 17) may suggest that the people finding their way on the mountains are shepherds.[300]

17 Jeremiah returns to the verb *listen*. He has commented previously on the disparity between the Judahites' words and the reality of their inner being (e.g., 12:2). Here, he reformulates the importance of a link between what they say and the way they think, *in the hidden places inside* which no one can see. If they will not truly listen, they will end up in the darkness of which he has spoken. Jeremiah goes on to describe how it will also affect him; the point is to try another approach to bringing home the terrible consequences if they refuse to give ear. *My whole being* (my *nepeš*) *will cry*, he will be so grieved at people's *exaltedness* (*gāʾôn* in v. 9, *gēwâ* here). Whereas exaltedness was previously Yahweh's gift, here it has become a self-confidence with which people make their own decisions about whom or how to worship. And the darkness to which exaltedness will lead is the darkness of *captivity* (*šābâ niphal*). It is the first reference in the scroll to going into captivity. Such will be the destiny of *Yahweh's flock*. A flock of sheep has no business making decisions about whether it will follow its shepherd.

d. About the Flock (13:18–22)

¹⁸*Say*^a *to the king and to her ladyship,*^b
  Get down low, sit.
Because your headship positions^c *are going down,*^d
  your splendid diadem.
¹⁹*The Negeb towns—they are being shut up,*
  and there is no one to open them.
Judah is being exiled, all of it—
  it is being exiled, completely.^e
²⁰*Lift up your eyes and look*^f
  at the people coming from the north.
Where is the flock that was given to you,^g
  your splendid sheep?
²¹*What will you say when someone*^h *appoints over you*ⁱ
  (and you yourself taught them)—
  over you guides, as head?
Contractions will take hold of you, won't they,
  like a woman in giving birth.

300. J. A. Thompson, *Jeremiah*, 369.

²²*And when you say to yourself,*
     "Why have these things happened to me?"—
*Because of the profusion of your waywardness your skirts*ʲ *are exposing*
     themselves,
your heels are suffering violation. ᵏ

a. LXX has a plural, assimilating to the more common usage in Jeremiah (e.g., 4:5).

b. LXX has "people in power."

c. For this understanding of *marʾăšôtêkem*, cf. Qimchi, in MG.

d. I take the *qatal* verbs in vv. 18–19, 22b as referring to the certain and imminent future; see the commentary.

e. MT has a section marker here. *Šəlômîm* is the plural noun "entire ones" used modally/adverbially (*HALOT* 1510b; *DCH*, 8:369).

f. The *ketiv*'s feminine singular verbs address Jerusalem (LXX adds "Jerusalem"). The *qere*'s plural verbs continue to address the king and queen.

g. Both the *ketiv* and the *qere* now use the feminine singular.

h. Tg assumes this is Yahweh. LXX has a plural, implying the impersonal construction.

i. LXX, Vg understand *pāqad* to mean "attend to" in the sense of "punish" (e.g. 5:9, 29), which makes sense in this colon but makes the jerky subsequent cola even harder to interpret and requires *ʿal* to have a different meaning there from here. For the meaning "appoint," cf. 49:19; 50:44.

j. LXX has "your back parts" (cf. Vg), which makes sense; Jeremiah has another catachresis or transferred epithet (cf. 5:16).

k. LXX "were made an example of" (*NETS* "made a spectacle of") perhaps suggests *DCH*'s *ḥāmas* III ("make bare"; cf. J. A. Emerton, "The Meaning of the Verb *ḥāmas* in Jeremiah 13,22," in *Prophet und Prophetenbuch: Festschrift für Otto Kaiser zum 65. Geburtstag*, ed. V. Fritz, K.-F. Pohlmann, and H.-C. Schmitt, BZAW 185 [Berlin: de Gruyter, 1989], 19–28).

Jeremiah's poetry suddenly becomes more concrete as he is bidden to address a king and his mother, though they are not identified. The king and the queen mother are to be deposed and replaced, the country is to be invaded, the towns are to be besieged, the city is to be shamed, and the people is to be taken into forced migration. The reason lies in the waywardness and unfaithfulness of the city and its people.

After that concrete beginning, then, the content of the section is familiar, but a further novelty is its use of a sequence of *qatal* verbs. Such verbs would usually refer to a past event, but it would be odd to urge the king and queen to come down from their thrones (v. 18) if they have already been deposed, and the description of a total exile as having already happened (v. 19) also raises eyebrows. Further, Jeremiah goes on to urge people to look at an invader coming (v. 20), which suggests that the attack is still future. Eventually, he speaks even more explicitly (in *yiqtol* verbs) as if the disaster lies in the future (vv. 21–22a) before closing with more *qatal* verbs.

In vv. 18–19, 22b, then, Jeremiah is using the *qatal* as prophets sometimes do, to refer to events that he can describe as having happened because they are so certain as to be actual. Yahweh has decided on them and initiated the process whereby they will take place, and the prophet has seen them. We have had possible examples of this usage earlier in the scroll (2:26; 5:6); this passage includes the first unequivocal ones.[301]

To put it linguistically rather than theologically, Jeremiah's usage reflects the fact that the verbal system in Hebrew does not focus on a difference between tenses as much as European languages do (as when we speak of past, present, and future verbs). The *qatal* denotes an actual event, the *yiqtol* a theoretical or possible event. In using a *qatal* verb, Jeremiah is indicating that he is talking about an actual event, not just a possibility. I translate the *qatal* verbs in this passage that refer to such events by an English present progressive (present continuous): *are going down, are being shut up, is being exiled, are exposing themselves, are suffering violation.* An advantage of the Hebrew usage is that people reading Jeremiah's scroll after the events to which his words could apply (esp. after 587) could give them past reference: king and queen had been deposed, Negeb town had been blockaded, Judah had been taken into exile, Jerusalem had been exposed. They had always been actual; after 587, they became visibly and experientially actual.

While MT makes another section break after v. 19, Jeremiah continues a tight 3-2 rhythm through v. 20. According to the *qere*, he continues the plural address in v. 20a pending a transition mid-verse to addressing Jerusalem and referring to its flock, which gives the section a verbal link with vv. 15–17. The section comes to a close with the threat of woman Jerusalem being exposed. It comprises six bicola, then a tricolon, then three more bicola.

18 Presumably, Yahweh is giving this commission to Jeremiah. The object of his bidding, simply *a king* and *her ladyship*, invites us not to identify them.[302] *Her ladyship* (*gəbîrâ*), more literally "the lady" (the feminine equivalent to "the lord"), is the queen mother, commonly a powerful figure in an ancient court and the power behind the throne (1 Kgs 15:13). In bidding the two of them to *get down low, sit, because your headship positions are going down,* Jeremiah would be announcing the imminent end of their rule (cf. 48:18; Isa 47:1; Ezek 26:16)—and announcing it to the people of Jerusalem if he made his declaration in the temple courtyard. The king and queen might be Jehoahaz and his mother; Jehoahaz was deposed by the Egyptians in 609 (2 Kgs 23:31–35). They might be Jehoiakim and his mother; Jehoiakim submitted to Babylonian control in 600 (2 Kgs 23:36–24:2). They might be Jehoiachin and his mother (2 Kgs 24:8–12; Jer 29:2); Jehoiachin was deposed by the

---

301. See D. E. Carver, "A Reconsideration of the Prophetic Perfect in Biblical Hebrew" (PhD diss., Catholic University of America, 2017), 216–17.

302. R. P. Carroll, *Jeremiah*, OTL, 302.

Babylonians in 597, and he and his mother were taken off to Babylon. They might be Zedekiah and his mother (2 Kgs 24:18); Zedekiah was taken off to Babylon in 587. The ambiguity of the possible chronological references in vv. 19–20 might further warn against trying to decide between these possibilities. In any case, the anonymity combined with the long list of possible candidates suggests that the text invites Judahites to see this declaration to a king and queen as a divine word that could apply more than once. If it had been fulfilled on one occasion, the fulfillment proved it was a word from Yahweh, and it encouraged one to expect that it would find fulfillment again.[303]

19 Similar possibilities arise in connection with Jeremiah's picture of trouble arising to the south. *The Negeb towns . . . are being shut up*: they have closed their gates because they are under pressure from hostile forces. And Jerusalem cannot come to their defense or break through to provision them: *There is no one to open them.* Among the scenarios that would fit, chronologically the first would be the aftermath of Josiah's death. After Pharaoh Neco defeated and killed him, he intervened in Judah from the south to depose his successor, Jehoahaz, whose father Josiah might have married his mother Hamutal from Libnah precisely "to shore up its southwestern borders against Egyptian pressure."[304] A much later possibility is that v. 19a reflects Edomite incursions into Judah. Then there is the series of invasions by Nebuchadrezzar in the reigns of Jehoiakim, Jehoiachin, and Zedekiah, which would fit the subsequent reference to exile. The word order with the subject before the verb might suggest that "even the Negeb towns" recognize that they are in trouble as the Babylonians advance from the north. Even an invader from the north might deal with the easier areas to the west and south before venturing into the mountains, as Sennacherib did (Isa 10:28–32 speaks metaphorically when he describes an invader approaching from the north, while Isa 36–37 implies a more literal account).[305] With the likely exception of Neco's action, any variant on these possibilities could threaten that *Judah is being exiled.* Following the first reference to being taken captive (*šābâ*) in v. 17, this is the first reference to being exiled (*gālâ*) since 1:1–3. *All of it—it is being exiled, completely* involves a hyperbole, though a telling one.

20a Jeremiah's further familiar warning could also link with a series of points in Jeremiah's time: there are *people coming from the north.* The fulfillment of the warning will be the arrival of Nebuchadrezzar and his forces to put pressure on or actually attack Jerusalem and defeat Jehoiakim, or depose

---

303. Cf. P. R. Ackroyd, "The Vitality of the Word of God in the Old Testament," in Ackroyd, *Studies in the Religious Tradition of the Old Testament* (London: SCM, 1987), 61–75; cf. B. S. Childs's comments on Isaiah in, e.g., *Old Testament as Scripture*, 325.

304. Sweeney, *I and II Kings*, 451.

305. Volz, *Jeremia*, 155.

Jehoiachin and take the Judahite leadership off to Babylon, or depose Zedekiah, devastate Jerusalem, and take more people off to Babylon. As usual,
Jeremiah's *lift up your eyes and look* need not imply they are actually at this
moment marching through Ephraim, hence the possibility that nothing
in vv. 18–20a refers to things that have happened on the ground yet. They
have all simply happened in Jeremiah's awareness of what the divine cabinet
has determined.

20b–21 This possibility receives support from what follows. The events
that are unfolding or will unfold in this way raise the question *where is the
flock given to you, your splendid sheep?* The *you* is feminine singular, which
will refer as it often does to Jerusalem (eventually named in the chapter's
last line).[306] The people are the flock for which Jerusalem has been a secure
fold, but they will be going off in a forced migration. Further, the deposing
of the king and his mother will mean that *someone appoints* other rulers *over
you*, not someone you choose as you chose Josiah and Jehoahaz (and perhaps
Jehoiachin). The rest of v. 21a is jerky, but it suggests Jerusalem has *taught*,
in the sense of welcomed or invited, people such as Assyria, Babylon, and
Egypt to act as its *guides*. It will find that these people, whom it wanted to
treat as allies and whom it supports, even as equals, are imposing authority
over it. Once again, Jeremiah holds before it a familiar but frightening image
applied elsewhere to Jerusalem: *Contractions will take hold of you, won't they,
like a woman in giving birth.*

22 Jeremiah has posed Jerusalem with a series of rhetorical questions in
vv. 20–21. Here is a question she will ask: *Why have these things happened to
me?* As far as Jeremiah is concerned, it is a rhetorical question; he thinks she
should know the answer, but he knows she needs to articulate it to herself.
It is *because of the profusion of your waywardness.* Nothing surprising there.
But the section draws to an end with another horrifying image, one with
a background in Hos 2:10(12) and one that Ezek 16 and 23 will develop ad
nauseam. Invasion and siege commonly issue in violation and rape, which
becomes an image for the fate of the city itself portrayed as a woman. Jeremiah perhaps takes a little of the edge off the horror of his language by
using a double euphemism. In reality, it is not *her skirts* that will expose
themselves but the body parts that her skirts are designed to conceal (there
is some irony in the fact that *exposing themselves, niglû*, comes from the verb
that meant *exiled, hoglāt*, in v. 19). It is not merely her *heels* that *are suffering
violation*. Only here are heels a euphemism for genitals instead of the more
usual "feet" (is she raped from behind?). It is disturbing that Jeremiah speaks
of such violence against a city personified as a woman, and it is possible to
think that the Bible should not talk about such things, but it is not clear that

306. Allen, *Jeremiah*, 163.

the proper reason for being disturbed is the possibility that it has encouraged violence against women.[307] Rather, it is that sexual violence is a reality in war and in other contexts whether or not Jeremiah talks about it, and Jeremiah makes it harder to avoid facing this reality that people would rather avoid thinking about. In vv. 18–27 as a whole, Jeremiah employs "the rhetoric of the monstrous-feminine . . . to horrify his audience"[308] and provoke a response from it.

e. About Exposure (13:23–27)

[23] *Can a Sudanese[a] change his skin,*
  or a leopard its spots?
You also can do good,[b]
  having been taught to do what is dire.
[24] *So I will scatter them[c] like stubble[d] passing on*
  to the wilderness wind.
[25] *This will be your lot,[e]*
  your measured portion from me (Yahweh's affirmation)
In that you put me out of mind
  and relied on deception.
[26] *So it is indeed I myself who am lifting your skirts over your face,[f]*
  and your humiliation will become visible.
[27] *Your acts of adultery, your neighings,*
  your whorish deliberateness,[g]
On the hills, in the open country—
  I have seen your detestable deeds.
Alas for you, Jerusalem!—
  you will not be clean
  after how long, still?[h]

a. LXX, Vg "Ethiopian" is misleading in terms of modern geography.

b. The verb reverts to masculine plural. LXX has the interrogative carrying over from v. 23a into v. 23b.

c. LXX "I scattered them" presupposes *waw*-consecutive instead of MTs simple *waw* (contrast Vg).

d. People might have to gather *qaš* for some purposes (Exod 5:7, 12); it is thus *stubble*, the bottom of the grain stalks, as opposed to chaff, the husks of the grain.

307. Fretheim, *Jeremiah*, 214.

308. A. Kalmanofsky, "The Monstrous-Feminine in the Book of Jeremiah," in Diamond and Stulman, *Jeremiah (Dis)placed*, 206.

e. Jeremiah reverts to feminine singular for vv. 25–27.

f. LXX "I will reveal your behind to your face" (cf. Vg) dissolves the euphemism, as in v. 22.

g. Initially, this series of noun phrases might seem to stand alone as exclamations, but the next line will suggest that they comprise anticipatory objects of the verb *I have seen*, in apposition to *your detestable deeds*.

h. MT has a marker here.

Yahweh begins again with a question to make people think; he will eventually return to the theme of exposure, which makes a link with vv. 18–22. The section comprises eight bicola with a closing tricolon. One pair of bicola run together in v. 25, another pair in v. 27a–b. The section unfolds in a sequence of expressions of offended indignation—sadness or puzzlement or hopelessness—and resolution to take action.

v. 23	Puzzled sadness
vv. 24–25a	Determined resolve
v. 25b	Offended indignation
v. 26	Determined resolve
v. 27a–b	Offended indignation
v. 27c	Puzzled sadness

23–24 Jeremiah jumps in a new direction at the beginning of another message, with a new image and even a new thought. The question *Can a Sudanese change his skin, or a leopard its spots?* may be a popular saying, though the presence of a number of such pithy sayings in the scroll might suggest that Jeremiah was something of an epigrammatist.[309] Sudan (*kûš*), south of Egypt, is an area where dark skins come to predominate. There is of course nothing wrong with being black or with being a leopard.[310] The point of comparison is that you are what you are. In effect, Jeremiah says, "You think they can change? In that case, you can change, too." Frighteningly, Jeremiah suggests that the Judahites are in the same position morally as they are. They cannot change. He is not implying a systematic theological point about whether people can change. He is as usual engaged in rhetoric,[311] implying "Prove me wrong!" The incentive to change is what will otherwise

---

309. C. Bultmann, "Jeremiah *epigrammatistes*," in *Prophecy in the Book of Jeremiah*, ed. H. M. Barstad and R. G. Kratz, BZAW 388 (Berlin: de Gruyter, 2009), 74–79.

310. But on the "of course," see M. Masenya, "'Can the Cushite Change His Skin . . . ?' Beating the Drums of African Biblical Hermeneutics," in Jonker, Kotzé, and Maier, *Congress Volume*, 285–301.

311. Fischer, *Jeremia*, 1:467–68.

follow: *So I will scatter them like stubble passing on to the wilderness wind* (see 4:11). Fortunately, "what is impossible for people is possible for God" (Matt 19:26),[312] as the story of the Sudanese politician (Acts 8:26–39) shows.[313]

25 Jeremiah reverts to addressing Jerusalem, for reasons that will emerge in a moment. That scattering is the future allocated to her, her *lot (gôrāl)*. The word commonly refers to a family's stretch of land, which fits the parallel description of it as *your measured portion from me.* A difference is that the family's land allocation was determined by lot and thus arbitrarily; it had nothing to do with what a family deserved. This allocation is different. It's not predetermined irrespective of merit. It reflects that fact that Jeremiah has often noted, that *you put me out of mind and relied on deception.* The antithesis between *me* and *deception* suggests that *deception* is virtually or actually a way of referring to the Master (e.g., 5:2, 31; 7:9; 20:6).

26 To put the consequences another way, Jeremiah reverts to the language of exposure. Here, its agent is explicit, and it's not the human conqueror. *It is indeed I myself who am lifting your skirts over your face* so that *your humiliation will become visible.* The focus of the action is not the sexual violation but the shame of bodily exposure; *your humiliation* is another way of referring to parts of the body that one instinctively keeps covered. "Shaming works because it stimulates fear" and thus horror.[314]

27a–b Yet the background of the action is quasi-sexual: it's the *whorish* activity and the *adultery* to which Jeremiah has often referred (e.g., 3:6–10), the frenzied *neighings* (5:8), all undertaken not in a moment of unexpected temptation but with *deliberateness (zimmâ).* Etymologically, this latter word simply denotes something one thinks about doing and decides to do, but most occurrences come in Leviticus and Ezekiel to denote a willful decision to engage in wrongful sexual activity. One might guess that most of the Jerusalemites whom Jeremiah attacks are respectable people engaged in what they see as responsible religious and political behavior, men faithful to their wives who would not dream of sexual impropriety. Jeremiah has to get them to see that their religious observances at the shrines *on the hills, in the open country* count as the kind of *detestable deeds* (4:1; 7:30) that they might condemn in people who lived less pure lives than they do. And Yahweh has *seen* them. The shamed naked female body at the end of Jer 13 contrasts with the respectable clothed male body at the beginning of the chapter. "Jeremiah displays the naked female body to persuade his audience to restore their relationship with God. He incorporates obscene nudity into his prophecy in

---

312. Jerome, *Jeremiah*, 87.
313. As Jerome notes elsewhere; see the quotations in Wenthe, *Jeremiah*, 111.
314. Kalmanofsky, *Terror All Around*, 13.

order to shock and shame Israel and to convince them once again to cleave to God's body like a fine linen loincloth."[315]

27c Jeremiah closes the chapter with an incoherent combination of exclamation and question, a kind of chain of aposiopeses. *Alas for you, Jerusalem*! Jeremiah says *alas* (*'ôy*) much more often than anyone else, though usually on someone's behalf in the form "alas for me/us." Here, he echoes Jerusalem's own incoherent *alas for me* in 4:31. Thus *alas* is an expression of sadness at least as much as anger. Neither Yahweh nor Jeremiah can get Jerusalem to turn: the section ends where it began in v. 23. In light of the critique in v. 27a–b, what is needed is that Jerusalem should seek to *be clean*, which would mean giving up its sexual/religious whoring and adultery. It has been going on for so long: how much longer will Jerusalem insist on continuing it? The expression *after how long* comes only here, but *how long* is an expression that recurs in protest prayers—sometimes incoherent ones involving aposiopesis like this one (Pss 6:3[4]; 90:13). So the question is an expression of protest, though on Yahweh's lips it may not be simply an expression of helplessness. It may imply "How long can this be allowed to continue" rather than simply "When will you seek cleansing?"[316] The answer will turn out to be, until 587.

C. PART 2C: DROUGHT, HUNGER, SWORD (14:1–17:27)

As parts 1, 2a, and 2b began by questioning Judah's assumptions about the exodus, the temple, and Sinai, part 2c begins by questioning its assumptions about prayer. After 13:23–27 made a plausible ending for one sequence of Jeremiah's messages, the phrase *What came as Yahweh's message to Jeremiah* comprises a curator's introduction to a further sequence. Jeremiah will include his own affirmation that Yahweh spoke *to me* in 14:11, 14; 15:1; 16:1; 17:19. The sequence unfolds as follows:

14:1–15:21	Four more sets of protests and responses between Yahweh, Jeremiah, and Judah
16:1–17:11	A series of confrontations and warnings about this country and domain
17:12–27	Another exchange between Judah, Jeremiah, and Yahweh with three ironies

315. A. Kalmanofsky, "Bare Naked," in Holt and Sharp, *Jeremiah Invented*, 62.
316. McKane, *Jeremiah*, 1:313–14.

1. Four More Exchanges (Protests and Responses) (14:1–15:21)

Whereas the voices of Yahweh and of Jeremiah speaking for Yahweh dominated Jer 13, the initiating voice of Judah and of Jeremiah speaking for Judah
dominates Jer 14–15. Decisive insights emerge through the dialogue between
God and prophet.[317]

a. The Dearths, the Plea, and the Response (14:1–12)

[1]*What came as Yahweh's message*[a] *to Jeremiah in the matter of the dearths.*[b]

[2]*Judah mourns,*
    her gateways—they fade away.[c]
People are in darkness on the ground,[d]
    Jerusalem's shout—it goes up.[e]
[3]*Their lords—they send their kids for water;*
    they come to the ditches—they don't find water.
They return, their containers empty—

---

317. See Rudolph's comment (*Jeremia*, 98) on 14:1–15:4.

they are shamed and humiliated, and they cover their head.^f
⁴*On account of the earth that's broken up,*^g
  because there has been no rain on the ground,
Farmhands are shamed—
  they cover their head.
⁵*Because even the hind in the open country—it gives birth,*
  but abandons^h *because there's no grass.*
⁶*The wild donkeys: they stand on the bare heights—*
  *they pant after wind like jackals.*ⁱ
Their eyes fail
  because there's no vegetation.

⁷*If our wayward acts aver*^j *against us,*
  Yahweh, act, for the sake of your name,
When^k *our turnings are many—*
  in relation to you we have done wrong.
⁸*Hope of Israel,*
  its deliverer in time of distress,
Why should you become like an alien in the country,
  like a traveler turning aside to stay the night?
⁹*Why should you become like someone at a loss,*^l
  like a strong man who cannot deliver?
But given that you are among us, Yahweh,
  and your name has been proclaimed over us, don't drop us.^m

¹⁰*Yahweh has said of this people:*

Truly, they like to drift,
  *in that they have not held back their feet.*ⁿ
But Yahweh: he does not accept them—
  he will now be mindful of their waywardness,
  and will attend to their wrongdoing.^o

¹¹*Yahweh said to me, Do not plead on account of this people, for good*
  things.

¹²*When they fast,*
  I will not be listening to their chant by way of plea.
When they make a whole offering and a grain offering,
  I will not be accepting them.
Because by sword and by hunger and by epidemic
  I am going to make an end of them.^p

a. K. Finsterbusch and N. Jacoby suggest that this jerky form of words (for which cf. 46:1; 47:1; 49:34) introduces a quotation; see "*šr*-Zitateinleitungssätze in Jeremia und 1QM," *VT* 65 (2015): 558–66.

b. LXX, Vg have "drought," for which the First Testament has more precise words, such as *ḥōreb* (50:38) and *ṣiyyâ* (Job 24:19; Jer 2:6 used it to denote desert). Plural *baṣṣārôt* comes only here; etymology suggests shortage or diminution, and the singular noun has such a more general meaning (Pss 9:9[10]; 10:1).

c. LXX has "were emptied"; Syr has "were dilapidated." Both verbs are used of both inanimate and animate subjects (McKane, *Jeremiah*, 1:316).

d. Lit. "they [which might be the gates, though they stand for the people] are dark to the ground."

e. The two lines work a-b-b'-a', with Judah and Jerusalem in the first and last cola. In addition, each line works internally a-b-b'-a' with the verbs on the outside and the nouns on the inside.

f. LXX lacks this colon, which v. 4b largely repeats.

g. An unmarked relative clause.

h. The infinitive absolute in place of a finite verb increases the force of a statement that is already strong (Volz, *Jeremia*, 161) and also suggests an incoherence at the statement's grimness.

i. LXX lacks "like jackals."

j. *'Ăwōnênû 'ānû*: the paronomasia suggests they are fulfilling their proper role. While *'ānâ* I usually means "answer," in many occurrences there is nothing for the speaker to be answering; in such cases it denotes a solemn attesting.

k. In effect "although," but it is doubtful whether *kî* should ever be translated thus. LXX, Vg have "because," which is theologically profound (see the commentary).

l. LXX implies *nirdām* "asleep" for MT's *hapax legomenon nidhām*—on which see *HALOT, DCH*.

m. MT has a section marker here. The reverse word order and asyndeton suggest that the previous clauses are subordinate to this final verb.

n. The asyndeton and reverse word order again suggest that this colon is subordinate to the first. The word order tempts LXX and Vg to see "their feet" as the object of the first verb. It would then mean "let wander," making good sense, but it would require *hiphil*, not *qal*.

o. The tricolon in v. 10 is identical with Hos 8:13b; LXX lacks the last colon. MT has a marker here.

p. MT has a section marker here.

Verse 1 creates some suspense because there is no message from Yahweh in vv. 2–6, nor in vv. 7–9; strictly, it comes only in vv. 10–12. The introduction in fact leads into "a poem of great compactness and intensity" in vv. 2–6,[318] describing the bleak and hopeless nature of the experience of drought. Unannounced, the poem leads into the people's explicit prayer in vv. 7–9, then

---

318. Holladay, *Commentary on Jeremiah*, 1:423. Y. Gitay contrasts it with Joel's more prosaic portrait of such a natural crisis: see "Rhetorical Criticism and the Prophetic Discourse," in *Persuasive Artistry: Studies in New Testament Rhetoric in Honor of George A. Kennedy*, ed. D. F. Watson, JSNTSup 50 (Sheffield: Sheffield Academic, 1991), 13–24.

into Yahweh's response in vv. 10–12. The section thus begins by hinting at the form of a liturgy of the kind that people might have used during a fast (such as the one referenced in 36:6) or in the context of famine (44:18; 52:6). But Yahweh's response turns it upside down. It becomes a kind of "counter-liturgy."[319] Thus part 2c of the scroll begins like parts 2a and b: by raising a question about the relationship between Yahweh and Judah. They may think that prayer makes a difference. Yahweh says, "Not necessarily."

The introduction announcing a message from Yahweh might make one infer that vv. 2–6 are a prophetic vision concerning something to come[320] or that *Yahweh's message* is a holistic expression covering the totality of Yahweh's communication, which interacts with what his people say (even the prayer that Yahweh rejects thus becomes part of his message).[321] The pathos of the description in vv. 2–6 does suggest an empathy and sense of grief on Yahweh's part that people have to go through what he makes them go through.[322] It's not explicitly a prayer; not only is the speaker not specified, but neither is any addressee, and Yahweh is not mentioned.[323] The verbs are *qatal* (the *qatal* verbs continue into v. 7 and v. 10), a quasi-stative usage describing "actions which are tantamount to states in that they occur in non-specific, i.e., typical or recurrent situations."[324] Whereas one might have expected such a poem to use a mournful rhythm (see 12:7–11a), actually its rhythm is quite uneven within the usual constraints (2-2, 2-3, 4-4, 3-4, 3-4, 2-2, 4-4, 3-3, 2-2). Perhaps that disorder itself gives expression to the disorder of the community's experience.

v. 1	Introduction
vv. 2–6	A description of people and animals dealing with the drought (four single bicola, two linked bicola, then three more single bicola)
vv. 7–9	A prayer (two pairs of bicola linked by enjambment, then two self-contained bicola)
vv. 10–12	Yahweh's response (an introduction followed by a bicolon and a tricolon, then another introduction followed by three bicola)

319. Holladay, *Commentary on Jeremiah*, 1:425. M. J. Boda suggests it marks a point in the transition from the lament form represented in the Psalter and the penitential prayer of the Second Temple period ("From Complaint to Contrition: Peering through the Liturgical Window of Jer 14,1–15,4," *ZAW* 113 [2001]: 186–97).

320. So Calvin, *Jeremiah*, 2:212.

321. Cf. Weiser, *Jeremia*, 129.

322. Fretheim, *Jeremiah*, 218.

323. W. A. M. Beuken and H. W. M. van Grol, "Jeremiah 14,1–15,9," in Bogaert, *Livre de Jérémie*, 313–14.

324. DG 57c.

1 The heading follows the pattern of the ones in 7:1; 11:1; 18:1; 21:1; 25:1, which mark transition points in the Jeremiah scroll. This example is distinctive in going on to state the subject, *in the matter of the dearths*. In this respect, it corresponds more closely to 46:1; 47:1; 49:34, with which it also shares an idiomatic quirk (see the translation note). The rare word *dearths* covers the drought that is the subject of 14:2–9 but also the other deprivations that Jer 14–17 refers to; the word recurs in 17:8. As was the case in 13:18, the "lack of an external referent in the section is an important point in its interpretation."[325] Its comment about understanding dearths and dealing with them relates not just to one situation. It needs taking into account on other occasions when the people of God experience drought, attack, or epidemic—and pray about it.

2 We know about the prospect of the earth mourning (4:28) and perhaps about the actuality (12:11). But mourning is more obviously a human activity, and here *Judah mourns*. Why? We do not discover immediately; Jeremiah simply restates the point: *Her gateways—they fade away*. The gates of a town or of a family's homestead refer by synecdoche to the town or homestead itself (e.g., Deut 5:14), and in turn the town or homestead refers to the people who live there. It is they who are fading away. Why? The next line simply restates the point again: *People are in darkness on the ground*. Darkness suggests the gloom of mourning (4:28; 8:21) in their faces and (as a metaphor for actual bereavement) in their dress. Literally, they are dark "to the ground"; in their grief they sink down and sit on the ground as one does when mourning. And *Jerusalem's shout goes up*, as it would in celebration on other occasions (Isa 42:11), but on this occasion it is an expression of grief (cf. Jer 46:12; Ps 144:14). But why?

3 The answer comes with a leap from the undefined to a concrete picture that omits any generalization. If there's a crisis in a community, the *lords*, the people with status and resources, will find ways to get by. But on this occasion, they have to *send their kids for water*, which suggests that their cisterns (on which Jeremiah has not been complimentary; see 2:13), in addition to their wells, are empty. Even the important people are getting desperate. "The heads of great families have sent their servants to scour the countryside" in search of water.[326] So the boys *come to the ditches*, perhaps the ditches dug to irrigate fields or terraces, and even there they *don't find water* and *they return, their containers empty*. No wonder *they are shamed and humiliated* when they get home. They have failed in their basic and vital task. *They cover their head*, rather than baring them as Westerners traditionally would, as another sign of grief (2 Sam 15:30; Est 6:12; it's almost the only way the verb *ḥāpâ qal* is used).

---

325. R. P. Carroll, *Jeremiah*, OTL, 308.
326. McKane, *Jeremiah*, 1:317–18.

4 Such is the problem in town or village. In the farmland, things are arguably more serious. If *the earth is broken up because there has been no rain on the ground,* people can't plow or sow. There will therefore be no vegetation for the animals, the barley and grain won't grow, and the fruit trees will wither. So *farmhands are shamed,* too, because they won't be able to produce what their bosses expect or to provide for their families or to take produce into the town to provide for its needs.

5–6 Once again the scene broadens. *Even the hind in the open country,* which is not where the hind would normally be, *gives birth but* against all the instincts of motherhood *abandons* its offspring *because there's no grass.* It can't look after itself, let alone them. Similarly, *the wild donkeys stand on the bare heights* wondering when there will be rain; *they pant after wind,* not searching for the whiff of a mate (2:24) but wondering if there is a hint of rain in the air, *like jackals* on the lookout for prey, or panting like dogs—not what one expects of donkeys.[327] But *their eyes fail*: they go blind, Jeremiah declares in the hyperbole that also comes in the Psalms in connection with human beings looking for God to act (e.g., Ps 69:3[4]). *There's no vegetation* and they have worn out their sight searching for it. There is no water (v. 3) because there is no rain (v. 4) and therefore no grass (v. 5) and no vegetation (v. 6).

7 Readers are left to work out that what follows is the prayer that Jeremiah imagines Judah praying in such circumstances. As the prayer puts it, Judah is like someone standing before the elders at the town gateway. Someone has an accusation—or rather accusations—to bring. Actually, it's not a person; it's the deeds themselves, the *wayward acts,* the deliberate straying onto other paths (5:25; 11:10; 33:8) that will do the testifying against Judah. The offenses are a matter of public record. There's no argument to be had. Yet the prayer begins with more than one irony. First, Jeremiah would surely regard the *if* in *if our wayward acts aver against us* as laughable if it were not tragic. Second, as far as one can imagine from things we have read, Jeremiah has no conviction that people would be praying this prayer; they would be on their way to the shrine to talk to the Master about the situation. And third, if they did pray it, he would not be able to imagine that they meant it. Yet fourth, the prayer is based on sound theology: *Yahweh, act, for the sake of your name,* which can suggest for the sake of your reputation (and this argument is a good one)[328] but also because of who you are (a more profound argument, and the one Jeremiah will shortly imply that people are using). Jeremiah goes on to have the people taking up one of his distinctive expressions: the *wayward acts* have been *our turnings* (2:19; 3:22), which indeed *are many.* It is a concrete indication that the prayer is one Jeremiah is devising for them rather than

327. Allen, *Jeremiah,* 169.
328. Cf. Rashi, in MG.

one of theirs that he is quoting. He expands their supposed confession into a trinity by having them also say *we have done wrong in relation to you* (ḥāṭā', the pseudo-acknowledgment in 3:25; 8:14 that will recur in 14:20; but contrast 2:35; 16:10). If vv. 2–6 are a quasi-protest psalm, then v. 7 deconstructs its logic. In a protest psalm, one pleads with Yahweh on the basis of not having acted in a way that makes it appropriate for Yahweh to bring calamity. This confession implies that it is quite appropriate for Yahweh to bring calamity.

8 The people spell out the implications of *for the sake of your name*: it is indeed not because they are committed to him (as people claim in a protest psalm) but because Yahweh is the *hope of Israel* (*miqwēh*, another distinctive Jeremiah word; see 17:13; 50:7). The *hope* may be subjective—he is the one in whom Israel hopes. But the parallelism suggests it is at least as much objective—he is the hope-worthy one, the one who fulfills hopes (LXX has "endurance") in that he is Israel's *deliverer in time of distress*. He has proved himself to be so in the past. So notwithstanding their waywardness, *why* now *should you become like an alien in the country, like a traveler turning aside to stay the night*, like a stranger who has no obligations to this country that he is just passing through and doesn't care about?[329]

9 More pointedly, is there a problem about your capacity to act as well as your motivation? *Why should you become like someone at a loss*, helpless or distracted? Yahweh is *like a strong man* (a *gibbôr*; cf. 32:18). The word commonly denotes a warrior, so it is pointed to describe this warrior as one *who cannot deliver*, especially after the earlier reference to *deliverance*. Perhaps Jeremiah imagines Judah meaning in v. 8 not that Yahweh has been its deliverance in the past but only that it hoped he would be its deliverance. Anyway, he is not fulfilling that hope. But the prayer closes with a statement of faith and hope that denies such an implication. *You are in our midst, Yahweh*—you are not just a casual passerby or a foreigner with big eyes that cannot see.[330] *Your name has been proclaimed over us*; we belong to you, like the temple (7:10, 11, 14, 30—though the link with Yahweh's comment about the temple might turn out to be unfortunate) or the city (25:29—that parallel might also turn out to be unfortunate). So *don't drop us* (*nûaḥ hiphil*). Don't just put us down and leave us there.

10 How could Yahweh resist such a prayer, given that he is one who answers prayer? "God's response introduced by the messenger formula does not correspond to expectations": instead of a declaration of forgiveness there is a declaration of judgment.[331] When Joel 2:12–17 has people praying this

---

329. Cf. Qimchi, in MG.

330. A saying in Côte d'Ivoire; see I. Coulibaly, "Jeremiah," in *Africa Bible Commentary*, ed. T. Adeyemo (Nairobi: Word Alive, 2006), 892.

331. Fischer, *Jeremia*, 1:479.

way, they get a positive response,[332] but Yahweh can resist this prayer with ease. He can see through it. They said *you . . . you . . . you.* He says, with the recurrent pejorative implication, *this people* (see, e.g., 5:23). The pejorative tone derives from the fact that *truly, they like to drift.* Whereas going astray suggests deliberately leaving the right path, drifting suggests wandering aimlessly and inconsistently. "In the sacred Scriptures, the feet of sinners are always moving."[333] The people have spoken with apparent purposeful intent, but Yahweh doesn't believe them. They are not suddenly starting to become focused and disciplined. *They have not held back their feet.* Not only will he therefore not accept their sacrifices (v. 12), he *does not accept them*— the people themselves. It is the only clear example of Yahweh ever saying he does not accept his people.[334] He is not going to forget their wayward acts, turnings, and wrongdoing (v. 7). On the contrary, *he will now* (that word is somewhat worrying) *be mindful of their waywardness.* And as usual, keeping something in mind means doing something about it: he will *attend to their wrongdoing.*

11 Yahweh has something else to say to Jeremiah. Given the Jeremianic language, it looks as if Jeremiah composed the previous prayer. Was he in some sense praying for the people? Anyway, Yahweh repeats the bidding *do not plead on behalf of this people* (7:16; 11:14). "The covenantal situation is so deteriorated that serious conversation between Yahweh and Judah is not possible. Yahweh withdraws from the conversation, for there is nothing more to talk about."[335] Might Yahweh also imply that he needs Jeremiah not to pray because he may find it hard to resist him? The bidding here adds *for good things*, a worrying specification. The people's wrongdoing is still withholding good things from them (5:25; 8:15). They are living in a time when prayer is impossible, a time of "unheil,"[336] non-salvation, disaster. Has nothing changed since the apparent move within Amos 7:1–8:6 from when Amos feels free to pray and then does not?[337] There is nowhere in the Bible that the imploring calling out to God is so fruitless and falls on such deaf ears.[338]

12 There is a further "on the contrary." As well as praying, people may *fast* and may *make a whole offering and a grain offering.* Both are costly actions—going without food and offering God the kind of sacrifice in which the entirety of the animal goes up to him, accompanied by the appropriate

332. D. R. Jones, *Jeremiah*, 205.

333. Jerome, *Jeremiah*, 90.

334. The equivalent words in Hos 8:13 may refer to them or may refer to their sacrifices.

335. Brueggemann, *Jeremiah 1–25*, 130.

336. W. H. Schmidt, *Jeremia*, 1:266.

337. See A. Schart, "The Book of Jeremiah and the Visons of Amos," *RevExp* 101 (2004): 277; more broadly, see Lalleman-de Winkel, *Jeremiah in Prophetic Tradition*, 209–33.

338. Fischer, *Jeremia*, 1:490.

grain offering (see Lev 1–2), as opposed to fellowship sacrifices in which the offerer shares when people join in a communion meal. But Yahweh *won't be listening to their chant* with which they accompany their fast. He *will not be accepting them*—the people or the sacrifices. These heartfelt, sincere, and sacrificial actions count for nothing when they are unaccompanied by a change in other aspects of life—for example, by giving up the inclination to hedge their bets by also seeking the Master's help. While Jeremiah does not suggest there is anything insincere about the people's turning to Yahweh, there is an unacceptable inconsistency or double-think about it. Far from accepting them, therefore, Yahweh has a threat in mind that makes more specific the threat in v. 10. To *sword* and *hunger* (see 5:12) he now adds *epidemic*; this unholy trinity will recur (e.g., 21:9; 27:8). They are the three great killers in war; it is entirely plausible that they would *make an end of* a people. Yahweh declares the intention to do so by means of them (cf. 9:16[15]), though of course he actually will not, even though the people do not turn.

b. The Prophets (14:13–18)

[13]*I said, Oh, Lord Yahweh, there, the prophets are saying to them, You will not see sword, and hunger—it will not happen to you, because things being truly well is what I will give you in this place.*[a]

[14]*Yahweh said to me: Deceit is what the prophets are prophesying in my name—I did not send them, I did not order them, I did not speak to them. A deceitful vision, divination that is vacuity, duplicity from their mind is what they are prophesying away to you.*[b] [15]*Therefore, Yahweh has said this about the prophets who are prophesying in my name when I did not send them and are saying, Sword and hunger—they will not happen in this country: With sword and with hunger those prophets will come to an end.* [16]*And the people that they are prophesying to will have been thrown*[c] *into the streets of Jerusalem in the face of the hunger and the sword, and there will be no one to bury those people—them, their wives, their sons, and their daughters. I will pour out their direness upon them.*

[17]*So you will speak this message to them:*

May my eyes run down with tears,[d]
  night and day, and may they not stop.
Because with a great shattering she has shattered,
  the young girl,[e] *my dear people,*
  with a very painful wound.[f]

¹⁸*If I were to go out to the open country,*
* there, people run through by a sword.*
If I were to come into the city,
* there, people sick with hunger.* ᵍ
Because both priest and prophet—
* they have roamed*ʰ *the country*
* but have not acknowledged it.* ⁱ

a. MT has a section marker here.

b. The *you* is plural. MT has a section marker here.

c. Lit. "will be [there] having been thrown."

d. LXX has Yahweh bidding Jeremiah to exhort the people to cry, which is more predictable in the context; Aq corresponds to MT.

e. See the translation note on 18:13.

f. The tricolon follows an a-b-b'-a' order, with the parallel descriptions of the catastrophe in the first and third cola forming a bracket around the whole and enveloping the parallel descriptions of *the young girl, my dear people* (lit. "the girl of the daughter of my people").

g. There is much flexibility about the use of *qatal* and *yiqtol* verbs in *if*-clauses (see, e.g., at length, *TTH* 136–55; briefly, *IBHS* 30.5.4). Here, the context suggests the *qatal* verbs denote a hypothetical present (cf. LXX, Vg, in their way).

h. *Sāḥar* can mean "trade," at least when it is in participial form (e.g., Gen 23:16; 37:28), and this pejorative connotation may hold here.

i. LXX, Vg take this colon as an unmarked relative clause, conforming it to, e.g., 15:14, but the different expression here with the *but* suggests a different meaning (e.g., 2:19, 23). Tg nicely renders "they did not seek": they did not ask any questions about what was going on or what God was doing. MT has a section marker here.

A second exchange follows. Whereas the first led from Judah to Yahweh to Jeremiah, this one simply involves Jeremiah and Yahweh. Jeremiah complains about prophets promising the people that all will be well and that they will not see sword and hunger—which makes a link with vv. 2–12. Yahweh agrees with his complaint and gives him another message confirming that all will not be well.

> vv. 13–16 An exchange between Jeremiah and Yahweh (prose)
> vv. 17–18 A message from Yahweh for Jeremiah to deliver (a bicolon
>   and a tricolon, then two more bicola and another tricolon)

13 Other prophets assure people that *sword* and *hunger* will not come; rather, things will be *truly well* for Judah—they won't even just be regularly well (4:10; 6:14; 8:11). Judah will enjoy *šālôm 'ĕmet*, well-being that can be relied on to continue. *In this place* might denote the temple, but it denoted the country the last time it occurred and it will denote the country the next time (7:20; 16:2), and that meaning fits here. *I will give you* sounds like a quotation from the actual words that these prophets utter in Yahweh's name. "The disputing of the *shalom* theology is a constant theme throughout the book of Jeremiah and a major issue of conflict between Jeremiah and other prophetic groups."[339] But is Jeremiah implying that Yahweh might be a little more sympathetic toward the people? It would be in keeping with the possible implication that Yahweh's prohibition on Jeremiah's praying presupposed that he might be tempted to answer Jeremiah's prayer.

14 What the braggadocious[340] prophets claim to be trustworthy Yahweh declares to be *deceit*. It links with the fact that he did not *send . . . order . . . speak to them.* He describes the status of their message in three ways, doubling each expression and varying the ways they are formulated. Paradoxically, they bring a *vision* all right (he does not deny its reality), but it is a *deceitful* one, more literally a vision of deceit or a vision from deceit (i.e., from the Master?). Second, it is *divination that is vacuity* (lit. "divination and vacuity," a hendiadys suggesting empty divination). Divination involves inferring future events from the observation of the stars or other natural phenomena, through which God was believed to be giving revelations. Maybe the double expression *divination that is vacuity* involves a tautology, given that Jeremiah likely views divination as inherently empty; Deut 18:10 simply says it's wrong. And third, their message is a matter of *duplicity* that simply comes *from their mind.* This phrase might also imply a tautology, presupposing that a vision that comes simply from the mind is therefore false. It did not come from their overhearing things that were said in Yahweh's cabinet (see further 23:9–40). At the end of the verse, Yahweh moves from *niphal* (*prophesying*) to *hithpael* (*prophesying away*), which hints at pejorative implications.

15–16 Given that Jeremiah's protest specifically concerns these prophets, Yahweh's response especially concerns them. *With sword and with hunger those prophets will come to an end.* But the people they deceive will share their fate. Yahweh reworks threats made before (see esp. 8:2). To *pour out their direness* neatly leaves ambiguous whether Yahweh refers to their dire behavior (which now receives its reward) or their dire fate (which rewards their behavior), and thus again invites reflection on the link between the two.

17 The subsequent message for the people does not belong with what follows in 14:19–15:9 (the verses "will not pass for a constituent part of a communal lament").[341] Although it facilitates a transition to that further protest-plea-

---

339. W. J. Wessels, "The Blame Game: Prophetic Rhetoric and Ideology in Jeremiah 14:10–16," *OTE* 26 (2013): 869, 876.

340. Mayer, *Commentary*, 378.

341. McKane, *Jeremiah*, 1:331 (though he actually treats them as part of what follows; contrast Bright, *Jeremiah*, 99).

threat sequence, it belongs with what precedes, as MT's section marker at the end of v. 18 recognizes (the mention of prophets along with priests in v. 18 supports the appending to vv. 13–16 to spell out once more the threat in v. 16). Once more, Jeremiah speaks of his tears, with the rhetorical significance of the reference particularly clear: as usual, the reason he talks about his tears is to encourage his hearers to take seriously the reason for his crying (otherwise, the introduction in v. 17a would be inappropriate).[342] On the other hand, it is Yahweh who commissions the tears, and *my people* much more often comes on Yahweh's lips,[343] so there is at least a hint that the grief they express is Yahweh's grief as well as Jeremiah's. The instruction is not simply that he should cry but that he should declare to his people, *May my eyes run down with tears, night and day, and may they not stop.* They need to understand that such prodigious crying will be the only adequate response to the reality he is about to describe. The city whose people he is to address is about to fall to pieces, to collapse, to *shatter*, as he has said before (4:6, 20; 6:1, 14; 8:11, 21; 10:17). Some of these earlier references indicate that Jeremiah shatters as city and people shatter, and his talk of crying here makes the same point. He is not separate from their fate and the reaction to it. But the point about mentioning it is to bring home to them its devastating nature. The city is like a woman struck down by *a very painful wound.* Jeremiah brings home the event's poignancy by describing her with the unparalleled elaborate expression *maiden daughter, my people* (Lam 2:13 is the nearest parallel). Yahweh as quasi-father wants Jeremiah as quasi-father to tell people how he feels about her, again so that they gain a sense of how terrible are the events that he threatens.

18 Jeremiah goes on to describe things in more down-to-earth fashion, though no less piercingly, as he asks his hearers to accompany him in their imagination on a tour of the crushed and suffering country that is about to become reality. In *the open country, there*, he points and asks his hearers to look: there are *people run through by a sword* as a result of the enemy army's rampaging. And in *the city, there*, he points again, are *people sick with hunger*, as happens when there are invasion and siege. Finally, to get back to the link with what preceded, the problem is that at present *both priest and prophet—they have roamed the country but have not acknowledged it.* "Something is happening here but you don't know what it is, do you, Mr. Jones" (Bob Dylan). "The religious establishment is bankrupt."[344]

---

342. Cf. McKane, *Jeremiah*, 1:329.

343. P. D. Miller, "Jeremiah," on v. 17.

344. M. Kessler, "From Drought to Exile: A Morphological Study of Jer. 14:1–15:4," in *Society of Biblical Literature Seminar Papers 1972*, ed. L. C. McGaughy (Missoula, MT: Society of Biblical Literature, 1972), 2:511, quoted in Allen, *Jeremiah*, 174.

c. The Wound and the Threat (14:19–15:9)

¹⁹*Have you actually rejected^a Judah,*
*   or Zion—has your spirit loathed her?*^b
Why have you struck us down
*   and we have no healing?*
Hoping for things to be well, but no good,
*   and for a time of healing, but there, terror.*^c

²⁰*We acknowledge our faithlessness, Yahweh,*
*   the waywardness of our ancestors.*
Because we have done wrong in relation to you,
*   ²¹don't disown us, for the sake of your name.*
Don't humiliate^d your honored throne,
*   be mindful, don't violate^e your pledge with us.*
²²Among the nations' empty things are there ones who make it rain,
*   or do the heavens—do they give downpours?*^f
You're the one, aren't you, Yahweh our God,^g
*   and we hope in you, because you—you made all these things.*^h

^{15:1}*But Yahweh said to me, If Moses and Samuel*ⁱ *were to stand before me, my spirit would not be directed toward this people*^j*—send them off from before my face, so that they go away.* ²*And when they say to you, "Where shall we go away to," you're to say to them, Yahweh has said this:*

People who are for death, to death,
*   people who are for sword, to sword,*
People who are for hunger, to hunger,
*   people who are for captivity, to captivity.*

³*And I will appoint over them four kin groups (Yahweh's affirmation):*

Sword to slay,
*   dogs to drag away,*^k
Birds of the heavens and animals of the earth
*   to eat and devastate.*^l

⁴*I will make them into something horrifying to all earth's kingdoms on account of Manasseh ben Hezekiah King of Judah, on account of what he did in Jerusalem.*^m

⁵*Because who will pity you, Jerusalem,*
*   who will bemoan you?*

Who will turn aside to ask[n]
　　about whether things are well for you?
[6]*You yourself have deserted me (Yahweh's affirmation)—*
　　you go backward.
So I'm extending my hand against you and devastating you—
　　I've got weary of relenting.[o]
[7]*I'm winnowing them with a winnower*
　　in the country's gateways.
I'm making childless, I'm wiping out my people,
　　on account of their paths from which they have not turned.[p]
[8]*Its widows are becoming more numerous for me*
　　than the sand of the seas.
I'm bringing for them, upon a youth's mother,[q]
　　a destroyer at midday.
I'm making fall upon them, suddenly,
　　shock[r] *and terror.*
[9]*One who bore seven fades away,*
　　she breathes out her life.
Her sun is setting while it's still daytime—
　　she is shamed and dismayed.
And the remainder of them I will give to the sword
　　before their enemies (Yahweh's affirmation).[s]

a. The infinitive precedes the finite verb, underlining the factuality of the action; the phrase recurs in the last line of Lamentations (5:22).

b. The line works a-b-b'-a', with place names juxtaposed at the center and elaborate verbal expressions on either side.

c. The line repeats from 8:15, with the addition of a *waw* at the beginning of the second colon; see the translation note and commentary on 8:15.

d. With BDB, I construe *tənabbēl* as *piel* from *nābēl* ("be foolish"), but there are several roots *nbl* of which readers may be reminded: *DCH*'s other three roots denote "wither/crumble," "be sacrilegious," and "act ignominiously."

e. See the translation note on 11:10.

f. On *rəbîbîm*, see the translation note on 3:3.

g. On this type of noun clause, see *IBHS* 16.3.3c; DG 1b; *TTH* 200; GKC 141h.

h. MT has a unit marker here.

i. Codex Alexandrinus of the Septuagint nicely adds "Aaron" (see Ps 99:6).

j. For the meaning of *'el*, cf. BDB, 40. *IBHS* 11.2.2 renders, "I have no heart for this people."

k. LXX, Vg "tear" is a loose translation.

l. There is nice poetic variation in the way the two lines work; it would have been easy to match the second bicolon to the first by saying "the birds of the heavens to eat and the animals of the earth to devastate."

m. Tg's explanation is that they did not repent like Manasseh (see 2 Chr 33:10–19).

n. The verses' 3-2 rhythm links *lišə'ōl* with the first colon and could encourage people to understand this word to mean "to Sheol," the place for which Jerusalem is bound.

o. LXX implies *hanniḥām* (*hiphil* from *nûaḥ*, "of leaving them alone, letting them lie") for MT *hinnāḥēm*, which makes for a nice link with 14:9 (Holladay, *Commentary on Jeremiah*, 1:421), though not a link that LXX makes with its translation.

p. An unmarked relative clause (Volz, *Jeremia*, 170).

q. After 587, readers might understand this colon to denote bringing upon a mother (Jerusalem) a youth (Nebuchadrezzar); see Blayney, *Jeremiah*, 71, 298.

r. Not the *'îr* meaning town (Vg, Aq, Sym) but a homonym (LXX; BDB, 735); the two nouns are thus a hendiadys: "terrifying shock" (Blayney, *Jeremiah*, 299).

s. MT has a section marker here.

Once again, Jeremiah invites people to imagine making a protest to Yahweh about his treatment of them, confessing their wrongdoing and pleading with him to stay in relationship with them, then hearing him declare that he will not listen to their prayers and is set on bringing even more devastating calamity. Maybe that exercise in imagination will push them into a proper turning. After 587, the section would offer to help people reflect on the reality that had partially fulfilled the threats and push them toward responding, to forestall a more thoroughgoing fulfillment. In this connection, a feature of the section is the variety of assumptions concerning Judah's responsibility for its policies and its destiny. It thus offers resources for reflection on the complex question concerning whether and how far people are responsible for the judgment that comes upon them and whether and how far they share in responsibility with past generations, even if (or perhaps precisely because) "laments cannot be pressed for their theological precision" (e.g., Ps 44:23[24]).[345] The section may be able to do so as a result of its bringing together material of diverse origins, though that possibility encourages readers to think about the interrelationship of the insights rather than excusing them from that reflection. It is an important reflection in connection with Britain's attitude to its former empire and to Brits whose background lies in countries within that empire, as well as for attitudes in the United States to the position of Native Americans and African Americans.

- Jeremiah portrays Judahites identifying with their ancestors in acknowledging waywardness (14:20). The nation is a corporate entity, a corporate reality. The present generation is entitled to be proud of the nation of which it is part, even though it played no part in making it what it is. Is there also a converse: "the corporate guilt of the nation accumulated through the generations"?[346] The third

345. Fretheim, *Jeremiah*, 225.
346. Bright, *Jeremiah*, 102.

and fourth generations benefit from the promises that were made to their ancestors and not to them (7:7, 14; 11:5; 16:15; 23:39; 24:10; 25:5; 30:3; 31:32; 32:22; 34:13). Does Yahweh also trouble the descendants for the wrongdoings of their ancestors, to the third and fourth generation?[347]

- Specifically, Yahweh will bring calamity to Judah *on account of Manasseh ben Hezekiah King of Judah, on account of what he did in Jerusalem* (15:4). The nuance implied by this statement is that the people as a whole pays a price for the actions of its leaders. While Westerners can hardly complain about this reality because we elect our leaders, Judahites might have done so since they did not. But a people and its leaders are bound up together whether or not people choose their leaders. They enjoy blessings through this relationship, and they experience troubles. The judgment that the analyses of Jeremiah himself are "altogether more profound" than those in 15:4[348] risks surrendering the insights expressed in the latter.
- The implication need not be that Yahweh will punish the second, third, and fourth generations irrespective of the nature of their own lives. It is this gloomy way of excusing oneself from responsibility for one's destiny that Jeremiah elsewhere outlaws (31:29). The confession Jeremiah puts on people's lips (14:20) has them identify their own faithlessness and waywardness with that of their parents. And the *because* that may be an addition in 15:5 safeguards any claim that the statement in 15:4 is unfair. *You yourself have deserted me*; that is why *I'm extending my hand against you* (15:6).
- Conversely, Lev 26:40–42 envisages that "they will confess their waywardness and their ancestors' waywardness in their trespass that they committed against me." Then "if by chance their foreskinned mind bows down and then they make amends for their waywardness, I will be mindful of my pledge with Jacob, and also my pledge with Isaac, and also my pledge with Abraham." Neither Jeremiah nor other parts of the First Testament could imagine that Israel might engage in serious turning and Yahweh might still insist on punishing them for their ancestors' wrongdoing.
- But an implication of 14:20 is that the ancestors' wrongdoings were so deeply ingrained that the children, grandchildren, and great-

---

347. D. R. Jones, *Jeremiah*, 212–13.

348. D. R. Jones, *Jeremiah*, 216; he sees this verse as a "gloss" reflecting a "Deuteronomistic judgment."

grandchildren never managed to throw them off.[349] And an implication of 15:4 is that the actions of one generation of leadership may be so far-reaching that subsequent generations of leadership may be unable to reverse them—as the Josiah story implies. "The boat was set to go over the falls a century earlier, and nothing that Israel, or its religious leaders (including Jeremiah) accomplished could finally do anything about such an eventuality."[350] Yet it's never over until it's over, and while this reality prompts reflection and understanding after 587, in the years leading up to that moment people are challenged to assume that their fate is not fixed and to act accordingly.

This sequence constitutes "a more vehement rerun" of 14:2–18,[351] with the balance between the elements putting less emphasis on the people's protest and plea and more on Yahweh's threat.

14:19	Judah's protest (three bicola, implicitly reacting to 14:17–18)
14:20–22	Judah's plea (five bicola—a similar length and dynamic to 14:7–9)
15:1–9	Yahweh's threat
vv. 1–4	(a prose framework around two linked pairs of bicola)
vv. 5–9	(twelve bicola; after the first, every line has a two-beat second colon)

Before their incorporation into this section, 14:19–22 might have already been one unit, and 15:1–4 and 5–9 look like two originally separate ones.[352]

14:19 Jeremiah again articulates Judah's protest, perhaps in light of events such as those of 597 or in light of the threats he has issued or (in the context in which this protest now appears in the scroll) in light of the message in vv. 17–18. The question *Have you actually rejected Judah?* is language Jeremiah himself could use on Judah's behalf, both because he often uses this verb (e.g., 6:30; 7:29) and because he often uses the idiom whereby one combines the infinitival and finite forms of a verb (e.g., 9:4[3]; 13:17). The protest is

349. So Qimchi, in MG.

350. Fretheim, *Jeremiah*, 228.

351. Allen, *Jeremiah*, 173.

352. E.g., Duhm (*Jeremia*, 130–32) sees 14:19–15:4 as of later origin than the material on either side.

Jeremiah's formulation of what Judah might be imagined as saying. On the other hand, the question *Has your spirit loathed Zion?* takes up an expression that is otherwise confined to Lev 26, where it refers both to the possibility of Yahweh's spirit loathing Israel and to the possibility of Israel's spirit loathing Yahweh. It also makes clear that on both sides, loathing does not imply only a feeling of disgust but an action that goes with it: loathing implies pushing away or throwing up. *Rejected* has the same implication: it means discarding, throwing away.[353] The objects of the throwing up/throwing away worryingly cover both nation (or people) and its religious center. Jeremiah has several times referred to Yahweh's striking Israel down and made clear the answer to the question *Why have you struck us down?* (2:30; 5:1–6). Thus, the word *healing* perhaps encouraged the repeating in v. 19b of the plaintive lament from 8:15; the word comes in Jeremiah only in these two places.

20–21 Jeremiah again goes on to articulate the explicit prayer that Judah prays or needs to pray, in language that reads like his formulation even if the substance is Judah's. In that case, he does so even though he knows they do not really understand the significance of their own words, so that the prayer is "a tragic exercise in futility."[354] One novelty is the plea *don't disown us*. The appeal and the familiar argument *for the sake of your name* are developed in the next line. It is developed first in the exhortation *don't humiliate your honored throne*. Yahweh's throne was Jerusalem in 3:17; here, that understanding fits the asking of a question about Zion in v. 19. Acting against the city means acting against his own kingly seat. The appeal is further developed in the positive exhortation to *be mindful* of *your pledge with us* and thus don't *violate* it. The references to throne and pledge compare (in reverse order) with the references to Judah and Zion in v. 19. The verbs carry some irony. On one hand, the people have reason to be worried about Yahweh being mindful (v. 10); and on the other, in light of 11:10, it takes some hutzpah to appeal to Yahweh not to violate his pledge with them. Reading this message in light of Jer 11 would suggest that Jeremiah is referring to the Moses pledge. But he also believes in the David pledge (33:19–22) and the parallelism with Jerusalem as Yahweh's throne points in this direction. Maybe he would see them as different iterations of the same commitment.

22 The confession Jeremiah puts on their lips has similar implications. If only they did ask the question, *among the nations' empty things* (8:19; 10:8) *are there ones who make it rain, or do the heavens—do they give downpours?* The alternative forms of the question suggestively juxtapose the roles and capacities of supernatural forces and of natural forces, as Jeremiah moves elsewhere

---

353. B. A. Levine, "When the God of Israel 'Acts-Out' His Anger: On the Language of Divine Rejection in Biblical Literature," in Kaltner and Stulman, *Inspired Speech*, 111–29.

354. Allen, *Jeremiah*, 174.

between these two ways of articulating the forces that bring calamity to Judah. The heavens can note and respond to events (2:12), but they cannot do anything on their own any more than nations can. While Jeremiah might have in mind astral powers,[355] he does not otherwise use the bare expression "heavens" to refer to them. "Doubtless there is some implanted power in the heavens" yet "the heavens do not of themselves give rain, but at the command of God."[356] Reference to Yahweh as the one who causes rain would be apposite in the context of references to drought, but war, not drought, is the background to this section, and Yahweh's sovereignty in nature and the gift of rain is of general importance every year.[357] *You're the one, aren't you, Yahweh our God.* Thus, *we hope in you, because you made all these things*—the rain and the downpours.

15:1 Once more, how could Yahweh resist this appeal? A declaration of forgiveness and a promise of relief and restoration must surely follow. Actually, Yahweh can again resist with ease. In this context, his reference to *my spirit* suggests a link to what precedes (14:19) and might have suggested the unit's incorporation here. *Moses and Samuel* could *stand before* Yahweh in meetings of his cabinet as participants and be successful as intercessors. Moses did so at Sinai (Exod 32–33; see also Num 14). Samuel did so at Mizpah and committed himself to interceding on an ongoing basis (1 Sam 7:8–9; 12:7–25). The unit more specifically suggests the picture of the people gathering before Yahweh to present their plea, like subjects coming before the king, and of Jeremiah fulfilling his role as their representative, as the mediator between people and King introducing them into his presence. But the King bids him, *send them off from before my face, so that they go away.* The verbs carry the irony of being exodus verbs.[358] If Jeremiah is a prophet like Moses, his Moses-likeness takes an upside-down form. In addition, *send off* and *go away* are the verbs for divorce in Deut 24:1–3 (the first though not the second comes in Jer 3:1).[359]

2–3 Where to? Yahweh's formulation could suggest that different fates are set for different people, though maybe one should not press the point. *Death* is to be most people's destiny. It might come by *sword* or by *hunger*, which often feature as a pair (e.g., 14:13, 15, 16, 18). To complete the two bicola, one might then expect a reference to epidemic (cf. 14:12), but the good news is that some people will be merely taken into *captivity*. In gruesome imagery, Yahweh appends a further formulation. *I will appoint over them four kin groups* of deathly experience; in case readers are inclined to doubt it,

---

355. R. P. Carroll, *Jeremiah*, OTL, 318.
356. Calvin, *Jeremiah*, 2:257; "except at your Word" (Tg).
357. McKane, *Jeremiah*, 1:332.
358. Holladay, *Commentary on Jeremiah*, 1:439–40.
359. Jindo, *Biblical Metaphor Reconsidered*, 115–16.

he offers his recurrent *Yahweh's affirmation*. First, there is again the *sword*, whose role of course is *to slay*, but slaying is not the end of the fate that Juda-hites are invited to look forward to. The second is that in the city, scavenger *dogs* will *drag* people's bodies *away*; it might be preliminary to eating them, but dogs enjoy playing with things, and eating comes in the next line. The third and fourth deathly experiences are ones that will attend to people who fall on the battlefield, scavenger *birds of the heavens and animals of the earth* who will *eat and devastate*.

4 When it happens, *all earth's kingdoms* will be around. The Babylonians will be able to stand for the kingdoms of the earth—they are the imperial power. But they will also be accompanied by the Edomites, the Moabites, the Ammonites, and others. And, says Yahweh, *I will make* the Judahites *into something horrifying* to them all. The extra piece of explanation is that it will happen *on account of Manasseh ben Hezekiah King of Judah, on account of what he did in Jerusalem*. Jeremiah has already had the Judahites acknowledging *the waywardness of our ancestors*. Elsewhere, Manasseh is chief of the guilty. Only Jeremiah refers to *Manasseh ben Hezekiah*; perhaps Hezekiah's positive reputation (cf. 26:18–19) heightens the disparaging of his son.[360] While it is Jeremiah's only mention of Manasseh, the comment fits the explanation for the fall of Jerusalem in 2 Kgs 23:26; 24:3. The last four kings of Judah are his grandchildren and great-grandchildren.

5 There follows another poetic unit that is presumably of separate origin. The *because* now makes a link with the preceding verses, and the question *about whether things are well* makes for a troubling link with 14:19. We know that Yahweh will not pity the people so as to hold back from bringing ca-lamity upon it (13:14); now he adds that there will be no one to *pity you, Jerusalem*, after the calamity. There will be no one to *bemoan you*: the word refers to the physical expression of grief by shaking the head, nodding, and quivering (4:1). No one will care enough to *turn aside to ask about you*. In other contexts, questions about who will do so would imply sympathy or protest. Here they are more like mockery.[361] Yet they also hint at a "divine ambivalence."[362] We need to "understand the words said to Jerusalem with much foreboding," like Jesus's words in Matt 23:37–38.[363]

6 Yahweh goes on to issue another accusation implying an answer to a question that might be raised by v. 4. No, the present generation cannot blame their parents, grandparents, and great-grandparents, even if they have

360. Calvin, *Jeremiah*, 2:270–71.
361. Holladay, *Commentary on Jeremiah*, 1:427.
362. Fretheim, *Jeremiah*, 228.
363. Origen, *Jeremiah*, 130, 131.

been deeply influenced by them.[364] *You yourself have deserted me*, Yahweh says to the city, again adding *Yahweh's affirmation*. That act of desertion lies behind Yahweh's act of desertion (7:29; 12:7). *You go backward*, away from where Yahweh points (7:24). So that's why *I'm extending my hand* in your direction *and devastating you*. The verbs are *qatal*, and I take them to refer to what Yahweh certainly intends (Vg has future-tense verbs; LXX has some past, some future; Tg has past) and translate them as present continuous (see the introduction to 13:18–22, pp. 354–55); there will be other examples of this in the next three verses. But after 587, it would be natural to connect them to what Yahweh had done. Yahweh's extending his hand is often good news (e.g., Exod 6:6), but not this time:[365] I have threatened to act in this way over the centuries and over recent decades and talked much of acting in wrath, but I have rarely done it. I have usually let you carry on kicking me in the teeth (it is the characteristic that makes Jesus an accurate incarnation of the God of Israel). I am now saying that enough is enough. *I've got weary of relenting* (on this word, see the commentary on 4:28).

7 Here are the frightening details. *Winnowing them with a winnower*, a pitchfork, ought to be a positive image; it's designed to achieve something good in getting rid of chaff. To make a related point, Yahweh previously denied that he was merely winnowing (4:11–12). Here, the stress lies on the flailing that the farmer does with his pitchfork. It's going to happen *in the country's gateways*, in each community and family. Thus, *I'm making* my people *childless* (Hebrew has a verb with this meaning as English does not, correlative to a word for "orphan"). *I'm wiping out my people* (cf. 1:10, though here the verb is *piel* as in 12:17). Once again, Yahweh provides his rationale: it will happen *on account of their paths from which they have not turned*. It's Jeremiah's standard accusation, which is also his standard implicit exhortation. Won't you listen, Jerusalem? Yahweh doesn't want to hear words of lament and confession, a turning that is a matter of words. He wants to see some turning that is a matter of paths.

8 As far as death is concerned, it is the men who pay more of the price in war, but it is therefore the women and children who live on as the bereaved. Instead of saying, "I am making its widows numerous," Jeremiah engages a circumlocution:[366] the invasion will mean that *widows are becoming more numerous for me than the sand of the seas*. The circumlocution is followed by an image that is grievous in light of its usual context (e.g., Gen 22:17; Hos 1:10 [2:1]). It implies a reversal of the promise to Israel's ancestors. So *I'm bringing for them, upon a youth's mother, a destroyer at midday*. Midday may suggest

364. Theodoret, *Ermeneia*, PG 81:596.
365. Weiser, *Jeremia*, 135.
366. Lundbom, *Jeremiah 1–20*, 728.

the time when one least expects an attack; for the sons who are involved in the battle, it means their life ends when it should be only half over.[367] For them, the day ends at midday. Either way, it will be as if people are hit by a calamity that no one could have expected: *I'm making fall upon them, suddenly, shock and terror.*

9 Suppose there is a mother with the great blessing of *seven* sons. She hears that all of them have been slain. It will not be surprising that she *fades away*. The recurrence of that word suggests the specific influence and reversal of the reference to seven sons and fading away in 1 Sam 2:5. Indeed, *she breathes out her life.* Her life is over, one way or another. For her, too, *her sun is setting while it's still daytime.* Instead of the pride and honor of being the mother of such an impressive family, *she is shamed and dismayed.* And supposing some people somehow survive, *the remainder of them I will give to the sword before their enemies.* Yes, vv. 5–9 are about "the end of Jerusalem."[368] Yahweh speaks of the execution of judgment, but his words give vv. 7b–9 "an overtone of lament."[369]

d. The Persecutors (15:10–21)

[10]*Alas for me, mother, that you gave birth to me,*
  a man involved in argument
  and a man involved in contention with the entire country.
Though I have not lent and people have not lent to me,
  everyone[a] *is slighting me.*[b]

[11]*Yahweh has said:*[c]

If I am not letting you loose[d] *regarding good things,*
  if I am not making fall upon you[e] *a time of dire things,*[f]
  a time of distress, with the enemy . . .[g]
[12]*Does iron break,*[h]
  iron from the north, and bronze?
[13]*Your resources and your stores I will make into plunder,*
  not for a price, but[i] *for all your wrongdoings and for all your territory.*
[14]*And I will make them pass*[j] *with your enemies*
  through a country you have not known.
Because a fire that has flared through my anger—

---

367. Weiser, *Jeremia,* 135.
368. Weiser, *Jeremia,* 134.
369. Beuken and van Grol. "Jeremiah 14,1–15,9," 320.

against you[k] *it will burn.*[l]

[15]*You yourself have acknowledged, Yahweh—*
    be mindful of me and attend to me,
    and take redress for me from my pursuers.
Do not, through your being long-tempered, take me—
    acknowledge my bearing reviling because of you.
[16]*Your words presented themselves, and I ate them;*
    your message[m] *became to me*
    a joy and the rejoicing of my mind.
Because your name was proclaimed over me,
    Yahweh, the God of Armies.[n]
[17]*I have not sat in the company of revelers and made merry—*
    before your hand I sat alone,
    because you filled me with condemnation.[o]
[18]*Why has my pain become eternal,*
    my wound grave, refusing to heal?
You've actually become[p] *to me like a deceptive thing,*
    water that can't be trusted.[q]

[19]*Therefore Yahweh has said this:*

If you turn and I turn you,
    before me you will stand.[r]
If you give out what is valuable rather than[s] *what is garbage,*
    you will be my very mouth.
Those people will turn to you;
    but you—you will not turn to them.
[20]*I will make you to this people*
    a bronze wall, fortified.
They will do battle against you, but they will not win over you,
    because I will be with you to deliver you, to snatch you away[t] *(Yahweh's*
        affirmation).
[21]*I will snatch you away from the hand of the faithless,*
    release you from the clutch of the terrifying.[u]

a. Lit. "all of it"; see the translation note on 6:13.

b. "Curse" (LXX) is too strong a translation of *qālal*; contrast *'ārûr* in 11:3. MT has a section marker here.

c. For MT *'āmar* (cf. Vg, Sym, Aq, Syr, Tg), LXX suggests *'āmēn* ("truly"), but this reading cannot lead into anything like the MT text that follows, where LXX's paraphrase may indicate that its translators were puzzled by the difficulties. One key question is the identity of the *you* in the following verses. Although in vv. 11–12 *you* could be either Jeremiah or Judah, it must surely be Judah in vv. 13–14 (against, e.g., Holladay, *Commentary on Jeremiah*, 1:455–57), and it is unlikely that the identity of *you* changes without announcement there (against, e.g., Lundbom, *Jeremiah 1–20*, 737); therefore *you* in vv. 11–12 is also Judah (cf. Reventlow, *Liturgie*, 210–28; also R. M. Paterson, "Reinterpretation in the Book of Jeremiah," *JSOT* 28 [1984]: 37–46). The unique brief opening *Yahweh has said* also does not look like an expression to introduce Yahweh's response to Jeremiah.

d. The *qere šērîtikā* look like a form from *šārâ*, which otherwise comes only in Job 37:3, where it means "let loose" (of lightning); cf. BDB. Rashi (in MG) compares Aramaic *šārā'* in Daniel; while it can positively suggest "release," it can also have a negative significance (Dan 5:6). The *ketiv* implies *šârôtikā*, which looks like a form from *šārar*, perhaps a byform of *šārâ* (*HALOT*), perhaps *DCH*'s *šārar* III ("treat with hostility/vex"). Vg, Aq, Tg imply *šē'ērîtikā* ("your remainder"), which generates the possibility that the word comes from the root *šā'ar*, spelled defectively in MT, and it could make good sense (cf. Qimchi, in MG), but a form from the rare *šārâ/šārar* more likely became assimilated to a form from *šā'ar* than vice versa. The assimilation does draw attention to the paronomasia with v. 9.

e. Tg implies, "I will make them get you to pray for them," which makes sense if the *you* is Jeremiah.

f. The two *if*-clauses without a protasis are a form of oath; see the commentary.

g. While the grammatically more straightforward translation would be "making fall upon you at a time of dire things, at a time of trouble, the enemy," this understanding leaves *'et-hā'ōyēb* high and dry at the end of the line. And *pāga'* is used in a variety of ways with *ba* (see BDB); I have taken the *ba* on *ba'ēt* to denote the object each time. For this usage in general, see *DCH*, 2:86; *HALOT*, 105b. LXX, Vg take *'et* as the preposition rather than the object marker.

h. I take *yārōa'* from *rā'a'* II as intransitive, as in 11:16, not as transitive (BDB).

i. LXX lacks *not* and *but*: the loss is indeed a price the people pay—for their wrongdoings.

j. For MT *wahă'abartî* (cf. Vg, Sym), LXX, Tg imply *wahă'abadtî* ("and I will make [you] serve your enemies"; cf. 17:4), which makes good sense.

k. The *you* becomes plural here.

l. MT has a section marker here. Verses 13–14 reappear in a variant form at 17:3–4.

m. The *ketiv* repeats the plural from the previous colon.

n. MT has a section marker here.

o. MT has a section marker here.

p. The infinitive precedes the finite verb, underlining the factuality of the action.

q. MT has a section marker here.

r. Vg has "if you turn, I will turn you, and you will stand before me," but this translation, shortening the protasis, does not fit the position of MT's "and." LXX ("if you turn, and I turn you, and you stand before me, and if you give out") adds an "and" and lengthens the protasis.

s. LXX, Vg translate *min* as "from."

t. LXX omits this second verb, eliminating the repetition.

u. MT has a marker here.

This fourth exchange within 14:1–15:21 starts with a protest by Jeremiah and ends with a robust response by Yahweh. It thus has a confrontational edge, like the exchange in 11:18–12:17, only more so. In 20:17–18, Jeremiah will be even more confrontational, but there will be no response from Yahweh—he lets Jeremiah have the last word. Here, Jeremiah first simply cries out loud about his current experience of persecution, which relates to the threats against Judah that he has to deliver. He then overtly protests to Yahweh about being required to keep delivering these threats that Yahweh never fulfills, which drives Yahweh to an equally strong response combined with a promise of protection that renews the promise at his commission.

This fourth exchange thus pairs with the second in moving between protests from Jeremiah to Yahweh and a response by Yahweh. But it does so in a more complex way that involves Judah so that it also pairs with the first and third exchanges. It is "part of the dialogical or trialogical dispute which illustrates in highly dramatic fashion the triangular relationship between YHWH, his people and their officials, and YHWH's prophet."[370]

vv. 10–18   Jeremiah's protest: his persecution
    v. 10   People's attacks (one tricolon and one bicolon)
    vv. 11–14   An appeal to Yahweh's threat to them (an introduction, a tricolon, and four bicola)
    vv. 15–18   Jeremiah's plea, his claim, and his accusation
       v. 15   the plea: one tricolon and one bicolon
       vv. 16–17   the claim: two tricola flanking one bicolon
       v. 18   the accusation: two bicola
vv. 19–21   Yahweh's response
    v. 19   Jeremiah needs to turn (an introduction and three bicola)
    vv. 20–21   Yahweh will protect (three bicola)

Yahweh's lines to Judah (vv. 11–14) and to Jeremiah (vv. 19–21) follow regular poetic form. Jeremiah's lines (vv. 10, 15–18) come to a similar length, but they are anarchic in a way that matches their content, comprising four tricola and five bicola. The effect is to underscore the tortuous nature of the exchange, with a contrast between Yahweh's relative calmness and the overflowing of Jeremiah's thinking and emotions. As a "prayerful conversation,"[371] it is quite something; Jeremiah's protest suggests "a wholly other world"[372] compared with what preceded. It overlaps with protests in the Psalms, though the comparison also serves to show how they are distinctive, and it compares with the cry of marginalized people in other contexts.[373]

---

370. H. Bezzel, "The Suffering of the Elect: Variations on a Theological Problem in Jer 15:10-21," in Barstad and Kratz, *Prophecy*, 53; he studies its possible development in this connection.

371. Pixley, *Jeremiah*, 53.

372. Weiser, *Jeremia*, 136.

373. See, e.g., K. Jesurathnam, "'Before I Formed You in the Womb of Your Mother': The Decentred World of Jeremiah and Dalits," *Bangalore Theological Forum* 34 (2002): 28–29;

- It begins (v. 10) with no address to Yahweh, like the account of Judah in 14:2–6; it is simply a protest.
- The quotation of Yahweh's words (vv. 11–14) functions a little like the recollection that can buttress a protest in a psalm; it could stand on its own, and the overlap between vv. 13–14 and 17:3–4 may mean that vv. 11–14 combine two originally separate messages that have been inserted between vv. 10, 15–21, which work without them.
- The plea (v. 15) eventually follows, with some suggestion of the three directions in which protests and pleas may work, in relation to "you," "me," and "them."
- The explicit recollection (vv. 16–17) functions like a claim to commitment in a protest psalm, further buttressing the plea.
- The closing question and accusation (v. 18) make for an unusual ending and contrast with statements of trust and hope in many psalms.
- Yahweh's response (vv. 19–21) is not the affirmative one for which a protester hopes, and it thus compares with his responses in 14:10–12, 15–18; 15:1–9; but it is now a response to Jeremiah himself that is confrontational but also open.

10 Rhetorically, Jeremiah addresses his *mother*, with sentiments that parallel those expressed at much greater length in Job 3.[374] One could not quarrel with his self-description. Within a few lines of the beginning of Jer 2 he was talking about Yahweh's *argument* with his people (2:9), and he has been presenting that argument through the scroll so far, though he will also point out that it is in their interests for him to do so (25:31; 50:34; 51:36). He is thus a man of *contention* (*mādôn*), a word that mostly comes in Proverbs. One can imagine people complaining about Jeremiah as an angry young man who indeed stirs up contention (e.g., Prov 15:18; 29:22), and he did protest about the leadership's failure to contend for people's rights (*dîn*, 5:28; 21:12; 22:16). He is caught in the conflict between Yahweh and Judah,[375] and he is arguing and contending with them, and they with him.

There is remarkable consistency between "the man" and "the message." The prophetic image portrays someone who stands opposed to the mainstream of contemporary thought, a "man of conflict" (15:10), for on every

---

Exploring Dalit Liberative Hermeneutics in India and the World (New Delhi: Christian World Imprints, 2015).

374. E. L. Greenstein sees "Jeremiah as an Inspiration to the Poet of Job," in Kaltner and Stulman, *Inspired Speech*, 98–110.

375. D. R. Jones, *Jeremiah*, 220.

level, whether political, societal, or religious—he is in conflict with the dominant opinions of his time.[376]

He is involved in controversy with everyone: priests, prophets, scribes, administration. *The entire country* knows it and talks about it, Jeremiah declares, hyperbolically; this is his reputation, and he does not like it. If he had been engaged in dealings whereby he *lent* to people who were in economic trouble and would want his debt repaid or whereby *people lent* to him because he was in economic trouble and they wanted him to repay, it might have led to conflict—but he hasn't been so engaged. There is no indication that he is talking about wrongful lending, maybe involving charging interest, or about forced foreclosure; but anyway, his claim makes for quite a contrast over against what he sees in the community (e.g., 5:1–5). Perhaps his comment about lending alludes to a proverbial saying,[377] equivalent to Shakespeare's "neither a borrower nor a lender be; for loan oft loses both itself and friend."[378] Yet *everyone*, the entire community, *is slighting me* (qālal piel): they are saying he is someone insignificant and irrelevant, or they are wishing him to be so.

11 Jeremiah here provides the background to that image of him as a man of argument and contention. While this declaration by Yahweh might have been one that Yahweh makes in response to Jeremiah's protest, in the context it looks more like an example of the kind of thing Yahweh has kept getting Jeremiah to say. The threat addresses Judah as "you" (see the translation note). Yahweh uses the form of oath whereby people express the wish that a terrible fate befall themselves if they fail to live up to what the *if*-clause refers to, and he uses the variant on that oath whereby they leave the actual wish unstated and taken for granted, just stating the *if*-clause.[379] A human being might complete the saying with "may God do this to me and may he do more" (e.g., 2 Sam 3:35). The translation thus runs out in an ellipsis, which corresponds to the way the Hebrew works. It also has some symbolic significance because there are questions about the verse's meaning as a whole, particularly its two verbs (see the translation notes). But the general point is clear. Yahweh is reiterating his repeated threat (whose delivery makes Jeremiah a man of contention) that he will bring about calamity on Judah, whose future is not going to be characterized by *good things* (cf. 14:11) but by *dire things* (cf. 11:11, 12, 14, 15, 17) and *distress* (cf. 4:31; 6:24).

---

376. J. Dubbink, "Getting Closer to Jeremiah: The Word of YHWH and the Literary-Theological Person of a Prophet," in Kessler, *Reading Jeremiah*, 26.

377. Duhm, *Jeremia*, 134.

378. Polonius's words in *Hamlet* 1.3.

379. See DG 156; Joüon 165; GKC 149; *IBHS* 40.2.2; the commentary on 22:6.

12 In what follows, there is little problem about the meaning of the words, though their reference is more elusive. The words *iron* and *bronze* recall the commission when Yahweh promised to make Jeremiah *an iron pillar* and *bronze walls over against the entire country* (1:18)—that *entire country* to which Jeremiah referred in v. 10. Continuing the reaffirmation of Yahweh's threat to Judah this way is a reminder, indirectly addressed to Jeremiah, about some facts that Yahweh has guaranteed. *Can iron break*, especially when it is *iron from the north*? Can *bronze* break? While the reference to the north will remind people of the invader from the north,[380] *iron from the north* could suggest a notably strong metal: the iron-mines on the Black Sea were well-known in this connection.[381] Yahweh's point is that Judah is not to make the mistake of thinking that it can defeat Jeremiah or dispose of him. He will not break. Yahweh guarantees it.

13–14 Yahweh backs up his threat to Judah with an anticipation of lines in 17:3–4. Perhaps their original setting was there and they have been brought back here by Yahweh or Jeremiah or Jeremiah's curators to amplify the recollection in vv. 11–12.[382] Talk of *your* (singular) *resources and your stores* suggests Yahweh is not addressing ordinary Judahites, prophets, or even priests, but the king. Jeremiah's many other references to resources commonly refer to the army, and the one to whom the resources belong is the king (e.g., 52:4, 8). Likewise, *stores* would denote the nation's assets overseen by him, which Yahweh also elsewhere warns will end up as *plunder* (20:5). The expression *not for a price* distinguishes this version of Yahweh's words from 17:3–4; it suggests, "I didn't get anything out of it, you know" (cf. Isa 52:3; Ps 44:12[13]). It was purely action undertaken *for all your wrongdoings and for all your territory*—that is, for your wrongdoings throughout your territory, suggesting that the entire country is implicated in the king's wrongdoing. He is its leader. Yahweh often focuses on Jerusalem, but the rest of the country should not think that he has not noticed what is happening elsewhere or that other parts of the country are safe. So Yahweh *will make* these resources and treasures *pass with your enemies through* (MT) or "will make you serve your enemies in" (LXX) *a country you have not known*. Lying behind this threat is not the anger of Jeremiah but the fact that a *fire has flared through my anger*. The words recur from Deut 32:22, which suggests they are being fulfilled here. Thus, *against you it will burn*.

---

380. Allen, *Jeremiah*, 181.
381. Blayney, *Jeremiah*, 299–300, with his reference to Strabo, *Geography* 12.3 (12.549).
382. Cf. G. V. Smith, "The Use of Quotations in Jeremiah xv 11–14," *VT* 29 (1979): 229–31 (though he takes vv. 11–12 as addressed to Jeremiah); see also M. H. Floyd, "Prophetic Complaints about the Fulfillment of Oracles in Habakkuk 1:2–17 and Jeremiah 15:10–18," *JBL* 110 (1991): 397–418.

15 Jeremiah himself starts again, picking up the protest he began in v. 10. Once more, his opening words take up from his commission:[383] *You yourself acknowledged* (cf. 1:5), so you should *be mindful of me* and also *attend to me*, another verb that Yahweh used on that commissioning occasion, though with a different meaning (1:10). *Take redress* (cf. 11:20) would be the concrete expression of mindfulness and attentiveness. Pursue (*rādap*) is a word of general meaning, but in a context such as this one it suggests something like persecution. It suggests people attacking someone when they have no warrant except that they violently oppose the person's convictions and public statements. Jeremiah's persecutors might be the king and his administration or might be people like the Anathoth community. And God's *being long-tempered* is a welcome characteristic when it works our way, but his being long-tempered with these people is a different matter. Jeremiah doesn't want Yahweh to *take* him—as is the case in English, that verb can be used to signify letting someone die or causing them to die (e.g., Gen 5:24; Ezek 33:4). Jeremiah picks up the verb *acknowledge* again: he needs Yahweh to *acknowledge my bearing reviling because of you*. Once more, to *acknowledge* means not merely recognizing something mentally, but taking action in light of what one knows. The same will be true of *reviling*. If reviling were merely words of insult, it might be harmless. But reviling is something that issues in action. While people can't take action against Yahweh, they can take action against his representative, so Jeremiah is worried.

16 Yet again, Jeremiah takes Yahweh and thus takes his readers back to his commission. *I'm putting my words in your mouth*, Yahweh had said (1:9). Yes, *your words presented themselves, and I ate them;*[384] *your message* (more literally, "your word," which thus makes a link with the previous colon) *became a joy to me and the rejoicing of my mind*. It is the only occasion on which he refers to joy in connection with being a prophet;[385] indeed, all his references to joy and rejoicing relate to their being taken away (7:34; 16:9; 25:10) until 33:11. "How could the word of God be so sweet and pleasant to the Prophet, when yet it was so full of bitterness?" But he knew they were

---

383. J. R. Lundbom draws some historical inferences from the link: see "Jeremiah 15,15–21 and the Call of Jeremiah," *SJOT* 9 (1995): 143–55.

384. W. L. Holladay suggests not only that Ezek 2:8–3:3 found its inspiration in these words but that Jeremiah uttered them to Ezekiel personally ("Had Ezekiel Known Jeremiah Personally?," *CBQ* 63 [2001]: 31–34). Elsewhere, Holladay wonders about Jeremiah's relationship with other prophets ("Jeremiah in the Midst of Prophetic Words," in *Geistes-Gegenwart: Vom Lesen, Denken und Sagen des Glaubens. Festschrift für Peter Hofer, Franz Hubmann und Hanjo Sauer*, ed. C. Niemand, F. Reisinger, and F. Gruber [Frankfurt: Lang, 2009], 67–80).

385. J. Bright, "A Prophet's Lament and Its Answer," *Int* 28 (1974): 65; cf. Lundbom, *Jeremiah 1–20*, 743.

Yahweh's words and Yahweh's message.[386] He was therefore okay about their negative implications, which were what led to the reviling. His acceptance of them also linked with the fact that *your name was proclaimed over me*, as it had been proclaimed over the temple and the people (7:10, 11, 14, 30; 14:9). It meant Yahweh owned him. Yahweh was his master. Therefore, he identified with his master's words. But also, therefore, Yahweh would protect him.

17 Jeremiah's commission has had implications for his way of life: *I have not sat in the company of revelers and made merry*. Reveling and merrymaking could suggest ordinary life occasions (cf. 16:2), or in this context festival celebrations. One day they will be appropriate again (30:19; 31:4), but not now. Jeremiah will not join in Thanksgiving or Christmas festivities: *Before your hand I sat alone, because you filled me with condemnation* (see the commentary on 10:10). He could not be involved in such events and keep quiet about the clash between what they presupposed and what he knew. Yahweh's hand can make prophets move or speak (1 Kgs 18:46; 2 Kgs 3:15) or it can hold them down (Isa 8:11), as happens to ordinary people (Pss 32:4; 39:10[11]).[387] So Jeremiah was filled with both joy (v. 16) and fury. No wonder he was torn apart. He may have appeared mentally ill.[388]

18 And there is no ceasing, because he has to keep declaring the coming of a monumental calamity that never arrives (perhaps a plaint like this one must antedate 597). We know from his messages that the city's fall is perpetually a present reality in his mind. He identifies with the city in this virtual-reality present suffering. He is stuck in a chronological limbo and feels now the *pain* that is *eternal* of a *wound* that is *refusing to heal* (6:7; 8:21–22; 14:17); *grave* is the word he will use later, of Judah's wound (30:12, 15). The dynamics of this reality reflect the divine long-temperedness of which v. 15 spoke. That long-temperedness is good news for Judah. But for Jeremiah, who has to keep declaring the imminence of a catastrophe that never comes, it means *you've actually become to me like a deceptive thing, water that cannot be trusted*. A spring like Gihon flows all year. It can be relied on. But from time to time, a spring that people think is reliable stops flowing. It deceives people into trusting its supply and lets them down. Such is Jeremiah's image for Yahweh's

---

386. Calvin, *Jeremiah*, 2:298. C. Bultmann views it as one indication that we should take greater account of the fact that Jeremiah was a poet as much as a prophet: see "A Prophet in Desperation? The Confessions of Jeremiah," in *The Elusive Prophet: The Prophet as a Historical Person, Literary Character and Anonymous Artist*, ed. J. C. de Moor, OTS 45 (Leiden: Brill, 2001), 83–93.

387. Allen, *Jeremiah*, 183.

388. P. R. Davies, "Reading Jeremiah," in *The One Who Reads May Run: Essays in Honour of Edgar W. Conrad*, ed. R. Boer, M. Carden, and J. Kelso, LHBOTS 553 (London: T&T Clark, 2012), 7.

deceptive unreliability in relation to him. Job said his friends were deceitful and unreliable that way (Job 6:14–21). Jeremiah says God is.

19 Now Yahweh responds. Once again, Jeremiah indicates how the protest-response relationship of prayer cannot be assumed to involve a simply positive and reassuring comeback from Yahweh. Lament "does not provide a formula that guarantees God's favorable response."[389] The four occurrences of *turn* associate the response with Yahweh's regular diction in Jeremiah, especially in 3:1–4:2. *If you turn* is the expression Yahweh used in addressing Israel in 4:2. The implication is that Jeremiah is in the same position as Israel. He has turned away from Yahweh, and he needs to turn back. There is another parallel, perhaps even more uncomfortable. In 3:1–4:2, Yahweh opened up the question whether he would have Israel back and never explicitly said that he would. Here, too, *I turn you* is the second part of the *if*-clause. In both contexts, Yahweh makes it impossible for the other partner (Israel or Jeremiah) to take anything for granted. The relationship between God and people or God and prophet is not contractual. Neither Israel nor Jeremiah can turn to Yahweh on the basis of simply knowing that they will be accepted. They have to turn because it is the right thing. The situation parallels that between two human beings when someone who has done wrong acknowledges their wrongdoing to the other party and waits anxiously to see what the reaction will be. Of course there is a sense in which people can be sure they will be accepted by Yahweh, because he cannot avoid being the kind of God he is. There is a sense in which he is not free: he is not free to be other than himself. Yet in both Jer 3 and 15, the rhetoric forbids people from taking Yahweh's acceptance for granted. There is an "if " on Yahweh's side as well as on theirs. On this occasion, the priority of Jeremiah's move and the secondary nature of Yahweh's contrast with the situation in 1:8.[390] But if Yahweh fulfills his *if* in response to Jeremiah's fulfilling his, then *before me you will stand.* That expression takes us back to 15:1, with the implication that Jeremiah will be able to stand in Yahweh's court and be Israel's advocate. But in this context, the other side to having that position has the emphasis. As well as articulating Israel's words to Yahweh, he will be able to articulate Yahweh's words to Israel—which the protest in vv. 15–18 has apparently imperiled. He will be free and under obligation to carry on preaching his uncompromising message, which is what is actually *valuable.* The Judahites would like him to preach *garbage,* about peace and good things. He has doubted whether Yahweh's declarations of intent can be trusted; Yahweh's threats have not come about, and Jeremiah doesn't think they are going to come about. He

---

389. P. J. Scalise, "The Logic of Covenant and the Logic of Lament in the Book of Jeremiah," *Perspectives in Religious Studies* 28 (2000–2001): 399.

390. Holladay, *Commentary on Jeremiah,* 1:464.

has thus fallen into taking the same view as his contemporaries. He needs to reaffirm his commitment to telling the truth. Then *you will be my very mouth*, if you go back to accepting the words put into your mouth by me (1:9) and uttering them. Jeremiah will then have the possibility of being as Godlike as he could ever be and achieving "the peak of all virtue."[391] Finally, in this verse, Yahweh goes back to mine further the inexhaustible potential of that verb "turn." *Those people will turn to you; but you—you will not turn to them.* Later stories in the Jeremiah scroll will tell of people turning to Jeremiah before and after 587 (Jer 37; 42). But Jeremiah is not to give in to the temptation to become a false prophet.

20–21 While the community might imperil Jeremiah by prevailing over him to give up on his message and to come to look at things their way, it could also imperil his life in a more down-to-earth way (Jer 38). Once again, Yahweh reverts to Jeremiah's commission and recycles words from 1:18–19,[392] though adding an extra reassurance in the verb *deliver you*. He goes on to give further precision to the repeated promise: specifically, *I will snatch you away from the hand of the faithless*. The formulation in familiar words is then complemented by less familiar ones (though cf. Job 6:23) in a line manifesting a tight parallelism that brings closure to the tumultuous exchange:

and	I will snatch	you	from	the hand of	the faithless
and	I will release	you	from	the clutch of	the terrifying

Release (*pādâ*; the conventional English translation "redeem" has different connotations) thus complements *snatch* with an expression that is novel in a Jeremianic context: only here and in 31:11 does Jeremiah use the verb, but both passages talk about being liberated from a kind of captivity. *Clutch* (*kap*) sharpens *hand*, and *terrifying* (*'āriṣ*) sharpens *faithless* (this word, too, occurs only once more in Jeremiah—applied to Yahweh in 20:11). Whereas *faithless* suggests objective wrongdoing, *terrifying* suggests such people's significance for those they threaten. Once more, Jeremiah gives an account of his agonizing not for his own sake, to let it all hang out, but to drive his hearers into looking at themselves. His protests are not ones that most readers should think to identify with, unless they are Dietrich Bonhoeffer or Martin Luther King Jr. The point about the record of the protests is to confront the people who caused the trouble, "to confront readers with their own past and the profoundly negative effects their words and deeds have had on God's own

---

391. John Chrysostom, *Baptismal Instructions* 6:19, quoted in Wenthe, *Jeremiah*, 123. Wenthe also gives two other quotations of this line from Jeremiah in Chrysostom.

392. Or, of course, provides the original formulation, which is then reworked in the account of Jeremiah's commission.

prophets (and leaders in every age!). Let readers not be too quick to make these laments their own! That appropriating move may be a subtle way of avoiding the indictment the prophet speaks."[393]

2. Confrontations and Warnings: This Country and Domain (16:1–17:11)

Jer 16–17 "intensifies the overall theme of 'plucking up and pulling down,'"[394] though without neglecting building and planting.[395] The question and re-sponse dynamic of Jer 14–15 disappears for a while; it will return in 17:12. Jer-emiah 16:1–17:11 is another sequence of units of separate origin. They contain an above-average number of references to *this country* or *my country*[396] or *this place* or the *domain* that belongs to Yahweh, which he shares with Israel but from which he intends to throw Israel out. This motif thus loosely holds together the series of messages, so perhaps they have been juxtaposed on that basis.

16:1–13   Four that have been provided with explicit links (*because* in vv. 5, 9; *all these things* in v. 10); they all relate to the suspen-sion of celebration in the country in light of the grim events that are to come

16:14–21   Three that take the edge off that discouraging message by promising a more positive future; they would be a special encouragement after 587, when the grim events had happened

17:1–11   Four that have a background in the thinking and form of Proverbs, which now explicitly or implicitly relate to Judah's situation in the monarchy's last decades

a. Joy and Favor Suspended Here (16:1–13)

[1]*Yahweh's message came to me:* [2]*You will not get yourself a wife,*[a] *and you will not have sons and daughters in this place.*[b] [3]*Because Yahweh has said this about*

---

393. Fretheim, *Jeremiah*, 243.
394. L. Stulman, *Jeremiah* (Nashville: Abingdon, 2005), 158.
395. Brueggemann, *Jeremiah 1–25*, 150.
396. Allen, *Jeremiah*, 188.

*the sons and about the daughters that are born in this place, and about their
mothers who bear them and about their fathers who father them in this country:*

⁴*They will die deaths from sicknesses*ᶜ—
  they will not be lamented.
They will not be buried—
  manure on the face of the ground they will become. ᵈ
By sword and by hunger they will come to an end,
  and their corpse will be food
For the bird in the heavens
  and for the animal on the earth. ᵉ

⁵*Because Yahweh has said this:*

Don't come into a house where there is a wake,
  don't go to lament and don't bemoan them.
Because I have gathered up my well-being from this people (Yahweh's
    affirmation),
  commitment and compassion. ᶠ
⁶*Big people and little people will die in this country—*
  they will not be buried.
People will not lament for them, they will not gash themselves,
  and they will not clip themselves for them.
⁷*They will not give a share to them*ᵍ *in mourning,*ʰ
  to console someone for a death.
They will not give them a consolation chalice to drink
  for his father or for his mother.
⁸*And into a house of feasting you will not come*
  to sit with them to eat and drink. ⁱ

⁹*Because Yahweh of Armies, Israel's God, has said this:*

Here am I, stopping from this place,
  before your eyes and in your time,
The voice of joy and the voice of rejoicing,
  the voice of groom and the voice of bride.

¹⁰*Then, when you tell this people all these things and they say to you, Why has
Yahweh spoken against us of all this great dire trouble, and what is our waywardness and what is our wrongdoing that we have done in relation to Yahweh
our God,* ¹¹*you will say to them, Because your ancestors abandoned me (Yah-*

weh's affirmation) and went after other gods, served them, and bowed down to them. Me they abandoned and my instruction they did not keep. ¹²And you yourselves have acted direly in acting worse than your ancestors, and there are you, going each one after the determination of his dire mind, so as not to listen to me. ¹³So I will hurl you from upon this country to a country that you have not known, you and your ancestors, and you will serve other gods there, day and night,ʲ in that Iᵏ will show you no favor.ˡ

a. In vv. 1–2a, LXX has, "And you will not get a wife, the Lord, the God of Israel, says," suggesting the independent shaping of MT and LXX as this message became part of the scroll.

b. MTᴬ has a section marker here.

c. The word order with the verb postponed, combined with the asyndeton, suggests that the first clause is subordinate to the second.

d. Here, the second colon is asyndetic and has the verb postponed, suggesting it is subordinate to the first. The line recurs from 8:2 where I treated it in that context as prose.

e. MT has a section marker here.

f. The *my* in the previous colon could carry over into this one. LXX lacks this colon and the next two.

g. Before or instead of *lāhem*, LXX, Vg may imply *lehem* ("bread"; cf. Isa 58:7), or bread may be the taken-for-granted object of the verb (cf. *pāraś* in Lam 4:4, though there *lehem* came in the parallel colon).

h. For MT *'ēbel*, Vg implies *'ābēl*, "a mourner."

i. MT has a marker here.

j. LXX lacks *day and night*.

k. LXX, Vg have "they"; Aq agrees with MT.

l. MT has a section marker here.

Jeremiah continues to speak of Yahweh's dealings with him, and the section develops the theme of staying alone and abstaining from revelry and merrymaking (15:17). He first relates how Yahweh commissioned another symbolic act like the one in 13:1–12a—or three symbolic acts,[397] all of which go against natural inclinations.[398] Here, Jeremiah does not describe fulfilling the commission, though a related similarity is that again there is therefore no record of people seeing Jeremiah fulfill it. While people would be aware of his staying single and not taking part in mourning or in feasting, and it is easy to imagine them asking why, the scroll does not record it. A symbolic act is an exercise in rhetoric at least as much as a stage in the implementing of something.[399] The account of Yahweh's message coming to him is the thing that counts, as an exercise in communication not just for his immediate acquain-

397. Volz, *Jeremia*, 180.
398. W. D. Stacey, *Prophetic Drama in the Old Testament* (London: Epworth, 1990), 143.
399. See K. G. Friebel, *Jeremiah's and Ezekiel's Sign-Acts: Rhetorical Nonverbal Communication*, JSOTSup 283 (Sheffield: Sheffield Academic, 1999), 82–99.

tances but for people reading the scroll. It is a story about "the flesh made word. . . . Jeremiah, generally active as performer and/or interpreter, has on this occasion become a (passive) stage object," turned into a sign. "Jeremiah's physicality (and in this narrative, his sexuality), must recede or be bracketed off in favour of textuality."[400] The account of the message's coming thus leads into explanations of its rationale rather than accounts of the fulfillment.

> vv. 1–4 Yahweh bids Jeremiah not to marry or have children (while vv. 1–3 are prose, v. 4 comprises four bicola, the second pair linked by enjambment)
> > v. 1 Jeremiah's introduction
> > vv. 2–4 Yahweh's message
> > > v. 2 The instruction
> > > vv. 3–4 The rationale
>
> vv. 5–8 Yahweh bids Jeremiah not to join in people's mourning (rationale and restatement comprising seven bicola)
> > v. 5a Jeremiah's introduction
> > vv. 5b–8 Yahweh's message
> > > v. 5b The instruction
> > > vv. 5c–7 The rationale
> > > v. 8 The instruction restated
>
> v. 9 Yahweh explains the rationale for the biddings (a pair of bicola linked by enjambment making a link with vv. 1–4 as well as with vv. 5–8)
> > v. 9a Jeremiah's introduction
> > v. 9b–c Yahweh's message: further rationale
>
> vv. 10–13 Yahweh instructs Jeremiah concerning what to say when people ask what lies behind that rationale, summarizing the message he has been commissioning Jeremiah to deliver over decades

1–2 The conventional-looking introduction again occurs in connection with a visual or experiential event where the more literalistic translation (Yahweh's message "happened" to me) might be apposite (see the commentary on 13:3). Yahweh requires the prophet's marriage status to serve his work as a prophet, as was the case with Hosea, Isaiah, and Ezekiel and with those who become eunuchs to serve God's reign (Matt 19:12). "Hosea married a harlot to demonstrate the corruption of Israel's relation to Yahweh, while [Jeremiah] married no one at all to demonstrate the end of Yahweh's rela-

---

400. M. Brummitt, "Recovering Jeremiah: A Thesis in Three Acts" (PhD diss., University of Glasgow, 2006), 209, 212, 213.

tion to Israel."[401] In a traditional society, people marry young, so maybe this instruction belongs to a time soon after Jeremiah's commission and before the Josianic reformation.[402] And in a traditional society, people do not deliberately stay single, so Yahweh's instruction is countercultural. It might call Jeremiah's masculinity into question.[403] Further, the Scriptures make a more integral link between marriage and having children than is usual in Western culture, and the second part of Yahweh's instruction is more radical and countercultural. It is the element developed in vv. 3–4. Having children was integral to God's purpose in creating the world—otherwise, the world was never going to be full or managed (Gen 1:26–28). Further, it was integral to God's purpose in commissioning and blessing Abraham and to the future of the people he had chosen, so a refusal to have children would imperil that future. Yahweh's command to Jeremiah would seem unscriptural and theologically incomprehensible.

3–4 Thus "in a move unparalleled in the Hebrew Bible, life is cut off before it begins" while "those unlucky enough to be born already will die unmourned, and those who should by rights have been their mourners will not be comforted."[404] The rationale for the command in v. 2 lies in the fate that lies ahead of the children and of the parents themselves *in this place* (Judah or Jerusalem) or *in this country* (a motif that will recur throughout this section). "These were not ordinary times"; Paul's advice about marriage presupposes the same conviction (1 Cor 7).[405] As often happens, Yahweh goes on to speak in more poetic form, with a broad parallelism between two descriptions of how people will die and what will happen to their bodies. Children and parents *will die deaths from sicknesses*; the subsequent appearance of *sword and hunger* suggests that *sicknesses* refers to epidemics, since epidemic, hunger, and war form a recurrent, unholy trinity (14:12; see the commentary there). But the emphasis lies on what happens afterward—or rather, on what doesn't happen. *They will not be lamented* and *they will not be buried* because there will be no one to undertake these loving responsibilities. Not to be lamented is not to be remembered or cared about, which (one could say) doesn't matter when you are actually dead but tends to matter when you are thinking about your death. If they are not buried, *manure on the face of the ground* is what *they will become* (see 8:2; 9:22[21]). Then there are the children and parents who *will come to an end by sword and by hunger* in the

401. Holladay, *Commentary on Jeremiah*, 1:469.

402. See M. A. Zipor, "'Scenes from a Marriage'—According to Jeremiah," *JSOT* 65 (1995): 85.

403. C. Carvalho, "Whose Gendered Language of God? Contemporary Gender Theory and Divine Gender in the Prophets," *Currents in Theology and Mission* 43 (2016): 14.

404. D. Lipton, "Food for the Birds," 127–28.

405. Lundbom, *Jeremiah 1–20*, 756.

context of the invasion that is to happen. They too will lie unburied so that *their corpses will be food for the bird in the heavens and for the animal on the earth* (cf. 7:33; 15:3). When they die, there will be no rest in Sheol, and quite some restoration work will be needed to get them ready for the resurrection day that Jeremiah doesn't know about.

5 Yahweh's *because* makes for a loose link with vv. 1–4, introducing another formulation that now expands on his point in vv. 1–4 and introducing another symbolic action. The *wake* (*marzēaḥ*) to which Yahweh refers is an event combining a vigil for someone who has died (hence the etymology of the word *wake*) with a commemorative meal.[406] The word comes otherwise only in Amos 6:7, where it refers more generally to a festive meal of a semi-religious kind, a little like an *agape* feast but perhaps more drunken. Here, indeed, Yahweh might initially seem to be referring to such a festive meal, but in the parallelism, the second colon makes explicit what kind of meal it is: an occasion to *lament* and *mourn*. If such meals deserved disapproval because of their self-indulgence or religious deviance, that problem is not Jeremiah's focus here, as it is not in v. 6b. If such occasions are important when someone dies in the community and one expresses one's sympathy and love for the family by joining them, why is Jeremiah to stand apart? In a moment, Yahweh will explain that standing apart will dramatize how there will be no such events in respect of deaths that are imminent. First, he explains why those deaths are going to happen, and he does so in terrifying words. *I have gathered up my well-being from this people.* Withdrawing *well-being* so that things are "not well" in a way that contrasts with the promises of other prophets is a familiar notion (e.g., 12:12; 14:19). To speak of gathering up this well-being is a sharp way to make the point, because gathering up (*'āsap*) often refers to death and burial (e.g., 8:2; 9:22[21]). Yahweh announces a funeral for well-being. To work out the implications, he adds reference to *commitment and compassion*, two of the most important aspects of his nature and his relationship with his people. On *commitment*, see 2:3 (and the commentary on it). *Compassion* (*raḥămîm*) is the plural of the word for a woman's womb, a link that the First Testament sometimes alludes to. Compassion is the feeling a woman has for the offspring of her womb. For Yahweh to gather up his compassion for Israel in order to bury it is to go against his motherly nature. The reference has all the more solemnity in the context of vv. 3–4 and 7.

6–7 Only after explaining the background and the implications of the deaths that are coming does Yahweh go on to refer to the deaths themselves. *Big people and little people will die in this country*; death will be no respecter of persons. Neither will the aftermath: *they will not be buried* because there will

---

406. See P. J. King, *Jeremiah: An Archaeological Companion* (Louisville: Westminster John Knox, 1993), 140–41.

be no one to do the burying. More concretely, there will be none of the observances that are part of mourning and a wake. *People will not lament for them, and they will not gash themselves or clip themselves for them.* These two common mourning practices are known from many cultures; what they meant varied from culture to culture. Deuteronomy 14:1 forbids them, presumably because Israel's neighbors engaged in them, and forgoing them was an aspect of Israel distinguishing itself. Here, Jeremiah is not concerned with the rights and wrongs of the practices but with the simple fact that people engaged in them as signs of mourning—and with the fact that death will be so omnipresent that no one will be left to undertake such rites. The same applies to noncontroversial practices. People *will not give a share to them with mourning to console someone for a death.* The sharing (more literally "splitting"—the breaking of bread) would be a gesture of fellowship and of generosity (cf. Isa 58:7); there will be none. Likewise, *they will not give them a consolation chalice to drink for his father or for his mother.* Motherhood, which should suggest progeny and hope, again conveys bereavement and barrenness (cf. 15:7, 10).[407]

8 To draw attention to these coming realities, Jeremiah is to embody now the way things will be then. While in this verse Yahweh may now be issuing a general prohibition about going into a house of feasting for some great celebratory occasion, the *house of feasting* may be simply another term for the *house where there is a wake* (which was literally "the house of a wake"), where one would *sit with them to eat and drink.* Either way, scandalously, Jeremiah will stand apart from such occasions. "He is no longer able to weep with those who weep and to rejoice with those who rejoice" (Rom 12:15).[408]

9 Yahweh goes on to make more concrete the rationale for his instructions. Gathering up well-being, making things not be well, will find expression in what happens to *the voice of joy and the voice of rejoicing,* the joyful and rejoicing voice. "When the church sins, God makes all joy and gladness to cease from it."[409] They are words Jeremiah associated with his commission in 15:16. But in combination with *the voice of groom and the voice of bride,* the words recur from a similar threat in a similar connection in 7:34. There, already, Yahweh had formulated his intention in terms of *stopping* the exercise of that voice *from this place.* It's going to happen *before your eyes and in your time.* The suffix *your* is plural: the symbolic action is Jeremiah's, but the message is Judah's.

10–13 "All these things" makes a link with what has preceded. Perhaps the entirety of vv. 1–13 does presuppose a time at the beginning of Jeremiah's activity (see the commentary on v. 2). Otherwise, it might seem mysterious or infuriating (or "almost comical"[410]) that people ask Jeremiah this ques-

407. Stulman, *Jeremiah*, 159.
408. McKane, *Jeremiah*, 1:368.
409. Jerome, *Jeremiah*, 101.
410. Wright, *Jeremiah*, 187.

tion whose answer he has been proclaiming for decades, and it might seem mysterious that it finds inclusion in the Jeremiah scroll. The resolution to the latter mystery might lie in v. 13. Yahweh has not previously used the strong verb *hurl* (*ṭûl hiphil*), which will recur in 22:26, 28; it occurs most often in connection with Jonah (Jonah 1:4, 5, 12, 15). And he speaks of hurling Judah *from upon this country*, a motif running through this section. Further, he matches the force of that verb with the chilling nature of his closing threat concerning how things will be in the country to which he projects people: *I will show you no favor.* Favor, or grace, is a key word that deserves setting alongside commitment and compassion; strikingly, however, it is a noun that Jeremiah does not otherwise use (except at 31:2), and even here he uses the *hapax legomenon ḥănînâ* rather than the regular word *ḥēn*.

In light of the passage, Calvin prays:

> Grant, Almighty God, that as we in various ways daily provoke thy wrath against us, and thou ceasest not to exhort us to repent,—O grant, that we may be pliant and obedient and not despise thy kind invitations, while thou settest before us the hope of thy mercy, nor make light of thy threatenings; but that we may so profit by thy word as to endeavor to anticipate thy judgments; and may we also, being allured by the sweetness of thy grace, consecrate ourselves wholly to thee, that thus thy wrath may be turned away from us, and that we may become receivers of that grace which thou offerest to all who truly and from the heart repent, and who desire to have thee propitious to them in Christ Jesus our Lord.[411]

b. Restoration, Cleansing, and Revelation Here (16:14–21)

[14]*Therefore there, days are coming (Yahweh's affirmation) when it will no longer be said, "Yahweh is alive*[a] *who got the Israelites up from the country of Egypt."* [15]*Rather, "Yahweh is alive who got the Israelites up from the northern country and from all the countries where he drove them away." I will return them to their land that I gave to their ancestors.*[b]

[16]*Here am I, sending for many fishers (Yahweh's affirmation) and they will*
  fish for them,
  and afterward I will send for many hunters and they will hunt for
    them,[c]
From upon every mountain and from upon every hill,
  and from the clefts in the cliffs.

411. Calvin, *Jeremiah*, 2:335.

¹⁷*Because, my eyes being on all their paths,*
they have not hidden themselves from my presence,^d
and their waywardness has not concealed itself from before my eyes.
¹⁸*I will recompense them first,*
double for their waywardness and their wrongdoing.
Because they have defiled^e *my country with their detestable corpses,*
with their offensive things they have filled my domain.^f

¹⁹*Yahweh, my force and my fort,*
my escape on the day of distress:
To you nations will come
from the ends of the earth and say:
Only deceit did our ancestors have as their domain,
something empty with nothing that could be any use in them.
²⁰*Can a human being make himself gods?*—
but they are not gods.
²¹*Therefore, here am I, getting them to acknowledge it*
on this occasion.
I will get them to acknowledge my hand and my strength,
and they will acknowledge that Yahweh is my name.^g

a. See the translation note and commentary on 4:2.
b. MT has a marker here. Verses 14–15 reappear in a variant form as 23:7–8.
c. If these lines are poetry, this one is a quite unusual 5-5 (or perhaps 4-1, 4-1).
d. LXX lacks this colon; Aq, Theod have it.
e. *Ḥālal*, which has a homonym meaning "run through"; see D. G. Garber, "A Vocabulary of Trauma in the Exilic Writings," in Kelle, Ames, and Wright, *Interpreting Exile*, 309–22. Its resonances would be significant here.
f. MT has a marker here. The subsection ends with a long 5-4 line, working a-b-b'-a'.
g. MT has a section marker here.

Deuteronomy has four ways of thinking about the catastrophe that would threaten Israel because of its waywardness and about its aftermath: total calamity within the country, transportation to another country, permanent confinement there, but also the possibility of return. There is some tension between them—they cannot all be true. In vv. 1–13, Jeremiah has emphasized the first but then spoken in terms of the second, with the possible implication that the third logically follows. Against all rhetorical expectations, he now speaks in terms of the fourth.[412] For how could Yahweh say what he said in

412. D. Rom-Shiloni, "Deuteronomic Concepts of Exile Interpreted in Jeremiah and Ezekiel," in C. Cohen et al., *Birkat Shalom*, 101–23; Rom-Shiloni infers that a promise such as that in vv. 14–15 must come from someone in the Judahite community in Babylon.

v. 13? Grace, along with compassion, commitment, and truthfulness, is an aspect of his nature (Exod 34:6); hence the fact that one who embodies the God of Israel is "full of grace and truthfulness" (John 1:14). Although Jeremiah makes little use of words such as grace, he has been presupposing and talking about this aspect of Yahweh's character when he has been urging Judah to turn back to Yahweh. He has been presupposing them even when he has been threatening Judah with Yahweh's anger or temper, notwithstanding his regretful reference to Yahweh's being long-tempered (15:15). This chapter describes the most massive dissolution of the society so far in Jeremiah. Fortunately, it also portrays grace in a more spectacular way.[413]

There follow three short messages that again reflect how Yahweh's threats are worse than his actions—or worse than his threats elsewhere. While he will throw Judah out of his country, he does not actually want people to serve other gods in the country to which he expels them, and he will show them his favor there. The first message is certainly prose; the second and third have some parallelism and rhythm.

> vv. 14–15 Yahweh will restore Israel to its land (a promise by Yahweh in prose)
>
> vv. 16–18 Yahweh will hunt down the people who have defiled his country and domain (a threat by Yahweh followed by rationale comprising two bicola linked by enjambment; then another threat followed by rationale comprising a tricolon and another pair of bicola)
>
> vv. 19–21 Yahweh will get the nations to acknowledge him (two linked bicola comprising address to Yahweh and introduction to the content of a confession by the nations, two comprising their confession, and two comprising Yahweh's response or comment)

Differences in form and imagery suggest that these three messages, which now form a "patchwork,"[414] were of separate origin. What happens when they are juxtaposed? Notwithstanding the *therefore*, vv. 14–15 constitute a contrast with what precedes, as they promise the return of Israel after its banishment in many countries. This message makes for a surprise, yet not a surprise in the context of the scroll's broader assumptions about Yahweh's relationship with Israel. Verses 16–18 return to the theme of reprisal for wrongdoing. Out of this context, one would assume that Israel is the object of the reprisal, but following on the first message, such a threat would be odd, and

---

413. Fischer, *Jeremia*, 1:537.
414. McKane, *Jeremiah*, 1:382.

the juxtaposition rather suggests that in this context it announces Yahweh's act of reprisal against the nations that have exiled Israel.[415] Again, while it is thus in one sense a surprise, it is not so in the broader context of the scroll's assumptions about Yahweh's activity in the world. Verses 19–21 thus offer another surprise over against the second message but again one that also fits the broader context of the scroll's assumptions. All three messages make sense in a post-disaster context as Yahweh's encouragements to the community that survives when the threat of exile in v. 13 has been implemented.

14–15 The *therefore* following on the threat in v. 13 is in one sense illogical[416] or may seem nonsensical.[417] But it does point to a deeper "theo-logic," like the "therefores" in Amos 3:2 and Ps 130:4.[418] The threat in vv. 10–13 cannot ultimately stand alone, as if it were Yahweh's last word. More immediately, the *therefore* may relate anticipatorily to the suffering to which Jeremiah alludes when he goes on to refer to *the northern country* and *all the countries where he drove them away*;[419] even in this message, there are both threat and good news.[420] One way or another, the declaration about no favor or grace leads into a declaration that new *days are coming*, a phrase that introduces good news about a day of deliverance here and in 31:27–30, 31–34.[421] When they come, *it will no longer be said, "Yahweh is alive who got the Israelites up from the country of Egypt."* That long-ago action was the original expression of grace; Jeremiah will refer to the way Israel then "found grace in the wilderness" (31:2) in his one use of the regular word for favor or grace. But now Jeremiah relativizes the exodus.[422] What will henceforth be said is that Yahweh *got the Israelites up from the northern country and from all the countries where he drove them away*. It will happen because *I will return them to their land that I gave to their ancestors.* And henceforth the promises that people make will appeal to the fact that *Yahweh is alive* who acted in this way. People who remain in Judah, Egypt, or Babylon or Ammon, Moab, or Edom can be reassured that the community in Judah is not finished. Their relationship with their ancestors is not merely their downfall but their future. The relationship between Yahweh's actions as threatened in v. 13 and as promised

415. Cf. Brueggemann, *Jeremiah 1–25*, 148–50.
416. Duhm (*Jeremia*, 141) comments about vv. 14–15, "How they got here, I don't know."
417. P. D. Miller, "Jeremiah," on the passage.
418. Wright, *Jeremiah*, 189.
419. Mayer, *Commentary*, 388.
420. Weiser, *Jeremiah*, 146.
421. C. Levin, "'Days Are Coming, When It Shall No Longer Be Said,'" in *Remembering and Forgetting in Early Second Temple Judah*, ed. E. Ben Zvi and C. Levin, FAT 85 (Tübingen: Mohr Siebeck, 2012), 105–24.
422. Fischer, *Jeremia*, 1:531.

in vv. 14–15 overlaps with that implied by Hos 11. The two accounts are not exactly parallel in that Hos 11 concerns whether Yahweh acts in wrath or in grace as opposed to whether his acting in wrath can be succeeded by acting in grace. But the dilemma or tension that Yahweh has to handle is the same. Yahweh is the God of grace. He is also the God who must take wrongdoing seriously. Yahweh makes explicit these two aspects to his character in his self-revelation in Exod 34:6–7. When his people do wrong, he is like a parent who has to keep deciding whether it is an occasion to be merciful or to be tough. Generally speaking, in the decades up to 587 he talks tough, but after 587 he can be free to talk mercifully.

16–17 The message of these two verses is familiar, but the context makes one rethink its significance, and its imagery is novel. While Isa 19:8; Ezek 47:10 refer to literal *fishers*, and Eccl 9:12; Hab 1:14 use fish in a simile, elsewhere only Amos 4:2 uses fishing as a metaphor for hostile action against people.[423] The two passages show that fishing is no fun for fish, notwithstanding Jesus's playful reworking of the metaphor. Likewise, the arrival of *hunters* is nothing for game animals to relax about. In the second line, the fish are forgotten and Yahweh focuses on the way animals in the wild may find nowhere to hide from an insistent hunter—*mountain* and *hill* and *clefts in the cliffs* will not be safe. So it will be when Yahweh sends out his hunters. And the hunters are able to rely not merely on their own *eyes* but on Yahweh's. The wild animals may know all the mountain *paths*, but Yahweh knows them too. So they will not be able to have *hidden themselves from my presence.* The reason for Yahweh's pursuit becomes explicit in the last colon: *their waywardness has not concealed itself from before my eyes*, either. The reference to waywardness hints at the metaphorical as well as literal point about *paths.*

18 Yahweh goes on to reformulate his commitment to action by means of another metaphor. The reprise of reference to *waywardness* along with the sharp change of metaphor might suggest that v. 18 was originally a separate threat from the one in vv. 16–17; the reprise has then led to the threats being juxtaposed. The new metaphor of *recompense* will recur in Jeremiah, usually in connection with Israel's attackers (e.g., 25:14; 50:29). This link points to a resolution of the puzzle concerning vv. 16–18. While the language in vv. 16–17 would make one think of Yahweh pursuing Judah (cf. Isa 2:19, 21),[424] vv. 16–17 then read oddly after vv. 14–15, as if they jump over vv. 14–15 to connect with vv. 12–13.[425] But the *recompense* image suggests that Yahweh is rather talking

---

423. S. Y. Cho suggests that the fishermen are Yahweh's supernatural aides ("The Divine Title 'Fisherman' in Jer 16:16," *JNSL* 35 [2009]: 97–105); but cf. T. R. Yoder, *Fishers of Fish and Fishers of Men: Fishing Imagery in the Hebrew Bible and the Ancient Near East*, Explorations in Ancient Near Eastern Civilizations (Winona Lake, IN: Eisenbrauns, 2016), 52–58.

424. D. R. Jones, *Jeremiah*, 234.

425. Rudolph, *Jeremia*, 112; Volz (*Jeremia*, 182) simply omits them.

about redress on the nations. A worker gets compensation at the end of the day, and Yahweh *will recompense them first*, in a negative sense, before restoring Judah (vv. 14–15) and before getting the nations to acknowledge him (vv. 19–21). He will recompense them *double*, maybe both *for their waywardness* and also for *their wrongdoing*, or maybe simply "quite enough." One might see the two expressions, *waywardness* and *wrongdoing*, spelled out in the reference to *detestable corpses* and *offensive things* in a neatly parallel bicolon structured a-b-c-c'-a'-b' (or, more broadly, a-b-b'-a'):

They have defiled	my country	with their detestable corpses;
with their offensive things	they have filled	my domain.

My country picks up from vv. 4 and 13; adding *my domain* leads into vv. 19–21 and 17:1–4. Like waywardness and wrongdoing, *detestable corpses* and *offensive things* may refer to the same thing. They are the things with which the nations have *defiled my country* when they came there with their dead gods; death always defiles, so dead gods are doubly defiling. They have *filled my domain* with them. But the doubling of the concrete description in terms of *detestable corpses* and *offensive things* may again correspond to or justify the doubling of recompense. Jeremiah has urged Yahweh to pour out his wrath on the nations (10:25); vv. 16–18 are Yahweh's response.[426]

19 There follows another message that is of independent origin from what precedes, is at surface-level in tension with it, yet reflects some theo-logic. Jeremiah first makes a confession and a statement of faith and hope. In general terms, the series of affirmations parallels the Psalms; indeed, it sounds like the beginning of a protest psalm.[427] Etymologically, the words for *force* and *fort* (*'ōz* and *mā'ôz*) may be unrelated, but they look as if they are related (the *mā-* is simply part of a noun formation), and it can be hard to tell which of the two connotations (strength and refuge) attaches to each word. The ambiguity is useful: a divine "fort" in whom you can take refuge needs to be someone who can be forceful on your behalf. To follow the order, Yahweh is one with force at his disposal who can therefore be a fort in which one can take refuge. In combination, the two words are a hendiadys: Yahweh is a strong refuge. While *force* is the more common word, an address to Yahweh as "my force" comes only here, though there are psalms that include the confession "Yahweh is my/our force" (Pss 28:7; 46:1[3]; 118:14) or "You are my fort" (Ps 31:4[5]). If there were any doubt whether the connotation "refuge" applies here, *escape* in the parallel colon makes it more explicit;

426. Fretheim, *Jeremiah*, 252.
427. Weiser, *Jeremia*, 147.

a psalm says, "You have been . . . an escape on the day of my distress" (Ps 59:16[17]), and David says, "You are my escape" (2 Sam 22:3). Jeremiah is acknowledging that *on the day of distress*, when he is under attack, Yahweh is the one who protects him. What is the point about the confession here? Does it reflect the way the Babylonians kept him safe in 587? Or is he pointing to the confession the nations need to make, not least in light of the threat in vv. 16–18 concerning their coming recompense? Does it stand in contrast with 10:25? The expectation that *nations will come from the ends of the earth* to acknowledge Yahweh also parallels the Psalms: "All the ends of the earth will turn to Yahweh; all the kin groups of the nations will bow down before him" (Ps 22:27[28]). They thus come to acknowledge the truth of the psalm's confession. But when the nations talk about *deceit* and *ancestors* and *domain* and *something empty* and *nothing that could be any use*, they use Jeremiah's language. He is providing the script for them.

20 The rhetorical question *Can a human being make himself gods?* with the yes-and-no answer *but they are not gods* (or "they are not God") corresponds to the declaration in 10:1–16, though the nations are also making the confession that Yahweh wishes Israel would make (2:5–11).[428] Yahweh is dealing with the nations as he deals with Israel. In effect, he often sets before Judah alternatives from which they have to choose: Hos 11 (noted in connection with v. 15) is an example, especially if one reads the whole chapter instead of stopping at v. 9. Here, Yahweh is setting alternatives before the nations. They must choose vv. 16–18 or vv. 19–21. Of course, they don't know about this choice; it is Judah that will know. Yahweh is setting before Judah the possibilities that lie open before the nations.

21 Yahweh responds by making a commitment to ensure that Jeremiah's statement of hope will come true. The sequence has an upside-down logic—one might expect the subsequent declaration to lead into Jeremiah's confession rather than respond to it. Again, the language is Jeremiah's in that he expends a lot of energy *getting* people *to acknowledge* Yahweh and loves to talk about the acknowledgment of Yahweh and about Yahweh's *hand* and *strength* and *name*. All four words came in 10:1–16, which closed with the declaration *Yahweh of Armies is his name*.

c. Forfeit Here (17:1–11)

¹*Judah's wrongdoing is written*
  with an iron stylus.
With a flint point it is engraved

---

428. Allen, *Jeremiah*, 193.

on the tablet of their mind and in relation to your altars' horns,
²*As their children are mindful of their altars and their totem poles,*
   by verdant tree, by lofty hills.
³*Mountain-dwellerᵃ in the open country,*
   your resources and all your stores I will make into plunder,
   your shrines, through wrongdoing, in all your territory.
⁴*You will drop them, and that through yourself,*
   from your domain that I gave you.
I will make you serve your enemies
   in a country that you have not known.
Because a fire you have kindled—
   *by my anger it will blaze for all time.*ᵇ

⁵*Yahweh has said this:*

Cursed is the man
   who relies on a human being,
And makes flesh his arm,
   and from Yahweh his mind turns aside.
⁶*He will be like a shrubᶜ in the steppe,*
   and he will not see when good things come.
He will dwell in scorched placesᵈ in the wilderness,
   *a salt country, with no one living there.*ᵉ
⁷*Blessed is the man*
   who relies on Yahweh
   and Yahweh will be his reliance.
⁸*He will be like a tree transplanted by water*
   and by a stream sending outᶠ its roots.
It is not afraidᵍ when heat comes,
   and its foliage will be verdant.
In a year of drought it is not anxious,
   and it does not cease producing fruit.

⁹*The mind is more deviousʰ than anything;*
   it's graveⁱ—who can know it?
¹⁰*I, Yahweh, am probing the mind,*
   examining the heart,
And givingʲ to an individual in accordance with his paths,
   *in accordance with the fruit of his practices.*ᵏ

¹¹*A partridgeˡ that incubatedᵐ but did not give birth—*
   someone who makes wealthⁿ but not by exercising authority.

In the middle of his days it will abandon him,
and at his end he will become a fool.

a. *Hărārî* otherwise occurs only as a designation of one of the thirty warriors (e.g., 2 Sam 23:33), where it might refer to an otherwise-unknown place called Harar or designate someone as a mountain-dweller (cf. Rashi, in MG). Similar forms appear in Gen 14:6; Ps 30:7(8), which suggest the meaning "mountain." Theod (see HUBP), Vg imply the easier plural *harărê*; this colon would then belong with the previous line.

b. MT has a section marker here. Verses 3–4 are a variant on 15:13–14. LXX lacks vv. 1–4 and the introductory colon to v. 5: see P.-M. Bogaert, "Jérémie 17,1–4 TM," in *La double transmission du text biblique: Études d'histoire du texte offertes en hommage à Adrian Schenker,* ed. Y. Goldman and C. Uehlinger, OBO 179 (Göttingen: Vandenhoeck & Ruprecht, 2001), 59–74.

c. Cf. Tg; LXX, Vg have "tamarisk," while BDB and *HALOT* have "juniper" (on the basis of a similar Arabic word), but tamarisk and juniper do okay in the desert, so they seem less likely. But much of the point lies in the paronomasia, *cursed* (*'ārûr*) is the *shrub* (*'ar'ār*) in the *steppe* (*'ārābâ*): plant, location, and destiny belong together.

d. Although *hărērîm* is a *hapax legomenon*, its root is familiar; LXX's "seaside" presumably refers to the Dead Sea (see the parallel colon; cf. McKane, *Jeremiah*, 1:390).

e. MT has a section marker here.

f. The line works a-b-c-d-d'-c'; the finite verb continues the participial construction.

g. The *qere* has *yir'eh* ("he will . . . see"), repeating v. 6; the *ketiv* more plausibly implies *yir'â* (cf. LXX, Vg).

h. Or "serpentine"; T. Novick, "*'qb hlb mkl w'nš hw' my yd'nw* (Jeremiah 17:9)," *JBL* 123 (2004): 535.

i. For MT *wə'ānuš*, LXX "and a man" implies *we'ĕnôš*. Vg "unfathomable" translates loosely in light of the parallelism.

j. LXX takes the infinitive to indicate purpose, but the *waw* suggests it continues the participial construction (cf. Vg).

k. MT has a section marker here.

l. Tg provides "like," but many proverbs work by simple juxtaposition (e.g., Prov 25:3, 11, 12, 14, 18, 19, 25, 26, 28).

m. LXX "gathered" presupposes the Aramaic verb *dāgar* (J. F. A. Sawyer, "A Note on the Brooding Partridge in Jeremiah xvii 11," *VT* 28 [1978]: 324–29).

n. A paronomasia: *'ōśēh 'ōśer*.

Yahweh continues to speak, confronting Judah about the deep-seated nature of its wrongdoing, but here 17:1–4 and (more concretely) 17:5–11 reflect the thinking of Proverbs and its use of imagery.[429] They are not a series of units that have simply strayed from their proper home in Proverbs but material that becomes another way of communicating the Jeremianic message about Judah and about the king. The medieval chapter division separating this section from what precedes reflects how 16:19–21 constituted a dramatic close to a chapter, though the juxtaposition of that material at the end of ch. 16

429. Cf. Rudolph, *Jeremia*, 85; Stulman, *Jeremiah*, 166.

with this material at the beginning of ch. 17 also implies that Judah is not responding to Yahweh as 16:19–21 expected of the nations. The verses form a sequence of subsections of separate origin but with common characteristics.

vv. 1–2   Critique of Judah (three bicola: the first two parallel, the second two linked by enjambment)

vv. 3–4   A threat of redress addressed to a mountain-dweller (a tricolon and three bicola)

v. 5a   Introduction

vv. 5b–8   Yahweh's words

   vv. 5b–6   A curse for the man who relies on humanity (four bicola)

   vv. 7–8   A blessing for the man who relies on Yahweh (a tricolon and three bicola)

vv. 9–10   Yahweh's insight into humanity's deviousness and his consequent action (three bicola, the latter two forming a pair)

v. 11   An aphorism about losing ill-gotten gain, followed by its interpretation (two bicola)

1 It is unusual for the text to jump straight in with no indication of the speaker; perhaps the curators were content to leave the unit that way because it is actually Yahweh who continues to speak, as he did in the preceding section. Likewise, the text does not initially identify an addressee, though what follows will make clear that Judah is the implicit, indirect addressee. The description of its deep-seated *wrongdoing* expresses the implications of what the scroll has said so far; it will continue to be justified by what happens up until 587 and afterward. Exodus and Deuteronomy describe Yahweh's commands being *written* on stone tablets, though they also indicate that ordinary writing would not work with this medium; they would need to be *engraved* (Exod 32:15–16). Proverbs 3:3 and 7:3 urge people to write them on the tablets of their mind. Yahweh here stretches the image still further: the problem is that it is Judah's *wrongdoing* that is thus written or engraved. This is done *with an iron stylus*, indeed *with a flint point*, which suggests the hardest possible engraving tool (the word might even mean diamond); Yahweh combines the ideas of writing and engraving. If his commands are written on the mind, they shape the behavior; if it is Judah's wrongdoing that is written there, it suggests that a commitment to wrongdoing has become ingrained there. "If this is so, where is the crazy old woman who claims that people can be without sin if they wish?"[430] The formulation is an alternative to asking whether a Sudanese can change his skin

---

430. Jerome, *Jeremiah*, 105, referring to Pelagius.

or a leopard its spots (13:23).[431] The problem is specifically a wrongdoing *in relation to your altars' horns*: whereas Judah was the subject in the first line, in Jeremiah it is regularly the addressee, and here the message switches to direct address to make sure people realize they are being confronted. Altars that people built to expiate wrongdoing were actually expressions of wrongdoing (Hos 8:11; cf. 11:13).[432] The link in particular with the altars' *horns* might be that someone accused of a capital offense could seek refuge by grasping the incense altar's horns (1 Kgs 1:50–51; 2:28); the message would thus be, "Don't think you have that place of refuge." Or the link might be that blood from a sacrifice would be spattered on the incense altar's horns, in particular on the Day of Atonement (Exod 30:10; Lev 4:7, 18, 25, 30, 34; 16:18); the reference could thus underscore the way the altars have reduced the prospect of Judah's finding expiation rather than increasing it.

2 Jeremiah makes more specific the point about *their altars* by referring also to *their totem poles* (*'ăšērâ*), wooden columns taking the form of figurines, in particular of the goddess Asherah (cf. 2:27; see the commentary there). They are *by verdant tree, by lofty hills* (e.g., 2:20; 3:6, 13), as was the case before Josiah's reformation. According to 2 Kgs 23, Josiah eliminated them; but *their children*, the next generation, *are mindful* of them and deeply attached to them.

3–4 It becomes clear that Yahweh is the speaker, and *mountain-dweller* (perhaps simply "mountain") is apparently a way of addressing Jerusalem, set in the midst of *the open country* of Judah. The action Yahweh intends in light of what he has bemoaned is to remove much of what Judah possesses. He repeats in a variant form the threat in 15:13–14 (see the commentary there): their attackers will take their resources and stores, all their national assets, as profit from their invasions. Here, Yahweh says Judah *will drop them* (*šāmaṭ*); ironically, he uses the term for forfeiting the repayment of a debt (*šəmiṭṭâ*, Deut 15:1–9; cf. Tg). The people will involuntarily and yet willfully (*through yourself*) forfeit their resources in the way they were supposed to forfeit them willingly and generously in the seventh year. The forfeit will include *your shrines, through wrongdoing, in all your territory*, which will thus appropriately fall away *from your domain that I gave you*, the domain that they had spoiled *with their detestable corpses, their offensive things* whose deceitfulness and emptiness even the nations are destined to recognize (16:19–20). Not only will *I make* your resources *pass with your enemies* (*'ābar hiphil*, 15:14) but *I will make you serve your enemies* (*'ābad hiphil* here) in a return to the people's status in Egypt (Exod 1:13; 6:5). And as a result of Yahweh's blazing anger, things will be that way *for all time*, as Yahweh adds in a final devastating

---

431. Calvin, *Jeremiah*, 2:356.
432. Thomas Aquinas, *Commentary on Jeremiah*; quoted in Schroeder, *Jeremiah*, 190.

variant on the formulation in 15:13–14. Fortunately, the translation "forever" (e.g., Vg *usque ad aeternam*), suggesting something that will last for eternity, gives a misleading impression. Like the English word *permanently*, the Hebrew term *'ad-'ôlām* can have varying reference. The context often suggests how permanent "for all time" will be. The expression denotes not "an absolute, timeless future" but "all thinkable, foreseeable future."[433] Commonly, it presupposes "until I have reason to change my mind," which safeguards against false confidence (cf. 7:7; 17:25; 25:5; 31:40; 32:40) but also against false despair (cf. 3:5, 12; 18:16; 23:40; 25:9, 12).

5 Jeremiah appends a further declaration that restates the point in more general terms, talking about humanity in general but applying in the context to Judah in particular. He makes explicit that it is a message from Yahweh, yet rather than as a message that Yahweh has uttered, it is expressed as an insight formulated by Jeremiah as if he were the kind of teacher whose insights appear in Proverbs. Like Proverbs, it speaks of a process built into the way the world works rather than one whereby Yahweh takes deliberate action. While it might thus be an existent piece of human insight that Yahweh turns into a message, it also corresponds in form and content to Moses's formulations in Deut 27–28. They describe as *cursed* anyone who commits certain acts (making an image being the first) and as *blessed* anyone who listens to Yahweh's commands. Proverbs does not use the cursed/blessed language, and more likely it is Jeremiah himself who formulates the lines this way. As is effectively the case in Deuteronomy, being cursed means losing a place in this *country* and ending up somewhere less hospitable. In form and imagery, the words also compare with Ps 1, whether the psalm is aware of Jeremiah or Jeremiah of the psalm or they are independent variants on a traditional formulation.[434] Comparing them draws attention to the difference in order, which corresponds to a difference in function in their contexts; in Jeremiah, the curse comes before the blessing (Ps 1 does not use "curse" language). The comparison also draws attention to Jeremiah's distinctive stress on reliance on Yahweh, a motif in Proverbs (e.g., 3:5; 16:20; 28:25; 29:25). In the Prophets, this is more an Isaianic motif than a Jeremianic one; Isa 31:1–3 brings together reliance, human beings, and flesh, and Isa 36 explores the motif of reliance on Yahweh. Yet in Jeremiah's time, the political context kept raising the question of the nation's reliance, through the period from Josiah's reign

433. Brueggemann, *Jeremiah 1–25*, 214.

434. See, e.g., G. Fischer, "Jeremia und die Psalmen," in *The Composition of the Book of Psalms*, ed. E. Zenger, BETL 238 (Leuven: Peeters, 2010), 469–78 (Fischer thinks the Psalms were influenced by Jeremiah rather than vice versa); W. L. Holladay, "Indications of Jeremiah's Psalter," *JBL* 121 (2002): 248–49; B. Gosse, "L'enracinement du livre de Jérémie dans le Psautier: Teil 2," *Biblische Notizen* 159 (2013): 39–40.

to Zedekiah's (and cf. 2:18). This difference in focus between Jeremiah and Ps 1 also draws attention to Jeremiah's description of the man as a *geber*, a macho man; in Ps 1, he is simply an *'îš*, a person. The macho man who *relies on a human being* thereby *makes flesh his arm*, his muscle. Such reliance is manifestly stupid because *flesh* (*bāśār*) is by definition weak—not a locus of sin, like flesh in Paul (*sarx*), but feeble (though vv. 1–2 in effect made the point that Paul will make by his use of *sarx*). In case you haven't got it, a third colon makes the correlative point about someone who relies on feeble humanity: *From Yahweh his mind turns aside* (*sûr*). Elsewhere, Jeremiah has implied defiance when he has used that verb (5:23; 6:28).

6 The nature of the environment down in *the steppe* (*hā'ărābâ*), the Arabah, the area around the Dead Sea, provides Jeremiah with simile and metaphor for describing the consequences of trusting humanity rather than Yahweh. A little distance away from the Jordan swell (12:5), nothing grows except a spindly *shrub*. There can be flourishing and fruitfulness up in the highland, but someone stuck down in the Arabah *will not see when good things come*. There need be nothing wrong with regular living in the wilderness, like Bedouin, but the man Jeremiah describes *will dwell in scorched places in the wilderness*, in the kind of area within the wilderness where there are not even little patches of grass that grow near a small water supply. It is *a salt country*; the Dead Sea in Hebrew is "the Salt Sea." The pervasiveness of its chemical deposits means nothing grows. No wonder there is *no one living there*. It contrasts so much with the country from which Judah will be hurled, which they have defiled (16:3, 13, 18). The allegory's implication is that disaster will follow if king and people think that their future lies in relying on a human being such as an Egyptian king.

7–8 Conversely, *blessed is the man who relies on Yahweh* and for whom *Yahweh will be his reliance*. The description of the blessing works with the same metaphorical framework as the description of the curse. The promise that this macho man *will be like a tree transplanted by water* corresponds to Ps 1:3 (except that it has "channels of water"); the cola about foliage and fruit also compare with Ps 1. In a neat a-b-c-c'-b'-a' comparison, the man will be

> like a tree
> > transplanted
> > > by water
> > > and by a stream
> > sending out
> its roots.

In the parallelism, the second colon makes more specific the key point about the location. It means the tree *is not afraid when heat comes*. With its paronomasia (see the translation note), that comment combined with the earlier reference to what the man of false reliance *will not see* makes for a comparison with Ps 40:3(4), which talks about what people will see and be afraid of (the same two verbs). The psalm also goes on to speak of the macho man who relies on Yahweh and has Yahweh as his reliance. It is testifying to the truth of what Jeremiah says, or Jeremiah is challenging Judah to live by what the psalm says. The location of the tree that symbolizes the man means that despite the heat, *its foliage will be verdant.* To restate the point about heat and about not being afraid, *in a year of drought it is not anxious.* And the key benefit of its location is that *it does not cease producing fruit.* The allegory's positive implication is that king and people need to rely on Yahweh for their fate; they will then have no need to be anxious about their political future. Jeremiah's declaration or promise is not that the faithful have an easy life, uncomplicated by challenges and problems. They have to face heat and drought.[435] But they are able to do so.

9 A further comment also has the form of a generalization that in broad terms compares with Proverbs. Eventually, this further comment will return to *fruit*, in a different connection from that in v. 8, but the verbal link might have encouraged the placing of this message here. Three lines make three interrelated points; each line is internally parallel. The first works a-b-c-a'-b'-c', the second a-b-c-d-c'-d', the third a-b-c-c'-d:

The mind	is more devious	than anything;
it	is grave—	who can know it?
I,	Yahweh,	am probing the mind,
		examining the heart,
and giving	to an individual	in accordance with his paths,
		in accordance with the fruit
		of his practices.

First, then, there is a problem about the human mind's deceptiveness. The description of the *mind* as *devious* (ʿāqōb) takes us back to 9:4(3) and in substance also to 12:2 (in a context with statements that stand in tension with vv. 5–8 here). What Judah says cannot be trusted. The parallel comment is that *it's grave* (ʾānûš); Jeremiah has the most occurrences of this unusual word, which usually qualifies the description of a wound or a sorrow (15:18; 30:12, 15) and will shortly describe the grim nature of the day of disaster that is coming (17:16). Here, it underscores the deviousness of which Jeremiah has spoken. Jeremiah's point is more specific than Gen 8:21; he is referring in particular to the deep-seated nature of the human mind as deceptive and

---

435. Stulman, *Jeremiah*, 169.

deceived. So *who can know it?* Even individuals who seek to be honest about themselves and their presuppositions may fail; we cannot even know our own minds.

10a But Yahweh can, the second line affirms. The problem is not a problem to Yahweh. While the First Testament often makes clear that Yahweh can have disappointments and surprises, Jeremiah's point here is that he can know whatever he chooses to know. Even if he is not by nature omniscient, he can be omniscient if he chooses. When he chooses to know what is in people's minds, he does so by looking—he finds things out, as human beings do. The difference is that there are no limits to what he can find out. He is thus one who is *probing* and *examining*, which takes us back to 6:27 and 9:7(6), but especially to 11:20. We are wise then to pray,

> Almighty God, unto whom all hearts be open, all desires known, and from whom no secrets are hid: Cleanse the thoughts of our hearts by the inspiration of thy Holy Spirit, that we may perfectly love thee, and worthily magnify thy holy Name; through Christ our Lord.[436]

10b The third line goes on to note that Yahweh can therefore deal with people in light of the truth they may try to conceal. The plea in the prayer quoted above is appropriate to this declaration. Either Yahweh cleanses and transforms or his people must be the victims of some unpleasant *giving* on his part. *Paths* is a good Jeremianic word, and nearly half the occurrences of *practices* (*ma'ālāl*) come in Jeremiah (e.g., 4:4, 18; 7:3, 5), so it constitutes a further indication that these Proverbs-like verses are Jeremiah's formulation. A subtlety about Jeremiah's chain of thought deserves noting. Christian spirituality sometimes affirms that God looks at the heart rather than the outward action or is interested in the inner attitude rather than the action. The Scriptures do not say so; God is interested in both and is not interested in attitudes that do not have corresponding actions—corresponding fruit, in fact. Jeremiah's point here is that God is not taken in when people say they will do or are doing one thing but are secretly planning or doing another.

11 The parable of the partridge involves two more internally parallel lines:

> A partridge that incubated   but did not give birth—
> someone who makes wealth   but not by exercising authority

But the two lines also function in the way that the two halves of a single line sometimes do: by raising a question that then receives an answer. How is this person like the partridge?

---

436. Thomas Cranmer's adaptation of a medieval Latin prayer; cf. Wright, *Jeremiah*, 202.

> In the middle of his days,   it will abandon him,
> and at his end   he will become a fool.

It is yet another Proverbs-like unit in that Proverbs likes to make parallels between the cosmos or nature on one hand and human beings on the other.

> The heavens regarding height, the earth regarding depth,
>   and the mind of kings—there's no exploring.
>   . . .
> Clouds and wind but no rain:
>   someone who takes pride in a false gift.
>   . . .
> A bad tooth and a wobbly foot:
>   confidence in someone who breaks faith on a day of pressure.
>   (Prov 25:3, 14, 19)

In each of these cases, the things in question are simply juxtaposed; there is no "like." They more resemble metaphors than similes. In this case, Jeremiah says in effect,

> Someone who makes wealth, but not by exercising authority,
>   is a partridge that incubated but did not give birth.

One significance about the order of the cola in Jeremiah is that the last word is *exercising authority* (*mišpāṭ*), which puts us on the track of a theme that underlies this entire section. The aphorism becomes the means of commenting on Jeremiah's expectations of a king,[437] the person with particular responsibility for exercising authority in Judah. While government is the responsibility of the entire Davidic household (21:12; cf. 22:3),[438] it is particularly the basis for Jeremiah's critique of Jehoiakim. He looked after himself well as king by exercising authority in a way that benefited him (*bəlōʾ mišpāṭ*, 22:13); Jeremiah's aphorism talks about doing well through not exercising authority (*lōʾ bəmišpāṭ*)—that is, in the proper fashion. The warning built into the aphorism is that in the end it will not pay. He will be like a bird that *incubated* chicks *but did not give birth* in the sense of seeing them hatch; the partridge perhaps figures in the aphorism because male partridges share in the incubating and subsequent caring for their mates' chicks.[439] With

---

437. K. Seybold, "Das 'Rebhuhn' von Jeremia 17,11," *Bib* 78 (1987): 57–73; Seybold notes that Duhm (*Jeremia*, 147) again wonders how it got here.

438. Mayer (*Commentary*, 392) takes this passage to refer to Jehoiachin.

439. See Lundbom, *Jeremiah 1–20*, 790.

the illegitimate wealth that the king gains, *in the middle of his days it will abandon him.* And Jehoiakim died at 36, halfway through what might have been the projected length of his life.[440] So *at his end he will become a fool* (*nābāl*), which might make people think about being a corpse (*nəbālâ*; cf. 16:18).[441] As this aphorism with its pointer toward the king closes off vv. 1–11, it confirms hints that Judah under its kingly leadership has been in focus through the section's Proverbs-like teaching. Perhaps it is the king who is the mountain-dweller, the macho man who declines to rely on Yahweh, the person who is incurably devious. "These innocent-looking affirmations hide the energy of prophecy."[442]

3. Another Exchange: Three Ironies (17:12–27)

[12]*An honored throne is on high—*
  from the first is our sacred place.[a]
[13]*Israel's hope, Yahweh:*
  all who abandon you will be put to shame.
The people who turn aside from me[b] *in the country will be written down,*
  because they have abandoned the fountain of living water—Yahweh.[c]

[14]*Heal me, Yahweh, so I may heal;*
  deliver me, so I may find deliverance,
  because you are my praise.
[15]*There, those people are saying to me,*
  "Where is Yahweh's message—
  it should come, please."
[16]*But I—I did not seek to escape from grazing*[d] *after you,*
  but a grave[e] *day I did not desire.*
You yourself know what goes out from my lips—
  it has been before your face.
[17]*Don't be a cause of breakdown to me—*
  you are my refuge on the day of dire trouble.
[18]*My pursuers should be shamed, and I—may I not be shamed;*
  they should break down, and I—may I not break down.
Bring upon them the day of dire trouble,
  and with a double shattering shatter them.[f]

---

440. Weiser, *Jeremia*, 152.
441. Craigie, Kelley, and Drinkard, *Jeremiah 1–25*, 229.
442. D. R. Jones, *Jeremiah*, 240.

[19]*Yahweh said this to me: Go[g] and stand at the People's Gateway by which the kings of Judah come in and by which they go out, and in all Jerusalem's gateways, [20]and say to them, Listen to Yahweh's message, kings of Judah, and all Judah, and all you who live in Jerusalem who come in by these gateways.[h]*
[21]*Yahweh has said this: Take care, for your own sake,[i] and don't carry a load on the Sabbath day or bring one through Jerusalem's gateways. [22]You will not take out a load from your houses on the Sabbath day and you will not do any work, but make the Sabbath day sacred, as I ordered your ancestors. [23]But they did not listen; they did not bend their ear. They stiffened their neck[j] so as not to listen[k] and so as not to accept restraint. [24]If you do listen[l] to me (Yahweh's affirmation) so as not to bring a load by this city's gateways on the Sabbath day, but to make the Sabbath day sacred so as not to do any work on it,[m] [25]then kings and officials, sitting on David's throne, riding on chariot and on horses, they and their officers will come by this city's gateways, the individual in Judah and the people who live in Jerusalem. And this city will live[n] for all time. [26]People will come from the towns of Judah, from around Jerusalem, from the region of Benjamin, from the foothills, from the highland, and from the Negeb, bringing whole offering, sacrifice, grain offering, and incense, and bringing a thanksgiving to Yahweh's house. [27]But if you do not listen to me so as to make the Sabbath day sacred and so as not to carry a load and come through Jerusalem's gateways on the Sabbath day, I will light a fire in its gateways. It will consume Jerusalem's citadels, and it will not go out.[o]*

a. In two asyndetic noun clauses arranged a-b-b'-a', the construct phrases frame the adverbial expressions (Holladay, *Commentary on Jeremiah*, 1:500–501), with the absolutes functioning adjectivally. The parallel with Ps 48:1–2(2–3) supports an understanding of them as clauses rather than as vocatives, with Vg and LXX, which read more briefly, "throne of honor on high, our sanctuary" (cf. Reventlow, *Liturgie*, 229–40).

b. For the *qere sûray*, the *ketiv* implies *yəsûray* ("the people restrained by me") or the construct *yəsûrê* ("the people restrained"; cf. *yāsar* in 2:19; 6:8; and *mûsār* in v. 23). LXX, Vg, Sym imply the construct *sûrê* ("the people who turn aside"); this line would then continue the confession begun in vv. 12–13a as the speakers declare the fate of such people.

c. MT has a section marker here. *Yahweh* comes at the end of the line, with the object marker *'et*, which turns the colon into one with five beats and adds to its emphasis.

d. For the construction, cf. GKC 119x. The participle *rō'eh* usually denotes a shepherd, but nowhere else is Jeremiah (or any other prophet) a shepherd, and "shepherding after you" is a tortuous expression. In Vg's understanding, Yahweh is the shepherd after whom Jeremiah is still going, which makes the construction more tortuous, and nowhere else in Jeremiah is Yahweh a shepherd. But the participle can refer to sheep grazing (e.g., Song 2:16; Isa 44:20), and the meaning is not so different in that case; cf. LXX "I have not tired of following after you" (D. R. Jones, *Jeremiah*, 247). For MT *mērō'eh* (from *rā'â*), Aq, Sym imply *mērā'â* (from *rā'a'*), meaning "from dire trouble."

e. For MT *'ānûš*, LXX, Vg imply *'ĕnôš* ("a human being's"; cf. v. 9).

f. MT has a section marker here.

g. The infinitive absolute is used as an imperative (cf. 2:2 and the note).

h. MT^L has a section marker here.

i. The preposition *bə* can denote the price to be paid for something, so *bənapšôtêkem* is close to implying "as the price for your lives."

j. LXX adds "more than their ancestors," as in 7:26, but the expression is even more confusing here than there since it is more explicit here that it is the ancestors whom Yahweh is describing.

k. For the *qere šəmôaʾ*, the *ketiv* implies the participle *šômēaʾ*, which is hard to make sense of and may just be a slip whereby letters were reversed (*šmwʿ* became *šwmʿ*).

l. The infinitive precedes the finite verb, underlining the factuality of the action.

m. For the *qere bô*, the *ketiv* implies *bāh* ("in it")—or the alternative spelling *bōh* (Craigie, Kelley, and Drinkard, *Jeremiah 1–25*, 238).

n. LXX, Vg have "be lived in," which is an implication (cf. BDB) but is not what the active verb says (Blayney, *Jeremiah*, 435).

o. MT has a unit marker here.

Jeremiah 14–17 comes to an end with a three-part section held together by verbal motifs: references to a throne, to sacredness, to abandoning, and to shame. While one commonly cannot know whether authors intend to incorporate suggestive juxtapositions into their work or whether the suggestiveness lies in the eye of the beholder, here the juxtaposition seems too big a coincidence to be accidental. In any case, it is present, whether or not it issued from conscious intention.

vv. 12–13   A confession incorporating the references to a throne, sacredness, abandoning, and shaming followed by a response affirming the confession (two bicola, then another bicolon)

    vv. 12–13a   The confession

    v. 13b   The response

vv. 14–18   A triple plea that incorporates reference to shaming and frames declarations about why Yahweh should respond[443] (two tricola and five bicola)

    v. 14   A plea for healing and deliverance and a confession of praise

    vv. 15–16   A protest and a confession of commitment

    v. 17   A plea for support and a confession of praise

    v. 18   A plea for the day of calamity to come

vv. 19–27   A prose commission to deliver a command about making the Sabbath sacred and about a throne

    vv. 19–20   The commission

443. Cf. Brueggemann, *Jeremiah 1–25*, 156.

vv. 21–22 The command: keep the Sabbath sacred
v. 23   The ancestors' failure to do so
vv. 24–26 The promise attached to obedience
v. 27   The threat attached to disobedience

12–13a Yahweh's *honored throne* and his *sacred place* can denote his palace in the heavens (e.g., Ps 11:4), but the words can also refer to their earthly equivalents, and here the *our* on *our sacred place* (the last syllable in the line) resolves any ambiguity. The confession enthuses over Yahweh's presence among his people, and the *our* suggests that Jeremiah is voicing Judah's faith. The confession is conceivable on Jeremiah's own lips, as is the declaration that *Yahweh is Israel's hope* (see 29:11; 31:17). It might thus refer to the temple, which Jeremiah does not disdain, but reference to the city would be more likely: the city was Yahweh's honored throne in 14:21; Jeremiah will refer to people coming and chanting *on Zion's height* (*mārôm*, as here) in 31:12; and *this place* was the city in 7:20. Describing temple or city as the sacred place *from the first* would be a hyperbole, though an understandable one; both have always been Israel's sacred place, ever since David's day. But it is more characteristic of Jeremiah to be raising questions about enthusiasm for or trust in temple or city (e.g., 7:1–15, where Shiloh was God's dwelling place *at the first*), so it would be surprising to discover him expressing unqualified enthusiasm for either. And when he talks elsewhere about Yahweh being *on high*, he refers to his being on high in the heavens (25:30). So vv. 12–13a do not really sound like Jeremiah.[444] And in 14:19–22, he recorded Judah pleading with Yahweh about *your honored throne* and affirming that they *hope in* Yahweh. So the confessions in vv. 12–13a are the people's confessions. Whereas the first three cola pick up phrases that might more directly use their words, the fourth makes them speak in Jeremiah's terms, and the declaration about people who *abandon you* makes a link with the aphorism preceding this confession, in v. 11. There is some irony or paradox in putting the word *abandon* on the people's own lips (and see, e.g., 16:11); the irony continues in the declaration that such people *will be put to shame* (e.g., 6:15; 8:12; 9:19[18]; 15:9).

13b Yahweh responds and confirms their declaration—again in Jeremianic terms, first as he designates the people who will be put to shame as *the people who turn aside from me in the country* (cf. 5:23; 6:28; 17:5). They *will be written down* as such, like Jehoiachin, who will be written down as childless

444. M. Metzger thus dates it as an affirmation of Zion from a later period than Jeremiah: see "'Thron der Herrlichkeit': Ein Beitrag zur Interpretation von Jeremia 17, 12f," in *Prophetie und geschichtliche Wirklichkeit im Alten Israel: Festschrift für Siegfried Herrmann zum 65. Geburtstag*, ed. R. Liwak and S. Wagner (Stuttgart: Kohlhammer, 1991), 237–62.

(22:30). The coup de grace in Yahweh's words comes, not surprisingly, in the last colon of vv. 12–13. Yahweh picks up their reference to abandoning but also repeats the formulation articulated against them in 2:13: *they have abandoned the fountain of living water*. When people hear that declaration, they might rerun the opening colon of the verse and remember that there are two words *miqweh*; one means hope, but the other means reservoir (e.g., Exod 7:19). Yahweh is both.

14 What follows involves a sudden leap; the scroll will not make a link with what precedes until v. 18. *Heal me, Yahweh, so I may heal* takes up from 15:18. Jeremiah continues to speak not about a personal illness or about wounds that have been inflicted on him by fellow-Judahites but about his anticipatory experience of Yahweh's shattering of Judah. Notwithstanding Yahweh's response to him in that earlier exchange, he is still devastated. Can Yahweh offer him no healing? Thus he goes on to plead for *deliverance* in keeping with the promise Yahweh gave him when speaking of healing earlier (15:20). In his anticipatory imagination, he continues to identify with the lament that Judah will cry out, *we haven't found deliverance* (8:20), and with its question: is Yahweh *the hope of Israel* or is he *like a strong man who cannot deliver* (14:8–9)? Jeremiah's affirmation that Yahweh is *my praise* pushes further that identification (cf. 13:11).

15 Paradoxically, part of Jeremiah's problem is still that the experience of Judah's shattering, which he has to keep embodying and talking about, continues to be anticipatory. The shattering never becomes a reality for Judah itself. And people continue to decline to take Yahweh's threat seriously. *"Where is Yahweh's message—it should come, please."* The *please* is the special barb.

16 Jeremiah could have been caught between two impossibilities. He could have sought to *escape from grazing after you*, but instead he became the sheep who followed Yahweh as shepherd. He might have said here that he had not rushed toward this relationship either; indeed he initially tried to resist it, though he gave up the attempt pretty quickly. Alternatively, he could have been the kind of person who is enthused about bringing doom-laden messages. But actually, *a grave day I did not desire*. When he described his own wound as grave (15:18), it was an aspect of his anticipation of the day of grave shattering (30:12, 15). He had not wanted that day to come. He had no delight in the idea of calamity coming on Judah. Is he fooling himself or thinking he can fool Yahweh? He has already characterized the human mind as grave in its deceptiveness and has asked rhetorically who can know it, and he has then recognized that Yahweh can see into it and look for the match between the inside of the person and the outward action (v. 9). Here, he acknowledges that *you yourself know what goes out from my lips—it has been before your face*. Maybe he refers especially to the prayers he has prayed for the people, notwithstanding Yahweh's instruction not to pray for them. They would be a particular indication that he had no desire for catastrophe to come to them.

17 Jeremiah can imagine a third (im)possibility. Way back at the beginning, when Yahweh issued his commission, he told Jeremiah he must not break down (1:17). But is Yahweh putting such pressure on him that *breakdown* is inevitable? Surely he cannot be doing so. *You are my refuge*: Jeremiah uses the noun only here; the confession recurs in the Psalms (e.g., Ps 142:5[6]). Yahweh must continue to be his refuge *on the day of dire trouble*, the moment when Judah's dire behavior meets its deserved redress. The day of Yahweh, which is darkness not light (Amos 5:18) and will be *a grave day* (v. 16), now becomes *a day of dire trouble*. Once again, in this plea, the distinction between present and future collapses. The day of dire trouble is still to come, but it's here now in Jeremiah's anticipatory experience. Jeremiah thus adds a fourth aspect to the basis of his plea. The first and last complement each other and the middle two complement each other.

> Yahweh is his praise (v. 14).
> People dismiss Jeremiah's warnings (v. 15).
> Jeremiah has been faithful to his commission, and Yahweh knows
>   it (v. 16).
> Yahweh is his refuge (v. 17b).

In a protest psalm, one may talk of what I am experiencing, what you (Yahweh) are doing or not doing, and what they (my troublers) are doing to me. Jeremiah has covered those three directions in the claims that back up his prayer: "You are my praise and my refuge; they are scorning; I neither sought to evade my commission nor improperly rejoiced in it" (cf. 15:15; see the commentary there).

18 At last there emerges the link with what preceded in this unit. The Judahites who have been declaring that people who abandon Yahweh will be put to shame, and the Judahites whose identity Yahweh has noted in this connection (v. 13) are the people who deride Jeremiah. They are *my pursuers*, and it is they who *should be shamed*, whereas *I—may I not be shamed*, which is what is happening at present. Jeremiah makes the point with its contrasts in a neatly parallel, long 4-4 a-b-c-d-a'-b'-c'-d' line:

> my pursuers   should be shamed   and I may I not be shamed
> they   should break down   and I may I not break down

They should have their falsity and their dire activity exposed to themselves and to the nations, while Jeremiah should be vindicated as the prophet who has been speaking the truth all along. The colon about breaking down fits with Yahweh's words back at the beginning (1:17). Jeremiah has to play his part in standing firm, but he needs a strength from outside to buttress his standing firm. Yahweh should *bring upon them the day of dire trouble, and with a double shattering shatter them*. Jeremiah originally had no desire for such a dire fate to come upon them, but he has come to identify with Yahweh's way of looking at them and at what must happen to them. He now does want to see their dire behavior meeting dire trouble, as Yahweh has said it must (on *double* shattering, see the commentary on 16:18). We know from things he has said already that he is grieved at the suffering that he recognizes must come to them, even while also accepting that it must come and being glad that he will thereby be vindicated; the Psalms and Paul make more explicit that they want to see their vindication in this way (e.g., Ps 35:26–27; 2 Tim 4:14).[445] He is conflicted, with a sense of turmoil that reflects Yahweh's.[446] As there are four aspects to the basis of Jeremiah's plea, so there are four aspects to the plea itself—two complementary pairs.

> Heal me, deliver me (v. 14a).
> Don't let me break down (v. 17a).
> Shame my persecutors (v. 18a).
> Bring upon them the day of trouble (v. 18b).

Whereas Yahweh has the last word in the exchanges in 11:18–12:17 and 14:13–15:21, Jeremiah has the last word here and in the succeeding exchanges in 18:1–20:18. The sequence compares and contrasts with (or is a converse of) Amos 7:1–9; 8:1–3, where twice Amos responds to Yahweh's revelation and twice lets Yahweh have the last word. Jeremiah continues to embody Judah's experience, and in telling Judah about it continues to seek to communicate with the people and to get them to turn. "The hostility he faces from human agents is matched by the silence of God. . . . God's silence to the poet corresponds to the absence of God announced to the whole people. God is no longer available either to Israel or even to the poet. The poet experiences the very absence that is the destiny of Israel."[447]

19–20 What follows makes for another sudden leap, into a commission like the ones in 7:1–14 and 11:1–13. We don't know which was *the People's Gateway*, but it was evidently one they shared with the royals when they came to the temple. Plural *kings* might be simply rhetorical,[448] though Judah

---

445. Allen, *Jeremiah*, 206.
446. Cf. Wright, *Jeremiah*, 204.
447. Brueggemann, *Jeremiah 1–25*, 158.
448. D. R. Jones, *Jeremiah*, 250.

did have five kings between 609 and 597 (see the commentary on 13:13). But the plural hints that Yahweh is not simply concerned with one king at one moment but with the line of kings in Judah, who on an ongoing basis are the bearers of a promise attaching to David (v. 25) and are responsible for seeing that the city is run in a way that matches Yahweh's expectations (as hinted by v. 11). The Jeremiah scroll wants to address that entire line, not just one representative. And Yahweh wants all the people to hear because they need to fall in with these expectations.

21 Jeremiah 7 and 11 have pressed the demands of Yahweh's pledge with Israel in general terms and in connection with many of the specifics in the Decalogue, such as murder, adultery, theft, swearing to deception, and burning offerings to other deities; Yahweh now adds another (honoring father and mother is the one practical command that remains unmentioned). His concern lies with something they need to *take care* about *for their own sake*. It might not seem to be in their interests to abstain from the activity that Yahweh here prohibits. The period (say) from 609 through 587 with its political upheavals, invasions, and experiences of drought and other dearth would be one of economic uncertainty; families might not be sure whether they would have enough to eat.[449] But at the end of his message, Yahweh will indicate a more cataclysmic way in which they will be imperiling their lives if they ignore what he says. What he requires is that they do *not carry a load on the Sabbath*. Nehemiah 13:15–22 makes more explicit the kind of load Yahweh refers to.[450] The plazas inside a town gateway were the location of pop-up markets where farmers could bring produce to sell, as they still are in Jerusalem.

22 The people who brought loads from their houses would be people such as jewelers, potters, bakers, and people engaged in "garage sales, tag sales, or Sabbath flea markets."[451] They should *not do any work*: they should not be engaged in their crafts at home as well as not bringing their products

---

449. Contrast R. P. Carroll's suggestion (*Jeremiah*, OTL, 368) that the passage suggests settled conditions.

450. On the possible development of this passage and its relationship to Exodus/Deuteronomy and Neh 13, see Fishbane, *Biblical Interpretation*, 131–34; J. Briend, "Le sabbat en Jr 17,19–27," in *Mélanges bibliques et orientaux en l'honneur de M. Mathias Delcor*, ed. A. Caquot, S. Légasse, and M. Tardieu, Alter Orient und Alte Testament 215 (Neukirchen: Neukirchener, 1985), 23–35; J. A. Gladson, "Jeremiah 17:19–27," *CBQ* 62 (2000): 33–40; R. Achenbach, "The Sermon on the Sabbath in Jeremiah 17:19–27 and the Torah," in *The Formation of the Pentateuch: Bridging the Academic Cultures of Europe, Israel, and North America*, ed. J. C. Gertz et al., BZAW 415 (Tübingen: Mohr Siebeck, 2016), 873–90; Rom-Shiloni "Actualization," 271–78.

451. Lundbom, *Jeremiah 1–20*, 806.

out to sell. They will thus *make the Sabbath day sacred*: here comes the link with vv. 12–13, with its reference to sacredness. The Scriptures provide a number of rationales for observing the Sabbath, such as its requiring heads of households to give their servants and their animals a break each week and its enabling people to enjoy rest and refreshment; but in speaking of making it sacred, Yahweh's command links with the description of his own act of creation. There (Gen 2:3), God made the seventh day sacred without indicating the implication that humanity should observe it. Here, Judahites are to observe it, and Yahweh implies it is not a novelty: *I ordered your ancestors* to make it sacred. As a command in the Decalogue, it is a fundamental aspect of Israelite life. There is a link between God making something sacred and his people doing so, a link applying to other objects such as the people and the temple. When God makes something sacred, he puts a claim on it; when human beings make something sacred, they recognize the claim. With the Sabbath, while every day belongs to God, the implication is that he has put a claim on this particular day, so people are to keep off it by not working. They thus imitate the pattern of his creation whereby he did a week's work and then stopped working for a day. If Gen 1:1–2:3 dates from the exile, the requirement here that Judahites observe the Sabbath and make it sacred would gain extra significance then, but there seems no particular reason to take this story in vv. 19–27 as fictional. Jeremiah does give more specificity to the Sabbath command given to Judah's ancestors by applying it to trade in Jerusalem. The extension fits the needs of the urban context that he addresses, though there is nothing very innovative about the move; Amos 8:5 has already presupposed the point.

23 But Judah's ancestors *did not listen; they did not bend their ear.* The plaint is the general one that Yahweh issued about the pledge (11:8), of which the Sabbath was part. *They stiffened their neck*, the additional plaint Yahweh made in connection with people's ignoring his priorities (7:26). They acted thus *so as not to listen* (16:12) *and so as not to accept restraint* (see 2:19–20, 30; and the translation notes and commentary there).

24–27 At this point, as at others, the community needs to turn its back on its ancestors' practice. It can then see the fulfillment of an idyllic picture of ongoing normal life; *this city will live for all time.* People will come from all over the country not just for trade but for worship. The Sabbath itself is not specially a worship day, and the focus here does not lie on an un-Jeremianic focus on "diligent prosecution of the cult."[452] Specifying the different parts of the country suggests the observance of the annual pilgrimage festivals. It implies the dimensions of Judah in Jeremiah's day

---

452. Bright, *Jeremiah*, 120.

before, for instance, the time when Edomites occupied the Negeb. But if the community takes no notice, *I will light a fire in its gateways*; the punishment would fit the crime since the gateways are the focus of the wrongdoing. But the fire will not stop there: *It will consume Jerusalem's citadels, and it will not go out.* While Jeremiah regularly implies an invitation to people to recognize that they have to choose between two destinies, here he explicitly lays alternatives before them in a way that is unusual. Evidently, observance of the Sabbath is of crucial importance. It will gain extra importance in the context of exile, and it will become a decisive marker of being the people of Yahweh. It does not imply legalism.[453] Jeremiah suggests two aspects of its significance: an economic one and a theological one. Willingness to set aside productive work and trade for one day each week suggests repudiating the assumption confronted by Karl Marx that economics is everything.[454] In good times, it suggests turning aside from coveting, the last of the commands in the Decalogue. In harder times, it suggests trusting God for what one eats, drinks, and wears (Matt 6:24–34). The economic significance of the Sabbath is thus its spiritual significance, which links with its theological significance, that (paradoxically) observing the Sabbath signifies a recognition that every day belongs to God. Giving tithes of one's possessions and thus holding back from using them signifies a recognition that all one's possessions come from God. It thus (again paradoxically) sanctifies them all. Keeping off of one day signifies a recognition that all one's time comes from God. It thus sanctifies all one's days. In both connections "this passage, like much else in Jeremiah, stakes everything on the centrality of God."[455]

D. PART 2D: CONCERNING PLANS AND COUNSELS (18:1–20:18)

The phrase *the message that came to Jeremiah from Yahweh* again signals a new compilation introduced by Jeremiah's curators, as it did in 7:1; 11:1; and (in similar words) 14:1; the next occurrence will be 21:1. The phrase thus introduces 18:1–20:18. The compilation brings together two sequences of material with stories about pots, postscripts to the stories, and related protests/prayers. The issue the stories raise concerns divine sovereignty, and they thus raise questions about possible understandings of the relationship between Yahweh's decision-making and Judah's decision-making. In the first sequence, the future is still open (the pot can be remade); in the second, it is closed (the pot is smashed). Before 587, the compilation would confront

---

453. Stulman, *Jeremiah*, 179.
454. Pixley, *Jeremiah*, 59.
455. Brueggemann, *Jeremiah 1–25*, 159.

the community with the necessity to take note of the challenge implied by the first sequence, before the closed future of the second set becomes a reality. After 587 it would summon the community to recognize the dynamic whereby things had worked out the way they had.

18:1–23	The potter: when your decisions can make a difference
18:1–12	Jeremiah and the potter: Yahweh's flexible plans
18:13–17	A verse postscript: Yahweh's assessment of Judah
18:18–23	A protest responding to what has preceded: an ultimate prayer
19:1–20:18	The pot: when it's too late
19:1–13	Jeremiah, the decanter, and Yahweh's counsel
19:14–20:6	A story postscript: the reaction, and the identity of the invader
20:7–18	Protests responding to what has preceded: two ultimate prayers

1. The Potter: When Your Decisions Can Make a Difference (18:1–23)

The motif of Yahweh's plans or counsel runs through Jer 18:

vv. 1–12	Yahweh can have plans concerning a nation, but whether they find fulfillment will depend on the nation's response; but Yahweh suspects that Judah will be determined to follow their own plans
vv. 13–17	What Israel has done and what Yahweh intends
vv. 18–23	The people who have their own plans for Jeremiah, related to questions about counsel; their counsel against Jeremiah and his response

As usual, the chapter's sections look as if they are of independent origin, but their shared theme links them in the scroll's arrangement.

a. Jeremiah and the Potter: Yahweh's Flexible Plans (18:1–12)

[1]*The message that came to Jeremiah from Yahweh:* [2]*Set to and go down to a potter's house. There I will get you to listen to my words.* [3]*So I went down to a potter's house, and there he was doing his work on the double stones.* [4]*The object that he was making with the clay would go to ruin*[a] *in the potter's hand, and he would make it again*[b] *into another object, as it was right in the potter's eyes to do.*[c]

427

⁵Yahweh's message came to me:

⁶Like this potter I can deal with you, can't I,
  household of Israel (Yahweh's affirmation).
There, like clay in the potter's hand,
  *so are you in my hand, household of Israel.*ᵈ
*⁷Momentarily,*ᵉ *I speak regarding a nation or regarding a kingdom*
  about pulling up and about pulling down and about wiping out.
⁸That nation turns from its faithlessness
  regarding which I spoke against it,
And I relent regarding the dire trouble
  *that I planned to do to it.*ᶠ
⁹And momentarily I speak regarding a nation or regarding a kingdom
  about building and about planting.
¹⁰It does what is dire in my eyes
  so as not to listen to my voice,
And I relent regarding the good
  *that I said to do to it.*ᵍ

*¹¹So now say, please, to each individual in Judah and regarding the people who live in Jerusalem: Yahweh has said this. Here am I, shaping dire trouble regarding you, and formulating a plan regarding you. Turn, please, each individual from his dire path. Make your paths and your practices good. ¹²But they will say,*ʰ *Futile, because it is after our own plans that we will go. Each individual, the determination of his dire mind we will act on.*ⁱ

a. The clause introduced by a *weqatal* is in effect a conditional clause (DG 113; *TTH* 148; Joüon 167b); another follows in v. 8.

b. On the *wayyiqtol*, see the translation note on 6:17.

c. MT has a marker here.

d. MT has a section marker here.

e. Tg has has "at one time," then "at another time" in v. 9, but there is no parallel for this meaning of *rega'* (rather, cf. 4:20, the only other occurrence in Jeremiah).

f. MT has a section marker here.

g. MT has a section marker here.

h. LXX, Vg have "they said" (cf. 13:11).

i. MT has a marker here.

Jeremiah tells another story about a symbolic action; in some aspects of its dynamic it resembles the story in 13:1–12a.[456] First, it pictures the way potters can do as they like with their clay when it goes wrong; Yahweh affirms that

456. Allen, *Jeremiah*, 213.

he can likewise do as he likes with Israel (vv. 2–6). After 597 or after 587, the story itself could bring an encouraging message. The fall of Jerusalem each time signified that the pot that Yahweh was shaping had gone to ruin—it was no good, and the potter was rolling up the clay into a ball and starting again. But at least he was starting again! So 597 or 587 needn't be the end. As was the case in 13:1–12a, the action is one that Yahweh commissions and Jeremiah goes on to undertake but that nobody witnesses. It works by becoming the subject of a story that people hear and are to imagine happening, not by being an event that they see. A distinctive feature is that Jeremiah is not the one who performs the symbolic action itself. It is a symbolic action that sets in motion the event that it portrays, but the person who sets the event in motion is the anonymous potter who doesn't realize what he is doing.

Yahweh's subsequent message (vv. 7–10) develops the account of his freedom in a way that goes beyond the story's implications, as the message in 13:1–12a related somewhat indirectly to the story. Here, the potter image doesn't obviously lead into the message, and the message doesn't obviously link with the image. Yahweh has two options concerning any nation, with everything depending on how they respond to him. In contrast to the story, the message suggests more explicitly that the final disaster hasn't yet happened. It envisages a nation or kingdom still having the option of turning from its faithlessness and avoiding a dire fate—or needing to maintain its faithfulness if it is to experience a more positive future. It's possible for people to assume that God's will is firmly fixed, that he is sovereign and all-knowing, that in light of his omniscience he decides what to do in the future, and that in light of his sovereignty he then makes it happen. Such convictions can be a basis for both comfort and despair. Like other prophets, Jeremiah makes different assumptions. He knows Yahweh is more flexible than this theology implies, and part 2d of the scroll thus begins like other parts, by questioning an assumption that Judahites might make.

Finally, Yahweh brings together his two themes; while we might have wondered if the message was an addition to the story made through the process whereby the scroll developed,[457] the eventual whole is indeed a whole. As the potter, Yahweh is shaping disaster for the Judahites, so they need to turn, but the trouble is they won't (vv. 11–12). Here, it is thus even more explicit that the final disaster to Judah hasn't yet happened. And here, Jeremiah sets the question of Judah's freedom and flexibility or lack of flexibility alongside that of Yahweh's. He has no doubt about Yahweh's flexibility; he has doubts about theirs. The section as a whole as we have it, then, fits well

---

457. On the possible development of the story, see C. Brekelmans, "Jeremiah 18,1–12 and Its Redaction," in Bogaert, *Livre de Jérémie*, 343–50.

before or after 597, combining challenge and encouragement. After 587, it would once again explain why things worked out the way they did.

v. 1	An introduction to this story and to Jer 18–20 as a whole
v. 2	A command from Yahweh, to go
vv. 3–4	An act of obedience by Jeremiah
vv. 5–6	A word of interpretation from Yahweh (an introduction and two bicola of prosaic verse)
vv. 7–10	A further word of interpretation from Yahweh (two sequences of three bicola of prosaic verse, each second and third linked)
v. 11	A command from Yahweh, to speak
v. 12	A prediction, about what will follow

1–4 The opening verse does double duty: the introduction to the story is also the introduction to the compilation (cf. 7:1). The practical background to the story (it is common to quote Duhm's description of it as "a very childish haggadah"[458]) is a feature of Jerusalem life that was presupposed by 17:19–27. City life generates or facilitates the emergence of specialist trades. No longer does every family need to bake its own bread; there are bakers where you can buy bread (37:21). Something similar applies to metalwork and to pottery. As was the case in the West until a couple of centuries ago, a man and his family would undertake their trade from home; the separation of home and work has not yet happened. Initially, all that Jeremiah knows is that he has to *go down to a potter's house.* In 22:1, *go down* presupposes that Jeremiah is in the temple area, and that implication may hold here (cf. also 36:12).[459] The temple area was often where he preached and hung out (cf. 36:5), and it would also therefore be a natural place for him to receive a commission from Yahweh. As was the case in 13:1–12a, an aspect of the dynamic of his work as a prophet is that he doesn't know everything all at once. Initially, he just has to go to the area where you would find a potter living, apparently in the lower (older, noisier) part of the city, the area nearer the water supply derived from the Gihon Spring and channeled along to the Siloam Pool, which a potter would need. The *double stones* were two pieces of shaped rock joined by a wooden shaft on which they could turn. With his feet, the potter moved the bottom stone and thus moved the top one on which he would manipulate the clay, as described in Sir 38:29–30.[460] Apparently, a potter's attempt to make

---

458. Duhm, *Jeremia,* 153; e.g., Weiser, *Jeremia,* 1:158.

459. Craigie, Kelley, and Drinkard, *Jeremiah 1–25,* 296.

460. See R. H. Johnston, "The Biblical Potter," *BA* 37 (1974): 86–106; see the picture on p. 100.

something didn't always work. The clay didn't become a pot. It somehow *would go to ruin*. The verb is the same one as in 13:7. In neither context does it suggest that someone is doing the ruining; the verb is *niphal* rather than *pual* or *hophal*, the explicitly passive verb forms. The potter doesn't cause the ruining; the shaping just doesn't work out for one reason or another. What the potter does is press the clay back into a ball and start again *as it was right in the potter's eyes to do*. He is not very troubled by what happens. It often happens. He just begins again.

5–6 It is at this point that the next stage in Yahweh's speaking happens. Yahweh is the potter. Israel is the pottery project that goes to ruin. The potter and clay image recurs elsewhere in the Scriptures, partly because it was a familiar feature of everyday life—the vast number of pottery fragments found in archaeological digs hints at how often people needed the potter's skill. The image thus appears in different connections in, e.g., Isa 29:15–16; 45:9; 64:8; Rom 9:20–21, and in Christian spirituality:

> Have Thine own way, Lord,
> Have Thine own way.
> Thou art the potter; I am the clay.
> Mold me and make me after Thy will,
> While I am waiting yielded and still.[461]

One thus has to be wary of reading into a passage implications of the image that do not apply in the passage in question. The notion of the clay having options is questionable, as Paul implies in Rom 9:20–21. "The subject strains the symbol as it focuses on human choice."[462] The clay cannot "help" how it turns out, as the land where the sower sows (Matt 13) cannot "help" what kind of soil it is. The point of these images lies not in the responsibility of clay or seed but in the potter's freedom and persistence and the sower's success. The potter does not throw away the clay he was working with and start again with a new ball of clay; he presses the clay back into a ball and reworks it. The respective theological implications of the two understandings would be radically different.[463] The good news for Judah is that Yahweh is not finished with it.

7 Yahweh makes a knight's move in what follows, as often happens in the interpretation of a dream or vision, which can take up some elements, ignore others, and introduce new motifs (see, e.g., Dan 2).[464] On its first

---

461. Wright, *Jeremiah*, 212.
462. Allen, *Jeremiah*, 216.
463. See the discussion in McKane, *Jeremiah*, 1:420–23.
464. Cf. D. R. Jones, *Jeremiah*, 255; and on interrelationships within Jer 18, see P. R.

occurrence in Jer 1:10, Yahweh's talk of *pulling up, pulling down,* and *wiping out* related to nations and kingdoms generally, and likewise Jonah assumes that the principle Yahweh here announces applies to a city such as Nineveh. Conversely, "God's dealings with his chosen people are not different in kind, in their moral and spiritual dynamics, from his dealings with any and every people."[465] Yet Yahweh speaks in the singular of *a nation* or *a kingdom,* and the context suggests that the terms refer to Israel or Ephraim or Judah. His point is that there is nothing final about his statements concerning the future. He speaks *momentarily,* for a moment. It is superficially a revolutionary statement, in that Yahweh's threats in Jeremiah have always sounded as if they were declarations about what was definitely going to happen. But their presupposition has always been that everything depended on what response the threat received. It was indeed a threat or warning: the point about it was to provoke a response that made its implementation unnecessary. Yahweh's relationship with his people is not like that of a judge in a Western law court, who pronounces a penalty that will be implemented no matter what the reaction of the guilty party. Yahweh's relationship with people is more like that of parents with their children. "God is depicted in Jeremiah 18 as sovereign, transcendent, *and* immanent."[466] He speaks first of a change of mind about bringing calamity. This first divine repentance is

> His true and proper repentance . . . the repentance in which He promises to go back and does in fact go back on warnings and even judgments which have already fallen. It is the repentance on account of which He sends His prophets, so that His people too may turn and thus lay hold of this promise and these benefits and confirm and justify God's gracious repentance. . . . That God is of such a nature that 'He repents of evil' is included with His grace, mercy, forbearance and clemency as one of His divine attributes.[467]

8 Everything depends on whether the nation in question *turns (šûb) from its faithlessness.* Yahweh may then *relent (nāḥam niphal).* Yahweh again juxtaposes the two Hebrew words that are sometimes translated "repent" (4:28 applies both to Yahweh; cf. Jonah 3:9). The first is an action word; the nature of the turning that is required has been made clear enough in Jeremiah's messages, which have spoken of faithlessness in religion, in pol-

---

Davies, "Potter, Prophet and People: Jeremiah 18 as Parable," *HAR* 11 (1987): 23–33; T. E. Fretheim, "The Repentance of God: A Study of Jeremiah 18:7–10," *HAR* 11 (1987): 81–92.

465. R. W. L. Moberly, *Prophecy and Discernment,* Cambridge Studies in Christian Doctrine (Cambridge: Cambridge University Press, 2006), 50.

466. J. Peckham, "The Passible Potter and the Contingent Clay: A Theological Study of Jeremiah 18:1–10," *JATS* 18 (2007): 136.

467. Barth, *CD* II, 1:498.

itics, and in social life. The second is also a feelings word; it can mean "find comfort" or "find relief." There is a suggestion that Yahweh breathes a sigh of relief when the nation's turning means he will not have to do the thing that he didn't really want to do. In theory, the principle he enunciates complicates the test of prophecy in Deut 18:15–22,[468] though there are (alas) no examples in the First Testament of Israel turning like the Ninevites and of a prophet like Jonah getting into trouble because his warning does not come true; Jeremiah's problem is that Yahweh's warnings fail to come true because he cannot bring himself to implement them even though Judah fails to turn.

9–10 A second possibility corresponds more closely to what Jeremiah has seen in the potter's house. In 1:10, it was natural to infer that pulling up/ pulling down and building/planting were successive operations, as they will be for Judah. Here they are alternative operations. Judah chooses which is to happen to it. Relenting turns out not to have those nice emotional overtones, and one has to "note then the kindness and severity of God" (Rom 11:22).[469]

11 After 587, it would be odd for the message to be formulated in terms of alternatives. Jeremiah's audience need to learn the lesson now, when the question is still open, and they need to learn it individually and corporately. Yahweh is *formulating a plan* against them—to use a regular way of making the point. Jeremiah first uses a more distinctive expression, which fits the context and at last makes for a link between the story in vv. 2–6 and Yahweh's message in vv. 7–10. Yahweh is indeed *shaping* something, like a potter (*yôṣēr*), though again Jeremiah shows how prophetic rhetoric can make knight's moves. The thing Yahweh is shaping is now utterly different. What he is shaping is *dire trouble* that corresponds to the people's *dire path*, which contrasts with making *your path and your practices good* so that they open up the way to the *good* of which v. 10 spoke. The good news is that it is specifically the bad-news shaping that can come to ruin in the potter's hand, if the people turn. It is this side to the twin possibilities in vv. 7–10 that Judah and Jerusalem need to take account of. To return to the earlier way of utilizing the image, the good news is that the potter is still working the clay. It can still be re-formed. Once it has become a pot, it will be too late (see 19:1–13).[470] But at the moment the pot has not been fired. Thus in the meantime, God says, "Do not despair."[471] The question is whether people will take action and disprove Jeremiah's prediction. "The linking of abso-

468. J. T. Hibbard, "True and False Prophecy: Jeremiah's Revision of Deuteronomy," *JSOT* 35 (2011): 339–58.

469. Origen, *Jeremiah*, 196.

470. Chrysostom, *Instructions to Catechumens* 1:4, NPNF 1, 9; cf. Wenthe, *Jeremiah*, 147.

471. Theodoret, *Ermeneia*, PG 81:608.

lute judgement with warning and exhortation to repentance is a common characteristic of much of the first part of the book [of Jeremiah]: apparently absolute statements, such as 18.1–11a, are alleviated by the warning and hortatory words of 18.11b."[472] The logical implication of the potter and clay analogy is that Israel is simply the clay in the potter's hand, totally subject to his manipulation. But Yahweh's challenge makes clear that this inference would be mistaken. The relationship between Yahweh and Israel is indeed a personal one, like the relationship between a parent and a grownup son or daughter or a professor and a student, not that between a traffic cop and a driver or a judge and an accused. Both parties have responsibility and power, and the question is how they implement their responsibility and power. Yahweh is prepared to become traffic cop or judge in due course and will do so. But the relationship has not reached that point yet, and he doesn't want it to (and even then, the image of the potter reworking the clay suggests the implication would not be final abandonment). The *please* each time suggests an "emotional urgency."[473]

12 Some hopes. "The tragedy of Judah's story is nowhere more poignantly set out than in the people's response to these words," whether they are defiant or despairing.[474] The end of the story overlaps with the end of the story in 13:1–12a, which incorporated a statement of fact: *But they haven't listened.* This story closes with a prediction that characteristically puts onto Judah's lips statements that they would never make in so many words but that are implied by the stance they will take. Either Yahweh or Jeremiah or both dare Judah to face the facts and own their own intentions—or prove him wrong. As an expression of Jeremiah's and Yahweh's lack of any expectation, the declaration also overlaps with 2:25: *futile, because it is after our own plans that we will go* compares with *futile, no, because I love foreigners, and it is after them that I will go*; the plans and the foreigners may refer to the same thing. "It's all over."[475] The final words also correspond to a formulation in the confrontation about Yahweh's pledge: *each individual, the determination of his dire mind we will act on* in this passage compares with *they went, each one, by the determination of their dire mind* (11:8). But the story does imply that it's still open to people to prove Yahweh and Jeremiah wrong. Once again, the words comprise a challenge when the future is still open; after 587, they will comprise an explanation.

---

472. P. R. Ackroyd, *Exile and Restoration: A Study of Hebrew Thought of the Sixth Century B. C.*, OTL (London: SCM, 1968), 52.

473. Holladay, *Commentary on Jeremiah*, 1:516.

474. P. D. Miller, "Jeremiah," on the passage.

475. Calvin, *Jeremiah*, 2:428.

b. A Verse Postscript: Yahweh's Assessment of Judah (18:13–17)

¹³*Therefore, Yahweh has said this:*

Ask, please, among the nations—
who has heard anything like these things?
*Something horrific*ᵃ *she has done, very much,*ᵇ
*young girl Israel.*ᶜ
¹⁴*Does the Lebanon snow abandon*ᵈ
*the crag in the open country?*ᵉ
*Or does the foreign water pull up*ᶠ*—*
the cold streams?
¹⁵*Because my people has put me out of mind—*
*to emptiness they burn sacrifices.*ᵍ
*They*ʰ *have made them collapse on their paths,*
age-long tracks,
So as to walk on byways,
*a path not built up,*ⁱ
¹⁶*So as to make their country a desolation,*
*age-long things to whistle at.*ʲ
Everyone who passes will be desolate at it,
and will shake his head.
¹⁷*Like the east wind I will scatter them*
before the enemy.
*Back and not face*ᵏ *I will let them see,*ˡ
*on their day of disaster.*ᵐ

a. *Something horrific* (*ša'ărurît*) issues from their exercise of their *determination* (*šərirût*, v. 12).

b. While "something very horrific" makes good sense, *mə'ōd* rarely qualifies a noun, and its separation from the noun makes this understanding even more difficult; LXX, Vg, Tg assume that *mē'ōd* qualifies the verb.

c. Hardly "the young girl of Israel"—that is, the city (so J. J. Schmitt, "The Virgin of Israel," *CBQ* 53 [1991]: 381–83). Further, *bətûlâ* does not mean "virgin" (see *DCH*): she is usually someone still living at home, and the charitable assumption would be that she is a virgin, but the word need not carry that connotation; here as commonly elsewhere it rather connotes a girl as vulnerable and precious to her father. So there is no semantic tension over the young girl actually being promiscuous.

d. Only here in the First Testament is *'āzab* followed by *min* ("from"), but *DCH* gives examples from Qumran.

e. LXX "breasts" implies a form from *šēd* for MT *śāday* (HUBP); Aq implies *šadday*, suggesting "Shadday's crag" (*CTAT* 2:621–22).

f. *Nātaš* makes for a catachresis; one might have expected *nāšat* ("dry up"; see BDB). See the commentary.

g. The asyndeton and the word order suggest that the second colon is subordinate to the first.

h. The plural apparently refers to the other deities to whom the singular *emptiness* refers.

i. This second colon alone has three stresses; a judiciously-placed hyphen could make it conform to the two-stress pattern of the section. Cf. Volz, *Jeremia*, 196; he notes that "not built up" is a single idea.

j. *Šărîqōt* might be intensive plural; the *ketiv šrwqt* is singular. The word seems onomatopoeic, comparing with English "shriek" (Craigie, Kelley, and Drinkard, *Jeremiah 1–25*, 247).

k. LXX lacks "back and not face"; omitting them makes v. 17 a single 4-4 line.

l. *'Er'ēm* looks more like a qal, but LXX, Vg, Tg take it as *hiphil*.

m. MT has a section marker here.

Verses 13–17 are the familiar kind of protest at Judah's unfaithfulness, leading into a warning about the terrible consequences that will follow. In origin, it will have formed an independent message; in this context its opening *therefore* marks it as illustrating the dire path and dire plan that vv. 2–12 described. And the picking up from 2:25 of the word *futile* in v. 12 now meshes with this section's links with Jer 2:

v. 13	cf. 2:9–13
v. 14a	cf. 2: 17, 19
v. 14b	cf. 2:13
v. 15a	cf. 2:32
v. 15b	cf. 2:17–18, 33
v. 17	cf. 2:27

The lines have the short, two-stress second colon characteristic of grieving prayers.

v. 13	Yahweh commissions Jeremiah to ask a rhetorical question (an introduction and two bicola)
v. 14	Yahweh spells out the question (two bicola)
vv. 15–16	Yahweh explains the question and points out the implications of the explanation (five bicola, the middle three linked)
v. 17	Yahweh asserts responsibility for those implications (two bicola)

13 The *therefore* indicates that this message now functions to put flesh on the preceding general statements about Judah's dire behavior and Yahweh's dire plan. It starts from the assumption that the prediction in v. 12 will find fulfillment and forms another invitation to imagine the future and therefore respond in such a way that it does not find fulfillment. Yahweh presupposes that there is something unparalleled and monstrous about the characteristic behavior of *young girl Israel*; at this point, he does not explain in what way it is so—to raise suspense (v. 15 will explain) or because it needs no explanation. Either way, people can just *ask . . . the nations* what they think.

14 Yahweh focuses rather on finding adequate metaphors to describe Israel's action. It is totally "unnatural."[476] To the far northeast from Ephraim (though not from Judah!) one could see Mount Hermon, a great *crag* surrounded by *open country*: "Lebanon is a great mountain and it is very broad in its summit; on it are fields and rocky caves where the sun's rays do not reach, so snow is constantly preserved there."[477] The snow thus lasts through the summer, doesn't it? It doesn't *abandon* its mountain. The verb is a telling one because abandoning is what Judah specializes in, as the scroll has noted from the beginning (1:16). The *foreign water* in that region, beyond the bounds of Israel itself, continues to seep underground toward Israel, even in the height of summer doesn't it? It doesn't *pull up* in the sense of stopping its flow, does it? This verb is an odd one to use but a telling one, familiar in the scroll from the beginning (1:10); it also came earlier in this chapter, in v. 7. In nature, the foreign water continues to run as *cold streams*, doesn't it? You've felt and drunk from those cold waters in the springs at Dan that form the beginning of the Jordan, haven't you? Or at least you've heard about them?

15 Yes, it does continue to flow. And by comparison, Israel's behavior is therefore indeed *something horrific* (v. 13) in that *my people has put me out of mind*. It is thus *to emptiness* that *they burn sacrifices*. There were *age-long tracks* that they were supposed to walk on (6:16), but that expression has become ironic: the empty deities have mysteriously beguiled them and *made them collapse on their paths* and sidetracked them onto paths that are age-long in a bad sense, paths that they insist on walking forever. These deities thereby get them *to walk on byways* that lead nowhere, on a path that is insecure, *not built up* so that they can walk it safely without falling into a ravine.

16 The gods of course did not see themselves as sidetracking people so that they walked on byways, and neither did they see themselves as acting *so as to make their country a desolation, age-long things to whistle at*. Yahweh implies an unfortunate comparison and link with the *age-long tracks* of v. 15: it will turn out that age-long tracks lead to age-long desolation. The horrified whistling will be heard because the real God will take action against them with the result that *everyone who passes will be desolate at it and will shake his head*.

---

476. W. H. Schmidt, *Jeremia*, 1:318.
477. Thomas Aquinas, *Commentary on Jeremiah*; quoted in Schroeder, *Jeremiah*, 199.

17 To get clearer how overwhelming it will be, think of a devastating hurricane from the east (see 4:11). Yahweh will bring such a hurricane. More literally, *I will scatter them* in that way *before the enemy*. Yahweh had promised to lift up his face and let it shine on Israel; on a day of threat and danger, Israel would turn to Yahweh's face and look for a sign that he will deliver them (e.g., Num 6:25–26; Ps 80:3[4], 7[8], 19[20]). They will find he has turned the other way: *Back and not face I will let them see on their day of disaster.* That will be the nature of the dire fate of which Yahweh spoke in v. 11, unless . . .

c. A Protest Responding to What Has Preceded: An Ultimate Prayer (18:18–23)

¹⁸*But they have said,*

Come, let's formulate plans against Jeremiah,
  because instruction will not fail from priest,
Or counsel from expert,
  or message from prophet.
*Come, let's strike him down with*ᵃ *the tongue,*
  *so that we may not*ᵇ *pay heed to any of his words.*

¹⁹*Pay heed to me, Yahweh,*
  *listen to the sound of the people who argue against me.*ᶜ
²⁰*Should what is dire be recompensed for what is good?—*
  because they have dug a pit for my life.
Be mindful of my standing before you
  to speak what is good concerning them,
  to turn your fury from them.
²¹*Therefore give their children to hunger*
  and pour them out to the power of the sword.
Their women should become childless and widowed,
  their men should become people slaughtered by death,
  their young men struck down by the sword in battle.
²²*A cry should make itself heard from their houses*
  because you get a horde to come against them suddenly.
*Because they have dug a pit*ᵈ *to capture me,*
  traps they have laid for my feet.
²³*You yourself, Yahweh, acknowledge*
  their entire counsel against me, for death.
Do not expiate their waywardness;
  their wrongdoing—do not blot it out from before you.

They should become people who have been made to collapse before you—
at the time of your anger, act against them.[e]

a. Or "on the tongue," to silence him (Syr; cf. B. A. Foreman, "Strike the Tongue: Silencing the Prophet in Jeremiah 18:18b," *VT* 59 [2009]: 653–57).

b. LXX lacks "not"; their point would then be that they will listen to him in order to have a basis for charging him (J. A. Thompson, *Jeremiah*, 441).

c. For MT *yarîbāy*, LXX, Tg imply *rîbî*, an easier reading whose meaning is little different (McKane, *Jeremiah*, 1:438), though it is then possible to see v. 20a as the content of the *rîb* rather than as Jeremiah's words (Holladay, *Commentary on Jeremiah*, 1:527–31).

d. Here the *ketiv* implies not *šûḥâ* as in v. 20 but *šîḥâ*, for which LXX *logon* implies *šîḥâ* (Craigie, Kelley, and Drinkard, *Jeremiah 1–25*, 251).

e. MT has a section marker here.

This third section in Jer 18 talks about the plans and the counsel that people are formulating against Jeremiah; in the context, they are a response to the typical Jeremianic critiques of vv. 1–17. So Jeremiah reports *plans* that compare and contrast with the one in v. 11. The reference to plans leads into a reference to the related idea of *counsel*, which appears in this section for the first time in the scroll. The word *counsel* then recurs (v. 23) with a similar meaning to that of plans. So vv. 1–17 provide the background to v. 18, and v. 18 provides the background to vv. 19–23 (MT has no break between vv. 18 and 19–23). Jeremiah reports the plans that he somehow knows about and pleads with Yahweh to put the planners down. Thus the sections within the chapter will be of separate origin, but the originally separate parts are juxtaposed in a way that makes them interconnect. While the report in v. 18 is prosaic, it can be laid out as bicola, which makes more obvious the continuity of vv. 13–17, 18, and 19–23.

v. 18   Jeremiah's report of the leaders' plans against him (introduction and three bicola, the first two linked)

vv. 19–23 Jeremiah's prayer

v. 19   An appeal to Yahweh to listen (one bicolon)

v. 20   A question expressing rationales for the plea (one bicolon, one tricolon)

vv. 21–22a A plea to Yahweh to see that they all die (bicola on either side of a tricolon)

vv. 22b–23a Statements expressing rationales for the plea (two bicola)

v. 23b–c A plea to Yahweh not to forgive but to act against them (two bicola)

18 How does Jeremiah know about these plots? Maybe Yahweh has told him, or maybe he has heard rumors, or maybe the background is the kind of events described in passages such as Jer 26 and 32. As usual, we have no way of knowing whether the historical background is the time of (say) Jehoiakim or Zedekiah, during both of whose reigns there were attempts to silence Jeremiah. Further, who are *they*? In the context, they are the *them* of v. 17, Judahites in general. Independently of the context, the verb might be virtually impersonal: there are people who have said what follows. In 20:6, there are *many* of them. But to *formulate plans* probably implies some vested interest, and it requires some power; in the story of Jesus's lynching, the people in general eventually take part, but the planning issues from the people with power and influence. Here, the people with power and influence would be *priest*, *expert*, and *prophet*, so they themselves may be the *they*. All were identified with the administration and the establishment; all have been subject to Jeremiah's critique, explicitly in his references to them and implicitly in his critique of religious, social, economic, and political policies that they advocate or support. That point links with the activities associated with the three groups. The business of a priest is *instruction* (*tôrâ*); while priests were responsible for leading worship in the temple every day, the focus here lies on the leadership they exercise by instructing people on what counts as proper worship, spirituality, and lifestyle (cf. Deut 17:8–11; 33:10). The business of an expert (*ḥākām*) is to give the king *counsel* about political decisions that need taking, though the same word has been used more generally for "smart" people (4:22; 8:8–9; 9:12[11], 17[16], 23[22]). The business of a prophet is to bring a message from Yahweh that has a more direct origin in Yahweh than the instruction based in tradition handed down from Moses or the advice reflecting the best human insight. The threefold declaration might be a kind of aphorism.[478] In principle, Jeremiah does not oppose any of the three, but in practice, he opposes all three because of the way they fulfill their roles. In denouncing priests, politicians, and prophets, he is attacking all the guardians of public weal; it is not surprising that he gets into trouble.[479] They return the compliment. *Come, let's strike him down with the tongue.* Their earlier reference to formulating plans indicates that they are not just going to throw insults at him but to make proposals about silencing him, action of the kind we will read in Jer 26 and 32. The last colon makes clearest that Jeremiah is again not reporting people's actual words but the implications of their words and actions.

19 Jeremiah's plea also implies the link between vv. 1–17 and vv. 19–23. His message concerns Yahweh's challenge to Judah; he gets in trouble for being the messenger. In light of what he somehow knows, he turns to Yahweh. Like many a protest prayer, he first urges Yahweh to listen. One aspect of the

---

478. Craigie, Kelley, and Drinkard, *Jeremiah 1–25*, 253.
479. Berrigan, *Jeremiah*, 82–83.

rhetoric of reporting this appeal to Yahweh is that people would themselves be used to praying this way. They need to see that they have put him in the position that they take when they pray. The specific appeal *pay heed* makes for a link with v. 18: they will not pay heed, but please will Yahweh do so?

20 Yahweh and Jeremiah's human audience have to see the wrongness in the attacks he has spoken of. He has been concerned about *what is good* for his attackers. It was his concern when he was lambasting them. Here, the second line implies that the good thing he was doing was praying for them, which was the means of seeking what was good for them. He was representing them in the meetings of the heavenly cabinet that he attended and took part in when he was *standing before you* (cf. the sequence in Ps 35:12–13). His aim was then *to turn your fury from them*, notwithstanding Yahweh's instructions not to do it. In light of such facts, how can *what is dire be recompensed for what is good*? This is what they are doing insofar as *they have dug a pit for my life*. It is again the way the Psalms talk (including Ps 35:7).[480] Here, at least, it is likely a metaphor for making plans against his life (see v. 23).

21–22 Therefore Jeremiah pleads for redress. How does one know what to pray for people? Part of the answer is that one prays for the things that God has signified he is interested in and committed to. And God has said that his wrath is to be poured out on the people. Jeremiah had not wanted it to happen, but he had found that he could not contain the divine wrath with which God had filled him, and God had told him it was to be poured out on little children, young men, women, and men—that it would bring battle, hunger, and sword, the loss of husbands and fathers and wives (e.g., 6:11–12; 9:20–21[19–20]; 14:12; 15:2, 7–9).[481] So Jeremiah is asking God to do what he has said he would do. His attackers themselves, their children, the women and the men and the young people in their families and community—they should all pay for the attackers' wrongdoing with their lives. The tricolon underlines the horrific comprehensiveness of the slaughter it portrays. As usual, the Scriptures work with the way families and communities are bound up together in their destiny; human beings are not simply separate individuals with separate destinies. Yahweh should *pour out* the children "like fruit or vegetables dumped from a basket onto a table under the watchful eye, and the knife, of the cook."[482] It would be as if the angel of death had taken over their houses, as happened to the Egyptians, to generate a terrible *cry* (Exod 11:6) or as if death has indeed climbed through people's windows. Jeremiah articulates his plea in a-b-c-d-c'-b'-d' parallelism in v. 22b:

480. Holladay ("Indications," 255–56) argues that Jeremiah knew Ps 35.
481. Wright, *Jeremiah*, 218.
482. Bright, *Jeremiah*, 125.

Because
    they have dug
        a pit
            for my capture
        traps
    they have laid
            for my feet

23 Yahweh might be tempted to forgive them—it was the good thing that Jeremiah has previously been seeking for them. He now wants Yahweh to resist that temptation: *Do not expiate their waywardness*. It is usually priests who expiate wrongdoing on people's behalf (e.g., Lev 16; this verse is the only occasion when Jeremiah uses the verb), but the provision for doing so comes from God, and in this connection he sets up the means of expiation. He makes arrangements whereby the community can *blot out* its wrongdoing *from before you*. Jeremiah leaps straight to that point, in a chilling parallelism, with the two verbs embracing the two nouns:

do not	expiate	their waywardness
their wrongdoing	from before you	do not blot out

God is not to make it happen. There should be no mercy. *They should become people who have been made to collapse before you.* "The picture thus conjured up is apparently that of a prisoner brought unceremoniously into the presence of one who is to determine his punishment and decide his fate."[483] Jeremiah is not presupposing that expiation and blotting out are impossible if the people turn from their faithlessness. He is presupposing that God is soft-hearted and tempted to forgive people independently of any change on their part, and he presses God not to do so. The inclusion of this horrifying prayer in the Scriptures implies that it was okay for Jeremiah to pray that way. How could it be, given that it stands in such contrast with other aspects of First Testament spirituality and theology? It contrasts with the merciful stance of Joseph in being willing to forgive his brothers for (more literally) digging a pit for his feet. There might be a number of considerations to take into account in answering that question.

(1)   As the commentary on vv. 21–22 already noted, all Jeremiah is doing is asking Yahweh to do what he said he would do. Wrath was not Jeremiah's idea. It was Yahweh's. His prayer parallels the equally

483. McKane, *Jeremiah*, 1:441–42.

horrifying Ps 137, which asks Yahweh to do what he had said he would do in Isa 13.

(2)   It reflects the fact that people can say anything to Yahweh. There are no limits to the outrageous prayers that one can pray. The point is not that the prayer then makes someone feel better. It is that prayer means giving things over to Yahweh in such a way that he becomes responsible for deciding what to do with them. (In this event, he more or less decided to do as Jeremiah said; Jeremiah's mixed feelings match Yahweh's mixed feelings.)

(3)   It reflects the fact that prayer is "the last resort of the helpless"[484] and the last resort of the powerless. People who possess power, wealth, or honor cannot pray this way. People under attack who have no way of defending themselves can do so. Prayer is an alternative to action, not least when action is impossible.

(4)   While the prayer is formally addressed to Yahweh, it is uttered and recorded for the overhearing of the people against whom Jeremiah is praying, as one of his devices for seeking to get them to turn to Yahweh. In his prayer, he is still seeking what is good for them, seeking to turn Yahweh's wrath from them by turning them away from being people who must be the victims of his wrath. It is encouraging to know that one is the subject of other people's prayers on one's behalf. It is even more galvanizing to know that one is the subject of other people's imprecatory prayers.

(5)   It thereby parallels the horrifying way Jesus speaks of his Father's punishment of his people, notwithstanding his prayer for his killers' forgiveness (e.g., Matt 21:33–41; 22:1–14; 23:29–36; 24:45–51; 25:14–30). As Jesus was not the first person to forgive enemies or talk of forgiving enemies, so he did not abolish within the Scriptures the notion of looking forward to their judgment (2 Thess 1:6–10; Rev 6:9–10).[485]

2. The Pot: And When It's Too Late (19:1–20:18)

The motif of the potter reappears. In Jer 18 it facilitated the point that the future was open; here it warns that it does stay open forever. Once more, the unit brings together material of diverse origin in order to expound its point:

---

484. O. Hallesby, *Prayer* (repr., Minneapolis: Fortress, 1994), 18.
485. Allen, *Jeremiah*, 220.

19:1–13	Again, the unit begins with a story that involves Jeremiah and something that is the work of a potter, and it has points of connection with the "postscript" to that preceding story comprising 18:13–17 (burning sacrifices to other gods, desolation, whistling)
19:14–20:6	Again, there is a kind of postscript to this story, itself in the framework of a continuation of the story of Jeremiah and the pot but focusing on a declaration of calamity to come
20:7–18	Again, the unit ends with prayers of protest of an extreme and shocking sort

a. Jeremiah, the Decanter, and Yahweh's Counsel (19:1–13)

[1]*Yahweh said this:*[a] *Go,*[b] *and acquire a decanter, made by a potter in earthenware,*[c] *with*[d] *some of the elders of the people and some of the elders of the priests.* [2]*Go out to the Ben-Hinnom Ravine, which is at the entrance to the Potsherd*[e] *Gate, and proclaim there the words that I speak to you.* [3]*Say: Listen to Yahweh's message, kings of Judah and people who live in Jerusalem.*[f]

Yahweh of Armies, Israel's God, has said this: Here am I, causing dire trouble to come on this place such that everyone who hears of it, his ears will quiver, [4]*since they have abandoned me, and made this place alien, and burned sacrifices in it to other gods that they had not acknowledged—they, their ancestors, and the kings of Judah—and filled this place with the blood of people who were free of guilt.* [5]*They have kept building the Master's*[g] *shrines to consume their children in fire as whole offerings to the Master, which I did not order and did not speak of; it did not arise in my mind.*[h]

[6]*Therefore, there, days are coming (Yahweh's affirmation) when this place will no longer be called "the Shameful Fireplace" and "Ben-Hinnom Ravine," but rather "Slaughter Ravine."* [7]*I will decant*[i] *the counsel of Judah and Jerusalem in this place and make them fall by the sword before their enemies and by the hand of the people who seek their life. I will give their corpse as food for the bird in the heavens and for the animal on the earth.* [8]*I will make this city into a desolation and a thing to whistle at—everyone who passes by it will be desolate and will whistle at all its wounds.* [9]*I will have them eat the flesh of their sons and the flesh of their daughters, and an individual will eat his fellow's flesh in the blockade and in the siege*[j] *with which their enemies and the people who seek their life besiege them.*

[10]*Then you will break the decanter before the eyes of the people who go with you* [11]*and say to them, Yahweh of Armies has said this: In this way I will break*

this people and this city, as one breaks a potter's object, which one cannot repair again. And in a shameful fireplace they will bury, because there is no room to bury. [k] [12]*So I will do to this place (Yahweh's affirmation) and to the people who live in it and make* [l] *this city like a shameful fireplace,* [13]*and the houses of Jerusalem and the houses of the kings of Judah will become like the place of "the Shameful Fireplace," unclean—to all the houses on whose roofs people have burned sacrifices for the entire heavenly army and poured libations to other gods.* [m]

> a. LXX adds "to me."
> b. The infinitive absolute is used as an imperative (cf. 2:2 and the translation note on it).
> c. *Ḥāreś* (the pausal form) makes for a paronomasia with *ḥarsît* (*potsherd*) in v. 2.
> d. In effect, the elders are further subjects of the command to *go*; see Rashi, in MG.
> e. For the *qere*'s *haḥarsît*, the *ketiv* implies *haḥarsût* or plural *haḥărāsôt*.
> f. LXX adds "and people who enter through these gates."
> g. As usual, LXX gives "Baal" a feminine article (see the translation note on 2:8).
> h. MT has a unit marker here.
> i. LXX has "slaughter."
> j. The hendiadys *bəmāṣôr ûbəmāṣôq* is also a paronomasia, and the subsequent *besiege* is the verb *ṣûq* from which that second noun comes, underlining the point further (I follow the NETS translation).
> k. LXX lacks v. 11b.
> l. The infinitive continues the finite verb; so again *poured* in the next verse (*TTH* 206; Joüon 124p).
> m. MT has a unit marker here.

One imagines the gossip in the potters' quarter: "First he comes in here and just sits all day, watching me and asking dumb questions and scaring away the customers. Then he goes away without buying so much as an egg-cup. Then he comes back later and buys a huge wine jar, the biggest I've made—and takes it to the rubbish dump and smashes it to bits! Weird or what?"[486]

The story has all the elements of a theatrical performance: a playwright/director (Yahweh), a stage, a performer, a prop, and an audience; and the members of the audience are witnesses to the performance and are actually onstage for it.[487] In this story, there is thus more implicit emphasis on the rhetorical significance of the sign-act.[488] Yet it is another variant on being not quite an account of a symbolic act (cf. 13:1–12a; 18:1–12). There is again

486. Wright, *Jeremiah*, 211.
487. M. Brummitt, "Recovering Jeremiah," 144, 174.
488. See Friebel, *Sign-Acts*, 115–24.

a divine commission to undertake an action—this time one that will be witnessed by some people and will involve an action that implements a divine
decision—but there is no account of Jeremiah's undertaking the action. The
act itself is not so crucial to what it pictures.[489] Maybe Jeremiah never did
what it says. The focus lies on the message associated with the action of
which Yahweh speaks. In the end, the emphasis in the story is on its being a
message to Judahites who hear it and are invited to imagine the event that is
commissioned but doesn't happen (in the way the story is told) and to listen
to the exhortation that is built on it. Either way, failing to report the act has
the effect of enabling the audience listening to the story to see themselves as
living between threat and fulfillment. It compromises the contrast between
the story of a potter who can rework the clay and the story of a pot that has
been baked and gets smashed. The implication is that it's still not too late.
But it's the eleventh hour. You must stop now. Hearing the story after 587,
however, would make one aware that Yahweh did decant the counsel.

As well as comparing with 13:1–12a and 18:1–12, the story compares with
7:29–34 in its condemnation of observances in the Ben-Hinnom Ravine, and
a number of the lines in 19:1–13 are more or less identical with lines there.
This story is in effect an expanded version of 7:29–34, though some motifs
there do not appear here, so it might be better to see the two passages as separate expansions of a common starting point. As is the case elsewhere when
the scroll incorporates two versions of some material, in the two contexts the
material fulfills different functions and brings different messages. The first
account of Yahweh's message about the Ben-Hinnom Ravine formed part of
the wide-ranging critique of Judah's worship in 7:1–8:3. There is thus some
analogy between 26:1–19 providing a narrative equivalent and background
to 7:1–15 and 19:1–13 providing a narrative equivalent and background to
7:29–34. Here, this second Ben-Hinnom Ravine passage forms part of the
interwoven report comprising part 2d of the scroll that concerns Jeremiah's
prophesying and the way he has to turn to Yahweh in the midst of it, and that
takes potter and pot as a motif.[490]

| vv. 1–3a | Yahweh's command to Jeremiah to go to the Ben-Hinnom Ravine and deliver a message |
| v. 1 | Jeremiah is to get a decanter (which will symbolize Yahweh's decanting Judah's counsel) and some witnesses |

---

489. Fretheim, *Jeremiah*, 284.

490. On different views of the possible development of the passage, see R. Gilmour,
"Reading Jeremiah 19:1–13," *Journal of the Hebrew Scriptures* 17/5 (2017).

vv. 2–3a	Jeremiah is to go to the Potsherd Gate (which draws attention to the fact that one cannot mend a broken pot) and deliver a message
vv. 3b–5	The message in outline
v. 3b	Yahweh's intention to bring calamity
vv. 4–5	The rationale
vv. 6–9	The message concerning Yahweh's intention in more frightening detail
vv. 10–13	Yahweh's command to Jeremiah to smash the decanter before the witnesses
v. 10	Jeremiah is to initiate the implementing of Yahweh's intention
vv. 11–13	Jeremiah is to explain again what it will signify

1 In Jer 1–10, *Yahweh has said this* invariably introduced a message for the people to whom Jeremiah speaks. Here it introduces Yahweh's instructions to Jeremiah (cf. 13:1; 15:19; 16:1, 9; 17:19); Jeremiah himself is more prominent in Jer 11–20. But there is no "to me" (as there is in 13:1); by implication, the story is told by someone else rather than by Jeremiah (cf. 19:14–20:6). In the instruction to *go and acquire a decanter made by a potter in earthenware* (also cf. 13:1), the rare word *decanter* and the specifying of *earthenware* relate to the message's delivery in v. 2 and to the symbolic action itself. Perhaps the taking up of phraseology from 13:1 explains the odd way whereby *some of the elders of the people and some of the elders of the priests* is attached loosely to the sentence, simply as further objects of the verb *acquire*. Elders of the people and of the priests are not common or technical terms. Whereas one might wonder at Yahweh or the narrator imagining that senior leaders in the community or in the priesthood would enthuse about being dragged into an expedition into the Ben-Hinnom Ravine that would surely mean trouble or controversy, 21:1 and later stories make that idea more plausible.[491] Anyway, Jeremiah needs only a few witnesses to report back to the administration, the people, and the priesthood (vv. 10–13), and maybe the ones who would accompany him would be sympathizers (cf. 26:17).

2 *The Potsherd Gate* to *the Ben-Hinnom Ravine* appears only here (see 2:23; 7:31; and the commentary there). Perhaps it was near the area where potters lived and was the gate that led to their dump. Nehemiah 2:13 mentions the Ravine Gate and the Trash Gate (not to be confused with what is now called the Dung Gate in the medieval walls of the Old City of Jerusalem—the city extended much further south in Jeremiah's day). Either would

491. Duhm, *Jeremia*, 169.

suit this story. Perhaps Potsherd Gate was not the gate's official or formal name,[492] but referring to it by this name appropriates the similarity of the words for potsherd and for earthenware (see the translation note). The name is also suggestive in connection with the action Jeremiah is to undertake, since the Potsherd Gate will be where he makes potsherds of his decanter.[493] While the apparently "unnatural" identification of the Ben-Hinnom Ravine by a gate[494] might reflect a desire to identify the relevant part of the ravine,[495] the similarity between the name and the symbolic act would be the more pressing point about referring to this particular gate.

3–4 Jeremiah is to proclaim there a message for the *kings of Judah and people who live in Jerusalem,* notwithstanding their not being present (addressing plural kings compares with 17:20; see the commentary there). Three implications follow. One is that Jeremiah's action is a little like the declaring of a verdict on an accused who is not in court (e.g., because of being on the run). The verdict is still valid, and the accused had better be wary of it. A second is that the witnesses will have the task of passing on the message. A third is that the story presupposes that kings and people will subsequently hear this message through someone's writing up the story. This incongruity over the audience may link with some incongruity over the story's references to *this place.* Elsewhere in the scroll *this place* can be the country, the city, or the temple. Here, in v. 6 at least, it must be the Shameful Fireplace, but in v. 12 it must be the city. In vv. 3–4, either reference is possible. Either the Ben-Hinnom Ravine within the city's environs or the city as a whole was part of Yahweh's domain (the expression would apply to both). And Judahites have *made this place alien* by their worship, by invoking alien gods, their alien empty things (5:19; 8:19), and by *shedding the blood of people who were free of guilt* (cf. 2:34; see the translation note and the commentary there)—which makes one think of Manasseh in the past and of Jehoiakim in the present (2 Kgs 21:16; 24:4; Jer 22:17). If *this place* is the city and not just the ravine, the slaying could include happenings within the city and in the temple as well as in the ravine and in shrines there, which would fit with the scroll's references elsewhere to such shedding of blood (2:34; 7:6; 22:3, 17; 26:15).[496] The consequence will be disaster such as will make *ears quiver* or ring, as they do when one hears something astonishing.

5–7 The continuation of Yahweh's declaration restates words from 7:31–33 (see the commentary there):

---

492. As Craigie, Kelley, and Drinkard hint (*Jeremiah 1–25*, 255).

493. Holladay, *Commentary on Jeremiah*, 1:536.

494. Bright, *Jeremiah*, 131.

495. Weiser, *Jeremia*, 1:167–68.

496. McKane, *Jeremiah*, 1:451–52.

Jeremiah 7 [see v. 30]	Jeremiah 19 [see v. 4]
31They have kept building shrines	5They have kept building the Master's shrines at the Shameful Fireplace,
which is in the Ben-Hinnom Ravine, to consume their sons and their daughters in fire, as whole offerings to the Master, which I did not order;	to consume their children[497] in fire, which I did not order and did not speak of;
it did not arise in my mind.	it did not arise in my mind.
32aTherefore, there, days are coming (Yahweh's affirmation) when no more will be said[498]	6Therefore, there, days are coming (Yahweh's affirmation) when this place will no longer be called
"the Shameful Fireplace" and "Ben-Hinnom Ravine" but rather "Slaughter Ravine."	"the Shameful Fireplace" and "Ben-Hinnom Ravine" but rather "Slaughter Ravine."
32bThey will bury in a shameful fireplace because there is no room.	11bAnd in a shameful fireplace they will bury because there is no room to bury.
33This people's corpse will be for food	7bI will give their corpse for food
for the bird in the heavens and for the animal on the earth, with there being no one disturbing them.	for the bird in the heavens and for the animal on the earth.
[see further v. 34]	[see further vv. 7a, 8–11a]

As is the case in 13:1–12a (and, for instance, in visions in Daniel), Yahweh's message is not an allegory in which there is a precise match between each element in the symbolic action and each element in the message (as there is with Jesus's interpretation of the sower parable in Mark 4). But there is more than one facet to the symbolic action's significance. A first facet emerges from Yahweh's having bidden Jeremiah to acquire a *decanter* (*baqbaq*), which is not a regular word for a regular jug (see only 1 Kgs 14:3). The decanter will match Yahweh's intention to *decant* (*bāqaq*) *the counsel of Judah and Jerusa-*

---

497. *Banêhem*, the same word as is translated *their sons* in the parallel passage where it is accompanied by *their daughters*.

498. The order here, which reflects the Hebrew syntax, differs from the more idiomatic English translation of 7:32 that I have given above.

lem in this place. He will pour the counsel out on the floor so that for practical purposes its contents no longer exist. Yahweh thus also picks up the word *counsel* from 18:18, 23. We know already that the Judahites have their plans and counsel and that these stand in tension with Yahweh's. Here, for the first time, the two counsels go head to head as Yahweh declares the intention to frustrate the Judahites' counsel. In further words that are part of the material in v. 7a that is distinctive to Jer 19 over against Jer 7, he declares that he will *make them fall by the sword before their enemies and by the hand of the people who seek their life*. In 18:18, *counsel* referred to the political policies that the king's advisers proposed for the nation's relationship with bigger powers such as Assyria, Babylon, and Egypt. This counsel will fail, with the result that the nation will experience defeat and decimation—as it did.

8–9 So passersby will respond with horror to what they see. Actually, they will do no such thing, because Jerusalem is not on a main road, which was at one level why it escaped destruction from Sennacherib in 701. The declaration that *everyone who passes by it will be desolate and will whistle at all its wounds* aims to drive Jerusalemites themselves to imagine the scene; whistling is not a sign of contempt but an expression of astonishment and horror. That people will *eat the flesh* of children and of fellow members of the community is an intentionally horrifying description of the depths to which they will be driven *in the blockade and in the siege* that will come to Jerusalem, *with which their enemies and the people who seek their life besiege them*. People will be starving and will not be able to hold themselves back from cooking and eating the flesh of people who have died. It is a standard threat (Lev 26:29; Deut 28:53; Ezek 5:10), and Lam 2:20; 4:10 implies its fulfillment.[499] Indeed, Josephus tells of a woman who killed her child in order to eat him.[500] It is hard to know how literally to take such a report; there is no doubt that it is designed to horrify. In the present context, the idea is another piece of rhetoric designed to drive Judah to its senses.

10–11 Yahweh moves from the proclamation Jeremiah must issue to the performative action he must undertake. People may have been aware of a practice known to us from Egypt a millennium or two earlier whereby Egyptian rulers might inscribe a clay statue, vase, or bowl with their enemies' names and then smash or otherwise spoil the object as a kind of enacted prayer that the enemies might be smashed.[501] Yahweh commissions Jeremiah to break the decanter as an action that will similarly initiate Yahweh's decanting the Judahites' counsel. The breaking is to take place before the

---

499. Blayney, *Jeremiah*, 318.
500. Josephus, *Jewish War* 4.3.4 §§201–19.
501. There is an example in *ANET*, 328–29.

eyes of witnesses so that it brings home to them and to people who receive their report the reality of what Yahweh intends to do. *In this way* (*kākâ*), a way that corresponds to the smashing you have just witnessed, *I will break this people and this city.* Yahweh's words thus point to yet another facet to the significance of the symbolic action and to the significance of mentioning the Potsherd Gate, the gate where you can find a mountain of pieces of broken pot. Because when one breaks a potter's object, one cannot repair it. That's the thing about pottery. The destruction of Jerusalem and of Judah will be definitive and final (of course it will not, actually). Yahweh's words also point to a significant difference between this story and the potter story in 18:1–12. You can press clay back into a ball and start again. You can't reshape a pot that's been fired. All you can do is throw it away. And when it then breaks, you can't put the pieces back together. The Jeremiah scroll is coming to describe the final, unalterable doom of the community.[502]

12–13 In theory *this place, this city,* and *the people who live in it* are very different from *the Shameful Fireplace,* but Yahweh speaks of them in a way that presupposes they have become confused. We don't know how many Jerusalemites frequented the Shameful Fireplace, but however many it was, its existence compromises the nature of Jerusalem itself. And Yahweh's action will so fill Jerusalem with death that it will become *like a shameful fireplace—* as unclean as death itself. Yahweh's action will have this effect on *the houses of Jerusalem and the houses of the kings of Judah.* They will become *unclean.* Really, they are unclean already, because they are *houses on whose roofs people have burned sacrifices for the entire heavenly army and poured libations to other gods.* The open roof area might be a natural place for any kind of household worship, including the pouring of drink offerings to which 7:18 referred (see the commentary there). It would be an especially natural place for making offerings to the heavenly army, whose worship appears in close association with the worship in Ben-Hinnom in 7:29–8:3 (cf. 32:29; 2 Kgs 23:12; Zeph 1:5).

b. A Story Postscript: The Reaction and the Identity of the Invader (19:14–20:6)

[14]*Jeremiah came from the Shameful Fireplace where Yahweh had sent him to prophesy, stood in the courtyard of Yahweh's house, and said to the entire people:*[a] [15]*Yahweh of Armies, Israel's God, has said this. Here am I, causing to come to this city and upon all its towns all the dire trouble that I have spoken of against it, because they have stiffened their neck so as not to listen to my words.*

---

502. Fischer, *Jeremia*, 1:603.

^{20:1}*Pashhur ben Immer the priest—he was appointee ruler in Yahweh's house—heard Jeremiah prophesying these things.* ²*Pashhur struck Jeremiah the prophet down and put him in the cell*^b *that was at the Upper Benjamin Gate, which was in Yahweh's house.* ³*The next day,*^c *Pashhur let Jeremiah out from the cell. Jeremiah said to him, Yahweh is naming you*^d *not Pashhur but rather All-Around-Is-Terror.*^e ⁴*Because Yahweh has said this: Here am I, giving you over to terror—you and all your friends. They will fall by the sword of their enemies, and your eyes will be looking. All Judah I will give into the hand of the king of Babylon. He will exile them to Babylon and strike them down with the sword.* ⁵*I will give over all this city's wealth, all its acquisitions, and all its valuables, and all the stores of the kings of Judah I will give over to their enemies' hand. They will plunder them, take them, and see that they come to Babylon.* ⁶*And you, Pashhur, and all the people who live in your house, you will go into captivity. To Babylon you will come, and there you will die, and there you will be buried, you and all your friends to whom you have prophesied by deception.*^f

a. MT has a section marker here.

b. *Mahpeket* otherwise comes only in 29:26; 2 Chr 16:10. LXX perhaps implies "dungeon," Vg "fetter," Tg "stocks," Sym "torture" (see Jerome, *Jeremiah*, 120–21). The implication is that he is chained up rather than made a public spectacle of.

c. LXX lacks *the next day*.

d. The *qatal* is performative (Allen, *Jeremiah*, 224); see 1:5 and the translation note on it.

e. LXX "migrant" (similarly, "migration" in v. 4) derives *māgôr* from *gûr* I rather than *gûr* III; Tg seems to derive it from *gûr* II ("gather together against"). MT has a unit marker here.

f. MT has a marker here. The references to *you and all your friends* form a framework around vv. 4–6; see Lundbom, *Jeremiah: A Study in Ancient Hebrew Rhetoric*, 62–63.

This new section has a distinctive importance in that it makes the first announcement that Babylon and its king will be Judah's conqueror and that Judah is destined to go into exile in Babylon. It also contains the first references to Jeremiah "prophesying" (the reference in 11:21 to his being told not to prophesy proves the rule) and the first to Jeremiah as a "prophet" since his commission. It is also the first actual reference to his delivering a message in the temple courtyard (though I assume that he often did so); in 7:1–2, he was bidden to stand in the temple gateway, and he presumably did, and 26:1–2 has Yahweh commissioning him to stand in the courtyard to deliver the message to which Jer 7 refers—when he turned out to be risking his life. So if we may connect some dots, this is the second such occasion, and he must know he is taking a risk.

The medieval chapter division recognizes that the verses relating Jeremiah's return to Jerusalem (19:14–16) continue straight on from 19:1–13, but it then separates them off from the verses relating the aftermath of that return, the meetings with Pashhur (20:1–6). MT begins its new unit at 19:14 and then runs straight into 20:1–18, with 19:14–20:6 comprising one section and 20:7–18 comprising another.

19:14	Jeremiah returns from Ben-Hinnom
19:15	Jeremiah proclaims Yahweh's message to the people
20:1–3a	Pashhur sets about Jeremiah and confines him overnight
20:3b–6	Jeremiah proclaims Yahweh's message to Pashhur

vv. 3b–4a	Yahweh is renaming Pashhur and acting in light of his new name
vv. 4b–5	Yahweh is giving over Judah and Jerusalem to the Babylonians
v. 6	Pashhur and his household and friends will die in Babylon

14–15 There is no reference to Jeremiah fulfilling his commission either to preach or to act, nor to the witnesses fulfilling theirs. Jeremiah returns from Ben-Hinnom, where he had gone *to prophesy*, and appears *in the courtyard of Yahweh's house* to deliver his customary message. In a sense, the two verses don't have any content of their own but simply make a bridge between 19:1–13 and 20:1–6.[503] The accusation that the Judahites *have stiffened their neck* makes a link with Jer 7 (see 7:26), though the words are even closer to being a repetition from 17:23. In the unfolding of the scroll, the two verses tighten the screw on the people and on the temple authorities—not because Jeremiah says something new but because of where and how he says it.

20:1 In First Testament times, there seems always to have been someone we might call "the chief priest," but there was no fixed way of describing him. The lack of a fixed title may link with the position's not having the power that the chief priest would have later, especially when there were no kings. Sometimes he is the head priest (e.g., 2 Chr 31:10; 34:9), sometimes the big priest (e.g., 2 Kgs 22:4; Neh 3:1), sometimes simply the priest (e.g., 2 Kgs 11:15; 2 Chr 34:14), sometimes the ruler of God's house (*nāgîd*; 1 Chr 9:11; 2 Chr 31:13; Neh 11:11). Pashhur is called by the compound expression *appointee ruler*, which comes only here; nowhere is the senior priest called appointee (*pāqîd*), and 2 Chr 24:11 has the construct phrase "the head priest's appointee." While the double expression might therefore be a unique description of the senior priest as *appointee* to which the later more familiar term *ruler* is added to clarify his position, more likely Pashhur was not senior priest. It's hard to fit him into the sequence of senior priests; according to 1 Chr 6:13–15 (5:39–41) in the time from Josiah to 587 the sequence goes from Hilkiah to Azariah to Seraiah to Jehozadak. More likely, he was the senior priest's representative, with responsibility for seeing that order was kept in the temple (cf. Tg). Immer was also the name of one of the Davidic priestly divisions (1 Chr 24:14).

2 Either way, in keeping with his position (29:26), Pashhur takes seriously his responsibility for ensuring that rogue prophets are not making a

---

503. McKane, *Jeremiah*, 1:449.

nuisance of themselves in the temple. He recalls Amaziah in Amos 7:10–17 but acts more forcefully. *Struck Jeremiah the prophet down* is a strong statement, as earlier occurrences of the verb (*nākâ hiphil*) indicate (e.g., 5:6). Yahweh is often the subject of this verb (e.g., 2:30; 5:3; 14:19; 21:6). Pashhur will see himself as doing God's work. And while congregations in the West are nowadays not so used to violence in church, there is a reason why a beadle or verger carries a ceremonial version of a mace as he attends on the minister. But Pashhur opens himself to the threat of unfortunate consequences, like Amaziah. The comparability of the two stories hints that they are examples of the recurrent potential for conflict between a properly commissioned minister with responsibility for good order and someone without that proper position who threatens to rock the boat.[504] The word translated *cell* indicates some form of confinement that could be imposed on a renegade for a night to teach him a lesson and get him to cool it (see the translation note). There was a Benjamin Gate in the city wall, leading into Benjaminite territory (37:12–13), but this is a Benjamin Gate to the temple courtyard, again presumably so-called because it was on the Benjamin side of the city; being a gate that was part of the temple complex, it would be higher up than the city gate.

3 Pashhur perhaps brings Jeremiah out for further trial.[505] When Jeremiah appears before Pashhur, we might expect that the priests' representative would give him some threat, an ultimatum.

> As, then, their authority was founded on the Law and on God's inviolable decree, Jeremiah might well have been much terrified; for this thought might have occurred to him,—"What can be the purpose of God? for he has set priests of the tribe of Levi over his Temple and over his whole people. Why, then, does he not rule them by his Spirit? Why does he not render them fit for their office? Why does he suffer his Temple, and the sacred office which he so highly commends to us in his Law, to be thus profaned? or why, at least, does he not stretch forth his hand to defend me, who am also a priest, and sincerely engaged in my calling?" For we know that God commands in his Law, as a proof that the priests had supreme power, that whosoever disobeyed them should be put to death.[506]

What actually happens is that "the voice of Pashhur is never heard again. Rather, Jeremiah speaks and is in obvious command of the situation even

---

504. P. D. Miller, "Jeremiah," on the passage.
505. Calvin, *Jeremiah*, 3:13.
506. Calvin, *Jeremiah*, 3:10.

though he is under restraint."[507] And consequences do follow for the unfortunate Pashhur, who maybe thought he was just doing his job and was being rather lenient compared with what happened on the occasion reported in Jer 26. In effect, the consequence is another symbolic action of a different kind. Names are important, especially when God determines them. *Nomen est omen*: a name is an announcement about the future, and in English at least, the word omen is ominous. Pashhur may be an Egyptian name, a compound incorporating the name of the god Horus,[508] and Jeremiah might have had fun with that fact if he had known, but it's a recurrent and quite respectable Israelite name (cf. 21:1), and Jeremiah makes nothing of it. There's no need to look for some way in which the new name links with the old one.[509] *All-Around-Is-Terror* takes up Jeremiah's warning to Judah in 6:25 (cf. 20:10; 46:5; 49:29). It sums up his ominous vision of the future that threatens Judah. While Israelite names sometimes express the commitment or conviction of the one who bears the name, or rather of his or her parents (Jeremiah perhaps means "Yahweh founded"),[510] specially-given names may rather refer to something external to the person for which they become a poster or a sign: for instance, A-Remainder-Will-Return (Isa 7:3) is not a statement about the personal significance of Isaiah's son who bears that name but a declaration of something he is designed to remind people of.[511] Further, giving someone a new name, as Jeremiah does, need not mean that Pashhur literally changes his name so that people actually address him as All-Around-Is-Terror any more than is the case with the other sons mentioned in Isaiah, God-Is-with-Us (though that might be) and An-Extraordinary-Counselor-Is-the-Warrior-God, the-Everlasting-Father-Is-an-Official-for-Well-Being (!) (Isa 7:14; 9:6). Rather, Pashhur becomes a poster for the facts about the imminent fate of Judah whose threat he has tried to suppress by arresting Jeremiah.

4 But because he has taken this action, he and people identified with him will themselves experience this fate. By his *friends*, Jeremiah perhaps denotes the fellow priests who identify with his position—possibly as opposed to the priests who accompanied Jeremiah to the Ben-Hinnom Ravine.[512] Perhaps *you and all your friends* carries a note of sarcasm. *And your eyes will be looking* may recognize and underline the pain of watching this happen and the necessity to acknowledge some responsibility for it, having taken a lead in discouraging the response to Jeremiah that might forestall the disaster. *Your*

---

507. P. D. Miller, "Jeremiah," on the passage.
508. See *HALOT*.
509. Weiser, *Jeremia*, 1:172.
510. See *HALOT*.
511. D. R. Jones, *Jeremiah*, 270.
512. Weiser, *Jeremia*, 1:172.

eyes will be looking. It is going to happen. You will see it with your own eyes. You will see it and grieve over it and have to recognize that you bear some responsibility for action that brings catastrophe not just to your friends but to *all Judah*. Yes, the name constitutes a warning not just to Pashhur but to the entire people (as it did in 6:25), who are also the people listening to this story. *All Judah I will give into the hand of the king of Babylon*. So far in the scroll, Jeremiah has frequently spoken of enemy invasion and of captivity and exile but has never named names. The monumental new point here is the identifying of the king of Babylon as the great invader and of Babylon as the location of people's exile (the king will not be named until 21:2). It is a turning point in the Jeremiah scroll. *He will exile them to Babylon and strike them down*: some will have the one fate, some the other. As Pashhur had struck down Jeremiah, so the Babylonian king will strike people down—but *with the sword*.

5–6 The city's resources will also go off to Babylon: *all . . . all . . . all . . . all*.[513] So will Pashhur himself, his family, and his "friends" (*all . . . all*). They will never come back. To die and not be buried is one threat to live with and one experience to avoid. To die and be buried away from the promised land is another. (But it looks as if Yahweh's bark is once again worse than his bite, given that members of Pashhur's family returned from Babylon in due course; see 1 Chr 9:10–13. Maybe they turned to Yahweh in Babylon.) The final clause adds a dramatic conclusion. Pashhur's "friends" are not just his peers. They are people *to whom you have prophesied by deception*. The story began with references to Jeremiah prophesying, the first references in the Jeremiah scroll; it closes with a reference to "false prophecy," the only other occurrence of the verb "prophesy" in Jer 15–22. Maybe Pashhur was simply a priest who prophesied, as a number of priests likely did. Or maybe Jeremiah speaks metaphorically: by trying to silence and discredit Jeremiah and his message, Pashhur was doing the same thing as the prophets who promised that things were going to go well for Judah. Either way, he prophesies *by deception*—which implies by the Master, whether he realizes it or not (5:31; see the commentary there). It implies trusting in deception (13:25, also *baššeqer*).[514] And actually, because he now becomes a poster (see the commentary on v. 3), his name will prophesy truly.[515]

---

513. Allen, *Jeremiah*, 228.

514. To be more precise, 13:25 and 20:6 have *baššāqer* because the word is at the end of the sentence.

515. D. R. Jones, *Jeremiah*, 270.

c. Protests Responding to What Has Preceded: Two Ultimate Prayers (20:7–18)

[7]*You inveigled[a] me, Yahweh; I got inveigled[b]—*
  you were strong toward me,[c] and you won.
I became something to laugh at all the time[d]—
  everyone[e] is mocking me.
[8]*Because as often as[f] I speak, I cry out—*
  violence and destruction I proclaim.
Because Yahweh's message became to me an object of reviling,
  and an object of derision all the time.
[9]*I would say: I will not be mindful[g] of him,*
  I will not speak any more in his name.
But it would become in my mind[h] like a burning fire,
  shut up in my bones.
I would be weary of holding it in—
  I couldn't win.
[10]*Because I have heard the report of many people,*
  "All around is terror": tell, let's tell of him!
Each one who wishes me well[i]—
  they are watching my step.[j]
"Perhaps he may be inveigled, and we may win over him
  and get our redress from him."
[11]*But Yahweh—he is with me,*
  like a terrifying strong man.
As a result, my pursuers—they will collapse;
  they won't win.
They will have been totally shamed, because they have not succeeded,[k]
  with disgrace for all time that will not be put out of mind.
[12]*So Yahweh of Armies, one who examines the faithful,*
  one who sees heart and mind,
May I see your redress from them,
  because to you I have rolled my argument.[l]
[13]*Sing to Yahweh,*
  praise Yahweh!
Because he has snatched the life of a needy person
  from the hand of people acting direly.[m]

[14]*Cursed be the day*
  that I was born on.
The day that my mother gave birth to me,

may it not be blessed.[n]
15 *Cursed be the person*
    that brought the news to my father,
"There is born to you a male child"—
    he made him so happy.[o]
16 *May that person become like the towns*
    that Yahweh overturned[p] *and did not relent,*
May he hear a cry in the morning
    and a blast at noon,
17 *The one who did not put me to death from the womb*[q]
    so that my mother became my grave
    and her womb pregnant for all time.
18 *Why actually did I go out from the womb*
    to see toil and sorrow,
    and my days would consume themselves in shame?[r]

a. For *pātâ piel*, LXX has "deceived," and Jerome glosses Vg "misled" as implying "deceived" (*Jeremiah*, 122); Aq has "charmed/enchanted." D. J. A. Clines and D. M. Gunn argue for "tried to persuade," though Yahweh did more than try; see "'You Tried to Persuade Me' and 'Violence! Outrage!' in Jeremiah xx 7–8," *VT* 28 (1978): 20–27.

b. The *niphal* suggests an intransitive or reflexive meaning.

c. Lit. "you were strong me"—the suffix is thus more like a dative than an accusative.

d. Lit. "all the day"; so also in the next verse.

e. Lit. "all of it"; see the translation note on 6:13.

f. Lit. "out of the enoughness/sufficiency/plentifulness of" (cf. 31:20; 48:27).

g. Vg has "make mention"; strictly, that meaning belongs to the *hiphil* rather than the *qal*, but BDB allows it for the *qal* here and at 23:36. LXX likewise has "I will not name the name," which A. R. P. Diamond suggests is one of the indications that LXX's version of the "confessions" is more communal and less prophetic; see "Jeremiah's Confessions in the LXX and MT," *VT* 60 (1990): 36.

h. LXX lacks "in my mind."

i. *Kōl 'ĕnôš šəlômî* ("every person of my well-being"; cf. 38:22).

j. Vg, Aq, Sym, Th translate "side."

k. *Hiśkîlû* from *śākal*, which resonates with *yikkāšəlû* from *kāšal* at the same position in the previous line: to collapse certainly means not to succeed.

l. MT has a section marker here.

m. MT has a section marker here.

n. The four cola in v. 14 have an a-b-b'-a' structure. While the earlier cola could be understood to be declaring that the day *is* cursed rather than it *should be* cursed (T. E. Fretheim, "Caught in the Middle: Jeremiah's Vocational Crisis," *WW* 22 [2002]: 357), the negative *'al* in this colon makes the jussive understanding more likely.

o. The four cola in v. 15 again have an a-b-b'-a' structure.

p. LXX, Tg add "in anger" (cf. Deut 29:22).

q. That is, "from [the time when I was still in] the womb."

r. MT has a unit marker here.

Jeremiah's protest and confession in vv. 7–13 follow on from the story in 19:14–20:6, though this link does not imply that they were originally connected. As is appropriate at this climactic point in the scroll, at the end of Jer 1–20, Jeremiah in effect recalls his commission back in Jer 1 and reviews the nature of his entire activity since he told of its beginning in 1:4–19. Whereas in 19:14–20:6 "Jeremiah stands wholly on the side of God, here he leans against him,"[516] and he is realistic and outspoken about the negative side to his work. But he goes on to testify to Yahweh fulfilling the promises that he made way back then, to affirm his assurance that Yahweh will see that his persecutors get their comeuppance, to pray that he will see it happen, and to give praise for the kind of rescue that 19:14–20:6 recorded. The subsection thus complements 19:14–20:6.[517] It is a psalm-like protest with a resolution, and both parts correspond to the story. Yahweh had responded to Jeremiah's first protests (11:18–12:6; 15:10–21) but not to his third (18:18–23), and he does not respond to this fourth one, but it has a distinctive dynamic that compares in some ways with the earlier dynamic. In effect, Jeremiah himself provides the response to his protest; further, this response corresponds to the way Yahweh has made his own response in action in 19:14–20:6. As far as his persecutors are concerned, Jeremiah "fervently prays that God's judgment be quickly forthcoming on the whole lot."[518] There is no sympathy for the people as a whole here; but a second stage will come in 20:14–18. Even though at one level vv. 7–13 simply express an aspect of Jeremiah's personal relationship with Yahweh, once again they appear in the scroll as part of the account of his work as a prophet and in connection with his fulfilling his commission. Like the rest of the scroll, they are designed to get people to heed his message.[519]

The subsection has many features of a protest psalm:

v. 7	Calling on Yahweh and protest at Yahweh's action, at the protestor's position, and at people's action (two bicola)
vv. 8–9	Protest at the protestor's position (five bicola)
v. 10	Protest at other people's action (three bicola)
v. 11	Declaration of confidence in Yahweh (three bicola)
v. 12	Plea (two linked bicola)
v. 13	Act of praise (two bicola)

516. Weiser, *Jeremia*, 1:174.
517. D. J. A. Clines and D. M. Gunn, "Form, Occasion and Redaction in Jeremiah 20," *ZAW* 88 (1976): 405.
518. Fretheim, *Jeremiah*, 289.
519. Cf. Berquist, "Prophetic Legitimation," 135–37.

The protest suggests a particular comparison with two psalms. On a broad canvas, it compares with Ps 22, which also begins in a distinctively abrupt and confrontational fashion (22:1–2[3–4]), develops its confrontation (22:3–21[5–23]), but then in the last part similarly reverses its stance to one of affirmation and praise (22:22–31[24–33]). It is a particularly profound example of a protest psalm that juxtaposes radical trust and radical remonstration. In more detail, Jeremiah's protest compares with Ps 31.

- The first line in Ps 31:13(14) is identical with the first line in v. 10.
- With "he snatched me from the hand of my enemies" (Ps 31:15[16]), cf. v. 13.
- With "I have become an object of derision" (Ps 31:11[12]), cf. v. 8.

A comparison of Jeremiah's protest with Ps 31 draws attention to the contrast whereby the psalm sets its complaint more systematically in the context of declarations of trust; Jeremiah is more forthright, though the two prayers end up in the same place. In each case, whether Jeremiah was directly influenced by the psalm or the psalm by Jeremiah, the comparison indicates on the one hand that Jeremiah is relating to Yahweh in the way that any Israelite under pressure might do—even if he is taking the freedom, boldness, and trust of Israelite prayer to an extreme—and on the other hand that any Israelite under pressure might take Jeremiah as a model of prayer.

Jeremiah 20:13 looks like a fine conclusion to a scroll. "This summons for praise would have been a perfect ending of the Pashhur-episode. If verse 13 would have been the final line of Chapter 20, then this episode could easily have been labelled: 'From prison to praise.'"[520] After v. 13, the move to a curse therefore makes for a "stark contrast,"[521] and people reading the Jeremiah scroll or hearing it read would surely then be bemused as well as shocked. Could Jeremiah still be speaking? Was his statement of praise ironic?[522] If vv. 7–13 indicate how he held together protest and praise, and even more if they give expression to the way he could be imagined talking to Yahweh while he was in the cell, how could vv. 14–18 relate to that dynamic? The tone is so different that it seems unlikely that it simply represents how Jeremiah himself felt on a bad day.[523] It is not a psalm-like protest, as vv. 7–13 are. The anguish and conflict he has expressed on his own account in that protest would not have made one expect an expression of torment of the kind that appears in vv. 14–18.

---

520. B. Becking, "Means of Revelation in the Book of Jeremiah," in Barstad and Kratz, *Prophecy*, 45.

521. W. H. Schmidt, *Jeremia*, 1:338.

522. C. J. Sharp, "Wrestling the Word: Submission and Resistance as Holy Hermeneutical Acts," *Anglican Theological Review* 97 (2015): 16.

523. J. Dubbink calls it "a critical expansion of 20.7-13" ("Jeremiah: Hero of Faith or Defeatist," *JSOT* 86 [1999]: 79).

So far in the scroll, Jeremiah has uttered two types of protest, both following the pattern of the Psalms. There have been protests he uttered in his own name, in light of people's attacks on him in response to the challenges and threats he keeps issuing. And there have been protests he uttered on Judah's behalf, expressing the way they were thinking or the way they ought to be talking to Yahweh rather than the way they actually were talking to him (14:2–9, 19–22). In vv. 7–18, he brings both kinds of protest to a climax, his own in vv. 7–13 and Judah's in vv. 14–18. The latter is "a cry of utter despair over the fate of people and city."[524] It represents how he feels as a Judahite and as a person who cares about his people and longs for them not to have to go through the fate he has been warning them of. By the end of Jer 11–20, "Jeremiah's fate and the fate of the nation converge symbolically so that what happens to him evokes and mimics the suffering of the people."[525] Thus in the last verse he speaks again of *sorrow* in connection with Judah's coming suffering (8:18) and of the *shame* with which Judah is threatened (2:26; 3:24, 25; 7:19). He wishes he had not been born because he wishes he had not seen Judah's destiny or been doomed to share it. He is torn apart by the hurt of Judah that he has experienced anticipatorily and vicariously. It is on Judah's behalf that he prays in this way as the scroll reaches a climax. Judah is fatally doomed (unless it responds). Yet "prays" is perhaps the wrong word. There is no appeal to Yahweh, as is the case in 14:2–6. It's more a lament about a situation that cannot be changed than a protest made to someone who might change it. In articulating this lament, once again Jeremiah seeks to pull Judah back from the brink as he invites it to look at its destiny this way. Perhaps after 587, people who recognized that Jeremiah had been right would be declaring their own curse on themselves in these words.[526]

Verses 14–18 are more varied in their prosody than vv. 7–13. They comprise six bicola, of which only the first two stand alone syntactically, though in substance they belong together. The third runs into the fourth, and the fifth runs into the sixth and into the tricolon that follows. The verses end dramatically with a double tricolon. There is almost no parallelism (only in v. 16b and in v. 17b within the tricolon); characteristically, the second colon in each line completes the first. There is parallelism between lines within v. 14, within v. 15, and within v. 16. The prosaic *that* (*'ăšer*) plays an unusual patterning role in vv. 14a, 14b, 15a, 16a. The outline of the section can be constructed with an a-a'-b-b' or an a-b-b'-a' pattern.[527]

524. R. P. Carroll, *Jeremiah*, OTL, 402.

525. O'Connor, "Jeremiah," 499.

526. M. C. Calloway, "Seduced by Method: History and Jeremiah 20," in Holt and Sharp, *Jeremiah Invented*, 16–33.

527. Craigie, Kelley, and Drinkard, *Jeremiah 1–25*, 278.

v. 14   Cursed be the day I was born (two bicola)
  vv. 15–16 Cursed be the messenger (two pairs of linked bicola)
v. 17   The reason for the curse (a tricolon continuing the pre-
        ceding bicolon)
v. 18   The reason for cursing the day (another, closing, tricolon)

7 Already, the three directions of a protest psalm feature: *you, I,* and *they.*
Jeremiah's opening verb (*pātâ*) has several connotations, which compound
to increase its forcefulness. In 1 Kgs 22:20–22 and 2 Chr 18:19–21, it suggests
a willful but well-intentioned deceiving of a prophet, and this understanding
prompts Origen into a long discussion that includes the observation that it
is better to be deceived by God than by the Serpent.[528] But Yahweh hardly
deceived Jeremiah. He was pretty open about how things would turn out for
him[529]—though Jerome suggests that Jeremiah refers to Yahweh's commissioning him to be a prophet to the nations, not to proclaim captivity for Jerusalem.[530] The verb can have sexual connotations, suggesting seduction (e.g.,
Hos 2:16[14]); if anything like this understanding is right, these might seem
"directly blasphemous words."[531] Another connotation of the verb is that of
treating someone as a simpleton (*pətî*), making a fool of them. Whichever
connotation attaches to the verb, Yahweh indeed overpowered Jeremiah in
commissioning him. "No words in the Classical Prophets show as plainly as
these that the Prophets in their demeanor and in their speech stand under a
divine compulsion."[532] When God comes on *strong,* who can stand firm? Yet
Jeremiah's second verb (*pātâ niphal,* not *pual*—almost "let myself be inveigled") implies that he accepts some responsibility for allowing Yahweh to turn
him into a prophet. In theory, he could have continued to resist, but he yielded
to Yahweh's enticement. He let Yahweh overcome his resistance. Jeremiah's
language points to the mystery of the relationship between divine sovereignty
or compulsion and human freedom or responsibility. The developing parallelism between the cola suggests some equivocality about that question:

> you inveigled   me   Yahweh I got inveigled
> you were strong toward   me   and you won

While Jeremiah's second verb does hint at his recognizing some responsibility for accepting his commission, the two verbs in the parallel colon all but

528. Origen, *Jeremiah,* 228.
529. Blayney, *Jeremiah,* 322.
530. Jerome, *Jeremiah,* 122.
531. Rudolph, *Jeremia,* 130.
532. Volz, *Jeremia,* 209.

withdraw that hint. The trouble is that Yahweh ended up making Jeremiah something for people to *laugh at*, something that the community was continually *mocking*. Here, the line has an a-b-c-c'-b'-a' pattern:

> I became
>> something to laugh at
>>> all the time
>>>> everyone
>>> is mocking
>> me.

If a person sends someone to undertake a task, then by definition they are not with them. "This polar tension . . . will be seen to lie at the heart of Jeremiah's dilemma as voiced in his confessions."[533]

8–9 Jeremiah's reasoning involves some hyperbole, but he is perhaps quoting what people said or how it seemed to him. Whenever he opened his mouth, it was to *cry out . . . violence and destruction*. He is always protesting about what is going on in the community (6:7; see the commentary there). He is so negative, so critical! And therefore *Yahweh's message became to me an object of reviling* (cf. 6:10), a reason to despise Jeremiah, and a cause of *derision*. He is in a no-win situation[534] in more than one sense. Yahweh has compelled him to serve him, but Yahweh doesn't lean on people to accept his message, nor does he fulfill its threats. "The gap between prediction and fulfillment has opened this space for this vocational crisis."[535] "The prophet's distress at being stuck between an insistent God and a resistant people" means that his inability to resist is "not a clinical compulsion, but a theological and vocational one."[536] He can try to be silent, but the power of the message is too great. There's quite a contrast with 15:16: *Your message became to me a joy and the rejoicing of my mind*.[537] The verse begins with *whenever* and ends with a repetition of *all the time*—the expression is a recurrent complaint in the Psalms (e.g., Pss 42:3[4], 10[11]; 44:15[16]; 56:1[2], 2[3], 5[6]).[538] At least, blessed is a man like Jeremiah who has no other basis for being reviled than God's message.[539] The reviling made him determine to give up delivering this message, but he *was weary of holding it in* (cf. 6:11; see the commentary there). He just couldn't.

533. J. G. Janzen, "Jeremiah 20:7–18," *Int* 37 (1983): 180.
534. Brueggemann, *Jeremiah 1–25*, 174.
535. Diamond, "Jeremiah," 568.
536. Fretheim, "Caught in the Middle," 351, 355.
537. Lundbom, *Jeremiah 1–20*, 856.
538. Holladay, *Commentary on Jeremiah*, 1:553.
539. Origen, *Jeremiah*, 237.

10 The *because* takes us back to the *reviling* and *derision*. Jeremiah has *heard the report of many people* repeating with scorn the phrase that sums up his message with its threat of invasion, *"All around is terror"* (v. 3). Did they pick up the phrase from Ps 31:13(14)? Did they give him that name, and did he then transfer it to Pashhur? (cf. also 6:25; 46:5; 49:29). Anyway, they are encouraging one another (he believes), *Tell, let's tell of him!* The talk may include his becoming a topic of amused conversation, but the lines that follow suggest there is more to it—at least public critique (they are hardly engaged in a conspiracy to inform on him, given that he was quite public in his proclamation; there was no need for a plot to report him to the authorities). The sense of being let down by people whom one trusted and who gave the impression of being trustworthy, *each one who wishes me well,* is another that recurs from the Psalms (Ps 41:9[10]). For one's friends to be *watching my step* ought not to mean they are hoping to see him fall over. Watching is usually a positive activity; your friends watch your back. But the Psalms also speak of a negative watching (Ps 56:6[7]). These "friends" are expecting him to get tripped up; indeed, he likely means that they are planning to trip him up, not just looking forward to it happening. As Yahweh had *inveigled* him and been able to *win over him,* his earthly opponents also want to do so. His language, with its "intratextual loop,"[540] may indicate how he stands in a hall of mirrors:[541] his friend Yahweh is his enemy, the message he wishes not to give he cannot help giving, his enemies pretend to be his friends, they are hoping to do what Yahweh has already done by inveigling him and defeating him, and they deserve to suffer redress, but they want to see redress from him. A story such as Jer 26 indicates what winning and gaining redress might look like, though the scheme fails.

11 Over against all that anguish, conflict, and fear, however, are some convictions. Again, this contrast resembles the dynamic of the Psalms. The key fact is that *Yahweh—he is with me,* as he had promised back at the beginning (1:8, 19). Yahweh's being with someone does not mean their having an inner sense of Yahweh's presence. Yahweh's presence is an objective and active one, as Yahweh had said at the beginning—*I am with you to snatch you away* (1:8, 19). Here the declaration is, *He is with me, like a terrifying strong man.* He is not *like a strong man who cannot deliver* (14:9). He is *the great God, the strong man, whose name is Yahweh of Armies* (32:18). LXX and Vg translate the word for *strong man* (*gibbôr*) as "warrior," which might seem worrying: do you want your God to be a warrior? Wouldn't you rather have a prince of peace? But a prophet or a people under pressure cannot afford the luxury of a prince of peace. They need someone ready and willing to rescue them.

---

540. M. A. Fishbane, *Text and Texture* (New York: Schocken, 1979), 98.
541. Holladay, *Commentary on Jeremiah*, 1:557.

They need someone terrifying (*ʿārîṣ*) whose fierceness matches that of their attackers (15:21). Jeremiah's *persecutors* are looking for him to *collapse*, but he knows that it is they who will. Their hopes and aims will not be fulfilled: *They won't win*. This fourth occurrence of the verb *win* (*yākōl*) brings a telling sequence to a positive climax:

- *You won* (v. 7): God's overpowering of Jeremiah
- *I couldn't win* (v. 9): Jeremiah's inability to hold back God's message, no matter what he suffers for speaking it
- *We may win* (v. 10): the nasty plans of Jeremiah's former friends, plotting to turn him over to the authorities
- *They won't win* (v. 11): Jeremiah's stubborn confidence that God will defend him and frustrate the plans of his enemies[542]

Yahweh had succeeded in overcoming Jeremiah, and Jeremiah has not succeeded in giving up his commission, but when his opponents hope to succeed in overcoming him, they will not succeed, precisely because Yahweh is with him.[543] Instead, *they will be totally shamed*. He will be proved to have been in the right. And their *disgrace* will last. *It will not be put out of mind*.

12 Jeremiah knows it is true; he needs Yahweh actually to implement it. His plea that Yahweh may do so restates an earlier confession and plea from 11:20 (see the commentary there):

> So Yahweh of Armies, one who exercises authority with
>   faithfulness,
>   one who examines heart and mind:
> May I see your redress from them,
>   because to you I have rolled my argument.

13 Imperatives such as *sing to Yahweh* and *praise Yahweh* are familiar from the beginning of a praise psalm and also from the beginning of a testimony psalm that gives thanks for Yahweh's act of deliverance. Here, that significance fits with the subsequent rationale: *because he has snatched the life of a needy person from the hand of people acting direly*. Could Jeremiah really have described himself as a needy person (*ʾebyôn*)?[544] The needy are another prominent feature in protest Psalms: they are the vulnerable, the endangered, the exposed, the people at risk (Pss 12:5[6]; 35:10; 140:12[13]). It is indeed not implausible for Jeremiah to see himself thus. In the present

542. Wright, *Jeremiah*, 227.
543. S. D. Snyman, "A Note on *pth* and *ykl* in Jeremiah xx 7–13," *VT* 48 (1998): 559–63.
544. McKane, *Jeremiah*, 1:481.

context, a confession of the kind that comes in v. 13 would fit the story in 19:14–20:6. But in vv. 7–12, we have come some distance from that story. A more plausible link is with the kind of protest psalm that closes with a commitment to sing to Yahweh when he has performed the act of rescue for which the psalm pleads (Pss 57:7[8]; 59:16[17]). The summons to song and praise is an anticipatory one: "My salvation is: I do not believe my disbelief."[545] It is to know that while Yahweh is the overwhelmingly powerful God (v. 7), he is also the personal and present God.[546] "The highest form of praise was not just to say nice things to God or about God. Rather real praise meant to acknowledge the reality and presence of God in all situations and circumstances, no matter how fraught with contradiction."[547] Further, Jeremiah here makes not a first-person commitment to praise but an imperatival call to praise, which makes explicit the connection between Jeremiah's anguish and prospective deliverance, and a community's response.[548] It indicates an assumption on Jeremiah's part that he has a community that will join in (cf. Ps 22:23[24]).

14 Jeremiah once said,

> Alas for me, mother, that you gave birth to me,
>> a man involved in argument
>> and a man involved in contention with the entire country.
>
> (15:10)

Cursed be the day that I was born on goes further and is more shocking. One can imagine that people listening to the scroll do not know what he could be talking about or why he could be expressing himself in this way. It will be v. 18 that comes nearest to making things more explicit, but Jeremiah's rhetoric holds back this clarification while it concentrates on expressing the torment. Meanwhile, it focuses on reminding readers (who don't yet know that they are the ones with whom he shares this anguish) of the joyous wonder that accompanies the birth of a baby, but contradicts it. People might be

---

545. Berrigan, *Jeremiah*, 88. Berrigan attributes the words to Graham Greene; according to L. Durán (*Graham Greene* [San Francisco: Harper, 1994], 97), the original words were, "The trouble is I don't believe my unbelief."

546. S. D. Snyman, "The Portrayal of Yahweh in Jeremiah 20:7–13," *HTS* 55 (1999): 176–82. P. S. Johnston considers these two aspects to Yahweh in Jeremiah from the opposite angle in "'Now You See Me, Now You Don't': Jeremiah and God," in *Prophecy and the Prophets in Ancient Israel: Proceedings of the Oxford Old Testament Seminar*, ed. J. Day, LHBOTS 531 (London: T&T Clark, 2010), 290–308.

547. Wright, *Jeremiah*, 228.

548. Davis Lewin, "Arguing for Authority," 115.

familiar with such a curse on one's birthday. Within the First Testament, Job 3 comprises a systematic such curse. A much more ancient Old Babylonian lament recounts how among the gods, a mother grieves over her son who has been killed:

> I am the mother who gave birth!
> Woe to that day, that day!
> Woe to that night! . . .
> The day that dawned for my provider,
> that dawned for the lad,
> my Damu!
> A day to be wiped out,
> that I would I could forget.
> You night [. . .] that should [never]
> have let it go forth,
> when my gendarmes [military recruiters] shamelessly
> made their way
> into my [presence].[549]

May it not be blessed is a litotes; v. 14 as a whole is the opposite of saying "happy birthday."[550]

15 "No one loves the messenger who brings bad news," says a messenger with some anxiety in Sophocles's *Antigone.* Don't shoot the messenger because you don't like the message, says the modern version. Shooting the messenger is a kind of symbolic act, as if one can kill the message by killing the messenger. So a curse on the messenger is a curse on the message. Jeremiah's declaration is a figurative one; he is not cursing an actual messenger, and a sense of indignation at his curse[551] misses the point, as is the case with curses in the Psalms.[552] The figurative nature of the curse is reflected in the way Jeremiah speaks as if there was a male messenger who brought a father news of a birth. While it might occasionally be the case (e.g., if the father is the king), generally the father would be sitting outside while the women of the community attend on his wife, and eventually one of the women brings him the news (a mother may not mind whether her baby is a boy or a girl; a father may be especially thrilled

---

549. T. Jacobsen and K. Nielsen, "Cursing the Day," *SJOT* 6 (1992): 188; cf. Lundbom, *Jeremiah,* 1:870.

550. McKane, *Jeremiah,* 1:486

551. Duhm, *Jeremia,* 168.

552. P. D. Miller, "Jeremiah," on the passage.

to have a son). There is no actual person who fulfills the role described here. Jeremiah is combining the events around a birth with a conventional image, that of a man bringing news after an occasion such as a battle (e.g., 1 Sam 4:12–17).

16–17 Jeremiah makes his point in another strong way by wishing on this figurative person a fate like that of Sodom and Gomorrah. He does so with some irony because the *towns* that are going to be *overturned* are the ones in which the Judahites live (see 19:15), about whose destiny Yahweh is not going to *relent* and act differently (e.g., 4:28; 15:6). Jeremiah has prayed for a *cry* to be heard from his persecutors' houses (18:22), and Yahweh has declared that he would not listen to them when they cry out (11:11–12). In his imagination, Jeremiah has heard the *blast* of war (4:19), and he has heard attackers resolving to go up at *noon* (6:4). Jeremiah underlines the point further in the grotesque and gruesome imagery that follows in v. 17. The illogic of expecting the messenger to kill the baby in the mother's womb further underscores the figurative nature of vv. 14–17.[553]

18 Jeremiah's prospective mood, then, is an awareness of *toil and sorrow* (8:18) such as will come with 587 and the destruction of city and temple.[554] *Shame* is Judah's destiny (3:25; 7:19). While Jeremiah wants to see redress on his enemies, it gives him no pleasure to contemplate the devastation of Judah. He longs that it should share his present awareness of what lies ahead of it, so that it may turn and Yahweh may relent.

E. PART 2E: ON KINGS AND PROPHETS (21:1–24:10)

The first half of Jeremiah draws nearer to a close with a compilation of messages having a double distinctive focus, on Judah's kings and prophets.[555] "Jeremiah 21–24 is foremost a treatise on leadership."[556] If Jer 18–20 was a climax to the scroll so far, then Jer 21–24 might be seen as an appendix or sidebar before we come to Jer 25. But it follows the pattern within the scroll in raising questions about the objects of Judah's trust; in this sense, it simply continues the scroll's sequence. And if the catastrophe seemed imminent in Jer 18–20, it is now even more imminent, or actually happening: in 21:1–10,

553. It also makes it unnecessary to ask whether Yahweh is the subject in v. 17; see J. R. Lundbom, "The Double Curse in Jer 20:14–18," *JBL* 104 (1985): 597.
554. Cf. Rashi, in MG.
555. On Jer 21–24 as a whole and its possible development, see J. B. Job, *Jeremiah's Kings: A Study of the Monarchy in Jeremiah* (Aldershot: Ashgate, 2006), esp. 15–37; and on its rhetoric, see Choi, "A New Heart."
556. Stulman, *Jeremiah*, 221.

the city is under siege. The chapters' presupposition is that Jerusalem's kings and its prophets might be the objects of its trust and hope, but if anything they are the cause of its imminent fall; "kings and prophets are the guilty men."[557] While focusing on the community's leadership, the material also interweaves shorter messages about the city and its people. The juxtaposition signals that the kings' and prophets' exercise of leadership has implications for city and people and for their destiny. Conversely, it suggests that city and people cannot simply congratulate themselves on not being kings or prophets; they are under judgment too. Further, it points to the fact that the addressees of part 2e as a whole (as of the rest of the scroll) are not merely kings and prophets but the entire people. Jeremiah fulfills a role that subverts the authority of their leadership.

Jeremiah 21–24 as a whole begins and ends with sections relating to the time of Zedekiah, Judah's last king, with the threat of sword, hunger, and epidemic, and with a contrast between Yahweh planning a dire fate rather than a good one and a good one rather than a dire one.[558] In between, it incorporates messages spanning several reigns and thus a number of years, though as usual we cannot date them precisely. In the context of the reign of Zedekiah and specifically of the siege of Jerusalem, the chapters would offer king, prophets, and people a final challenge and choice. After 587, it would implicitly explain why a dire fate fell on the city. In this context, particular significance would attach to its promises for the future regarding kings (23:5–6) and regarding the people as a whole (23:7–8; 24:4–7). It falls into two major parts:

> 21:1–23:8   About kings (and their people)—in order, except that Zedekiah comes first
>
> 23:9–24:10 About prophets (and their people)—naming no names, though Jer 27–29 associates tension among prophets with Zedekiah's reign

1. About Kings (and Their People) (21:1–23:8)

Since the preface to the scroll (1:1–3), no contemporary kings have been named except Josiah in 3:6, but part 2e now mentions a series of kings. Thus, whereas it is impossible to date the messages in Jer 2–20 to the reigns of specific kings, the situation now changes. The kings do not come in a chronolog-

---

557. R. P. Carroll, *Jeremiah*, OTL, 404.
558. Allen, *Jeremiah*, 237.

ical sequence; the last Judahite king comes first. Further, even when naming names, the chapters speak five times about David's throne, David's household, and the Davidic tree (21:12; 22:2, 4, 30; 23:5); in Jer 2–20, there were just two references to David (13:13; 17:25). Jeremiah 21–24 is concerned with the vocation and failure of the Davidic line, with its having turned the gift into a guarantee.[559] "The Jeremiah tradition singles out the Davidic kings . . . as the primary architects of the national calamity of 587."[560] The time of reckoning has come for them.[561] It makes one inclined to pray,

> Grant, Almighty God, that since thou didst formerly take such heavy vengeance on the impiety of thine ancient people, that thou didst not spare even kings, . . . O grant, that we at this day may continue in obedience to thy word, and not so kindle thy vengeance against us.[562]

While the unit is thus concerned with the Davidic line's danger, it is also concerned with its promise. Throughout the scroll, the messages have been more threats and promises than predictions, and this characteristic is even clearer in the threats and promises relating to the kings.

The treatment of the kings that begins with Zedekiah implicitly almost ends with him (23:5–6), operating in the manner of a movie that first tells the audience where the story is going before backtracking to indicate how it got there. While many individual sections address the individual kings, their audience will have been the community as a whole, and the community is more directly the audience of the compilation.

21:1–10		About Zedekiah and about city and people
	21:1–7	Zedekiah
	21:8–10	City and people
21:11–22:9		About David's household and about city and people
	21:11–22:5	David's household
	22:6–9	City and people
22:10–30		About three kings and about city and people
	22:10–12	Shallum/Jehoahaz
	22:13–19	Jehoiakim
	22:20–23	City and people

---

559. Achtemeier, *Jeremiah*, 70.

560. A. Varughese, "The Royal Family in the Jeremiah Tradition," in Kaltner and Stulman, *Inspired Speech*, 320.

561. Fischer, *Jeremia*, 1:672.

562. Calvin, *Jeremiah*, 3:142.

a. Zedekiah (and the City) (21:1–10)

¹*The message that came to Jeremiah from Yahweh when King Zedekiah sent to him Pashhur ben Malkiah and Zephaniah ben Ma'aseyah the priest, saying,* ²*Inquire on our behalf of Yahweh, please, because Nebuchadrezzar*[a] *King of Babylon is doing battle against us. Perhaps Yahweh will act with us*[b] *in accordance with all his extraordinary deeds, and he will withdraw*[c] *from against us.*[d]

³*Jeremiah said to them, You will say this to Zedekiah.*[e] ⁴*Yahweh, the God of Israel,*[f] *has said this. Here am I, turning aside the instruments of battle that are in your hand,*[g] *with which you are doing battle with the king of Babylon and*[h] *with the Chaldeans*[i] *who are blockading you from outside the wall. And I will gather them*[j] *into the middle of this city.* ⁵*I myself will do battle with you with a hand stretched out and with a strong arm and with anger*[k] *and with fury and with great rage.* ⁶*I will strike down the people who live in this city, both human being and animal—in a great epidemic they will die.* ⁷*And afterward (Yahweh's affirmation) I will give Zedekiah King of Judah and his servants and the people, those who remain*[l] *in this city from the epidemic, from the sword, and from the hunger into the hand of Nebuchadrezzar King of Babylon,*[m] *into the hand of their enemies, and into the hand of the people seeking their life. He will strike them down through*[n] *the mouth of the sword—he will not spare them, he will not pity, and he will not have compassion.*[o]

⁸*And to this people you will say,*[p] *Yahweh has said this: Here am I, putting before you the path to life and the path to death.* ⁹*The person who stays in this city will die by sword, by hunger, and by epidemic.*[q] *But the person who goes out and falls away to the Chaldeans who are blockading you, he will live. His life will be his as loot.*[r] ¹⁰*Because I have set my face against this city for something dire, not for something good (Yahweh's affirmation).*[s] *Into the hand of the king of Babylon it will be given, and he will consume it in fire.*[t]

a. LXX lacks the name. It is spelled in various ways in the OT (see BDB). While a form such as *Nəbûkadne'ṣṣar* that appears in English as Nebuchadnezzar is the most familiar, a form such as *Nəbûkadre'ṣṣar*, which predominates in Jeremiah and Ezekiel, is closer to Akkadian *nabu-kudurru-uṣur* (with its own variants), a prayer or confession: "Nabu protect(s) the eldest son"; cf. J. Goldingay, *Daniel*, WBC 30, rev. ed. (Grand Rapids: Zondervan, 2019), 136, on Dan 1:1.

b. LXX lacks *with us*.

c. *Ya'āleh* could be parsed as *hiphil* with Yahweh as subject ("and make him withdraw"), which is in any case the implication.

d. MT^L has a section marker here; MT^A has it after v. 3.

e. LXX adds "King of Judah."

f. LXX lacks *the God of Israel*.

g. LXX lacks *that are in your hand*.

h. LXX lacks *with the king of Babylon and*.

i. More precisely, the *kaśdîm*; the switch from *ś* to *l* sometimes happens in Akkadian. *Kaśdîm* is the term both for the country and for the people; I take it to denote the people when it has the article, as here, but it is more ambiguous when it is anarthrous.

j. LXX lacks this verb.

k. LXX lacks *and with anger*.

l. The *waw* attached to the participle is explicative rather than meaning "and": the expression sums up the groups rather than adding the remainers as another group.

m. LXX lacks *into the hand of Nebuchadrezzar King of Babylon*.

n. LXX, Vg have "with," but the preposition is *lə*.

o. LXX has "they will strike them down" and then makes Yahweh the subject of the rest of the sentence. It is a noteworthy example of the detailed differences between LXX and MT in this section of Jeremiah; see R. D. Wells, "Indications of Late Reinterpretation of the Jeremianic Tradition from the LXX of Jer 21 1—23 8," *ZAW* 96 (1984): 407.

p. This verb is singular: that is, this message is one to Jeremiah from Yahweh, perhaps originally separate from the one that precedes.

q. LXX lacks the reference to epidemic.

r. LXX adds "and he will live," as in 38:2.

s. LXX lacks *(Yahweh's affirmation)*.

t. MT has a section marker here.

As MT's section markers suggest, the story comprises three parts:

vv. 1–2   Zedekiah sends aides to consult Yahweh through Jeremiah

vv. 3–7   Jeremiah gives the aides an uncompromising threat of catastrophe

vv. 8–10   Jeremiah adds a promise to individuals if they abandon the city

1 The introduction follows the pattern in 2:1; 7:1; 11:1; 14:1; 18:1, again combining a preface to this part with an introduction to the particular story that follows. Once more, an account of a message from Jeremiah may link with a report elsewhere in the scroll of the occasion when he gave it (e.g., 7:1–15; 26:1–24); this passage and the stories in Jer 37 and 38 may relate to the same event.[563] Each time, the presupposition is that Zedekiah has rebelled against

563. But M. Avioz connects Jer 21 and 37 with earlier and later occasions in the city's final siege ("The Historical Setting of Jeremiah 21:1–10," *AUSS* 44 [2006]: 213–29).

Nebuchadrezzar, presumably by defaulting on the payment of tribute and/ or by entering into a treaty with the Egyptians, and Nebuchadrezzar has come to blockade the city to put Zedekiah in his place (52:3b–4). Jeremiah 32–34 and 37–38 then relate to various moments in the siege. While previous chapters have often portrayed attacks on Jerusalem as if they were actually happening, the "as if" is important; mostly or entirely, they portray what Jeremiah sees in his imagination and shares with people as a warning of what is coming. Here for the first time we are in the midst of actual events.[564] It will turn out that this siege indeed leads to the city's fall and destruction and to the capture of Zedekiah, though no one knows it yet; the time is maybe late 589 or early 588, and there is still the possibility that Nebuchadrezzar may go away. The story brings not only the first mention of any contemporary king since 3:6 but also the mention of Judah's very last king, with a kind of appropriateness at the beginning of the unit on kings (on Zedekiah, see "Background," p. 4). In addition, it opens with a mention of someone called *Pashhur*, which makes for a link with Pashhur the priest in the previous chapter;[565] the name is common enough. The link contains some irony. There, Pashhur the priest was attempting to silence Jeremiah. Here, Pashhur and another priest are coming to consult him. But this Pashhur will turn out to be no improvement on the previous one (38:1–4). This Pashhur seems also to have been a priest (Neh 11:12), though it's odd that here the noun is attached only to *Zephaniah*, another name that recurs in the First Testament. Perhaps it reflects Zephaniah's senior status, suggested by the way he appears in 29:25, 29 (which chronologically preceded the present episode); he appears again in a similar connection in 37:3, and most solemnly in 52:24. Both Pashhur and Zephaniah function as the king's aides, hinting at the extent to which the clergy would be identified with the administration. On the other hand, it is noteworthy that Zedekiah does not send to one of the other prophets, who are also identified with the administration (see Jer 27–28). Perhaps he already has his doubts about them; perhaps their messages have already been discredited; perhaps he is hedging his bets, like the kings in 1 Kgs 22; perhaps he is demonstrating the (understandable) vacillation that will recur in further stories about him in the Jeremiah scroll. But the section makes no negative comment on Zedekiah.[566]

2 *Inquire* is what a king would do of the different entities that are his resources (8:2; 10:21), especially in a war situation.[567] The verb covers divi-

---

564. Stulman, *Jeremiah*, 205.

565. See especially Rudolph, *Jeremia*, 135.

566. On the mixed assessment of Zedekiah, see, e.g., J. B. Job, *Jeremiah's Kings*, 99–119.

567. H. M. Barstad, "Prophecy in the Book of Jeremiah and the Historical Prophet," in *Sense and Sensitivity: Essays on Biblical Prophecy, Ideology and Reception in Tribute to Robert*

nation by its various means; Yahweh's prophets are the means that Yahweh approves, but Israelites often looked elsewhere. The scroll here makes its first reference to Nebuchadrezzar (see the translation note); the lateness of this introduction puts him in his place, too. He had paid Jerusalem a visit in 601 and had besieged the city in 597, but a siege during Zedekiah's reign will be the blockade that began in about 589 and issued in the city's fall and destruction in 587. The implication here is that Zedekiah's inquiry takes place at an early stage in the blockade. The question he raises and the precedents to which it appeals are fine ones. He makes the scroll's only reference to Yahweh's *extraordinary deeds* (*niplā'ōt*), though the verb lying behind that noun (*pālā'*) appears significantly in 32:17, 27. The exodus is the great instantiation of these extraordinary deeds (Exod 3:20), and the story may raise the question whether Jerusalem can "claim" the story in Exodus.[568] But the Psalms often reminded king and people that these wonders were not confined to the distant past (e.g., Ps 107:8, 15, 21, 31). And everybody knew that Yahweh had delivered Jerusalem in an extraordinary way from Sennacherib a century previously (see Isa 37). Zedekiah thus follows the example of his great-great-grandfather Hezekiah, who commissioned his aides to ask the prophet to pray, and he received a message—containing good news. Zedekiah's appeal to such precedents implies the assumption that the relationship between Yahweh and Israel is still in force.[569] It also indicates that he is not just asking Jeremiah to request information from Yahweh about what is going to happen. *Inquire* (*dāraš*) suggests "both oracle and intercession";[570] it has the double meaning attaching to the English verb "seek," which is often used to translate the Hebrew word.[571] Zedekiah is asking Jeremiah to pray for the city, as Tg makes explicit and as is explicit in 37:3. *On our behalf* (*ba'ădēnû*) often suggests intercession: Yahweh used this preposition in bidding Jeremiah not to intercede for Judah (7:16; 11:14).

3–4 Jeremiah can speak as if he knows what might happen and how it should be prevented, but also as if he knows what will happen.[572] The story

Carroll, ed. A. G. Hunter and P. R. Davies, LHBOTS 348 (London: Sheffield Academic, 2002), 90.

568. D. Rom-Shiloni, "Facing Destruction and Exile: Inner-Biblical Exegesis in Jeremiah and Ezekiel," *ZAW* 117 (2005): 192–94.

569. Calvin, *Jeremiah*, 3:53.

570. Volz, *Jeremia*, 217.

571. See further R. Thelle, "*drš 't-yhwh*: The Prophetic Act of Consulting Yhwh in Jeremiah 21,2 and 37,7," *SJOT* 12 (1998): 249–56.

572. M. J. de Jong, "Rewriting the Past in Light of the Present: The Stories of the Prophet Jeremiah," in *Prophecy and Prophets in Stories*, ed. B. Becking and H. M. Barstad, OTS 65 (Leiden: Brill, 2015), 124–40.

makes no reference to Jeremiah inquiring of Yahweh. It presupposes the self-evident nature of Yahweh's response. While it is in one sense a shocking moment in the scroll's unfolding, especially in the concrete nature of the message at this point, it is in keeping with everything we have read. Yahweh not merely declines to come to Judah's support; he intends to work against Judah and take the side of *the Chaldeans.* They were a people from southern Babylonia to whom Nebuchadrezzar's father Nabopolassar belonged and who were the ruling caste in Babylonia in the sixth century, but in the First Testament, *Chaldeans* is the regular word for the people of Babylonia in general.[573] Yahweh says he will act as if he is interfering to divert Judahite arrows so that they miss their targets.[574] It will be as if the weapons have gained a life of their own. Perhaps it is the weapons that he intends thus to *gather . . . into the middle of this city*, or perhaps it is the Babylonians that he intends to gather in this way. The verb is the one he used when he commissioned his aides to *go, gather every animal of the open country—bring them to devour* (12:9). The turning of the Judahites' weapons is paralleled by the turning of the Babylonians from outside to inside.[575]

5 By means of the weapons or the Babylonians, not only will Yahweh frustrate the Judahites' battling: *I myself will do battle with you.* Yahweh, too, recalls the exodus.[576] He will again act *with hand stretched out and with a strong arm* (e.g., 32:21; Exod 6:6; Deut 4:34; 5:15, though Jeremiah here reverses the description of hand and arm). He had not been especially angry with Egypt at the exodus, but now he is expressing *anger* and *fury* and *rage.* In another context, the message could be read positively: Yahweh could be doing battle with Judah in the sense of being on Judah's side and acting with anger against Nebuchadrezzar.[577] But any ambiguity in his words disappears. The angry, fury, and rage are the ones Deut 29:27 warned of. Hand and arm are exercised against Judah, not on Judah's behalf.

> The Exodus tradition functions as the common denominator for both the King's officials and the prophet. . . . However, in polar contrast to the officials' request for hope and salvation, Jeremiah reuses the same historical tradition to crush the long-standing analogy portraying God as Savior.

---

573. Cf. Goldingay, *Daniel*, 155, on Dan 1:4.

574. See H. Weippert, "Jahwekrieg und Bundesfluch in Jer 21 1–7," *ZAW* 82 (1970): 396–409.

575. Holladay, *Commentary on Jeremiah*, 1:569.

576. Cf. Duhm, *Jeremia*, 169–70.

577. Craigie, Kelley, and Drinkard, *Jeremiah 1–25*, 286–87.

The prophet introduces a completely opposite notion in which God is the main foe of His people.[578]

"If the proclamation of holy war gave heart to the fighters, the reversal of the motif would achieve the opposite."[579]

6–7 The inbuilt perils of siege will be Jerusalem's downfall, though Jeremiah lists the three great perils in unconventional fashion. First, there will be *a great epidemic*, another reversal of the exodus (Exod 9:3, 15). It will affect animals as well as the human beings with whose fate the fate of animals is interwoven, who suffer through human guilt.[580] "The Chaldeans will do battle with you from outside and I will do battle with you by a great epidemic."[581] Then, later, there will be *sword* and *hunger* until there is another reversal as the Judahites are given into the hand of their attackers—whereas Yahweh had once given nations such as the Canaanites into Israel's hand.[582] Their vanquishers, the people *seeking their life*, will not only be *the Chaldeans*; and we know from subsequent reports that Moab, Ammon, and Edom will be involved. Like Yahweh (13:14) and as Yahweh's agent, Nebuchadrezzar *will not spare them, he will not pity, and he will not have compassion.* The triad of verbs is the last of a series of triads: anger/fury/great rage; king/servants/people; epidemic/sword/hunger; Nebuchadrezzar/enemies/people seeking their life; spare/pity/have compassion. As usual, God will thus be at work, though through human agents. But "'if God be against us . . .' Nebuchadnezzar is the least of their problems."[583] In the culmination of the event in 587, things did not work out as one might have expected from this message, which is an indication that the message does not come from after the actual fall of the city,[584] though that context might make the message more positive (at least Yahweh was in control).[585] If anything, the circumstances of Zedekiah's capture and its aftermath will be worse. A literal fulfillment of Jeremiah's warning would have been a mercy.

8 As often happens, inquiring of Yahweh produces not only an answer to the plea and a response to the question (unwelcome ones in both cases on this occasion) but also a reframing of the question or a supplementary answer to an unasked supplementary question. Suppose there are people who

---

578. Rom-Shiloni, "Facing Destruction and Exile," 194.

579. R. P. Carroll, *Jeremiah*, OTL, 409.

580. Calvin, *Jeremiah*, 3:59.

581. Qimchi, in MG.

582. P. D. Miller, "Jeremiah," on the passage.

583. Wright, *Jeremiah*, 233, 234.

584. McKane, *Jeremiah*, 1:494.

585. So C. M. Maier, "God's Cruelty and Jeremiah's Treason: Jeremiah 21:1–10 in Postcolonial Perspective," in Maier and Sharp, *Prophecy and Power*, 133–49.

are willing to dissociate themselves from Zedekiah and his policies. Maybe Pashhur and Zephaniah are such people, or they are willing to become such people in light of what Yahweh has said. Is it inevitable that they are caught up in the imminent catastrophe? While we are unwise to read into Jeremiah a modern Western preoccupation with theodicy, Jeremiah's rider to his declaration about catastrophe relates to such questions. When people are told that disaster is coming, individuals have to see if they can take charge of their destiny, not just let themselves be swallowed by it if there is a way they can evade it. Yahweh offers to enable them to do so: *Here am I, putting before you the path to life and the path to death.* Jeremiah is taking up words from Deut 30:15, 19: "See, I have put before you today life and what is good, death and what is dire. . . . Life and death I have put before you." But he tweaks the words he takes up, as he often does. One way he does so is by reworking the antithesis as *the path to life and the path to death* in light of the importance of the motif of *path* in his own message (e.g., 2:36; 3:21; 6:16). His phraseology thus differs from Deuteronomy's, though the idea of walking on Yahweh's path is also important there (e.g., Deut 13:5[6]; 31:29), and in between those two references to life and death, Deut 30:16 speaks of walking on Yahweh's paths. But Jeremiah is the only person in the Scriptures who explicitly speaks of "the path to life" and "the path to death." He does so in a more specific sense than the phrase later gains.[586] The antithesis became important as a way of summarizing a theme that does recur in the Scriptures. In the late first century AD and thus within New Testament times, the *Didache* begins, "There are two ways, one of life and one of death," and it expounds these over its first six chapters, though without referring to Jeremiah.[587]

9 That link draws attention to other ways in which Jeremiah is tweaking Deuteronomy. He makes the words a challenge to individuals rather than to the people as a whole. Further, the path Deuteronomy is talking about is the path of commitment to Yahweh, which is indeed commonly the connotation of the word in Jeremiah, but here the person who walks the path to life is *the person who goes out and submits to the Chaldeans who are blockading you.* People who stay in the city will be looted by the Babylonians, but anyone who leaves will in effect deprive the Babylonians of their loot: *His life will be his as loot.* It has been called a sarcastic, proverbial saying (cf. 39:18; 45:5),[588] and it may be proverbial, but there seems no reason to think that it undervalues the notion of being able to hold onto one's life. Either way, the person who holds onto life stands in contrast with the person who walks the path to death, *the person who stays in this city,* who *will die by sword, by hunger,*

586. Volz, *Jeremia*, 219.
587. But see Wenthe, *Jeremiah*, 160–61.
588. Rudolph, *Jeremia*, 136.

and by epidemic. It is a mind-boggling statement in its own right, but all the more when one sees it as Jeremiah's revisionist reworking of Deuteronomy. "'Choose exile and live!' seems to be Jeremiah's call to the people"; the exhortation could eventually be open to a negative ideological understanding in respect of the attitude it takes to the ordinary people left behind in 587.[589] But in the context of Jeremiah's exhortation, it stands with these people, because dissociating oneself from Zedekiah and accepting Yahweh's action against Jerusalem implies affirming the right path and repudiating the wrong path in that other sense on which Jeremiah and Deuteronomy agree. One might then perceive it as consistent both with Deuteronomy's speech and with Jeremiah's speech elsewhere.

10 The frightening closing word *fire* will recur three times in the next section, in 21:12, 14; 22:7. Jeremiah's stance would sound like a political position and also an act of treachery. And "it is hard, oh so hard, to resist the crowd in times of collective enthusiasm for 'national defense.'"[590] It is likely that there were or had been pro-Egyptian and pro-Babylonian parties in Jerusalem—Judahites who thought that the city's political future lay either with Egypt or with Babylon. Jeremiah is not pro-Babylonian as a political stance; his stance is a theological position.[591] And elsewhere he declares Yahweh's judgment on Babylon at great length. Nor does he say that the future lies with a community in Babylon rather than a community in Judah; his message is not one that the later community in Babylon could claim as supporting it rather than the "left-behind" community back in Judah.

b. David's Household (and the City) (21:11–22:9)

[11]*And regarding*[a] *the household of the king of Judah:*
Listen to Yahweh's message, [12]*household of David. Yahweh has said this:*

Make decisions in the morning[b] *with authority,*[c]
    snatch away one who has been robbed from the hand of the fraud
So that my fury does not go out like fire
    and burn with no one to put it out,
    in the face of the dire nature of your practices.[d]

[13]*Here am I, regarding you,*[e] *you who sit in the valley,*
    a crag[f] *in the flatland (Yahweh's affirmation),*[g]

589. M. Masenya, "Invisible Exiles? An African–South African Woman's Reconfiguration of Exile in Jeremiah 21:1–10," *OTE* 20 (2007): 764.
590. Pixley, *Jeremiah*, 68.
591. Fretheim, *Jeremiah*, 311–12.

People who say, "Who will get down[h] against us,
who will come into our refuges?"
[14]*I will attend to you*
in accordance with the fruit of your practices (Yahweh's affirmation).[i]
I will set fire to its forest,
and it will consume everything around it.[j]

[22:1]*Yahweh said this: Go down to the house of the king of Judah and speak there*
this message. [2]*Say, Listen to Yahweh's message, king of Judah who sits on David's*
throne—you, your servants, and your people who come through these gateways.[k]
[3]*Yahweh has said this: Exercise faithful authority; snatch away one who has*
been robbed from the hand of the fraud; resident alien, fatherless, and widow—
do not abuse; do not do violence; the blood of one who is free of guilt[l]—do not
shed, in this place. [4]*Because if you do act[m] on this message, then kings sitting*
for David on his throne will come through the gateways of this house, riding on
chariotry and on horses, he, his servants, and his people.[n] [5]*But if you do not*
listen to these words, by myself I am swearing[o] (Yahweh's affirmation) that a
ruin is what this house will become.[p]

[6]*Because Yahweh has said this about the house of the king of[q] Judah:*

You are Gilead to me,
the head of Lebanon.
If I do not make you a wilderness,
towns that are not lived in . . . [r]
[7]*I will sanctify[s] devastators against you,*
an individual and his implements.
They will cut down your choice cedars[t]
and let them fall into the fire.

[8]*Many[u] nations will pass by this city and will say, one person to his fellow: On*
what account did Yahweh act in this way to this great city? [9]*And they will say:*
On account of the fact that they abandoned the pledge of Yahweh their God and
bowed down to other gods and served them.[v]

a. LXX lacks *and regarding.*

b. Perhaps implying "morning by morning," but for that meaning one would expect not
labbōqer but *labbəqārîm* or *labbōqer labbōqer* (BDB; cf. Zeph 3:5).

c. LXX and Vg translate this colon as if the expression were an established one such as
ʿāśâ mišpāṭ (5:1; 7:5; 22:3, 15), *dibber mišpāṭ* (1:16; 4:12), or *šāpaṭ mišpāṭ* (1 Kgs 3:28; Ezek
16:38), meaning "exercise authority/give judgment," but here the verb is uniquely *dîn*; further, in the morning comes between verb and noun. I infer that *mišpāṭ* is used adverbially
(cf. Deut 16:18, as Vg recognizes there).

d. The *ketiv* has "their practices." LXX lacks this colon.

e. The second-person pronoun and the participle that follows are now feminine singular.

f. For MT *ṣûr*, LXX implies *ṣôr* ("Tyre"), which could be some sort of insult, maybe suggesting self-confidence, or could mean LXX takes vv. 13–14 as a prophecy against a foreign nation (McKane, *Jeremiah*, 1:511).

g. LXX lacks (*Yahweh's affirmation*).

h. LXX "terrify" (cf. Vg) derives *yēḥat* from *ḥātat* rather than *nāḥēt*.

i. LXX lacks this line.

j. MT^L has a section marker here.

k. MT^L has a section marker here.

l. See the translation note on 2:34.

m. The infinitive precedes the finite verb, underlining the expectation.

n. LXX has "they . . . their . . . their."

o. The *qatal* is declarative/performative—a speech act (see 1:5 and the note).

p. MT has a marker here.

q. The Cairo Codex of the Prophets lacks *the king of*.

r. The *ketiv nwšbh* is perhaps a feminine plural form (CTAT 2:636–37). On the if-clause, see the translation note on 15:11 and the commentary on 22:6.

s. LXX interprets as "bring on"; cf. its interpretation at 6:4.

t. Lit. "the choicest of your cedars."

u. LXX lacks *many*.

v. MT has a section marker here.

These next subsections could be read as addressed to Zedekiah, and they would certainly be challenges Jeremiah could issue to him and to the city in his day.[592] They would again indicate that it's never too late for the administration to get its act together and forestall Yahweh's judgment. But in themselves, these subsections stand back from the preceding explicit focus on the last king and his fate, and it's plausible to imagine that they originally addressed earlier kings. The scroll omits any specific reference and lets them be statements, exhortations, threats, and promises relating to kings in general: Josiah, Jehoahaz, Jehoiakim, Jehoiachin, Zedekiah. King and people stand before two alternatives.[593] And while there was no original link between 21:1–10 and 21:11–14, the juxtaposition would apply to Zedekiah a point about royal priorities in general.[594] After 587, the verses would offer implicit explanation for the city's fall but also promise that the Davidic line might have a future if it meets their challenge.

After a preface, the section brings together five separate units:

592. Allen, *Jeremiah*, 236.

593. W. H. Schmidt, *Jeremia*, 2:11.

594. R. Irudaya, "A Prophetic Call against War: A Politico-Theological Study of Jeremiah 21:1–14," *Info on Human Development* 29/1 (2003): 6.

21:11b–12 A challenge and warning to David's household (a bicolon and a tricolon, linked)

21:13–14 A challenge and a warning to Jerusalem (four bicola, two linked)

22:1–5 A challenge, a promise, and a warning to an unnamed king of Judah (prose)

22:6–7 A warning about the palace of an unnamed king of Judah (four bicola)

22:8–9 A warning about the fate of Jerusalem (prose)

Jer 22:1–7 is largely a part-prose and part-verse equivalent to 21:11–14:[595]

21:11–14	22:2–7
[11b]listen to Yahweh's message	[2]listen to Yahweh's message
[12]household of David	king of Judah who sits on David's throne . . .
Yahweh has said this	[3]Yahweh has said this
make decisions, in the morning, with authority	exercise faithful authority
snatch away one who has been robbed	snatch away one who has been robbed
from the hand of the fraud	from the hand of the fraud . . .
	[5]if you do not listen to these words . . .
so that my fury does not go out like fire	[7b]they will cut down your choice cedars
and burn with no one to put it out in the face of the dire nature of your practices	and let them fall into the fire
[13a]here am I, regarding you, you who sit in the valley,	[6b]you are Gilead to me
a crag in the flatland (Yahweh's affirmation) . . .	the head of Lebanon . . .
[14b]I will set fire to its forest, and it will consume everything around it.	

595. N. Mastnjak, *Deuteronomy and the Emergence of Textual Authority in Jeremiah*, FAT 2. Reihe 7 (Tübingen: Mohr Siebeck, 2016), 21–26.

11a These words will be paralleled by the briefer preface to 23:9–40; they are an introduction to the three sections about kingship that occupy 21:11–23:8 as a whole. *Household* (*bayit*) will occur with more than one of its senses in this section. Here *household of the king of Judah* suggests the Judahite line of kings, who in Jeremiah's day are closely related within that household: they comprise Josiah, three of his sons, and one of his grandsons.

11b–12 The exhortation to *listen* is plural, and in origin it might be a bidding to the current king and his administration (cf. 22:2). But in the broader context of this passage, it suggests the line of kings as a whole; *the household of David* will then be this line. The reference to David draws attention to their right to reign as kings and to the promise attaching to David's household (2 Sam 7). It might also draw attention to the obligation resting on this household. Judahites might think that Yahweh's promise to David and his line had no obligations attached to it—that the promise was unconditional. But 2 Sam 7 did not say so; if anything, it pointed in the opposite direction in that it warned of trouble for David's offspring if he behaved in a wayward fashion. Psalms 72 and 132:12[596] suggest the same implication in positive form: being the Davidic king means implementing faithful authority for the people. It was the best thing David ever did, just after Yahweh gave him that promise (2 Sam 8:15).[597] Do it, says Yahweh, "in the morning, before you occupy yourselves with eating and drinking and with the things that you need"[598] (cf. 2 Sam 15:2), and certainly "before that by drinking and excess he had made himself unfit to judge aright."[599] Jeremiah has already talked about exercising *authority* (5:1; 7:5) and about the faithful exercise of *authority* (4:2; see the commentary there), but it is these sections on the kings that include "the greatest concentration of the word *mišpāṭ*."[600] Here, once again, Jeremiah tweaks the formulation (see the translation note). In the parallel colon, one might have expected reference to faithfulness, but he replaces that general notion with the concrete obligation to *snatch away one who has been robbed from the hand of the fraud*, which gives specificity to the idea of exercising authority.[601] The *fraud* is the person who finds ways of robbing someone of their home or their land so that their life, along with that of their family, is in desperate danger. A primary obligation of government is to exercise authority in such a way as to *snatch* them *away* from that danger. "Among all the commandments that might have been cited in these oracles against the

---

596. Brueggemann, *Jeremiah 1–25*, 197.
597. Qimchi, in MG.
598. Qimchi, in MG.
599. Mayer, *Commentary*, 402.
600. Bracke, "Justice," *WW* 22 (2002): 387.
601. McKane, *Jeremiah*, 1:510.

kings, repeatedly choosing those that have to do with the exercise of abusive power against the weak and needy is remarkable. We know all too well how easy it is for people in power (and those who evaluate them!) to focus on other concerns."[602] If the community does not operate on that basis, Yahweh will see that disaster follows. If it tolerates the kind of society in which the powerful can enrich themselves and the weak lose everything they have, then Yahweh will take action against the community. One might fear that the weak themselves will then suffer; but they have already lost everything and have nothing to lose.

13–14 While there is no formal mark of an ending after vv. 11b–12 or of a new beginning here, the usual address in the feminine singular to the city and the change in imagery and focus indicate that this subsection is another separate short message, which gives city as well as administration something to think about (like vv. 8–10 in relation to vv. 1–7). *Here am I regarding* (*'el*) *you* (cf. 50:31; 51:25) is a slightly less overtly aggressive expression than "here am I against (*'al*) you" (23:30–32), but the phrase's implications are still aggressive. In the threat, the key word is *crag*. It otherwise comes only in 18:14 to refer to Mount Hermon, which indicates that Jeremiah is talking about a mountain that would seem seriously impressive to the people who are addressed. In Jeremiah's day, Jerusalem was surrounded by a deep *valley* so that it resembled a tell standing out from a plain, like Lachish or Hazor— though Jeremiah can also use similar language of Moab (48:8, 28–29). There on its mountain, Jerusalem can *sit* enthroned like a queen.[603] Its people could feel secure: *"Who will get down against us? Who will come into our refuges?"* Oddly, while Jerusalem is surrounded by valleys, it is also surrounded by higher mountains from which an attacker might come down. But the city had survived Sennacherib's invasion, which would seem to justify the confidence expressed here. Perhaps that deliverance had made people believe in the "inviolability of Zion."[604] Such confidence will not survive Yahweh's attentiveness. The reference to people's *practices* makes for a link with vv. 11b–12 and implies a reminder to the city as a whole that it must not infer from those verses that it can just blame the administration for what happens in it and to it. Another aspect of the city's justified pride could be the forest around Jerusalem or the city's forest-like building style (e.g., 1 Kgs 10:17, 21), but a forest is also vulnerable to fire (cf. vv. 10, 12). Fire is a fright, and forest fire a particular fright. The medieval chapter division makes a break at this point and might thus suggest that there were four answers to Zedekiah's inquiry

602. Fretheim, *Jeremiah*, 314.
603. Weiser, *Jeremia*, 1:187, 188.
604. Craigie, Kelley, and Drinkard, *Jeremiah 1–25*, 293.

in 21:1–2 about whether there is any hope for the city, a question which "he probably wishes he had not asked":[605]

21:3–7   No.
21:8–10   The wise will leave the city.
21:11–12 Put things right in the city.
21:13–14 No.

22:1–3 People also *go down* to the palace if they are in the temple, which is at the high point of the city and is where Jeremiah might naturally receive messages from Yahweh (cf. 18:2; see the commentary there). While the implicit reference to the temple might make one infer that *these gateways* are those of the temple (cf. 7:2), v. 4 will make it more likely that they are the palace gateways. That understanding is already encouraged by the reference to the *king*, his *servants*, and his *people*—in other words, his staff. Here, the bidding to them amplifies the one in 21:12 (see the comparison in the introduction to 21:11–22:9, p. 481). It also compares with something Jeremiah enunciated earlier for the people in general (7:3–7; see the commentary there). Much of the elaboration corresponds to regular Jeremianic concerns, though *abuse* (*yānâ hiphil*) comes only here in Jeremiah (the *qal* appears in 25:38; 46:16; 50:16). The verb expresses a particular disquiet about ill-treatment of resident aliens in passages in the Torah such as Exod 22:21(20); Lev 19:33; Deut 23:16(17).

4 The big novelty now is that Yahweh attaches a further promise to the fulfillment of the bidding—or rather, reaffirms the original promise to David for kings who fulfill the conditions. There are or there will be *kings sitting for David*—sitting as people who belong to David, as David's.[606] Such *kings sitting . . . on his throne will come through the gateways of this house, riding on chariotry and horses, he, his servants, and his people*. Jeremiah implies that it is not just the king who will rejoice in this fact. The rest of Judah will rejoice too, like British people celebrating a coronation. But if there is no *mišpāṭ ûṣədāqâ*, the palace will burn down.

5 Human beings swear by someone or something other than themselves that acts as a guarantor of their oath; they are then asking God, in particular, to note the oath and to act against them in case of default. Yahweh is saying, "It is as if I will punish myself if I fail to do as I say"; or "it will be as if I have stopped being me."[607] Yahweh's oath once again presupposes that it's still not over. The king still has a chance to turn. Once again, there is no record of Jeremiah delivering this message, a reminder that it is recorded to

---

605. Brueggemann, *Jeremiah 1–25*, 186.
606. Joüon 130g.
607. Cf. J. Goldingay, *Genesis* (Grand Rapids: Baker, 2020), 357, on Gen 22:16.

encourage the entire community to remember what Yahweh expects of the kings of Judah and their administration.

6 Yahweh goes on to restate the threat concerning Jerusalem and the king's house in particular. He is apparently addressing the palace (the *you* is second-person masculine singular). What Yahweh meant by *you are Gilead to me* would not be immediately obvious. Is it an insult, suggesting the impiety of the northern kingdom (e.g., Hos 6:8) that led to its invasion and devastation?[608] Or is it a compliment (e.g., Song 4:1)? The parallel reference to *the head of Lebanon* points in the second direction; Gilead (cf. 8:22) and Lebanon were the locations of famous forests. So the logic is, I rejoice in you as I rejoice in Gilead and Lebanon, or you remind me of Gilead and Lebanon (cf. the reference to a forest in 22:14). For Yahweh, Jerusalem was their equal. Nevertheless, about Jerusalem that he has affirmed in this way, Yahweh is prepared to take another of those oaths whereby people wish a terrible fate on themselves if they fail to live up to what the *if*-clause refers to but that leave the actual wish unstated and taken for granted (cf. 15:11; see the commentary there). So Yahweh's *if I do not* is a very strong way of saying there is no doubt that I will *make you a wilderness, towns that are not lived in*. While Yahweh is rhetorically addressing the palace in Jerusalem and the city itself, he is comparing it with a wilderness that has a number of towns in it. The devastation will happen notwithstanding his high esteem of city and palace in its magnificence.

7 So *I will sanctify devastators against you*. It is a doubly extraordinary resolve. He will not only send devastators; he will sanctify them, as Jeremiah had imagined Yahweh or the shepherds urging the sanctifying of war against Jerusalem (6:4) and as Jeremiah had urged him to sanctify the wrongdoers (12:3; see the commentary there). Once again, the imagery of Yahweh commissioning a war is used against Judah. Its attackers will be like the foresters who felled the trees of Lebanon for the building of the "forest" which the temple sometimes seemed to be and who thus gave majesty to the palace. They and their tools will now be dedicated to this destructive task. The *cedars* came; they will go. They will feed the *fire* that Yahweh ignites (21:14). The "hall for the exercise of authority" (*'ulām hammišpāṭ*), magnificently paneled in cedar (1 Kgs 7:7), has in effect already been vacated, so it might as well be destroyed.[609]

8–9 Once more, Jeremiah turns to say something about the city itself. While Jeremiah rhetorically pictures foreigners asking the question, it is really the question Judah will need to ask and needs to think about now so as not to have to ask it then. The rhetoric is similar to that in 18:16; 19:8. The question and answer figure compares with one in Ashurbanipal's annals: "Whenever

---

608. Theodoret, *Ermeneia*, PG 81:620.
609. P. D. Miller, "Jeremiah," on the passage.

the inhabitants of Arabia asked each other: 'On account of what have these calamities befallen Arabia?' (they answered themselves:) 'Because we did not keep the solemn oaths (sworn by) Ashur, because we offended the friendliness of Ashurbanipal, the king beloved by Ellil!"[610] Jeremiah's version likewise speaks of the wrongdoing in the people's stance toward their God, adding at the end of this section a further explanation for the threats in 21:11–22:7. And Jeremiah's wording compares with a threat in Deuteronomy:

Jer 22:8–9	Deut 29:24–26(23–25)
Many nations will pass by this city and will say, one person to his fellow:	All the nations will say,
On what account did Yahweh act in this way to this great city? Why this great angry wrath? And they will say:	on what account did Yahweh act in this way to this country? And they will say,
On account of the fact that they abandoned the pledge of Yahweh their God	On account of the fact that they abandoned the pledge of Yahweh, the God of their ancestors,
which he solemnized with them when he got them out of the country of Egypt, and went and bowed down to other gods and served them.	and served other gods and bowed down to them.

It has in common with Deuteronomy the reference to the pledge committing the people to be loyal to Yahweh (the first since 11:1–17); a major difference is the lack of reference to the exodus in Jeremiah, though Deuteronomy also goes on to say more about Yahweh's anger and about the exile that it envisages.

c. Three Kings (22:10–30)

[10]*Don't cry about a dead man,*[a]
   don't bemoan him.

---

610. *ANET*, 300.

Cry and cry[b] for the man who is going,
 because he will not return anymore
 and see the country of his birth.[c]

[11]*Because Yahweh has said this regarding Shallum ben Josiah King of Judah, who was reigning in place of Josiah his father, who has gone out from this place: He will not return there anymore,* [12]*because[d] in the place where they have exiled him, there he will die, and this country he will not see anymore.[e]*

[13]*Oh, one who builds his house without faithfulness,*
 his lofts without the exercise of authority,
His fellow he makes serve[f] for nothing—
 his wages he does not give him,
[14]*Who says, "I will build myself a house of some size[g]*
 and enlarged[h] lofts,"
And cuts[i] for it a set of windows,[j]
 both paneled with cedar and painted[k] with vermilion:
[15]*Will you reign because you are energetic[l] with cedar?[m]—*
 your father—he ate and drank, didn't he.
He exercised faithful authority,
 then things were good for him.
[16]*He made decisions for powerless person and needy person,*
 then things were good;
 that is acknowledging me, isn't it (Yahweh's affirmation).[n]

[17]*Because you have no eyes or mind*
 except for what can be grabbed,
For the blood of someone free of guilt,[o] to shed,
 for fraud and for crushing, to implement.[p]

[18]*Therefore Yahweh said this regarding Jehoiakim ben Josiah King of Judah:*

They will not lament for him,
 "Oh, my brother," or "Oh, sister."
They will not lament for him,
 "Oh, lord," or "Oh, his majesty."[q]
[19]*With a donkey's burial he will be buried*
 by being dragged and thrown out[r]
 outside Jerusalem's gateways.[s]

[20]*Go up[t] to the Lebanon and cry out,*

487

in the Bashan raise your voice.
Cry out from Abarim,[u]
   because all your friends have shattered.
[21]*I spoke to you when you were relaxed*[v]—
   you said, "I will not listen."
This has been your way from your youth,
   because you have not listened to my voice.
[22]*All your shepherds—wind will shepherd them,*
   and your friends—into captivity they will go.
Because then you will be shamed and disgraced,
   on account of all your dire behavior.[w]
[23]*You who sit*[x] *in the Lebanon,*
   nested among the cedars, how you have been favored,[y]
When contractions come to you,
   writhing like a woman giving birth.

[24]*I am alive*[z] *(Yahweh's affirmation): if Coniah*[aa] *ben Jehoiakim King of Judah were a signet on my right hand—that*[bb] *from there I would tear you off.* [25]*I will give you into the hand of the people who are seeking your life, into the hand of the people before whom you are fearful, into the hand of Nebuchadrezzar King of Babylon, and*[cc] *into the hand of the Chaldeans.* [26]*I will hurl you and your mother who bore you into another country where you were not born and where you will die.*[dd] [27]*To the country where they are lifting up their spirit to return, they will not return.*[ee]

[28]*Is he a despicable shattered pot,*[ff]
   this man Coniah,
   or a container that no one wants?
Why has he been hurled out, he and his offspring,[gg]
   thrown out to a country that they did not know?

[29]*Country, country, country, listen to Yahweh's message.*[hh] [30]*Yahweh has said this:*

Write down this person as deprived,[ii]
   a man who will not succeed in his days.
Because no individual from his offspring will succeed,
   sitting on David's throne,
   and ruling again in Judah.[jj]

   a. For MT *ləmēt*, LXX perhaps implies *lammēt* (Duhm, *Jeremia*, 174).

b. In this further example of an infinitive combining with a finite verb, the infinitive comes second, which is classically seen as suggesting continuation rather than simply intensification; see the comments in *IBHS* 35.3.1d.

c. MT has a section marker here.

d. For *kî*, the Cairo Codex of the Prophets reads *kî ʾim* ("rather"; cf. LXX, Vg).

e. MT has a section marker here.

f. *ʿĀbad bə* regularly has a quasi-*hiphil* meaning (see *DCH*, 6:213b; cf. Jer 25:14; 30:8; 34:9, 10). Cf. English "work them."

g. Lit. "a house of measures/extents/sizes."

h. Presumably, *məruwwāḥîm* comes from *rûaḥ* II, but it's nice to picture Jeremiah imagining Jehoiakim also linking the word with *rûaḥ* I and thinking of it as airy (Qimchi, in MG).

i. The *qatal* verb continues the participial construction.

j. *Ḥallûnāy* with its -*āy* ending would be a singular noun of the kind noted in GKC 86i (Allen, *Jeremiah*, 248), but perhaps the *waw* on the next word is really the ending of this word, which then means "its windows."

k. The infinitive absolute *māšôaḥ* follows the participial significance of *sāpûn* earlier in the colon (DG 103a).

l. On *mətaḥăreh*, see the translation note on 12:5. Here, LXX assumes it has the usual meaning of *ḥārâ* ("be angry").

m. For MT *bāʾārez*, LXX has "with Ahaz."

n. In vv. 13–17, LXX has a further series of differences from MT that give the two versions a different cast (see Wells, "Indications," 407–9).

o. See the translation note on 2:34.

p. MT has a section marker here.

q. LXX precedes the four cola with "Woe to this man" and then lacks *or "Oh, sister"* and *or "Oh, his majesty."*

r. The two infinitive absolutes function like adverbs; see *IBHS* 4.6.2b, 35.3c.2a; DG 102; GKC 113h; but Joüon 123r compares with the continuing of a finite verb by an infinitive and describes the usage as defining circumstances.

s. MT has a section marker here.

t. The verbs in vv. 20–23 are second-person feminine singular.

u. Tg interprets the geography in light of v. 23; all three places then refer to Jerusalem itself.

v. LXX "in your transgression" makes explicit that it was a careless sense of security.

w. With paronomasia, the verse begins *kol rōʿayik* and ends *kōl-rāʿātēk*. LXX "all who love you" generates a different paronomasia by deriving the latter not from *rāʿaʿ* but from *rāʿâ* II, as opposed to *rāʿâ* I. In contrast, Aq, Sym derive the opening *rōʿayik* from *rāʿâ* II and translate "your companions."

x. The *qere yōšabt* looks like a mixed form, a cross between *yōšebet* and the archaic second person *yāšabtî* implied by the *ketiv* (GKC 90n); compare and contrast 10:17, and the parallel *qere* and *ketiv* variation in the next colon.

y. LXX, Vg have "you will groan," deriving the unique form *nēḥant* from *ʾāḥan* rather than *ḥānan*.

z. See the translation note and commentary on 4:2.

aa. *Konyāhû*; alternative forms of the king's name include *yəkônyâ*, *yəkonyāhû*, or *yəkônyâ* and *yəhôyākîn*, *yəhôyākin*, or *yôyākîn*; these combine the short form of the name of Yahweh with a form of the verb *kûn* and mean "Yahweh endures" or "Yahweh makes endure." Qimchi (in MG) suggests that this short form is pejorative, though Duhm (*Jeremia*, 179) notes parallels such as Jeberechiah = Berechiah, and R. P. Carroll (*Jeremiah*, OTL, 437) wonders if it is affectionate.

bb. The *kî* strengthens the apodosis after the *if*-clause (DG 121 remark 2).

cc. LXX lacks *into the hand of Nebuchadrezzar King of Babylon, and*.

dd. The verb is plural.

ee. MT has a marker here.

ff. *'Eṣeb* means *pot* only here, but the parallelism supports this understanding, though Isaac Abravanel's understanding that it means "hurt" (*Commentary on the Latter Prophets*, as paraphrased by Rosenberg, *Jeremiah*, 1:184) at least points to a paronomasia.

gg. LXX lacks the reference to the offspring, one of a number of ways in which LXX is shorter and simpler than MT in vv. 28–30.

hh. MT^L has a section marker here.

ii. Vg, Syr, Tg infer that *'ărîrî* means "deprived of children," which the context will go on to support. Initially, the colon may simply raise a question ("deprived of what?"), which the following cola will go on to answer. LXX has "banished."

jj. MT^A has a unit marker here.

After the message about Zedekiah and about the Davidic household in general, the scroll adds messages relating to the three kings between Josiah and Zedekiah while also incorporating one further message to Jerusalem:

vv. 10–12	Shallum (Jehoahaz): a forewarning (a bicolon and a tricolon, then prose)
vv. 13–19	An eventually named son of Josiah (Jehoiakim): a critique and a forewarning (six bicola and a tricolon: the first four bicola run together as an extended vocative and run into the fifth; then four bicola, with the opening two running into each other, and a tricolon)
vv. 20–23	Jerusalem: an oblique forewarning, a critique, and a direct forewarning (eight bicola, with the last two running into each other)
vv. 24–30	Coniah (Jehoiachin): a forewarning (prose, then a tricolon and two bicola, then a bicolon and a tricolon)

Yahweh declares what is to happen to the three kings and to the city. While there is sharp critique of Jehoiakim and of Jerusalem, the more consistent feature of the four units is the forewarning about what is to happen rather than explanation in terms of wrongdoing. Though 2 Kgs 23:31–24:17 explains the wrongdoing in a routine way, Jehoahaz and Jehoiachin each had only three months in which to do something terrible. Having not critiqued Zedekiah in 21:1–10 and having named no names in 21:11–22:9, Jeremiah does not critique Jehoahaz or Jehoiachin and so explain their exile, and he expresses approval of Josiah. His entire critique lands on Jehoiakim's head. The messages will presuppose the criteria by which Yahweh evaluates Judah's kings, by which the people might do some evaluating, and on which they might think about whom they put on the throne when they have the chance (it was they who chose Jehoahaz and perhaps Jehoiachin: 2 Kgs 23:30; 24:6). But the focus lies on the tragedy that will fall on each king. The entire story of Judah's last kings "evokes only weeping and sadness."[611] Thus what holds together vv. 10–30 is "not only disdain for Judah's rulers but also the language of lamentation."[612] The people who listen to these declarations about their kings need to understand what the declarations say about their own future, which is also the direct topic of the Jerusalem unit.

10–12 Jeremiah does not name the subject of v. 10, and the lines could be proverbial. *Going* is vague and could in itself refer to being about to die as opposed to being dead.[613] It is vv. 11–12 (as the messages are juxtaposed) that clarifies the point about v. 10 for people who could not work out that they relate to the time just after Josiah's unexpected death in battle at the age of thirty-nine. The exhortation not to grieve for the king would be scandalous in any context, though one should not take Jeremiah too literally as banning grief for Josiah; his exhortation resembles Jesus saying that people must hate their parents if they are to follow him (and see 2 Chr 35:24–25, ironically with a reference to Jeremiah composing laments). Nevertheless, the injunction would be shocking if Josiah was people's hero for asserting Judahite independence in relation to Assyria and for undertaking his religious reformation. Josiah's successor was his fourth son, whose birth name was Shallum (1 Chr 3:15) but who was enthroned as Jehoahaz. He was then immediately deposed by the Egyptians—which perhaps indicates that he had supported his father's anti-Egyptian policy and that this commitment had been the reason for people supporting his succeeding to the throne. Pharaoh Neco took Jehoahaz off to Egypt, which will be the destination of the *is going* in Jeremiah's message and the destination of the *has gone out from this place*; it suggests some irony because the verb (*yāṣā'*) is used often for Israel going out *from* Egypt.[614] People can be told not to grieve for Josiah because there is now something else to grieve. "Jeremiah reversed normal practice—usually it is the dead who are mourned, not those who are still alive. But Jeremiah bids them to weep for Jehoahaz, who will never return to his native land. He speaks of him as though he were already dead."[615] The expression *anymore* . . . *anymore* . . . *anymore* tolls through the message. His irreversible deportation

---

611. P. D. Miller, "Jeremiah," on the passage.

612. Stulman, *Jeremiah*, 211.

613. McKane, *Jeremiah*, 1:523–24.

614. Craigie, Kelley, and Drinkard, *Jeremiah 1–25*, 307.

615. W. J. Wessels, "Josiah the Idealised King in the Kingship Cycles in the Book of Jeremiah," *OTE* 20 (2007): 866.

is his tragedy. He never did come back (2 Kgs 23:32–34). His destiny was repeated by Jehoiachin and Zedekiah; indeed, out of the immediate context, one could take the banished king to be either of these two.[616]

13–14 In place of Jehoahaz, the Egyptians put on the throne his older brother Eliakim, whom the Pharaoh renamed Jehoiakim. The renaming is ironic, as it is a more explicitly Yahwistic name for a king who was not very Yahwistic; renaming would be simply an expression of Pharaoh's authority. "Jehoiakim was Jeremiah's great foe; the statement about him is thus distinctively sharp and disdainful."[617] Again, Jeremiah begins without indicating whom he is talking about. *Oh* (*hôy*) announces that he is expressing horror, which would typically relate to someone's death (actual or expected) or to someone's despicable behavior such as might presage or deserve death (cf. vv. 18; 23:1; 30:7; 34:5; 48:1; 50:27).[618] Here, both connotations are appropriate, in what precedes and in what follows. Jeremiah is expressing horror at *one who builds his house without faithfulness* and will do so through vv. 13–14 until we come to a *you* in v. 15. Whether or not he was supposed to deliver this message to Jehoiakim himself, vv. 10–12 suggests that the messages here are designed to address Judah about their kings' destiny in Jehoahaz's day and now in Jehoiakim's day and in any other king's day. The trouble with Jehoiakim is apparently that he decides it's time to remodel the palace on a scale more appropriate (as he thinks) to the king of Judah, or to build a new palace (see the commentary on 6:1). The *lofts* will be rooms on the roof, which is a regular feature for a Middle Eastern house, but he goes about the project at the expense of being fair to his subjects. Admittedly, such dynamics always apply; they are an aspect of what Samuel warned people about kings (1 Sam 8), and the original Davidic and Solomonic palaces must have been built using resources that could have been shared among the people. Jeremiah might not have objected to the remodeling project in itself, given that people often don't mind resources being spent on their kings and presidents and perhaps feel they get some reflected glory from the expenditure. His problem is the two ways in which the project stands in tension with a commitment to *faithfulness* in the *exercise of authority*. First, it involves the use of unpaid conscript labor. First Kings 5 doesn't indicate whether Solomon's conscript workers got paid or just had to abandon their farms while they were engaged in the work. With Jehoiakim, this is explicit. Second, it's *his fellow*, his fellow-Israelites, that *he makes serve for nothing*. The neatness of the poetry contrasts with the out-of-order nature of the action:

---

616. So, respectively, Qimchi, in MG; and Jerome, *Jeremiah*, 131.
617. Volz, *Jeremia*, 224.
618. See H.-J. Zobel, "הוֹי, *hôy*," *TDOT* 3:359–64.

> Oh, one who builds his house without faithfulness,
> his lofts without the exercise of authority.

The international political situation would add to the objectionable nature of the expense of the project alongside the pressure of having to pay tribute to Egypt or Babylon as the political situation changed.[619] In v. 14, Jeremiah goes on to express distaste for the project's extravagance in two more neatly parallel lines.

15 After the four lines that were syntactically one long preamble, Jeremiah comes to a searching question in an unusually long 5-4 line whose cola do not obviously interconnect. Jehoiakim assumes that imposing architecture, *being energetic with cedar*, is a sign of royal majesty that will stand him in good stead for the future. He will have an impressive palace from which to enjoy a long reign.[620] But his exercise of initiative contrasts with the way his father made his mark.[621] Over against Jehoiakim's assumptions, Jeremiah sets some facts about Josiah. Josiah did okay in life; eating and drinking sums up the necessities of a good life. He "lived well enough," as they said of Jesus in contrast to John the Baptizer (Matt 11:19).[622] But what was the basis of his enjoying those necessities? He attended to the true kingly priorities and then found that things worked out well for him (until he took on Pharaoh Neco). The parallelism between the cola and lines in v. 15 works in a complex and subtle way. *Will you reign as king?* and *Your father . . . didn't he?* constitute parallel beginnings of cola. But *you are energetic with cedar* then finds its complementary, contrasting statement in *he exercised faithful authority*; and *he ate and drank* finds its parallel in *then things were good for him*. Jehoiakim works for his own glory. He is engaged in "political idolatry."[623]

16 With more straightforward parallelism between lines, Jeremiah now uses the less common verb for *made decisions* (*dîn*), then spells out its implications as he did in 21:12. It means making decisions for the *powerless* person (*'ānî*, Jeremiah's only reference to the powerless) and for the *needy person* (*'ebyôn*, who did come earlier in 2:34; 5:28; also 20:13 as a self-description).

---

619. Katho, "To Know and Not to Know Yhwh," 126. Katho goes on to compare the way modern monarchs and presidents like to multiply residences.

620. Cf. Rashi, in MG.

621. Qimchi (in MG) interestingly takes the father to be David, as Tg may imply in using the expression *malkā' qadmā'â 'ābûk*; the First Testament does say that David "implemented the faithful exercise of authority" (2 Sam 8:15), which it does not say of Josiah.

622. Bright, *Jeremiah*, 142.

623. B. Katho, "Jeremiah 22: Implications for the Exercise of Political Power in Africa," in *Interpreting the Old Testament in Africa: Papers from the International Symposium on Africa and the Old Testament in Nairobi*, ed. M. Getui, K. Holter, and V. Zinkuratire, Bible and Theology in Africa 2 (New York: Lang, 2012), 157.

Jehoiakim's father accepted those royal obligations, and *things were good*—as v. 15 said. The unexpected third colon then throws in a devastatingly important prophetic assumption. "Knowing me" (*hada'at 'ōtî*) means *acknowledging me*. It is not a matter of an intimate person-to-person relationship or an insight into truths about God—though Jeremiah and Yahweh also believe in these things. It's about acknowledging in the sense of recognizing and accepting someone's authority. Acknowledgment of Yahweh (cf. 2:8; 4:22; 9:3[2], 6[5], 24[23]) lies in making decisions in the way vv. 15–16 describe. "Not everyone who says to me, Lord, Lord, will enter the kingdom of the heavens, but the person who does the will of my Father in the heavens" (Matt 7:21); Jeremiah here defines what that will is.[624] "Piety leads men to all the duties of love."[625] The criterion for determining whether leaders acknowledge God is not whether they profess belief in God or go to worship but whether they see that decisions get made in the interests of the powerless and needy person; and if a nation is a democracy, the same criterion determines whether this nation counts as one that acknowledges God.[626] Verses 15–16 are "a stunning act of social criticism, the most poignant of its kind in the entire Bible."[627]

17 There is worse to be said about Jehoiakim, a further nuancing of what Jeremiah has already said. It was not only by compelling people to do the work for nothing that Jehoiakim could improve his accommodation. And it was not only by neglecting his vocation to be the supreme court that he failed to exercise faithful authority. Like the powerful people Jeremiah lambasts elsewhere, Jehoiakim used the legal system to defraud people of their land or houses, which he could then appropriate. He did so by defrauding them of their lives, in the famous manner of Ahab (1 Kgs 21). With more impressive hyperbole, Jeremiah declares that it was the only thing that his *eyes or mind* focused on; the pathetic account of Ahab's initial frustration with Naboth (1 Kgs 21:1–4) provides an illustration of that focus that would be funny if it did not have such terrible consequences. The only thing Ahab or Jehoiakim could see and the only thing they could think about was *what can be grabbed* (cf. 6:13).

18–19 In the Prophets, *Oh* (v. 13) often leads into *therefore* (cf. 23:1–2). As happens when one member of the community issues an accusation against another and the elders who have gathered in the village square issue their judgment, a remonstration by Yahweh leads into a declaration of intent regarding the consequences of the facts described in vv. 13–17. Elijah confronted Ahab with a grisly account of the death he would die for getting Naboth killed. Jeremiah jumps beyond Jehoiakim's death to the aftermath that he invites

---

624. Theodoret, *Ermeneia*, PG 81:621.
625. Calvin, *Jeremiah*, 3:107.
626. Pixley, *Jeremiah*, 71–72.
627. Brueggemann, *Jeremiah 1–25*, 192.

Jehoiakim and the listeners to imagine. No one will be sorry when Jehoiakim dies. Perhaps the first line imagines people consoling his brothers (Jehoahaz and Zedekiah) and his sisters. It will turn out that he is only 36 when he dies in 598, so it would be quite possible for his mother still to be alive and to need consoling, too. But they *will not lament for him* as their *lord* and as *his majesty*. They will do so formally, but they won't mean it, because they will resent the life he has lived and the rule he has exercised. He will have no state funeral. His death will be treated more like the death of a *donkey*. Maybe you strip a dead donkey of its hide, but then you throw its carcass out; a donkey's burial is a non-burial. As usual, Jeremiah is not predicting literal events but painting a vivid imaginary picture; 2 Kgs 24:1–7 may imply that Jehoiakim died a natural death, though it does not mention his burial (as do 21:18, 26; 23:30). But his reign was marked by trouble from the Babylonians and from the Arameans, Moabites, and Ammonites, and he did die when he was only in his thirties.

20 Once more, Jeremiah tantalizes slightly by not identifying whom he is addressing, though the feminine singular puts the people on the track of identifying his target—it's them. He turns for a moment from the kings to address the city, as he did in 21:8–10 and 22:6–9. Once more, the juxtaposition of this message with the previous one could make the audience think about the implications of the king for the city but also encourage it not to kid itself that it can simply blame the king for the city's state. It has to accept some responsibility. Metaphorically speaking, Jerusalem is to go and climb a mountain from which it can cry out so that its cry can be heard. The places lie to the north and east, and Jeremiah lists them in north-south order: *Lebanon* (which can denote Mount Hermon), *Bashan* (the Golan Heights— perhaps he imagines one of the hills that stand higher than the main plain), and *Abarim* (the highland opposite Jericho, from which Moses had his view of the promised land). The city will need to utter a cry of pain that everyone hears, because *all your friends have shattered*. They will be allies such as the ones with whom Judah joined in Jehoiakim's day in the rebellion that prompted Nebuchadrezzar's visit in about 601 (2 Kgs 24:1)—either they have been defeated, or Jeremiah pictures them as defeated. Jerusalem is therefore in deep trouble. The association of Aram, Moab, and Ammon with that visit (2 Kgs 24:2) suggests a reason for Jeremiah's naming Lebanon, Bashan, and Abarim: these peoples occupy those areas to the north and east.

21 Babylon's rise meant a reversal of the good times that people had been enjoying in the recent past, when Jerusalem was doing well—times of security and relaxation (*šalwâ*). Assyria's decline had left Judah freer to control its own destiny and not required to pay tribute to a superpower. It would have been nice if in that time it had been faithful to Yahweh, as for a time in Josiah's day it was. But prosperity and relaxation may work the opposite way. And Jerusalem had not been much inclined to *listen* to Yahweh. Like "knowing," listening implies an attentiveness that issues in action—namely, doing what Yahweh says. But the Jeremiah scroll has been full of critique of Judah for doing the opposite. *Your youth* takes us back to 2:2 but also to 3:24–25; the commitment of 2:2 was short-lasting.

22–23 So the community's leaders will be blown away, like *shepherds* who are being herded instead of herding. A parallel fate will encompass its *friends*, those allies who have shattered. The parallelism perhaps implies that being taken into captivity is a more literal description of what being blown away by the wind will mean. It will be the final shaming and exposure of Judah's leaders that Jeremiah has consistently threatened. It will prove that their religious, political, and social policies were misguided, as he has consistently said. At the moment, Jerusalem sits *in Lebanon*, as it were, with the glory of the forest that surrounds it or of its forest-like cedar-paneled buildings (Lebanon is functioning as a metaphor in a different way from v. 20). Jerusalem is like a bird with its nest in the trees, quite secure.[628] Yes, *how you have been favored*! But maybe there is a hint of worry in that observation (cf. 16:13; see the commentary on 16:13 and on 16:14–15). In light of the next colon, the comment is ironic.[629] The unusual verb form for *you have been favored* looks worryingly like a word that could mean "you have groaned" (see the translation note). Certainly there is something to worry about in the threat that follows, as Jeremiah again compares the travail that will come to Jerusalem with the labor pains of *a woman giving birth* (6:24; 13:21).

24 The scroll returns to kings, and turns finally and explicitly to *Coniah*, an alternative name for Jehoiachin (see the translation note), who figures in Jeremiah more often than any other named king.[630] Although he was unmentioned in 1:1–3, he apparently became a focus of the Judahite hopes with which 52:31–34 implies some sympathy. We know from 28:1–4 that there was at least one prophet in Jerusalem promising that Yahweh in his faithfulness to Jerusalem and to David's line would bring Jehoiachin and the other exiles back. Meanwhile, the advantage of reigning for only three months (before being deposed and transported to Babylon) is that people have no chance to discover your weaknesses, in contrast to what happened with his successor, his uncle, the hapless Zedekiah, who had lots of opportunity to make mistakes and show his inadequacy. Here, in connection with the teenage Jehoiachin, Yahweh swears a solemn oath analogous to an Israelite oath beginning "Yahweh is alive." On an Israelite's lips it would imply, "Yahweh is alive and he will take action if I am lying" (see the translation note and com-

628. Foreman, *Animal Metaphors*, 241–44.

629. Lundbom, *Jeremiah 21–36: A New Translation with Introduction and Commentary*, AB 21B (New York: Doubleday, 2004), 152.

630. Job, *Jeremiah's Kings*, 97.

mentary on 4:2). How frightening to have Yahweh himself taking such an oath! Jeremiah goes on to invite his hearers to think of Yahweh as having a *signet* ring, which is a most valuable possession. People seal documents with their signet ring. It's comparable to a list of one's passwords and personal information. Yahweh says to think of his signet ring as on *my right hand*, the hand that for most people is the more powerful. Now, says Yahweh. If you, Coniah, were that ring (Jeremiah speaks as if Yahweh is addressing the king himself), with the implication that I identify with you, I would *tear you off* and give you over, like someone giving over credit card information and passwords to a thief. Why will Yahweh act in this way to Jehoiachin? What has he done to deserve it? Jeremiah will raise that question in v. 28, though only rhetorically. He will not answer it, because the message isn't really about the king and his destiny and deserts. It's about the people and its destiny and deserts.

25–27 The message apparently presupposes that Jehoiakim has indeed died and Jehioachin has succeeded him. Within three months, Nebuchadrezzar is at the gates, Jehoiachin has surrendered, and Nebuchadrezzar has taken him off to Babylon with the rest of the Jerusalem leadership and put Zedekiah in his place (2 Kgs 24:8–17). So this threat belongs in that three-month period. Whether or not 23:18 referred to the young king's mother, who is no doubt a power behind the throne, Jeremiah here does refer to her. In due course, Jehoiachin gets released from prison in Babylon (52:31–34), but as far as we know, he never returns to Judah.

28 The poetic verses that follow presuppose his being deposed and taken to Babylon. They, too, address his people in Jerusalem rather than the deposed king himself. The opening image recalls 19:1–13: Jehoiachin is like the pot that Jeremiah was once told to smash. It's no use to anyone. Is that all there is to Jehoiachin? Either way, Jehoiachin is going into exile. *Why*? Here is where Jeremiah asks this question but gives no answer. And who are these *offspring*? Jehoiachin is only a teenager, so Jeremiah is perhaps talking about offspring he may have, preparing the way for vv. 29–30.

29 The scroll makes one further addition to the message about Jehoiachin, now explicitly addressing Judah as a whole. It's important that the country listens. "The triplet signals by its insistent personification on the part of the prophet that place from which Jehoiachin's presence and future is excluded."[631] Jehoiachin shares in his people's waywardness, but he is no more and no less guilty than they are, and the declaration about his fate relates to their guilt and fate, not to his in isolation.[632]

---

631. D. J. Reimer, "On Triplets," 209.

632. M. H. Patton, *Hope for a Tender Sprig: Jehoiachin in Biblical Theology*, BBRSup 16 (Winona Lake: Eisenbrauns, 2016), 58–69.

30 The message links with the mention of his offspring (v. 28). It doesn't say he won't have children, and Babylonian records refer to his having five sons, for whose provision the record was kept,[633] while 1 Chr 3:17–18 lists seven, one of whom was an ancestor of Jesus (Matt 1:12). The message does say that he should be registered as childless.[634] Yahweh is "imagining scribes at his side, ready to take dictation."[635] Any children Jehoiachin has will not be in the register, in the citizen list.[636] Certainly no one from his line sat on David's throne and ruled in Judah (the kings in the second and first century came from the clan of Levi). Yet it can hardly be a coincidence that Yahweh later promises to make Jehoiachin's grandson his signet ring, in the only other reference to Yahweh having a signet ring (Hag 2:23). Evidently, he does not intend to implement this threat;[637] *b. Sanhedrin* 37b sees Jehoiachin's having children as indicating that exile can make expiation for everything (cf. Isa 40:1–2). No, Yahweh is not done with the promise to David. Nevertheless, v. 30 is "a summons to write down for posterity the hard destiny of Jehoiachin, to place on permanent record that he was a luckless king, stripped of his kingship, deposed and banished, one whose fortunes would never be reversed, who would never taste success nor have the satisfaction of restoration." There is thus a "wonder and terror" about his destiny.[638] And no one should dream of attaching hopes to him.

d. A Good Shepherd, a Faithful Shoot, a New Exodus (23:1–8)

¹*Oh,*ᵃ *shepherds wiping out*ᵇ
    *and scattering the flock of my*ᶜ *shepherding (Yahweh's affirmation).*ᵈ

²*Therefore Yahweh, Israel's God, has said this about the shepherds who shepherd my people:*ᵉ

You are the ones who scattered my flock;
    you drove them away and did not attend to them.
Here am I attending to you
    *for the dire nature of your practices (Yahweh's affirmation).*ᶠ
³*I myself will collect the remainder of my flock*

633. See *ANET*, 308.
634. Rudolph, *Jeremia*, 143.
635. Lundbom, *Jeremiah 21–36*, 163.
636. W. J. Wessels, "Jeremiah 22,24–30," *ZAW* 101 (1989): 244.
637. Qimchi, in MG.
638. McKane, *Jeremiah*, 1:551, 552.

from all the countries where I have driven them away.
I will return them to their habitat,
and they will be fruitful and increase.
[4]*I will set up shepherds over them, and they will shepherd them;*
they will not be afraid anymore, they will not break down,
and they will not need to be attended to (Yahweh's affirmation).[g]

[5]*There, days are coming (Yahweh's affirmation)*
when I will set up for David a faithful[h] shoot.[i]
He will reign as king and will show understanding;[j]
he will exercise faithful authority in the country.
[6]*In his days, Judah will find deliverance,*
and Israel—it will dwell in confidence.
And this is his name by which one will call him:
Yahweh is our faithfulness.[k]

[7]*Therefore, there, days are coming (Yahweh's affirmation) when people will no longer say, "Yahweh is alive*[l] *who got the Israelites up from the country of Egypt."* [8]*Rather, "Yahweh is alive who got up, who got the offspring of Israel's household from the northern country and from all the countries to which I drove them away." And they will live on their soil.*[m]

a. See the commentary on 22:13.

b. BDB takes *məʾabbədîm* as a virtually unique occurrence of *ʾābad piel*, meaning "loose, cause to stray," but Jeremiah often uses the verb with the more horrifying meaning (e.g., 12:7; 15:7).

c. LXX has "their."

d. MT[A] has a section marker here.

e. I follow Volz (*Jeremia*, 231) in laying out vv. 2b–6 as verse.

f. Yahweh's double paronomasia underlines the point. He repeats the paronomasia from 22:22: the shepherds (*rōʿîm*; words from this root come four times in vv. 1–2a) have done what is dire (*rōaʿ*). Then he comments that they have not attended to the sheep, so he will attend to the shepherds, using this verb (*pāqad*) in two different connections; a third will follow in v. 4.

g. MT has a section marker here.

h. "Rightful" might be a plausible connotation of *ṣaddîq* (McKane, *Jeremiah*, 1:561); the subsequent reference to *ṣədāqâ* then reframes what it means to be *ṣaddîq*.

i. LXX *anatolē* can mean "shoot" but more often means "dawn," a suggestive connotation here; see J. Lust, "Messianism and the Greek Version of Jeremiah," in *VII Congress of the International Organization for Septuagint and Cognate Studies*, ed. C. E. Cox, SCS 31 (Atlanta: Scholars, 1991), 89–99; G. R. Lanier, "The Curious Case of *ṣmḥ* and *anatolē*," *JBL* 134 (2015): 505–27. Tg has "an anointed one" (*māšîaḥ*).

j. For *śākal*, see the translation note and commentary on 10:21.

k. MT has a marker here. Verses 5–6 recur in a variant form in 33:14–16.

l. See the translation note and commentary on 4:2.

m. MT has a marker here. In LXX, vv. 7–8 come after v. 40; they recur in a variant form from 16:14–15. On the relationship of MT and LXX in Jer 23 more broadly, see R. D. Weis, "Jeremiah amid Actual and Virtual Editions: Textual Plurality and the Editing of the Book of Jeremiah," in *The Text of the Hebrew Bible and Its Editions: Studies in Celebration of the Fifth Centennial of the Complutensian Polyglot*, ed. A. Piquer Otero and P. A. Torijano Morales, Supplements to the Textual History of the Bible 1 (Leiden: Brill, 2017), 370–99.

The collection of messages focusing on kings comes to an end with three promises. In keeping with the challenges and threats in 21:1–22:30, these promises do not confine themselves to the subject of a king. The middle one relates directly to that theme. The third concerns the people as a whole. The first has an ambiguous relationship with the theme. It's about shepherding, but it's about shepherds (plural) and implicitly about Yahweh shepherding. Thus the promise section as a whole underplays any promise of a future king in a way that matches what precedes: no descendant of Jehoiachin will occupy David's throne. Yahweh's promise to David must stand, but when and how it may find fulfillment is not to be a preoccupation. Yahweh is focused more broadly on good shepherding and on gathering the exiles.

All three promises make sense between 597 and 587 or afterward. All three saw some fulfillment in the later decades of that century, though the fulfillment is partial, as regularly happens with God's threats and promises. It's typical of both threats and promises not only to use picture language that cannot be pressed but also to portray things in ultimate terms rather than terms that will find fulfillment in the course of events within this age. But later decades will see God making a return to Judah possible (in fulfillment of Jeremiah's promises; see 2 Chr 36:22; Ezra 1:1). Leaders such as Sheshbazzar, Zerubbabel, Jeshua, Ezra, and Nehemiah will shepherd the community. One of them will be a grandson of Jehoiachin whom Yahweh promises to make his signet ring (Hag 2:23) and whom he comes close to designating as the shoot (Zech 6:9–13), though both Christian and Jewish exegetes can oppose that understanding in association with their differing convictions about the Messiah[639] ("messianic" would also be an unwise term to use to describe Jeremiah's promises).[640] The fact that the threats and promises find a degree of fulfillment warns and encourages the people of God to be sure that they will find ultimate fulfillment and to respond to them appropriately.

639. See, e.g., Theodoret, *Ermeneia*, PG 81:628; Mayer, *Commentary*, 409, noting the address to the twelve clans in James 1:1, which implies that the church is the fulfillment of the promise in vv. 1–4; Altschuler, *Mesudat David* on vv. 5–6, in MG; also Isaac Abravanel, *Commentary on the Latter Prophets*.

640. B. Becking, "Messianic Expectations in the Book of Jeremiah?" in Lundbom, Evans, and B. A. Anderson, *Jeremiah*, 93–112.

vv. 1–4   The good shepherd
 vv. 1–2b   Accusations (two bicola separated by a resumptive
    introduction)
 v. 2c   A declaration of intent to take punitive action
    (one bicolon)
 vv. 3–4   A declaration of intent to take restorative action
    (two bicola and a tricolon)
vv. 5–6   The faithful Davidide (four bicola)
vv. 7–8   The new exodus (prose)

1 While Judah's *shepherds* would include its sequence of kings over the past fifteen years (Jehoahaz, Jehoiakim, Jehoiachin, Zedekiah), in the scroll "shepherds" has also included the rest of its leadership, including prophets, priests, and scribes (e.g., 2:8; 10:21). The horrible irony here is that Judah's own shepherds have been behaving like the foreign shepherd/kings (6:3; 12:10). Leaders easily become misleaders. Two days after Hitler's installation, 26-year-old Dietrich Bonhoeffer gave a radio broadcast (strangely cut short by the broadcasting authorities) on "The Younger Generation's Altered View of the Concept of Leader [*Führer*]," in which he spoke of the ease with which this happens.[641] *Wiping out* and *scattering* seems an illogical sequence, like taking into captivity and killing (20:4); some of the flock would be wiped out, some would scatter. Jeremiah's challenge, with its parallelism, is designed to pile up images. Elsewhere, wiping out and scattering are Yahweh's actions (e.g., 15:7; 18:17), but Yahweh's freedom as Israel's shepherd to act thus does not imply that his under-shepherds can—perhaps rather the opposite. It's not, after all, a shepherd's natural activity. Jeremiah underlines the scandalous nature of the shepherds' action by describing the people as *the flock of my shepherding* (cf. Pss 74:1; 79:13; 100:3; also 95:7, "the people of his shepherding, the flock of his hand"). The Judahites are used to singing about the flock in this way.

2 Instead of being *shepherds who shepherd*, they *scattered my flock*. To put it more forcefully in the parallelism, they *drove them away*, which sounds even more deliberate and hostile; it again corresponds to Yahweh's declarations concerning his own action (8:3; 16:15). To say *you did not attend to them* is therefore an understatement, but it prepares the way for Yahweh's correlative, also understated but frightening comment: *Here am I attending to you for the dire nature of your practices.*

3 As is often the case in the First Testament, wrongdoing requires both redress on the wrongdoers and rescue and restoration for their victims. So the chief shepherd will also take this second action. If he will eventually

---

641. Dietrich Bonhoeffer, *No Rusty Swords: Letters, Lectures, and Notes, 1928–1936* (London: Collins, 1965), 202; cf. Berrigan, *Jeremiah,* 93.

reverse the action of his under-shepherds, why did he not attend to them earlier? The Scriptures have no answer to that question except Paul's comment in Rom 9 that he is God and you are not, so shut up; though one might add that God is like a parent who hesitates to intervene in his (adult) children's lives because they need to run them for themselves. But in due course, he says, *I myself will collect the remainder of my flock.* He thus introduces a verb (*qābaṣ piel*) that will recur in this connection (29:14; 31:8, 10; 32:37) and at last gives more positive resonances to a noun (*šə'ērît*) that has been used only with negative ones (6:9; 8:3; 11:23; 15:9; see the commentary there, esp. on 6:9). Admittedly *remainder* is still not a very encouraging word; but Yahweh goes on to develop his promises. First, *I will return them to their habitat*: the sheep and shepherding image continues, and the word for habitat (*nāweh*) can imply pasture as well as a secure place to live. Second, *they will be fruitful and increase.* It will be like a new beginning of creation (Gen 1)[642] and a repeat of what God did for Israel's ancestors (Exod 1:7).[643]

4 They will still need shepherds, but Yahweh will now see that the *shepherds* are people who *will shepherd*—properly, by implication. The promise goes on: the sheep *will not be afraid any more* or *break down*. They will not *need to be attended to.* Vg translates this verb (*pāqad niphal*) "be missing," which can be its implication, but the verb earlier meant *attend to*, and Yahweh thus uses it to complete a triple paronomasia.

5 The second promise takes up Yahweh's commitment to David. So far, the Jeremiah scroll has taken a confrontational stance to the David of the day, though it has also envisaged the continuance of the Davidic monarchy if there is response to the confrontation (13:12–14; 21:11–12; 22:1–30). The positive nature of this promise has no precedent in the scroll, though it will recur especially in 33:17–26 (see the commentary there); beyond these two passages, "there is not a great deal more about the 'ideal king' in Jeremiah, although there is plenty about actual kings."[644] To say that *days are coming* (cf. 7:32; see the commentary there) gives people no assurance about the date and hardly even hints whether it will be very soon or some years away. It does give them the assurance that what it threatens or promises will definitely happen. Describing it as an eschatological promise[645] might again not clarify things, but it does imply "a decisive break in the history of the Davidic monarchy" with "no connection in terms of historical probabilities between the present circum-

---

642. K. D. Mulzac, "'The Remnant of My Sheep': A Study of Jeremiah 23:1–8 in Its Biblical and Theological Contexts," *JATS* 13 (2002): 140.

643. Holladay, *Commentary on Jeremiah*, 1:615.

644. D. J. Reimer, "Redeeming Politics in Jeremiah," in Barstad and Kratz, *Prophecy*, 128.

645. Cf. Rudolph, *Jeremia*, 147.

stances and the future hope."⁶⁴⁶ David's line is a tree that is about to be felled or has been felled, if the promise comes from after 587. So, as well as setting up new shepherds, Yahweh promises *I will set up for David a faithful shoot*. The hearers' ears might prick up at that adjective (*ṣaddîq*), which is not one that Jeremiah uses often as Isaiah, Psalms, and Proverbs do (only 12:1, of Yahweh; 20:12, of Jeremiah himself). In this sense, the idea of a faithful king is a new one. Yet Jeremiah has often critiqued the administration as well as the people in general for a lack of faithfulness. And the last king of Judah was called Zedekiah (*ṣidqîyāhû*), which means "Yahweh is my faithfulness." Yet faithfulness was not embodied in Zedekiah's reign. Yahweh's promise invites people to smirk and to rejoice that this failure is not the end of the story. Neither was Zedekiah someone who would *show understanding* in a variety of senses— political and religious. This Davidic shoot will do so. His understanding will express itself in the exercise of *faithful authority in the country*, that recurrent expectation (e.g., 22:3). He will embody the awareness that leadership means not only going for a goal and caring for the people one leads but the faithful exercise of authority.⁶⁴⁷ In other words, if Jeremiah might seem to be undermining his own assault on the monarchy, he makes sure he is not doing so by presupposing that any monarchy that Yahweh could shore up would be quite different from the one he has critiqued. And maybe the promise points not just to one king but to a new royal line that will fulfill that charge.⁶⁴⁸

6 Thus, whereas Judah met with calamity in the time of Zedekiah and other kings in Jeremiah's day, in this king's day Judah will *find deliverance*. Otherwise put, *Israel . . . will dwell in confidence*. Both *Judah* and *Israel* might here refer to the people of God as a whole; vv. 7–8 will fit this understanding.⁶⁴⁹ But in parallelism, they usually refer to the Southern and Northern Kingdoms. So here, Jeremiah raises his eyes and raises his people's eyes to think not only about Judah but also about Ephraim. In the parallelism, as the reference to Ephraim goes beyond the reference to Judah, *dwell in confidence* (or with a sense of security) goes beyond *find deliverance*. This promise recurs in the Torah (Lev 25:18–19; 26:5; Deut 33:12) and will recur in Jeremiah (32:37; 33:16). Finally, Yahweh says, this king's name will be *Yahweh is our faithfulness* (*yhwh ṣidqēnû*); attentive hearers who know Zedekiah smirk again. LXX encourages the smirk by making the name *Iōsedek*, a more precise reversal of its *Sedekia*. Thus "the . . . last king of Judah *does* appear in the text, but then

646. McKane, *Jeremiah*, 1:561.

647. W. J. Wessels, "Leader Responsibility in the Workplace: Exploring the Shepherd Metaphor in the Book of Jeremiah," *Koers* 79 (2014).

648. Allen, *Jeremiah*, 259.

649. Allen, *Jeremiah*, 259.

by way of not mentioning his name." And the name of the new king is not "'Yhwh *my* righteousness' but 'Yhwh *our* righteousness'. . . . The audience is being involved, it is their righteousness, their salvation, which is at stake."[650] (There are no known actual Israelite names of this kind with a first-person plural suffix;[651] the name Immanuel tests the rule, but the suffix on *'immānû* is not possessive and it, too, is no one's actual name.)

7–8 That aspect of the middle promise leads into the final one that explicitly concerns the people's destiny, in accordance with the recurrent pattern in 21:1–23:8. Once again, Yahweh declares that *days are coming*, and once again people in the Second Temple period could see something but not everything by way of fulfillment of his promise. People did not stop celebrating the exodus in favor of celebrating the return from exile, and that return was not as spectacular as the departure from Egypt and coming to Canaan—at least as the Torah tells that story. But Yahweh did make it possible for people to come back, and they did *live on their soil*, a new note in this version of the promise that came earlier in 16:14–15.

2. About Prophets (and Their People) (23:9–24:10)

As the first compilation of messages in part 2e focused on kings but also had messages for Judah, the second focuses on prophets but also has a message for Judah. But whereas the "kings" compilation interwove its messages, the "prophets" compilation focuses more on the prophets in 23:9–40, then on Judah in 24:1–10.

a. About Prophets (23:9–40)

⁹*Regarding the prophets.*[a]

My mind within me has shattered,
all my bones have trembled.[b]
I have become like someone drunk,[c]
like a man wine has overcome,
In[d] *the face of Yahweh*
and in the face of his sacred words.[e]
¹⁰*Because adulterers—*

---

650. J. Dubbink, "Cedars Decay, a Sprout Will Blossom: Jeremiah 23:5–6," in *Unless Someone Guide Me . . . : Festschrift for Karel A. Deurloo*, ed. J. W. Dyk (Maastricht: Shaker, 2001), 162, 164.

651. Cf. Holladay, *Commentary on Jeremiah*, 1:619.

the country is full.[f]
Because in the face of an oath[g] the country mourns,[h]
    the wilderness pastures have dried up.
Their crushing[i] has become dire,
    their strength not right.
[11]Because both prophet and priest—they are polluted;
    even in my house I have found their dire action (Yahweh's affirmation).
[12]Therefore their path will become for them
    like slippery tracks in the dark.
They will be pushed down and they will fall on it,
        because I will make dire trouble come on them,
        the year of their being attended to (Yahweh's affirmation).

[13]Yes,[j] in the prophets of Samaria
    I saw something nasty:
They prophesied away[k] by the Master[l]
    and led my people Israel astray.[m]
[14]And in the prophets of Jerusalem
    I saw something horrific:
Committing adultery and going by deception,
    and grasping[n] the hand of people who behave direly,[o]
    so that they have not turned,[p] an individual from his dire behavior.
They have become to me, all of them, like Sodom,
    the people who live in it, like Gomorrah.[q]

[15]Therefore Yahweh of Armies has said this about the prophets:

Here am I, making them eat wormwood
    and drink poisoned water.
Because from the Jerusalem prophets
    has gone out pollution to the entire country.[r]

[16]Yahweh of Armies has said this. Do not listen to the words of the prophets.

The people who are prophesying to you—
    those people are filling you with emptiness.
A vision out of their mind they speak,
    not from Yahweh's mouth,
[17]Saying and saying[s] to people who disown[t] me,
    "Yahweh has spoken:[u]
    'Things will be well for you.'"
And [to] everyone who walks by the determination of his mind,
    they have said: "Dire fortune will not come to you."

¹⁸*Because who has stood in Yahweh's cabinet,ᵛ*
   so he might see and listenʷ to his message—
who has paid heed to my messageˣ and listened?ʸ

¹⁹*Here is Yahweh's storm—*
   fury has gone out.
A storm is whirlingᶻ—
   on the head of the faithless it will whirl.
²⁰*Yahweh's anger will not turn,*
   until his acting on and until his implementing his mind's intentions.
In the later days,
   *you will have true insight into it.*ᵃᵃ

²¹*I did not send the prophets,*
   but they themselves ran.
I did not speak to them,
   but they themselves prophesied.
²²*If they had stood in my cabinet,*
   they would enable my people to listenᵇᵇ to my words,
And they would get them to turn from their dire path,
   *from the dire nature of their practices.*ᶜᶜ

²³*Am I a God nearby (Yahweh's affirmation)*
   *and not a God far away?*ᵈᵈ
²⁴*If an individual hides in a hiding place,*
   do I myself not see him (Yahweh's affirmation).
The heavens and the earth—
   I fill them, don't I (Yahweh's affirmation).

²⁵*I have listened to what the prophets who prophesy deception in my name have said: "I've had a dream, I've had a dream."* ²⁶*How long—will there be in the mind of the prophets who prophesy deception, prophets with duplicity in their mind,* ²⁷*who think to get my people to put my name out of mind with their dreams that they recount, an individual to his fellow, as their ancestors put my name out of mind through the Master . . .* ᵉᵉ

²⁸*The prophet who has a dream with him*
   should recount a dream.
And the one who has my message with him
   should speak my message in truth.

What does straw have with grain? (Yahweh's affirmation).

²⁹*My message is like this, isn't it: like fire (Yahweh's affirmation),*
and like a hammer that shatters a crag.^{ff}

³⁰*Therefore here am I, against the prophets (Yahweh's affirmation) who steal my words, an individual from his fellow.* ³¹*Here am I, against the prophets (Yahweh's affirmation) who get their tongue and utter an affirmation.*^{gg} ³²*Here am I, against the prophets of deceptive dreams (Yahweh's affirmation): they tell them and lead my people astray with their deceptions and with their wild words when I myself didn't send them and didn't command them, and they are no use to this people at all*^{hh} *(Yahweh's affirmation).*

³³*So when this people or the prophet or a priest asks you, What is Yahweh's burden? you will say*ⁱⁱ *to them, What is the burden?*^{jj} *I will hurl you away (Yahweh's affirmation).* ³⁴*The prophet or the priest or the people that says "Yahweh's burden"—I will attend to that individual and to his household.* ³⁵*Thus you are to say, an individual to his fellow and an individual to his brother, "What has Yahweh averred"*^{kk} *or "What has Yahweh spoken."* ³⁶*Yahweh's burden you are not to be mindful of*^{ll} *any more, because the burden—it will be for the person with his*^{mm} *message. But you will pervert the words of the lively God, Yahweh of Armies, our God.* ³⁷*You are to say this to the prophet, "What has Yahweh averred to you?" or "What has Yahweh spoken?"* ³⁸*But if you say, "Yahweh's burden," therefore Yahweh has said this: Since you have said this thing, "Yahweh's burden," and I sent to you, "You will not say: Yahweh's burden,"* ³⁹*therefore here am I; I will forget you: lifting you up,*ⁿⁿ *I will hurl you away, and the city that I gave to you and to your ancestors, from before my face.* ⁴⁰*I will put upon you reviling for all time and disgrace for all time, which will not be put out of mind.*^{oo}

a. LXX "among the prophets" perhaps links *lannəbi'îm* to the preceding verse (v. 6 in LXX); cf. *NETS*. Vg "to the prophets" identifies it as a heading. Tg "because of the prophets" links it to what immediately follows. On LXX and MT in Jer 23, see Weis, "Jeremiah amid Actual and Virtual Editions."

b. BDB and *DCH* take *rāḥəpû* as a *hapax legomenon*, distinguishing *rāḥap* I from *rāḥap* II, which has just two First Testament occurrences. *HALOT* has only one root *rāḥap*, which encourages a comparison of this verb with the occurrence in Gen 1:2; see Calvin, *Jeremiah*, 3:157–58.

c. For MT *šikkôr*, LXX "broken" implies *šābûr*.

d. Lit. "from" here and in the next colon.

e. LXX "in the face of splendor of his glory" suggests *mippənê hădar kəbôdô*, perhaps under the influence of Isa 2:10, 19, 21 (Duhm, *Jeremia*, 182).

f. LXX lacks this line.

g. For MT *'ālâ*, LXX implies *'ēlleh* ("these things"). Tg takes *'ālâ* to refer to (false) oaths, like *šāba'* (e.g., 5:7), which pairs neatly with the reference to adultery (Mayer, *Commentary*, 409).

h. See 12:4 and the translation note there.

i. LXX, Vg take *mərûṣâ* to mean "course, race"; see the commentary, and see 8:6 and the translation note there. Tg takes it to mean "desire," from *rāṣâ*.

j. The initial *û* looks forward to the parallel, resumptive *û* in v. 14 (Duhm, *Jeremia*, 184).

k. See the commentary on 14:14.

l. As usual, LXX gives "Baal" a feminine article (see the translation note on 2:8); so also in v. 27.

m. MT^L has a section marker here.

n. The finite verb continues from the infinitives (DG 76b).

o. Syr "their friends" derives *mərē'îm* from *rā'â* rather than *rā'a'*; it thus nicely anticipates vv. 27, 30.

p. *Ləbiltî* is unusually followed by a *qatal* rather than an infinitive, as in 7:8 (LXX implies the usual construction), suggesting an aim that has been fulfilled (see further 27:18 and the translation note there).

q. MT has a marker here.

r. MT has a unit marker here.

s. An infinitive combines with a participle, the infinitive coming second (compare and contrast 22:10).

t. *Committing adultery* (v. 14) is *nā'ap*; *disown* is *nā'aṣ*. In letters as in reference, the two are close to each other; the one implies the other.

u. For MT *limənā'ăṣay dibber yhwh*, LXX implies *limənā'ăṣê dəbar yhwh* ("who disown Yahweh's message"), which loses the parallelism between vv. 17a and 17b.

v. In a related context in Amos 3:7, *sôd* means "plan"; cf. Aq, Sym, Tg here (and LXX's less transparent *hypostēma*; Theod's *hypostasis*); see Jerome, *Jeremiah*, 142. But in Jer 6:11; 15:17, *sôd* means an assembly, and *stand* suggests that meaning here.

w. For MT's *wəyērē' wəyišma'* (which might be jussive), Vg, Syr imply *wayyar' wayyyišma'* ("and has seen . . . listened"); so also LXX for the first verb (it lacks the second).

x. The *ketiv* implies *dəbārî* ("my message," the more difficult reading) for the *qere dəbārô*.

y. MT has a section marker here. An intricate parallelism and enjambment run through vv. 16b–18. The opening colon in v. 16b is the heading for what follows. In v. 17, the two lines are parallel, with v. 17aα paralleled by v. 17bα and v. 17aβ–γ paralleled by v. 17bβ. A variant parallelism within another tricolon appears within v. 18, as v. 18a is paralleled by v. 18b.

z. Masculine *sa'ar* complements feminine *sa'ărâ* in the parallel line, while the *hithpolel* participle of *ḥûl* will be complemented by the *qal* in the parallel colon.

aa. Verses 19–20 reappear in a variant form as 30:23–24. Without them, vv. 16–18, 21–22 run more smoothly.

bb. LXX implies a *qal* verb rather than a *hiphil* and again implies a *waw*-consecutive, as in v. 18.

cc. MT has a section marker here.

dd. The *min* on *miqqārōb/mērāḥōq* ("from near/from far") has lost the idea of separation (BDB, 578, 581). LXX lacks the initial interrogative *ha* and translates this line as a statement, perhaps a more straightforwardly orthodox theological declaration, though it could imply a threatening message of a different kind (compare Theod and contrast Aq, Sym).

ee. The sentence, which began incoherently with the double interrogative, runs out without coming to an end syntactically.

ff. MT has a section marker here. LXX spreads the bicolon over three cola; see F. H. Polak, "Jer. 23:29–An Expanded Colon in the LXX?" *Textus* 11 (1984): 119–23.

gg. LXX "slumber their slumber" derives verb and noun from *nûm*, not inappropriately in the context and given that the verb *nā'am* (denominative from the frequent noun *nə'um*) comes only here. Was it invented by Jeremiah? (Bright, *Jeremiah*, 153).

hh. The infinitive of *yā'al* (*hiphil*) precedes the finite verb, underlining the factuality of the action.

ii. *You* is singular on the first two occasions in v. 33a, addressing Jeremiah; henceforth it is plural, addressing the people, prophet, and priest who were mentioned in v. 33a, except for a further isolated singular in v. 37 that apparently addresses a notional individual among them in the way one can in English by using the word "you" to mean "one."

jj. For MT *'et mah maśśā'*, Vg has "why do you have a burden"; LXX implies *'attem hammaśśā'* ("you are the burden"), which makes good sense.

kk. On *'ānâ* here and in v. 37, see the translation note on 14:7.

ll. For MT *tizkərû*, LXX has "name"; see the translation note on 20:9.

mm. Lit. "the person of his message/word." Vg takes *his* to denote "his own," but the sentence makes more sense if it denotes Yahweh's.

nn. Once more, an infinitive follows a finite verb. But given that the finite verb comes from *nāśâ*, the spelling of the infinitive *nāśō'* (rather than *nāśōh*) is anomalous. As a form from *nāśā'*, it ought to mean lend (*nāśā'* I) or delude (*nāśā'* II). On the other hand, for the finite verb, LXX, Vg, Aq, Sym presuppose forms from *nāśā'*, which is more what one might have expected in this subsection with its focus on *maśśā'*. MT's expression thus involves a mixed form as well as a paronomasia in the combination of finite verb and infinitive (for which cf. 8:13 and 48:9 and the translation notes there). But here, the infinitive functions as a finite verb and leads into the finite verb that follows.

oo. Verses 7–8 come here in LXX.

Instruction will not fail from priest or counsel from expert or message from prophet (18:18). Jeremiah had some problems with priests and experts, but alongside the kings it was the prophets that he had most reason to talk about, and he needed to distance himself from them even though—or because—he was in some sense a prophet himself. The account of his altercations with Hananiah (28:1–17) suggests that he would have looked like a prophet. He used the forms of speech that prophets used (Hananiah, too, spoke like someone bringing messages from the King; see 28:2). He performed symbolic deeds as they did. The expression "word of Yahweh" is not original to a prophet such as Jeremiah and might be introduced into his words later.[652] But once it is there, a theology of the word emerges from 23:9–40.[653]

The word *prophet* (*nabî'*) in the First Testament is harder to define than the words "priest" or "expert" (or "king"), though it is easier to understand when set against those other nouns. A priest's role is to offer instruction

---

652. C. Levin, "The 'Word of Yahweh,'" in *Prophets, Prophecy, and Prophetic Texts in Second Temple Judaism*, ed. M. H. Floyd and R. D. Haak, LHBOTS 427 (London: T&T Clark, 2006), 42–62.

653. Fischer, *Jeremia*, 1:710.

(*tôrâ*) based on a body of accepted instruction or teaching that priests received from previous generations (whether already in writing or still as oral teaching) and that issues in an expanding body of instruction or teaching that came to be *the* Torah. Priests worked out what to say to people on the basis of what they had received. An expert (*ḥākām*, conventionally "wise") also speaks on the basis of a body of accepted insight, and there need be no conflict between a prophet and the experts any more than between a prophet and the priests,[654] but the background of their insight lies more overtly in ordinary worldly events and human experience rather than in the authority of a key figure such as Moses, though it could include empirical data that Western people find bizarre, such as the phenomena that divination studies. A prophet may take into account both these bases, but overtly his message comes from a sense of receiving something directly from God (see "Yahweh's Message Came," pp. 3–5). There could no doubt be conflict between priests and between experts about truth and about what should be done, and there was such conflict between prophets. In Israel, the problem of discerning between prophets who do and who do not speak truly was an issue more or less ever since prophecy came into being and up until the destruction of Jerusalem, and also later in Zech 13.[655] It is a characteristic feature of prophecy in Israel, where it takes a distinctive form in which prophets at least agree that they all speak in the name of the one God.[656] Jeremiah 27–29 portrays it as particularly a problem between 597 and 587, in Jerusalem and in Babylon, when Judahites lived with the question whether Yahweh's wrath had finally poured out and restoration could now be expected. The texts do not refer to its being a problem in the aftermath of 587, when there were no longer prophets disagreeing over whether disaster was coming. Perhaps

654. M. Gilbert. "Jérémie en conflit avec les sages?" in *Le livre de Jérémie: Le prophète et son milieu. Les oracles et leur transmission*, ed. P.-M. Bogaert, 2nd ed., BETL 54 (Leuven: Peeters, 1997), 105–18, 427–28.

655. With which A. Lange links the development of the debate documented in the Jeremiah scroll (*Vom prophetischen Wort zur prophetischen Tradition: Studien zur Traditions- und Redaktionsgeschichte innerprophetischer Konflikte in der Hebräischen Bibel*, FAT 34 [Tübingen: Mohr Siebeck, 2002], 278–306; cf. J. Hill, "The Book of Jeremiah MT and Early Second Temple Conflicts about Prophets and Prophecy," *Australian Biblical Review* 50 [2002]: 28–42).

656. See H. B. Huffmon, "The Exclusivity of Divine Communication in Ancient Israel," in *Mediating between Heaven and Earth: Communication with the Divine in the Ancient Near East*, ed. C. L. Crouch, J. Stokl, and A. E. Zernecke, LHBOTS 566 (London: T&T Clark, 2012), 67–81. It has been a problem through church history and in First Testament interpretation: see S. B. Tarrer, *Reading with the Faithful: Interpretation of True and False Prophecy in the Book of Jeremiah from Ancient to Modern Times*, JTISup 6 (Winona Lake, IN: Eisenbrauns, 2013).

587 largely discredited prophecy and for centuries prophets were widely assumed by definition to be false.[657] It seems unlikely that this compilation issued from a post-587 context, though it would have been instructive for Judahites thinking through the implications of the catastrophe. More likely, the compilations on kings and on prophets issued from the reign of Zedekiah, though dating the origin of the individual subsections is a different (and unanswerable) question.

Like the compilation of messages about kings, the compilation about prophets is interwoven with messages relating to the people as a whole, paralleling the combination in 21:1–23:8. Like the reproach of kings, the reproach of prophets is important for the people as a whole; they are not invited to feel superior just because the prophets are being critiqued.

> vv. 9–12   A testimony to being overwhelmed, an indictment of the country with the implication that prophets and priests are identified with it, and a warning of calamity (eight bicola, the second leading into the third, concluded by a tricolon)
>
> vv. 13–15   A parallel indictment working by the opposite logic, that prophets are misleading people into waywardness, and another warning of calamity (two linked bicola, then a bicolon leading into a tricolon, then a single bicolon, then a resumptive introduction followed by two bicola)
>
> vv. 16–18   An exhortation not to listen to the prophets backed by a further indictment of them on the basis of the origin of their messages in their own minds (after the introduction, two bicola leading into a tricolon, then another bicolon leading into another tricolon[658])
>
> vv. 19–20   A warning of fiery action on Yahweh's part, which in the context is the warning that follows up that indictment (four bicola)
>
> vv. 21–22   A resumptive declaration about the prophets related to the indictment: they are self-propelled (three bicola)
>
> vv. 23–24   A resumptive declaration related to the warning: God can reach everywhere (three bicola)
>
> vv. 25–32   Another resumptive indictment about the prophets being self-propelled followed by warnings (prose incorporating three bicola and a one-colon saying)

657. A. Catastini, "Who Were the False Prophets?" *Henoch* 34 (2012): 330–66.

658. See the translation note on v. 18.

vv. 33–40 A warning about Yahweh's burden: twice Jeremiah describes a circumstance and issues the warning, then at
greater length he issues an instruction and follows it up
with a warning in case of disobedience (prose)

9a The introduction parallels 21:11, which led into comments on a sequence
of kings in Jeremiah's day; this introduction leads into comments on a sequence of prophets in Jeremiah's day, though without naming them as it did
the kings.

9b–d The first subsection opens in Jeremiah's typically oblique way,
though it begins to indicate the link with the introduction and with the subsections that will follow. The words recall lament psalm language,[659] though
it will emerge that Jeremiah is not protesting his treatment by Yahweh or by
other people. Reading these lines in light of the introduction could suggest
that Jeremiah is shattered by the prophets (Tg) or by the waywardness he
speaks of, but before coming to the description of waywardness, he indicates
the actual reason for his dismay. It is not that he is in the midst of losing his
youthful naivety[660] or shattered by the experience of being addressed by
Yahweh; he is not referring to an experience of being taken out of himself,
of ecstasy,[661] or of "intensity of inspiration."[662] It's the content of Yahweh's
address that has this effect on him. He is once again testifying to the staggering effect of Yahweh's message, which he calls Yahweh's *sacred words*. It
is perhaps surprising that this phrase does not recur in the First Testament
(Ps 105:42 refers to "his sacred word," alluding to Yahweh's promise) given
the awe-inspiring nature of the fact that God has spoken. God has spoken!
The *sacred words* that "unman the prophet are the words of Yahweh in vv.
10–12."[663] He had talked about the effect of Yahweh's message on his *mind*
and *bones* in 20:9, and he picks up the theme again.[664] Once more, Yahweh
does not respond to his lament, but in any case, its function is to speak to the
Judahites, and specifically to their prophets (and priests).

10 Grievously, the matters on which Yahweh has spoken are on one hand
wrongdoing (*because adulterers—the country is full*) and on the other an oath
(*the country mourns, the wilderness pastures have dried up*). Jeremiah has referred to literal adultery in the context of reference to other wrongdoing

---

659. Weiser, *Jeremia*, 1:207.
660. Volz, *Jeremia*, 235.
661. See, e.g., the discussion in Fretheim, *Jeremiah*, 332.
662. D. R. Jones, *Jeremiah*, 304.
663. McKane, *Jeremiah*, 1:569.
664. Holladay, *Commentary on Jeremiah*, 1:624.

(7:9), but adultery is more often an image for religious unfaithfulness (e.g., 3:8–9), and that understanding makes sense here.[665] There is therefore some irony or poetic justice if adultery issues in drought, because attentiveness to other deities was designed to ensure a good harvest rather than to prevent it. "Jeremiah's polemic against Baal is founded on the idea that Yahweh is the creator who in his power and might can take away that which Baal supposedly can provide and is hailed for." Further, "On the one hand he is the one who blesses creation, but on the other the one who curses it."[666] Jeremiah's reference to his inner shattering may suggest that drought and crop failure are at the moment visionary realities that are perceptible to his mind and imagination rather than empirical realities visible to anyone. But the shattering presupposes that they will become empirical realities. The *oath* hangs over the country. And the reason (to put it another way) is the *crushing* of people, the exercise of oppressive *strength* against them. Once again Jeremiah associates religious faithlessness with faithlessness within the community in the action that strong people take against weak people instead of acting on their behalf. The adulterers are also crushers.

11 How is it possible? Prophet and priest collude with or encourage the people with power in their acts of oppression, Jeremiah implies, as he has implied before. To restate the accusation of adultery as it applies to them in particular, *they are polluted* (*ḥānēp*), the term Jeremiah associated with whoring and adultery in 3:1–10 (see the commentary there). They don't just engage in their wrongdoing out in the city. They exercise their ministry in the temple itself. Maybe Jeremiah refers simply to their teaching or maybe to their facilitating acts of oppression such as child sacrifice. If the reference to adultery refers to literal marital unfaithfulness, it corresponds to the way leaders in the church get involved in adultery and other forms of sexual immorality, like other leaders in society. One way or another, "'the goodly fellowship of the prophets' was not all that goodly."[667]

12 They will therefore pay a price. They think they have a safe *path* to walk, but they will find it resembles *slippery tracks* along a mountain slope that are even more dangerous *in the dark*. And they won't just fall. They will *be pushed down*. By Yahweh? Yes, they *will fall* because *I will make dire trouble come on them*—again the dire action of which v. 11 spoke meets with dire

---

665. See W. J. Wessels, "Prophets at Loggerheads: Accusations of Adultery in Jeremiah 23:9–15," *AcT* 31 (2011): 346–62.

666. W. J. Wessels, "God the Creator: Contrasting Images in Psalm 65:10–14 and Jeremiah 23:9–15," *OTE* 23 (2010): 855, 856.

667. Achtemeier, *Jeremiah*, 75 (see further p. 57 in this commentary). The quotation comes from the fourth-century hymn called the "Te Deum."

THE BOOK OF JEREMIAH

consequences. Yahweh imagines Jeremiah praying the prayer in Ps 35:5–8 and declares that he will ensure that it is fulfilled. He will see to it personally: no divine aid here as there is in that prayer.

13 There follows an originally separate subsection relating just to prophets, restating the same themes. One can see why the curators might have juxtaposed the two messages, as this one also talks about adultery and about pollution. Once again there is a link with Jer 3, now in the comparing of Ephraim/Samaria and Judah/Jerusalem and their respective prophets. Jeremiah imagines faithful Judahites looking up north and seeing something *nasty* (*tapillâ*)—literally, something unsavory or tasteless (Job 6:6). The "rather mild epithet"[668] might seem an understatement as a way of describing prophets who *prophesied by the Master* and thus *led my people Israel astray*. But the litotes makes for a contrast when Jeremiah continues as he does in the next verse.

14 Because what Jeremiah sees in Jerusalem is not just nasty but *horrific* (cf. 5:30). How is it worse? The answer again overlaps with the unfavorable correlation of Ephraim and Judah in Jer 3. There the point was that one might have thought Judah would learn something from what happened to Ephraim. Here, Jeremiah applies that point to the prophets. They too are involved in *committing adultery and going by deception* in unfaithfulness to Yahweh and an inclination to follow the Master of Deception. Jeremiah does not say they were overtly following the Master, as the Ephraimites' prophets did. Perhaps they thought they were serving Yahweh. If so, Jeremiah again sees them as having such a perverted understanding of God that they are in effect serving the Master. "Baal is not viewed as a single deity but as a whole stock of ideas leading away from Yahweh."[669] The prophets are religious leaders in the community whose vocation was to set people on the right path and draw them away from the wrong one, but instead they are involved in *grasping the hand of people who behave direly*. They are encouraging their unfaithfulness or failing to confront it in such a way as to strengthen them and push or pull them on in their way of behaving. The result is that *people do not turn*. In Yahweh's eyes, Jerusalem is *like Sodom* or *like Gomorrah*. When Isaiah drew that analogy, he associated it with Judah's being decimated like Sodom and Gomorrah (Isa 1:9–10). Jeremiah invites people to make the same association. But Sodom and Gomorrah is what the community has come to resemble *to me*, and it had better assume that its future will have the same resemblance. With some irony, Zedekiah's staff comment elsewhere that Jeremiah is *weakening the hands* of the men who are seeking to defend the city (38:4): "The poet understands well the enormous power of religion to legitimate public

668. R. P. Carroll, *Jeremiah*, OTL, 455.
669. Jeremias, "Hosea Tradition," 29.

514

policy. The religious leadership which opposes Jeremiah legitimates public policy uncritically, and in so doing it generates more wickedness."[670] And then "it is the very proximity of corruption to YHWH's presence in the temple that makes YHWH into an agent of overthrow."[671] In competing with the prophets Jeremiah is engaged in "a life and death battle."[672]

15 *Therefore Yahweh of Armies has said this* is "probably the most characteristic 'form' of prophetic utterance,"[673] here used against the prophets who used it themselves (28:2). Yahweh has announced that, to be more explicit and again with poetic justice, he is going to act like the "demonic host" at a banquet[674] and give the wrongdoers the same food and water as their people. The threat previously made to the people is here applied to *the prophets* (see 9:15[14] and the translation note and commentary there). "Yahweh will provide a meal of poisonous herbs to be washed down with a poisonous draught"[675] or with a drink from the undrinkable waters of the Dead Sea.[676] And Jeremiah gives a reason that links to vv. 9–12: the prophets are the source of a *pollution* that affects *the entire country*.

16 The third subsection is indirectly a further indictment of the prophets, but directly an exhortation not to listen to them. The indictment comes in the exposition of the reason, and it works by referring to the origin of the prophets' words, which explains the problem about their content. People should *not listen to the words of the prophets* because they *are filling you with emptiness*. The verb *filling you with emptiness* (*hābēl hiphil*) comes from the noun meaning emptiness, one of Jeremiah's favorite words to describe other gods (see 2:5 and the translation note and commentary there). How are people to determine whether the prophets' *vision* comes *out of their minds* and *not from Yahweh's mouth*? The antithesis suggests the link between a vision that someone sees because Yahweh reveals it and a message that someone shares because Yahweh speaks it into the prophet's ear.

17 It's easy to tell the difference, Jeremiah implies. To put it in the terms of vv. 9–15, the criterion is, are they people who have colluded with or even encouraged religious adultery? To put it a different way, are they colluding with or encouraging *people who disown me*, with the person who is *walking by the determination of his mind* and is thus praying to anyone he feels like in any way that seems a good idea? Are they promising such people that *things will be well* and that *dire fortune* will not come to them?

670. Brueggemann, *Jeremiah 1–25*, 202.
671. Moberly, *Prophecy and Discernment*, 72.
672. Volz, *Jeremia*, 237.
673. D. R. Jones, *Jeremiah*, 307.
674. Rudolph, *Jeremia*, 151.
675. McKane, *Jeremiah*, 1:576.
676. Moberly, *Prophecy and Discernment*, 72.

18 If they are, there is a contrast with someone such as Jeremiah *who has stood* in attendance on Yahweh *in Yahweh's cabinet* and has thus *seen and listened to his message*; once again, Jeremiah combines the visual and the oral. Such a prophet *has paid heed to his message and listened* rather than paying attention to the Master and listening to him. The appropriate question to ask of a prophet, then, is "Whom have you been listening to?" Yahweh's cabinet (*sôd*) is the meeting of Yahweh and his staff that reviews events in the world, decides on action to take, and commissions envoys to undertake it (e.g., 1 Kgs 22:19–22; Ps 82:1; Isa 6:1–8). It is a very different gathering from the ones Jeremiah mentions elsewhere (*sôd* recurs in 6:11; 15:17).[677] The appeal to membership in Yahweh's cabinet is perhaps a surprise given that he portrayed his commission as a one-on-one event.[678] It need be no more a "mythological" idea[679] than the idea of God and the idea that God is not the only being in the supernatural realm. It is a model that helps one conceptualize the reality of God, of God's working through other supernatural beings, and of human servants of God being involved in the processes whereby God decides on and implements decisions about the world. The motif of Jeremiah's attending this cabinet presupposes that it is possible for human beings to be in one place bodily but in another place in their minds. It is a familiar experience to sense that someone is with us in body but that "really" they are "somewhere else," and the potential for this separation has found new expression through the invention of the telephone and through the development of video-conferencing and the like. Yahweh can summon Jeremiah into a cabinet meeting in which Jeremiah takes part in his mind while still being physically in Jerusalem.[680] It is likely not illuminating to refer to it as ecstatic experience and more illuminating to think of it as an experience in the imagination, as long as we do not infer that it is therefore imaginary. Through this invitation, Jeremiah learns about the cabinet's decisions and plans. And he is clear that the *šālôm*-prophets have not done so; otherwise they would not be speaking of the future in the way they do. They may speak in good faith, but the criterion that determines whether they have spoken Yahweh's message is not the subjective experience that they can speak of (any more than is the case with Jeremiah). It is how their words fit with the nature of the theological and moral relationship between Yahweh and Israel.[681]

677. J. A. Thompson, *Jeremiah*, 497.

678. K. M. Rochester, "Prophetic Ministry," 245.

679. D. R. Jones, *Jeremiah*, 309.

680. P. J. Scalise sees this experience as the nearest to a vision that Jeremiah speaks of: see "Vision beyond the Visions in Jeremiah," in Hayes and Tiemeyer, *"I Lifted My Eyes and Saw"*, 47–58.

681. Weiser, *Jeremia*, 1:211.

19 So the community is the victim of prophetic misleading. It might then have inferred that it bears no responsibility for wandering away from Yahweh. It just followed where it was led. This further vision implicitly urges it to see that Yahweh has closed off this avenue of excuse. To fill in the dots between vv. 16–18 and 19–20, Judah needs to see the calamity that is coming as a consequence of the people's following the prophets' leading. It is *a storm* that *is whirling on the head of the faithless*—that is, of people in general, not just their prophets.

20 Jeremiah's threat anticipates a parable of Jesus such as the rich man and Lazarus (Luke 16:19–31) that portrays the threatening purpose that his Father will implement for his people. Neither Jeremiah nor Jesus is talking about "the end of the days" (Tg), the ultimate End, but neither are they talking simply about the future in a general sense. Jesus is referring to a time after the rich man's death, and Jeremiah is talking about the time of Yahweh's *acting on* and *implementing his mind's intentions* and thus bringing about the semi-ultimate catastrophe. He is then looking beyond it to "the aftermath of the judgment,"[682] the time when "it's over."[683] He is inviting people to picture the time *in the later days* when they will then *have true insight into* God's basis of operation. "When the final moment of captivity arrives, the exulting conqueror prevails over you, and he binds your hands with the rattling of chains, then 'you will understand.'"[684] But like the Trojans, who didn't realize what the wooden horse concealed, they will then "become wise too late."[685] "There are two ways to learn, and the second is the hard way."[686] So they need to open themselves to the insight now.

21 Jeremiah reverts to speaking directly of the prophets and restates his point from vv. 16–18 in a variant order. Maybe vv. 21–22 were the original continuation of vv. 16–18. Jeremiah here starts from the presupposition that a prophet is an envoy sent by a king, running to fulfill a commission. These prophets run as if they had been sent, but they hadn't. They speak in the manner of a prophet relaying a message from the king, "My lord has said this," but actually their King had not spoken to them. Yahweh makes the point in neat parallel lines (they may be two 2-2 lines or two 4-4 cola making one line):

> I did not send the prophets, but they themselves ran.
> I did not speak to them, but they themselves prophesied.

682. McKane, *Jeremiah*, 1:583.

683. Bright, *Jeremiah*, 152.

684. Jerome, *Jeremiah*, 143.

685. Mayer, *Commentary*, 411; this proverb first appears in Cicero, *Letters to His Friends* 6.16.1.

686. Allen, *Jeremiah*, 267.

First, there was not divine sending, but there was running; then (when they got to the destination) there was not divine speaking, but there was prophesying.

22 Yahweh picks up the earlier imagery but tightens the screw. He had spoken of the origin of the prophets' words in their own minds, which issues in their promising people that Yahweh would be with them and contrasts with what would have been the case if they had been in attendance at a cabinet meeting. Here he again presupposes the origin of their words in their own initiative, which links with their not having attended such a meeting, then adds the indictment that they thus confirm people in their waywardness. Earlier, they told people that something dire was not their destiny; here, they fail to get people to turn from their dire path. "How could a prophet confuse his own word with God's word? How could a prophet fail to speak condemnation to the sinful, covenant-breaking situation?"[687] By struggling to give people hope in difficult times.[688] By avoiding the idea that the service of God that he thought he was offering wasn't service of God at all. By thinking that God was near his people and committed to them. By thinking that God was committed to carrying them and forgiving their waywardness. By believing that Yahweh's covenantal relationship with his people was pure grace, an expression of unconditional love on God's part.[689] Because in this situation, it's easy to tell prophets who haven't been sent or addressed, who haven't *stood in my cabinet*. They are prophets who don't urge people to *turn*. The juxtaposition of vv. 21–22 with vv. 19–20 makes a nice (or rather frightening) link in the use of that verb. You don't turn; my anger doesn't turn. The responsibility of the prophets is thus a terrifying one. In other words, Jeremiah's logic is not "I have been in attendance at the cabinet, which is how you can know that my message about Yahweh's wrath against the adulterous community is true"; the community could not evaluate such a claim.[690] The logic is, "I have delivered a message about Yahweh's wrath against the adulterous community, which is how you can know that I have been in attendance at Yahweh's cabinet." The First Testament assumes that telling true from false prophecy is not so difficult, because the criteria for the discernment are theological and moral.[691] Maybe it's significant in this connection that Jeremiah's messages

---

687. Craigie, Kelley, and Drinkard, *Jeremiah 1–25*, 345.

688. Pixley, *Jeremiah*, 73.

689. R. E. Manahan, "A Theology of Pseudoprophets: A Study of Jeremiah," *Grace Theological Journal* 1 (1980): 77–96.

690. Cf. W. J. Wessels, "Prophet versus Prophet in the Book of Jeremiah," *OTE* 22 (2009): 746.

691. Cf. B. S. Childs, *Old Testament Theology in a Canonical Context* (Philadelphia: Fortress, 1986), 141.

can often be seen to be reflecting the Torah.[692] "If the prophets had had access to the council their message would have been different from the empty visions with which they encouraged the wicked."[693] The argument is not that listening in on the cabinet's deliberations means a prophet is successful, as Jeremiah's story shows. It is that listening in on those deliberations means a prophet is confrontational when confrontation is appropriate.[694] "Failure to hear the word of the Lord [is] a moral and not a hermeneutical failure."[695] At the moment, the test of prophecy in Deut 18:21–22 cannot vindicate Jeremiah or the other prophets. They would say that "it is Jeremiah's message of judgment that reveals him to be a false prophet."[696] He would claim that the test in Deut 13:1–5(2–6) provides a test that works. And the fact that Jeremiah and not the other prophets gained a place in the Scriptures reflects the way events proved that he spoke the truth[697] and did fulfill the test in Deut 18:21–22.

23 A further juxtaposition again has Yahweh speaking more generally and closing off excuses from the community as a whole. The First Testament rarely speaks of Yahweh being spatially *nearby* (*qārōb*). It does speak of Yahweh coming near when people need him to do so (Deut 4:7), and it speaks much of people being able to come near to Yahweh. The electrical holiness of Yahweh might make the idea of perpetual nearness implausible or scary (cf. Heb 12:29). At the same time, the First Testament speaks frequently of Yahweh's name or face being present with the people, which is a way of speaking about nearness that safeguards a little against that problem. Maybe here Yahweh talks about being nearby because the Judahites think in those terms, especially in connection with his real presence in the temple (cf. 7:1–15), but the point he wants to make is that even if he is spatially nearby, that presence does not confine him. He is also *a God far away*. "The 'near God' against whom the prophet inveighs here is the God of the false prophets." As Christians can easily imply, people thought that God was constantly and easily available to them and that his will could be easily equated with their own desires. "By contrast, the 'distant God' was a God whose word could not be

692. See D. Rom-Shiloni, "Prophets in Jeremiah in Struggle over Leadership, or Rather over Prophetic Authority?," *Bib* 99 (2018): 363–70.

693. R. P. Carroll, *Jeremiah*, OTL, 463.

694. Fretheim, *Jeremiah*, 337–38, contrasting the inference R. P. Carroll goes on to draw in *Jeremiah*, OTL, 463 (earlier, "A Non-Cogent Argument in Jeremiah's Oracles against the Prophets," *Studia Theologica* 30 [1976]: 43–51; also "Halfway through a Dark Wood," in Diamond, K. M. O'Connor, and Stulman, *Troubling Jeremiah*, 77–78); see further Moberly, *Prophecy and Discernment*, 83–88.

695. S. E. Fowl and L. G. Jones, *Reading in Communion: Scripture and Ethics in Christian Life*, Biblical Foundations in Theology (London: SPCK, 1991), 91.

696. Diamond, "Jeremiah," 567.

697. Brueggemann, *Jeremiah 1–25*, 201.

manipulated or horsetraded. It was a word which invaded human experience from beyond with overwhelming power."[698] "In the end, the different image of God separates Jeremiah from his opponents more than anything else."[699]

24 Jeremiah specifically draws an inference that is similar to the point made in Ps 139 and Amos 9. There's nowhere people can go that means they escape from his presence and attention, which can be good news or bad news. *If an individual hides in a hiding place, do I myself not see him*? Don't think you can hide from Yahweh. Yahweh is omniscient, or at least capable of being omniscient. *The heavens and the earth—I fill them, don't I?* Yahweh is omnipresent. It is "a remarkable affirmation against all trivializing of God."[700] There is nothing there that the prophets would have disputed. But they haven't seen a frightening implication.

25 Whereas the first half of the section *regarding the prophets* comprised a sequence of short units in verse that have been strung together, the second half comprises just two longer units that are mostly prose. They again restate Yahweh's critique of the prophets as people who share their own thinking and claim that it represents Yahweh's thinking when it does nothing of the sort. This first subsection focuses on dreams, which have not been mentioned before. Elsewhere in the First Testament (esp. in Genesis and Daniel) and in the New Testament, dreams are a means of God speaking, as they are among other peoples, though none of the prophets refer to dreams except Joel, who is positive (2:28 [3:1]), and Jeremiah, who is unfailingly negative (27:9; 29:8). In the New Testament, Jude 8 is also negative about dreams.[701] Jeremiah's negative attitude gives us no answer to a question about his attitude in principle to dreams. We simply get his dismissal of the only dreams that matter in the context, as is the case if we ask what might be Jeremiah's attitude in theory to temple worship, prayer, or sacrifice. In connection with dreams, in his time the rule laid down in Deut 13:1–5(2–6) would again be significant and suggests a background for his polemic. Yahweh's first objection to the prophets' dreams relates to *my name*. Reporting them with the claim that they report a message from Yahweh means they are "taking Yahweh's name in vain," attaching Yahweh's name to something false, something phony (Exod 20:7). Dreams are the stock-in-trade of prophets who encourage people to follow *the Master*, to follow *deception* (*šeqer*).

26–27 Yahweh asks in exasperation *how long* they will go on in this way—he speaks like Israelites protesting to him about things that affect them (e.g.,

---

698. W. E. Lemke, "The Near and the Distant God: A Study of Jer 23:23–24 in Its Biblical Theological Context," *JBL* 100 (1981): 554.

699. J. Jeremias, "Remembering and Forgetting: 'True' and 'False' Prophecy," in Ben Zvi and Levin, *Remembering and Forgetting*, 52.

700. Holladay, *Commentary on Jeremiah*, 1:640.

701. Cf. Jerome, *Jeremiah*, 177.

Ps 13:1–2[2–3]). As he implied in making the contrast in vv. 13–14, the Judahite prophets didn't see themselves as *thinking to get my people to put my name out of mind*, but it is what they were doing because their understanding of Yahweh was so perverted that it no longer counted as an understanding of Yahweh. Jeremiah's comment again implies the assumption that the criteria for distinguishing true prophets from false prophets are moral and theological. Whether or not they quite realize it, the other prophets serve a different god. They serve the Master. They serve deception.

28–29 Yahweh's second objection to their dreams is that, in the present context at least, there is an absolute contrast between having *a dream* and having *my message*.[702] Admittedly, "the divine word versus the dream factor is only on the surface of it and not the heart of the matter. . . . The conflict is between word and word. . . . These prophets proclaim *šālôm šālôm* (6:14; 8:11; 23:17; cf. 4:10), which is really *ḥālōm ḥālōm*, 'dream dream.'"[703] Only with *my message* can *truth* (*ʾĕmet*) be associated: the observation refers as much to the truthfulness of the message as to the truthfulness of the messenger. Truthfulness is the opposite of the *deception* or *duplicity* to which v. 26 referred. The prophets' dreams are *straw*, lacking in substance or value or protein; Yahweh's message is wheat—substantial and valuable and upbuilding. The relationship between chaff and wheat parallels that between deception and truthfulness, the one empty and worthless, the other valuable.[704] To put it another way, *my message is like fire* or *like a hammer that shatters a crag*. The images are frightening and worryingly unspecific in the way they affirm the destructive act that Yahweh intends to perform by speaking his message through Jeremiah, which contrasts with the wellbeing that the other prophets promise that God's message will bring. God's message is frighteningly sword-like (Heb 4:12). The implication is not that God's message is always fiery and shattering, but in this context, it has that nature and function.[705]

30 Beginning with v. 30, three further verses form a conclusion to this subsection and also an interim conclusion to the material on the prophets as a whole, though they make two new points and may again be of separate origin. In the arrangement of 23:9–40, they form a warning that issues from the indictment in vv. 25–29 while also adding extra indictment to back up the warning. They begin in a fashion that is again worryingly vague: the warning is simply, *Here am I, against the prophets*. But what more worryingly comprehensive statement could Yahweh make? It contrasts with his encouragingly comprehensive "I am/will be with you" (1:8, 19; 15:20). There follows

---

702. Allen, *Jeremiah*, 270–72.
703. R. P. Carroll, *Jeremiah*, OTL, 470, 471.
704. Rashi, in MG.
705. Fretheim, *Jeremiah*, 339.

a critique of the prophets as people *who steal my words, an individual from his fellow.* Are they taking up positive promises uttered by Jeremiah and by other prophets whose authenticity Jeremiah would recognize and quoting those positive promises outside of their more confrontational context? Or are they adapting them, for instance by turning Jeremiah's declaration that Yahweh will break Moab (48:38) into a declaration that he will break Nebuchadrezzar (28:2)?[706] Or are they stealing them in order to hide them? Or is *my words* ironic—does their message consist of deceptive words that Yahweh plants on the lips of the prophets as an act of judgment? Or does it consist of words that are allegedly Yahweh's? Or does *my words* simply mean that they attach their own words to the kind of introductory words that Yahweh and Jeremiah use?

31-32 The second critique would restate that last possibility: they *get their tongue*; they (as it were) take hold of their own tongue and use it to *utter an affirmation* as if their words came from Yahweh. The expression *Yahweh's affirmation* is one that Jeremiah often uses. A third critique then restates points from vv. 21–29 but adds that the prophets' deceptive words are *wild* (*paḥăzût*, a noun) like turbulent water (Gen 49:4) that could carry people away to destruction (see Judg 9:4). To switch to a litotes,[707] their words *are no use to this people at all.* It is Jeremiah's recurrent critique of recourse to the Master and his accoutrements (cf. 2:8, 11; 7:8; 12:13; 16:19).

33 The closing subsection is a tour de force centering on the word *burden* (*maśśā'*). It represents the "culmination of Yhwh's frustration."[708] Yahweh expresses that frustration by taking up the form of speech where a person such as a priest discusses a question to which someone needs an answer (cf. Hag 2:10–14). There is thus an irony in the form of the message as well as in the way it works with that word *burden*. Perhaps we should see Jeremiah as utilizing homonyms, one meaning an utterance (something one lifts up one's voice to utter; cf. Isa 13–23), the other meaning a load that someone lifts up, with both coming from the verb meaning "lift up" or "carry" (*nāśā'*).[709] Jeremiah imagines someone asking him about Yahweh's *burden* in the sense of his utterance or message. (In v. 37, *you*—singular—will be any individual prophet, but initially the obvious assumption is that Yahweh is addressing Jeremiah himself; see the translation note on v. 33.) The implication is not that the message is burdensome in the sense of being bad news and that the

---

706. So Nicholas of Lyra, as quoted in Schroeder, *Jeremiah*, 220.

707. McKane, *Jeremiah*, 1:595.

708. W. J. Wessels, "I've Had It with You: Jeremiah 23:33–40 as Culmination of YHWH's Frustration," *OTE* 25 (2012): 761.

709. So BDB; see further M. J. Boda, "Freeing the Burden of Prophecy: *Maśśā'* and the Legitimacy of Prophecy in Zech 9–14," *Bib* 87 (2006): 338–40.

person might be asking the question seriously or derisively, but either way it's an act of imagination on Jeremiah's part. There is no need to assume that people would actually ask Jeremiah, of all people, such a question, partly because they would know the kind of dusty answer they would likely get (though in desperation, Zedekiah once does so, in Jer 37). Anyway, Jeremiah is instructed to pretend to misunderstand them or to twist their words so as to take them to refer to what is burdensome to Yahweh. The answer is thus that they are the burden in that other sense and that he intends to throw the burden off, to *hurl you away*.

34–37 People are therefore forbidden to talk about Yahweh's burden in the sense of Yahweh's message. The ban is "not just terminological fussiness"[710] but a kind of symbol of the fact that they are the burden. Instead they are to talk in terms of what Yahweh has *averred* or *spoken*. Fancy theological or "spiritual" terms are thus discouraged—or at least this one is. Don't pretend to talk about Yahweh's burden, because the way you talk shows that you don't know what it is. You are not a *person with his message*. Only the person who really lifts up that burden—a person such as Jeremiah—is allowed to use this language.

38–40 If people ignore this instruction, it will give further proof that they don't know what they are talking about and further reason for Yahweh to *forget lifting you up*. The expression is convoluted and ambiguous (see the translation note). It makes use of the link between the noun for burden and the word for "lift up" or "carry," and the image of lifting up or carrying Israel can have more than one meaning. It can suggest carrying Israel as one carries a child or carrying Israel's wrongdoing (i.e., forgiving). Either way, Yahweh's threat is frightening. It will mean he will throw off this burden, *hurl you away*; that verb repeats from v. 33, with which it thus forms a bracket around vv. 33–40. He will hurl them away *from before my face* so that he can no longer see them. And his action will issue in *reviling for all time* (cf. 20:8) and *disgrace for all time, which will not be put out of mind* (he virtually repeats the phrase from 20:11). It thus makes for neat poetic justice, as v. 27 reported that the prophets had got his people to put his name out of mind like their ancestors.

b. Two Lots of Figs (24:1–10)

[1]*Yahweh got me to look: there, two receptacles of figs positioned in front of Yahweh's palace (after Nebuchadrezzar King of Babylon took into exile Jeconiah*[a] *ben Jehoiakim King of Judah, the officials of Judah, craftworker,*[b] *and smith*[c]

---

710. McKane, *Jeremiah*, 1:599.

from Jerusalem and made them come to Babylon),[d] [2]*one receptacle very good figs, like first-ripe figs, one receptacle very dire figs that couldn't be eaten because of being dire.*[e] [3]*Yahweh said to me, What are you looking at, Jeremiah? I said, Figs—the good figs very good figs, the dire ones very dire that couldn't be eaten because of being dire.*[f]

[4]*Yahweh's message came to me.* [5]*Yahweh, the God of Israel, has said this: Like these good figs, so I will have regard to the Judahite exile group that I have sent off from this place to the country of Chaldea,*[g] *for good.* [6]*I will set my eye on them for good and enable them to return to this country. I will build them up and not smash, I will plant them and not pull them up.* [7]*I will give them a mind to acknowledge me, because I am Yahweh. They will be a people for me and I—I will be God for them, because they will turn to me with their entire mind.*[h]

[8]*But like the dire figs that couldn't be eaten because of being dire (because Yahweh has said this), so I will make Zedekiah King of Judah and his officials and the remainder in Jerusalem, the people remaining in this country and the people who are living in the country of Egypt—*[9]*I will make*[i] *them something horrifying,*[j] *something dire, to all the kingdoms of the earth, an object of reviling, an example, a taunt, and a formula of slighting in all the places where I will drive them away.* [10]*I will send off against them sword, hunger, and epidemic until they come to an end from upon the land that I gave to them and to their ancestors.*[k]

a. On this form of the name, see the translation note on 22:24.

b. *B. Sanhedrin* 38a and *Gittin* 88a derive *ḥārāš* from *ḥāraš* II instead of *ḥāraš* I; it would then denote people who are silent in listening to teachers of Torah, which was so important in Babylon.

c. Outside the context of reference to events in 597 (29:2; 2 Kgs 24:14, 16), *masgēr* means "prison," which fits the meaning of the verb *sāgar* ("shut"); cf. LXX "prisoners" (which might plausibly imply "hostages"; see Bright, *Jeremiah*, 193), Vg "imprisoners," and Tg "sentries" or "locksmiths." Blayney (*Jeremiah*, 358) suggests "armorers," craftsmen who make armor to enclose the body. *B. Sanhedrin* 38a and *Gittin* 88a (see previous note) take them to be teachers who can close off discussion. LXX also has "the wealthy," which would be a fair inference from 2 Kgs 24:14–15.

d. The parenthesis interrupts the flow of the sentence and may be a clarifying elaboration based on 2 Kgs 24:15–16.

e. MT has a marker here.

f. MT has a unit marker here.

g. See the translation note on 21:4.

h. MT has a section marker here.

i. *Nātan* in v. 8 never reached its syntactical goal, and this recurrence resumes it, but the repetition makes for paronomasia with the repeated word for fig, *ta'ēnâ*; see J. H. Walton, "Vision Narrative Wordplay and Jeremiah xxiv," *VT* 39 (1989): 508–9.

j. LXX has "something scattering" and lacks "something dire." V. 9a corresponds to 15:4a except for this extra element in MT, but LXX translates it more literally there; McKane (*Jeremiah*, 1:611) sees the influence of the last phrase in v. 8.

k. MT has a unit marker here. With vv. 8–10, cf. 29:17–19.

In the immediate context, 24:1–10 contributes to the way Jer 21–24 combines attentiveness to Judah's leaders (kings and then prophets) and to the community as a whole that is affected by them and cannot evade responsibility for its destiny by appealing to their guilt. Retrospectively, as well as closing off the sequence in Jer 21–24, this final episode in part 2 of the scroll pairs with the scroll's introduction (1:4–19): this chapter, too, is a prose testimony by Jeremiah in which he speaks of seeing something, in which Yahweh engages in a question-and-answer conversation with him about what he is looking at, and in which Yahweh speaks of building, smashing, planting, and pulling up. It links more broadly with Jeremiah's message in preceding chapters: the antithesis of good and dire, the description of the country as *this place*, the reference to *the remainder*, and the phrase *sword, hunger, and epidemic*. Prospectively, it links with the stories about Jeremiah and the other prophets in Jer 27–29, where vv. 8–10 actually reappear in a variant form as 29:17–19; it illumines and is illumined by them. In Judah and in Babylon, prophets such as the ones who are the subject of 23:6–40 encouraged their communities to believe that the tragedy in 597 was now a thing of the past and that Yahweh was with them and would soon restore them. Jeremiah urged both communities to see that this promise involved whistling into the wind. There was worse calamity to come. Jeremiah 24 encapsulates that fact.

On the basis of this message, supporters of Jehoiachin rather than Zedekiah could claim Jeremiah was on their side.[711] Or, after 587, Judahites in Jerusalem and in Babylon could see that Jeremiah's declarations had found fulfillment.[712] Or the Babylonian community could later use this message against the Jerusalem community[713] (though by then the good figs of the Babylonian community would have been joined by the bad figs of the post-597 Judahite community, which would complicate such appeals). Or people who returned from exile could use it against people who never went into exile[714] (with the same complication). Or they could use it against the community in Egypt[715] (whose presence there likely reflects the relationship with Egypt that successive Judahite administrations had cultivated or reflects Egypt's role as a place of refuge). Ezra 1–6 reports tensions between the two communities over who counts as faithful and who does not; Jer 24 could be used as a bargaining chip in that context (see "The Persian Period: A Fourth Horizon?," pp. 17–20).

But in itself, the chapter shares with the preceding chapters of the scroll

---

711. Cf. Allen, *Jeremiah*, 278.
712. Jerome, *Jeremiah*, 149.
713. E.g., C. J. Sharp, "Sites of Conflict," in Kelle, Ames, and Wright, *Interpreting Exile*, 369.
714. R. P. Carroll, *Jeremiah*, OTL, 487.
715. Nicholson, *Preaching to the Exiles*, 110.

the aim of getting Judah to turn to Yahweh and thus to forestall the disaster that otherwise hangs over it—which vv. 8–10 describe with devastating clarity. In this sense, it is hardly true that "the ideology of Jer 24 has no parallels in the book."[716] Actually the word *ideology* obscures rather than clarifies its point. Its message straightforwardly confronts the Jerusalem community among whom Jeremiah lives. Jeremiah indeed speaks here not of salvation or disaster for the entire community but of salvation for one group and disaster for another;[717] he does so because Jer 24 makes sense "as arising out of an *ad hoc* message, directed to a particular situation in which it was necessary to indicate that the exiles were not automatically to be regarded as condemned and the community in Jerusalem and Judah as vindicated."[718] Its stance coheres with that expressed in Ezek 11 at about the same time in the 590s. There, Ezekiel (one of the people taken off to Babylon in 597) describes the community in Judah as people convinced that the community in Babylon are people who have been abandoned by Yahweh, condemns their waywardness, declares that catastrophe is coming upon them, and promises that Yahweh will restore the exiles. Here, Jeremiah issues an equivalent message in Judah itself, expressing the same promise that the exiles will receive a new mind and that *they will be a people for me* and *I will be God for them*. Both chapters point to three audiences for their message: Jeremiah, the Jerusalem community, and the exile community,[719] but Ezekiel speaks to the people in Babylon, Jeremiah to the people in Judah.

> vv. 1–3   What Yahweh enabled Jeremiah to see
> > vv. 1–2   A vision (incorporating a note on the date)
> > v. 3   A question and answer
> vv. 4–10   What Yahweh said to Jeremiah
> > vv. 4–7   A promise about the exile group
> > vv. 8–10   A threat about the Jerusalem community

1a While the chapter will fit with what has preceded, it begins with a new image, and it has a distinctive focus. As was the case in 1:11–14, from Jeremiah's opening words one would not be able to tell whether Yahweh draws his attention to something and then enables him to look at it in a new way

716. C. M. Maier, "The Nature of Deutero-Jeremianic Texts," in Najman and Schmid, *Jeremiah's Scriptures*, 121; she then dates it in the Persian period.

717. W. H. Schmidt, *Jeremia*, 2:59.

718. Ackroyd, *Exile and Restoration*, 55. While the chapter may have been expanded (see the translation notes on vv. 1, 9 and, e.g., Holladay, *Commentary on Jeremiah*, 1:654–55), possible expansions do not suggest specific links with any of those later contexts or significances.

719. Volz, *Jeremia*, 249.

or whether he enables him to see something in his mind's eye. Figs are an important food in Israel, a chief source of sweetness (see the translation note and commentary on 11:5). Are they sitting in baskets for sale, having been brought in by a farmer? But it would then be odd that they are *in front of Yahweh's palace*, the temple (see the commentary on 7:4). Are they in pans, ready for turning into syrup? (*Dôd*, the word for *receptacle*, more often means a cooking pan.) Have they been brought to the temple as an offering of firstfruits? Is that why Yahweh is looking at them and evaluating them?[720]

1b A devastating moment has recently passed, the Babylonian conquest of Jerusalem in 597 and the forced migration of all the leadership that the Babylonians could lay their hands on. Second Kings 24:10–16 gives a more extensive list, while Jer 27–29 and Ezekiel indicate that the group included priests and prophets, and some verses from Jer 23 reappear in Jer 29. The Jeremiah scroll does not talk about Nebuchadrezzar's siege and capture of Jerusalem in 597, which led to the plundering of the temple, the deportation of its leadership, and the replacement of Jehoiachin by Zedekiah. They are described in 2 Kgs 24:10–17 and in the Babylonian Chronicle, the Babylonian administration's official record of events:

11. The seventh year: In the month Kislev, the king of Akkad mustered his army and marched to Hattu.
12. He encamped against the city of Judah and on the second day of the month Adar he captured the city (and) seized its king.
13. A king of his own choice he appointed in the city, (and) taking the vast tribute he brought it into Babylon.[721]

Texts that are thought to relate to King Esarhaddon's Egyptian campaign some decades earlier have lists of skilled workers transported to Assyria, including physicians, diviners, goldsmiths, cabinet-makers, charioteers, drivers, bowmen, shield-bearers, veterinarians, singers, bakers, brewers, fishermen, cartwrights, shipwrights, and blacksmiths.[722] One can see that an equivalent transportation from Jerusalem would have devastating implications for the life of the city. Here, the Jeremiah scroll first mentions the *king* and his *officials*. Then there are *craftworker* and *smith*; they are the kind of people who could be useful in repairing the city after its siege and

720. Mayer, *Commentary*, 414.
721. A. K. Grayson, *Assyrian and Babylonian Chronicles* (Locust Valley, NY: Augustin, 1975), 102; cf. *ANET*, 594. The Babylonians referred to their empire as Akkad (Gen 10:10) after the name of an ancient capital city.
722. See *ANET*, 293.

fitting it out for further acts of rebellion, so it was smart to remove them. The disaster was a fulfillment of warnings Jeremiah has continually issued, but hardly anyone believed him. Many of the reactions expressed in Lamentations, presumably from a decade later, would already be reactions at this first fall of the city:

> Listen, please, all you peoples,
>   see my pain.
> My girls and my young men
>   went into captivity. (Lam 1:18)

> He brought right to the earth, made ordinary,
>   the kingdom and its officials. (Lam 2:2)

> The breath of our lungs, Yahweh's anointed,
>   was captured in their traps,
> The one of whom we had said, "In his shade
>   we will live among the nations." (Lam 4:20)[723]

2-3 *First-ripe figs* are ones that come to fruition in spring and are thus a special, succulent delight after the dreariness of winter (Hos 9:10; Mic 7:1). These figs are as good as those (Jeremiah compares them with first-ripe ones—he doesn't say they *are* first-ripe ones). *Very dire figs that couldn't be eaten* doesn't mean they are rotten but rather that they are sour or tough. They lie at the other end of the culinary spectrum from the good figs; no other book in the Bible contrasts *very good* and *very dire* as these verses do.[724] The oddness of a receptacle full of bad figs in front of the temple encourages the impression that Jeremiah refers to a seeing that happened in a vision. As was the case with the watcher cane and the fanned pot (1:11, 13), it would not be obvious what the figs represented nor what was signified by the difference between the quality of the two lots of figs. The question and answer (v. 3) implicitly underlines that point by its unrevealing nature. One would initially assume that *good* and *dire* referred to their inherent quality, but the chapter will eventually suggest that "good" signifies "not their characteristics but their destiny."[725] It refers to a good fate as opposed to a dire fate.[726]

4 Jeremiah's testimony, *Yahweh's message came to me*, confirms that the

---

723. The language reflects convictions attached to Yahweh's commitment to the line of David. In 597, their embodiment was Jeconiah/Jehoiachin; in 587 it will be Zedekiah.

724. Fischer, *Jeremia*, 1:715.

725. Rudolph, *Jeremia*, 158; cf. Reventlow, *Liturgie*, 87–94.

726. Allen, *Jeremiah*, 276.

significance of the figs was not self-evident to him; first he knew that Yahweh was drawing his attention to the figs or presenting the image of figs to his mind's eye, then Yahweh needed to reveal what they signified. He also here implies that this revelation from Yahweh is not just for him: like everything else in the scroll, it is a message for the community.

5–6 It turns out that the figs stand for the Jerusalem community and the exile community. The new focus in Jer 24 is the Judahites' enforced division into people who were taken off to Babylon in 597 and people who were able to stay behind in Jerusalem. It is easy to imagine that those who were able to stay behind could assume that those who were taken off were not merely the unlucky ones but also the ones who deserved exile. They were the ones with no future; their fate was permanent. Applied to them, the image of bad figs could confirm that assessment. Without making any comment on the first possibility, characteristically Yahweh turns the second assumption upside-down, while also reversing a threat like the one in Amos 9:4.[727] Deuteronomy 28:11 promises that the community that lives in obedience to Yahweh will find that Yahweh singles it out for good. Yahweh here makes the surprising declaration about the exiles that they will actually be treated like good figs: *I will set my eye on them for good*. He will make it possible for them to return to Judah and he will fulfill for them the declaration that he made about the significance of Jeremiah's work way back at his commissioning (1:10). There has been smashing and pulling up, but "exile does not seal its victims' fate."[728] *I will build them up and not smash, I will plant them and not pull up.* Neither his words at the time of that commission nor these words are set in relation to what they deserve—to whether they are in themselves bad figs. They simply express his intention.

7 Another surprise follows, except that it is not really a surprise. It would be remarkable if Yahweh had implied that the exiles were in themselves good guys. He has consistently inspired Jeremiah to castigate the entire community of which they were part. He still maintains that assessment. But, by implication, there is no point simply restoring them to Judah so that they can carry on living the way they did before. Yahweh declares the intention to transform them in their relationship with him, a transformation that they need no more and no less than the Jerusalem community. He will treat them as nice figs even though there is no indication that they are better than the nasty figs. It will be an expression of his setting his eye on them for good. Jeremiah has talked much about the community's acknowledgment of Yahweh, but regularly in the negative (e.g., 2:8; 4:22; 9:3[2]). He has talked much about their mind, again in negative terms

727. Schart, "Book of Jeremiah," *RevExp* 101 (2004): 280.
728. Stulman, *Jeremiah*, 220.

(e.g., 3:10, 17; 5:21, 23). He has recalled how Yahweh set up an arrangement whereby he would become God for them and they would become a people for him, but it didn't work (7:23; 11:4). He has urged his people to circumcise their minds (4:4) but also expressed doubt about their capacity to do good (13:23).[729] Now he will do something about it. And they will *turn to me with their entire mind*. His declarations leave unclear the relationship between his action and their action, between his giving them a new mind and their turning with that mind. How does God go about changing the nature of someone's mind in a way that will have this result? Is he like a neurosurgeon performing an operation on someone's brain so that their behavior changes? If Jeremiah implies an answer to this question, it lies in the movement from v. 6 to v. 7. When Yahweh sets his eye on the (undeserving) exiles for good, enables them to return to Judah, builds them up, and plants them, it will be an astonishing expression of his generosity and commitment such as will bring about the acknowledgment and turning of which he speaks. Jeremiah 31:31–34 has similar implications. In Deut 30:1–10, too, Moses speaks of Israel turning to Yahweh in exile, of Yahweh taking them home, and of Yahweh transforming their attitudes. That order contrasts with the order in Jeremiah, though Moses is no more unequivocal about the relationship between cause and effect or about the order of events than Jeremiah (English translations are inclined to help things along by including words such as "then"). Both Moses and Jeremiah speak of a transformation by Yahweh, a turning by Israel, and a return from exile, but between them they leave unexplained the mysterious relationship between these three.[730] If "the future belongs to the exilic community that refuses both *assimilation* into Babylonian definitions of reality and *despair* about the prospect of return,"[731] Yahweh will need to take action to bring that about, and so will they. In the context of Jeremiah's confrontation of the community that remains in Jerusalem, the promise relates to the 597 exiles whom they despise; in due course it will become a promise for "all Israel's clans," even for Ephraim as well as Judah (30:22; 31:1, 33–34; 32:38–40).

8 One can imagine another possible aspect to the Jerusalem community's stance in relation to the exiles. Notwithstanding the horror of what happened in 597, they might be breathing a sigh of relief that Yahweh has implemented the wrathful threats that they had not believed. At least it was now over. Not

---

729. Brueggemann, *Jeremiah 1–25*, 210.

730. Cf. G. E. Gerbrandt, *Deuteronomy*, Believers Church Bible Commentary (Harrisonburg, VA: Herald, 2015), 475–78.

731. W. Brueggemann, "A Second Reading of Jeremiah after the Dismantling," *Ex auditu* 1 (1985): 164.

so, says Jeremiah. Previous chapters of the scroll have talked about the *remainder* that would be left after the coming catastrophe, and not necessarily in positive terms (6:9; 8:3; 15:9; but contrast 23:3). The beginning of Jer 21–24 warned specifically that Yahweh would give over to Nebuchadrezzar the people *remaining* after 597, including Zedekiah (21:7). *Remaining* and *remainder* or remnant (as it is traditionally translated) are not usually positive ideas in Jeremiah. The people *living in the country of Egypt* will be people who had moved to Egypt previously or who took refuge there in anticipation of the 597 siege. Jeremiah 44:1 suggests that there was quite a Judahite diaspora there before 587, and this comment provides background to the account in Jer 42–44 of more people taking refuge there (cf. also 26:21). But recourse to Egypt for help or refuge is always questionable.[732] Politically, the background in this verse is the inclination to continue assertions of independence of the kind that the scroll will later describe.[733]

9–10 Yahweh now particularly applies to the remaining community in Jerusalem his warnings about their being turned into *something horrifying* (15:4) or *dire* (e.g., 1:14; 4:6; 6:1) or an object of *reviling* (23:40). The potential of those warnings has not been exhausted by the events of 597. To make it worse, Yahweh adds threats that appear in Deut 28:37: the community is destined to be an *example* of what can happen to a people, a *taunt* that might be used, a means of *slighting* a people (cf. Deut 28:45): "You look as bad as Jerusalem after it was destroyed!" People should not think that their compatriots have been driven off but that they themselves have escaped: Yahweh will bring about that fate *in all the places where I will drive them* (Deut 28:37 speaks similarly of "all the peoples where Yahweh will propel them"). They are to be the victims of the threats in Deuteronomy attached to people who ignore Yahweh's standards. They are going to *come to an end*.[734] To say that the community is an embodiment of slighting is virtually to curse it (cf. the references to curses in Deut 28). And if this curse were relayed to the Babylonian community, it could be an encouragement to it.[735] But Jeremiah is in Jerusalem, and it is the Jerusalemites who will hear about the curse. Why, then, is there a promise of restoration for the exiles and not for them? Why

732. Cf. Calvin, *Jeremiah*, 3:246.

733. Katho ("To Know and Not to Know," 299–307) reads the chapter against the background of equivalent dynamics in the Congo.

734. If the prophetic scroll reflects the Torah rather than vice versa and if Deut 28 reached its final form sometime after 587, then Jer 24 did too. But maybe Yahweh's words come from the 590s (in which this message is set) and reflect an earlier version of what appears in Deut 28. On these questions, see, e.g., Mastnjak, *Deuteronomy*, 93–133.

735. See J. S. Anderson, "The Metonymical Curse as Propaganda in the Book of Jeremiah," *BBR* 8 (1998): 1–13.

are the bad figs a picture of their future while the good figs portray the exiles' future? Why does Yahweh take sides? There is no basis for distinguishing between what each community deserves.[736] The point of the message is to get home to the Jerusalemites the inevitability of their paying the price for their wrongdoing if they continue in it, though also to hint at the basis for hope.[737] It would be sensible to turn now, but the declarations about the Babylonian community will open up possibilities for the Jerusalemites after 587. They can ask whether such declarations apply to them too.

736. R. J. R. Plant, *Good Figs, Bad Figs: Judicial Differentiation in the Book of Jeremiah,* LHBOTS 483 (London: T&T Clark, 2008), 87–89.

737. W. J. Wessels, "Jeremiah 24:1–10 as a Pronouncement of Hope," *OTE* 4 (1991): 397–407.

AN INTERIM CONCLUSION (25:1–38 [LXX 25:1–13; 32:1–24])

Jeremiah 25 brings the first half of the Jeremiah scroll to a climax and conclusion. The opening of the chapter dates it in 604, twenty-three years after Jeremiah's commission. As the chapter marks the halfway point in the Jeremiah scroll, then, it also more or less marks the midpoint in Jeremiah's activity, which extended from the mid-620s through to the mid-580s. Although there were seventeen years to pass until the final fall of Jerusalem, 604 saw the burning of Jeremiah's first, cumulative scroll (Jer 36) and thus saw Judah's reaching what will turn out to be the point of no return. In addition, Jer 25 marks the transition from chapters dominated by messages in poetry to chapters dominated by stories. The chapter is a "hinge" in the scroll,[1] "the central axis around which the entire book revolves."[2] Further, so far the scroll has been dominated by messages warning of disaster, whereas from now on there will be more promises of restoration and renewal.[3] The first half included only understated notes declaring that Yahweh will not bring a total end to Judah's story (e.g., 4:27; 5:10, 18) and in due course some brief promises (16:14–15; 23:1–8; 24:4–7). One should not exaggerate the nature of the transition: a sequence of worrisome stories will come next (Jer 26–29), but they will be followed by chapters of promises (Jer 30–33), then another, longer sequence of worrisome stories (Jer 34–44) will be followed by a longer set of chapters that are better news for Judah (Jer 45–51) until the scroll closes with a final horrifying story but also a note of hope (Jer 52).

Jeremiah 25 marks the most spectacular divergence between MT and LXX of Jeremiah. After vv. 1–14 in MT, there appear in LXX six chapters declaring how Yahweh will bring calamity on other nations—chapters that appear as Jer 46–51 in MT. In addition, differences between the detailed text of MT and LXX are especially noticeable in Jer 25—usually by LXX's lacking phrases that appear in MT. So MT has expanded the text underlying LXX, or LXX has abbreviated MT's text, or both are independent recensions of an earlier version of the chapter.[4] Further, the three sections of the chapter in the MT

1. M. Kessler, "Jeremiah 25,1–19: Text and Context: A Synchronic Study," *ZAW* 109 (1997): 46; "The Function of Chapters 25 and 50–51 in the Book of Jeremiah," in Diamond, K. M. O'Connor, and Stulman, *Troubling Jeremiah*, 66.

2. K. A. D. Smelik, "An Approach to the Book of Jeremiah," in Kessler, *Reading Jeremiah*, 9; cf. M. Kessler, "The Scaffolding of the Book of Jeremiah," in Kessler, *Reading Jeremiah*, 57–66; R. E. Clements, "Jeremiah's Message of Hope," in Kessler, *Reading Jeremiah*, 145; also R. D. Patterson, "Bookends, Hinges, and Hooks," 109–31.

3. Wright, *Jeremiah*, 271.

4. See, e.g., L. Laberge, "Jérémie 25,1–14: Dieu et Juda ou Jérémie et tous les peuples," *Science et Esprit* 36 (1984): 45–66; G. Fischer, "Jer 25 und die Fremdvolkersprüche," *Bib* 72 (1991): 474–99; J. W. Watts, "Text and Redaction in Jeremiah's Oracles Against the Nations,"

version look as if they are messages of separate origin that the scroll's curators have brought together. Each of them declares that calamity is coming for
Jerusalem and for other peoples, but they do so in three different ways.

vv. 1–14	A climactic warning in prose about coming disaster, in which Jeremiah makes a critical moment the occasion to review his prophesying over twenty-three years; Judah is especially in focus, but other nations appear in the closing promise of reversal for Babylon
vv. 15–29	Another prose expression of these declarations of intent to bring calamity on Jerusalem, Babylon, and also other nations in due course, using the image of a chalice; the opening *because* makes a link between two messages that were separate in origin
vv. 30–38	A compilation of four declarations in poetry, of separate origin, that again declare the intention to bring calamity but now put more (perhaps exclusive) focus on the other nations rather than on Judah

A. A CLIMACTIC WARNING (25:1-14)

[1]*The word that came to Jeremiah about the entire people of Judah in the fourth
year of Jehoiakim ben Josiah King of Judah (i.e., the first year of Nebuchadrezzar
King of Babylon),*[a] [2]*which Jeremiah the prophet spoke*[b] *to the entire people of
Judah and toward all the people who lived in Jerusalem.*

[3]*Since the thirteenth year of Josiah ben Amon King of Judah, and until this
day, yes, twenty-three years, Yahweh's word has come to me. I've spoken to you,
speaking assiduously,*[c] *but you haven't listened.* [4]*Yahweh*[d] *would send to you all
his servants the prophets, sending assiduously,*[e] *and you haven't listened, you
haven't bent your ear to listen:* [5]*Please turn, each person, from his dire path and
from the dire nature of your practices, and you will live*[f] *on the land that Yahweh
gave to you and to your ancestors from all time and to all time.* [6]*Do not go after
other gods, to serve them and bow down to them, and do not irk me*[g] *with the
things your hands have made, and I will not act direly to you.* [7]*But you haven't*

CBQ 54 (1991): 432–47; A. Aejmelaeus, "Jeremiah at the Turning-Point of History: The
Function of Jer. xxv 1–14 in the Book of Jeremiah," *VT* 52 (2002): 459–82; S. Gesundheit,
"The Question of LXX Jeremiah as a Tool for Literary-Critical Analysis," *VT* 62 (2012):
29–57; E. Silver, "Framing the Oracle of a Seventy-Year Servitude: Early Contestation of
the Jeremian Legacy in the Vorlage of the LXX of Jeremiah 25:1-7," *CBQ* 78 (2016): 648–65.

listened to me (Yahweh's affirmation), so that you've irked me with the things your hands have made, with dire results for you.[h]

[8]*Therefore Yahweh of Armies has said this: Since you haven't listened to*[i] *my words,* [9]*here am I, sending and getting all the kin groups*[j] *from the north (Yahweh's affirmation), and for*[k] *Nebuchadrezzar King of Babylon, my servant, and having them come against this country and against the people who live in it—and against all these nations around.*

I will devote[l] *them and make them into a desolation, a thing to whistle at, wastes*[m] *for all time.* [10]*I will wipe out from them the sound of rejoicing and the sound of joy, the sound of groom and the sound of bride, the sound of millstones*[n] *and the light of lamp.*[o] [11]*This entire country will become a waste and desolation.*

These nations will serve the king of Babylon for seventy years. [12]*But at the fulfillment of the seventy years, I will attend to the king of Babylon and to that nation (Yahweh's affirmation) regarding their waywardness, and to the country of Chaldea,*[p] *and I will make it into a desolation for all time.* [13]*I will cause to come on that country all the words that I have spoken against it, everything that is written in this document, which Jeremiah prophesied against all the nations.* [14]*Because they have put them into serfdom, those people,*[q] *too—many nations and big kings.*[r] *I will recompense them in accordance with their action and what their hands have made.*[s]

a. LXX lacks the synchronism with Nebuchadrezzar and Babylon, along with the similar references in vv. 9, 11, 12; it also lacks *Jeremiah the prophet* in v. 2, and in v. 3 *Yahweh's word has come to me* and *but you haven't listened.*

b. On the *'ăšer* clause, see the translation note on 1:2.

c. See the translation note and comment on 7:13; the expression comes again in the next verse.

d. LXX has "I" verbs in vv. 4–5 (and "my" for *his*; it also lacks *to listen*), which leads more smoothly into v. 6.

e. For *'aškēm*, the Cairo Codex of the Prophets has the expected infinitive *haškēm.*

f. More literally, "turn . . . and live"; the paronomasia *šûbû . . . ûšəbû* suggests the link between the two verbs (Volz, *Jeremia*, 253).

g. The *yiqtol* verb continues the imperative. The message makes an unannounced transition to Yahweh speaking; such transitions are not unusual in Jeremiah.

h. MT has a marker here. LXX lacks *(Yahweh's affirmation)* and the rest of the verse.

i. LXX has "believed."

j. LXX has "a kin group."

k. Taking *'el* here as the sign of the accusative would make the sentence smoother; see M. I. Gruber, "'*el* = '*et*: An Unrecognized Lexeme in Biblical Hebrew," in *Marbeh Ḥokmah: Studies in the Bible and the Ancient Near East in Loving Memory of Victor Avigdor Hurowitz*, ed. S. Yona (Winona Lake, IN: Eisenbrauns, 2015), 269–81.

l. LXX, Vg, Tg have words suggesting "eliminate"; Aq, Sym *anathematizō* better corresponds to *ḥāram* (hiphil). But see the commentary.

m. For *ûlǝḥorbôt*, LXX "and for disgrace" implies *ûlǝḥerpat*. MT's plural (compare English "ruins") is intensive, suggesting "total waste" (Lundbom, *Jeremiah 21–36*, 248).

n. LXX "the fragrance of perfume" perhaps reflects confusion between Greek *murou* (perfume) and *mulou* (mill stone) (R. P. Carroll, *Jeremiah*, OTL, 492).

o. Repointing *'ôr nēr* as *'ûr nir* ("tilled land") makes a link with what follows; see D. Grossberg, "Pivotal Polysemy in Jeremiah xxv 10–11a," *VT* 36 (1986): 481–85.

p. See the translation note on 21:4.

q. *Hēmmâ* adds emphasis to the suffix on *bām* (GKC 135g).

r. Vg, Aq, Theod "they [have] served" gives *'ābad* its usual meaning (cf. v. 11); the verb's subject would then be the *many nations and big kings*, and the object would be the Chaldeans. But Tg has "made them serve," the regular meaning of *'ābad bǝ* (see 22:13 and the translation note there). The subject is then the Chaldeans, and *many nations and big kings* qualifies *those people*. Rashi (in MG) takes the *qatal* verb as an anticipatory *qatal* (see the introduction to 13:18–22, pp. 354–55), indicating that the nations will turn the Chaldeans into serfs. With the same result, Theod has "will serve": i.e., the Chaldeans will serve the many nations.

s. MT has a marker here. LXX lacks v. 14, a difference related to the deviation between MT and LXX over the location of the messages about different nations, which LXX includes here.

The section opens by noting the significance of this year in Judah's history and in international politics. It made this moment one for Jeremiah to issue an urgent challenge to his people to think about how Yahweh has been speaking to them over the past two decades and about their response and to offer a chilling interpretation of current events. The new Babylonian king is Yahweh's servant, through whom he is going to fulfill his intention to take action against Judah (though he is *only* Yahweh's servant, and his time will come).

vv. 1–2	Introduction
vv. 3–7	The message, part one: the indictment
v. 3	Review: Jeremiah's prophesying and people's response
vv. 4–6	Review: the prophets' prophesying and people's response
v. 7	Resumptive review: people's response to Yahweh
vv. 8–11a	The message, part two: the consequence
vv. 8–9a	Yahweh's summons to Nebuchadrezzar
vv. 9b–11a	Yahweh's action against Judah
vv. 11b–14	The message, part three: the limitation—Babylon's time will come

Much of the review recycles expressions that the scroll has made familiar:

- Verses 4, 8 repeat from 7:13, 25–26.
- Verse 5 repeats from 7:7; 16:21; 18:11.
- Verses 6–7 repeat from 1:16; 7:6, 19; 13:10.
- Verses 9, 11 repeat from 1:15; 7:34; 16:16; 18:16.
- Verse 10 repeats from 1:10; 7:34; 16:9.

The summary sometimes repeats precise phrases, sometimes takes up words and formulates the statement slightly differently. Either way, the effect is indeed to recapitulate Jeremiah's message over these decades in brief fashion.

1–2 The opening, *the word that came to Jeremiah*, compares with the introductions in 7:1; 11:1; 14:1; 18:1; 21:1, and the continuation *about the entire people of Judah* compares in particular with 21:1 in adapting the opening phrase so that it becomes a more dedicated introduction to Jer 25. The reference to *the entire people* (cf. 19:14) again indicates that everybody needs to listen to the message—not just people such as kings and prophets who were the direct focus in Jer 21–24. The reference to Judah expands on that point, though the addition of *all the people who lived in Jerusalem* is a reminder that they will bear the brunt of the calamity. More significant is the date, *the fourth year of Jehoiakim* as king of Judah, which is also *the first year of Nebuchadrezzar* as king of Babylon, the year 604. This significant date will recur in 36:1; 45:1; 46:2. Though "seemingly innocuous," it "signals the arrival of Nebuchadrezzar's reign of terror and the end of Judah's preexilic world."[5] Daniel 1:1 refers to Jehoiakim's third year; differences between such dates are a nightmare to understand—they issue in part from differences in the way Judah and other peoples calculated years.[6] In 605, Nebuchadrezzar had defeated the combined Assyrian and Egyptian forces at the Battle of Carchemish, which decisively established Babylon as a superpower.[7] On the subsequent abdication and death of his father Nabopolassar, Nebuchadrezzar became king. While the audience might not be expected to know about Carchemish, they would be able to work out the significance of this year marking the accession of the king who (politically and militarily speaking) will determine their fate. Whereas Assyria's decline had left Judah in control of its own affairs, Judah will now again become a tribute state. Politically, one could say that the interaction between Babylonian desire to control the Levant and Judahite desire

---

5. Stulman, *Jeremiah*, 226. See further J. Hill, "The Construction of Time in Jeremiah 25 (MT)," in Diamond, K. M. O'Connor, and Stulman, *Troubling Jeremiah*, 146–60.
6. See, e.g., Allen, *Jeremiah*, 284–85.
7. See, e.g., Lipschits, *Fall and Rise of Jerusalem*, 11–35.

to maintain its independence generates a clash of interests and a conflict that Judah can only lose. Theologically, one could say that Josiah's reformation had not brought about a sufficiently profound change in Judah's religious commitment and community life to forestall the necessity of Yahweh taking action against it, and Babylon proves to be Yahweh's means of taking the action. Jeremiah 20:4-6 had made that fact explicit for the first time, though we don't know whether chronologically the Pashhur clash preceded or followed 604. Either way, here for the first time Babylon is named as the northern enemy that was mentioned but not identified in passages such as 1:14 and 13:20. So 605 and 604 are turning points; hence also the action described in Jer 36. In effect, the message related here summarizes the contents of the scroll to which Jer 36 refers (and thus the contents of Jer 2-6, if we can see those chapters as going back to that scroll). The relationship between Jer 25 and 36 (message and story) thus compares with the relationship between Jer 7 and 26. The link with Jer 36 also suggests another significance in the reference to *the entire people of Judah* and *the people who lived in Jerusalem*. According to 36:5, Jeremiah cannot personally deliver the message, and it is Baruch who does so. Jeremiah 36 focuses on Baruch's delivering it to the king and his staff but also, and first, describes his reading it to the entire people of Jerusalem and the people who have come from the Judahite towns on a fast day.

3-7 The message will summarize Jeremiah's preaching over more than two decades (see 1:2), as is suggested by its recycling expressions from earlier chapters (see the list in the introduction to vv. 1-14 and the commentary on them). The summary here is that the message has been an exhortation to *please turn, each person, from his dire path*. There have not actually been a huge number of exhortations in the scroll (but see esp. Jer 3). Prophets commonly presuppose that Yahweh's message needs no explicit bidding to "turn" in order to indicate that Yahweh's statements of intent are not merely information about the future but warnings to which people need to respond. There is thus no tension between "denouncing the corruption (moral, social, religious) of the city and its people" and being "a preacher of repentance" who "announced the possibility of turning rather than the inevitability of destruction."[8] But people have not turned in response to the prophet. "His work had been useless."[9] Yahweh has been long tempered for many years,[10] and Jeremiah's *speaking assiduously* has matched Yahweh's *sending assiduously* (cf. 7:25). Only here is Jeremiah the subject of this expression. "Twenty-three years of truth-telling: nothing accomplished. . . . Still the 'system' remains

---

8. As R. P. Carroll implies in *Jeremiah*, OTL, 491.

9. Calvin, *Jeremiah*, 3:257.

10. Theodoret, *Ermeneia*, PG 81:636.

intact." But Jeremiah did not give up; and "what nobler life than one passed in heroic vindication of truth."[11]

8–9a Yahweh explicitly replaces Jeremiah as speaker, giving greater authority to what now follows.[12] A revolutionary new statement comes in the description of *Nebuchadrezzar King of Babylon* (cf. 21:2; 22:25) as *my servant*; Yahweh's speech "teems with robust and even shocking images."[13] "The devil and all the ungodly serve God."[14] The expression *my servant* is familiar enough. It can refer, among others, to Abraham, Moses, and Isaiah (e.g., Gen 26:24; Num 12:7; Isa 20:3) and especially to David (e.g., 2 Sam 3:18; 7:5, 8; 1 Kgs 11:13; 14:8; 2 Kgs 19:34; 20:6; Ps 89:4[3], 21[20]). But the current Davidic king has become rebel rather than servant, and Nebuchadrezzar's becoming king and becoming Yahweh's servant is when Davidides such as Jehoiakim cease to be king or Yahweh's servant.[15] The designation reflects more than Jehoiakim's failure. The people as a whole have resisted one sending and will now be on the receiving end of another sending. They have resisted one set of servants; they will not be able to resist this servant.[16] It is thus a reproach to them to call Nebuchadrezzar Yahweh's servant; it reflects the way they have ignored God's "real" servants.[17] So the person who is serving Yahweh now, without being aware of it, is the imperial authority. In general terms, the idea is not novel; Isa 10:7–32 spoke analogously about the Assyrian king, and Isa 44:24–45:7 will speak analogously about the Persian king who will bring some fulfillment of this chapter's declarations concerning the fall

11. Berrigan, *Jeremiah*, 103, 108.

12. O'Connor, "Jeremiah," 509.

13. Lundbom, *Jeremiah 21–36*, 315.

14. Calvin, *Jeremiah*, 3:270.

15. K. Schmid, "Nebukadnezars Antritt der Weltherrschaft und der Abbruch der Davidsdynastie: Innerbiblische Schriftauslegung und universalgeschichtliche Konstruktion im Jeremiabuch," in *Der Textualisierung der Religion*, ed. J. Schaper, FAT 62 (Tübingen: Mohr Siebeck, 2009), 150–66; cf. "Nebuchadnezzar and the End of the Davidic Dynasty: History and Historical Construction in the Book of Jeremiah," *Proceedings of the Irish Biblical Association* 36–37 (2013–14): 1–16; also "Nebuchadnezzar, the End of Davidic Rule, and the Exile in the Book of Jeremiah," in *The Prophets Speak on Forced Migration*, ed. M. J. Boda et al., AIIL 21 (Atlanta: Society of Biblical Literature, 2015), 63–76; Brueggemann, "Jeremiah," 141. If the description issued from a textual error (W. E. Lemke, "'Nebuchadrezzar My Servant,'" *CBQ* 28 [1966], 45–50), it was an error of great moment. The designation comes only in MT; it might suggest a more positive attitude to Babylon among the "1.5 generation" of Judahite exiles (J. Ahn, *Exile as Forced Migrations: A Sociological, Literary, and Theological Approach on the Displacement and Resettlement of the Southern Kingdom of Judah*, BZAW 417 [Berlin: de Gruyter, 2010], 113).

16. Wright, *Jeremiah*, 264.

17. Calvin, *Jeremiah*, 3:266.

of Babylon. But it is new terminology. It does not imply a relationship that is "intimate" and not just "instrumental";[18] Yahweh does not talk to Nebuchadrezzar, and Nebuchadrezzar does not talk to Yahweh. Yahweh is just using Nebuchadrezzar. But there are other implications in the description. It implies that Judah should not worry too much about Nebuchadrezzar. He is simply Yahweh's servant.[19] And Jeremiah will go on to affirm that his service has a limited duration. He is not the end of the story. Jacob is not to be afraid because it can still be called *my servant* (30:10; 46:27, 28) and Yahweh has not given up on the idea of David being *my servant*;[20] he will not break his pledge with David *my servant* (33:21, 22, 26). Yet further, one might put the stress on the *my* in *my servant*. Nebuchadrezzar thought he was the servant of Nabu, as the one who gave him "the just scepter to provide for all the inhabited world."[21] He didn't realize whose servant he really was. A further disturbing note is the observation that in this connection, Judah's waywardness will have negative implications for *all these nations around*—the *these* is anticipatory of the list to come later in the chapter.[22] It is perhaps not surprising; it parallels the way Yahweh's bringing trouble on Judah affects not only the leaders whom one might see as directly responsible for its waywardness but also the people as a whole, children as much as grown-ups. Yahweh's action commonly involves collateral damage, through humanity's being bound up in the web of life together. While politically the nations could seem just the unlucky victims of "the spillage of the invasion into adjacent states,"[23] theologically the implication is that the failure of the people of God to respond to God can have implications for other people.

9b A further revolutionary statement comes in Yahweh's declaration of intent to *devote them*. What follows indicates that *them* refers to *this country* and *the people who live in it*; Jeremiah will come back to the fate of the *nations* in v. 12. The verb (*ḥāram*) denotes giving something over to Yahweh (e.g., a piece of land) in unqualified and irreversible fashion (e.g., Lev 27:29). It most commonly refers to a devoting that means killing; it especially applies to devoting the proceeds of war. Whether or not the verb's sacral connota-

---

18. So J. Hill, *Friend or Foe? The Figure of Babylon in the Book of Jeremiah MT*, BibInt 40 (Leiden: Brill, 1999), 206.

19. K. A. D. Smelik, "My Servant Nebuchadnezzar," *VT* 64 (2014): 109–34.

20. R. de Hoop, "Perspective after the Exile: The King, 'bdy, 'My Servant' In Jeremiah—Some Reflections on MT and LXX in Exile," in *Exile and Suffering: A Selection of Papers Read at the 50th Anniversary Meeting of the Old Testament Society of South Africa OTWSA/OTSSA, Pretoria August 2007*, ed. B. Becking and D. Human, OTS 50 (Leiden: Brill, 2009), 105–21.

21. R. Da Riva, *The Twin Inscriptions of Nebuchadnezzar at Brisa* (Vienna: Institut für Orientalistik, 2012), 55.

22. Rudolph, *Jeremia*, 160.

23. Allen, *Jeremiah*, 286.

tion gets lost in such contexts (see the translation note), Yahweh is turning on its head the instruction he once gave to Israel about its treatment of the Canaanites, portraying for Judah "a fantastic landscape of horror inspiring ruin and devastation."[24]

10–11a Jeremiah includes a fourth telling and unprecedented phrase. *The sound of rejoicing and the sound of joy, the sound of groom and the sound of bride* (7:34; 16:9) are here complemented by *the sound of millstones and the light of lamp* (cf. Rev 18:22–23). The disaster will terminate not merely the occasional community rejoicing that accompanies a wedding but the entirety of community life. Milling flour is the first task of the day, and it is a noisy business; the lighting of a lamp marks the onset of evening. The cessation of both suggests gloom.[25] If there is no milling and no light, there is no food, no eating, and no life.

11b–12 *These nations* are then the *nations around* to whom v. 9a referred. Whereas their desolation may last forever (v. 9b; cf. 15:14; 17:4—but one should allow for hyperbole) a limit is set to Babylon's suzerainty. Its time will come. Yahweh's promise relates directly not to the Judahites' time in Babylon but to the time of Babylon's ruling the world. In due course, Yahweh will *attend* to it for its *waywardness*, and it too will become a *desolation*. The First Testament consistently treats nations such as Assyria and Babylon both as Yahweh's agents and as destined to receive his attention for their waywardness. Thus theologically, Jeremiah is both pro- and anti-Babylonian; Babylon is "both Yahweh's servant (v. 9), and the one destined to drink last of all from the cup of wrath (v. 26)."[26] *Seventy years* is not a term for a lifetime in the First Testament, even in Ps 90:10, which refers to seventy or eighty. Seventy suggests a full number (e.g., Exod 15:27; 24:1, 9; Judg 1:7; 8:30; 1 Sam 6:19; 2 Sam 24:15; 2 Kgs 10:1; Ezek 8:11), a substantial number but not an infinite one. Babylon will rule the nations for so long that hardly anyone alive will see the end of that rule, but its end will come. And seventy is not a number that suggests precision—seventy as opposed to sixty-nine or seventy-one. In an Assyrian inscription, Marduk declared that Babylon would lie waste for seventy years, though he later changed his mind.[27] Jeremiah's point may include the conviction that Yahweh does not operate that way, at least not randomly—only in response to people's turning (18:1–11). As it turned out, Babylonian hegemony did last for about seventy years, which

---

24. Diamond, "Jeremiah," 578.

25. Blayney, *Jeremiah*, 339.

26. Diamond, "Jeremiah," 578.

27. D. D. Luckenbill, "The Black Stone of Esarhaddon," *AJSL* 41 (1924–25): 166–67. M. Leuchter suggests that Jeremiah is drawing people's attention to this inscription ("Jeremiah's 70-Year Prophecy and the Atbash Codes," *Bib* 85 [2004], 503–22).

naturally encouraged reflection on this figure. There are then various ways of determining the beginning and ending of the seventy years. And because the end of Babylonian hegemony meant the possibility of Judahites returning from exile and the possibility of the restoration of city and nation, seventy years becomes a term for Israel's affliction (2 Chron 36:21; Zech 1:12; 7:5; Dan 9:2).[28]

13–14 Yahweh's expectations of Babylon are evidently not unlike his expectations of Judah, and its fate will be the same. On one hand, Babylon is critiqued for its oppression. On the other, it is critiqued on account of *what their hands have made* (cf. vv. 6, 7). I take *this document* to be the Jeremiah scroll as a whole;[29] the reference is like the allusions that I occasionally make to this commentary. But this is where LXX locates the material about individual nations that comprises MT Jer 46–51 (LXX Jer 26–31) (see the introduction to Jer 46–51, p. 822), and *this document* could then refer to those chapters.

B. THE CHALICE (25:15–29 [LXX 32:1–15])

[15]*Because Yahweh, the God of Israel, has said this to me. Get this chalice of wine (fury)*[a] *from my hand and make them drink it,*[b] *all the nations that I am sending you to.* [16]*They will drink and reel*[c] *and go crazy because of the sword that I am sending among them.*

[17]*So I got the chalice from Yahweh's hand and made them drink it, all the nations that Yahweh sent me to:* [18]*Jerusalem and the towns of Judah, its king and its officials, to make them a desolation and a ruin, a thing to whistle at and a formula of slighting, this very day;*[d] [19]*Pharaoh King of Egypt, his servants, his officials, his entire people,* [20]*and the entire multiethnic group;*[e] *all the kings of the country of Uz,*[f] *all the kings of the country of the Philistines (Ashkelon, Gaza, Ekron, and the remains of Ashdod),* [21]*Edom, Moab, the Ammonites,* [22]*all the kings of Tyre, all the kings of Sidon, the kings of the shores that are across the sea,* [23]*Dedan, Tema, and Buz,*[g] *all the people who are clipped at the forehead,* [24]*all the kings of Arabia, all the kings of the multiethnic group*[h] *who dwell in*

28. See, e.g., J. Nogalski, "These Seventy Years: Intertextual Observations and Postulations on Jeremiah and the Twelve," in *History, Memory, Hebrew Scriptures: A Festschrift for Ehud Ben Zvi*, ed. I. D. Wilson and D. Edelman (Winona Lake, IN: Eisenbrauns, 2015), 248–50; J. Applegate, "Jeremiah and the Seventy Years in the Hebrew Bible," in *The Book of Jeremiah and Its Reception*, ed. A. H. W. Curtis and T. Römer, BETL 128 (Leuven: Peeters, 1997), 91–110. J. Hill sees the Jeremiah scroll itself as speaking of an "unended exile" ("'Your Exile Will Be Long': The Book of Jeremiah and the Unended Exile," in Kessler, *Reading the Book of Jeremiah*, 149–61).

29. Lundbom, *Jeremiah 21–36*, 251.

the wilderness, ²⁵*all the kings of Zimri, all the kings of Elam, all the kings of Media,* ²⁶*all the northern kings who are near or who are far in relation to each other—all the kingdoms of the earth that are on the face of the land. And the king of Sheshach,*ⁱ *he will drink after them.*

²⁷*You will say to them:*ʲ *Yahweh of Armies, the God of Israel, has said this. Drink, get drunk, throw up, fall, and don't get up again*ᵏ *because of the sword that I am sending among you.* ²⁸*When they refuse to get the chalice from your hand to drink, you will say to them, Yahweh of Armies has said this: you will definitely drink.*ˡ ²⁹*Because here am I: against the city over which my name is proclaimed, I am beginning to bring dire trouble, and you, you will really be free of guilt?*ᵐ *You will not be free of guilt, because a sword I am calling against all the people who live on earth (an affirmation of Yahweh of Armies).*

a. In apposition to what precedes, *fury* looks like a word of explanation to ensure readers understand what the wine symbolizes.

b. The *qatal* verb continues from the imperative (DG 76a; Joüon 119l).

c. LXX renders *gāʿaš* as "throw up," and *HALOT* notes other scatological possibilities. But *qāyāʾ*, which definitely means "throw up," comes in v. 27; Vg, Aq, Sym, Tg assume something like "reel."

d. LXX lacks *and a formula of slighting, this very day;* on the latter phrase, see the translation note on 11:5.

e. Lit. "mixture"; also in v. 24.

f. LXX lacks *all the kings of the country of Uz.*

g. LXX has "Ros" for *Buz.*

h. LXX lacks *all the kings of Arabia* (*ʿărāb*), which is similar to *all the kings of the multi-ethnic group* (*hāʿereb*) and also *all the kings of Zimri* in v. 25. J. G. Janzen suggests a conflate reading here ("Double Readings in the Text of Jeremiah," *HTR* 60 [1967]: 438).

i. LXX lacks *and the king of Sheshach, he will drink after them.* Sheshach is an alternative name for Babylon (Tg; cf. 51:41): the second letter of the (consonantal) alphabet, *b*, is replaced by the second from the end, *š*, and the eleventh letter, *l*, is replaced by the eleventh from the end, *k*. R. C. Steiner revives the view that the alternative name was used to disguise the writer's anti-Babylonian sentiments; see "The Two Sons of Neriah and the Two Editions of Jeremiah in the Light of Two Atbash Code-Words for Babylon," *VT* 46 (1996): 74–84.

j. MT has a marker here, adding to the sense of drama about v. 27 (see the commentary).

k. The *yiqtol* verb continues the imperative.

l. The infinitive precedes the finite verb, underlining its actuality; the usage recurs in the next verse.

m. *Nāqâ niphal* (see the translation note on the adjective *nāqî* at 2:34); there is no interrogative marker, but the context suggests that the clause is a question (DG 152a; *TTH* 119γ; GKC 150a; Joüon 161a).

Verses 15–29 expand on vv. 12–14, detailing the nations to whom disaster is coming and using the image of the chalice in doing so. The verses relate a visionary experience on Jeremiah's part that compares with the visionary experience in 1:4–10. His getting hold of the chalice parallels that commission when Yahweh touched him in quasi-physical fashion. It's not actually physical like the events related in Jer 13, 18, and 19, where other people could have seen the journeys with the shorts, the visit to the potter, and the breaking of the decanter (though the stories do not say that people did see them). Here, no one would have seen the action. But the effect is similar. On one hand, Yahweh and Jeremiah are doing something that puts Yahweh's will into effect. And on the other, people get to know about it because Jeremiah tells the story. Thus it's "not an acted sign, but an appeal to the imagination."[30] By telling the story, Jeremiah delivers the message to Judah. As far as we know, the nations would never know about it; it is designed for the Judahites and it is significant for them in various ways. While "God's prophets today may well be similarly called to speak to the nations,"[31] more certainly and more comparably, they will be called to speak about the nations to the people of God, like Jeremiah, and to remind it that God's judgment begins with his family (1 Pet 4:17).

While vv. 15–29 connect with what precedes, they move in a different direction. In vv. 12–14, Babylon was in focus, and the other nations were its victims. Here, the other nations are the victims of Yahweh's fury, presumably with the implication that they deserve dire trouble. The section thus makes for a further link with the account of Jeremiah's commission. Here he is *the nations' prophet* whom Yahweh is *sending* and who is appointed *over the nations, yes, over the kingdoms, to pull up and to pull down and to wipe out and to smash* (1:10). The two aspects of their destiny correspond to Judah's: they are both victims from whose attackers Yahweh will take redress and wrongdoers against whom Yahweh takes action.

vv. 15–16	Jeremiah reports how Yahweh commissioned an action: what he is to do
vv. 17–26	Jeremiah reports how he did as he is told, giving a list of the nations affected
vv. 27–29	Jeremiah elaborates on the commission: what he is to say

The sequence (commission, action, interpretation) compares with that in 18:1–12.[32]

30. D. R. Jones, *Jeremiah*, 329.

31. Pixley, *Jeremiah*, 77.

32. Lundbom, *Jeremiah 21–36*, 256. M. DeRoche sees the passage as originally poetry ("Is Jeremiah 25:15–29 a Piece of Reworked Jeremianic Poetry?," *JSOT* 10 [1978]: 58–67).

15–16 The *because* makes for a link between this section (which was originally independent) and what precedes, and makes clear that it elaborates on it. Drinking wine from a chalice as a symbol of receiving something from Yahweh is likely not a new image (e.g., Pss 16:5; 23:5; 116:13), and even the image of the chalice as toxic may not be new (e.g., Pss 11:6; 75:8[9]; Hab 2:16; also Isa 19:14 without specific mention of a chalice). The image may have background in conventions associated with treaty-making between a big power and a subordinate power. In treaties, the subordinate power often had to curse itself in specific ways against the possibility that it should not keep its word, and many of the self-curses find parallels in the statements of doom in Jeremiah and elsewhere—statements of doom for Israel of the kind that appear here in v. 10, but especially statements of doom for other nations. They include the land being ravaged so that it becomes just a place where animals live and the devastation being so great that passing nations shudder in horror. A treaty between Esarhaddon and an underling includes the prospect of being poisoned, and refers to drinking from a common chalice as one aspect of an oath-taking ceremony.[33] It would not be surprising if "the cup would be one of gladness as long as the vassal was faithful, but it would become a cup of reeling and staggering in the case of revolt."[34] Jeremiah extensively develops the negative chalice image (cf., e.g., Isa 51:17–23; Ezek 23:31–34; also Lam 4:21); it is perhaps also presupposed by the picture of pouring out wrath (e.g., 6:11; 10:25; 14:16; Hos 5:10; Pss 69:24[25]; 79:6). Maybe the wine is spiked, or maybe the nations are simply forced to drink too much; either way they *reel and go crazy* like a drunk. Yahweh already commissioned Jeremiah to make the Judahites drunk, with devastating consequences (13:12–14), and the image of Yahweh as the demonic host at a banquet recurs from 23:15 (cf. 51:39). A good host will make sure that his guests are well-plied with wine. But this banquet will resemble an occasion when plotters have been planning a coup and the guests are too drunk to be able to resist the sword when it comes. More literally, the pouring out of Yahweh's fury means he is *sending* a *sword* among them (cf. 9:16[15]; 24:10); only Ezekiel uses the word *sword* more often than Jeremiah (e.g., Jer 14:11–18; 15:1–9).

17–18 Further aspects of the overlap but distinctiveness in relation to vv. 1–14 become clear in the list of Yahweh's victims. First, Judah itself appears;

---

33. See *ANET*, 534–41.

34. T. G. Smothers, "A Lawsuit against the Nations: Reflections on the Oracles against the Nations in Jeremiah," *RevExp* 85 (1988): 550; he refers to D. Hillers, *Treaty Curses and the Old Testament Prophets*, Biblica et Orientalia 16 (Rome: Biblical Institute, 1964), 41–79. For other theories of the origin of the image, see Keown, Scalise, and Smothers, *Jeremiah 26–52*, 278–79.

Jeremiah describes its fate in familiar terms (see v. 9; also 18:16; 19:8; 22:5; 24:9). In Jeremiah's vision, the disaster comes *this very day*; the implication need not be that in real time the year is 597 or 587 as opposed to 604, but it may be. Jeremiah perhaps depresses his listeners; they thought they were about to hear about trouble threatening their adversaries, for a change, but instead they get the same old same old. Putting Judah at the head of what was supposed to be a list of foreign nations compares with the casual insertion of Jerusalem in the list in Isa 13–23 (see Isa 22) or the placing of Judah and then Ephraim at the climax of Amos 1:3–2:16.

19–26 There is not much encouragement, either, in the transition to talk of Egypt, because Judah viewed Egypt as its recurrent best hope; the term *multiethnic group* will refer to foreigners living in Egypt who were there for trade (for instance) or had taken refuge there as Judahites did.[35] The subsequent list roughly corresponds to the peoples covered by Jer 46–49.

- *Uz*, however, does not feature in Jer 46–49; it might cover peoples to the southeast (it is associated with Esau/Edom in Gen 36:28; Lam 4:21; and cf. Job 1:1) or to the northeast (it is associated with Aram in Gen 10:23).
- *The country of the Philistines* (see Jer 47) covers peoples to the southwest. Ashdod had been besieged and eventually conquered by Psammeticus I, father of Neco, a few years previously;[36] Gath, unmentioned, had been destroyed by the Assyrians a century previously.
- *Edom, Moab,* and *the Ammonites* (see Jer 27:3; 48–49) returns to the southeast and east, moving from south to north. Such peoples have been Judah's allies,[37] so there continues to be little encouragement here, though Moab and Ammon will shortly join with Babylon in attacking Judah (2 Kgs 24:2).
- *Tyre, Sidon* (see 27:3; 47:4), and the other seacoast peoples move to the northeast, and talk of peoples *across the sea* looks to Cyprus and Turkey and perhaps to Phoenician colonies further west such as Carthage.
- *Dedan, Tema,* and *Buz, all the people who are clipped at the forehead* (see 9:26[25]), and *Arabia*, with *the multiethnic group who dwell in the wilderness* take one across the desert to the east. The wilderness dwellers would also cover Kedar and "the encampments" in 49:28–33.

35. Mayer, *Commentary*, 417.
36. Herodotus, *Histories* 2.157.
37. Calvin, *Jeremiah*, 3:266.

- *Elam* and *Media* and the unknown *Zimri* looks further in that direction.
- Almost finally, Jeremiah refers to the *northern kings*, which would cover Damascus (49:23–27) and the peoples listed in 51:27.

One way or another, Jeremiah has covered peoples in every direction, *all the kingdoms of the earth*, in a movement that broadly starts nearer home and gradually moves to nations on the edge of Judah's world. Geographical logic and rhetorical force both take the passage finally to the nation that everyone would think of first as deserving Yahweh's eventual attention. The unexpected substitute name *Sheshach* (see the translation note) is hardly an attempt to conceal reference to Babylon, which is explicitly mentioned often enough. It is perhaps snide, adding to the sense of climax. No, Babylon's king will not escape.

> The text is a kind of Old Testament depiction of the universal judgment day, when the Lord will judge "all flesh." Precisely because so many of the nations mentioned here seem remote from the biblical story or remote from the interests of the God of Israel, the text makes its particular claim about the lordship of Yahweh. The rule of the Lord of Israel is set within the affairs of nations and peoples, and there is no community outside of the sovereign activity of that God. We encounter here no narrow stream of holy history but a view of universal history that insists that the workings of divine justice are not confined to those who are called out and elected to God's service. All human communities are called to account, and even the mightiest have no final autonomy. The political leaders who seem to be in charge of the affairs of the world stand under a higher power, whether they are aware of it or not. . . . In the interactions of nations, in the conflicts and upheavals, a transcendent governance is manifest.[38]

But the message still concerns the present world; in this sense it's not "apocalyptic."[39]

27–29 Jeremiah's elaboration on the commission belongs logically with vv. 15–16, but the order in which the report unfolds means that these verses bring the section to a climax. The commission indicated the significance of the visionary-symbolic action, though it did so only in general terms, and it might seem to raise some questions—at least, Yahweh now answers some questions. As he fulfills his commission, what is Jeremiah to say to the nations about how long-lasting the drunkenness will be, about what happens if they refuse to drink, and about why it's happening to them as well as to Judah, which is Yah-

---

38. P. D. Miller, "Jeremiah," on the passage.
39. R. P. Carroll, *Jeremiah*, OTL, 503, uses that word four times.

weh's and Jeremiah's chief concern? In dealing with these matters, Jeremiah enhances the sense of climax with a double introduction: *You will say to them: Yahweh of Armies, the God of Israel, has said this.* The argument is now explicit, in *a fortiori* or *qal wahomer* form: if Yahweh is bringing dire trouble on his own city, how can he stop there when other peoples are just as deserving? His logic is not that they have ill-treated Judah. Most of them are faraway peoples who have nothing to do with Judah. The passage is not about redress. It's about Yahweh taking action against waywardness. In effect, Jeremiah is saying "all have sinned and fallen short of God's glory" (Rom 3:23). None of them can say they are free of liability and guilt and therefore exempt from punishment. "The universal extent of the thinking about judgment to the entire world of peoples hangs together here with the extent and intensity of the concept of God."[40]

C. THE PROPHECY (25:30–38 [LXX 32:16–24])

[30]*So you—you will prophesy all these things to them. You will say to them:*

Yahweh—from on high he roars,
  from his sacred lair he gives voice,
  he roars, yes roars,[a] against his habitat.
A shout like treaders he avers,[b]
  to all the people who live on earth.

[31]*A din has come to the end of the earth,*
  because Yahweh has an argument against the nations.
He is entering into the exercise of authority regarding all flesh;
  the faithless—he has given them to the sword (Yahweh's affirmation).[c]

[32]*Yahweh of Armies has said this:*

There, dire trouble is going out from nation to nation,
  a big storm stirs from the furthest parts of the earth.[d]
[33]*There will be people run through by Yahweh on that day,[e]*
  from the end of the earth to the end of the earth.
They will not be lamented
  and they will not be gathered.[f]
They will not be buried—
  manure on the face of the ground they will become.[g]

[34]*Howl, you shepherds, cry out,*

40. Weiser, *Jeremia*, 2:234.

grovel,[h] *lords of the flock.*
Because the days for your slaughtering have been fulfilled, and your
> *scatterings,*[i]
> *and you will fall like a valuable vessel.*[j]
[35]*Flight will fail from the shepherds,*
> *escape from the lords of the flock.*

[36]*The sound of the shepherds' cry,*
> *the howl of the lords of the flock,*
> *because Yahweh is destroying their pasture.*
[37]*The meadows where things were well have become still,*
> *in the face of Yahweh's angry blazing.*
[38]*He has abandoned his lair like a lion,*
> *because their country has become a desolation,*
In the face of the oppressor's blazing,[k]
> *in the face of his angry blazing.*[l]

a. The infinitive precedes the finite verb, underlining the factuality of the action.

b. See the translation note on 14:7.

c. MT has a section marker here.

d. This colon is a variant on 6:22b.

e. LXX has "Yahweh's day," which draws attention to the fact that MT speaks in terms of Yahweh doing something in ordinary time, within history, but offers a significant theological comment on such action within history.

f. LXX lacks this line.

g. V. 33c combines phrases from 8:2 and 16:4.

h. G. R. Driver's translation of *pālaš hithpael*; see "Studies in the Vocabulary of the Old Testament I," *JTS* 31 (1929–30): 275–76; cf. Holladay, *Commentary on Jeremiah*, 1:681, and see also *DCH*.

i. *Ûtəpûṣôtîkem* (lacking in LXX) looks like a mixed form, a cross between a verb and a noun, between "and your scatterings" and "and I will scatter you" (Allen, *Jeremiah*, 282).

j. For MT *kikəlî*, LXX implies *kə'ēlēh* ("like rams"), which fits the context.

k. LXX has "the big sword" (partly assimilating to 46:16; 50:16), then lacks the final colon. Vg takes the word for oppressor, *hayyônâ* as its homonym, "the dove."

l. MT has a unit marker here.

A third time, Yahweh makes his declaration about bringing calamity. Whereas the first section put the main stress on disaster for Judah but also included the nations, and the second included Judah but put more stress on the nations, here stress lies mainly on the nations; Judah is present, but its presence is understated. This final section brings together four poetic units:

> vv. 30–31 A lion roars (an introduction, a tricolon, and three bicola)
> vv. 32–33 A big storm stirs (an introduction and four bicola, the latter
> two with enjambment)

vv. 34–35 Shepherds are slaughtered and scattered (three bicola)
vv. 36–38 A pasture is destroyed (a tricolon and three bicola, the last two with enjambment)

30–31 In Jer 4:7; 5:6, the northern invader was attacking Judah, but he was always the front man for Yahweh; now Yahweh is the lion that *roars*. The roar comes not from Zion, as in Amos 1:2; 3:8, but from the heavens, *from on high*. While his *sacred lair* (*māʿôn*) could simply denote his dwelling and could refer to the temple, the noun can denote an animal's den, which makes sense in this context, and it more often denotes his heavenly abode, which also makes sense in the parallelism. In fact, he roars *against* his earthly *habitat* (*nāweh*), which can also denote a fold or abode more broadly (e.g., 10:25; 31:23), but most occurrences refer to the abode of animals, especially sheep (e.g., 23:3; 33:12; 49:19, 20; 50:7, 19, 44, 45). Here, Jeremiah speaks a little quixotically, as if the habitat or fold belongs to the lion. The thing signified is affecting the formulation of the metaphor: Judah's country does belong to Yahweh. His roaring *against his habitat* adds to the significance of the fact that the roar does not come *from* Zion.[41] Arguably, Amos is not so different, as there the roar from Zion also becomes a roar at Zion; Jeremiah reverses the sequence, with Zion as the object first and the other nations later. Either way, there is no escape from this message for Israel. Jeremiah does not maintain the lion image: Yahweh becomes a man shouting as loudly as someone treading grapes, which people do with loud enthusiasm (48:33; Isa 16:10). So Jeremiah is again being quixotic: this shout is a solemn, aggressive, forceful one that sounds to the entire earth. One might have thought that the nations were simply to be witnesses to Yahweh's action against Judah. Actually, it transpires that the *din* Yahweh causes with his loud voice is to reach the entire earth because he has an argument with it (here, Jeremiah may be adapting Hos 4:1). He wishes to confront its people in court in order to enter into the exercise of authority in relation to them (cf. 2:35; see the commentary there). They are not just witnesses or members of the court. The middle two lines of vv. 30–31 work a-b-b'-a', with the cola about averring and about an argument being parallel, as are the intervening two cola:

> A shout like treaders he avers
>> to all the people who live on earth.
>> A din has come to the end of the earth
> because Yahweh has an argument against the nations.

41. Craigie, Kelley, and Drinkard, *Jeremiah 1–25*, 374.

He wants to meet up with them in court, but the case is already decided. In his mind, he has already *given them to the sword* (the *qatal* is anticipatory; see the introduction to 13:18–22, pp. 354–55). It is not because they are simply unlucky. They are *the faithless*. Yes, "all have sinned and fallen short of God's glory" (Rom 3:23; see the commentary on v. 29). So it is not just Judah that is the object of Yahweh's attack. Once again, Jeremiah obscures the line between the chosen people and the rest of the world. "Both Jews and Greeks, all are under sin" (Rom 3:9).

32–33 The second unit restates the point. It begins again from the worldwide nature of what Yahweh intends but moves to another image: *A big storm stirs from the furthest parts of the earth.* The worldwide reference contrasts with the Judah reference of 6:22b. No, it is not just Judah that will be the storm's victim (23:19). *From the end of the earth to the end of the earth* makes the same point, as it repeats a phrase from 12:12, where it denoted "from the end of the land to the end of the land." It's worldwide but, once more, not apocalyptic.[42] Jeremiah again pictures people *run through* by the sword, and like Judahites, their suffering will not cease with their death (see 8:2; 16:4).

34–35 Once again, Jeremiah changes the imagery in what looks like a third originally separate unit. As elsewhere, *shepherds* refers to leaders, the *lords of the flock* which comprises the people they are in charge of and are supposed to care for. In this context, they are the leaders of the nations, though given Judah's inclusion in vv. 15–29, Judahite leaders might be rash to assume that the warning does not apply to them. They are to *grovel* in anguish and degradation; the verb usually refers to rolling in dirt or ash (6:26). They will do so in light of their awareness that their days are numbered. Instead of their flock being slaughtered or scattered (10:21; 23:1–2), they will be slaughtered or scattered. The idea of the fall and shattering of a valuable vessel is a compressed image. One looks after a valuable pot because of its importance, to make sure it does not fall, and one looks after it more carefully than an everyday one. These leaders think they are valuable and important (Tg has them "coveted like valuable vessels"), but they will fall. There will be no escape. *Flight will fail from the shepherds* as "flight will fail from the swift" in Amos 2:14.

36–38 The final unit also works with the shepherd imagery but takes it in another direction. Now the shepherds are distraught not because of what is happening to them but because of what is happening to their pasture, as shepherds would be. Shepherds would be distraught; their pasture's well-being is vital to their work. One is then to imagine the nations' leaders lamenting what has happened to their countries. They had been pasturing in *meadows where things were well* (meadows of *šālôm*), but Yahweh has burned

---

42. Volz, *Jeremia*, 395.

up these meadows with his wrath. There are no shouts of shepherds or bleatings of sheep now. It's a shame they didn't cry out to God before the dire trouble came rather than leaving it until afterwards.[43] The unit closes with a return to the image of Yahweh as the lion. Jeremiah knows that the lion has *abandoned* (in the sense of left, gone out from) his lair, because he can see the results in his mind's eye: the *country has become a desolation* when it should be meadow. "Farms, gardens, businesses, the exercise of crafts, the exchange of contracts, weddings, meetings, festivals, enjoyments, and the like"[44]—it's all ceased. The unit, the section, the chapter, and the first half of the Jeremiah scroll come to an end with a solemn and horrifying emphasis on Yahweh's destructive wrath.[45] Yes, "the text is a kind of Old Testament depiction of the universal judgment day."[46] One might compare teaching such as Jesus's in Matt 24–25 or Paul's in 2 Thess 1; Jeremiah's emphasis here on Yahweh being active in the present and in history is a reminder that Jesus and Paul had a similar expectation and were not talking merely about a distant future end-of-the-world event.

43. Isaac Abravanel, *Commentary on the Latter Prophets.*

44. Theodoret, *Ermeneia*, PG 81:641.

45. E. K. Holt, "King Nebuchadrezzar of Babylon," in Diamond and Stulman, *Jeremiah (Dis)placed*, 217–18.

46. P. D. Miller, "Jeremiah," on vv. 19–26.

III. PART THREE: THE DIE CAST AND THE POSSIBILITY OF RESTORATION (26:1–36:32)

Jeremiah 26 sees a sharp, unannounced transition from messages to stories, which will dominate the rest of the scroll—at least through Jer 26–45. These twenty chapters comprise parts 3 and 4 of the scroll as a whole. Part 3 (Jer 26–36) is framed by stories about the time of Jehoiakim, but the bulk of them (Jer 27–29 and 32–34) concern the time of Zedekiah. The stories are mostly gloomy, but in the middle of part 3 is a series of promises and stories about the restoration of Judah and Ephraim.

26 Jehoiakim: how Jeremiah almost lost his life
 27–29 Zedekiah: Jeremiah, the envoys, the prophets, and the exiles
  30–31 Undated: turnarounds for Judah and Ephraim
  32–33 Zedekiah: a gesture of confidence in a desperate context
 34 Zedekiah: a threat and a promise; a promise, a failure, and a threat
35–36 Jehoiakim: how the Rechabites kept their word and how Jeremiah lost his scroll

The threats in the first half of the scroll "practice against the dramatized Jerusalem community a withering hostility toward hope."[1] It is in this context that "the deferral of hope" which has characterized the first half of the scroll makes room for "the revival of hope."[2]

A. PART 3A: STORIES ABOUT PROPHETS (26:1–29:32 [LXX 33:1–36:32])

Although Jer 26 marks a switch from messages to stories, the theme picks up from where Jer 1–25 almost ended, in that part 3a speaks of prophets Yahweh sent, prophets he did not send, and the difference between them, and goes on to spell out the implications of the *seventy years* declaration in 25:11–12. It comprises four stories.

---

1. A. R. P. Diamond, "Deceiving Hope: The Ironies of Metaphorical Beauty and Ideological Terror in Jeremiah," *SJOT* 17 (2003): 39.

2. J. G. McConville, *Judgment and Promise: Interpretation of the Book of Jeremiah* (Leicester: Apollos, 1993), 43, 79.

Jer 26   Jeremiah almost loses his life after confronting the Juda-
          hites in the temple

Jer 27   Jeremiah bids Judah submit to Babylon and not expect the
          temple artifacts' speedy return

Jer 28   Hananiah loses his life after confronting Jeremiah in the
          temple

Jer 29   Jeremiah bids the exile community to settle down and not
          expect their speedy return

The four chapters thus follow an a-b-a'-b' sequence, with each element in the second pair of chapters going beyond the first in the manner of parallelism: the threat of a prophet's death and an actual prophet's death, then the nonreturn of accoutrements and the nonreturn of people. Chronologically, Jer 26 is set at the beginning of Jehoiakim's reign, but Jer 27–29 is set in Zedekiah's time, and these three chapters also have linguistic features in common that suggest they had a common origin before they became part of the Jeremiah scroll.[3] They usually have the spelling Nebuchadnezzar rather than Jeremiah's usual Nebuchadrezzar (but with some variation among manuscripts), they often spell names such as Jeremiah with the ending *-yah* instead of the more usual *-yahu*, and they call Jeremiah *the prophet* more often than the Jeremiah scroll usually does. They are formulated "against the revolutionary movement in the year 594"[4] and they reflect "conflicting theologies of hope."[5]

1. *How Jeremiah Almost Lost His Life (26:1–27:1a [LXX 33:1–24])*

[1]*At the beginning of the reign of Jehoiakim ben Josiah King of Judah, this word came*[a] *from Yahweh.*

[2]*Yahweh has said this: Stand in the courtyard of Yahweh's house and speak against*[b] *all the towns of*[c] *Judah, the people who are coming to bow down in Yahweh's house, all the words that I'm ordering you*[d] *to speak to them—don't cut out a word.* [3]*Perhaps they will listen and turn, each from his dire path, and I will relent concerning the dire thing that I am intending to do to them in the face of the dire nature of their practices.* [4]*So you will say to them: Yahweh has*

---

3. On their possible development, see F. L. Hossfeld and I. Meyer, *Prophet gegen Prophet: Eine Analyse der alttestamentlichen Texte zum Thema: wahre und falsche Propheten*, Biblische Beiträge 9 (Freiburg: KBW, 1973), 90–111; F. L. Hossfeld and I. Meyer, "Der Prophet vor dem Tribunal: Neuer Auslegungsversuch von Jer 26," *ZAW* 86 (1974): 30–50; Lange, *Vom prophetischen Wort*, 224–60; Sharp, *Prophecy and Ideology in Jeremiah*, 54–62, 103–24.

4. Volz, *Jeremia*, 255.

5. Stulman, *Jeremiah*, 243.

said this. If you do not listen to me so as to walk by my instruction that I have put before you, ⁵listening to the words of my servants the prophets whom I am sending to you, sending them assiduouslyᵉ—but you haven't listened—⁶then I will make this house like Shiloh, and this city I will make into a formula of slighting for all the nations on earth.ᶠ

⁷*The priests and the prophetsᵍ and the entire people heard Jeremiah speaking these words in Yahweh's house. ⁸Then, as Jeremiah finished speaking all that Yahweh had ordered him to speak to the entire people, the priests and the prophets and the entire people took hold of him, saying: You will definitely die.ʰ ⁹Why have you prophesied in Yahweh's name: Like Shiloh—so will this house become; and this city—it will be a waste, without anyone living there? So the entire people congregated against Jeremiah in Yahweh's house. ¹⁰The Judahite officials heard these things, went up from the king's house to Yahweh's house, and sat in the entrance of Yahweh's gateway (the new one).ⁱ ¹¹The priests and the prophets said to the officials and to the entire people: A death sentence for this man, because he has prophesied against this city, as you have heard with your ears.*

¹²*Jeremiah said to all the officials and to the entire people: Yahweh—he sent me to prophesy to this house and to this city all the words that you have heard. ¹³So now, make your paths and your practices good, and listen to the voice of Yahweh your God, so that Yahweh may relent regarding the dire thing that he has spoken against you. ¹⁴Me—here am I, in your hand. Do to me in accordance with what is good and in accordance with what is right in your eyes. ¹⁵Yet you will definitely acknowledge that if you are going to put me to death, that it is the blood of a man free of guilt that you are putting upon yourselves and against this city and against the people who live in it, because in truth Yahweh sent me to you to speak in your ears all these words.ʲ*

¹⁶*So the officials and the entire people said to the priests and to the prophets: There is no death sentence for this man, because it is in the name of Yahweh our God that he has spoken to us.*

¹⁷*Some people from among the elders of the country got up and said to the entire assembly of the people, ¹⁸Micahᵏ the Morashtite, he was prophesying in the days of Hezekiah King of Judah, and he said to the entire people of Judah:*

Yahweh of Armies has said this:

*Zion—as open country it will be plowed,
 Jerusalem—ruins it will become,
  the mountain of Yahweh's house—shrinesˡ in a forest.*

¹⁹*Did Hezekiah King of Judah and all Judah actually put him to death?ᵐ He was in awe of Yahweh, wasn't he, and he sought Yahweh's goodwill,ⁿ and Yahweh*

relented of the dire thing that he had spoken of against them. But we are going to undertake a big dire action against ourselves.

[20]*Also, a man was prophesying away*[o] *in Yahweh's name, Uriah ben Shemaiah from Kiriath-jearim. He prophesied against this city and*[p] *against this country in accordance with all Jeremiah's words,* [21]*and King Jehoiakim and all his strong men*[q] *and all his officials heard his words. The king*[r] *sought to put him to death, and Uriah heard and was afraid.*[s] *He fled and came to Egypt.* [22]*But King Jehoiakim sent men to Egypt, Elnathan ben Achbor and men with him, to Egypt.*[t] [23]*They got Uriah out of Egypt and made him come to King Jehoiakim. He struck him down with the sword and threw his corpse into the graves of the ordinary people.*[u]

[24]*However, the hand of Ahikam ben Shaphan—it was with Jeremiah so that no one could give him into the hand of the people to put him to death,*[v] [27:1]*at the beginning of the reign of Jehoiakim ben Josiah King of Judah.*[w]

a. Syr adds "to Jeremiah," a more predictable reading.

b. The chapter alternates between *ʿal* and *ʾel* with an "odd" fluidity (McKane, *Jeremiah*, 2:661). I have translated *ʿal* either *against* or *upon* except in vv. 5 and 15, but *ʾel* also as *against* or *concerning* in vv. 3, 5, 9, 11b, 12b, 15, 19, as well as *to*.

c. LXX lacks "the towns of."

d. The *qatal* verb is declarative/performative, denoting what Yahweh is doing at this moment (see 1:5 and the translation note there).

e. See the translation note and commentary on 7:13.

f. MT has a marker here.

g. To make explicit the contrast with *prophets* in v. 5, LXX calls them "false prophets," as it did in 6:13 (see the commentary on 6:13 and 2:8); this translation recurs in 28:1; 29:1, 8.

h. The infinitive precedes the finite verb, underlining the factuality of the action. This idiom recurs in v. 15.

i. MT has a section marker here. Tg, Syr, and some MSS of LXX and Vg have "the entrance of the new gateway of Yahweh's house" as in 36:10, a more predictable reading.

j. MT has a section marker here.

k. The *ketiv* has "Micaiah"; cf. 1 Kgs 22.

l. LXX has singular; cf. 7:31.

m. In a question, the infinitive absolute before the finite verb perhaps differs slightly in implication from the use in vv. 8 and 15 (DG 101a).

n. On *ḥālâ*, see the commentary.

o. *Nābāʾ hithpael* as in 14:14; 23:13; 29:26–27, not *niphal* as in vv. 11, 12, 20b and elsewhere. There can hardly be a pejorative implication for the narrator, though possibly he hints at the view of the people who will attack Uriah.

p. LXX lacks *against this city and*, which in MT underlines the parallel between Uriah and Jeremiah.

q. LXX lacks *and all his strong men*; they appear with Hezekiah's officials in 2 Chr 32:3, so their mention here adds to the parallel (and contrast) with Hezekiah (Keown, Scalise, and Smothers, *Jeremiah 26–52*, 4).

r. LXX has "they."

s. LXX lacks these two verbs.

t. LXX omits v. 22b. The overlap within the verse may indicate that MT combines two readings; see S. Talmon, "Double Readings in the Masoretic Text," *Textus* 1 (1960): 180.

u. LXX has "the grave of the children of his people"—his family tomb.

v. MT has a unit marker here.

w. MT makes *at the beginning of the reign of Jehoiakim ben Josiah King of Judah* the beginning of Jer 27, but Jer 27 goes on to refer to an event in Zedekiah's reign. Reading "Zedekiah" for *Jehoiakim* (so Syr and some medieval Hebrew MSS; see *BHS*) solves the problem, but it looks like a later correction; see S. W. Crawford, J. Joosten, and E. Ulrich, "Sample Editions of the Hebrew Bible," *VT* 58 (2008): 365. I take it as a chronological footnote to Jer 26. It joins the occurrence in 26:1a in forming a bracket around the chapter; cf. A. C. Osuji, *Where Is the Truth: Narrative Exegesis and the Question of True and False Prophecy in Jer 26–29 (MT)*, BETL 214 (Leuven: Peeters, 2010), 121. Jerome (*Jeremiah*, 166) takes the whole of 27:1 as a footnote to Jer 26, but the closing *lēʾmōr* in 27:1b excludes this understanding.

Jeremiah 26 tells the story of what issued from Jeremiah's delivering the message about the temple recorded in Jer 7.[6] Its underlying question is, can a prophet really announce disaster (*Unheil*) against Jerusalem?[7] The account of Jeremiah's commission in 1:4–19 warned that he would be under attack but promised that Yahweh would protect him. Did he get attacked, and did he get protected? In this first story in Jer 26–29, Jeremiah gets into trouble that might lead to his death but gets out of trouble and escapes the threat to his life. As the beginning of the second half of the Jeremiah scroll, it is a narrative equivalent to 1:4–19, giving another picture of Jeremiah's danger and safety.[8] It also fits with the general nature of Jer 1–25, which has suggested that Jeremiah lived a risky life. He was against everyone—king, people in government, priests, prophets, ordinary people. This story is interested in what happens to Jeremiah at the hands of his people for the same reason as the poetry in Jer 11–20. He brings Yahweh's message by embodying what happens to that message as well as by declaring it. And Jer 26 tells a story about people's response to Yahweh's message. "The issue is not so much conflict among the prophets or between Jeremiah and his public as it is the fate of Jeremiah's message, seen now as the true word of God. Will the word be heeded or ignored?"[9] The story's implication is similar to that of the poetry. It indicates how Yahweh's word was not silenced.

6. On the relationship between the two chapters, see, e.g., Holt, "Jeremiah's Temple Sermon," 73–87.

7. Fischer, *Jeremia*, 2:23.

8. Stulman, *Jeremiah*, 236.

9. B. O. Long, "Social Dimensions of Prophetic Conflict: Jeremiah versus Hananiah," in *Anthropological Perspectives on Old Testament Prophecy*, ed. R. C. Culley and T. W. Overholt, *Semeia* 21 (1981): 41.

The account is intelligible as an account of how Jeremiah's trial could actually have proceeded,[10] but "the art of storytelling is on display here."[11] The story unfolds in two acts.[12]

26:1–11   Act 1: How Jeremiah gets into trouble that might lead to his death

26:1–6   Scene 1: How Yahweh commissions Jeremiah to threaten disaster to temple and city. In the context of the scroll, little that we don't already know happens in this scene.

(a)   Yahweh gives Jeremiah a typical commission to make the kind of critique that he has been making for decades.

(b)   His specific threat is the one he issued in 7:1–15, except that the city now features.

26:7–11   Scene 2: How priests, prophets, and people determine to have Jeremiah put to death. In a way, nothing new happens here either, in that the scroll has already reported threats on Jeremiah's life. But this declaration of intent is more concerted.

(a)   It involves two of the main power groups, the priests and prophets, and also the people as a whole; the first part of the scene ends with the entire people gathered aggressively around Jeremiah.

(b)   It then involves the palace officials, who are nearer to having the authority to decide on a death penalty, with the king hovering in the background; the second part of the scene ends with another declaration that Jeremiah should be put to death, though the people have changed sides.

The plot thus builds tension through act 1.

---

10. R. Westbrook, *Law from the Tigris to the Tiber* (Winona Lake, IN: Eisenbrauns, 2009), 2:425–38.

11. M. H. McIntire, "A Prophetic Chorus of Others: Helping Jeremiah Survive in Jeremiah 26," *RevExp* 101 (2004): 302; see further H. Brichto, *Toward a Grammar of Biblical Poetics: Tales of the Prophets* (New York: Oxford University Press, 1992), 226–30.

12. Osuji (*Where Is the Truth*, 124) has an overlapping analysis.

26:12–16   Act 2: How Jeremiah gets out of trouble and escapes the threat to his life

26:12–15   Scene 1: How Jeremiah urges the officials and the people not to put him to death. In his commission, Yahweh told Jeremiah he must stand firm and say what Yahweh bids him say, and here he does so. His argument is

      (a)   Yahweh sent him;

      (b)   they must turn, and Yahweh will relent of his threat;

      (c)   they can put him to death, but they will be shedding innocent blood;

      (d)   Yahweh sent him—really.

26:16   Scene 2: How officials and people determine that he should not be put to death because he spoke in Yahweh's name

26:17–27:1a   Three postscripts or codas[13]

The tension in the story is thus resolved. The story has answered the question that underlies it: Jeremiah did get attacked, but he stood firm and he did escape. It could thus have ended with v. 16, but its answer has raised some further questions.

26:17–19   Question 1: What really made the assembly change its mind?

Another group of players, the elders, appeared, with a reminder about Micah, who spoke in similar terms to Jeremiah, and about how Judah responded to him.

26:20–23   Question 2: Do prophets always get rescued in that way?

No; here is a story about how the king himself put another prophet to death. This coda underscores the fact that Jeremiah was in real danger.

---

13. It has been suggested that these three units in the story are additions to the original version; see, e.g., F.-L. Hossfeld and I. Meyer, "Der Prophet vor dem Tribunal," 30–50; I. Meyer, *Jeremia und die falschen Propheten: Redaktionsgeschichtliche Studien zum Jeremiabuch*, OBO 13 (Göttingen: Vandenhoeck & Ruprecht, 1977), 15–45; W. McKane, "Jeremiah and the Wise," in *Wisdom in Ancient Israel: Essays in Honour of J. A. Emerton*, ed. J. Day, R. P. Gordon, and H. G. M. Williamson (Cambridge: Cambridge University Press, 1995), 143–46.

26:24–27:1a Question 3: So was Yahweh fulfilling his side of the commission in 1:4–19?
Yes, though it was Ahikam who did the work.

Those questions are thereby answered, though as usual, the answers themselves raise more questions: Who are these elders, what is the king's attitude
to the attack on Jeremiah, who is this Ahikam, and what did he do? (see
the commentary).

Who would be interested in this story? Who would the curators want
to listen to it? It vindicates both Jeremiah and Yahweh, relating how both
parties were faithful to the terms of the relationship set up nearly twenty
years previously. That implication would hold even if, perhaps especially
if, it also implies that Yahweh is active via human agents such as the pro-
vincial elders and Ahikam. Set at the beginning of Jehoiakim's reign and at
the beginning of the second half of the scroll, it opens up how things will
be in Jehoiakim's and Zedekiah's reigns. It would provide a further basis
for people to take Jeremiah's message seriously in the reign of Jehoiakim,
when the story is set, or any time up to 587—or after 587, when the possibility of taking this message seriously had a new profile. It also suggests that
the people as a whole, the officials of Judah, and the king (all of whom in
different ways have an ambiguous position in the story) need to make up
their minds what stance they will take to Jeremiah's message. And people
in positions of leadership or influence, such as Ahikam and the elders, need
to accept responsibility to stand up and be counted. On the other hand,
the community needs to be wary of priests and prophets, who have made
up their mind about their stance; they were powerful groups in the time of
Jehoiakim, as well as in the time of Zedekiah (even though many had been
taken off to Babylon). After 587, the prophets are discredited, but Jeremiah
has to continue to be courageous in speaking boldly and continues to be
under pressure.

1 Historically, Jehoiakim's reign is a "watershed" moment,[14] and the *beginning* of his reign in 609 is thus a telling moment. *Beginning* may be a quasi-
technical expression, denoting the part-year that precedes the first full calendar year of his reign. The famous fourth year (25:1) has not yet arrived, but
evidently any positive results from Josiah's reformation have disappeared,
possibly because it would be known and evident from the beginning that

14. G. E. Yates, "Narrative Parallelism and the 'Jehoiakim Frame': A Reading Strategy
for Jeremiah 26–45," *JETS* 48 (2005): 275; cf. G. E. Yates, "'The People Have Not Obeyed':
A Literary and Rhetorical Study of Jeremiah 26–45" (PhD diss., Dallas Theological Seminary, 1998), 138–39.

Jehoiakim was unsympathetic to his father's reforms.[15] According to 2 Kgs 23:31–37, the Egyptians made Jehoiakim king in place of his brother Jehoahaz, presumably on the assumption that he would toe the Egyptian line, as his father had not and as they plausibly assumed Jehoahaz, as the people's choice to follow Josiah, would not. And Jehoiakim does pay tribute to Egypt and ensure that the people shell out to make it possible. Given how Jehoiakim's reign would turn out, this story lays out the stance Jeremiah will need to take to that reign and constitutes an introduction to the dynamics of the next decade or two, on which subsequent stories will expand.

2 Jeremiah is to stand in the public space in front of the temple proper to deliver a message to the crowd. The occasion is evidently some special one when people from all over Judah are present—a festival or a fast. Perhaps they would be aggravated that they come all this way for a festival and then get lambasted by a prophet.[16] While Yahweh often tells Jeremiah to communicate all his words, only here does he add the apparently redundant gloss *do not withhold a word*, which reminds one of Moses (Deut 4:2; 12:32 [13:1]). Yahweh's bidding hardly implies a worry that Jeremiah might be tempted to do so; it rather underlines the importance of the mission and heightens the drama.

3 As usual, Yahweh's threats aim not merely to inform them of a fate that will follow come what may, but to get them to *turn*—though that aim is usually implicit rather than explicit, as is the case in Jonah's preaching and in the exposition of the point in 18:1–12. The openness of Yahweh's stance and the reality of Yahweh's hopes are suggested by his *perhaps* (cf. Luke 20:13).[17] On the other hand, while the possibility of relenting takes up 18:1–12, the *perhaps* recognizes that it cannot be taken for granted; Yahweh can get tired of relenting (15:6). Formally, the two elements of the message are different from the ones that characterize Jeremiah's poetic messages, which classically comprise (a) an indictment, (b) a threat, often introduced by a "therefore." Here the elements are:

(a)   You must listen and turn from your dire path.
(b)   Then I will relent of my dire threat.

4–6 Yahweh spells out his message again, more in keeping with that other pattern, but at slightly greater length, though still briefly. "By radically abridging the sermon to three verses (26:4–6), the narrator himself

---

15. J. A. Wilcoxen, "The Political Background of Jeremiah's Temple Sermon," in Merrill and Overholt, *Scripture in History and Theology*, 151–66.

16. Calvin, *Jeremiah*, 3:329.

17. Jerome, *Jeremiah*, 162.

ironically disregards Yahweh's warning not to trim a word. This procedure reveals, of course, that the sermon is not the point of interest here."[18] In light of the abbreviation, the reference to the city is noteworthy as an addition in relation to 7:1–15. The summary does not include the positive promises that attach to turning in 7:3–7, only the implication that Yahweh will cancel the threats expressed in 7:8–15.

> (a) If you don't listen and walk by my instruction and listen to my prophets (as you have not),
> (b) then I will implement my intention to devastate temple and city.

Yahweh thus mentions two sources, or vehicles, of his speaking to his people: his instruction (see 2:8; 6:19; 8:8; 16:11) and the words of his prophets (mentioned in a positive connection in 7:25; 25:4). One walks by the instruction by listening to the prophets. Further, "people hear about walking in Yahweh's law from the priests, but it is the prophets who call for a return to the law when the way has been lost."[19] A difference over against 7:25 and 25:4 is that there Yahweh spoke of having sent prophets in the past; here he speaks of an ongoing and thus present *sending*. It is a sending that puts the people listening to the story into the position of needing to think about the way they are responding to prophets who are speaking to them now. It suggests the prayer:

> Grant, Almighty God, that as thou hast been pleased not only to make known thy will once by the Law, but also to add more light by thy holy prophets . . . that we may not be deaf nor tardy to hear, but promptly submit ourselves to thee, and so suffer ourselves to be ruled by thy word, that through our whole life we may testify that thou art indeed our God, we being thy people.[20]

7 One would have expected a reference to Jeremiah delivering his message, but there is none. The chapter's dynamics compare with those of 13:1–11 (where there is no reference to people seeing or hearing about Jeremiah's symbolic act), 19:1–13 (where there is in addition no reference to his undertaking the act), or 25:15–29 (where there is no mention of an actual chalice or of anyone drinking). Part of the logic is the fact that all the stories are

---

18. K. M. O'Connor, "'Do Not Trim a Word': The Contributions of Chapter 26 to the Book of Jeremiah," *CBQ* 51 (1989): 620.

19. Lundbom, *Jeremiah 21–36*, 288.

20. Calvin, *Jeremiah*, 3:337.

designed to speak to listeners. Further, although Jer 26 is a story about Jeremiah, it is "less concerned with the prophet himself than with the forces surrounding him," with "the society of Jerusalem in the twilight years of the Judean monarchy."[21]

8 The mention of *the priests and the prophets* bears an ironic relationship to what has preceded, because Yahweh's teaching was the business of the priests, and Yahweh's word was the business of the prophets (cf. 18:18), but these priests and prophets have not been encouraging people to walk by Yahweh's teaching and have not been declaring words that actually came from Yahweh—hence their taking a lead in the hostility to Jeremiah. At this stage, the people as a whole are also involved; they have been well-taught. Their words carry an irony, because the people who are liable to the death penalty are the people who go after other gods and encourage Israel to do so.

9a But Jeremiah "announces the violation of the inviolable."[22] It's not surprising there is a reaction. How could Jeremiah claim that Yahweh was saying such a thing? Yahweh would surely not declare that temple and city were going to be destroyed. They are places he has made a commitment to—for example, in Ps 132:13–14. Jeremiah's words clash specifically with Ps 78:67–68, which speaks of Yahweh replacing Shiloh with Zion. (Theories vary over whether those psalms would be earlier or later than this story, but the knowledge that Yahweh had made a commitment to city and temple would in any case be a reality in Jeremiah's day; it had been vindicated a century earlier in their deliverance from Sennacherib.) Jeremiah must be being insolent and presumptuous in making such a declaration in Yahweh's name, and such speaking makes one liable to death (Deut 18:20).

9b-10 The description of how the people *congregated* against Jeremiah sums up vv. 7–9a, though it carries its own irony—they were supposedly gathered in the temple as a different kind of congregation. The royal palace is down the hill from the temple, so the royal officials go up to the temple from there. Tg calls this gateway the eastern gateway, which could refer to the one in 2 Kgs 15:35,[23] the newest gateway as far as we know. It will feature again in 36:10; we don't know whether it is the gateway mentioned in 20:2. One might wonder why the officials weren't in the temple,[24] but their late appearance heightens the drama. Temple security wasn't their business, and deciding blasphemy cases wasn't the king's business (cf. 1 Kgs 21).[25] On the

---

21. Leuchter, *Polemics of Exile*, 25.

22. Diamond, "Jeremiah," 580.

23. See further C. T. R. Hayward, *The Targum of Jeremiah: Translated, with a Critical Introduction, Apparatus and Notes*, The Aramaic Bible 12 (Edinburgh: T&T Clark, 1987), 121.

24. Calvin, *Jeremiah*, 3:343.

25. Volz, *Jeremia*, 95.

other hand, what follows is not a formal trial,[26] and given that Jeremiah is in danger of lynching, it might not be unreasonable for the officials to come to investigate when they hear, or hear of, a disturbance.

11 Jeremiah has spoken of what Yahweh will do and of what they must do. They leave out Yahweh, and they leave out their own responsibility.[27] "His opponents do not claim that his word is false, only that it is prohibited."[28] But "here religion stands against religion. Both parties believe they can claim the weight of the tradition for themselves."[29] The narrator does hint that the people as a whole are less committed to getting Jeremiah put to death than the priests and prophets are, and v. 16 will confirm this hint.

12–16 Jeremiah responds with a bold statement whose implication is that Yahweh's having sent him means he has not committed a capital offense.[30] On that basis, he simply reaffirms his message, then declares that he speaks *in truth* about having been sent. So he has not spoken with presumption and does not fall foul of Deut 18:19–22.[31] It's not really a defense but an assertion. He speaks with authority (cf. Matt 7:29). But he affirms that they will deserve death if they put him to death. Whereas there might have seemed to be an impasse, puzzlingly the argument comes to a conclusion. The people as a whole and the officials are somehow persuaded; they do come out well from the story.

17–18 Chronologically and logically, the intervention of *the elders of the country* likely belongs before v. 16 and explains it;[32] First Testament stories often work like movies in moving forward and then backward in time and giving people the result of events and then the events themselves by way of explanation. The elders who appear as additional participants in the drama would be senior figures in towns such as Bethlehem, Hebron, Morashah, and Lachish—members of the decision-making body there who are present because people from all over Judah are in Jerusalem for the feast or fast. Perhaps the implication is that leaders in the Judahite towns are less degenerate than Jerusalem leaders. It may be no coincidence that they appeal to what happened to Micah, a prophet from one of their towns. His warning comes

26. See the discussion in McKane, *Jeremiah*, 2:676–81.

27. P. D. Miller, "Jeremiah," on the passage.

28. W. Brueggemann, *Jeremiah 26–52*, International Theological Commentary (Grand Rapids: Eerdmans, 1991), 8.

29. Weiser, *Jeremia*, 2:240.

30. Duhm, *Jeremia*, 213. Consideration of his guilt or otherwise does not correspond to prescriptions in Deut 18; see M. Malan and E. E. Meyer, "Jeremiah 26–29: A Not So Deuteronomistic Composition," *OTE* 27 (2014): 921–22; contrast C. F. Mariottini, "The Trial of Jeremiah and the Killing of Uriah the Prophet," *JBQ* 42 (2014): 27–35.

31. Fischer, *Jeremia*, 2:34.

32. Allen (*Jeremiah*, 294) thus translates "some of the country elders had stood up."

in Mic 3:12. The only other occurrence of *ruins* (*'iyyîm*) apart from Mic 1:6 comes in Ps 79:1 (perhaps it also refers back to Mic 3:12).

19 *He sought Yahweh's goodwill* is, more literally, "he got Yahweh's face to be pleasant or sweet." The verb *ḥālâ piel* often denotes the attempt to get someone to be favorable or merciful when one has surrendered any right to favor or mercy and deserves chastisement: on Sinai, Moses turns to Yahweh in this way, and it leads to Yahweh relenting (Exod 32:11–14). While this connotation fits here, there is no reference in Micah or in 2 Kings to Hezekiah's seeking Yahweh's goodwill, though in general terms it fits the story's dynamics (see 2 Kgs 18:3–6; 19:14–19; 20:1–3). But anyway, the elders don't quite say that turning to Yahweh was what led to Yahweh's relenting. What they do imply is that their ancestors knew that Yahweh's declaration of inescapable doom did not mean what it said.[33] "The text assumes that repentance is the proper response to harsh words of destruction."[34] "Everything hinged on the way prophecy was received."[35] And in the years up to 587, the story would urge the administration to follow Hezekiah's example.[36]

20–21 There is no indication of the chronological relationship between what now follows and what preceded; the relationship is thematic. The chapter recognizes that not every prophet escapes as Jeremiah did. The vignette reminds people of what might have happened and of an alternate possibility regarding the way the main plot line might have developed.[37] It brings out what had been "the perilous, indeed deadly, gravity of Jeremiah's situation."[38] Jeremiah 26 turns out to be "a story of three prophets."[39] Kiriath-jearim ("Forest Town," modern Abu Ghosh) is ten miles west of Jerusalem; maybe it's significant that Uriah is another person like Micah and the elders (and Jeremiah) who's not a Jerusalemite. Jehoiakim's attitude to Uriah stands in contrast with Hezekiah's to Micah. It presumably has political implications.

---

33. Diamond, "Jeremiah," 581; cf. D. N. Freedman and R. Frey, "False Prophecy Is True," in Kaltner and Stulman, *Inspired Speech*, 82–87.

34. W. L. Kelly, "Deutero-Jeremianic Language in the Temple Sermon: A Response to Christi M. Maier," in Najman and Schmid, *Jeremiah's Scriptures*, 143.

35. R. E. Clements, "Prophecy Interpreted: Intertextuality and Theodicy—A Case Study of Jeremiah 26:16–24," in Goldingay, *Uprooting and Planting*, 41.

36. C. Hardmeier, "Die Propheten *Micha und Jesaja* im Spiegel von Jer xxvi und 2 Regum xviii–xx," in Emerton, *Congress Volume*, 172–89.

37. H. S. Pyper, "'Whose Prophecy Is It Anyway?' What Micah 3:12 Is Doing in Jeremiah 36," in *Far From Minimal: Celebrating the Work and Influence of Philip R. Davies*, ed. D. Burns and J. W. Rogerson, LHBOTS 484 (London: T&T Clark, 2012), 373.

38. Schmidt, *Jeremia*, 2:79.

39. J. Dubbink, "A Story of Three Prophets: Synchronic and Diachronic Analysis of Jeremiah 26," in *Tradition and Innovation in Biblical Interpretation: Studies Presented to Professor Eep Talstra on the Occasion of His Sixty-Fifth Birthday*, ed. W. T. van Peursen and J. Dyk, SSC 57 (Leiden: Brill, 2011), 19.

Uriah *prophesied . . . in accordance with all Jeremiah's words*, and we know the kind of thing Jeremiah said about Jehoiakim (22:13–19). It's therefore not surprising if the king declined to let Uriah get away with it.[40] The king got no mention in vv. 10–19, which raises the question of what his attitude was to Jeremiah; this vignette points toward an answer Jeremiah needs to be wary of. But in the Jeremiah scroll, Jeremiah and Jehoiakim never meet—presence and absence are reversed in Jer 36.[41]

22–23 Elnathan appears again in 36:12, 25 urging Jehoiakim not to burn the 604 scroll. The contrast points to the tricky position of a king's staff in being under obligation to him and his policies but also being under obligation to take Yahweh seriously (see the references to the *officials* in, e.g., 1:18; 2:26; 8:1; 24:8; 32:32; 36:11–19; 37:14–15; 38:1–4). Here his job is to get Uriah extradited.[42] Taking refuge in the country whose leader had put Jehoiakim on the throne turned out not so wise.[43] The graves of the ordinary people who had no family tomb were apparently in the Kidron Ravine (2 Kgs 23:6): Uriah "was not only persecuted whilst he lived, but his persecutors . . . denied unto him the honour of a Prophets buriall."[44] Although Jer 26 implies a promise about Yahweh's message, it acknowledges ambiguities in that connection. People's response to Yahweh's word varies. It may be negative (the priests and prophets) or positive (the elders, Ahikam) or hard to assess (the officials). The king is ambivalent; the people vacillate. Everything depends on the way human beings respond to situations, and Yahweh's word sometimes does get silenced. Yahweh is the subject of the sending and the speaking at the beginning of the story, and the subsequent story refers back to him in that connection. He also declares the intention to act in light of people's response to his message, and the subsequent story refers back to that intention. But in between the giving of the commission and the implementing of the intention (outside the frame of the story), Yahweh is the subject of no verbs. Yahweh leaves things to the human beings, watching what goes on and hoping for the best (*perhaps*, v. 3); Jeremiah sees himself as in the people's hands. He escapes; Uriah doesn't. Uriah received a prophet's "reward" (Matt 5:10–12).[45] Peter escapes; James doesn't (Acts 12).[46] The account of Jesus's arrest and

---

40. Cf. J. Kegler, "The Prophetic Discourse and Political Praxis of Jeremiah," in *God of the Lowly: Socio-historical Interpretations of the Bible*, ed. W. Schottroff and W. Stegemann (Maryknoll, NY: Orbis), 47–56.

41. R. P. Carroll, *Jeremiah*, OTL, 514.

42. Bright, *Jeremiah*, 171.

43. J. Applegate, "Narrative Patterns for the Communication of Commissioned Speech in the Prophet: A Three-Scene Model," in *Narrativity in Biblical and Related Texts*, ed. G. J. Brooke and J.-D. Kaestli, BETL 149 (Leuven: Peeters, 2000), 86.

44. Mayer, *Commentary*, 420.

45. Dearman, *Jeremiah*, on the passage.

46. Jerome, *Jeremiah*, 165.

trial also has this story as its background.[47] God does not rescue Jesus, as he does not rescue Uriah. But he does restore him to life—indeed he bestows on him resurrection life so that it may be possible for both Jeremiah and Uriah in due course to share it.

24 This *hand* contrasts with the hand in v. 14. As there is no chronological sequence whereby vv. 17–19 follow v. 16 chronologically or vv. 20–23 follow either v. 16 or vv. 17–19, so it is with v. 24 following vv. 19–23. But v. 24 does link with v. 16 in the same way vv. 17–19 do: it provides another bit of explanation for why v. 16 worked out the way it did. The First Testament's first and instructive reference to Ahikam comes in the account of Josiah's reformation (see 2 Kgs 22:12–14). For readers of this scroll, mention of him will also make a connection with Jeremiah's link with his son Gedaliah (39:14; 40:5–16). People listening to the story in different times might know about those links and about Ahikam's famous father, Shaphan. The family will be important through parts 3 and 4 of the Jeremiah scroll:[48]

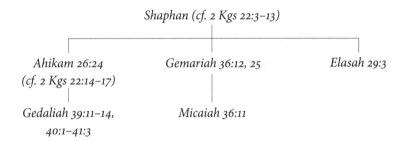

Shaphan (cf. 2 Kgs 22:3–13)

Ahikam 26:24 (cf. 2 Kgs 22:14–17)   Gemariah 36:12, 25   Elasah 29:3

Gedaliah 39:11–14, 40:1–41:3   Micaiah 36:11

One significance of Ahikam coming at the end of the story was perhaps that everyone knew him. The structure of the simple sentence is noteworthy: almost, "Guess who made sure Jeremiah was okay?" Other references to him would make one think that he was one of the officials in vv. 10–16, and this verse suggests he played a key role among them in rescuing Jeremiah. "There has been no repentance," and thus "the larger issue [Jeremiah's] preaching exposed has been sidestepped."[49] But "this simple, unelaborated statement provides an effective climax to the chapter"[50] in giving the last word to Jeremiah's rescue rather than Uriah's death.

27:1a This closing expression pairs with 26:1a in forming a bracket around the story (see the translation note).

---

47. See the detailed comparisons in Keown, Scalise, and Smothers, *Jeremiah 26–52,* 33–34; Lundbom, *Jeremiah 21–36,* 300–301.

48. See Lipschits, *Fall and Rise of Jerusalem,* 84–88. Cf. L. Boadt, *Jeremiah 26–52, Habakkuk, Zephaniah, Nahum,* Old Testament Message 10 (Wilmington, DE: Glazier, 1982), 15.

49. Pixley, *Jeremiah,* 86.

50. D. R. Jones, *Jeremiah,* 345.

2. Jeremiah Bids Judah Submit to the Babylonians
(27:1b–22 [LXX 34:2–22])

^{1b}*This word came to Jeremiah from Yahweh.*^a ²*Yahweh has said this to me. Make yourself restraints and shafts and put them on your neck.* ³*And send them off*^b *to the king of Edom, to the king of Moab, to the king of the Ammonites, to the king of Tyre, and to the king of Sidon by the hand of envoys, the ones who are coming*^c *to Jerusalem to Zedekiah King of Judah.* ⁴*Give them this order for their lords. Yahweh of Armies, the God of Israel, has said this: You will say this to your lords.* ⁵*I am the one who made the earth and the human beings and the animals that are on the face of the earth,*^d *with my great energy and with my bent arm, and I give it to whoever is right in my eyes.*^e ⁶*So now I myself*^f *am giving all these countries into the hand of Nebuchadnezzar King of Babylon, my servant.*^g *Even the living things in the open country, I am giving them to him to serve*^h *him.* ⁷*All the nations will serve him, his son, and his grandson, until the time for his country comes, him too, and many nations and big kingdoms put him into serfdom.*ⁱ ⁸*The nation and the kingdom that do not serve him (Nebuchadnezzar King of Babylon),*^j *the one that does not put its neck to the king of Babylon's shaft: with sword and with hunger and with epidemic I will attend to that nation (Yahweh's affirmation) until I have finished them off by his hand.* ⁹*And you: do not listen to your prophets, to your diviners, to your dreams, to your mediums, or to your augurs, who are saying to you, "You will not serve the king of Babylon."* ¹⁰*Because it's deception that they are prophesying to you, in order to remove you far from upon your country, and I drive you away and you perish.*^k ¹¹*But the nation that lets its neck come to the king of Babylon's shaft and serves him—I will leave it*^l *on its land (Yahweh's affirmation), and it will serve it*^m *and dwell on it.*

¹²*And to Zedekiah King of Judah I spoke in accordance with these words: Let your necks come to the king of Babylon's yoke; serve him and his people*ⁿ *and live!* ¹³*Why should you die, you and your people, by sword, by hunger, and by epidemic, as Yahweh has spoken regarding the nation that will not serve the king of Babylon?* ¹⁴*Don't listen to the words of the prophets who are saying to you, "You will not serve the king of Babylon," because it's deception that they are prophesying to you.* ¹⁵*Because I did not send them (Yahweh's affirmation), and they are prophesying in my name for deception, in order that I may drive you away and you perish, you and the prophets who are prophesying to you.*

¹⁶*And to the priests and to this entire people I spoke: Yahweh has said this. Don't listen to the words of the prophets who are prophesying to you, "There: the objects from Yahweh's house are being returned from Babylon any day now."*^o *Because it's deception that they are prophesying to you.* ¹⁷*Don't listen to them— serve*^p *the king of Babylon, and live. Why should this city become a waste?*^q ¹⁸*But*

if they're prophets and if Yahweh's word is with them, they should please press Yahweh of Armies so that the objects that remain in Yahweh's house and the house of the king of Judah and in Jerusalem would not have come[r] to Babylon.[s] [19]Because Yahweh of Armies has said this regarding the pillars and concerning the reservoir[t] and concerning the stands[u] and concerning the rest of the objects that remain in this city,[v] [20]which Nebuchadnezzar King of Babylon did not get when he took into exile Jeconiah[w] ben Jehoiakim King of Judah from Jerusalem to Babylon, and all the gentry[x] from Judah and Jerusalem.[y] [21]Because Yahweh of Armies, the God of Israel, has said this concerning the objects that remain at Yahweh's house and the king of Judah's house and Jerusalem: [22]To Babylon they will be brought, and there they will be until the day I attend to them (Yahweh's affirmation) and I have them go up and I return them to this place.[z]

a. V. 1a is the conclusion to Jer 26 (see the translation note on v. 1a). As an introduction to Jer 27, v. 1b compares with the introductions in 7:1; 11:1; 18:1; 21:1.

b. The Lucianic recension of the Septuagint lacks *them* and thus implies "send word," but it is hard to parallel this usage of *šālaḥ piel* (cf. Duhm, *Jeremia*, 127–28), and the omission of the suffix perhaps reflects a sense that a literal sending of the restraints and shafts was implausible.

c. Vg has "who have come," but the regular use of the participle to suggest something that is happening or is about to happen fits Jeremiah's not proceeding to meet up with them. Whereas the noun is anarthrous, the participle has the article, but there are parallels for such inconcinnities; see DG 42 remark 2, 112 remark 1; GK 126w. LXX adds "to encounter them," using a noun cognate with its verb in v. 18; it presumably refers to Jeremiah's confronting the envoys, though it fits poorly into LXX's sentence.

d. LXX lacks *and the human beings . . . on the face of the earth*, perhaps by homoioteleuton.

e. Yahweh's verbs *made* (*'āśâ*) and *give* (*nātan*) echo the ones with which he commanded Jeremiah in v. 2 (there translated *make* and *put*): the prescription for Jeremiah's action anticipated and corresponds to this account of Yahweh's action (Allen, *Jeremiah*, 307).

f. LXX lacks *so now* and *myself*.

g. For *my servant*, LXX has "to serve him." On the tricky questions raised by those expressions, see W. McKane, "Jeremiah 27,5–8," in Fritz, Pohlmann, and Schmitt, *Prophet und Prophetenbuch*, 98–110; McKane, *Jeremiah*, 2:688–89. J. Stökl suggests that the difference between the MT and LXX text is an illustration of two different evaluations of Nebuchadnezzar that appear in different texts; see "Nebuchadnezzar: History, Memory and Myth-making in the Persian Period," in *Remembering Biblical Figures in the Late Persian and Early Hellenistic Periods: Social Memory and Imagination*, ed. D. V. Edelman and E. Ben Zvi (Oxford: Oxford University Press, 2013), 265. See also B. Gosse, "Nabuchodonosor et les évolutions de la rédaction du livre de Jérémie," *Science et Esprit* 47 (1995): 177–87; more generally on LXX in relation to MT in Jer 27–28 (LXX 34–35), see R. D. Wells, "Dislocations in Time and Ideology in the Reconceptions of Jeremiah's Words," in Goldingay, *Uprooting and Planting*, 322–50.

h. LXX translates "work for"; so also in vv. 9, 11, 12 (though contrast the previous note).

i. See the translation note on 25:14. LXX lacks v. 7.

j. LXX lacks *that do not serve him (Nebuchadnezzar King of Babylon)*, perhaps by homoioteleuton.

k. LXX lacks *and I drive you away and you perish.*

l. *Wəhinnaḥtîw* is set over against *wəhiddaḥtî* (*I drive you out*) (Keown, Scalise, and Smothers, *Jeremiah 26–52*, 51–52).

m. That is, the nation will serve the land, as the genders of verb and nouns make clear; but LXX has the land serving the nation.

n. LXX lacks from *and his people* through the end of v. 14a, perhaps by homoioteleuton.

o. Lit. "now, tomorrow." LXX lacks these words.

p. The verbal sequence is thus asyndetic and more urgent than the sequence in v. 12.

q. In place of v. 17, LXX simply has "and I did not send them."

r. *Bō'û* is a mixed form, the consonants of a *qatal* and the pointing of a *yiqtol*; the unusual nature of a *qatal* here (see 23:14 and the translation note on it) makes it the more likely reading.

s. MT has a unit marker here. LXX lacks *so that . . . Babylon.*

t. Lit. "sea."

u. LXX lacks the references to pillars, reservoir, and stands.

v. LXX lacks *that remain in this city.*

w. On this form of the name, see the translation note on 22:24.

x. LXX lacks *Nebuchadnezzar* and *ben Jehoiakim King of Judah* and from *all the gentry* to the end of v. 21.

y. MT^L has a section marker here.

z. MT has a unit marker here. LXX lacks *and there they will be* to the end of the verse.

The further account of Yahweh commissioning Jeremiah to perform a symbolic act with no account of his doing so is again an invitation to a Judahite audience to imagine the act and respond accordingly. The story is set more than a decade later than Jer 26, soon after the events of 597 and Zedekiah's accession to the throne (see 28:1). Nebuchadnezzar's authority in Babylon and over the Levant has become a reality. Envoys from neighboring nations have come to Jerusalem, perhaps to persuade Judah to join in another assertion of independence from Babylon. The symbolic act represents submission to Nebuchadnezzar, which Jeremiah urges on them and on Judah. The object involved in the representation is an ox yoke comprising shafts or poles and ropes; the story in Jer 28 that follows has Jeremiah wearing a shaft and another prophet breaking it. Following on Nebuchadnezzar's successful siege of the city, plundering of the temple, and exile of King Jehoiachin and officials, priests, prophets, craftworkers, and other important people in 597, Jer 27 and 28 focus on the fate of the artifacts that he took off to Babylon rather than on the possible return of the people, which will feature in Jer 29. Certainly, the return of a king would cause complications, but maybe this focus would seem snide to readers. Jeremiah 27 and 28 urge Judah to accept that the exiles are not going to come back soon—contrary to the promises of other prophets. Thus the chapters belong together, though each can stand on its own. In the aftermath of 597 or of 587, both stories about symbolic actions would have brought a message to their Judahite audience as well as signifying and implementing the action that Yahweh was declared to be taking.[51]

Why would Yahweh bother with the temple accoutrements? It matches the considerable attention that he gives to such matters in connection with the wilderness sanctuary (Exod 25–40). In any context (the 590s, the time after 587, or the Persian period), the focus of either the LXX or the MT version of this story on the plundering and return of things from the temple speaks to an important theme. Although the Jeremiah scroll has been able to face the loss of the pledge chest with equanimity (3:16), it apparently views the temple's accoutrements as vital. They are symbols of Yahweh's presence with his people and of his involvement with them, he has affirmed their significance in that connection, and they have fulfilled that function for centuries. While attitudes to the temple have gone wrong and imperiled it (7:1–15), this dynamic does not mean the temple loses significance. The city's eventual capture and destruction, the temple's devastation, and the exile of many of the people could seem to introduce an unbridgeable caesura into Israel's story, but the temple accoutrements could contribute to the bridging of that caesura. They will stand for continuity between the First Temple and the Second Temple.[52] The false promises of the other prophets do illustrate how important these things were to Judah, and Yahweh's promises take into account the longing and anxiety about continuity that his people would have. "What seems to stand on the margins, the cultic vessels from Yahweh's house, is in the temple theology a sign for the work of the punishing, liberating, merciful, and powerful God."[53]

After an introduction, the chapter comprises three main sections concerning three related messages:

vv. 2–11   A message for the kings of neighboring peoples: submit to Nebuchadnezzar until his time comes, and don't listen to your advisers who say otherwise

vv. 12–15 A message for Zedekiah: submit to Nebuchadnezzar if you want to live, and don't listen to your prophets who say otherwise

51. Friebel, *Sign-Acts*, 136–54.

52. Fretheim, *Jeremiah*, 386; cf. P. R. Ackroyd, "The Temple Vessels," in *Studies in the Religion of Ancient Israel*, ed. G. W. Anderson et al., VTSup 23 (Leiden: Brill, 1972), 166–81.

53. J. Schreiner, "Tempeltheologie im Streit der Propheten: Zu Jer 27 und 28," *BZ* 31 (1987): 14.

vv. 16–22 A message for priests and people:
don't listen to your prophets who say that the temple objects are coming home soon; everything else is going to go to Babylon until I attend to them

Each section refers to serving the king of Babylon, to the good that will come from doing so and the trouble that will come from not doing so, and to falsehood. But the story also works in a narrative equivalent to staircase parallelism in poetry, by which the second colon in a line partly repeats the first but also takes things further, and a third colon may repeat the dynamic:

- The first message rhetorically addresses the neighboring powers and refers to their prophets, diviners, and augurs; it distinctively speaks of Yahweh's lordship as creator over the entire world and his giving authority to Nebuchadnezzar for a limited time.
- The second message repeats the exhortation about submission but directly addresses Zedekiah and applies it to Judah, referring to its prophets.
- The third message addresses priests and people, begins with a reference to Judah's prophets who ought to be interceding for the city, and declares that more plundering is otherwise destined to happen before Yahweh makes it possible for things to return.

MT's version is over one-third longer than LXX's. As usual, this may reflect accidental omissions in LXX or expansion in MT (see the translation notes).[54] Whereas LXX's text makes no reference to the possibility that Yahweh may restore Judah, MT's version affirms that Nebuchadnezzar's Babylon will not last forever and that there is a prospect of the temple objects eventually returning. The implication might be that LXX's text reflects the message as Jeremiah gave it in the 590s whereas MT's text reflects the way Jeremiah or his curators repreached the message after 587; if one makes a comparison with the Gospels, LXX's version is then more like Mark, MT's more like Matthew.

1b It will become explicit in v. 3 that we are now in the reign of Zedekiah, and it seems that 28:1 is a retrospective note to this chapter (see the translation note there). We are therefore at the beginning of his reign, and the chapter

---

54. E. Tov includes a retroversion of the LXX text into Hebrew in "Exegetical Notes on the Hebrew Vorlage of the LXX of Jeremiah 27 (34)," *ZAW* 91 (1979): 73–93. But A. van der Kooij argues that LXX has abbreviated MT ("Jeremiah 27:5–15," *JNSL* 20 [1994]: 59–78).

lays down the challenge for his reign as Jer 26 laid down the challenge for Jehoiakim's.

2 This prophetic sign is the fundamental motif on which Jer 27–28 is built. Yahweh commands Jeremiah to undertake a symbolic action that overlaps with 13:1–11 (where Yahweh commissions him to undertake an action that he could and did literally undertake), with 19:1–13 (where Yahweh commissions him to undertake an action that he could literally take but where there is no direct report of his doing so), and with 25:15–29 (where Yahweh commissions him to undertake an action that could only be imaginary, and in imagination he does undertake it). Here, the action looks potentially realistic and this-worldly: the *restraints* or ropes and the wooden *shafts* are the two parts of an ox yoke (see 2:19–20 with the translation note and commentary). While it would most commonly be an ox that wore a yoke, which attached it to the plow, a human being might wear a yoke in order to carry a load in a balanced way, and conscript workers, slaves, or prisoners might be compelled to wear one.[55] The action is thus plausible, but it looks only semi-literal; it's hard to imagine Jeremiah putting on multiple sets of restraints and shafts.

3 Jeremiah 28 does suggest that Jeremiah actually made one shaft and put it on, but the shaft evidently stayed in Jerusalem. Sending off shafts and ropes to other kings was thus imaginary or was represented in some way before the envoys: does Jeremiah gatecrash their meeting?[56] Perhaps this story indicates that sometimes a prophet did deliver a message to a foreign nation.[57] But anyway, the chapter doesn't refer to Jeremiah doing as Yahweh said. Whether or not he did, the point as usual lies in the recounting of this message to Judahite listeners. Although it is formally addressed to the five kings, it is designed for Judahites to overhear. The first three nations are the peoples east of the Jordan; the other two are on the coast in the far northwest. The five appear together as in 25:21–22a. They would all be peoples in whom Nebuchadnezzar was interested, because a main route south to Arabia ran east of the Jordan, while Tyre and Sidon were gateways to Mediterranean trade. Jeremiah does not say why the envoys have come. It might be a "courtesy" visit at the beginning of Zedekiah's reign, not long after he has been put on the throne by Nebuchadnezzar. Or it might reflect these peoples' contemplating a declaration of independence from Babylon and coming to lean on Zedekiah to join them (cf. Isa 7), which would fit with Yahweh's

---

55. Foreman, *Animal Metaphors*, 193–94.

56. Wright, *Jeremiah*, 281.

57. P. R. Raabe, "Why Prophetic Oracles against the Nations," in *Fortunate the Eyes That See: Essays in Honor of David Noel Freedman*, ed. A. B. Beck et al. (Grand Rapids: Eerdmans, 1995), 252.

bidding them to submit to Babylon in this chapter. It might be surprising if Zedekiah would contemplate rebellion, as he was put on the throne by Nebuchadnezzar,[58] but he did rebel a few years later (52:3).

4–5 Yahweh's assertion about his identity and power makes sense in the context of his sending a message to these foreign peoples, whether the sending is pretend or actual. Even if his message goes only to Judah, the plausibility of Jeremiah's prophecy about Nebuchadnezzar depends on the truth of this assertion. Yahweh can arrange things so that Nebuchadnezzar acts in a way that fulfills Yahweh's purpose, because he is both *the God of Israel* and the one who *made the earth and the human beings and the animals.* The creation context suggests animals in general (e.g., 16:4; 19:7), but the reference to animals of the wild in v. 6b may imply that the reference here is to farm animals (cf. 9:10[9]; 21:6). Yahweh made the world *by my great energy* (kōaḥ, an inherent ability to do as one likes). And he did so *by my bent arm* (a physical capacity to act as one wishes, like a man wielding a tool such as a hammer, but also frequently an arm that wields a symbol of power such as a scepter). The two expressions reappear in connection with creation in 32:17, but they first come together in connection with Yahweh's getting Israel out of Egypt in Deut 9:29, while 2 Kgs 17:36 makes the same connection in explaining the fall of Samaria. So Yahweh's energy and authority are one, expressed in creation and in political events. He can act in events because he has the same qualities as he expressed in creation. And he can give the resources in the world he made to whomever he wishes. He decides who *is right in my eyes.* The expression does not imply the person who is upright in Yahweh's eyes (as Nebuchadnezzar possibly was not) but the person who seems right in a particular context for a particular purpose: 18:4 is the verb's one other occurrence in Jeremiah (cf. also the related adjective in 26:14; 40:4–5).

6 And giving control of Israel's world to Nebuchadnezzar is what is right to Yahweh, what suits him, *now.* "Now" might imply that it need not be forever; this extra note in MT would constitute even better news for the Judahites after 587 (see the translation note).[59] Even the animals of the wild are to serve him. It is precisely because they serve him that they can be a lethal danger to Judah (12:9); they are the metaphorical and literal ravagers of the land under Yahweh. So Nebuchadnezzar is *my servant.* That description in 25:9 has already nuanced the point: he is Yahweh's servant in that he is the means of implementing the purpose of *the God of Israel* for Judah. Perhaps Judahites who were in Babylon or who later had come back from Babylon might therefore be able to claim that they stood in the context of Yahweh's

58. R. P. Carroll, *Jeremiah*, OTL, 530.
59. See Allen, *Jeremiah*, 307.

purpose.[60] There is no implication that Nebuchadnezzar sees himself that way. The entirety of Yahweh's message in vv. 2–11 relates to Yahweh's purpose for Judah, which is the entity that the message addresses indirectly but primarily and perhaps exclusively. "How unfortunate it is for Israel when in comparison with Israel Nebuchadnezzar is called 'the servant of God'!"[61] What Nebuchadnezzar is going to do, he is going to do; Yahweh is prepared to use it. "God, in siding with Babylon, places a divine imprimatur on the imperialistic policies and campaigns of Nebuchadnezzar."[62] As the God who made the world, then, he can do as he wishes with great empires and with little local powers. Jeremiah does not imply that he always does as he wishes with all those empires and powers, only that he can do it when he wishes. Whether and how he does so will depend on how he is prosecuting his purpose for Israel at a given moment. At the same time, outside the framework of this message, the way he is prosecuting his purpose for Israel relates to his purpose for empires and other powers by a feedback mechanism. Perhaps that point follows from Nebuchadnezzar's being Yahweh's servant, in that a master has obligations to his servant—he cannot simply use him.

7 The serfdom is not short term. In the event, Nebuchadnezzar's son and grandson did succeed him, though the succession was messy; his successors were his son Amel-Marduk, his son-in-law Nergal-sharezer, his grandson Labashi-Marduk, and then Nabonidus, who was unrelated to his dynasty. But Yahweh's declaration concerns a time frame rather than a family sequence. It is related to his declaration that the exile will last seventy years. The rule of Nebuchadnezzar's line will be relatively long-lasting, it will extend to two or three generations, it will go beyond the time of most people alive in the 590s, yet it will not last forever—only *until the time for his country comes* and he becomes serf rather than master. Yahweh does not quite say that the contemporary serf-master relationship will be reversed, and it will not be, in that the replacement of Babylon by Medo-Persia brought no greater freedom or power to the six peoples that feature in this message than they had under Nebuchadnezzar.

8 While it is clear why Yahweh wants Judah to submit to Nebuchadnezzar, it's not clear why he wants the other peoples to do so, unless their resistance to Nebuchadnezzar is in danger of leading Judah astray. We have to recall again that the real recipient of this message is Judah itself. Yahweh's warning to the five peoples is really a warning to Judah not to sell its soul to them. The dynamic of Yahweh's speaking though Jeremiah continues the dynamic of his speaking in Isa 13–23, whose point was to get Judah neither to trust nor fear

60. R. P. Carroll, *Jeremiah*, OTL, 532.
61. Jerome, *Jeremiah*, 167.
62. Fretheim, *Jeremiah*, 387.

other peoples in its world. It fits that the formula to describe the trouble that will come to the five peoples (*with sword and with hunger and with epidemic*) is the same as the formula applying to Judah. But the inclusion of Tyre among the five illustrates how there are limits to the extent to which in practice Yahweh uses his power. Tyre successfully resists his intention that Nebuchadnezzar should conquer it (Ezek 26–29), as the fall of Babylon happens in a different way from Yahweh's declarations in Jeremiah, Ezekiel, and Isa 40–55.

9 Kings such as these five have a range of resources to aid them in formulating policies. The string of terms suggests a tone anticipating the tone of the list of experts in Dan 2, which is perhaps both impressed and skeptical. Distinguishing between some of them is guesswork. *Prophets* were people who could bring the king messages from God that aided him in making decisions. *Diviners* (*qōsēm*) worked out what might be going to happen on the basis of omens such as unusual meteorological phenomena or other strange natural happenings. *Dreams* implies people who shared their own significant dreams or could interpret the king's dreams. *Mediums* (*'ōnēn*) communicated with people who had passed to discover what was going to happen. *Charmers* (*kaššāp*) were people skilled in incantations that could cause or prevent calamities. The kings are not to trust any of them when they counsel resistance to Babylon.

10–11 Again Jeremiah makes the point in the way he would express things to Judah—which is what he is really doing; he's not really interested in what happens to Edom, Moab, Ammon, Tyre, and Sidon. The nations' prophets are *prophesying falsehood* (as Judahite prophets do; e.g., 5:31; 14:14; 23:25–26, 32). They are not consciously seeking to bring disaster, but insofar as they willfully ignore a message from Yahweh about rebelling against Nebuchadnezzar, they are in effect trying to bring about the downfall of their people and to make Yahweh act against them. Yahweh neatly combines their responsibility and his sovereignty. *They* will be removing their people from their homeland; *he* will be driving them out. Both king and people will thus *perish*. But acting as Yahweh says will have opposite results. There are three. Instead of driving the nation out, *I will leave it on its land*. It will thus *dwell on it*. The most interesting verb is the middle one: it will *serve* the land, as Yahweh originally intended in shaping the first human being. A further implication of his words is that, as usual, "judgment is not a fate" for Judah or for any nation. It "can live even now if only it will live under the judgment which has already come upon it, if only it will bring itself under that judgment instead of resisting it."[63]

12–13 Jeremiah now reports how he did address the king of Judah, whom the envoys had come to see. It is to Zedekiah that he actually speaks in light

63. Barth, *CD* IV, 1:470.

of Yahweh's word to him in v. 1, the word relating to the symbolic act; he has reported no speaking to the envoys, because the real point about the chapter is his speaking to Judah. But his plural *your necks* and his plural verbs (all the second-person verbs in vv. 12–15 are plural), followed up by *you and your people*, make explicit that he is not just talking about or to the king. Did the Judahites want Zedekiah, who was the Babylonian nominee, on the throne in place of Jehoiachin? Either way, his confrontation might be "one of the most courageous and outrageous acts of Jeremiah's ministry," going far beyond the temple sermon. It might seem an act of subversion (cf. 38:4).[64] He advocates a "policy of appeasement" in relation to Babylon.[65] Conversely, if Zedekiah was inclined to rebel, he would view Jeremiah as undermining his position, not least by talking to the entire people in this way. And for them, that they have to *serve his people* is a solemn charge.[66] On the other hand, whereas the message formally designed for the envoys talked about death and being finished off and perishing, now Jeremiah also talks about being able to *live* (cf. 21:9; later, 38:2, 17, 20).

14–15 To Zedekiah and Judahites, furthermore, he speaks only of not listening to other *prophets*. He makes no reference to other possible resources, notwithstanding earlier negative references to divination and dreams (e.g., 14:14; 23:32; and cf. 7:30–8:3). In Jer 27–29, the problem he faces is the phenomenon of prophets with different visions. With regard to them, he repeats the critique of v. 10, then backs it up with the declaration from Yahweh that he didn't send them (cf. 23:21, 32) and that they are both *prophesying deception* and *prophesying for deception.* Deception is not only the content of their message (it is a "fantasy"[67]) but even its aim. To say they are prophesying *for* deception also recalls Jeremiah's use of *deception* as virtually a surrogate for the Master (e.g., 5:3, 31).

16 Jeremiah finally turns explicitly to *priests* and *people* in order to focus on a concrete feature of the prophets' promises, which also links with his message to the five kings. After the successful siege of the city and transporting of *objects from Yahweh's house* in 597, one can imagine the temptation to think that maybe Jeremiah had been right after all in declaring that trouble was coming, but that the trouble had now come and surely Yahweh would now let the objects from the temple come back. But there is to be no return, Yahweh says, certainly not *any day now.* The talk of the temple objects would link with his addressing the priests, and they would also be in the mind of the people gathered in the temple courtyard where Jeremiah would deliver his

---

64. D. R. Jones, *Jeremiah*, 347.
65. Rudolph, *Jeremia*, 174.
66. Calvin, *Jeremiah*, 3:393.
67. Brueggemann, *Jeremiah 26–52*, 20.

message. He will also be intending that the people he mentions in the third person, *the prophets*, should overhear the message that is directly addressed to priests and people.

17 Not least for the people's sake, he incorporates reference to the city as well as the temple. And he goes on to his last reference in the chapter to service, a recurrent motif. The key theological notion in this connection is Nebuchadnezzar's being Yahweh's servant (v. 6). When someone is the servant of a king or a King, it gives them authority. So the animals of the wild are to serve Nebuchadnezzar (v. 6); they will thereby serve Yahweh. All the nations will serve him in the sense of accepting his authority (v. 7). To refuse to do so is to collude with a lie (v. 14), and people who do refuse will find themselves in trouble with the master whom Nebuchadnezzar serves (vv. 8, 9, 13). But if Judah, at least, does serve Nebuchadnezzar, it will be the key to life (vv. 12, 17). Thus there are paradoxes embedded in the motif of service. Another is that people who submit to serving Nebuchadnezzar will also therefore be privileged to serve their own land (v. 11). Nebuchadnezzar's position as servant is not voluntary. Not only does he not know it is his position; by implication, he would have no interest in serving Yahweh. He is interested only in serving himself. Thus in due course he will be turned from servant with authority to servant or serf of the people over whom he has exercised authority (v. 7). Jeremiah's language about Nebuchadnezzar overlaps with Paul's in Rom 13:1–7: the authority of governments comes from God, and people should submit to it. The authority is "God's servant for your good." Paul's comment relates to a different sort of context, and Jeremiah's relates to his specific context. But they share the notion of the authority of the imperial power as God's servant in contexts where people would not be enthusiastic about it. And they share the assumption that precisely the notion of servanthood means that authorities do not have carte blanche to do as they like, nor will God tolerate their doing so—because they are his servants.

18 As far as the objects from the temple are concerned, Jeremiah adds that anyway the prophets ought to be concentrating on something else: on lobbying Yahweh on the community's behalf (*pāgaʿ*; see the commentary on 7:16). "These two things are united—teaching and praying. Then God would have him whom he has set a teacher in his Church, to be assiduous in prayer."[68] A prophet stands between God and people and mediates both ways. The link between prophecy and prayer is given paradoxical witness when Yahweh tells Jeremiah the prophet that he is not to pray (see 7:16; 11:14; 14:11–12; 15:1). Whether they pray for the people to whom they (allegedly) bring Yahweh's message is a test of whether they are true prophets.[69] While

---

68. Calvin, *Jeremiah*, 3:406.
69. Thompson, *Jeremiah*, 536.

the *please* is as usual a little sarcastic, it need not signify that Jeremiah doesn't mean his exhortation, which also supports the idea that one shouldn't be literalistic in interpreting those reports of being bidden not to pray for Judah. A further sting in his comment comes near the end, in that there is some ambiguity over whether he is talking about the way they should have prayed (in which case the community would not have lost the temple objects) or about the way they should pray (so that it doesn't experience further losses). In the context of the 590s, both ideas are significant, and when Jeremiah's words are read after 587, they will have telling new significance. Either way, people ought not to be thinking about the things that they say are coming back. They ought to be asking whether they bear any responsibility for the loss of them and thinking about the prospect of the remaining temple accoutrements joining them. It will not just be these objects. As v. 17 MT referred to city as well as temple, here MT refers also to things in *the house of the king of Judah and in Jerusalem*: so people reading this prophecy in its MT form after 587 may be reassured that their loss was somehow covered by Yahweh's sovereignty—and v. 22 will then assure them that this sovereignty will also cover their return.

19–20 There is more to add in connection with the temple. Beyond the easily portable things, other objects of value will fall to Nebuchadnezzar in 587. There are the two *pillars* of bronze standing in front of the temple, the bronze *reservoir* for priestly ablutions standing in the middle of the temple's inner courtyard, and the ten bronze *stands* that may also have related to ablutions. Jeremiah 52:17–23 will relate how Nebuchadnezzar did have them broken up so that the bronze could be taken to Babylon and recycled, and it will give detail on how he also took there *the remainder of the objects that remain in this city*. In a superficial sense, it is surprising that there are any such objects that Nebuchadnezzar did not take along with *Jeconiah ben Jehoiakim and all the gentry*, as 2 Kgs 24:13–16 could give the impression that Nebuchadnezzar emptied the city in 597. But both 2 Kgs 24–25 and the Jeremiah narratives indicate that 2 Kgs 24 speaks hyperbolically—as indeed do 2 Kgs 25 and Jer 52 themselves in their account of what happened in 587.

21–22 Do Yahweh's words presuppose that the fall of Jerusalem is inevitable? If one locates Jeremiah and his listeners in the 590s, it is not inevitable—all talk about its inevitability continues to carry the implicit qualification "unless you turn." If one locates Jeremiah and his listeners after 587, then it is inevitable—it has happened. And what went to Babylon in 597 and what will go in 587 will then be there for as long as Yahweh decides. But three more verbs add a note of promise: Yahweh will *attend*, will *have them go up* and leave Babylon, and will have them *return* to this place—this city or this temple. All three verbs come in Ezra 1:1–3; 2:1 in the account of the fulfillment of these promises. Jeremiah's words thus illustrate how every prophetic scroll that talks about a coming, final calamity also talks about a promise for beyond calamity. One of my first Old Testament teachers, Alec Motyer, who died not long before I began this commentary, liked to say that a prophet who simply spoke of judgment would be a false prophet. No First Testament prophet is portrayed that way. So it would seem unwise to assume that Jeremiah did not envisage restoration after disaster, even in the 590s. In this connection, the Jeremiah scroll's account of the disagreement between Jeremiah and other prophets concerns not *whether* there will be restoration but *when* there will be restoration.

3. How Hananiah Lost His Life (28:1–17 [LXX 35:1–17])

[1]*So it happened that year, at the beginning of the reign of Zedekiah King of Judah.*[a]

In the fourth year,[b] *in the fifth month, Hananiah*[c] *ben Azzur the prophet, who was from Gibeon, said to me in Yahweh's house before the eyes of the priests and the entire people:* [2]*Yahweh of Armies, the God of Israel, has said this. I am breaking*[d] *the yoke of the king of Babylon.* [3]*In yet two years' time*[e] *I am going to bring back to this place all the objects from Yahweh's house that Nebuchadnezzar King of Babylon got from this place and made come to Babylon.*[f] [4]*And Jeconiah*[g] *ben Jehoiakim King of Judah*[h] *and the entire exile group from Judah who were coming to Babylon, I am going to bring back to this place (Yahweh's affirmation),*[i] *because I will break the king of Babylon's yoke.*

[5]*Jeremiah the prophet said to Hananiah the prophet before the eyes of the priests and before the eyes of the entire people*[j] *who were standing in Yahweh's house—*[6]*Jeremiah the prophet said,*[k] *Yes, may Yahweh act in this way—may Yahweh implement your words that you have prophesied, by bringing back the objects from Yahweh's house, and the entire exile community, from Babylon to this place.* [7]*Yet listen, please, to this word*[l] *that I am going to speak in your ears and in the ears of the entire people.* [8]*The prophets who were before me and before you from of old, they prophesied regarding many countries and concerning big kingdoms, about battle and about dire fortune and about epidemic.*[m] [9]*The prophet who prophesies of things being well—when the prophet's word comes about, the prophet can be acknowledged as one whom Yahweh sent in truth.*

[10]*But Hananiah the prophet got the shaft from on the neck of Jeremiah the prophet and broke it.* [11]*And Hananiah said before the eyes of the entire people: Yahweh has said this. In this way I will break the yoke of Nebuchadnezzar King of Babylon in yet two years' time*[n] *from on the neck of all the nations.*

Jeremiah the prophet went on his path.[o] [12]*The word of Yahweh came to Jeremiah after Hananiah the prophet had broken the shaft from on the neck of Jere-*

miah the prophet: [13]*Go,*[p] *and say to Hananiah: Yahweh has said this. Wooden shafts you broke, but you will make*[q] *in their place iron shafts.*[r] [14]*Because Yahweh of Armies, the God of Israel, has said this. It is an iron yoke that I am putting on the neck of all these nations, for serving Nebuchadnezzar King of Babylon, and they will serve him. Even the living things of the open country I am giving to him.*[s]

[15]*And Jeremiah the prophet said to Hananiah the prophet, Listen, please, Hananiah: Yahweh didn't send you and you—you have made this people rely on deception.* [16]*Therefore Yahweh has said this. Here am I, sending you off from on the face of the land—this year you are going to die, because it is a lie*[t] *that you have spoken regarding Yahweh.*[u]

[17]*Hananiah the prophet died that year,*[v] *in the seventh month.*[w]

a. The references to *the beginning of the reign of Zedekiah* and to *the fourth year* look as if they should refer to the same time, which is difficult. I take the first sentence to refer back to the story in Jer 27 as the opening clause in 27:1 refers back to the story in Jer 26; the next sentence then dates the story that now begins; cf. Qara, in MG.

b. The *qere šānâ* is absolute; the *ketiv šnt* is construct (see GK 134p).

c. *Ananias* in LXX, anticipating the story of another deceitful Ananias in Acts 5 (Allen, *Jeremiah*, 315).

d. The *qatal* verb is declarative/performative, denoting what Yahweh has decided to do and is thus in effect doing at this moment; so also the verbs in v. 14 (see 1:5 and the translation note on it).

e. Lit. "two years days"; cf. v. 11; Gen 41:1; 2 Sam 13:23; 14:28. The contexts do not suggest "two full years," which would incidentally reduce the force of Hananiah's point here. There is no difference in connotation between "two years days" and simply "two years," as there is not in English between "two years" and "two years' time."

f. LXX lacks v. 3b.

g. On this form of the name, see the translation note on 22:24.

h. LXX lacks *ben Jehoiakim King of Judah.*

i. LXX lacks *I am going to bring back to this place (Yahweh's affirmation).*

j. LXX has priests and people in the reverse order, which might suggest reference to the priests standing in the temple in the course of their service and keeping an eye on what went on (J. Renkema, "A Note on Jeremiah xxviii 5," *VT* 47 [1997]: 253–55).

k. The *waw*-consecutive is resumptive in relation to the incomplete sentence in v. 5 (Volz, *Jeremia*, 262).

l. LXX has "listen to the word of the Lord," which thus designates this message as more than simply Jeremiah's somewhat mocking comment.

m. LXX lacks *and about dire fortune and about epidemic.* MT's unique sequence contrasts with "sword, hunger, and epidemic" in, e.g., 27:8, 13; it is one of a number of variant but related phrases (see, e.g., 5:12).

n. LXX lacks *Nebuchadnezzar* and *in two years' time.*

o. MT has a unit marker here.

p. The infinitive absolute is used imperatively (cf. 2:2 and the translation note there).

q. LXX has "I will make," which makes sense in light of what follows.

r. The plurals in this verse take up the plurals in Jer 27, referring to yokes for the different nations (v. 14).

s. LXX lacks *Nebuchadnezzar* and *and they will serve him. Even the living things of the open country I am giving to him.*

t. There are two or three homonyms *sārâ* linking with two or three roots but with related meanings: rebellion, falsehood, and apostasy (see *DCH*). In this context, the parallelism with v. 15 suggests falsehood.

u. LXX lacks *because it is a lie that you have spoken regarding Yahweh.*

v. LXX lacks *Hananiah the prophet* and *that year.*

w. MT has a unit marker here.

The story of a confrontation between Hananiah and Jeremiah parallels Jer 26. That story related how Jeremiah told people, priests, and prophets that Yahweh was going to bring about the wasting of the temple; as a consequence, they declared he was to be put to death, but it didn't happen. This story relates how Hananiah tells Jeremiah, priests, and people that Yahweh is going to bring about a restoration of the temple; as a consequence, Jeremiah declares that he is to be put to death, and it happens. The story also follows on Jer 27. There, Yahweh told Jeremiah to model the submission of the city to Nebuchadnezzar's authority and urged it to submit to that authority rather than perish. Here Hananiah tells the people that Yahweh is bringing about Nebuchadnezzar's downfall and models that downfall, but as a result, he does perish.

The account of a prophet's death in Jer 28 thus stands over against the account of a prophet's escape from death. Neither event is attributed to Yahweh, but Jeremiah's escape is implicitly a fulfillment of Yahweh's promise to protect him, and Hananiah's death happens in fulfillment of a declaration that Jeremiah attributes to Yahweh. The Hananiah story thus provides another take on the relationship between prophecy and the danger of death, a recurrent motif in the scroll but one that has featured particularly in Jer 26–27. On one hand, priests, prophets, and people have made death threats to Jeremiah (26:7–24). On the other, Jeremiah has made death threats to people who resist submission to Babylon on the basis of the promises of other prophets (27:8, 10, 13, 15). Here, the link between prophecy and death finds a new expression. It is not the discouraging prophet who dies, but the encouraging one. There is then a link with a motif that is especially prominent in Jer 11–20: the community's opposition to Jeremiah and Jeremiah's experience of rejection is an embodiment of what is going on between the community and Yahweh. In this story, the death of Hananiah for contradicting Yahweh as he brings his encouraging message is an embodiment of the community's destiny if it heeds that message.

Once again, the art of storytelling is on display in this narrative describing how a prophet with an encouraging message drops dead. It is a story characterized by unpredictable and shocking drama, all within seventeen verses. After the retrospective summary of what had happened at the beginning of Zedekiah's reign (v. 1a), it relates:[70]

vv. 1b–11a	Act 1: How Hananiah issued a challenge to Jeremiah's message
vv. 1b–4	Scene 1: How, three years later, Hananiah delivers an encouraging message. There is nothing surprising about this first scene, which gives concrete dramatic expression to generalizations about prophets that have featured in chapters such as Jer 23 and 27. Hananiah's message does contradict what Jeremiah said in the previous chapter, so that dramatically the question it raises is, how will Jeremiah respond to this message?
vv. 5–9	Scene 2: How Jeremiah expresses disbelief about Hananiah's being sent by Yahweh. Again, there is nothing surprising in Jeremiah's response except perhaps in his positive assessment of the idea of Hananiah's promise finding fulfillment, but the audience within the story and the audience listening to the story may well wonder what will happen now, or they may assume that nothing will now happen until time indicates which prophet was sent by Yahweh.
vv. 10–11a	Scene 3: How Hananiah breaks Jeremiah's symbolic yoke. The third scene contains a slight surprise and a dramatic development. The slight surprise is that Jeremiah is actually wearing a yoke of the kind to which 27:2 referred. Although v. 1 made a chronological link with Jer 27 and Hananiah has referred to a yoke in vv. 2–4, we might have forgotten that commission. The dramatic development is that Hananiah breaks Jeremiah's yoke, which might indeed seem menacing. Hananiah is not merely opposing Jeremiah and contradicting what the audience know is Yahweh's own word. He is acting in a way designed to thwart what Yahweh's symbolic action portends and puts into effect. The audience's mouth opens. What will

70. Osuji (*Where Is the Truth*, 198) gives an overlapping analysis of the story.

	happen now? (Although dramatically this scene be- longs here as the climax of act 1, it would make sense if chronologically it followed vv. 1–4.)
vv. 11b–14	Act 2: How Jeremiah issued a challenge to Hananiah's message
v. 11b	Scene 1: How Jeremiah goes home. The immedi- ate answer to the question of what will happen is "not much." Jeremiah has no response in action or word to Hananiah. The audience within the story may think that Hananiah has won, and the audi- ence of the story may continue to wonder what will happen now.
vv. 12–14	Scene 2: How Yahweh gives Jeremiah a discouraging message. The further answer is also "not much." Yah- weh gives Jeremiah a message that is devastating in its implications yet simply a reaffirmation of what he and Jeremiah usually say. The audience will assume that it is obvious what will now happen: Jeremiah will deliver the message.
vv. 15–17	Act 3: How Jeremiah issued a warning to Hananiah and it came true
vv. 15–16	Scene 1: How Jeremiah tells Hananiah that Yahweh will put him to death. The story now surprises and shocks. There is a dramatic jump in that Jeremiah does not do as he was told in vv. 12–14, though chapters in the scroll often omit how Jeremiah fulfills commissions he is given (27:1–11 was an example). The scroll moves easily between being prolix (in the way it indulges in repetition and drives its point home) and being elliptical and fast-moving and thus leaving the audience to fill in the gaps. Here, as well as not relating how Jeremiah passed on the message announced in vv. 12–14, it goes on to relate how Jeremiah gives a dreadful message of which we have not been told. The audience within the story goes home talking about it. The audience of the story listens intently.
v. 17	Scene 2: How Hananiah dies. The narrative closes with a stark, understated denouement that leaves the audience to think about its implications and about all the things that remain unsaid.

The event and the story would bring a message home in the context in which the story is set, the years when the fall of Jerusalem threatens the community. After 587, the story would provide further evidence that Jeremiah was right and further grounds for taking his message seriously now.[71] As was the case in Jer 27, MT's version is rather longer than LXX's.

1 Although the story that will now unfold is more or less self-contained, it connects with Jer 27, and the opening makes that link with its retrospective allusion to *the beginning of the reign of Zedekiah*. But that allusion leads into a reference to *the fourth year* of his reign, about 594. We are thus on the way from the 597 disaster to the siege that led to the city's final fall, though of course no one at the time knows when or even that the other shoe will eventually fall. For this period, the Babylonian Chronicle reports rebellions against Nebuchadnezzar in Babylon:

> 21. The tenth [year: the king of Akk]ad stayed home. From the month Kislev until the month Tebet *there [was]* a rebellion in Akkad.
> 22. [. . .] . . . he put his large [army] to the sword (and) conquered his foe.
> 23. [. . .] He marched [to] Hattu. The kings and . . . [. . .] . . .
> 24. [*came*] and [*he received*] their vast booty. He returned to B[abylon].[72]

We have noted that it would not be surprising if nations like the ones represented by the envoys in Jer 27 engaged in initiating such a rebellion and seeking to draw in Zedekiah, whose visit to Babylon this year (51:59–64) might then be part of the aftermath. *To me* indicates that Jeremiah continues to speak, though the first-person speech holds only for this opening verse. While a Qumran document in Aramaic called "A List of False Prophets" (4Q339) uses the actual expression *nby'y šqr'* and names Ahab, Zedekiah, Shemaiah, and Hananiah,[73] in Jer 28 Hananiah is simply a *prophet*, like Jeremiah; the story keeps adding this description *a prophet* to his name as it does to Jeremiah's name. The generalizations about prophets we have read in the scroll so far could make us think of them as charlatans who were obviously deceivers. This story disabuses readers of that assumption. It would not be

---

71. See H.-J. Stipp's comments (on the reconstructed original version of the story) in "Zwei alte Jeremia-Erzählungen: Jeremia 28 und 36. Fallstudien zum Ursprung der Jeremia-Erzähltradition," *Bib* 96 (2015): 321–32.

72. Grayson, *Chronicles*, 102.

73. *DSS* 2:708–9; cf. Lundbom, *Jeremiah 21–36*, 330.

immediately obvious that Hananiah was a fraud.[74] Coming from Gibeon, he is almost a neighbor of Jeremiah, and for people listening, the two prophets are two Benjaminites who look the same, act the same, and speak the same. The narrative does not suggest that there was a clear distinction between institutional and freelance prophets, central and peripheral prophets,[75] or nationalistic and independent prophets, nor that either Hananiah or Jeremiah belongs to one such group rather than its opposite. Apparently, Hananiah sets up the confrontation with Jeremiah, which is designed to be public: he brings his message to Jeremiah *before the priests and the entire people*. Once again, the scene is the temple courtyard, and once again the gathering may imply a communal event, perhaps a specially called fast; there is no regular event in the fifth month. Or perhaps *the entire people* simply means "all the people who were there at the time" because it was a regular place to hang out or because they had gathered for a family event such as a sacrifice. While this narrative is the scroll's first account of a confrontation between prophets, one may assume that it was not uncommon for there to be a number of prophets pronouncing messages in the temple courtyard and for their messages to be contradictory. They would be the prophets whom ordinary people might consult about something personal or familial, perhaps having recourse to ones they knew might give them the kind of answer they wanted. They would also be the prophets whom the administration might consult, partly on the same basis (27:9, 16; 37:3, 17). In other words, prophets would not offer their messages only on their own initiative.

2–4 Hananiah introduces his message the same way as Jeremiah: *Yahweh of Armies, the God of Israel, has said this.* There is no indication that he was insincere: "Intentionality is no longer a criterion for discernment of distinction between Hananiah and Jeremiah, and thus between so-called false and true prophets generally."[76] He may well have been "conscious of a prophetic call"[77] and "we have no grounds for thinking that Hananiah was not really convinced that he spoke Yahweh's word,"[78] even though "surely these words ought to have been like a thunderbolt to him, laying prostrate

---

74. Fretheim, *Jeremiah*, 391.

75. R. P. Carroll, *Jeremiah*, OTL, 548; cf. R. R. Wilson, *Sociological Approaches to the Old Testament*, Guides to Biblical Scholarship (Philadelphia: Fortress, 1984), 67–80.

76. J. A. Sanders, "Hermeneutics in True and False Prophecy," in *Canon and Authority: Essays in Old Testament Religion and Theology*, ed. G. W. Coats and B. O. Long (Philadelphia: Fortress, 1977), 22; following G. Quell, *Wahre und falsche Propheten* (Gütersloh: Bertelsmann, 1952); see further J. A. Sanders, "Jeremiah and the Future of Theological Scholarship," *Andover Newton Quarterly* 13 (1972): 133–45.

77. T. W. Overholt, "Jeremiah 27–29: The Question of False Prophecy," *Journal of the American Academy of Religion* 35 (1967): 244; cf. Overholt, *Threat of Falsehood*, 38.

78. Rudolph, *Jeremia*, 179.

his perverseness."[79] He uses the same performative form of speech as Jeremiah when he says in Yahweh's name, *I am breaking* (lit. "I have broken"). His image, *I am breaking the yoke of the king of Babylon*, comes from Jer 27; he takes it up in order to counter what Jeremiah had said about this yoke and what it symbolized. In effect, Jeremiah had declared that Nebuchadnezzar and his successors would have peoples under his yoke for several generations, for seventy years, for the lifetime of anyone who was listening, and had said that people should submit to him like an ox submitting to its master's yoke. Hananiah declares that there is a different word from Yahweh. His difference from Jeremiah is not over whether there is hope for Judah's future. Both prophets know there is. But Hananiah declares there is to be restoration now, and Hananiah emphasizes the miraculous nature of what Yahweh will do.[80] Within two years, the temple accoutrements are to come back; their mention makes a further link with Jer 27. "Two years—or seventy years. Who is to be believed?"[81] In addition, the other king and the exiles (unmentioned in Jer 27) are to come back. That declaration directly contradicts Jeremiah (see 22:26–27). It might constitute a mixed message to Zedekiah. The temple objects coming back would be good news, but the other king?[82] You could call Hananiah anti-Babylonian (and risking his life with Zedekiah)[83] and Jeremiah pro-Babylonian. Jeremiah deconstructs the distinction between insiders and outsiders if it means Judahites over against Babylonians, for instance, because some of the insiders are enemies and some of the outsiders are Yahweh's servants.[84]

5–7 Everyone's *eyes* are on Jeremiah *standing in Yahweh's house* in the sense of standing in its courtyard. On the basis of what we have read in the Jeremiah scroll so far, we might guess that in general terms it would be no surprise that a prophet such as Hananiah would be bringing an encouraging message in this context, though its specificity might be new. And the crowd would likely know that Jeremiah saw things differently. Initially, then, they might be taken aback at Jeremiah's reaction, but he soon makes clear that he had been speaking ironically—even if in another sense wistfully (cf. 1 Kgs 22:15). "Jeremiah, the prophet of bad news, prays that his own hard truth is false and that Hananiah's pleasant word is the truth."[85] The confrontation between the two prophets continues to play out *before the eyes of the priests and before the eyes of the entire people*.

---

79. Calvin, *Jeremiah*, 3:414.
80. See Rom-Shiloni, "Prophets in Jeremiah," 355–63.
81. Berrigan, *Jeremiah*, 120.
82. Boadt, *Jeremiah 26–52*, 23.
83. R. P. Carroll, *Jeremiah*, OTL, 542–43.
84. L. Stulman, "Insiders and Outsiders in the Book of Jeremiah," *JSOT* 66 (1995): 65–85.
85. Searcy, "A People," 337.

8-9 Jeremiah's historical observation involves more hyperbole. It most obviously doesn't cover Isaiah, in whose tradition Hananiah could see himself to stand; he could claim that he was declaring the fulfillment of promises such as Isa 9:4(3); 10:27; 14:25.[86] Thus "the curious thing is that considered apart from its historical context, there is nothing particularly 'false' about Hananiah's message."[87] Conversely, one could wonder if "the issue of true and false prophecy turns upon Jeremiah's relationship to the older Isaiah tradition."[88] But Jeremiah's generalization had been broadly true of prophets ever since the split between Judah and Ephraim, not least of the prophets whose messages came to be collected in scrolls such as those associated with Amos, Micah (quoted in 26:18), and Hosea (whose influence one can see in Jeremiah). Even if Hananiah identified with Isaiah, he was being selective in his appeal. While these prophets did bring messages of trouble for *many countries and big kingdoms,* including the likes of Babylon, in the present context Jeremiah more likely refers to such nations as Yahweh's agents in bringing *battle, dire fortune,* and *epidemic* to Israel (cf. LXX, Vg). So when someone such as Hananiah makes promises about things *being well,* don't believe it until you see it.

10-11a Once again, the crowd wonders what will happen next, and Hananiah provides them with another symbolic act. "Hananiah . . . is convinced, imaginative, and intransigent. . . . Unfortunately, it is far easier to break a symbolic yoke than it is to override Yahweh's tough verdict."[89] We don't know if Yahweh intended Jeremiah to make six literal yokes in 27:2; Jeremiah evidently had at least made one yoke, and he is wearing it. As a symbolic act, as usual it is not merely an image of something that should or will happen. Insofar as Yahweh commissioned it, the act is Yahweh's means of implementing his intention that Nebuchadnezzar should rule over Judah. As a symbolic act, then, Hananiah's breaking the yoke is also Yahweh's (alleged) symbolic act. Hananiah's message concerns not merely Judah but *all the nations,* the kind of nations whose representatives appeared in Jer 27. Such a symbolic act would usually precede or accompany the message related to it (cf. Jer 13; 19; 27).[90] Here, the narrative holds back the account of Hananiah's breaking of the yoke to bring act 1 to a climax.

11b Yet again, the crowd wonders, but Jeremiah simply goes away. Is he thrown into uncertainty by Hananiah's certainty?[91] Would it look like an ad-

---

86. Cf. Lundbom, *Jeremiah 21–36,* 333.

87. Overholt, "Jeremiah 27–29," 244; cf. Overholt, *Threat of Falsehood,* 40.

88. Sweeney, *Form and Intertextuality,* 92.

89. Brueggemann, *Jeremiah 26–52,* 27.

90. Keown, Scalise, and Smothers, *Jeremiah 26–52,* 54.

91. Cf. M. Buber, *On the Bible* (repr., Syracuse, NY: Syracuse University Press, 2000), 166–71.

mission of defeat? Or is he simply going home to wait for Hananiah's promise to be falsified? That intention would fit with the criterion in Deut 18:21–22. The meeting between Hananiah and Jeremiah is a classic embodiment of the clash between prophets, where two messages (and symbolic actions) simply confront one another. There is no formal way of telling who is the true prophet, though the criteria implicitly lie behind vv. 8–9 (they were also implicit in 23:9–40). If there is a clash between the theological and moral commitments of a people and the stance a prophet is taking to that people and its future, it shouldn't be so hard to tell that the prophet speaks falsely, and time will tell. In the meantime, Jeremiah has nothing else to say. Nor does Yahweh give him something to say. Paradoxically, "Jeremiah's silence reinforces his credentials as a true prophet. . . . Jeremiah only speaks prophetically when a word of God has been put on his lips." He will not speak until Yahweh gives him something to say.[92]

12–14 But later (who knows how much later?) Yahweh gives him something else to say, again as a message to him—there is no reference to another public confrontation, though the audience listening to the story is able to imagine it. Hananiah has broken one yoke; he is to make another to replace it. He must renounce his false message and become a convert to the message that Jeremiah has been delivering, and he must show he has done so by an action that reverses his previous one. Iron is a substance with connotations that are both positive (Yahweh has made Jeremiah an iron man, 1:18) and negative (Israel once suffered in an iron furnace, 11:4). An iron yoke would be more substantial than a wooden one, and impossible to break. It would be an even more certain expression of Yahweh's intent and implementation of that intent. Yahweh presumably speaks figuratively in saying that Hananiah must make a yoke of this intractable material. As with Jeremiah's symbolic acts, one should not be literalistic about Yahweh's word. Indeed, the important thing is the metaphorical iron yoke that Yahweh is making, whose significance (*Even the living things of the open country I am giving to him*) uses the same words as 27:6 to repeat its point.

15–16 So Jeremiah speaks to Hananiah again, but says something quite different from the message that appears in vv. 13–14. While it is not unusual for the Jeremiah scroll to leave unstated the delivering of a message, it is unusual for it to report the delivering of a different message. Did Jeremiah devise this message and Yahweh then fulfill it (cf. Num 16)?[93] More likely, the audience is expected to infer that it was part of what Yahweh said to Jeremiah so that the narrative again follows a sequence that has a dramatic effect. Hananiah's

---

92. P. Gallagher, "Discerning True and False Prophecy in the Book of Jeremiah," *Asia Journal of Theology* 28 (2014): 9–10.

93. So Isaac Abravanel, *Commentary on the Latter Prophets*.

association with *deception* carries with it a threat: *Yahweh didn't send you* (but you behaved as if he had), so he is *sending you off from on the face of the land.* The warning would carry the connotation of being thrown out of the country (cf. 7:14; 20:6; 27:14–15), but the reference to land (*'ădāmâ*) rather than country (*'ereṣ*) carries an ambiguity. While *land* can refer to country (12:14; 24:10; 27:10–11), it also suggests the earthy land from which humanity was formed and on which people live and die. Jeremiah hints at that broader meaning that makes his threat more frightening. After all, *deception* also links with death (e.g., 14:14–15; 20:6). Jeremiah also uses a rare word for *lie* (*sārâ*; see the translation note); he picks it up from Deut 13:5(6), which makes death the sanction for a prophet who lies. Prophets who bring encouragement are people who turn the community away from Yahweh, and that dire action carries the same sanction (see also Deut 18:20).[94] The implication may not be that a court should impose the death penalty; whereas Jeremiah's opponents thought so (Jer 26), Jeremiah seems not to.[95] There are many acts to which that sanction is attached, and the First Testament does not seem to envisage the human implementing of capital punishment for them. Rather, the guilty person lays himself or herself open to being struck dead by Yahweh. That threat is usually expressed in general terms, and it can easily be discounted. Here, the threat that *you are going to die* with *this year* attached to it outdoes Hananiah's two-year promise[96] and also raises the stakes for Jeremiah, for Hananiah, and for Yahweh.

17 "If Jeremiah is a shocker, Yahweh is nothing less."[97] Fulfillment comes not in two years or one year but in two months. "Hananiah's death provides further proof of the falsehood of his oracles as well as the truthfulness of Jeremiah's."[98] He had dishonored Jeremiah, but in the end it is he who is shamed.[99] There is an irony in Hananiah's name, which means "Yahweh is gracious." It's not a designation just for a person but for a type of prophecy.[100] But "the profound appeal of Hananiah's message . . . continues to disturb confidence about the reader's own present" given "the enduring temptation to claim the LORD's promises" and to trust and hope independently of facing questions God raises about the reader's life.[101]

---

94. On links and contrasts with the material in Deuteronomy on false prophecy, see Malan and E. E. Meyer, "Jeremiah 26–29," esp. 923–25.

95. Bright, *Jeremiah*, 203.

96. Diamond, "Jeremiah," 585.

97. Berrigan, *Jeremiah*, 118.

98. Stulman, *Jeremiah*, 248.

99. M. W. Bartusch, "From Honor Challenge to False Prophecy: Rereading Jeremiah 28's Story of Prophetic Conflict in Light of Social-Science Models," *Currents in Theology and Mission* 36 (2009): 455–63.

100. Fischer, *Jeremia*, 2:79.

101. Keown, Scalise, and Smothers, *Jeremiah 26–52*, 58–59.

4. Jeremiah Bids the Exile Community to Settle Down (29:1–32 [LXX 36:1–32])

[1]These are the words in the document that Jeremiah the prophet sent from Jerusalem to the rest of[a] the elders of the exile community, to the priests, to the prophets, and to the entire people that Nebuchadnezzar had taken into exile from Jerusalem to Babylon,[b] [2]after Jeconiah the king, her ladyship, the overseers[c] (the officials of Judah and Jerusalem[d]), craftworker, and smith went from Jerusalem, [3]by the hand of Elasah ben Shaphan and Gemariah ben Hilkiah, whom Zedekiah King of Judah sent to Nebuchadnezzar[e] King of Babylon, to Babylon.[f]

[4]Yahweh of Armies, the God of Israel, has said this to the entire exile community that I took into exile from Jerusalem to Babylon. [5]Build houses and settle. Plant orchards and eat their fruit. [6]Get wives and father sons and daughters. Get wives for your sons. Your daughters—give them to husbands so that they may give birth to sons and daughters.[g] Become many there; do not become few. [7]Inquire after the welfare of the town[h] where I have taken you into exile. Plead with Yahweh on its behalf, because in its welfare there will be welfare for you.[i] [8]Because Yahweh of Armies, the God of Israel,[j] has said this. Your prophets who are among you and your diviners should not delude you. Do not listen to your dreams that you are generating.[k] [9]Because it is with deception that they are prophesying to you in my name—I did not send them (Yahweh's affirmation).

[10]Because Yahweh has said this. At the behest[l] of the fulfillment of seventy years for Babylon, I will attend to you, and I will implement for you my good word, by bringing you back to this place. [11]Because I myself—I acknowledge the plans that I[m] am making for you (Yahweh's affirmation), plans about things being well and not for dire trouble, by giving you a future and a hope.[n] [12]You will call me and you will go,[o] you will plead with me, and I will listen to you. [13]You will have recourse to me, and you will find, because you will inquire of me with your entire heart. [14]I will let myself be found[p] by you (Yahweh's affirmation). So I will bring about your restoration[q] and collect you from all the nations and from all the places where I have driven you away (Yahweh's affirmation) and bring you back to the place from where I exiled you.[r]

[15]Because you have said, "Yahweh has established prophets for us in Babylon . . ."[s] [16]Because Yahweh has said this regarding the king who is sitting on David's throne and regarding the entire people that is living in this city, your brothers who did not go out with you into exile. [17]Yahweh of Armies has said this. Here am I, sending off against them sword, hunger, and epidemic. I will make them like nasty figs that are not eaten because they are dire. [18]I will chase after them with sword, with hunger, and with epidemic, and make them into something horrific to all the kingdoms of the earth, an oath, a desolation, a thing to whistle at, and an object of reviling among all the nations to which I have driven them away, [19]on account of the fact that they have not listened to my

591

*words (Yahweh's affirmation)—people to whom I sent off my servants the prophets, sending them assiduously,*ᵗ *but you did not listen (Yahweh's affirmation).*

²⁰ *So you, listen to Yahweh's word, entire exile community that I sent off from Jerusalem to Babylon.*ᵘ ²¹*Yahweh of Armies, the God of Israel, has said this regarding Ahab ben Koliah and regarding Zedekiah ben Maʿaseiah, who are prophesying deception to you in my name. Here am I, giving them into the hand of Nebuchadrezzar*ᵛ *King of Babylon. He will strike them down before your eyes.* ²²*From them a formula of slighting will be obtained for the entire exile group from Judah that is in Babylon, saying "May Yahweh make you like Zedekiah and like Ahab, whom the king of Babylon roasted in fire"—*²³*since they acted with villainy in Israel and committed adultery with their neighbors' wives and spoke a word in my name, deception*ʷ *that I had not ordered them. I am the one who knows,*ˣ *and a witness (Yahweh's affirmation).*ʸ

²⁴*Regarding Shemaiah the Nehelamite, you*ᶻ *are to say:* ²⁵*Yahweh of Armies, the God of Israel, has said this. Since you are the one who sent documents in your name to the entire people that is in Jerusalem,*ᵃᵃ *to Zephaniah ben Maʿaseiah the priest, and to all the priests,*ᵇᵇ *saying,* ²⁶*"Yahweh himself has made you priest in succession to Jehoiada the priest, so that there should be appointees for Yahweh's house apropos anyone who is crazy or is prophesying away, and so that you would put him into the cell,*ᶜᶜ *into restraint.*ᵈᵈ ²⁷*So now, why have you not denounced Jeremiah the Anathothite, who is prophesying away for you?* ²⁸*Because consequently he has sent to us in Babylon to say, 'It will be a long time. Build houses and live there, plant orchards and eat their fruit . . .'"* (²⁹*Zephaniah the priest*ᵉᵉ *read this document in the ears of Jeremiah the prophet.)*ᶠᶠ

³⁰ *So the word of Yahweh came to Jeremiah:* ³¹*Send to the entire exile community, saying, Yahweh has said this regarding Shemaiah the Nehelemite. Since Shemaiah has prophesied to you but I myself did not send him, and he has got you to rely on deception,* ³²*therefore Yahweh has said this. Here am I, attending to Shemaiah the Nehelemite and to his offspring—he will not have anyone living among this people and he will not see the good things that I am going to do for this people (Yahweh's affirmation), because it is a lie that he has spoken against Yahweh.*ᵍᵍ

a. LXX lacks *the prophet* and *the rest of.* The background to the latter word may be that some of the elders had passed or that some elders were still in Jerusalem.

b. LXX lacks *that Nebuchadnezzar had taken into exile from Jerusalem to Babylon.*

c. LXX, Vg have "eunuchs" for *sārîsîm,* which is the meaning in, e.g., Isa 56:3–4; but more commonly, the word simply denotes officials (cf. Tg, Theod). The phrase that follows (with no "and" preceding it) clarifies the point.

d. For *of Judah and Jerusalem,* LXX has "and every free person," which suggests the *ḥōrîm,* the *gentry* mentioned in 27:20 MT (see *HALOT*).

e. LXX lacks *Nebuchadnezzar.*

f. MTᴸ has a section marker here.

g. LXX lacks *so that they may give birth to sons and daughters*.

h. LXX has "country," which might seem to make more sense (Duhm, *Jeremia*, 229).

i. MT^L has a unit marker here.

j. LXX lacks *of Armies, the God of Israel*.

k. *Ḥālam* is here uniquely *hiphil*.

l. Lit. "at the mouth."

m. LXX lacks *I acknowledge the plans that I*, perhaps by homoioteleuton.

n. A hendiadys meaning "a hopeful future" (Rudolph, *Jeremia*, 184). LXX lacks *by giving you a future and a hope*.

o. LXX lacks *call me and you will go*. MT's accents link these two verbs, suggesting a going back from exile (Allen, *Jeremiah*, 321).

p. LXX "I will appear" might imply *wənir'ētî* for MT *wənimṣē'tî*. Was MT influenced by Isa 55:5 (Duhm, *Jeremia*, 231)? But HUBP sees LXX's text as theologically motivated. Tg has "I will be inquired of."

q. For the *qere wəšabtî 'et šəbûtkem*, the *ketiv* implies *wəšabtî 'et šəbîtkem*. Vg, Tg translate "bring back your exile"; LXX lacks the phrase but translates similarly when it occurs at 30:3. There seems no way out of the assumption that in this expression, the qal of *šûb* is transitive, as if it were *hiphil*; the usage is virtually confined to this compound phrase (see, e.g., *HALOT*). The rendering in LXX, Vg, Tg links the noun with the verb *šābâ*, which fits most occurrences of the phrase, but not, e.g., Job 42:10. More likely, the noun derives its meaning from its similarity to *šûb*: the phrase is "a sonorous expression of *šûb* with a cognate accusative" (Lundbom, *Jeremiah 21–36*, 355). It would include bringing back your exile, but it implies more. A. T. Morrow and J. F. Quant argue that the phrase's background lies in Deut 30:3; see "Yet Another New Covenant: Jeremiah's Use of Deuteronomy and *šbyt/šwb šbwt* in the Book of Consolation," in Lundbom, Evans, and Anderson, *Jeremiah*, 170–90.

r. LXX lacks *(Yahweh's affirmation)* to the end of the verse.

s. MT^L has a section marker here.

t. See the translation note and commentary on 7:13.

u. MT^L has a section marker here. LXX lacks vv. 16–20.

v. LXX lacks *of Armies, the God of Israel*; *ben Koliah*; *ben Maʿaseiah, who are prophesying deception to you in my name*; and *Nebuchadrezzar*. In MT Jer 27–29, *Nebuchadrezzar* is spelled thus only here.

w. LXX lacks *deception*.

x. For the *qere hayyôdēaʿ*, the *ketiv* implies *hû yōdēaʿ* (Rudolph, *Jeremiah*, 187); the meaning is the same.

y. MT^L has a section marker here (29:9b–31:35a is missing from MT^A).

z. *You* is singular.

aa. For *Yahweh of Armies . . . to the entire people that is in Jerusalem*, LXX has "I did not send you in my name."

bb. LXX lacks *and to all the priests*.

cc. See the translation note on 20:2.

dd. *Ṣînōq* comes only here; *HALOT*, *DCH* suggest a neck iron.

ee. LXX lacks *the priest*.

ff. LXX lacks *the prophet*. MT^L has a unit marker here.

gg. LXX lacks *(Yahweh's affirmation), because it is a lie that he has spoken against Yahweh*. MT^L has a section marker here.

In the a-b-a'-b' arrangement of Jer 26–29, this fourth chapter in the sequence corresponds to Jer 27. Whereas Jer 27 addressed people in Jerusalem but presupposed their interest in the question of the return of temple objects that Nebuchadnezzar had taken to Babylon, Jer 29 addresses people whom Nebuchadnezzar had taken to Babylon but presupposes their interest in the question of their own return to Jerusalem. Both messages would be significant for both communities even though they focus on one or the other. Like Jer 27, this chapter urges the community to accept that the situation is not going to change in the immediate future, though it promises that it will change in due course, and it confronts prophets who are bringing a message contrary to Jeremiah's. At the same time, it follows on from Jer 28, if not as tightly as Jer 28 followed on from Jer 27. Its encouragement to people to settle down suggests that the chronological context is the same as that in Jer 27–28, the early years after 597 when Nebuchadnezzar transported a substantial Judahite group to Babylon. Like Jer 28, the chapter takes up the theme of *šālôm* and closes with a reference to the *lie* (*sārâ*) that a prophet has spoken—this word comes only six other times in the First Testament. Its contents thus correspond to those of one of Jeremiah's oral messages, but Jeremiah is now "prophesying by mail,"[102] necessarily if he could not appear in person.[103] One would not know that they were the contents of a written missive if the introduction had not said so, but prophecy by letter is a known phenomenon in the ancient world.[104]

"Despite the pivotal role given to the exile in biblical scholarship, only a few biblical texts directly address the experience of deportation and exile." Perhaps "the lack of concentrated focus on the experience of deportation in the Bible suggests an inability to deal with this period or an intentional suppression of the experiences of deportation." Jeremiah 29 is thus a rare example of a text that deals with this issue, offering the exiles "strategies for constructing home away from the homeland. The prophet writes to a community displaced by imperial action while at the same time using the resources of the empire to transmit the message." Key to these strategies is the notion of hybridity, "a strategic disruption of dominant power that turns power back on itself through the appropriation of forms, expressions, and structures of that power. . . . Hybridity remains ambivalent, contradictory, and unpredictable." But it thereby "poses threats to dominant power."[105]

---

102. Allen, *Jeremiah*, 323.

103. K. van der Toorn, "From the Mouth of the Prophet: The Literary Fixation of Jeremiah's Prophecies in the Context of the Ancient Near East," in Kaltner and Stulman, *Inspired Speech*, 191–202.

104. M. Dijkstra. "Prophecy by Letter," *VT* 33 (1983): 319–22.

105. S. V. Davidson, *Empire and Exile*, 130, 152, 155, 156.

In a broad sense, Jer 29 comprises a letter or letters, though it does not use either of the Hebrew words for letter (*'iggeret* and *ništawān*) that come in Chronicles, Ezra, and Nehemiah, and it contains none of the salutations or closing phrases that characterize letters.[106] It is "an embedded Hebrew letter."[107] The introduction simply calls it a document, the word that will recur in 30:2; LXX and Vg call it a book; Jerome calls it a booklet.[108] It actually combines more than a single missive; v. 24 marks a new start and v. 30 another new start. Verses 24–29 imply that a prophet among the exiles has written back to Jerusalem in light of Jeremiah's letter, and vv. 30–32 is Yahweh's response to his message. But the chapter is not simply a chronological report of a round of correspondence. It is jerky, and it doesn't provide listeners with the links they need to make straightforward sense of the correspondence. Really, only vv. 4–23 are a straightforward missive; vv. 24–32 as well as vv. 1–3 are a curator's compilation of notes relating to a second round of communication.[109] The absence of vv. 16–20 from LXX might suggest it is an addition; in the chapter as a whole, MT is one-third longer than LXX.[110]

The chapter parallels Jer 26–28 in being jerky, leaving gaps, and putting things in dramatic rather than chronological order. It requires listeners to work hard to understand the sequence of events, like a television drama jumping between scenes and times.[111] Another reason for the jerkiness is the intention that the community in Jerusalem as well as in Babylon should see its significance. Jeremiah affirms neither the people left behind in Jerusalem nor the people taken off to Babylon. Both are equally inclined to listen to the wrong voices and to trust in Yahweh's promises in misguided ways. While the chapter would thus speak to both communities in the 590s, it would also speak to them after 587. After 539, when people were free to move back to their families' former homes in Judah, it would give neither community a basis for taking a superior stance in relation to the other.

106. See D. Pardee, *Handbook of Ancient Hebrew Letters*, Sources for Biblical Study 15 (Chico, CA: Scholars, 1982).

107. M. L. Miller, *Performances of Ancient Jewish Letters: From Elephantine to MMT*, Journal of Ancient Judaism Supplement 20 (Göttingen: Vandenhoeck & Ruprecht, 2015), 160.

108. Jerome, *Jeremiah*, 857.

109. On the possible development of the chapter and of its place in Jeremiah, see, e.g., McKane, *Jeremiah*, 2:744–48; on the coherence of the chapter itself, G. Büsing, "Ein alternativer Ausgangspunkt zur Interpretation von Jer 29," *ZAW* 104 (1992): 402–8.

110. R. de Hoop includes a reversion of LXX into Hebrew in his study of the relationship of the two versions, "Textual, Literary, and Delimitation Criticism," in *The Impact of Unit Delimitation on Exegesis*, ed. R. de Hoop, M. C. A. Korpel, and S. E. Porter, Pericope 7 (Leiden: Brill, 2008), 29–62.

111. M. L. Miller (*Performances*, 160–86) considers further the performance aspect to Jer 29.

1–2 The preamble presupposes Nebuchadnezzar's siege and capture of Jerusalem in 597 and the transportation of the city's leadership and key resource people (see the commentary on 24:1). As the rest of the chapter will show, there was evidently communication between Judahites in Jerusalem and in Babylon, though the distance was nearly a thousand miles and the journey would thus take two or three months. The message would be written on papyrus and rolled up so that it became a *məgillâ*, a scroll, the word that recurs in Jer 36.[112] Although in numbers the *exile community* was not so large (3,023 according to 52:28), the comprehensive list of the addressees of the *document* underscores what a significant group it was. *Elders*, *priests*, and *prophets* are people we hear about in Ezekiel. Even apart from Ezekiel himself, who has

---

112. On papyrus and other aspects of writing in connection with Jeremiah, see Lundbom, *Jeremiah 21–36*, 586–87, 602–3.

not had his commission yet (see Ezek 1:1–3),[113] the prophets there need not all be ones offering false hopes.[114] The list works in a somewhat random fashion, continuing in v. 2 with a further catalog supplementing and overlapping with v. 1; the total compilation gives the listeners a comprehensive impression. The second catalog covers people we already know a little about: we are familiar with *Jeconiah* and with *craftworker* and *smith* from 24:1, and the *overseers* will be the same people as the *officials* in that verse, while *her ladyship* will be the queen mother of 22:26.

3 Communicating over that distance would be monumentally expensive and hardly practicable for a private individual, but the king would need to communicate with his boss in Babylon (cf. 51:59–64) and send taxes,[115] and Jeremiah is able to slip something into a diplomatic pouch.[116] He can do so because the *Shaphan* family is evidently sympathetic to Jeremiah; maybe its support helped to make up for the opposition of his own family.[117] *Elasah* is apparently the brother of Ahikam (26:24); Shaphan and *Hilkiah* were both involved in the process that led to Josiah's reformation (2 Kgs 22). Even if the two sons identified with the principles that were accepted by Zedekiah's father but not by him, apparently it didn't stop him using them. Indeed, maybe Zedekiah would be only too glad to have Jeremiah tell Jehoiachin and company to stay in Babylon.[118]

4–5 Whereas v. 1 had the curators describing Nebuchadnezzar as taking the Judahites into exile, Jeremiah has Yahweh claiming to have done so. His further doubly key phrase in this initial instruction is the exhortation to *build* and *plant*, which compares and contrasts ironically with Yahweh's undertaking to build and plant, beginning in 1:10. Is this building and planting their implementing of Yahweh's undertaking? Was that undertaking less good news than it seemed—as it is to take place in Babylon? Or is their building and planting an interim foretaste of his doing so? Another comparison and contrast lies in the addition of the bidding to *build houses and settle* and to *plant orchards and eat their fruit*, which will recur in v. 28. Such actions indicate settling down for a while. It takes time for trees to grow and bear fruit. In the West, we might similarly speak of buying a house rather than renting.

113. Cf. Jerome, *Jeremiah*, 177.

114. Calvin, *Jeremiah*, 3:443. Tg calls them "scribes" and then has "prophets of deception" in v. 8, "teachers" in v. 15, and simply "prophets" in v. 19.

115. So Nicholas of Lyra; see the excerpt in Schroeder, *Jeremiah*, 228; also Mayer, *Commentary*, 423.

116. Thompson, *Jeremiah*, 545.

117. See B. O. Long's comments ("Social Dimensions," 45–47) on a prophet's family networks.

118. Calvin, *Jeremiah*, 3:446–47.

At the same time, the exhortation implies making a home in a way that resists simple assimilation to the empire.

6 Here, but not in v. 28, a series of further exhortations follows. Building, planting, marrying, having children, watching your children grow up and marry and have children: they are aspects of the full life Israelites would want to live. But not *here*. Yet the young men are not to postpone finding a wife until they get back to Jerusalem, and having married, they are not to wait to have children. If people have children who are growing up, they are to help them find wives and husbands so they can engage in the same process. It will thus be "Generation 1.5" who will really have to do it.[119] Which takes you to a third generation, one that corresponds to the three generations of Nebuchadnezzar's rule (27:7). They are to become many *there*, in Babylon.[120] They may be captives, but they are free where they are; they are not imprisoned. Maybe Nebuchadnezzar sees them as hostages; maybe they were useful. Maybe ordinary Babylonians would not have welcomed these foreigners, these forced migrants.[121] Does the exhortation imply a nonviolent stance in relation to one's foes?[122] Does it imply intermarriage?[123] The opponents of Ezra and Nehemiah might appeal to it in that connection. Or is "the emphasis on the founding of familial institutions in a new geopolitical context . . . a fitting point of order for a group that had been subject to the trauma of captivity and transplantation into an alien social world"?[124] It is thus another way to resist the empire and "create an ethnic enclave within the empire." The family becomes "a symbol of resistance."[125] Either way, there's quite some difference here from the negative connotations of the idea of exile in a heathen land (Amos

---

119. Ahn, *Exile as Forced Migrations*, 107–58.

120. Keown, Scalise, and Smothers, *Jeremiah 26–52*, 62.

121. Cf. B. Katho, "Seek the Peace of the City . . . for in Her Peace There Shall Be Peace for You (Jeremiah 29:4–9)," *OTE* 26 (2013): 349–50.

122. So D. L. Smith, "Jeremiah as Prophet of Nonviolent Resistance," *JSOT* 43 (1989): 95–107; cf. D. L. Smith, *The Religion of the Landless* (Bloomington: Meyer Stone, 189), 127–38.

123. See Ames, "Cascading Effects," 183–84; H. Weippert, "Fern von Jerusalem: Die Exilsethik von Jer 29,5–7," in *Zion: Ort der Begegnung. Festschrift für Laurentius Klein zur Vollendung des 65. Lebensjahres*, ed. F. Hahn et al., BBB 90 (Bodenheim: Hanstein, 1993), 127–39; W. E. March, "Guess Who Is Coming to Dinner! Jeremiah 29.1–9 as an Invitation to Radical Social Change," in *God's Word for Our World: Biblical Studies in Honor of Simon John De Vries*, ed. D. L. Ellens et al., LHBOTS 388 (London: T&T Clark, 2004), 1:200–210.

124. M. Leuchter, "Personal Missives and National History: The Relationship between Jeremiah 29 and 36," in *Prophets, Prophecy, and Ancient Israelite Historiography*, ed. M. J. Boda and L. M. W. Beal (Winona Lake, IN: Eisenbrauns, 2013), 280.

125. Davidson, *Empire and Exile*, 163, 165.

7:17; Hos 9:3).[126] "Let Babylon become the place of *šālôm*! Let it become a new Judah!"[127] The community is to grow, not shrink. Whereas people could think that the Abrahamic (and creation) promise and commission no longer apply, actually they do. Jeremiah has to fight on two fronts, both against frivolous hope and against despondency,[128] and his exhortation is both a constraint and an encouragement. One reason why people such as the Assyrians and Babylonians transported people such as the Judahites was that they needed workers; the need and the action anticipated the way the United States and Britain encouraged immigration from Mexico and from the Caribbean. It meant that Judahites who took Jeremiah's advice were able to do well in Babylon, which also meant it was hard to persuade them to return to Judah when they had the chance.

7 Refugees are thus to become residents, though not citizens.[129] They are to commit themselves to the town where they live. Being concerned for its welfare might suggest participating in its economic life.[130] They are to *inquire after the welfare of the town*—that is, to pray about it,[131] to *plead with Yahweh on its behalf*. What has been three times forbidden to Jeremiah in connection with his own people is encouraged for the exiles in connection with the foreign state.[132] The Babylonians didn't believe in Yahweh, so "if [the exiles] did act on the instruction to pray, it would be a sign of trust in Yahweh's ability to have an effect on people who do not even worship Yahweh."[133] Praying for the imperial city on the basis of what one knows is the real truth about God and the world also incidentally destabilizes that city in reality and in one's own thinking.[134] If Jeremiah implies that the exiles are all in the vicinity of one town, then it is presumably Tel Aviv on the Kebar Canal (Ezek 3:15), southeast of Babylon itself. But surely they were not, and Jeremiah doesn't imply it. His instruction applies to whatever town they live in. Jeremiah's exhortation might seem to clash with other things that peo-

---

126. Rudolph, *Jeremia*, 182–83.

127. Katho, "Seek the Peace of the City," 363.

128. Weiser, *Jeremia*, 2:261.

129. Wright, *Jeremiah*, 291.

130. So E. Bons, "'Work for the Good of the City to Which I Have Exiled You': Reflections on Jeremiah's Instructions to the Exiles in Jer 29:5–7," *Anales de Teología* 19 (2017): 7–22.

131. See S. Wagner, "דָּרַשׁ, *dāraš*," *TDOT* 3:293–307. The reference to the town extends the overlap with Deut 20:5–10; see A. Berlin, "Jeremiah 29:5–7: A Deuteronomic Allusion," *HAR* 8 (1984): 3–11.

132. Fischer, *Jeremia*, 2:95.

133. W. J. Wessels, "Patience, Presence and Promise: A Study of Prophetic Realism in Jeremiah 29:4–7," *Verbum et Ecclesia* 37 (2016): 5.

134. Cf. Davidson, *Empire and Exile*, 167–68.

ple know Yahweh has said. But it fits with Jeremiah's picture of Nebuchadnezzar instead of the Davidic king being Yahweh's servant at the moment, with that picture nevertheless not being Yahweh's or Jeremiah's final word (33:19–26). Likewise, his exhortation contrasts with the promise in Ezek 28:25–26.[135] Parallels of language in Isa 65:18–23 suggest that the prophet whose voice lies behind that passage knew about this letter;[136] that message hints that this one could be reversed. Jerusalem has been the place where Yahweh was accessible, and people were used to praying for its welfare (Ps 122); Jeremiah is not contradicting that awareness. He knows that Yahweh intends to destroy Babylon, and people in Babylon will look forward to that event in their prayers (Ps 137).[137] Yet paradoxically, that assumption can coexist with the exhortation to pray for your enemies. It's in your interests, Jeremiah says (cf. 1 Tim 2:1–2).[138] Whereas the Psalms, then, associate the welfare of Israel with Jerusalem, an implication of Jeremiah's message is that the exiles (who are keen to get back there) might have to ask whether "the success of any future prophetic intercession on their [own] behalf is dependent upon a petition for the welfare of Babylon. The šālôm of the community in exile is bound up with the šālôm of their oppressors." For the time being, for the exiles, "Babylon had replaced Zion as the center of the order of creation." So "the removal of šālôm from Jerusalem . . . did not call the notion of the order of creation itself into question. A restoration of šālôm was still possible, though under changed conditions. Jeremiah's exhortation of the exiles to build houses and plant gardens, to marry and bear children was in fact a call for their renewal."[139] It's almost as if he is saying, "Let's not have too much singing Ps 137." His language in these verses has come to be generalized in connection with Christians' commitment to the town where they live; but the particularities of the context in which Yahweh gives this instruction are important.

8–9 The problem in the background of the exhortation is that there are people in Babylon as in Jerusalem who have a faith in Yahweh and a knowledge of his promises that makes them hopeful that they will not be in Babylon for long enough to make it worthwhile to do the things of which vv. 5–7 spoke. They are tempted to believe the opposite message to that in

---

135. D. Rom-Shiloni, "Ezekiel and Jeremiah," 223–27.

136. B. D. Sommer, "New Light on the Composition of Jeremiah," *CBQ* 61 (1999): 649–51.

137. Volz, *Jeremia*, 273.

138. Theodoret, *Ermeneia*, PG 81:649.

139. J. P. Sisson, "Jeremiah and the Jerusalem Conception of Peace," *JBL* 105 (1986): 440–41; cf. Fischer, "Is There *Shalom* or Not?," 365–66; Ahn, *Exile as Forced Migrations*, 127; H. Gossai, "Jeremiah's Welfare Ethic and the Challenge to Imperial Protocol," in *Postcolonial Commentary and the Old Testament*, ed. H. Gossai (London: T&T Clark, 2019), 258–74.

vv. 5–7, which comes from their *prophets*, *diviners*, and *dreams* (see 14:14; 23:25–32; 24:9; and the commentary there). But they with their talk of Yahweh soon fulfilling his promises to his people actually *delude* (*nāšā'*; see 4:10 and the commentary on it). To put it in Jeremiah's regular terms, they are *deception* (*šeqer*). Yahweh *did not send them*: it is the "Cantus firmus of his performance."[140]

10–11 As Jer 28 has implied, the difference between Jeremiah and other prophets is not over whether Yahweh will break Babylon and bring the exiles back but about the time scale. Whereas the figure of seventy years underscored the direness of the community's fate in 25:11, here "judgment and hope are held together in the figure of the seventy years" (again, it is the length of Babylonian power, not directly of Judahite exile). Neatly, Yahweh takes up the verb *attend to* in this connection, which can mean to take action for or take action against (e.g., 21:14; 23:2, 12; 25:12). And neatly, Yahweh takes up the language of formulating plans, to which the same applies. He has talked about plans before: *Here am I, shaping dire trouble regarding you, and formulating a plan regarding you* (18:11).[141] But now, "against both illusionary expectation and despairing resignation, Jeremiah speaks of God's powerful governance which both settles into exile and ends exile."[142] Jeremiah does not say that the timing is dependent on the Judahites (in Jerusalem or Babylon) turning to Yahweh. If they do turn now, one can imagine that Yahweh might restore them now. But Jeremiah is clear that Yahweh's ultimate purpose is not dependent on their response. Yahweh has plans whose fulfillment will emerge from his long-range purpose, not from what his people deserve. His final intention is not to bring about *dire trouble* (*rā'â*) but to *implement* a word that is *good* (*ṭôb*). His *plans* thus relate to *a future and a hope*, a hopeful future: the phrase contrasts with previous occurrences of the word *future* (*'aḥărît*), which denoted an end with negative connotations (5:31; 12:4; 17:11; 23:20).[143] "The first half of the letter [vv. 4–14] is about *shalom*: first the anticipated *shalom* of the Babylonian exiles (v 7); then the eventual *shalom* of Jerusalem (v 11)."[144] Yahweh's references to his action and their turning reflect a key tension in Jeremiah and elsewhere in the Scriptures. Their seeking and Yahweh's acting are interwoven, but not in a way that is open to any kind of cause-effect explanation.[145]

---

140. Hossfeld and Meyer, *Prophet gegen Prophet*, 112.

141. P. D. Miller, "Jeremiah," on the passage.

142. Brueggemann, *Jeremiah 26–52*, 38.

143. D. R. Jones, *Jeremiah*, 364.

144. Lundbom, *Jeremiah 21–36*, 347.

145. K. A. D. Smelik, "Letters to the Exiles: Jeremiah 29 in Context," *SJOT* 10 (1996): 288; he notes that R. P. Carroll (*Jeremiah*, OTL, 558–59) divides the two ideas between two sources.

12–13 Is the possibility of prayer suspended until the end of the seventy-year period?[146] Fortunately, v. 7 has already made clear that prayer is possible even now. People will not find Yahweh inaccessible or hard to find.[147] The exile offers the chance of a new life,[148] but Jeremiah's account of the form that restoration will concretely take focuses on the prayer relationship between Yahweh and Israel. He uses five terms to describe their side to this relationship. They will *call*, they will *go*, they will *plead*, they will *have recourse*, and they will *inquire*. Calling, the most general expression, covers worship, proclamation, and prayer (3:4, 19; 10:25; 11:14; 33:3) and denotes something that people can do anywhere. But *go* and *plead* (*pālal hithpael*) suggest physically coming to the temple, the place where they know they can find Yahweh but to which they have no access at the moment; they will then approach Yahweh in the way one approaches any king, in order to bring a plea to the person in authority who has the power to grant it. The reference in v. 7 made clear that pleading is regularly something one does for other people, not for oneself. It went along with an exhortation to *inquire* (*dāraš*); *have recourse* (*bāqaš piel*) has similar meaning. Both imply coming to Yahweh to discover what his will is and to lay hold of the resources that he can make available. Yahweh closes his description of what turning to him will look like with a reference to *your entire heart* or mind or will, a similar phrase to the one Moses uses about turning to Yahweh in exile in Deut 4:29.[149] Yahweh then has just two verbs to describe his side of the relationship. The first is *listen*. Like other verbs, such as "know/acknowledge" and "remember/be mindful," *listen* does not denote something that simply happens inside a person's head. When human beings listen, it means they respond and obey. Jeremiah uses the verb in this connection more than anyone (e.g., vv. 8, 19, 20). When Yahweh is the subject, too, it means responding; and in a context like this one, it means doing what the supplicant asks. Given the scores of occurrences with human beings as subject, this rare occurrence with Yahweh as subject has all the more force. Yahweh's other verb is not one of which he is subject in v. 13: it comes as a promise people will *find* him.

14 Here that verb *find* becomes one of which Yahweh is subject. He will be findable (*māṣā' niphal*) to them. Yahweh continues in a way implying some fruitful ambiguity or openness. *I will bring about your restoration.* Understanding this restoration in light of vv. 12–13 could suggest that the prayer

146. R. R. Wilson, "Resources of Jeremiah in Daniel 9," in *Sibyls, Scriptures, and Scrolls: John Collins at Seventy*, ed. J. Baden and E. J. C. Tigchelaar, JSJSup 175 (Leiden: Brill, 2016), 1396–98.

147. Fretheim, *Jeremiah*, 405.

148. Fischer, *Jeremia*, 2:112.

149. See G. Vanoni, "Anspielungen und Zitate innerhalb der hebräischen Bibel: Am Beispiel von Dtn 4, 29; Dtn 30,3 und Jer 29,13–14," in Gross, *Jeremia und die "deuteronomistische Bewegung*," 383–95; Vanoni also sees Deut 30:3 behind the passage.

relationship there described is an aspect of the restoration. But understanding vv. 12–13 in light of the exposition of the restoration here could suggest that the prayer is directed toward that restoration. Yahweh may not respond to prayer for restoration now, but in two or three generations' time he will do so. Bringing about restoration thus means terminating and reversing judgment.[150] Either way, in the context of the 590s or 580s, people in Judah or in Babylon could see this promise as something for their children to look forward to. In the later Babylonian period, it would more and more count as a promise to lay hold of. In the Persian period, people who had known the return from exile and the rebuilding of the temple would naturally focus on the first understanding. Yahweh spells out the restoring of fortunes in terms of the return of the exiles on a broader canvas than merely that of Babylon: *I will collect you from all the nations and from all the places where I have thrown you out* (the theme of collecting and returning appears in Ezekiel as well as in Jeremiah).[151]Again, after 587, that promise will have clear resonance, and if a version of the Jeremiah scroll containing this chapter was available to Jeremiah's community or its descendants in Egypt, then this version of Yahweh's promise might be significant for them.

15 "We are astonished (but not really) to learn that purveyors of false hope have sprung up among the exiles as well."[152] Are they claiming a fulfillment of Deut 18:15, 18? The *because* in v. 15 links not backward but forward, with vv. 20–32. But the continuity will be disturbed for a while by vv. 16–19, which jump in a different direction before coming back to the subject.

16–19 Understanding the chapter thus becomes more complicated as it goes off on a tangent from which it will eventually return, like Paul in Romans. The message of vv. 16–19 corresponds to that of Jer 24. Is it designed to encourage the exiles, or to take the Jerusalemites down a peg or two, or both? It points to the possibility that this "letter" is meant for the Jerusalemites to hear (as the *you* in the closing verb suggests). They have to choose between 29:16–19 and 27:12–15, and they choose by deciding which prophets to believe. Jeremiah's comment on the Davidic king is devastatingly direct, and it would seem to support Jehoiachin over against Zedekiah. The same applies to its comment on the Jerusalemites over against the exiles, though Jeremiah is equally dismissive in relation to Jehoiachin and the exiles. Even more sleight of hand might be required to get a letter that included vv. 16–19 into Zedekiah's diplomatic bag.[153]

---

150. J. M. Bracke, "*šûb š°bût*: A Reappraisal," *ZAW* 97 (1985): 233–44.

151. J. Lust, "'Gathering and Return' in Jeremiah and Ezekiel," in Bogaert, *Livre de Jérémie*, 119–42, 428–30.

152. Berrigan, *Jeremiah*, 123.

153. See Volz, *Jeremia*, 269.

20–22 As Jeremiah's critique in vv. 16–19 ended with the Jerusalemites declining to listen to the prophets Yahweh had sent, it brought us back to the subject of v. 15 with its reference to prophets. It has also softened up the exiles before confronting them. There turn out to be some particular reasons for the letter occupying the first half of the chapter (further anticipating Paul's letters) as Jeremiah now speaks of individuals concerning whom he has received information. The names are new, the critique is familiar, and the threat corresponds to the situation. One can imagine that Nebuchadnezzar would be unenthusiastic about Judahite prophets making promises in Babylon along the lines of the promises Hananiah is making in Jerusalem, and if he executed these prophets, he might be unconsciously acting as Yahweh's servant. But *roasted in fire* is not a natural way to describe burning someone to death, and burning to death is not a regular form of execution in Babylon. The language rather suggests a metaphorical roasting (*qālâ*) as an appropriate fate for a son of Koliah (*qôlāyâ*)—as his becoming a formula for slighting (*qəlālâ*) is also appropriate. So who knows what (if anything) Jeremiah has literally in mind and what actually happened to these two men.

23 The critique combines the innovative with the familiar. Only here does Jeremiah speak of *villainy* (*nəbālâ*), which suggests a willful rejection of the claims implied by one's society's ethical and religious principles. A number of the word's occurrences denote gross sexual wrongdoing (Gen 34:7; Judg 19:23–24; 20:6, 10; 2 Sam 13:12–13), and these villains indeed *committed adultery with their neighbors' wives* but also *spoke a word in my name, deception that I had not ordered them.* Their villainy found expression in their lives and in their ministry. In declaring that he is *the one who knows*, Yahweh might be signaling that he is aware of activities that by their nature the offenders wanted to keep secret. Yet Jeremiah's other references to adultery (e.g., 7:9) may mean that the community was broad-minded and tolerant and that they didn't worry too much about secrecy. Yahweh's declaration about knowing then confronts their failure to think about the implications of their behavior. Either way, Yahweh is in a position to act as *witness* in a court case about this waywardness. In a hearing at the city gate, the elders make decisions on the basis of what witnesses say, and the notion of witnesses includes what Western conventions might call an accuser. Before the heavenly court, Yahweh will be in a position to give eyewitness testimony that is bound to mean a guilty verdict. "How many of our own flock, like Ahab and Zedekiah, prophesy falsehood in the name of the Lord, commit foolishness in Israel and commit adultery with the wives of their fellow citizens who were born of the very same city, the church!"[154] Quite a few, to judge from what one hears.

---

154. Jerome, *Jeremiah*, 181.

24 The missive now lurches in another direction; again the chapter's sequence recalls the jumpiness of episodes in a television drama.[155] The audience has to hold in its mind the reference to *Shemaiah* until we eventually discover why Yahweh has something to say about him and associate what we discover there with what Jeremiah has just said in vv. 21–23 about Ahab and Zedekiah and with what he said in vv. 8–9 about the prophets among the exiles in general. Then we will understand the entire drama. The speaker might be Yahweh and the addressee Jeremiah, or the speaker might be Jeremiah and the addressee a messenger.

25 As we try to work out what is going on, first we discover that Shemaiah is among the exiles and that he has been taking advantage of that diplomatic bag, like Jeremiah. While the use of the plural *documents* might not mean anything (v. 29 will use the singular, and see Isa 39:1 for the plural), it is a noteworthy difference over against v. 1, and the phrase *to the entire people that is in Jerusalem, to Zephaniah ben Ma'aseiah the priest and to all the priests* may suggest that he copied his memo generously. He wanted everyone to know.

26–28 In particular, he wants to lean on Zephaniah (see 21:1) as senior priest so that he gets a grip of Jeremiah, though the story in Jer 21 would make Zephaniah's heart sink at the suggestion. Shemaiah reminds Zephaniah that he stands in the succession of Jehoiada, the tough-minded and tough-acting priest who got a grip of things in the reign of Athaliah and saw to her killing and that of the priest who served the Master (2 Kgs 11:15–20).[156] It is the last clearly-approved slaying in Judah's story up to 587. That link is one pointed reason for referring to him. In addition, he had set up the positions of appointee guards in the temple (*pᵊquddôt*; 2 Kgs 11:18). In Jeremiah's day, the priests are thus in the temple as *appointees* (*pᵊqiddîm*) to have oversight of affairs there, which is the description of Pashhur in 20:1. And one of their responsibilities is to exercise that oversight in connection with *anyone who is crazy or is prophesying away*, which (from Shemaiah's perspective) includes Jeremiah. There's no need to infer that Jeremiah went about speaking in tongues or behaving in odd ways; Shemaiah is simply being insulting about his message. Jeremiah should be put in the cells again (cf. 20:2). At least, he should be *denounced* (*gā'ar*), which is no trivial matter: it somehow puts an end to things, like shaming. When Yahweh denounces the sea or the nations (e.g., Pss 9:5[6]; 80:16[17]; 104:7; 106:9), it stills or silences them.[157] It is

---

155. Duhm (*Jeremia*, 234) calls it an "unparalleled muddle"; but see C. Hardmeier, "Jer 29, 24–32—'eine geradezu unüberbietbare Konfusion'? Vorurteil und Methode in der exegetischen Forschung," in *Die Hebräische Bibel und ihre zweifache Nachgeschichte: Festschrift für Rolf Rendtorff zum 65. Geburtstag*, ed. E. Blum et al. (Neukirchen: Neukirchener, 1990), 301–17.

156. Jerome, *Jeremiah*, 182.

157. A. A. Macintosh, "A Consideration of Hebrew *g'r*," *VT* 19 (1969): 471–79.

Zephaniah's neglect of his responsibility that has led to Jeremiah's being free to send these scandalous messages to the exiles.

29 The explanation that Zephaniah *read this document in the ears of Jeremiah* explains the background to Yahweh's giving Jeremiah the message that vv. 25–26 began to introduce, so that chronologically the order of events is

- Zephaniah gives Jeremiah free rein;
- Jeremiah writes to the exiles;
- Shemaiah complains;
- Zephaniah reports the complaint to Jeremiah;
- Yahweh gives Jeremiah something to say in response.

Did Zephaniah's reading the message count as a rebuke, or was he rather sympathetic to him?

30–32 In light of the unchronological order of events in vv. 24–29, the curators provide a resumptive introduction to Yahweh's message. The initial critique of Shemaiah is the usual one: *I myself did not send him* and *he has got you to rely on deception*. The sanction that will follow also matches other sanctions: he and his family will lose their place in Yahweh's people, and (with poetic justice) they will not see the fulfillment of the promises whose timescale Shemaiah himself questions. Perhaps he will not have children, or perhaps his children will not succeed him in his position of leadership. The *(Yahweh's affirmation)* as an encouragement really to believe what the prophet says is the eighth in the chapter, above average even for Jeremiah. The closing critique is then the distinctive one from the end of Jer 28, a final indication that Shemaiah functions in the same way as Hananiah, as a "Jeremianic anti-type."[158]

B. PART 3B: AT LAST, A FOCUS ON HOPE (30:1–33:26)

Whereas Jer 1–24 and 25 focused on challenge and threat and Jer 25 and 26–29 incorporated a little further indication that disaster will not be the end, Jer 30–33 adjusts the balance and concentrates more on the prospect of a positive future. Individual messages in Jer 30–31 reflect the themes, motifs, and images of the rest of the scroll; they also have substantial links with Hosea and Isa 40–55.[159] Their distinctiveness lies in their focus on promise rather than threat. Yahweh's moving in this direction in the messages he gives to Jeremiah fits his original declaration that Jeremiah was to be involved in

---

158. M. Leuchter, *Polemics of Exile*, 47.
159. Lundbom, *Jeremiah 21–36*, 371–76.

building and planting as well as in pulling down and pulling up (1:10). The declaration reverberates in this document (31:28). Yet the chapters' promises are slightly incongruous in their setting, in that Jer 30–33 follows chapters set in the context of a threatening time, the aftermath of 597 and the beginning of Zedekiah's reign, and it does not suggest that the context is inherently more hopeful. So the setting of the messages in the Jeremiah scroll invites readers to link them with the dark days of Zedekiah's reign, to imagine Yahweh making his promises when the future is bleak. Indeed, the scroll "repeatedly deals with the relationship between present suffering, further danger, and future salvation."[160]

Jeremiah 30:1–3 relates how Yahweh commissioned Jeremiah to write down the messages that will follow in Jer 30–31 about Yahweh's restoration of the people and the country. It will be a "booklet of consolation" or "comfort";[161] Jer 36 gives us a general picture that can enable us to imagine the writing of this document. Jeremiah 32–33 then relates events late in Zedekiah's reign during the last months before the fall of Jerusalem, when the situation is at its most bleak and Yahweh bids Jeremiah engage in a symbolic act that is a sign of his commitment to the restoration of the people and the country. In Jer 30–33 as a whole, then, the scroll manages "to pack all the hopeful elements into the siege period, so that even before the city had fallen its future rise should be announced."[162] Whereas we might have expected the vision of a new future to come at the end of the scroll, it actually comes as "a glowing centre, a hidden life, yet to emerge in historical specificity."[163]

The implication is not that the messages themselves necessarily come from this chronological context, or from any one chronological context. The scroll might include messages Yahweh gave Jeremiah over decades that he did not then generally share because they would surely compromise his threats, and the focus on Ephraim in Jer 31 has raised the question whether much of its material has a context back in the beginning of Jeremiah's work. So the document would parallel the 604 scroll in collecting Jeremiah's messages over several decades.[164] Here, too, messages will have been collected and up-

---

160. Keown, Scalise, and Smothers, *Jeremiah 26–52*, 83.

161. Duhm, *Jeremia*, 237.

162. R. P. Carroll, *Jeremiah*, OTL, 634.

163. O'Connor, "Jeremiah," 512.

164. See Volz, *Jeremia*, 277–302 (he calls the chapters "Prophecy of Salvation for the Northern Kingdom"); Rudolph, *Jeremia*, 188–89. Holladay (*Commentary on Jeremiah* 2:155–71) systematically analyzes the material as having an origin in Jeremiah's preaching to Ephraim in Josiah's day, applied to Judah and updated by Jeremiah on the eve of 587 and then redacted later. See also, e.g., J. Unterman, *From Repentance to Redemption: Jeremiah's Thought in Transition*, JSOTSup 54 (Sheffield: Sheffield Academic, 1987), 38–53; M. A. Sweeney, "Jeremiah 30–31 and King Josiah's Program of National Restoration and Religious

dated as Yahweh's message in the later context, and here, too, it is questionable whether we can work our way back behind it to an earlier version.

But 30:1–3 gives no date for this commission. When Yahweh commissioned Jeremiah to write the 604 scroll (36:1–7), he was unable to preach publicly. This other scroll might have issued from a time when he was in custody and unable to preach in person (cf. 32:1–2; 33:1). The document has the exiles especially in mind (30:3); maybe the time has now passed when Jeremiah had to discourage the 597 exiles from being immediately hopeful. Or its contents might suggest a time after the fall of Jerusalem, when Jeremiah would be in a position to start bringing a message about restoration in Judah. Jeremiah 30–31 then comprises a message designed for people traumatized by the experience they have gone through.[165] It would complement the story in 2 Kings, with its more exclusive focus on the catastrophe itself and its relative lack of encouragement.[166] Within the Jeremiah scroll, the transition to Jer 30–31 parallels Ezekiel's move from the drift of Ezek 4–24 (in the time of Zedekiah) to the orientation of Ezek 33–48 (when news of the fall of Jerusalem has arrived). The setting in which people prayed the prayers in Lamentations (whatever it was) would provide a context for the delivery of these messages, and it would fit their resonances with prayers in the Psalter. The account of Jeremiah's own life after the city's fall as he moves from Jerusalem to Mizpah to Egypt could thus also provide a setting for his delivering them. There is a striking echo of "to build and to plant" at Mizpah (42:10). It is also easy to imagine the compiling of the document in Egypt and the sending of copies to Jerusalem and Babylon and to imagine curators in any of these locations developing its contents as they may have developed the rest of the contents of the eventual scroll. All these possibilities are possibilities, guesses between which we do not have a basis to judge.

While the writing of documents that is mentioned in the Jeremiah scroll is partly practical, it is also a symbolic and performative act,[167] a sign-act.[168]

Reform," *ZAW* 108 (1996): 569–83; N. Lohfink, "Der junge Jeremia als Propagandist und Poet," in Bogaert, *Livre de Jérémie*, 35–68; Leuchter, *Josiah's Reform*, 70–86. For critique and alternative proposals, see, e.g., T. Odashima, *Heilsworte im Jeremiabuch: Untersuchungen zu ihrer vordeuteronomistischen Bearbeitung*, BWANT 125 (Stuttgart: Kohlhammer, 1989); W. McKane, "The Composition of Jeremiah 30–31," in Fox et al., *Texts, Temples, and Traditions*, 187–94; M. A. Halvorson-Taylor, *Enduring Exile: The Metaphorization of Exile in the Hebrew Bible*, VTSup 141 (Leiden: Brill, 2011), 43–106. On the differences between MT and LXX in Jer 30–31, see B. Becking, "Jeremiah's Book of Consolation," *VT* 44 (1994): 145–69.

165. See, e.g., L. J. Claassens, "The Rhetorical Function of the Woman in Labor Metaphor in Jeremiah 30–31," *Journal for the Theology of Southern Africa* 150 (2014): 67–84.

166. G. Galil, "The Message of the Book of Kings in Relation to Deuteronomy and Jeremiah," *BSac* 158 (2001): 406–14.

167. R. P. Carroll, *Jeremiah*, OTL, 568–69.

168. So Keown, Scalise, and Smothers, *Jeremiah 26–52*, 88.

The documents that eventuate (36:32; 51:59–64) are not given to anyone. The point lies in the writing at least as much as in the existence of an immediate audience. The documents implement the events of which they speak. They are the guarantee that Yahweh's word will find fulfillment. But recording their writing thus also assures readers that the events of which they speak will take place, and it establishes that events that followed, such as people's freedom to return to Judah and rebuild temple, city, and community, did fulfill Yahweh's will and Jeremiah's words (all of which also applies in 25:13 regarding the document it refers to). It is for such a future readership that this document is copied into the Jeremiah scroll as a whole. It is also significant for them in connection with aspects of it that remain to be fulfilled. The incorporation of these documents in the wider Jeremiah scroll also means they are available to Israel on an ongoing basis. Whatever happened to produce this particular document, what emerged would continue to speak to people in Judah, in Babylon, and in Egypt over subsequent decades and centuries.

"Both Jews and Christians pervert this passage, for they apply it to the time of the Messiah; and when they hardly agree as to any other part of Scripture, they are wonderfully united here; but . . . they depart very far from the real meaning of the Prophet."[169] For people who are not living in the traumatic circumstances of the early sixth century, these chapters

- invite us to enter into the life, suffering, and prospects of people living through those decades; as is the case with any exercise in empathetic historical imagination, it is impossible to predict what will be the fruit of doing so;
- invite us to think about the life of the people of God in the 530s and 520s and through the Second Temple period as they lived with these chapters, sometimes seeing them fulfilled and rejoicing in what Yahweh was doing in fulfillment of his promises, while sometimes seeing them unfulfilled and continuing to live in hope;
- provide us with ways of looking at how God's activity in Jesus did bring the fulfillment of some of these promises and how the promises continue to indicate agendas to which God is committed;
- offer us resources for looking at the way God acts in relation to his people now;
- present us with images for picturing what the final consummation of God's purpose will look like.

169. Calvin, *Jeremiah*, 4:6, referring to Jer 30:4–6, though by 30:9, Calvin says the prophecy has become messianic (13); see, e.g., Qimchi, in MG (though Rashi relates it to the exile); Nicholas of Lyra (see the excerpt in Schroeder, *Jeremiah*, 234).

Six times, 30:1–31:22 says *Yahweh has said this*; these introductions divide it into six sections. While each section incorporates a message from Yahweh in the narrow sense, they also incorporate words of Jeremiah, of Ephraim, and of Rachel; they thus illustrate how the idea of a message being Yahweh's word can have a broad meaning. As well as providing listeners with a signpost regarding the structure of the chapters, the introductions constitute a reminder to them that they are to treat the whole as a "divine word."[170] Another pattern in the document's arrangement is that the gender of the addressees alternates:

30:5–11	masculine	30:12–17	feminine
30:18–31:1	masculine	31:2–6	feminine
31:7–14	masculine	31:15–17	feminine
31:18–20	masculine	31:21–22	feminine

Israel thus appears as clan head Jacob, comprising men who have lost their manliness (30:5–11); as Zion, abandoned by her lovers (30:12–17); as clan head Jacob, whose city will be rebuilt (30:18–31:1); as young girl Israel, still loved and destined to rejoice (31:2–6); as firstborn son Ephraim, still cared for by his Father (30:7–14); as weeping mother Rachel, promised she will see her offspring again (31:15–17); as prodigal son Ephraim, for whom his father still has compassion (31:18–20); and as young girl Israel, urged to stop wavering and embrace her destiny (31:21–22).

1. Introduction to the Document (30:1-4 [LXX 37:1-4])

¹*The word that came to Jeremiah from Yahweh.*
²*Yahweh, the God of Israel, has said this: write for yourself all the words that I have spoken*ᵃ *to you in a document.* ³*Because there, days are coming (Yahweh's affirmation) when I will bring about the restoration*ᵇ *of my people Israel and Judah (Yahweh has said). I will bring them back*ᶜ *to the country that I gave their ancestors so that they possess it.*ᵈ
⁴*So these are the words that Yahweh spoke regarding Israel and regarding Judah.*

a. Qimchi (in MG) in effect implies that the *qatal* is anticipatory (see the introduction to 13:18–22, pp. 354–55): Yahweh is referring to the messages he is about to give.
b. See the translation note on 29:14; here, however, Vg takes *šəbût* to mean "restoration."

170. R. P. Carroll, *Jeremiah*, OTL, 596.

c. *Wahăšibōtîm* makes for a paronomasia with *wəšabtî šəbût*, notwithstanding the previous note on the meaning of that phrase.

d. MT^L has a unit marker here.

1–2 *The word that came to Jeremiah from Yahweh* is a common marker of a new sequence in the Jeremiah scroll; the next occurrences will come at 32:1; 34:1; 34:8. Here, it leads into a substantial introduction to Jer 30–31, signifying the new stage in the Jeremiah scroll as a whole. As usual, "although Jeremiah is the one addressed . . . , the real recipient of the word-event is not the prophet but the people" (cf. v. 4).[171] The commission anticipates 36:2, though it also thereby highlights the question of what is the *all*? Verse 3 will give the answer.

3–4 The document's contents relate to *the restoration of my people Israel and Judah*, which will be the subject of Jer 30–31. *I will bring about the restoration* "states the theme" of the chapters,[172] though it "lacks specificity"; *restoration* is initially spelled out in the promise to *bring them back to the country that I gave their ancestors*, which "makes concrete the programmatic theme of reversal" by embodying it in the promise of a return to the land. This promise is "the central, quintessential hope of the Jeremiah tradition" that "gives materiality to biblical faith; it concerns real life in the world" in that land is indispensable to human life, human identity, and human hope.[173] The introduction presupposes that the people have been thrown out of their land; in other words, in reality or in imagination, it sets the promises in a context after 597 or after 587. The people it refers to are exiles, perhaps in Babylon, in Egypt and elsewhere, rather than the people left behind in Jerusalem—though many of the messages that follow would be significant in Jerusalem, too. Jeremiah's task is to encourage the devastated people with the reassurance that the catastrophe is not the end. *Days are coming* (7:32; 9:25[24]; 16:14; 19:6; 23:5, 7; 31:27, 31, 38; 33:14; 48:12; 49:2) suggests certainty but gives no indication of time scale. And the subject of the chapters that follow is *my people*, spelled out as *Israel and Judah* (cf. 36:2). That phrase rules out the claiming of the promises by (for instance) any one group of exiles. And if (some of) the messages originally related to Ephraim in particular, then they are now adapted so as to apply to Judah too. Reference to *Israel and Judah* began in Jer 3, where the association was an association in faithlessness, and so it has usually been (5:11; 11:10, 17; 13:11), but Jeremiah has also spoken of the restoration of both households (23:6). He will now develop that motif. He doubles the reference in vv.

171. B. A. Bozak, *Life "Anew": A Literary-Theological Study of Jeremiah 30–31*, AnBib 122 (Rome: Pontificio Istituto Biblico, 1991), 28.

172. Volz, *Jeremia*, 289.

173. Brueggemann, *Jeremiah 26–52*, 47.

3 and 4, in case you were not sure you heard it right the first time. Israel and Judah will once again *possess* the country: the verb is one that characterizes Deuteronomy. It occurs in the promises in Deut 30:1–10, which presuppose the context of exile; indeed, "the whole of the Book of Consolation can be viewed as a prophetic expansion in full poetic colour of the expectation and promise expounded in Deuteronomy 30:1–10."[174]

2. *A Reversal for Zion (30:5–31:1 [LXX 37:5–38:1])*

The first chapter of promise starts realistically with the toughness of the situation in Judah to which something new needs to be said and sets the "new thing" over against the toughness. Each of its three sections has Yahweh acknowledging the trauma and hurt that he has brought about by the action he has taken in his wrath against his people in their waywardness. Each sets against that acknowledgment his promise that he is bringing renewal and well-being.

30:5–11	Trembling and terror give way to relief and release
30:12–17	Injury and pain give way to regeneration and healing
30:18–31:1	Restoration and compassion displace fury and incomprehension

a. Trembling Terminated (30:5–11)

⁵*Because Yahweh has said this.*

The voice of trembling we have heard, ᵃ
  terror, and there is no well-being.
⁶*Please ask and look*
  whether a male gives birth.
Why have I seen every man,
  his hands on his haunches like someone giving birth,
  and [why] have all faces turned to greenness?
⁷*Oh,* ᵇ *because that day is big,*
  so that there is none like it.
A time of distress it is for Jacob; ᶜ
  and from it he will find deliverance? ᵈ

⁸*On that day (an affirmation of Yahweh of Armies):*

174. Wright, *Jeremiah*, 301.

I will break his yoke from upon your neck,
    *your restraints*ᵉ *I will tear off,*
    *and foreigners will not make him into a serf*ᶠ *anymore.*
⁹ *They will serve Yahweh their God,*
    and David their king,
    *whom I will set up for them.*ᵍ

¹⁰ *So you, don't be afraid, my servant Jacob (Yahweh's affirmation),*
    don't panic, Israel.
Because here am I, delivering you from far away,
    and your offspring from their country of captivity.
*Jacob will return and be quiet,*ʰ
    will relax, with no one making him tremble,
    ¹¹ *because I will be with you (Yahweh's affirmation) to deliver you.*

*Because I will make an end among*ⁱ *all the nations*
    where I have scattered you.
Yet of you I will not make an end,
    *but restrain you through the exercise of authority,*ʲ
    *and certainly not treat you as free of guilt.*ᵏ

a. LXX has "you will hear," which matches v. 6 and makes the text easier.

b. For MT *hôy* (on which see the commentary on 22:13), LXX implies *hāyû* ("were") and attaches it to the previous line.

c. The first three cola in v. 7 are noun clauses; in the absence of verbs, one has to infer the time reference from the context. While v. 6 would suggest past, past ill fits the fourth colon and what follows in vv. 8–11.

d. LXX and Vg take this clause in the obvious way as a statement, but the transition within the line is then harsh. The word order perhaps supports the idea that it is an unmarked question (B. Becking, *Between Fear and Freedom: Essays on the Interpretation of Jeremiah 30–31*, OTS 51 [Leiden: Brill, 2004], 139); see the translation notes on 3:1; 25:29. Either way, a positive affirmation about deliverance follows in vv. 8–11.

e. LXX has "their neck, their restraints"; see the commentary.

f. See the translation note on 22:13.

g. MTᴸ has a section marker here.

h. The subject separates *wəšāb* from *wəšāqaṭ*, which makes it unlikely that the phrase means "he will again be quiet."

i. As Vg (and LXX at 26:28 = MT 46:28) recognizes, v. 11a has *bə*, but v. 11b has the object marker.

j. *Lammišpāṭ* usually means "for the exercise of authority" or "for the making of a decision," which fits even Isa 28:26 with the verb *yāsar*, but here the meaning must be similar to *bəmišpāṭ* in 10:24 (see the translation note).

k. MTᴸ has a unit marker here. LXX lacks vv. 10–11; it has them at 46:27–28 (which came earlier in the LXX order, as 26:27–28). On *nāqâ* piel, see the translation note on the adjective *nāqî* at 2:34; the infinitive precedes the finite verb, underlining the (negative) factuality of the action. Tg takes *nāqâ piel* to mean "empty out" in accordance with its possible etymo-logical meaning and with the *niphal* in Isa 3:26 (Blayney, *Jeremiah*, 366).

"Fearful dread is portrayed, as it is often pictured in Jeremiah."[175] While the portrayal of trembling and terror could match the aftermath of 597, Jer 27–29 suggested how during the reign of Zedekiah, Jeremiah combined promise and challenge/threat, whereas vv. 5–11 comprise a message offering promise without any warning of further catastrophe. Such a message may more likely link with the final disaster in 587. The portrayal suggests that calamity is in the midst of happening, which could imply a setting in the siege that will lead to Jerusalem's fall, but it promises that the end will not be the end. It goes on to offer "a study in contrasts."[176]

> v. 5a   Introduction
> vv. 5b–7   A lament at Jacob's situation in light of the disaster that hangs over him (four bicola plus a tricolon at the center)
> vv. 8–9   Yahweh's promise of freedom for Jacob from one servitude to accept another (an introduction followed by two tricola)
> vv. 10–11 Yahweh's further encouragement (two bicola and a tricolon, then another bicolon and a tricolon)

5a The introduction parallels the introduction to 14:1–12. As happened there, Jeremiah will in fact go on to talk about what he has heard and seen; we get Yahweh's actual message in relation to those facts in vv. 8–11. What Jeremiah has heard and seen thus constitutes background to that message, yet it is also part of it.

5b It might be misleading to speak in terms of what Jeremiah has seen and heard; what he describes is people's reactions to things that one might have seen and heard. It compares with the Psalms in this respect. We discover that people are *trembling* and beset by *terror,* but not what has caused those reactions; we are not even told who is doing the trembling and panicking. Insofar as we learn anything objective of that kind, it is a negative: *There is no well-being.* Coincidentally, perhaps, but significantly, this comment follows on a sequence of references to well-being in 23:17; 25:37; 28:9; 29:7, 11. The prophets' promises of well-being have indeed failed. Read in light of Jer 2–6, a description of this kind would denote something Jeremiah has seen in imagination, but here the context with the promises and encouragements that will come in vv. 8–11 suggests he is referring to what is now actually happening in fulfillment of those earlier visions that sought to forestall disaster. But following the pattern of those visions, he speaks not merely

175. W. H. Schmidt, *Jeremia*, 2:111.
176. B. A. Bozak, *Life "Anew"*, 34.

objectively (people are trembling and terrified . . .) but subjectively (*I have heard . . . seen . . .*). He thereby also conveys the empathy of the prophet and of Yahweh toward the people who are experiencing trembling and terror. He and Yahweh know about the suffering of the people to whom he brings Yahweh's message. "Even God is taken aback at the severity of the suffering of the people."[177] There is no "I told you so" here, though there will be some later. Nor is there an emphasis on waywardness or an urging of repentance; their time is before the catastrophe, when it can still be avoided.[178] Jeremiah draws later audiences into that empathy, too, and into the awareness of Yahweh's empathy. In the Antiochene crisis in the 160s, for instance, when we know people were reading Jeremiah (see Dan 9), Jeremiah draws them into a realization that Yahweh has heard and seen.

6 While women have reason to feel fearful and anxious about giving birth, in the First Testament *trembling* and *terror* are not associated with giving birth but with battle. Thus v. 6 adds another image; Jeremiah takes up wording from Isa 19:16. It was supposed to be what happened to Israel's foes (Deut 2:25), but it is happening to Israel (cf. the vision in 6:24–25). Jeremiah pictures men afraid and consumed by anxiety in light of the prospect of defeat, and the position they then adopt resembles that of a woman in the midst of giving birth. They are turned in on themselves, hunched up, themselves adopting a fetal position, the color drained from their faces. The word for *man* (*geber*) suggests someone who would normally be rather macho, but such valor has gone. The tricolon underlines the point.[179]

7 The terror-making crisis is visibly on its way, and the reaction of fear relates to the frightening reality of the day that is dawning. The word *day* almost deserves a capital D. Jeremiah is talking about a day of huge significance, a day of military and political catastrophe, a *time of distress* (see 14:8, which goes on to talk about deliverance; 15:11). In 16:19, it is *a day of distress*, an embodiment of Yahweh's day, a day *big* in importance because of its frightening nature (Joel 2:11, 31; Zeph 1:14; Mal 4:5). *Distress* is another expression associated with childbirth (4:31; 6:24; 49:24). Such terror and trembling were supposed to be the destiny of Israel's foes; Jeremiah uses the expression "Yahweh's day" only in connection with the Egyptians (46:10). In this message about restoration, we might have hoped that through vv. 5–7 he was describing their fate. Only now is *Jacob* identified as the person over-

177. Fretheim, *Jeremiah*, 416.
178. B. Lindars, "Rachel Weeping for Her Children," *JSOT* 12 (1979): 51–52.
179. For feminist reflection on this imagery, see C. J. Sharp, "Mapping Jeremiah as/in a Feminist Landscape," in Maier and Sharp, *Prophecy and Power*, 48–50; L. J. Claassens, "'Like a Woman in Labor': Gender, Queer, Postcolonial and Trauma Perspectives on Jeremiah," Maier and Sharp, *Prophecy and Power*, 117–32.

whelmed by terror. *And from it he will find deliverance?* Is there any prospect that Yahweh will prevent that day arriving?

8 The imagery changes; vv. 8–9, with their new introduction, could originally have been a separate promise,[180] though they fit the context. In the context, Yahweh's first response picks up the phrase *that day* and neatly reworks it: that day becomes the day of liberation. The imagery picks up from Jer 27–28. Submit *your neck* to Nebuchadrezzar's *yoke* and *serve* him and his people, Jeremiah had said; he had been commissioned to make *restraints* in this connection (27:2, 12). *Break his yoke from upon your neck?* That was Hananiah's talk (28:2, 4, 11). *You served alien gods?* Okay, *you will serve foreigners* (5:19). Yahweh is causing them to do so. But Jeremiah has also indicated that the submission and service were to be temporary. They might last some seventy years, or two or three generations, but not forever. Yahweh will terminate that arrangement. "A hope against divine violence has been displaced by a hope *in divine violence.*"[181] *On that day* and *his yoke from upon your neck* echo Isa 10:27;[182] it is now a promise relating to Babylon. *That day* is that day. There is something to look forward to. Jeremiah portrays "God's wrath as salvation for Israel."[183]

9 So Israel's restraints are torn off. Domination by the empire is not the end of the story. But it would be misleading to say that Israel is simply set free. Neither Testament pictures people being liberated from bondage so that they do as they like. They are taken out of one service to fulfill another, as happened at the exodus. Yahweh's words in v. 8 thus have a different resonance. He had complained, *long ago you broke your yoke; you tore off your restraints, and said, "I will not serve"* (2:20; see the translation note and commentary on 2:19–20). Now, *they will serve Yahweh their God*, and serve *David their king, whom I will set up for them.* The 587 catastrophe will mean they have no king of their own, but Yahweh has promised that David will reign again (17:25; 22:4; 23:5, where Yahweh speaks in terms of "setting up"; 33:14–26). The people's expectations need to be political as well as material.[184] If it should seem that people simply are being delivered from one servitude to another, there is some reassurance in those promises that express Yahweh's expectations of the Davidic king as himself Yahweh's faithful servant (33:14–26).

10a–b A further promise, also perhaps originally independent of the

180. A. Rofé, "David Their King (Whom God Will Raise)," in *Leshon Lemuddim: Essays on the Language and Literature of the Hebrew Bible in Honour of A. A. Macintosh*, ed. D. A. Baer and R. P. Gordon, LHBOTS 593 (London: T&T Clark, 2013), 130–35; cf. Becking, *Between Fear and Freedom*, 135–64.

181. Diamond, "Deceiving Hope," 39–40.

182. *CTAT*, 2:682.

183. Fretheim, *Jeremiah*, 424.

184. Brueggemann, *Jeremiah 26–52*, 49.

present context, continues both from vv. 5–7 and from vv. 8–9. Instead of trembling and being terrified, *don't be afraid, my servant Jacob . . . ; don't panic, Israel.* Verse 10a comprises neatly parallel bicola:

> So you, don't be afraid, my servant Jacob (Yahweh's affirmation),
>   don't panic,   Israel.
> Because here am I,   delivering you from far away,
>   and your offspring   from   their country of captivity.

The encouragement in vv. 10–11a as a whole outlines:

v. 10a	An exhortation not to be afraid
v. 10bα	An assurance that Yahweh is present
v. 10bα–β	A promise that he is going to act
v. 10c	A description of what will follow
v. 11a	A rationale

Its promise of deliverance has the elements of a pattern that recurs elsewhere, especially in Isa 40–55 (e.g., 41:8–13), though the phrases are also Jeremianic (1:8, 17; 15:20).[185] Perhaps the prophet who speaks in Isa 40–55 picked up and developed phrases from Jeremiah, or perhaps these verses pick up phraseology from Isa 40–55 and constitute a later addition to the Jeremiah scroll, or perhaps both prophets work within a familiar tradition. The prophecy's form goes back to that of a priest bringing reassurance and encouragement to an individual (which is the way the message speaks)[186] or to that of prophetic oracles among other peoples;[187] it has been adopted and adapted so as to bring the same warm encouragement to the community. We have heard about servant Nebuchadrezzar, and we will shortly hear about servant David (25:9; 27:6; 33:21–26); here for the first time we hear about *servant Jacob.* On its first appearances in Isa 40–55 (in 41:8–9), *my servant* signifies the master's commitment to his servant Israel, which is the context here. Yet the servant language also picks up from vv. 8–9, where it relates to the servant's commitment to his master (cf. Isa 42:1–4). If the community is going to serve Yahweh, then as Yahweh's servant it has nothing to be afraid of. Masters look after their servants. They will be involved in *delivering* them, in fact: so the answer to the incredulous question about *deliverance* in v. 8 is yes, though the deliverance will come after the time of distress; it will not forestall it. Deliverance is another motif in Isa 40–55, as is *here am I* followed

---

185. J. M. Berridge, *Prophet, People, and the Word,* 184–98.
186. Bright, *Jeremiah,* 286.
187. Becking, *Between Fear and Freedom,* 155–61.

by a participle (43:19, though it's also another expression that recurs in Jeremiah), and the return of the people's *offspring* (Isa 43:5) from *far away* (43:6; 49:12) and from *captivity* (49:24–25).

10c–11a The promise about returning, being quiet, and relaxing, *with no one making him tremble* is a more distinctive promise that picks up from v. 5. Yahweh looks beyond the return to the life Israel will live subsequently. The promise leads into a third colon, providing the undertakings with some backing: *because I will be with you (Yahweh's affirmation) to deliver you.* Yahweh recycles phrases applied to Jeremiah himself in 1:19; 15:20. Presence and deliverance mean both that the bringing back will happen and that the security back in the land will be a reality. If the reference to deliverance in v. 7bβ does not take Jacob "through night to the light,"[188] then the section as a whole with this closing promise in v. 11a does so.

11b–c Yes, *I will make an end among all the nations where I have scattered you.* Yahweh picks up the terms of 9:16(15). There, scattering meant making an end of them, and Yahweh is in the midst of fulfilling that threat. Yet he has also said that he would not make an end of them (4:27; 5:10). Here, he squares the circle by talking about making an end *among* the nations; making an end *among* them doesn't count as making an end *of* them there. Deliverance will be possible; there will be something to deliver. Yahweh's action against Jacob means to *restrain* them, correct them, as Jeremiah imagined them asking him to (10:24; and cf. 6:8 and the noun in 2:30; see the translation note and commentary on 2:19–20, 30). He will *certainly not treat you as free of guilt.* He is referring to the discipline and chastisement in which he is engaged at the moment. But he hasn't annihilated them. Apart from this verse and the parallel 46:28, the only occurrences of the infinitive that comes here are in Exod 34:7; Num 14:18; and Nah 1:3. Like the Nahum reference, Jeremiah is taking up that key statement about Yahweh from Sinai and from Kadesh. Yahweh's self-description is what is evident in the calamity that has come to Judah. But it's subordinate to compassion and commitment.

b. You Deserve Your Injuries, but I Will Heal (30:12–17)

[12]*Because Yahweh has said this.*

Indeed,[a] your[b] injury is grave,[c]
  your striking down severe.
[13]*There is no one making decisions for you[d] in connection with the sore[e]—*
  means of healing, new growth, there is none for you.
[14]*All your friends have put you out of mind;*

188. Rudolph's heading for vv. 5–7 (*Jeremia*, 189).

you they do not inquire after.
Because with a striking down by an enemy I have struck you down,
with correction by someone fierce, [f]
On account of the multiplying of your waywardness,
your wrongdoings being numerous. [g]
[15] *Why do you cry out because of your injury,*
your pain grave?
On account of the multiplying of your waywardness,
your wrongdoings being numerous,
I did these things to you. [h]

[16] *Therefore, all the people who consume you—they will be consumed,*
all your foes, all of them—they will go into captivity. [i]
Your plunderers will become plunder,
all your spoilers I will give as spoil.
[17] *Because I will make regeneration grow up for you,*
and your strikings down—I will heal you (Yahweh's affirmation),
Because "Driven away" they have called you:
"It's Zion, [j] *which there is no one inquiring about."* [k]

a. Taking the *lə* as emphatic (F. Nötcher, "Zum emphatischen lamed," *VT* 3 [1953]: 380).

b. *Your/you* is feminine singular throughout vv. 12–17.

c. For MT *'ānûš*, LXX's "I raised up" may suggest a form of or an interpretation in light of Hebrew *nāśā'*.

d. For *dān dînēk*, cf. 5:28; 22:16.

e. On *māzôr*, see *DCH*.

f. LXX, Vg "fierce correction" implies *mûsār* for MT *mûsar*, but the construct fits the parallelism.

g. The *qatal* continues the infinitival construction here and in the next verse (*TTH* 118).

h. LXX lacks v. 15.

i. LXX has "they will eat their own flesh"; HUBP suggests a combination of a different reading or misreading and some consequent adaptation.

j. For MT *ṣiyyôn*, LXX implies *ṣêd* ("prey").

k. MT[L] has a section marker here.

Like vv. 5–11, these verses start from the suffering and anguish of the community. They constitute a concentrated expression of the theme of affliction that recurs in Jeremiah.[189] In isolation, one might take them as the suffering and anguish of the city after 587, but the sections on either side suggest a moment when the city's fall is imminent but has not quite happened, so this section may issue from the same setting. In the midst of disaster, then, Yahweh seeks

189. J. Muilenberg, "The Terminology of Adversity in Jeremiah," in *Translating and Understanding the Old Testament: Essays in Honor of Herbert Gordon May*, ed. H. T. Frank and W. L. Reed (Nashville: Abingdon, 1970), 47.

to get people to face facts, but he also promises that the calamity will not be the end. When disaster strikes, people naturally ask why it has happened, and often there is no explanation. On this occasion, the answer lies in Zion's waywardness. Crying out as if the calamity were undeserved is therefore out of order. "Jeremiah speaks not out of indignation but with firmness born out of exasperation."[190] Yet that robust response is not all Yahweh has to say. With apparent illogic, *therefore* he will put down Zion's attackers and restore it. Thus "the major image of the poem" is "woundedness turned to healing."[191]

v. 12a	Introduction
vv. 12b–14a	The community's plaint (three bicola)
vv. 14b–15	Yahweh's response (a) (three bicola and a tricolon)
vv. 16–17	Yahweh's response (b) (four bicola)

12-13 The introduction again implies that Yahweh speaks, as in due course v. 14b will confirm. But in the three lines he is reflecting back what the people themselves would be saying in their prayers or in their laments to one another. The addressee, too, is unnamed, but it is feminine singular, and the last colon in the section will at last name *Zion*. She is a woman who has been done *grave injury*, struck down in a *severe* way. It might have been an accident, nobody's fault. But *there is no one making decisions for you in connection with the sore* implies an analogy with someone who has been injured; it takes the view that somebody is to blame and ought to be accepting responsibility for seeing to her medical care (cf. Exod 21:18–19). But nobody is doing so. Thus there are no *means of healing*, no *growth* of new flesh and skin (cf. 8:22; the city also spoke like a woman in these terms in 10:19–20). "No court will take up Israel's 'lost cause.'"[192]

14a Yahweh begins to hint at a transition to some different imagery. Never mind the person who made it happen. *All your friends have put you out of mind* too. *You they do not inquire after.* Nobody cares (cf. 15:5, 18). But *friends* ('āhab piel participle) has bad connotations (see 22:20, 22). Actually, it suggests Judah's allies, who would be responsible for the wounding. It suggests the usual suspects—Moab, Edom, Ammon. So there's an irony in saying they don't care. Of course they don't. Further, *friends* can also suggest lovers, and this woman is one who has often been accused of unfaithfulness and wrongful loving (2:25).

14b-15 Yahweh gets more explicit, in several directions. A plaint like the one lying behind vv. 12–14a would often charge him with being the cause of the problem or being the one who ought to be doing something about it and isn't. The plaint's not doing so has thus raised a little suspense: who is the cause and why is he being neglectful? First, he himself now claims respon-

190. Brueggemann, *Hopeful Imagination*, 37.
191. Bozak, *Life "Anew"*, 57.
192. Fretheim, *Jeremiah*, 420.

sibility for the wounding. Indeed, it's no slight wound. He *struck . . . down*; the verb (*nākâ hiphil*), which lies behind the noun in v. 12, often implies killing. Like their so-called friends, he has behaved like an enemy. If his action was designed to be corrective or disciplinary (cf. v. 11), it was *correction by someone fierce*. It was exercised with an intensity that implied abandoning compassion (cf. 6:23). The parallelism works neatly in an a-b-c-d-b'-c' pattern to clash with the harsh message:

because	with a striking down	by an enemy	I have struck you down
	with correction	by someone fierce	

The Psalms commonly accuse Yahweh of being responsible for his people's suffering and claim there is no reason for it. Here Yahweh affirms responsibility and asserts that there is good reason—as happens in Lamentations and in Isa 40–66. That factor behind the events of 597 and 587 is the one commonly denied by those Psalms. As happens in Isa 40–66, Yahweh answers back. His action responded to *the multiplying of your waywardness* and *your wrongdoings being numerous*. When people have been attacked without cause (and thus have a basis for arguing that the elders should require their assailant to pay their medical expenses), they have reason to *cry out* (*zāʿaq*) like Israel in Egypt (Exod 2:23). Zion cannot cry out in that way *because of your injury* and because of how *grave* is *your pain*: it brought its trouble on itself. The rationale is the same as the logic when Yahweh tells Jeremiah not to pray for the people (e.g., 15:1).[193] The last colon sums up the middle line in v. 14 and thus completes a chiasm in vv. 14b–15, another piece of poetic neatness that clashes with the subject matter:

> v. 14b   I struck you down.
>   v. 14c   It happened because of your waywardness.
>   v. 15a   So why are you crying out because of your injury?
>   v. 15bα–β   It happened because of your waywardness.
> v. 15bγ   I did these things to you.

16 Yahweh goes in for a magnificently illogical *therefore*, as he sometimes does (cf. 15:19; 16:14; see the commentary there). Given that Zion can't claim to deserve anything different from Yahweh, vv. 16–17 "are constructed to make a detailed and deliberate counterpoint to the preceding."[194] What does

---

193. P. D. Miller, "Jeremiah," on the passage.
194. W. Brueggemann, "The 'Uncared for' Now 'Cared for' (Jer 30:12–17)," *JBL* 104 (1985): 423.

the *therefore* imply? At the moment, "Yahweh's motivation is obscure,"[195] but one must be wary of smoothing out such incongruities[196] and be prepared to wait for the answer to questions. Meanwhile, Yahweh simply asserts that the *people who consume you* were unwittingly Yahweh's agents, but they were behaving fiercely for their own reasons, and *they will be consumed*. The *foes who took Zion into captivity* (in the person of her children) *will go into captivity*. The *plunderers will become plunder*, the *spoilers* will become *spoil*. As is commonly the case in the First Testament, the calamity is the mirror image of the wrongdoing; here the parallelism underlines the point:

> Therefore   all the people who consume you   they will be
> consumed
> all your foes all of them   they will go into captivity
> Your plunderers   will become as plunder
> all your spoilers   I will give   as spoil

The first three cola also point to a natural process of justice built into how life works. It is not exactly a matter of the punishment fitting the crime, as there is no reference to crime or punishment. But the last colon also affirms that Yahweh claims responsibility for the working of this process as he did for the wounding. Only here does the principle of an eye for an eye come in, and it is Yahweh who implements the principle, not Zion.

17 Is reparation what Zion wants? It wasn't the implication of where we began in v. 12. Punishing the attackers will not deal with Zion's cries. "The 'wounds' of Jerusalem (19.8) must be healed."[197] They will be. Again, Yahweh speaks in neat parallelism, without the clash we have noted, and with an a-b-b'-a' sequence at the center (verb-noun-noun-verb) whose reversal mirrors the reversal in the action:

> I will make grow
> regeneration for you
> and your strikings down
> I will heal

The God who struck also bandages. He will make new flesh and new skin grow where the injury is. He will heal the wounds that issued from his

---

195. Diamond, "Jeremiah," 590.

196. W. van Heerden, "Preliminary Thoughts on Creativity and Biblical Interpretation with Reference to Jeremiah 30:12–17," *OTE* 6 (1993): 348.

197. B. Gosse, "The Masoretic Redaction of Jeremiah," *JSOT* 77 (1998): 79.

striking down. There is to be miraculous healing of "a hopeless case."[198] The logical link in the first line—the *because*—is again not especially logical, but the closing line with its further *because* may meet the desire for logic and answer the question raised by the *therefore*, not least through making a link with the earlier reference to someone *inquiring about*.[199] It relates to the passage's "poetics of absence."[200] If people are calling Zion *driven away*, outcast, they can hardly be faulted; driving away is what Yahweh has often threatened (e.g., 27:10, 15; 29:14, 18). Here Yahweh faces the painful results of what he had to do to his people. He hears other people describing them that way, and it means he has to take restorative action. Even if Zion deserves there to be no one inquiring about her, Yahweh cannot tolerate it forever. The Jeremiah scroll has imagined people walking past the ruined city and expressing their horror and commenting on the reasons for it (18:16; 19:8; 22:8–9). It now imagines them needing to change their tune. The "name" *driven away* will indeed be reversed (Isa 62:12).[201]

c. A Restored City and Relationship (30:18–31:1)

[18]*Yahweh has said this.*

Here am I, bringing about the restoration of Jacob's tents;
  on his dwellings[a] *I will have compassion.*
A city will be built up on its tell,
  a citadel[b]*—it will sit for the exercise of authority for him.*[c]
[19]*Thanksgiving will go out from them,*
  the voice of revelers.
I will make them many—they will not become few;
  I will honor them—they will not be belittled.[d]
[20]*His children will be as they were of old,*
  his assembly[e]*—it will stand established before me.*
I will attend to all his oppressors;
  [21]*his lord will come from him.*

198. Lundbom, *Jeremiah 21–36*, 401.

199. Brueggemann, "The 'Uncared For' Now 'Cared for,'" 425; it is one of the indications that vv. 12–17 do integrally belong together (Becking, *Between Fear and Freedom*, 165–87).

200. Sharp, "Mapping Jeremiah as/in a Feminist Landscape," 48; she notes how prominent is *'ên* ("there is no") as a "marker of absence" in Jeremiah (cf. vv. 5, 10).

201. Lundbom, *Jeremiah 21–36*, 402, citing B. Halpern, "The New Names of Isaiah 62:4," *JBL* 117 (1998): 639.

His ruler—he will go out from his midst,[f]
  and I will bring him near and he will come up to me.
Because who will be the one who has pledged his heart
  to come up to me? (Yahweh's affirmation).[g]
[22]*So you will be a people for me,*
  and I—I will be God for you.[h]

[23]*Here is Yahweh's storm—*
  fury has gone out.
A storm is raging—
  on the head of the faithless it will whirl.
[24]*Yahweh's angry blazing will not turn*
  until his acting on and implementing his mind's intentions.
In the later days,
  you will have insight into it.[i]

[31:1]*At that time (Yahweh's affirmation):*

I will be God for all Israel's clans[j]
  and they—they will be a people for me.[k]

a. LXX "his imprisonment" perhaps issues from understanding *šəbût* (*restoration*) to mean "captivity" (McKane, *Jeremiah*, 2:774); LXX also lacks *tents* in the first colon.

b. LXX, Vg, Tg have "temple," but there are no other occurrences of this meaning for *'armôn*.

c. The nearest parallel to the unique *'al mišpāṭô yēšēb* is Isa 28:6; I take the suffix to refer to Jacob.

d. LXX lacks this colon.

e. LXX "testimonies" suggests *wə'ēdōtāw* (cf. 4QJer[c]; HUBP) from *'ēdâ* (or a form from *'ēdût*) connected with *'ûd* (cf. 44:23) rather than *'ēdâ* connected with *yā'ad*.

f. Tg has "their king" and "their anointed."

g. On the line's syntax, see *TTH* 201; Joüon 144a.

h. MT[L] has a section marker here. LXX lacks v. 22.

i. Verses 23–24 reappear in a variant form from 23:19–20.

j. LXX has "for the clan of Israel."

k. MT[L] has a section marker here.

Like vv. 5–11 and vv. 12–17, this third section both faces catastrophe and promises restoration, but here, the elements come in reverse order until this section, too, comes to a climax with a promise of a restored relationship between the people and Yahweh.

30:18a   Introduction

30:18b–21	Promise of restoration of city and community (eight bicola)
30:22	Promise of restoration of the relationship between people and Yahweh (one bicolon)
30:23–24	Threat of Yahweh's angry blazing (four bicola)
31:1a	Renewed introduction
31:1b	Promise of restoration of the relationship between people and Yahweh (one bicolon)

The section illustrates in an extreme form the scholarly disagreement over attributing and dating messages in Jeremiah, especially in Jer 30–31: does it come from Jeremiah in the time of Josiah[202] or Jeremiah after 597[203] or Jeremiah after 587[204] or curators in the Persian period[205] or curators in the Maccabean period?[206] My assumption is that, set in the context of Jer 30, it is another message that we are invited to see against the background of the suffering that preceded the city's fall in 587. Whatever is the correct answer, "if in verses 5–11 we saw the panic of people who had no hope of being rescued, in verses 12–17 we hear the cries of people who had no hope of being healed,"[207] and this last section presupposes a community that would not be able to imagine the rebuilding of its city, of itself, or of its relationship with Yahweh.

18 While this time the introduction leads straight into a promise of restoration, it will turn out that the audience should not take too much for granted. Whereas vv. 12–17 spoke of the material and physical restoration of Judah but did so metaphorically, this section speaks more literally. It begins with one of Jeremiah's signature phrases, *bringing about restoration*; Yahweh's withholding of *compassion* is now reversed. It applies the idea of restoration first to people's homes, the *tents* or *dwellings* that have been devastated in the course of the attacks of Judah's adversaries on the towns of Judah and on Jerusalem. *City* and *citadel* could both be collective[208] (Jeremiah has often referred to cities), and speaking of restoring tents perhaps promises a return of the good old days. The promises presuppose destruction that reduces towns to ruins, but Israelites are used to the idea that towns get destroyed and then their people build up again on their ruins. It will happen, even

---

202. E.g., Volz, *Jeremia*, 290–91.
203. See Fretheim, *Jeremiah*, 414.
204. E.g., Allen, *Jeremiah*, 339.
205. E.g., R. P. Carroll, *Jeremiah*, OTL, 584.
206. Duhm, *Jeremia*, 241.
207. Wright, *Jeremiah*, 306.
208. Rudolph, *Jeremia*, 193.

though Deut 13:16(17) declared that an apostate town could never be built up again but would simply stay a tell; Yahweh revokes his own law.[209] In addition to the rebuilding of people's homes, there will be a new *citadel* (6:5; 9:21[20]; 17:27) from which the administration will exercise authority for the community again.

19 The transformation will be such as to inspire thanksgiving and reveling that will emerge from the new city's homes. Merrymaking will make for quite a contrast with the present voices (vv. 5, 15), and Jeremiah's own holding back from *revelers* (15:17) will no longer be necessary. When Yahweh forgives and restores his people, he thereby opens their lips for praise again (Ps 51:15[17]).[210] Not long before—if we may imagine this promise set just before the final catastrophe—Yahweh had bidden the 597 community in Babylon to become *many* and not *few* (29:6), implying a fulfillment of his promise to Abraham. Now he promises that he himself will ensure it happens in Jerusalem. As they increase, their belittling or slighting (26:6; 28:8; 29:22) or shame will be replaced by *honor*.

20a There will thus be a return to the way things were *of old*. *Jacob* in v. 18a continues to be the referent of *his* through v. 21a. *His children* have been struck down (2:30; cf. 10:20); the reference is not to young people but to the people as a whole who are his descendants. Now they will flourish again. They had flourished *of old*, back at the beginning of Israel's story, when there had been a fulfillment of that promise to Abraham. On the eve of the exodus, the *children* of Jacob/Israel had become *many* (Exod 1:7; cf. Deut 26:5). Now there will be a fulfillment again. Thus Judah's *assembly* will be in a position to meet and carry out its responsibilities, as it was in "the time of Moses and David":[211] the term *assembly* (*'ēdâ*) first appears in connection with the exodus story (Exod 12), and most of its occurrences come in the subsequent narrative of Israel's journey from Egypt toward the promised land. It's hard to distinguish clearly between the assembly as the decision-making body of Israel and the assembly as a worshiping congregation,[212] though that difficulty may imply a distinction that is alien to the First Testament. Here, the context with its references to city and citadel suggests a decision-making body, but *before me* suggests a congregation.

20b–21 Notwithstanding the flourishing (in fact, as a consequence of it), *oppressors* (*lāḥaṣ* participle) were also a problem *of old* (see Exod 3:9; the

---

209. G. Fischer, "A New Understanding of the Book of Jeremiah," in Najman and Schmid, *Jeremiah's Scriptures*, 38. The word *tell* otherwise occurs only in 49:2; Josh 8:28; 11:13.

210. Calvin, *Jeremiah*, 4:38.

211. Duhm, *Jeremia*, 242.

212. See D. Levy, J. Milgrom, and H. Ringgren, "עֵדָה, *'ēdâ*," *TDOT* 10:468–80.

related noun appears in Deut 26:7). It will not be surprising if they are a problem again; it is part of the pattern of Israel's life. But it's not something to worry about too much, because Yahweh will once more *attend* to the matter (see Exod 3:16, 19). He will see that Jacob's people has its *lord*, Jeremiah's alternative term for "shepherd" in 25:34–36. A Moses-like, shepherd-like figure will again emerge from among them to take the lead under Yahweh in dealing with the oppressors. Thus *his ruler . . . will go out from his midst. Lord* and *ruler* might be ways of avoiding calling this leader the king,[213] in keeping with the avoidance of that word in some other contexts; and *from his midst* might link with the principle in Deut 17:15. But both words often have more general reference, and they come together in the plural in 2 Chr 23:20 in connection with Jehoiada's organizing the enthronement of Joash. So they could refer more generally to overlords and governors. The point that Yahweh does make is that he will give the ruler access to him: *I will bring him near, and he will come up to me*. The first might make him more than Moses (Exod 3:5) and the priests and Levites whom Moses brought near to Yahweh at the beginning (e.g., Exod 40:12, 14). The priests, too, were people who could *come up* to Yahweh (Exod 19:22), though there was another sense in which only Moses could do so (Exod 24:2). But Yahweh's invitation will make it possible for the ruler to be someone who *pledges his heart to come up to me*. Otherwise (to paraphrase Yahweh's words), "who would gamble his life" to do so?[214] So the emergence of this leader from their midst and Yahweh's welcome of him into close access is a further undergirding of the community's safety.

22 Thus the relationship between Yahweh and Israel will be restored, as 24:7 envisaged, and will again become what it was designed to be *of old*, back at the beginning (cf. 7:23; 11:4; Exod 6:7). In the context, the implication is that Yahweh will indeed keep the commitment that he has just described—but also that they will need to keep theirs.

30:23–31:1 All that prospect is future. Meanwhile, Jeremiah repeats 23:19–20 in a slightly variant form—a serious reminder about the need for Jacob's people to keep their commitment. But whereas earlier the prospect functioned "to terrify the constituency of Jeremiah's prophetic opponents," here "it serves as an anchor for the message of restoration."[215] Finally, Jeremiah repeats 30:22 in a slightly varied form with a reference to *all Israel's clans*: which leads neatly into what now follows. (Repetitions in the Jeremiah scroll are not accidental or dumb.)

---

213. Duhm, *Jeremia*, 242.
214. Bright, *Jeremiah*, 280.
215. Diamond, "Deceiving Hope," 34.

3. A Reversal for Ephraim (31:2–22 [LXX 38:2–22])

Whereas the concrete references to Zion and thus implicitly to Judah in 30:5–31:1 were not surprising, one would not have predicted the concrete references to Samaria and Ephraim that now appear in 31:2–22. This passage names Ephraim four times—twice as many times as in Jer 1–30 altogether (4:15; 7:15). In another sense, it is not surprising that Jeremiah should have something to say about Ephraim. While his own coming from Benjamin might make him inclined to wonder about Ephraim's destiny, a vision for the future of Ephraim alongside that of Judah is a motif in the scroll of the Jerusalemite Ezekiel. The rationale there is a conviction about Yahweh's commitment to twelve-clan Israel, and that rationale would apply in Jeremiah, too. Again, there are links between Jeremiah and Hosea, and Hosea the Ephraimite expounds the conviction that Yahweh continues to be committed to Ephraim. While Judahites might be dismissive of Ephraim's future, from a self-centered angle they might also reflect on the importance of the principle that Yahweh stays committed to his people even when they are wayward. An implication of Paul's argument in Rom 9–11 is that the community that believes in Jesus cannot think of God abandoning his ancient people without imperiling its own security (he could then abandon the church, too). The same argument would apply to Judahites who did not continue to expect Yahweh to be faithful to Ephraim. So for a variety of reasons, it is not surprising that Jeremiah's vision for the future in the 590s or 580s includes Yahweh building and planting for Ephraim as well as Judah. While 3:18 does envisage Judah and Ephraim together returning to their homeland, 31:2–22 fits how 30:1–31:40 as a whole implies a vision of the deliverance and destiny of the two households as the people of God; 31:23–40 will take it further.[216]

While rhetorically Jeremiah addresses Ephraim here (e.g., in vv. 3–6), there is no Ephraimite assembly to which he can literally deliver his message, and the chapters speak of no community to whom he can send a letter. The message is intended for—well, Israel, the people of God as a whole. The first direct audience will be people in Judah, but among them are refugees from Ephraim who could rejoice at the encouragement and the promise. Beyond Northern refugees in Jerusalem and people living just north of the city, the Ephraimites might include descendants of people who escaped deportation, descendants of forced migrants from other parts of the Assyrian Empire (the Samarians of Ezra-Nehemiah), and descendants of the Ephraimite clans living in Mesopotamia (while vv. 2–6 make no reference to such Ephraimites, vv. 7–22 speak of people returning from there). Jeremiah has a vision, and Yahweh has an intention for them.

216. Weiser, *Jeremia*, 2:275.

Yahweh's promises to Ephraim raise the question of whether and how his promises find fulfillment.

- The Jeremiah scroll (specifically Jer 18) has indicated that Yahweh does not always implement his declarations of intent, because they are part of a relationship with his people. They are threats and promises whose fulfillment depends on the response they meet with.
- As with other promises and threats, these declarations of intent belong to Ephraim in Jeremiah's day; fulfillment in the life of the "ten lost tribes" millennia later hardly counts as fulfillment of these promises.
- During the Second Temple period, a flourishing community developed throughout the territory of what had once been Ephraim, a community that welcomed Jesus more enthusiastically than people in the territory of old Judah.
- If that community comprised descendants of forced migrants from Assyria as much as people of original Israelite ethnicity, one might see that development as an enhanced fulfillment of Yahweh's promises rather than a failure of them.

As was the case in 30:5–31:1, declarations that *Yahweh has said this* function as introductions to the three sections of this unit, vv. 2–6, 7–14, and 15–22 (this last includes a resumptive extra occurrence of the wording). While 30:5–31:1 may incorporate material from an earlier stage in Jeremiah's activity, when he spoke of Yahweh's purpose for Ephraim, any such reference was well-disguised in its reworking for incorporation in 30:1–31:40. In 31:2–22, the reference to Ephraim is explicit, though again nothing points directly to the time of Josiah; the material is embedded in the document of promises relating to the eve or aftermath of 587.

a. Building and Planting (31:2–6)

[2]*Yahweh has said this.*

It found favor[a] *in the wilderness—*
 the people of[b] *those who survived the sword.*[c]
Israel, in going[d] *to attain rest:*[e]
 [3]*"From long ago,*[f] *Yahweh let himself be seen by me."*[g]
Yes, with age-long love I loved you;[h]
 as a result I led you along with commitment.[i]
[4]*Once again I will build you and you will build yourself up,*

young girl Israel.[j]
Once again you will take up your hand-drums[k]
 and go out with the whirl of[l] *revelers.*
[5]*Once again you will plant vineyards*
 on the mountains of Samaria.
Planters will have planted and will begin to eat,[m]
 [6]*when there is a day.*
Watchers will have called
 on the highland of Ephraim:
Get up, let's go up to Zion,
 to Yahweh our God.[n]

a. LXX "I found warmth" (cf. the substance of 2:2) implies *ḥōm* for MT *ḥēn*.

b. LXX implies *'im* for MT *'am*.

c. The word order puts the subject at the end and thus puts emphasis on it; the next colon works the same way (*TTH* 208.4).

d. In effect, the infinitive functions as a finite verb (GK 113dd).

e. *Rāga' hiphil* is inwardly transitive (see GK 53d, e, f) as in Deut 28:65; Isa 34:14; cf. Vg. LXX "to destroy" perhaps takes the verb as *raga'* I and understands it in light of the previous colon (HUBP).

f. Cf. Tg. LXX has "from far away," but in the context the rarer time reference (see BDB; Diamond, "Jeremiah," 590) works better. Vg is ambiguous, like the Hebrew.

g. For *lî*, LXX implies *lô*, "to him," an easier reading. Tg assumes that the speaker is Jerusalem (cf. the fem. sing. *you* in vv. 3b–6); Rashi (in MG) assumes that Jeremiah speaks.

h. *You* is feminine singular throughout vv. 3–6.

i. The two nouns used adverbially, *with love* and *with commitment*, enclose the line as a whole.

j. See the translation note on 18:13.

k. Not tambourines (with metal dangles), which had not been invented (Lundbom, *Jeremiah 21–36*, 416–17).

l. LXX "the congregation of" implies *qahal* for MT *məḥôl*; there is a similar variation in v. 13. Aq, Vg imply MT.

m. *Ḥālal piel* in such contexts denotes being free to treat something as ordinary rather than sacred, as it is for its first years (Lev 19:23–25). LXX "and praise" implies *wəhallēlû*.

n. MT[L] has a unit marker here.

While it eventually emerges that Jeremiah here turns to Ephraim, the point becomes clear only in vv. 5–6. At first, Judahites might take the message as a further encouragement to them, and they might have mixed feelings when they eventually have to rethink vv. 2–4.

v. 2a	Introduction
vv. 2b–3	Yahweh recollects his commitment to Israel over the years (three bicola)
vv. 4–6	Yahweh reaffirms his commitment in the present context of Ephraim's need (six bicola, the last two linked)

2 Once again, the introduction invites the listeners to take the whole section as Yahweh's word, even though it will be a while before Yahweh speaks.[217] In the actual message, the subsequent opening words themselves take us back to the beginning of the main part of the Jeremiah scroll in 2:1–3. There, Yahweh recalled how tough things were for Israel *in the wilderness* after Yahweh had got them out of Egypt. "Wilderness as a place . . . serves as an imaginative theater for conceptualizing God's consistency in bringing grace into future desolations."[218] They *survived the sword* there too. It is an ironic expression in that it usually denotes foreign people who did not survive Israel's onslaught upon them (but Isa 1:9 uses it the other way). The sword was not the means whereby the Egyptians attempted to put Israel down, notwithstanding Exod 18:4, though perhaps there and here the sword is a metonymy. It does seem likely that swords were involved in Exod 17:8–13, as they were in Exod 32:27–29! That last link resonates with Yahweh's recollection in Jer 2 and with Jer 30, though there is no reference to Israel's waywardness in this section. *The sword* could also remind readers of the sword Jeremiah often threatens (e.g., 6:25; 9:16[15]) and that Ephraim has especially experienced.[219]

3 In Jer 2, Yahweh talked about *commitment* and *love*; here, he talks initially about *favor* or grace, then about *love*, and then about *commitment*. There, however, it was Israel's commitment and love. Here it is his own grace, love, and commitment; he is recalling his attitude to Israel, as opposed to Israel's attitude to him. And there the point was to recall how short-lived Israel's commitment and love were; here the point is to recall how consistent have been his grace, love, and commitment over the years. When Israel was on its way *to attain rest* in the promised land, then, and settle and relax there after escaping the vulnerability of its life in Egypt and of its journey through the wilderness, Yahweh had *let himself be seen*, had appeared (*rā'â niphal*). I take Israel to be the *me*. His appearance (*mar'eh*) had accompanied Israel (Num 9:15–16) *from long ago*. It was not just an experience confined to that long-ago time. He has been showing himself ever since those far-off days at the beginning of Israel's story, leading Israel along like a farmer leading an ox, and with commitment, not the harshness that could be characteristic of a less caring farmer. It has been *with an age-long love* that he has loved Israel, he confirms in responding to Israel's words about his letting himself be seen. *Age-long* thus rephrases *from long ago*,[220] though what follows indicates that Yahweh would be happy to accept the ambiguity of the expression that could denote a love that extends for all time forward as well as backward. The expression *age-long love*—love of the age, love of all time—comes only here,

217. Weiser, *Jeremia*, 2:283.
218. A. T. Abernethy, "Theological Patterning in Jeremiah," *BBR* 24 (2014): 155.
219. K. H. Wynn, "Jeremiah 31:1–6," *Int* 68 (2014): 185.
220. Volz, *Jeremia*, 292.

though the more or less synonymous expression "commitment for all time" is frequent (classically, see Ps 136). Anyway, how can there be love that is not age-long in both directions, especially when predicated of God?[221] Whereas on the edge of the promised land, the job of a preacher such as Moses is to issue challenges about commitment and to discourage people from taking God's love for granted, in the midst of disaster the preacher's job is to issue reminders that there is a sense in which love can be taken for granted and that the story of God's relationship with his people shows it to be so. Thus

> whenever despair presents itself to our eyes, or whenever our miseries tempt us to despair, let the benefits of God come to our minds, not only those which we ourselves have experienced, but also those which he has in all ages conferred on his Church, according to what David also says, who had this one consolation in his grief, when pressed down with extreme evils and almost overwhelmed with despair, "I remember the days of old." (Psalm 143:5) So that he not only called to mind the benefits of God which he himself had experienced, but also what he had heard of from his fathers, and what he had read of in the books of Moses. In the same manner the Prophet here reminds us of God's benefits, when we seem to be forsaken by him; for this one thought is capable of alleviating and comforting us.

Those narratives about what God did in the past are not "obsolete," because "'whatsoever is written,' says Paul, 'has been written for our instruction, that through the patience and the consolation of the Scripture we might have hope.' (Romans 15:4)."[222]

4 Yahweh includes no description of the people's desperate situation and anxiety such as came in 30:5–31:1, but he presupposes it by virtue of the nature of these promises. If he is to *build once again* and they are to become *revelers* once again and to *plant once again*, there must have been some pulling up and pulling down (1:10). Yahweh now makes explicit that the *you* in v. 3 and the addressee in v. 2 was *young girl Israel*. He will build her up, and she will build herself up: the double use of the verb implies the double agency involved. It will happen only because he makes it possible, but it will happen only because she does the work. Rebuilding will then mean rejoicing, music, and reveling, as in 30:18–19.

5–6 For a third time, Yahweh says *once again*. But now comes the surprise: the planting will take place *on the mountains of Samaria*, on the terraces constructed on the sides of hills for the growing of vines and fruit trees. *Young girl Israel* is not a personification of the exodus people as a whole but of Ephraim, as Israel was in 30:3–4 and in Jer 3 (also, e.g., 5:11; 11:10, 17; 13:11; 23:13). For

---

221. Barth, *CD* IV, 2:758.
222. Calvin, *Jeremiah*, 4:57, 58.

Ephraim, too, Yahweh's past love and commitment do not belong only to the past. Building and planting applies to Ephraim too. *Samaria* usually denotes the city that was the long-time capital of Ephraim (cf. 41:5), standing on a hill but also surrounded by hills, to which the expression *mountains of Samaria* might refer. But *Samaria* can designate the Northern Kingdom as a whole (e.g., 2 Kgs 17:24, 26; 23:19 in Josiah's time); this reference makes sense here. On a wide front, the Samarian hill country will see *vineyards* flourishing and their owners free to eat from them. *The highland of Ephraim* will then mean more or less the same thing as *the mountains of Samaria*, but the point of the reference is different and perhaps a surprise, or perhaps not. The mountains now become the vantage point on which lookouts can stand. Such lookouts are commonly defensive or aggressive (4:16), but here there is a peace dividend. Instead of warning people about invasion, they are urging them to worship. "The rebuilt community is one in which work and worship are integrated."[223] Henceforth, it will not be merely stray Ephraimite refugees who come to Zion in this connection. In Jeremiah's imagination and in Yahweh's intention, they have already begun to do so (the verbs translated future perfect in vv. 5–6 are *qatal*). Specifically, the link with planting and harvesting suggests that the lookouts are urging people to go up to Jerusalem for the pilgrimage festival. It is the practice that Jeroboam terminated by establishing the sanctuaries at Bethel and Dan as Ephraim's festival locations. If these messages of Jeremiah's do go back to Josiah's time, then they cohere with his ambition to see Ephraim acknowledging Jerusalem. In the present context, the renewal of a relationship with Yahweh and of a fullness of life that Judah and Ephraim will share does not mean an acceptance of the religious views that Ephraim has been maintaining over recent centuries, even in a cleaned-up version that gives up the worship of the Master or gives up worship of Yahweh that is tainted by a theology associated with the Master. Ephraim will be recognizing Zion as the place Yahweh chose. In Jeremiah's picture, it is not a burdensome duty but a joy. "Universalism" can combine with a view of "Zion as the centre of worship in the coming salvation."[224]

b. Redeeming and Restoring (31:7–14)

[7]*Because Yahweh has said this.*

Chant for Jacob with joy,
shrill about the head of the nations.
Make it heard, praise, and say:

223. R. P. Carroll, *Jeremiah*, OTL, 590.
224. D. R. Jones, *Jeremiah*, 396.

"Deliver[a] your people, Yahweh,
the remainder of Israel."
[8]*Here am I, enabling them to come*
from a northern country.
I will collect them from the furthest parts of the earth,
among them blind and lame.[b]
The pregnant and the one giving birth, together—
a great assembly, they will return here.
[9]*With crying they will come,*
and with prayers for grace[c] *I will lead them.*
I will enable them to go to wadis with water,
by a level path on which they will not tumble.
Because I have become a father to Israel,
and Ephraim is my firstborn.[d]

[10]*Listen to Yahweh's word, nations,*
tell on shores far away.
Say, the one who dispersed Israel will collect him,
and guard like a shepherd his flock.
[11]*Because Yahweh has redeemed Jacob,*
restored him[e] *from a hand too strong for him.*
[12]*They will come and chant on Zion's height,*
and shine at[f] *Yahweh's good things,*
Because of new grain and because of new wine and because of fresh oil,
and because of the young of flock and cattle.
Their life will become like a watered garden,
and they will not ever again be faint.
[13]*Then a girl will rejoice in dancing,*
young men and old men together.[g]
I will change their mourning into joy,
comfort them and enable them to rejoice, away from their sorrow.
[14]*I will drench the priests' life with fatness,*
and my people will be full of my good things (Yahweh's affirmation).[h]

a. LXX implies "Yahweh has delivered," and 4QJer[c] has *hwšy'*. In the Babylonian period, it would be an anticipatory *qatal* (see the introductory comment on 13:18–22); in the Persian period, it would rejoice in what Yahweh actually had done (to invert the comment in Holladay, *Commentary on Jeremiah*, 2:184).

b. For *bām 'iwwēr ûpiśēaḥ*, LXX "on the Passover festival" implies *bēmô'ēd pesaḥ*, a nice reading, though it would be a shame to lose MT's.

c. LXX "consolations" (cf. Aq, Sym) implies *tanḥûmîm* for MT *taḥnûnîm*.

d. MT[L] has a section marker here.

634

e. The verb is simple *waw* plus *qatal*, being a parallel description of the act in the first colon, not a description of a further act.

f. Vg has "flow to" (cf. LXX), Tg "delight themselves in"; see the commentary.

g. For *yaḥdāw*, LXX repeats "will rejoice," implying *yaḥdû*. Aq, Vg imply MT.

h. MT^L has a section marker here.

As the section again begins once more to speak of *Jacob* and *Israel*, we will be wise not to make assumptions about the referent of those names. In due course, our hesitancy is rewarded: Yahweh is continuing to speak about Ephraim. Here, the verses begin from Ephraim's dispersion in a land far away and promise Yahweh's deliverance. Ephraim's metaphorical or literal weakness or vulnerability will not hold him back. He will lead them safely on their journey and provide for them extravagantly on an ongoing basis when they get back home. Once more, he pictures them flocking to Jerusalem for the festivals to praise Yahweh for what he has done.

v. 7a	Introduction
vv. 7b	Praise and plea to Yahweh to deliver Israel (a bicolon and a tricolon)
vv. 8–9	Yahweh's responsive promise: he will enable Israel to come back (six bicola)
vv. 10–11	Challenge to the nations to note Yahweh's promise (three bicola)
vv. 12–14	Further exposition of the promise: the praise they will give for his blessing (six bicola, the first two linked)

This section has many points of connection with Isa 40–66. If Jer 30–31 comes in part from the Persian period, then the points of connection indicate a knowledge of those chapters; if Jer 30–31 comes from the time just before or just after 587, the dependence is the other way around.

7 The section's opening is doubly surprising: the commission from Yahweh is a commission to engage in addressing Yahweh, and the opening line makes one expect simply an act of praise, but the second line includes a prayer. The combination recalls the nature of praise and prayer in the Psalms, where praise often leads into prayer and prayer is hardly possible without praise. Joy and praise are the appropriate stance before Yahweh, but the tricolon recognizes that a plea also needs to be uttered in connection with *the head of the nations*. While the parallelism in the first line would at first suggest that Jacob is the head of the nations, and Jeremiah will later call Babylon the last of them (50:12), at the moment Babylon is surely the head and Ephraim is

merely the *remainder* of what it once was. It is therefore not surprising that a plea follows the praise. So the plea *deliver* links with the reference to *the head of the nations*, and the phrase *the remainder of Israel* heightens the point. There is or there will be not much left of Judah (6:9; 8:3; 15:9; 23:3; 24:8), but it is much more obvious that there is not much left of Ephraim through its being defeated and exiled over a century ago.

8 Yahweh looks that fact in the face and promises to deliver. The remaining Ephraimites are in *a northern country*, away in old Assyria. How could they come back? Yahweh will enable them to do so. They are scattered there. He will *collect* them, as he will collect the scattered remains of Judah; this same verb (*qābaṣ piel*) expressed Yahweh's promise to Judah (23:3; 29:14), and behind that reference is the promise in Deut 30:3. It's a very different arrival *from a northern country* and *from the furthest parts of the earth* than the one threatened in 6:22.[225] That one spoke of death, this one speaks of life.[226] What, he will collect all of them, the weak and the tired ("give me your tired, your poor, your huddled masses yearning to breathe free")? Yes, *the blind and the lame, the pregnant and the woman giving birth*. If Yahweh brings them all, indeed *a great assembly* (or "congregation"—a *qāhāl*) *will return here*.

9 Why will there be *crying*? Perhaps it is a joyful weeping[227] because they cannot believe what is happening, having thought they would never have the chance to return. But the parallelism indicates that the crying will be accompanied by *prayers for grace* (the two expressions came as a construct phrase in 3:21); Jeremiah then makes a suggestive jump as Yahweh promises that he will *lead them* with these prayers for grace. The prayers will meet with his response and thus become interwoven with his leading. Suppose they set off and wonder if they will really be able to make it? Yahweh will ensure that they find wadis with water in them, such as they will need in order to make such a journey, and that their paths are level so they don't fall (he speaks metaphorically or metonymically; cf. the picture in 6:15, 21; 8:12). It's the way a shepherd cares for his flock, but the reason he gives is that he has also *become a father to Israel* and that Ephraim (at last the naming) is actually his firstborn son. It is a climactic statement, after which MT[L]'s section marker encourages a pause for breath. The surprising nature of both statements points to their distinctive metaphorical nature. Yahweh has always been father to Israel as a whole, at least since the exodus (Hos 11); further, there are several candidates ahead of Ephraim for designation as firstborn within Israel. But Yahweh is making a new commitment to being Ephraim's father and acting as such at this moment, and he will treat

225. Weiser, *Jeremia*, 2:285.
226. R. P. Carroll, *Jeremiah*, OTL, 591.
227. Jerome, *Jeremiah*, 192.

Ephraim as if he is his firstborn, without there being an implication that he neglects other sons (among whom people adopted into sonship through Jesus might be included).[228]

10 Yahweh goes on to address the *nations*. He did so in 6:18 to shame Judah over the catastrophe he was bringing as the penalty for its wayward-ness—though as a way of bringing the reality home to Judah itself. Here he does so to encourage Ephraim about the renewal he is bringing. If Yahweh draws the nations' attention to it, it must be real, otherwise he will make a fool of himself! He restates the promises from v. 8 in case people haven't heard them or believed them, and he also once again affirms responsibil-ity for bringing about the catastrophe and confirms the intention to bring about the restoration. Yahweh is the one God; there is no evil power bringing trouble and then a benign power reversing it. He *dispersed* (*zārâ piel*), like a farmer winnowing grain so as to disperse the chaff (4:11; 15:7; 49:32, 36; 51:2). It's ridiculous to think of collecting the husks that blew away. Yet Yahweh intends to *collect* what he scattered as useless: he repeats the verb from v. 8. Beyond that collecting, he will *guard them like a shepherd his flock*; he also restates promises from v. 9 again in case they are not sure they have heard right. They are indeed his *flock*, and he is their *shepherd*.

11 He backs up his promise further with two key verbs. In Deuteronomy, *redeemed* is an exodus word. Behind it is the idea of being in the power of someone from whom one cannot break away, of being in inescapable serf-dom; redemption thus requires a strong hand (Deut 7:8; 9:26; 13:5[6]; 15:15; 24:18). Jeremiah tweaks the image: the one from whom Yahweh redeems Israel is one whose *hand* is *too strong for him* (cf. Ps 35:10). Yahweh will have thereby *restored* them, another exodus word (Exod 6:6; 15:13), especially picked up in Isa 40–55 (e.g., 43:1; 44:22–23). Restoring again links with ser-vitude: a restorer is a member of one's family who has resources that he is willing to use to set relatives free from a bondage into which reversals have taken them. Redeeming and restoring speak both of Yahweh's power and of his commitment. When Yahweh speaks in the past tense of redeeming and restoring, people could hear him as recalling what he indeed did at the exo-dus, which is a pattern for what he will do now, or as speaking of his future redeeming and restoring of Ephraim that is so definite it can be spoken of as actual; he is in the midst of doing it (cf. 28:2 and the translation note on it, ironically because there Hananiah is fooling himself).

12 What will follow parallels the close of vv. 2–6. Ephraim *will come and chant on Zion's height*, as all Israel was supposed to do. People came on pil-grimage festivals in connection with the harvest as well as the exodus, and so they will here. Jeremiah neatly uses a verb with two possible meanings,

228. Barth, *CD* II, 2:203.

as he will in 51:44 (cf. Isa 2:2; Mic 4:1). *Nāhār* means a stream, and one might imagine people streaming to Zion (*nāhar* I). But a homonym (*nāhar* II) means *shine*, and the context suggests it is the primary idea here. Taking Ephraim back to its homeland will be only the beginning of the story, as when Yahweh took Israel to Canaan at the beginning. There will be *Yahweh's good things* to beam over. They are spelled out in the rest of the verse. *New grain, new wine,* and *fresh oil* are the immediate fruits of the harvest. The idea is not that they would be growing on Zion but that people would rejoice in them there, as they represent a fulfillment of the promise in Deut 7:13. In slightly different words, that promise also refers to *the young of the flock and cattle,* which suggests the same point with regard to the animals: they, too, are an aspect of the fruitfulness that the imagery brings before people's eyes. The third line makes explicit that the beginning will not be the end but only the start of something ongoing, *a life* that is *like a watered garden,* with no danger that people will *ever again be faint* because the harvest has failed.

13–14 So there will be *dancing, joy,* and *comfort* to replace *mourning* (e.g., 12:4, 11; 14:2) and *sorrow* (e.g., 8:18; 20:18) because there is no more of the anxiety, sadness, and grief of a life where there is not enough to eat and people languish. Even *the priests* (about whom Jeremiah has had few good words to say)[229] will enjoy the lusciousness of the offerings that people are now in a position to bring, as the people are *full of my good things.* The "idyllic images of a pastoral life" in these verses are "worthy of a Breughel."[230] Perhaps the lavishness of the priests' share in the offerings is an indication of the abundance of the people's blessing,[231] but perhaps the priests are there because they are an integral and accepted aspect of Israel and of Yahweh's relationship with Israel.[232]

c. Turning and Compassion (31:15–22)

[15]*Yahweh has said this:*

A voice is making itself heard on a height,[a]
  wailing, most bitter crying.[b]
Rachel crying over her children,
  refusing to take comfort over them,
  because "There is no one."[c]

---

229. "What the priests are doing here, no one knows" (Volz, *Jeremia,* 280).
230. R. P. Carroll, *Jeremiah,* OTL, 588.
231. Allen, *Jeremiah,* 347–48.
232. See further L.-S. Tiemeyer, "The Priests and the Temple Cult in the Book of Jeremiah," in Barstad and Kratz, *Prophecy,* 233–64, esp. 256.

¹⁶*Yahweh has said this:*

Restrain your voice from crying,
  your eyes from tears.
Because there is payment for your work (Yahweh's affirmation):
  they will return from the enemy's country.
¹⁷*So there is hope for your future (Yahweh's affirmation):*
  *the children will return to their territory.*ᵈ

¹⁸*I have clearly heard*ᵉ *Ephraim bemoaning himself:*ᶠ

"You have restrained me and I am under restraint,
  like a calf not trained.
Turn me, so that I may turn,
  because you are Yahweh, my God.
¹⁹*Because after my turning,*ᵍ *I relented;*
  *after my humbling myself,*ʰ *I struck my thigh.*
I am shamed, and yes, I am disgraced,
  because I have carried reproach since my youth."

²⁰*Ephraim is a precious son to me, isn't he,*
  or a child that is delighted in.
*Because as often as*ⁱ *I have spoken against him,*
  I would definitely be mindful of him still.
That's why my insides have been in turmoil for him—
  *I would definitely have compassion for him (Yahweh's affirmation).*ʲ

²¹*Set up markers for yourself,*ᵏ
  *put "bitterness"*ˡ *for yourself.*
Apply your mind to the highway,
  *the path that you walked.*ᵐ
*Turn, young girl Israel,*ⁿ
  turn to these, your towns.
²²*How long will you vacillate,*
  turning daughter?
*Because Yahweh has created a new thing in the country:*ᵒ
  *a female can turn her arms around a man.*ᵖ

a. *Bərāmâ* (cf. Vg). LXX "in Ramah" implies *bārāmâ*; the place name Ramah regularly has the article (Neh 11:33 is the one exception), like Los Angeles, and thus strictly means "The Height."

b. See the translation note on 6:26.

c. MTᴸ has a section marker here. The singular makes a link with the story of Jacob and Rachel and their family in Gen 37:30; 42:13, 32, 36; 44:26, 30, 34—which is also the context in which there is much talk of *payment* (S. E. Brown-Gutoff, "The Voice of Rachel in Jeremiah 31," *Union Seminary Quarterly Review* 45 [1991]: 184); see the commentary on v. 16.

d. MT^L has a section marker here.

e. The infinitive precedes the finite verb, underlining the factuality of the action.

f. Cf. LXX. Vg "wander" assumes another aspect of the range of meanings of *nûd*; perhaps we are invited to hear both meanings (Holladay, *Commentary on Jeremiah*, 2:189).

g. LXX "my imprisonment" (cf. 30:18) implies *šibyî* for MT *šûbî*.

h. Vg takes the *niphal* infinitive *hiwwāḏǝ'î* to mean "my being instructed" as if it were *hophal* (cf. BDB), while LXX has "my knowing" as if it were *qal*. I take the verb as *DCH*'s *yāda'* II.

i. See the translation note on 20:8.

j. MT^L has a section marker here. In v. 20b–c, two successive lines have a *qatal* verb followed by a *yiqtol*, and each time the *yiqtol* verb is preceded by its infinitive, underlining the fact to which it refers. I take both *yiqtol* verbs to refer to the past and as having past imperfect significance.

k. *Your/you* in vv. 21–22 is feminine singular.

l. *Tamrûrîm* recurs from v. 15; cf. Tg. Rashi (in MG) links the word rather with *tāmār* ("palm tree") and takes it as another word for a marker or signpost, but this seems a stretch. LXX simply transliterates both nouns.

m. For the *qere hālākt*, B. Becking reads the *ketiv hlhkty* as Yahweh's first-person reference to his return to Canaan ("The Return of the Deity," in Amit et al., *Essays on Ancient Israel*, 53–62).

n. Cf. v. 4; and see the translation note on 18:13.

o. LXX "created salvation for new planting" perhaps suggests the influence of Isa 43:19; 61:11 (HUBP).

p. MT^L has a section marker here. Tg has "the people, the house of Israel, shall pursue the Law."

Verses 15–22 comprise three units respectively offering comfort to a bereaved mother, reassurance to a guilty son, and encouragement to a wavering daughter. They thus address Rachel as Ephraim's mother (vv. 15–17), Ephraim as Yahweh's son (vv. 18–20), and young Israel as Yahweh's daughter (vv. 21–22). All three address Ephraim directly or indirectly, they have overlapping concerns, and they use overlapping language. Their differences suggest that they are of separate origin, so they were brought together by the curators and are signaled as belonging together by the common introduction in v. 15a.

v. 15a	Introduction to vv. 15–22
vv. 15b–17	A report about Rachel, an introduction to a message for her, and the message (a bicolon and a tricolon, then three bicola)
vv. 18–20	An introduction to a report about Ephraim, its reflection, and Yahweh's comment (four bicola, then three more)
vv. 21–22	A challenge to young girl Israel to turn (five bicola)

15 Once again, *Yahweh has said this* marks the beginning a section that will eventually be a direct word from Yahweh but starts with the human words to which Yahweh will respond. A contrast with vv. 2–6 and 7–14 is that there Yahweh started from the positive, the challenge involved in the idea of Ephraim's restoration then being more prominent in vv. 7–14 than in vv. 2–6; this third section faces the challenge at the beginning. In addition, from the beginning, Jeremiah signals that the subject is the northern clans. "Jerusalem has listened too long to its own immediate crisis. Now it is invited … to listen to a much older, much more pathos-filled voice."[233] Jeremiah invites the audience to imagine a voice of pain—*wailing, most bitter crying*. Who could it be? It is the voice of Rachel, mother of Joseph, grandmother of Ephraim and Manasseh, and mother of Benjamin, who died and was buried "on the way to Ephrath" (Gen 35:19–20). There was thus a place known as Rachel's tomb in Benjamin (1 Sam 10:2), and perhaps the implication here is that it was near Ramah; the question where Rachel was actually buried is complicated (Gen 35:19–20 also refers to Bethlehem), but for Jeremiah's purposes, it is unnecessary to resolve it. The point is that at a place known as Rachel's tomb, she could be imagined *crying* as her *children* trudged off into exile after the fall of Samaria in 721. Indeed, Jeremiah does not explicitly refer to her tomb and need not imply that location. The vision reflects or imagines the mourning of people who had somehow escaped the 721 exile and were still bemoaning their exiled fellow-Ephraimites.[234] Representing them, Rachel sits *on a height* (see the translation note) grieving over their loss. They are all gone. "Cicero, when treating of the highest ornament of an oration, says that nothing touches an audience so much as when the dead are raised up from below."[235]

16–17 The word of Yahweh in the stricter sense now begins, addressing Rachel. She need neither cry out in pain nor let her tears flow. Genesis associates the word *payment* (*śeker*) with Jacob, the man who loved Rachel: Leah links Issachar's name with this word, and Jacob and Laban use it in connection with Jacob's serving Laban (Gen 30:18, 28, 32, 33; 31:8). Like Jacob, Rachel thinks she has earned nothing for the work of mothering that cost her frustration, sadness, labor, and eventually death. But her mother's *payment* lies in the life of her children; she will see the payment, because they will come back. *So there is hope for your future.* "Rachel had lost her own life in giving life to Benjamin, and through him to the people of Israel and Judah. Now she watched again as life and a future slipped away. She saw no hope.

---

233. Brueggemann, *Jeremiah 26–52*, 64.

234. Allen, *Jeremiah*, 348.

235. Calvin, *Jeremiah*, 4:92. See the treatise formerly attributed to Cicero, *Rhetorica ad Herennium* 53; and Cicero, *Orator ad M. Brutum* 25.

She accepted no comfort."[236] Yahweh declares that there is reason for hope. "The Lord's answer to Mother Rachel's prayer is a kind of resurrection."[237]

18 After yet another introduction to what follows, "the lament of the mourning clan mother is followed by a lament of another kind."[238] It again expresses deep feelings, not those of a woman's terrible maternal loss but of a man's regret for a "disgraceful youthful past."[239] One would not immediately know whether the *I* was Yahweh or Jeremiah, but v. 20 will indicate it is Yahweh. Ephraim is not bemoaning someone else (as in 15:5; 16:5; 22:10) but himself; *bemoaning* (*nûd hithpael*) is a body-word, suggesting rocking or swaying or shaking the head. Yahweh has subjected him to tough discipline, as he has Judah (*yāsar*, 2:19–20; see the translation note and commentary there). But arguably Ephraim's discipline has been much harsher. A calf would wear ropes as restraints to train it; so Yahweh has treated Ephraim. The move to the language of turning (*šûb*) almost makes the audience smirk: it is the language that runs through Jer 3 with its comparison and contrast between Ephraim and Judah in that connection. Jeremiah again works with the potential of this verb. Ephraim has recognized that he needed discipline, needed to turn, but as a not-yet-trained calf, he hasn't done so. He recognizes that Yahweh is his God (quite a recognition for the Ephraim whom Jeremiah has described so far). But he needs Yahweh to turn him, to complete the training operation. Then Ephraim will turn. Jeremiah again presupposes that there is something Yahweh needs to do for people and something they have to do, the relationship between the two being mysterious. The Anglican collect for this week as I write runs:

> Almighty God, who alone can bring order to the unruly wills and affections of sinful humanity: give your people grace so to love what you command and to desire what you promise, that, among the many changes of this world, our hearts may surely there be fixed where true joys are to be found.

19 Part of the background is Ephraim's recognition that he had turned (away); but at least he has recognized it and has *relented* (unlike Judah in 8:6, where "turning away" features on either side of the reference to relenting). He has acknowledged his turning and has *struck* his *thigh*. The two expressions spell out aspects of the nature of relenting. It means looking at things a different way (a traditional English translation is "change one's mind"). It

---

236. F. A. Niedner, "Rachel's Lament," *WW* 22 (2002): 409.
237. P. D. Miller, "Jeremiah," on the passage.
238. Weiser, *Jeremia*, 2:288.
239. R. P. Carroll, *Jeremiah*, OTL, 598.

also implies a reaction in the realm of feelings, here suggested by a physical action; beating one's chest might be another equivalent. Ephraim continues to spell out the nature of the change he claims when he recognizes the reality of shame and disgrace and of the reproach that has been hurled at him without him taking any notice. He is not now just shrugging his shoulders at a narrow-minded prophet like Jeremiah. He knows that reproach goes back to the beginning of his story, as Jer 2–3 again suggests. *Reproach since my youth* (lit. "the reproach of my youth") makes for an unhappy contrast with *your youthful commitment* ("the commitment of your youth," 2:2).[240] "Before I was afflicted I went astray. . . . It was good for me that I was afflicted" (Ps 119:67, 71).[241] He has reached the point where he can say, "Father, I have sinned" (Luke 15:21).[242]

20 Initially, it might almost seem as if Yahweh has not listened to Ephraim's disdaining of himself, though perhaps in a good way. He doesn't even directly reply to Ephraim. Whom is Yahweh addressing? Jeremiah? Judah? The nations? Of course, it doesn't matter, because within the rhetoric of the poem, he is speaking for Ephraim to overhear (and in the next level of that rhetoric, for Judah to hear). Yahweh reminds the listeners that he is Ephraim's father (v. 9); Ephraim is a son whom he treasures like a valuable possession. He would not be so stupid as to lose him or throw him away. Yahweh delights in him, like a vineyard owner delighting in the plants he tends in order to get them to grow fruitfully. Ephraim is an important investment for Yahweh. Yahweh is not just being fatherly. His words suggest that he has been listening. He cares about this calf. He has been training it for a purpose, as a father trains his son and disciplines him so the son will be useful on the farm and will be able to take over when his father is past it. Yahweh's speaking against Ephraim was not simply punitive. Even while speaking his disciplinary words, he was still being mindful of him. It doesn't mean Yahweh is a cool and calculating father. *My insides have been in turmoil for him.* The verb (*hāmâ*) can denote the groan of someone in distress (4:19; 48:36) or the roar of the sea (5:22; 6:23; 31:35; 50:42; 51:55); on the only occasion when *my insides* is the subject, it refers to the anxiety of a lover in troubling circumstances (Song 5:4). Here, the significance of the turmoil and inner rumbling is clarified by the parallelism: it is the bodily reflex of his compassion. The word for *insides* (*mēʿîm*) can refer to the womb (e.g., Isa 49:1) or to the origin of a child inside its father's body (e.g., Gen 15:4), and the word for *compassion* (*rāḥam piel*) links with the more technical word for the womb (*reḥem*), which suggests that fatherly (and motherly) imagery continues. In

240. D. R. Jones, *Jeremiah*, 394.
241. Theodoret, *Ermeneia*, PG 81:664.
242. Rudolph, *Jeremia*, 197.

a scene in the movie *Chariots of Fire*, the runner's tough trainer listens alone to a radio broadcast of his protégé's race and rejoices ecstatically when he wins. Such is Yahweh's involvement with his son.

21 For a third time in vv. 15–22, there is a switch to a new addressee; this time it is unannounced but signaled by the addressee's now being feminine singular. Once more, her identity is held back until the third line. The lines hint at a systematic ambiguity: they are talking about a literal return to Canaan and also about a moral and religious return to Yahweh. *Markers* (ṣiyyûn) come only here and in 2 Kgs 23:17; Ezek 39:15, where they indicate markers drawing attention to a tomb, to help people avoid going too close if they want to avoid defilement. Here, the parallelism suggests that the signpost that reads *"bitterness"* is a warning about what defiles and what is death-dealing, perhaps as an encouragement to grieve over it.[243] Israel has not cared enough about such questions over the years; hence Jeremiah's earlier comments on things being bitter, not least in their consequences (2:19; 4:18). That link makes one reflect on the etymological connection between *markers* and Yahweh giving orders (ṣāwâ piel). So Israel needs to think about its *highway*, the *path* it has walked in the past. *Young girl Israel* must *turn*, which takes us back to this motif in Jer 3. Then Yahweh adds a bidding to her to return to *her towns*, which indicates how systematically he is talking at two levels. Ephraim needs to think about the religious and moral path it was long walking and about the bitter journey into exile that issued from that walking, and it needs to make sure it abjures that path as it also undertakes the journey back home on which Yahweh invites it.

22 Yahweh underlines the point with the exhortation not to *vacillate* and with a double further recycling of the image of turning. The image has suggested returning to Yahweh, returning to the right path, and returning to the homeland, but the same verb can denote turning away from Yahweh and from the right path. In the final line, Jeremiah outdoes himself in his capacity for the enigmatic with his declaration that *a female will turn her arms around a man*. Both the puzzling nature of the line and its lack of verbal link with the context raise the question whether it is an aphorism that Jeremiah has adopted.[244] The book of Proverbs illustrates how aphorisms can be elliptical and baffling to someone outside the cultural context.[245] The first colon is not

---

243. See E. E. Kozlova, "Grave Marking and Wailing: Ritual Responses to the Babylonian Crisis in Jeremiah's Poetry (Jer 31, 21)," *SJOT* 31 (2017): 92–117.

244. Duhm, *Jeremia*, 251; he adds, "What it means, no one knows." Rudolph (*Jeremia*, 198) notes that "in ancient times it gave occasion to whole monographs"; R. P. Carroll (*Jeremiah*, OTL, 601–5) lists possibilities. A. O. Bellis calls it "an intentionally ambiguous, multivalent riddle-text" ("Jeremiah 31:22b," in Goldingay, *Uprooting and Planting*, 5–13).

245. See also the Latin American aphorisms in E. Tamez, *When Horizons Close: Rereading Ecclesiastes* (Maryknoll, NY: Orbis, 2000), 146–54, which Tamez is able to explain.

so difficult: *Yahweh has created a new thing* uses language that recurs in Isa 40–55 in a similar connection to Jer 30–31 (see the translation note). That context indicates how the focus in talk of creating in the First Testament (*bārā'*) lies on the extraordinary sovereign action of God, which achieves something that breaks bounds and shatters expectations. *New* then spells out the verb's implications. In Isa 40–55, the two words relate to putting down Babylon, freeing Judahites to return to their homeland, and restoring Jerusalem—the same context as Jer 30–31. In isolation, the second colon expresses astonishment at the way a woman may surround a man (*sābab polel*): when it happens, one could call it a new thing that Yahweh has created. There are many senses in which a woman might do so in different contexts. Here, part of the aphorism's attractiveness is its use of this verb meaning "surround," which makes for a paronomasia with *šûb*.[246] In the context, the female is presumably the turning girl, young girl Israel, who reappears from v. 4. The macho man (*geber*)[247] reappears from 30:6, where the *female* also pairs with the *male*. In 30:5–6, the males are behaving like women. At the close of the double poetic sequence in 30:5–31:22, the woman is playing the man[248] or is united with the man as a mark of the end of the disruption of exile.[249] Miraculous indeed is the new thing of which this entire section speaks with its movement from grieving Rachel to new creation. "God's power is greater than the power of sorrow-bringing forces."[250] Tg has for this last line, "Behold, the Lord is creating a new thing upon the earth: the people, the house of Israel, will pursue the Torah." Matthew 2:16–18 uses v. 15 to throw light on the death of the babies of Bethlehem that resulted from Jesus being born there; then "Christians, almost with one consent" explain v. 22b as "the virgin carrying the infant Christ in her womb," which is "deservedly laughed at by the Jews."[251] Yet this application of v. 22 is no more outrageous than Matthew's application of v. 15. "Ignoring altogether the original context of the passage, he uses Rachel's lament to suggest a correspondence between the suffering of the children of Israel in exile . . . and the suffering of the

---

246. Mayer, *Commentary*, 433.

247. B. W. Anderson, "'The Lord Has Created Something New,'" *CBQ* 40 (1978), 464–65.

248. Holladay, *Commentary on Jeremiah*, 2:195.

249. B. Becking, *Between Fear and Freedom* (Leiden: Brill, 2004), 221–25. See further among feminist studies P. Trible, "The Gift of a Poem: A Rhetorical Study of Jeremiah 31:15–22," *Andover Newton Quarterly* 17 (1977): 271–80; D. Sawyer, "Gender-Play and Sacred Text: A Scene from Jeremiah," *JSOT* 83 (1999): 99–111.

250. B. Becking, "'A Voice Was Heard in Ramah,'" *BZ* 38 (1994): 242.

251. Calvin, *Jeremiah*, 4:116. Calvin would know Nicholas of Lyra's comments along these lines (see the excerpt in Schroeder, *Jeremiah*, 249). Jerome (*Jeremiah*, 198) implies this understanding in a low-key way, though Theodoret (*Ermeneia*, PG 81:665), starting from LXX's plural "people will go about in salvation," applies it to the apostles.

children of Israel under Herod."[252] Subsequently the Holocaust means that "never merely peripheral for Jews, the weeping Rachel has moved into the center."[253] In all these examples, believers find illumination from their texts and show how the inspired application of a text that has little to do with its original meaning can be fruitful.

4. A Reversal for Israel and Judah (31:23-40 [LXX 38:23-40])

The final collection of promises in Jer 30–31 is a compilation of seven short messages that were originally separate but now constitute a series of promises about Jerusalem (the first and last) and about Israel as a whole (the middle five). Whereas 30:5–31:22 could be imagined against the background of Judah's context just before 587, this unit implies that the catastrophe has happened. And whereas Jeremiah has often projected himself and his people into that situation as a way of seeking to forestall the event itself by getting them to turn, these prosaic sections give the impression that the calamity has indeed taken place, and they imply a series of questions people might then worry about. But there is no way of knowing whether the questions and the answers belong to the period immediately after the city's fall or come from a decade or two later, nor whether they come from Jeremiah himself or his curators. The implicit questions are

- Will Judah ever see blessing again?
- Will Israel and Judah ever see building and planting?
- Will people continue to pay the price for the previous generation's waywardness?
- Will Israel and Judah fall into the same waywardness as they did previously?
- Will Israel die out as a people?
- Will Israel be cast off forever because of what it has done?
- Will Jerusalem ever be rebuilt?

The messages thus promise:

---

252. Knowles, *Jeremiah in Matthew's Gospel*, 52.

253. E. L. Fackenheim, "The Lament of Rachel and the New Covenant," *Cross Currents* 40 (1990): 342. C. Ritter surveys the appropriation of vv. 15–17 in *Rachels Klage im antiken Judentum und frühen Christentum: Eine auslegungsgeschichtliche Studie*, Arbeiten zur Geschichte des antiken Judentums und des Urchristentums 52 (Leiden: Brill, 2003).

vv. 23–26	Yahweh will bless the city
vv. 27–28	Yahweh will build and plant
vv. 29–30	Redress will issue from the present, not the wrongdoing of the past
vv. 31–34	Yahweh will solemnize a new pledge
vv. 35–36	Israel will never cease as a nation
v. 37	Yahweh will never cast Israel off
vv. 38–40	The city will be rebuilt

Their framework is prose, though the unit incorporates some poetic lines, like 1:4–19, and introductory expressions such as *Yahweh has said this* or *there, days are coming* look like the markers between sections. These recurrent introductory phrases buttress the reassurance Yahweh offers. *Yahweh has said this*: whether the promises come from Jeremiah or from his curators, they come from Yahweh. *There, days are coming* (sometimes backed up by *Yahweh's affirmation*): the promise does not indicate that the restoration is imminent, but it does indicate that it is certain. All but one of the "answers" to the implicit questions come in the first person from Yahweh, yet he speaks about the people in the third person,[254] giving the impression that they had not been addressing him with their questions but just murmuring them to themselves or to each other. Are people too traumatized to address their questions to Yahweh? They are in a similar position to the Israelites in Egypt, who were groaning and crying out in a way that Yahweh heard whether or not their cry was addressed to him (Exod 2:23–25).

a. The Renewal of Blessing (31:23–26)

[23] *Yahweh of Armies, the God of Israel, has said this. People will again say this word in the country of Judah and in its towns when I have brought about their restoration:*

Yahweh bless you, faithful habitat,[a]
  sacred mountain!

[24] *Judah and all its towns, together, will live in it, farmhands and [people who] travel*[b] *with the flock.* [25] *Because*

I am drenching the weary person,
  and every person [that] is faint I am filling.[c]

---

254. Fretheim, *Jeremiah*, 438.

²⁶*"At this I woke;*
I saw, and my sleep was nice for me."^d

a. For *yǝbārekǝkā*, LXX "[be] blessed" implies the familiar *bārûk*; LXX also lacks *pasture*. Aq, Sym have "the Lord bless you who dwells in faithfulness."

b. The elliptical unmarked relative clause resembles one in 2:8 (see the translation note there); there is another unmarked relative clause in the next verse (Rudolph, *Jeremia*, 198).

c. The *qatal* verbs are anticipatory, denoting what Yahweh has as good as done (see the introduction to 13:18–22, pp. 354–55). The two positive verbs enclose the line as a whole and thus disempower the two negative adjectives.

d. MT^L has a section marker here. Metrically, it is more natural to link *I saw* with the first colon (so MT), but the sequence (*I woke* and then *I saw*) would then be odd.

23 If Yahweh is to bring about the *restoration* of Israel and Judah after the catastrophe of 587, one central necessity is the restoration of Zion. It would be vital to Ephraim as well as to Judah, but the beginning of this section of material from the context of Judah after 587 focuses on the importance of that restoration to *Judah* and thus to *its towns*. Rhetorically, Jeremiah jumps beyond the destruction (which makes the blessing impossible) and the current experience of it and also beyond the renewal to the way things will then be and beyond the way things will then be to the way people will be able to respond to it. He thus invites his audience into a double leap of imagination. They know that Zion is a key to blessing. Yahweh made a commitment to living there (even if he has abandoned his home there at the moment); people come to pray and praise there (even if there are severe limitations on the extent to which they can do so at the moment). Blessing is supposed to emanate from there. So the other side of restoration, people will again urge Yahweh to bless Zion in the sense of making it a source of blessing. Zion as a *faithful habitat* is a complex idea. A habitat (*nāweh*) is the abode of sheep and shepherd; in this case, the people's abode is thus Yahweh's abode. The faithfulness that characterizes it would be Yahweh's faithfulness (*ṣedeq*; see on *ṣǝdāqâ* in the commentary on 4:2). Yahweh's faithfulness will have brought about the restoration, but there will also be need of the people's faithfulness if the dynamics of the relationship between God, place, and people are to work better than they have. Jeremiah's phrase recalls the description of the renewed and purified Jerusalem as faithful city (Isa 1:26). Further, it is the *sacred mountain*, the place that especially belongs to Yahweh. Faithfulness as a personal, moral, and community commitment on one hand and sacredness as a metaphysical or ontological state on the other hand complement each other. Yahweh is the distinctively faithful one; it is an aspect of his being the sacred one. Yahweh is the distinctively sacred one; it finds expression in his faithfulness. These dynamics find expression in his shepherdly home.

24–25 The story in Ruth begins with the fact that the people of *Judah and* *all its towns* cannot always *live in it*, in Judah; sometimes, rains and harvest fail and there is nothing for people or animals to eat. Having a Babylonian army foraging on everything in sight would have the same effect. Judah's farmland and pasturage after 587 would be in a state of devastation. But the restoration will make life possible again both for farmers and for shepherds. The lowly expression *farmhands* suggests laborers rather than people who have their own land, and *people who travel with the flock* might then be mere shepherd boys rather than the shepherds to whom the flock belongs.[255] These two groups would be the people who do the hard work and who are thus most likely to get *weary* and *faint* (people in exile got weary and faint, as Isa 40:28–31 notes,[256] but there is no pointer to a reference to the exiles here). *A fortiori*, if they will be okay, anyone will be. Jeremiah has again conveyed the result before he describes the cause: people will be able to live and work in Judah because Yahweh is already in the midst of providing for them abundantly. Over against *weary* and *faint* (cf. v. 12) are set *drenching* (cf. v. 12) and *filling*.

26 The first-person *I* has evidently changed.[257] Tg paraphrases the speaker's comment, "Because of this news about the days of consolation that are destined to come, I woke up, and saw; I went to sleep again, and my sleep was nice for me." It adds that these are Jeremiah's words, but they look more like a quotation from the weary and faint person, like the unannounced quotation in v. 3.[258] When the restoration happens, such a person will react thus. It will be like dream becoming reality (cf. Ps 126).[259] In the present context, the words suggest encouragement brought by the dream before it becomes reality so that the dynamics parallel those regarding exiles in Isa 40:27–31.

b. New Sowing (31:27–28)

[27] *There, days are coming (Yahweh's affirmation) when I will sow Israel's household and Judah's household with human seed and animal seed.* [28] *As I have watched over them to pull up and to pull down, to smash*[a] *and to destroy and to do something dire, so I will watch over them to build up and to plant (Yahweh's affirmation).*

    a. LXX lacks the first three verbs.

    255. Holladay, *Commentary on Jeremiah*, 2:196.
    256. Qimchi, in MG.
    257. On different possibilities regarding who speaks, see H. Leene, "Jeremiah 31,23–26 and the Redaction of the Book of Comfort," *ZAW* 104 (1992): 349–51.
    258. Keown, Scalise, and Smothers, *Jeremiah 26–52*, 128–29.
    259. Duhm, *Jeremia*, 251.

27–28 A triple introduction undergirds this promise: *There* (can't you see it?), *days are coming* (they are assured, and they are on the way) *(Yahweh's affirmation)* (you don't just have to believe me). The promise constitutes an appropriate accompaniment to the preceding one. It reaffirms that Yahweh is not concerned only with Judah, in case vv. 23–26 gave us that impression. And it offers an assurance about the productiveness of both human beings and animals, neither of which could be taken for granted. In offering this assurance, Yahweh affirms that *to build up and to plant* will now replace *to pull up and to pull down, to smash and to destroy and to do something dire.* The last phrase is an addition to the original instantiation of the threat (1:10), but it picks up a note that featured in the same context (1:14), and it became one of Jeremiah's characteristic expressions. "The five negative verbs have all been fully enacted. There is no more threat in them." God has watched over or "monitored" their fulfillment (1:12) until the warning of destruction was "fully actualized." That declaration is the backdrop for the positive promise that follows. Thus the message "places us between a death already wrought and a resurrection only anticipated."[260] Yahweh announces "the new creation of the people of God."[261] Yahweh's wrath has poured out on humanity and animal (7:20; 21:6). Now Yahweh announces new life.

c. Present Redress (31:29–30)

[29]*In those days, people will no more say,*

It's the parents who ate[a] *unripe fruit,*[b]
   but it's the children's teeth that go numb.

[30]*Rather, an individual, for his own waywardness, will die—any human being who eats the unripe fruit, his teeth will go numb.*[c]

    a. The *qatal* can be used in descriptions of recurrent situations and thus in aphorisms (*IBHS* 30.5.1c; *TTH* 12; *DG* 57c; Joüon 112d) so that the contrast with the *yiqtol* in Ezek 18:2 is not significant (contrast R. R. Hutton, "Slogans in the Midst of Crisis: Jeremiah and His Adversaries," *WW* 10 [1990]: 232).
    b. LXX has, specifically, "unripe grapes," but see *HALOT*.
    c. MT[L] has a section marker here.

   260. Brueggemann, *Jeremiah 26–52*, 67–68.
   261. Weiser, *Jeremia*, 2:292.

29 This saying recurs in Ezek 18:2, where Ezekiel's response is dated about 592 (to judge from 8:1) and thus in the same period as the one in which the Jeremiah scroll sets Jer 30–31. The conviction it expresses continues to be maintained after 587 (see Lam 5:7). Many kinds of fruit gain their sweetness through the last stage of their growth to maturity; it is tempting to eat them early, but one may not find it as pleasant as one anticipated. It may leave a nasty taste in the mouth, and it has an effect on tooth enamel.[262] The background of the aphorism's implication is then that children often pay the price for their parents' waywardness. Judahites experiencing pulling up, demolition, overthrow, destruction, and dire experiences in general are interpreting them as the consequence not of their own wrongdoing but of the previous generation's wrongdoing.

30 One might expect Jeremiah simply to say it isn't so and to draw attention to the teaching that runs through the Torah that people are responsible for their own lives. One person cannot be punished for another's wrongdoing. Never did First Testament faith think of humanity as so corporate that individuals had no responsibility for their own decisions. And Jeremiah has made clear that the present generation is quite guilty. They are wayward. But he doesn't point out those facts. He knows that the aphorism is half right. Parents do influence their children and make a difference to their destiny, for good and for ill. If the present generation's parents had not indulged in the kind of worship, politics, and community life that Jeremiah has critiqued, maybe their children would not have done so. Jeremiah knows that "Yahweh attends to parents' waywardness in connection with children" (Exod 20:5; 34:7), and he will shortly refer to the fact (32:18; cf. 15:4). The message thus "introduces into the images of a great and prosperous future a chill note about the human condition."[263] While not denying the half-truth in the aphorism, however, Jeremiah does say that things will be different in future. How will that be? He implies that there are two forms of corporate and individual relationship and responsibility, a vertical one and a horizontal one. The aphorism relates to the vertical one, about which he says nothing at this point because he focuses on the horizontal one. He implies that people are inclined to make excuses for themselves on the basis of the reality of corporate relationship and responsibility as well as on the basis of what the previous generation did, and he challenges them to work with the fact that Yahweh treats individuals as individuals. Yet "it is not the case that theodicy will be henceforth individualized; rather it is the new nation of Israel and

---

262. B. Becking, "Sour Fruit and Blunt Teeth: The Metaphorical Meaning of the *Māšāl* in Jeremiah 31,29," *SJOT* 17 (2003): 8.

263. R. P. Carroll, *Jeremiah*, OTL, 609.

Judah created by Yahweh which makes the great change possible"[264] (which takes us to the vertical relationship). The next section will make that point and will answer the question of how things will work in a different way in the future.[265]

d. A New Pledge (31:31–34)

[31]*There, days are coming (Yahweh's affirmation) when I will solemnize with Israel's household and with Judah's household a new pledge,* [32]*not like the pledge that I solemnized with their ancestors at the time when I grasped hold of them by their hand to get them out of the country of Egypt, the pledge that they violated, when I myself was husband to them*[a] *(Yahweh's affirmation).* [33]*Because this is the pledge that I will solemnize with Israel's household after those days (Yahweh's affirmation):*

I am putting[b] *my instruction inside them,*
and on their mind I will write it.
And I will be God for them,
and they will be a people for me.

[34]*And they will no more teach, an individual his neighbor and an individual his brother, "Acknowledge Yahweh," because they will acknowledge me, all of them, from the littlest of them to the biggest of them (Yahweh's affirmation).*

Because I will pardon their waywardness,
and of their wrongdoing I will no more be mindful.[c]

a. The verb is *bāʿal* ("be lord," Vg); see the commentary on 3:14a. Tg "I took pleasure in them" sees positive implications in the verb; LXX "I neglected them" is a pejorative version deriving from the context and suggesting neglect because they violated the pledge (McKane, *Jeremiah*, 2:819).

b. LXX has a future verb, while MT has a *qatal*, which I take as anticipatory (see the introduction to 13:18–22, pp. 354–55) rather than as referring back to the Sinai covenant; so A. Schenker, *Das Neue am neuen Bund und das Alte am alten: Jer 31 in der hebräischen und griechischen Bibel*, FRLANT 212 (Göttingen: Vandenhoeck & Ruprecht, 2006); cf. G. Walser, "Jeremiah 38:31–34 (MT 31:31–34)," in *XIV Congress of the International Organization for Septuagint and Cognate Studies, Helsinki, 2010*, ed. M. K. H. Peters, SCS 59 (Atlanta: Society of Biblical Literature, 2013), 369–380; earlier, H. Tita, "'Ich hatte meine Tora in ihre Mitte gegeben': Das Gewicht einer nicht berücksichtigte Perfektform in Jer. xxxi 33," *VT* 52

264. McKane, *Jeremiah*, 2:816.
265. Weinfeld, "Jeremiah and the Spiritual Metamorphosis," 40.

(2002): 551–56; contrast H.-J. Stipp, "Die Perikope vom 'Neuen Bund' (Jer 31:31–34) im Masoretischen und Alexandrinischen Jeremiabuch," *JNSL* 35 (2009): 1–25.

c. MT^L has a section marker here. Again, the two verbs embrace and nullify the two nouns.

31 As in v. 27, the triple introduction undergirds the implausible promise—one Yahweh might not fulfill in the next few months but certainly will fulfill sooner rather than later. To *solemnize* a pledge is literally to "cut" it; Jer 34 will clarify the background to that expression. A *pledge* is then a solemn commitment that one party makes to another or that two parties make to each other (see the commentary on 11:1–17). Yahweh again makes explicit that he is talking about a relationship with Israel as a whole, Ephraim and Judah.

32 He had *grasped hold of them by their hand to get them out of the country of Egypt*, which one might have thought would generate appreciation and a responsive commitment. But it hasn't. The Jeremiah scroll has indicated clearly that the pledge between Yahweh and Israel is not working; 11:1–17 has made the point, but every chapter has made it evident without using the "pledge" language. It was so notwithstanding the fact that Yahweh had married them—not in the egalitarian, mutual-relationship sense that appears in the Song of Songs but in the sense of a patriarchal marriage. By marrying Israel's household, Yahweh had come to have authority over them; he had become their master (see 2:2–3; 3:14a and the commentary there). He had earned the right to have expectations of them. But they have declined to fulfill his expectations. They have thereby *violated* the pledge (see 11:10 and the translation note on it). Jeremiah makes no distinction between Ephraim and Judah or between Judahites in Babylon, Egypt, or Jerusalem in this respect.

33 So that pledge didn't work; Israel needs a new one. It's an iconoclastic view, like many of Jeremiah's views.[266] Unfortunately for Yahweh, Israel's unfaithfulness doesn't release him from faithfulness to his side of the relationship; commitment (*ḥesed*) means continuing to be faithful (see 2:2 and the commentary on it). From the nature of who he is, then, emerges the necessity to solemnize a new, improved pledge *after those days* and years of violation. The problem is not that there was something wrong with the instruction tied to the first pledge; Israel did not need new instructions. The problem was that Yahweh and Moses had written them only on stone (Exod 32–34) and on a scroll (Deut 31:9–13). They addressed people from outside. They were not internalized. What Yahweh is now doing is *putting my instruction within them and writing it on their mind*—the *within* might apply to the people corporately or individually. Normally, a mother doesn't need

266. P. L. Redditt, "When Faith Demands Treason: Civil Religion and the Prophet Jeremiah," *RevExp* 101 (2004): 236.

to be told to look after her baby. She is hardwired to do so. Yahweh is now intending to hardwire Ephraim and Judah with his instruction in this way. Perhaps there is a link with the idea that Israel will not miss the pledge chest (3:16–17), which contained the tablets inscribed with Yahweh's instruction; if the tablets are now inscribed on the people's mind, perhaps they will not need the stone version.[267] If we ask what *my instruction* refers to,[268] there is no need to assume that the expression denotes any particular instantiation of Yahweh's expectations, such as the Ten Words. The word *instruction* (*tôrâ*) never had fixed reference—it changed as circumstances and contexts required its formulation in new ways.[269] It denoted whatever Yahweh's instructions were. The point is that in the past, it is Israel's wrongdoing that has been written on the tablet of its mind (17:1); through Yahweh's doing this new thing, matters will be different. Then, *I will be God for them and they will be a people for me*. In one sense, there will be nothing new there; Yahweh is picking up the language of Sinai and the basis on which the relationship already worked (7:23; 11:4; cf. 30:22; 31:1). But the relationship will now function properly. The new pledge will not be "fragile."[270]

34a If Yahweh's instruction is inscribed onto Israel's corporate mind, it will transform the way people relate to each other. At the moment, individual Israelites have to urge each other to do what is right, and they have not been so inclined. So far in Jeremiah, references to neighbors and brothers have been predominantly negative (e.g., 9:4–8[3–7]): neighbors and brothers are people who cheat and deceive each other.[271] Priests and prophets teach people, but their teaching cannot be relied on. Parents teach children (Deut 11:19), but in practice it tends to mean they teach them waywardness (vv. 29–30). People don't teach each other to *acknowledge Yahweh* (see 1:5 and the translation note on it). As knowing or acknowledging Yahweh's path (5:4–5) means people living in light of what they know (walking on this path—not merely being aware of where the path is), so knowing or acknowledging Yahweh means living in light of whom people know (living in recognition of

267. Weinfeld, "Jeremiah and the Spiritual Metamorphosis," 25.

268. See F. Adeyemi, *The New Covenant Torah in Jeremiah and the Law of Christ in Paul*, StBibLit 94 (New York: Lang, 2006).

269. Fretheim, *Jeremiah*, 443; further, T. E. Fretheim, "Law in the Service of Life: A Dynamic Understanding of Law in Deuteronomy," in *A God So Near: Essays on Old Testament Theology in Honor of Patrick D. Miller*, ed. B. A. Strawn and N. R. Bowen (Winona Lake, IN: Eisenbrauns, 2003), 190–99.

270. R. P. Carroll, "Inscribing the Covenant: Writing and the Written in Jeremiah," in *Understanding Poets and Prophets: Essays in Honour of George Wishart Anderson*, ed. A. G. Auld, JSOTSup 152 (Sheffield: Sheffield Academic, 1993), 66.

271. Katho, "To Know and Not to Know Yhwh," 343.

who Yahweh is and of what he expects, not merely being aware of who he is or having a warm personal relationship with him). Jeremiah said of Josiah:

> He exercised faithful authority,
>> then things were good for him.
> He made decisions for powerless person and needy person,
>> then things were good;
>> that's acknowledging me, isn't it. (22:15–16)

All Israel and Judah will now live this way, little people and big people; it will be a spectacular reversal of 5:1–5. There will be "no more blockheads with memories like sieves."[272] Perhaps he speaks hyperbolically,[273] like Paul in 1 Thess 4:9.[274]

34b How will Yahweh do it? Perhaps the answer lies in this further undertaking. Once again, 5:1–7 suggests some background; there, Yahweh spoke about *pardon* and determined not to grant it. Here he determines to grant it. People no more deserve pardon than before, but Yahweh intends to relate to them in a different way. Perhaps the implication is that the destruction of Jerusalem and the exile will count as enough punishment for their waywardness (cf. Isa 40:1–2). Fulfilling his promises to bring Ephraim and Judah back to the land and enabling them to restore city and temple will be a sign of his willingness to pardon and not be *mindful* of the *wrongdoing* that has accumulated over the centuries. Maybe it will be the astonishing nature of that pardon and willful forgetting that reaches into the heart of Israel in a way that Yahweh has never gained access to it before and causes his expectations to be written into people's minds so that now they live up to them.

Although *days are coming* (v. 31) may imply that the fulfillment of Yahweh's promise may not come immediately, it does imply that its fulfillment will come reasonably soon, as is the case with the occurrences of that expression in vv. 27 and 38. Otherwise, these promises have little significance for Jeremiah's audience. The assumption that it gives them something to look forward to coheres with what happened over subsequent decades. Some exiles did come back to Jerusalem and did rebuild the temple, and during the Second Temple period, Israel did come closer to living by Yahweh's instruction than it had done before. His first four basic requirements were to bow down to Yahweh alone, to foreswear images, to revere Yahweh's name, and to keep the Sabbath. Israel began to live by those expectations as if they were written into their minds in a way they had not previously. The exodus led into the pledge-

---

272. McKane, *Jeremiah*, 2:826, summarizing Duhm, *Jeremia*, 257.
273. Calvin, *Jeremiah*, 4:139.
274. B. P. Robinson, "Jeremiah's New Covenant: Jer 31,31–34," *SJOT* 15 (2001): 199.

making as an event that was unmerited and an act of grace. The restoration will lead into a new pledge-making as an event that is positively undeserved and an act of more radical grace. "Forgiveness is more than a characteristic of the new covenant; it is the very basis of the astonishing workings of God. Divine forgiveness makes possible inner transformation, intimacy with God, and an inclusive community that delights in faithful living."[275] "It is in fact this forgiveness that will allow newness in the relationship."[276]

Yahweh's relationship with Israel depends on Israel's commitment in response to Yahweh's commitment. Israel's commitment was not forthcoming; hence his "breaking down and pulling up." Inscribing his instruction into their minds will mean that this problem does not recur. Will Israel no longer need to give its attention to keeping its commitment? Is Yahweh replacing a relationship that was conditional on obedience with an unconditional relationship? Jeremiah does not use any "if" language, though talk of conditionality moves to a different metaphor from written on stone/written on the mind, and in reflection on metaphors, one has to be wary of an equivalent to "totality transfer" in connection with the meaning of words.[277] Nor is it the case that the relationship was supposed to be reciprocal before but is now one-sided, a matter of Yahweh acting and Israel having no reciprocal obligation. The covenant will continue to involve obedience to Yahweh's instruction, but that obedience will now be "natural."

> The elements are exactly the same as in that covenant with Abraham, Moses and Joshua which is normative for the Old Testament as a whole. The formula "I will be your God, and ye shall be my people" is emphatically endorsed. . . . The relationship of God with Israel, which is the substance of the covenant, is not held up, that is to say, arrested, and set aside and destroyed. . . . [But] the form in which it was revealed and active in all the events from the exodus from Egypt to the destruction of Israel and Judah was such that in it the faithfulness and power of Yahweh seemed always to be matched and limited by the perpetually virulent and active disobedience and apostasy of the covenanted people. . . . The circle of the covenant which in its earlier form is open on man's side will in its new form be closed: not because men will be better, but because God will deal with the same men in a completely different way, laying His hand, as it were, upon them from behind, because He Himself will turn them to Himself. To His faithfulness—He himself will see to it—there will then correspond

---

275. Stulman, *Jeremiah*, 274.

276. B. Katho, "The New Covenant and the Challenge of Building a New and Transformed Community in DR Congo," *OTE* 18 (2005): 120; cf. J. Krašovec, "Vergebung und neuer Bund nach Jer 31,31–24," *ZAW* 105 (1993): 428–44.

277. J. Barr, *The Semantics of Biblical Language* (London: Oxford University Press, 1961), 218.

the complementary faithfulness of His people. The covenant—God Himself will make it so—will then be one which is mutually kept, and to that extent a foedus dipleuron.[278]

Jeremiah 31:31-34 does not open up the question of the relationship between active obedience and instruction inscribed on the mind. Jeremiah 24:7 has come closer to doing so, though it remains a little ambiguous: *I will give them a mind to acknowledge me, because I am Yahweh. They will be a people for me and I—I will be God for them, because they will turn to me with their entire mind* (cf. also 32:38-40). Formulations in other documents are similar. Deuteronomy 30:1-11 asserts that Israel must turn back to Yahweh and obey him with its entire mind and that Yahweh will circumcise its mind so that it loves him and obeys him. In the context of its discussion of the saying about sour fruit, Ezek 18:31 urges the Israelites to get themselves a new mind, while Ezek 36:26-27 promises that Yahweh will give them a new mind and thus get them to follow his commands.[279] The Qumran community spoke much of covenant and sometimes of the "new covenant" into which members of the community entered (e.g., Damascus Document 6:19; 8:21; 19:34; 20:12).[280] The Qumran Community Rule sees its people as the new covenant people

278. Barth, *CD* IV, 1:33-34. Foedus dipleuron (two-sided covenant) is a term from Reformed controversy over the relationship of covenant, grace, and obedience. Barth goes on to note that the link between covenant and forgiveness did hold already in the First Testament times, but it will now be more visible and not obscured by human resistance to God's grace. See further J. N. Moon, *Jeremiah's New Covenant: An Augustinian Reading*, JTISup 3 (Winona Lake: Eisenbrauns, 2011).

279. On the possible influence of Ezekiel on Jer 31:31-34, see, e.g., B. Gosse, "La nouvelle alliance de Jérémie 31,31-34," *ZAW* 116 (2004): 568-80 (also Gosse, "La nouvelle alliance et les promesses d'avenir se référant à David dans les livres de Jérémie, Ezéchiel et Isaïe," *VT* 41 [1991]: 419-28); H. Leene, "Ezekiel and Jeremiah," in *Past, Present, Future: The Deuteronomistic History and the Prophets*, ed. J. de Moor and H. R. van Rooy, *OTS* 44 (2000): 150-75.

280. *DSS* 1:558-61, 578-79; see, e.g., B. Nitzan, "The Concept of Covenant in Qumran Literature," in *Historical Perspectives: From the Hasmoneans to Bar Kokhba in the Light of the Dead Sea Scrolls*, ed. D. Goodblatt, A. Pinnick, and D. R. Schwartz, STDJ 37 (Leiden: Brill 2018), 85-104; E. J. Christiansen, "The Consciousness of Belonging to God's Covenant and What It Entails according to the Damascus Document and the Community Rule," in *Qumran between the Old and New Testaments*, ed. F. H. Cryer and T. L. Thompson, JSOTSup 290 (Sheffield: Sheffield Academic, 1998), 69-97; S. E. Porter and J. C. R. de Roo, eds., *The Concept of the Covenant in the Second Temple Period*, JSJSup 71 (Leiden: Brill 2003); S. Hultgren, *From the Damascus Covenant to the Covenant of the Community: Literary, Historical, and Theological Studies in the Dead Sea Scrolls*, STDJ 66 (Leiden: Brill, 2007); T. R. Blanton, *Constructing a New Covenant: Discursive Strategies in the Damascus Document and Second Corinthians*, Wissenschaftliche Untersuchungen zum Neuen Testament 2/233 (Tübingen: Mohr Siebeck, 2007); J. J. Collins, *Beyond the Qumran Community* (Grand Rapids: Eerdmans, 2010). On different opinions in Second Temple Judaism, see also, e.g., D. D. Swanson, "'A Covenant Just Like Jacob's,'" in *New Qumran Texts and Studies: Proceedings of the First*

but also urges them to live in accordance with Yahweh's commands. The New Testament Letter to the Hebrews sees its people as the new covenant people but also urges the importance of obedience and the danger of forgoing one's salvation. None of these writings clarify how God will go about inscribing his expectations onto his people's mind in such a way as to make it "natural" to fulfill them; all imply that their readers have an active part to play in fulfilling them and that playing this active part is essential to their being the new covenant people. Jeremiah 31:31–34 implies the same assumption rather than the implication that Ephraim and Judah can now do as they like without imperiling their position.

The assumption at Qumran and in the New Testament that the new covenant is a reality for their communities does not imply that they see the promise as having found complete fulfillment; indeed, the way they talk about the new covenant implies the assumption that it has not. It resembles other promises Yahweh makes through Jeremiah. Christians then need to note two further considerations. It is not clear that Christians are hardwired with Yahweh's instructions any more than Ephraim and Judah were, even after the outpouring of the Holy Spirit. We still need to teach each other, and we still contravene basic commandments quite a lot. The new covenant is "an ideal which has not yet been realized" though "it at least serves as a standard by which we may measure ourselves, a goal which we may all strive to attain."[281] So we look forward to God's completing the fulfillment of this promise, as of others.[282] Further, it is not the case that "the use of this text in Heb. 8:8–13; 9:15–22; and 10:16–17 provides a basis for a Christian preemption of the promise," as if it does not belong to the Jewish people.[283] In quoting it, "Hebrews seems not to draw any negative conclusions regarding the relationship of the Jewish people to God."[284] The interpretation of vv. 31–34 in Hebrews is similar to Matthew's interpretation of v. 15. Everything depends on whether you start from Jeremiah and ask what God was saying to Israel in the text or whether you start from Jesus and move backward.[285]

Meeting of the International Organization for Qumran Studies, ed. G. J. Brooke with F. García Martínez, STDJ 15 (Leiden: Brill, 1994), 273–86.

281. M. L. King Jr., "The Significant Contributions of Jeremiah to Religious Thought," in *The Papers of Martin Luther King Junior* (Berkeley: University of California, 1992), 1:194.

282. W. E. Lemke, "Jeremiah 31:31–34," *Int* 37 (1983): 183–87.

283. Brueggemann, *Jeremiah 26–52,* 72–73; cf. R. Rendtorff, *Canon and Theology* (Edinburgh: T&T Clark, 1994), 196–206.

284. Fretheim, *Jeremiah,* 449.

285. T. M. Willis, "'I Will Remember Their Sins No More': Jeremiah 31, the New Covenant, and the Forgiveness of Sins," *Restoration Quarterly* 53 (2011): 1–15; W. Kraus, "Die Rezeption von Jer 38:31–34 (LXX) in Hebräer 8–10," in *Text-Critical and Hermeneutical Studies in the Septuagint,* ed. J. Cook and H.-J. Stipp, VTSup 157 (Leiden: Brill, 2012),

e. Israel's Permanence (31:35–36)

35 Yahweh has said this.ᵃ

One who gives the sun as a lightᵇ by day,
   the decrees regardingᶜ moon and stars as a light by night,
Who stillsᵈ the sea when its waves roar—
   Yahweh of armies his name:
36 If these decrees can pass away from before me (Yahweh's affirmation),
   the offspring of Israel can cease also
   from being a nation before me, for all the days.ᵉ

a. LXX has v. 37 before vv. 35–36.
b. Tg "to give light" here and in the next colon parses *lə'ôr* as a verb rather than a noun.
c. LXX lacks *the decrees regarding*.
d. Tg, Syr thus take the verb as *rāgaʿ* II as in v. 1, not *rāgaʿ* I ("stir up"; so LXX, Vg); the subsequent *waw*-consecutive is then epexegetical (*TTH* 75–76; *IBHS* 33.2.2; Joüon 118j).
e. MT has a section marker here.

35–36 Might one fear that Israel would go out of existence? One might have that anxiety in the aftermath of 587. Ephraim could seem all but obliterated as a people, and the same fate could seem to threaten Judah. In responding to the question, Yahweh points to two aspects of his sovereignty. Both count as *statutes*: they are definitely fixed. First, there is the regular patterned movements of sun, moon, and stars. "The day continually dawns for man, and the sun, moon and stars which indicate the separation of day from night shine for him" in order that he may know that he has time and place when "the Word of God is spoken to man, and judges him, and becomes his radically saving and preserving promise, and summons him to pray for the grace of God."[286] Second, there is the rising and falling of the sea. This second line is identical to Isa 51:15aβ–b. Jeremiah 4:23–26 earlier shared a nightmare vision of Yahweh letting or causing creation to collapse; these verses are "an antithesis" to that vision.[287] When it is in the midst of finding fulfillment, the declaration that the apparently disorderly and chaotic rising and falling of the sea's waves is under divine control might be a more obvious reassurance than pointing to the regularities of each day.[288] In a disturbingly new situ-

447–62. C. Locatell also documents the use of this passage in debates over infant baptism in "Jeremiah 31:34, New Covenant Membership, and Baptism," *Scriptura* 114 (2015): 1–14.

286. Barth, *CD* III, 1:164.

287. W. Brueggemann, "Jeremiah: Creatio in Extremis," in *God Who Creates: Essays in Honor of W. Sibley Towner*, ed. W. P. Brown and S. D. McBride (Grand Rapids: Eerdmans, 2000), 157.

288. Calvin, *Jeremiah*, 4:146.

ation, it is an innovative, new way to ground Yahweh's commitment.[289] As people look questioningly to the future, Yahweh affirms "the indissoluble nature of salvation."[290]

f. Israel's Security (31:37)

[37] *Yahweh has said this.*

If the heavens above can be measured[a]
    and earth's foundations can be fathomed below,
I also can reject all Israel's offspring
    because of all that they have done (Yahweh's affirmation).[b]

a. LXX "raised" implies *yārumû* for MT *yimmaddû*, a plausible misreading in light of the parallel colon—all the more as LXX there translates *wəyēḥāqərû* as "be lowered."
b. MT has a section marker here.

37 Might Yahweh simply cast off Israel? Jeremiah has come close to giving the impression that he could, though he has safeguarded against the possibility with qualifications on his declarations about the end (4:27; 5:10, 18; most recently 30:11). Again, the moment when Nebuchadrezzar is at the gates or has demolished them is one where reassurance would especially be needed.

g. The City's Rebuilding (31:38–40)

[38] *There, days are coming[a] (Yahweh's affirmation) when the city will be built up for Yahweh from the Hananel Tower to the Corner Gate.* [39] *The measuring line will go out further, straight over Garob Hill, and it will turn to Goah.* [40] *The entire vale—corpses and fat[b]—and all the fields[c] as far as the Kidron Wadi, as far as the Horses Gate corner on the east, will be sacred for Yahweh. It will not be pulled up and it will not be smashed again ever.[d]*

a. Only the *qere*, not the *ketiv*, has *are coming*.
b. Vg "ash."
c. For the *qere's šədēmôt*, the *ketiv* has *šrmwt*, a slip emerging from the similarity of *d* and *r*. Vg, Sym "open land of death" implies *śədēh māwet* ("cemetery"), an appropriate

289. H. B. Huffmon, "The Impossible: God's Word of Assurance in Jer. 31:35–37," in *On the Way to Nineveh: Studies in Honor of George E. Landes*, ed. S. L. Cook and S. C. Winter, ASOR Books 4 (Atlanta: Scholars, 1999), 172–86.
290. Rudolph, *Jeremia*, 204.

description of the area (M. R. Lehmann, "A New Interpretation of the Term *šdmwt*," *VT* 3 [1953]: 361–71); at least one can imagine readers noting a paronomasia.

d. MT has a marker here.

38–40 One last time, the promise begins with that threefold reassurance *there, days are coming (Yahweh's affirmation)*. Again, one recalls that in the aftermath of 587, it might seem that Jerusalem is finished. The consolation document comes to a resounding if down-to-earth end with this promise. Yahweh has said *I will sow* and *I will solemnize* (vv. 23, 31), and one might have expected "I will build" (cf. v. 4). *The city will be built up for Yahweh* constitutes a different kind of assurance. People will have to do the work, but the fact that the city is rebuilt *for Yahweh* is an implicit guarantee that it will happen—not because every human project that claims to benefit Yahweh can make that assumption, but because Yahweh underwrites this one. It will be the work of Nehemiah that sees the fulfillment of the promise, though the particulars here link only slightly with the Nehemiah story, and the boundaries Jeremiah describes cover a wider area than Nehemiah's city.[291] Partly on the basis of that account, geographers and archaeologists locate the *Hananel Tower* at the northeast corner of the city, north of the Temple Mount, in the area of the Sheep Gate (Neh 3:1; 12:39) and thus in the region of the later Antonia Fortress. It then follows to locate the *Corner Gate* at an equivalent northwest point of the city, in the area of the later David's Tower (2 Chr 25:23; 26:9). To begin with these two points might make sense given the fact that the city's northern limits were its especially vulnerable side, since they were not protected by valleys, as the other sides were—though the remaining boundaries do not take that consideration into account. If the account of the city's walls continues in the same counterclockwise direction, *Garob Hill* would be at the city's southwest corner and *Goah* on its southern boundary or southeast corner, though the places are otherwise unknown. The Horse Gate (Neh 3:28) was then on the eastern side of city and temple, perhaps just below the southeastern corner of the temple, so that it takes us back near the Hananel Tower and completes the circuit. Meanwhile, *vale* and *fields* refer to the Hinnom Valley to the south, stretching across to the Kidron Wadi on the east. The Kidron Valley fields makes one think of the terraces with olive trees, though it is also an area characterized by tombs and graves. *Corpses* fits in particular with 7:32–33; they would be the remains of the Assyrian or Babylonian besiegers of the city (cf. Tg). It could also sug-

291. For what follows, see J. Simons, *Jerusalem in the Old Testament* (Leiden: Brill, 1952), 231–33, who gives particular consideration to 31:38–40. More generally, see, e.g., D. Bahat, *The Illustrated Atlas of Jerusalem* (New York: Simon and Schuster, 1990), 30–33; M. Ben-Dov, *Historical Atlas of Jerusalem* (New York: Continuum, 2002), 84–88.

gest victims of the human sacrifices in the Hinnom Valley to which 7:30–31 referred. *Fat* suggests the area where the fat-soaked ashes from the temple sacrifices were dumped (e.g., Lev 4:12). The promise combines the well-known, the unknown (to us), and also the extraordinary and scandalous in the way these areas come to be part of what is *sacred for Yahweh*. If we may see a kind of parallelism between vv. 38–40 and 23–26, then vv. 38–40 go beyond vv. 23–26. Not only is the mountain sacred; so are the surrounding lower vale and the open lands. If only it were the case that the city had not been pulled up or smashed again ever!

5. *The Acquisition of Land (32:1–44 [LXX 39:1–44])*

It is now explicitly Zedekiah's tenth year, the siege of Jerusalem has begun, and its destruction is imminent. The story invites readers in Judah or Babylon or Egypt after 587 to picture Yahweh drawing Jeremiah in that context into a gesture of confidence in Yahweh's underwriting of Judah's future, and it further invites them to believe in that future with him. The chapter thus relates Jeremiah's acquisition of a parcel of land. But it goes on to become a subtle, complex, and dramatic exposition of key themes concerning Yahweh's involvement with the land and Israel's attitude to it and concerning the necessity of Yahweh's taking redress and engaging in restoration. "Chapter 32 contains a salvation promise for the Judahite land."[292] But "the perplexity of [vv. 16–25] is mirrored more broadly in the tension between two contrasting motifs that run through the unit, the handing over of Jerusalem to the enemy (vv. 3, 24–25, 28, 36, and 43) and the renewed purchase of land in Judah (vv. 15, 25, and 43–44)"; the two motifs are juxtaposed in v. 25 and again in vv. 43–44. The tension between them also reflects how "home determines one's identity, sense of self, and sense of place" and how "the report of Jeremiah's purchase of property and the transmission of that symbolic action within the literary structure of the book of Jeremiah confront the reality of empire as it threatens the nation's sense of place." Jeremiah's purchase is "an act of nationalist resistance to the empire."[293] The comment "Buy the field; declare yourself friend of creation (and of the Creator); indict the destroyers of an ecology blasted and degraded by war"[294] provides another illustration of a question emerging from a different context finding illumination in the text (see the commentary on 31:22).

292. Weiser, *Jeremia*, 2:300.

293. S. V. Davidson, *Empire and Exile: Postcolonial Readings of the Book of Jeremiah*, LHBOTS 542 (London: T&T Clark, 2011), 55, 56.

294. Berrigan, *Jeremiah*, 136.

While narratively the story of Jeremiah acquiring the land forms the chapter's center of attention and MT has a unit marker after v. 15, "the length of the final section [vv. 26–44] and its climactic position indicate that the unit's focus lies here."[295] "The sermon is everything."[296] The chapter's form compares with that of chapters in John's Gospel that start from an event in Jesus's life and make it the jumping off point for reflection on his significance that they present as Jesus's own teaching. In Jer 32, maybe Jeremiah recorded his prayer and the message he received from Yahweh in response to it, so that it all goes back to a time before the fall of the city. Or maybe Jeremiah cast his subsequent reflection into the form of a prayer and a message so that Jeremiah acted as his own John. Or maybe his curators have done so in the manner of John; the chapter's framework presents itself as coming from the curators, who speak about Jeremiah in the third person in vv. 1–5 and v. 26.[297] Again in anticipation of chapters in John, Jer 32 unfurls with some subtlety and sometimes requires listeners to fill in gaps. And like Jer 26, for example, one aspect of this subtlety is its unfurling in a way that is sometimes movie-like and dramatic rather than chronological: after the story of the land's acquisition ends in v. 15, the chapter goes back to a point in between vv. 14 and 15 as Jeremiah raises a question to which v. 15 has presupposed an answer.[298]

The unit unfolds:

vv. 1–5   The curators provide background to the story indicating how bleak things are in Jerusalem and summarize the chapter's point (v. 5)

vv. 6–15   Jeremiah relates how he acquires the land and summarizes the significance of his action (v. 15)

vv. 16–25   Jeremiah relates the prayer he had prayed when he didn't know what the point of this action was

vv. 26–44   The curators report Yahweh's response to Jeremiah
    vv. 26–35   Why he is undertaking his dire action
    vv. 36–41   How his dire action will be followed by good
    vv. 42–44   How his good action will embody what Jeremiah's symbolic action exemplifies

295. Allen, *Jeremiah*, 364–65.

296. D. R. Jones, *Jeremiah*, 405

297. On the possible development of the chapter, see, e.g. D. Rom-Shiloni, "The Prophecy for 'Everlasting Covenant' (Jeremiah xxxii 36–41)," *VT* 53 (2003): 201–23.

298. E. Di Pede notes that Jer 32 begins a series of narrative surprises running through Jer 32–45: see "Surprises et rebondissements en Jr 32–45 au service de l'intrigue et du message prophétique," in *La surprise dans la Bible: Festschrift Camille Focant*, ed. G. van Oyen and A. Wénin, BETL 247 (Leuven: Peeters, 2012), 77–88.

In vv. 16–44, the lines are rhythmic and incorporate some parallelism, and I lay them out as poetic lines. At many points, LXX's text is shorter than MT's. Whereas elsewhere this difference may often indicate that MT has expanded an earlier version of the scroll, here LXX may have often accidentally abbreviated an earlier version.[299]

While in a narrow sense, vv. 1–15 are the chapter's concrete story, Jer 32 as a whole also comprises a story about an interaction between Yahweh and Jeremiah. If a story is a narrative with a tension that needs resolving or a question that needs answering, then this story's implicit question is whether the coming catastrophe will simply mean the end of Judah or whether Yahweh will really bring about Judah's restoration after the catastrophe that looks inevitable. In handling that question, it focuses on a dialogue between Jeremiah and Yahweh, and it thus compares with the dialogues between Jeremiah and Yahweh in Jer 11–20, though it is less agonized. The comparison extends to the way Jeremiah's life forms part of the way Yahweh brings his message to Judah before 587 and the way the record of his activity speaks after the catastrophe. These features issue in the possibility of reading the chapter by focusing on its main character, Jeremiah, on the narrator as the teller of the story and on the nature of his story, or on the community listening to the text—both the first audience and later audiences.[300]

a. The Background (32:1–5)

[1]*The word that came to Jeremiah from Yahweh in the tenth year of Zedekiah King of Judah (it was the eighteenth year of Nebuchadrezzar).* [2]*The king of Babylon's force were then blockading Jerusalem, and Jeremiah the prophet was confined in the court of the guard, which was at the house of the king of Judah,* [3]*where Zedekiah King of Judah had confined him, saying, "Why are you prophesying: Yahweh has said this. Here am I, giving this city into the hand of the king of Babylon, and he will capture it,* [4]*and Zedekiah King of Judah—he will not escape from the hand of the Chaldeans, because he will definitely be given*[a] *into the hand of the king of Babylon, his mouth will speak with his mouth and his eyes will see his eyes,*[b] [5]*to Babylon he will make Zedekiah go, and there he*

---

299. So A. G. Shead, *The Open Book and the Sealed Book: Jeremiah 32 in Its Hebrew and Greek Recensions*, JSOTSup 347 (London: Sheffield Academic, 2002).

300. E. Talstra and R. Oosting, "Jeremiah 32: A Future and Its History—Actualisation in Writing and Reading," in *African and European Readers of the Bible in Dialogue: In Quest of a Shared Meaning*, ed. G. O. West and H. De Wit, Studies of Religion in Africa 32 (Leiden: Brill, 2008), 208.

will be until my attending to him (Yahweh's affirmation)—when you people do
*battle with the Chaldeans, you will not succeed."*c

> a. The infinitive precedes the finite verb, underlining the factuality of the action.
> b. The *ketiv* implies *ʿênô* ("his eye"), which the *qere ʿênāyw* perhaps corrects.
> c. MT has a unit marker here. LXX lacks *until my attending . . . succeed.*

While the chapter opens by setting up the expectation of a message from God
(and it will eventually provide one), it then moves sideways into a lengthy
diversion on the message's background so that the first word it offers is from
the king who has just confined Jeremiah in prison.[301] Chronologically, the
sequence of events is

- Babylonian forces are blockading Jerusalem (v. 2a)
- Yahweh gives Jeremiah a message about the fall of the city and Ze-
  dekiah's exile to Babylon (vv. 3b–5)
- Jeremiah delivers this message, but Zedekiah claims to have no idea
  of the reason for it (v. 3a)
- Zedekiah confines him to the court of the guard (v. 2b)
- Yahweh gives Jeremiah another message (v. 1)

This account indicates how bleak things are. But "the Prophet here declares,
that though he was shut up in prison, the Word of God was not bound"
(2 Tim 2:9).[302]

1–2 The setting, then, is the final siege of Jerusalem before its fall in 587.
In itself, *blockading* (*ṣûr*) simply implies making it impossible for resources
to get into the city or for people to leave, and thus trying to wear it down.
It needn't signify active attempts to take the city; the Babylonians are just
sitting there. Verse 24 will indicate that something more forceful is on the
way, but vv. 6–15 will show that, within the city, some semblance of normal
life continues. To a degree, it is even true for Jeremiah. Jeremiah 37 (which
relates an earlier incident) indicates that he had earned the hostility of powerful people in Jerusalem by continuing to deliver the message that is about
to be related here, and v. 2 may imply that he is at least partly in protective
custody, in an "open prison."[303]

3–5 How rhetorical is Zedekiah's why? On a number of occasions, Jeremiah mediated Yahweh's message to Zedekiah, sometimes because he asked

---

301. Pixley, *Jeremiah*, 104.
302. Calvin, *Jeremiah*, 4:158, 159.
303. McKane, *Jeremiah*, 2:837.

for it, sometimes when he did not (see Jer 21; 27; 34; 37; 38). And "every time Jeremiah gave him the same basic message—'this city is doomed, and so are you'—until Zedekiah could repeat the prophet's words from memory. But if he knew the words of Jeremiah by heart, he certainly did not take them to heart as the word of God."[304] For the audience's sake, if not for Zedekiah's sake, the answer to his "why" will feature in vv. 16–44. Grammatically, it's ambiguous whose mouth and eyes will do the speaking and looking when the two kings meet, but there is no doubt that Nebuchadrezzar will be the active agent when he issues sentence on Zedekiah for leading Judah in an attempt to declare independence. In theory, then, references to mouth and eyes suggest privilege and intimacy: Yahweh spoke with Moses mouth to mouth (Num 12:8, the only other occurrence of the phrase except for 34:3); "eye to eye" comes only here and in 34:3, though "face to face" is an expression for such intimacy (e.g., Exod 33:11; Deut 34:10). So there is a sardonic implication in Jeremiah's words, a grim irony in the reference to Zedekiah's eyes (see 39:5–7), and a sardonic ambiguity about the reference to Yahweh *attending* to Zedekiah there, traditionally "visiting" him.[305] It will be the point at which Zedekiah's sons find that "death is God's final visitation on a person in this life."[306]

b. Jeremiah Acquires Some Land (32:6–15)

[6]*So Jeremiah said: Yahweh's word came to me.* [7]*Here is Hanamel ben Shallum, your uncle, coming to you to say, "Acquire for yourself my land which is in Anathoth, because you have authority regarding restoration, by acquiring it."* [8]*And Hanamel, my uncle's son, came to me in accordance with Yahweh's word,*[a] *to the court of the guard, and said to me, "Please acquire my land that is in Anathoth, which is in the country of Benjamin, because you have authority regarding the possession and the restoration—acquire it for yourself."*

So I acknowledged that it was Yahweh's word, [9]*and I acquired the land that was in Anathoth*[b] *from Hanamel, my uncle's son. I weighed out the silver to him, seventeen sheqels of silver,* [10]*wrote in a document, sealed it, charged witnesses, and weighed out the silver on scales.* [11]*I got the acquisition document, both the*

---

304. Wright, *Jeremiah*, 341.

305. C. Begg argues for a positive understanding in "Yahweh's 'Visitation' of Zedekiah," *Ephemerides Theologicae Lovanienses* 63 (1987): 113–16; see further J. Pakkala, "Zedekiah's Fate and the Dynastic Succession," *JBL* 125 (2006): 443–52. J. Applegate ("The Fate of Zedekiah," *VT* 48 [1998]: 155) emphasizes the intrinsic ambiguity of the passage.

306. Denis the Carthusian, *Enarratio in Jeremiam*, in *Opera Omnia* (Montreuil: Typis Cartusiae S. M. de Pratis, 1900), 9:235; cf. Schroeder, *Jeremiah*, 261.

*sealed one (the rule and the decrees)*ᶜ *and the one left open,* ¹²*and gave the document*ᵈ *(the acquisition) to Baruch ben Neriah son of Mahseiah before the eyes of Hanamel my relative*ᵉ *and before the eyes of the witnesses who had written in the acquisition document, before the eyes of all the Judahites who were sitting in the prison courtyard.* ¹³*I ordered Baruch, before their eyes:* ¹⁴*Yahweh of Armies, the God of Israel, has said this. Get*ᶠ *these documents, this acquisition document, both the sealed one*ᵍ *and this left open one (a document),*ʰ *and put them in an earthenware container so that they may last a long time.*ⁱ ¹⁵*Because Yahweh of Armies, the God of Israel, has said this: houses, lands, and vineyards will once again be acquired in this country.*ʲ

a. LXX lacks *in accordance with Yahweh's word.*

b. LXX lacks *that was in Anathoth.*

c. LXX lacks *(the rule and the decrees)*, which fits uneasily in the sentence. It is a legal phrase similar to ones that recur in Deut 5:31(28); 6:1.

d. *Hassēper* has the article here, so it can't be construct like simple *sēper* in the phrases on either side.

e. Verse 9 had *ben dōdî*, meaning *my uncle's son*, but on its own here, *dôd* has to have this broader sense (LXX has "my uncle's son" here).

f. The infinitive absolute functions as an emphatic imperative (see 2:2 and the translation note on it).

g. LXX lacks *both the sealed one.*

h. The translation *open one (a document)* reflects the jerky nature of the text: whereas in v. 12 *sēper* had an article that it didn't need, here it is anarthrous where it needs an article.

i. MTᴸ has a section marker here.

j. MTᴸ has a unit marker here.

The section resumes from v. 1 after the digression in vv. 2–5. Jeremiah relates how he acquired a parcel of land that belonged by right to his family but had apparently become lost to it or was in danger of becoming lost to it.

vv. 6–7	Jeremiah receives a message about an appeal that will come from his cousin
v. 8a	The appeal comes
vv. 8b–14	Jeremiah accedes to the appeal, describing the process in great detail
v. 15	Jeremiah receives a message from Yahweh explaining the action

Although vv. 6–15 are thus a self-contained and complete story, from v. 16 it will become clear that they are also just the beginning of the longer story occupying Jer 32 as a whole. They open up the question that the chapter as a whole has to answer, the tension it has to resolve. It will also transpire that

v. 15 is an anticipatory summary of what will follow in the rest of the chapter. As a story that relates a symbolic or sign-act, it compares and contrasts with a number of earlier stories in the scroll.

- Yahweh commissions the act, as usually happens in such sign-act stories about Jeremiah (though not 51:59–64).
- The act symbolizes the message attached to it, like the depositing of the shorts in Jer 13, the shaping of the pot in Jer 18, and the breaking of the decanter in Jer 19.
- The act also exemplifies the event it anticipates, like Jeremiah's holding back from marriage and from mourning in Jer 16.
- The act perhaps also initiates the event it represents, like the breaking of the decanter and the yoke in Jer 19 and 28.
- The act takes place before other people, like the breaking of the decanter and the yoke and unlike the depositing of the shorts, which functions as a symbolic act only for Jeremiah and for people who hear the story.
- The story records the implementing of the act, as happened with the depositing of the shorts and the shaping of the pot; contrast the stories about the breaking of the decanter, the imposition of the yoke in Jer 27, and the drinking of the wine in the vision in Jer 25.
- The story explains the significance of the act only after the act is over, as is the case with the depositing of the shorts; contrast the breaking of the decanter.

6–8a The introduction resumes from v. 1. While Jer 37 relates an earlier attempted visit by Jeremiah to Anathoth during a break in the siege, there is no need to hypothesize that Hanamel somehow came from there to Jerusalem to see Jeremiah; many people might have taken refuge in the city as the Babylonians approached. The story implies a situation in Anathoth approximately like that envisaged in Lev 25 and paralleled in Ruth; Lev 25:34 and Num 35:1–8 relate more specifically to the situation of Levitical families. In Ruth (to read between the lines), a failure of the harvest has required Elimelech to take out a loan in order to feed his family, then to surrender his land when he couldn't repay the loan. Perhaps the Babylonian invasion had put Jeremiah's extended family into similar circumstances or the Babylonians had taken over some of its land. If Shallum were still alive, presumably it would be he as the head of the household who would have taken out a loan and been unable to repay; Hanamel would then need to try to do something about the situation. But his calling it *my land* may mean his father has died. Moreover, it's thirty-eight years since Yahweh's commission of Jeremiah in 626, so Jeremiah must be at least in his late fifties, and it's unlikely that either Hilkiah or Shallum is still alive. Perhaps Jeremiah is first in line to act as redeemer or restorer by paying off the debt, or perhaps there has been some other person like Mr. So-and-So in Ruth 4:1 who has refused or been unable to do so. The imminent fall of Jerusalem would surely make Jeremiah hesitate to part with his silver to acquire land that neither he nor anyone else might ever be able to use (an unlikelihood that, ironically, Jeremiah is more prepared than most people to treat as a certainty). The tension between Jeremiah and his extended family in Anathoth presupposed in Jer 11–12 would provide another potential disincentive to his acting as restorer. So it is just as well that Yahweh makes it hard for Jeremiah to say no and compels him to acknowledge that *it was Yahweh's word*. Jeremiah agrees to do as the Torah expected. To speak of him "buying" the land might be misleading. In theory, Israelites cannot own land because it belongs to Yahweh; he lets them live on it and use it, but they cannot buy or sell it. The question is who controls the land.[307] Yet once people have got used to the idea of acquiring or surrendering control of land in a way that involves silver changing hands, this subtlety might not have been in the front of people's minds. Nevertheless, Hanamel's use of the terms *possession* and *restoration* indicates that he thinks within the Torah's framework and hopes that Jeremiah will do so. *Possession* (from the verb *yāraš*) is what Yahweh gave the Israelites when they arrived in Canaan. *Restoration* (from the verb *gā'al*) is what happens when the land comes back to the family to which it was allocated in the first place. And Jeremiah does agree to exercise his responsibilities and rights as the closest relation in terms of the restorer notion.[308]

8b–9a The reference to Jeremiah's acknowledgment and his consequent action make clear that Yahweh's message (v. 6) had implications beyond the information that Hanamel was coming. The information did not mean Jeremiah had to say yes. It might simply have given him time to prepare to say no and deliver a stinging declaration about this being no time for such action given that Yahweh was about to bring about disaster as a consequence of Judah's wrongdoing. More likely, the implication is that Jeremiah must say yes because the Torah expects it. He must be like Boaz, not like Mr. So-and-So. Yahweh makes it difficult for Jeremiah to say no, notwithstanding the political situation and the family dynamics. Jeremiah's later reference in v. 25 to what Yahweh had said to him confirms this implication. Yahweh expected him to agree to take the action that would keep the land in the family, in line

307. W. R. Domeris, "Jeremiah and the Poor," in Goldingay, *Uprooting and Planting*, 56–58.
308. W. R. Domeris, "The Land Claim of Jeremiah," in Diamond and Stulman, *Jeremiah (Dis)placed*, 149.

with the Torah; perhaps the idea would be that he could then let Hanamel continue to farm it. So the picture is not of Jeremiah having the right to make an advantageous real estate investment but of his having the right to do the correct thing by the family. Indeed, "when Jeremiah redeems the field, he is not just doing a favor for his cousin; he is taking possession of a piece of Israel's inheritance from the LORD (vv. 22–23, 41)."[309] Yet one also wonders "if Jeremiah expects the land to be lost just as the loincloth was ruined and the earthenware jug broken, a symbol of coming judgment."[310]

9b The sheqel is a measure of weight; money as such has not been invented, and the value of things would be calculated in terms of the value attached to a sheqel's weight (about half an ounce) of silver or gold. We don't know whether seventeen sheqels was a usual amount for whatever was the size of the plot of land. And we don't know where Jeremiah got seventeen sheqels of silver from: Was his own immediate family better off than Hanamel's? Or did he makes some money prophesying? First Samuel 9:7–8 might imply that it was only the price of sixty-eight prophecies.

10–12 Parallels with documents from Egypt suggest that the contract was written twice on the same piece of papyrus. One half was rolled up and sealed in wax with Jeremiah's seal and the seals of the witnesses. The parenthetical expression *the rule and the decrees* suggests that it became the official copy, the legal copy, drawn up according to law. The other half was rolled up but left unsealed so it could easily be consulted.[311] The reference to Baruch at this point in the story is his first appearance in the Jeremiah scroll, but chronologically his appearance in Jer 36 happened two decades before (on Baruch, see the commentary on Jer 36). In effect, the role of a scribe overlapped with that of a lawyer, and a scribe's status might compare with that of a lawyer in the Western world.[312]

13–15 *Ordered* is an eyebrow-raising verb; it makes Jeremiah sound a little like God.[313] Presumably, Jeremiah entrusts the document to Baruch for safekeeping because he was himself confined to the palace courtyard. The point about an earthenware container is that it can be sealed tight so as to prevent air getting to the documents; it is the form of storage used for the Qumran documents, many of which could thus remain in reasonable condition for two millennia. But the expression *a long time* (lit. "many days"), which recalls 13:6, is of more than mere practical chronological significance. Like the expression "days are coming" (e.g., 31:27, 31, 38), it implies a time that is

---

309. Keown, Scalise, and Smothers, *Jeremiah 26–52*, 152.

310. P. D. Miller, "Jeremiah," on the passage.

311. See B. Porten, "Aramaic Papyri and Parchments," *BA* 42 (1979): 74–104.

312. See the Egyptian documents "In Praise of Learned Scribes" and "The Satire on the Trades" (other than that of the scribe!) in *ANET*, 431–34.

313. S. Macwilliam, "The Prophet and His Patsy: Gender Performativity in Jeremiah," in Maier and Sharp, *Prophecy and Power*, 173–88.

certain to come but is not around the corner. It leads into the explicit inter-pretation of the symbolic act whose point at last emerges in v. 15. Jeremiah is doing the right thing by his family and by the Torah, but in doing so, he is also giving expression to something else relating to the information about the background to his action, in vv. 2–5. *Once again*, moreover, takes up the *once again* in 31:4a, 4b, 5a, 23. And to speak of *houses, lands, and vineyards* is really to make a promise about every aspect of regular Judahite life. "The whole prophecy is contained in v. 15."[314] The presence of witnesses is also significant in this connection. In addition to the document being witnessed and Baruch being present as a witness, so are the other Judahites in the palace courtyard. They are witnesses not merely to a real estate transaction but to this sign event and thus to Jeremiah's dramatizing what Yahweh is going to do, as "the prophet puts his money where his mouth is."[315] It is also the first time we have heard Yahweh saying anything like the statement in v. 15, so it makes for a jaw-opening closure for the story, though it will also turn out to be a cliffhanger for the chapter's continuation.

c. Jeremiah Quizzes Yahweh (32:16–25)

[16]*I pleaded with Yahweh after I had given the acquisition document to Baruch ben Neriah.*

[17]*Oh, Lord Yahweh, there:*

You're the one who made the heavens and the earth
    by your great energy and by your extended arm.
Anything—it's not too extraordinary for you,
    [18]*exercising commitment to thousands*
But repaying the waywardness of parents
    into the lap of their children after them.
Great, strong God,
    Yahweh of Armies his name,
[19]*Great in counsel*
    and plentiful in deed,
You whose eyes are appointed
    over all the paths of human beings,
To give to an individual in accordance with his paths

---

314. D. R. Jones, *Jeremiah*, 409.
315. D. Steele, "Jeremiah's Little Book of Comfort," *Theology Today* 42 (1985–86): 476; cf. Lundbom, *Jeremiah 21–36*, 525.

and in accordance with the fruit of his practices![a]
²⁰*You who set out signs and portents*
   in the country of Egypt until this day,
Both among Israel and among human beings
   you made for yourself a name this very day.[b]
²¹*You got your people Israel out*
   from the country of Egypt,
With signs, with portents, with a strong hand,
   with an extended arm, and with great fear.[c]
²²*You gave them this country,*
   which you promised to their ancestors to give them,
A country flowing with milk and syrup,[d]
   ²³*and they came and took possession of it.*
But they didn't listen to your voice,
   and by your instruction[e] *they did not walk.*
All that you commanded them to do
   they didn't do.
So you have made come upon them
   all this dire trouble.
²⁴*There are the ramps,*[f]
   which have come to the city for capturing it.
The city is given into the hand of the Chaldeans,
   who are battling against it,
   in the face of sword and hunger and epidemic.
So what you spoke has happened,
   and there are you, looking.[g]
²⁵*And you—you have said to me,*
   Lord Yahweh,
Acquire for yourself the land for silver
   and charge witnesses—
   and the city is given into the hand of the Chaldeans![h]

a. LXX lacks this colon.

b. On this phrase, see the translation note on 11:5.

c. LXX, Syr, Sym, Tg imply *mar'eh* ("sight") for MT *môrâ*; cf. Deut 4:34; 26:8 for the same confusion (HUBP).

d. See the translation note and commentary on 11:5.

e. The *ketiv* and LXX have "instructions."

f. Vg takes *sōlalôt* to denote siege engines, but etymology supports *ramps* as at 6:6; cf. LXX "the crowd" (climbing via the ramps?).

g. LXX lacks this colon.

h. MT^A has a section marker here.

Here, Jeremiah eventually comes to a question implied by vv. 1–14, to which he has already presupposed an answer in v. 15. If the chapter works chronologically, then, this section indicates some doubt about that answer; more likely, the chapter now gives us the background to the answer. Either way, the entirety of the rest of the chapter functions for the audience as explanation and reinforcement for the declaration and (especially after 587) as an answer to questions it would raise for them.

At one level, Jeremiah's prayer follows a common First Testament pattern in that the bulk comprises praise of Yahweh; only in its closing lines does it come to its particular concern. After the introduction, it consists of fifteen bicola (of which eleven are self-contained) and five tricola.

v. 16	Introduction
v. 17a	Address
vv. 17b–18b	Yahweh the creator, involved with the generations in commitment and redress (three bicola, the second and third linked)
vv. 18c–19	Yahweh of Armies, watching over the paths of human beings (four linked bicola)
vv. 20–21	Yahweh the God who got Israel out of Egypt with great fear (two pairs of bicola)
vv. 22–24b	Yahweh who gave Israel its country but is now bringing dire trouble upon it (two linked bicola, four bicola, and a semi-closing tricolon)
vv. 24c–25	Yahweh as the one who, in this context, has bidden Jeremiah acquire land! (two bicola and a closing tricolon)

The dynamic of the praise manifests a distinctive profile. Sequences of cola alternate between giving straightforward acknowledgment of Yahweh for his power and generosity and more ambivalent acknowledgment of his power and chastisement; the stress is increasingly on the punitive.[316] The sequences acknowledging generosity and chastisement increase in length (six cola, then eight, then eight again, then eleven) until they reach the horror of the *dire trouble*, with the *ramps* that herald the city's *capturing* and the people's experience and expectation of *sword and hunger and epidemic*. There they are before Yahweh's eyes, and it is in this context that Yahweh has bidden Jeremiah buy land. Verses 17–24b thus constitute a huge raising of suspense before we come to vv. 24c–25. The expressions of praise for Yahweh's generosity and faithfulness carry an irony; they are undermined by the lines that draw attention to Yahweh's acts of redress. The acknowledgment they make thus bears an internal contradiction: "You can do what you like, but . . ." People sometimes question Yahweh's allowing some catastrophe to fall on his people; Jeremiah's question is almost the obverse. He has no

---

316. Allen, *Jeremiah*, 368.

problem with the catastrophe, but why then commission the crazy purchase? His asking the question shows how prayer is the way to raise theological questions, as doxology is the way to do theology. It's one reason why prayer is a hermeneutical key to understanding biblical books.[317] In portraying this dynamic in the relationship between Yahweh and Israel as the background for prayer, vv. 16–25 compare with the prayers in Neh 9 and Dan 9, where a leader prays for his people.[318] At surface level, Jeremiah is quizzing Yahweh about a question that concerns him individually, but he is also praying on his people's behalf as he undertakes his purchase not for his sake or merely for his family's sake but for his people's sake. And of course, it is another matter whether Jeremiah himself is agonizing over the question at all. He knows the answer to it. As usual, he is engaged in rhetoric, in communication, in seeking to enable Judah before or after 587 to understand Yahweh's ways.

16–18b *Oh*, or it could be "Oh no!" or "Alas!" Jeremiah begins, as he does when he is discombobulated (1:6; 4:10; 14:13). His prayer opens by acknowledging Yahweh as creator and as involved in people's lives. He repeats his distinctive observation that Yahweh's *great energy and extended arm* were key not only to Israel's deliverance from Egypt but also to his making *the heavens and the earth* (cf. 10:13; 27:5).[319] It is obvious when one thinks about it, but it is nevertheless a distinctively Jeremianic point. In this context, the point about creation and power leads into a related comment about everyday life, which can be the context in which people experience things that are *extraordinary* (*pālā' niphal*) and that embody a *commitment* that extends *to thousands*—presumably thousands of generations, as is the case in the commandment (Exod 20:5–6). The trouble is that the commandment also notes that Yahweh's energy finds expression in *repaying the waywardness of parents into the lap of their children.* Yes, Yahweh is merciful, but he also punishes.[320] Whatever 31:29–30 implies, Jeremiah does not take it to imply a disagreement with the commandment. One might ask whether the tension between this prayer and 31:29–30 suggests that the prayer comes from Jeremiah's curators rather than Jeremiah himself; Jeremiah is then not in tension with himself. But this hypothesis mainly just moves the question along, as it

317. G. Fischer, "Gebete als hermeneutischer Schlüssel zu biblischen Büchern," in *Congress Volume Ljubljana 2007*, ed. A. Lemaire, VTSup 133 (Leiden: Brill, 2010), 219–237; cf. B. Rossi, *L'intercessione nel tempo della fine: Studio dell'intercessione profetica nel libro di Geremia*, AnBib 204 (Rome: Pontificio Istituto Biblico, 2013).

318. Cf. Weinfeld, *Deuteronomy*, 42.

319. See M. D. Terblanche, "Yahweh Is the Creator of (Heaven and) Earth: The Significance of the Intertextual Link Between Jeremiah 27:5 and 32:17," *OTE* 27 (2014): 637–50.

320. M. D. Terblanche, "Jeremiah 32:17–18a: The Great and Powerful God Shows Steadfast Love to Thousands, but Punishes Sin," *OTE* 30 (2017): 157.

raises the question of the tension within the scroll itself. And it surrenders the theological possibility of considering the interrelationship between the way one generation influences the destiny of another and the way every generation is responsible for its destiny.

18c–19 The second sequence continues from the first in speaking of Yahweh's involvement with humanity as a whole, but it suggests a move to speaking about Yahweh's involvement in the affairs of the nations. He is *Yahweh of Armies*, a title that Jeremiah and other prophets love. He is the God who has all power at his disposal. It coheres with calling Yahweh *the strong God*, the warrior God who doesn't lose his battles, who is thus the *great* God—not only great in strength, as he needs to be, but *great in counsel*, as he also needs to be. He can formulate plans and implement them so as to be also *plentiful in deed*. Jeremiah once again moves toward the more solemn. His *eyes are appointed over all the paths of human beings*: he has his eye on you, which can be great news. But the position of his eyes means he can *give to an individual in accordance with his paths and with the fruit of his practices*. *Practices* always means bad practices in Jeremiah, and he has referred elsewhere to this *fruit* (17:10; 21:14); the phrase suggests dire habits issuing in dire action and dire action receiving a dire reward.

20–21 The prayer goes on to Yahweh's getting Israel out of Egypt and into the promised land, which involved *signs and wonders* of the kind Deuteronomy rejoices in (e.g., Deut 6:22; 26:8). Jeremiah's reference to the exodus emphasizes how it constituted a demonstration of who Yahweh was. He *set out* these signs and wonders in a way that everyone could see them, *both among Israel and among human beings* in general; in Egypt and *until this day*, they continue to give testimony to Yahweh. Thus *you made for yourself a name* that continues to be known *this very day*. Jeremiah goes on to restate what Yahweh did in words that take up Deut 26:8: "Yahweh got us out from Egypt with a strong hand and with an extended arm and with great fear and with signs and with wonders." The signs and wonders thus reappear from v. 20 and the extended arm from v. 17, where it was associated with creation. But in this context, the difference between Jeremiah's words and Deuteronomy's words is that *great fear* now brings the account of the exodus to its climax.[321]

22–24b Jeremiah continues with his virtual quotation from Deut 26:9 and 15: "He gave us this country . . . as you promised to our ancestors, a country flowing with milk and syrup." Moses had spoken of "when you come into the country that Yahweh your God is giving you . . . and you take possession of it" (Deut 26:1); Jeremiah can now turn those words into past tense. However, whereas Moses could look forward to people saying, "I have listened to the voice of Yahweh my God—I have done in accordance with all that you com-

---

321. Fischer, *Jeremia*, 2:204.

manded me" (Deut 26:14), Jeremiah has to point out that this didn't happen. To put it in his own characteristic terms, *by your instruction they did not walk.* Consequently, Yahweh has *made come upon them all this dire trouble.* From that characteristic Jeremianic language, Jeremiah moves to being more concrete about how things thus worked out. *There are the ramps* for the attackers to climb up as they attack the city that is also weakened by injury, hunger, and illness. If the city has not yet actually fallen (as the context of Jeremiah's prayer suggests), it has as good as fallen.

24c-25 Yahweh can see it, and he is looking at it, isn't he? "Jeremiah's effusive emphasis on God's power and omniscience in the earlier verses of the prayer ironically renders God's authority in the present moment fragile."[322] Yahweh has to keep alert until the end of his people's prayers. Psalm 89 builds up its praise for thirty-seven verses before it comes to the accusation that retrospectively undermines all that has preceded (Ps 89:38[39]). Jeremiah's act of praise is indeed a huge raising of suspense. At last we come to the point of the prayer—though there is no prayer in the narrow sense. Given that you can see what is going on, in proper redress for the city's waywardness, what's with your commissioning me to exchange the silver that might come in useful for some land that won't? I know you can't stop now, so what's with the acquisition of land?[323] There is again a gap that the audience has to fill. Jeremiah has not recorded an actual commission to acquire land, only a promise that Yahweh attached to land. "Verse 25 converts the promise of v. 15 into an imperative. But the prayer appears to end in v. 25 with a puzzlement. . . . What can it mean? . . . Is it serious? Is it possible? Shall it be acted upon?"[324] "Not even the prophet can easily believe his utopian visions."[325] But anyone can ask God whether he really means something, though it's good if the questioner is also prepared to say, "Not as I wish, but as you do" (Matt 26:39).[326]

d. Yahweh Replies: First, the Bad News (32:26-35)

[26]*Yahweh's word came to Jeremiah.*

[27]*Here am I, Yahweh,*
  the God of all flesh—

322. C. J. Sharp, "Buying Land," 165–66.
323. Fretheim, *Jeremiah,* 460.
324. W. Brueggemann. "A 'Characteristic' Reflection on What Comes Next (Jeremiah 32.16–44)," in *Prophets and Paradigms: Essays in Honor of Gene M. Tucker,* ed. S. B. Reid, LHBOTS 229 (Sheffield: Sheffield Academic, 2009), 25.
325. Diamond, "Jeremiah," 591.
326. Fretheim, *Jeremiah,* 461.

for me, is there any deed too extraordinary?[a]
[28] *Therefore Yahweh has said this.*

Here am I, giving this city[b]
  into the hand of the Chaldeans
  and into the hand of Nebuchadrezzar[c] *King of Babylon, and he will*
      take it.
[29] *The Chaldeans will come,*
  the people who are battling against this city.
They will set this city on fire
  and consume it with the houses
On whose roofs people offered sacrifices to the Master
  and poured libations to other gods
  in order to irk me.
[30] *Because the Israelites and the Judahites*
  have been doing only[d] *what was dire in my eyes,*
From their youth, because the Israelites
  have been only irking me
  with the things their hands have made (Yahweh's affirmation).[e]
[31] *Because directed toward*[f] *my anger and my wrath—*
  so this city has been for me,
From the day that they built it
  until this day,
So as to remove it from before my face
    [32] *for all the dire behavior of the Israelites and the Judahites,*
Who acted to irk me,
  they, their kings, their officials,
Their priests, their prophets,
  the individuals in Judah, and the people who live in Jerusalem.
[33] *They turned the back of their neck to me,*
  not their face,
When I was teaching them, teaching assiduously,[g]
  but there were none of them listening to accept restraint.
[34] *They set out their detestable things in the house that is called by my name,*
  against it, to defile it.
[35] *They built the Master's shrines,*
  which are in the Ben-hinnom Ravine,
To make their sons and their daughters pass through to the Shameful
    King,[h]
  which I did not order them and did not arise in my mind,
To do this offensive thing,
  in order to make Judah do wrong.[i]

a. The middle colon closes *kol-bāśār* (any and every flesh); the third colon closes *kol-dābār* (any and every deed).

b. For *here am I, giving this city*, LXX has "this city will definitely be given over" (cf. 34:2).

c. LXX lacks *Chaldeans and into the hand of Nebuchadrezzar*; Vg simply lacks *Nebuchadrezzar*.

d. With LXX, I take *'ak* to mean *only* rather than "indeed" (though LXX suggestively links the *only* with the subject rather than the verb); so too in the next line—*only* fits the rest of the indictment.

e. LXX lacks *because the Israelites . . . (Yahweh's affirmation)*.

f. For this translation of *'al*, see BDB, 757.

g. See the translation note and commentary on 7:13.

h. *Mōlek* (see the commentary); LXX "to the king" implies *melek*.

i. MT has a section marker here.

Yahweh's response begins where the prayer almost began, then leaps to where the prayer almost finished and focuses there.

v. 26	Introduction
v. 27	Yahweh's self-introduction (one tricolon)
v. 28a	Resumptive introduction
vv. 28b–29	Yahweh confirms his intention to have the Babylonians destroy the city (an opening tricolon, a bicolon, and a bicolon linked to a semi-closing tricolon)
vv. 30–35	Yahweh elaborates on the waywardness that brings this redress
vv. 30–32	They have acted to provoke me in the city (a bicolon linked to a tricolon, and five linked bicola)
vv. 33–35	They have acted to cause offense in worship (two linked bicola, a bicolon, and three linked bicola)

26–27 The curators' introduction to Yahweh's reply picks up the phraseology of the introduction to the chapter, as none of the intervening introductions have done. Is this the real *word that came to Jeremiah from Yahweh* of v. 1?[327] Anyway, Yahweh starts by confirming Jeremiah's early comment: "Yes, you're right, there is no limit or constraint on what I can do." He picks up the reference at the beginning of Jeremiah's prayer to his creation of the entire world by affirming that he is *the God of all flesh* and the God who is capable of all things. What is the implication? Does it make for an inauspicious start to his response? Is giving Jerusalem into the Babylonians' hand an example of the extraordinary things that Yahweh can do? How does Yahweh's comment relate to the extraordinary things of which Zedekiah himself speaks in 21:2 in the context of the siege? Is Yahweh's self-introduction a hint

327. So Allen, *Jeremiah*, 365.

that defeat and loss might not be his last word? Or might there be things that God cannot do, ignoring the monstrous behavior of Judah being one of them?[328] Jeremiah and the audience have to listen on to discover the answer to these questions.

28–29 In the first instance, the answer is gloomy. Rather than suggesting that defeat and loss might not be Yahweh's last word, his response points in that opposite direction. Yes, he is giving the city into the hand of the Chaldeans. And there will be some poetic justice about the action he takes. The city's destruction means the burning down of its houses, which are made of mud brick and wood. And it is these houses on whose roofs the Judahites have customarily *offered sacrifices to the Master and poured libations to other gods* (see 19:13), so it's appropriate, isn't it? It's as if they were deliberately trying *to irk me*.

30–32 They certainly succeeded. Twice more, Yahweh picks up the word *irk* (*kāʿas hiphil*), a favorite verb in Jeremiah (7:18, 19; 8:19; 11:17; 25:6, 7; 44:3, 8) and in 1 and 2 Kings (e.g., 2 Kgs 17:11, 17; 22:17; 23:19). It suggests getting someone worked up; it is the opposite of being calm and unperturbed. It is what Peninnah did to Hannah by finding it too easy to have babies (1 Sam 1:6–7). It implies a concentration of negative emotion—not a polite annoyance but an overwhelming passion, a furious rage.[329] What gets Yahweh thus worked up is the attention his people pay to gods other than him. It's been characteristic of Israel all its life. The city's life has been consistently *directed toward my anger and my wrath* since the day it was built, as if it was aiming to make Yahweh destroy it. The charge applies wherever you look and whomever you look at, as Jeremiah has often indicated—kings, officials, priests, prophets, ordinary individuals, in the city or in the rest of Judah. Yahweh twice throws in reference to *Israelites* in the sense of the Northern Kingdom to make sure he has covered all bases. Let no one say that he has no rationale for letting Nebuchadrezzar take the city. Has Jeremiah overstated Yahweh's rage? Has Yahweh overstated it? There is certainly some hyperbole here. But maybe the even-more-concrete account of people killing their children and burning them as offerings, which will come in v. 35, deserves some over-the-top rage. And at least the wild nature of Yahweh's fury in this first stage of his response to Jeremiah's prayer will be accompanied by further wildness in the enthusiasm with which he will go on to speak of restoration. There is nothing moderate about Yahweh.

33–35 His rage is in part a response to people's refusal to respond to his reaching out to them. He offered them his teaching and did so *assiduously*, but they gave him the back of their neck rather than their face. He tried to apply

---

328. T. E. Fretheim, "Is Anything Too Hard for God?," *CBQ* 66 (2004): 231–36.
329. See F. Stolz, *TLOT*, 2:622–24.

correction or discipline or restraint to them (cf. 2:19–20, 30; see the translation notes and commentary there). They would have none of it. He had set his house in their midst and let his name be attached to it, with the implication that he in person is identified with it; and if one takes into account its originally being their idea, the point becomes more forceful. Their response was twofold. They filled it with means of worship that were disgusting because of what they implied about him. And they also built shrines for the Master in the Ben-hinnom Ravine. To what he said in 7:30–31, Yahweh adds that they *make their sons and their daughters pass through to the Shameful King*. They make them pass through fire (Deut 18:10; 2 Kgs 16:3; 17:17; 21:6; Ezek 20:31), which might not be too bad if it means coming out the other side. But they are not passing through in order to come back home but in order to cross over to the Shameful King; the expression is another term for what Jeremiah elsewhere calls incinerating their sons and daughters (7:31). The Shameful King is a distinctively First Testament version of the name of the King of Sheol.[330] He would be regularly known in Hebrew as *melek*, "King" (see the translation note), but Jeremiah spells the name *mōlek* and thus makes this name an example of the First Testament's casting a judgment on something by respelling it: compare "Tophet," the *Shameful Fireplace* (7:31; see the translation note there; also 3:24 and the commentary on it). He is the Shameful King, associated with the shamefulness of worship of the Master.

e. Yahweh Replies: Second, the Good News of Reaffirmation (32:36–41)

[36]*But now, therefore, Yahweh, the God of Israel, has said this with regard to*[a] *this city of which you people are saying, "It's given into the hand of the king of Babylon with sword, with hunger, and with epidemic":*

[37]*Here am I, collecting them from all the countries*
    where I have driven them,
In my anger and in my wrath
    and in great rage.
I will return them to this place
    and let them dwell in confidence.
[38]*They will be a people for me*
    and I—I will be God for them.
[39]*I will give them one mind*
    and one path,[b]

---

330. See J. Day, *Molech: A God of Human Sacrifice in the Old Testament*, University of Cambridge Oriental Publications 41 (Cambridge: Cambridge University Press, 1989).

To be in awe of me for all the days,
and it will be good for them and for their descendants after them.
40*I will solemnize for them a pledge for all time*
that I will not turn from them
in my doing what is good to them. c
Awe for me I will put in their mind
so that they do not turn away from me.
41*I will rejoice over them in doing what is good to them,*
and I will plant them in this country in truthfulness
with my entire mind and with my entire spirit. d

> a. On *'el*, see BDB, 40, under section 6; the distance from the verb and the fact that Yahweh does not address the city works against translating simply "to."
> b. In both cola, for MT *'eḥād*, LXX implies *'aḥēr* ("another").
> c. LXX lacks this colon.
> d. MT has a section marker here.

By this point in Jer 32, the audience is entitled to be bewildered, like Jeremiah himself. The chapter began with a reminder of how discouraging the situation was in Jerusalem (vv. 1–6) and then related how Jeremiah was pushed into acquiring some land (vv. 7–15). Jeremiah described how confused he was by the clash between the deservedly discouraging situation and the command that he explicitly associated with Yahweh (vv. 16–25). Yahweh did not reduce Jeremiah's confusion when he confirmed at some length that the city's deliverance to Nebuchadrezzar was religiously inevitable, and the curators did not reduce the audience's bewilderment by reporting Yahweh's words (vv. 26–36). The first half of Yahweh's response to Jeremiah has thus again raised suspense. Now at last, there comes some good news and resolution.[331]

v. 36   Introduction to a sequence of promises
v. 37   The first promise: I will reestablish the people in the land
          (three bicola, the first two linked)
vv. 38–39 The second promise: the relationship will be real; I will
          reshape their mind (three bicola, the latter two linked)
v. 40   The second promise reaffirmed (a tricolon and a bicolon)
v. 41   The first promise reaffirmed (a tricolon)

The promise thus works in an a-b-b'-a' pattern, and in the manner of parallelism, the resumptive set of promises in vv. 40–41 go beyond the first.

---

331. See further J. Applegate, "'Peace, Peace, When There Is No Peace': Redactional Integration of Prophecy of Peace into the Judgement of Jeremiah," in Curtis and Römer, *Jeremiah and Its Reception*, ed. A. H. W. Curtis, BETL 128 (Leuven: Peeters, 1997), 51–90.

36 Jeremiah initially gives no hint that Yahweh is now moving from talk of catastrophe to talk of restoration. Beginning with *therefore* was something to worry about in v. 28, as it often is in Jeremiah (e.g., 25:8; 28:16; 29:32). But there has been an occasional different, illogical-looking *therefore* (16:14; 30:16), and it will turn out that v. 36 is an instance of it. Yahweh "moves from the certainty of judgment to an uncertain future"[332] in a positive sense, or from certainty of judgment to a certain positive future.

37–38 Who are the *them*? In the immediate context, they would be the *you* of v. 36, which fits the focus on Judah in vv. 42–44 and the reference to returning to *this place* (cf. 27:22; 28:1–6). But grammatically, *them* suggests a reference back to the Israelites and Judahites of vv. 30–35, which would fit the broader concern with both Ephraim and Judah in Jer 30–31 and the promise in v. 38 (cf. 31:31–34). Either way, the promise cannot be limited to a particular group such as the exiles of 597 or the people about to be exiled after the city's fall. It goes on to refer to a driving off to *all the countries*, which indicates the broad perspective on the scattering that has featured earlier (e.g., 16:15; 23:3, 8; 29:10). It has Ephraim as well as Judah in mind, and it refers to or includes the broader driving off of Judah that will follow the city's fall. One way or another, when they *dwell in confidence* back in the land, unthreatened by people like Nebuchadrezzar, and become *a people for me* who have Yahweh as *God for them*, they will prove "the good fortune of the people whose God is Yahweh" (Ps 144:15).[333]

39 In vv. 31–34, Yahweh has already implied that there is more he needs to do for the vision expressed in v. 38 to find fulfillment. Here, he reformulates the promise in 31:31–34. In this context, *one mind and one path* could suggest the oneness of Ephraim and Judah as one people. The double expression suggests the necessary combination of right attitude, thinking, and emotion with right action—what Paul will call "willing and acting for what pleases him" (Phil 2:13).[334] Jeremiah has made clear that actually the people have long had *one mind and one path*, but not in a good way, so LXX's "another mind and another path" is what Israel also needs. But *one mind* also resonates with the prayer to "unify" my mind (*yāḥad* piel; Ps 86:11),[335] *one path* resonates with the exhortation in Deut 5:29,[336] and *one* also resonates with Deut 6:4; Jeremiah is pointing toward a oneness of mind and path in a commitment to the one Yahweh.

40 Yahweh reaffirms this second promise by continuing the reformulation of 31:31–34 as he speaks now of the pledge lasting *for all time* (see 17:4

---

332. Stulman, *Jeremiah*, 279.

333. Calvin, *Jeremiah*, 4:215.

334. Calvin, *Jeremiah*, 4:219.

335. P. M. Lasater, "Law for What Ails the Heart: Moral Frailty in Psalm 86," *ZAW* 127 (2015): 652–68.

336. Fischer, *Jeremia*, 2:212.

and the commentary on it). The Sinai pledge has not so lasted. Like the earlier formulation, this phrase does not imply that the pledge is unconditional in the sense that Yahweh is giving Israel permission to do as it likes without having any fear of imperiling its relationship with Yahweh (a logic equivalent to the logic that Paul questions in Rom 6). Yahweh is giving Israel one mind and path, and it will result in Israel's living in submissive awe, which Yahweh restates as an awe that will mean *they do not turn away from me*. It is an aspect of solemnizing with them a pledge that will last because of the way it is set up. He will not *turn* from them (*šûb*), revoking his commitment; they will not *turn away* from him (*sûr*), turning aside to other deities.

41 Yahweh is a person of much enthusiasm who acts with great strength of feeling, and our being people of passion reflects our being made in his image. The passion in rejoicing over his people (cf. Deut 28:63; 30:9; Isa 62:5; 65:19; Zeph 3:17) parallels the passion of his furious anger with them in v. 37, though he doesn't rejoice in bringing redress.[337] Zedekiah's questions in vv. 3–5 implied that acting in wrath might be one of the things that were impossible for Yahweh (see vv. 17, 27), but it's not so.[338] Yet anger doesn't come from his heart (Lam 3:33) but from somewhere nearer the edge of his person. He will be relieved to be able to give up wrath and give in to rejoicing. He picks up again one of his characteristic verbs in Jeremiah: *I will plant them in this country*, from which he will have cast them out. There are thus two sides to Yahweh's promise: "Yahweh offers covenant and field."[339] And he will plant them *in truthfulness*. While their truthfulness will be needed, as v. 40 has implied, the last word is with his truthfulness, because he will act *with my entire mind and with my entire spirit*. There is another resonance in relation to Deuteronomy, of a profoundly imaginative kind. Yahweh expects his people to turn to him with its entire mind and spirit (Deut 30:10); it will be a response to his relating to them with his entire mind and spirit. Yahweh thereby hints at another means whereby Israel's necessary transformation will happen as Yahweh's instruction comes to be written into its mind (Jer 31:33–34).

f. Yahweh Replies: Third, the Good News about Land (32:42–44)

⁴²*Because Yahweh has said this:*

As I have caused to come to this people
*   all this great dire trouble,*
So I am causing to come for them

337. So Calvin, *Jeremiah*, 4:226.
338. Fretheim, *Jeremiah*, 464.
339. Berrigan, *Jeremiah*, 140.

all the good that I have spoken of for them.
⁴³*So the land in this country will be acquired,*
of which you people are saying, •
"It's a desolation, without human being or animal—
it's given into the hand of the Chaldeans."
⁴⁴*People will acquire fields for silver,*
with writing in a document and sealing
and charging witnesses,
In the country of Benjamin and in the areas around Jerusalem,
in the towns of Judah, in the towns in the highland,
In the towns in the foothills, and in the towns in the Negeb,
because I will bring about their restoration (Yahweh's affirmation).^a

a. MT has a unit marker here.

While vv. 36–41 might, in broad terms, have resolved the tension that has pervaded this chapter, Jeremiah will hardly have forgotten the question he raised: What about his acquisition of the piece of land? These closing verses come back to that question.

v. 42a	A resumptive introduction to further promises
v. 42b–c	Resumptive general promise: I will bring good things instead of dire things (two linked bicola)
vv. 43–44	A specific promise: people will acquire land instead of writing it off (two linked bicola then a tricolon and two bicola, all linked)

42 First, Yahweh summarizes his undertaking in general terms (cf. 31:28). The *because* reflects how his promise of restoration is at least as much part of his message as his threat of desolation, so that in a paradoxical way, the threat's fulfillment is also a guarantee of the promise's fulfillment. According to *B. Makkot* 24b, Rabbi Akiva was quite happy to rejoice over the ruins of the temple, which had been destroyed in his day in AD 70, because the fulfillment of the threat of its destruction had paved the way for the fulfillment of the promise of its rebuilding, and it could do so again.[340]

43–44 Yahweh goes on to take up Jeremiah's question. Yahweh's encouragement to Jeremiah to do his duty by the cousin who perhaps thought he was taking him for a ride linked with Yahweh's commitment to ensuring that normal life would return to Judah. Yahweh starts with Benjamin and the region around Jerusalem, and thus the area of particular concern in vv. 1–15, but his undertaking with regard to this area applies to a return to normal life

340. Allen, *Jeremiah*, 371.

throughout the country. The good news incorporates visible signs.[341] The analysis of its geography compares with 17:26; *the towns of Judah* are spelled out as comprising *the towns in the highland* south of Jerusalem such as Bethlehem and Hebron, *the towns in the foothills* to the west and southwest such as Lachish, and *the towns in the Negeb* such as Beersheba. The promise implicitly raises but does not clarify questions about the future of Ephraim, which is unmentioned here, about the relationship between Jerusalem and the rest of Judah,[342] about the relationship between the towns and the country,[343] about the relationship between people who return from exile and people who never leave,[344] and about the relationship between people thousands of years later with rival claims to this land.[345] But Jer 32 has provided its answer to the particular question that was its concern. Its answer had in fact been presupposed back in v. 15; everything since has been examining the question that was raised by vv. 7–14. Given that v. 15 summarized the implications of vv. 16–44, chronologically the declaration in v. 15 now follows. People on the eve of the fall of Jerusalem have to accept their immediate fate, but they need not despair. And people hearing the curators' story after 587 who cannot yet see a community characterized by one mind and one path or cannot yet see planting are invited to believe that they will see them.

6. Some Vital Afterthoughts (33:1–26 [LXX 40:1–13])

Chapter 33 comprises a series of six separate promises from Yahweh that further supplement Jer 30–32. They do again incorporate the somber as well as the hopeful, but they increase further the emphasis on the positive.

vv. 1–9	I will bring healing to Jerusalem and restoration to Judah and Ephraim
vv. 10–11	Rejoicing and praise will again resound in Jerusalem
vv. 12–13	Flocks will pasture again all over the country

341. Fischer, *Jeremia*, 2:216.

342. Volz, *Jeremia*, 309–10.

343. See G. H. Wittenberg, "The Vision of Land in Jeremiah 32," in *Earth Story in the Psalms and the Prophets*, ed. N. C. Habel, The Earth Bible 4 (Sheffield: Sheffield Academic, 2001), 129–42.

344. See H. M. Barstad, *The Myth of the Empty Land: A Study in the History and Archaeology of Judah during the "Exilic" Period* (Oslo: Scandinavian University Press, 1996); subsequent discussion in O. Lipschits and J. Blenkinsopp, eds., *Judah and the Judeans in the Neo-Babylonian Period* (Winona Lake, IN: Eisenbrauns, 2003).

345. See J. Stegeman, "Reading Jeremiah Makes Me Angry," in Peursen and Dyk, *Tradition and Innovation*, 45–67; "Remembering the Land: Jeremiah 32 and in Palestinian Narrative and Identity," *Kirchliche Zeitgeschichte* 26 (2013): 41–54.

vv. 14–18   I will see that David and Levi have successors minister-
            ing for Ephraim and Judah
vv. 19–22   Those promises will be as sure as my pledge with day
            and night
vv. 23–26   I will show my compassion for the descendants of Abra-
            ham, Isaac, and Jacob

The promises express Yahweh's commitments regarding the "public, historical, sociopolitical future of the community," resolutely contradicting the
people's present condition "against all apparent limitations imposed by 'realism.'"[346] The chapter is full of blossoming, flourishing hope.[347]

The six promises divide into two sets. The first three begin by painting an
even grimmer picture than previous chapters. The toughness of the situation
in Jerusalem is especially clear in the first, which is the longest and the most
concrete and which one would have thought came from after the city's fall.
But its introduction makes a link with the same context as Jer 32, suggesting
that the subsequent description relates to the dark days before that final
fall. The second and third promises work by taking up familiar themes and
undertakings, but they add distinctive references to the ruined state of the
city, which is their background. Here, too, the inference that the city has
fallen might be false if the messages simply presuppose the grimness of the
situation, even as the catastrophe still draws near.

The fourth, fifth, and sixth messages leave behind concrete portrayal and
references to wasting, desolation, and ruin, to focus on the future of Yahweh's
promise to David and to the Levites. These promises, too, might come from
before or after 587 and from Jeremiah or his curators. They form a distinctive
set of messages that appear in MT but not LXX,[348] which at least suggests
that their incorporation into the scroll happened later than that of vv. 1–13,
but they contain no pointer to a date beyond the Babylonian period. If MT
and LXX represent separate recensions of an earlier version of the scroll,
then their being only in MT no more indicates that their origin is later than
is the case when Luke's expansion of Mark's story is longer than Matthew's.
Uncertainties about their origin are anyway countered by the scroll's invitation to read them in the context of Jerusalem on the eve of the city's fall.

346. Brueggemann, *Jeremiah 26–52*, 92.

347. Fischer, *Jeremia*, 2:219, 223.

348. It is ironic, then, that D. Ortlund suggests that the passage "provides such a unique cluster of pivotal biblical-theological themes that it forms a one-of-a-kind canonical intersection"
through the entire Scripture ("Is Jeremiah 33:14–26 a 'Centre' to the Bible?" *EvQ* 84 [2012]: 120).

a. I Will Bring Healing and Purification to Judah and Ephraim (33:1–9)

[1]*Yahweh's word came to Jeremiah a second time; he was still confined in the court of the guard.*

[2]*Yahweh has said this, the one who is doing it,*[a]
Yahweh who is shaping it to establish it—
Yahweh is his name.
[3]*Call to me and I will answer you,*
and I will tell you big things,
inaccessible things that you have not acknowledged.[b]

[4]*Because Yahweh, the God of Israel, has said this about the houses in this city and about the houses of the kings of Judah that have been pulled down. Regarding the ramps and regarding the sword—*[5]*people coming*[c] *to do battle with the Chaldeans and to fill them with the corpses of the human beings whom I have struck down in my anger and in my rage, and in that I have hidden my face from this city because of all their dire action:*

[6]*Here am I, making regeneration grow up for it and healing;*
I will heal them and reveal to them
abundance of well-being with[d] *truthfulness.*
[7]*I will bring about the restoration of Judah*
and the restoration of Israel.
I will build them up as at the first
　　[8]*and purify them from all their waywardness with which they did*
　　　　wrong to me.
I will pardon[e] *all their acts of waywardness with which they did wrong to*
　　me
and with which they rebelled against me.
[9]*It will be for me a joyful name,*
praise and splendor,
For all the nations of the earth
that hear all the good
that I am doing to them.
They will be in awe and they will tremble
because of all the good and because of all the well-being
that I am doing for it.[f]

a. LXX has "making earth," perhaps assimilating to 10:12 (HUBP) and changing the drift of the verse (cf. Amos 4:13; 5:8–9; 9:5–6). Vg has a future participle and Tg a past verb, while Syr has "made you . . . shaped you . . . established you," also changing the drift of the verse.

b. MT has a marker here.

c. LXX lacks [*people*] *coming* (*bā'îm*), which makes the text easier. Sym, Th have "to the sword of the people coming."

d. Lit. "and"; I take the phrase as a hendiadys for "truthful well-being" (14:13).

e. LXX has "I will not remember."

f. MT has a section marker here.

While the combination of verse and prose recurs in Jeremiah (e.g., vv. 14–18), this section is the first where lines of verse provide the opening "text" which the rest of the section expounds. The opening poetic lines promise extraordinary things that Yahweh will do if people call on him. The middle verses of prose explain the background, the destruction and slaughter in Jerusalem, which people know about or can envisage; the verses function to raise suspense. The closing verses spell out what the extraordinary things will be: a restoration that will bring healing, well-being that can be relied on, upbuilding, purification, and pardon, such that will make the world marvel.

> v. 1   The curators' introduction
> vv. 2–3   Yahweh's self-introduction, invitation, and promise about revelation (two tricola)
> v. 4a   Jeremiah's introduction to the message that follows
> vv. 4b–5 The background to the main message
> vv. 6–9   The main message, spelling out the implications of the two tricola
>> vv. 6–8   Yahweh's acts of restoration (a tricolon and three bicola)
>> v. 9   The consequences in the response of the nations (a bicolon and two tricola)

1 "What themes become important to a prisoner, punished as he is for the crime of truth-telling? . . . Imprisonment is the credential of Jeremiah" (cf. Phil 1:7, 13–14; 2 Tim 1:8; Rev 1:9).[349] The opening verse introduces vv. 2–9 in particular but drifts into becoming an introduction to the chapter as a whole.

2 The two tricola are both difficult, but they are thought-provoking where they are clear. They do not identify *this* or *it*. But such a *this* (lit. "thus") regularly refers to what follows, so here it will refer to v. 3 and/or to vv. 4–9, which spell out v. 3. And *it* will refer to these verses' revelations about what is happening and is going to happen in the life of prophet and people. It is indeed something that Yahweh *is doing* or is going to do, something Yahweh

349. Berrigan, *Jeremiah*, 141, 142, 144.

is shaping (*yāṣar*) or is going to shape. Shaping suggests the work of a potter, and it is usually a positive operation, though Jeremiah has spoken of shaping in a negative way (18:11). *To establish* (*kûn hiphil*) is also usually a positive operation; Jeremiah used this verb of creation (10:12). Is the catastrophe that is unfolding something Yahweh is doing, shaping, establishing? But the ease with which participles in Hebrew, as in English, can denote what someone is going to do (Vg has all future participles in v. 2) means that Yahweh might be looking beyond the catastrophe and speaking about positive doing, shaping, and establishing. *Yahweh is his name.* Yes, it comes from him. Is that all he means?

3 The second tricolon begins to spell out the implications of the first. Its own elusiveness stems from the identity of the *you.* Is it Jeremiah?[350] But why would Yahweh be issuing such an invitation to him, especially at this point in time? And what would the *big* and *inaccessible things* be? We have read lots of big and formerly inaccessible things in the scroll so far, not least in chs. 30–32, and there are no new such revelations to follow here.[351] There is nothing apocalyptic in Jer 33.[352] But in the scroll so far, Jeremiah as prophet has sometimes stood for the people, and calling and being answered is designed to be an aspect of the people's relationship with Yahweh (e.g., Pss 4:1[2]; 102:2[3]; 120:1; 138:3). Jeremiah will later speak of Yahweh answering them when he prays for them and of him telling them what Yahweh says (42:4). So here, *you* at least includes Judah. It is the people as an entity whom Yahweh will *tell big* and *inaccessible things that you have not acknowledged* (more likely than things they have not known, since arguably he has also given Judah all his good news already). Whoever is the *you*, the promise *I will answer you, I will tell you big things, inaccessible things* makes the audience think again about v. 2, where doing, shaping, and establishing are verbs that apply naturally to Yahweh's constructive acts. (It was from this verse that William Carey was preaching in 1792 when he formulated his trademark saying "Expect great things from God; attempt great things for God" and thereby "brought modern Christian missions to birth."[353]) Doing, shaping, and establishing are the encouraging big things that Yahweh will talk about here (cf. Isa 48:6). Those verbs recall how Yahweh both shapes light and creates darkness, makes well-being and dire fortune (Isa 45:7)—which for Judah are now going to come in the opposite order.

350. B. Rossi (*L'intercessione*, 331–34) sees Yahweh as now giving Jeremiah the permission to pray that he had long withheld.
351. Rudolph, *Jeremia*, 215.
352. Weiser, *Jeremia*, 2:311.
353. Keown, Scalise, and Smothers, *Jeremiah 26–52*, 175.

4–5 So what are these things? Yahweh moves from the broad, general, nebulous, and possibly encouraging to the concrete, definite, tangible, and definitely agonizing realities of the community's current experience, to which prose is perhaps appropriate. The focus is no longer the action Jeremiah took in Jer 32 and the destiny of land outside the city but the city's own desperate state, which was also a background concern in Jer 32. The implication may be that ordinary people have had to tear down their homes, perhaps because they were just inside the walls and stood in the way of defenders. And people living in palaces have perhaps had to surrender the stone of which the palaces were made to shore up the walls (but plural *houses* might simply imply one many-roomed palace). The stone and the mudbrick might also be materials to throw down on attackers. In vv. 4b–5, the syntax is incoherent, an appropriate mirror of the circumstances Jeremiah is describing; perhaps we shouldn't try too hard to make sense of it.[354] The implications are evident: people who have stood on the walls to defend the city have lost their lives in doing so, or are about to lose their lives if Yahweh speaks anticipatorily. It's as if they came there in order to lose their lives thus. Perhaps the corpses of other people who died were also laid here because it was impossible to leave the city to bury them in the proper places.[355] And Yahweh asserts responsibility for what has been happening, in two ways. Actively, it was he who struck the defenders down, not the Chaldeans. And passively, the Chaldeans were able actually to do so because Yahweh had hidden his face from the city. Its well-being depended on Yahweh lifting his face over it and shining over it (Num 6:25–26), like a king smiling over someone and seeing that they do well. But if the king refuses to see a suppliant, turning his face away, the person's security and protection disappear. "The hiding of the divine face is a metaphor of anger and destruction, of Yahweh's withdrawal of his protection and favour" (cf. Isa 8:17; 54:8; 63:6).[356] The efforts described in vv. 4b–5a are useless when v. 5b lies behind the problem.[357]

6–7a Fortunately, however, vv. 4–5 were only the negative backdrop to what follows. While *it* and *this* in v. 2 perhaps referred immediately to the present or imminent calamity, they also overflowed in their reference to the *big, inaccessible* things that Yahweh would tell people about if they called and that he is actually going to tell them about anyway. He first speaks in terms of the familiar image of the city as like an individual who has been mugged; Yahweh will be like a healer. He will bring *regeneration* to it, like the new flesh

354. McKane, *Jeremiah*, 2:855.
355. Holladay, *Commentary on Jeremiah*, 2:225.
356. R. P. Carroll, *Jeremiah*, OTL, 633.
357. Stulman, *Jeremiah*, 281.

that needs to *grow up* where there is a wound; Hebrew can thus use the word regeneration (*'ărukâ*) figuratively, like the English word, as Jeremiah does in 8:22; 30:17 (concretely in Neh 4:7[1]). The same applies to *healing* (8:15; 14:19). Actually, healers can't do much; they can't make healing happen. But as Yahweh has been the mugger, so *I will heal them*; again compare 30:17, whose wording reappears here and whose promises are summarized more briefly here. He can make healing happen. "I am Yahweh who heals you" (Exod 15:26) is "the divine Magna Carta in the matter of health and all related questions."[358] *Abundance of well-being with truthfulness*, well-being that can be relied on and that will last, adds to that promise, which is spelled out further in the familiar terms of v. 7a. Truthful well-being was what the other prophets had been promising (14:13), and now Jeremiah promises it. "The same God who in the catastrophe implements his unrelenting judgment . . . at the same moment reveals the implementing of salvation."[359] The other side of calamity, Jeremiah reclaims the beliefs that had led Judah astray, almost as if he vindicates his opponents.[360] "How do we move from 'there is no peace' [no *šālôm*, no well-being] to announcing 'peace' and 'good news'? . . . Peace is not possible until there is a dismantling of the holy city and an embrace of exile as the place of God's newness."[361]

7b–8 Yahweh restates the point in terms of another familiar image, the rebuilding of the community. From the beginning, Jeremiah knew that there was to be demolition but then building up (1:10). As individual wounded people will need literal healing, the city will need literal rebuilding, but in both cases, Yahweh focuses on the metaphorical. The city's restoration, the bringing into existence of a new Jerusalem, is "holistic";[362] it involves the physical and the spiritual. In connection with the rebuilding, Yahweh will also need to *purify* and *pardon*, two further different images for Yahweh's dealing with the consequences of the people's dire lifestyle. Yahweh has three images for the dire acts that purification and pardon have to deal with: they are acts of waywardness (*'āwôn*, leaving the right path), of rebellion (*peša'*, defying the king's authority), and of wrongdoing (*ḥāṭā'*; these acts especially are the ones that issue in a need for purification—a purification offering is a *ḥaṭṭā't*). Only here does Jeremiah refer to purifying (*ṭāhar* piel), which is arguably harder than pardon because it means removing the stain that the dire action has caused and that people continue

---

358. Barth, *CD* III, 4:369.
359. Weiser, *Jeremia*, 2:312.
360. Cf. Diamond, "Jeremiah," 593.
361. Brueggemann, *Like Fire*, 177.
362. Fretheim, *Jeremiah*, 474.

to carry. The undertaking corresponds to the appeal elsewhere for Yahweh to expiate wrongdoing—which Jeremiah urges Yahweh not to do (18:23). The people are like someone who has killed a person, whose blood can be seen on the killer's hands and body; indeed, they *are* such killers (e.g., 22:17; 26:20–23; 32:35). The Scriptures suggest several ways for dealing with stain, which are familiar from everyday life. Stains disappear with time (e.g., Lev 15); major stains take longer, part of the significance of the exile's lasting seventy years. One may cover a stain so it is no longer visible (Pss 32:1; 85:2[3]). One may cut out an offensive stain, an aspect of what Yahweh is doing in destroying Jerusalem. Yet evidently, the punishment involved in the city's fall will not have constituted redress such as makes cleansing unnecessary.[363] Who could say what calamity could count as adequate purification? Would only the total destruction that Yahweh has often threatened be enough? But perhaps one may somehow zap away stain, in a magical kind of way (2 Kgs 5; Ps 51:1[3]), as the offerings prescribed in Leviticus zap away minor stains; this is perhaps what Yahweh here declares he can do. Given that both the concept and the action of pardoning are easier, in a sense, as a king or president has power to pardon crimes or acts of rebellion, does pardon have that magical effect, rendering a person into someone who never did the act?

9 Marvelous consequences will follow for Jerusalem (the verb is feminine, like the city). The implication of its restoration, purifying, and pardon will be that Yahweh can look on it with pleasure as he cannot now. At the moment, the very name makes him angry (he doesn't even utter it in this section, though he will in the next). But then *it will be for me a joyful name*, and also *praise and splendor*. Yahweh picks up the phraseology of 13:11 (and behind it Deut 26:19) and declares that it will come true for Jerusalem. He made no reference to *the nations* back there, but now he adds that they will acknowledge Yahweh's act of restoration, which will affect not only *it* (Jerusalem, v. 6) but *them* (Judah and Israel, v. 7, who also appeared in 13:11 alongside Jerusalem). The nations have been imagined asking horrified questions and making horrified comments about the city's fall (18:16; 19:8; 22:8–9; 25:9; 30:17); now they are imagined being astounded at its restoration. Jerusalem is destined to be the city on a hill that cannot be hid and the means by which blind eyes are enabled to see (cf. 3:17). It does not have to turn itself into that city any more than Jeremiah had to speak directly to the nations in order to be a prophet to the nations. God will bring it about.[364]

---

363. R. P. Carroll, *Jeremiah*, OTL, 635.
364. Barth, *CD* IV, 3:57.

b. Rejoicing and Praise Will Again Resound in Jerusalem (33:10–11)

[10] *Yahweh has said this. Once again there will make itself heard in this place (of which you are saying, "It's a waste, without human being, without animal"), in the towns of Judah and in the streets of Jerusalem that are desolate (without human being, without anyone living there, and without animal),* [11] *the voice of joy and the voice of rejoicing, the voice of groom and the voice of bride, the voice of people saying,*

Confess Yahweh of Armies,
  because Yahweh is good,
  because his commitment is for all time,

bringing a thank-offering to Yahweh's house. Because I will bring about the restoration of the country as at the first, Yahweh has said.[a]

> a. MT has a section marker here.

10–11 This second message takes up familiar phrases and images and re-works them. Yahweh's first word does so: *once again* (*'ôd*) echoes 31:4a, 4b, 5a, 23; 32:15. That expression summarizes the reversal that Yahweh promises. Jeremiah had been not unfairly accused of saying that the city *will be a waste, without anyone living there* (26:9). *Without human being or animal* had been the people's own phrase just now (32:43). Here, five times, Yahweh uses that word *without* (*'ên*) in describing the city's deprivation. The *entire country has become desolate* (12:11), Yahweh has observed. I am putting an end to *the voice of joy and the voice of rejoicing, the voice of groom and the voice of bride*, he has declared (16:9; cf. 7:34; 25:10). While people were used to chanting, "Confess him . . . because Yahweh is good, his commitment is for all time" (Ps 100:4–5), they are hard words to utter at the moment. But Jeremiah has promised that people will again be *bringing a thanksgiving to Yahweh's house* (17:26). In light of vv. 4–9, it is noteworthy that Yahweh makes no mention of bringing purification offerings; they will now be people who acknowledge Yahweh rather than sinners.[365] Finally, Yahweh has often promised that he will *bring about the restoration of the country*, and he will have done so. Yes, all the negatives will be reversed and the positives fulfilled. There is nothing that has been *inaccessible* here, but much that they have *not acknowledged* (v. 3). As healing and upbuilding would involve purification and pardon (vv. 6–8), here the rejoicing of ordinary life and of worship stand alongside each other. It is the combi-

---

365. Qimchi, in MG.

nation that makes for the reestablishment of true human life in the city. "The resumption of social life is intimately linked to the resumption of life with God."[366]

c. Flocks Will Pasture Again All Over the Country (33:12–13)

[12]*Yahweh of Armies has said this. Once again there will be in this place—the ruin without human being or animal—and in all its towns the habitat of shepherds resting a flock.* [13]*In the towns in the highland, in the towns in the foothills, in the towns in the Negeb, in the country of Benjamin, in the area around Jerusalem, and in the towns of Judah, the flock will once again pass under the hands of the counter, Yahweh has said.*[a]

a. MT has a section marker here.

12–13 The same dynamic recurs. Yahweh again picks up the language of ruin without human beings or animals but moves away from the city to the country and its towns, and speaks in a way that recalls Yahweh's promise that people will again say, *Yahweh bless you, faithful habitat* (31:23). They will again rest their flock there. *Once again* (that word recurs twice more), Yahweh casts his eye over all the regions of Judah; listing them again suggests Judah in its entirety. In 17:26, the listing related to their bringing offerings, in 32:44 to their acquiring land. Each time, he reaffirms this promise in a different connection. Here it confronts and reverses the *without* of vv. 10 and 12, which is now sixfold (and reverses the vision in 9:10[9]).[367] Yahweh imagines shepherds all over the country counting sheep and rejoicing in their increase, with no implication that shepherd or Yahweh will want or need to weed out the bad ones (Lev 27:32–33; Ezek 20:37–38). Usually, town being turned into pasturage is a negative image (e.g., 4:26; 22:6), but not here.[368] Sheep will now "safely graze" as they have not been able to.[369]

---

366. Brueggemann, *Jeremiah 26–52*, 97.

367. Volz, *Jeremia*, 313.

368. Keown, Scalise, and Smothers, *Jeremiah 26–52*, 172; they infer that the shepherds and sheep are leaders and people.

369. R. P. Carroll, *Jeremiah*, OTL, 634, contrasting with his comment noted in connection with 6:3.

d. David and the Levites Will Have Their Successors Ministering for Ephraim and Judah (33:14–18)

¹⁴ *There,* ᵃ *days are coming (Yahweh's affirmation) when I will implement the good word that I spoke for the household of Israel and for the household of Judah.*

¹⁵ *In those days and at that time:*
I will make a faithful branch shoot for David,
and he will exercise faithful authority in the country.
¹⁶ *In those days, Judah will find deliverance,*
and Jerusalem—it will dwell in confidence.
This is what one will call it:
Yahweh is our faithfulness. ᵇ

¹⁷ *Because Yahweh has said this:*

There will not be cut off for David
an individual sitting on the throne of the household of Israel.
¹⁸ *And for the priests, the Levites, there will not be cut off*
an individual before me making a whole offering rise,
Burning a grain offering,
and offering a sacrifice, for all the days. ᶜ

a. LXX lacks vv. 14–26.
b. MT has a section marker here.
c. MT has a marker here.

For the second set of promises in vv. 14–26, Jerusalem remains in focus, but Jeremiah moves away from his attentiveness to its embattled or ruined and desolate state, and the promises now relate specifically to the fulfillment of Yahweh's commitment to David and to Levi. The deposing of the Davidic king and the destruction of the temple in 587 would provide a natural background for these promises in the decades that followed, though it is also possible to imagine them as Yahweh's message to Judah with the approach of the calamity that would predictably terminate priestly practice and dissolve the monarchy. Jeremiah had long been implicitly or explicitly threatening these developments and had also implicitly or explicitly promised the restoration of the temple and its worship and the restoration of the Davidic monarchy.

v. 14 Introduction
vv. 15–16 Promises regarding David and regarding Judah and Jerusalem (a tricolon and two bicola)

v. 17a   A resumptive introduction
vv. 17b–18   Promises regarding David and regarding the Levites
                (a bicolon and two linked bicola)

14–15 The *good word* that Yahweh will *implement* is one with positive implications for *the household of Israel* as well as *the household of Judah*. The first promise about David reworks 23:5–6, with some abbreviation and suggestive modification:

²³:⁵There days are coming Yahweh's affirmation	¹⁵In those days and at that time
when I will set up for David a faithful shoot	I will make a faithful branch shoot for David
He will reign as king and will show understanding	
he will exercise faithful authority in the country	and he will exercise authority in the country
⁶In his days Judah will find deliverance	¹⁶In his days Judah will find deliverance
and Israel it will dwell in confidence	and Jerusalem it will dwell in confidence
And this is his name by which one will call him	And his is what one will call it
Yahweh is our faithfulness	Yahweh is our faithfulness

Once again, Jeremiah presupposes that the Davidic tree is about to be felled but that even a felled tree can see new growth. So, Yahweh promises, *I will make a faithful branch shoot for David*. The idea parallels Isa 11:1,[370] though the precise imagery is different: Isaiah speaks of a bough and a limb (*ḥōṭer* and *nēṣer*), Jeremiah of a branch or shoot (*ṣemaḥ*); the terms are roughly synonyms, but the words are different. One modification to the earlier version in 23:5 is that v. 15 adds the verb *ṣāmaḥ*, from which *ṣemaḥ* comes (lit. "I will make a shoot shoot out" or "I will make a branch branch out"). The only other occurrence of *ṣemaḥ* in this connection is Zech 3:8; 6:11–12, where Zechariah seems to be picking up the image from Jeremiah and combining it with others. Zechariah also uses Jeremiah's verb, and there is one other text where the verb recurs in this connection, Ps 132:17. Now 23:5–6 and 33:14–17 are more or less the only Davidic promises in Jeremiah. While their general points of connection are with Isaiah, they also link with the promise to David in 2 Sam

---

370. On Jeremiah's dependence on Isa 11:1–16, see M. A. Sweeney, "Jeremiah's Reflection on the Isaian Royal Promise," in Goldingay, *Uprooting and Planting*, 308–21.

7 (to which Kings and Chronicles recurrently refer back) and in Pss 89 and 132. In his own way, then, Jeremiah is implying a connection with the promise to David presupposed in Samuel-Kings, in Isaiah, and in some Psalms. But as is the case in 23:5–6, if he might seem to be undermining his own assault on the monarchy, he makes sure he is not doing so by indicating that any monarchy that Yahweh could shore up would be different from the one he is putting down: David's shoot *will exercise faithful authority.* Further, Yahweh now omits the declaration that *he will reign as king and will show understanding,* which along with the addition of the promise to the Levites, reduces the significance of the Davidic figure.[371] The double change suggests a comparison and contrast with the situation in Judah at the beginning of the Persian period. There, a Davidic shoot does rule in Judah but doesn't reign as king. And Zechariah sets the senior priest alongside the Davidic shoot, though he speaks more about him as an individual than about the priests in general. One might see this dual arrangement as a fulfillment of Jeremiah's promise or infer that this promise comes from a time around the transition from Babylonian to Persian rule.

16 Noteworthy further modifications of the earlier version of the promise are the replacement of Israel (i.e., Ephraim) by Jerusalem, though v. 14 has already affirmed that this promise has positive implications for Israel as well as Judah. The name *Yahweh is our faithfulness* is also applied to Jerusalem rather than to the shoot. "This chapter celebrates Jerusalem as the key to Yahweh's purpose for Israel,"[372] which is not an idea that would seem very plausible just before or just after 587. The idea that the city will be the locus of faithfulness would also seem implausible. A human community will go by the name "Yahweh is our faithfulness" and will be characterized by trust and commitment![373]

17 Less systematically, the second promise about David also reflects phraseology that has occurred elsewhere. Jeremiah has declared of Jehoiachin:

> No individual from his offspring will succeed,
>> sitting on David's throne,
>> and ruling again in Judah. (22:30)

If anything, that threat implies that Davidic rule will continue in Judah, not that the Davidic monarchy will cease. Here in v. 17, Yahweh makes explicit that the declaration about Jehoiachin does not mean that there will never

---

371. See J. Erzberger, "Jeremiah 33:14–26: The Question of Text Stability and the Devaluation of Kingship," *OTE* 26 (2013): 663–83.

372. Allen, *Jeremiah*, 374.

373. P. D. Miller, "Jeremiah," on the passage.

again be a Davidic king, picking up the wording of the promise as Solomon articulated it in 1 Kgs 8:25 (see also 2:4; 9:5).

18 Yahweh goes on to affirm a matching undertaking about the Levites that takes up the formulation of the Davidic promise. Once again, *there will not be cut off*. Both undertakings relate to the Jerusalem focus introduced into the reworked promise in vv. 15–16—that is, Jerusalem will know the rule of David and the ministry of the Levites. So Jeremiah is not only confirming the promise about David in 1 Kings, he is also providing the Levites with a matching promise. It is the first time in the First Testament that David and the Levites appear together; the collocation will be characteristic of Chronicles. Further, like the references to kings, previous references to priests and sacrifices in the Jeremiah scroll have been more or less uniformly negative, though 31:14 undertook something in this connection. So this promise is even more novel than vv. 14–17. Whereas the undertaking that relates to David links with material in Samuel-Kings but not with Deuteronomy, the expression *the priests, the Levites* is characteristic of Deuteronomy (17:9, 18; 18:1; 24:8; 27:9); Chronicles (and usually Ezra and Nehemiah) refers to "the priests and the Levites." An aspect of the distinctive nature of this promise in vv. 14–18, then, is to combine the interests of Deuteronomy (which speaks of *the priests, the Levites* and doesn't refer to David or to a divine commitment to a king) and the interests of Samuel-Kings and Isaiah (which refer to Yahweh's promise to David but not to *the priests, the Levites*). While a collocation of Davidic leadership/covenant and Levitical leadership/covenant comes to feature in Second Temple times, that collocation does not correspond to the one that features here: for instance, here there is no mention of Moses, Aaron, Phinehas, Zadok, or even Levi himself, only of the Levites as a group (contrast Sirach 45).[374] And the responsibility of the Levites relates purely to worship; it is the descendant of David who will exercise political leadership. There is no vision for the leadership of a senior priest in the community, not even of the kind of leadership exercised by Joshua alongside Zerubbabel (see, e.g., Hag 1:1, 12, 14; Zech 6:11–12).

e. Those Promises Are as Sure as Yahweh's Pledge with Day and Night (33:19–22)

[19] *Yahweh's word came to Jeremiah.* [20] *Yahweh has said this. If you people could annul my pledge in connection with the day and my pledge in connection with the night, so that daytime and night would not happen at their time,* [21] *also my pledge could be annulled with David my servant so that he would not have a son*

---

374. See further Tiemeyer, "Priests and the Temple Cult," 233–64.

reigning on his throne, and with the Levites, the priests,[a] *my ministers.* [22]*That which cannot be counted, the army of the heavens, and cannot be weighed, the sand in the sea, so I will make many the offspring of David my servant and the Levites ministering to me.*[b]

a. Only here does this form of the phrase occur (contrast v. 18). Allusions to familiar phrases sometimes incorporate the inversion of words; see Leuchter, *Polemics of Exile*, 78. It can bring readers up short and push them to pay attention (P. C. Beentjes, "Inverted Quotations in the Bible: A Neglected Stylistic Pattern," *Bib* 63 [1982]: 523).

b. MT has a section marker here.

19–22 Yahweh reaffirms and reformulates the promise regarding David and the priests, the Levites, and leaves himself with even less wiggle room. This message and that in vv. 23–26 are explicitly described as given to Jeremiah, so if they actually come from his curators rather than from Jeremiah himself, they compare with the book of Daniel's attributing visions to Daniel that were "inspired" by Daniel and his visions but had no direct link with Daniel.[375] Only here does the First Testament refer to a pledge in connection with day and night, though the image compares with Yahweh's promises in Gen 8:21–9:17. They both refer to day and night and to a pledge, though they do not relate the two to each other. This pledge is not simply an aspect of God's creation of the world. After human waywardness skewed things in the world (Gen 3), time "is a different, a new time," and there is a new promise attaching to it.[376] The possible link with Gen 8–9 also suggests a link with Jeremiah's frightening vision in 4:23–25, which itself recalls Gen 6–9. Judah's sin led to a dissolution of creation like that in Genesis; Yahweh's act of restoration presupposes a stability of creation.[377] David now regains his position as *my servant*, which had been transferred to Nebuchadrezzar,[378] while only here and in 52:18 does Jeremiah refer to *ministers* or to people *ministering (māšar)*. The word suggests the work of a priest in relation to offerings; it is again a term that comes in Deuteronomy (10:8; 17:12; 18:5, 7; 21:5). The further encouragement of the images in v. 20 works by taking up promises that elsewhere apply to the people as a whole (e.g., 31:37; Gen 15:5; Hos 1:10 [2:1]) and applying them to David and the Levites. It is a wild hyperbole; Israel would not find it beneficial to have that many descendants of David or Levi.

375. P.-M. Bogaert suggests that vv. 14–26 as a whole are a rereading of earlier verses from Jeremiah: see "*Urtext, text court et relecture,*" in Emerton, *Congress Volume*, 236–47; cf. M. Sjöberg, "Inner-Biblical Interpretation in the Redaction of Jeremiah 33:14–26," in Bautch and Knoppers, *Covenant in the Persian Period*, 175–93.

376. Barth, *CD* I, 2:47.

377. H. Lalleman, "Jeremiah, Judgement and Creation," *TynB* 60 (2009): 15–24.

378. R. P. Carroll, *Jeremiah*, OTL, 638.

f. Yahweh Will Keep His Commitment to the Offspring of Jacob and of David (33:23–26)

²³*Yahweh's word came to Jeremiah.* ²⁴*You have seen what this people has spoken, haven't you: "The two kin groups that Yahweh chose—he's rejected them." So my people—they despise it from still being a nation, before them.*ᵃ ²⁵*Yahweh has said this. My pledge in connection with daytime and night, the decrees regarding heavens and earth, if I have not set them up:* ²⁶*also the offspring of Jacob and David my servant I could reject so as not to get rulers from his offspring for the offspring of Abraham, Isaac, and Jacob. Because I will bring about their restoration and have compassion on them.*ᵇ

    a. The Lucianic recension of the Septuagint, Theod, and Syr have "before me," an easier reading assimilating to 31:36 (Allen, *Jeremiah*, 374). MT has a section marker here.

    b. MT has a marker here.

23–24 The final promise stands back and speaks more generally, though puzzlingly. The dismissive words ascribed to *this people* would make sense on the lips of the besieging Babylonian army, but there is no parallel for calling the Babylonians *this people*. The term must surely denote the community with which Jeremiah is involved and to which he speaks, which he commonly calls by this expression. But who are *the two kin groups that Yahweh chose* but *has rejected*? The "choice" language is again Deuteronomy's, not Jeremiah's, but the "reject" language is Jeremiah's (e.g., 6:30; 7:29; 14:19; 31:37), so he could hardly fault people who use "reject" language.

- Understood in light of the way Jeremiah spoke earlier, the two kin groups could be the households of Ephraim and Judah (e.g., 31:27, 31; 33:14) or Judah and Benjamin (cf. 32:44; 33:13);[379] *this people* is then talking about itself in saying with understandable gloom (just before or after 587) that Yahweh has rejected them. In effect, Jeremiah would be quoting from the kind of prayers that appear in Lamentations, which people were praying in the aftermath of 587 and which articulated the conviction that Yahweh had or might have "actually rejected us" (Lam 5:22). But it does not seem likely that *my people—they despise it from still being a nation, before them* refers to their attitude to themselves.
- One might infer from v. 26 that the two kin groups are Jacob and David, but they make for an odd pair; David's kin group is part of Jacob.
- In earlier prophets, *Jacob* can refer to Ephraim (Hos 10:11; Amos

379. Denis the Carthusian, *Enarratio in Jeremiam*, 244; cf. Schroeder, *Jeremiah*, 277.

3:13; 6:8; 7:2, 5; 9:8; Mic 1:5); it would then be the line of David and the people of Ephraim that *this people*, Judah, is dismissing. This understanding would make sense, but the context offers no concrete pointer to this being a unique reference for Jacob in Jeremiah.

- Rather, understanding the reference in light of vv. 14–22 suggests that the two kin groups are the descendants of David and Levi, which fits another expression of grief in Lamentations: "He has despised king and priest" (Lam 2:6). That verb *despise* (nā'aṣ) recurs here, as it came in one of Jeremiah's strongest expressions concerning rejection (14:21). So Yahweh is reassuring Judah that David and the Levites still count as *my people* and as a *nation* for him.

25–26 Yahweh repeats and reworks the previous analogy so that he speaks again of his pledge regarding the sequence of *day and night* but now also of the cosmic laws that apply to *heavens and earth*, and he applies the analogy to the people and their kings. The contemporary descendants of Jacob (that is, the people of Israel) are still part of *the offspring of Abraham, Isaac, and Jacob*. It is to state the obvious but in a significantly novel way within Jeremiah.[380] The descendants of Abraham, Isaac, and Jacob will share again in the life of a people ruled by David, share in Yahweh's act of *restoration* and in Yahweh's *compassion*. Who could believe that "the principalities of death do not have the last word"?[381]

The promises about David and the Levites raise background questions: how and when did Jeremiah or his curators come to combine these themes and expressions? They also raise foreground questions. "Despite its strong words, the promise has not come true. A Davidic kingship never existed any more, and with the destruction of the Second Temple priesthood came to an end."[382] Yahweh let Nebuchadrezzar his servant terminate the Davidic monarchy after fulfilling his original promise to David for about four hundred years; over the subsequent two and a half millennia, he has not done so. For a short time in the second century, Jewish kings did sit on David's throne, but they were not descendants of David.[383] Two centuries later, in a metaphorical sense, a descendant of David from Nazareth emerged as king of the Jews (see esp. Luke 1:32), but he never sat on David's throne, and he was not very fond of being designated as king.

---

380. C. Lombaard, "The Strange Case of the Patriarchs in Jeremiah 33:26," *AcT* 35 (2015): 36–49.

381. Berrigan, *Jeremiah*, 145.

382. Rudolph, *Jeremia*, 219.

383. This consideration alone makes it seem unlikely that the message would be designed to support the Hasmoneans (Duhm, *Jeremia*, 276).

As for *the priests, the Levites,* within decades of Yahweh's making this promise about them, they were indeed making these *offerings* in the restored temple, and they did so for six centuries, but then a further and final destruction of Jerusalem terminated these offerings, and they have not been made for two millennia. It is again possible to say that the man from Nazareth functioned metaphorically as a priest, though his Judahite and Davidic lineage that enabled him to be metaphorically designated "the root" as well as "the offspring" of David (Rev 22:16) was also the reason why he could not be seen as the fulfillment of this promise concerning specifically Levitical priests. Hebrews presupposes this fact in its systematic exposition of his position as something more like a Melchizedek priest.

Alongside the Christian understanding that Jesus was king and priest, at least as promising an approach to considering the foreground of these promises emerges from the New Testament declarations that the community that belongs to Jesus is itself "a sacred priesthood" appointed "to offer up spiritual sacrifices acceptable to God through Jesus Anointed" and is indeed "a royal priesthood" (1 Peter 2:5, 9). The last phrase links with both sides to the promise in Jeremiah but takes its terminology from Exod 19:6, where Yahweh declares that Israel is "a kingdom of priests" or a "priestly kingdom" (*mamleket kōhənîm,* which LXX translates obversely as "a royal priesthood"). The Jesus community does not come to replace Israel in that position, but it does come to share in that position with Israel. An implication of Exod 19:6 is that Israel *was* a priesthood and a kingdom before it *acquired* priests and kings; the First Testament makes no mention of priests among Yahweh's people until after that declaration, and kings come on the scene in Israel only rather later.

When the Jesus community becomes such a royal priesthood, can this event count as a fulfillment of Jeremiah's promise? The Jeremiah scroll has made two earlier promises about things that would last *for all the days* (31:36; 32:39), and it has much more often used the expression *for all time* (*lə'ôlām* or simply *'ôlām*). This expression is not always good news (e.g., 17:4; 18:16; 25:9). Fortunately, the small print associated with it qualifies it with expressions such as "depending on how you respond to this promise/threat" and thus "until I change my mind" (see 18:1–12). When it is good news, it might seem that such qualifications undo everything positive about an undertaking. But it does not have that effect because of who Yahweh is. He does not change his mind randomly. He does not lie and change his mind like a human being (Num 23:19). Because of who he is, he could change his mind in order to do something more generous than he said, but not something meaner. The fulfillment of these promises in Jer 33:14–18 is of that kind. The promises to David and to Levi are more than fulfilled as Yahweh implements through Jesus his original intention for Israel as a whole to be a royal priesthood.

Yahweh's promises also have an interim implication. Critiquing institutions such as monarchy and priesthood is all very well, but societies need structures. Second Temple Judah needed Davidic governors like Zerubbabel, priestly governors like Ezra, and priestly kings like the Hasmoneans—it needed something. People who critique militarist and unjust institutions have to discuss peaceful and egalitarian ones too.[384] And subsequently to New Testament times and ironically, the church reestablished something like priesthood and monarchy within itself, not least in what became known as the monarchical episcopate, and the arrangement continues in churches that have senior pastors, while the Jewish community has lived contentedly for two millennia without priests or leaders who have authority over congregations.

C. PART 3C: STORIES IMPLYING A REVERSION TO REALITY (34:1–36:32 [LXX 41:1–43:32])

The three sequences that comprise part 3 of the scroll began with gloomy stories (Jer 26–29), moved to something more promissory (Jer 30–33), and now come to a gloomy conclusion with more stories. The setting indicated in 34:1 denotes a background in the same period as Jer 32–33 in what will turn out to be the final crisis in the life of Jerusalem and the reign of Zedekiah, but the chapter soon indicates that it does not maintain the note of encouragement that appeared in Jer 30–33. We are "back to reality."[385] In its tone, Jer 34 thus returns to Jer 27–29, with two messages that do imply a stage when the situation is not quite final. Jeremiah 35–36 then takes us further back, into the reign of Zedekiah's brother, which had been the background to Jer 26. So Jer 34–36 as a whole completes "the concentric frame around Jeremiah's book of hope by reversing the temporal setting from the tenth year of Zedekiah during the final siege of Jerusalem back to the fourth year of Jehoiakim."[386]

It comprises four units:

34:1–7 A threat and a promise from the time of Zedekiah
34:8–22 A story about Zedekiah and a threat from his time
35:1–19 A threat and a promise from the time of Jehoiakim
36:1–32 A story about Jehoiakim and a threat from his time

---

384. Pixley, *Jeremiah*, 107.
385. Fretheim, *Jeremiah*, 483.
386. Diamond, "Jeremiah," 593–94.

1. A Threat and a Promise from the Time of Zedekiah (34:1–7 [LXX 41:1–7])

[1]The word that came to Jeremiah from Yahweh, with Nebuchadrezzar King of Babylon and his entire force, and all the kingdoms of the earth ruled by[a] his hand, and all the peoples,[b] battling against Jerusalem and against all its towns. [2]Yahweh, the God of Israel, has said this. Go,[c] and say to Zedekiah King of Judah: say to him, Yahweh has said this. Here am I, giving this city[d] into the hand of the king of Babylon, and he will consume it in fire. [3]You yourself will not escape from his hand because you will definitely be captured.[e] Into his hand you will be given. Your eyes—they will look at the eyes of the king of Babylon. His mouth—it will speak to your mouth.[f] To Babylon you will come. [4]Yet listen to the word of Yahweh, Zedekiah King of Judah. Yahweh has said this about you. You will not die by the sword;[g] [5]in peace you will die. Like the burnings for your ancestors, the previous kings that were before you, so people will burn for you.[h] "Oh,[i] lord," they will lament for you. Because a word I myself have spoken (Yahweh's affirmation).[j]

[6]Jeremiah the prophet spoke to Zedekiah the king of Judah all these words in Jerusalem, [7]with the king of Babylon's force battling against Jerusalem and against all Judah's towns that were left[k]—at Lachish and at Azekah, because they were left among the towns of Judah as fortified towns.[l]

a. Lit. "the rule of."

b. For *and all the kingdoms of the earth ruled by his hand, and all the peoples*, LXX has simply "and all the earth ruled by him."

c. The infinitive absolute is used imperatively (cf. 2:2 and the translation note on it), which would add useful emphasis given that Jeremiah does not usually go to see a king unsummoned.

d. For *here am I, giving this city*, LXX has "this city will definitely be given over" (cf. 32:28).

e. The infinitive precedes the finite verb, underlining the factuality of the action.

f. Some MSS of LXX lack this sentence, perhaps by haplography (Lundbom, *Jeremiah 21–36*, 551).

g. LXX lacks this clause.

h. MT *yiśrapū-lāk* hardly justifies Vg "burn you"; and Israel did not practice cremation.

i. See the commentary on 22:13.

j. MT has a section marker here.

k. LXX has "and against Judah's towns."

l. MT has a unit marker here.

The first, brief unit is short and its message not very specific about the context it implicitly presupposes. Further, for the most part it repeats the content and even the words of 32:5.[387] This similarity puts us on the track of the

387. D. R. Jones, *Jeremiah*, 425.

way the rhetoric of Jer 34 as a whole parallels Jer 32 and in part thus proceeds dramatically rather than chronologically. The act of communication between Jeremiah/Yahweh and Zedekiah in this first unit differs from others, where Zedekiah takes the initiative (21:1–7; 37:3–10, 17–21; 38:14–28). Here, "the prophet is pictured as Yahweh's envoy going fearlessly into the palace."[388] The unit then functions as a lead-in to vv. 8–22, which begin and end with Zedekiah, illustrate how he fails to *listen to the word of Yahweh*, clarify aspects of the ambiguity of vv. 1–7, and might explain why the promise in vv. 4–5 gets compromised.[389] This unit makes a link with what precedes that is not only chronological but substantial: it continues to moderate threat with promise and thus to offer some hope in dark days. But in light of subsequent events, it conveys some irony, or at least raises questions about fulfillment. What we will come to know about Zedekiah's later experience will remind us that Yahweh's warning and promise here function in the same way as other threats and promises. As well as being ambiguous, they are not statements about what will inevitably happen. They constitute a challenge to respond. Thus the unit needs to be read at two levels. It reports a message Jeremiah gave to Zedekiah, which needs to be read in the context of the situation in 589/588. But the curators are telling the story later about the giving and delivering of this message, and vv. 6–7 imply a context after the city's fall, so that the unit is itself a message to the community in that context, inviting people in that context to think about the message and its ambiguity.

> v. 1   The curators' introduction
> vv. 2–5   Yahweh's message:
>   vv. 2–3   Threat
>   vv. 4–5   Promise
> vv. 6–7   The curators' report of Jeremiah's delivery of the message

LXX's version is shorter than MT, but in this chapter, there are more instances where LXX may have accidentally or deliberately shortened MT.[390]

1 The opening expression *the word that came to Jeremiah from Yahweh* can mark the beginning of major compilations within the Jeremiah scroll. The phrase is then qualified by words that give it a particular setting, as will happen again at v. 8 and as happens at 32:1 and 35:1. The note identifying the

388. Volz, *Jeremia*, 318.
389. Keown, Scalise, and Smothers, *Jeremiah 26–52*, 178–79.
390. See, e.g. the translation notes on vv. 3b and 8 and McKane's survey of views on vv. 10–11 (*Jeremiah*, 2:871). On the possible development of the section, see H.-J. Stipp, "'In Frieden wirst du sterben': Jeremias Heilswort für Zidkija in Jer 34,5," in *"Vom Leben umfangen": Ägypten, das Alte Testament und das Gespräch der Religionen. Gedenkschrift für M. Görg*, ed. S. J. Wimmer and G. Gafus, Ägypten und das Altes Testament 80 (Münster: Ugarit, 2014), 173–81.

context of the message uses terms that are simultaneously less and more threatening than Jer 32–33. The Babylonian army is not yet besieging Jerusalem, and *all its towns* also suggests it is not even focused on Jerusalem yet (see further vv. 6–7). The time is thus earlier than the one presupposed in vv. 8–22 (cf. 37:5). It recalls the time presupposed by Jer 27, the other exception to the rule about Jeremiah going to see Zedekiah only when summoned. It was in Jer 27:6–7 that Yahweh declared, *I myself am giving all these countries into the hand of Nebuchadrezzar King of Babylon, my servant. . . . All the nations will serve him.* Here, the introduction draws attention to the magnitude of the threat that consequently issues from *Nebuchadrezzar King of Babylon.* He is indeed thus the man *by his hand* ruling *all the kingdoms of the earth* and *all the peoples.* He has come to Judah with *his entire force.* And he is *battling against Jerusalem and against all its towns.* Technically, it would be these other peoples, not the king of Babylon himself, as v. 21 implies; he stays in his base at Riblah (38:17–18; 39:5).[391] Nevertheless, if you are Zedekiah, you are entitled to be worried. The three occurrences of *all* would underscore the point, and the two more occurrences in vv. 6–7[392] will emphasize it further.

2 Yahweh has a message for him; three times vv. 1–2 affirm that what follows comes from Yahweh. First the bad news, restating the message of 32:3–5 (though chronologically, that passage looks back on this one): Zedekiah's worst fears are going to be realized. Jerusalem is going to fall, because Yahweh is giving it away to Nebuchadrezzar. It will be set on fire, as often follows when cities are captured.

3 Zedekiah himself *will not escape from his hand*: Yahweh keeps issuing this threat (32:4; 38:18, 23) in a telling anticipation of how escape is what Zedekiah will vainly seek when the city falls (39:4–5; 52:7–8). *You will definitely be captured*: and he was (52:9). *Your eyes—they will look at the eyes of the king of Babylon.* It is an "eerie anticipation" of his fate in Jer 39.[393] *His mouth—it will speak to your mouth.* There will be irony in the fulfillment of that declaration (39:5–7; 52:9–11), which will involve events worse than his worst fears.

4 There are ways in which events might be less awful than his worst fears. Four more times in vv. 4–5 Jeremiah affirms that what follows comes from Yahweh. First, *listen!* Why would he do so? That question links with one aspect of the ambiguity of vv. 4–5. Jeremiah consistently lays before people a way of death and of life and implicitly or explicitly urges them to choose the latter. Evidently, neither threats nor promises have inevitability attached to them. Everything depends on how people respond, for good or ill. Here,

391. Weiser, *Jeremia*, 317.
392. Brueggemann, *Jeremiah 26–52*, 104.
393. Leuchter, *Polemics of Exile*, 83.

at least, there are ways in which the grimness of the coming events might be mitigated for Zedekiah himself if he listens. *You will not die* in battle. Given the flexibility of Hebrew *yiqtol* verbs, perhaps Yahweh means "you need not die" in battle; similar possibilities attach to the verbs that follow.

5 Yahweh continues to be ambiguous: in *šālôm* you will die. MT's verse division suggests a new sentence with the implication that things will be good when you die. Babylon can be the place where there is well-being for Judahites (29:7). But in slightly different words, his father Josiah had been told he would die in *šālôm* (2 Kgs 22:20). What did Huldah mean, and did it happen? Could Zedekiah ever think things were well after he had presided over his city's fall, watched his sons be executed, had his eyes seared out, then lived through the rest of his life in prison (52:9–11), unlike his nephew (52:31–34)? If we ignore MT's verse division, Yahweh is suggesting something less fulsome than "dying with things being well"; he is drawing a contrast between dying by the sword and thus in war, which will not happen, and dying in peace, which as far as we know did happen. *You will not die by the sword; in peace you will die* is thus a "syntactical chiasm."[394] Yahweh does not promise that Zedekiah will rest with his ancestors, which will be strictly impossible in Babylon. But he will be properly buried. People will *lament* his death, sighing *Oh, lord*, which was by no means what Jeremiah had promised his brother (22:13–19). Snidely, Yahweh takes up the verb *burn* from v. 2 in speaking of the *burnings* that will mark Zedekiah's death. The story of Asa's death (2 Chron 16:11–14) clarifies the nature of the burnings: while the funeral rite might include burning incense so that its smoke rises and suggests prayers ascending to God (Ps 141:2; Rev 8:3–4), these burnings will rather be funeral pyres. The message closes with a final reminder that it comes from Yahweh. The *word* is "a promise, a pledge."[395] It's up to Zedekiah to listen to it, and his response will determine how things turn out. *I will attend to him*, Yahweh had said, ambiguously (32:5). Verses 3–5 spell out what his attentiveness might mean without resolving the ambiguity. Zedekiah indeed looked in the eyes of the king of Babylon and listened to him speak, and he was taken off to Babylon. We don't know how he died or how people mourned him.

6–7 Did Jeremiah do as he was bidden? And how did Zedekiah react? This footnote records Jeremiah's delivery of the message and also makes more explicit its context, before the city's final siege. The king of Babylon has dealt with nearly all the easy targets. He is now focusing on two key towns in the foothills. Lachish is the most impressive fortified city after Jerusalem; Azekah is halfway from Lachish to Jerusalem. We have a collection of

394. Lundbom, *Jeremiah 21–36*, 551.
395. Duhm, *Jeremia*, 279.

ostraca from Lachish that apparently come from just before the fall of that city and of Jerusalem itself and thus from 589/588.[396] A number are letters from a subordinate to his superior officer in Lachish, and one mentions being unable to see fire signals from Azekah, which might mean that Azekah has fallen.[397] The curators do not tell us Zedekiah's response to Jeremiah's delivering *all these words* to Zedekiah when he is still *in Jerusalem*. But an audience listening to the story in the aftermath of 587 hardly needs to be told; they know what happened. They know what choices Zedekiah made, even though the outworking of other aspects of vv. 4–5 may not yet be clear. The story helps them understand why things worked out the way they did. In addition, the omission leaves that audience and later readers in the same position as Zedekiah, with the two possibilities open, and it puts the choice before them too.[398]

2. A Story about Zedekiah and a Threat from His Time (34:8–22 [LXX 41:8–22])

[8] *The word that came to Jeremiah from Yahweh after King Zedekiah solemnized a pledge with the entire people that was in Jerusalem*[a] *to proclaim for themselves*[b] *a release,* [9] *to send off each individual his Hebrew servant and each individual his Hebrew maidservant, free, so that they wouldn't make them serve as a Judahite, each individual his brother.* [10] *All the officials and the entire people that came into the pledge listened*[c] *so as to send off, each individual, his servant and each individual his maidservant, free, so that they didn't make them serve anymore. So they listened and sent them off,*[d] [11] *but they turned back after this and turned the servants and the maidservants back that they had sent off free.*[e] *They forced them to be servants and maidservants.*[f]

[12] *Then Yahweh's word came to Jeremiah from Yahweh.* [13] *Yahweh, the God of Israel, has said this. I myself solemnized a pledge with your ancestors on the day of my getting them out from the country of Egypt, from a household of servants:* [14] *At the end of seven*[g] *years you will send off, each individual, his Hebrew brother who has sold himself*[h] *to you and has served you six years—you will send him off free from being with you. Your ancestors didn't listen to me. They didn't bend their ear.* [15] *But you yourselves turned today and did what was right in my eyes in proclaiming a release each individual to his neighbor. You solemnized a*

---

396. See *ANET*, 321–22.

397. See Z. B. Begin, "Does Lachish Letter 4 Contradict Jeremiah xxxiv 7?," *VT* 52 (2002): 166–74.

398. Berrigan, *Jeremiah*, 149.

pledge before me in the house over which my name is proclaimed. [16]*But you have turned back and defiled my name and turned back, each individual his servant and each individual his maidservant, whom you had sent off free for themselves. You have forced them to become servants and maidservants for you.*[i]

[17]*Therefore, Yahweh has said this. You yourselves have not listened to me in proclaiming a release, each individual to his brother and each individual to his neighbor. Here am I, proclaiming a release to you (Yahweh's affirmation)—to sword, to epidemic, and to hunger.*[j] *I will make you into something horrific to all the kingdoms of the earth.* [18]*I will give the men who overstepped my pledge, who didn't implement the words of the pledge that they solemnized before me,*[k] *the calf*[l] *that they cut into two and passed between the parts—*[19]*the officials of Judah, the officials of Jerusalem,*[m] *the officers,*[n] *the priests, and the entire people of the country*[o] *who passed between the parts of the calf:* [20]*I will give them into the hand of their enemies, into the hand of the people who are seeking their life.*[p] *Their corpse will become food for the bird of the heavens and for the animal of the earth.* [21]*Zedekiah King of Judah and his officials I will give into the hand of their enemies, into the hand of the people who are seeking their life, into the hand of the king of Babylon's force who are withdrawing from against you.* [22]*Here am I, issuing a command (Yahweh's affirmation), and I will turn them back to this city. They will battle against it, take it, and consume it in fire, and the towns of Judah I will make into a desolation, with no one living there.*[q]

a. LXX has simply "with the people." Lundbom (*Jeremiah 21–36*, 558, 560) attributes this and other LXX shortfalls more to LXX haplography than MT expansion.

b. Dative of disadvantage (Rudolph, *Jeremia*, 220); but *lə* in connection with this action recurs throughout the story.

c. For *wayyišmə'û*, LXX nicely implies *wayyāšûbû* ("turned").

d. LXX lacks "free . . . off."

e. LXX lacks "and turned . . . free."

f. MT has a marker here.

g. LXX has "six"; see the commentary.

h. While *mākar niphal* can be passive (e.g., Ps 105:17), here a reflexive sense applies: "Deuteronomy 15 does not take the needs of the owner as point of departure, but that of the predicament of the person who has sold himself," and the same is true of Jer 34 (M. D. Terblanche, "Jeremiah 34:8–22: A Call for the Enactment of Distributive Justice," *AcT* 36 [2016]: 153).

i. MT has a section marker here.

j. Tg has "from" rather than *to* each time.

k. For MT *lipnay*, Aq implies *lipnê* ("in front of the calf"), which generates a syntactically smoother reading.

l. One would initially translate, "I will make the men [into or like] the calf"—quite a severe threat (e.g., Rudolph, *Jeremia*, 224); but the verb rendered *I will give* (*wənātattî*) recurs at the beginning of v. 20 and looks resumptive there, so more likely the reference to the calf involves an anacoluthon (Holladay, *Commentary on Jeremiah*, 2:242).

m. LXX omits *the officials of Jerusalem*.

n. See the translation note on 29:2.

o. On *the people of the country*, see the translation note on 1:18.

p. LXX lacks *into the hand of the people who are seeking their life* here and in v. 21.

q. MT has a unit marker here.

This second message in part 3c emerges from a story with a socio-ethical background in an aspect of the way some traditional peoples provided a safety net for families in economic trouble. The head of such a household could secure a loan from another household. If unable to repay the loan, he could put junior members of the family and eventually himself into servitude to the other family. In Israel, the Torah presupposes that six years of such servitude would pay off the debt, but this story implies that, in practice, householders might hold onto their bondservants, perhaps because they had nowhere to go if they were released—hence the fine print in the rules in Exod 21:2–6 and Deut 15:12–17. The fifty-year provision of Lev 25 also relates to the difficulty of seeing that householders observed these guidelines. Among other peoples in Israel's world, occasional proclamations by kings, especially at the beginning of their reigns, have the same background. The provisions show that having good laws is one thing; living by them rather than evading them is another. Anyone can agree that we should care for needy people; nobody wants to compromise their living standards in this connection. We'd like the government to do it, which, in a way, might be what Zedekiah tries to do in this story.

vv. 8–11	The curators' introduction to Jeremiah's message and its background
v. 12	The curators' resumptive introduction to Jeremiah's message
vv. 13–22	Jeremiah's message:
vv. 13–16	Yahweh's review of events:
vv. 13–14a	How Yahweh made a pledge with the ancestors
v. 14b	How they failed to listen
v. 15	How the present generation turned
v. 16	How they then turned back
vv. 17–22	Yahweh's consequent intentions:
vv. 17–18	He will grant a release and make them a horror
vv. 19–20	He will see to their slaughter
vv. 21–22	He will surrender Zedekiah to the Babylonians

The story's dynamics have points of comparison with some other stories in the scroll. Like some other accounts of symbolic actions, it includes a commission to pass on Yahweh's message; like some of these actions, it includes no account of his doing so. The curators again tell the story as a message to Judahites after 587 in a way that functions to explain the fall of Jerusalem; vv. 21–22 are its climax. And it parallels Jer 32 in telling its story in dramatic fashion rather than wholly in chronological order, raising questions and (sometimes) answering them later.[399]

8 The mere fact that householders had bondservants does not imply that they were doing anything wrong. For the audience of the story, the information about the proclamation would raise the question of the nature of the proclamation and the reason for it but not answer this question. Indeed, the information would point in one or two directions that are different from the answer that, by implication, Yahweh eventually provides. First, the story refers to the king solemnizing a pledge and making a proclamation for which there is no provision in the Torah, though it recalls the action of Zedekiah's father in 2 Kgs 23 and it parallels proclamations other kings in Israel's world might make, especially at the beginning of their reigns.[400] Second, Zedekiah leads the entire city in a pledge *to proclaim a release* to bondservants—he did not solemnize it to them but along with them. *Release* (*dərôr*) comes only in this chapter and in Lev 25:10 (which prescribes that every fifty years there should be a release or return of land that has been mortgaged because people were in economic trouble), Ezek 46:17 (which refers to that year), and Isa 61:1 (which uses it as a metaphor). Thus the passage is talking about something that is a cross between the freeing of servants after six years, the releasing of land after fifty years, and the proclamation of release by a king about which we know from other ancient sources. Zedekiah's action does not correspond to any single formulation in the Torah.[401]

9 The implicit basis for this act of release is that a bondservant is a *brother*, a member of your extended family. Yahweh has no problem in principle with

---

399. Cf. K. A. D. Smelik, "The Inner Cohesion of Jeremiah 34:8–22," in *Torah and Tradition: Papers Read at the Sixteenth Joint Meeting of the Society for Old Testament Study and the Oudtestamentisch Werkgezelschap, Edinburgh, 20th July – 23rd July 2015.*, ed. K. Spronk and H. Barstad, OTS 70 (Leiden: Brill, 2017), 239–50.

400. From the previous millennium, see "The Edict of Ammisaduqa," *ANET*, 526–28; J. J. Finkelstein, "Ammiṣaduqa's Edict and the Babylonian Law Codes," *Journal of Cuneiform Studies* 15 (1961): 91–104.

401. P. D. Miller, "Jeremiah," on the passage; cf. M. Kessler, "The Law of Manumission in Jer 34," *BZ* 15 (1971): 105–8; J. Berman, "The Legal Blend in Biblical Narrative (Joshua 20:1–9, Judges 6:25–31, 1 Samuel 15:2, 28:3–25, 2 Kings 4:1–7, Jeremiah 34:12–17, Nehemiah 5:1–12)," *JBL* 134 (2015): 110–11; M. Leuchter, "The Manumission Laws in Leviticus and Deuteronomy: The Jeremiah Connection," *JBL* 127 (2008): 635–53.

temporary servitude for debt; the question is whether people treat their servants as brothers (as Leviticus and Deuteronomy both urge) and thus (for instance) release them when the time comes. Here, the curators initially refer to the bondservants as Hebrews, a designation that came to convey some irony. For Christians, "Hebrews" is a natural way to refer to Israelites or Jews, but within the First Testament its usage matches that of related words in other ancient languages that are not so much ethnic or religious terms as sociological ones. It's the word that another nation would use to describe an Israelite living as an outsider among them, not a word Israelites would normally use of themselves.[402] The reference to the pledge incorporates a reminder that bondservants are not outsiders. Householders could fall into thinking of them as outsiders, when their bondservants are people who have lost possession of their land. But they are Judahites. They are brothers and sisters.

10 The chapter does not indicate why the city agreed to the pledge. It might be a response to some challenge to take the Torah seriously, if people expected Yahweh to change his mind about surrendering the city to the Babylonians—a challenge like Jeremiah's exhortation about the Sabbath (17:19–27). Or it might be designed to free the servants to fight.[403] Or it might be designed to bolster the servants' commitment to the city and discourage them from defecting to the Babylonians.[404] Or it might be a more cynical result of households being aware that they had no great use for servants when the city was under siege. The servants could not labor in the fields, and the cost of feeding them exceeded their usefulness; *for themselves* may hint that the decision was selfish.[405] Would they have taken account of the expectations in Deut 15:13–14? Could they have done so during a siege?[406] And where would the servants go? Would it be feasible to get back to their own lands and homesteads during a blockade?

11 The story does not answer such questions; it is interested in the fact that, for some reason, the heads of households changed their minds. *They turned back after this and turned the servants and the maidservants back*: the curators repeat the verb *turn*, with its wide range of meanings that Jer 3 made

402. See, e.g., D. E. Fleming, "Hebrews," in *Dictionary of the Old Testament: Historical Books*, ed. B. T. Arnold and H. G. M. Williamson (Downers Grove, IL: InterVarsity, 2005), 386–90.

403. Blayney, *Jeremiah*, 382.

404. M. L. Wisser ("the Malbim") in his *Commentary on Biblical Literature* (c. 1874), as quoted in Rosenberg, *Jeremiah*, 2:280.

405. R. A. Jacobson, "A Freedom That Is No Freedom: Jeremiah 34 and the Sabbatical Principle," *WW* 22 (2002): 396–405.

406. R. P. Carroll, *Jeremiah*, OTL, 648.

use of. Perhaps they missed them as workers; perhaps the servants were only too willing to return if they had lost their source of food and a roof over their heads. But the curators say that they *forced* them (*kābaš*), the word used in Gen 1:28; Esth 7:8;[407] and the similar context of Neh 5:5. Thus the entire story would speak to the Neh 5 situation.[408]

12–13 The account of the pledge and the reneging have been a long periphrasis through vv. 8b–11, with no mention of Yahweh or of Jeremiah. It has thus raised the question what Yahweh and Jeremiah will have to say about the events described. The delay between the word's announcement and its revealing parallels that in Jer 32. The pledge was just something that was going on in which neither Yahweh nor Jeremiah was involved. Whatever was the background, the reneging is the action that spurs Yahweh into involvement. Now the rhetoric goes into reverse, with the great stress on Yahweh's speaking in vv. 12–13a. Initially, it's the involvement of a *pledge* that draws him in. *I myself* sets up a contrast with *for themselves* in v. 8. But instead of answering the questions that vv. 8–11 raise for the curious reader, Yahweh first sets the event in the context of the pledge he himself solemnized in connection with getting the Israelites released from a household of servants.

14 He goes on (secondly) to set the event in the context of one of the requirements of that pledge, that they would let their own servants go after six years, further complicating the relationship of the story to the passages in the Torah that we have noted. Exodus 21:2–6 presupposes that bondservants gain their freedom after six years, which will mean six years after they individually committed themselves to their servitude; the seventh year will not be the same for all bondservants. Deuteronomy 15 presupposes that every seven years there is a general remission of debts; the seventh year is the same for all bondservants. That difference may link with the quirk that Yahweh refers to release at *the end of seven years*, whereas Exod 21 and Deut 15 imply that the release comes after six years. Possibly, Yahweh simply speaks idiomatically; *at the end of seven years* means "at the end of the seven-year period" which means "in the seventh year." One might compare the statement that God finished work on the seventh day (Gen 2:2), when, more literally, he finished on the sixth. But Yahweh's wording may link with the reference to the end of the seventh year in Deut 31:10, the occasion of the septennial reading of the Torah; and it's been suggested that 590 was the seventh year,

---

407. Holladay, *Commentary on Jeremiah*, 2:241.
408. S. Chavel, "'Let My People Go': Emancipation, Revelation, and Scribal Activity in Jeremiah 34.8–14," *JSOT* 76 (1997): 93–95.

when the reading of the Torah would have been due.[409] This consideration adds to the indications that the unit is not working with one theory or process concerning the release of bondservants or assuming that Zedekiah and his contemporaries would be doing so. Having introduced this reference to the seven-years rule, Yahweh then (thirdly) adds that the community's action matches the way it has always behaved.

15–16 To release these servants would have meant "to accept a loss that will not be recovered,"[410] to deny that economic considerations—considerations of profit—have the final word. It's hard to maintain that stance. Yahweh elaborates on the community's waywardness in this connection. He has already confirmed the implied critique of it in the preamble in vv. 8–11, that its reneging took no account of the fact that a bondservant is a *brother*, a member of your extended family. He now adds (fourthly) that the servant who is your brother is also your *neighbor*, a fellow member of the community. Here, it is the word *neighbor* that is set over against *Hebrew* (which has a prominent place in Deut 15:12). The implication is that while Israelites over the years have not fulfilled the requirement to release their bondservants after six years, they have *turned today*. Chronologically it wasn't *today*, but the word suggests another resonance from the rules about remission, where it appears twice (Deut 15:5, 15): today is the day when one hears Yahweh's word and does what it says. Within Jeremiah, the word *turned* is significant—the word that recurred in Jer 3. The usage here again makes clear that turning or repentance does not mean (or does not merely mean) feeling sorry or saying you are sorry. It means turning around. The Judahites *did what was right in my eyes in proclaiming a release individually to his neighbor*. It was real turning;[411] maybe they did give them means of support for their lives outside the provision of their "adopted" family. How amazed and how excited would Jeremiah have been—and Yahweh too. There is joy in heaven over one sinner who repents (Luke 15:7, 10). The Judahites showed how serious they were by solemnizing their pledge *before me in the house over which my name is proclaimed*, like Josiah (2 Kgs 23:3). But then they *turned back* again and *turned* the people *back* and *forced them to become servants and maidservants* again. As the solemnizing of the pledge before Yahweh added to its force, so going back on their commitment meant (fifthly) that they *defiled my name* (*ḥālal piel*). Defiling the country was bad (16:18), but defiling or desecrating

409. So Archbishop James Ussher, *The Annals of the World* (London: Crook and Bedell, 1658), 90; cf. Blayney, *Jeremiah*, 382. For modern theories along these lines, see Keown, Scalise, and Smothers, *Jeremiah 26–52*, 186–87. L. S. Fried and D. N. Freedman argue that it was the jubilee year ("Was the Jubilee Year Observed in Preexilic Judah?," in J. Milgrom, *Leviticus 23–27* [New York: Doubleday, 2001], 2257–70).

410. Pixley, *Jeremiah*, 110.

411. Fretheim, *Jeremiah*, 489.

Yahweh's name . . . To invoke Yahweh's name as you make a commitment to do something is to recognize the extraordinary, special nature of that name because it refers to the great God. To go back on that commitment is to treat Yahweh as ordinary, as nothing.

17-20 The indictment invites the audience to stop asking the interesting questions raised by vv. 8–11 and instead to ask a more urgent one: what would Yahweh do in light of this indictment? It thus leads into a threat. Actually, the audience knows the answer to that question—they have been on the receiving end of Yahweh's fulfilling the threat. In a strange way, the story brings them good news: there was a reason for the catastrophe that came on the city, which Jeremiah had kept saying would come upon it. Yahweh continues to inspire Jeremiah with his wordsmithing. You have pulled back from *proclaiming a release*? Okay, *here am I, proclaiming a release to you*: the punishment will fit the crime.[412] The declaration leads into a reference to Jeremiah's favorite trio, *sword, epidemic*, and *hunger* and to one of his favorite fates, becoming *something horrific to all the kingdoms of the earth* (15:4; 24:9; 29:18). Then, momentarily, he returns to this specific situation. They *overstepped my pledge*? They *did not implement the words of the pledge that they solemnized before me*? Then he adds a useful spelling out of what this solemnizing involved: a *calf that they cut into two and passed between the parts*. The one other passage in the First Testament that illumines their formal oathtaking procedure is Gen 15:7–20. It will have involved bringing a calf and dismembering it so that they could walk through the midst of the pieces of the calf while saying, "May my fate be the same as this calf's if I do not keep this pledge that I am making"; hence the expression *solemnized a pledge* is literally "cut a pledge." The entire people had prayed to be dismembered, and they will be. There is a treaty dating from the eighth century inscribed on rock, made with the king of Arpad and found near Aleppo, that includes among its sanctions the prayer that the king of Arpad and his courtiers should be cut up as "this calf is cut up" (the number and variety of the curses indicate that they are metaphors, but the calf seems literal).[413] In another treaty with the Assyrians, the king of Arpad prays that he, his family, his officials, and his people may have their heads torn off in the same way as the lamb sacrificed in connection with the ceremony has its head torn off.[414] The punishment will symbolically fit the crime. The pledge said, "May we be cut up as this animal was cut up." The consequence

---

412. P. D. Miller, "Sin and Judgment in Jeremiah 34:17–19," *JBL* 103 (1984): 611–13.

413. *ANET*, 660. A. S. Kapelrud questions whether people would be familiar with an analogy between the fate of the animal and their prospective fate ("The Interpretation of Jeremiah 34, 18ff," *JSOT* 22 [1982]: 138–40); if not, Yahweh's introducing it would be the more frightening.

414. *ANET*, 532–33.

of contravening it is to be released to death as they released the servants to servitude.[415] In this connection, Yahweh returns to familiar Jeremianic lingo: they will lose their lives to their enemies, *their corpse will become food for the bird of the heavens and for the animal of the earth.*

21 Finally, Yahweh gives the audience a further snippet of information on the precise context of the episode. Nebuchadrezzar has relieved his initial blockade of Jerusalem in order to go and fight the Egyptians (37:5). Apparently, it was this relief that stimulated the householders to go back on the release of the bondservants. Normality could now return. Did the relief mean people could return to their land holding and needed their servants again? Did they infer that Yahweh had responded to their turning? What was Zedekiah's role in the reversal? Was he simply going along with it and manifesting the indecision that he shows in his relationship with Jeremiah, for which he and his people pay a high price? The turning back indicates some illogic. People have forgotten that "Torah obedience within covenantal fidelity is the canon of national security. Prophecy is its advocate, with responsiveness to the prophetic mission the sign of covenantal fidelity."[416]

22 The forgetting drives Yahweh into issuing a command to the king of Babylon, who is (after all) his servant. The servant may not realize that he is responding to a command fulfilling Yahweh's purpose, but he is again doing so. "The entire history of the world revolves around the Law and the people of the Law."[417] The empire is always selfish, but God sometimes harnesses its selfishness. There is therefore one more *turn back* to report, the turn that the audience has experienced. It maybe reminds them that they have some turning to do.

3. A Reminder About the Rechabites and a Promise from Their Time (35:1–19 [LXX 42:1–19])

¹*The word that came to Jeremiah from Yahweh in the days of Jehoiakim ben Josiah King of Judah.* ²*Go*ᵃ *to the Rechabites' household*ᵇ *and speak with them;*ᶜ *have them come to Yahweh's house to one of the rooms and give them wine to drink.*

³*So I got Jaazaniah ben Jeremiah, the son of Habazzaniah, his brothers, all his sons, and the entire household of the Rechabites* ⁴*and had them come to Yahweh's house to the room of the sons of Hanan ben Igdaliah,*ᵈ *a man in touch*

415. Wright, *Jeremiah*, 361–62.
416. Diamond, "Jeremiah," 593.
417. Duhm, *Jeremia*, 284.

with God,[e] which is next to the officials' room, which is above the room of Maaseiah ben Shallum, a threshold guardian. [5]*Before the members of the Rechabites' household I put pitchers full of wine and chalices, and said to them, "Drink some wine."* [6]*But they said, "We don't drink wine, because Jonadab ben Rechab our ancestor ordered us: You will not drink wine, you or your descendants, for all time.* [7]*And a house you will not build, seed you will not sow, a vineyard you will not plant. You will not have it. Because you will dwell in tents all your days, in order that you may live many days on the face of the land where you're residing.* [8]*We have listened to the voice of Jehonadab[f] ben Rechab our ancestor in all that he ordered us, so as not to drink wine all our days, we, our wives, our sons, and our daughters,* [9]*and so as not to build houses for us to dwell in, and not to have[g] vineyard and field and seed.* [10]*So we've dwelt in tents, and we've listened and acted in accordance with all that Jonadab our ancestor ordered us.* [11]*But when Nebuchadrezzar King of Babylon advanced into the country, we said, Come on, let's come to Jerusalem, from before the Chaldeans' force and before Aram's[h] force. So we've dwelt in Jerusalem."[i]*

[12]*Then Yahweh's word came to Jeremiah.[j]* [13]*Yahweh of Armies, the God of Israel, has said this. Go and say to the individual in Judah and to the people living in Jerusalem: Won't you receive restraint so as to listen to my words? (Yahweh's affirmation).* [14]*It was implemented, the words of Jehonadab ben Rechab,[k] in that he ordered his descendants not to drink wine. They haven't drunk until this day, because they listened to their ancestor's order.[l] But I—I spoke to you, speaking assiduously,[m] and you didn't listen to me.* [15]*I sent to you my servants the prophets, sending assiduously, to say, "Please turn, each individual from his dire way. Make your practices good, don't go after other gods and serve them, and dwell[n] on the land that I gave to you and to your ancestors." But you didn't bend your ear, you didn't listen to me.* [16]*Because the descendants of Jehonadab ben Rechab implemented their ancestor's order that he gave them, but this people—they have not listened to me.[o]*

[17]*Therefore, Yahweh, the God of Armies, the God of Israel, has said this. Here am I, causing to come to Judah and to all the people who live in Jerusalem all the dire trouble that I spoke against them, since I spoke to them and they didn't listen, I called to them and they didn't answer.*

[18]*But to the Rechabites' household, Jeremiah said: Yahweh of Armies, the God of Israel, has said this. Since you listened to the order of Jehonadab your ancestor and kept all his orders and acted in accordance with all that he ordered you,[p]* [19]*therefore Yahweh of Armies, the God of Israel, has said this:[q]*
There will not be cut off an individual for Jonadab ben Rechab
  standing[r] before me, all the days.[s]

a. The infinitive absolute is used imperatively; so also in v. 13; cf. 2:2 and the translation note on it.

b. Rather than their "house," as they were presumably camped out in the city (Thompson, *Jeremiah*, 616), and *bayit* means *household* in vv. 3, 5.

c. LXX lacks *and speak with them*.

d. LXX has Gedaliah, a more familiar name.

e. Lit. "man of God"; see the commentary.

f. Contrast the spelling in v. 6; both spellings recur in the chapter in MT (LXX and Vg have only the short form). Cf. the alternating of names such as Jehoram and Joram elsewhere.

g. Lit. "and there will not be for us"; the finite verb (oddly singular, following the three nouns) continues the infinitival construction.

h. LXX has "the Assyrians'"; Syr has "Edom's."

i. MT has a unit marker here.

j. LXX has "to me"; the whole of vv. 3–19 thus becomes Jeremiah's words. L. J. de Regt sees this difference as an example of how MT and LXX can be more or less dramatic in their presentation of Jeremiah ("The Prophet in the Old and New Edition of Jeremiah," in *The New Things: Eschatology in Old Testament Prophecy. Festschrift for Henk Leene*, ed. F. Postma, K. Spronk, and E. Talstra [Maastricht: Shaker, 2002], 173).

k. *The words of Jehonadab ben Rechab* have the object marker as if the verb were "people implemented" (LXX translates the verb thus); see DG 95a; Joüon 128b.

l. LXX lacks *until this day because they listened to their ancestor's order*.

m. See the translation note and commentary on 7:13; the usage comes again in the next verse.

n. The further imperative expresses the consequences of the imperatives earlier in the sentence (GK 110i; Joüon 116f).

o. MT^L has a section marker here.

p. MT^L has a section marker here.

q. LXX has a different and much briefer version of vv. 17b–19a, which has vv. 18–19 continuing to address Judah rather than addressing the Rechabites.

r. Tg renders "ministering."

s. MT has a unit marker here.

Part 3 moves toward the completion of the chiasm comprising Jer 26–36 as it moves backward from the reign of Zedekiah to the reign of Jehoiakim, and the curators tell of another of Jeremiah's symbolic acts with its associated message as a further example of how "people and events are transformed into signs and symbols" in the Jeremiah scroll.[418] The event issues in a commission to go and speak to the people of Judah and Jerusalem and in a renewed promise for the Rechabites, but there is again no account of the message being passed on or of the story being told to the Judahites, though there were implicitly some witnesses for the event as there were for the smashing of the chalice in Jer 19. Within the framework of the storytelling, the curators quote

---

418. Diamond, "Jeremiah," 595. C. H. Knights makes a particular comparison with 18:1–11 ("The Structure of Jeremiah 35," *ExpT* 106 [1994–95]: 142–44).

Jeremiah's account of events in vv. 3–11 or perhaps simply tell that section of the story in a more vivid way, as if Jeremiah were speaking.

In the unfolding of chapters 26–36, this story pairs with 34:8–22.[419]

- It is a *word that came to Jeremiah from Yahweh*, its background is pressure on the city from Nebuchadrezzar, and it is set in the reign of one of Judah's last two most notorious kings.
- It works dramatically rather than chronologically, raises questions that it will answer only later if at all, and contains a message for Judah but no account of the message's delivery.
- It has a context in an event in the temple, and it suggests a contrast between two groups—the Rechabites refusing wine in accordance with their ancestor's word over against the householders' failing to free servants in accordance with their own word and Yahweh's.
- It portrays the Rechabites as consistent and steadfast, the householders as fickle and unreliable.
- It makes an *a fortiori* contrast between people who would live by their ancestor's word and people who would not even live by their God's word, setting a story about fidelity over against a story about a breach of fidelity.[420]
- It incorporates an indictment (*then Yahweh's word came to Jeremiah*, v. 12) followed by a threat (*therefore Yahweh has said this*, v. 17).
- It complements a message relating to what Yahweh said in the provisions of the Torah and one relating to what Yahweh said through prophets.
- It talks about listening, bending ears, and turning, issues a promise to people who listened that contrasts with the threat to people who didn't listen, and complements the threat involving parody with a promise involving parody.
- The story's implicit listeners are again the curators' audience after 587, for whom it explains why the calamity happened; they overhear the message Yahweh addresses to the Judahites of Jehoiakim's day and in their imagination see the symbolic event.

v. 1	The curators' introduction to the message that came to Jeremiah
v. 2	The message

419. See further E. A. Martens, "Narrative Parallelism and Message in Jeremiah 34–38," in *Early Jewish and Christian Exegesis: Studies in Memory of William Hugh Brownlee*, ed. C. A. Evans and W. F. Stinespring, Homage Series (Atlanta: Scholars, 1987), 33–49.

420. Weiser, *Jeremia*, 319, 323.

vv. 3–11   Jeremiah's account of the action he then took:
    vv. 3–5   How he took some Rechabites to a temple room and offered them wine
    vv. 6–10   How and why they refused
    v. 11   How they came to be in Jerusalem at that time
    v. 12   The curators' introduction to a message that then came to Jeremiah
vv. 13–17   The message for Judah and Jerusalem
    v. 13a   The introduction
    v. 13b   A commission to go speak to the people
    vv. 13c–16   A challenge and rebuke to them for their disobedience
    v. 17   A threat of calamity to come as a consequence
v. 18a   The curators' introduction to Jeremiah's message for the Rechabites
vv. 18b–19   The message for the Rechabites
    v. 18b   A commendation
    v. 19   A promise of blessing to come as a consequence

Once again, at different points variation between LXX and MT may issue from haplography or just a desire for succinctness, as was the case in Jer 34.[421]

1–2 The story again begins with an introduction raising as many questions as it answers. *In the days of Jehoiakim* is a bit vague. What are *the Rechabites* doing in Jerusalem, given that they foreswore living in the city? Do they live as one household, so are there not a huge number of them? Why is Jeremiah to tempt them with alcohol? And why is the temple the proposed venue for the experiment? Nor will the chapter explain everything and make everything obvious, even though (in MT) it is prolix in detail.[422]

3–4 The story segues into a report expressed in the form of Jeremiah's own words, as happened in Jer 27–28. Jaazaniah and his brothers are apparently the senior figures in the Rechabite household, Jaazaniah being "the head of the brotherhood."[423] Like a church, the temple complex had a number of rooms, functioning as stores, vestries, meeting rooms, and offices (see Neh 13:4–5), and the entire family assembles in one of them—which confirms that they are not a big group. Hanan is *a man in touch with God*, literally "a man of God"; it would be nice to assume that he was a man of God in

---

421. Lundbom, *Jeremiah 21–36*, 571–80; contrast W. McKane, "Jeremiah and the Rechabites," *ZAW* 100 (1988): 106–23.
422. McKane, *Jeremiah*, 2:886.
423. Duhm, *Jeremia*, 285.

the English sense, but this connotation does not attach to the expression *'îš hā'ĕlōhîm* (for which see, e.g., 2 Kgs 1–9). It may suggest he was a prophet (Tg), which could explain his having an office at the temple, where prophets exercised their ministry to people; his *sons* might be people he was training, like "the sons of the prophets" in 2 Kgs 1–9. His room's location near those of a threshold guardian and of the officials marks it out as important, though the officials might not enthuse about Jeremiah's commandeering a room in the temple. They might be especially unhappy for a collection of people comparable to "first-generation Quakers, Mennonites, Shakers,"[424] a "scruffy bunch" of teetotal alternative-lifestyle folk, to be offered free drinks by God's prophet, "and it's all happening in church."[425] Perhaps Jeremiah had the event take place in a room visible to people in the temple area for maximum publicity (cf. 36:10),[426] or perhaps, on the contrary, he staged the event in a side room for privacy even while making it one that happened in Yahweh's presence. The *guardian* was presumably one of the three senior figures in the priestly body of threshold guardians (see 52:24), who appear in a number of passages in 2 Kings in connection with collecting offerings and looking after things in the temple (2 Kgs 12:9; 22:4; 23:4; 2 Chr 34:9).

5–7 Perhaps Hanan or Maaseiah could also produce wine from the temple store. One way or another, anyway, Jeremiah produces the wine, and not in small quantities. He is not testing the Rechabites in the sense of seeking to discover whether they will stand by their principles.[427] For the purposes of the message they will help him to convey, it is important that he can presuppose that they will stand firm. Their having come to live in the city might seem to make this a more hazardous assumption than it would once have been, but if they were living in tents in Jerusalem, maybe they could claim they had not been involved in compromise. Anyway, they duly refuse the wine and give some explanation for their stance. Jeremiah did not need the explanation, and maybe neither did the audience of this story. It is there to make explicit the background to what follows. Their ancestor Jonadab/ Jehonadab (a different Jonadab from the one in 2 Sam 13) otherwise appears only in 2 Kgs 10:15–27, where he supports Jehu in cleaning out worship of the Master from Samaria. This locates him in the 840s and thus indicates that the Rechabites had been a group for over two centuries.[428] Rechab belonged to the Kenites (1 Chr 2:55), the same group as Moses's father-

---

424. Berrigan, *Jeremiah*, 150.
425. Wright, *Jeremiah*, 363.
426. So Isaac Abravanel, *Commentary on the Latter Prophets*.
427. So Rudolph, *Jeremia*, 227.
428. See further H. B. Huffmon, "The Rechabites in the Book of Jeremiah and Their Historical Roots in Israel," in Lundbom, Evans, and Anderson, *Jeremiah*, 191–210.

in-law, who were adopted into Israel and evidently became "a hard-core Yahwistic clan,"[429] in Samaria rather than in Judah. They were Bedouin-like[430] coppersmiths, metalworkers, and/or sheep herders, which links with the commitments that they describe to Jeremiah but would make them seem in various ways "exotic" in Jerusalem.[431] Their "adoption" and their commitment to Yahweh did not mean that they had an allocation of land; they remained resident aliens.[432] They were in a position like that of Abraham.[433] But Jonadab had promised them that living as he prescribed would ensure that they could continue to live on the land where they dwelt as resident aliens (*gûr*): it is the first time Jeremiah has used the verb (though concern for the resident alien featured in 7:6; 14:8; 22:3), but it will recur when Jeremiah has to go off to live in Egypt in Jer 42–44. It's not clear whether they were especially loyal to Yahweh, as Jonadab was, or whether they liked the simple life,[434] but living as they did would mean they didn't look as if they were trying to take over land. The comparison and contrast between Jonadab's promise and the one attached to the fifth commandment is instructive: "in order that you may make long your days on the land that Yahweh your God is giving you" (Exod 20:12).

8–11 Their claim is couched in terms that will suit Yahweh's aims, though the story does not yet answer the question why Yahweh is engaged in this drama. The Rechabites do add a piece of information explaining their presence in Jerusalem. The invasion is perhaps the one in 2 Kgs 24:1–2, an episode in Nebuchadrezzar's ongoing assertion of authority in the region that took place in about 600. It did not issue in a siege of Jerusalem and it might not have involved the presence of Nebuchadrezzar in person any more than the city's fall in 587 did. But in prospect, it could seem a serious threat to a group of tent-dwellers, though one might see some irony in their moving to Jerusalem "since Jerusalem has become the last place where safety is to be had."[435]

12–17 Now the story comes to explain Yahweh's commission to Jeremiah, beginning with another complex and repeated account of how Yahweh speaks and issues the commission. For the last time, Yahweh picks up another of Jeremiah's favorite words, *restraint* (*mûsār*; cf. 2:19–20, 30; see the translation note and commentary there). It suggests holding someone

---

429. M. Leuchter, *Polemics of Exile*, 95.

430. Volz, *Jeremia*, 325.

431. S. V. Davidson, "'Exoticizing the Otter': The Curious Case of the Rechabites in Jeremiah 35," in Maier and Sharp, *Prophecy and Power*, 189–207.

432. Rashi, in MG.

433. Qimchi, in MG.

434. Theodoret, *Ermeneia*, PG 81:681.

435. Diamond, "Jeremiah," 585.

back from what you don't want them to do, or chastising and correcting them when they do it. One wonders whether the Rechabites would be an object of curiosity or laughter in Jerusalem. Yahweh turns such attitudes upside-down. They have something to teach. Yahweh goes on to reprove the people in terms characteristic of Jeremiah and Deuteronomy: *speaking assiduously*; *you didn't listen*; *I sent to you my servants the prophets*; *turn from your dire way*; *make your practices good*; *don't go after other gods and serve them*; *the land that I gave to you*; *you didn't bend your ear*; and so on.[436] The reference to other gods is especially noteworthy because, with 32:29, it's the only such reference between 25:6 and 44:3; and so is the reference to the spoken, prophetic word as opposed to the Torah. From the indictment, the regular consequences will follow, with further, sometimes ironic links to indictments and threats elsewhere (e.g., 7:13, 27; 11:11, 14; 33:3).

18–19 In contrast to the threat, there is a promise for the Rechabites, who offer "a case study in fidelity" to set against the case study in infidelity in Jer 34.[437] While "such clear-cut, unambiguous categories of 'good guys' and 'bad guys' are easy to fault,"[438] pedagogically many people find them helpful and encouraging. Yahweh does not imply that the Rechabites' lifestyle is preferable to the regular Judahite lifestyle, though their commitment to a simple and carefree life merits reflection: "Everyone who keeps those laws should have the title 'son of Jonadab ben Rechab.'"[439] Yahweh's point is rather that they did what they were bidden to do. If only Judah would do the same! Thus he gives them a "parody" of his promise to David and to the Levites (see 33:17–22)[440]— as if they were as important as them! They will not be reigning like David or offering sacrifice like the Levites, but they will be *standing before me*, which is what servants do in their position of privilege and access as they attend on their master (7:10; 15:1, 19; 18:20; 40:10). For the Rechabites, this promise is a reward for faithfulness rather than one made in spite of failure.[441] As is the case with those other promises, we have a hard time knowing what cash value they turned out to have. "There was *infinitely* more hope for this fringe group than for mainstream Judaism";[442] yet we hear virtually nothing about them in Second Temple times except the paradoxical note in Neh 3:14, which raises the question what a Rechabite is doing building the walls of Jerusalem. The

---

436. See D. R. Jones, *Jeremiah*, 434–35.
437. Brueggemann, *Jeremiah 26–52*, 104.
438. Stulman, *Jeremiah*, 293.
439. Theodoret, *Ermeneia*, PG 81:681.
440. Pixley, *Jeremiah*, 112–13.
441. Keown, Scalise, and Smothers, *Jeremiah 26–52*, 194.
442. Allen, *Jeremiah*, 393.

Mishnah (m. Ta'anit 4:5) does report that the Rechabites had a place on the roster for bringing wood to the temple for the altar fire.

4. A Story about Jehoiakim and a Threat from His Time (36:1–32 [LXX 43:1–32]

[1]*In the fourth year of Jehoiakim ben Josiah King of Judah, this word came to Jeremiah[a] from Yahweh.* [2]*"Get yourself a scroll document, and you will write in it all the words that I have spoken to you about Israel[b] and about Judah and about all the nations from the day I spoke to you, from the days of Josiah[c] and until this day.* [3]*Perhaps the household of Judah may listen to all the dire trouble that I am planning to do to them, in order that they may turn each one from his dire path and I may pardon their waywardness and their wrongdoing."[d]*

[4]*So Jeremiah summoned Baruch ben Neriah, and Baruch wrote from Jeremiah's dictation all Yahweh's words that he had spoken to him, on the scroll document.* [5]*Jeremiah ordered Baruch: "I'm under restraint[e]—I can't come to Yahweh's house.* [6]*So you are the one who will come[f] and read out Yahweh's words in the scroll that you have written from my dictation, in the ears of the people in Yahweh's house on a fast day. And also in the ears of all Judah that come from their towns you will read them out.* [7]*Perhaps their prayer for grace will fall[g] before Yahweh and they may turn each one from his dire path. Because the anger and the fury is great of which Yahweh has spoken concerning this people."* [8]*Baruch ben Neriah acted in accordance with all that Jeremiah the prophet ordered him by reading out Yahweh's words in the document in Yahweh's house.[h]*

[9]*So in the fifth[i] year of Jehoiakim ben Josiah King of Judah, in the fifth month, the entire people in Jerusalem and the entire people who came from the towns of Judah proclaimed a fast before Yahweh in Jerusalem.[j]* [10]*And Baruch read out Jeremiah's words in the document in Yahweh's house, in the room of Gemariah ben Shaphan the scribe, in the upper court, at the entrance of the new[k] gateway of Yahweh's house, in the entire people's ears.*

[11]*Micaiah, the son of Gemariah ben Shaphan, listened to all the words of Yahweh from the document* [12]*and went down to the king's house to the scribe's room. And there, all the officials were sitting there: Elishama the scribe, Delaiah ben Shemaiah, Elnathan ben Achbor,[l] Gemariah ben Shaphan, Zedekiah ben Hananiah, with all the officials.* [13]*Micaiah told them all the words that he had listened to as Baruch read out in the document in the people's ears.* [14]*Then all the officials sent Jehudi ben Nethaniah, the son of Shelemaiah ben Cushi, to Baruch to say, "The scroll which you read out in the people's ears—do get it in your hand, go."*

So Baruch ben Neriah got the scroll in his hand and came to them. [15]*They said to him, "Sit down,*[m] *please, and read it out in our ears."* [16]*Then, when they had listened to all these words, they were fearful,*[n] *each one toward his neighbor, and they said to Baruch,*[o] *"We must definitely tell*[p] *the king all these words."* [17]*Baruch himself they asked, "Tell us, please, how you wrote all these words from his dictation."* [18]*Baruch said to them, "From his dictation he would read out all these words to me, with me writing on the document in ink."*[q] [19]*The officials said to Baruch, "Go hide, you and Jeremiah. No one is to know where you are."* [20]*And they came to the king in the courtyard, but the scroll they deposited*[r] *in the room of Elishama the scribe.*

They recounted all these words in the king's ears. [21]*So the king sent Jehudi to get the scroll, and he got it from the room of Elishama the scribe. Jehudi read it out in the king's ears and in the ears of all the officials who were standing around the king,* [22]*with the king sitting in the winter house in the ninth month,*[s] *with a brazier before him ignited.*[t] [23]*Then, as Jehudi read out three or four columns, he*[u] *would rip it with a scribe's knife and throw it*[v] *into the fire that was in the brazier, until the entire scroll had come to an end in the fire that was in the brazier.* [24]*The king and all his servants who were listening to all these words were not fearful, and they did not rip their clothes.* [25]*Moreover Elnathan, Delaiah, and Gemariah—they interposed with the king not*[w] *to burn up the scroll, but he didn't listen to them.*[x] [26]*The king ordered Jerahmeel, the king's son, Seraiah ben Azriel, and Shelemaiah ben Abdiel*[y] *to get Baruch the scribe and Jeremiah, but Yahweh hid them.*[z]

[27]*Yahweh's word came to Jeremiah after the king's burning up the scroll with the words that Baruch had written from Jeremiah's dictation:* [28]*Again, get yourself another scroll and write on it all the earlier words that were on the earlier scroll that Jehoiakim King of Judah burned up.* [29]*And about Jehoiakim King of Judah you are to say, Yahweh has said this: You are the one who burned up this scroll, saying, Why have you written in it, "The king of Babylon will definitely come and devastate this country and make human being and animal cease from it"?*[aa] [30]*Therefore, Yahweh has said this about Jehoiakim King of Judah: He will not have someone sitting on David's throne. His corpse, it will have been thrown out to the heat by day and to the cold by night.* [31]*I will attend, for him and for his offspring and for his servants, to their waywardness.*[bb] *I will let come on them and on the people who live in Jerusalem and on the individual in Judah all the dire trouble of which I spoke to them, but they did not listen.*[cc]

[32]*So Jeremiah*[dd] *got another scroll and gave it to Baruch ben Neriah the scribe, and he wrote on it from Jeremiah's dictation all the words in the document that Jehoiakim King of Judah had burned up in the fire. There was also added to them many words like them.*[ee]

a. LXX has "to me."

b. LXX has "Jerusalem," not *Israel*, perhaps because Ephraim would not be of interest to the presumed Egyptian setting of LXX's text (Holladay, *Commentary on Jeremiah*, 2:255).

c. LXX has "Josiah King of Judah."

d. MT has a section marker here.

e. Lit. "restrained" or "barred" (Bright, *Jeremiah*, 176, 179); see the commentary.

f. LXX omits *so you are the one who will come.*

g. LXX translates "mercy for them will fall"; see the commentary.

h. MT has a marker here.

i. For MT *haḥămišît*, LXX implies *hašəmînît* ("eighth")

j. LXX also has "and the household of Judah."

k. Tg has "eastern," as at 26:10.

l. There are variants in LXX in connection with the names of Delaiah and Elnathan.

m. For MT *šēb*, LXX and Tg imply *šub* ("repeat").

n. LXX "took counsel" may imply *pāḥərû* (cf. HUBP and *DCH*, 6:678, for the root).

o. LXX lacks *to Baruch.*

p. The infinitive precedes the finite verb, underlining the necessity.

q. LXX lacks *in ink* (*baddəyô*), a hapax legomenon in the First Testament but known from later Hebrew and Aramaic. MT has a marker here.

r. The *waw*-consecutive is anomalous, as the depositing preceded the coming to the king.

s. LXX lacks *in the ninth month.*

t. *Wə'et-hā'â . . . məbō'eret* has the object marker before the passive verb; see the translation note on 35:14. See also *IBHS* 25.1b; DG 94 remark 6 (though GK 117l thinks that a verb such as "he had" is presupposed); and J. Barton, "Traces of Ergativity in Biblical Hebrew," in Provan and Boda, *Let Us Go Up to Zion*, 33–44. LXX "with a fire in a brazier" makes for a more regular construction.

u. Jehudi or Jehoiakim? If it is Jehudi, he is acting on Jehoiakim's behalf.

v. The infinitive absolute continues the finite verb construction.

w. LXX Vaticanus and Sinaiticus lack the *not* (Diamond, "Jeremiah," 597)!

x. LXX lacks *but he didn't listen to them.*

y. LXX lacks *and Shelemaiah ben Abdiel.*

z. LXX has "they were hidden," an aorist passive as in v. 19; Volz (*Jeremia*, 330) sees the MT reading as a dittograph of the subsequent *wayəhî*. MT has a marker here.

aa. MT has a marker here.

bb. LXX lacks *to their waywardness.*

cc. MT^L has a section marker here.

dd. LXX has "Baruch" and then lacks *and gave it to Baruch ben Neriah the scribe.*

ee. MT has a marker here.

The final story in part 3 of the Jeremiah scroll completes the chiasm comprising Jer 26–36. It also relates to the same year as Jer 25 and pairs with it in its historical significance. The two chapters thus compare with Jer 7 and 26 as complementary reports of the same event. As well as pairing with Jer 25, the chapter forms a pair with Jer 45, which bears the same date. And like Jer 25, it faces both ways: in addition to concluding its chiasm, it leads into Jer

37–44 by suggesting how decisions taken in Jehoiakim's day bore their dire fruit over the next twenty years.

Jeremiah 36 relates to a key year in the history of Western Asia, the year Nebuchadrezzar became king of Babylon and won significant military victories, establishing his position and Babylon's position (see the commentary on Jer 25, esp. vv. 1–2). In that historical context, the opening of the chapter sets up the question that the story will need to answer. The achievements of Josiah's reformation have not lasted, and Jehoiakim has encouraged a reversion to the traditional ways of Ephraimite and Judahite kings. Yahweh does not intend to put up with the situation forever. The question is, will the people of Judah see the error of their ways? The chapter explores the question by telling a story in five acts in "one of the great narratives, not only of the book of Jeremiah but also in the whole Bible."[443]

vv. 1–8	Act 1: How Jeremiah has Baruch read to the people a collected version of Jeremiah's messages
vv. 1–3	Scene 1: Yahweh commissions Jeremiah to write down his messages
v. 4	Scene 2: Jeremiah dictates them to Baruch
vv. 5–7	Scene 3: Jeremiah commissions Baruch to go read them out
v. 8	Scene 4: Baruch does so
vv. 9–14a	Act 2: How Baruch undertook the reading: the narrative gives more information on it and continues to the consequences
vv. 9–10	Scene 1: Baruch reads the scroll in the people's hearing (we do not discover what the people thought)
vv. 11–13	Scene 2: Micaiah goes to the palace with news of what Baruch has done
v. 14a	Scene 3: Officials in the palace send for Baruch
vv. 14b–19	Act 3: How Baruch reads the scroll to the officials
vv. 14b–15	Scene 1: Baruch reads the scroll to them
v. 16	Scene 2: They panic and realize they must tell the king
vv. 17–19	Scene 3: They quiz Baruch and tell him to go hide

443. R. P. Carroll, "Manuscripts Don't Burn—Inscribing the Prophetic Tradition: Reflections on Jeremiah 36," in *"Dort ziehen Schiffe dahin . . .": Collected Communications to the XIVth Congress of the International Organization for the Study of the Old Testament, Paris 1992*, ed. M. Augustin and K.-D. Schunck, Beiträge zur Erforschung des Alten Testaments und des Antiken Judentums 28 (Frankfurt: Lang, 1996), 31.

vv. 20–26	Act 4 How the officials tell the king, who destroys the scroll
v. 20	Scene 1: They go tell the king about the scroll
v. 21	Scene 2: The king sends for it
vv. 22–24	Scene 3: The king has it read and burns it piece by piece
v. 25	Scene 4: The officials fail to stop him
v. 26	Scene 5: The king tries to get Jeremiah and Baruch arrested but fails
vv. 27–32	Act 5: How Jeremiah dictates an enlarged replacement version of the scroll
vv. 27–28	Scene 1: Yahweh commissions Jeremiah to rewrite the scroll
vv. 29–31	Scene 2: Before he does so, Yahweh gives Jeremiah an extra message for Jehoiakim
v. 32	Scene 3: Jeremiah duly re-dictates the scroll and adds to it

Like Jer 32, the chapter thus unfurls with some subtlety. It sometimes requires listeners to fill in gaps and sometimes plays out in dramatic rather than chronological order. Thus act 1 raises a question and closes by summarizing the fulfillment of Jeremiah's commission relating to that question, though without establishing the answer. It has Yahweh telling Jeremiah to get a scroll and write, but Jeremiah assumes he can employ a scribe or secretary and can get him to read out the scroll; and presumably some if not all of the explanation in scene 3 took place chronologically before the dictation in scene 2. Act 2 likewise goes back to fill in the details of Baruch's fulfillment of his commission before resuming the movement toward answering the original question. Within act 3, there is a dramatic delay between their realization that they must tell the king and their actually doing so as they quiz Baruch (which perhaps came chronologically before their realization). Within act 4, there is another dramatic delay between their reporting to the king and his reading the scroll, because they don't take the scroll with them. In contrast, things then proceed briskly and vividly; the officials' failed attempt to stop the king is reported after it actually takes place. Act 5 brings a conclusion but leaves the audience with a further series of questions, partly related to the one with which we started. Is the people's fate sealed even though they have had no opportunity to respond to Yahweh's initial question? When did Jeremiah dictate additions to the scroll, and how could he do so without being commissioned? What were the additions, and how do they relate to any form of a Jeremiah scroll that the audience knows?

Maybe the scroll got lost or destroyed in the course of the city's fall in 587, as presumably happened to the pledge chest. And maybe it's a coincidence that Jer 2–6 comprises an organized collection of Jeremiah's messages that would make sense in the context of the story told in Jer 36. Or maybe Jer 2–6 goes back to the scroll whose origins this story tells. It's a guess, but it makes sense (see "Unity of Composition," p. 7).

The story is told about Baruch, so he is unlikely to be its author.[444] A scribe's expertise would be a necessary though not a sufficient qualification for writing the kind of stories that appear in Jeremiah and in a work such as 1 and 2 Kings; in other words, the authors of those works would likely be scribes. But there is no indication that Baruch in particular had any hand in the writing up of Jeremiah's story and preaching beyond taking down dictation on this occasion. Nor does the wealth of circumstantial detail in the story establish that it must rest on eyewitness testimony. Writers of fiction may provide a wealth of circumstantial detail. Here the detailed information on people's thinking and conversations suggests that the story is the imaginative creation of a skilled writer, though this consideration, too, does not establish that it is a piece of imaginative fiction dramatizing the theological significance of events in Jehoiakim's day (a little like Gen 1 or Gen 2) rather than an account of a historical event that an author has re-created with the aid of imagination (a little like John 5 or John 6).[445] The wealth of plausible circumstantial detail may suggest that the storyteller lived close to the place and time of which it speaks (e.g., in Jerusalem, Mizpah, or Egypt in the Babylonian period).[446] One can imagine the author writing up the story after 587, when it would function as another account and explanation of why the city fell.

A further feature of the story is that people who knew the Josiah story in 2 Kings would see that Jer 36 is an upside-down version:[447]

444. See further Y. Hoffman, "Aetiology, Redaction and Historicity in Jeremiah xxxvi," *VT* 46 (1996): 181.

445. McKane (*Jeremiah*, 2:910–12) notes the shortfall in scholarly discussion of how far literary artistry and historical concern are compatible or must be in tension.

446. See J. A. Dearman's discussion of the implications of the names in Jer 36, in "My Servants the Scribes," *JBL* 109 (1990): 403–21.

447. C. D. Isbell, "2 Kings 22:3–23:24 and Jeremiah 36," *JSOT* 8 (1978): 33–45; G. J. Venema, *Reading Scripture in the Old Testament: Deuteronomy 9–10; 31, 2 Kings 22–23, Jeremiah 36, Nehemiah 8*, OTS 48 (Leiden: Brill, 2004), 95–137. C. Minette de Tillesse sees the development the other way around: the Josiah story was shaped in part as a contrast with the Jehoiakim story ("Joaqim, repoussoir du 'Pieux' Josias," *ZAW* 105 [1993]: 352–76).

2 Kgs 22–23	Jer 36
Yahweh had ordered the writing of a scroll	Yahweh orders the writing of a scroll
The scroll comes to be known in the temple	The scroll comes to be known in the temple
The head priest and Shaphan find the scroll	Shaphan's son hears the scroll read[448]
(the first of three readings)	(the first of three readings)
Shaphan tells the king	The officials in the palace tell the king
Shaphan reads the scroll to the king	Jehudi reads the scroll to the king
The king listens to the words of the scroll	The king and his staff do not listen
The king rips up his clothes	The king rips up the scroll
The king is aware of Yahweh's great wrath	Jeremiah is aware of Yahweh's great wrath
Later, the king burns objects of false worship	The king burns the scroll
The king consults a prophet about what to do	The king orders the arrest of the prophet
Yahweh says that the king will not see disaster	Yahweh says that the king will see disaster
and that the king will die in well-being	and that the king will die in humiliation

Many features of Jer 36 lack an equivalent in the Josiah story or are distinctive to the Jehoiakim story. The Jehoiakim story concerns a prophetic scroll rather than a Torah scroll. It concerns the nations as well as Israel. The event portrays the priests, secretaries, and officials in more ambiguous light and portrays an implicit difference of stance between them and the king and his court. But the similarities suggest that one significance of the Jehoiakim story is that he appears as an anti-Josiah. Josiah is not his father. This aspect of Jer 36 adds further nuance to the significance of the story after 587. It answers the question, how could things have gone so wrong when they seemed to be going so right a few decades ago? The one-word answer is Jehoiakim.[449] In

448. Dearman ("My Servants the Scribes," 410) notes the detailed interplay with the scribes' names, partly via 26:22, 24.

449. H. M. Wahl suggests how the Shaphan family continued to develop the story in Egypt ("Die Entstehung der Schriftprophetie nach Jer 36," ZAW 110 [1998]: 365–89); see also C. Hardmeier, "Zur schriftgestützten Expertentätigkeit Jeremias im Milieu der Jerusalemer Führungseliten (Jeremia 36)," in Schaper, Textualisierung der Religion, 105–49.

this context, it might also take further the logic of 16:1–9, as Jeremiah himself is almost absent from the story and "interest turns from the personality of the prophet to *the book of Jeremiah*."[450] "The scroll has taken the place of the freely spoken prophetic word."[451] In this connection, the story makes for a contrast or counterbalance to the comment in 8:8 about writing as falsifying, about writing as deformation.[452]

Some differences between LXX and MT may again result from haplography, some from LXX's deliberate simplifying, some from MT's elaborating the earlier text that lies behind both versions.

1–2 In this key year, Yahweh issues a new commission to Jeremiah; the audience is perhaps expected to recall from 25:1 why this year is important or to remember it from what they know. Baruch is to get not merely a regular *document*, which might be just a page (e.g., 3:8; 29:1; 30:2; 32:10), but a *scroll*, something long enough to need rolling up when it has been written on (codices—that is, books of the kind that the Western world is familiar with—did not come into use until the Roman period). The documentation of Yahweh's messages through Jeremiah over two decades will require much more than the equivalent of one page. At Mari on the Euphrates in the second millennium, prophecies were written down as they were uttered,[453] and one can imagine it happening in Judah, but the First Testament makes no reference to such a practice, and there would have been less reason or context for writing down the subversive prophecies of someone like Jeremiah. There is reason to do so to provoke a crisis now. Yahweh could have Jeremiah go and repeat them orally, but writing them down and then reading them is another symbolic act and speech act.[454] The text is initiated by God; it intends to evoke drastic change; it is wrought in and through human fidelity; and it is designed for public propagation (but its reception will be mixed).[455] *All the words* is a hyperbole; what Jeremiah produces is a cross section of his entire message that can be read out in one go (indeed, three times in one day), which is what Jer 2–6 comprises. It is to cover *Israel* and *Judah* and

450. Brueggemann, *Jeremiah 26–52*, 129; cf. Brummitt, "Recovering Jeremiah," 236.

451. T. Römer, "From Prophet to Scribe: Jeremiah, Huldah and the Invention of the Book," in *Writing the Bible: Scribes, Scribalism and Script*, ed. P. R. Davies and T. Römer (Durham: Acumen, 2015), 91.

452. R. P. Carroll, "Manuscripts Don't Burn," 37.

453. A. Schart, "Combining Prophetic Oracles in Mari Letters and Jeremiah 36," *JANES* 23 (1995): 75–93; see *ANET*, 623–32.

454. M. Kessler, "The Significance of Jer 36," *ZAW* 81 (1969): 381–83; J. G. McConville, "Divine Speech and the Book of Jeremiah," in *The Trustworthiness of God: Perspectives on the Nature of Scripture*, ed. P. Helm and C. R. Trueman (Leicester: Apollos, 2002), 18–38.

455. W. Brueggemann, "Haunting Book—Haunted People," *WW* 11 (1991): 62–68.

all the nations. That it should talk about Judah is natural. The reference to (Northern) Israel, Ephraim, is striking, but Ephraim has been significant for Judah because Judah needed to learn from its story (Jer 3) and because it is still part of Israel as the people of Yahweh along with Judah, as Jer 31 has presupposed. The reference to the nations reflects how the destiny of Judah and Ephraim interacts with the activity of the nations, both the big imperial powers and the little peoples who are Judah's neighbors. Jeremiah 2–6 does not refer to nations with the specificity that Jer 46–51 will (and cf. Jer 25), but it does speak of Egypt and Assyria, of the unnamed northern invader, and of "the nations."

3 *Perhaps* is a natural word to find on human lips (v. 7; cf. 20:10; 21:2). Here, it again comes on Yahweh's lips, at a point and in a connection that matches 26:3. At one level, Yahweh maybe knows the answer to the question he raises, but the verse indicates that the future really is open, interactions between Judah and Yahweh are real, Judah has real freedom and responsibility to decide how it will respond to Yahweh, and its response will make a real difference to what happens. Yahweh is prepared to undertake another investigation to see "whether the Jews were healable" because he never gets "wearied" of asking the question; he never gives up hope.[456] In a sense, the final calamity is inevitable (36:31). But it's never over until it's over. And Yahweh will watch anxiously for the response to his reaching out to his people. He wants them to *turn* because he wants the chance to *pardon*. Sometimes, he speaks as if pardon comes first and turning is a response; 31:31–34 might be an example. The risk with that way of operating is that it can seem to trivialize wrongdoing and undervalue human responsibility. So sometimes he operates the other way. You can't predict which way he will work in any given context. You can't assume pardon without turning, but neither can you exclude it. Verse 7 will nuance the point further. So v. 3 opens up a question that will eventually receive a doubly troubling answer. No, they won't turn, but it is the king's action rather than theirs that will express it—so that the *each one* (*'îš*) is especially disquieting.

> Though the words are inked-in, need we assume that the ink is indelible? The narrative suggests not. The divine command, "Take a roll of scroll and write on it," (36. 2) is supported by the divine justification: "perhaps (*'wly*) the house of Judah will hear of all the evil (*hrʻh*) I am planning to do to them, in order that they will each turn away from their evil (*hrʻh*) ways so that I may forgive them for their iniquity and their sin" (36. 3). Yhwh's *perhaps* indicates, if not indecisiveness, a future that remains *undecidable*, open. Thus, for the present, the list of evils remains just that, a list, and

---

456. Calvin, *Jeremiah*, 4:345.

one that can still be erased. . . . The *perhaps* evokes *the I would prefer not to* of which Derrida makes this comment: "It evokes a future without either predicting or promising; it utters nothing fixed, determinable, positive, or negative." . . . Paradoxically, the success of the scroll will effectively erase its content: the people's return from their evil ways will render its plans unfulfilled.[457]

4 While Baruch played a mundane role in Jer 32, chronologically that incident took place later than this one; as far as we know, this commission is the first contact between Jeremiah and Baruch. In Jeremiah's day, people will have had enough basic literacy to write their names and so on, and someone with a priestly background like Jeremiah could have written down his messages for himself. Maybe it would be natural to employ a professional secretary or scribe (*sōpēr*), as authors in the United States used to get someone to type their manuscripts. But the question why Jeremiah employed Baruch in this way is one of the questions raised earlier in the story and answered subsequently (in v. 5). While there will have been many scribes or secretaries in Jerusalem (three more are mentioned in Jer 36–37 and 52), they will have had varying religious commitments (see 8:8) and varying degrees of commitment even if they worshiped Yahweh alone. Jeremiah commissions someone who will need to be willing to do more than take down dictation (see vv. 5–19; also 45:1–5). In one sense, his role is prosaic, but it will involve danger, and he may end up guilty by association, as Jer 43 and 45 will imply.

5–6 As Yahweh had said nothing about someone other than Jeremiah writing the scroll, he had also said nothing about someone other than Jeremiah reading it. Here, Jeremiah explains both matters: he cannot go to the temple, so he has to get Baruch to write a scroll that he can then read out. But the clarification only raises a further question: Why or how is Jeremiah *under restraint*? If the answer to that question lies within the story, it might be that Yahweh is holding him back (Yahweh is often the subject of this verb, *'āṣar*) because it would be even more dangerous for him to go in person than it is for Baruch, but the use of this expression elsewhere in Jeremiah (33:1; 39:15) suggests he was under house arrest or in custody. While any community event would provide an occasion when the large number of people would be present in the temple, a fast would be an occasion appropriate to his somber message.[458]

7 Jeremiah's explanation restates the question in v. 3; the expression *they may turn each one from his dire path* recurs. It thus confirms that it is the issue

457. Brummitt, "Recovering Jeremiah," 302–3, with a quotation from J. Derrida, *The Gift of Death* (Chicago: University of Chicago, 1995), 75.

458. Calvin, *Jeremiah*, 4:348.

with which the story is concerned, though it also thereby underscores the doubly troubling nature of the answer we will eventually discover. This second *perhaps* complements the one in v. 3. If a *prayer for grace* (*təḥinnâ*) falls before someone, it involves both that people pray such a prayer and that God or a human being accepts it (37:20; 38:26; 42:2, 9). Jeremiah here expresses first the hope that a prayer for grace may fall before Yahweh and only then the hope that *they may turn each one from his dire path*. The stress thus lies on their reaching out to Yahweh in these two ways, in their prayer and in their turning. "There are two things mentioned as necessary in order to obtain pardon,—prayer, and turning." There must be both.[459] Yahweh has wondered whether they will turn, and Jeremiah wonders whether they will turn. The story will get sidetracked, and we will never discover whether they would, because the king will hijack the process and show how grievously effective the action of leaders can be. Or to put it another way, the action of the king determines what counts as the response of the people. Leadership is a frightening thing.

8 The narrative goes on to summarize Baruch's action in what could seem like the end of a story, in a formal sense. But in substance, it is only the end of the beginning. Yahweh asked a question and uttered his *perhaps*, and vv. 4–8 have not answered it; in this sense, they cannot stand on their own.

9 The storyteller now begins to elaborate things. The collocation of the dates in vv. 1 and 9 would suggest that it's nearly a year before Baruch's opportunity arrives. Admittedly, Israel had more than one way of understanding the beginning of the year, like Western peoples, so that for different purposes or at different times the year began in spring or fall; v. 1 might presuppose the fall system whereas v. 9 uses the spring system in accordance with Exod 12:2. The reading could then have happened only a few weeks after the commission.[460] But in any case, the point about the reference to *the fourth year* noted in the introduction to this chapter (see especially 25:1; 46:2) is that Yahweh's commission relates to the political and historical context of the accession of Nebuchadrezzar. That event will turn him into Yahweh's servant, with devastating implications for Judah if it continues to ignore Jeremiah. On the basis of the year starting in the spring, the ninth month is around December. There is no set fast at that time, though m. Ta'anit 1:5–6 prescribes fasts for this month if the rains have not yet come,[461] and this fast might relate to such a need (see 3:2–5; 14:1–12). But the ninth month can also be known as Kislev (Zech 7:1), and the Babylonian Chronicle records:

459. Calvin, *Jeremiah*, 4:351.

460. See further the commentary on 41:1–3 below; and Lundbom, *Jeremiah 37–52*, 189, though his comments imply that this understanding would generate a clash with the Babylonian Chronicle's dating of events.

461. Volz, *Jeremia*, 331.

In the first year of Nebuchadrezzar in the month of Sivan he mustered
his army
and went to the Ḥatti-territory, he marched about unopposed in the
Ḥatti-territory until the month of Kislev.
All the kings of the Ḥatti-land came before him and he received their
heavy tribute.
He marched to the city of Askelon and captured it in the month of
Kislev.
He captured its king and plundered it and carried off [spoil from
it....]
He turned the city into a mound and heaps of ruins and then in the
month of Sebat he marched back to Babylon.[462]

So the fast happens in the month the Babylonians sacked Ashkelon, forty
miles away, though we don't know if the audience could be expected to know
about that collocation of dates in the way it perhaps could be expected to
recognize the broad political, historical, and theological context suggested
by the date in v. 1.

10 The words are Yahweh's words (vv. 2, 4, 6); they are also *Jeremiah's
words*. The story not only gives us clues about the origin of the Scriptures;
it has already suggested the purpose of reading them out, which is to get the
people of God to pray and to change (v. 7). The Shaphan priestly family plays
an important role in events from the time of Josiah to 587 and afterward,
beginning with their support for Josiah's reformation, so it might not be surprising if they were sympathetic to Jeremiah's work and would be happy for
Jeremiah's aide to use one of their offices. Their stance draws our attention to
the need not to be too sweeping in our interpretation of Jeremiah's critique
of "the priests." It was common for priests also to be secretaries or scribes;
they would need writing skills for their work, not least in putting rules into
writing as part of the process involved in the development of the written
Torah. Apparently, some of the temple rooms faced out onto the courtyard
where people would gather on a feast or festival occasion and where Jeremiah
would have preached (cf. 35:4?). Jeremiah has regularly communicated with
the people by standing in the courtyard, but maybe communicating with
the entire crowd on a fast day made it necessary to use one of these rooms
as a pulpit.

11–14a On the other hand, while the story envisages the entire household of Judah listening to the message, the key factor as the story unfolds
is the king knowing about it. Evidently, Micaiah was in his father's office
while his father was in a meeting down in the palace. Were they discussing

---

462. D. J. Wiseman, *Chronicles of Chaldaean Kings* (London: British Museum, 1956), 69.

the potential political and military crisis just noted in connection with v. 9? But in the story, their absence adds to the suspense and the drama. There is nothing new in what Jeremiah says via Baruch, but there will be an extra intensity about it. Micaiah, there on his own, would be unable to avoid listening to the entirety of Jeremiah's message and then going down to the palace (lower down the slope of the city from the temple) to tell them what he has heard. One might guess that Micaiah is a trainee priest in his twenties while his father is a middle-aged priest involved in leadership. If Elishama is *the scribe* and has an office in the palace, it suggests he is a senior figure in the administration, and the other people in the meeting are presumably also senior figures. The names Elishama, Gemaryahu ben Shaphan, Jerahmeel son of the King, and Berachyahu ben Neriyahu the scribe appear among many others on clay seals ("bullae") that have materialized in excavations from Jerusalem in the period of the 587 destruction; these names seem to be the same as those of *Elishama, Gemariah, Jerahmeel* (v. 26), and Baruch.[463] *Jehudi* is more of an errand boy; his extraordinarily long name ends with the word that suggests someone of Sudanese origin who has been adopted into Judah.[464] There is further dramatic delay as these officials have to send for Baruch and the scroll, because Micaiah hasn't brought them with him. The writing and the sending of Baruch mean that Jeremiah can go by means of his scroll where he could not go in person, from his living quarters to the temple complex to the offices in the palace to the king's throne room, from private space to public space to otherwise inaccessible official space to the royal audience chamber and back to the personal space where he dictates a new copy of the scroll.[465] It is thus a scroll, not a prophet or even a scribe (though "the proliferation of secretaries" is noteworthy),[466] that Jehoiakim eventually has dealings with. The scroll becomes a character in the story, independent and autonomous, able to speak across geographical and temporal distances as a prophet cannot.[467]

14b-16 The story continues to unfold dramatically. There was the scene in the temple, then the first scene in the scribe's office, then a third scene there. Why were the officials fearful when the scroll said what Jeremiah had

463. N. Avigad, "Jerahmeel and Baruch," *BA* 42 (1979): 114–18; Y. Shiloh and D. Tarler, "Bullae from the City of David," *BA* 49 (1986): 196–209.

464. Holladay, *Commentary on Jeremiah*, 2:258.

465. V. H. Matthews, "Jeremiah's Scroll and Linked Zones of Communication," *Biblical Theology Bulletin* 39 (2009): 116–24.

466. M. Brummitt and Y. Sherwood, "The Tenacity of the Word," in Hunter and Davies, *Sense and Sensitivity*, 11; cf. M. Brummitt and Y. Sherwood, "The Fear of Loss Inherent in Writing," in Diamond and Stulman, *Jeremiah (Dis)placed*, 56.

467. C. L. Eggleston, *"See and Read"*, 96–98.

been saying for twenty years?[468] Was it simply a fear about the scroll's implications for the nation? Were they fearful because they could guess the king's reaction? Would they be in trouble for giving Jeremiah a platform? Were they fearful for Baruch and Jeremiah? But the comment on their fearfulness communicates how objectively frightening Jeremiah's message was. Might they hope it could push Jehoiakim into a change of policy?[469] In relation to the question in v. 3, their reaction may suggest just the response one would have hoped for. It thus generates anticipation about how the king will react.

17–20a The story continues to unfold in dramatic rather than chronological order and to maintain suspense as it now has the officials asking Baruch about the scroll's origin. Baruch's testimony "spells out that written prophecy is not simply records of revelation but the very substance of revelation, containing the exact same divine Word that lives in the mouth of the prophet."[470] Their question would belong chronologically before their determining to go and tell the king. Perhaps they were then afraid that the scroll would get confiscated, or perhaps they simply deposited the scroll in the place where scrolls were kept, but again the point in the drama is that the outworking of events will be prolonged as the king has to send for the scroll. Their advice to Baruch implies that the constraints on Jeremiah would not stop him hiding, and it confirms their sympathy for Jeremiah. There are two levels at which a king might be concerned about a prophet. A king might think that a prophet is simply not the real thing; he might be more convinced by a prophet such as Hananiah. He might nevertheless then be aware that a prophet like Jeremiah is bad for morale; politically, he might seem to be taking the Babylonians' side, like a traitor. And a king might not be clear in his own spirit which level he is working with, like Ahab in 1 Kgs 22. The Uriah story (26:20–23), perhaps from just a year or two before this one, would make clear the wisdom of the officials' advice to Baruch. But that precedent also draws attention to the ambivalence of their position as royal officials;[471] it was Elnathan who had accepted Jehoiakim's commission to extradite Uriah. These are people with official positions and people with minds that know Jeremiah to be right. They are caught between Jeremiah and Jehoiakim. If the original version of this story were told in a context not unlike the one it describes, it would serve to support Jeremiah.[472]

---

468. R. P. Carroll, *Jeremiah*, OTL, 660.

469. Cf. Brueggemann, *Jeremiah 26–52*, 132–33.

470. Leuchter, "Jeremiah," 178.

471. J. Erzberger, "Jr 36: Moïse et Jérémie en dispute sur la tradition," *Transversalités* 129 (2014): 38.

472. H.-J. Stipp, "Zwei alte Jeremia-Erzählungen," 332–47.

20b–23 The author continues to tell the story dramatically, relating (unnecessarily) how the king sent for the scroll and how the officials are standing in the position of aides while the king sits with his servants. "Each reading of the scroll effects a greater reaction."[473] The author goes on to paint a picture of the scene, with the king keeping warm with the aid of his firebowl. It was almost the middle of winter, and it would likely be cold (cf. Ezra 10:9); the temperature in Jerusalem gets down to freezing, and it snows every few years. Perhaps it is therefore unlikely that the king holds his meetings out of doors, though this practice might ensure that they were over quickly; if the *courtyard* (v. 20a) is inside, perhaps the firebowl is one brought inside rather than there being a fixed fireplace in the palace. But anyway, the firebowl serves the story. A scribe's knife would be a tool for sharpening a pen (hence the English word "penknife," which KJV uses) or for scratching out a mistake. If the scroll was of skin rather than papyrus, then the king was using it to cut the sutures between the pieces that made up the scroll.[474] Either way, "if Jehoiakim had simply grabbed the whole scroll and thrown it in the fire, it could have gone down as an act of impulsive rage. But no. . . . Jehoiakim's act was cold, systematic, repeated."[475] The king is aiming to cut Jeremiah and Yahweh down to size. Burning is a key activity of Jehoiakim as it had been of Josiah (2 Kgs 23:4, 6, 11, 15, 16, 20).[476] Jehoiakim is indicating his rejection of and contempt for the message and also seeking to ensure that it doesn't get implemented. Writing the scroll was another of Jeremiah's symbolic acts, and Jehoiakim's destruction of it is yet another, paralleling Hananiah's symbolic act in Jer 28.[477] Once there are curated collections of Jeremiah's messages, the story would suggest a desire to destroy them.[478] "There is tremendous risk involved in abandoning one's writing."[479] So Jehoiakim becomes "the first [person] we read of, that ever offered to burn the Bible," though fortunately "'forever, O Lord, thy Word is stablished in heaven,' saith David" (Ps 119:89).[480] But on one hand, "the Church and the Synagogue have always, Jehoiakim-like, cut out passages and consigned them to the brazier";[481] and on the other, the practice is built into the notion of critical approaches to biblical study.

---

473. P. D. Miller, "Jeremiah," on the passage.

474. R. L. Hicks, "*Delet* and *mᵉgillāh*: A Fresh Approach to Jeremiah xxxvi," *VT* 33 (1983): 46–66.

475. Wright, *Jeremiah*, 375.

476. J. Erzberger, "Jr 36," 36.

477. Lundbom, *Jeremiah 21–36*, 604.

478. M. Leuchter, "Jehoiakim and the Scribes: A Note on Jer 36,23," *ZAW* 127 (2015): 320–25.

479. C. J. Sharp, "Jeremiah in the Land of Aporia," in Diamond and Stulman, *Jeremiah (Dis)placed*, 41.

480. Trapp, *Commentary*.

481. R. P. Carroll, as quoted in Brummitt and Sherwood, "Tenacity of the Word," 27.

24–26 Part of the point in referring to the fearfulness of that group of officials now emerges: it contrasts with the lack of fearfulness on the part of the king and his *servants,* the palace staff who are identified with him in a way that the priestly officials are not. The mixed reaction of the Judahite establishment parallels Jer 26.[482] These officials were willing to collude with the ripping of the scroll but not to rip their clothes.[483] Ripping one's clothes and thus making oneself look like someone to whom something terrible has happened is a sign of grief. The note about the officials' advice again comes in dramatic rather than chronological order; it functions to underline the enormity of his action and it fits with the fear they had, which he lacks. Given that Jehoiakim is only about thirty (2 Kgs 23:36), Jerahmeel could hardly be his actual son. Possibly "king's son" means a member of his staff; a number of seals give the title "son of the king" after the name (see the translation note and commentary on vv. 11–14a). "Daughters of the king" appear in 41:10, suggesting members of the royal court. Seraiah and Shelemiah then, along with Jerahmeel, would be members of the palace staff who are identified with the king and his policies and who try to find Jeremiah and Baruch. The two men had presumably taken their own steps to hide (see v. 19; the verb is the same), but they needed Yahweh's protection, too, and *Yahweh hid them.* The statement carries enormous emphasis because such a narratival statement with Yahweh as the subject—except ones about Yahweh speaking—is rare, even "quite unique in the book of Jeremiah."[484] Solemnly, the next one that is at all similar will be 52:3, but that chapter will go on to tell us how Yahweh did it. Here, the storyteller piques our curiosity and declines to satisfy it. The statement's laconic nature also compares with 28:17.[485]

27–28 Jehoiakim had indulged in a magnificent gesture, and it might have seemed a successful one if he had been able to arrest Jeremiah. Even then, it would not stop Yahweh bringing about a fulfillment of the scroll's words. But at least it would stop Jeremiah's traitorous and morale-imperiling talk. We don't know whether Jeremiah was inhibited from preaching in public henceforth. The story is more interested in the deeper aspect to the significance of Jehoiakim's action. If it could seem that Jehoiakim had forestalled the fulfillment of Yahweh's threats, it is not so. "Jeremiah rewrites the scroll, sealing Jehoiakim's judgment."[486] Jeremiah has not lost his memory. "By the end of Part III the fate of Jerusalem and Judah is determined by the ashes of

---

482. Stulman, *Jeremiah,* 297.
483. Calvin, *Jeremiah,* 4:370.
484. R. P. Carroll, *Jeremiah,* OTL, 661.
485. D. R. Jones, *Jeremiah,* 446.
486. M. L. Brown and P. W. Ferris, *Jeremiah, Lamentations,* The Expositor's Bible Commentary (Grand Rapids: Zondervan, 2010), 328.

that scroll lying under the king's brazier. . . . The king may burn the scroll, but he cannot prevent its contents becoming operative"; indeed, it is his symbolic act that "releases the fatal word."[487]

29–30 Jehoiakim will pay a price for his contempt of Yahweh's message. Dramatically, only at this point does the story give us the gist of the scroll's contents—its threat of a totally destructive invasion from Nebuchadrezzar. Jehoiakim's contempt for this threat is the background to a double extra threat addressed to him personally, which contains no surprises for anyone reading the Jeremiah scroll sequentially. As usual, one should not take the threats too literally. His son (see 22:24–30) did succeed him, though not for long. And the anticipatory account of his death differs from the previous one (22:18–19). The throwing out of his corpse is appropriately similar to the actual fate of Uriah (26:23), and also to the king's action with the scroll (v. 23). The subsequent imagery links slyly with the fact that it is freezing cold at the time of the event (winter is *ḥōrep*, heat is *ḥōreb*). The account of his actual death in 2 Kgs 24:6 does not suggest that it corresponded to either of the imaginative threats of it. The chapter does not clarify whether the extra threat reached Jehoiakim; it is for the audience to hear, as is suggested by the transition to a third-person formulation in v. 30. But "the king who would destroy scripture is herewith included in scripture."[488]

31 Instead of preventing the fulfillment of Jeremiah's threats, "by burning the original scroll, Jehoiakim . . . has ironically unleashed the threatened doom upon himself and the nation as their ineluctable fate."[489] The scroll's burning is an ironic sign or cause of the city's burning.[490] "The violence done to the scroll in Jer 36 tears at the relationship between the king and people of Judah and their divine suzerain. Cutting the scroll uncuts the covenant; burning the scroll burns the palace, temple, and city."[491] The story thus comes to a "tragic conclusion"[492] as it "relates the tragedy" that Yahweh's word "met with so little response."[493] The story has now answered the question that v. 3 opened up, though its answer would cause unease in cultures that like to think of people and leadership as having separate responsibilities and destinies. His servants can hardly complain that they are enveloped in his fate.

---

487. R. P. Carroll, *Jeremiah*, OTL, 663; "Part III" refers to Jer 26–36.

488. Berrigan, *Jeremiah*, 155.

489. Diamond, "Jeremiah," 597.

490. P. J. Scalise, "Scrolling through Jeremiah: Written Documents as a Reader's Guide to the Book of Jeremiah," *RevExp* 101 (2004): 216.

491. N. B. Levtow, "Text Production and Destruction in Ancient Israel," in *Social Theory and Israelite Religion: Essays in Retrospect and Prospect*, ed. S. M. Olyan, Resources for Biblical Study 71 (Atlanta: Society of Biblical Literature, 2012), 125.

492. Volz, *Jeremia*, 334.

493. M. Kessler, "Form-Critical Suggestions on Jer 36," *CBQ* 28 (1966): 399.

Things may seem harder for the people in general, but the story reminds the audience again of the solemn way in which the fates of leaders and people are interwoven. "Within a brief period of four years, Jehoiakim's regime nails the coffin shut on the Judean nation."[494] Perhaps people get the leader they deserve; there are no complaints in Lamentations that it wasn't our fault but the king's fault. Here, "ominously there is no reference to repentance (*šûb*) as there was in the initial scene."[495] It is the audience for the story after 587 that will need to do the turning of which Jer 34 spoke rather than seeking, literally or metaphorically, to destroy the scroll.

32a The new writing is a new symbolic action. "God will not leave the king scroll-less, even if the king wants no scroll."[496] Reciting the written text functions "to make it a legal 'witness' against those to whom it has been read out"; rewriting it functions "to produce a durable record of the oracles of YHWH as proof to be used, now and in the future, against the nation and the king."[497] The writing is thus "a theological/religious act." Yahweh speaks, but in addition, Yahweh commissions the writing down.[498] And it means "the word of YHWH . . . prevails against obstacles, even the king himself,"[499] who brings its curse on himself.[500] Further, the writing makes it possible for people after 587 (for instance) to receive the same message as people in 604, with its challenge but also its hope. Though the question of the extent of the contents of the scroll is "muddy waters,"[501] Jer 2–6 would work as an answer to the question, and if it wasn't Jer 2–6, we don't know what it was. Must the scroll have existed when the story was told, otherwise the story would deconstruct?[502] Does the story open a window onto the process of the formation of the book of Jeremiah?[503] Or does this assumption simply reflect our desire for information on the subject?

32b The story closes with a further intriguing piece of information, and a surprise given the lack of any divine instruction to add anything (contrast vv. 1–2 and the warnings in, e.g., Deut 4:2).[504] "Even as [Jehoiakim] tries to

494. Stulman, *Jeremiah*, 296.

495. Dearman, "My Servants the Scribes," 408.

496. Brueggemann, *Jeremiah 26–52*, 138.

497. J. Schaper, "On Writing and Reciting in Jeremiah 36," in Barstad and Kratz, *Prophecy*, 146.

498. Eggleston, *"See and Read"*, 164; see further 16–48.

499. F. Hartenstein, "Prophets, Princes, and Kings: Prophecy and Prophetic Books according to Jeremiah 36," in Najman and Schmid, *Jeremiah's Scriptures*, 72.

500. Hartenstein, "Prophets, Princes, and Kings," 89.

501. McKane, *Jeremiah*, 2:901.

502. K. van der Toorn, *Scribal Culture*, 174.

503. Weiser, *Jeremia*, 330.

504. Eggleston, *"See and Read"*, 122.

reassert his own conception of his circumstances on the events, the words of the scroll mock his efforts."[505] As Hananiah will attempt to frustrate the message of judgment embodied in a yoke by destroying the yoke, Jehoiakim attempts to destroy the message, literally, *in the fire*. But in Jer 28, a yoke of iron is Yahweh's last word, and the end of this scene introduces a new expanded scroll.[506] If Jeremiah has already dictated all the messages Yahweh had given him, the extra messages must be ones he received later; one might then guess that they appear within Jer 7–24. Thus "this final notice about the reconstitution and expansion of the scroll has been the focal point of much speculation, carrying implications for the scribal craft as the vehicle for the divine word originally conveyed through prophecy."[507]

But again, the theories are attempting to answer questions that emerge from our interests rather than from pointers in the Jeremiah scroll itself.

505. A. Deken, "Does Prophecy Cause History? Jeremiah 36: A Scroll Ablaze," *OTE* 30 (2017): 651.

506. Keown, Scalise, and Smothers, *Jeremiah 26–52*, 207.

507. M. Leuchter, "Jehoiakim and the Scribes," 320; ironically, he goes on to add to the speculation.

IV. PART FOUR: THE CALAMITY AND THE AFTERMATH
(37:1–45:5 [LXX 44:1–51:35])

Part Four comprises a semi-continuous series of stories relating to a crucial period of four or five years between 589/588 and 585, from just before the fall of Jerusalem through the disaster itself to the aftermath in Judah and in Egypt—though there are no dates attached to the last events narrated, and maybe the period was longer. While it alludes to the fate of the Judahites who went to Babylon or stayed in Judah or took refuge in places such as Ammon, it gives no direct account of this fate. It focuses on how Jeremiah himself first goes to stay in Mizpah and then goes with a group of Judahites to Egypt, where he delivers a final message. Whereas the Jeremiah scroll has previously put its stories in a dramatic order, with backward and forward chronological movement, it now makes a transition to something more like continuous narrative order as it relates the last stages of its interwoven story of Judah's fate and Jeremiah's activity. A series of themes run through the narrative:

- People ask Jeremiah for a message from Yahweh but ignore it when they get it.
- They impose constraints on Jeremiah, but he survives (and so do his allies).
- Jeremiah continues to deliver Yahweh's message, and it comes true.
- Babylon is Yahweh's agent in bringing calamity but is merciful when people cooperate with it.
- The disobedience of the Judahite community in Egypt means there is no hope for it.
- Events reflect the interweaving of "choice and destiny."[1]

The narrative's ending with Jeremiah in Egypt reflects the scroll's general focus on the way Yahweh speaks through Jeremiah to the Judahites; Egypt is where he continues that activity after the fall of Jerusalem and the Mizpah debacle. We might guess that a storyteller developed the narrative in Egypt as things began to settle down there. The Jeremiah scroll never tells us about Jeremiah's later years and his death, as it does not tell us about his birth and early years. Its focus lies on the message and the activity, not on the man, and from this angle, Jer 44 makes an appropriate end to his story. The narrative then found its way into the Jeremiah scroll there or wherever else the scroll came into existence, and this process would be part of the background to the

---

1. McConville, *Judgment and Promise*, 111.

743

emerging of the two versions of the scroll that lie behind LXX and MT.[2] And the narrative has practical implications for Judahites in Judah and Babylon as well as in Egypt, such as:

- Accept your position as a people that deserved the calamity that came upon you.
- If you are the messenger, stay firm and trust Yahweh.
- Be responsive to Yahweh's message when it comes.
- Pay attention to the message that Jeremiah brought.
- Submit to the imperial authority rather than rebelling against it.

Were there other reasons for composing a narrative dismissive of the Judahite community in Egypt? A few decades later there was tension between different groups within Judah,[3] but the account of these tensions does not refer to Judahites from Egypt. And from papyri discovered at Elephantine in Upper Egypt we know of Judahites whose theology would have horrified Jeremiah, but these papyri come from a century or two later from another place, and anyway their authors seem to have got on okay with the establishment in Judah.[4] So it requires considerable connecting of dots to suppose that (e.g.) Judahites who had been in Babylon composed this narrative to discredit Judahites in Egypt. While the narrative portrays Jeremiah taking a confrontational stance to Judahites in Egypt, he earlier took a confrontational stance to the community in Judah itself. Maybe Judahites in Egypt could write self-critically, as Judahites in Judah and in Babylon could. The

2. On the two versions of Zedekiah's story in Jer 37–40 MT and 44–47 LXX, see S. L. Birdsong, *The Last King(s) of Judah: Zedekiah and Sedekias in the Hebrew and Old Greek Versions of Jeremiah 37(44):1–40(47):6*, FAT 2/89 (Tübingen: Mohr Siebeck, 2017); and on the first two chapters, R. D. Weis, "The Textual Situation in the Book of Jeremiah," in *Sôfer Mahîr: Essays in Honor of Adrian Schenker*, ed. Y. A. P. Goldman, A. van der Kooij, and R. D. Weis, VTSup 110 (Leiden: Brill, 2006), 269–93.

3. See the comments on "Unity of Composition" in the Introduction to this commentary.

4. See, e.g., ANET, 491–92; *The Context of Scripture: Canonical Compositions, Monumental Inscriptions, and Archival Documents from the Biblical World*, ed. W. W. Hallo and K. L. Younger (Leiden: Brill, 2003), III:116–217; B. Porten, *Archives from Elephantine* (Berkeley: University of California, 1968); Porten, "The Jews in Egypt," in *The Cambridge History of Judaism*, ed. W. D. Davies and L. Finkelstein (Cambridge: Cambridge University Press, 1984), 372–400; B. Becking, "Yehudite Identity in Elephantine," in *Judah and the Judaeans in the Achaemenid Period*, ed. O. Lipschits et al. (Winona Lake, IN: Eisenbrauns, 2011), 403–19; G. Granerød, *Dimensions of Yahwism in the Persian Period: Studies in the Religion and Society of the Judaean Community at Elephantine*, BZAW 488 (Berlin: de Gruyter, 2016); C. Cornell, "The Forgotten Female Figurines of Elephantine," *Journal of Ancient Near Eastern Religions* 18 (2018): 111–32.

story of the community's origins was then generated within that community, and it urged that if it carried on the way it was, death was its destiny. In fact, the Judahite community came to thrive over the years. The Septuagint is usually assumed to have had its origin in the flourishing Jewish community in Alexandria. Egyptian Jews were among the Jews at Pentecost in Acts 2, and an Egyptian, Apollos, was a key leader among Jews who came to believe in Jesus (Acts 18:24; 1 Cor 3:6).[5] It would be nice to imagine that the community had heeded Yahweh's challenge, though Josephus implies that its later thriving reflects forced migration after the dissolution of Alexander's empire.[6]

Part Four outlines:

37:1–21	Zedekiah consults Jeremiah; Jeremiah is locked up
38:1–28a	Jeremiah is locked up; Zedekiah consults Jeremiah
38:28b—39:14	The city falls, and the fates that follow
39:15–18	A promise of safety for Ebed-melech
40:1–12	A new start at Mizpah, the Watchtower
40:13–41:18	Things begin to fall apart
42:1–43:13	Yahweh's direction given and rejected
44:1–30	A final confrontation, exhortation, and warning
45:1–5	A promise of safety for Baruch

A. PART 4A: LAST CHANCES, CALAMITY, AND A FOOTNOTE FOR EBED-MELECH (37:1–39:18 [LXX 44:1–46:18])

The first three chapters in part 4 tell of the last days of Jerusalem before it falls to the Babylonians, and then of the actual fall of the city. Jeremiah 37–38 focuses on a series of consultations between Jeremiah and the hapless King Zedekiah, in which Zedekiah more than once asks Jeremiah what he thinks is going to happen and if there is any hope, and Jeremiah more than once gives him messages from Yahweh that Zedekiah does not wish to hear. Jeremiah 39 relates how the city can hold out no longer and how the Babylonians capture Zedekiah himself when he tries to escape. The three chapters close with a message of encouragement for an African servant of the king who had rescued Jeremiah from possible death. While the narrative as a whole is mostly chronological, an overlap between the end of Jer 39 and the beginning of Jer 40 marks a key transition moment. Jeremiah 39 ends with Jeremiah entrusted to Gemariah and with the message for Ebed-melech relating to his action

---

5. Wright, *Jeremiah*, 404.
6. *Antiquities* XII.1.

narrated in Jer 38; Jer 40 backtracks in order to give a longer account of how Jeremiah comes to be with Gemariah, which leads into what then follows. Thus Jer 37–39 and 40–45 form the two parts of the narrative as a whole.

1. *Zedekiah Consulting Jeremiah; Jeremiah Locked Up (37:1–21 [LXX 44:1–21])*

1 Zedekiah ben Josiah came to reign as king instead of Coniah ben[a] Jehoiakim; Nebuchadrezzar King of Babylon made him king in the country of Judah. 2 But he, his servants, and the people of the country[b] did not listen to the words of Yahweh that he spoke by means of Jeremiah the prophet.

3 King Zedekiah sent Jehucal ben Shelemiah and Zephaniah ben Maaseiah, the priest, to Jeremiah the prophet, saying, "Please plead on our behalf with Yahweh our God" 4 (when Jeremiah was coming in and going out among the people[c] and they had not put him in a house of confinement, 5 and when Pharaoh's force had gone out from Egypt and the Chaldeans who were blockading Jerusalem[d] had heard the news of them and had withdrawn from Jerusalem).[e] 6 Yahweh's word came to Jeremiah the prophet. 7 Yahweh the God of Israel has said this: This is what you are to say[f] to the king of Judah who is sending you to me to inquire of me. There, Pharaoh's force that is going out to you as a support will return to its country, Egypt,[g] 8 and the Chaldeans will return and do battle against this city, and they will capture it and consume it in fire.[h] 9 Yahweh has said this. Don't deceive yourselves and say, "The Chaldeans will definitely go[i] from against us," because they will not go. 10 Even if[j] you had struck down the entire force of the Chaldeans who are doing battle with you, and people who have been skewered remain among them, each one in his tent, they will set to and consume this city in fire.

11 When[k] the Chaldean force had withdrawn from against Jerusalem in the face of Pharaoh's force,[l] 12 Jeremiah went out from Jerusalem to go to the region of Benjamin to undertake a sharing[m] from there among the people. 13 He was at the Benjamin Gateway, and the man in charge[n] was there; his name was Irijah ben Shelemiah, son of Hananiah. He seized Jeremiah the prophet, saying, "You're falling away to the Chaldeans." 14 Jeremiah said, "Lies![o] I'm not falling away to the Chaldeans." But he didn't listen to him. Irijah seized Jeremiah and made him come to the officials. 15 The officials were incensed at Jeremiah: they struck him down and put him[p] in a confinement house,[q] the house of Jonathan the secretary, because they made it into[r] a detention house 16 when Jeremiah came to the cistern house, to the cellars.[s]

Jeremiah[t] lived there for a long time.[u] 17 Then King Zedekiah sent and got him. The king asked him in his house, in secret, "Is there a word from Yahweh?"

*Jeremiah said, "There is," and said, "Into the hand of the king of Babylon you will be given over."*ᵛ

¹⁸*Jeremiah said to King Zedekiah, What have I done wrong to you, to your servants, and to this people that you have put*ʷ *me into a house of confinement?* ¹⁹*Where are your prophets who prophesied to you, "The king of Babylon will not come against you and against this country"?* ²⁰*So now listen, please, my lord king. Please may my prayer for grace fall before you. Don't send me back to the house of Jonathan the secretary, so I don't die there.* ²¹*So King Zedekiah gave an order, and they appointed Jeremiah to the court of the guard, and to give him*ˣ *a round of bread daily from the bakers' street until all the bread from the city came to an end.*

*So Jeremiah lived in the courtyard of the guard.*ʸ

a. LXX lacks *Coniah ben*; a straight transition from Jehoiakim to Zedekiah suggests that 36:30 is literally fulfilled (R. P. Carroll, *Jeremiah*, OTL, 670). On the form of the name Coniah, see the translation note on 22:24.

b. On *the people of the country*, see the translation note on 1:18.

c. For MT *hā'ām*, LXX implies *hā'îr* ("the city").

d. LXX lacks *who were blockading Jerusalem*.

e. MT has a unit marker here.

f. The verb is plural, so it is addressed to the aides.

g. The double expression is odd and may reflect a conflate text (Holladay, *Commentary on Jeremiah*, 2:265).

h. MT has a marker here.

i. The infinitive precedes the finite verb, underlining the factuality of the action.

j. On the use of *kî 'im*, see *TTH* 143.

k. For *wəhāyâ* ("and it happened"), one would have expected *wayyəhî*; see the translation note on 3:9.

l. MT has a section marker here.

m. The *hiphil* of *ḥālaq* I (*ḥālaq* II in *HALOT*) comes only here. LXX has "buy," which would imply acquiring a share (HUBP sees the influence of 32:8, 44), but one would then expect the *qal*; Aq, Sym, Th convey the same implication. But Vg, Tg have "divide up," a more plausible understanding of the *hiphil*. An audience might hear resonances of the other *ḥālaq*, which would suggest that Jeremiah was slipping off (cf. Qimchi, in MG)—as Irijah thinks.

n. Lit. "the master of charge/appointment." *Pəqidut* is a *hapax legomenon*, with the same potential range of meanings as *pəquddâ* (cf. BDB); thus Tg has "the man appointed." LXX "with whom he stayed" perhaps reflects *pāqad*'s meaning "visit" (HUBP).

o. *Šeqer*, one of Jeremiah's signature expressions, meaning "deception."

p. The two simple *waw* verbs suggest a spelling out of their being incensed as opposed to denoting consequent actions (Volz, *Jeremia*, 336–37). *Sebirin* (alternative readings that had been proposed but that the Masoretes do not accept) have the expected *waw*-consecutives.

q. LXX lacks *a confinement house*.

r. Vg has "he had been placed over."

s. *Ḥānût* comes only here. In later Hebrew, it means a tent or shop (*DTT*); Aq has "workshop" (cf. Vg; see further the notes in F. Field, *Origenis Hexaplorum quae supersunt* [Oxford:

Clarendon, 1867], 2:682). BDB suggests a vaulted room, which a cistern might be. Perhaps *cistern house* (cf. Exod 12:29) is an anticipatory clarifier of the unusual word (*cistern* will recur in Jer 38), or perhaps the cellars led to the cistern.

t. LXX lacks *Jeremiah*, which in MT is an indication that a new section begins here.

u. MT^L has a unit marker here.

v. MT^L has a section marker here.

w. The verb is plural (singular in LXX, Vg).

x. LXX takes the infinitive as continuing the finite verbs (cf. GK 113z); it would then seem to imply a once-for-all giving (Joüon 123x), though there are comparable unusual simple *waw* verbs in vv. 11 and 15. Conversely, Vg translates the previous waw-consecutive *wayyapqidû* (*they appointed*) as if it were also subordinate to "he ordered" (see BDB, 845; *HALOT*, 1011a).

y. MT's lack of any marker at the end of Jer 37 is noteworthy, especially since markers multiply through Jer 38; see the commentary on 38:1.

After the introduction, the first story in part 4 is actually a triple one, an account of three confrontations between the administration and the prophet.

vv. 1–2	An introduction setting up the question that this first story will begin to handle
vv. 3–10	Zedekiah sends aides to get Jeremiah to pray; Jeremiah gives them a discouraging message
vv. 11–16a	Jeremiah tries to go to Anathoth; Irijah arrests him and puts him in a tough form of detention
vv. 16b–21	Zedekiah asks Jeremiah if there is a word from Yahweh; Jeremiah gives him a confrontational response, but Zedekiah does ease his conditions

Verses 1–2 are an introduction to 37:3–39:17, perhaps added when a curator brought together the stories in 37:3–39:17. In the rest of the chapter, "the times are . . . desperate"[7] and "fear dominates each scene";[8] the stories reflect how it is possible to be "frozen by fear."[9] In this context, they have in common a less definitive or more sympathetic stance in relation to the people involved in events.

- Zedekiah asks Jeremiah to pray for the city; it's not explicit how one should evaluate this plea.
- Yahweh responds to Jeremiah's "inquiring" of him; it's not explicit

7. Fretheim, *Jeremiah*, 512.
8. Stulman, *Jeremiah*, 305.
9. Dearman, *Jeremiah*, in his comments on Jer 38.

whether Jeremiah's inquiring counts as "praying" despite being forbidden to pray,[10] and there is no report of Zedekiah's reaction.

- After the temporary relief of the city, Jeremiah seeks to venture out to Anathoth; it's not clear exactly what he is going to do there or whether he is coming back.
- Irijah suspects he is defecting, and one can hardly blame him for this inference.
- The officials angrily put Jeremiah into detention, which is also an understandable reaction.
- Zedekiah again asks Jeremiah if there is a word from Yahweh; is it significant that there is no account of Jeremiah consulting Yahweh or of the word that follows being a word from Yahweh?
- Again, there is no account of Zedekiah's reaction.
- Jeremiah's subsequent complaint is understandably testy.
- Zedekiah's response is reasonably gracious and generous.

The chapter thus reflects the tension that sometimes obtains between the clarity with which one can look back on events with hindsight (vv. 1–2) and their ambiguity as people live through them (vv. 3–17). Something of this ambiguity will continue through Jer 37–45 and will thus encourage reflection by the audience that listens to this sequence of stories in the situation after 587—perhaps initially in Mizpah, then in Egypt.

The stories in vv. 3–10 and 11–21 look independent of each other in origin, and within vv. 3–10 the parenthetical background information in vv. 4–5 looks like a bit of clarification added when the curators compiled the chapter.

1–2 From Jer 36, there is a chronological jump from 604 to 597, from Jehoiakim's fourth year to his death, the first fall of Jerusalem, the first exile, and the banishment of Jehoiakim's successor. But dramatically and substantially, there is some continuity. These opening verses make a link with Jehoiakim as one of Zedekiah's predecessors (and brother), and begin not only with the king but with his *servants* and *the people* who had listened to the 604 scroll (36:6–14, 24, 31). They go on to note that in Zedekiah's day, these Judahites did not listen to Jeremiah, which is where the previous chapter almost finished (36:31). The introduction thus both links backward and looks forward to the chapters that will follow, with their theme of people's unwillingness to listen to the prophet. It gives readers a clue to reading the narrative as a whole, which will provide an answer the question, "So how

---

10. Cf. M. Roncace, *Jeremiah, Zedekiah, and the Fall of Jerusalem: A Study of Prophetic Narrative*, LHBOTS 423 (London: T&T Clark, 2005), 37.

did they fail to listen?" Nebuchadrezzar has put yet another of Josiah's sons on the throne in Judah in place of his nephew Coniah/Jehoiachin. He has perhaps assumed that Jehoiachin would continue the policies of Jehoiakim his father, who was inclined to assert Judahite independence from Babylon, and he would hope that his own appointee would be more subservient. The overloaded expression *reign as king* underscores the replacement of that younger Davidide, whom some people would doubtless still see as the real king, now the king in exile. But the expression also conveys an irony: "The last days of Judah are ostensibly ruled over by Zedekiah," but "his rule . . . is of little importance, given the larger events of international politics" in which Babylon and Egypt battle for sovereignty in the region and about which Jeremiah can speak because he knows what Yahweh is doing. But Zedekiah's deeper problem is not his relative powerlessness but that unwillingness to *listen*.[11] Nebuchadrezzar might also hope that the presence of a hostage Judahite community in Babylon, including the ex-king and along with the articles taken from the temple, would be a disincentive to assertions of independence. For different reasons, Jeremiah will urge the Jerusalem community in that direction. But the instinct to insist on one's freedom is too strong. Zedekiah's regime "floundered and self-destructed through its opposition to and rejection of the Jeremianic mission," which was willing to be in service to "the success of Babylonian imperial designs."[12]

3–5 The chapter fast forwards from 597 to 589/588. Nebuchadrezzar has been campaigning in the Levant and blockading Jerusalem, but then Pharaoh Hophra (cf. 44:30 and the commentary) has emerged from Egypt to contest Nebuchadrezzar's attempt to assert sovereignty in the area that historically and logically belongs in Egypt's sphere of influence. Judah can see the Egyptian action as a help to it (v. 7), without asking whether being under Egypt's heel is better than being under Babylon's. The scenario presupposed here may also be the background to Lachish Ostracon 3, which refers to a Judahite commander apparently on a mission to Egypt (see the commentary on 34:6–7).[13] So Nebuchadrezzar has had to give up his blockade in order to pay attention to Pharaoh. This development is good news for Judah, but how good? Zedekiah sends aides to consult Jeremiah over the question; Jeremiah is apparently not under house arrest, as he will be shortly. *Jehucal ben Shelemiah* is another name that occurs on a seal from this period, as does Shelemiah's name itself.[14] *Zephaniah* took part in the mission related in 21:1–2 and

---

11. Brueggemann, *Jeremiah 26–52*, 138, 139.
12. Diamond, "Jeremiah," 598.
13. See *ANET*, 322.
14. See the commentary on 36:11–14a.

in the exchanges between Jeremiah and the 597 exiles reported in 29:29–32, while *Maaseiah* appeared in 35:4. To be more precise, Zedekiah sends them to get Jeremiah to pray. Prayer that the relief may be more than temporary would be appropriate, and it is a prophet's job to pray. But references to prophets praying can imply praying for guidance (32:16; 42:2–4, 20), and Yahweh understands Zedekiah to have sent the men "to inquire of me" (v. 7).[15] The parallel with Hezekiah sending aides to get Isaiah to pray (2 Kgs 19) draws attention to the difference between the two stories[16]—almost the only similarity is the verb *plead* (*hithpallēl*), which compares with the noun "plea" (*təpillâ*) in the Hezekiah story. There, the king and his aides are distraught at the attackers' blasphemy, their appearance matches their agitation, and the prophet's response is a promise rather than a threat. But we know from v. 2 that Zedekiah won't take any notice of what Yahweh says.

6–10 Perhaps wisely, Zedekiah has not actually asked for a message from Yahweh, but he gets one. The Egyptian venture will be short-lived. The Egyptians will return to Egypt and the Babylonians will return to . . . Jerusalem, to take the city. Zedekiah presupposes that the Egyptians are concerned to bolster Judahite autonomy in relation to Babylon; Ezek 17:15 relates how he asked for such help. But the Egyptians would not want Judah to have too much autonomy in relation to Egypt itself. While Jeremiah does assume that the Egyptians will be no match for the Babylonians, it would be misleading to describe him as pro-Babylonian and anti-Egyptian; the basis for his advice to Zedekiah is theological rather than political or military. He knows that Yahweh has designated Nebuchadrezzar as his servant. While his message is all about what the Egyptians and the Babylonians will do, not about what Yahweh will do (contrast the formulation in 21:3–7),[17] the basis for his declarations is the fact that *Yahweh has said this*. The words about what will happen are all Yahweh's words (vv. 6, 7, 9). Jeremiah undergirds the point by his closing comment: even if the Babylonian army was reduced to a battered remnant (the related verb *remain* occurs), it would still summon up the energy to fulfill Yahweh's declarations. If Yahweh is going to bring about a miracle, it will be to ensure that the city falls, not that it gets saved.[18]

15. See 21:1–2 and the commentary on it.
16. A. R. P. Diamond, "Portraying Prophecy: Of Doublets, Variants and Analogies in the Narrative Representation of Jeremiah's Oracles—Reconstructing the Hermeneutics of Prophecy," *JSOT* 57 (1993): 111–14. C. Hardmeier sees the Hezekiah narrative as composed in Jeremiah's day and as in dialogue with this chapter: see *Prophetie im Streit vor dem Untergang Judas: Erzählkommunikative Studien zur Entstehungssituation der Jesaja- und Jeremiaerzählungen in II Reg 18–20 und Jer 37–40*, BZAW 187 (Berlin: de Gruyter, 1990).
17. Fretheim, *Jeremiah*, 514.
18. Diamond, "Jeremiah," 599.

Again, the prospects thus contrast with events at the time of Sennacherib and Hezekiah. The future will resemble the occasion when Yahweh delivered a large Judahite force into the hand of a small Aramean one (2 Chr 24:24) rather than when he delivered a large Midianite force into the hand of a small Israelite one (Judg 7).[19] As often happens, the scroll does not record Jeremiah's delivery of the message to the aides or to Zedekiah; it appears in the scroll for the benefit of the audience that knows it came true.

11-12 The withdrawal of the Babylonian blockade means that people can go in and out of the city. The action Jeremiah is consequently trying to take could be related in some way to the events described in Jer 32. His supervising some sharing out in the family fits with the position Hanamel gives him there. Perhaps Jeremiah is the senior member of the family in which his father Hilkiah and Hanamel's father Shallum were brothers (see the commentary on 32:6–8a); and perhaps some sorting out of the estate needs doing. *The people* might refer either to the people of Anathoth, in the midst of whom the business needs to be conducted, or to Jeremiah and Hanamel's more immediate family.

13 But the story is not very interested in clarifying what Jeremiah is going to do. His undertaking just happens to be the reason why he is off to Anathoth through the *Benjamin Gateway*, the gateway that leads straight into Benjaminite territory (it would have been in the area of the medieval city's Damascus Gate). He gets apprehended there by *the man in charge*, the officer with senior authority in the area, on the reasonable suspicion that he intends (at least in due course) to follow his own advice that people should surrender to the Babylonians; they had been encamped north of the city and perhaps have a rump position there. The officer, offended by Jeremiah's suspected "defeatism,"[20] is apparently the brother of Jehucal in v. 3 (and 38:1) and perhaps uncle of Jehudi, if his grandfather is the same Shelemiah (36:14). It's too much to think that Hananiah might be the prophet of Jer 28;[21] Shelemiah and Hananiah are both common names.

14-16a It would be understandable if someone like Irijah thought of Jeremiah as pro-Babylonian, and if that description were fitting, going over to the Babylonians could be quite appropriate. Actually, Jeremiah's stance is more subtle. But evidently, Jeremiah did not convince Irijah or *the officials* in the palace who were less sympathetic to him than the officials in Jehoiakim's day (see Jer 26; 36) and were the victims of his tongue in the present context (32:32; 34:19, 21; 38:4, 25). Apparently the authorities have commandeered

19. Allen, *Jeremiah*, 406.
20. Rudolph, *Jeremia*, 237.
21. So Rashi, in MG.

(part of?) the house belonging to a secretary (perhaps a secretary of state); possibly Jonathan and his family had been among the people taken off into exile in 597.[22] The house had a convenient subterranean facility (see the translation note), and they could conveniently turn it into a place of detention. It made "a kind of ultimate black hole."[23]

16b–17 It looks as if Jeremiah would have been in his place of confinement for longer had Zedekiah not wanted to consult him; perhaps the Babylonians are on their way back, in fulfillment of Jeremiah's earlier warning. The Jeremiah scroll portrays Zedekiah as a weak character compared with his father and his brothers, and 2 Kgs 24–25 is compatible with this picture. His chief characteristic is that he keeps asking Jeremiah the same question but not taking any notice of the answer; he also has difficulty making a decision and sticking to it or standing up to his staff (Jer 21; 34; 38). So here he asks his standard question but keeps it a secret. Does his secrecy imply he is open to accepting whatever Jeremiah may say?[24] Further, "in the question 'Is there?' something characteristic comes to expression": you can't assume there will be a word from God. God's word is not at human disposal.[25] But the narrative implicitly contrasts Zedekiah with Jeremiah, who does not give up straight talking when he escapes from the dungeon for what may be only a moment.

18–21 Zedekiah's irresolution works in Jeremiah's favor. The *cellars* in Jonathan's house (and perhaps especially the *cistern*) were evidently no more fun than the one in Malchiah's house, of which Jer 38 will speak; perhaps the officials really left Jeremiah there to starve.[26]

2. Jeremiah Locked Up; Zedekiah Consulting Jeremiah (38:1–28a [LXX 45:1–28a])

¹*Shephatiah ben Mattan, Gedaliah ben Pashhur, Jucal ben Shelemiah, and Pashhur ben Malchiah*ᵃ *heard the words that Jeremiah was speaking to the entire people:*ᵇ ²*Yahweh has said this. The person who stays in this city will die by sword, by hunger, and by epidemic,*ᶜ *but the person who goes out to the Chaldeans will live. His life will be his as loot.*ᵈ *He will live.*ᵉ ³*Yahweh has said this. This city will definitely be given into the hand of the king of Babylon's*

22. Duhm, *Jeremia*, 300.
23. McKane, *Jeremiah*, 2:929.
24. Roncace, *Jeremiah*, 53–54.
25. W. H. Schmidt, *Jeremia*, 2:208.
26. Rudolph, *Jeremia*, 237.

force. He will capture it. ⁴*The officials said to the king, He should please be put to death, this man,*^f *because as a result he is weakening the hands of the people engaged in the battle, the people who remain in this city, and the hands of the entire people by speaking to them in accordance with these words. Because this man is not inquiring after the well-being of this people—rather about something dire.* ⁵*King Zedekiah said, There, he is in your hand, because the king cannot overcome you in a thing.*^g ⁶*So they got Jeremiah*^h *and threw him into the cistern (of Malchiah, the king's son),*ⁱ *which was in the prison courtyard. They put Jeremiah in with ropes.*^j *There was no water in the cistern, but mud, and Jeremiah sank into the mud.*^k

⁷*Ebed-melech the Sudanese, a man who was an overseer*^l *(he was in the king's house), heard that they had put Jeremiah into the cistern. The king was sitting in the Benjamin Gateway.* ⁸*Ebed-melech went out from the king's house and spoke to the king.* ⁹*My lord king,*^m *these men have acted in a dire way in all that they have done to Jeremiah the prophet, in that they have thrown him into the cistern. He's dead*ⁿ *in his situation*^o *because of hunger (because there was no more bread in the city).* ¹⁰*So the king ordered Ebed-melech the Sudanese: Get thirty*^p *people into your charge from here, and get Jeremiah the prophet up from the cistern before he dies.* ¹¹*So Ebed-melech got the people into his charge*^q *and came to the king's house to below the store. From there, he got worn clothes and worn rags and put them into the cistern to Jeremiah, with ropes.*^r ¹²*Ebed-melech the Sudanese said to Jeremiah, Put the worn clothes and rags under your armpits, please, under the ropes. Jeremiah did so,* ¹³*and they drew Jeremiah up with the ropes and got him up from the cistern.*

So Jeremiah lived in the prison courtyard,^s ¹⁴*and King Zedekiah sent and got Jeremiah the prophet to him at the third entrance that was in Yahweh's house. The king said to Jeremiah, I'm going to ask you something. Don't hide anything from me.* ¹⁵*Jeremiah said to Zedekiah, When I tell you, you will actually put me to death,*^t *won't you, and when I counsel you, you will not listen to me.* ¹⁶*So King Zedekiah promised Jeremiah in secret:*^u *Yahweh is alive,*^v *who made this life for us: if I put you to death or if I give you over into the hand of these people who are seeking your life . . .*^w

¹⁷*So Jeremiah said to Zedekiah:*^x *Yahweh, the God of Armies, the God of Israel, has said this. If you do go out*^y *to the officers of the king of Babylon, you yourself will live and this city—it will not be consumed in fire. You and your household will live.* ¹⁸*But if you do not go out to the officers of the king of Babylon, this city will be given into the hand of the Chaldeans, they will consume it in fire, and you will not escape from their hand.*^z

¹⁹*King Zedekiah said to Jeremiah, I am anxious about the Judahites who have fallen away to the Chaldeans, in case they give me over into their hand and they assault me.*^{aa} ²⁰*Jeremiah said, They will not give you over. Listen to*

Yahweh's voice, please, regarding what I am going to say to you, so that things will be good for you, and you yourself may live. ²¹*But if you are going to refuse to go out, this is the thing that Yahweh has enabled me to see:* ²²*There, all the women who remain in the house of the king of Judah being made to go out to the officers of the king of Babylon, and there, the women saying:*^{bb}

They have seduced you and overcome you,
 the men who were your allies.
Your feet were stuck in a swamp—
 they turned away back.

²³*And they are making all your wives and your children go out to the Chaldeans, and you yourself will not escape from their hand.*^{cc} *Because by the hand of the king of Babylon you will be taken, and this city you will consume*^{dd} *in fire.*^{ee}
 ²⁴*Zedekiah said to Jeremiah, No one must know of these words, and you will not die.* ²⁵*So when the officials hear that I have spoken with you and they come to you and say to you, Tell us, please, what you spoke to the king*^{ff}—*do not conceal it from us, and we will not put you to death. So what did the king say to you?* ²⁶*you will say to them, I was submitting my prayer for grace before the king so as not to make me return to the house of Jonathan to die there.*^{gg} ²⁷*And all the officials came to Jeremiah and asked him, and he told them, in accordance with all these words that the king ordered. So they left off from him, because the thing had not made itself heard.*^{hh}
 ^{28a}*So Jeremiah lived in the courtyard of the guard until the day when Jerusalem was captured.*ⁱⁱ

a. LXX lacks the reference to Pashhur ben Malchiah.
b. MT having had no marker before 38:1, MT^L has a section marker here. LXX lacks *entire*.
c. LXX lacks the reference to *epidemic*.
d. See 21:9 and the commentary on it.
e. MT has a section marker here.
f. *This man* has object marker; see the translation note on 35:14.
g. For the construction, cf. Ps 13:4(5). Vg rather takes *dābār* as the verb's object, suggesting "cannot attain a thing with you" (cf. *DCH*), but one would then expect the pointing *'ittəkem* rather than MT's *'etkem* (perhaps also implied by LXX; cf. BDB). The word order also works against this understanding.
h. LXX lacks *so they got Jeremiah.*
i. On nouns with the article followed by a proper noun, see GK 127f.
j. LXX lacks *with ropes.*
k. MT has a section marker here.
l. See the translation note on 29:2, and T. Parker, "Ebed-melech as Exemplar," in Goldingay, *Uprooting and Planting*, 253–59. LXX lacks *a man who was an overseer.*

m. LXX lacks *my lord king* and then has Ebed-melech accusing the king: "You have acted . . ."

n. The *wayyiqtol* is anomalous (*IBHS* 33.3.1f); perhaps the implication is "he's as good as dead" (cf. Tg; *TTH* 79).

o. Lit. "in his place."

p. One medieval MS has "three," which is more the kind of number that one would expect, but such a text-critical substitution "ranks as one of the least supportable emendations in the entire book of Jeremiah [no small accolade] and betrays a painfully unimaginative reading of the text" (Lundbom, *Jeremiah 37–52*, 72).

q. LXX lacks *into his charge*.

r. LXX lacks *with ropes*.

s. MT has a section marker here.

t. The infinitive precedes the finite verb, underlining the factuality of the action.

u. LXX lacks *in secret*.

v. See the translation note and commentary on 4:2.

w. MT has a section marker here. LXX lacks *who are seeking your life*. On the *if*-clause, see the translation note on 15:11.

x. MT^A has a section marker here.

y. The infinitive precedes the finite verb, underlining the factuality of the action.

z. MT has a section marker here. LXX lacks *from their hand*.

aa. MT^L has a unit marker here. LXX, Vg, Tg have "mock," but *ʿālal* denotes something more physically painful.

bb. I translate the participles as present, on the assumption that they represent what Jeremiah saw in his vision; cf. LXX; Duhm, *Jeremia*, 306.

cc. LXX lacks *from their hand*.

dd. For MT *tiśrōp*, LXX, Tg "will be consumed" implies the more predictable *tiśśārēp* (cf. v. 17), whose unimaginative nature as an emendation ranks with "three" for "thirty" in v. 10. Vg "he will burn" (cf. 21:10) implies *yiśrōp*.

ee. MT has a marker here.

ff. LXX has "what the king said to you."

gg. MT has a unit marker here.

hh. MT^L has a unit marker here.

ii. MT^L has a section marker here.

This second story in Jer 37–39 parallels the first in relating how Zedekiah consults Jeremiah about what is going to happen and Jeremiah gives him bad news. In a variety of ways and in the manner of parallelism, this second story heightens the first and complements it.[27]

- The officials exercise their own initiative and make their own speech.
- Zedekiah is a more central figure.
- Zedekiah is in a greater state of indecision and fear.

27. Fischer, *Jeremia*, 2:329.

- Jeremiah is likewise in a greater state of fear and hesitancy.
- In place of Irijah as accuser and assailant, Ebed-melech emerges as Jeremiah's ally and rescuer.

Jeremiah 37–38 exemplifies how the Scriptures can include more than one version of a story that has overlapping motifs, such as the accounts of creation, Yahweh's self-revelation to Moses, the emergence of Saul as king, the emergence of David as king, the deliverance of Judah from Sennacherib, Jesus's miraculous feeding of several thousand people, and the bestowing of the Holy Spirit on his followers. It may be hard to know whether the stories relate to different events or are varying accounts of the same event. If they are varying accounts, the dissimilarities will reflect how authors have been inspired to generate different vivid and instructive narratives on the basis of some basic facts that the stories have in common, of some complementary theological insights, and of some imagination. It may not matter too much; in this case, either way, "the art of story-telling" is a key feature of the two chapters,[28] and the Jeremiah scroll evidently wants the audience to pay attention to both versions. The inclusion of both draws attention to the key themes that they have in common and to their individual features.

Actually, this unit is a third one involving Jeremiah, Zedekiah, and some of his officials during the siege of Jerusalem. All three manifest overlapping motifs:

- Zedekiah sends officials to ask Jeremiah to approach Yahweh on the city's behalf (21:1–2; 37:3–5).
- Jeremiah passes on Yahweh's message that the Babylonians will capture the city and that people should surrender to them now if they want to live (21:3–10; 37:6–10; 38:2–4, 17–18).
- Believing Jeremiah is a traitor, some officials put him into life-threatening detention in a cistern (37:11–16; 38:4–6).
- Zedekiah agrees to rescue Jeremiah from the cistern (37:18–21a; 38:7–13).
- Zedekiah consults Jeremiah in secret (37:17; 38:14–27).
- Jeremiah ends up in the prison courtyard instead of the cistern (37:21; 38:28).

A comparison of the three stories also draws attention to their distinctive features. While 21:1–10 focuses on the message to Zedekiah and 37:1–21

---

28. R. P. Carroll, *Jeremiah*, OTL, 683.

focuses on developments in the context of the Egyptians' intervention and the Babylonians' consequent temporary withdrawal, 38:1–28 focuses on its four characters, on the dilemmas or challenges they face, and on the ways they deal with them:

- The first character is actually a group, the four officials. They correctly perceive that Jeremiah is expecting disaster for Jerusalem, not well-being, and that his message has a negative effect on people who are trying to defend the city. Their problem would be solved if they accepted Jeremiah's message, but as long as they reject it, their action makes sense. And how are they to be sure that he is a prophet who tells the truth rather than one whose word is deceptive?[29]

- Zedekiah is king, but his words and actions reflect how monarchy has its checks and balances, like democracy. He is dependent on the collaboration of other leaders and on consensus over how to deal with issues. It would be more the case if many people maintain an allegiance to his deposed predecessor.[30] So he is torn between doing what the officials say and doing what he knows is right. As well as being in a tricky position in relation to the nation's officials, he is in a vulnerable position in relation to ordinary members of his own people who find fault with his policy. His position as a Babylonian appointee could make for a further complication. And he is in a more vulnerable position than anyone in relation to the attacking military forces in case of the failure of the city's attempts to survive their assault. In addition, he is subject to a frightening account from Jeremiah of what the future holds if he maintains his current policy and of the responsibility he will have for the disaster Jeremiah says is coming (*This city you will consume in fire*). The chapters thus portray Zedekiah with more sympathy than critique.[31] He is "a desperate king living in desperate times."[32]

- Ebed-melech is the one new character in the story, the kind of unambiguous hero who appears from time to time to play a bit part in the scroll's drama, like Ahikam or Baruch. He is a foreigner, like Rahab or Ruth or Uriah; the brief story about him draws atten-

---

29. D. R. Jones, *Jeremiah*, 459–60.

30. Thompson, *Jeremiah*, 638.

31. M. C. Calloway, "Telling the Truth and Telling Stories: An Analysis of Jeremiah 37–38," *Union Seminary Quarterly Review* 44 (1991): 256; cf. H.-J. Stipp, "Zedekiah in the Book of Jeremiah," *CBQ* 58 (1996): 627–48.

32. M. Leuchter, *Polemics of Exile*, 117.

tion to his ethnicity three times, twice more than is strictly necessary[33] (compare the way the Ruth story keeps noting that she is a Moabite). He shines a negative light on the Israelite characters in the story by the unambiguous way he perceives a challenge and responds to it. While he might be a foreign diplomat based in the palace, the way he knows his way around it (v. 11) may rather suggest that he is simply a member of the king's household staff. Either way, he shines a light on the way the Judahites with political power go about exercising it.

- As for Jeremiah himself, on one hand the officials' account and later his dialogue with Zedekiah indicate that he continues to fulfill his commission with resolution. But fulfilling his commission imperils his life. It makes him hesitant to continue to do so, especially when it is quite ineffective—why risk his life for nothing? He is then put on the spot by Zedekiah, who wants him to be economical with the truth in what he says to the officials about their conversation, and he does as instructed. One might make three other observations about this last point. First, being economical with the truth means not saying everything; it doesn't mean lying. Second, the Scriptures don't disapprove of vulnerable people lying to people with power over them (e.g., Exod 1:15–21; James 2:25). But third, the story offers no moral evaluation of Jeremiah any more than of the other characters in the unit, either positive or negative. It is not concerned with a moral question. Its focus lies on the toughness of the situation that Jeremiah faces and of the way things work out.

What applies to Jeremiah in this connection applies to the other characters. The unit offers no negative evaluation of Zedekiah, the officials, or Jeremiah, nor any explicit positive evaluation of Ebed-melech (who will get his commendation in 39:15–18). Like 37:3–21, in its openness and obliqueness it thus stands in tension with the judgment in 37:1–2, and it functions to give further resources to the story's audience in Mizpah or in Egypt as people reflect on what they have gone through and what they are going through.

The twofold plot sequence of this unit corresponds to that of Jer 37:

vv. 1–13a   Some officials put Jeremiah in a cistern in the prison courtyard

---

33. Weis, "Textual Situation," 278; though one should note that the First Testament often "unnecessarily" repeats epithets—Jeremiah is three times called "the prophet" in this chapter.

vv. 1–6   The officials take their action because of his message

vv. 7–13a   Ebed-melech, the Sudanese overseer, gets him rescued

vv. 13b–27   Zedekiah secretly quizzes Jeremiah about what is going to happen now

vv. 13b–18   Jeremiah hesitates to speak because he is afraid of Zedekiah

vv. 19–23   Zedekiah expresses his fear of the Judahites

vv. 24–27   Zedekiah swears Jeremiah to secrecy

v. 28a   The curators provide a concluding link to what follows

1–3 The story starts without introduction, which would suggest that it carries on chronologically from Jer 37. At first, the implication would then apparently be that Jeremiah continued preaching to the entire people even when he was in the prison courtyard (LXX's lack of the word *entire* hardly resolves that difficulty). More likely, either this story is separate from and parallel to the one that precedes or the opening sentence refers to what these officials (as they will be called in v. 4) had heard before his confinement. It would have been entirely plausible for them to have heard it: the account of his message virtually repeats words from the parallel passage in 21:7–10 and from 32:3–4 (cf. also, e.g., 27:8, 12–13; 34:17–22). Jehucal (with the longer spelling) appeared in 37:3, and maybe Gedaliah's father is the Pashhur of 20:1–6, while Pashhur ben Malchiah appeared in a similar connection in 21:1. The names of Gedaliah ben Pashhur and Jucal/Jehucal ben Shelemiah have appeared on Jerusalem seals (see the commentary on 36:11–14a). Shephatiah ben Mattan is otherwise unknown.

4–6 Again, it is easier to assume that the officials' worry relates to a situation when Jeremiah is free to cause trouble in the city than a situation when he is already in custody; the officials' concern parallels Irijah's, which led to his bringing Jeremiah to "the officials" earlier (37:13–14). But "the nearer the catastrophe approaches, so much more critical does the position of the imprisoned prophet also become."[34] Talk of executing Jeremiah first came in Jer 26, at the beginning of Jehoiakim's reign. So he has been living with this threat for twenty years. And in vv. 1–13 as a whole, "death is the grim leitmotif":[35] the threatened death of the city and the threatened death of the prophet, which would be designed to avert it but would be more likely to ensure it. "When the leadership opposes the prophetic mission, they reveal the depth of national religious decay."[36] But the leaders are not so wrong in their account of Jeremiah's preaching. He does keep talking about *something dire* as opposed to *well-being* as the city's destined and proper fate.

34. Weiser, *Jeremia*, 2:346.
35. Allen, *Jeremiah*, 412.
36. Diamond, "Jeremiah," 600.

And his preaching would indeed discourage the city's defenders. The king's comment shows that an Israelite monarch does not have absolute power; like a president or prime minister, he cannot always get his way. Naturally, the prison courtyard also had a cistern, and apparently a more unpleasant one than Jonathan's. "As Jeremiah reaches his nadir, the drama in the plot reached its peak: what will happen to Jeremiah now?"[37] The cistern belonged to one Malchiah (cf. v. 1), "the king's son." Second Kings 24:18 suggests that Zedekiah is too young for his actual son to be the owner of a cistern. Maybe "king's son" is a title (see the commentary on 36:24–26).

7–8 The First Testament refers to a number of Africans and other foreigners serving in the Israelite army or in other capacities; 2 Sam 18:21–32 tells of another impressive Sudanese. Foreigners might immigrate as escaped slaves and might be welcome because they would be less tempted to disloyalty.[38] Perhaps Ebed-melech's outsider status somehow enabled him to see the barbarism of the officials' action in a way that Judahites could not.[39] In these chapters, "the foreigners frame the offenses of the native people."[40] Ironically, the king is presumably sitting *in the Benjamin Gateway* deciding on cases that are brought to him, and Ebed-melech has one for him to consider. A town gateway is the regular place where disputes and questions are sorted out by the community's senior members (e.g., Ruth 4; Isa 29:21; Amos 5:10, 12, 15). In Jerusalem, the king, with his responsibility for the faithful exercise of authority (*mišpāṭ ûṣədāqâ*) would have some responsibility for such procedures. With further irony, it is a foreigner who embodies what an Israelite king, a faithful shoot for David, is supposed to be in this connection.[41] Second Samuel 15:2–6 perhaps implies that in normal times the king would oversee the procedures rather than personally implementing them, though these are not normal times. But the Benjamin Gateway in particular is also a "symbolic space": it is where Irijah arrested Jeremiah (37:13).[42]

9–13a There is an ellipsis somewhere in the logic of the reference to bread (so it is unlikely to be a gloss,[43] because glosses should smooth things, not complicate them): if there is no more bread, everyone is going to die of starvation. Maybe Ebed-melech is exaggerating the dimensions of a food shortage that makes people ignore Jeremiah's needs, or maybe Ebed-melech hopes

---

37. Roncace, *Jeremiah*, 76.

38. See further Lundbom, *Jeremiah 37–52*, 70.

39. Mayer, *Commentary*, 446.

40. E. K. Holt, "The Potent Word of God: Remarks on the Composition of Jeremiah 37–44," in Diamond, K. M. O'Connor, and Stulman, *Troubling Jeremiah*, 167.

41. W. L. Widder, "Thematic Correspondences between the Zedekiah Texts of Jeremiah (Jer 21–24; 37–38)," *OTE* 26 (2013): 491–503.

42. Roncace, *Jeremiah*, 86.

43. Volz, *Jeremia*, 341.

that Zedekiah won't notice the illogic in his argument[44]—and he doesn't. Thirty people is way more than is needed for the task, but it could be a wise size of gang if the officials are going to oppose the project.[45] Apparently, the palace has a junk room beneath the storeroom, and it is from there that Ebed-melech gets the padding to protect Jeremiah from rope burn.

13b–16 As happened in Jer 37, Jeremiah does not now gain his freedom, but he does live in less unpleasant confinement. In due course, Zedekiah surreptitiously arranges to see him. *The third entrance that was in Yahweh's house* was presumably a private way into the temple from the palace. Jeremiah guesses that Zedekiah's question, which sounds as if it ought to be novel if it is the topic for a secret meeting, is actually the same old question, in response to which Jeremiah will have to make something like the same old statement that got him into the cistern and in danger of death before. Further, in response to it Zedekiah will presumably take the same amount of notice he usually does. Distinctive to Jeremiah's objection is his describing his potential response as giving *counsel* (*yāʿas*; Jeremiah otherwise uses the verb only in 49:20, 30; 50:45). Counsel is usually the business of the king's advisers (18:18). The use of this verb indeed reflects the political and military implications of any advice Jeremiah will give.

17–18 Jeremiah does restate the message that got him sinking into the mud; see vv. 2–3 and compare 21:9–10; 32:3–4; 34:2–3. But the possible results of Zedekiah's turning have changed. There is no promise here that the city can avoid surrendering to Nebuchadrezzar, as Jeremiah earlier implied. Yahweh's message yesterday may not be his message today. Circumstances change, and the message changes; Yahweh's word works in dialogue with historical and political factors. The change in Yahweh's word is a sign that the fall of the city is now inevitable. The verses "drive the foregone conclusion even more sharply toward its completion."[46] But Zedekiah can hope to avert the worst consequences of conquest by a voluntary submission.

19–20 Zedekiah therefore has a different question. What if the Chaldeans hand him over to the Judahites who have already surrendered? The existence of such a group is quite a revelation. Are they people who did as Jeremiah said, people who have followed Jeremiah's exhortation to go out and submit to the Babylonians? Or have they just done so because the situation seemed hopeless? Either way, they almost sound like a kind of alternative Judahite government, a government in (nearby) exile.[47] Maybe they will want to punish Zedekiah for not having done the same himself earlier and saved every-

---

44. Thompson, *Jeremiah*, 640.

45. Lundbom, *Jeremiah 37–52*, 72.

46. Fretheim, *Jeremiah*, 524.

47. See Lipschits, *Fall and Rise of Jerusalem*, 93–97, who sees here the background to Gedaliah's Mizpah community and administrative center.

one some suffering. Jeremiah's response is quite a promise. If it's too late for Yahweh to deliver the city, it is not too late for him to look after people who turn to him and do as he says.

21–23 Jeremiah also nuances his promise that surrender will be the best thing for Zedekiah himself. He has heard women chanting some lines by way of a taunt song.[48] The contemptuous lines of verse give more precision to the basis for the assault that Zedekiah is anxious about. In real time, the women have not begun chanting yet, but in his awareness of what Yahweh is going to bring about, Jeremiah has heard them. Formally, the lines are a lament in 3-2 rhythm, but in substance they are indeed a taunt, like Isa 14:4b–21.[49] Zedekiah should surely not have been so stupid, the women imply. The king is going to be shamed by what happens to the city, by what happens to the women, and further shamed by the women themselves.[50] He needs to remember how women pay a terrible price when their men get defeated in war, a fact that is also a further cause of shame to the men themselves. Zedekiah has let himself be deceived by his *allies* ("the men of your *šālôm*"); *they have . . . overcome you, the men who were your allies* corresponds to Obad 7. The Egyptians let him down in the end as Jeremiah said they would, and he has also been overcome by his own officials (v. 5). He really is somewhat pathetic. While the word for *swamp* comes only here, sinking in a quagmire is an image elsewhere for being overwhelmed by a potentially fatal predicament from which one cannot extricate oneself (Pss 40:2[3]; 69:14[15]).[51] Such a plight engulfed Zedekiah. It was supposed to be a mess that one's friends helped one to get out of; Zedekiah's friends had high-tailed it out instead (cf. 37:9). He is just as sunk in the mud as Jeremiah—or rather, whereas Jeremiah has just escaped from the mud, Zedekiah is still in it and will never escape it.[52] In his summary prose description of the humiliating calamity that is imminent, Jeremiah makes no reference to Yahweh's activity. While Yahweh reveals what will happen, the agency is human. Jeremiah's warning comes as a devastating conclusion in this connection: you, Zedekiah—not Yahweh, not the Chaldeans—*this city you will consume in fire*. "The torch was not applied by Zedekiah,"[53] but he was responsible for the torching.

24–28a Zedekiah, oddly, is more concerned about his officials than about the Babylonians. The story shifts from focusing on Jeremiah's fears to fo-

---

48. Volz, *Jeremia*, 345.

49. Holladay, *Commentary on Jeremiah*, 2:290.

50. Roncace, *Jeremiah*, 107–8.

51. On the question of dependence either way, see B. Ego, "'In meinem Herzen berge ich dein Wort': Zur Rezeption von Jer 31,33 in der Torafrömmigkeit der Psalmen," *Jahrbuch für Biblische Theologie* 12 (1997): 277–89; B. Gosse, "Le Psaume 40 et le livre de Jérémie," *ZAW* 117 (2005): 395–404.

52. B. Green, "Sunk in the Mud: Literary Correlation and Collaboration between King and Prophet in the Book of Jeremiah," in Holt and Sharp, *Jeremiah Invented*, 34–48.

53. Calvin, *Jeremiah*, 4:449.

cusing on Zedekiah's, expressed in the spoken words that carry most of the freight through Jer 37–38.[54] Ironically, the king is now seeking Jeremiah's protection from the officials. Further, to protect himself, Jeremiah must not repeat the message that the officials know he consistently preaches.[55] The narrative half-implies that Zedekiah recognizes the truth in the message, but he is "politically incapable of doing what he knows to be theologically correct."[56] He is "sympathetic to Jeremiah and Yahweh's word but unable to obey."[57] In the response he suggests to Jeremiah's potential cross-examiners, the prospect of the cistern at Jonathan's house returns, and if we take into account the fact that he actually does do what v. 26 says (cf. 37:20), Jeremiah tells no lies; he just doesn't tell the officials everything.[58]

3. The City Falls, and the Fates That Follow (38:28b—39:14 [LXX 45:28b—46:14])

[38:28b] *When Jerusalem was captured:*[a] [39:1]*in the ninth year of Zedekiah King of Judah, in the tenth month, Nebuchadrezzar King of Babylon came with his entire force to Jerusalem and blockaded it.*[b] [2]*In the eleventh year of Zedekiah, in the fourth*[c] *month, on the ninth of the month, the city was broken open.*[d] [3]*All the officials of the king of Babylon came in and sat in the middle gateway: Nergal-sarezer*[e] *(samgar*[f]*), Nebu Sarsechim*[g] *(rab-saris*[h]*), Nergal-sarezer (rab-mag*[i]*), and all the remainder of the officers of the king of Babylon.*[j]

[4]*When Zedekiah King of Judah saw them, he and all the people who had been engaged in the battle, they fled. They went out by night from the city by the road to the king's garden through the gateway between the double walls. He went out by the road to the Steppe,* [5]*but the Babylonian force pursued them, and they overtook Zedekiah in the Jericho steppes. So they got him and made him go up to Nebuchadrezzar King of Babylon at Riblah in the region of Hamath, and he spoke out authoritative decisions with him.*[k] [6]*The king of Babylon slaughtered Zedekiah's sons at Riblah before his eyes; and all the gentry from Judah the king of Babylon slaughtered.* [7]*Zedekiah's eyes he blinded, and he shackled him with bronze chains*[l] *to make him come to Babylon.*

54. T. M. Willis, "'They Did Not Listen to the Voice of the Lord': A Literary Analysis of Jeremiah 37–45," *Restoration Quarterly* 42 (2000): 71.

55. R. P. Carroll, *Jeremiah*, OTL, 689.

56. Brueggemann, *Jeremiah 26–52*, 152.

57. Applegate, "Fate of Zedekiah," 307.

58. Fretheim, *Jeremiah*, 519.

[8]*The king's house and the housing of the people*[m] *the Chaldeans consumed in fire, and the walls of Jerusalem they pulled down.* [9]*The rest*[n] *of the people who remained in the city and the people who had fallen away, who had fallen away to him—the rest of the people who remained,*[o] *Nebuzaradan*[p] *the chief of the guards*[q] *took into exile in Babylon.* [10]*But some of the people who were poor, who had nothing, Nebuzaradan the chief of the guards allowed to remain in the country of Judah; he gave them vineyards and tillage*[r] *on that day.*

[11]*Nebuchadrezzar King of Babylon gave orders*[s] *concerning Jeremiah by means of Nebuzaradan*[t] *the chief of the guards:* [12]*"Get him and keep your eyes on him, and don't do anything dire to him. Rather, as he speaks to you, so act with him."* [13]*So Nebuzaradan the chief of the guards sent, he and Nebushazban*[u] *(rab-saris), Nergal-sarezar (ram-mag), and all the senior officers of the king of Babylon—*[14]*they sent and got Jeremiah from the prison courtyard and gave him over to Gedaliah ben Ahikam, son of Shaphan, to let him go out to his house.*[v] *So he lived*[w] *among the people.*[x]

a. MT has a unit marker here, but 38:28b looks more like an introduction to Jer 39 than a postscript to Jer 38.

b. MT[L] has a section marker here.

c. Vg has "fifth" (and lacks the reference to the ninth of the month), assimilating to 2 Kgs 25:8.

d. Whereas 2 Kgs 25:4 has the *niphal* verb *wattibāqaʿ*, which could imply the city opening the gates, the verb here is *hophal hobqəʿâ*, which suggests the Babylonians forcing them open; see the discussion in Rudolph, *Jeremia*, 244.

e. A Hebraized version of the name appearing in the list of "The Court of Nebuchadnezzar" in *ANET*, 308.

f. In MT's punctuation, this word is the beginning of another name, but the Babylonian word *simmagir* suggests a duty carried out by an officer of Nebuchadrezzar (*HALOT*, 759).

g. MT links the name *nəbû* with *samgar*, but both possibilities in the previous note suggest that LXX is right to link it with *śarsəkîm*; the resultant name is then a compound noun like Nebuchadrezzar (Hendel and Joosten, *How Old?*, 114; see their references).

h. In Hebrew, this title suggests "chief officer," but it is apparently a Hebraized version of a similar Akkadian title (see BDB, 913; *HALOT*, 769b–70a, 1172–73).

i. Another title for a senior officer (*HALOT*, 543a, 1172–73), distinguishing this Nergal-sarezer from the one mentioned earlier. A Nergal-sarezer (Neriglissar) eventually succeeded Nebuchadrezzar as king of Babylon.

j. LXX lacks vv. 4–13.

k. See the translation note on 1:16.

l. The dual *nəḥuštayim* commonly means *bronze chains* (BDB) holding together the two legs and feet.

m. Lit. "the house of the people." The expression comes only here; it is equivalent to *all the houses in Jerusalem* and *every house of a big person* in 52:13.

n. *Yeter* is a synonym of words such as *šəʾērît*, but it never makes the transition to becoming a word with positive connotations (K. D. Mulzac, "Ytr as a Remnant Term in the Book of Jeremiah," *Journal of the Adventist Theological Society* 19 [2008]: 3–17).

o. For *the rest of the people who remained*, 52:15 has an unusual expression for *the rest of the crowd*, which the curators might be paraphrasing here.

p. A Hebraized version of a name meaning "Nabu has given offspring"; cf. BDB, *HALOT*.

q. Lit. "executioners" or "butchers."

r. For the MT *hapax legomenon yəgēbîm*, Vg, Th "cisterns" implies *gēbîm*.

s. The *waw*-consecutive is used loosely, as this action must precede that in v. 10.

t. This name also appears in the list of "The Court of Nebuchadnezzar" in *ANET*, 308, as Nabuzeribni.

u. A Hebraized version of a name meaning "May Nabu deliver me"; cf. BDB, *HALOT*.

v. Lit. "let him go to the house," which can mean simply "let him go home" (Vg; cf. Hag 1:9).

w. Vg takes the *waw*-consecutive clause as continuing the infinitive.

x. MT has a section marker here.

As the sequence of narratives continues, this unit begins in the same context as Jer 37–38—the Babylonian blockade and siege of Jerusalem that started in 589/588—and seamlessly moves on chronologically to the city's actual fall in 587. It compares and contrasts with the accounts of the event in Jer 52 and 2 Kgs 25.[59] Here, the city's fall is just one further stage in a story that will continue in Jer 40–44. Coming in the middle of things, it takes rather matter-of-fact form after all the "metaphor, cosmic imagery, prose commentary, poetic utterance, symbolic acts, foreshadowing, and hyperbole" that have been used to prepare readers for an event that would shake the heavens and the earth,[60] "the primary horror galvanizing all the mythopoetic energy of the scroll."[61] Only the incidental references to "that day" (vv. 10, 16, 17) might hint at something more. The narrative relates the dreadful nature of what happens to Zedekiah without comment, letting it speak for itself; we view the event through Zedekiah's own eyes, not the narrator's.[62]

The setting of 38:28b–39:18 within Jer 37–44 suggests at least part of the reason for the distinctive nature of this version of the story of the city's fall. Like 38:1–28a, it focuses on the fate of four figures—the same three individuals but a different group of people.

> 38:28b–39:3 Background: the city's fall
> 39:4–7   The fate of Zedekiah

59. In this volume, the commentary on Jer 52 tabulates the similarities and differences between the three accounts.

60. Stulman, *Jeremiah*, 319.

61. A. R. P. Diamond, "Interlocutions: The Poetics of Voice in the Figuration of YHWH and His Oracular Agent," *Int* 62 (2008): 55.

62. Cf. Roncace, *Jeremiah*, 119.

The account of the four key figures again manifests a series of ambiguities, which in part derive from the unit's not beginning with an explicit judgment on Zedekiah and on the city, equivalent to 52:1–3 and 2 Kgs 24:18–25:3. While Jer 39 does stand under the shadow of 37:1–2 and its implicit provision of a key to understanding the unit, Jer 39 itself makes no reference to Yahweh until its closing paragraph relating a message for Ebed-melech, and the distance from 37:1–2 increases the tension between that judgment and the ambiguities of this unit. Jeremiah 39 thus raises the following questions.

- How are we to evaluate the flight of Zedekiah and his forces (and their implied abandonment of him, explicit in 52:8)? And how are we to understand Zedekiah's meeting with Nebuchadrezzar and the brutal actions of Nebuchadrezzar that contrast with Jeremiah's promises to Zedekiah in 32:3–5, a few months earlier (which referred to no conditions)? And how are we to relate the meeting and the actions with the further promises (containing no conditions) a few months before in 34:2–5? A few years previously, 27:20 had also issued a warning about the fate of the gentry (in the only other reference to them in Jeremiah) that was less gloomy than their actual fate here.
- What is the implication of the further difference from Jer 52, the absence of any reference to the fate of the temple? And how are we to understand the forced migration of people who had surrendered along with the people who had stayed in the city, notwithstanding Jeremiah's promise to people who surrendered? Are these people who "fell" involuntarily (cf. 6:15; 8:12; Lev 26:7–8, 36)? On the other hand, what is the implication of the further difference from Jer 52 that here the poor people who had not surrendered are allowed to remain in Judah and are *given* vineyards and fields rather than left as vinedressers and farmhands (presumably to work for the Babylonians)? These events link with the promise in 27:11; but how do they link to the distinction between good and bad figs in Jer 24?
- Why does Nebuchadrezzar give a special order concerning Jeremiah? Since Nebuchadrezzar is Yahweh's servant, it's quite appropriate that he should look after another of Yahweh's servants.[63] And

---

63. Fretheim, *Jeremiah*, 532.

maybe Nebuchadrezzar knows that Jeremiah has been urging the city to surrender. This bit of the story increases our sympathy for Irijah and the officials who saw Jeremiah as a traitor. The passing on of Jeremiah to Gedaliah is difficult to understand; we will need to read on in Jer 40 to understand the sequence of events, as Jer 39–40 again proceeds in dramatic rather than chronological order.

We will consider Ebed-melech in relation to 39:15–18.

38:28b—39:3 The account of the city's fall in 52:4–6 (virtually identical with 2 Kgs 25:1–3) will overlap with this account and provide additional information on Nebuchadrezzar's blockade of the city and his eventual active siege. The tenth month implies December 589 or January 588; the city's fall took place in July 587. In place of some of the detail in 52:4–6, this version provides information relating to the fate of Jeremiah (see v. 13). While it's likely that Nebuchadrezzar showed up at Jerusalem for the initiation of the blockade, v. 5 shows that he didn't stay. The Babylonians presumably besieged the city from the north, the side not protected by valleys, and made the breach in the city's walls on that side, where the middle gateway would likewise be located. Coming in and sitting down there would signify taking up a position of authority. It's not quite a fulfillment of the declaration in 1:15, but it's something similar.[64] Jeremiah has referred to *the officials* in 38:17, 22; now the key ones are named. *Samgar*, *rab-saris*, and *rab-mag* all seem to be terms for Babylonian officers, equivalent to expressions such as commandant, general, and senior officer, but we don't know their precise meaning, and neither would the audience.

4–5a Presumably, what issued in the flight was not specifically the sight of the Babylonian leaders sitting there after the Babylonian forces broke through the walls but the more general sight of the Babylonian forces themselves, perhaps on the previous night when the city's collapse was evidently imminent. The expression *the double wall* would again suggest the north side of the city, where a later tradition came to identify the quarry just east of the modern Damascus Gate as "Zedekiah's Cave," his secret escape route.[65] More likely, however, as the Babylonians prepared to enter on the north and sit in a gateway there, Zedekiah and his troops prepared to leave through a gateway on the southeast that led into the steep slopes of the Kidron Ravine, which might be less guarded and would lead toward Jericho. The description of the location fits the references in Neh 3:15 to a wall and a pool at the king's garden, in 2 Chr 32:5 to Hezekiah building an extra wall outside the old city

---

64. Rashi, in MG.
65. Rosenberg, *Jeremiah*, 2:312.

wall in connection with safeguarding the city's water supply, and in Isa 22:11 to a double wall and a pool resulting from construction in Hezekiah's time.[66] While the Babylonians were surrounding the city (cf. 52:7), they were perhaps focusing on the push to enter the city from the north and not paying attention on other sides, or perhaps *all the people who had been engaged in the battle*, who accompanied Zedekiah, were able to evade or overcome any Babylonian lookout posts on that southeast side. The Steppe, the *ʿărābâ*, strictly refers to the desert area south of the Dead Sea, but here it may take in the region north of the Dead Sea, including the area around Jericho. Presumably, Zedekiah was aiming to get across the Jordan to take refuge in Ammon, Moab, or Edom (cf. 40:11; 41:15). But he and his company failed; maybe the Babylonian forces would be fitter than the Judahites, who would be weakened by fighting and by shortage of food.

5b–7 Zedekiah "ran for his life, but not fast enough."[67] The king would be a main focus of the Babylonians' interest. He had led the rebellion, and Nebuchadrezzar would want him to pay for it—again to act as a deterrent to other people's leaders. Riblah is on the main route from Egypt or Canaan to Mesopotamia, a convenient location for a Babylonian king to have his base in an area less isolated than Jerusalem. It is two hundred miles from Jericho, a straight shot up the Jordan Valley into the Bekaa Valley if the Babylonian forces chose to go that way. Nebuchadrezzar's *authoritative decisions*, or "judgments" (*mišpāṭîm*), would be his decisions about Zedekiah's punishment for his rebellion (52:3, 9). But the audience might recall that authoritative decisions was a subject that Yahweh talked about way back (4:12), and Jeremiah too (12:1). Nebuchadrezzar is making his own decisions, but without realizing it, he is implementing Yahweh's decisions. Slaughtering Zedekiah's sons would ensure that no one could think of putting them on the throne. Blinding Zedekiah would incapacitate him; it is an action known to have been taken against people such as slaves or war captives.[68] Jeremiah 52:11 adds that Nebuchadrezzar put Zedekiah in prison in Babylon until his death. The *gentry* (*ḥōrîm*; cf. 27:20) had apparently accompanied the fighters, mistakenly thinking they would thus do better than they would by waiting for the city's fall. Perhaps Zedekiah and the gentry were willing to forfeit the fulfillment of a less grim fate by attempting to run rather than staying when the city was about to fall.

8–9 The scroll continues to offer its distinctive account of the fall. *Pulled down* has extra resonance: the story is recording the fulfillment of Yahweh's

66. See H. Wildberger, *Isaiah 13–27*, A Continental Commentary (Minneapolis: Fortress, 1997), 367–70.
67. Brueggemann, *Jeremiah 26–52*, 288.
68. Lundbom, *Jeremiah 37–52*, 88–89.

threat that goes back to Jeremiah's commission (1:10). Something similar applies to the account of how the Babylonians *consumed* the city *in fire* (e.g., 37:8, 10; 38:18) and *took* people *into exile* (e.g., 13:19; 20:4). The account first summarizes the destruction more briefly than Jer 52 and 2 Kings 25, omitting reference to the burning of the temple. In contrast, the summary relating to the people taken into exile then contains some redundancy; the second occurrence of *the rest of the people who remained* functions as a summary of the group taken off. According to 52:28–30, this group was relatively small, but here the scroll encourages the impression that the entire people is transported and the city left empty. The calamity was as great as Yahweh said it was going to be, though people who went into exile in Babylon might also suggest the implication that the future lies with them.[69]

10 In a further distinctive formulation compared with 52:16, the scroll goes on to a delicious irony. Only in 5:4 has Jeremiah referred to *the poor* (*dallîm*), people who don't have land and therefore have no way of being self-sufficient; there, he initially professed to think that they were distinctively people who didn't acknowledge Yahweh. The passage then incorporated its own irony as he came to recognize that the same applied to the important people. One expression of the latter's failure to acknowledge Yahweh is their treatment of needy people (2:34; 5:28), and the protection of the powerless and needy was a special responsibility of a king such as Zedekiah (22:16). So who brings about the fulfillment of that obligation? A foreigner![70] The Babylonians become "almost benevolent overlords."[71] A great reversal of destinies takes place, going beyond the aborted move in 34:8–16 and effecting a fulfillment of 6:12.[72] The poor are not merely conscript labor for the Babylonians, as in isolation 52:16 might imply;[73] Nebuzaradan *gave them vineyards* and *tillage*. By implication and with further irony, these might be vineyards and land that had belonged to them but had been taken from them over the years. It would not have been a topic for rejoicing among the landholders who were being forced into exile.[74] The poor will feature further as part of Gedaliah's responsibility (40:7). In association with vineyards, the unique word *tillage* (*yāgēb*; a related participle comes in 52:16) might refer to the terraces on which olives and other fruit were cultivated. In light of earlier links, the closing expression *on that day* would also carry some resonance. It can denote the epoch-making

69. Brueggemann, *Jeremiah 26–52*, 156.

70. Wright, *Jeremiah*, 389.

71. M. E. Biddle, "The Redaction of Jeremiah 39–41 (46–48 LXX)," *ZAW* 126 (2014): 232.

72. Weiser, *Jeremia*, 2:356.

73. J. N. Graham, "'Vinedressers and Plowmen,'" *BA* 47 (1984): 55–58; cf. Allen, *Jeremiah*, 420; "vinedressers and plowmen [lit. tillers]" is the text at 52:16.

74. Calvin, *Jeremiah*, 4:69.

day when Yahweh acts to effect the fulfillment of his purpose in bringing about catastrophe and new creation, which will also be the implication in the reference to the day of Jerusalem's fall in vv. 16 and 17 (cf. 4:9; 25:33; 30:7–8; 48:41; 49:22, 26; 50:30). It is not merely that Nebuzaradan took his action at that chronological time; giving landless people vineyards and tillage is an aspect of the restoration of Jerusalem and Judah.

11–14 Like everybody else, Jeremiah is simply the object of Babylonian actions; he does nothing.[75] While it wouldn't be surprising if Nebuchadrezzar's intelligence-gathering procedures discovered that Jeremiah had been encouraging Zedekiah and his people to surrender to him, it would be unlikely that he would be dealing with this matter personally. But the story hints at another point about the fulfillment of Yahweh's word (e.g., 1:18–19; 15:20–21). The names of the officers overlap with but differ from the ones that appeared in vv. 3, 11, and 13.[76] The next chapter will tell us more about Nebuzaradan's dealings with Jeremiah and about Gedaliah (a different Gedaliah from the one in 38:1), who evidently did not flee with Zedekiah and escaped the fate of other people who surrendered or stayed in the city. It will also imply that Jeremiah *lived among the people* in Gedaliah's house (*with him*; 40:6) rather than returning to his own house in (nearby) Anathoth.

4. A Footnote Message for Ebed-melech (39:15–18 [LXX 46:15–18])

[15]*Yahweh's word had come to Jeremiah*[a] *when he was confined*[b] *in the prison courtyard.* [16]*Go*[c] *and say to Ebed-melech the Sudanese: Yahweh of Armies, the God of Israel, has said this. Here am I, causing my words to come about for this city, for something dire, not for something good. They will happen before you on that day.*[d] [17]*But I will rescue you on that day (Yahweh's affirmation). You will not be given over into the hand of the people before whom you are fearful,* [18]*because I will definitely enable you to escape.*[e] *By the sword you will not fall. Your life will be yours as loot,*[f] *because you've relied on me (Yahweh's affirmation).*[g]

a. The word order ("To Jeremiah had come . . .") avoids a *waw*-consecutive in a context where the meaning required is pluperfect (Allen, *Jeremiah*, 418).

b. LXX lacks *when he was confined*.

c. The infinitive absolute is used imperatively; cf. 2:2 and the translation note on it.

d. LXX lacks this sentence.

e. The infinitive precedes the finite verb, underlining the factuality of the action.

75. Roncace, *Jeremiah*, 128.

76. See, e.g., P.-M. Bogaert, "Les généraux babyloniens selon Jérémie (LXX 46,3; TM 39,3 et 13) et selon Flavius Josèphe (Ant. Jud. X,135)," *RB* 123 (2016): 519–35.

f. See 21:9 and the commentary on it.

g. MT has a marker here.

This message for Ebed-melech brings Jer 37–39 to an edifying climax. As a promise to Baruch will come in Jer 45 and not where we might have expected it, at the end of Jer 36 (or even here), a promise to Ebed-melech comes here and not in Jer 38 where we might have expected it—especially as Yahweh apparently gave it to Jeremiah then. And it fits here as an aspect of the story's account of what happened to the key players. The message's location here contributes to bringing the first part of the Jer 37–45 narrative to a close, as the location of the message for Baruch will contribute to bringing the entire narrative in Jer 37–38 to a close.[77] Like the preceding paragraph about Jeremiah's joining Gedaliah, the message for Ebed-melech thus comes out of chronological order. But whereas that paragraph relates to what follows, this message relates chronologically to what has preceded.

15–18 Evidently, being *confined in the prison courtyard* didn't stop Jeremiah paying visits outside, as his earlier detention would have done (unless we should not press the meaning of *go* and it could cover sending a message); the courtyard was a kind of open prison.[78] Placed here, the report of Jeremiah's message follows the account of the events that have fulfilled the first part of the declaration. Ebed-melech will have seen the city's *dire* rather than *good* fate come about. By implication, he also will have seen the promise fulfilled. *That day* has arrived (see the commentary on v. 10). As often happens, the story gives no account of Jeremiah's delivering the promise to him. For the audience, it is enough to include the promise; the audience also knows that the day arrived and that threat and promise have been fulfilled. There was no reference to fear in 38:7–9, but it would be odd if Ebed-melech didn't have any fear; the reference also recalls 1:8 and the promises that follow there. The encouragement and promise that apply to Jeremiah apply to Ebed-melech too. Nor was there any statement that Ebed-melech *relied on me* in 38:7–9, but it would explain the courage presupposed by 38:7–9. The message's closing declaration is thus a double surprise: this foreigner was someone who trusted in Yahweh even though he was scared—and it would be quite reasonable to be scared, whether he was scared of the Babylonians or of the king and his officials. "Such trust rules out fear" (see 17:7–8).[79] In both respects, this paragraph thus provides an informative footnote to 38:7–13.

77. K. D. Mulzac, "Is Jeremiah 39:15–18 Out of Order?" *AUSS* 45 (2007): 69–72.

78. D. R. Jones, *Jeremiah*, 466.

79. R. P. Carroll, *Jeremiah*, OTL, 697.

The blessings of the one whose help is the God of Jacob,
whose hope is in Yahweh his God! (Ps 146:5)

The blessings of the people whose God is Yahweh! (Ps 144:15)[80]

B. PART 4B: THE AFTERMATH, AND MISSED CHANCES (40:1–44:30 [LXX 47:1–51:30])

Jeremiah 39 is one of several points where the Jeremiah scroll could have come to a satisfactory end. Jeremiah's warnings have been fulfilled, he is safe, and the chapter closes with an encouraging word for the person who trusts in Yahweh. Actually, we are less than halfway through Jer 37–45. The narrative now goes on to tell of the arrangements made for the administration of the ongoing community in Judah implied by 39:10–14, then of how there is no end to the willingness of some people to make things worse in Judah. Their action takes Jeremiah to Egypt, where he ends up berating them for their further demonstration of stupidity, which threatens to bring about the end of their community.

1. A New Start at Mizpah, the Watchtower (40:1–12 [LXX 47:1–12])

[1]*The word that came to Jeremiah from Yahweh after Nebuzaradan the chief of the guards sent him off from The Height[a] when he got him; he was shackled[b] in chains among the entire exile group from Jerusalem and Judah who were being taken into exile to Babylon.*
    [2]*So the chief of the guards got Jeremiah[c] and said to him, "Yahweh your God—he spoke of this dire thing for this place, [3]and he has made it come about.[d] Yahweh has acted as he spoke,[e] because you[f] did wrong in relation to Yahweh and did not listen to his voice, and this thing has happened[g] to you. [4]So now, here, I am releasing you[h] today from the chains that are on your hand. If it is good in your eyes to come with me to Babylon, come, and I will keep my eye on you. But if it is dire in your eyes to come with me to Babylon, hold back—look at the entire country before you—regarding what is good and regarding the thing that's right in your eyes to go there, go."[i] [5]But he did not yet respond.[j] "Or go back[k] to Gedaliah ben Ahikam, the son of Shaphan, whom the king of Babylon has appointed over the towns[l] of Judah—go back with him among the people, or anywhere it is right in your eyes to go—go." So the chief of the guards gave him provisions and[m] supplies and sent him off, [6]and Jeremiah came to Gedaliah*

ben Ahikam at The Watchtowerⁿ and lived with him among the people who remained in the country.^o

⁷*All the officers from the forces that were in the open country and their men heard that the king of Babylon had appointed Gedaliah ben Ahikam over the country and that he had appointed with him men and women and little ones, some^p of the poor of the country, of the people who had not been taken into exile to Babylon.* ⁸*They came to Gedaliah at The Watchtower: Ishmael ben Netaniah, Johanan and Jonathan the sons of Kareah,^q Seraiah ben Tanhumeth, the sons of Ephai^r the Netophethite, Jezaniah the son of the Maacathite, they and their men.* ⁹*Gedaliah ben Ahikam, the son of Shaphan, promised them and their men, "Don't be afraid of serving^s the Chaldeans—stay in the country and serve the king of Babylon, and things will be good for you.* ¹⁰*Me, here am I, staying at The Watchtower to take up my position^t before the Chaldeans who will come to us. You, gather wine and summer fruit and oil and put it in your containers and stay in your towns that you have taken over."* ¹¹*All the Judahites who were in Moab and among the Ammonites and in Edom and in all the countries also heard that the king of Babylon had given Judah a remainder group and that he had appointed Gedaliah ben Ahikam, the son of Shaphan, over them.* ¹²*So all the Judahites came back from all the places where they had scattered and came to the country of Judah to Gedaliah at The Watchtower and gathered very much wine and summer fruit.*^u

a. See the translation note on 31:15.

b. LXX lacks *shackled*.

c. On the Aramaic-style use of *lə* to mark the object, see GK 117n; DG 94 remark 8.

d. Tg "came" translates *wayyābë'* as if it were *qal*.

e. LXX lacks *and he has made it come about* and *as he spoke*.

f. The *you* is plural through v. 3.

g. On the simple *waw* construction, see the translation note on 37:15; here, the verb restates *Yahweh has acted*.

h. The *qatal* verb is declarative/performative, a speech act (see 1:5 and the note). The *you* is now singular.

i. LXX lacks *But if . . . go*.

j. Cf. Prov 1:23 for this meaning of *šûb* (*DCH*, 8:283a; McKane, *Jeremiah*, 2:1000–1001). The *yiqtol* compares with the use after *ṭeren* (GK 107c).

k. For MT *šubâ*, Vg implies *šəbâ* ("live").

l. LXX has "country."

m. LXX lacks *provisions and*.

n. Like *hārāmâ* in v. 1, *hammiṣpâ* is a place name with the article.

o. MT has a marker here.

p. I take the *wə* as explicative—that is, the men, women, and children are the poor people.

q. LXX has simply "Johanan ben Kareah."

r. The *ketiv*, LXX, Aq, Vg imply "Ophai."
s. For MT *'ăbôd*, LXX implies *'abdê* ("the servants of") as in 2 Kgs 25:24.
t. Lit. "stand."
u. MT has a marker here.

Even though Jer 39 might have made a satisfactory end for the Jeremiah scroll, like any ending it would leave readers wondering what happened afterward. What happened to Zedekiah and to the exile community in Babylon and to the city of Jerusalem? Actually, the scroll does not answer those questions. Who is this Gedaliah, and where is his house? What is Jeremiah doing staying with his people? And is there a future for Judah? These questions it does pick up, while also in due course taking the story in a new direction that one would not have guessed. If the original audience of the story in Jer 37–44 was in Egypt, then the chapters that follow provide the answer to the question "How did we get here?" and 40:1–12 forms a crucial hinge in that story. In moving forward, the story once again backtracks slightly. While 39:11–14 summarized Jeremiah's fate following on the fall of Jerusalem as an aspect of bringing that facet of the narrative to an end, 40:1–6 now tells us more about how things worked out for him in this connection as an aspect of opening up where the narrative will now go. In turn, 40:7–12 broadens the focus as the narrative becomes the story of the remainder community centered on Mizpah. Through 40:7–41:18, Jeremiah gets no mention, and we do not discover the nature of *the word that came to Jeremiah from Yahweh* (40:1) until 42:1–22. Jeremiah 40–41 thus gives us the background to that message and to the events involving Jeremiah that will follow.

v. 1	An introduction, setting up expectations that will not be realized until Jer 42
vv. 2–6	How Jeremiah got from Jerusalem via The Height to The Watchtower
vv. 7–12	How Judahite fugitives came to make a new start under Gedaliah at The Watchtower

1 The opening phrase *the word that came to Jeremiah from Yahweh* functions in part to advertise that we are beginning a new section within the scroll, and it is quite usual for this phrase to be qualified by a time reference such as follows here (see 32:1; 34:1, 8; 35:1). But this time reference is distinctively lengthy and turns out to gain a significance of its own—as background not to a message that follows (because the message will not come until 42:1–22) but to a subsequent narrative. By way of expansion on 39:11–15, we learn that Nebuzaradan and his colleagues did not send Jeremiah off straight from the prison courtyard to Gedaliah's house. Initially, he was just one of the Jerusalem captives who were on their way to Babylon but were encamped at a waystation. *The Height*, Ramah, is five miles north of Jerusalem on the main road toward Riblah and Babylon, within Benjamin and just past Anathoth, and only a mile or two from The Watchtower, Mizpah, on which more in a moment.

2–3 The audience might infer that what follows is indeed *the word that came to Jeremiah from Yahweh* announced by v. 1, as the storyteller now has Nebuzaradan preaching an impeccable Jeremianic sermon to Jeremiah.

> A strange speech to come from an Heathen man, but God used his tongue to say thus, the more to confound the Jews that were guilty of that which he charged them withal, that now at the least in their misery they might be moved to repent, which they would not do in their prosperity, as Balaams Asse sometime rebuked his foolishness.[81]

Put another way, Nebuzaradan functions as a servant of Yahweh, like his master.[82] Dramatically, Jeremiah's thinking is confirmed through the mouth of the Babylonian.[83] It would be wooden to focus on the plausibility or implausibility of Nebuzaradan preaching in this way; the point is the content of his words and the dramatic and rhetorical impact of portraying them coming from the mouth of a foreigner (cf. 22:8–9).[84] He recalls the virtuous foreign kings in Chronicles acknowledging Yahweh's power and justice and even speaking like a disciple of Jeremiah.[85]

4–5 Nebuzaradan's *so now* follows logically: Jeremiah had been the one through whom Yahweh spoke the message that Jeremiah's people ignored, and therefore he should not be in chains as they should. Jeremiah can choose where he goes. Nebuzaradan's laying out of the options is more discursive than his sermon. He seems to offer Jeremiah three alternatives. He can go to Babylon, or he can go anywhere in Judah, which would presumably include retirement in Anathoth, taking up the family landholding of which we have heard in Jer 32 and 37; apparently Jeremiah does not warm to either of these possibilities. Or as a third possibility, he can *go back to Gedaliah ben Ahikam, the son of Shaphan*, which recalls Jeremiah's debt to Gedaliah's father (see 26:24). The reference to Gedaliah's grandfather also draws attention to the leadership role of the Shaphan family in Jerusalem over some decades (see

81. Mayer, *Commentary*, 450.
82. Keown, Scalise, and Smothers, *Jeremiah 26–52*, 235.
83. Weiser, *Jeremia*, 2:358.
84. R. P. Carroll, *Jeremiah*, OTL, 699.
85. Ben Zvi, "Voice and Role of a Counterfactual Memory," 181–82.

esp. 2 Kgs 22:3–14; Jer 36:10–12). The accounts indicate that their attitudes were closer to those of Josiah and Jeremiah than to those of Jehoiakim and Zedekiah, an implication that might lie behind Gedaliah's being someone the Babylonians believed they could work with.

6 Jeremiah chooses the third option. We do not discover his reasons, but it would imply staying in public life with the man who is the de facto governor of Judah[86]—though actually calling him "governor" would be anachronistic.[87] His decision is another indication that we should not read too much into his having spoken ten years previously of the exiles as the good figs and as the community with which the future lies. There is a future at *The Watchtower*, Mizpah; Jeremiah's choice might imply a validation of an ongoing community there.[88] The site of Mizpah may be Nebi Samwil[89] or may be Tell en-Nasbeh.[90] Both are north of Jerusalem, two or three miles from Ramah, *The Height*. Each is claimed to make better sense than the other geographically in light of the story as it will unfold. Nebi Samwil (the traditional site of Samuel's tomb) has a more impressive location to be called a watchtower. Archaeological investigations of Tell en-Nasbeh have produced more concrete results, including the indications that the site suffered no sixth-century destruction, which would make it a convenient location for a political headquarters,[91] and also that it was the nearest to a flourishing (or at least functioning) location within the Judahite "post-collapse" society.[92]

7–12 Whereas vv. 1–6 were an independent unit in the story, what follows is a variant on part of the last chapter of 2 Kings (it does not come in Jer 52):[93]

86. It's therefore hard to see Jeremiah as embracing his marginal position as a means of resisting the dominant power of the empire (S. V. Davidson, "Chosen Marginality as Resistance in Jeremiah 40:1–6," in Diamond and Stulman, *Jeremiah (Dis)placed*, 150–61; cf. Davidson, *Empire and Exile*, 88–129).

87. E. Peels, "The Assassination of Gedaliah," in Becking and Human, *Exile and Suffering*, 87. On Gedaliah's position, see further O. Lipschits, *Fall and Rise of Jerusalem*, 88–97.

88. J. Hill, "Jeremiah 40:1–6," in *Seeing Signals, Reading Signs: The Art of Exegesis*, ed. M. A. O'Brien and H. N. Wallace, LHBOTS 415 (London: T&T Clark, 2004), 137.

89. Holladay, *Commentary on Jeremiah*, 2:294–95; Y. Magen, "Nebi Samwil," *BAR* 34 (2008): 36–45, 78–79.

90. J. R. Zorn, "Mizpah," in Arnold and Williamson, *Dictionary of the Old Testament: Historical Books*, 701–5; "Jeremiah at Mizpah of Benjamin," in Lundbom, Evans, and Anderson, *Jeremiah*, 69–92.

91. Boadt, *Jeremiah 26–52*, 103.

92. See the survey in K. Valkama, "What Do Archaeological Remains Reveal of the Settlements in Judah during the Mid-Sixth Century BCE?," in Ben Zvi and Levin, *Concept of Exile*, 39–59.

93. McKane (*Jeremiah*, 2:994–96) also analyzes the similarities and differences of the LXX text of the passage.

Jer 40:7–12	2 Kgs 25:22–24
	[22]The people that remained in the country of Judah whom Nebuchadnezzar King of Babylon allowed to remain: he appointed over them Gedaliah ben Ahikam son of Shaphan.
[7]All the officers of the forces who were in the open country and their men heard that the king of Babylon had appointed Gedaliah ben Ahikam over the country and that he had appointed with him men and women and little ones, some of the poor of the country, of the people who had not been taken into exile to Babylon.	[23]All the officers of the forces and their men heard that the king of Babylon had appointed Gedaliah.
[8]They came to Gedaliah at The Watchtower: Ishmael ben Netanyah, Johanan and Jonathan the sons of Kareah, Seraiah ben Tanhumeth, the sons of Ephai the Netophathite, and Jezaniah the son of the Maacathite, they and their men.	They came to Gedaliah at The Watchtower: Ishmael ben Netanyah, Johanan ben Kareah, Seraiah ben Tanhumeth the Netophathite, and Jaazaniah the son of the Maacathite, they and their men.
[9]Gedaliah ben Ahikam, the son of Shaphan, promised them and their men, saying, "Don't be afraid of serving the Chaldeans— Stay in the country and serve the king of Babylon and things will be good for you.	[24]Gedaliah promised them and their men and said to them, "Don't be afraid of the servants of the Chaldeans. Stay in the country and serve the king of Babylon and things will be good for you.

The story begins to unfold in a way suggesting good prospects for the Judahite community making a new start in Judah.[94] The reference to putting Gedaliah in charge of the ordinary people who were not taken into exile, including people who had lost their land, picks up the note in 39:10 as the account of Nebuzaradan and Jeremiah picked up 39:11–14. If a relatively small number of people has been taken off to join the 597 exiles in Babylon (52:29), a significant number now feel safe about returning from places where they have taken refuge. The officers and their men are presumably members of the army that had been defending Jerusalem, serving under the command of Zedekiah, "each one a potential warlord."[95] They are also people who had cut and run from Zedekiah when he fled (52:8) and have been keeping out of the way around Judah as weeks have passed since the city's fall. They might take a number of attitudes to the new situation, even if for practical purposes they can see what public stance they need to take. Of Ishmael ben Netaniah and Johanan ben Kareah we shall hear more in 40:13–43:6, but no more of Johanan's brother Jonathan or of Seraiah ben Tanhumeth. The sons of Ephai come from a village near Bethlehem and thus not too far from Jerusalem (Ezra 2:21–22; Neh 7:26; 12:28–29). The name Jezaniah comes in 2 Kgs 25:23 as Jaazaniah and appears in that form with the title "servant of the king" on a seal from Tell en-Nasbeh,[96] though the name ("Yahweh listens") is common (e.g., Jer 35:3; 42:1; Ezek 8:11; 11:1). Maacah was a small Aramaean kingdom east of the Jordan in the area that technically belonged to Manasseh (Josh 13:11–13; see also 2 Sam 10:6–8); presumably his family had moved to Judah, perhaps after the Assyrian conquest, but like Ebed-melech or Uriah the Hittite, he is known as a foreigner even while being accepted within Judah.

Gedaliah urges them all to take the stance that Jeremiah had urged earlier: submit to Babylon's authority. Jeremiah's promise from before 587 (27:11) may still apply. They should trust Gedaliah to mediate between them and the Babylonians; he will "stand before" the Babylonians like Moses and Samuel standing before Yahweh (15:1)[97] or like Jeremiah himself standing there (15:19; 18:20). Most tellingly, he will be like Nebuzaradan himself standing before Nebuchadrezzar (52:12). A person can stand before a king only on the basis of having been commissioned to do so, but people who have been so

94. C. R. Seitz, "The Crisis of Interpretation over the Meaning and Purpose of the Exile," *VT* 35 (1985): 78–97; Ackroyd, *Exile and Restoration*, 57.

95. Allen, *Jeremiah*, 432.

96. There is a picture in J. R. Zorn, "Mizpah: Newly Discovered Stratum Reveals Judah's Other Capital," *Biblical Archaeology Review* 23 (1997): 35.

97. Rudolph, *Jeremia*, 248.

commissioned can do so with confidence as they fulfill their responsibility. The Babylonians trust Gedaliah to oversee the Judahites; the Judahites can trust him, as one of them, to look after their interests. "Although much has been uprooted and demolished, the oath of Gedaliah represents a time to build and to plant."[98] The city fell in about July, so the months that follow would see a natural harvest, notwithstanding the country's devastation by war. The Judahite military and the landless families returning from *all the countries* (quite a hyperbole) can therefore profit from the land that people have abandoned in preparation for the winter that will follow. It will be a different gathering from the grim one that Jeremiah commissioned in 10:17. "There is a comparative calm after the storm."[99] Thus they *gathered very much wine and summer fruit.* "Is the crop not a blessing, . . . a sign of a new beginning?"[100] Maybe they themselves do not count as bad figs?[101] It looks like a new start, the beginning of a fulfillment of the promises in Jer 30–31; "a new age is beginning."[102] On the other hand, there is no talk of turning back to Yahweh, and Ezek 33:23–29 suggests a gloomy understanding of the Judahites' stance in relation to Yahweh.[103] Neither is there any talk of Yahweh turning to them.

2. *Things Begin to Fall Apart (40:13–41:18 [LXX 47:13–48:18])*

[13] *Now Johanan ben Kareah and all the officers from the forces that were in the open country came to Gedaliah at The Watchtower* [14] *and said to him, "Do you actually acknowledge*[a] *that Baalis King of the Ammonites—he has sent Ishmael ben Nethaniah to strike you down dead?"*[b] *But Gedaliah ben Ahikam didn't believe them.* [15] *So Johanan ben Kareah—he said to Gedaliah in secret at The Watchtower, "Please, I will go and strike down Ishmael ben Nethaniah and no one will know—why should he strike you down dead, and all Judah that have gathered to you scatter, and the remainder of Judah perish?* [16] *But Gedaliah ben Ahikam said to Johanan ben Kareah, "Don't do this thing, because you're speaking lies about Ishmael."*[c]

---

98. K. Bodner, *After the Invasion: A Reading of Jeremiah 40–44* (Oxford: Oxford University Press, 2015), 39.

99. Bodner, *After the Invasion*, 14; rather surprisingly, he is referring to Jer 40–44 as a whole.

100. W. H. Schmidt, *Jeremia*, 2:241.

101. M. Leuchter, "Group Identity and Scribal Tradition In Jeremiah," *JHS* 18/1 (2018): 54–55.

102. R. P. Carroll, *Jeremiah*, OTL, 705

103. Fretheim, *Jeremiah*, 536.

[41:1]*Then in the seventh month, Ishmael ben Nethaniah, son of Elishama, who was of royal descent, came, he and the king's senior people,*[d] *he and ten men with him, to Gedaliah ben Ahikam at The Watchtower, and they ate a meal there together at The Watchtower.* [2]*But Ishmael ben Nethaniah got up, he and the ten men who were with him, and struck down Gedaliah ben Ahikam the son of Shaphan with the sword and put him to death,*[e] *the one whom the king of Babylon had appointed over the country.* [3]*And all the Judahites who were with him (with Gedaliah)*[f] *at The Watchtower, and the Chaldeans who were present there (the men of battle), Ishmael struck down.*

[4]*On the second day after the putting of Gedaliah to death, when no one knew,* [5]*men from Shechem, from Shiloh, and from Samaria came, eighty men, trimmed of beard, torn of clothes, having gashed themselves, with grain offering and incense in their hand to bring to Yahweh's house.* [6]*Ishmael ben Nethaniah went out to meet them from The Watchtower, crying as he was going.*[g] *As he encountered them,*[h] *he said to them, "Come to Gedaliah ben Ahikam."*[i] [7]*Then, as they came into the middle of the town, Ishmael ben Nethaniah slaughtered them, into the middle of the cistern,*[j] *he and the men who were with him.*[k] [8]*But ten men who were present among them—they said to Ishmael, "Don't put us to death, because we have stores in the open country—wheat, barley, oil, and syrup." So he held back and didn't put them to death among their brothers.* [9]*Now the cistern where Ishmael threw all the corpses of the men whom he struck down by means of Gedaliah*[l] *was the one that King Asa made on account of Baasha King of Israel. It was the one that Ishmael ben Nethaniah filled with skewered men.*

[10]*Ishmael took captive all the remainder of the company that was at The Watchtower, with the king's daughters and all the people who remained at The Watchtower*[m] *for whom Nabuzaradan the head of the guards had appointed Gedaliah ben Ahikam. Ishmael ben Nethaniah took them captive*[n] *and went to cross over to the Ammonites.*[o] [11]*But Johanan ben Kareah, he and all the officers in the forces who were with him, heard the entire dire thing that Ishmael ben Nethaniah had done,* [12]*and got all the men and went to do battle with Ishmael ben Nethaniah. They found him at the great waters that are at Gibeon.* [13]*Then, when the entire company that was with Ishmael saw Johanan ben Kareah and all the officers in the forces who were with him, they were glad.* [14]*The entire company that Ishmael had taken captive from The Watchtower turned around*[p] *and went back again*[q] *to Johanan ben Kareah.* [15]*But Ishmael ben Nethaniah—he escaped with eight men from before Johanan and went to the Ammonites.*[r]

[16]*Johanan ben Kareah and all the officers in the forces who were with him got all the remainder of the company that he had taken back from Ishmael ben Nethaniah from The Watchtower after he had struck down Gedaliah ben Ahikam*[s]*—men, men of battle, women, little ones, and eunuchs,*[t] *whom he took back from Gibeon.* [17]*They went and stayed at Chimham's*[u] *Field,*[v] *which was*

near Bethlehem, on the way to coming to Egypt, [18]*in the face of the Chaldeans, because they were afraid in the face of them because Ishmael ben Nethaniah had struck down Gedaliah ben Ahikam whom the king of Babylon had appointed over the country.*[w]

a. The infinitive precedes the finite verb, underlining the question.

b. Lit. "to strike you down as a self/life."

c. MT has a section marker here.

d. LXX lacks *he and the king's senior people.*

e. LXX lacks *ben Ahikam the son of Shaphan with the sword and put him to death.*

f. LXX lacks *with Gedaliah.*

g. Lit. "going, to go, and crying" (see GK 113u; DG 101 remark 3). LXX has the men crying as they went, which makes more straightforward sense.

h. LXX lacks *as he encountered them.*

i. MT[L] has a section marker here.

j. On the elliptical construction, see GK 119gg.

k. LXX lacks *he and the men who were with him.*

l. Lit. "by the hand of Gedaliah"; cf. the extended usage of *bəyad* in 37:2; 39:11; 50:1. LXX implies *bôr gādōl* ("[was] a large cistern"), which is easier.

m. LXX lacks *and all the people who remained at The Watchtower*; MT may be a conflate text (Janzen, "Double Readings," 440).

n. LXX lacks *Ishmael ben Nethaniah took them captive.*

o. MT has a section marker here.

p. LXX lacks *they were glad. The entire people that Ishmael had taken captive from The Watchtower turned around.*

q. Lit. "they repeated and went"; that is, I take *wayyāšubû* as an auxiliary verb (Volz, *Jeremia*, 353; see GK 120d).

r. MT has a section marker here.

s. LXX lacks *ben Nethaniah from The Watchtower after he had struck down Gedaliah ben Ahikam.*

t. In this context, *sārîsîm* will be eunuchs (contrast 29:2; 34:19; Rudolph, *Jeremia*, 252).

u. The *ketiv* has *kmwhm*, apparently a slip.

v. LXX takes *gērût* as a place name, but Vg, Sym rather derive it from *gûr*, suggesting a place where people might camp temporarily (see BDB, 158; *DCH*, 2:375), while Aq "sheep-folds" might link with David's grant of land to Chimham (2 Sam 19:31–40; cf. Tg; *HALOT*).

w. MT has a marker here.

Gedaliah had appeared like a bright star in the night for the grieving Juda-hites.[104] But it turns out that the hopeful picture presented by 40:1–12 was a false dawn. Gedaliah is assassinated, and the rest of the community focused on Mizpah flees; arguably, "these two chapters are the saddest in the whole book of Jeremiah."[105] Three distinctively human figures and two unfortunate groups of people dominate this next episode of the story.

104. Volz, *Jeremia*, 354.
105. Dearman, *Jeremiah*, on Jer 41–42.

- Gedaliah turns out to be less wise than we thought and pays with his life for being too trusting.
- As a man with a claim to be in a position to exercise power, Ishmael is ambitious and ruthless in disposing of Gedaliah, but he is not far-seeing enough.
- Johanan knows things and knows what action to take, and he acts decisively, but in the end he is not sure what to do next.
- Some worshipers from Ephraim find themselves in the wrong place at the wrong time, though some of them know how to talk themselves out of trouble.
- The Judahites at The Watchtower switch between being the protected charges of Gedaliah, then of Ishmael, then of Johanan, but are never in a position to shape their own destiny.
- Jeremiah must have been around (see 40:6; 42:1–3) but does not feature in the story. We cannot answer the question of where he was; the effect in the story is to underline how events unfold without his or Yahweh's involvement in this "world . . . of shattering of dreams, of lost potential, of blood and violence."[106] Thus "what remains to be told of the history of Jeremiah seems to set the seal of failure on the work of his life."[107]

The unit is another where MT is much longer than LXX and where some differences may indicate MT expansion of an earlier version[108] while some may reflect LXX's rationalization of a version that it judged prolix.[109]

40:13–16 The opening of the story makes for a transition between 40:1–12 and 41:1–18. Linked to 40:1–12, it forms one unit in the Aleppo Codex and in the medieval chapter divisions in printed Bibles and so makes for a worrying contrast with the near-idyllic[110] picture of the new community that has preceded. In relation to what follows, with which it forms a new unit in MT[L], it provides vital background. But it leaves unanswered as many questions as it raises.

---

106. E. Ben Zvi, "The Voice and Role of a Counterfactual Memory in the Construction of Exile and Return," in *The Concept of Exile in Ancient Israel and Its Historical Contexts*, ed. E. Ben Zvi and C. Levin, BZAW 404 (Berlin: de Gruyter, 2010), 169–88 (184).

107. J. Skinner, *Prophecy and Religion: Studies in the Life of Jeremiah* (Cambridge: Cambridge University Press, 1922), 335.

108. See R. D. Wells, "The Amplification of the Expectations of the Exiles in the MT Revision of Jeremiah," in Diamond, K. M. O'Connor, and Stulman, *Troubling Jeremiah*, 272–92.

109. See further the discussion in McKane, *Jeremiah*, 2:1013–22.

110. R. P. Carroll, *Jeremiah*, OTL, 705.

- Is Johanan offering Gedaliah intelligence (does he ask, "Do you know?")? In that case, how did he get this piece of intelligence? Or is he asking why Gedaliah isn't taking account of what he knows ("Do you acknowledge?")?
- Why does the Ammonite king want to kill Gedaliah? Is it simply because Gedaliah represents Babylon's assertion of authority in the area, for which Baalis would have no more enthusiasm than Zedekiah? Ezekiel 21:18–32 portrays Ammon as one of Nebuchadrezzar's potential targets,[111] and Zedekiah was likely on the way to Ammon when he fled.[112] Or maybe Baalis would like to take over Judah with Ishmael as his puppet.[113] A seal from what would have been ancient Ammon that may refer to Baalis suggests that his name is an Ammonite equivalent to Isaiah (that is, it comprises the name of the deity combined with the verb meaning "save").[114]
- Why would Ishmael be willing to kill Gedaliah? That question will find some clarification in 41:1. Maybe he would say he didn't think Judah should submit to Babylonian government in the hands of someone who had given up on Yahweh's promise to David.[115]
- What is the link between Baalis and Ishmael? Perhaps 27:2–3 points toward an answer: Ammon, Moab, and Edom have made common cause with Judah in relation to the Babylonians.
- Why didn't Gedaliah believe Johanan, especially on the assumption that he knew of Ishmael's royal connections? His father knew the danger a leader could be in (26:24). Did he have suspicions about Johanan himself, which may be justified by subsequent events (40:15; 41:16–17)?[116] Was he trusting Yahweh because a story like that of his father and Jeremiah (and the one involving his uncle Gemariah in Jer 36) showed that Yahweh could be trusted? Or did he think that the Judahite survivors were now united? Why didn't he consult Yahweh, as one can imagine even Zedekiah doing (21:1; 37:3; 38:14) and as Johanan eventually will (42:1)?
- Where is Jeremiah when all this is going on? Why didn't Yahweh reach out to Gedaliah by means of Jeremiah? Jeremiah's silence and

111. D. R. Jones, *Jeremiah*, 471.
112. Bright, *Jeremiah*, 253.
113. So Isaac Abravanel, *Commentary on the Latter Prophets*.
114. See L. G. Herr, "The Servant of Baalis," *Biblical Archaeologist* 48 (1985): 169–72; B. Becking, "Inscribed Seals as Evidence for Biblical Israel?" in *Can a "History of Israel" Be Written?*, ed. L. L. Grabbe, JSOTSup 245 (Sheffield: Sheffield Academic, 1997), 80–82.
115. Boadt, *Jeremiah 26–52*, 104.
116. Lundbom, *Jeremiah 37–52*, 114–15.

absence mirrors God's silence and absence.[117] Both lack an explanation in the story.

The action and inaction of each of the characters in the story promote reflection for the audience, not least by declining to answer those questions.

41:1 The time of year is background in two ways to the events that follow. First, the seventh month (September-October) is marked by the Feast of Sukkot at the end of the harvest season; it is also thus the beginning of the new year, on another way of working the calendar. A reference to the harvest season fits the encouragement to gather the fruits of the harvest in 40:10. It would be nice to know what year it is: has the Judahite community had a year to settle down under Gedaliah's administration, or more? If Jerusalem fell in 587, is this 586? Apparently, the information that follows about Ishmael and Nethaniah is more significant. A secretary called Elishama appeared in 36:12, where he might easily count as one of Jehoiakim's *senior people* (*rabbîm*). Further, David had a son called Elishama (2 Sam 5:16), so maybe his line is the one whereby Ishmael counted as someone *of royal descent* (a list of David's sons such as the one in 2 Sam 5 reminds us that there were hordes of such people). Anyway, "the royal genealogy forms a segue to murder."[118] The meal in which Ishmael takes part may then be a combination of harvest festival and celebration of the exodus (Sukkot combined those two) and also a state dinner, a kind of diplomatic occasion, which might somehow explain why Jeremiah was not there. The expression *came . . . to Gedaliah ben Ahikam at The Watchtower* (cf. also 40:13) is a "grim parody" of 40:6.[119]

2-3 Gedaliah's father had played a part in ensuring that Jeremiah did not share the fate of Uriah (26:24); no Ahikam preserves Gedaliah himself. One aspect of the Jeremiah scroll's significance (like that of 1 and 2 Kings) is to help people make sense of the fall of Jerusalem by showing how it issued from Israel's turning away from Yahweh. As the point is often put, it's about theodicy.[120] But like 1 and 2 Kings, the scroll also recognizes that this explanation is only partial. "Jeremiah's silence in the face of Gedaliah's assassination is akin to the narrative silence over the death of Josiah in 2 Kings."[121] This story ensures that the Jeremiah scroll deconstructs—in a good way. It assures its readers that things make sense, but it also recognizes that sometimes they don't. "The Gedaliah fiasco" bears witness to human brutality and gratuitous

117. Stulman, *Jeremiah*, 322; cf. L. Stulman, "Jeremiah as a Polyphonic Response to Suffering," 311–16.
118. Bodner, *After the Invasion*, 57.
119. Allen, *Jeremiah*, 433.
120. See, e.g., "Unity of Composition," pp. 10–11.
121. Diamond, "Jeremiah," 609.

suffering. Its "counter-theodicy" recognizes how the world and the life of the people of God are "a fissured and broken place . . . that seems at times to be morally irrational and expressly evil" and from which God is absent. God is not engaged in the violence (as the participants likely believe he is), but he allows the voice of the violated to be heard.[122] The story suggests the ruthlessness and enormity of Ishmael's act of terror or terrorism[123] by noting how first he and his men joined in this meal, then killed Gedaliah and the rest of the Judahite and Babylonian administration who were there for the dinner. It illustrates how banquets are dangerous occasions (e.g., Gen 21; Esth 1; Dan 5; Judith 12–13). It also adds further to the rationale for the action by Ishmael and his co-conspirators: "Excuse me, Gedaliah was appointed by the Babylonians, and his household is full of Babylonian military and Judahite collaborators!" The *all* is a hyperbole; there were evidently Judahites at Mizpah who were not at the dinner (see v. 10). Second Kings 25:25–26 has a much briefer equivalent to vv. 1–3 and then summarizes the rest of the story in Jeremiah.

4–5 *The second day* will mean the next day, so no one yet knows what happened late the previous night when other people had gone to bed. People arrive from Ephraim—not from any old Ephraimite towns but from the place where Israel confirmed its pledge relationship with Yahweh back in Moses's day, from the place where the pledge chest had been, and from the town that had been Ephraim's long-time capital and now gives the province its name.[124] In other circumstances, their arrival would be a further sign of the fulfillment of Jeremiah's promises (see 31:2–22), and of the continuing effectiveness of Josiah's reformation (2 Kgs 23:19–20). The fulfillment would be noteworthy, even miraculous, even though the sad state of the temple would moderate any rejoicing over it. The pilgrims embody both encouragement and grimness. In this Sukkot season, they bring grain offerings and frankincense to offer. Is there a sanctuary at Mizpah where they will make their offerings? We know of none.[125] Rather, they are on their way to the temple in Jerusalem. The account in Ezra 1 of returning Judahites initiating the restoration of the temple indicates both that its devastation terminated the regular round of sacrifice and that devastation does not mean destruction, as if the walls have been pulled down. Some form of prayer and offering might continue—as Lamentations may presuppose. The devastation does mean that the pilgrims

---

122. Stulman, *Jeremiah*, 327–28. Stulman adds that the story "refutes the theodicy argument in the book," but this formulation seems an oversimplification that is the mirror image of the idea that the book exists to assure people that everything makes sense. Stulman himself discusses "Jeremiah as a Polyphonic Response to Suffering" in the chapter so titled in *Inspired Speech*, 302–18.

123. Fischer, *Jeremia*, 2:379.

124. Rudolph, *Jeremia*, 252–53.

125. Cf. Mayer, *Commentary*, 452.

come bearing the marks of grief, which also suggests that they are coming to Yahweh in an attitude of penitence (cf. Zech 7:5; 8:19); the seventh month additionally includes the Day of Atonement. They are turning to Yahweh not just in their hearts but in their appearance and with their offerings and their pilgrimage. Trimming one's beard or trimming one's hair and gashing oneself are generally forbidden, especially to priests, in Lev 21:1–5; Deut 14:1, but Jer 16:6 is not against gashing in principle, and the rules in the Torah likely relate to these being practices associated with praying to other gods. The story does not imply disapproval of the pilgrims in this connection.

6–9 Their turning to Yahweh contrasts with the further enormity of Ishmael's conscience-less meeting that pretends to identify with their grief and then kills them. Did he hope to frame them for the massacre and kill them on that basis?[126] Or was their execution another aspect of his commitment as a Judahite and a Davidide? Or did he want to appropriate the stores and offerings they were carrying? For some of them, their turning gets compromised—though one could hardly blame them for their way of evading death. Maybe the further supplies were hidden on the way, or maybe the surviving pilgrims refer to more extensive stores laid by for the coming winter back in places like Shiloh, only a day's journey away. The Judahite murderer throws the corpses of the Ephraimites who wanted to worship in Jerusalem into a cistern dug by a Judahite king who was faithful to Yahweh and needed to resist an Ephraimite king who was not (1 Kgs 15).

10–14 Is Ishmael's strategy to lead a resistance movement in exile from east of the Jordan? With some irony, people who had escaped being taken captive into exile by Nebuchadrezzar now find themselves taken captive into exile by a prince of their own. The irony might be especially apparent to the king's daughters, an interesting feature in the story's cast. Presumably they are not just Zedekiah's daughters; one might think of them more broadly as "the women of the court."[127] Apparently, Johanan and the other army officers did not live in The Watchtower—Gedaliah had bidden them to settle in the towns that they were able to occupy because the inhabitants had gone (40:10). But news reaches them before Ishmael can get far. Gibeon is on the mountain ridge before one descends down into the Jordan Valley to get to Ammon. It is only a couple of hours away on either theory of The Watchtower's location (see the commentary on 40:4–6). Whatever Ishmael's rationale for being at that location, his caravan seems still to be preparing for the journey ahead, by the well-known pool at Gibeon—another ironic reference (see 2 Sam 2). While a Mizpah at Tell en-Nasbeh is more obviously on the route for travelers from Ephraim to Jerusalem, it is not the obvious way to flee from Tell

126. Wisser ("the Malbim"), *Commentary on Biblical Literature*.
127. D. R. Jones, *Jeremiah*, 471.

en-Nasbeh to Ammon. But the narrative may not be very interested in the geographical location of The Watchtower or in Ishmael's reasons for taking the route he took; it is more interested in that ironic link with 2 Sam 2.

15 From there, Ishmael makes his escape. Relentlessly and point by point, the story has built up a portrait of him as a villain without principle, boundary, or shame. He became the agent of the king of one of Israel's traditional foes, he took part in a plot to murder a fellow-Judahite who had been appointed by the imperial authority that Yahweh had placed over Judah, he ignored the likely implications for the surviving Judahite community, he joined in a celebratory meal with Gedaliah as if they were friends and brothers, he struck him down along with other fellow-Judahites and Babylonians, he presented himself in the guise of someone grieving over such an event and inveigled some pilgrims into unwittingly surrendering their lives to him, he let some of the pilgrims escape with their lives because he could get some stores from them, he filled with his victims' corpses a cistern dug for very different reasons, and he attempted to take off as his captives the Judahites who had escaped his sword. The story does not seek to understand him or his motives, nor to suggest how he lived with himself; "surely there are few more murky villains in the Hebrew Bible."[128] As well as being just a villain, it might seem that "Ishmael has effectively killed off any positive future in the homeland."[129] Perhaps Judahites hearing the story in Babylon could later say to themselves, "Aha, the future belongs to us, not to those people that Jeremiah called the bad figs," though the story does not make that point.[130] It is a more wide-ranging, suggestive, and far-reaching narrative than merely a tale designed to support one group by putting another group down.[131]

16 As the story has built up its portrait of the villainous Ishmael, it has also built up point upon point a portrait of Johanan as its hero,[132] though also without suggesting an understanding of the man; and this portrait deconstructs over the next chapter or two. But Johanan is so far a man of insight, worth, and honor who has sought to get Gedaliah to safeguard his own position, has shown that he cares about the future of the community and not just about Gedaliah (41:15),[133] has been prepared to take preemptive action in order to save Gedaliah

---

128. Bodner, *After the Invasion*, 157.

129. R. P. Carroll, *Jeremiah*, OTL, 713.

130. Cf. W. Oswald, "Jeremiah and Moses," in *"My Spirit at Rest in the North Country" (Zechariah 6.8): Collected Communications to the XXth Congress of the International Organization for the Study of the Old Testament, Helsinki 2010*, ed. M. Augustin and H. M. Niemann, Beiträge zur Erforschung des Alten Testament und des antiken Judentum 57 (Frankfurt: Lang, 2011), 267.

131. Biddle ("Redaction of Jeremiah 39–41," 228–42) suggests that it is designed to support a lay governor such as Nehemiah over against the necessity for rule to be Davidic.

132. R. P. Carroll, *Jeremiah*, OTL, 711.

133. McKane, *Jeremiah*, 2:1004–5.

and the community, is then prepared to take ex post facto action when Gedaliah forbade the preemptive action, and has won the rejoicing, welcome, and commitment of Ishmael's captives. But after his successful rescue mission, what on earth is he now to do to see to the future of the Judahite community?

17–18 Is there some illogic about his fear of the Babylonians when he has taken action against the man who killed their appointee and their military?[134] Yet Gedaliah had been the one to "stand before" the Babylonians on their behalf; they have lost their representative with the Babylonians.[135] One can hardly blame Johanan for guessing that the Babylonians may not be too discriminating in their reprisals against anybody who looks like Judahite leadership. His immediate action is to move the company's base from Mizpah, where the Babylonians will know where to find them, to somewhere obscure where they may not. By the time of the fall of Jerusalem, Judah had likely lost control of the Negeb (cf. 13:19) to the Edomites, who are now at the "zenith" of their power[136] (hence the promises in Obadiah as well as Jer 49). So Bethlehem is effectively Judah's southern boundary, and *Chimham's Field*, only a ten-mile journey from Gibeon, would make as safe a place to take refuge as could be found. The location would be *on the way to coming to Egypt*, and fleeing to Egypt would take the company in the only direction that was outside Babylonian imperial control,[137] though v. 17 need not imply that the company was yet set on making that move. For the immediate future, it has simply *stayed* in the Bethlehem area. But will that refuge do if the Babylonians start looking for them? Can they assume the right to stay in Chimham's Field? The word for *Field* may hint at a place where people could reside temporarily (see the translation note).

3. Yahweh's Direction Given and Rejected (42:1–43:13 [LXX 49:1–50:13])

The end of Jer 41 has hinted where the story will go from here, but the process whereby people now make their next move is convoluted as well as tragic. After Ishmael's acts of assassination and massacre, the company led by Johanan has taken refuge as far south within Judah as it can go, in the direction of Egypt, but there is nothing fixed about a move there. Once again, the community faces a decision.[138]

---

134. Leuchter, *Polemics of Exile*, 125–26.

135. Qara, in MG.

136. A. Lemaire, "Edom and the Edomites," in *The Books of Kings: Sources, Composition, Historiography and Reception*, ed. A. Lemaire and B. Halpern, VTSup 129 (Leiden: Brill, 2010), 240.

137. Thompson, *Jeremiah*, 661.

138. Fischer, *Jeremia*, 2:399.

There are again many detailed differences between MT and LXX, usually involving MT being more wordy. Maybe sometimes MT has introduced more wordiness into an earlier version, sometimes LXX has deliberately reduced wordiness or omitted phrases by accident.

a. The Judahites Ask for Direction (42:1–6)

[1]*All the officers in the forces, with*[a] *Johanan ben Kareah*[b] *and Jezaniah*[c] *ben Hoshaiah*[d] *and the entire company, small and big, came up* [2]*and said to Jeremiah the prophet, "Please, may our prayer for grace fall before you: plead on our behalf with Yahweh your God on behalf of this entire remainder, because we remain as a little thing from being much (as your eyes see us),* [3]*so that Yahweh your God may tell us the path that we should go on and the thing that we should do."* [4]*Jeremiah the prophet said to them, "I have listened. Here am I, I am going to plead with Yahweh your God*[e] *in accordance with your words. Every word that Yahweh answers you, I will tell you—I will not withhold anything from you."* [5]*So those people—they said to Jeremiah, "May Yahweh be against us a true and trustworthy witness if in accordance with everything that Yahweh your God sends you for us, so we do not act.* [6]*Whether it is good or dire, to the voice of Yahweh our God, to whom we*[f] *are sending you, we will listen, in order that things may be good for us, because we listen to the voice of Yahweh our God."*[g]

a. Explicative *waw*.

b. LXX lacks *ben Kareah*; so also in v. 8.

c. LXX implies Azariah as in 43:2, where MT implies that Azariah is Jezaniah's brother.

d. This Jezaniah is thus a different person from Jezaniah the son of the Maacathite in 40:8; we noted in the commentary there that Jezaniah/Jaazaniah is a common name. LXX implies Maaseiah (whom it also has in 43:2); cf. 21:1; 29:21, 25; 35:4; 37:3, and elsewhere—it seems also to be a common name, sometimes with spelling variation. Perhaps there were three names in an earlier version of this text and these have become "telescoped" in MT (Allen, *Jeremiah*, 427; cf. *CTAT* 2:746–47).

e. LXX has "our God" (*NETS* has "your God"), a suggestive difference, though it loses something of the "vigor of the exchange" (Lundbom, *Jeremiah 37–52*, 130).

f. The *ketiv 'ānû* is a Postbiblical Hebrew equivalent to the regular *'ānaḥnû* (*qere*) (BDB, 59).

g. MT has a marker here.

In the trickiness of their situation, with the prospect of reprisals from the Babylonians, the company know what they must do; they must ask for Yahweh's instructions.

vv. 1–3   The company ask Jeremiah to inquire of Yahweh for them
v. 4   Jeremiah agrees
vv. 5–6   They promise to do whatever Yahweh says

1 The rescue of the captives had solved one problem, and the company has found somewhere to stay for a while, but it has to ask the question what it should do in the medium and longer term. So the *entire company* (!) . . . *came up* to Jeremiah. Presumably, he was among the people whom Ishmael took captive, whom Johanan rescued, and who moved on to the Bethlehem area. Etymologically, *came up* (*nāgaś*) denotes drawing near; the verb suggests approaching someone or something when there is reason not to take for granted the right to do so. Its one preceding occurrence in Jeremiah (30:21) expresses the point vividly. It carries some irony, given where the story is going to lead, suggesting a deference to Jeremiah that will not be forthcoming subsequently. It is only the first such irony in vv. 1–6. But "the leadership of the community . . . seems to have run out of options," and "after 587 as before 587 Jeremiah is consulted when the community knows nowhere else to turn," though in both contexts it doesn't like his response.[139]

2–3 The company's approach to Jeremiah with a petition to *plead on our behalf to Yahweh your God* thus repeats the appeal Zedekiah made in 37:3— though at least he said "our God"—which did not issue in taking any notice of the message that then came from Yahweh. "Behind the narrative of the simple request lie many innuendoes,"[140] one of which is that "intercession is wasted on people who promise to obey Yahweh's word and then end up not obeying it."[141] Repeating the familiar noun *remainder* and the related verb *remain*, Johanan and company add the expression *a little thing* (*məʿaṭ*), which indicates a contrasts with the *much* (*harbēh*) that Judah once was. Deuteronomy 28:62–63 warned people that this diminution could happen using the same words. It's not obvious that the speakers have made the link with that threat, but the audience might make it. The verbal link helps explain the hyperbole. The audience will recognize that *this entire remainder*

139. Brueggemann, *Jeremiah 26–52*, 173.
140. Holladay, *Commentary on Jeremiah*, 2:298.
141. Lundbom, *Jeremiah 37–52*, 129.

which will go off to Egypt does not comprise everyone still residing in Judah as a whole.[142] The exile in 587 did not empty the land, and neither will the departure of the present group; Nebuchadrezzar will exile more in a couple of years (52:29–30). Anyway, the company needs to ask, what is the *path* we should now go on? They are not asking about the best route to Egypt. Their question presupposes that they don't know what to do next, but they will know that going to Egypt is one option.

4–6 Jeremiah responds in the way they would have hoped, and the company makes a commitment of the kind it should. Is Jeremiah now free to pray for them?[143] Unfortunately, it's often the case that the record of a commitment of this kind is but preliminary to an account of how people fail to keep their word (e.g., Exod 24:3–7). The people's reference to Yahweh's witness (!) will turn out to be ironic (see v. 19).

b. Yahweh Gives Them Direction, Promises, and Warnings (42:7–18)

[7]*Then, at the end of ten days, Yahweh's word came to Jeremiah.* [8]*So he called to Johanan ben Kareah and to all the officers in the forces who were with him, and to the entire company, small and big,* [9]*and said to them, Yahweh the God of Israel to whom you sent me to let your prayer for grace fall before him,*[a] *has said this.* [10]*If you again*[b] *stay in this country, then I will build you up and not smash, I will plant you and not pull up, because I have relented over the dire thing that I did to you.* [11]*Don't be afraid before the king of Babylon, before whom you are afraid—don't be afraid of him (Yahweh's affirmation), because I am with you to deliver you and to rescue you from his hand.* [12]*I will give you compassion, and he will have compassion*[c] *on you and will let you go back*[d] *to your land.*

[13]*But if you're going to say, "We will not stay in this country," in order not to listen to the voice of Yahweh your God,* [14]*saying, "No,*[e] *because to the country of Egypt we will come, where*[f] *we will not see battle, and the sound of the horn we*

---

142. But H.-J. Stipp warns against underestimating their statement, as if "the myth of the empty land" was devised only much later, in "The Concept of the Empty Land in Jeremiah 37–43," in Ben Zvi and Levin, *Concept of Exile*, 103–54. See also A. Faust, "Deportation and Demography in Sixth-Century B. C. E. Judah," in Kelle, Ames, and J. L. Wright, *Interpreting Exile*, 91–103; O. Lipschits, "Shedding New Light on the Dark Years of the 'Exilic Period,'" in Kelle, Ames, and J. L. Wright, *Interpreting Exile*, 57–90; and for the myth of the empty land, R. P. Carroll, "The Myth of an Empty Land," in *Ideological Criticism of Biblical Texts*, ed. D. Jobling and T. Pippin, Semeia 59 (Atlanta: Scholars, 1992), 79–93; Barstad, *Myth of the Empty Land*. The origin of the phrase lies in the image of southern Africa that nineteenth-century European settlers liked to convey.

143. Rossi, *L'intercessione*, 346–62.

will not hear, and for food we will not be hungry, and we will stay there," [15]*so now therefore listen to Yahweh's word, remainder of Judah. Yahweh of Armies, the God of Israel,*[g] *has said this. If you actually set*[h] *your faces toward coming to Egypt and come to reside there,* [16]*then it will happen: the sword that you are afraid of—it will there overtake you in the country of Egypt, and the hunger that you are anxious about—it will there stick after you in Egypt, and there you will die.* [17]*And then*[i] *all the people*[j] *who have set their faces to come to Egypt to reside there will die by sword, by hunger, and by epidemic.*[k] *They will have no one surviving or*[l] *escaping before the dire thing that I am going to let come upon them.*[m] [18]*Because Yahweh of Armies, the God of Israel*[n] *has said this. As my anger and*[o] *my fury poured on the people who lived in Jerusalem, so my fury will pour on you when you come to Egypt. You will become an oath, a desolation, a form of slighting, and an object of reviling, and you will not again see this place.*

a. LXX lacks *the God of Israel to whom you sent me to let your prayer for grace fall before him.*

b. For MT *šôb*, LXX, Vg imply *yāšôb* ("if you do [stay]," an infinitive preceding the finite verb, underlining the point); the double use of the same verb is what one would more usually expect.

c. For *wəriḥam*, LXX, Vg imply *wəriḥamtî* ("I will have compassion").

d. For MT *wəhēšîb*, LXX implies *wahăšibōtî* ("I will let you go back") as in 23:3; 29:14; Aq, Vg imply *wəhōšabtî* ("and I will let you live").

e. LXX lacks *saying, "No".*

f. For *'ăšer*, meaning "where," see BDB, 82; cf. Vg.

g. LXX lacks *remainder of Judah* and *of Armies the God of Israel.*

h. The infinitive precedes the finite verb, underlining the factuality of the action.

i. Lit., "and then they will happen"; plural *wayihyû* is assimilated to the plural subject (DG 72 remark 2; GK 112y).

j. LXX also has "and all the resident aliens," implying *zārîm*, perhaps derived from *zēdîm* in 43:2 (Duhm, *Jeremia*, 323)—though HUBP notes that LXX does not imply *zēdîm* there.

k. LXX lacks *and by epidemic* here and in v. 22.

l. LXX lacks *surviving or.*

m. MT[L] has a section marker here.

n. LXX lacks *of Armies, the God of Israel.*

o. LXX lacks *my anger and.*

vv. 7–8	Yahweh gives Jeremiah a message, and Jeremiah summons them to hear it
vv. 9–18	The message
v. 9	Introduction
vv. 10–12	If they stay in Judah, Yahweh will build them up and protect them
vv. 13–14	But if they decide to go to Egypt . . .
v. 15a	Resumptive introduction

vv. 15b–17 . . . they will die
v. 18a Resumptive introduction
v. 18b Wrath will fall on them as it did before

7–9 The story again shows how a prophet may have to wait to discover what Yahweh has to say (cf. 28:12). It is a striking necessity given that the basic message when it comes might seem predictable and mostly expresses itself in quite predictable terms.[144] But a promise of deliverance with an encouragement not to be afraid is a common response to somebody's prayer[145] (and the kind of message a false prophet might bring), which could make a prophet especially concerned to listen carefully in a meeting of the cabinet (23:18) to what Yahweh has to say.[146] And maybe it would be good for the people to be kept on tenterhooks, too, and not take responses for granted.[147]

10 The message puts some if-then alternatives before the company, a short version of the kind of if-then alternatives that appear in Deut 28. As there, there is first a positive one, which thus also compares with the way Jesus talks to his disciples: "If you forgive people their offenses, your heavenly Father will also forgive you" (Matt 6:14; see the commentary on 7:13–14). Whereas Jeremiah had once told people *not* to stay where they are if they want to have a future (38:2), now he tells the remaining Judahites to *stay* where they are if they want to have a future. But like the earlier bidding, it challenges people to do the thing that looks implausible. As with the earlier bidding, Jeremiah attaches implausible divine undertakings to it. Here, they pick up some standard yet therefore important promises. In 1:10, the verbs came with a double stress on the negative: there were twice as many negative verbs, and they all came first and threatened to drown out the positive verbs, as was not inappropriate in that setting. Here, the stress is on the positive. All six verbs also came in 31:28 in a more positive context. But the recurrence of the four verbs from 24:6 in the version we have here is especially noteworthy. It indicates that they apply not only to people who were taken off to Babylon as the "good figs" but also to these people who would seem to count among the "dire figs." To the statement about building and planting, Yahweh adds an even more striking declaration, *I have relented over the dire thing that I did to you*, the destroying of Jerusalem. Relenting (*nāḥam niphal*) could have various implications. It could mean regretting an action and therefore refraining from taking it if one could have the time over again. It could mean being con-

144. Diamond, "Jeremiah," 605.
145. P. D. Miller, "Jeremiah," on the passage.
146. Thompson, *Jeremiah*, 665.
147. Theodoret, *Ermeneia*, PG 81:695.

soled or comforted by virtue of having taken the redress that needed taking.[148] It could suggest regretting what happened because Nebuchadrezzar's tough action was excessive—though Yahweh speaks of what he did, not of what Nebuchadrezzar did.[149] It could suggest regretting the necessity to do it—but it was a necessity. The context here suggests that the point lies in Yahweh's intention not to act that way again.[150] Arguably, the key characteristic of relenting is that one gives up one form of action to take on another[151]—usually by giving up action that brings trouble and thus showing mercy. Relenting is "the language of possibility and renewal."[152] Yahweh is affirming that he will not have the Judahite community suffer more. He is committed to its future. But the company needs to listen on to vv. 13–18, where they will discover that Yahweh is not unconditionally turning his back on doing something *dire*. They would be unwise to assume that he has unequivocally relented as opposed to declaring that he will relent if they stay.

11–12 Yahweh's intention renders unnecessary the understandable fear to which 41:18 referred. The fear's seriousness is underlined by the three references to it. Yahweh again picks up familiar promises, *to deliver you and to rescue you from his hand*, applying to the company undertakings that had started off as promises to Jeremiah (15:20). *I will give you compassion* is less of a stock expression (but see 33:26) and just as exciting in its own right. The promise *he will have compassion on you* is revolutionary. Jeremiah has otherwise spoken in such terms in the negative (6:23; 21:7). It is now another way of indicating that Yahweh has relented. Yahweh can make the empire the agent of compassion.[153] It was a favor for which Solomon asked in his prayer for the exiles at the temple dedication (1 Kgs 8:50); once again, such favors apply not just to exiles (as they do in that prayer) but to people who stay in Judah. People who have had to take refuge in Chimham's Field will not have to stay there forever; Nebuchadrezzar will make it possible for them to return to their own stretch of land.

---

148. So Vg, Sym, Th. LXX's *anapepaumai* may have the same implication or may simply mean desisting.

149. M. E. Biddle, "Contingency, God, and the Babylonians: Jeremiah on the Complexity of Repentance," *RevExp* 101 (2004): 247–65.

150. Cf. Tg "turned."

151. See H.-J. Fabry, "נחם, *nḥm*," *TDOT* 9:342. It's like taking redress as opposed to revenge (e.g., 11:20) in being at least as much an action word as a feelings word (Volz, *Jeremia*, 360).

152. R. P. Carroll, *Jeremiah*, OTL, 716.

153. W. Brueggemann, "At the Mercy of Babylon: A Subversive Rereading of the Empire," *JBL* 110 (1991): 6.

13–16 "This all *seems* so simple."[154] But there is the alternative possibility, expressed as a negative if-then, which also corresponds to the way Jesus talks: "If you do not forgive people, neither will your Father forgive your offenses" (Matt 6:15). Like Moses in Deut 28, Jeremiah accompanies the promises with correlative warnings, which take more space. In effect, he sets two paths before them, as he did before Zedekiah: the path to life and the path to death (21:8; cf. Deut 30:19). But he makes the point in his own way; the warnings are partly distinctive to this passage, partly corresponding to earlier passages in the scroll. The *if*-clause is actually a double one, which relates to the possibility that was flagged in 41:17. Yahweh can imagine that people don't want to *see battle* and or *hear* the *sound of the horn* announcing the approach of an attacking army (4:19, 21). They don't want any more of the correlative experience of being *hungry* to which Jeremiah has often referred (e.g., 5:12; 14:12–18). Actually, ignoring Yahweh's message will mean experiencing exactly the perils of which Jeremiah has often spoken: sword and hunger will follow the people. In the terms of metonymy, the sword will *overtake* them as the Babylonian army overtook Zedekiah (39:5) and hunger will *stick after* them like a pursuing army (e.g., Judg 20:42, 45), as Deut 28:21, 60 warned of illness and epidemic sticking to them. Deuteronomy 17:16 declared that they were never to go back to Egypt, and Jeremiah has hinted at lots of reasons for this (2:6, 18, 36; 9:26[25]; 24:8; 25:19; 26:21–23).[155]

17–18 To fit even more closely with Jeremiah's regular warnings, the people will *die by sword, by hunger, and by epidemic*. No one will survive or escape the further *dire thing* that will follow the dire thing that Yahweh relents of (v. 10). It is a "stinging" judgment.[156] Wrathful anger will pour out again (cf. 7:20; 21:5; 32:31, 37; 33:5). They will again become *an oath, a desolation, a form of slighting, and an object of reviling* (cf. 29:18; 24:9). If they turn their backs on Judah, Yahweh will ratify their action.

c. Yahweh Gives Them a Rebuke (42:19–22)

[19] *Yahweh has spoken*[a] *against you, remainder of Judah—do not come to Egypt—acknowledge definitively*[b] *that I am bearing witness*[c] *against you today*[d] [20]*that you deceived, at the cost of your lives,*[e] *when you yourselves sent me to Yahweh your God,*[f] *saying, "Plead on our behalf with Yahweh our God, and in accor-*

---

154. Stulman, *Jeremiah*, 334.

155. See G. E. Yates, "New Exodus and No Exodus in Jeremiah 26–45," *TynB* 57 (2006): 1–22.

156. K. D. Mulzac, "Śrd as a Remnant Term," 46.

*dance with everything that Yahweh our God says, so tell us and we will act." *[21]*I have told you today*[g] *and you haven't listened to the voice of Yahweh your God, even concerning anything with which he sent me to you.* *[22]*So now, you should acknowledge definitively that by sword, by hunger, and by epidemic you will die*[h] *in the place where you want to come to reside.*[i]

a. Tg, Vg, Th imply *dəbar* ("[Yahweh's] word") for MT *dibber*.

b. The infinitive precedes the finite verb, underlining the factuality of the action; cf. v. 22.

c. The *qatal* is declarative/performative, a speech act (see 1:5 and the translation note on it).

d. LXX lacks *that I am bearing witness against you today*.

e. The *hiphil* of *tāʿâ* ought to be transitive, but whom are they deceiving? Jeremiah? Yahweh? Perhaps we should see the verb as "inwardly transitive" (cf. GK 53d–f; *DCH*, 8:657–58). Vg has the people deceiving themselves, which in a sense they are, but the preposition on *bənapšôtêkem* makes that understanding of the construction unlikely. LXX "in yourselves" is a bit insipid. For "at the cost of" or "against," cf. 2 Sam 23:17; 1 Kgs 2:23.

f. LXX lacks *to Yahweh your God*, and *our God* later in the verse.

g. LXX lacks *I have told you today*, and *your God, even concerning anything* later in the verse.

h. LXX simply has "so now by sword and by hunger you will die."

i. MT has a section marker here.

19–22 After Jeremiah's passing on the message about direction for the future, there is a jump to these verses in which he testifies to the company, upbraids them, and challenges them. He speaks as someone who stands in court *bearing witness against* the company. They summoned Yahweh as a witness in v. 5; Jeremiah now makes Yahweh a witness against them.[157] He has stood in the gathering of Yahweh and his aides where he is supposed to speak on behalf of Yahweh's people, but now he has to give a report that works against them. They had asked him to pray and to inquire, but their action shows they never really intended to take any notice. Maybe they didn't know it; human beings are complicated creatures. The threats he has issued will therefore be fulfilled. *You have deceived* (Him? Yahweh? Themselves?) and done so *at the cost of your lives*, because it's going to mean that *by sword, by hunger, and by epidemic you will die in the place where you want to come to reside.* Two chapters remain in the story in Jer 37–44, but Jeremiah's message in vv. 19–22 "essentially seals the fate of the survivors from Judah."[158] His rebuke presupposes that the company has given a negative response to his message, which will be given concrete expression in its setting out for Egypt, but the narrative has not recorded the response. Something must have happened

157. Volz, *Jeremia*, 361.
158. Keown, Scalise, and Smothers, *Jeremiah 26–52*, 253.

between Jeremiah's passing on the message and his critiquing the company for ignoring it. That oddity puts the scroll's audience on the track of seeing that at this point, the sequence in Jer 42–43 may be dramatic rather than chronological. To put it another way, vv. 19–22 raise the question, how did Jeremiah know they had rejected his message? The next section of the story will provide the answer.

d. The Judahites Reject the Message (43:1–3)

¹*Then, when Jeremiah had finished speaking to the entire company all the words of Yahweh their God*ᵃ *with which Yahweh their God had sent him to them, all these words,*ᵇ ²*Azariah ben Hoshiah said, with Johanan ben Kareah and all the arrogant*ᶜ *people, saying*ᵈ *to Jeremiah, "It's lies that you are speaking*ᵉ*—Yahweh our God did not send you to say, You will not come to Egypt to reside there.* ³*Because Baruch ben Neraiah is inciting you against us in order to give us into the hand of the Chaldeans, to put us to death or to take us into exile in Babylon."*

a. LXX lacks *their God* here and again later in the verse.

b. MT's section marker here implies reading v. 1 as a self-contained sentence: "It happened when Jeremiah finished . . . all these words."

c. LXX lacks *arrogant*.

d. The participle does not fit the structure of the sentence; its syntax breaks down.

e. LXX lacks *that you are speaking*.

1–2 If this account of the company's response provides the background to 42:19–22, then *all the words* refers to the message in 42:7–18. Either way, maybe it's significant that someone other than hero Johanan takes the lead in rejecting Jeremiah's message. But he does evidently tag along, as do a collection of *arrogant* people. The word (*zēd*) implies being willful or presumptuous. It's not a common word; nearly half its occurrences come in Ps 119, where it denotes "an attitude that is not compatible with submission to God's word" and also "carries with it a propensity for slander," both of which implications fit the occurrence here.[159] Further, there are two suggestive occurrences of the verb "act arrogantly" in connection with the Israelites wanting to go back to Egypt (!) when they are disturbed by the report of their spies (Neh 9:16–17) and with their then going up into Judah to attempt to take the country when Yahweh has told them not to (Deut 1:43). The people here accuse Jeremiah of telling lies (*šeqer*), which is their implicit critique of Moses in that context. With some irony, it is also explicitly Jeremiah's favor-

---

159. Bodner, *After the Invasion*, 112.

ite insult, and in addition it was his recent response to Irijah and Gedaliah's response to Johanan (37:14; 40:16). Each time, the word suggests no mere ordinary untruth but something deceptive and false that carries deep peril. The point is underscored by the declaration *Yahweh did not send you*. There is no more fundamental claim that Jeremiah makes than that Yahweh sent him (e.g., 1:7; 25:4; 26:5, 12, 15; 29:19) and no more fundamental critique that he makes of other prophets than that Yahweh did not send them (e.g., 23:21, 32; 27:15; 28:15; 29:9). The company is categorizing Jeremiah as a prophet like Hananiah.

3 Explaining Jeremiah's prophecies in terms of his secretary's influence rather than Yahweh's sending is a further class-one insult. It is the first we know about Baruch being part of the company. The accusation now carries irony because for more than a century scholars have attributed to Baruch a key creative role in the generation of the Jeremiah scroll, despite the fact that the only role the scroll attributes to him is looking after a document, taking Jeremiah's dictation, and reading it out (Jer 32; 36; 45).[160] Nor does the scroll give any indication that Baruch (or Jeremiah) supports the Judahite community in Babylon as opposed to the community in Judah or in Egypt or that the narrative wants us to understand him that way.[161] The desperate accusation does go on to underline the depth of the community's realistic anxiety about its potential fate, either death or transportation. If the Babylonians identified it with the assassination of the Babylonian administrator, then the two possibilities that the community has so far managed one way or another to avoid (though many Judahites have not) open up before it.

e. They Move to Egypt (43:4-13)

[4]*So Johanan ben Kareah,*[a] *with all the officers in the forces and the entire company, did not listen to the voice of Yahweh by staying in the country of Judah.* [5]*Johanan ben Kareah and all the officers in the forces got the entire remainder of Judah who had come back from all the countries where they had scattered*[b] *to reside in the country of Judah*[c]—[6]*men, women, and little ones, and the king's daughters, and every individual that Nebuzaradan the chief of the guards*[d] *had left with Gedaliah ben Ahikam, the son of Shaphan, and Jeremiah the prophet, and Baruch ben Neraiah.* [7]*And they came to the country of Egypt because they did not listen to Yahweh's voice; they came to Tahpanhes.*[e]

160. Cf. Bodner, *After the Invasion*, 113-14.
161. McKane, *Jeremiah*, 2:1064; for such a view, see, e.g., Brueggemann, *Jeremiah 26-52*, 183-86.

[8]*Then the word of Yahweh came to Jeremiah in Tahpanhes.* [9]*Get big stones in your hand and bury them in mortar*[f] *in the brickwork*[g] *that's at the entrance to Pharaoh's house in Tahpanhes, before the eyes of Judahite people.* [10]*You will say to them, Yahweh of Armies, the God of Israel*[h] *has said this. Here am I sending and getting Nebuchadrezzar, King of Babylon, my servant,*[i] *and I will set*[j] *his throne upon these stones that I have buried.*[k] *He will extend his scepter*[l] *over them.* [11]*He will come and strike down the country of Egypt:*

People who are for death, to death,
   people who are for captivity, to captivity,
   people who are for sword, to sword.

[12]*I will set*[m] *fire to the houses of the gods of Egypt.*[n] *He will consume them and take them captive. He will grasp*[o] *the country of Egypt as a shepherd grasps his coat, and go out from there with things being well.* [13]*He will break up the columns of the sun house which is in the country of Egypt,*[p] *and the houses of the gods of Egypt*[q] *he will consume in fire.*[r]

a. LXX lacks *ben Karaeh* here and in the next verse.

b. LXX lacks *from all the countries where they had scattered.*

c. LXX lacks *of Judah.*

d. LXX lacks *the chief of the guards.*

e. MT has a section marker here.

f. For MT's *hapax legomenon* bammeleṭ, Aq, Th, Vg may imply *ballāṭ* ("in secret/under cover"), though covering/frame/casing is the meaning of *malṭēṭ* itself in Postbiblical Hebrew (*DTT*, 789).

g. *Malbēn* is also a *hapax legomenon* in whatever is its precise meaning here; in its one other occurrence in 2 Sam 12:31, it relates to brick manufacturing. LXX lacks *in mortar in the brickwork that's.*

h. LXX lacks *of Armies, the God of Israel.*

i. LXX lacks *my servant.*

j. LXX implies *wəśām* ("and he will set").

k. LXX implies *ṭāmāntā* ("you have buried").

l. Akkadian *šippiru* suggests the meaning of the *hapax legomenon* šaprîr (*ketiv* šaprûr; see *HALOT, DCH*). Tg has "palace" or "armory"; LXX has "weapons"; Vg has another word for "throne"; they seem to be guessing from the context or on the basis of the word's similarity to the root *šāpar*, which suggests splendor.

m. LXX, Vg imply *wəhiṣṣîl* ("he will set").

n. LXX has "of their gods."

o. Vg, Tg have "wrap on/cover oneself" on the assumption that the verb is BDB's *ʿāṭâ* I. LXX "delouse" here and later in the verse apparently assumes *ʿāṭâ* II and presupposes that he is specifically grabbing at lice; see *DCH*, and, e.g., J. A. Emerton, "Lice or a Veil in the Song of Songs 1.7," in Auld, *Understanding Poets and Prophets*, 127–40. This understanding seems more "ingenious" than plausible (J. van Doorslaer, "Sicut amicitur pastor pallio suo . . . ," *CBQ* 13 [1951]: 319).

p. For *which is in the country of Egypt*, LXX has "in Heliopolis."
q. LXX has "and their houses."
r. MT has a marker here.

The account of how the company comes to Egypt comprises two elements:

vv. 4–7	The move to Tahpanhes	
vv. 8–13	A message from Yahweh for the people at Tahpanhes	
v. 8	Introduction	
vv. 9–13	The message	
v. 9	An instruction: get some stones and embed them	
v. 10a	A resumptive introduction	
vv. 10b–13	A declaration of intent relating to the stones:	
v. 10b	Nebuchadrezzar will come	
vv. 11–13	He will strike down Egypt	
v. 11	He will strike down the people	
v. 12a	He will destroy its temples	
v. 12b	He will grasp the country	
v. 13	He will destroy its temples	

4–6 Whatever Johanan's degree of initiative in connection with the rejection of Jeremiah's message, he retains responsibility for the company's leadership. The story then emphasizes the significance of the company that he led, not so much in connection with its size but in connection with its comprehensiveness: *all the officers*; *the entire company*; *the entire remainder*; *from all the countries*; *men, women, and little ones*; *king's daughters*; and in case we have forgotten anyone, *every individual*—plus Jeremiah and Baruch. It is ironic that the people who had scattered are described as having returned in order to *reside* (*gûr*) as temporary residents (cf. 42:15, 17, 22; 43:2); one imagines they thought they were returning to stay (*yāšab*), to live permanently in Judah (cf. 42:10, 13, 14). While the narrative does emphasize the company's comprehensiveness, even if one doesn't allow for hyperbole, it need not imply that all Judahites had returned to Judah from their scattering nor that all Judahites who had returned had been put under Gedaliah's charge by Nebuzaradan.[162] It's talking about everyone who had returned and who had been among the ones under Gedaliah's oversight. The mention of Jeremiah and Baruch raises questions on both sides. Why did they take them? Did they compel them? Why would they? Would the two of them have preferred not

---

162. Thompson, *Jeremiah*, 669.

to go? ("Jeremiah went knowing that this would not have God's blessing."[163]) Perhaps the story simply assumes that both the leadership and these two individuals would accept that this community just is a community. Whatever the community does or whatever happens to it, Jeremiah and Baruch are part of it and part of its destiny. And one can perceive God's merciful providence at work in their taking Jeremiah: it meant that through Jeremiah, God can keep offering mercy to them even through reproaching them with their rebelliousness.[164]

7 Tahpanhes (see 2:16) was near Egypt's northeastern border—a kind of twin for Bethlehem on Judah's southern border, with a two-hundred-mile journey in between. It would be a natural place for the Judahites to stop with a sense of safety at the end of their trek.

8–9 Yahweh commissions one last symbolic act (that we know of) from Jeremiah. Like some other such acts, this sign is to have witnesses. But as with some other such acts, the scroll does not recount how Jeremiah did as he was told. And as with some other such acts, the narrative's point is to convey something to the people listening to this story as they imagine the scene. Would they be wondering what the Egyptians would have thought? Did the palace have no guards?[165] Maybe it was not occupied at the time.[166] It would not be Pharaoh's only palace, and "palace" may be a misleading expression. It was more like a government building or frontier fortress, though also an official residence for Pharaoh when he was visiting. There was a similar building at the other end of Egypt, on the southern border, at Elephantine, and in interpreting texts from there, A. E. Cowley suggests that "government house" is a more appropriate way to think of it.[167] But anyway, maybe the enacted parable was enacted in a parabolic way, like Ezekiel's equivalent acts (see the commentary on 13:3–5). *Bury* (*ṭāman*) often suggests hiding something (cf. 18:22); it recurred in connection with the symbolic act when Jeremiah had to hide some shorts (13:4, 5, 6, 7), and the idea here is likely similar. The stones are not being buried so as to be kept from view but deposited somewhere secure and out of sight until the time comes for them to be brought out into the open. They are a kind of guarantee that Nebuchadrezzar will come and set his throne there. This building on the Egyptian border symbolizes Egyptian power and the sense of security it could offer to a crowd of Judahite

---

163. Boadt, *Jeremiah 26–52*, 110. See further H.-J. Stipp, "Die Verschleppung Jeremias nach Ägypten," *VT* 64 (2014): 654–63.

164. Oecolampadius, *In Hieremiam*; cf. J. J. Tyler, *Jeremiah, Lamentations*, Reformation Commentary (Downers Grove, IL: InterVarsity, 2018), 389.

165. Duhm, *Jeremia*, 326.

166. Lundbom, *Jeremiah 37–52*, 144.

167. A. E. Cowley, *Aramaic Papyri of the Fifth Century B. C.* (Oxford: Clarendon, 1923), 5.

refugees, but Nebuchadrezzar's arrival will put Egyptian power in its place and terminate the security that seemed to come from taking refuge there.[168]

10–11 The act is a sign that anticipates Yahweh's fulfilling an intention he has formulated. Back in 25:9 and 27:6, he spoke of sending (for) and getting kin-groups from the north, and specifically *Nebuchadrezzar King of Babylon, my servant*, to exercise authority and bring catastrophe upon Judah and upon other nations. Nebuchadrezzar is unwittingly Yahweh's agent in doing so. It's the first reference to his being Yahweh's servant since 25:9 and 27:6; he has the same role as there. First, he is going to exercise authority. Then he is going to bring calamity. Johanan and company think they have evaded such further catastrophe by moving to Egypt, but they have not done so. Yahweh will act in the same way again, setting up thrones again before a conquered people (cf. 1:15). Jeremiah goes on to express that point by reformulating phrases from 15:2:

15:2	43:11
People who are for death, to death,	People who are for death, to death,
people who are for sword, to sword,	people who are for captivity, to captivity,
People who are for hunger, to hunger,	people who are for sword, to sword.
people who are for captivity, to captivity.	

One way or another, there is no escape. People will be like someone fleeing from a lion and being met by a bear (Amos 5:19).[169]

12 In the way Yahweh speaks in vv. 11–12, he moves in a disorienting fashion between referring to what he himself will do and what Nebuchadrezzar will do, and LXX sometimes has "he" or "you" where MT has "I." The switching and variation may reflect text-critical issues or differences between the two editions of the scroll. It may reflect the way a prophet moves easily between talking of Yahweh as "I" or as "he."[170] It also points to two sets of theological assumptions and convictions, both of which have something to be said for them. What happens issues from Yahweh and his decisions; it also issues from Nebuchadrezzar and his decisions. Yahweh's decisions are implemented through Nebuchadrezzar. Nebuchadrezzar is unwittingly doing Yahweh's work. The link between the two emerges in another way in the juxtaposed references to Yahweh showing compassion and Nebuchadrez-

---

168. Allen, *Jeremiah*, 440.
169. P. D. Miller, "Jeremiah," on the passage.
170. Cf. Duhm, *Jeremia*, 327.

zar showing compassion (42:12). In the present text, "the alternatives have arisen, in part, because of the convergence of human and divine agency that is at the heart of this story. The politics of the nations is the politics of God; the divine sovereignty is manifest over and through human sovereigns."[171]

13 The final verse of the chapter completes a second sequence in the portrayal of calamity in vv. 11–13:

v. 11	country and people	v. 12a	religious institutions
v. 12b	country and people	v. 13	religious institutions

If one assumes some continuity between these verses, Yahweh could be referring to further structures in Tahpanhes.[172] Columns or obelisks are a key feature of Egyptian religious architecture, and one would expect there to be examples at Tahpanhes, where the sun god Re would be worshiped. But LXX plausibly assumes that the expression *sun house* refers to Heliopolis, Sun City, on the Nile a hundred miles to the southwest, on the northeastern side of modern Cairo. A broadening of horizon here at the end of Jer 43 would fit the further broadening of horizon in 44:1. Either way, the expression *which is in the country of Egypt* distinguishes this sun house from Beth Shemesh in Judah. Heliopolis, then, takes its name from being the sanctuary of the sun god, though its local name was "The Pillars." There is still a seventy-foot-high obelisk there, which had been there for over a thousand years by Jeremiah's day (two other obelisks from there were taken to London and New York, where each is known as Cleopatra's Needle). While vv. 11–13 talk about catastrophe coming on Egypt, in the context the point about the proclamation is its significance for Judahites who have been so foolish as to take refuge there. The lines are a working out of 42:16–18. Yahweh is giving expression to his inclination to snatch away from his people the things in which they trust more than they should, so that they learn to put all hope and trust in him. The Judahites thought they could escape from the Babylonians by going to Egypt, but Yahweh warned them that the Egyptians were going to be caught by the same calamities. "There is no sufficiently secure defense against impending calamities, apart from true repentance."[173] As usual, Jeremiah's declaration saw a form of fulfillment, but not one that exactly or fully corresponded to the picture he gave. In the 37th year of his reign (568/567), Nebuchadrezzar invaded Egypt and engaged with Pharaoh Amasis,[174] though according to what seems to be the Egyptian version of events, Amasis won

---

171. P. D. Miller, "Jeremiah," on the passage.

172. Cf. Holladay, *Commentary on Jeremiah*, 2:302.

173. J. Pappus, *In Omnes Prophetas* (Frankfurt: Spiessius, 1593), 117; cf. Tyler, *Jeremiah*, 388.

174. See the text in *ANET*, 308.

a crucial battle against the "Asiatics."[175] It was a raid, not an occupation,[176] which fits the prophecy. In a more radical way, Sun House "was demolished, destroyed, and stopped when the Lord Christ was incarnated and came to this world."[177]

4. A Final Confrontation, Exhortation, and Warning (44:1–30 [LXX 51:1–30])

[1]*The word that came to Jeremiah regarding all the Judahites who were living in the country of Egypt, living in Migdol, in Tahpanhes, in Memphis,*[a] *and in the country of Pathros.*[b]

[2]*Yahweh of Armies,*[c] *the God of Israel, has said this. You yourselves have seen the dire thing that I let come on Jerusalem and on all the towns of Judah. There they are, a ruin this day, and there is no one living in them,* [3]*in the face of the dire thing that people did to irk me by going to burn offerings*[d] *so as to serve*[e] *other gods that they had not acknowledged—they and you and your ancestors.* [4]*I sent to you all my servants the prophets, sending assiduously,*[f] *saying, "Please do not do this offensive thing that I repudiate."*[g] [5]*But they didn't listen, they didn't bend their ear, so as to turn from their dire action, in order not to burn offerings to other gods.* [6]*So my fury, my anger, poured and blazed against the towns of Judah and against the streets of Jerusalem, and they have become a ruin, a desolation, this very day.*[h]

[7]*So now Yahweh, the God of Armies, the God of Israel,*[i] *has said this. Why are you doing such a dire thing to yourselves, to cut off for yourselves man and woman, child and baby, from within Judah, in order not to leave yourselves a remainder,*[j] [8]*by irking me with the actions of your hands by burning offerings to other gods in the country of Egypt where you are coming to reside, in order to cut it off for yourselves and in order to become a form of slighting and an object of reviling among all the nations on earth?* [9]*Have you put out of mind the dire actions of your ancestors, the dire actions of the kings of Judah, the dire actions of its wives,*[k] *your own dire actions,*[l] *and the dire actions of your wives, which they took in the country of Judah and in the streets of Jerusalem?* [10]*They have not been crushed*[m] *until this day and they have not been in awe.*[n] *They have not walked by my instruction or*[o] *by my decrees that I put before you and before your ancestors.*[p]

---

175. See K. Jansen-Winklein, "Die Siegesstele des Amasis," *Zeitschrift für ägyptische Sprache und Altertumskunde* 14 (2014): 132–53.

176. Rudolph, *Jeremia*, 259.

177. From Ephrem the Syrian's commentary on Jeremiah, as quoted in Wenthe, *Jeremiah*, 241.

[11]*Therefore Yahweh of Armies, the God of Israel,*[q] *has said this. Here am I, setting my face against you in respect of something dire, to cut off all Judah.* [12]*I will get the remainder of Judah who set their faces to come to the country of Egypt to reside there, and they will entirely come to an end in the country of Egypt—they will fall by the sword, and by hunger they will come to an end—little and big, by sword and famine they will die. They will become an oath, a desolation, a form of slighting, and an object of reviling.*[r] [13]*I will attend to the people who live in the country of Egypt as I attended to Jerusalem by sword, by hunger, and by epidemic.* [14]*There will not be one who escapes or survives of the remainder of Judah, the people who have come to reside there in the country of Egypt, or to turn back to the country of Judah, people who are lifting up*[s] *their spirits to turn back to live*[t] *there, because they will not turn back, except people who escape.*[u]

[15]*All the men who knew that their wives were burning offerings to other gods, and all the women who were standing by, a big assembly, and the entire company that were living in the country of Egypt in Pathros, answered Jeremiah:* [16]*The word that you have spoken to us in Yahweh's name: we are not listening to you.* [17]*Because we will definitely act on*[v] *every word that has gone out from our mouth, in burning offerings to the Queen*[w] *of the Heavens and pouring libations to her, as we did, we ourselves, our ancestors, our kings, and our officials, in the towns of Judah and in the streets of Jerusalem; and we were full of food, we were doing well, and nothing dire did we see.* [18]*But since the time we stopped burning offerings to the Queen of the Heavens and pouring libations to her,*[x] *we have lacked everything, and by sword and by hunger we have come to an end.* [19]*And when we are burning offerings to the Queen of the Heavens and pouring libations to her,*[y] *it's not apart from our husbands that we have made loaves to image her*[z] *and to pour libations to her, is it.*[aa]

[20]*Jeremiah said to the entire company, against the men, against the women, and against the entire company who were answering him with a word:* [21]*The incense that you burned in the towns of Judah and in the streets of Jerusalem, you, your ancestors, your kings, your officials, and the people of the country: of them Yahweh has been mindful, and he has brought them to mind, hasn't he.* [22]*And Yahweh could*[bb] *no longer carry it in the face of the direness of your practices, in the face of the offensive things that you did. So your country became a ruin, a desolation, and a form of slighting, without anyone living there*[cc] *this very day.* [23]*In the face of the fact that you burned offerings and that you did wrong in relation to Yahweh and did not listen to Yahweh's voice, and by his instruction and by his decrees and by his declarations you did not walk: that's why this dire thing has befallen you this very day.*[dd]

[24]*Jeremiah said to the entire company and to all the women: Listen to Yahweh's word, all Judah that is in the country of Egypt.*[ee] [25]*Yahweh of Armies, the God of Israel, has said this. You and your wives,*[ff] *you have both spoken with*

your mouths and with your hands have fulfilled it: "We will definitely act on our promises that we have made to burn offerings to the Queen of the Heavens and to pour libations to her." You may definitely implement your promises, you may definitely act on your promises. gg

²⁶*Therefore, listen to Yahweh's word, all Judah who are living in the country of Egypt. Here am I, I am swearing*hh *by my great name (Yahweh has said): If my name is any more proclaimed in the mouth of any individual in Judah, saying, "The Lord Yahweh is alive,"*ii *in the entire country of Egypt . . .* ij ²⁷*Here am I, watching over them in respect of something dire and not of something good. Every individual from Judah who is in the country of Egypt will come to an end by sword and by famine until they are finished off.* ²⁸*The people who survive the sword—they will return from the country of Egypt to the country of Judah, few in number. But the entire remainder of Judah who are coming to the country of Egypt to reside there will acknowledge whose word gets implemented, mine or theirs.*kk

²⁹*This will be the sign for you (Yahweh's affirmation)*ll *that I am going to attend to you in this place, in order that you may acknowledge that my words against you will definitely get implemented*mm *in respect of something dire.* nn ³⁰*Yahweh has said this. Here am I, I am giving Pharaoh*oo *Hophra King of Egypt into the hand of his enemies, into the hand of the people who are seeking his life, as I gave Zedekiah King of Judah into the hand of Nebuchadrezzar King of Babylon his enemy, the one seeking his life.*pp

a. LXX lacks *in Memphis*.

b. MT^L has a section marker here.

c. LXX lacks *of Armies* and *this day* later in the verse.

d. See the translation note and commentary on 1:16.

e. LXX lacks *so as to serve*, later in the verse implies *yəda'tem* ("you had not acknowledged") for MT *yədā'ûm*, and lacks *they and you and your ancestors*.

f. See the translation note and commentary on 7:13.

g. See the translation note on 12:8.

h. On *this very day* (which recurs in vv. 22 and 23), see the commentary on 11:5a. MT has a section marker here.

i. LXX lacks *the God of Israel*.

j. See 6:9 and the commentary on it.

k. Elsewhere, *nāšāyw* denotes "his wives," but there is no antecedent for "his"; rather, Judah is the antecedent. Aq implies *śārāyw* ("its officials"; Allen, *Jeremiah*, 443; cf. 8:1); LXX implies *śārêkem* ("your officials"), assimilating to vv. 17, 21.

l. LXX lacks *your own dire actions*.

m. Th understands *dākā' pual* metaphorically ("made contrite"); see the commentary. LXX, Tg have "they have not stopped [their dire behavior]," which is perhaps a loose translation. Vg, Aq, Sym "been cleansed" links the verb with the Aramaic equivalent of Hebrew *zākâ*.

n. LXX lacks *and they have not been in awe.*

o. LXX lacks *by my instruction or.*

p. MT has a section marker here.

q. LXX lacks *of Armies, the God of Israel.*

r. LXX has a shorter version of vv. 11–12.

s. Tg nicely has "deceive themselves," implying a form of *nâšā'* (cf. 37:9) rather than *nāśā'.*

t. LXX lacks *to live.*

u. MT has a marker here.

v. The infinitive precedes the finite verb, underlining the factuality of the action—three times more in v. 25 and in v. 29.

w. On the word's form, see the translation note on 7:18.

x. LXX lacks *and pouring libations to her.*

y. The finite verb continues the participial construction.

z. LXX lacks *to image her.*

aa. MT has a marker here.

bb. *Yiqtol yûkal* implies an ongoing inability (Volz, *Jeremia*, 367, comparing GK 107b) rather than indicating that the line contains a waw-consecutive whose *waw* is separated from its verb (Rudolph, *Jeremia*, 262; see *TTH* 85).

cc. LXX lacks *without anyone living there.*

dd. LXX lacks *this very day.* MT has a section marker here.

ee. LXX lacks *all Judah that is in the country of Egypt.* MT^L has a section marker here.

ff. For MT *'attem ûnəšêkem*, LXX implies *'attēnâ hannāšîm* ("you wives"), which better fits the feminine verbs that follow.

gg. MT has a marker here.

hh. The *qatal* verb is declarative/performative, a speech act; see 1:5 and the translation note on it. On Yahweh's swearing, see the commentary on 22:5.

ii. See the translation note and commentary on 4:2.

jj. On the *if*-clause, see the translation note on 15:11. M. Leuchter suggests a link between Jeremiah's declaration and the clash between different groups who all saw themselves as Jewish in Ezra ("The Exegesis of Jeremiah in and beyond Ezra 9–10," *VT* 65 [2015]: 62–80).

kk. LXX lacks *mine or theirs.*

ll. LXX lacks *(Yahweh's affirmation).*

mm. LXX lacks *in this place . . . implemented.*

nn. MT has a marker here.

oo. LXX lacks *Pharaoh.*

pp. MT has a section marker here.

"Jeremiah 44 comes at the very nadir of Judaean political fortunes, with the last gasp of life in Judah squeezed out by the assassination of Gedaliah and the subsequent flight from the anticipated Babylonian reprisals. Now in Egypt, the fugitive community receives an oracle of judgment from Jeremiah."[178] In this final message, the horizon broadens as Jeremiah addresses the entire Judahite community in Egypt, spread over a much broader area than merely

---

178. D. J. Reimer, "Redeeming Politics," 125.

Tahpanhes; indeed, the focus lies on Upper Egypt, the far south. The chapter offers no indication of how much later the message came in relation to the arrival of Johanan's group in Tahpanhes. Jeremiah 24:8 referred to the presence of other Judahites in Egypt before Jeremiah's arrival, and we know from the Elephantine Papyri about a Judahite community in Upper Egypt a couple of centuries later.[179] But the background to and chronology of such Judahite presence in Egypt is a matter of guesswork. What is definite is that "Egypt is portrayed as a place of despair for Israel" in Jer 37–44.[180]

While one can conceive of Yahweh giving Jeremiah a message addressed (at least rhetorically) to the entire Judahite community in Egypt, it seems implausible that Jeremiah made the journey of several weeks to have a meeting with the Pathros community as described in this chapter or that they came to Tahpanhes to meet him. More likely, Yahweh later inspired one of the curators of Jeremiah's work to compose this imaginative account that expresses Yahweh's challenge to the Pathros community and to the Judahite community in Egypt in general, conveying what a "difficult and hopeless task" Jeremiah had in Egypt.[181] The report's including no account of Jeremiah delivering the message in vv. 2–14 fits with its being an imaginative and rhetorical account. The chapter thus forms a first coda to Jer 37–43; Jer 45 will form a second coda. In the context of the Jeremiah scroll as a whole, the two chapters pair with Jer 1. As the curators composed that opening chapter to introduce Jeremiah's work, so they composed Jer 44–45 to close it, and Jer 44 sums up Yahweh's critique of Judah over the decades as well as critiquing the Pathros community.

The main body of the message twice follows a threefold sequence that is similar to the outline structure of Jer 2–6, which comprised confrontation in terms of what has been happening, exhortation to change, and warning of the calamity that will otherwise follow. Over against Jer 2–6, this chapter is distinctive for incorporating a response by the community in between the threefold formulations, and then a closing sign.

v. 1	The curators' introduction
vv. 2–6	Confrontation: Jeremiah rehearses the story of the Judahite community's unfaithfulness and the price it paid
vv. 7–10	Exhortation (*so now*): Jeremiah urges people therefore to stop being unfaithful in the same way
vv. 11–14	Warning (*therefore*): Jeremiah threatens people with disaster

179. See the introduction to part 4 (pp. 744–45).
180. G. Galvin, *Egypt as a Place of Refuge*, FAT 2/51 (Tübingen: Mohr Siebeck, 2011), 132.
181. Weiser, *Jeremia*, 377.

vv. 15–19   The men and the women of Pathros retort that they did better when they were serving the Queen of the Heavens, so they are not going to stop

vv. 20–23   Confrontation: Jeremiah repeats his rehearsal of the story

vv. 24–25   Exhortation: Jeremiah sarcastically urges people to carry on being unfaithful

vv. 26–28   Warning (*therefore*): Jeremiah reformulates his threat of disaster

vv. 29–30   Jeremiah promises a sign that Yahweh will be taking action

The chapter is repetitive in MT's version, which is not an indication that it has been expanded.[182] Some writers repeat themselves, saying the same thing twice in slightly different words or even in the same words—the same words. "It may be that by shortening the text . . . we shall arrive at a slimmer and better narrative," but the disparity between different scholars' attempts at shortening raises questions about whether a slimmer version would be a more original one;[183] it might be "better" only in matching expectations that come from a different cultural context. LXX's text is also shorter, as usual, perhaps because of being based on a shorter version, because of deliberately cutting down some of the wordiness, and/or because of accidental omission.[184]

1 Yahweh now has a message for *all the Judahites in Egypt*, not simply the people in Tahpanhes with whom Jeremiah came, who were the immediate focus in the previous chapter. *Migdol* was a name of some significance for Judahites because of its connection with the exodus (Exod 14:2; Num 33:7), though there may have been more than one Migdol. The word's etymology suggests it was a tower or fortified place (cf. 2 Sam 22:51; and the more common *migdāl* in, e.g., Jer 31:38); the word was apparently adopted into Egyptian usage from a Semitic background. But the mention in the exodus story suggests a place in northeast Egypt, and in Ezek 29:10; 30:6, Migdol stands for the far north of Egypt. It was thus not far from Tahpanhes, but even nearer the Egyptian border.[185] Migdol to Syene is the Egyptian equiva-

---

182. Lundbom, *Jeremiah 37–52*, 155.

183. McKane, *Jeremiah*, 2:1085.

184. The translation notes, as usual, draw attention to many of the points where LXX is shorter, though by no means to all of them.

185. See E. D. Oren, "Migdol," *BASOR* 256 (1984): 7–44; J. K. Hoffmeier, "The Search for Migdol of the New Kingdom and Exodus 14:2," *Buried History* 44 (2008): 3–12.

lent of Dan to Beersheba, and places are here listed from northeast to south. Memphis[186] had once been Egypt's capital, and it remained an important city whose location in the north, in Lower Egypt, gave it importance when Egypt was subject to invasion by Assyria, Babylon, or Persia. Migdol, Memphis, and Tahpanhes will recur together in 46:14. Pathros complements Memphis as a name for Upper Egypt (hence the expression *the country* or "region" *of* Pathros); the name comes from an Egyptian term meaning southland.[187] So Migdol/Tahpanhes suggests the far north/northeast, Memphis suggests Lower Egypt, and Pathros suggests Upper Egypt. The message indeed addresses Judahites in the entire country.

2–6 Whereas some Egyptian Judahites had experienced the fall of Jerusalem while others had taken refuge in Egypt earlier, they have all in some sense *seen* it. They all know about it. And broadly, they have all been involved in the religious commitment that generated the calamity, even if they escaped before the ax fell. Jeremiah's confrontation takes up and summarizes his confrontation of people throughout the scroll, not least way back at the beginning, where he threatened "dire trouble" to come on them (see 1:16).[188] The arraignment also recalls Huldah's indictment in 2 Kgs 22:16–17.[189] The section works chiastically:

> v. 2   Yahweh brought dire trouble, ruin, to Jerusalem and Judah
> > v. 3   It issued from Judah's dire action
> > > v. 4   Yahweh sent prophets to obviate this development
> > v. 5   But people didn't turn from their dire action
> v. 6   Yahweh brought ruin to Jerusalem and Judah

Thus "the prophets are not a threat against Israel, not a negative force, but are God's gracious gift through which repentance and forgiveness might occur."[190] Yet how odd that the Judahites took the truculent Jeremiah with them; what trouble they brought on themselves by doing so! "They undermine their own plans of muting and skirting the voice of God." But in Jeremiah, "Yahweh follows the people to Egypt and is not about to cave in to their prodigal stance."[191] *The towns of Judah* and *the streets of Jerusalem* omits reference to Yahweh's house; the chapter will later make explicit that it is attacking religious ob-

---

186. On the name Memphis, see the translation note on 2:16.
187. See BDB.
188. Wright, *Jeremiah*, 402–3.
189. Holladay, *Commentary on Jeremiah*, 2:287.
190. Brueggemann, *Jeremiah 26–52*, 194, 195.
191. Stulman, *Jeremiah*, 345.

servances that characterize family and personal spirituality rather than the temple. Although Jeremiah has occasionally referred to wrongs within the society, the focus of the scroll's concern continues to be the community's un-faithfulness to Yahweh rather than people's unfaithfulness to one another. It's said that inequality increases during peace time and reduces during war and other such crises (though Jer 34 may testify to an exception). Maybe there is less mutual faithlessness to critique in the aftermath of 587. Conversely, catastrophe and loss may test people's commitment to God and issue in their turning in other directions from the conviction they professed when times were easier—as the Job story presupposes.

7–10 While confrontation continues, it merges into exhortation. Jeremiah repeats much of the sequence of vv. 2–6, now as present reality and danger: a dire thing (v. 7), irking Yahweh by burning offerings (v. 8), refusing to take any notice of Yahweh (vv. 9–10). The implicit exhortation is dominated by rhetorical questions that express bewilderment and invite people to look at themselves from outside so that they see the inexplicable nature of their actions. A *why* question runs through vv. 7b–8 and then a simply incredulous *have you* question runs through v. 9. The questions reuse familiar Jeremianic formulations but introduce innovative notes. The danger of the community's dire behavior is to *cut off for yourselves* the entire family of Judah, including people of both sexes and the children on whom the future depends. You will thus not *leave yourselves* a remainder. The dire behavior consists in continuing to burn offerings to other gods in the same way they did in Judah in the years that led up to the catastrophe. Will they never learn? *Slighting* and *reviling* tellingly take up the warning in 24:8–9, which included reference to people who would go to Egypt after the fall of Jerusalem, and the double reference to wives trailers critique that will be developed in vv. 24–28. To say that people *have not been crushed* is surprising, as they obviously have been—but evidently not enough, or they haven't recognized the fact. "The remnant has learned nothing from their national crushing at the hands of the Babylonians."[192] They haven't internalized it. It's the only First Testament passage where the verb (*dākā'/dākâ*) clearly suggests something happening to people's attitudes that issues in awe and thus in responsiveness.

11–14 The warning again recycles previous warnings but updates them with the contextual threat that Judahites in Egypt will not be able to return to Judah when they want to. The entire community is going to be terminated in Egypt. They ought not to have set their faces to go there; Yahweh will set his face against them so that they will not be able to go back when they *are lifting*

192. Bodner, *After the Invasion*, 134.

up their spirits to turn back to live there (cf. 42:17). In that connection, a further parallel with Jer 2–6 appears: warnings of total destruction get qualified (cf. 4:27; 5:10, 18). *There will not be one who escapes or survives* is unequivocal. But Jeremiah adds *except people who escape*. Is this phrase a later addition, to take the edge off the talk of total annihilation? What understanding of the resultant text as a whole was in the mind of the person who added the phrase? The jolting clash between the opening of the verse and its closing still stands. Maybe that jolting is the point, whether the phrase is original or is a later addition. The opening declaration is designed to have a traumatic effect on the audience; the closing phrase can minister to people who have been appropriately traumatized by the declaration. It opens up the possibility of hope to people who respond in the appropriate way to Jeremiah's warning. As usual, the point about declaring inevitable calamity is to forestall it.[193]

15–18 Whether or not Jeremiah had ever been to Migdol or Memphis, the scroll here portrays him as being far away from Tahpanhes in the south, in Pathros. The reference to a big assembly of people living in Pathros makes it more likely that the chapter portrays the meeting happening there than that it portrays a company from there coming all the way to Tahpanhes. The Pathros community respond forthrightly in declining to accept Jeremiah's confrontation (they don't see the history the way he does), his exhortation (they don't intend to change), or his warning (which doesn't match their experience in the past). Their religious stance identifies with that described in 7:16–20 (see the commentary there). It coheres with our knowledge of the later Elephantine community whose location could count as Pathros, which was not very orthodox by the standards of the Torah. Whereas the group that brought Jeremiah with them at least went through the motions of acknowledging Jeremiah and being open to Yahweh's message to them (42:1–6), the Pathrosites do not. Life had worked out well for them until they changed their religious practice, and they intend to continue with it. Perhaps Josiah's reformation would have stopped offerings to the Queen of the Heavens after 622, but 609 and the following years saw a series of reversals and problems for Judah, and if this sequence of developments is the background, some plausibility attaches to their analysis,[194] to which a twenty-first-century gender-based reading may also be sympathetic.[195] The

---

193. R. R. Hutton, "Slogans in the Midst of Crisis," 234.

194. Cf. Rudolph, *Jeremia*, 261. On the link with Josiah's reform, see Y. Hoffman, "History and Ideology: The Case of Jeremiah 44," *JANES* 28 (2001): 43–51.

195. Cf. C. J. Sharp, "Gender and Subjectivity in Jeremiah 44," in *Women and Exilic Identity in the Hebrew Bible*, ed. K. E. Southwood and M. A. Halvorsen-Taylor, LHBOTS 631 (London: T&T Clark, 2018), 75.

disagreement between women and prophet illustrates how "using experiences and 'facts' to explain ideological positions" doesn't work. One's "prevenient theology" is what makes it possible to interpret an event such as what happened in 587: people could share the same experience but disagree about its meaning.[196] Jeremiah's approach to discerning the difference between prophets (23:9–40) made a parallel assumption: his theology and ethic underlay his evaluation of the other prophets.

19 Although the passage refers to the same religious commitment as 7:16–20, its angle on that commitment is different. There, it was described as a family observance; here, the women speak of it as especially theirs.[197] They do associate their husbands with it. The necessity to do so coheres with the requirements about vows in Num 30: the male head of the household was responsible for its financial viability, so women could not make commitments that had economic implications without their husbands' agreement.[198] Whereas Jeremiah thinks there is a problem about adding gods to their religious service, they think the problem is subtraction.[199] Perhaps they worshiped Yahweh and saw no clash with also worshiping his consort.[200] Or perhaps their not mentioning Yahweh means they have eliminated him from their religious world so that Yahweh will answer in kind, "essentially disowning the community."[201]

20–23 In response, Jeremiah reaffirms his message with its three elements. In keeping with the nature of parallelism, the second version takes the first further at each point. In his confrontation, he adds that Yahweh *could no longer carry* the people's wrongdoing. He could no longer bear it. He is able to carry people's wrongdoing for a long time and not make them pay the price for it, but there comes a time when toleration goes too far against the other side to his moral nature that requires him to take wrongdoing seriously. *Carry* (*nāśā'*) is the First Testament's regular word for "forgive" (that is, "forgive" in English translations usually represents that Hebrew word). This passage is the only time the Jeremiah scroll uses the verb *carry* in this connection: it

---

196. R. P. Carroll, *Jeremiah*, OTL, 739. In this context, "ideological" is not so different from "theological"; but on "ideological" in this connection, see further W. Brueggemann, "The 'Baruch Connection': Reflections on Jeremiah 43:1–7," *JBL* 113 (1994): 405–20.

197. At last we get a woman's voice, S. V. Davidson comments in "'Every Green Tree and the Streets of Jerusalem': Counter Constructions of Gendered Sacred Space in the Book of Jeremiah," in George, *Constructions of Space IV*, 121–27.

198. Blayney, *Jeremiah*, 406.

199. Diamond, "Jeremiah," 607.

200. See, e.g., J. E. Harding, "The Silent Goddess and the Gendering of Divine Speech in Jeremiah 44," in Maier and Sharp, *Prophecy and Power*, 208–23.

201. Leuchter, *Polemics of Exile*, 132; he infers that Jeremiah leaves no scope for the community to turn and that the chapter presupposes that the future lies only with the Babylonian community.

prefers the word that rather means "pardon" (*sālaḥ*; 5:1, 7; 31:34; 33:8; 36:3; 50:20; see the commentary on 5:1). The implication is that Yahweh had been continually forgiving Judah, continually carrying its wrongdoing and not making Judah carry responsibility for it and therefore not bringing calamity upon it. He had been turning a blind eye to it. But there came a time when he said, "That's it."

24–25 The distinctive note in the exhortation is the irony or sarcasm with which it closes. The community had done as it said it would, and it may continue to do so. *You may definitely implement your promises, you may definitely act on your promises.* Yahweh takes up the biting sarcasm of 7:21, following on his critique of people making offerings to the Queen of the Heavens in that context, and gives expression to it in a new way.[202]

26–27 The third element in the pattern is the warning. The declaration that no one will take Yahweh's name on their lips in making an oath follows in two ways from what has preceded. To put it sardonically, they won't do so because they won't be doing anything; they will have been consumed by sword, panic, and epidemic. But not taking Yahweh's name on their lips is also a devastating description of their loss of identity. More specifically (in a way that follows directly from what preceded), they won't be taking Yahweh's name on their lips in making solemn promises. It is an expression of poetic justice in light of earlier references to promises in the name of the Queen of the Heavens and offerings to the Queen of the Heavens (vv. 17, 25). They have chosen the name to put on their lips in connection with their promises; Yahweh confirms it. The warning further takes up Yahweh's talk of watchfulness, which will revert again from being good news (see 31:28) to being bad news. Yahweh has described himself as collecting the Judahites "from all the countries where I have driven them" (32:37). He has specifically spoken in these terms to the 597 exiles in Babylon (29:14). Does the waywardness of the Egyptian community exclude it from this promise? Is that waywardness such that it "annuls any such hope"?[203]

28 But once again, the declaration of total annihilation is compromised by an unexpected qualification: *The people who survive the sword—they will return from the country of Egypt to the country of Judah few in number.* Likewise, whereas v. 14 declared that there would be no remainder, here *the entire remainder of Judah who are coming to the country of Egypt to reside there will acknowledge whose word gets implemented, mine or theirs.* They cannot do that acknowledging if they have simply been annihilated. Clashes within these verses put us on the track of the need not to be literalistic or wooden in understanding the text. The prophecy's author was not stupid, and neither was

202. Holladay, *Commentary on Jeremiah*, 2:304.
203. So Keown, Scalise, and Smothers, *Jeremiah 26–52*, 265.

the audience (well, except that they were theologically and morally stupid). The author was engaged in persuasion, which worked by setting possible scenarios before the audience—the audience for whom Jer 44 was composed as well as the audience within the scene it describes.

29 The promise of a sign is another respect in which vv. 20–30 go beyond vv. 2–14. And it implies a more explicit recognition that the debate between Jeremiah and his audience (or the chapter's author and its audience) cannot be resolved by appeal to empirical experience. As well as depending on a theology and an ethic, Jeremiah's argument depends on a hope Yahweh gives people—not in the subjective sense of hopefulness but in the objective sense of something that is going to happen (one might say the argument is subject to eschatological verification). It depends on a promise that coheres with the theology and the ethic and forms an aspect of the total perspective within which Yahweh wants people to live. At the end of Jeremiah's final message directly addressed to Judah, for the first time Yahweh promises the Judahites a sign. It is a sign like the one he gave Moses (Exod 3:12), not the ones he gave the Israelites and the Egyptians (e.g., Exod 4:8–9, 17, 28, 30): that is, there is nothing to see now, but there is a statement about the future that will be fulfilled. It is the combination of word and event that constitutes the sign. As with that sign for Moses, only afterward will it be empirically clear that Yahweh is now doing something. And as with the Exodus signs, the sign's object is the acknowledgment of Yahweh that will or should follow when the declaration has been implemented. The promise of a sign is another indication that one should not be literalistic in interpreting the prophecy's declarations about the entire community being annihilated, because the promise presupposes there will be Judahites in Egypt to see the sign.

30 The sign is the equivalent of the death knell for Hananiah in 28:16.[204] As was the case there, Jeremiah could not prove his interpretation was correct; it does depend on later verification. Perhaps the lack of any note concerning the sign's implementing, which contrasts with the Hananiah story, indicates that (far from being a prophecy given after the event)[205] this chapter derives from before the implementing. The declaration concerns the destiny of Pharaoh Hophra, the king of Egypt (the Greek version of the name was Apries), who reigned from about 589 to 570. In a way, it picks up the declaration in 43:10–13, though without making a link with an invasion by Nebuchadrezzar (on which see further 46:13–24). Indeed, the comparison with Zedekiah's fate implicitly excludes such a link. Herodotus (*Histories*, 2:169) and Diodorus Siculus (*Historical Library*, 1:68) relate the death of

204. Diamond, "Jeremiah," 607.
205. So, e.g., Rudolph, *Jeremia*, 263.

Hophra, who was father-in-law of Amasis (see the commentary on 43:10–13). They give different accounts of his end, but both relate how he met his death at the hands of Amasis's agents.

5. A Footnote Message for Baruch (45:1–5 [LXX 51:31–35])

[1]*The word that Jeremiah the prophet spoke to Baruch ben Neraiah when he wrote these words on a document from Jeremiah's dictation in the fourth year of Jehoiakim ben Josiah King of Judah.*[a]
[2]*Yahweh the God of Israel has said this to you, Baruch.* [3]*You have said,*

Oh, please, me,
  because Yahweh has added suffering to my pain.[b]
I am weary with my groaning;
  relief I have not found.[c]

[4]*You are to say this to him.*[d] *Yahweh has said this.*

Here, what I built up, I am smashing,
  and what I planted, I am pulling up (that is, the entire country).[e]

[5]*So whereas you for yourself,*[f] *you seek*[g] *big things—don't seek them, because here am I, letting something dire come upon all flesh (Yahweh's affirmation). But I am giving you your life as loot in all the places that you go to.*[h]

a. MT[L] has a section marker here.

b. Vg translates, "added suffering to my suffering," which gives the right impression; see the commentary.

c. The 2-2 line thus takes a-b-b'-a' form. For *relief* (*mənûḥâ*), Tg has "prophecy," which presupposes the idea of Yahweh's spirit resting (*nûaḥ*) on people so that they prophesy (Num 11:25–26) and implies that Baruch's complaint concerns not being able to be a prophet (cf. Rashi, in MG).

d. Yahweh is now addressing Jeremiah, whereas in v. 3 he spoke as if addressing Baruch, but even there he was actually doing so by telling Jeremiah the message to give Baruch; one should not make heavy weather of the "convoluted nature of the exchange" (Keown, Scalise, and Smothers, *Jeremiah 26–52*, 272).

e. LXX lacks *(that is, the entire country)*; Tg adds "of Israel"; see the commentary.

f. "You seek big things for yourself" would give a misleading impression; cf. Allen, *Jeremiah*, 450; Joüon 133d; see the commentary.

g. GK 150a and Joüon 161a take this as a question.

h. MT has a marker here.

A message for Baruch forms a second coda to the narrative in Jer 37–43. It has several points of connection with what has preceded.

- The date in v. 1 makes a link with Jer 36. Whereas one would not have been surprised if a message for Baruch had appeared in association with that chapter, like Jer 36 it appears in an odd chronological place here, following material relating to later events.
- Located here, however, vv. 2–3 suggest a link with the nearer narrative at 43:3. Baruch had to hide when he associated himself with Jeremiah the first time; now he is being blamed for Jeremiah's message!
- Located here, likewise, v. 4 makes a link with the message about building up, tearing down, planting, and pulling up in 42:10, which led into that accusation against him, as well as with 1:10 and other passages that use this language.
- Further, located here, v. 5 suggests a link with 39:15–18. There, Yahweh gave Jeremiah a message for his other supporter, Ebed-melech, to whom he also spoke of the dire fate coming on Judah and to whom he promised that he would keep his life as spoil.
- The last phrase in v. 5, referring to places where Baruch might have to go, is now illumined by the fact that he is in Egypt. Yahweh has kept his word for twenty years so far.

Once more, there is no account of Jeremiah's delivering the message, which is again included in the scroll not merely as a personal word for Baruch but as a message with something to say to the audience. Like Jeremiah's recounting of his protests to Yahweh (his "confessions"), this account of the message that speaks to Baruch's anguish testifies to the price that secretary as well messenger pay for doing their work, and thus speaks to their listeners' treatment of them and of the message they bring from God. And it indirectly draws attention in a new way to the nature of the message that disturbs Baruch and should have disturbed the audience.[206] Reading on into Jer 46–51 will indicate that it also looks forward to what follows. Like Jer 25 and Jer 36, it is both an end and a beginning. It faces both ways.

1 What are *these words*? In light of the date that follows, they cannot be the preceding words in Jer 44. And in light of the big gap since Jer 36, they can hardly be the words that Baruch took down that year whose story came in

---

206. See further M. A. Taylor, "Jeremiah 45: The Problem of Placement," *JSOT* 37 (1987): 79–98.

Jer 36. The answer to the question will emerge only in 46:1–2.[207] The verse again presupposes the quite humble (though vital) role that Baruch fulfilled: it does not suggest that he or scribes like him were the kind of people who generated the content of a prophetic scroll.[208]

2–3 What v. 2 calls something that *Yahweh the God of Israel has said* begins by quoting Baruch's own words. The dynamic parallels 14:1–12, though here Yahweh's making explicit that he is quoting Baruch makes it not quite as dramatic. It does raise a little suspense as we await Yahweh's actual message (see the commentary on 14:1). The protest attributed to Baruch comprises two psalm-like lines, like Jeremiah's protests in Jer 11–20. One should therefore not be literalistic about the language. But while psalmic language often speaks in three directions, in terms of I (the protester), you (Yahweh), and he/they (human attackers), Baruch speaks only of I and he (Yahweh). Psalms can also include reference to Yahweh in the third person, but one wonders whether this protest that compares with a plaint such as Isa 40:27 is a little worrying in not addressing Yahweh at all. Baruch's point about *suffering* and *pain* is not that he first felt pain and then felt suffering; his innovative form of expression is a kind of hendiadys suggesting that Yahweh has been piling suffering and pain onto him.[209] While we have heard about Baruch being in danger (Jer 36) and subject to denunciation (Jer 43), his extravagant language suggests he is not simply talking about his own pain but praying as Jeremiah does, out of his people's anguish or on the basis of his identification with them. In the 604 context (see Jer 25; 36), he would be anticipatorily grieving about the suffering that is coming to them. In the context of the prayer's placement in the scroll, he would be grieving about the suffering they have now experienced and also about the further suffering of which Jer 44 has spoken.

4 As was the case with Jeremiah's protests, Yahweh's response indicates that a protest prayer cannot assume a positive response. Indeed, as was the case with Jeremiah's protests, Yahweh's response takes a form that is quite complex in content.[210] It neither simply sympathizes nor simply negates but presses Baruch to look at matters within a different framework, and it does so in a way that twists and turns. Actually, Baruch gets three responses. The first is to say, "Tough." Baruch is right about Yahweh's intentions. Only here does Jeremiah have Yahweh refer to his past building and planting, to be replaced

207. This logic works only for MT, since Jer 46–51 comes earlier in LXX; there, Jer 45 (LXX 51:31–35) leads straight into Jer 52.

208. P. House, "Investing in the Ruins: Jeremiah and Theological Vocation," *JETS* 56 (2013): 12.

209. McKane, *Jeremiah*, 2:1097.

210. See P. J. Scalise, "Baruch as First Reader: Baruch's Lament in the Structure of the Book of Jeremiah," in Goldingay, *Uprooting and Planting*, 291–307.

by tearing down and pulling up, as opposed to promising or implying that there is building and planting to come. In addition, Yahweh adds the solemn footnote referring to *the entire country*.

5 The second response makes things worse: Yahweh forbids Baruch from praying, as he more than once forbade Jeremiah. Don't ask Yahweh to do *big things*. *Seek* (*biqqēš*) suggests prayer (e.g., Ezra 8:21), like "inquire after" (*dāraš*, notably 29:7). The context suggests praying for big things not for himself in some way (what would they be?) but for Judah, big things such that Yahweh earlier promised (33:3; cf. Pss 71:19; 106:21). There are no great promises of restoration in part 4 of the Jeremiah scroll like the ones in part 3.[211] It's not going to happen. *Something dire* is what is going to happen. But then comes the point where Yahweh's word becomes typically oblique. Usually, he speaks of something dire for Judah, but he can speak of dire things coming upon other peoples (e.g., 25:32), and here the calamity is to come *upon all flesh*, which need not simply imply Judah. It even makes one reconsider that expression *the entire country* (*kol hā'āreṣ*, v. 4), which could mean "the entire world."[212] In isolation, one might not think too much about that broader understanding of the phrases in vv. 4 and 5, but the next verse (46:1) and what it introduces could make one think further. What will now follow will add to the significance of locating Jer 45 at this point and of locating the messages about other nations here and not following Jer 25, where they appear in LXX. So the double possibility raised by vv. 4 and 5 is both of more trouble for Judah (which fits the time since 604 and fits Jer 44) and of trouble for the nations that have brought trouble to it (which Jer 46–51 will go on to declare). In the meantime, however, and thirdly, Baruch does get an unequivocal promise for himself, something by way of a positive answer to a protest, for which people hope when they dare to pray. At least, don't worry about your own fate, says Yahweh. He will make sure that Baruch is safe, as he more than once said in different terms to Jeremiah (1:19; 15:20–21). Yahweh's promise compares more precisely with his undertaking to Ebed-melech, which he kept; to Baruch, he had added *in all the places that you go to*, and Baruch is doing okay in Egypt.[213] As usual, a promise about *loot* should not be undervalued, as if it were a small thing. For soldiers, loot is a big thing (see 21:9 and the commentary on it).

---

211. Yates, "Narrative Parallelism," 280.

212. Cf. C. R. Seitz, "The Prophet Moses and the Canonical Shape of Jeremiah," *ZAW* 101 (1989): 21–25; B. Gosse, "Jérémie xlv et la place du recueil d'oracles contre les nations dans le livre de Jérémie," *VT* 40 (1990): 145–51.

213. Fretheim, *Jeremiah*, 571.

V. PART FIVE: MESSAGES ABOUT OTHER PEOPLES
(46:1–51:64 [LXX 26:1–31:44])

Many Western readers might prefer the prophetic scrolls without the prophecies about God bringing disaster to other nations, but Jer 46–51 especially reflects Jeremiah's fulfillment of his commission to be a prophet regarding the nations. His words to Hananiah would make an appropriate epigraph to the chapters: *The prophets who were before me and before you from of old, they prophesied regarding many countries and concerning big kingdoms, about battle and about dire fortune and about epidemic* (28:8). There are several aspects to the logic of their inclusion and several questions to which the messages about other nations might be the answer.

Prophecies about other nations are integral to prophecy in Israel's world; a major function of prophecy was to assure a people and its monarch that their god was going to protect them, give them victory, and put down their enemies. Such prophecies may be the oldest prophetic material that there is.[1] While the structure of the Jeremiah scroll may present "the judgment of Judah as a paradigm for the rest of the nations,"[2] the history of prophecy that lies behind the presence of these messages in the various prophetic scrolls suggests that the prophecies about Israel have their origin in a way of thinking and speaking about the nations, not the opposite. With prophecy, as with priesthood and kingship, Yahweh takes something from Israel's world and adapts it to his purpose. He does so in different ways in different prophetic scrolls. In Amos, prophecies about other nations soften up Ephraim for the prophet's confrontation of Ephraim itself. In Isa 1–39, they underscore a concern that Judah should neither rely on other nations nor be afraid of them, and they form part of a movement from Judah itself being the focus (Isa 1–12) to the world becoming the horizon (Isa 24–27). In Ezekiel, they form part of the transition from confrontation and threat (Ezek 1–24) to promise and hope (Ezek 33–48).

Theologically, it would not be surprising if Yahweh wanted Israel to be aware that he was involved in the nations' affairs and not just in Israel's, even when their lives did not impact Israel's. He was not just Israel's local God. Whereas Christians may be content not to think about their God being involved in the results of (say) the two World Wars, the Korean War, the Algerian War, the India-Pakistan war, the Vietnam War, the Falklands War, and the Iraq War, the First Testament suggests that Yahweh wanted Israel to

---

1. R. P. Carroll, *Jeremiah*, OTL, 751. See, e.g., J. H. Hayes, "The Usage of Oracles against Foreign Nations in Ancient Israel," *JBL* 87 (1968): 81–92.

2. J. Hwang, "The *Missio Dei* as an Integrative Motif in the Book of Jeremiah," *BBR* 23 (2013): 500.

think about such events. There are many ways of understanding wars. They may (for instance) be a people's way of seeking independence, of extending power, of gaining wealth, of resisting an aggressor, or of resolving disputes over territory. They may seem just to be meaningless. Prophecies concerning the nations declare that in some cases, at least, there was a supernatural aspect or significance to them.

In Jeremiah, whereas this collection of prophecies about the nations appears almost at the end of the scroll in MT, in LXX it appears in the middle, following on Jer 25. We do not know whether either order is more original or whether they represent ways in which different curators assembled Jeremianic material; either position makes sense.[3] In LXX Jeremiah, they spell out the declaration of calamity for the nations in 25:1–13. In relation to Judah, they then contribute to an alternation of confrontation (2:1–25:13), promise (25:14–32:24), confrontation (33:1–36:32), promise (37:1–40:13), confrontation (41:1–51:35). In MT Jeremiah, they instead follow on Jer 45 and come with other material focusing on events after 587, in Jer 37–45 and 52. On one hand, they thus do not interrupt Jeremiah's material relating to Judah, as Jer 26–45 follows on Jer 25. And on the other, they make the Jeremiah scroll (almost) close with a worldwide horizon and, in the promise about putting down the great agent of destruction and exile, make for a transition from bad news for Judah to good news for Judah after the false dawn in Jer 30–33.

The chapters do not give much consideration to reasons for the trouble that comes to the different peoples. The focus is more on the fact of calamity than on the reasons. The point about the chapters thus compares and contrasts with the argument of Rom 1–3. There, Paul's argument is that the gentile world is wayward and so is the Jewish people, and thus both deserve judgment. Here, the background of the argument is that Israel is wayward and deserves judgment, and the chapters move from Israel to the world. The combination is the same, but the order is the reverse. And here, the focus lies on the fact of trouble coming rather than the reasons for it, whereas Romans pays as much attention to the reasons as to the trouble itself.

Unlike the messages that confront Judah, these chapters refer little to Yahweh's wrath or anger (49:37; 51:45), and "the use of accusation and indictment" is "extremely laconic."[4] This shortfall further highlights how the really guilty party in Jeremiah is the people of Yahweh. Israelite prophecy

3. For discussion, see, e.g., M. Haran, "The Place of the Prophecies against the Nations in the Book of Jeremiah," in *Emanuel: Studies in Hebrew Bible, Septuagint, and Dead Sea Scrolls in Honor of Emanuel Tov*, ed. S. M. Paul et al., VTSup 94 (Leiden: Brill, 2003), 699–706; H.-J. Stipp, "Das eschatologische Schema im alexandrinischen Jeremiabuch," *VT* 64 (2014): 484–501; J. W. Watts, "Text and Redaction," 432–47.

4. Diamond, "Jeremiah," 611.

focuses on critique of the prophets' own people. Jeremiah does speak of Yahweh's taking redress for the nations' wrongdoing (46:10; 50:15, 28; 51:6, 11, 36), exposing and shaming false confidence and trust in defensive and religious resources (46:24; 48:1, 7, 29; 49:4, 16), acting against expansionist ambitions (46:8), and vindicating his being the only real God (48:7). With regard to imperial powers such as Egypt and Babylon in particular, if the prophecies have a focus, it lies on these nations' preoccupation with their own grandeur. Yahweh is declaring that he will see that imperial powers with their confidence and expansive aims do not stay in position forever. With some irony, Babylon is the agent of calamity in Jer 46–49 and the victim of it in Jer 50–51. But the logic of including other powers—Judah's neighbors and the representative eastern ones—is simply that they become illustrations of Yahweh's being sovereign in the entire world of nations. Some of the messages concern distant peoples that do not impinge on Judah (49:23–39), and these messages give no reason for the calamity that is coming on their subjects, which raises the question whether "prophecies of judgment" is at all the right way to describe the messages about other nations. Little in the descriptions of the different nations' destinies and faults applies distinctively to particular peoples or appears in distinctive forms in different prophets. A number of verses, lines, and phrases recur between the messages about different peoples within Jer 46–51 and between Jeremiah and other prophetic scrolls; different prophets perhaps used a shared store of such messages in articulating what Yahweh had to say about the different peoples.

In what context might Jeremiah have delivered these messages? There is a marked concentration of the dating of messages in Jer 46–51 (46:2; 47:1; 49:34; 51:59),[5] which suggests that they do belong in concrete historical and political contexts. An indication within the scroll is the visit of the envoys from countries such as Ammon, Moab, and Edom in the context of a possible rebellion against Babylon (Jer 27). One can imagine a prophet like Hananiah or Jeremiah uttering a message in a political setting in the narrow sense (that is, a meeting of kings and their staffs) or in the temple courts in an attempt to influence public opinion. The subsequent involvement of these peoples in attacking and conquering Jerusalem would provide another natural context for a prophet to have something to say about Yahweh's intentions concerning them. But Jer 27, again, does not suggest that Jeremiah's message there is designed to suggest good news for Judah, and Jer 46–49 gives little indication that its messages are somehow good news for Judah, though Jer 50–51 is different. Like the messages about other peoples in Amos, the messages in Jer 46–51 include virtually no indications that the nations are being punished for what they have done to Israel. While this motif does appear in the message

5. P. R. Raabe, "What Is Israel's God Up To?," 233.

about Ammon and at one or two points in the gargantuan message about Babylon, it features not at all in the messages about Egypt, Moab, Edom, Damascus, Kedar, and Elam. Further, the prophecies are not just about putting other nations down, and a title such as "Oracles against the Nations" also gives a misleading impression. The nations are the recipients of promises (46:26; 48:47; 49:6; 49:39) and of sympathy (47; 48). And the promises of restoration for different nations rule out chauvinism. Restoration, not judgment, is God's last word.[6] Jeremiah was, after all, commissioned "to build and to plant" as well as "to pull up and pull down" (1:10), for them as well as for Judah.[7] For them, unlike Judah, there is no exhortation to repentance or promise that judgment can be escaped.[8] But that characteristic reminds us that these messages were not addressed to the nations themselves but to Judah; it also reminds us of the point implicit in Jonah, that the lack of explicit exhortation to repentance may accompany an implied challenge to repentance rather than preclude it.

The placing of the passages together might seem to imply that they are similar, but they manifest a variety of tone, form, and approach; they are "in no way standardized."[9] Typically, they describe an army experiencing defeat, a calamity arriving from the north; it comes as Yahweh's day, and the result is shame. But they vary in length, complexity, unity, chronological specificity, rationale, and relationship to Judah. As is the case with their position in the scroll as a whole, the order of the messages in MT and LXX differs:

MT		LXX	
46:2–28	Egypt	25:14–19	Elam
47:1–7	Philistia	26:1–28	Egypt
48:1–47	Moab	27:1–28:64	Babylon
49:1–6	Ammon	29:1–7	Philistia
49:7–22	Edom	29:8–23	Edom
49:23–27	Damascus	30:1–5	Ammon
49:28–33	Kedar and Hazor	30:6–11	Kedar and Hazor
49:34–39	Elam	30:12–16	Damascus
50:1–51:64	Babylon	31:1–44	Moab

LXX thus has the message about Babylon in the middle of the sequence while MT has it at the end, and opinions again differ on whether one version of the

---

6. See P. D. Miller, "Jeremiah," for his "Reflections" on Jer 46–51.

7. Fretheim, *Jeremiah*, 575, 577.

8. J. G. Amesz, "A God of Vengeance? Comparing Yhwh's Dealings with Judah and Babylon in the Book of Jeremiah," in Kessler, *Reading the Book of Jeremiah*, 99–116.

9. Holladay, *Commentary on Jeremiah*, 2:313.

order is older than the other. LXX's order looks random, whereas there is a broad geographical and theological logic about MT's. It

- begins from the south and west, with Egypt (the nearest regional superpower, Judah's recurrent resource of military support, and the geographical location of Jer 43–44) and Philistia;
- goes on to Judah's neighbors to the east, beginning with the most substantial set of messages concerning Moab and then moving to Ammon and Edom;
- moves to Damascus, Kedar, Hazor, and Elam, peoples further away that were of no significance for Judah but point to Yahweh's lordship over all the nations, not just great powers and neighbors of Judah;
- finally comes to Babylon, the most substantial collection, the most important nation for Judah, and the agent of its downfall, which Jer 52 will go on to relate.

The MT sequence means that in the first half "Babylonian imperial predation still furthers Yahweh's own imperial designs" while in the second half "the Babylonian beast . . . goes to the ground as its Yahwistic master treats it to the same fate as the rest of the world,"[10] even though the scroll then does actually close with the account of the Babylonian destruction of Jerusalem.

A. PART 5A: INTRODUCTION, AND EGYPT (46:1–28)

Part 5 begins with a one-line introduction to the set of passages about the other nations. Following on Jer 43–45, a unit about Egypt then makes an apposite beginning to the messages about different nations. The unit comprises two substantial poems followed by two brief but important footnotes:

vv. 2–12	A message about Egypt on the eve of the battle between Egypt and Babylon at Carchemish, declaring that Egypt will lose
vv. 13–24	A message about Egypt concerning an invasion by Nebuchadrezzar that will issue in disaster, exile, and shame
vv. 25–26	A summary declaration that Yahweh will give Egypt over to Nebuchadrezzar but will subsequently restore the country

10. Diamond, "Jeremiah," 610.

vv. 27–28   A summary promise to Israel that he will likewise take
              action against it and scatter it but will subsequently
              bring it back

Like other messages about the nations, the unit offers little insight on
the rationale for bringing calamity on Egypt. As an act of redress (v. 10), it
might be a belated act of redress for Egypt's treatment of the Israelites back
at the beginning of their story or a redress for the recent killing of Josiah by
Neco and its related interference in Judah's life; its imposition of Jehoiakim
as king was not exactly a favor (2 Kgs 23:31–37). Yet there is no indication
that the message attacks Egypt because it is Judah's enemy. Perhaps it relates to Egypt's opposing Nebuchadrezzar as Yahweh's servant. Most likely,
Yahweh attacks it because of its self-confident, arrogant pretensions (cf. vv.
7–8, 12). It had imperial designs, and Yahweh is inclined to be against empires. Hearing such a message proclaimed in the temple courts, Judahites in
Jehoiakim's day might be given food for thought about the folly of treating
Egypt as a potential resource and support. After 587, Judahites might be
encouraged about the prospects of their own eventual freedom, restoration,
and independence.

1. Introduction; and Before the Battle of Carchemish (46:1–12 [LXX 26:1–12])

¹*What came as Yahweh's word*ᵃ *to Jeremiah the prophet concerning the nations.*

²*Regarding Egypt.*

*About the force of Pharaoh Neco,*ᵇ *king of Egypt, which was at the River Euphrates at Carchemish, which Nebuchadrezzar King of Babylon struck down
in the fourth year of Jehoiakim ben Josiah*ᶜ *King of Judah.*ᵈ

³*Get ready breastplate and shield,*
   advance for battle!
⁴*Harness the horses,*
  set to, cavalry!
Take your stand in helmets,
  polish the lances,
  put on the armor!

⁵*Why have I seen*ᵉ—
  they are shattered,

they are falling back.
Their strong men—they were being struck down,[f]
  they have fled, fled.[g]
They didn't turn round—
  all around was terror (Yahweh's affirmation).
[6]*The quick is not to flee,*
  the strong man is not to escape.
To the north, by the side of the River Euphrates,
  they have collapsed, fallen.

[7]*Who is this who goes up like the Nile,*
  like the rivers whose water surges?
[8]*Egypt that goes up like the Nile,*
  like the rivers whose water surges.[h]
It said, I will get myself up[i]—*I will cover earth;*
  I will obliterate town and[j] *people who live in it.*
[9]*Go up, horses,*
  dash, chariot,
  the strong men are to go out,
Sudan and Put,
  who grasp breastplate,
Ludites, who grasp,
  who direct[k] *bow.*

[10]*That day*
  will belong to the Lord Yahweh of Armies,[l]
A day of redress,
  for taking redress from his adversaries.[m]
Sword will consume and be full,
  will soak in their blood.
Because the Lord Yahweh of Armies[n]
  will have a sacrifice[o]
  in a northern country at the River Euphrates.

[11]*Go up to Gilead and get ointment,*
  young girl,[p] *Miss Egypt!*
It is to no effect that you have done much[q]—
  means of healing, new growth, there is none for you.
[12]*Nations have heard your humiliation;*[r]
  of your shout the earth is full.[s]
Because strong man has collapsed on strong man—
  together the two of them have fallen.[t]

a. On the jerky form of the words, see the translation note on 14:1.

b. For MT *nəkô*, Tg suggests a connection with *nākeh* ("lame")—perhaps a snide reinterpretation rather than an indication that Tg read the text differently.

c. LXX lacks *ben Josiah*.

d. Rudolph (*Jeremia*, 268) interestingly suggests that this time reference applies to 46:2–49:33 as a whole, but the suggestion involves some emendations of the text.

e. LXX lacks *have I seen*.

f. I take the *yiqtol* verb as past imperfect in significance.

g. Lit. "[in] flight they fled"; the combination of two forms of the root is "a signature Jeremiah construction (cf. 11:18; 14:17; 15:19; 17:14; 20:7; 30:16; 31:4, 18)" (J. R. Lundbom, "Language and Rhetoric in Jeremiah's Foreign Nation Oracles," in Lundbom, Evans, and Anderson, *Jeremiah*, 214).

h. LXX lacks this colon.

i. The form *'a'ăleh* has to be an inwardly transitive *hiphil* (the *qal* would be *'e'ĕleh*); cf. the translation note at 2:26. It might "magnify the arrogance of the boast" (Lundbom, *Jeremiah 37–52*, 197).

j. LXX lacks *town and*.

k. *Dārak* suggests treading on the bow to increase its tension and thus its reach (Altschuler, *Mesudat David*, in MG); J. A. Emerton argues rather for "string" ("Treading the Bow," *VT* 53 [2003]: 465–86).

l. LXX has "to the Lord our God."

m. Tg has "from his people's adversaries."

n. LXX has simply "the Lord."

o. Tg has an ordinary word for "killing."

p. See the translation note on 18:13.

q. The *qere* reads *hirbêt*; the *ketiv* implies *hirbêtî*. The parallel in 30:13 suggests that the following colon makes a clause in itself (Lundbom, *Jeremiah 37–52*, 204); for the absolute use of the verb, cf. Exod 30:15; Prov 13:11; 1 Chr 4:27.

r. LXX implies *qôlēk* ("your voice") for MT *qəlônēk* (cf. Vg, Aq, Sym), which works well with the parallelism but may be assimilated to it (Sharp, "Take Another Scroll and Write," 493).

s. The genders are all masculine in the first colon and all feminine in the second, perhaps underscoring the "global picture" (*CHP*, 125).

t. MT has a unit marker here.

Following the introduction to all of the messages about other nations in v. 1, v. 2 introduces the messages about Egypt. The first message comprises two parallel parts, both relating to Egypt's involvement in a battle; the second half goes over the same ground as the first, in the manner of the parallelism within a poetic line. Each half starts from the situation before the battle and, in the imagination, bids the Egyptian army to get ready or watches it getting ready (vv. 3–4, 7–9). It then leaps forward chronologically to give an imaginative account of the Egyptian army in a state of utter and hopeless defeat (vv. 5–6, 10–12). Neither half describes the battle itself; the message focuses on the preparation and the aftermath. There would be more point to the message if it preceded the event rather than describing it afterward, and one can imagine Jeremiah delivering it in the temple courts, perhaps as rumors circulated about an expected battle.

v. 2   An introduction in prose
vv. 3–6   Part one
    vv. 3–4   A bidding to the army to get ready: two bicola and a closing tricolon, every colon parallel, every colon with two stresses after the first, communicating a breathless haste that corresponds to the contents of the section
    vv. 5–6   A portrait of the army's state after the battle: an opening tricolon and four bicola, every colon again two stresses except for the next to last; there is again thus a breathless anxiety about the section that conveys a sense of panic
vv. 7–12   Part two
    vv. 7–9   A report of the army's going up for the battle followed by a further bidding: three more usual bicola, then for the bidding another tricolon and two bicola in which every colon is two stresses, with that breathless affect
    vv. 10–12 A declaration about the significance and the nature of the day of battle: three bicola and a tricolon, then another portrait of the state of things after the battle, in four bicola

The message's poetry and content both compare with the messages with which the Jeremiah scroll begins: Jeremiah's vision of calamity coming on Egypt parallels his vision of calamity coming on Judah. The Egyptian army is making ready for battle like the northern army making ready to invade Judah as Jeremiah portrayed it. But it is now operating not against Judah but against Egypt, the nation that Judah sometimes hoped would be its protector in such situations. When the message urges Egypt to get ready for battle, it does so ironically; it portrays its military preparations as actually useless. Rhetorically, the message makes the point dramatically by the way each of its halves leaps from preparations to the aftermath of cataclysmic defeat. Terror is all around, as it was for Judah.

Babylon's defeat of Egypt at Carchemish in 605 initiated the era in which it was the great power (albeit for only a few decades). Modern readers might see the victory as predictable and inevitable. It wasn't. Egypt was a bigger nation than Babylon; the message emphasizes its army's size. Humanly speaking, Judah wasn't stupid in seeing it as an ally and protector that Judah could rely on. The message assumes that there are sometimes occasions that Yahweh decides to treat as his occasion; some days he decides to treat as his day (v. 10). It is one consideration that makes history unpredictable.

1–2 Following an introduction to all of the messages about the nations in v. 1, *regarding Egypt* introduces the unit on Egypt as a whole (48:1 fulfills the same function for its unit). The continuing introduction then relates what will follow in vv. 3–12 to the time when *the force of Pharaoh Neco, king of Egypt, was at the River Euphrates at Carchemish* near Aleppo, on the Syrian-Turkish border, which had been a key city in the Assyrian Empire. It was encamped there as part of an attempt in association with the Assyrians to thwart a Babylonian takeover as the imperial power, and specifically the big power west of the Euphrates—and thus as Judah's overlord. The year and the occasion is the decisive one to which Jer 25, 36, and 45 refer (see the commentary on 25:1–2). While the message belongs to the time before the battle, the curators' introduction belongs to the time after *Nebuchadrezzar King of Babylon* (as he would become a year later) *struck down* that force. The Babylonian version of events during the twenty-first year of his father Nabopolassar's reign relates:

> The king of Akkad stayed home (while) Nebuchadnezzar (II), his eldest son (and) the crown prince, mustered [the army of Akkad]. He took his army's lead and marched to Carchemish which is on the bank of the Euphrates. He crossed the river [to encounter the army of Egypt] which was encamped at Carchemish. [. . .] They did battle together. The army of Egypt retreated before him. He inflicted a [defeat] upon them (and) finished them off completely. In the district of Hamath the army of Akkad overtook the remainder of the army of [Egypt which] managed to escape [from] the defeat and which was not overcome. They [the army of Akkad] inflicted a defeat upon them (so that) a single (Egyptian) man [did not return] home. At that time Nebuchadnezzar (II) conquered all of Ha[ma]th.[11]

No doubt the Babylonian Chronicle speaks hyperbolically in describing total annihilation, as Jeremiah does. But perhaps not surprisingly, we don't have Neco's version to check it by.[12]

3–4 The provision of the introduction means anyone reading the scroll can know what the message is about. Judahites listening to Jeremiah in the temple courtyards might initially have no idea or might be aware that this

---

11. Grayson, *Chronicles*, 99.

12. On the thinness of data on Neco, see H. M. Barstad, "Jeremiah the Historian," in *Studies on the Text and Versions of the Hebrew Bible in Honour of Robert Gordon*, ed. G. Khan and D. Lipton, VTSup 149 (Leiden: Brill, 2012), 91–94.

decisive event was imminent and might know that its result would be decisively important for them. Yahweh gives them insight about it. Jeremiah does not indicate who is commissioning the warriors—he or their commander or Yahweh. The point is the actual commission. Nor does Jeremiah make clear whose warriors are being commissioned or whose warriors are running for their lives—Babylon's or Egypt's. Which way the listeners understood it would make a difference to their potential response. Some would be glad to hear of the comeuppance of the Egyptian army and king that had defeated and killed Josiah. But the Egyptians had put Jehoiakim on the throne in place of his brother Jehoahaz, and official Judahite policy was likely pro-Egyptian. People who saw the Egyptians as potential allies and supporters would not welcome the idea of an Egyptian defeat. So the message works with the elusiveness that often characterizes prophecy expressed in poetry. It makes people listen and requires them to listen on if they are to get the point. The exhortation compares with the exhortations to Judah in 4:5–6; 6:1–6, which were ironic in the opposite direction as they urged Judah to prepare to be attacked.

5 Jeremiah has a further vision (perhaps in the strict sense, but perhaps not) of the battle's results. The message leaps forward, and jumps throughout v. 5 in a sequence of two-beat cola. First, Yahweh or Jeremiah ironically asks *why have I seen* what I have seen. God or prophet has seen four stages of disaster. First, those brave fighters who were commissioned: *they are shattered*, demoralized, traumatized by the engagement. As a result, *they are falling back*, retreating, letting the other side push them back. But not fast enough: *their strong men*, their supposed tough warriors, *were being struck down*. Not surprisingly, finally, they simply *fled*. One would like one's brave warriors then to regroup, but *they didn't turn round* and reengage with the enemy. They simply attempted to hightail it. In this chapter, ridicule is Jeremiah's "chief weapon."[13] But one can hardly blame these soldiers: *all around was terror*. Again, there is a parallel with the way things are or threaten to be for Judah (6:25; see also 20:3, 10; 49:29). They were surrounded by terrifying forces and a terrifying fate.

6 Whereas they hoped to take flight and get away, the enemy is not going to let them, or Yahweh is not going to let them. Jeremiah expresses this determination in two neat parallel cola and then in two internally parallel cola:

the quick	is not to flee
the strong man	is not to escape
to the north	by the side of the River Euphrates
they have collapsed	fallen

The legendary *north* stands not merely for a place in terms of literal geography where certain nations lived, but for the home of fabled forces that could

---

13. J. J. Jackson, "Jeremiah 46: Two Oracles on Egypt," *HBT* 15 (1993): 141.

consume anyone's world (cf. 1:14). Yet the reference to an enemy coming from the north is also often down to earth,[14] and here the confrontation happens all too literally *to the north, by the side of the River Euphrates.* There, the warriors *have collapsed, fallen.* In anticipation, Jeremiah has seen it with mock incredulity. He invites Judah to see it with real incredulity, but also as a reality that confronts Judahite commitments and Judahite policy. The mockery of Egypt would not only imply Egypt's disgrace; it would also disgrace people in Judah who were counting on Egypt as a counterbalance to Babylon.[15]

7–9 Only with the second version of the story is it explicit who is fighting; Jeremiah initially makes the point in three neatly parallel lines in vv. 7–8 and follows it with seven more cola in "two-beat 'battle' rhythm."[16] It was the Egyptians who had been routed and humiliated. The imaginary portrait now collapses the process that led to the battle; it was four years ago that Neco headed out of Egypt to assert himself at the Euphrates, on the march that Josiah tried to forestall. Having swatted that fly, Neco had established his semi-permanent position at Carchemish and dared Nebuchadrezzar to dispute it. Nebuchadrezzar has done so, to great effect. If Jeremiah's listeners are not convinced (or even if they are), let them think about it and use their imaginations again. Let them picture the Pharaoh's magnificent army advancing northeast from Egypt to Mesopotamia, as tumultuous a flood as the Nile itself, and in the manner of the Assyrian flood that Jeremiah and his audience would know more about.[17] It had advanced with such confidence, as Judah is in a position ruefully to recall. The Babylonians and Medes—how are they going to resist the might of Egypt and Assyria? Once again, an unidentified commander-in-chief urges on the forces, which come not merely from Egypt itself but from Sudan (that is, the country south of the First Cataract) and Put (perhaps Libya, perhaps Somalia—which fits its mention alongside Sudan) and Lud (for which the same two possibilities apply).[18] Yet with the formulation's irony, Yahweh also hints at why Egypt must be put down, its pretension to *cover earth* and its intention to *obliterate town and people who live in it.* Carchemish did finally put an end to Egypt's ambition

---

14. Jones, *Jeremiah*, 493.

15. Holladay, *Commentary on Jeremiah*, 2:318. See further C. de Jong, "Deux oracles contre les nations: Reflets de la politique étrangère de Joaqim," in Bogaert, *Livre de Jérémie*, 369–79.

16. *CHP*, 382.

17. J. R. Huddlestun, "'Who Is This That Rises Like the Nile?' Some Egyptian Texts on the Inundation and a Prophetic Trope," in Beck et al., *Fortunate the Eyes That See*, 360–63.

18. See D. T. Adamo, "The Portrayal of Africa and Africans in the Book of Jeremiah," *In die Skriflig* 52 (2018).

to *cover earth*; it determined who was going to rule the Levant and therefore who was going to be Judah's nemesis.

10 So far, Jeremiah has simply portrayed the earthly dynamics of the coming battle. Only with the second stanza of the second half of the message does the prophet/poet name the agent behind what happens. He thus now "identifies the real enemy of Egypt," both in the sense of the one against whom Egypt is asserting itself and the one who will defeat Egypt; and he identifies the one whose plan is being fulfilled in this engagement. It is neither Egypt's nor Babylon's plan.[19] It is Yahweh who commissions the Egyptian army. Or perhaps Yahweh jumps on the engagement and takes charge of it. Initially, Jeremiah resumes the perspective of someone for whom the event is still future, his perspective when he delivers this message. The day that is coming is *that day*. There is no antecedent "that day" for Jeremiah to be referring back to; *that day* is Yahweh's day. Putting down Egypt will be an aspect of the implementing of Yahweh's final purpose, which is associated with *that day* and can become reality from time to time in history. Thus the day that is coming *will belong to the Lord Yahweh of Armies*, an apposite title in this war context. *That day* threatens Egypt as it threatens Judah, and *a day of redress* threatens Egypt as redress threatens Judah (cf. 5:9; see the commentary there). Does *sword will consume and be full, will soak in their blood* imply that Yahweh's adversaries are more the military and the administration than the ordinary Egyptian people? It will be as if *the Lord Yahweh of Armies* is having *a sacrifice*. That is how bloody it will be. Characteristically, Ezekiel turns Jeremiah's one-word image into an allegory (Ezek 39:17–20; cf. also Zeph 1:7–8).

11–12 Jeremiah reverts to the rhetoric of vv. 5–6, whereby Yahweh's imagination jumps to the aftermath of the engagement, to the situation beyond the flight and the striking down of which vv. 5–6 spoke. There are all those bodies. Maybe some of them are not dead yet. In theory, the Egyptians could send first responders for medicines. We know that Gilead is the direction to look, but also that its ointment will be no more use to Egypt than to Judah (see 8:22; see the commentary there). There are no effective *means of healing* and there is *no new growth . . . for you* (cf. 30:13; see the commentary there). Once again, Egypt's destiny is the same as Judah's. The same principle applies to Egypt's *humiliation* (cf. 13:26). For Judah, it was to be visible like a woman's exposure; for Egypt, it will be audible in its demoralized warriors' panicked *shout*, which makes for another parallel with Judah, though in a different connection (14:2). There is yet another parallel in the picture of the way the warriors have *collapsed* on one another, *together* (6:21).

19. Pixley, *Jeremiah*, 136.

2. *Before Nebuchadrezzar's Invasion of Egypt (46:13–24 [LXX 26:13–24])*

13 *The word that Yahweh spoke to Jeremiah the prophet regarding the coming of Nebuchadrezzar King of Babylon to strike down the country of Egypt.*

14 *Tell it in Egypt, make it heard*[a] *in Migdol,*
make it heard in Memphis and in Tahpanhes!
Say, "Take your stand, get yourself ready,
because the sword has consumed around you!"
15 *Why has your great champion*[b] *bowed down?*[c]*—*
he has not stood, because Yahweh has thrust him down.
16 *He has done much collapsing*[d]*—*
yes, one individual has fallen on his neighbor.
People said, "Set to,
we'll go back to our people,
To the country of our birth,
in the face of the sword of the oppressor."[e]
17 *There they gave*[f] *Pharaoh*[g] *the king of Egypt the name,*
"A noise who let the appointed time pass."

18 *I am alive:*[h] *an affirmation of the King,*
Yahweh of Armies his name,[i]
That,[j] *like Tabor with the mountains,*
and like Carmel with the sea, one will come.
19 *Things for exile—make them for yourself,*
you who sit as Miss Egypt.
Because Memphis—it will become a desolation;
it will fall in ruins,[k] *with no one living there.*[l]
20 *A lovely, lovely heifer, Egypt—*
a horsefly[m] *from the north has come, come.*[n]

21 *Its mercenaries within it, too,*
like bullocks from the stall,[o]
Because they—they too have turned round—
they have fled altogether—they have not stood.
Because their day of disaster has come upon them,
the time of their being attended to.
22 *Its sound like a snake*[p] *as it goes*
when they go in force:[q]
With axes they have come to it,
like fellers of trees.

²³*They have cut down its forest (Yahweh's affirmation),*
  when it could not be explored,
When they were more than locust,
  and there was no counting of them.
²⁴*Miss Egypt has been shamed,*
  given into the hand of the northern people.

 a. LXX lacks *in Egypt, make it heard* and later in the verse lacks *and in Tahpanhes*.
 b. The two singular verbs and the singular suffix on *thrust him down* suggest that *'ab-bîreykā* is a plural of majesty.
 c. LXX "has Apis fled" suggests *nās ḥap* for MT *nišḥap* (*HALOT*, 339), with *'abbîreykā* then the subject of the second colon.
 d. One would expect an infinitive, not a participle, for *collapsing*; but on the construction, see *CTAT*, 2:613–17. Vg, Aq give the *hiphil* verb its more usual causative significance ("he has multiplied the collapsing one[s]"), but singular *kôšēl* is difficult. For MT *hirbâ* (*much*) LXX implies *hămônkā* ("your crowd [is collapsing]").
 e. The phrase is more likely a construct than an anarthrous noun qualified by a participle with the article (GK 126w); the phrase recurs in 50:16, and the participle came in a related expression in 25:38 (see the translation note there). LXX implies *hayyəwāniyyâ* ("the Greek").
 f. Lit. "called." For MT *qārə'û*, LXX, Vg imply imperative *qirə'û*.
 g. LXX adds "Neco," indicating a link with the same event as vv. 2–12.
 h. See the translation note and commentary on 4:2.
 i. For *the King, Yahweh of Armies his name*, LXX has simply "the Lord God."
 j. The *kî*-clause indicates the content of the oath implied by v. 18a.
 k. See the translation note on 2:15.
 l. MT has a section marker here.
 m. Etymologically, a stinger; behind the metaphor may be the Greek myth of the goddess Io, who can take the form of a heifer, gets pursued by a horsefly, and takes refuge in Egypt (D. E. Gershenson, "A Greek Myth in Jeremiah," *ZAW* 108 [1996]: 192–200).
 n. LXX lacks the repetition of *lovely*, and for the closing repetition implies *bā' bāh* ("has come upon it") for MT *bā' bā'*.
 o. Lit. "of the stall," where they were fattened up.
 p. Vg derives *nāḥāš* from *nḥš* III ("copper, bronze").
 q. LXX suggests *bəḥûl* ("in sand") for MT *bəḥîl*, which links neatly with the reference to a snake.

The Egyptians are now engaged with Nebuchadrezzar not in a battle a long way from home but within Egypt, as victims of invasion. The curators again provide an introduction (v. 13), and the message again moves imaginatively between the prospect and the actuality of the crisis, but in a different order from that in vv. 3–12. Here, Yahweh first ironically urges the Egyptians to get ready for a last stand, in the context of an invasion already under way (vv. 14–17), then asserts his guarantee that he is taking action and urges the Egyptians to get ready for exile (vv. 18–19). In the second half, he once more starts from the picture of an invasion that is under way (vv. 20–21) and finally speaks as if defeat has overwhelmed the nation (vv. 22–24). The message might link with events just after the battle at Carchemish or with Nebuchadrezzar's campaigns in 588 that ultimately led to the fall of Jerusalem, or with his campaign in 601—though it did not bring an Egyptian defeat (see the introduction to 47:1–7, p. 843). *Qatal* and *yiqtol* verbs again alternate in vv. 14–24, suggesting that the perspective switches between a portrayal of an attack that has begun and an announcement of an attack that is going to happen; it is sometimes difficult to tell which perspective applies. My understanding is:

> vv. 14–17 The invasion has begun, and the mercenaries have fled
> vv. 18–19 The invasion is certain because Yahweh says so
> vv. 20–21 The invasion has begun, and the mercenaries have fled
> vv. 22–24 The invasion has taken place, and Egypt is shamed

Like vv. 2–12, the message rhetorically urges warriors to get on with their responsibilities and in doing so makes use of irony and sarcasm. Over against vv. 2–12, it brings its message home by means of a series of metaphors that add to its opacity: Egypt the heifer, its mercenaries as bullocks, its army slithering off like a snake, another army as tree-fellers. An army and the nation it represents may not only be vulnerable when it goes a long way from home on a campaign; it may not even be safe after it slinks back home. The message adds to the first one the fact that Yahweh is capable of defeating the gods that allegedly protected a nation such as Egypt, as well as seeing that the nation itself gets defeated. One point about the message's metaphors is that they form part of a sarcastic portrayal of these deities. There is the champion that collapses because Yahweh puts him down (in v. 15, LXX is more specific; see the translation note). There is the heifer that is vulnerable to the horsefly. There is the snake that slithers away at the arrival of the foresters. The message may also point to further human factors in Babylon's becoming the great empire and Egypt's failing to fulfill expectations: certainly Nebuchadrezzar was a great leader, and Jeremiah puts a scathing indictment on the lips of Pharaoh's mercenaries. Whichever Pharaoh it is, the message's Judahite audience might be inclined to take him seriously as king, but they and he need to come to terms with the fact that there is another King (vv. 17–18).

13 Whereas v. 2 connected vv. 3–12 with a specific occasion that it is easy to link with known historical events, v. 13 gives no such date, and we cannot be sure which possible Babylonian invasion of Egypt this message presupposes. It might have been an aspect of the aftermath of the Carchemish battle, or Nebuchadrezzar's campaigns that led to the fall of Jerusalem, or the events referred to in connection with 44:29–30[20]; it would then initially be

20. See ANET, 308; Wiseman, *Chronicles of Chaldaean Kings*, 94–95; and for the other possibilities, Keown, Scalise, and Smothers, *Jeremiah 26–52*, 287–88.

a message for the Judahite community in Egypt. But the introduction's lack of specificity supports the possibility that the message does not relate to a specific expected invasion any more than a number of the other messages in Jer 46–51. In other words, Yahweh gives Jeremiah a vision of a projected invasion of Egypt by Nebuchadrezzar. Like many prophecies, it is then not a kind of advance video of an actual invasion but an imaginary and imaginative picture of what calamity could mean for Egypt. Its following on vv. 2–12 perhaps implies that the fulfillment of that vision and the factuality of that defeat provide grounds for taking this vision seriously and holding onto it whether or not it saw anything like a fulfillment.

14 The message begins with an ironic exhortation to towns in Lower Egypt with which we are familiar from 44:1 (there is no mention of Pathros). After the move of Johanan's group, the message would have particular force for them. *Memphis*, as the key city in Lower Egypt, pairs with the name of *Egypt* itself, and the line also pairs Migdol and Tahpanhes as two fortress towns in northeastern Egypt that would be affected early on by an invasion. Memphis was the location of a temple devoted to Apis (Herodotus, *Histories*, 2:153; see v. 15).[21] The assumption may be that Yahweh is addressing his aides, or local lookouts who would exhort the towns to get ready for the attack that is coming—though the imperatives in v. 14b are singular and suggest an exhortation to each town or to the nation as a whole. But the exhortation jumps forward and speaks as if the invasion has already begun and the invader has already engaged with Egyptian forces. One reason why the exhortation is ironic is that the engagement and the defeat (*the sword has consumed around you*) mean that the towns' fate is sealed. As in vv. 2–12, only the prose introduction identifies the Egyptians' foe as Babylon, and specifically Nebuchadrezzar (in due course vv. 20 and 24 will refer to the northern people), though there is no one else to invade Egypt in Jeremiah's day.

15 It is apparently Jeremiah who asks the rhetorical question. LXX convincingly implies that the *great champion* is the Egyptian god Apis, symbolized by a live bull and/or a bull image (see the translation note). Perhaps the bull had been brought into battle, like the Israelite pledge chest in 1 Sam 4. The problem for the Egyptians, as for the Israelites on that occasion, is that this stratagem has failed. The army has collapsed; the bull has collapsed. The Babylonians and Egyptians would assume that the battle was being fought under the patronage of their respective gods; Jeremiah perhaps implies that the messengers are to explain to the people in the three towns that there is another deity involved.

16–17 Because it is Yahweh who has brought about the Egyptian army's collapse. The description again suggests that it included many foreigners (cf.

21. M. Jones, "The Temple of Apis in Memphis," *Journal of Egyptian Archaeology* 76 (1990): 141–47.

v. 9), who fled in the midst of the battle. Like modern migrants, they likely came to Egypt looking for food and work, coming from countries where famine was common. Why should they stand firm when death threatens them here too? They might as well be at home.[22] *Dulce et decorum est pro patria mori?*[23] Even if it is true, it doesn't apply to dying for someone else's country. The mercenaries actually brought even more shame on Egypt, and specifically on Pharaoh. Their cry is, "Pharaoh the king of Egypt is a king of confusion."[24] That is his *name.* If the invasion dates to the time of Apries, Jeremiah might be putting a fair assessment on their lips.[25] But it may not imply a judgment specific to him; it recalls Isaiah's taunt about Egyptians whose assistance is useless and who are just Rahab[26] sitting around instead of flailing and thrashing as Rahab the monster was supposed to (Isa 30:7).

18 Their imagined comment leads neatly into Yahweh's claim for himself. He sets his *name* as the real *King* against the snide *name* given to *Pharaoh the king;*[27] nothing more needs be said about the so-called king of Egypt. The real King who now speaks is the one who will bring to Egypt the leader of the invasion and the battle, the also so-called (but not named) king of Babylon.[28] The chronological perspective changes back to the time when the invasion has not yet happened. Nebuchadrezzar will march southwest from Mesopotamia past Mount Tabor and past Mount Carmel, impressive like those hills that stand out in the context of the mountains and plain around, and like the sea at Carmel's foot.

19 So get ready, Egypt. Once more, Jeremiah portrays Egypt's fate by analogy with Judah's; actually, it is unlikely that Nebuchadrezzar would be taking Egyptians into exile. With further irony that would not be known even to Jeremiah, Egypt's description as a queen enthroned but about to lose her throne anticipates the portrayal of Babylon itself in Isa 47. *A desolation,* a city that *will fall in ruins, with no one living there* again recalls Judah's prospective fate (2:15).

20-21 The *heifer* (*'eglâ*) might make one think again of Apis, in a snide way since Apis was a bull, not a heifer; the masculine form of the word (*'ēgel*) is also a word for an animal image as worshiped in Israel (a heifer might

22. Cf. Qimchi, in MG.
23. "It is sweet and proper to die for one's country" (Horace, *Odes* 3.2.13); cf. Berrigan, *Jeremiah,* 178.
24. Calvin, *Jeremiah,* 4:650.
25. J. K. Hoffmeier, "A New Insight on Pharaoh Apries from Herodotus, Diodorus and Jeremiah 46:17," *Journal of the Society for the Study of Egyptian Antiquities* 11 (1981): 165-70.
26. The monster associated with Egypt is *rahab,* not the *rāḥāb* of Josh 2.
27. J. Goldingay, "Jeremiah and the Superpower," in Goldingay, *Uprooting and Planting,* 65-67.
28. Cf. Fischer, *Jeremia,* 2:489-90.

rather represent Hathor or Isis).[29] What follows suggests that the heifer represents Egypt; but the heifer is going to be stung to death by the northern *horsefly* that has already arrived. Jeremiah retains the metaphor in comparing Egypt's mercenaries (cf. v. 9) to fatted calves. He repeats the point from v. 16 about these warriors, who (in the manner of mercenaries) have *fled* and not *stood*—just like Apis (v. 15). Repeating the last verb retrospectively adds to the insulting of Apis. He's no better than Egypt's mercenaries.

22–23 The last unit is the most opaque, both because of the interweaving of verb tenses and because of the combining of metaphors—the snake, the tree-fellers, the locusts. *It* is feminine and refers again to Miss Egypt, the heifer, now a snake that is apparently trying to slither off silently. But the snake can be a figure for divinity in Egypt as in Canaan, specifically in Thebes (see v. 25), and this simile could remind some people of that link. So like the heifer, the snake could stand for Egypt and its divinities. But the snake *goes* off in slithery fashion; the parallel colon then describes the contrasting Babylonian army whose soldiers *go in force*. The snake's slithering away contrasts with the army's forceful march. Otherwise put, its slithering away responds to the arrival of a corps of metaphorical foresters (perhaps the snake is seeking to escape through the forest undergrowth). The woodcutters *have cut down* the Egyptian *forest* which *could not be explored* (that is, could not be quantified); the forest might stand for literal woodland, for the Egyptian army, or for wooden-paneled monumental buildings. The Babylonian army could cut it down even though it was as numerous as a horde of locust. The synagogue lectionary sets this Jeremiah passage alongside a reading from the Torah that includes Exod 10:3–20, with which it makes a neat link.[30]

24 The message closes with another horrifying image. Miss Egypt *has been shamed* by her ignominious defeat and surrender and has been *given into the hand of the northern people*, in both respects like Judah, but also in a corporate equivalent to something like the experience of a woman becoming the sexual victim of a conquering force.[31] The implied agent lying behind the *niphal* participle in the last colon is Yahweh himself, who is the great giver in a bad way as well as in a good way (the *niphal* came in this connection in, e.g., 21:10; 32:24–25; 38:3, 18; see also 44:30). Yes, Egypt is as vulnerable as Judah to Yahweh's surrendering it to the northern people (e.g., 1:13–15; 3:18; 4:6; 6:1, 22).

---

29. G. Galvin, *Egypt as a Place of Refuge*, 154.

30. M. A. Fishbane, *Haftarot*, The JPS Bible Commentary (Philadelphia: Jewish Publication Society, 2002), 97.

31. R. P. Carroll, *Jeremiah*, OTL, 771.

3. Two Encouraging Footnotes (46:25–28 [LXX 26:25–28])

[25]*Yahweh of Armies, the God of Israel, has said:*[a] *Here am I, attending to Amon*[b] *of Thebes,*[c] *and upon Pharaoh, upon Egypt, upon its gods, upon its kings, upon Pharaoh,*[d] *and upon all who rely on him,* [26]*and I will give them*[e] *into the hand of the people who seek their life, into the hand of Nebuchadrezzar King of Babylon, and into the hand of his servants. But afterward, it will dwell as in former days (Yahweh's affirmation).*[f]

[27]*But you, don't be afraid, my servant Jacob,*
   don't panic, Israel.
Because here am I, delivering you from far away,
   and your offspring from their country of captivity.
Jacob will return and be quiet,
   will relax, with no one making him tremble.[g]
[28]*You, don't be afraid, my servant Jacob (Yahweh's affirmation),*
   because I will be with you.
Because I will make an end among all the nations
   where I have driven you.
But of you I will not make an end,
   but I will restrain you through the exercise of authority,
   and I will certainly not treat you as free of guilt.[h]

a. LXX lacks *Yahweh of Armies, the God of Israel has said.*
b. Vg, Tg have "noise," as if the Hebrew were *hāmôn.*
c. For MT *minnō', LXX implies *bənāh* ("her son"). Syr has "Amon of the water" (cf. the description of Thebes in Nah 3:8). Vg, Tg have "Alexandria," which fits the later historical situation.
d. LXX lacks *upon Egypt, upon its gods, upon its kings, upon Pharaoh.*
e. LXX lacks *and I will give them.*
f. MT has a marker here.
g. MT has a marker here.
h. Verses 27–28 repeat 30:10–11 in a slightly variant form; see the translation notes there. MT has a section marker here.

Two separate footnotes close off the Egypt unit. The first reaffirms that Nebuchadrezzar will take action against Egypt but then promises Egypt's restoration. The second repeats an earlier promise of Israel's restoration to its homeland. The juxtaposition is suggestive. Destruction is not Yahweh's last word for Egypt and banishment is not Yahweh's last word for Israel.

25–26 Yahweh's affirmation makes a comprehensive declaration of intent with regard to Egypt, summing up the prosaic implications of vv. 2–24. It begins with another assertion of authority in relation to an Egyptian deity, this time Amon—once the top god of Egypt, though not as prominent in Jeremiah's time. The reference to Thebes (a key city in Upper Egypt) and its deity complements the earlier reference to Memphis (a key city in Lower Egypt) and its deity. Whereas vv. 2–12 and 13–24 focused on the empirical reality of battle and invasion while also affirming Yahweh's involvement, vv. 25–26 focus on Yahweh's initiative and action. Nebuchadrezzar is simply Yahweh's unwitting beneficiary. It is the first time that he is named within the actual messages in the unit, but the name comes in a message that itself takes prose form; so far, the name has never come in the poetry in the Jeremiah scroll (though it will come in the poetry in Jer 48–51). Such names are prosaic; metaphors communicate more, though they may leave the audience guessing more. The prose and poetry in the scroll thus complement each other. The message in vv. 13–24 implied that it would be stupid people who *rely on Pharaoh*; this message makes the point explicit. In the years running up to 587, the people relying on Pharaoh would include the Judahite administration; subsequently, they would include Johanan's group.[32] The unexpected feature of the message is the closing promise, though it fits Jeremiah's original commission. As a prophet concerning nations and kingdoms, Jeremiah was commissioned to build and plant as well as pull down and pull up. While nations and kingdoms could just have been background to building and planting for Israel, in retrospect, at least, Yahweh's worldwide lordship makes it not surprising to find a promise to restore Egypt. The message does not spell out the promise's cash value in the variegated way that Isa 19:18–25 does. It does suggest a freedom for Egypt to be itself, but with the possible implication that it will not be a great empire again and thus be either resource or threat to Judah (cf. Ezek 29:13–16).[33]

27–28 The second footnote restates 30:10–11. A notable difference is the verb *driven* (instead of "scattered"), which also came in passages such as 32:37. The promise that Yahweh is *delivering you from far away* gains extra resonance following on the chapters relating how Judahites ended up in Egypt. It stands in some creative tension with the threat that no Judahites will ever return from Egypt and adds heft to the qualification on that threat in 44:28. One might see it as contrasting with, correcting, complementing, or clarifying what precedes, or as strengthening the message of deliverance and judgment implicit in Jer 46–51 as a whole.[34]

---

32. Weiser, *Jeremia*, 2:395.

33. Qimchi, in MG.

34. E. Peels, "'But Fear Not, O Jacob My Servant': Place and Function of the Salvation Oracle Jeremiah 46:27–28 MT," in *Biblical Hebrew in Context: Essays in Semitics and Old Testament Texts in Honour of Professor Jan P. Lettinga*, ed. K. van Bekkum, Gert Kwakkel, and Walter H. Rose, OTS 74 (Leiden: Brill 2018), 114–29.

The oracle of Yahweh against Egypt has made the world a safe place for Israel. . . . Both the great power and the beloved community are given futures, and the two futures are not incompatible. It is as though the poem witnesses to and sanctions a moment in geopolitics which is chaotic and disruptive, when power is turned loose against all established normalcies. The poem, in the end, envisions a settled normalcy when all the powers are back in their proper places and proper perspectives. When that happens, Jacob can resume its life.[35]

B. PART 5B: NEIGHBORS AND DISTANT PEOPLES (47:1–49:39)

There now come four messages (or collections of messages) relating to Judah's neighbors on the west (Philistia) and on the east (Moab, Ammon, and Edom)—the four that appear together in 25:20b–21 and appear as a group in Ezek 25. They will be followed by two messages about faraway peoples, Kedar/Hazor and Elam.

1. Philistia (47:1–7 [LXX 29:1–7])

¹*What came as Yahweh's word*[a] *to Jeremiah the prophet about the Philistines, before Pharaoh struck down Gaza.*[b]

²*Yahweh has said this.*

Here, water is rising from the north
  and becoming[c] *a flooding wadi.*
It floods the country and what fills it,
  the town and the people who live in it.
Humanity cries out,
  and all the people who live in the country howl.
³*At the sound of the pounding of the hooves of his mighty steeds,*
  at the noise of his chariotry, the din of its wheels,[d]
Fathers have not turned their faces to children
  because of the slackening of hands,
⁴*On account of the day that has come*
  for destroying all the Philistines,
For cutting off from Tyre and Sidon
  every surviving helper.

35. Brueggemann, *Jeremiah 26–52*, 229–30.

Because Yahweh is destroying the Philistines,
   the remainder of Caphtor's shore.[e]
[5]*Clipping has come to Gaza,*
   Ashkelon has been rendered still.[f]
You remainder of their vale,[g]
   how long will you gash yourself?[h]

[6]*Oh, sword of Yahweh,*
   how much longer will you not be quiet?
Gather yourself into[i] *your sheath,*
   rest, be still!
[7]*How can you be quiet,*[j]
   when Yahweh has given it an order?
For Ashkelon and for the seacoast—
   there he has appointed it.[k]

a. On the jerky form of the words, see the translation note on 14:1. For v. 1, LXX simply has "regarding the foreigners."

b. MT has a section marker here.

c. The *waw*-consecutive continues the participial construction.

d. The 4-4 cola (unique in the poem) convey the relentless thundering. I follow MT's versification in seeing v. 3a as the beginning of a new sentence.

e. LXX lacks *the Philistines* and *Caphtor's*.

f. LXX has "thrown out"; on this verb here and in v. 6, see the translation notes on 6:2; 8:14.

g. For MT *'imqām*, LXX implies *'ănāqîm* (cf. Josh 11:22).

h. MT[L] has a section marker here.

i. In MT[L], *'al* is a slip for *'el*.

j. LXX, Vg have a third-person verb, which matches the parallel colon.

k. MT has a marker here.

At first sight, the introduction to the Philistia poem would imply that Egypt brought calamity to the Philistines, but the poem itself speaks of trouble from the north, and the Babylonian Chronicle records Nebuchadrezzar's taking Ashkelon a year after defeating Neco at Carchemish (see the commentary on 25:9). Chronologically, then, Jer 47 follows at least on 46:2–12. The attack from the south might have happened some time before the northern one; Herodotus (*Histories*, 2:159) has Neco conquering Gaza, possibly in 609 on the expedition that included his victory over Josiah. Or it may relate to an Egyptian campaign following Nebuchadrezzar's action in about 601. That year, Nebuchadrezzar marched on Egypt itself but was apparently repulsed by Neco, so that Nebuchadrezzar needed to go home and regroup. The Babylonian Chronicle thus goes on:

In the fourth year the king of Akkad mustered his army and marched
  to the Ḫatti-land. In the Ḫatti-land they marched unopposed.
In the month of Kislev he took the lead of his army and marched to
  Egypt. The king of Egypt heard (it) and mustered his army.
In open battle they smote the breast (of) each other and inflicted great
  havoc on each other. The king of Akkad and his troops turned back
  and returned to Babylon.
In the fifth year the king of Akkad (stayed) in his own land and gathered
  together his chariots and horses in great numbers.[36]

Like Judah, then, one way or another Gaza came under attack more than
once over a relatively short period, but its location in an area fought over by
the two great powers made it vulnerable (whereas Judah brought trouble
on itself).[37]

Like 46:14–24, the poem can be ambiguous about whether it is describing
something that is happening or will happen or has happened, but it makes
sense understood as describing something that has begun to happen in the
poet's imagination. It parallels 46:3–12 in starting from a portrait of events as
purely humanly-caused (vv. 2–4a) then segueing into an emphasis on Yahweh's causation (vv. 4b–7). It gives even less hint of the reasoning behind
Yahweh's action or regarding his reasons for telling Judah of his intention. It
simply asserts that the worldly event of which a northern adversary is the human agent is something that Yahweh wills. If one were to ask what reflection
the poem might generate in wise Judahites, then they might see it as a warning about resisting Nebuchadrezzar.[38] They might ask whether it has a background in Yahweh's relationship with the Philistines and ask about Judah's
relationship with them: it was Yahweh who brought the Philistines to the Levant from Caphtor (Amos 9:7), yet they came to occupy land that Yahweh had
designated to Israel. The LXX translation of Philistines as "foreigners"—more
literally "other tribe people"—might reflect a sense that they were "foreigners
living within the borders of Israel."[39] While their location on the coastal route
from the north and northeast to the south and southwest would make them
vulnerable to the interest of the powers on either side, they would also be of
interest to Judah because the obvious line of access to Jerusalem lay from their
direction, as it still does. It was presumably in that connection that Hezekiah
had invaded Philistia and taken control of the area (2 Kgs 18:8). But in a tit for
tat action, in the course of putting down Hezekiah's rebellion against Assyria,

36. Wiseman, *Chronicles of Chaldaean Kings*, 71.
37. Lundbom, *Jeremiah 37–52*, 233.
38. See McKane's discussion in *Jeremiah*, 2:1153–54.
39. McKane, *Jeremiah*, 2:1141.

Sennacherib had given over swathes of Judahite territory to the kings of the Philistine towns.[40] Yahweh's promises about the Philistines in Ezek 25:15–17 (also 16:27) could suggest that these events may still rankle in Jeremiah's day and indicate that Yahweh does intend to take redress from the Philistines on Judah's behalf. The undertaking in Ezekiel comes in the context of similar statements about Judah's other neighbors Moab, Ammon, and Edom, as it does in Jer 47–49 (and for Judah in the fifth century, a promise about Philistia being put in its place would be good news: see, e.g., Neh 4:7). To connect the dots, then, this present vision would parallel the visions in Ezekiel as an affirmation of Yahweh's commitment to take redress on Philistia. But if Judahites engaged in such reflections, they were indeed connecting widely spaced dots. Jeremiah himself does not describe the attack on Philistia as an act of judgment or suggest that the Philistines have done anything to deserve what happens except be in the wrong place at the wrong time. It simply asserts once more that something that one might see as a random event within world history (like the events in Dan 11) is one in which Yahweh's sovereignty is at work. One might perceive the event as implicitly an implementing of Nebuchadrezzar's commission to be Yahweh's servant in exercising authority over the world in which Israel lives (25:19–21). Centuries ago, Israel and Philistia were serious independent forces that could therefore fight serious battles with each other, but now they are just "pawns of the great powers."[41] But even over matters that have nothing to do with Israel, Yahweh is sovereign and may be taking action for reasons that human beings do not know.

There seems no reason to see the poem as eschatological or apocalyptic.[42] After an introduction, it comprises a portrayal of the attack, then a protest and a response:

v. 1	Introduction
vv. 2–5	A portrayal of the attack
v. 2	More metaphorically: the flood and the wailing
vv. 3–4	More literally: the invasion and the destruction
v. 5	The aftermath: the grieving
v. 6–7	A protest and a response
v. 6	The protest
v. 7	The response

After the introduction, the poem comprises fourteen neat bicola, most of them illustrating various forms of parallelism. They are thus tighter than

40. See the Sennacherib Annals, *ANET*, 288.
41. Brueggemann, *Jeremiah 26–52*, 231.
42. Contra Duhm, *Jeremia*, 342–44.

Jeremiah's usual poetry, but they compare with his usual poetry in their use of imagery, rhetorical questions, apostrophe (addressing a nonhuman subject), and the imaginative portrayal of a catastrophe in a way that brings home its horror. They use expressions appearing elsewhere in Jeremiah: the flooding forces (v. 2; cf. 46:7–8); the trouble from the north (v. 2; see, e.g., 1:13–15; 4:6; 6:1, 22); the drooping hands (v. 3; cf. 6:24; 38:4). Like some other Jeremianic poems, this one starts abruptly, in the middle of things, without indicating speaker or audience (neither of which is ever identified) or subject, and with an unidentified "he" playing a key role.

1 The information in this opening verse, relating to and making a link with trouble from the south that came on a different occasion from that implied by the poem itself, might add to the pressure on Judah not to think that Neco's capture of Gaza heralded a serious reassertion of Egyptian power, which could work in Judah's favor.[43]

2 With a little irony in the context, Jeremiah pictures an invader flooding from the north as 46:7–8 pictured the Egyptian army flooding from the south (but Isa 8:7–8 also already portrayed the Assyrians flooding through Judah). As the flood in 46:7–8 suggested the Nile, this one suggests the Euphrates. And in contrast to that flood, this one succeeds in overwhelming its victims. Indeed, it resembles the frightening and overwhelming reality of a flash flood that can turn an empty wadi into a raging torrent, as if the country and the towns are an encampment in the dry river bed that get unexpectedly engulfed and made to cry out in panic.

3–5 Jeremiah goes on to give a more literal but still imaginary account of the invasion and its results, which include men being so paralyzed that they cannot even scoop up their children so as to take them to safety. Their failing to do so is "inconceivably unnatural," though the description has a near parallel in the behavior of animals in 14:5[44]—which, if anything, adds to the horror. It anticipates the reference to women eating their babies in Lam 2:20. The antecedent of *his* is not identified (presumably it is Nebuchadrezzar), and only in v. 4 is Philistia identified as his victim. The Philistines on the southwest coast are associated with the Phoenicians of Tyre and Sidon on the northwest coast, who follow Philistia, Edom, Moab, and Ammon in 25:20–22; the implication here is that the Philistines could be allies to the Phoenicians, who have therefore lost their potential allies. Amos 9:7 refers to the Philistines as from Caphtor, which counts as a foreign shore and may

---

43. H. J. Katzenstein, "'Before Pharaoh Conquered Gaza' (Jeremiah xlvii 1)," *VT* 33 (1983): 249–51; E. Peels, "'Before Pharaoh Seized Gaza': A Reappraisal of the Date, Function, and Purpose of the Superscription of Jeremiah 47," *VT* 63 (2013): 308–22.

44. Holladay, *Commentary on Jeremiah*, 2:338.

denote Crete. While as usual the poem speaks hyperbolically when it refers to *destroying all the Philistines*, it is noteworthy that kings of Tyre, Gaza, Sidon, and Ashdod came to be members of Nebuchadrezzar's court in their exile.[45] And the wasting of Philistia is portrayed as sufficiently devastating to warrant Jeremiah seeing Gaza as simply characterized by *clipping*, the cutting of the hair that was a mark of mourning (cf. 16:6; 41:5), and Ashkelon as being *rendered still* by the devastation that has come to it. Further, Jeremiah can inquire rhetorically of the rest of the Philistine plain in the terms of another rite that signifies mourning: *How long will you gash yourself?* (cf. 16:6; 41:5).

6–7 The protest that follows is an implicit exhortation to the slaughtering sword to get itself back into its sheath—more literally, to the swordsman to put it back there. Is the protester Jeremiah or an imaginary someone from Philistia? The *oh* is an expression of horror (see the commentary on 22:13); any normal person would want to see an end to this slaughter. The bidding comes to a close with a repetition of a verb from v. 5: Ashkelon has been rendered still or is being rendered still, so please, the sword must now be still. Enough already! As usual, the *how long* question is rhetorical, though not for the usual reason. The protesting question is simply the deceptive lead-in to the devastating reply in v. 7. It was Yahweh who gave the order for the slaughter, and it must continue until he says, "Enough."

2. Moab (48:1–47 [LXX 31:1–44])

Moab forms a mirror image of Judah on the other side of the Jordan, between Ammon and Edom. Like Judah, on one side it extends alongside the Dead Sea a thousand feet below sea level. Its territory then climbs steeply to three thousand feet above sea level, like Judah's, to country that is quite fertile; but it then climbs higher. Judah on the west gives way to the Mediterranean Sea; Moab on the east gives way to the Arabian Desert.[46]

Until we come to Babylon in Jer 50–51, the Moab chapter is the most substantial collection of messages about another nation in Jeremiah. The extensive treatment of Moab fits the broader prominence of Moab in the First Testament. Moab features more often than Ammon or Edom (less often than Philistia, but Philistia's references cluster more in the Saul and David stories), so it is not odd that the Jeremiah scroll should give it so much attention. The messages' theme, in line with that of the messages about other nations, is simply that Yahweh intends to bring calamity on Moab, though they close

---

45. *ANET*, 308.

46. See, e.g., J. M. Miller, "Moab and the Moabites," in *Studies in the Mesha Inscription and Moab*, ed. J. A. Dearman, Archaeology and Biblical Studies 2 (Atlanta: Scholars, 1989), 1–40.

with a line promising subsequent restoration. Like Jer 46–47, the chapter's rhetoric works with an alternation between the literal and the metaphorical and also with an alternation between the general and the specific and concrete (it names many individual places). These two reinforce each other. But it does not give dates or incorporate information that would enable one to guess at their context, as much of Jer 46–47 does. In line with the messages about other nations, some might relate to an imminent or current invasion or defeat, some might relate to an invasion or defeat that has already happened, some might issue simply from the prophet's insight regarding what Yahweh is going to do at some time. The curators have collected the messages in a way that does not enable readers to reconstruct possible references. Within Jeremiah's lifetime, one can imagine messages about Moab functioning to discourage Judah from continuing in forms of worship influenced by Moabite religion (2 Kgs 23:13), from joining with Moab in rebelling against Babylon (Jer 27:3), and from thinking that Yahweh was going to do nothing about Moab's involvement in attacks on Judah in the decades leading up to 587 (2 Kgs 24:2). But the distinctive length of the chapter suggests that there is more to its significance than those links that also apply to other peoples.

The poems refer to many places in Moab, a number of which appear in an inscription or stele commissioned two centuries previously by Mesha, king of Moab, which illumines the Moabite perspective on its god, Chemosh, and also illumines issues that arise in Jer 48. The Mesha inscription reads:

(1) I am Mesha, son of Kemosh[-yatti], the king of Moab, the Dibonite. (2) My father was king over Moab for thirty years, and I, I was king after my father. And I made this high place for Kemosh in Karchoh as h[eight of deliverance], (3) because he delivered me from all kings and (4) because he has made me look down on all my enemies. Omri, (5) the king Israel, oppressed Moab for many days, for Kemosh was angry with his land. (6) And his son succeeded him. And he said—he too—I will oppress Moab. In my days he did [so]. (7) But I looked down on him and on his house, and Israel has gone to ruin, yes has gone to ruin for ever! Omri had taken possession of the wh[ole la]nd (8) Medeba. And he lived there in his days and half the days of his son, forty year. (9) But Kemosh [resto]red it in my days. And I built Baal Meon and I made in it a water reservoir. And I bui[lt] (10) Kiriathaim. And the men of Gad lived in the land of Ataroth from ancient times and the king of (11) Israel built Ataroth for himself. And I fought against the city and I captured it, and I killed all the people [from] (12) the city as a sacrifice for Kemosh and for Moab. And I brought back the fire-hearth of DWDH and I ha[ul]ed (13) it before the face of Kemosh in Kerioth. And I made the men of Sharon live there, as well as the men of (14) Maharith. And Kemosh said to me: Go, take Nebo from

Israel! And I (15) went in the night and I fought against it from the break of dawn until noon. And I (16) took it, and I killed [its] whole population: seven thousand [ma]le citizens and aliens, females citizens and [aliens] (17) and servant girls. For I had put it to the ban for Ashtar Kemosh. And from there I took the [ves-] (18) sels of YHWH. And I hauled them before the face of Kemosh. The king of Israel had built Jahaz (19) and he stayed there during his campaigns against me. And Kemosh drove him away before [my] face. (20) [And] I took from two hundred men of Moab, all its division and I led it up to Jahaz and I have taken it (21) in order to add it to Dibon. I was the one who built Karchoh, the wall of the wood and the wall of (22) the citadel. And I was the one who built its gates. And I was the one who built its towers. And (23) I was the one who built the house of the king. And I was the one who made the double reser[voir for the spri]ng in the innermost part (24) of the city. Now, there was no cistern in the innermost part of the city, in Karchoh, but I said to all the people: Make, (25) each one of you, a cistern in his house. And I was the one who cut out the moat for Karchoh by means of Israelite (26) prisoners. And I was the one who built Aroer. And I was the one who made the military road in the Arnon. (27) I was the one who built Beth Bamoth, for it was destroyed. And I was the one who built Bezer, for [it lay in] ruins. (28) [And the me]n of Dibon stood in battle-order, for all Dibon, they are in subjection. And I was the one who became (29) ki[ng over] hundred in the cities which I added to the land. And I was the one who built (30) [Beth Mede]ba and Beth Diblathaim and Beth Baal Meon and I brought there (31) [. . .] flocks of the land. (32) [. . . And] Kemosh said to me: Go down, fight against Horonaim! And I went down. (33) [. . . And] Kemosh [resto]red it in my days [. . .] from there [. . .].[47]

Mesha's understanding of Chemosh parallels Jeremiah's understanding of Yahweh.[48] Illustrating the "close affinity between Israelite and Moabite beliefs,"[49] Mesha believes that Chemosh is a god involved in history and in relationships between different nations and is committed to Moab. He is a god who gets angry at aggression toward his people and merciful toward his people. He has guided Mesha about when to attack aggressors and delivered Mesha from his attackers, and thus given him honor rather than shame. In light of this act of deliverance, Mesha built Chemosh a sanctuary at Karchah.

47. From A. R. van der Deijl, *Protest or Propaganda: War in the Old Testament Book of Kings and in Contemporaneous Ancient Near Eastern Texts*, SSN 51 (Leiden: Brill, 2008), 304–9.

48. See further G. L. Mattingly, "Moabite Religion and the Mesha' Inscription," in Dearman, *Studies in the Mesha Inscription*, 211–38.

49. R. P. Carroll, *Jeremiah*, OTL, 795.

He dedicated the spoil of the battle to Chemosh while also killing the men in the battle but devoting the women and girls to Ashtar Chemosh, which might be another designation for Chemosh or might denote a partner goddess.[50] There was presumably more to Mesha's theology than appears in the inscription as there was more to Jeremiah's theology than appears in Jer 48, but these elements are similar. The question at issue would not be the correct way to understand deity but the truth about whether Chemosh actually was God or whether Yahweh was.

Much of Jer 48 shows marked similarity to Moab material in Isaiah and Numbers:[51]

[5]because at the ascent to Luhith with crying goes up	because at the ascent to Luhith with crying they go up it[52]
because on the Horonaim descent the great distress of the outcry at the breaking people have heard	because on[53] the Horonaim road people raise an outcry at the breaking (Isa 15:5)
[29]we have heard of Moab's majesty very majestic	we have heard Moab's majesty very majestic[54]
his exaltedness and his majesty his majestic nature and the loftiness of his mind	his majestic nature and his majesty
[30]I . . . acknowledged (Yahweh's affirmation) his excess	and his excess
but his oracles were not right not right have they acted	his oracles were not right
[31]as a result over Moab I will howl for Moab, all of it, I will cry out about the people of Kir-heres	therefore Moab will howl for Moab, all of it will howl[55] for the raisin-blocks of[56] Kir-hareseth
one could murmur	you could murmur, stricken indeed (Isa 16:6–7)
[32]with more than the crying of Jazer I will cry for you	as a result I will cry with crying for Jazer

---

50. See H.-P. Müller, "Chemosh," *DDD*, 186–89.

51. Wildberger (*Isaiah 13–27*, 127–29) lays out the parallels in Hebrew.

52. Where Jer 48:5 has *bekî*, Isa 15:5 has *bô*.

53. Isa 15:5 lacks the explicit preposition *bə*.

54. Isa 16:6 has the *hapax legomenon gē*'; Jer 48:29 has the usual *gē'eh*.

55. Isa 15:5 also has "my heart cries out for Moab."

56. Isa 16:7 has *la'ăšîšê*, but Jer 48:31 has *'el 'anšê*, "a milder reading" (Holladay, *Commentary on Jeremiah*, 2:343).

Sibmah vine	Sibmah vine (Isa 16:9)[57]
you whose tendrils passed to the sea,	its shoots extended, passed to the sea
while as far as the sea Jazer they reached	as far as Jazer they reached (Isa 16:8)[58]
upon your summer fruit and upon your cut grapes	upon your summer fruit and upon your grain[59]
a destroyer has fallen	a shout has fallen
[33]rejoicing and gladness gather themselves up	rejoicing and gladness gather themselves up[60]
from the orchard from the country of Moab	from the orchard
in the vineyards they are not chanted, shouted	
I have made wine cease from the presses	wine in the presses
no one treads with a shout—	no treader treads
the shout is not a shout	I have made the shout to cease (Isa 16:9–10)
[34]from the outcry of Heshbon as far as Elealeh	Heshbon and Elealeh cry out
as far as Jahaz they have given their voice	as far as Jahaz their voice has made itself heard (Isa 15:4)
from Zoar as far as Horonaim Eglath-shelishiyah	his fugitives as far as Zoar Eglath-shelishiyah (Isa 15:5)
because the water of Nimrim too— it also becomes desolation	because the water of Nimrim— it will become desolation[61] (Isa 15:6)
[35]I will make cease for Moab (Yahweh's affirmation)	Moab has wearied himself at the shrine
anyone making an offering at a shrine	(Isa 16:12)
and burning a sacrifice to his god	
[36]as a result my heart for Moab—	as a result my insides for Moab—
like pipes it will moan	like a guitar it will moan
my heart for the people of Kir-heres	my soul for Kir-heres (Isa 16:11)
like pipes it will moan	

57. Isa 16:9 has *gepen*; Jer 48:32 has *haggepen*.
58. Isa 16:8 has these cola in a different order.
59. Isa 16:9 has *qəṣîrēk*; Jer 48:32 has *bəṣîrēk*.
60. Isa 16:10 has a masculine verb; Jer 48:33 has a feminine verb.
61. Isa 15:6 has simply *məšammôt*; Jer 48:34 has *liməšammôt*.

as a result the surplus he made, they
have perished

[37]because every head, clipping   on all his heads, clipping
and every beard, cutting   every beard, cutting
on all hands, gashes
and on hips, sack   on his hips they have bound sack
[38]on all the roofs of Moab and in its   on its roofs and in its squares
squares
all of him, lamenting   all of him howls (Isa 15:2–3)
[43]terror and pit and trap   terror and pit and trap
against you who live in Moab (Yah-   against you who live in the earth—it
weh's affirmation)   will happen
[44]the person who flees in the face of   the person who flees at the sound of
the terror   the terror
will fall into the pit   will fall into the pit
and the person who climbs out of   and the person who climbs out of
the pit   the pit
will be caught in the trap   will be caught in the trap (Isa
     24:17–18)

[45]because fire—it has gone out from   because fire—it has gone out[62] from
Heshbon   Heshbon
a flame from within Sihon   a flame from the town of Sihon
it has consumed Moab's brow   it has consumed Ar of Moab[63]
the skull of the people destined for   the lords of the shrines at the
tumult   Arnon[64]
[46]oh, for you, Moab   oh, for you, Moab
the people of Chemosh has perished   people of Chemosh, you have
     perished
because your sons have been taken   he gave your sons as fugitives
as captives
and your daughters into captivity   and your daughters into captivity[65]
     (Num 21:28–29)

The existence of several related versions of prophecies about Moab's fate
draws further attention to Moab's importance for Yahweh and for Israel. Once

---

62. Num 21:28 has a masculine verb; Jer 48:45 has a feminine.

63. Num 21:28 has a *qatal* verb; Jer 48:45 has a *waw*-consecutive. Num 24:17 has "it will smash the brow of Moab."

64. Num 24:17 has "the foundation [*qarqar*] of all the people of Seth" (if "foundation" is the meaning of *qarqar* and if *šēt* denotes Seth), while *scalp* in Jer 48:45 is *qodqōd*.

65. In Num 21:29, *captivity* is *šəbît*; in Jer 48:46, it is *šebî* then *šibyâ*.

the Canaanites could be discounted, Moab was the most important of Israel's neighbors until Jeremiah's day, though Edom then got a whole scroll to itself in Obadiah when it inherited this position. Related to this fact was an ongoing dispute over territory throughout Israel's history, from its beginnings at least until the eighth century, reflected in the Mesha Stele as well as in the First Testament. It makes explicit the long-standing conflict between Moab and Israel over the territory north of the Arnon, a conflict sharper and longer than conflicts between Israel and its other neighbors, which may underlie the greater prominence of Moab in Isaiah and Jeremiah and the general absence of explicit links between the messages and specific historical contexts; they constitute general promises that Yahweh will eventually deal with Moab.

These geographical considerations suggest another aspect to the rationale behind Moab's prominence in Jeremiah's messages about the nations. Yahweh is promising to take back the land in the formerly Amorite territory north of Moab, which he claimed at the time of Israel's arrival in the area and allocated to Reuben and Gad. The same logic lies behind the focus on Edom in Obadiah and elsewhere, since the Babylonian period saw Edom taking over considerable Judahite land. While we cannot locate all the places mentioned by Mesha or by Jeremiah, the places that are due for devastation about whose location we are reasonably sure lie north of the Arnon, in the territory that Yahweh claims but that Moab has moved into—perhaps recalling that they had lived in this area in a yet earlier time. It is therefore not surprising that Yahweh repeats a number of times that Moab would be removed from this territory he claimed. The arrival of the Assyrians and then of the Babylonians changed the dynamics of the tensions between Moab and Israel, but it did not abolish them. Yahweh does not take action against Moabite territory south of the Arnon, which he gave to Moab (Deut 2:9). The references to Aroer on the Arnon in this connection are significant; Aroer marks the northern boundary of Moab proper and the distinction between north and south. Where Jer 48 mentions places south of the Arnon, in Moab proper, it mentions them as places where Moabites are naturally grieving over what has happened in the north, but not as places that have themselves been devastated.

There is thus also nothing surprising if versions of Yahweh's declarations about Moab were recycled in different contexts. Isaiah 15–16 might then reflect reworking of Jer 48, or Isa 15–16 (and Isa 24 and Num 21–24) and Jer 48 might both reflect reworking of an earlier version of these declarations that did not survive, or Jeremiah might be using Isa 15–16; 24 and Num 21–24 in something like the form we have them. I take this last, simplest possibility as my working hypothesis. The dating of all this material is uncertain,[66] and it points to another possibility, that the curators have also brought together

66. See, e.g., Bright, *Jeremiah*, 322; Holladay, *Commentary on Jeremiah* 2:346–49; Wild-

other messages from Yahweh about Moab from before Jeremiah's day as well as material from other prophets and theologians in Jeremiah's day and in subsequent decades. But we cannot distinguish between material that came from Jeremiah and material that came from elsewhere.

Several of these possibilities imply that here and maybe elsewhere Yahweh is reaffirming old promises about Moab; their not having been finally fulfilled was a reason for holding onto them and reaffirming them (not for abandoning them). Calvin's prayer fits:

> Grant Almighty God, that we may learn, not only to consider thy judgments when they appear before our eyes, but also to fear them whenever they are announced, so that we may implore thy mercy, and also repent of our sins and patiently bear thy paternal chastisements and never murmur when thou sparest for a time the ungodly.[67]

The links with Numbers and Isaiah are sometimes serendipitous, which may suggest they emerge from an acquaintance with the promises as proclaimed from time to time orally rather than from consultation of a written scroll. Elements in these promises stuck, and sometimes substantial phrases and lines reappear in a form that reflects conscious or unconscious modification. It would be inappropriate to assimilate the Jeremiah text to Isaiah and Numbers or vice versa unless there seemed reason to think that one version had become corrupted; LXX Jeremiah here is also different in detail from MT Jeremiah, as elsewhere. Each version is valid in its own right; I comment on Jeremiah MT while documenting in the notes some differences from LXX and from the material in Isaiah and Numbers.[68]

While the frequent transitions in the chapter suggest that it comprises a collection of messages rather than a single long message, and one certainly cannot get a picture of an enemy fighting one battle against Moab,[69] the dividing lines between units are often difficult to identify, and different commentators offer varying analyses of the chapter's structure. The chapter thus parallels Jer 2 in the way it brings together a collection of prophecies, often juxtaposing units that complement each other. Their sequence is thus not random, but personal impressions are involved in dividing the chapter into meaningful units.[70] In addition, while most of the messages are in

---

berger, *Isaiah 13–27*, 124–25; J. Blenkinsopp, *Isaiah 1–39: A New Translation with Introduction and Commentary*, AB 19 (New York: Doubleday, 2000), 297–98.

67. Calvin, *Jeremiah*, 5:33.

68. J. I. Woods lays out Jer 48 MT and LXX synoptically, then comments on the differences between the two, in *Jeremiah 48 as Christian Scripture* (Cambridge: Clarke, 2011), 25–66.

69. Cf. Duhm, *Jeremia*, 345; he calls the chapter a "strange anthology."

70. Thus my divisions hardly ever correspond to Lundbom's (*Jeremiah 37–52*, viii-ix), Allen's (*Jeremiah*, 477–78), or Holladay's (*Commentary on Jeremiah*, 2:349–53).

verse, they incorporate some prose footnotes, and it is sometimes hard to discern whether we are reading prosaic verse or poetic prose. Their language contains many expressions and rhetorical figures that recur throughout the Jeremiah scroll; they seem no less and no more likely to be of the same authorship as other material in it.[71]

The chapter's main theme is an affirmation that Yahweh will act against Moab and that the effect on Moab will be devastating. It manifests considerable sympathy toward Moab in this connection, but the expressions of sympathy seem ironic; they are a way of underlining the depth of the catastrophe.[72] No doubt Yahweh really does grieve at the need to bring such calamity to Moab, as he grieves at the need to bring calamity to Judah. And the chapter does close with a reverse irony: Yahweh promises Moab's restoration in the same terms as he promises Judah's restoration. Any Judahite celebration of Moab's comeuppance must give way finally to celebration of its restoration.

a. Moab Broken (48:1–10)

[1]*Regarding Moab.*

Yahweh of Armies, the God of Israel, has said this.

Oh, on account of Nebo, that it has been destroyed,
  Kiriathaim has been shamed,[a] captured.
The fortress has been shamed, shattered—
  [2]*there is no glory about Moab anymore.*
In Heshbon, people intended something dire against it:
  "Get going, let's cut it off from being a nation.
Madmen, too, you will be rendered still[b]—
  after you the sword will go."

[3]*The sound of an outcry from Horonaim:*
  "Destruction, a great breaking!"
[4]*Moab has been broken,*
  its little ones[c] have let their outcry be heard.
[5]*Because at the ascent to Luhith[d]*
  with crying, crying goes up.[e]
Because on the Horonaim descent,
  the great distress of the outcry at the breaking, people have heard.

71. See Lundbom, "Language and Rhetoric," 212–19.
72. See the discussion of Isa 15–16 in this connection in B. C. Jones, *Howling over Moab: Irony and Rhetoric in Isaiah 15–16*, SBLDS 157 (Atlanta: Scholars, 1996), 113–61, 231–41.

⁶*Flee, save your life,*
  *and become*ᶠ *like Aroer*ᵍ *in the wilderness!*
⁷*Because on account of your relying on what you have made and on your*
    *stores,*ʰ
  you too will be captured.
*And Chemosh*ⁱ *will go out to exile,*
  his priests and his officials together.
⁸*The destroyer will come to every town,*
  *no town*ʲ *will escape.*
The vale will perish,
  the flatland will be laid waste (what Yahweh has said).
⁹*Give a rosette*ᵏ *to Moab*
  *because it is to go out ruined.*ˡ
Its towns—they will become desolate,
  from having no one living in them.
¹⁰*Cursed the one who does Yahweh's work treacherously,*
  *cursed*ᵐ *the one who holds back his sword from blood.*

a. LXX lacks this verb.

b. Or "made to weep"; see the translation notes on 6:2; 8:14.

c. For ṣəˁîreyhā, LXX implies ṣôˁārâ ("as far as Zoar"); cf. Isa 15:5.

d. For the qere luḥit (cf. Isa 15:5), the ketiv implies luḥôt.

e. The expression is perhaps a synecdoche for "people go up crying" or "people cry as they go up."

f. The verbs and suffix in the first colon were masculine plural; this verb looks feminine plural, but it might have been understood as masculine with an energic ending (see Bright, *Jeremiah*, 314; on the general notion of energic forms, see GK 48bc; Joüon 61f).

g. Aq, Vg take ˁărôˁēr to denote a desert shrub (see BDB), and MT may invite readers to see both meanings here (cf. CTAT 2:778–80). LXX implies ˁārôd ("a wild donkey").

h. For MT's double expression, LXX simply has "fortifications"; the presence of just one word would make for a more plausible colon (four stresses instead of five), but what that one word would be is a matter of guesswork. The suffixes in this line are feminine singular.

i. The ketiv kmyš corresponds to the Ebla spelling (IBHS 1.6.3l; cf. Müller, "Chemosh," 186–87); and compare the name of the city Carchemish.

j. LXX lacks town.

k. Rashi (in MG) takes ṣîṣ to mean wings, an extension of its meaning a lock of hair or a tassel in Aramaic (DTT, 1279; ṣîṣit in Hebrew), which would fit if nāśāʾ in the next colon means "fly" (see BDB); but see the next note. W. L. Moran suggests "salt" on the basis of a similar Ugaritic word meaning "salt field" ("Ugaritic ṣîṣûma and Hebrew ṣîṣ," Bib 39 [1958]: 69–71). LXX implies ṣiyyôn ("marker"; cf. 31:21), here suggesting a gravestone (see BDB). Aq, Sym have "flower" or "shoot."

l. The phrase nāṣōʾ tēṣēʾ parallels 8:13 and 23:39 (see the translation notes there) in combining the idiom whereby an infinitive precedes a finite verb with paronomasia; nāṣāʾ is a byform of nāṣâ ("fall in ruins"; see the translation note on 2:15), chosen (or invented) for the similarity to yāṣāʾ ("go out").

m. LXX lacks the repeated cursed.

This first sequence comprises an imaginary lament, perhaps a funeral lament, at a calamity that is coming or has come upon Moab; it goes on to include imaginary exhortations to people to flee therefore from the disaster area. The disaster issues from people's trust in their human-made religion focused on Chemosh, who will be going into exile. The sequence comes to an end with a curse on the devastation's agents if they do not do their work properly.

v. 1a–b   A double introduction

vv. 1c–2   A grieved portrayal of the northern towns' destruction as if already actual (four bicola)

vv. 3–5   An account of the horrified and grieved reaction to this event in the south (four bicola)

vv. 6–9   An exhortation to people in the south to flee from the calamity coming (seven bicola)

v. 10   A curse on people who do not do this destructive work thoroughly (one 5-4 bicolon)

1–2 *Regarding Moab* signals the subject of Jer 48 as a whole, while *Yahweh of Armies, the God of Israel, has said this* then introduces the first in the collection of messages. The beginning of the actual message, *oh*, can be the beginning of a lament at someone's death; it is "the ominous death knell that sounds for Moab"[73] (see the commentary on 22:13). *Nebo* is near the top of the mountain ridge in the north of northern Moab, one of whose peaks is the Mount Nebo of Deut 34. *Kiriathaim* is another town in the same area. *The fortress* is likely a term to describe this town, one that implies some irony— Kiriathaim has turned out not to have the strength that *fortress* suggests. The parallel colon makes a parallel point about *Moab* in general, the reference to its *glory* linking with the double reference to being *shamed*. *Heshbon* is also quite far north, northeast of Nebo. The reference to the unnamed invaders then introduces a paronomasia: *intended* is ḥāšəbû, so Heshbon was a fitting place for people to implement an intention to *cut . . . off* Moab's life as *a nation*. *Madmen* may be the site now known as Dimneh, further north again, near Rabbah. Whatever its location, its fate again links with its name, perhaps in more than one way. "Be still" is dāmam/dāmâ, whose meaning overlaps with the idea of devastation (see the translation note); in addition, dōmen is dung, and madmēnâ is a dung pit. So this first description of devastation refers to a series of places quite far north in northern Moab, the part of Moab that Yahweh had allocated to Israel, including a place near that mountain where Moses surveyed the promised land and then died.

3–5 In contrast, but complementing that description, four lines report the turmoil brought by the news of it in southern Moab, from what Juda-

---

73. Woods, *Jeremiah 48*, 227.

hites might see as Moab proper. The country as a whole is riven by a series of canyons running down to the Dead Sea from the peak of Moab's eastern ridge. *Horonaim* was on one of these descents. Verse 34 implies that it was in the far southeast, near the southern end of the Dead Sea. So we move from the north in vv. 1–2 to the far south here. The mention of *Luhith* inside the double mention of Horonaim suggests that Luhith is at the top of the Horonaim ascent.[74] The comment on the *destruction* in the north picks up the verb *destroyed* from v. 1, while the general comment about Moab that follows likewise picks up the reference to Moab in v. 2. The message underlines things with its double reference to the *outcry* that has been *heard* and to *breaking* and being *broken*. To make the portrayal worse, it is the outcry of *the little ones* that the prophet hears and reports. Then the final colon adds *great distress* (more literally, "distresses") to the doubled reference to *outcry* and *breaking* (and *heard*) so that the account gains force both from the repetition and from this new element that contributes to an unusual triple noun expression (distresses of the outcry of the breaking—with a third reference to breaking). The lines are a carefully wrought piece using poetic form to bring home their point to the Judahites.

6 Although the actual disaster has so far affected only northern Moab, those horrified mourners in southern Moab would be unwise to assume that they will be exempt from the same experience. The exhortation to *flee* thus follows from what precedes. It does not constitute the content of the outcry (which would be a protest rather than a piece of advice) but an exhortation addressing the people who have voiced the outcry and need to take action for themselves in light of it. *Aroer* is a town on the Arnon, a river flowing into the Dead Sea from the east that can be seen as the northern boundary of Moab proper (Num 21:13; Deut 2:36; 3:12; 4:48). It would be the place through which news of the troubles in the north would come in order to reach the south. It is still a functioning city in v. 19, so the threat of becoming like Aroer is puzzling. But it appears in another prophecy about a foreign nation in a comment about its being destroyed and abandoned and just an abode for flocks (Isa 17:2), so here, becoming like Aroer might be another snide idea. It would link with *'ărô'ēr* also being a word for a desert shrub. On the other hand, *wilderness* commonly does not imply lifeless desert but pasturage, and the idea here might be that at least being an abode for flocks would be something. One way or another, though, the towns in the south need to take action if they are to avoid the fate of the towns in the north.

7 Whereas *you* in v. 6 was plural, now it is feminine singular. The prophecy speaks to Moab corporately (Moab was feminine singular in v. 4). For the

74. See C. Ben-David, "The 'Ascent of Luhith' and the 'Road to Horonaim,'" *Palestine Exploration Quarterly* 133 (2001): 136–44.

first time, a reason is given for the dire fate that is coming on Moab. *Relying on the wrong thing* is an important theme in Jeremiah. Judah's problem is that it has relied on deception one way or another (7:4; 13:25; 28:15; 29:31). Mistaken reliance is key to life and death for other peoples, not just for Israel. Moab's false reliance is the same as Judah's. The expression *what you have made* (*ma'aśeh*) regularly refers to divine images (e.g., 1:16; 10:3, 9; 25:6, 7). In association with that word, *stores* might be the valuable accoutrements of a shrine (e.g., 2 Kgs 24:13). The next line, with its reference to Chemosh, makes more explicit the reference to religious reliance. It might seem more excusable for Moab to rely on its religion and its religious artifacts than it is for Judah, but here the prophecy cuts it no slack (and perhaps the prophet would like to imagine the Judahites listening to this prophecy working out for themselves that, if Moab is guilty and in deep trouble in this connection, *a fortiori* they are more guilty and in deeper trouble). As the Mesha inscription presupposes, *Chemosh* is Moab's deity as Yahweh is Israel's. But Chemosh does not have the power to save his people; rather, he and his ministers inevitably share their fate. The formulation of this point overlaps with a comment in Amos 1:15 concerning Ammon: "Their king will go to exile, he and his officials together." The prophet may hint at a further point: Chemosh going into exile means Moab's conquerors taking his image back home with them. Relying on *what you have made* and on *your stores* gives people a false sense of security: these things may actually make them vulnerable to attackers who would like to appropriate them. Such reliance is tactically unwise as well as religiously and theologically wrong.

8–10 The prophet goes on to generalize the account of the coming destruction. The *destroyer*, the destruction's agent, is not identified, like the northern enemy earlier in Jeremiah. In 604 and the following decades, it could be assumed that Nebuchadrezzar is this agent, but as elsewhere, the prophecy's lack of specificity means it is not limited to this reference, and in origin it might be earlier or later. Either way, every *town* will experience his coming, as will both *vale* and *flatland*—the Jordan Valley and the high plateau. Sardonically, then, the prophet urges unnamed hearers (Yahweh's aides, if we should attempt to identify them) to give Moab a coronet to compensate for its ruined state as it goes off into exile. It is perhaps the same unnamed agents whom v. 10 indirectly urges to do their destructive work thoroughly, though the exhortation has been "claimed" by various subsequent readers.[75] It may presuppose that Yahweh doesn't enjoy commissioning such work; it is alien to him (Isa 28:21), and it doesn't come from his heart (Lam 3:33). He knows that no normal person wants to engage in killing, so sometimes his agents have to be spurred on.

75. Woods, *Jeremiah 48*, 188–216.

b. Retrospect and Prospect (48:11–17)

[11]*Moab at rest from his youth,*
  quiet on his lees:
He has not been emptied from vessel to vessel,
  into exile he has not gone.[a]
As a result his taste has stood in him,
  and his aroma—it hasn't changed.[b]

[12]*Therefore, there, days are coming (Yahweh's affirmation):*

I will send off tippers for him, and they will tip him out;
  his vessels they will empty,[c]
  their jars they will break up.
[13]*And Moab will be shamed because of Chemosh*
  as the household of Israel was shamed
  because of Beth El, their reliance.

[14]*How could you say,*[d]
  "We are strong men,
  forceful men for the battle?"
[15]*Moab has been destroyed,*
  into its towns people have gone up.
The choicest of its young men—
  they have gone down to the slaughter.
(An affirmation of the King,
  Yahweh of Armies his name).[e]

[16]*Moab's disaster*[f] *near coming,*
  its dire fate—it hurried fast.
[17]*Condole with him,*[g] *all you who are around him,*
  all who acknowledge his name.
Say, "How the vigorous scepter has been broken,
  the splendid mace."

a. The line works a-b-b'-a' so that *into exile* makes for a shocking beginning to the parallel second colon.

b. MT has a section marker here. This line also works a-b-b'-a', but the parallelism contains no such shocks.

c. For MT *yārîqû*, LXX implies *yādēqqû* ("they will crush," BHS), which makes for good parallelism.

d. The next verse, with its past reference, suggests that this *yiqtol* does not have simple future reference.

e. LXX lacks this line.

f. LXX has "day," not inappropriately (46:21 had *day of disaster*).

g. Moab becomes masculine singular, as in vv. 11–13, after being feminine singular in vv. 14–15.

The second sequence starts again from Moab's current state and its past, then issues a warning of how the future will contrast with the past, its four subsections once more working with the contrast and movement between past, present, and imminent, imagined future:

> v. 11   A retrospective (three bicola)
>
> vv. 12–13 Yahweh's declaration of intent (an introduction and two tricola)
>
> vv. 14–15 An alternative imaginary retrospective (a tricolon, two bicola, and an extra bicolon affirming that Yahweh speaks)
>
> vv. 16–17 Another alternative imaginary retrospective (three bicola)

11 The first retrospective takes the long view. Later sections of the chapter will pick up the theme of vines, grapes, and wine, in recognition of Moab's being wine country, and this sequence starts from the same aspect of its reputation. Moab is like a bottle of good wine that has been allowed to sit and mature in its vat. *Lees* are the remains of the yeast from grape skins. Leaving the wine on the lees for too long spoils it (cf. Zeph 1:12),[76] but leaving it undisturbed for a while enables it to develop flavor and aroma. This wine has not been poured from one vessel to another: Moab has not been "disturbed" by being taken into exile (like Ephraim, say, if the prophecy dates from around 604, or like Judah if it dates from later). But including that word *exile* sets up a worry. And in any period, for Judahites, this retrospective raises the question of why. It half implies a protest like the ones that lie in the background of Pss 49 and 73.

12–13 Actually, things are not going to stay that way. In itself, the arrival of *tippers* would not be bad news; the word could suggest people who decant the wine from vats into individual bottles. But these tippers are more like vandals who deliberately pour away the contents of the vat. They not only *empty the vessels*; they *break* them. The poem goes on to interpret the allegory, which spells out the implications of that brief reference to exile in v. 11. Once again, it critiques Moab's false *reliance* and derides *Chemosh*, as

---

76. See W. D. Barker, "Wine Production in Ancient Israel and the Meaning of *šəmārîm* in the Hebrew Bible," in *Leshon Limmudim*: *Essays on the Language and Literature of the Hebrew Bible in Honour of A. A. Macintosh*, ed. D. A. Baer and R. P. Gordon, LHBOTS 593 (London: T&T Clark, 2013), 268–74; he thinks v. 11a implies the spoiling has happened, but v. 11b suggests it hasn't.

in v. 7. Here, the critique is more specific. Chemosh, the supernatural object of their reliance, cannot protect his people; therefore, they *will be shamed*. With another acerbic note, addressed to the poem's actual audience, it adds a comparison with Ephraim and its reliance on Beth El. There are texts that refer to a god called Beth El, the name being apparently shortened from a form such as El of the house of El. This allusion is the First Testament's only clear reference to Israelite worship of a god with this name, though passages such as Amos 3:14 may have the same implication.[77] Beth El would be a title for the senior god that people worshiped—Ephraimites might have seen it as "really" an alternative way of worshiping Yahweh when they worshiped at Bethel. But the fall of Ephraim was an exposure of their reliance, which actually constituted recourse to another deity. The reference to Ephraim and its fall would again fit a time such as 604 and the context of Jeremiah's critique of Ephraim as he seeks to stop Judah going the same way. Indeed, parallels in Jeremiah's language to describe Moab and its fate and Judah and its fate could bring home to Judah that it could be "at risk of becoming an outsider, becoming 'Moabite,'" and that "the only hope for the weeping Rachel and the boasting Judean 'Moab' alike is to yield to the God who alone is capable of inscribing the covenant directly on the human heart."[78]

14–15 In light of what is going to happen and has already happened in the vision's imagination as v. 15 will describe it, this further cutting question relates to what the Moabites thought they were—in effect, it is another critique of their false reliance. They have always seen themselves as a strong collection of fighters. But events will belie the claim that v. 14 would once have implied. The content of the question comes in parallel 2-2 cola in v. 14, and they lead into parallel 2-2 bicola in v. 15a–b that breathlessly describe the grimness of what has happened (what will have happened), then yet another 2-2 bicolon in v. 15c, where the statement of visionary imagination is underlined by a particularly strong variation on the common "Yahweh's affirmation." The "report" that *Moab has been destroyed* is thus amplified by the explanation that unnamed enemy fighters *have gone up into its towns*. "Going up" commonly implies an invasion or attack; towns are regularly located on hills, and in Israel, invaders commonly have to "go up" into its highland country. Here, that verb opens the way for an unhappy contrast: the defeat means *the choicest of its young men*, the people on whom Moab's future military viability depends, *have gone down—down to the slaughter*.

---

77. See W. Röllig, "Bethel," *DDD*, 173–75.

78. C. J. Sharp, "Embodying Moab: The Figuring of Moab in Jeremiah 48 as Reinscription of the Judean Body," in *Concerning the Nations: Essays on the Oracles against the Nations in Isaiah, Jeremiah and Ezekiel*, ed. A. Mein, E. K. Holt, and H. C. P. Kim, LHBOTS 612 (London: T&T Clark, 2016), 108.

16–17 In another imaginary retrospective, the first colon in isolation would seem to be referring to the present, but the parallel colon makes clear that the line refers to the sudden way the *disaster* fell on Moab. In this imagined future, then, its neighbors are urged to *condole with* Moab. They are people who *acknowledge his name*, who know and respect Moab and are shocked by what has happened, especially as its *dire fate* is here specified as its loss of independence. The *scepter* or *mace* stood for a nation possessing leadership that could act with power in its world. Moab's symbol of power could be seen as not only *vigorous* but also *splendid*, like impressive bejeweled ceremonial insignia carried in a procession. In the imagined future, it is *broken*. The recurrence of that verb overlaps in significance and resonances with occurrences such as the ones in vv. 4, 25, and 38. The breaking of the scepter symbolizes the breaking of the nation. In reality, Moab's breaking would hardly be an eventuality that its neighbors would regret much, so the figure rather suggests to Moab what it will itself need to regret. To the poem's Judahite audience, it is a reality over which it might in theory console Moab—but more realistically it might need to see the event as another warning against allying with Moab.

c. What Has Happened? (48:18–25)

[18]*Go down from honor, sit in thirsty ground,*[a]
   you who sit as Miss Dibon.
Because the destroyer of Moab has gone up to you—
   he has devastated your fortresses.
[19]*By the road, stand and look out,*
   you who sit as Aroer.
Ask the man fleeing and the woman escaping,
   say, "What has happened?"
[20]*Moab is shamed because it has shattered—*
   howl, cry out.
Announce at the Arnon
   that Moab has been destroyed.

[21]*A decision has come to the flatland*[b] *region,*
   to Holon, to Jahzah,
Upon Mephaath, [22]*upon Dibon, upon Nebo,*
   upon Beth-diblathaim, [23]*upon Kiriathaim,*
Upon Beth-gamul, upon Beth-meon,
   [24]*upon Kerioth, upon Bozrah,*
Upon all the towns in the country of Moab,

far and near.
²⁵*Moab's horn has been cut off,*
  *his arm—it has been broken (Yahweh's affirmation).*ᶜ

    a. Lit. "in the thirst"; cf. the use of the related adjective in Isa 44:3.
    b. *Mišpāṭ* has come to *mîšōr.*
    c. LXX lacks *(Yahweh's affirmation).*

The sequence manifests a similar dynamic to vv. 1–10, presupposing the same realities of theological geography. Once more it starts in the middle of things, presupposing that the ax has fallen in northern Moab and issuing two exhortations relating to the need to face that fact. It then goes on to catalog the towns that have been devastated.

> vv. 18–20 Biddings to Dibon and Aroer, with parallel descriptions in the biddings (six bicola in three pairs)
> vv. 21–25 A report of what has happened that explains and responds to the biddings (four linked bicola making one sentence and one more summarizing bicolon)

18 We are again *in medias res*. Whereas vv. 1–2 started from devastation in the far north of northern Moab, vv. 18–20 focus on two key towns at the southern end of that region. *Dibon* is five miles north of Aroer; both are not far north of the Arnon and located on the King's Highway, a main international north-south route up the Rift Valley. Dibon was where the Mesha Stele was found, and in that ninth-century inscription, Mesha describes himself as a Dibonite. Although it was north of the Arnon, at this time, at least, it was the Moabite capital. The poetic apostrophe addresses this key Moabite city to urge it to recognize its reduction from a position of *honor* to a position described elsewhere as sitting in the dirt or reduced to wilderness, and here described as sitting in dry, *thirsty ground*. The poem again juxtaposes how the Moabite city must *go down* because *the destroyer of Moab has gone up* to conquer it (the destroyer is again unidentified; see v. 8 and the commentary on it).

    19–20 Like Dibon, Aroer is personified as a woman. It is a place that south-bound fugitives from Dibon would pass as they fled toward southern Moab, a little like Ephraimites fleeing south to Judah after the Assyrian invasion. The poem imagines people asking the fugitives *what has happened*. Interpreted literalistically, it is a foolish question, especially in a town from which people would be able to see and hear things. Its rhetorical point is to draw attention to something horrific having happened. What follows in v. 20 is the answer to the question; perhaps we are to think of it as the fugitives' own answer. Its implication is, "If Dibon has fallen, the entire tableland has been overrun."[79]

79. Lundbom, *Jeremiah 37–52*, 279.

21–24 These prosaic lines come in the midst of a poetic account of the imagined past devastation of Moab; they can be laid out as rhythmic lines. As the destroyer is unnamed but the audience likely know who he is, so the agent of decision-making is unspecified but the audience definitely knows (or is supposed to know) that Yahweh is the one who makes this kind of authoritative decision (*mišpāṭ*; see the commentary on 1:16; 4:2). We cannot locate most of the places named in the list, but it is evident that they are intended to convey the impression of an event affecting the entire country, as the last phrases in v. 24 make clear. In particular, *flatland* or plateau suggests the entire northern region (cf. v. 8), and the locations we can identify are all north of the Arnon.

25 The anticipatory description of calamity on Moab which closes this sequence takes up imagery different from that in v. 17, it restates the same point. The devastation in Moab has an effect like cutting off an animal's horn; its horn is key to its aggressive action and therefore a symbol of its power. Or it has an effect like that of breaking a human being's arm, which is also key to the person's aggressive action and therefore a symbol of their power. This visionary sequence again portrays Moab as totally broken.

d. Wine and Arrogance (48:26–32)

[26]*Get him drunk, because against Yahweh he got big;*
  Moab will overflow[a] with his vomit,
  and he too will become an object of fun.

[27]*Hasn't Israel been the object of fun for you?[b] Has he been found among thieves,*
that at all your words[c] against him you shake your head?[d]

[28]*Abandon towns, dwell in the cliff,*
  you who live in Moab.
Be like a pigeon that nests
  in the sides of the mouth of a gorge.[e]
[29]*We have heard of Moab's majesty,*
  very majestic,
His exaltedness and[f] his majesty,
  his majestic nature and the loftiness of his mind.
[30]*I myself have acknowledged (Yahweh's affirmation) his excess,[g]*
  but his oracles[h] were not right—not right have they acted.

[31]*As a result, over Moab I will howl,*
  for Moab, all of it, I will cry out.
About the people of Kir-heres[i] one could murmur,[j]

[32]*with more than the crying for Jazer.*[k]
I will cry for you, Sibmah vine,
  you whose tendrils passed to the sea.
While as far as the sea, Jazer[l] *they reached,*
  upon your summer fruit and upon your cut grapes a destroyer has
    fallen.

a. *Sāpaq* usually means "clap" (cf. 31:19; and LXX "with his hand"), but this meaning makes poor sense here; I take the verb as *DCH*'s *sāpaq* V, *HALOT*'s *sāpaq* II.

b. The absence of an apodosis following the *'im* clause suggests that *'im* is an interrogative—and again in the next clause (Joüon 161d).

c. See the translation note on 20:8, though here *middê* introduces a noun rather than a verb. LXX lacks *at all your words.*

d. While it's possible to lay out v. 26 as a tricolon, it's virtually impossible to read v. 27 as poetry. For MT *titnôdād*, LXX "made war" suggests *titgôdēd* (*BHS*).

e. LXX has past tense verbs throughout this verse.

f. LXX lacks *his exaltedness and.*

g. *'Ebrâ* and related words usually denote anger but can refer to other forms of "overflowing" or unrestrained self-expression. LXX, Tg imply *'ăbōdātô* ("his work").

h. *Baddîm* can refer to the words that someone speaks or to the people who speak the words. As they are here the subject of "act," the latter is more likely (see the commentary).

i. LXX "Kiradas" might imply that its real name was *Kir-ḥādāš*, "New City."

j. LXX has imperative verbs in v. 31.

k. Cf. Blayney, *Jeremiah*, 419.

l. Tg, Aq, Sym have "sea of Jazer," which would presumably refer to the Dead Sea; but how could it be given that name?

This sequence is jumpier than the previous two; it more evidently combines material of diverse origin. The curators have collated material interweaving two motifs, wine and majesty; the first line introduces them. It returns to the present (the trouble being explicitly in the future), issues exhortations to Moab's potential destroyers, and recalls a rationale for the trouble, which the prose sentence nuances. In vv. 28–30, the prophecy issues an exhortation to Moab itself in light of the calamity that is portrayed as imminent; it also elaborates on the rationale that necessitates it. Then, in vv. 31–32, it reacts to what indeed happens to Moab as a consequence. Much of vv. 29–32 reworks messages about Moab in Isa 15–16 (see the introduction to this chapter, pp. 850–51).

vv. 26–27	Moab must be made to get drunk, because Moab got big and contemptuous (a tricolon and a prose sentence)
vv. 28–30	Moab must flee, because its majesty will mean its downfall (five bicola)
vv. 31–32	Moab's wine production is ruined, and Moab cries from north to south (a tricolon and four bicola)

26–27 The bidding starts from the real present, and an unnamed voice (perhaps Jeremiah's) urges unnamed actors (in his time, it would be the Babylonians) to take a form of action that recalls the chalice in 25:15–29. In this chapter's context, it links with the wine motif in vv. 11–13, to which vv. 31–32 will return. The problem is that Moab *got big*; in theory, there is nothing wrong with getting big, but it tends to imply a rivalry with Yahweh's importance (cf. Ezek 35:13), as is explicit here: Moab got big *against Yahweh*, "asserted autonomy from Yahweh."[80] The advantage of getting him drunk is that it will turn him into something pathetic. It will be an act of poetic justice. How did Moab get too big for its boots and treat Israel as *an object of fun*, something to laugh at, something to scorn? The general context for this chapter suggests it was by Moab's casual and contemptuous occupation of land that Yahweh claimed and had allocated to Israel. Given that the Torah makes the Arnon the boundary between Israel and Moab, places such as Aroer and Dibon (as well as the many other places in the north that have been mentioned) were located in areas that Moab had taken over. These lines are thus a further rare example of a prophecy providing a rationale for Yahweh's bringing calamity to a foreign people and a rare reference to the foreign nation's relationship with Israel in this connection. The development of the rationale involves suggesting that Moab was without excuse. It had treated Israel cynically and scornfully, hadn't it? Israel hadn't done anything that made it deserve Moab's encroachment, had it? It hadn't stolen land from Moab, had it? The land to the north that the Torah saw as Israel's had not belonged to Moab at the time but to some Amorites who unwisely took on Israel. Moab just threw out its scornful words, shook its head in further scorn ("Pathetic Israel can't stand up to me!"), and took what it wanted.

28–29 The poetic lines that follow look separate in origin, but juxtaposed with what now precedes in the context, they eventually elaborate on the point about Moab's getting big. Yahweh's agents' job is to get Moab drunk— metaphorically. Moab will therefore be wise to get out of town to avoid having to drink the spiked chalice. To be more literal, if an invader is coming and there is no chance of defeating him, it's sensible to hide. When a bird is scared, it takes refuge in a cleft in a cliff, where most threats can't reach it, and human beings sometimes do the same (4:29). Moab might thus seek refuge in the clefts of a canyon such as the Arnon. As if it were feasible, as if there were a place where one could escape Yahweh's reach! And it's an ignominious thing to have to run for your life; it contrasts with the *majesty* and *loftiness* to which Moab aspires, with Moab's getting big. Majesty and loftiness *of mind* or of attitude are further terms that don't have to imply arrogance (Moab's territory, towering up from the Jordan Valley, was physically impressive).

---

80. Brueggemann, *Jeremiah 26–52*, 240.

But they easily do so (e.g., Lev 26:19, of Israel!). Isaiah 2 has already spoken at some length about hiding in the rocks when Yahweh's majesty confronts Judahite majesty.

30 *Excess* makes explicit the pejorative implications of the reference to Moab's majesty, exaltedness, and loftiness. The excess expresses itself in *his oracles* which were *not right* and did not do right. *Oracles* (*baddîm*) here thus refers to people who bring oracles and mislead Moab into the action it takes. While the word is the Hebrew version of an Amorite word for such diviners, it is also, nicely, a homonym of a Hebrew word for babblers or babblings,[81] as Jeremiah's audience would know. Is the babbling what Moab said about Israel and Yahweh? (again see vv. 26–27). If so, its excess also expresses itself in how Moab *acted* in relation to Israel and Yahweh, which also *was not right*. Like Judah, Moab manifested that "pride in the form of the self-help which is forbidden to man,"[82] and "this pride is a disaster waiting to happen."[83] Yahweh got to know about it, recognized its reality, and determined to do something about it.

31a Therefore, there will be reason for lamenting what will now happen. Like the leap between preparation for battle and aftermath of defeat in 46:2–12, there is here a leap between facts requiring action and grief over the consequences of the events that follow, but no immediate description of what those events will be. The poem jumps straight to the words of someone speaking like a friend of Moab who is overcome by the horror of what is going to happen to it, who will condole with it in the way v. 17 said to. It will make him *howl* and *cry out* (vv. 31b–32 will add *murmur* and *cry* in the sense of weep). Who speaks? Who is the *I*? Back in v. 30, Yahweh was the *I*, and in v. 33 Yahweh must be the *I*, so he must be here. He is both the one who takes action against Moab and the one who declares his grief over the consequences. Theologically, one can perceive a profundity here, though rhetorically it seems likely that Yahweh's declarations of grief at what happens to Moab are designed to underline its horror; it is an event to which the natural response would be horror.

31b–32 *Kir-heres* is traditionally identified with modern Kerak, on the King's Highway. It appears as Kir-hareseth in 2 Kgs 3:25, where it is apparently the Moabite capital, and this identification would here make it stand appropriately for Moab as a whole, or for southern Moab as a whole.[84] Ety-

---

81. See *HALOT*.

82. Barth, *CD* IV, 1:473.

83. Lundbom, *Jeremiah 37–52*, 288.

84. But K. A. D. Smelik questions these assumptions and argues for the north (*Converting the Past: Studies in Ancient Israelite and Moabite Historiography*, OTS 28 [Leiden: Brill, 1992], 85–89).

mologically, the name should mean "Pottery (or Potsherd) Wall (or City),"
which might generate a grin in Hebrew. Jazer stands for the northern region
of Moab in Num 32:1–3 and may do so here. Evidently, *Sibmah* can be associated with viniculture, and the poem pictures vines from Sibmah stretching
across to *the sea*—presumably the Dead Sea, the sea that begins below Jazer.
Stretching across to the sea is a sign of their flourishing. A destroyer falling
on vineyards is a horrifying idea at the best of times, but Sibmah is "a met-
onymic expression for the wine country and cultivated land of Moab,"[85] as
is suggested by the subsequent reference to *summer fruit* and *cut grapes*. The
threat suggests the invader devastating the land's entire produce.

e. Worship Replaced by Wailing (48:33–39)

[33]*Rejoicing and gladness gather themselves up*
  from the orchard,[a] *from the country of Moab—*
  I have made wine cease[b] *from the presses.*[c]
No one treads with a shout—
  the shout is not a shout.
[34]*From the outcry of Heshbon as far as Elealeh,*
  as far as Jahaz they have given their voice,
From Zoar as far as Horonaim,
  Eglath-shelishiyah.
Because the water of Nimrim—
  it also becomes desolation.

[35]*I will make cease for Moab (Yahweh's affirmation) anyone making an*
    offering at a shrine
  and burning a sacrifice to his god.
[36]*As a result, my heart for Moab—*
  like pipes it will moan.
My heart for the people of Kir-heres—
  like pipes it will moan.

As a result, the surplus[d] *he made—*
  they have perished,[e] [37]*because every head, clipping,*
  and every beard, cutting.
On all hands, gashes,
  and on hips, sack.
[38]*On all the roofs of Moab and in its squares,*

85. Volz, *Jeremia*, 414.

all of it, lamenting.^f
Because I have broken Moab,
like an object no one wants (Yahweh's affirmation).
³⁹*Oh, how it has shattered—wail;*
oh, how Moab has turned his back in shame.
Moab will become an object of fun,
something shattering to all the people around him.^g

a. LXX lacks *from the orchard.*
b. LXX lacks *I have made* and *cease.*
c. The asyndeton and the word order with the object preceding the verb suggest that this colon is subordinate to what precedes it.
d. *Yitrâ* comes only here and in Isa 15:7; but the common masculine *yeter* denotes what is left over, in a negative sense (39:9) or a positive one (Isa 56:12). In the context here, the positive sense is appropriate (cf. vv. 32–33).
e. While the move from feminine singular to masculine plural is jerky, it is possible with a collective (DG 25). But the construction is less harsh if this colon and in particular this verb is treated as the lead-in to v. 37.
f. LXX lacks this colon.
g. MT has a section marker here.

In the fifth sequence, celebration and sacrifice give way to outcry and wailing. Much of the material reworks verses from Isa 15–16 (see the introduction to this chapter, pp. 851–52).

vv. 33–34	Moab loses any reason to celebrate (an opening tricolon and four bicola)
vv. 35–36b	Moab's desolation and outcry in response to Yahweh's stopping its worship (three bicola)
vv. 36c–39	Moab's grief and lament in response to Yahweh's breaking it (an opening tricolon and five bicola)

33–34 The poem links with what precedes in taking up the motif of harvest. The grape harvest is an occasion of great celebration, but the catastrophe this poem envisages will mean there is no celebration. *I have made wine cease from the presses* means there will not be enough grapes for them to get as far as sitting on the lees (v. 11). So *rejoicing and gladness gather themselves up like someone dying* (e.g., Deut 32:50). There will be no celebratory *shout*; no shout at all really—nothing to shout about in a positive way. Put otherwise, the shout will be an *outcry*, a protest that sounds throughout the country—*all of it*, as v. 31 said; the three lines of v. 34 spell out the point once more in terms of some geographical specifics. Even if the northern region chiefly experiences the devastation, the *outcry* comes not only from there (from Heshbon, Elealah, and Jahaz in the distant north) but also in the far south (from Zoar,

Horonaim, and *the water of Nimrim*—evidently one of the perennial rivers flowing from the ridge to the Dead Sea, not just a wadi). Perhaps the average Judahites would have no more clue about Moabite geography than modern Western readers, but they might know the basics, and even if they lacked that degree of knowledge, it would not prevent their appreciating the force of this poem's account of the outcry that sounds out from the entire country because of its desolation.

35-36b The juxtaposition with vv. 33-34 suggests one or two possible points of connection in these lines. The failure of a harvest would make sacrifice impossible: there is nothing to bring. The failure of a harvest makes it especially necessary to pray, but one result of the desolation is that there is no one to go and pray. Given that the *I* of v. 35 must be Yahweh, it is also Yahweh who is doing the moaning in v. 36. As was the case in v. 31, there is presumably some irony in the grief Yahweh expresses. Moab's being unable to offer sacrifice is a horrific aspect of the disaster that has come upon it, a horror that would make anyone grieve. *Kir-heres* stands in parallelism with Moab within the two lines of v. 36a, which fits the assumption that it is the Moabite capital, as in v. 31.

36c-37 Every year, farmers hope for a *surplus* in their harvest. They need it for bartering so they can get hold of things they need but cannot produce, for saving in case next year's harvest fails, and for being generous to people like Elimelech and Naomi who show up because there is trouble the other side of the Jordan (one should hardly leave Jer 48 without remembering Ruth).[86] Moab has good agricultural land, and vv. 32-33 have implied that there have been good harvests, as the Ruth story presupposes. They have now ceased. Thus (in the poet's imagination) the good things that Moab enjoyed *have perished*. The evidence is the way its people are mourning the disaster. Cutting one's hair short instead of letting it flow, trimming one's beard that is otherwise a sign of seniority and honor, gashing one's hands (still a sign of distress in a Western context), dressing in an undignified manner: they are all signs of the grief one feels and expresses when someone has died.

38-39 While one obvious response to disaster is to have recourse to the shrine (v. 35), Moabites knew that their gods could also be accessible at home and in the city. *Lamenting on all the roofs* thus suggests not merely the roof as a place where people gather socially, like the backyard. It is a place where one reaches out to the gods (cf. 19:13; 32:29). Lamenting in the *squares* also suggests gatherings that involve prayer and offerings, as Jeremiah speaks of Judahites making offerings in the streets of the city (44:17, 21). In the prophet's vision, the nation's distraught prayer reflects Yahweh's having *broken Moab*. The image of Moab as broken recalls vv. 3, 4, 5, 17, and 25, as well as

---

86. Oecolampadius, *In Hieremiam*, on the passage; cf. Tyler, *Jeremiah*, 421.

the threat to Judah in 19:11, while the image of *an object no one wants* recalls Jehoiachin in 22:28. Yes, broken Moab will become *an object of fun*, something to laugh at with scorn (cf. vv. 26–27). Yet the laughter will be a kind of schadenfreude, a rejoicing in someone else's misfortune that semi-conceals a fear that one will have the same experience. Moab's *shattering* (cf. vv. 1, 20) will have a shattering effect on anyone who sees it (cf. 1:17; 8:9; 17:18; 23:4; 30:10; 46:27—this verb comes more often in the Jeremiah scroll than in any other book). Perhaps Jeremiah's portrayal of it might have a shattering effect on people who seek to imagine it with him. The exclamation *how* (*'êk*) is another of Jeremiah's signature expressions; it can be an explanation "of lamentation . . . or of satisfaction,"[87] and both could apply here (cf. 50:23; 51:41).

f. An Eagle, a Trap, a Fire (48:40–46)

⁴⁰*Because Yahweh has said this.*

There, like an eagle one will sweep,
    *and spread his wings toward Moab.*ᵃ
⁴¹*The towns*ᵇ *are being captured,*
    *the strongholds—they are being seized.*ᶜ
The heart of Moab's strong men will become
    on that day
    *like the heart of a woman in labor.*ᵈ
⁴²*Moab will be laid waste as a people,*ᵉ
    because against Yahweh he got big.

⁴³*Terror and pit and trap*ᶠ
    *against you who live in Moab (Yahweh's affirmation).*ᵍ
⁴⁴*The person who flees in the face of the terror*
    will fall into the pit.
And the person who climbs out of the pit
    will be caught in the trap.
Because I will bring to it, to Moab,
    the year of their being attended to (Yahweh's affirmation).

⁴⁵*In the shelter of Heshbon,*
    people fleeing have halted, out of energy.
Because fire—it has gone out from Heshbon,
    *a flame from within Sihon.*ʰ

---

87. BDB, 32. *'Êkâ* in v. 17 was more unequivocally doleful (cf. Lam 1:1; 2:1; 4:1, 2).

It has consumed Moab's brow,
the skull of the people destined for tumult.[i]
⁴⁶*Oh, for you, Moab,*
the people of Chemosh has perished!
Because your sons have been taken as captives
and your daughters into captivity.[j]

a. LXX lacks this line.

b. LXX, Vg take *haqqəriyyôt* as the name of a specific town, as in v. 24, but here it has the article.

c. A neat a-b-b'-a' line, with the second colon going beyond the first (see the commentary).

d. LXX lacks v. 41b.

e. Lit. "from [being] a people."

f. *Paḥad, paḥat, paḥ.*

g. LXX lacks *(Yahweh's affirmation).*

h. 2QJer has "from Sihon's town," assimilating to Num 21:28.

i. Lit. "people of tumult."

j. Verses 45b–46 correspond to Num 21:28–29; LXX lacks vv. 45–46.

The imagery changes again for the final sequence, which also reverts to more explicit talk of invasion and conquest and segues from taking up the warnings from Isa 15–16 in the previous two sequences to taking up warnings from Isa 24 and Num 21 (see the introduction to this chapter, p. 852). The compilation of messages in this chapter opened its warnings with *hôy*; it almost closes them with *'ôy*. Further, the intermingling of images with which it closes, along with its reworking of prophetic warnings from elsewhere, combine to take the chapter to a forceful near-conclusion. The three units within this last sequence begin from three images:

vv. 40–42   An eagle (a prose introduction, two bicola, a tricolon, and another bicolon)
vv. 43–44   A trap (four bicola)
vv. 45–46   A fire (five bicola)

40–42 If one is to identify the *eagle*, it denotes Nebuchadrezzar (cf. Ezek 17), but Jeremiah is more interested in the eagle-like or vulture-like nature of the conqueror than his identity (cf. Deut 28:49). The point is the conqueror's swoop, which will issue in the capture of *towns*, even fortified *strongholds*. It will terrify Moab's alleged *strong men*, its warriors, with the kind of fear that properly possesses a woman who is having a baby and knows it may be the death of her. The first two lines are thus neatly parallel in different ways. The first is an example of staircase parallelism in which the second colon presupposes some elements in the opening colon but then takes things further.

there	like an eagle	one will sweep
and will spread	his wings	toward Moab.

The Hebrew word order makes the aural link between the two middle words, *like an eagle* (*kannešer*) and *his wings* (*kənāpāyw*). The next line is another a-b-b'-a' bicolon:

they are being captured	the towns
the strongholds	they are being seized.

In v. 41b, the extra middle colon in the tricolon adds a further note of significance to what happens. This day is no ordinary day, and this battle is no ordinary battle. It is *that day*, Yahweh's day, a day when Yahweh is implementing his ultimate purpose (see the commentary on 46:10). Only here, as the chapter draws to its close, is the catastrophe that comes on Moab given this significance (cf. 46:10, 21 for Egypt; 47:4 for Philistia; 49:22 for Edom, when the complete formulation recurs; 49:26 for Damascus; perhaps a little less explicitly, 50:27–31 for Babylon). The threat of being *laid waste* corresponds to v. 8; and the reasoning corresponds to v. 26.

43-44 The second metaphor works with an image that directly applies to an animal that someone wants to catch, or metaphorically to an individual human being upon whom some unscrupulous plotter has designs (18:22; Pss 119:110; 140:5[6]). A *trap* for an animal could mean a *pit* disguised by brushwood that the animal fell into, and traps for human beings would also benefit from disguise, though Jeremiah works the imagery in a different way. Imagine how, with a sigh of relief, you climb out of the pit—then you get caught in a trap. There is no escape (cf. Amos 5:18–19). Jeremiah may, then, be affirming that no individual Moabites will escape when *the year of their being attended to* arrives; or he may be applying to the nation as a corporate entity the image that applies directly to the individual. Either way, there is nowhere to run, nowhere to hide.

45a The sequence in due course makes a transition to a third image. Like a trap, fire is a significant literal reality, not least in the context of invasion and war. While towns get set on fire accidentally in peace time, attacking and defending them in war often means playing with fire. Here, the literal reality again becomes a metaphor. So the first line describes one result of Moab's invasion by a foreign army, by the eagle. An invasion sometimes results in people from rural areas taking refuge in towns, and Heshbon would be a natural refuge for people from the northern region. As happens a number of times in the chapter, the logic in v. 45 is then elliptical—the *because* does not provide a clear link. The deficit relates to the role of v. 45a as the prophet's introduction to a reworking of Num 21:28–29, which occupies vv. 45b–46. The *because* is part of the text as it appears in Num 21:28, where it makes a different link.

45b–46 The quotation from Numbers contains several levels of irony. In their context in Numbers, the lines refer directly to the conquest of northern Moab by Sihon, whose capital was the northern city of Heshbon. It was then by virtue of defeating Sihon that Israel came to be in control of this territory that had once belonged to Moab. In this context, the lines mock Moab for that earlier defeat but also speak anticipatorily of a further defeat threatening Moab. Only in an indirect sense will the fire have its origin in Heshbon: perhaps a northern invader will first take this key northern city, which then becomes the starting point for bringing devastation to Moab as a whole that in a sense repeats that of Sihon. Jeremiah's words deviate from the ones in Num 21:28 and 24:17 and introduce a mixed metaphor. *Consumed* fits the reference to fire that precedes it, but not the reference to Moab's head (*brow* and *skull*) that follows; in Num 24:17, the verb is "shattered." But the verb corresponds to a message about Moab in Amos 2:1–2, which describes how fire "will consume" Moab and adds that Moab will die "in tumult," which is also Jeremiah's image here. Once, Moab's offspring became captives to Sihon; now, they will be captives to another invader.

g. But Disaster Is Not the End (48:47)

[47]*But I will bring about the restoration*[a] *of Moab in the aftermath of the time (Yahweh's affirmation).*
 As far as this is the decision about Moab.[b]

    a. See the translation note on 29:14.
    b. MT has a section marker here. LXX lacks vv. 45–47.

The entire series of messages about Moab has been unfailingly bleak (if you are the Moabites) or encouraging (if you are the Judahites looking for Moab to be put down). The last bicolon puts things in reverse. Even if Yahweh's expressions of grief throughout the chapter were designed to add to the impression that a horrific fate was coming on Moab, this last line affirms that taking redress is not Yahweh's last word. Yahweh applies to Moab the same promise he applies to Israel. Applied to Moab in this context, it generates a neat contrast with v. 46 as *šebî* (*captives*) and *šibyâ* (*captivity*) give way to *šabtî šəbût* (*bring about . . . restoration*).[88]

---

    88. Brueggemann, *Jeremiah 26–52*, 246.

3. *Ammon (49:1–6 [LXX 30:1–5 or 17–21])*

¹*Regarding the Ammonites.*

Yahweh has said this.

Did Israel have no sons,
   had he no one entering into possession?
*Why did their King Milcom*ᵃ *dispossess Gad*ᵇ
   and his people come to live in its towns?

²*Therefore, there, days are coming (Yahweh's affirmation):*

I will make the battle shout heard
   *against Rabbah of the Ammonites.*ᶜ
It will become a desolate tell,
   *its daughter-villages*ᵈ—*they will be set on fire,*
   *and Israel will dispossess its dispossessors (Yahweh has said).*ᵉ

³*Howl, Heshbon, because Ai has been destroyed;*
   cry out, daughter-villages of Rabbah.
Put sack around you and lament,
   *run to and fro in the fences.*ᶠ
*Because their King Milcom*ᵍ—*he will go into exile,*
   his priests and his officials together.
⁴*Why do you glory in the vales*
   (flowing your vale)?
*You, miss, one who is turning,*ʰ *one who relies on her stores:*
   "Who will come against me?"
⁵*Here am I, letting there come against you*
   *terror (an affirmation of the Lord Yahweh of Armies)*ⁱ *from all the*
      people around you.
*You will scatter,*ʲ *each in his own direction,*
   *with no one collecting a wanderer.*ᵏ

⁶*But afterward I will bring about the restoration*ˡ *of the Ammonites (Yah-*
   *weh's affirmation).*ᵐ

   a. *Their King Milcom* represents simply *malkām* in MT, while LXX, Vg have Melkom;
see the commentary.
   b. Some LXX MSS have "Gilead" (the geographical term) instead of *Gad* (the clan that
lived there).

c. LXX lacks *of the Ammonites.*

d. For MT *bənôteyhā*, LXX implies *bāmôteyhā* ("its shrines").

e. LXX lacks this colon.

f. LXX lacks this colon. For MT *gədērôt*, Tg, Syr imply a form from *gādad* meaning "companies."

g. See the translation note on v. 1.

h. For MT *šôbēbâ*, Sym implies *šəbûyâ* ("exiled"); Vg has "charming" as in 6:2 (HUBP).

i. LXX has simply "said the Lord."

j. The *you* is now plural.

k. LXX lacks *a wanderer.*

l. See the translation note on 29:14.

m. MT has a marker here. LXX lacks v. 6. Different editions of the LXX have the messages concerning Ammon, Edom, Damascus, and Kedar/Hazor in different orders.

It is not surprising that Ammon, as another of Israel's neighbors, should appear in the messages about other nations. The Israelites knew they were related to the Ammonites as to the Moabites (Gen 19) and that they were not to have designs on their land, which Yahweh had given them (Deut 2). And as the Israelites knew that Ammon and Moab were related (again, see Gen 19), it is not surprising that Ammon should follow Moab in these messages. Like Moab, Ammon was involved in the political discussions related in Jer 27; like Moab, Ammon was a people Yahweh and Nebuchadrezzar used to seek to bring Judah to heel (2 Kgs 24:2); and like Moab, Ammon was a refuge for Judahites when Nebuchadrezzar invaded Judah (Jer 40:11; 41:10). Unlike Moab, Ammon was (allegedly) involved in intrigue in Judah after the invasion (Jer 40:14), but Israel's relationship with Ammon had not been fraught in an ongoing way like its relationship with Moab, which both makes the focus of this message surprising and helps explain its specifics.

The message has four sections:

v. 1	A double introduction and an accusatory question (two bicola)
v. 2	An introduction and a declaration of intent (a bicolon and a tricolon)
vv. 3–5	An exhortation to Ammon presupposing that the disaster is on its way (three bicola, a double bicolon, and two more bicola)
v. 6	A promise of restoration (prose)

Verses 1–2 and 3–5 could stand on their own and might be of separate origin, with v. 6 an added footnote.

1 After the curators' introduction to the message as a whole and the prophet's own introduction, the prophet asks a double rhetorical question. Jeremiah often uses this device to drive the addressees to think and to acknowledge they are at fault (e.g., 8:4–5, 19, 22), but in a context such as this one, it operates indirectly. In effect, it invites the Judahites who are the actual audience to ask what answer the Ammonites might give to these questions. The answer is less obvious than it might seem, and it might seem painful.[89] The area of Gad as an Israelite clan was across the Jordan, between the Jordan and Ammon itself. It included much of the area that had been subject to dispute between Moab and Israel. We have no information on when Ammon took the action described in v. 1b, but it would be plausible to link it with the Assyrian invasion of Ephraim in 734 (see 2 Kgs 15:29), which involved transporting people from the area east of the Jordan. This event would have given the Ammonites a chance to horn in on former Israelite territory, even before the more catastrophic events of 722.[90] After all, once the Gadites had been taken off by the Assyrians, as later happened to Ephraim as a whole, who are the *sons* who might be *entering into possession*? The implication of the first rhetorical question in this verse is thus ironic: it would be quite a statement of faith to think of Israel having sons who would again live in the Gad area. Is the further suggestion that Ammon ought have left it empty for when some Israelites come back? On the assumption that there are no valid answers to his questions, however, Yahweh has reason to take action against Ammon—which would (for instance) be a challenge to Judahites who were being invited to join in an alliance with the Ammonites. The language of possession and dispossession is the language regularly used of Israel's original arrival in the land, and the implication of the language is that Ammon is reversing that process. *Milcom*, the god of Ammon, was equivalent to Chemosh for the Moabites and Yahweh for the Israelites.[91] While we have some artifacts that refer to Milcom, we do not have any material analogous to the Mesha inscription that tells us how the Ammonites understood him, but we may assume that he was thought of in similar terms to Chemosh. Etymologically, the name Milcom is presumably related to the Semitic word for king. While the First Testament sometimes has the proper spelling Milcom (e.g., 2 Kgs 23:13) and sometimes uses the pejorative form Molech (with vowels suggesting "shameful"), here the name is vocalized *malkām*, which generates the meaning *their King*: hence the double translation above.

2 In redress for the Ammonites' taking over Gad's territory, then, Yahweh will bring about the destruction of the Ammonite capital and its *daughter-*

---

89. Lundbom, *Jeremiah 37–52*, 315.

90. C. W. Tyson alternatively suggests a link with events between 597 and 587; see *The Ammonites: Elites, Empires, and Sociopolitical Change (1000–500 BCE)*, LHBOTS 585 (London: T&T Clark, 2014), 120–21.

91. E. Puech, "Milcom," *DDD*, 575–77.

villages, and with "poetic justice"[92] Israel will take over its territory. The capital is Rabbah, which will be the site of Philadelphia in Greek and Roman times, one of the ten cities of the Decapolis, and in modern times the location of the Jordanian capital, Amman. The daughter-villages would be the communities not far away from the capital that lived in symbiotic relationship with it. The relatively small size of Ammon would mean that there were not as many self-contained towns spread over the country as there were in Moab; Ammon was more like Judah in its last decades, with its one city. Jeremiah does not name the agent of Ammon's promised destruction, we have no record of such an event, and the Israelites never repossessed the area. Calvin notes that this prophecy was not fulfilled "except under the kingdom of Christ";[93] it is neat to observe that crowds from the Decapolis followed Jesus (Matt 4:25).

3 We have already come across *Heshbon* as located in the far north of the area that had belonged to the Amorites and was then disputed between Moab and Israel; apparently it could also sometimes count as Ammonite territory.[94] We do not know the location of *Ai*, whose name is the same as that of the town whose story is told in Josh 7–8. It is always *hāʿay*, with the article, and the name resembles the Hebrew word for a ruin (ʿî), so perhaps some town's actual name has been reworked into this noun that promises its destiny, or perhaps the word refers to Rabbah itself. The survivors of its destruction are sardonically invited to *run to and fro* in panic *in the fences* or little stone walls of the villages—or the sheep pens. The reason is the same one as applied to Chemosh in 48:7. Jeremiah thus "demonstrated the idols' feebleness, because they too with the worshipers went away captive."[95]

4 The chiding and threatening of Ammon compare and contrast with the chiding and threatening of Moab. Ammon has reason to be proud of its *vales* that are *flowing* with milk and syrup like Israel's (e.g., 11:5; 32:22), as Moab has reason to be proud of its vineyards and orchards, but taking them for granted will turn out to be unwise. Ammon is like Israel, a *miss . . . who is turning* (31:22). In some sense, she is guilty for turning away from Yahweh and *relying on her stores* like Moab (48:7). Following on the brio of the implication that Ammon has turned away from Yahweh, it makes sense to assume that the treasures are again the artifacts associated with her faith. So the question *Who will come against me?* is a statement of her confidence in Milcom.

5 Yahweh has an answer to her rhetorical question, an answer that sardonically takes up her own words. "*Who will come against me?*" I'll show you

92. P. D. Miller, "Jeremiah," on the passage.

93. Calvin, *Jeremiah*, 5:70.

94. It is one indication that vv. 1–5 might be in origin a Moab prophecy; see E. A. Knauf, "Jeremia xlix 1–5: Ein zweites Moab-Orakel im Jeremia-Buch," *VT* 42 (1992): 124–28.

95. Theodoret, *Ermeneia*, PG 81:728.

who or what will come against you. Again, Yahweh talks about *terror* (cf. 48:43–44). He semi-articulates who are the agents he will use in bringing calamity—people like the Moabites themselves to the south, the Arameans to the north, and the desert peoples to the east, of whom this chapter will go on to speak. The Ammonites too will *scatter* in all directions, like Judah (40:12; 43:5). But whereas Yahweh will *collect* the Judahites (23:3; 29:14; 31:8, 10; 32:37), no one will collect the Ammonite *wanderer*.

6 Which would be a devastating conclusion were it not for the actual conclusion, similar to Moab's (48:47). "Both Ammon's immediate fate (devastation) and Ammon's long-term destiny (well-being) . . . are in the hands of Yahweh."[96] In the message about Ammon, Jeremiah sounds especially like Hananiah,[97] but this footnote subverts that impression. Addressed to the Judahites, it reminds them not to get proud, as if they will be the only ones who get to be restored.[98]

4. Edom (49:7–22 [LXX 29:8–23 or 30:1–16])

7 Regarding Edom.

Yahweh of Armies has said this.

Is there no good sense in Teman anymore,
*   has counsel perished from insightful people,* [a]
*   has their good sense gone bad?* [b]
8 Take flight, be turned back, go deep to live, [c]
*   people who live in Dedan.*
Because the doom of Esau [d]
*   I am letting come* [e] *upon him, the time when I am attending to him.* [f]
9 If grape-pickers came to you,
*   they wouldn't let gleanings remain.*
If robbers in the night—
*   they'd devastate what they needed.* [g]
10 Because I myself am stripping Esau,
*   exposing his hiding places,*
*   and should he hide,* [h] *he will not be able to.*
His offspring is being destroyed,

96. Brueggemann, *Jeremiah 26–52*, 250.
97. W. H. Schmidt, *Jeremia*, 2:305.
98. Theodoret, *Ermeneia*, PG 81:728.

his relatives and his neighbors—and there will be none of him.
[11]*Abandon your orphans, I will keep them alive,*
 and your widows—they can rely on me.[i]

[12]*Because Yahweh has said this:*

There, people for whom there has been no decision that they should drink the chalice will actually drink it. And you are one who will actually be free of guilt? You will not be free of guilt. Rather you will actually drink.[j] [13]*Because by myself I am swearing*[k] *(Yahweh's affirmation) that a desolation, an object of reviling, a desert,*[l] *and a form of slighting is what Bozrah will become. And all its towns— they will become ruins for all time.*

[14]*A message from Yahweh I have heard,*
 and an envoy sent among the nations:
Collect together and come against it,
 set to for battle!
[15]*Because there, least among the nations I am making you,*
 most despised among humanity.
[16]*Your dreadfulness!—it has deceived you,*
 the arrogance of your mind.
You who stay in the hides in the cliff,
 who seize the height of the hill:
Because you have put your nest high, like the eagle—
 from there I will get you down (Yahweh's affirmation).[m]

[17]*So Edom will become a desolation—*
 everyone who passes by it will be desolate.
He will whistle at all its wounds,[n]
  [18]*as at the overturning of Sodom and Gomorrah and its neighbors*
   (Yahweh has said).
No one will live there,
 no human being will reside in it.[o]
[19]*There, it will be as when a lion goes up*
 from the Jordan swell into a permanent habitat.
Because I intend to hustle him[p] *out of it,*
 and whoever is chosen for it I will appoint.
Because who is like me,
 who summons me?
Who on earth is the shepherd
 who can stand before me?[q]

²⁰*Therefore listen to Yahweh's counsel,*
  which he has determined for Edom,
*His intentions, which he has devised*ʳ
  for the people who live in Teman.
*If the flock's boys don't drag them away,*ˢ
  if their habitat isn't desolate at them . . . ᵗ
²¹*At the sound of their fall, the earth is shaking,*
  *an outcry—at the Sea of Reeds its sound is making itself heard.*ᵘ
²²*There, like an eagle one will go up,*
  *he will soar and spread his wings against Bozrah.*ᵛ
The heart of Edom's strong men will become
  on that day
  *like the heart of a woman in labor.*ʷ

a. Vg, Tg, Aq, Sym "sons" understandably derives *bānîm* from *bēn* rather than from *bîn*. No doubt Judahite children were "subjected to endless moralistic injunctions employing this word-play" (Holladay, *Commentary on Jeremiah*, 2:375).

b. The line's opening interrogative also applies to the second and third cola.

c. For MT's imperative verbs, Aq implies *qatal*; cf. Sym for the third verb.

d. For *'ēśāw*, LXX "he made" implies *'āśâ*.

e. The *qatal* verb is declarative/performative—a speech act (see 1:5 and the translation note on it); so also in vv. 10, 13, 15.

f. The further declarative/performative verb depends on the construct noun (GK 130d).

g. For MT *hišḥîtû dayyām*, LXX "they will place their hand" implies *yāśîtû yādām*.

h. I take *wənehbâ* as qatal and as hypothetical (see the general discussion in *TTH* 136–55, esp. 155); or it might be a participle ("hiding, he will not be able").

i. MT has a section marker here. Tg has Yahweh addressing Israel in this line.

j. LXX has a shorter version of this verse; three times an infinitive precedes a finite verb, underlining the point.

k. See the translation note on v. 8; and on Yahweh's swearing, see the commentary on 22:5.

l. LXX lacks *a desert*.

m. LXX lacks *(Yahweh's affirmation)*.

n. V. 17b repeats from 19:8; v. 18a will repeat in a variant form in 50:40.

o. V. 18 overlaps with Isa 13:19–20.

p. Lit. "I intend to be speedy, run him" (the first verb is cohortative).

q. MTᴸ has a section marker here.

r. *Counsel* is *'ēṣâ* and *determined* is *yā'aṣ*; then, *intention* is *maḥăšābâ* and *devised* is *ḥāšab*.

s. LXX suggests taking the verb impersonally: "if people do not drag them away, the little ones of the flock"; contrast Vg.

t. On this form of oath, see the translation note on 15:11.

u. Verses 19–21 will reappear in a slightly different form as 50:44–46; for the comparison, see the commentary there. The verbs are anticipatory: see translation note c on 50:3.

v. For *boṣrâ*, LXX "its fortresses" implies *mibṣārehā*.

w. MT has a marker here.

The unit has five sections with an introduction.

v. 7a	Introduction
vv. 7b–11	An exhortation to Edom to have the good sense to run for its life (an introduction; a tricolon and four bicola; a resumptive tricolon and two bicola)
vv. 12–13	An introduction and an oath to make Edom drink the chalice (prose)
vv. 14–16	A testimony to having heard Yahweh commissioning Edom's attackers (two linked bicola, two self-contained bicola, and two more linked bicola)
vv. 17–19	Yahweh's declaration about how he will act against Edom (seven bicola)
vv. 20–22	An exhortation to unnamed listeners to listen to Yahweh's plans (two linked bicola, three self-contained bicola, and a closing tricolon)

A message about Edom completes the treatment of Judah's eastern neighbors; as Ammon lies north of Moab, Edom lies south, and thus south and southeast of the Dead Sea and of Judah. The greater length of the Edom unit compared with the Ammon unit reflects Edom's greater importance to Judah, especially in the context of its moving in on land in southern Judah beginning in the sixth century. Further, Israel knew the Edomites as even closer relatives than the Moabites and Ammonites—their descent goes back to Jacob's brother Esau (v. 8).[99] And Edom had sometimes been allied with Israel or under Israel's sovereignty (see 2 Sam 8; 2 Kgs 3; 8). Like Moab and Ammon, Edom appears in the consultations in Jer 27 and becomes a refuge for Judahites at the time of the Babylonian invasion. Like the Moab chapter, the Edom unit has close points of contact with another prophetic text—in this case the Edom prophecy in Obadiah.

Jer 49	**Obadiah**
[9]If grape-pickers came to you,	[5]If robbers came to you,
they wouldn't let gleanings remain.	if plunderers in the night,
If robbers in the night—	how you are silenced—
they'd devastate what they needed.	they'd rob what they needed,
	wouldn't they?
	If grape-pickers came to you,

99. See L. Haney, "Yhwh the God of Israel . . . and of Edom?" in Goldingay, *Uprooting and Planting*, 78–115.

883

they wouldn't let gleanings remain,
would they?[100]

14A message from Yahweh I have heard,

and an envoy sent among the nations:

Collect together and come against it; set off for battle!

15Because there, least among the nations

I am making you,

most despised among humanity.

16Your dreadfulness! It has deceived you—

the arrogance of your mind.

You who stay in the hides in the cliff,

who seize the height of the hill:

saying inside, "Who can get me down to earth?"

Because you have put your nest high, like the eagle—

from there I will get you down (Yahweh's affirmation).

1A message—we have heard from Yahweh,

and an envoy sent among the nations:

Set off; let us set off against it for battle!

2Because there, least among the nations

I am making you;

you will be most despised among humanity.

3The arrogance of your mind,

it has deceived you.

You who stay in the hides in the cliff,

the height of the hill,

4if you make it high like the eagle,

if your nest is set among the stars,

from there I will get you down (Yahweh's affirmation).

Again, one prophecy may be dependent on the other or they may be mutually dependent on an earlier scroll or on oral material. Alongside the detailed differences, the major dissimilarity is that Obadiah emphasizes Edom's guilt for its violence to Israel, for which Yahweh will take redress, whereas Jer 49 makes no mention of this motif. Insofar as there is a basis for Yahweh's action in Jer 49, it is simply Edom's self-confidence. This difference suggests that Jer 49 might come from before 587 whereas Obadiah comes from after 587. It seems more likely that Obadiah added the motif of redress than that Jeremiah removed it.

All five sections could have been messages delivered in Jerusalem on different occasions, though the *waw*-consecutive opening vv. 17–19 makes a link with vv. 14–16 that might be original, and the *therefore* opening vv. 20–22 makes a link with vv. 17–19 that might be original.

100. The Obadiah version of this section is thus longer than the Jeremiah version, and it has two of the cola as rhetorical questions instead of statements, but the substance is the same.

7–8 After the curators' introduction to the unit as a whole and the prophet's introduction to vv. 7–11, Jeremiah again begins with a rhetorical question—a triple question, and one that piques the audience's curiosity. It perhaps presupposes that the Edomites had a reputation for being smart (Job and his friends came from there), Teman "happily being a kinde of University, but now there were none wise enough to save their City."[101] Their insight is "soon to be conspicuous by its absence."[102] The insight that would be appropriate in the context is the political and diplomatic kind that is the object of critique elsewhere in the Prophets and will prove useless in a context where Yahweh is deciding what is going to happen.[103] So how do the Edomites give the impression of having lost their senses? Because they ought to be running for their lives, and they are not. Three more or less synonymous imperatives match the three more or less synonymous questions. The third has a hint of irony—going deep suggests having insight.[104] The three verbs raise more questions for the audience. Why will good sense mean taking flight? Because there is disaster on the way for Edom, brought about by Yahweh and constituting the moment when Yahweh will *attend to him*; it will not be friendly attention. *Teman* is an area within Edom (Job's friend Eliphaz was a Temanite); we do not know its exact location, though the parallelism in Amos 1:12 with Bozrah, in the north of Edom, may imply that Teman was in the north. *Dedan* was to the south, and could thus pair with Teman (Ezek 25:13), symbolizing Edom's southern extent. It was actually in Arabia (Isa 21:13), and here the reference may be to Dedanite caravans that would be wise to get back home.[105]

9–11 Imagine a couple of forms of theft. Imagine people stealing your grape harvest. When people harvest their grapes, they are supposed to leave some for needy people; thieving grape-pickers don't operate that way. Robbers will devastate everything to get what they want. Yahweh intends to operate the same way toward Edom. With the self-contradiction that doesn't bother Jeremiah's rhetoric, after urging the Edomites to flee, Yahweh tells them it will be no use. With further self-contradiction, he tells them he will annihilate the entire people, including their offspring, so there will be no future for the nation; then he notes that there will therefore be no relatives and neighbors to look after children and widows, but it's okay, because he will look after them. God is, after all, the father of orphans and defender of widows (Ps 68:5[6]).[106]

---

101. Mayer, *Commentary*, 446.

102. Allen, *Jeremiah*, 496.

103. McKane, *Jeremiah*, 2:1215.

104. E. Assis, *Identity in Conflict: The Struggle between Esau and Jacob, Edom and Israel*, Siphrut 19 (Winona Lake, IN: Eisenbrauns, 2016), 95–96.

105. Holladay, *Commentary on Jeremiah*, 2:375.

106. J. Bugenhagen, *In Ieremiam*, on the passage, as quoted in Tyler, *Jeremiah*, 426.

Possibly the offer is snide, but if so, Yahweh leaves himself open to being taken seriously; it will be no use his saying, "I didn't mean it."

12–13 In many contexts, peoples that don't deserve calamity do experience it. Among them would be some of Nebuchadrezzar's victims (Judah of course does not count as one of them; they deserve it, all right). While some of Nebuchadrezzar's actions linked with his being Yahweh's servant and meant he was unconsciously implementing Yahweh's will, some of them are solely him implementing his own decisions and they are simply tolerated by Yahweh. But Edom cannot expect to escape scot-free. By implication, it deserves the calamity coming to it, though for Edom there is even less indication of the reasons than there was for Moab or Ammon, and much less indication than in Obadiah with its stress on the wrong Edom has done to Judah. The *chalice* is the symbol from 25:15–29, and the threat of being made into *a desolation, an object of reviling, a desert, and a form of slighting* is a variant on threats that apply there to other nations and to Judah (25:9, 18) and elsewhere simply to Judah (29:18; 42:18; 44:12). *Bozrah*, just southeast of the Dead Sea (to be distinguished from the Moabite Bozrah in 48:24), was the Edomite capital.

14–16 The *message* Jeremiah hears is not one addressed to him but one he overhears, a message to unnamed warriors—either supernatural or human. The subsection's point is again to announce a threat to Edom that Judah thereby hears about, another threat to reduce Edom to nothing. Here alone there comes a hint of the reason for the action. Edom's *dreadfulness*, its frightening, horrific nature, consists in the *arrogance of* its *mind*, which has *deceived* it. It thought it had so much insight and good sense and could determine its own destiny. It thought it was safe, and its physical location encouraged that assumption. It's not so. The fault Yahweh finds is similar to the one found in Moab.

17–18 Actually, Edom will experience a desolation matched by the desolation it brings into the minds of people appalled by the sight of it. Edom will end up like *Sodom and Gomorrah* (see the commentary on 23:14): it will have been so devastated that no one can live there. Sodom and Gomorrah are on the edge of Edomite territory, or even within the area Edom now occupies, so geographically the location of the comparison is especially apposite.[107] The horrified *whistle* of these people passing by is again an aspect of the general fate of the nations and of other peoples (25:9, 18) and a match for the whistle at Judah's fate (19:8; 29:18).

19 There were few permanent settlements within striking distance of the *Jordan swell* (see the commentary on 12:5). So the image of a raid by a *lion* is a nightmare one, a picture of something people could believe would never

---

107. Boadt, *Jeremiah 26–52*, 134–35.

happen. The *habitat* (*nāweh*) might be the place where sheep lived, the place where shepherds lived, or the place where human beings lived (see the commentary on 10:25; 25:30): on any understanding, the image is scary. A lion is a recurrent image for a devastating, irresistible attacker, and Tg assumes it stands for a military commander here. Only rarely is it a straight image for Yahweh. But what follows suggests this reference in v. 19. To be more literal, Yahweh will *hustle* Edom out of its homestead and give it to anyone he cares to. It will be another expression of poetic justice and a comforting image for Judahites if the Edomites were already hustling them out of their land in southern Judah. And after he takes action, no one *summons* him (*yāʿad hiphil*): that is, no one can issue him with a date for a court appearance to explain himself. To revert to the lion image, no *shepherd* is going to be able to stop *me* having my way with the sheep.

20-21 The *therefore* is not a link that marks the transition from indictment to sentence but the introduction to an alternative spelling out of the threats that have preceded. Again and again in the message about Edom, Yahweh keeps reiterating his threat of violent destruction. "Jeremiah's prophecy against the Edomites is filled with repetition: of images, of antagonists, of forms of destruction, even of the wording of entire verses" (which is a trait it shares with Jer 50 and Obadiah) in a way that generates the opposite of pleasure—"counterpleasure."[108] In substance, this final subsection connects with the opening one in picking up the word *counsel*. These two references form a frame around vv. 7–22. All that we have been reading in vv. 7–22 has been the counsel or plan that Yahweh has *determined* for Edom—or against Edom. After that statement about Yahweh's counsel and his *intentions*, Jeremiah reverts to the shepherd imagery of v. 19, though he takes it in a new direction. It will require only the most junior of shepherd boys to drag away the corpses of the Edomite "sheep," whose *habitat* will be appalled at what has happened to them at the "hands" of the lion. One might then think that it will be the "land" of Edom that will *shake* at *the sound of their fall*, but the parallelism suggests that it is *the earth* (*hāʾāreṣ*) that will do so. The *sound* will be heard as far away as Egypt.

22 Thus Edom's fate will parallel Moab's (see 48:40-41). In the context of vv. 17–19, one might also take the eagle to be Yahweh, but in that previous application of this image to Moab, it was the unnamed human attacker. Is it significant that Yahweh promises no restoration for Edom, such as he did for Moab and Ammon?[109] It fits the pattern of First Testaments threats about Edom (Ezek 25:12–14; 35; Joel 3:19; Amos 1:11–12; Obad). It is therefore neat

---

108. R. Graybill, "Jeremiah, Sade, and Repetition as Counterpleasure in the Oracle against Edom," in Holt and H. C. P. Kim, *Concerning the Nations*, 128–29.

109. So Calvin, *Jeremiah*, 5:112–13.

to recall the promise about the widows and orphans, and to recall that the Idumeans converted to Judaism[110] and that crowds of them came to Jesus (Mark 3:7–8).

5. *Damascus (49:23–27 [LXX 30:12–16 or 29–33])*

²³*Regarding Damascus.*

Hamath is shamed, and Arpad,
  because it is bad news that they have heard.
They have dissolved—in the sea,ᵃ there is anxiety,
  it cannot be quiet.
²⁴*Damascus has become weak,*
  it has turned its face to flee.
Panic—it has grasped hold of it;
  pressure and contractions—it has seized her like a woman giving birth.ᵇ
²⁵*How has the praiseworthy city notᶜ been abandoned,*
  the town I have celebrated?ᵈ
²⁶*Therefore its young men will fall in its squares,*
  all its men of battle will be stillᵉ
  on that dayᶠ (an affirmation of Yahweh of Armies).ᵍ
²⁷*I will set fire to the walls of Damascusʰ*
  and it will consume the fortresses of Ben-hadad.ⁱ

a. LXX lacks *in the sea*. Tg "like people who go down to the sea" implies *ka* for MT *ba*, an easier reading.
b. LXX lacks this colon.
c. Vg lacks *not*.
d. Lit. "the town of my celebration"; LXX, Aq, Sym, Th, Tg, Vg lack "my."
e. See the translation note on 6:2.
f. LXX lacks *on that day*.
g. LXX lacks *of Armies*. This verse recurs in a slightly variant form in 50:30.
h. This colon corresponds to Amos 1:14a, except for the change in the city's name.
i. MT has a marker here. This colon corresponds to Amos 1:4b.

Damascus was the most important city in Aram (Syria), a significant neighbor of Ephraim but not of Judah. Among the subjects of the messages in Jer

---

110. Josephus's account (*Jewish Antiquities* 13.9.1) suggests forced conversion; but see, e.g., the discussion in A. Kasher, *Jews, Idumaeans, and Ancient Arabs: Relations of the Jews in Eretz-Israel with the Nations of the Frontier and the Desert During the Hellenistic and Roman Era (332 BCE – 70 CE)*, Texte und Studien zum Antiken Judentum 18 (Tübingen: Mohr Siebeck, 1988), 44–78.

49–51, Aram alone did not appear in Jer 25. Jeremiah 35:11 referred to the Rechabites' observation that Aramean forces joined with the Babylonian forces putting pressure on Judah in about 600 (cf. 2 Kgs 24:2).

After the introduction, the message comprises five bicola, then a resumptive tricolon and one more bicolon.

23 Hamath is a major city-state in northern Syria, and Arpad is one in the far north; the two come as a pair elsewhere (e.g., Isa 10:9). The picture of these northern cities hearing bad news raises suspense as we wait to hear what the bad news is and thus to discover how they are *shamed*. It is evidently really bad news: the two cities have *dissolved*, or melted or gone soft. The verb is usually a metaphor; literally, it can refer to the softening of the ground by rain. In the terms of a contradictory metaphor, the cities are churned up like the sea, and there is no quieting of their disturbed state.

24 It transpires that the same is true of the leading Aramean city, in the southwest ("capital" is probably not the right term, since it is not clear that Aram was one political unit). Mention of Hamath and Arpad simply prepares the way for the message's real subject.[111] It actually concerns Damascus, as was indicated by the introduction, but the introduction perhaps comes from the curators, and people in Jerusalem hearing the prophet declaim the message would have had to wait to discover its reference. The alarm in Damascus is the cause of the northern cities' shame; it is because "Damascus has lost its nerve" that "Hamad and Arpad are demoralized."[112] The chief city (and thus by implication the nation as a whole) *has become weak* and therefore incapable of resisting an attacker, and it is inclined to *flee*. Its people are inclined to abandon it. They are in that state of panic that can overcome a woman who is about to have a baby and who knows it may be the death of her. In Jeremiah's imagination, at least, the three cities' inhabitants know that invasion and disaster are imminent. If we read the prophecy in light of the reference in v. 28a, we might guess that it relates to Nebuchadrezzar's attack on Aram just before his invasion of Judah in 597.

25 It is regrettable that they have not *abandoned* the city. Are the descriptions of it part of the explanation? It is *the praiseworthy city*, one that has been a source of admiration, "the chief city of Syria, so pleasantly situated, so rich and luxurious, that one compares it to Corinth or Ephesus."[113] It was "a fruitful oasis on the edges of the Syrian wilderness."[114] It's the kind of description

---

111. Weiser, *Jeremia*, 2:419.
112. McKane, *Jeremiah*, 2:1230–31.
113. Trapp, *Commentary*, on the passage.
114. P. D. Miller, "Jeremiah," 357 (English updated).

that Judahites might give of Jerusalem.[115] Who is the *I* who so admires the city? The surprising clarification will come in v. 27. It might mean that Yahweh is here being compassionate, or that he is being sarcastic so that the line is a "taunt";[116] the line raises similar questions to the ones raised by v. 11.[117]

26–27 It would have been wise to abandon the city, because staying will mean its defenders lose their lives when the calamity overtakes it. The message gives no hint regarding the human agent of any siege or of setting fire to the city, the frequent concomitant of siege and capture. Its focus is that behind any human agent will be Yahweh, which matches the additional note that turns v. 26 into a tricolon by declaring that the event will take place *on that day* (cf. 46:10; see the commentary there). The dynamic parallels the pattern in the Moab and Edom messages (48:41; 49:22) whereby that extra phrase forms part of the lines that bring the message to a close. Yahweh gives no hint of the reasons for his action. The message thus compares and contrasts with Amos 1:4 and 14. While the wording in v. 27 corresponds to those verses, the context there does give reasons for Yahweh's action. As is characteristic of Jer 46–51, this announcement focuses on the fact, not the explanation. The name *Ben-hadad* designates the king as a son of the god Hadad. It is the name or title of a number of Syrian kings in the First Testament (it was a different Syrian king in Amos's day).The reference here is not to a particular individual king but to whoever is king at the time, to "the ruling house in Damascus."[118]

6. Kedar and Hazor (49:28–33 [LXX 30:6–11 or 23–28])

[28]*Regarding Kedar and regarding the Hazor kingdoms,*[a] *which Nebuchadrezzar King of Babylon struck down.*

Yahweh has said this.

Set to, go up to Kedar,
   destroy the Easterners![b]
[29]*Their tents and their flock they will get,*
   their tent cloths and all their things.
Their camels they will take off for themselves,
   and they will call out about them,
   "All around is terror!"

115. McKane, *Jeremiah* 2:1234.
116. Keown, Scalise, and Smothers, *Jeremiah 26–52*, 334.
117. *CTAT*, 2:812.
118. Holladay, *Commentary on Jeremiah*, 2:381.

³⁰ *Take flight, flee,* ^c
go deep to live, you who live in Hazor (Yahweh's affirmation).
Because Nebuchadrezzar ^d *King of Babylon*
  has determined counsel against you;
  he has devised an intention against them. ^e

³¹ *Set to, go up, to a nation at peace,*
  living in confidence (Yahweh's declaration). ^f
It has no gateways and no bars—
  alone they dwell.
³² *Their camels will become plunder,*
  their horde of livestock, spoil.
I will scatter to every wind the people clipped at the forehead,
  from all its sides I will let their disaster come (Yahweh's affirmation).

³³ *Hazor will become an abode of jackals,*
  a desolation for all time.
No individual will live there,
  no human being will reside in it. ^g

    a. For MT *mamləkôt ḥāṣôr*, LXX "courtyard queen" implies *malkat ḥāṣēr*; "courtyard" recurs in LXX in vv. 30, 33.
    b. The verbs are plural.
    c. LXX lacks *flee*.
    d. LXX lacks *Nebuchadrezzar*.
    e. The *qere 'ălêkem* ("against you") looks an easier reading than the *'ălêhem* implied by the *ketiv*.
    f. LXX lacks *(Yahweh's declaration)*.
    g. MT has a section marker here.

As Aram was a major group of city-states to the north of Judah, Kedar was a major group of tribes in the northern Arabian Desert, to the east of Judah, Edom, Moab, Ammon, and Aram. Kedar and its desert neighbors feature in Assyrian and Babylonian sources—"quite often, in fact, because they were attacked and despoiled by a succession of Assyrian and Babylonian armies."[119] Here, the message about them focuses on "the idiosyncracies of the tribes' seminomadic lifestyle."[120] Once again, Yahweh does not say why he issues the destructive commission.

    119. Lundbom, *Jeremiah 37–52*, 353; he refers to *ANET*, 284, 286, 291–92, 297–301, which record the Assyrian campaigns against and plundering of tribes in Arabia.
    120. Allen, *Jeremiah*, 500.

After the double introduction, the unit about Kedar comprises two parallel messages, perhaps originally separate.

vv. 28–29 A commission to attack Kedar and an anticipation of its reaction (two bicola and a tricolon)

v. 30 An exhortation to the Kedarites to flee (a bicolon and a tricolon)

vv. 31–32 Another commission to the attackers and another anticipation (four bicola)

v. 33 A declaration about what will result (two bicola)

Both messages (or both parts of the message) thus begin with a bidding to unnamed agents to *set to* and *go up* against a people, and both then identify the initiator of the action—Nebuchadrezzar in the first, Yahweh in the second. In combination, the two units suggest the two levels of decision-making and initiative involved in what happens.[121]

28a While Kedar is familiar as the name of a group of tribes, *Hazor kingdoms* is more puzzling. There are several places called Hazor in Canaan; the background to the multiplicity is the name's link with *ḥāṣēr*, meaning enclosure, courtyard, or settlement. Perhaps, then, the Hazor kingdoms are a collection of more settled Arabian tribes associated with Kedar, or a subset of it, each with its own king. The Babylonian Chronicle records Nebuchadrezzar's attack on Arab tribes and his taking plunder during the year before his invasion of Judah in 597.[122]

28b–29 The message begins by commissioning some people to undertake such an attack; without the curators' introduction, once again a Judahite audience would not know who is addressed. *Easterners* is a general-purpose First Testament name for the peoples east (and northeast and southeast) of Canaan, peoples in Arabia and Mesopotamia, so it works in the parallelism. All Kedarites are easterners, though not all easterners are Kedarites. While one can imagine the attackers making off with the things mentioned in v. 29, if that were its point, one might expect v. 29 to continue to address them, as "you." It is more straightforward to take the "they" to refer to the attackers' victims. As in the Damascus message, Jeremiah imagines them aware of their danger and needing to take evasive action. They are in a state of panic: Jeremiah puts the familiar cry *all around is terror* onto their lips (see 6:25; 20:3, 10; 46:5). But they are not pictured as paralyzed like the Arameans. Hearing

---

121. So P. D. Miller, "Jeremiah," on the passage.
122. Grayson, *Chronicles*, 101; *ANET*, 564.

of an invading force's approach, they will pack up their homes and hightail it, perhaps thinking they have more chance of escaping Nebuchadrezzar than more settled peoples have.

30 The second part of this poetic unit encourages them to do so. The explanation reuses the formulations of vv. 8, 20, applying them now to Nebuchadrezzar's counsel and intentions rather than Yahweh's. Metaphorically, the Hazorites need to dig deep to find a hiding place. There is again some contradiction in Yahweh's commissioning attackers and also bidding their potential victims to flee, but as usual the tension works rhetorically to underline the point to the audience—both commands draw attention to the calamity that threatens.

31 Yahweh's second commission takes rather cynical form. The nomadic Kedarites aren't the kind of peoples who fight to develop a significant empire, like Assyrians or Babylonians. They keep to themselves, live away from the habitat of the great civilizations, and expect to be able to take their security for granted. They don't live in towns with gates and bars with which the gates can be kept firmly shut. The description has to presuppose that they have forgotten the number of occasions when imperial forces have attacked them and plundered them.

32-33 Their undefended settlements will be a pushover. Unless they manage to take the evasive action of which v. 29 spoke, they, their camels, and their livestock will be easy prey. There will be some poetic justice in what happens if they gained much of their livestock from plundering (Judg 6:1-6).[123] The description *clipped at the forehead* recurs from 9:26(25); 25:23. Dramatically, almost at the end of the message, suddenly Yahweh's *I* makes an appearance, as it did at the end of the Damascus message. Yahweh is not only the distanced commissioner of this action but the scatterer of unprotected nomads, as there he was the one who set on fire the fortifications of city-dwellers. The description of the consequences again applies to this other people the fate that hangs over Judah (e.g., 10:22; 34:22) as well as Edom (49:18) and Babylon (50:39-40).

7. Elam (49:34-39 [LXX 25:14-19])

[34]*What came as Yahweh's word*[a] *to Jeremiah the prophet regarding Elam at the beginning of the reign of Zedekiah King of Judah.*[b]
   [35]*Yahweh of Armies has said this.*
   Here am I, breaking the bow of Elam, the kernel of its strength. [36]*I will let come to Elam four winds from the four corners of the heavens. I will scatter*

123. Lundbom, *Jeremiah 37-52*, 354.

them to all these winds; the nation will not exist where Elam's fugitives do not come. [37]*I will break Elam down before their enemies, before the people who seek their life, and I will let a dire fate come upon them, my angry blazing (Yahweh's affirmation).*[c] *I will send off the sword after them until I have finished them off.*[d] [38]*And I will put my throne in Elam and obliterate from there king and officials (Yahweh's affirmation).* [39]*But in the aftermath of the time I will bring about the restoration of Elam (Yahweh's affirmation).*[e]

a. On this jerky form of the words, see the translation note on 14:1.

b. LXX has the phrase about Zedekiah in the last line of the Elam unit.

c. LXX lacks *(Yahweh's affirmation)* here and in the next verse.

d. One might read LXX's infinitive as distancing Yahweh from the action and suggesting a more benign understanding of God; see H.-J. Stipp's discussion of the possible difference between the concept of God in MT and LXX in Jeremiah ("Gottesbildfragen in den Lesartendifferenzen zwischen dem masoretischen und dem alexandrinischen Text des Jeremiabuches," in *Text-Critical and Hermeneutical Studies in the Septuagint*, ed. J. Cook and H.-J. Stipp, VTSup 157 [Leiden: Brill, 2012], 242).

e. MT has a marker here.

Before coming to Babylon, Jeremiah refers in a prose message to a third, further-away power, making a trio with Aram and Kedar that parallels the Moab-Ammon-Edom trio. Elam was beyond even Babylon, east of the Persian Gulf, between Babylon and Persia, in the southwestern part of modern Iran. It was thus the furthest away of the peoples covered by Jer 46–51. It had been an important civilization in earlier millennia, though its great days were past. Like the Kedarites, the Elamites were often in conflict with the Assyrians, and they sometimes allied with Babylon in resisting Assyrian power, but the decline of Assyria saw them falling under Median hegemony. There are no specifics in this message about Elam, and once again no reasons for Yahweh's action. Elam "stands at the remotest edge of the prophet's knowledge";[124] all he can do is use its name (five times). But the geographical dynamic suggests an assertion that Yahweh is lord of the nations, even ones so far away and unrelated to Judah.[125] The Kedar/Hazor and Elam messages are the clearest indications that these messages do not concern matters that Judah might be interested in. Yahweh is a bigger God with a bigger horizon than Judahites might think. The messages parallel the challenges to the heavens and the earth to worship Yahweh; he claims a universal authority whether or not people recognize it. And "the claim that is inherent in these oracles concerning other nations, oracles that are often addressed quite directly to them, is all the more radical if they were not spoken in their presence."[126]

124. Holladay, *Commentary on Jeremiah*, 2:387.

125. Cf. H. G. L. Peels, "God's Throne in Elam," *OTS* 44 (2000): 216–29.

126. P. D. Miller, "Jeremiah," in his reflections on Jer 46–51.

34 The introduction locates the message in the same general period as vv. 28–33, though slightly later. The Babylonian Chronicle tells of a campaign by Nebuchadrezzar in about 595 in which an attack on Elam would fit.[127]

35–39 The Elamites' reputation as bowmen recurs from Isa 22:6. But the distinctive feature of the message is the focus on Yahweh's action, expressed in a series of first-person verbs:

- I am breaking (v. 35): Elam's bow is strong, but not strong enough.
- I will let come (v. 36): the four winds will do their work, but they are Yahweh's agents.
- I will scatter (v. 36): the destinations cannot be calculated or limited.
- I will break down (v. 37): their enemies will do their work, but they implement Yahweh's will.
- I will let come (v. 37): a dire fate issues from Yahweh's angry blazing.
- I will send off (v. 37): even the reference to the sword mentions no human warrior.
- I will put (v. 38): the phrase otherwise applies only to Nebuchadrezzar in 43:10 (but see 52:32).
- I will obliterate (v. 38): this action makes it possible for Yahweh to take charge.
- But I will bring about (v. 39): suddenly the *I* goes from negative to positive.

C. PART 5C: BABYLON, AND THREE CONCLUSIONS (50:1–51:64)

As it is not surprising that the Jeremiah scroll eventually includes a set of messages concerning other nations, so it is not surprising that this set of messages comes to a climax with Babylon, the great power in Jeremiah's time that brought about the fall of Jerusalem. The messages come in two chapters of announcements concerning Babylon's own fall and associated announcements promising restoration for Israel.[128] Nor is it surprising that the Babylon material is so substantial, comprising a compilation of such material that is almost as extensive as the messages relating to all the rest of the nations that are covered by Jer 46–49. With these messages about Babylon, the Jeremiah scroll comes to a climax with its assertion of the preem-

---

127. Grayson, *Chronicles*, 102; see further Lundbom, *Jeremiah 37–52*, 362.

128. M. K. Chae emphasizes the hopeful aspect to the arrangement ("Redactional Intentions of MT Jeremiah Concerning the Oracles against the Nations," *JBL* 134 [2015]: 577–93).

inence of Yahweh over the world power.[129] "The very size of this collection shows the special nature of Babylon among the nations. This is *the* empire; it cannot be treated like just another nation."[130] Commentators belonging to imperial nations such as Britain or the United States may dislike what might seem the chapters' "obsessional antagonism towards the national enemy."[131] But the chapters might seem different when read through the eyes of people from Kenya in the 1950s or Nicaragua in the 1980s. "Revenge fantasies"—in this case, imagining Yahweh taking redress—can be a strategy for survival.[132]

The material on Babylon is followed by a brief conclusion to the messages about other nations, pairing with the introduction to them in 46:1 (51:58b), a coda about a last act of Jeremiah in relation to Babylon (51:59–64a), and a conclusion to Jeremiah's message as a whole (51:64b).

1. Introduction (50:1 [LXX 27:1])

[1]*The word that Yahweh spoke regarding Babylon, regarding the country of Chaldea,*[a] *by means of Jeremiah the prophet.*[b]

a. *Kaśdîm* can refer both to Chaldeans and to Chaldea; in phrases such as "the country of" and "the people who live in," I take it to refer to Chaldea (cf. expressions such as "country of Judah," "country of Egypt"). See further the translation note and commentary on 21:4.
b. LXX has a much shorter version of the verse.

This opening to the chapters rather suggests that they come from Jeremiah himself, an impression confirmed and developed in the story that follows (51:59–64). As is the case with the Jeremiah scroll as a whole (see the discussion "Unity of Composition" in the introduction to this commentary, pp. 5–26), there are several ways one might interpret this impression.

- Is it a fiction? Did all the material come from prophets and scribes other than and later than Jeremiah?[133] I have no theological objection to this suggestion, given that God can inspire fiction, but I find it somehow implausible.
- Does it indicate that every message in the chapters came from Jere-

129. Fischer, *Jeremia*, 2:630.
130. Pixley, *Jeremiah*, 144.
131. R. P. Carroll, *Jeremiah*, OTL, 814.
132. A. Kalmanofsky, "'As She Did, Do to Her': Jeremiah's OAN as Revenge Fantasies," in Mein, Holt, and H. C. P. Kim, *Concerning the Nations*, 109–27; but H. S. Pyper critiques the chapters' implicitly quietist stance in "Postcolonialism and Propaganda in Jeremiah's Oracles against the Nations," in Mein, Holt, and H. C. P. Kim, *Concerning the Nations*, 145–57.
133. See, e.g., Rudolph, *Jeremia*, 297–99.

miah himself? It may be so, but there would then be a contrast with the way the Scriptures usually work. For instance, the Gospels give us different adapted versions of Jesus's teaching in Matt 5–7 and Luke 6 (and teaching that is different again in John) rather than transcripts.

- The mainstream scholarly view is that Jeremiah's curators, too, provide adapted versions of his teaching. These chapters then provide both actual words of Jeremiah, words of Jeremiah that the curators have supplemented, and words that have been developed by the curators themselves and by other prophets. Being the mainstream scholarly view does not mean this assumption is right, but I take it as my own working assumption. Here as elsewhere, the scroll presents us with an adapted version that the curators have been inspired to formulate.

A further mainstream scholarly assumption is that we can go on to work out which elements within the chapters actually came from Jeremiah and which came from his curators or other prophets. I do not work with this assumption, since the criteria for making such distinctions seem questionable. For instance:

- If the content or style or vocabulary of a message matches that of other messages from Jeremiah, it need not mean it comes from Jeremiah.
- If the content or style or vocabulary of a message does not match that of other messages from Jeremiah, it need not mean it does not come from Jeremiah.
- A passage's looking like a later insertion into the message in which it appears need not mean that someone other than Jeremiah made the insertion.
- A passage's being poetry rather than prose need not indicate that it comes from Jeremiah, and its being prose rather than poetry need not preclude its coming from Jeremiah.
- A passage's being a reworking of a passage from earlier in the scroll neither indicates nor precludes its coming from Jeremiah.
- A passage's being a reworking of a passage from another prophetic scroll need not preclude its coming from Jeremiah.
- When the prophecies in Isa 40–55 talk to their audience about Cyrus the Great as a figure of the present, it is one of the concrete indications that the authorship of Isa 40–55 can be distinguished from the work of Isaiah ben Amoz and that the chapters come from a later century. There are no parallel concrete indications of later authorship in Jer 50–51 (or elsewhere in the Jeremiah scroll).

The chapters' not suggesting criteria for distinguishing between Jeremiah's words and the words of his curators is one reason why scholars come to different conclusions regarding which are which. Fortunately, the messages' authorship need not make a difference to their meaning, and they are intelligible without our being able to identify their author. I am therefore agnostic on the question of authorship, here as elsewhere in this commentary, and in referring to "Jeremiah," I conflate the actual Jeremiah and whoever may be channeling him.

One lack that generates uncertainty about the messages' origin is that Jer 50–51 does not have dates or other historical references, unlike the preceding messages to Kedar/Hazor and Elam. This feature raises the question whether "Babylon comes to represent more than the historical Babylon and becomes here the ultimate enemy of YHWH, the entity that stands under an almost cosmic judgment,"[134] which could then be a factor in the development of awareness of and study of the problem of evil in the Hebrew Bible.[135] This fact might link with the absence of any prospect for Babylon's restoration to parallel the promise of restoration for, for example, Egypt and Moab.

On the other hand, the chapters do refer concretely to the Medes and related peoples (51:11, 27–28), and Babylon's coming to represent something beyond the historical Babylon may be more an aspect of the chapters' reception over the centuries than part of the meaning they would have had for Jeremiah, his curators, and the people who first heard the scroll read. This reception includes the influence of Jeremiah in the New Testament, with its references to Babylon, and in particular its expectation that God will put down Rome. That contemporary Babylon will drink from the chalice full of Yahweh's anger, will fall cataclysmically, and will be turned into a place where demons dwell and into one haunted by all kinds of unclean birds (Rev 18:2). "The event so dramatically portrayed in chapters 50–51 was the necessary prelude to the historical future for Judah that had been promised in chapters 30–33. And similarly, the event portrayed in Revelation 18, in language richly borrowed from Jeremiah, is the necessary prelude to the eternal future for the whole creation that we glimpse in Revelation 21–22."[136]

In the dynamic of the first half of the Jeremiah scroll, the prophet speaks initially of an unidentified aggressor from the north who will bring Jerusa-

134. R. I. Thelle, "Babylon in the Book of Jeremiah (MT)," in Barstad and Kratz, *Prophecy*, 216–17; cf. J. Hill's (*Friend or Foe?*) thesis that the notion of metaphor is key to understanding Babylon in Jeremiah.

135. Y. Hoffman, "Jeremiah 50–51 and the Concept of Evil in the Hebrew Bible," in *The Problem of Evil and Its Symbols in Jewish and Christian Tradition*, ed. H. G. Reventlow and Y. Hoffman, JSOTSup 366 (London: T&T Clark, 2004), 14–28.

136. Wright, *Jeremiah*, 436.

lem's downfall (e.g., 1:13–15; 3:18; 4:6; 6:1, 22) and only later names Babylon as the aggressor (20:1–6). Jeremiah 50–51 manifests a parallel dynamic. Initially, the chapters speak solely of an aggressor from the north who will bring Babylon's own downfall (50:3, 9, 41); only later do they name names (51:11, 27–28). The Medes had arisen to great power status in the region during the same period as the Babylonians, and the two powers had worked together to encourage the downfall of Assyria. From the late seventh century they then coexisted, with the Median empire extending in an arc northwest, north, northeast, and east of the Babylonian Empire. During the period after Babylon became Judah's de facto overlord (beginning, say, after Nebuchadrezzar's victory in the Battle of Carchemish in 605), it would thus take no great political acumen or divine revelation to work out that if anyone was going to put down the Babylonians, it could be the Medes. When it happened, in the mid-sixth century, Cyrus the Great was able to combine the Median and Persian empires, and it was they that in due course put paid to Babylon. While some of the messages in Jer 50–51 may then derive from prophets who were channeling Jeremiah, their referring only to the Medes and not to the Persians is one pointer suggesting that these poems come from the period before the Medo-Persian empire became a reality. The references to Ararat, Minni, and Ashkenaz (51:27) also make sense in the context of the early or mid-sixth century and not later.[137]

The coda to the chapters in 51:59–64 does specifically date Jeremiah's original Babylon scroll in 594, three years after the first plundering of the temple and the first exile of Judahites to Babylon. Although Jeremiah wrote this scroll in order to have it thrown into the Euphrates, the reference to *all these words* (51:60), words that still exist, implies that he produced a second copy, as he did of the 604 scroll. The story of his writing the scroll implies that he had been speaking about the destiny of Babylon and about the significance of that destiny in connection with the future of Judah for some years up until 594. This statement fits with the unsurprising fact that Jer 25 has him speaking of these questions in 604, when Babylon had just become the imperial power and Nebuchadrezzar had just become its king. Over the next twenty years, until we lose track of Jeremiah in Egypt, it would be surprising if he did not have further things to say about these questions, and not surprising if he or his curators added them to any scroll he compiled in 594. Indeed, a number of the units in Jer 50–51 imply that the fall of Jerusalem has happened, though the interpretation of these statements is tricky and they may be anticipatory references to that event. This latter possibility is supported by the messages' ability also to speak as if the fall of Babylon has happened. Such messages seem to be anticipatory references to a future event. They

137. See Keown, Scalise, and Smothers, *Jeremiah 26–52*, 363–64.

speak in vividly imagined terms that suggest no knowledge of what actually happened in 539, as they show no awareness of Persia being on the horizon and do not compare with the passages about Cyrus in Isa 44–45. The final dated event to which the Jeremiah scroll refers is the release of Jehoiachin in 562, but it does then refer to "all the days of his life" after that release, which might imply some passage of time (it also refers in 52:11 to the day of Zedekiah's death, but it gives no indication of whether it had happened). One might then hypothesize that the 550s or 540s are the period in which Jer 50–51 reached its final form.[138]

The question of dates links with another aspect of the scroll's contents. There is a contrast between Jeremiah's message about Babylon and Nebuchadrezzar in Jer 50–51 and Jeremiah's elsewhere seeing Nebuchadrezzar as Yahweh's servant and requiring Judah to submit to Babylon (e.g., Jer 27–29). This contrast is a wide-canvas version of his combining the two attitudes in the same context in Jer 25. There, too, he spoke of Nebuchadrezzar as Yahweh's servant, but also of Yahweh as planning in due course to "attend to" the Babylonians, make them drink a chalice full of divine wrath, and turn their country into a wasteland. Yahweh's double attitude corresponds to the two sides he expresses in connection with Assyria in Isa 10:5–19.[139] In speaking of Babylon in Jer 27–29, too, he "repeatedly anticipates that city's demise."[140] Theologically, there is no tension between Jeremiah's urging a policy of submission to Babylon in Jer 25 and promising that Yahweh will take redress on Babylon in Jer 50–51. And whereas 29:10 has Jeremiah saying that Babylon would fall after seventy years while 51:33 has him say that it will happen in *yet a little while*, one cannot press the significance of that latter phrase (compare Isa 10:25; 26:20; 29:17; Hagg 2:6–7; and similar tensions within the New Testament), or, for that matter, of the former.

Pragmatically, however, there is a tension between the two aspects of the message attributed to Jeremiah, a tension that itself has two facets. It is misleading to speak of Jeremiah's stance in that other context as pro-Babylonian,

138. Again, see "Unity of Composition," pp. 5–26; "Authorship and Date," pp. 27–36. S. Frolov argues that 52:31–34 in their 2 Kings version must date from within Evil-merodach's reign from 562 to 560 and thus that 2 Kings reached its final form by that date ("Evil-Merodach and the Deuteronomist: The Sociohistorical Setting of Dtr in the Light of 2 Kgs 25,27–30," *Bib* 88 [2007]: 174–90); the same argument would suggest that the Jeremiah scroll reached its final form by that date.

139. Boadt, *Jeremiah 26–52*, 139. R. P. Carroll (*Jeremiah*, OTL, 843) questions this analogy on the grounds that Isa 10:5–19 accuses Assyria of excessive zeal, but actually its argument seems to concern arrogance—as is the case in Jer 50–51.

140. M. Leuchter, "Sacred Space and Communal Legitimacy in Exile: The Contribution of Seraiah's Colophon (Jer 51:59–64a)," in Boda et al., *Prophets Speak on Forced Migration*, 84.

even if pro-Babylonian politicians in Jerusalem could claim his support for their policies. It "reduces the whole issue to a shallow and simplistic level of political alignment, as if Jeremiah was simply the pawn of one of the squabbling factions in Jerusalem."[141] On the other hand, the public proclamation of prophecies such as the ones in Jer 50–51 would hardly have issued in "honourable treatment under the patronage of the empire" (39:12–14; 40:4–6).[142] But maybe we should not assume that Babylon took that much notice of the rantings of a small-time prophet whom Judah itself did not take seriously. It is perhaps more problematic that the proclamation of these messages to the Judahite communities either in Jerusalem or in Babylon in the years leading up to 587 would surely compromise the effectiveness of the message that Jeremiah otherwise preaches in Jer 27–29 and elsewhere.[143] It would make him sound like Hananiah.[144] This consideration might support the assumption that 51:59–64 does not imply a public reading of this scroll (see the commentary there). It would fit 51:59–64 if the series of messages were chanted as a form of prayer or as something like a curse that might be Yahweh's means of implementing the calamity of which they speak.[145] If we should not assume that Jer 50–51 reflects Jeremiah's public preaching in the decades up to 587, nevertheless it does suggest the aim of communicating with Judahites, perhaps in congregational meetings in Judah or Egypt or Babylon after 587 (50:5 pictures Jeremiah delivering that message in Jerusalem).

> The Prophet adopts various modes of speaking, and not without reason, because he had to thunder rather than to speak; and then as he spoke of a thing incredible, there was need of no common confirmation; the faithful also, almost pining away in their miseries, could hardly entertain any hope. This is the reason why the Prophet dwells so long and so diffusely on a subject in itself not obscure, for there was not only need of amplifying, but also of great vehemence.[146]

Behind Jeremiah's various modes of speaking, one can perceive a number of modes of speaking from the community's everyday life, with which the audience would be familiar and which supports the assumption that ultimately the messages were designed for the Judahites to hear. There will be varying

---

141. Cf. Wright, *Jeremiah*, 438–39; and the commentary on 21:10 above.

142. R. P. Carroll, *Jeremiah*, OTL, 816.

143. K. A. D. Smelik, "The Function of Jeremiah 50 and 51 in the Book of Jeremiah," in Kessler, *Reading Jeremiah*, 87–98.

144. See M. Köszeghy, *Der Streit um Babel in den Büchern Jesaja und Jeremia*, BWANT 173 (Stuttgart: Kohlhammer, 2007).

145. Cf. R. P. Carroll, *Jeremiah*, OTL, 842, 847, 855.

146. Calvin, *Jeremiah*, 4:197.

relationships between the way these forms of speech worked in everyday life and the way the prophet has adapted and transformed them. A message may thus adopt and adapt a form such as

- an announcement by a messenger bringing news of distant events (e.g., 50:2);
- an announcement or warning by a prophet about coming political events, with advice about the necessary action (e.g., 50:3, 8–10, 41–46; 51:6–10, 45–58);
- a promise given by a priest or prophet in response to a plea from their people (e.g., 50:4–7, 17–20, 33–34; 51:34–44);
- a confrontation or warning by a prophet or priest, given in connection with people's wrongdoing (50:11–13);
- a commission by a commander-in-chief to his army (50:14–16, 21–32; 51:1–5, 11–14, 20–28);
- a curse uttered by a priest or prophet (50:35–40);
- and a praise song (51:15–19).

The messages thus cover topics such as threats to Babylon, commissions of attackers, and promises to Israel, but as with the rest of the Jeremiah scroll, the arrangement is not systematic. The curators do not put together all the threats or all the promises or all the treatments of a particular theme. While on occasions they juxtapose messages that speak in similar ways, at other points the arrangement seems random. In this respect, the unit compares with chapters such as Jer 2 and Jer 48. I infer that the curators sometimes juxtaposed messages that went well together and were mutually illumining but sometimes simply fitted things in where they could or worked with already existent smaller collocations. One can discern some points at which the chapters bring together related material:

- 50:2–20 gives prominent attention to the restoration of Ephraim and Judah and interweaves this theme with the provision of reasons for Yahweh's action against Babylon.
- 50:21–32 comprises three commissions to Babylon's attackers and provides a number of reasons for Yahweh's action that relate to Yahweh himself rather than to Israel's needs or destiny.
- 50:33–46 comprises threats of Babylon's fall that work especially by restating prophetic messages appearing elsewhere in the Jeremiah scroll or in other prophetic scrolls.
- 51:1–33 is a more miscellaneous collection, perhaps framed by the introductory and closing "Yahweh has said this" statements; I have

treated it as two compilations, with the song of praise in vv. 15–19 forming a climax to the first and the dramatic apostrophe in vv. 20–23 opening the second.

- 51:34–44 is a protest by Zion about Nebuchadrezzar's treatment of it and a response by Yahweh.
- 51:45–58a comprises two exhortations to leave Babylon and two sets of reasons based on the fact that "days are coming."[147]

The emphases of the chapters are:[148]

- Yahweh intends to put Babylon down himself; he assures the Judahites that imperial power and oppression will not last forever (50:2–3, 23, 39–40; 51:25–26, 41–43, 54–58).
- He will thereby show who is really God and expose the powerlessness of the Babylonian gods and the images that represent them (50:2, 34, 44; 51:17, 47).
- Given that he works in the world and works through human agencies, he will act by military means using the nations and armies of the region (50:3, 9, 41–43; 51:1–3, 11–12, 27–28).
- He will take redress on Babylon for its wrongdoing in relation to him (50:11, 14–15, 24, 28, 29–32; 51:11, 24).
- As one who "acts on behalf of those who cannot defend themselves,"[149] he will treat Babylon the way Babylon treated Israel and other nations—and the way he himself treated Israel (50:15, 22–23; 51:35–36, 49).
- He intends to enable Ephraim and Judah to return to Yahweh, to Zion, and to their land (50:4–7, 17–20, 33–34; 51:10).
- Given that "there is a time to settle and a time to flee,"[150] Jer 29 represented the first "time," but Judahites now need to be willing and ready to leave Babylon (50:8; 51:6, 45, 50).

Near the end of the two chapters comes a protest prayer of Judah's and a response from Yahweh promising action (51:34–44).

---

147. My understanding of the chapters' structure thus compares with those of K. T. Aitken, "The Oracles against Babylon in Jeremiah 50–51," *TynB* 35 (1984): 25–63; and A. O. Bellis, *The Structure and Composition of Jeremiah 50:2–51:58* (Lewiston, NY: Mellen, 1995).

148. Cf. Wright, *Jeremiah*, 433–36.

149. Stulman, *Jeremiah*, 385.

150. Wright, *Jeremiah*, 440.

But, even when it is implicit, both compositions are a series of impassioned responses to equally impassioned grievances. The whole is a testimony that "God heard their groaning . . . and God took notice of them" (Exod 2:24–25). It was to be heard by those who pleaded for the punishment of their oppressors, as in Ps 83:9–17(10–18). The promises of homecoming in ch. 50 correspond to the petitions, "Do good to Zion in your good pleasure; rebuild the walls of Jerusalem," in Ps 51:18(20). The promises of the people's vindication in ch. 51 correspond to the wish in Ps 79:10, "Let the avenging of the outpoured blood of your servants be known among the nations before our eyes" (cf. Ps 58:10[11] and esp. 137:8 concerning Babylon). And the promises of Yahweh's own vindication, also in ch. 51, implicitly answer laments that Judah's God, too, had suffered loss amid Judah's suffering, as Pss 74:4–8 and 79:1 protest. . . . A host of grief-stricken prayers find their divine amen in chs. 50–51.[151]

Indeed, "a good liturgy of the events of the sixth century would read 50–51 *after* the reading of the book of Lamentations."[152]

2. *The Fate of Flock, Lions, and Shepherds (50:2–20 [LXX 27:2–20])*

[2] *Tell among the nations and make it heard,*
   lift up a banner and make it heard.[a]
Do not conceal, say:
   "Babylon has been captured.
Bel has been shamed, Merodach shattered,
   its idols shamed, its fetishes shattered."[b]
[3] *Because a northern nation is going up*[c] *against it—*
   that one will make its country into a desolation.[d]
There will be no one living in it—
   human being and animal alike[e] *are fleeing, going.*[f]

[4] *In those days and at that time (Yahweh's affirmation):*[g]

The Israelites will come,
   they and the Judahites together.
Crying as they go,[h] *they will go,*

---

151. Allen, *Jeremiah*, 509. Cf. B. Gosse, "L'enracinement du livre de Jérémie dans le Psautier: Teil 1," *Biblische Notizen* 158 (2013): 41–44.
152. R. P. Carroll, *Jeremiah*, OTL, 834; cf. Allen, *Jeremiah*, 509.

and Yahweh their God they will have recourse to.
[5] *To Zion they will ask the way,*
   their faces toward here: "Come!"[i]
They will join themselves to Yahweh in a pledge for all time
   that will not be put out of mind.[j]
[6] *A flock that were lost, my people became*[k] —
   their shepherds led them astray.
On the mountains they turned them back[l] —
   from mountain to hill they went.
They put their resting-place out of mind —
   [7] *all the people who found them consumed them.*

Their adversaries said:

We will not incur liability,[m]
   on account of the fact that they did wrong toward Yahweh,
   the faithful habitat, their ancestors' hope,[n] *Yahweh.*[o]

[8] *Flee*[p] *from within Babylon,*
   from the country of Chaldea, get out,[q]
   be like the he-goats before the flock.
[9] *Because there, I am stirring,*
   getting to go up[r] *against Babylon,*
An assembly of big[s] *nations*
   from a northern country.
They will line up in relation to it —
   from there it will be captured.
Its arrows will be like those of a bereaving[t] *strong man —*
   they will not turn back empty.
[10] *Chaldea will become spoil —*
   all its spoilers will be full (Yahweh's affirmation).[u]
[11] *Because you celebrate, because you are merry,*[v]
   you plunderers of my domain,
Because you jump like a heifer threshing,[w]
   bellow like stallions,[x]
[12] *Your mother is being greatly shamed,*
   the one who gave birth to you is being confounded.[y]
There, the end of the nations:
   wilderness, desert, and steppe.[z]
[13] *Because of Yahweh's fury it will not live;*[aa]
   it will become a desolation, all of it.

Everyone passing by Babylon will be desolate
  and will whistle at all its wounds.

¹⁴*Line up against Babylon all around,*
  *all you who direct*ᵇᵇ *the bow.*
Shoot at it, don't spare an arrow,
  *because it has done wrong in relation to Yahweh.*ᶜᶜ
¹⁵*Shout against it all around;*ᵈᵈ
  it is giving its hand.
Its towers are falling, its walls are smashing,
  *because it is Yahweh's redress.*ᵉᵉ
Take redress upon it;
  as it did, do to it.
¹⁶*Cut off sower*ᶠᶠ *from Babylon,*
  and the one who seizes the sickle at harvest time.
*In the face of the oppressor's*ᵍᵍ *sword,*
  an individual to his people, they will turn their face;
  *an individual to his country, they will flee.*ʰʰ

¹⁷*Israel is a sheep that was detached,*
  that lions have driven away.
First the king of Assyria devoured it,
  and this was the end:
  *Nebuchadrezzar*ⁱⁱ *king of Babylon got its bones.*ʲʲ

¹⁸*Therefore Yahweh of Armies, the God of Israel,*ᵏᵏ *has said this:*

Here am I, attending
  to the king of Babylon and to his country
  as I attended to the king of Assyria.
¹⁹*And I will return Israel to its habitat,*
  *and it will pasture in the Carmel and the Bashan.*ˡˡ
*In the highland of Ephraim and the Gilead*ᵐᵐ
  its appetite will be full.

²⁰*In those days and at that time (Yahweh's affirmation):*ⁿⁿ

*It will be sought, the waywardness of Israel,*ᵒᵒ *but there will be none,*
  and the wrongdoings of Judah, but they will not be found,
  *because I will pardon whomever I let remain.*ᵖᵖ

a. LXX lacks this colon.
b. LXX has a distinctive version of this line; D. J. Reimer notes it as one where MT may

906

manifest a hardening attitude toward Babylon (*The Oracles against Babylon in Jeremiah 50–51* [San Francisco: Mellen Research University Press, 1993], 135–36, 152).

c. The *qatal* verb is now anticipatory, a usage related to the declarative/performative (see the introduction to 13:18–22, pp. 354–55; see also 1:5 and the translation note on it). The usage recurs in vv. 12 and 15.

d. The asyndeton and the word order with the subject preceding the verbs suggest that this colon is subordinate to the previous one. So also in vv. 3b, 6–7 (3×), 9, 10.

e. Lit. "from human being even to animal."

f. On this verb, see note p. LXX lacks *fleeing, going*.

g. LXX lacks *(Yahweh's affirmation)*.

h. Lit. "going and crying" (two infinitives).

i. For MT *bōʾû*, LXX, Vg, Aq, Tg imply varying easier readings.

j. MT^L has a section marker here.

k. The *qere* has plural, the *ketiv* singular.

l. The *qere* has a *qatal* verb, *šôbəbûm*; the *ketiv* implies the adjective *šôbābîm* ("turning back"), as in 3:14, 22.

m. LXX "we will not forgive them" suggests the verb *nāśāʾ* rather than *ʾāšam*.

n. And/or their well; see P. J. P. Van Hecke, "Metaphorical Shifts in the Oracle against Babylon (Jeremiah 50–51)," *SJOT* 17 (2003): 71–73.

o. LXX lacks *Yahweh*. MT has a section marker here.

p. Whereas one would expect *nudû* (from *nûd*) to mean "wander," that meaning does not lead well into the decisiveness implied by the next two cola; some occurrences of *nûd* seem to treat it as a byform of *nādad*, which makes better sense here (9:10[9] has *nādad*).

q. The verbs come at either end of v. 8a, which has an a-b-bʹ-aʹ pattern. For the *qere*'s imperative *ṣēʾû*, the *ketiv* implies jussive *yēṣəʾû* ("they are to get out").

r. LXX lacks *getting to go up*.

s. LXX lacks *big*.

t. For MT's *maśkîl* (cf. Vg, Aq), LXX, Sym imply *maśkîl* ("insightful").

u. LXX lacks *(Yahweh's affirmation)*.

v. The *ketiv* has feminine singular verbs throughout v. 11.

w. For MT *dāšâ* from the verb *dûš*, LXX, Vg imply *dešeʾ* ("[on] grass").

x. The simple *waw* suggests two simultaneous actions.

y. LXX's "your mother for good" is a puzzle; HUBP considers approaches.

z. LXX lacks *desert and steppe*.

aa. See the translation note on 17:25.

bb. See the translation note on 46:9.

cc. LXX lacks this colon.

dd. LXX lacks *all around*.

ee. Tg has "Yahweh's people's redress," and it might indeed give Judah some satisfaction to see that Babylon goes through the experience of destruction that Jerusalem went through, but Jeremiah does not think in these terms, and neither does Judah take the redress. Yahweh takes the redress (through the northern army) for what Babylon did in relation to him.

ff. For MT *zōrēaʿ* (cf. Aq, Sym), LXX "seed" implies *zeraʿ*.

gg. For MT *yônâ*, LXX has "Greek," implying *yəwāniyyâ* (cf. 46:16).

hh. MT has a section marker here.

ii. LXX lacks *Nebuchadrezzar*.

jj. MT has a marker here.

kk. LXX lacks *of Armies, the God of Israel*.

ll. Tg appropriately paraphrases "a fruitful and fat land." LXX lacks *and the Bashan.*

mm. For Tg's rendering ("the sanctuary"), 22:6 provides the background (C. T. R. Hayward, *The Targum of Jeremiah: Translated, with a Critical Introduction, Apparatus and Notes*, The Aramaic Bible 12 [Edinburgh: T&T Clark, 1987], 181).

nn. LXX lacks *(Yahweh's affirmation).*

oo. This phrase has the object marker as if it were the object of the passive verb.

pp. LXX continues, "in the country, says the Lord." MT^A has a unit marker here.

Verses 2–20 comprise a sequence of six messages that were originally independent. Two features are distinctive of this first sequence. One is the prominence it gives to the restoration of Ephraim and Judah, which it does not directly link with the fate of Babylon, but which does implicitly link with it. That restoration means something physical, material, and geographical; it also means a restoration of the people's relationship with Yahweh and with each other. The other distinctive feature is Yahweh's reasons for bringing calamity on Babylon. The calamity will mean the exposure of their idols' powerlessness; it will also be an act of redress for their plundering Yahweh's own domain in Canaan and enjoying doing so.

vv. 2–3   Yahweh's commissioning an announcement of Babylon's fall (five bicola)

vv. 4–7   Yahweh's promise that Israel will return to him and to its country (an introduction, seven bicola, a resumptive introduction, and a closing tricolon)

vv. 8–13   Yahweh's urging people to leave Babylon in light of its coming capture and his confrontation of Babylon itself (an introductory tricolon, two linked bicola, three bicola, and three sets of three bicola, the middle set being linked)

vv. 14–16 Yahweh's commission to Babylon's attackers (six bicola and a closing tricolon)

vv. 17–19 The background and Yahweh's declaration of intent (a bicolon and a tricolon; then a resumptive introduction, an opening tricolon, and two bicola)

v. 20   A promise that Israel's waywardness will not be a problem in the future (an introduction and a tricolon)

2 The opening lines summarize the main point of Jer 50–51. As is often the case in Jer 46–51, the prophet issues a commission whose speaker and addressees are unnamed, though the curators' introduction in v. 1 implies that we should assume Yahweh to be the speaker. The addressees are not military figures who are to implement Yahweh's intention, as they were in 49:28 and 31, but messengers who are to announce that this decision has been implemented. So Yahweh invites Jeremiah's actual hearers to imagine that the fall of Babylon has happened. These actual hearers are presumably Judahites in Jerusalem or Egypt, or in Babylon itself. They are to imagine the messengers hastening from Babylon around its empire to tell people the news. Whereas lifting up a *banner* or standard would be a literal reality in connection with commissioning an army, here it is a figure of speech—messengers do not literally lift up a banner. It is an image for making the news publicly available in a context where Babylon itself might like to *conceal* it; that verb is a litotes. There is another level to the figure of speech. In reality, the fall has not yet happened, so the talk of lifting a banner and making something heard and not concealing it suggests both the image of actual messengers who will one day announce Babylon's fall when it has actually happened and the paradoxical idea that the certainty of Babylon's fall needs to be proclaimed now, among the Judahites; it needs to be believed in by the message's actual audience. "Let all take notice of the good news; there shall be a general jail delivery."[153]

There are two aspects to the news that will eventually be announced. First, there is the news that *Babylon* itself *has been captured*—which raises the questions of how and by whom. But before we get a sort-of answer to those questions, Yahweh moves on to a corollary that is at least as important: *Bel has been shamed, Merodach shattered*. Bel is named in the First Testament only here, in 51:44, and in Isa 46:1, each time in a similar context (Bel appears further in LXX in its version of Daniel and in the Letter of Jeremiah). *Merodach* appears only here, though his name features in compound names (e.g., 52:31); it forms an alternative way of pronouncing the god conventionally referred to in English as Marduk. Both *Merodach* and *Bel* refer to the supreme Babylonian god, the supreme god of the Babylonian world by virtue of being the supreme god of the imperial capital. Strictly speaking, Merodach is a name while Bel is a title related to *baʿal*; it also means "master."[154] When Jerusalem fell, Yahweh seemed to have been defeated and shamed. The fall of Babylon will mean that Marduk has been defeated, *shamed*, and *shattered*. He will not have been able to defend his city. The three verbs *captured*, *shamed*, and *shattered* came together in regard to Moab in 48:1; the latter two verbs came together in 8:9; 48:20, 39. These two apply both to the god himself and to the images that represented him. *Idols* and *fetishes* come only here in Jeremiah. *Idols* (ʿāṣāb) is a word Hosea likes; *fetishes* (gillûlîm) comes mostly in Ezekiel. Both are potentially mean words: etymologically *idols* suggests at best something manufactured, at worst something causing

153. Trapp, *Commentary*, 358 (spelling updated).
154. See T. Abusch, "Marduk," *DDD*, 543–49; Abusch notes that there are various ways of vocalizing the name, and the Hebrew version does not seem to be pejorative like Molech (see the commentary on 32:35).

pain and toil; *fetishes* at best suggests mere blocks of wood, at worst lumps of feces. In Hebrew as in English, *shattered* (*ḥātat*) can nicely refer both to a physical shattering (e.g., 14:4) and to an inner shattering (e.g., 1:17; 17:18). Likewise, *shamed* can denote both a public shaming by events and an inner shaming that internalizes the public shaming. And there is a mutual interplay between what happens to the god and to his images. The god is emotionally or mentally shattered, or should be, as his image is physically shattered; and the idol is shamed as the god whom it allegedly represents is shown to have no reality that corresponds to his reputation.

3 Jeremiah makes a transition to speaking overtly about the future (see the translation note), and at last there comes some sort of explanation of who will have captured Babylon and will have thereby shamed and shattered it and its god. It is only a sort-of explanation, because it names no names, as 51:11, 27–28 will eventually do. With some irony, the conqueror is simply designated as someone from the north, which was Jeremiah's description of Jerusalem's conqueror until he eventually named Babylon. As the dynamic in Jer 50–51 parallels that in Jer 2–20, Babylon becomes Judah's doppelgänger.[155] Its coming devastation will correspond to that of Judah and other threatened peoples (see, e.g., 2:15; 33:10; 49:13, 33; see the commentary there). Now, "the new 'foe from the north' makes the old 'foe from the north' helpless, wretched, and devastated."[156] Geographically, it would be even clearer and more literal that Babylon's attackers come from the north if they were the Medes than was the case with Judah and the Babylonians. But as was the case earlier, designating the conqueror as a northern nation is as much a symbolic as a geographical statement (see 1:14 and the commentary on it).

4 Chronologically associated with the fall of Babylon, Ephraimites and Judahites will come to Zion. Indeed, when vv. 4–5 are heard "in tandem" with vv. 2–3, for Jer 50–51 "two main themes are put in bold relief."[157] One might say that "the entire 'message' of this literature is given in a nutshell in the first five verses."[158] Implicitly, there might be need for a causal link between the two events; for various reasons, a Judahite return from Babylon presupposes Babylon's fall. But even more than the description of Babylon falling to an attack from the north, the description in vv. 4–7 is not just talking in down-to-earth terms about a return from exile. It works in a different

155. R. Thelle, "Babylon as Judah's *Doppelgänger:* The Identity of Opposites in the Book of Jeremiah," in Mein, Holt, and H. C. P. Kim, *Concerning the Nations,* 77–94; cf. Reimer's concluding comments to his study of forms and imagery in Jer 50–51 (*Oracles against Babylon,* 240).

156. Brueggemann, *Jeremiah 26–52,* 261.

157. Lundbom, *Jeremiah 37–52,* 376.

158. M. Kessler, *Battle of the Gods: The God of Israel versus Marduk of Babylon. A Literary/Theological Interpretation of Jeremiah 50–51,* SSN 42 (Assen: van Gorcum, 2003), 71.

framework—indeed, a series of different frameworks. First, it is talking about Ephraimites and Judahites together, like Jer 30–33. The background to Yahweh's promise, then, is a vision of the destiny of the entire people of Israel and of a return of Ephraimites who had been transported by Assyria as well as Judahites who had been transported by Babylon. And *together* goes behind not only the exile that followed 722 but the split between the two peoples that happened two centuries previously. *Crying* also picks up from 31:9. In this context as in that one, crying does not denote simply sadness (cf. 22:10; 31:15; 48:32; though it may imply contrition, cf. Ezra 10:1) but a more mixed emotion—a response to something deeply moving and so marvelous that it seems too good to be true. People can have recourse to Yahweh in exile (29:13), but Jeremiah here speaks of a recourse to Yahweh associated with returning from exile.

5 One reason is that Zion remains the place to which he made a special commitment (3:14; 8:19; 31:6, 12; four more references will follow in Jer 50–51). People are not going merely to Jerusalem, the city and the place where people live; they are going to Zion, the place where the temple is. Human beings like having special places where they can be sure of meeting with God, and Yahweh mercifully made Zion such a place. Actually, people are coming *here*: apparently Jeremiah and his audience are in Jerusalem.[159] Another reason for referring to *recourse* to Yahweh in this connection is implicit in the prediction in v. 5b, which presupposes the collapse of the pledge that once obtained between Israel and Yahweh (see 11:1–17; on the image of a *pledge*, see the introduction to 11:1–17, pp. 315–16). It's really scandalous to think that they will need to *join themselves to Yahweh*—that verb elsewhere refers to foreigners becoming worshipers of Yahweh (Isa 14:1; 56:3, 6; Zech 2:11[15]). But they will indeed need to. Jeremiah underlines the point by speaking of *a pledge for all time* (picking up from 32:40), unlike the pledge that Israel annulled. And he adds that it is one *that will not be put out of mind*, so that this phrase is attached to something much more pleasant than it previously was (20:11; 23:40). Will it not be put out of mind by Yahweh or by them? Either way, the rebellion that led to disaster and the disaster itself are not going to recur, ever.

6 How did they come to be far away, and how did that pledge get annulled, and how did they cease to be joined to Yahweh and to become like foreigners? Israel, *my people*, are a flock, but they became *a flock that were lost*. How could it have happened? Because *their shepherds*, the kings, priests, and prophets, *led them astray*. They took them over *mountain* and *hill*, which ought to be no problem, because the hillsides are where the pasture is, but here the mountains stand for the shrines, the "high places," which were often

159. Lundbom, *Jeremiah 37–52*, 375.

at elevated positions on hills and mountains. Thus the flock *put out . . . of mind* (that verb again) *their resting-place*. The term denotes the abode where (for instance) sheep can sleep safely (e.g., Isa 65:10), which in the allegory denotes the Zion to which they are now returning.

7 The consequence of the sheep abandoning their safe resting-place is that they can be caught, killed, and eaten. To be less allegorical, Israel was vulnerable to adversaries such as Assyria and Babylon. Jeremiah invites his audience to imagine these adversaries defending their action with complete plausibility. To use Jeremiah's expression, they were acting as Yahweh's servants; no guilt can attach to their action. The guilt is Israel's for abandoning Yahweh, whom Jeremiah imagines the adversaries describing in two telling images. Yahweh is their *faithful habitat*, another expression taken up from Jer 30–31 (see 31:23 and the commentary on it). Jeremiah transfers the image from Zion to Yahweh himself. And he adds that Yahweh is the people's *hope* (cf. 14:8; 17:13)—*their ancestors' hope* and therefore one who they know can be taken as their hope, if they think about their ancestors' story. Jeremiah portrays the Babylonians as understanding things that Israel has not yet understood—both the reality of their wrongdoing and the reality and nature of their God.[160]

8 Placed here, this exhortation takes up from vv. 2–7 in several ways: it issues some urgent imperatives to some unnamed addressees, like v. 2; it does so in connection with the coming fall of Babylon to a force from the north; it speaks of Babylon's shame; and it takes up the image of a flock. Out of its context in the scroll, the addressees might be any people (at least, any foreign people) in Babylon—its function would then be simply to underline the magnitude and the certainty of the city's fall. In its context in the scroll, it puts pressure on Judahites who are quite settled and happy in Babylon (cf. Isa 48:20). Yahweh urges them to leave, as his agents once urged Lot and his family to leave Sodom (Gen 19).[161] Perhaps the macho he-goats are the first to push their way forward when the shepherd lets the flock out from its pen. Perhaps the idea is that people should not be looking over their shoulder to see if someone else is on the move.[162] Tg takes the exhortation to imply that they should be like officers at the head of the people, "strutting without fear or fright."[163]

9–10 *Stirring* (*'ûr hiphil*) is the First Testament's common verb for the arousing of a major power to take action against Babylon (e.g., Isa 13:17; 45:13). It will actually be *an assembly of big nations*, a collaboration of peoples (Medes, Persians), who will put Babylon down. Here, Yahweh describes how they will *line up* as an army so that the city will be *captured* (cf. v. 2). In a

160. Brueggemann, *Jeremiah 26–52*, 261.
161. Allen, *Jeremiah*, 513.
162. H. Bullinger in his sermon on this passage, as quoted in Tyler, *Jeremiah*, 438.
163. Qimchi, in MG, as paraphrased by Rosenberg, *Jeremiah*, 2:383.

grisly image, the archers are like hunters whose arrows will certainly hit their target. So will warriors turn wives into widows and children into orphans. Thus the people of *Chaldea*, the former spoilers, *will become spoil*.

11–12a The people who *will become spoil* (v. 10) are the people who currently celebrate being *plunderers of my domain* (*naḥălâ*; see the commentary on 2:7). It will be so even while they claim they are only doing what their victims deserve (v. 7). So they are further victims of poetic justice. Jeremiah's vivid imagery for their celebratory plundering (v. 11b) is his way of making the point that Isa 47:6 makes in the context of a different vivid image. Yes, when their mother city is defeated, it will be *shamed* and *confounded*.

12b–13 The unique expression *the end of the nations* links by contrast with Babylon's being *the head of the nations* (31:7). Hebrew has no word for "empire," and *nations* sometimes functions as such a word would; this connotation makes sense here. Jeremiah is proclaiming the end of the Babylonian Empire in *wilderness, desert, and steppe*, the kind of grim landscape that Yahweh once had to bring Israel through (2:6). As in v. 3, the development of this description in v. 13 reuses standard descriptions of disaster that have already applied to Judah (e.g., 4:27; 19:8).[164]

14–15 Another originally separate message begins again with imperatives, this time the kind addressed to unnamed warriors; eventually Jeremiah will tell us that the implementers of these commands will be the Median army, but at the moment they are anonymous. He develops the figure of commissioning attackers in a sustained way through six of the seven lines that comprise the message, and in doing so broadens the nature of the exhortations. Three cola urging on the bowmen dominate v. 14, but the fourth colon repeats the charge from v. 7 (where it was an excuse). The next verse has overlapping dynamic. First, three cola issue an exhortation to fighters generally; the second and third describe the victory that is unfolding. *Giving its hand* is elsewhere a term for committing oneself or making a pledge, like "shaking hands" in English, though from a position of weakness (e.g., Ezek 17:18; Lam 5:6).[165] Jeremiah is imagining Babylon making alliances to defend itself against the coalition of attackers that previous verses have described— as (ironically) Assyria made alliances when the Babylonians and Medes (!) were attacking it. The fourth colon is then another *because* clause, a corollary of the preceding *because* colon. Babylon has done wrong in relation to Yahweh (v. 14); so Yahweh will take *redress* (see the commentary on 5:9). Redress involves more poetic justice. The punishment is to fit the crime.

16 A further bidding expresses vividly though more abstractly an aspect of the recurrent threat regarding the devastation of cultivated land

---

164. Cf. Gosse, "Masoretic Redaction of Jeremiah," 79.
165. Keown, Scalise, and Smothers, *Jeremiah 26–52*, 366.

(e.g., v. 12). In keeping with the rhetoric of vv. 14–15, Yahweh again issues a commission to Babylon's attackers, this time to *cut off* the people involved in agriculture. The first line covers the two ends of their work, sowing and harvesting, and thus implicitly everything that happens in between. Cutting off could mean killing, but the second line implies that wise farmworkers will evade slaughter. Much agricultural work in Babylonia was undertaken by foreigners whom Babylon had transported, Judahites included, and they will be able to recognize the moment when it is wise and possible to *flee* home.

17 The message in vv. 17–20 again picks up the sheep image from vv. 6–7 and 8–10, but once more it takes it in a different direction. Israel is now not the victim of its own shepherds nor the flock hightailing it out of Babylon but the single victim of Assyrian and Babylonian *lions*. The double identification of the attackers underlines how *Israel* here refers to the one nation, notwithstanding its division into Ephraim and Judah. The point is further underscored by its being called a single *sheep*—or goat; the word (*śeh*) can refer to either. Either way, in the First Testament and in material reality, a single sheep suggests vulnerability. Here the single sheep became *detached* from the flock and came to be at the mercy of several lions.[166] One cannot press the metaphor to establish what is the flock here, though the implication may be that the Israelites thought they had been treated harder than people such as Edom, Moab, and Ammon. The point Jeremiah makes is rather the grizzly picture of its first being vulnerable to Assyria, who essentially *devoured* it, then to Nebuchadrezzar, who chewed its bones.

18–19 Yahweh has already *attended to the king of Assyria*; he will do the same to *the king of Babylon and to his country*. Once again, the country that benefits from its leader's actions also pays the price for them. But the point about the threat is that it will enable *Israel* (again Jeremiah refers to the entire nation) to *return to its habitat*. This term regains its more literal reference (contrast v. 7), one especially appropriate in the context of the sheep image. The reference is spelled out in the parallel cola with their allusion to *pasture*. Metaphor also returns in the naming of the four great fertile regions, which are not especially literal pasture, but for literal Israel they will be indeed places where *its appetite* can *be full*.

20 Again picking up the dynamic of Jer 30–31, a further promise adds relational provision to material provision, in keeping with the principle that both are required in connection with human need and divine care. The messages in vv. 2–19 have made clear that Israel's sufferings stem from its *waywardness*. There is some subtle ambiguity about the promise. Is there no waywardness to be found because all waywardness will be pardoned? Or is the promise

166. Foreman, *Animal Metaphors*, 84.

914

that no waywardness will be manifested, as a result of the creative potential of being pardoned and restored? The latter logic might fit 31:31–34.

3. Challenges That Yahweh Accepts (50:21–32 [LXX 27:21–32])

[21]*Against the country—Double Bitterness:*[a]
go up against it,
and toward the people who live in Attention.[b]
Put to the sword and devote[c] *after them*[d] *(Yahweh's affirmation);*
act in accordance with all that I have ordered you.[e]
[22]*The sound of battle in the country,*[f]
a great breaking!
[23]*How*[g] *it*[h] *is splitting and breaking,*[i]
the hammer of the entire earth!
How it is becoming a desolation,
Babylon among the nations!
[24]*I am trapping you,*[j] *yes, you are being captured, Babylon,*
but you yourself do not acknowledge it.
You are being found, yes, you are being seized,
because against Yahweh you issued a challenge.
[25]*Yahweh is opening his store*
and getting out his instruments of condemnation.
Because that is the work of the Lord Yahweh of Armies[k]
in the country of Chaldea.

[26]*Come to it from end to end,*[l]
open up its granaries.
Pile it up like heaps[m] *and devote it—*
there is not to be a remainder of it.
[27]*Put all its bullocks*[n] *to the sword—*
they are to go down to the slaughter!
Oh, them, because their day is coming,
the time of their being attended to![o]
[28]*The sound of people fleeing and escaping*
from the country of Babylon,
To tell in Zion of the redress of Yahweh our God,
redress for his palace.[p]

[29]*Make it heard toward Babylon to archers,*[q]
all who direct a bow!
Camp against it all around—

there must not be[r] people who escape.
Recompense it in accordance with its deed—
   in accordance with all that it did, do to it.
Because it was arrogant in relation to Yahweh,[s]
   to Israel's sacred one.
[30] *Therefore its young men will fall in its squares;*
   all its men of battle will become still[t]
   on that day[u] (Yahweh's affirmation).[v]

[31] *Here am I toward you, arrogance (an affirmation of the Lord Yahweh*
      of Armies[w]),
   because your day has come,
   the time when I am attending to you.[x]
[32] *Arrogance will collapse and fall,*
   with no one to lift it up.
I will set fire to its towns[y]
   and it will consume everything around it.[z]

a. The article on *hā'āreṣ* works against the translation "the country of Double Bitterness" (Lundbom, *Jeremiah 37–52*, 402). LXX "bitterly" understands *mərāthaim* adverbially.

b. LXX takes *pəqôd* to mean "attend to."

c. On this verb, see the commentary on 25:9b.

d. The elliptical expression generates assonance across three words, *ḥarōb wəhaḥărēm 'aḥărêhem* (*CTAT*, 2:829).

e. MT has a section marker here.

f. LXX also has "of the Chaldeans."

g. See the commentary on 48:39.

h. Tg interprets *it* as "the king," but this requires some inference; the verb's masculine gender may derive from the masculine word for *hammer* (*paṭṭîš*).

i. The *qatal* verbs are again anticipatory (see the translation note on v. 2); there are further examples in vv. 23b–25 and 31.

j. LXX has a third-person plural verb.

k. LXX lacks *of Armies*.

l. *Miqqēṣ* (lit. "from end") elsewhere refers to time, but *miqqāṣâ* and *miqqāṣeh* can have the broader meaning (cf. 51:31; Gen 47:2; Ezek 33:2); Sym understands "all of you." On the text of the colon, see *CTAT*, 2:829–31.

m. For MT *kəmô 'ărēmîm*, LXX "like a cave" implies *kəmô mə'ārāb*; Vg "in heaps" implies *bəmô 'ărēmîm*.

n. For MT *pāreykā*, LXX "its fruit" implies *piryāh* (LXX then derives the verb from *ḥārēb*, "be dry"). Tg appropriately paraphrases "its strong men."

o. MT has a section marker here.

p. LXX lacks this colon.

q. Whereas LXX, Vg, Tg give *rabbîm* its usual meaning, "many," the parallel colon suggests "archers" (cf. Job 16:13).

r. The *qere* presupposes the presence of *lāh* ("of it"), also, as in v. 26.

s. Tg has "against the people of the Lord"; cf. the note on v. 15.

t. See the translation note on 6:2.

u. LXX lacks *on that day*.

v. MT has a marker here. The verse is a slight variant on 49:26.

w. LXX has simply "of the Lord."

x. The (anticipatory) *qatal* verb (see the translation note on v. 2) depends on the construct noun (GK 130d).

y. For MT *'ārāyw* (cf. Aq), LXX has "its forest" (implying *ya'ărô*) as in 21:14b, of which this line is a slight variant.

z. MT has a section marker here.

This second section of messages comprises three further commissions to Babylon's attackers. The commissions compare with vv. 14–20, but they have two linked characteristics over against vv. 1–20. The section more or less gives up making any references to Israel; its focus lies simply on the catastrophe Yahweh intends to bring to Babylon. And it incorporates a number of reasons for this action on Yahweh's part, whose rationale does not relate to Israel's needs or destiny.

> vv. 21–25 Yahweh's commission is a response to Babylon's challenge to him (an opening tricolon and eight self-contained bicola)
>
> vv. 26–28 Yahweh's commission concerns an act of redress in connection with his palace (six bicola, the last two linked)
>
> vv. 29–32 Yahweh's commission initiates a rebuke to Babylon's arrogance (four bicola and a semi-closing tricolon, then a resumptive tricolon and two bicola)

21 Yet again, Yahweh commissions an attacker against Babylon (this time the verbs are singular). It is the first occasion when Babylon is given a substitute name: *Double Bitterness*, or Merathaim. The name recalls the Babylonian place name Marratu, which suggests bitter water, but Jeremiah turns it into a Hebrew word that makes a comment on Babylon as a place characterized by double bitterness, like Judah: *how dire and bitter* (*mar*) had Judah's behavior been (2:19). The name could also make people think in terms of "Double Rebellion" ("rebel" is *mārâ*); the words "rebel" and "bitter" came close together when Yahweh said that Judah *has rebelled against me. . . . This is your direness, because it's something bitter* (4:17, 18). As we know already from v. 18, Babylon is therefore about to receive *Attention* (*pəqôd*) of an unwelcome sort (see v. 27). Here, too, Jeremiah takes up a Babylonian name, that of a tribe called Puqudu (which also appears in Ezek 23:23). So the doubly bitter/rebellious people is about to be attended to. The second line puts great emphasis on total annihilation: (a) *put to the sword*, (b) *devote*, which suggests elimination, and (c) in case there is any doubt, make sure you go *after them* and get the last of them. Don't let there be any survivors. And in this connection, *act in accordance with all that I have ordered you.*

22–25 Yet again Jeremiah imagines things happening, now in fulfillment of the commission in the previous verse, and he seeks to get the audience to imagine it. Babylon has been *the hammer of the entire earth*, but that hammer is now *splitting and breaking*. Then, rhetorically, Yahweh addresses Babylon itself, which brings the point home to Jeremiah's Judahite audience in a new way: Yahweh has laid a trap for Babylon. It is *being captured*, and like an animal that walks into a trap, it doesn't realize. As is the case with the Judahite leadership, "Something is happening here but you don't know what it is, do you, Mr. Jones" (Bob Dylan; see the commentary on 14:18). How encouraged Judahites could be now by this "mock lament"![167] Jeremiah adds one of the occasional pieces of rationale that characterize this section: *because against Yahweh you issued a challenge.* Babylon thought it could assert itself against Yahweh—for instance, by invading his palace (v. 28). It is about to find that it was mistaken. Yahweh is *getting out* the weapons whereby he will give practical expression to his *condemnation* (see the commentary on 10:10). Such *work* does not come naturally to him; it is strange or alien (Isa 28:21). But in circumstances such as the present ones, it is the necessary *work of the Lord Yahweh of Armies.*

26–27 In that connection, Jeremiah or Yahweh again reverts to commissioning destroyers. The prophecy seems at first to be speaking once more in terms of the country's food supplies, with the commission leaping over the military attack to the aftermath; while an invading army commonly scoops up a country's food supplies to feed itself, here the victors are commissioned to engage in pointless total destruction that will make ongoing life impossible. But the subsequent instruction to *pile it up like heaps and devote it* then suggests that the talk of *granaries* was a metaphor. It is Babylon itself that is to be piled up like grain and destroyed. Likewise, the *bullocks* stand for the nation's warriors (cf. Isa 34:7; Ezek 39:18, which also talk about slaughter). *Their day* is a distinctive expression, but having a day of their own is not good news. It is *the time of their being attended to.* As the exclamation *how* (v. 23) can suggest either lamentation or satisfaction or both (it is "an ironic lament"),[168] the exclamation *oh* (*hôy*) can signify either protest (22:13) or grief (22:18) but in this context may also suggest both (see the commentary on 22:13).

28 One again has to be wary of literalism in interpreting Jeremiah's hyperbole. If the northern army has annihilated the entire people, there are no

167. Kessler, *Battle of the Gods*, 88.
168. Weiser, *Jeremia*, 2:438.

fugitives escaping to Zion. But Jeremiah allows for such escapees, presumably Judahites, who are the means of again articulating that Yahweh's action against Babylon counts as redress and here make concrete the reason for the redress and the nature of that challenge that Jeremiah referred to in v. 25. People cannot expect to attack the king's or the King's *palace* (on this word, see the commentary on 7:4) and get away with it. While it is to be expected that the redress will be a comfort to the Judahites, Jeremiah wants them to see it as a proper response to the Babylonians' treating Yahweh with contempt. The assault on the temple might be that of 597 or 587, and might relate to the assault having actually happened or to the event that Jeremiah knows will happen.

29-30 A third commission follows. Logically, it goes behind the preceding one and it has a particular focus. It begins with a commission to commissioners: that is, Yahweh bids his aides to go and tell the northern army's *archers* to get on with their job of firing arrows at the city's defenders to provide cover for the engineers building ramps and undermining gates and walls.[169] Both archers and engineers will *camp against it all around*, but the focus lies on the archers, who are to form a vast company to surround Babylon in order that they can also make sure that no one escapes. Everyone will be shot. The commission's burden thus parallels and amplifies vv. 26-27. It will be appropriate *recompense* for what the city itself did, which is now expressed in terms of being *arrogant* (see the commentary on 43:2). Its self-confident assertiveness clashes with Yahweh's being *Israel's sacred one*. Jeremiah uses the title conventionally translated "the holy one of Israel," which is characteristic of the book of Isaiah but also occurs in Pss 71:22; 78:41; 89:18(19). You cannot mess with someone who is sacred; it provokes a response. In addition, Yahweh's being *Israel's* sacred one makes attacking Israel unwise, like invading his domain or palace. Underestimating him is unwise. Like Israel, Babylon has made this mistake and will pay the price.

31-32 The scroll juxtaposes another message, taking up the theme of *arrogance*, which becomes a kind of title for Babylon.[170] Babylon is arrogance incarnate and, yes, it is about to pay the price. "Arrogance typically has a short life."[171] Likewise, the message picks up the idea of people having their day, in the bad sense. It will be *the time when I am attending to you* (cf. v. 27).

---

169. Thompson, *Jeremiah*, 742-43.

170. *You* is masculine singular, and Isaac Abravanel (*Commentary on the Latter Prophets*) neatly identifies Belshazzar as the embodiment of arrogance, though the pronoun may simply reflect the gender and number of *zādôn*.

171. Lundbom, *Jeremiah 37-52*, 413.

4. Threats That Yahweh Repeats (50:33–46 [LXX 27:33–46])

³³ *Yahweh of Armies*^a *has said this.*

The Israelites are oppressed,
   and the Judahites, together.
All their captors took strong hold of them^b—
   they refused to send them off.
³⁴ *Their restorer*^c *is strong—*
   Yahweh of Armies his name.
He will definitely argue^d *their case*
   in order to give rest to the earth
   and to give unrest^e *to the people who live in Babylon.*

³⁵ *A sword against Chaldea (Yahweh's affirmation)*^f
   toward the people who live in Babylon,
   toward its officials and toward its experts!
³⁶ *A sword toward the oracles,*^g *and they will become fools;*^h
   a sword toward its strong men, and they will shatter!
³⁷ *A sword toward his horses and toward his chariotry,*ⁱ
   and toward the entire foreign group that's within it,
   and they will become women!
A sword toward its stores, and they will be plundered—
   ³⁸ *a desert*^j *toward its water, and it will dry up.*^k
Because it is a country of images,
   and because of their dreadful objects^l *they will go crazy.*^m
³⁹ *Therefore creatures from the desert will live with creatures from foreign*
      *shores,*ⁿ
   and ostriches will live in it.
It will not live^o *again, ever;*
   it will not dwell for generation after generation.^p
⁴⁰ *As at God's overturning of Sodom,*
   and of Gomorrah and of its neighbors (Yahweh's affirmation),
No one will live there,
   no human being will reside in it.^q

⁴¹ *There, a people is coming from the north,*
   a big nation and many kings—
   they stir themselves from the furthest parts of the earth.
⁴² *Bow and sabre they grasp hold of,*
   they are fierce, and they have no compassion.
The sound of them—it's like the sea that roars,
   and on horses they ride,

Drawn up like an individual for battle,
  against you, Miss Babylon.
⁴³ *The king of Babylon has heard the news of them*
  and his hands have drooped.
Distress has grasped hold of him,
  writhing like a woman giving birth. ʳ

⁴⁴ *There, it will be as when a lion goes up*
  from the Jordan swell into a permanent habitat.
Because I intend to hustle him out of it,
  and whoever is chosen for it I will appoint.
Because who is like me,
  who can summons me?
Who on earth is the shepherd
  who can stand before me?
⁴⁵ *Therefore listen to Yahweh's counsel*
  that he has determined for Babylon,
His intentions that he has devised
  for the country of Chaldea.
If the flock's boys don't drag them away,
  if the habitat isn't desolate at them . . .
⁴⁶ *At the sound when Babylon is being seized,* ˢ
  the earth is shaking,
  and an outcry among the nations—it is making itself heard. ᵗ

a. LXX lacks *of Armies*.

b. The asyndeton and the word order with the object preceding the verb suggest that this colon is subordinate to the next.

c. Aq, Sym nicely render "the one who is near them."

d. The infinitive precedes the finite verb, underlining the point; it is formed like an infinitive construct rather than an absolute (which is more typical), enhancing the assonance of *rîb yārîb 'et-rîbâ* (Joüon 123q).

e. The verbs *hirgîaʿ* and *hirgîz* (give rest/unrest) are nicely alliterative while contradictory in meaning; both look like *qatals* but are actually infinitives (see GK 53l).

f. LXX lacks *(Yahweh's affirmation)*.

g. See the translation note and commentary on 48:30.

h. LXX lacks this colon.

i. LXX additionally repeats "a sword toward its strong men."

j. *Sword* is *ḥereb*; *desert* is *ḥōreb*.

k. LXX "will be shamed" suggests *yēbōšû* rather than *yābēšû*.

l. For MT *'êmîm*, LXX "islands" implies *'iyyîm*, which comes in the next colon.

m. For MT's *hithpoel yithōlālû*, LXX, Vg, Tg "glory" implies *hithpael yithallālû* (4:2).

n. *Ṣiyyîm* and *'iyyîm* (*creatures, foreign shores*) rhyme, like *tōhû* and *bōhû* in 4:23 and Gen 1:2 (Holladay, *Commentary on Jeremiah*, 2:420), with similar implications.

o. See the translation note on 17:25.

p. LXX lacks this colon.

q. Verse 40 repeats 49:18 (see the translation notes and commentary there) in a slightly different form.

r. Verses 41–43 repeat 6:22–24 (see the translation notes and commentary there) in a slightly different form; see E. Peels, "'Against You, Daughter of Babylon': A Remarkable Example of Text-Reception in the Oracle of Jeremiah 50–51," in Peursen and Dyk, *Tradition and Innovation*, 31–44.

s. LXX, Vg translate loosely "at the sound of the seizing"; *nitpaśâ* is actually a finite verb dependent on the construct noun (cf. Joüon 129p).

t. MT has a section marker here. Verses 44–46 repeat 49:19–21 (see the translation notes and commentary there) in a slightly different form.

The last section of Jer 50 is dominated by a sequence of threats that continue to declare the coming fall of Babylon and do so especially by restating older prophetic messages.[172] An implication of this feature is the assumption that a message from Yahweh may not be "done" when it has applied in one context or to one people. It is almost to be expected that it would apply in others and to others.[173]

vv. 33–34   Yahweh will act as he did in the exodus story, as Israel's restorer and advocate (an introduction, three bicola, and a closing tricolon)

vv. 35–40   Yahweh charges a sword, which leads into a reworking from Isa 13 and Jer 49 (a bicolon framed by two tricola; then six bicola, the last two linked)

vv. 41–43   A people is coming from the north, described by reworking 6:22–24 (an opening tricolon, a bicolon, two linked bicola, then two bicola)

vv. 44–46   Yahweh intends to hustle Babylon like a lion, a reworking from 49:19–21 (four bicola, two linked bicola, a bicolon, and a closing tricolon)

The four messages thus complement each other in the background they presuppose:

- in the exodus story;
- in the message about Babylon in Isaiah;

---

172. A. O. Bellis, "Poetic Structure and Intertextual Logic in Jeremiah 50," in Diamond, K. M. O'Connor, and Stulman, *Troubling Jeremiah*, 179–99.

173. Cf. P. R. Ackroyd, *Studies in the Religious Tradition of the Old Testament* (London: SCM, 1987), 61–75.

- in a message about Judah from much earlier in the Jeremiah scroll;
- and in a message about Edom from the immediately previous chapter in Jeremiah.

33 Initially, this sequence returns to the logic of Yahweh's action. Whereas vv. 21–32 described it as redress and recompense in response to Babylon's action and stance toward Yahweh himself, now it becomes a response to Babylon's action in relation to Israel. *Oppressed* (*'āšaq*) more precisely means treated fraudulently (7:6; 21:12), and vv. 33b–34 suggest an awareness of this connotation. Jeremiah takes the reality of fraudulence and oppression within a community, whereby the powerful cheat the needy out of their rights, and make it an image for the way Assyria and Babylon have treated Israel as a whole. Ephraim and Judah had simply insisted on their independence, on being in control of their own destinies, but Assyria and Babylon first took them captive and then *refused to send them off*: the phrase recalls a much earlier experience (Exod 4:23; 7:14).[174] Actually, the Judahites will turn out to be happy in Babylon and not enthusiastic about returning to Judah when they have the chance, but this irony hardly changes the wrong involved in the imperial powers' domination of the region.

34 What Israel needed in Egypt was someone to act as its *restorer* (see the commentary on 31:11). Fortunately it had someone (Exod 6:6; 15:13), and someone with a *strong* hand (Exod 3:19; 6:1; 13:3, 9, 14, 16). And fortunately, Israel again has a restorer, who is indeed *strong*; the adjective (*ḥāzāq*) links with the verb in v. 33b (*ḥāzaq hiphil*). *Yahweh of Armies is his name* underlines the point. The task of a restorer may involve taking up someone's case in a meeting of the elders at the town gate; the account of Boaz in Ruth 4 provides an example. Yahweh will fulfill this moral obligation, too (Ps 74 also brings together talk of Yahweh restoring and of his taking up Israel's case).[175] If we may press the image, Yahweh is appearing in a meeting of the heavenly powers and arguing Israel's case there—the prophecy sets aside any thought of Israel's having deserved what happened to it. The broader context is that the neat byproduct of Yahweh's action against Babylon is also to *give rest to the earth* as a whole that is Babylon's victim, because it will *give unrest to the people who live in Babylon* itself. The promise stimulates a prayer:

---

174. Thompson, *Jeremiah*, 743–44.

175. B. Gosse, "Jérémie 50,33–40, en relation avec les psaumes d'Asaph et deutéro-Asaphites et le livre d'Isaïe," *BN* 158 (2013): 4–6.

Grant, Almighty God, that, as thou hast deigned once to take us under thy protection, we may always raise up our eyes to thine infinite power, and that when we see all things not only confounded, but also trodden under foot by the world, we may not yet doubt but that thy power is sufficient to deliver us, so that we may perpetually call on thy name, and with firm constancy so fight against all temptations, that we may at length enjoy in thy celestial kingdom the fruit of our victory, through Jesus Christ our Lord.—Amen.[176]

35–37a One might see this next declaration of Babylon's doom as a response to vv. 33–34.[177] It begins as a kind of curse, a little like Mercutio's "a plague o' both your houses,"[178] except that when Yahweh utters a curse, it is certain to come true. A *sword* will fall. Jeremiah has spoken many times of a sword as the means of bringing death. Here, it is to come on the people as a whole, then on those within the people who make its political decisions and formulate its political policies, then on its *oracles* in the sense of the ministers who bring messages from a god about what is going to happen and what should therefore be done to avoid it (if it is bad news); Yahweh will see to the frustrating of their revelations so that *they will become fools*. Then it is to come on the supposed *strong men* who defend the city so that *they will shatter*, physically but perhaps also in morale, like their deities (v. 2; see the commentary there). It will come on *his* (the king's?) *horses* and *chariotry* and *the entire foreign group that's within it*—which in this context suggests a force of foreign mercenaries. They *will become women*, like Egypt's mercenaries who cannot be relied on to stand firm when things get overwhelmingly dangerous (46:16, 21).

37b–38a The content of the curse has already suggested that we should not be literalistic in interpreting the *sword*, as if it wielded itself. The point now becomes clearer: the sword stands for the fighter bearing the sword, who will plunder Babylon's armory and resources. A final toggling of the language abandons the sword image for the image of desert or drought that will come upon Babylon's water supply, which is also the key to its being able to irrigate its fields. It is an ironic and devastating threat, because Babylon straddled the Euphrates, and water was the last thing it thought it needed to worry about.

38b In adding a reason for the curse, the message comes to have a similar shape to that of vv. 33–34. There, the argument was that Babylon will fall because Yahweh is strong; here the argument is that Babylon will fall because it is

---

176. Calvin, *Jeremiah*, 4:205.

177. So A. O. Bellis, "The New Exodus in Jeremiah 50:33–38," in *Imagery and Imagination in Biblical Literature: Essays in Honor of Aloysius Fitzgerald, F. S. C.*, ed. L. Boadt and M. S. Smith, CBQ Monograph 32 (Washington, DC: Catholic Biblical Association, 2001), 157–68.

178. W. Shakespeare, *Romeo and Juliet*, Act III, Scene 1; cf. Lundbom, *Jeremiah 37–52*, 419.

a country of images and its images are weak, inadequate to the challenge lying
before them. They will not be able to protect Babylon from sword or drought.
Indeed, the Babylonians' devotion to them will issue in sword and drought.
Yahweh declared earlier that the nations *will go crazy* because of the sword he
sends among them (25:16); the same logic applies. It is because the Babylonians'
reliance on them will have this dreadful result that the images are *dreadful objects*. There is no reason to think that the Babylonians were afraid of their images
or the gods they represented, though in reality they should be afraid.

39–40 The message in vv. 35–40 closes with a development of the point
about desert and drought. It begins with a reference to creatures whose
names do not correspond to actual species but rather link with desert and
foreign shores and thus suggest creatures that are alien, eerie, and frightening. Ostriches appear elsewhere in the company of such creatures of the
wild or of the desert (e.g., Isa 34:13–15; 43:20; Lam 4:3). The message makes
its point by adopting phrases that appear elsewhere in prophecy. One can
compare vv. 39–40 with declarations about Babylon in Isa 13:19–22 and about
Edom in Jer 49:18 (see also 49:33):

Jer 50:39	Isa 13:19–22
	as at God's overturning of Sodom and of Gomorrah
therefore creatures from the desert will	
live with creatures from foreign shores	
and ostriches will live in it	
it will not live again, ever	it will not live ever
it will not dwell for generation after generation	it will not dwell for generation after generation . . .
	creatures from the desert will lie down there . . .
	ostriches will dwell there . . .
	jackals in its castles

Jer 50:40	Jer 49:18
as at God's overturning of Sodom and of Gomorrah and of its neighbors	as at the overturning of Sodom and Gomorrah and its neighbors
(Yahweh's affirmation)	(Yahweh has said)
no one will live there	no one will live there
no human being will reside in it	no human being will reside in it

925

Though we cannot be sure about the direction of the adopting, the parallels indicate how prophecies interact with each other. If Yahweh has spoken once in a particular way, his message will not be just a random one-off revelation but an expression of his typical or ongoing purpose. So there will be no surprise when it turns out to be illuminating in a different context, as happens with the Moab prophecy in Jer 48. Thus prophecies may come in wholly fresh words or may come in familiar words, and both processes can produce compelling and frightening results.

41–43 The dynamic continues with a message that applies to Babylon the message to Judah in 6:22–24:

50:41–43	6:22–24
[41]there a people is coming from the north	[6:22]there a people is coming from a northern country
a big nation and many kings	a big nation
they stir themselves	it stirs itself
from the furthest parts of the earth	from the furthest parts of the earth
[42]bow and sabre they grasp hold of	[23]bow and sabre they grasp hold of
they are fierce, and they have no compassion	it's fierce, and they have no compassion
the sound of them—it's like the sea that roars	the sound of them—it's like the sea that roars
and on horses they ride	and on horses they ride
drawn up like an individual for battle	drawn up like an individual for battle
against you Miss Babylon	against you Miss Zion
[43]the king of Babylon has heard the news of them	[24]we have heard the news of it
and his hands have drooped	our hands have drooped
distress has grasped hold of him	distress has grasped hold of us
writhing like a woman giving birth	writhing like a woman giving birth

The impact of the message would be enhanced for anyone who had heard the version in 6:22–24. It offers the reassurance that the grimness of what Yahweh intends for Judah will also overwhelm Babylon,[179] and in particular its king.[180] Conversely, anyone in Judah who first heard the message about Babylon and rejoiced in it could be devastated by the realization that the same fate hangs over Judah. One could see 6:22–24 as in effect one of the prophecies about a foreign nation applied to Judah.[181]

179. W. Brueggemann, "At the Mercy of Babylon," 7–8.
180. Qimchi (in MG) again finds Belshazzar here.
181. Cf. Holt, "Meaning of an *Inclusio*," 181–205.

44–46 The section dominated by the reworking of earlier prophecies closes with a restatement of the threat concerning Edom in 49:19–21, which thus continues from the reworking of 49:18 in v. 40:

50:44–46	49:19–21
[50:44]there, it will be as when a lion goes up	[49:19]there, it will be as when a lion goes up
from the Jordan swell into a permanent habitat	from the Jordan swell into a permanent habitat
because I intend to hustle him out of it	because I intend to hustle him out of it
and whoever is chosen for it I will appoint	and whoever is chosen for it I will appoint
because who is like me	because who is like me
who can summons me[182]	who can summons me
who on earth is the shepherd	who on earth is the shepherd
who can stand before me	who can stand before me
[45]therefore listen to Yahweh's counsel	[20]therefore listen to Yahweh's counsel
that he has determined for Babylon	that he has determined for Edom
his intentions that he has devised	his intentions that he has devised
for the country of Chaldea	for the people who live in Teman
if the flock's boys don't drag them away	if the flock's boys don't drag them away
if the habitat isn't desolate at them	if their habitat isn't desolate at them
[46]at the sound when Babylon is being seized	[21]at the sound of their fall
the earth is shaking[183]	the earth is shaking
and an outcry among the nations	an outcry at the Sea of Reeds
it is making itself heard	its sound is making itself heard

Once again, Jeremiah's reworking of earlier messages indicates that there is system in Yahweh's operating and that his hearers would be unwise to assume that he is simply predicting what they will read in the newspapers about Edom or about Babylon. The fall of Jerusalem was not the kind of event that prophets pictured; nor were the fall of Babylon, the fall of Edom, the fall of Antiochus Epiphanes, the coming of the Messiah, or the fall of Jerusalem in AD 70. Prophecies are not predictions inspired by God but imaginative and imaginary scenarios inspired by God so that they have the capacity to give a

---

182. Whereas 49:19 has the spelling *yōʿîdennî*, 50:44 has *yôʿidennî*.
183. Whereas 49:21 has the usual *qal* verb, 50:46 has the *niphal*.

true impression of the significance of the event to which they refer and thus to provoke an appropriate response whereby people turn to God.

5. *The Faithful and Powerful God (51:1–19 [LXX 28:1–19])*

¹*Yahweh has said this.*

Here am I, stirring against Babylon,
  and toward the people who live in "The midst of those who rise against
      me,"ᵃ
  a devastating wind.
²I will send off aliensᵇ against Babylon and they will winnow it,
  and strip its country,
When they have beenᶜ against itᵈ all around
  on the day of dire fortune.
³Toward [the one who] will direct, the one who will direct his bow,ᵉ
  toward [the one who] will get himself up in his armor:ᶠ
Do not spare the young men—
  devote its entire army.
⁴They will fall, run through, in the country of Chaldea,
  thrust through in its streets.
⁵Because Israel and Judah has not been widowed
  through its God, through Yahweh of Armies,
Because their country—it was full of liability
  through Israel's sacred one.ᵍ

⁶Flee from within Babylon—
  save, each individual, his life.
Don't become stillʰ through its waywardness,
  because it is a time of redress.
For Yahweh it is a remuneration
  with which he is recompensing it.
⁷Babylon was a gold chalice in Yahweh's hand,
  getting the entire earth drunk.
In that nations drank of its wineⁱ—
  as a result, nationsʲ are crazy.
⁸Suddenly Babylon is falling and breakingᵏ—
  howl over it!
Get ointment for its wounds—
  perhaps it may heal.
⁹We are healing Babylon,

but it has not healed.
Abandon it, let's go,
  each to his country.
Because the decision about it has reached to the heavens,
  it has risen to the skies.
[10] *Yahweh has made great faithfulness go out for us*[l]—
  come, let us recount in Zion
  the action of Yahweh our God.[m]

[11] *Polish the arrows,*
  fill the quivers!

(Yahweh is stirring the spirit of the kings of Media,
  because against Babylon his intention is to devastate it.
Because that will be Yahweh's redress,
  redress for his palace.)[n]

[12] *Toward the walls of Babylon lift up a standard,*
  establish a strong watch.
Set up watchmen,
  prepare ambushes.
Because Yahweh is both intending and acting on
  that of which he spoke toward the people who live in Babylon.
[13] *You who dwell*[o] *by abundant water,*
  abundant in stores:
Your end is coming,
  the measure for[p] *your cutting off.*[q]

[14] *Yahweh of Armies has sworn by his life:*

Though I have filled you with humanity like locust,[r]
  they will chant a shout against you.[s]

[15] *Maker of earth by his energy,*
  establisher of the world by his smartness,
  who by his insight stretched the heavens:
[16] *With the sound of his giving a roar of water in the heavens,*
  and his causing billows to go up from the end of the earth,
Lightnings with the rain he makes,
  and he causes wind to go out from his stores.
[17] *Every human being shows himself stupid through his knowledge,*
  every goldsmith is put to shame through his image.

Because his model is deception;
there is no spirit in them.
[18] *They are empty, a work for mockery—*
at the time of their being attended to, they will perish.
[19] *Not like these is Jacob's share,*
because he is the shaper of everything.
And it is the clan that is his domain:
Yahweh of Armies is his name. [t]

a. For MT *lēb-qāmāy*, LXX has "the Chaldeans" (cf. Tg); "the other ancient versions seem greatly perplexed, and differ in their interpretation of this passage" (Blayney, *Jeremiah*, 139). MT's expression comes from substituting the Hebrew equivalent of ABC by ZYX; thus *ksdym* (Chaldeans) becomes *lbqmy* (cf. v. 41 and the translation note on 25:26). Jeremiah then provides these consonants with some vowels, generating a phrase that makes a point about Babylon; see the commentary.

b. For MT *zārîm*, Aq, Sym, Vg imply *zōrîm* ("winnowers"), and LXX implies *zēdîm* ("arrogant people") with a related different reading of the subsequent verb; cf. McKane, *Jeremiah*, 2:1296.

c. For MT *hā'û*, LXX "woe" implies *hôy*.

d. LXX has "Babylon."

e. On the verb, see the translation note on 46:9.

f. MT involves an ellipsis in each colon. For *wə'el* each time, Vg implies *wə'al* ("he is not to direct . . . not to take a stand"); Tg has a negative in the first clause—a grammatically easier reading that would be an instruction relating to Babylonian defenders. On the complexity of the textual tradition, see *CTAT*, 2:839–41.

g. LXX has "sacred things."

h. On this verb, see the translation note on 6:2.

i. The asyndeton and the word order with the object preceding the verb suggest that this colon is subordinate to the next.

j. LXX, Vg lack this second *nations*.

k. The *qatal* and *wayyiqtol* verbs are anticipatory (see the translation note on 50:3); there are further examples in vv. 11–13.

l. Like Hebrew *ṣidqōtênû*, Tg's *zkwtn'* could be numerical plural or intensive/abstract plural (see *DTT*). On the assumption of intensive/abstract, LXX not inappropriately has "his judgment," repeating *krima* from v. 9, while Aq's *tēn dikaiosynēn autou* spells out the word's implications. But Vg's *iustitia nostra* (cf. Sym) is misleading; see the commentary.

m. MT[A] has a section marker here.

n. LXX "his people" is an inner-LXX slip for *naou autou*.

o. The feminine singular *šōkant* looks like a cross between *qatal šākant* and participle *šōkenet*, while the *ketiv* implies the archaic *šākantî*; see the translation notes on 2:19, 20.

p. Lit. "the cubit of," a unique use of *'ammat*; LXX "truly" implies *'ĕmet* (cf. Aq).

q. Cf. Vg; *HALOT*. For MT *biṣ'ēk*, LXX "into your guts" implies *bəmē'ayik*. Aq, Sym assume the regular meaning of *beṣa'* ("what can be grabbed," 6:13; 8:10; 22:17).

r. LXX, Vg "because I will fill" implies that the colon refers to the huge attacking army (cf. Tg), but one would then expect *'im lō'* (cf. Rudolph, *Jeremia*, 308) rather than simply *'im*. The construction is illustrated by a parallel in 2 Kgs 5:20 (Thompson, *Jeremiah*, 754), though here it is clearer that *kî* and *'im* are separate rather than being a compound expression. *Kî* (lit. "that") introduces the content of the oath. The *if*-clause then indicates something Yahweh intends to do, but it is *qatal* because it is the condition for the apodosis in the next colon, which constitutes the point of the oath.

s. MT has a section marker here.

t. MT has a marker here. Verses 15–19 repeat from 10:12–16; see the translation notes and commentary there. The only noteworthy difference is that 10:16 has *Israel* in the penultimate colon.

Yahweh formulates his intentions regarding Babylon, in new ways, and again urges people to be ready to abandon the city for their own safety, while Jeremiah buttresses his affirmations and his exhortation with reminders of Yahweh's unparalleled power as creator and his commitment to Israel. "Each of the three first sections emphasizes that the annihilation of Babylon is Yahweh's will; the fourth adds to it that he has the power for that."[184]

vv. 1–5   Yahweh's declaration of intent about an attack on Babylon (after an introduction, an opening tricolon and seven bicola, with six in pairs)

vv. 6–10   An exhortation to flee from Babylon in light of Yahweh's coming action (ten bicola, then a closing tricolon)

vv. 11–14 An exhortation to Babylon's attackers, with a disclosure of their identity (a bicolon, two bicola in parenthesis, three bicola, two linked bicola, then a resumptive introduction and a bicolon)

vv. 15–19 A song of praise concerning Yahweh as the creator whose domain is Israel (an opening tricolon, two linked bicola, then five bicola)

1–2 The introduction *Yahweh has said this* corresponds to the beginning of the messages about Philistia, Ammon, and Kedar (47:2; 49:1, 28), and it will have encouraged the medieval provision of a chapter break at this point, but there is no marked new beginning here in relation to what precedes.[185] Once again, Yahweh speaks of *stirring up* attackers on *Babylon* (cf. 50:9). But the further description of the calamity to come then glosses Babylon with the phrase *the midst* (lit. the "heart" or "mind") *of those who rise against me*. The letters of that phrase (*lbqmy*) are a reverse paronomasia on the name Chaldeans (see the translation note). But in addition, "by a kind of bonus,"[186] the letters can be vocalized so that *those who rise against me*

184. Rudolph, *Jeremia*, 305.
185. Duhm, *Jeremia*, 366.
186. McKane, *Jeremiah*, 2:1295.

makes another comment on Babylon's offensiveness and on the reason for bringing catastrophe upon it—another way of describing the Chaldeans as people who do wrong in relation to Yahweh or issue a challenge to Yahweh or invade Yahweh's palace or act arrogantly toward Yahweh (50:14, 24, 28, 29). In describing the calamity, Yahweh takes up the image of *a devastating wind* and indicates the nature of its devastating work as he develops the image, with a further paronomasia.[187] *Aliens* (*zārîm*) will devastate Babylon, but in terms of the image in v. 2, they will be winnowers (*zōrîm*; see the translation note). For winnowing, one needs a breeze, but this wind will be a gale that blows away wheat as well as chaff. Yahweh's declaration about Babylon again corresponds to his threat against Judah (4:11–12). Verse 11 will shortly identify the alien winnowers, while 2 Chr 36:22–23 and Ezra 1:1–2, in referring to Jeremiah, will describe how Yahweh "stirred the spirit (*rûaḥ*) of Cyrus" (whom one could indeed call a devastator) to commission Judahites to go and rebuild the temple.

3–4 Jeremiah reverts to speaking literally, though with some elusiveness (see the translation note). The people who fulfill the function of the wind are the foreign archers in their armor. They are no more to *spare* the young Babylonian fighters than they are to spare their arrows (50:14); rather, they are to *devote* the Babylonian forces. After *devote*, one hardly needs the word *entire*, which thus underscores the grisly reality that the verb presupposes; each time Jeremiah uses this verb in connection with Babylon (cf. 50:21, 26), he adds some such expression to underline the point. If the audience wants to imagine the implications in even more down-to-earth gruesome terms, v. 4 outlines them.

5 The *because* perhaps makes a contrast between the coming fate of Babylon and the past fate of Israel. One might think that Israel has indeed been *widowed* in the sense of abandoned by its husband.[188] Whereas being widowed in a Western context may be chiefly a cause of grief and sorrow, in a traditional society the male head of a family is key to its security and livelihood, and widowhood threatens vulnerability and starvation. The second *because* might then indicate why Babylon is going to be widowed,[189] but the sequence of clauses more likely suggests that it indicates why such abandonment of Israel would have been justifiable: Israel's land was full of wrongdoing, and thus of guilt, and thus of *liability* (*'āšām*). Jeremiah uses this noun only here, though with some irony it follows up an occurrence of the related verb (50:7). There, Israel's attackers were imagined reassuring themselves that they would incur no liability because Israel deserved the chastisement

187. Qimchi, in MG.
188. R. P. Carroll, *Jeremiah*, OTL, 838.
189. Qimchi, in MG.

of which they were the executors—and they were right that Israel *was full
of such guilt* through following other deities, *through* (that is, in relation to)
Israel's sacred one. There is further irony, since Jeremiah's earlier reference
to Yahweh as Israel's sacred one (50:29), also the only other occurrence in
Jeremiah, related to Babylon's arrogance toward Yahweh as Israel's sacred
one. Israel is just as guilty, but this guilt has not issued in Yahweh's turning
it into a widow.

6 In the context, this new message that begins with another exhortation
to leave Babylon because of the coming calamity is addressing the Judahites
there, but (rhetorically at least) it might also address other foreigners such
as merchants doing business in Babylon.[190] Yet again, the wording links ironically with what precedes: when the Babylonians *become still* (50:30), you
don't want to join them, do you? You don't want to be present when Yahweh
takes *redress* upon Babylon (cf. 50:28) for its waywardness, when he gives
Babylon its *remuneration*, when he is *recompensing* Babylon (cf. 50:29). There
might have seemed nowhere safer than Babylon.[191] Actually there was nowhere more dangerous.

7 Jeremiah returns to the imagery of 25:15–29, where the chalice went
from *Yahweh's hand* to Jeremiah's hand for the nations to drink from, though
here Jeremiah uses the image in a different way. This *chalice* is *gold*, which
would make *the entire earth* feel even more honored to drink from it. It stands
for an empire "politically powerful and culturally dazzling."[192] But the chalice
not only gets them drunk; it makes them *crazy* (cf. 50:38).

8–10 Now is the moment of the great reversal. Babylon is "the butler who got
sick."[193] If we are to be literalistic, the people urged to dress Babylon's wounds
are foreigners in its midst, which will again mean not least the Judahites, exercising a ministry like Jonah's to Nineveh—or Daniel's to Nebuchadrezzar and
Belshazzar![194] But their task is hopeless, and anyway the exhortation is perhaps
sarcastic.[195] The wounds are fatal, because of Yahweh's *decision* (*mišpāṭ*; see
1:16; 4:2 and the commentary there). This decision Yahweh has made about
Babylon *has reached to the heavens, it has risen to the skies.* The next line clarifies
this declaration. Yahweh's steadfast commitment and faithful decisions, which
reach the heavens and the sky, the high mountains and the great deep, issue in
deliverance for his people (Ps 36:5–6[6–7]; cf. Pss 57:10[11]; 108:4[5]). Yahweh's
decision about Babylon is such a decision, one whereby *Yahweh has made great*

---

190. Qimchi, in MG.

191. Calvin, *Jeremiah*, 4:240.

192. McKane, *Jeremiah*, 2:1300.

193. Kessler, *Battle of the Gods*, 106.

194. Duhm, *Jeremia*, 368.

195. Isaac Abravanel, *Commentary on the Latter Prophets*, as paraphrased by Rosenberg,
Jeremiah, 2:396.

faithfulness go out for us. Therefore, our obligation as Judahites is to get back to *recount in Zion the action of Yahweh our God.* Jeremiah invites people to imagine chanting a thanksgiving psalm.[196] As usual, the faithfulness to which Jeremiah refers is thus not Israel's faithfulness (of which it had shown little) or vindication (of which it had deserved little) but Yahweh's faithfulness that emerged from his commitment, the great faithfulness or faithful acts proclaimed in Judg 5:11; 1 Sam 12:7; Ps 103:6; Dan 9:16; Mic 6:5.

11 Another new message begins. Jeremiah once again addresses Babylon's imagined attackers, specifically its archers. Here, they have not left home yet; they are to start preparing for a march. The exhortation gives way to a background comment that looks like a later insertion into the exhortation, but it's an important insertion because it reveals these attackers' identities. The dynamic of Jer 50–51 follows that of the opening chapters of Jeremiah, where first there was mention of an attacker from the north, then the identification of the attacker, though it may again promote the reflection, "Well, yes, who else could it be?" *Stirring* (*'ûr hiphil*) was the verb used of the coalition of unnamed nations in 50:9 and of the unidentified wind (*rûaḥ*) in 51:1; it was the language used in Isa 10:26 of Assyria (though there the verb was *polel*) and in Isa 13:17 of the Medes. The reworking of Isa 13:19–22 in 50:39–40 makes it plausible to think of Jeremiah here alluding to Isa 13:17. To speak of stirring up the *spirit* (*rûaḥ*, as in v. 1) suggests both arousing the energy and awakening something inside a person that might surprise them, which fits the language in 2 Chr 36:22 and Ezra 1:1. The plural *kings* hints at a recognition that the Median Empire is a coalition, like the Babylonian Empire. These kings will be the means of exacting *Yahweh's . . . redress for his palace,* of which 50:28 spoke.

12 The leadership of the attacking army is to *lift up a standard* to muster the troops for an advance on Babylon, initially simply to blockade the city and prevent anyone going in to bring provisions or getting out to escape— hence the *ambushes.* As Yahweh formulated an intention and acted against Jerusalem (Lam 2:17), so he is *intending and acting* against Babylon.[197]

13 Jeremiah turns to address Babylon itself. It might think it could last out a long blockade. It doesn't have to worry about its water supply, like most cities; and it apparently has a substantial grain supply. But it is deceiving itself. Etymologically, the *end* of something (*qēṣ*) is the point at which it is "cut off" (*qāṣaṣ*), and maybe Jeremiah plays with that fact when he glosses his reference to the *end* with an apparent metaphor in the expression that refers more literally to "the cubit [at which] you are cut off," a different verb

196. Cf. Duhm, *Jeremia*, 368.
197. R. P. Carroll, *Jeremiah*, OTL, 839.

for cutting off (*bāṣaʿ*) and a more technical expression suggesting that "the cutting of the web from the loom is a figure for death" (cf. Isa 38:12).[198]

14 Yahweh's oath (cf. Amos 6:8) backs up Jeremiah's declaration. Yahweh's words could signify that he intends to send a huge army to Babylon, but the construction more likely refers to his already having made Babylon the monumentally huge city that it was (see the translation note). Either way, he will see that a shout issues within it and against it that will echo his own shout in 25:30 (cf. also 48:33).

15–19 The announcement of Babylon's end underscored by Yahweh's oath issues in an appropriate song of praise.[199] Its description of Yahweh reiterates from 10:12–16 (see the commentary there); it proclaims his power and wisdom as the creator[200] and thus backs up the claims he has been making in vv. 11–14. "To confess the Holy One in such circumstances as the maker of everything . . . must have seemed to many, even many Israelites, as whistling in the dark."[201] But here, these lines assert that he has the capacity to do as he says, and has the motivation to do so, given the fact that Jacob is *his domain*.

6. The Shatterer Shattered (51:20–33 [LXX 28:20–33])

[20]*You,*[a] *a shatterer for me—*
   of battle instruments:[b]
I used to shatter nations with you,[c]
   and devastate kingdoms with you.
I used to shatter horse and its charioteer with you,
   and shatter chariot and its charioteer with you.
[22]*I used to shatter man and woman with you,*
   and shatter elder and youth with you.[d]
I used to shatter young man and young girl[e] *with you,*
   [23]*and shatter shepherd and his flock with you.*
I used to shatter plowman and his pair with you,
   and shatter governors and overseers with you.
[24]*But I will pay back Babylon*
   and all the people who live in Chaldea,
For all their dire dealing,
   which they did in Zion before your[f] *eyes (Yahweh's affirmation).*[g]

---

198. Bright, *Jeremiah*, 356.
199. Kessler, *Battle of the Gods*, 113.
200. Brueggemann, "Jeremiah: Creatio in Extremis," 163.
201. Pixley, *Jeremiah*, 152.

²⁵*Here am I in relation to you,*
 devastator mountain (Yahweh's affirmation),[h]
 the devastator of the entire earth.
I will extend my hand against you
 and roll you from the cliffs
 and make you a burnt mountain.
²⁶*People will not get from you*
 a cornerstone or foundation stone
 because you will be a total destruction for all time (Yahweh's
  affirmation).

²⁷*Lift up a standard in the earth,*
 sound a horn among the nations,
 sanctify nations against it.
Make it heard to kingdoms[i] *against it:*
 Ararat, Minni, Ashkenaz.
Appoint a marshal[j] *against it,*
 get horse to go up like bristling[k] *locust.*
²⁸*Sanctify nations against it,*
 the kings[l] *of Media,*
Its governors and all its overseers,
 and every country that it rules.
²⁹*The earth is quaking and writhing,*[m]
 because Yahweh's intentions are being implemented against Babylon,[n]
To make the country of Babylon
 a desolation, without anyone living there.
³⁰*The strong men of Babylon are ceasing to do battle—*
 they are sitting in the fortresses.
Their strength is drying up—
 they are becoming women.
People are setting fire to its dwellings,
 its bars are breaking.
³¹*Runner runs to meet runner,*
 messenger to meet messenger,
To give the message to the king of Babylon
 that his city has been captured from end to end.[o]
³²*The fords—they have been seized,*
 the marshes[p]*—people have set them on fire,*
 the men of battle—they are panicking.[q]

³³*Because Yahweh of Armies, the God of Israel,*[r] *has said this:*

Miss[s] Babylon is like a threshing floor
at the time of its treading.
Yet a little while
and the time of harvest will come for it.

a. *You* is again masculine singular, and Qimchi (in MG) assumes that Yahweh addresses the king of Babylon, but the gender may again derive from the associated noun—here *mappēṣ*—and the *you* may continue to be Babylon itself.

b. This phrase is the object of *shatterer* (cf. LXX, Vg, Tg) in a broken construct chain (cf. Isa 19:8).

c. LXX, Vg give the sequence of *waw*-consecutives their usual future time reference; *you* would then need to be the Medes or their king (cf. v. 28 LXX). But the role described is not elsewhere theirs but Babylon's past role, so more likely the verbs are past imperfect in significance.

d. LXX lacks this colon.

e. See the translation note on 18:13.

f. The *your* is plural.

g. MT has a section marker here.

h. LXX lacks *(Yahweh's affirmation)*.

i. Sym has "kings."

j. *Ṭipsār* apparently derives from an Akkadian word for a scribe; Vg simply transliterates it, LXX has "siege engines," and Tg has "people who make war." BDB (381) compares *šōṭēr*, which also implies the "military function of those skilled in writing."

k. Likewise, the versions imply puzzlement about this rare word, for which see Job 4:15.

l. LXX has singular "king."

m. Tg "be sick" derives *tāḥōl* from *ḥālâ* rather than from *ḥûl*.

n. The *qatal* and *wayyiqtol* verbs are anticipatory (see the translation note on 50:2); there are further examples in vv. 30 and 32.

o. See BDB and the note on 50:26. But LXX attaches this phrase to the next line.

p. LXX has "communities" and *HALOT* "forts," which seem more plausible than the usual meaning of *'ăgammîm*.

q. MT has a section marker here.

r. LXX lacks *of Armies, the God of Israel*.

s. For MT *bat*, LXX "the houses of the king of" implies *bottê melek*.

Verses 20–33 is a further miscellaneous collocation of messages, with a strong beginning in Yahweh's confrontation of his erstwhile agent of shattering and devastation.

vv. 20–24	A warning to Babylon the shatterer (six bicola, then two further linked bicola)
vv. 25–26	A warning to Babylon the devastator (three tricola)
vv. 27–33	A commission to Babylon's attackers (two tricola framing eleven bicola, including four in two pairs, then a resumptive introduction and two bicola)

20–23 Yahweh again speaks to Babylon and recalls the role he has given it in the past. In this poem "of astonishing intensity and discipline,"[202] the image of the shatterer compares with the more concrete image of the club, applied to Assyria (Isa 10:5) and to Moab (Jer 48:17). The hammer song also matches the sword song of 50:35–38.[203] Here, the unique term *shatterer* links with the verb that will be repeated. Suggesting someone who would break things to pieces (cf. 13:14; 22:28; 48:12), it is a more fearful image for Babylon's role in 25:8–29. "In a way, this little poem summarizes the whole message of Jeremiah,"[204] except that here "Yahweh . . . presents no argument, no indictment, no reasons—giving only a single-minded judgment via some unspecified agent to the nations and kingdoms of the world."[205]

24 But Yahweh's using Babylon in this way has now come to an end, and the experience is to be directed onto Babylon itself. In making this point, Yahweh turns to addressing the Judahites about Babylon in a side comment rather than continuing to speak to Babylon. The dynamic compares with that in v. 11; here as there, the side comment looks like an insertion into the context of the address to Babylon, yet one that plays an important role as "the window through which the rest of the subsection is meant to be viewed."[206] The actual audience for Jeremiah's entire message is Judahites, so rhetorically the change is a move from letting them "overhear" Yahweh addressing Babylon to directly addressing them about Babylon. There is a power about the indirect address; there is another sort of power about the direct address. If they should be unsure whether the message about Babylon is really a piece of good news that is actually meant for them, then the switch makes the point explicit. The reference to what the Babylonians did *in Zion before your eyes* conveys particular poignancy. Judahites exiled to Babylon in 587 or slouching off to Egypt two or three years later and Judahites who never left or who fled across the Jordan: they all saw it.

25–26 But it was simply a side comment, and there follows a further message addressing Babylon, with a declaration that the years of its being devastator and shatterer (cf. v. 21) are indeed over. While it's clear that Babylon is a means of devastation, and that *of the entire earth*, the address to a *mountain* is more surprising. It might simply be a metaphor for Babylon as huge, strong, and domineering. But *devastator mountain* (*har hammašḥît*; lit. "mountain of devastation" or "mountain of the devastator") comes in 2 Kgs 23:13 in connection with Josiah's reformation, referring to the mountain ridge

---

202. Brueggemann, *Jeremiah 26–52*, 272.
203. Boadt, *Jeremiah 26–52*, 145.
204. Pixley, *Jeremiah*, 153.
205. Lundbom, *Jeremiah 37–52*, 456.
206. Allen, *Jeremiah*, 528.

opposite Jerusalem, or part of it, where Solomon built shrines for his wives' deities. Its familiar name is the Mount of Olives, though that term comes in the First Testament only in Zech 14:4. The area is covered in olive trees, and its alternative name is then "mountain of anointing" (*har hammišḥâ*; e.g., m. Rosh Hashanah 2:4).[207] The title in 2 Kgs 23:13 is a pejorative variant of this name, denoting the mountain as a place that had been devastated by the rites conducted there or that would bring devastation on Judah or that would be devastated by Yahweh's action against it. In taking up this designation, Jeremiah passes a similar verdict on Babylon. While Babylon is not literally a mountain, metaphorically it is a place equivalent to the devastator mountain that Judahites knew. It is a place devastated by the service of gods such as Bel and due to be devastated for its service of Bel, and (as the next colon notes) a place that had caused devastation all over its world. Yahweh goes on to let the metaphor be triply mixed. The mountain comes to be located on *cliffs*. Momentarily, we should perhaps forget the picture of Babylon *as* a mountain and think of it sitting *on* a height, from which it is thrown off and turned into a burnt-out mountain—which will suggest the destructive conflagration of the city, so complete that there will be nothing to recycle. Genesis 11:3 shows an awareness that in literal terms there was no stone in Babylon.[208]

27–28 In a further message related in substance through not in imagery, Yahweh once again commissions aides to charge an army to march against Babylon, with a dramatic series of imperatives: *lift up, sound, sanctify, make it heard, appoint, get . . . to go up*, and *sanctify* again—this last significant repeated verb frames the entire enterprise. There is no doubt that the northern attacker is doing Yahweh's work. There is another sacred engagement to be undertaken, like the one Yahweh commissioned against Judah (cf. 6:4; 22:7). Whereas such commissions have previously implied a single nation's army, against Babylon something more substantial is perhaps needed or appropriate. Babylon has been the sacred army; now it is to be the victim of a sacred army. *Ararat, Minni, and Ashkenaz* (Uraṛtu, Mannai, and Ašguzas or Scythia)[209] are peoples north of Assyria (in eastern Turkey and Iran), and they are thus appropriate referents for talk of a northern army. They are within the broad parameters of the sixth-century Median Empire; it is their kings who are *the kings of Media*.

29–32 *The earth* (or "the land"—of Chaldea) *is quaking* in anticipation of this army's arrival, and its military is paralyzed; at least, such a reaction will

---

207. Holladay, *Commentary on Jeremiah*, 2:425. English translations of the Mishnah render the name loosely as "Mount of Olives."

208. Duhm, *Jeremia*, 370. Tg interprets the stones metaphorically as kings and rulers.

209. See Lundbom, *Jeremiah 37–52*, 463–64. The application of the name Ashkenaz to an area within Europe and of the term Ashkenazi to European Jews came about in the medieval period.

be appropriate. The account in these verses operates like a camera spotting different things going on and presenting them in an appropriately jumbled montage. Breaking down of the city's gateway bars, for instance, would precede the invaders setting fire to its houses. The account of the runners or messengers parodies the commitment and efficiency of the imperial communication system. The arrival of intelligence would be expected to have the effect noted in 50:43. *Fords* and *marshes* are features of the Euphrates outside the city; their capture would precede the breaking down of bars and burning of houses. It would be the reeds in the marshes that the army would set on fire, perhaps "to cut off escape and to burn out fugitives who might have sought refuge there."[210] The montage conveys an impression of chaos, confusion, and turmoil. According to Herodotus (*Histories* 1.191), Cyrus's actual capture of Babylon did involve the Persians taking its people unawares, and because of the city's great size, the outer parts of it were overcome while the inhabitants of the middle part knew nothing of it.[211]

33 Once more, Jeremiah and Yahweh stand back and return to the present. The introduction to v. 33 perhaps closes off vv. 1–33 (see v. 1). You can tell when harvest is due: the threshing floor has been prepared by being cleared and trodden down, and it sits waiting for the threshers to arrive. Babylon's time really is coming, as surely as harvest time comes.

7. *Zion's Lament (51:34–44 [LXX 28:34–44])*

[34]*He consumed me, confounded me,*[a]
  did Nebuchadrezzar king of Babylon—
  he rendered me an empty dish.
He swallowed me like a monster,
  filled his belly with my treats, rinsed me off.[b]

[35]*The violence done to me and my body*[c] *be on Babylon,*
  says the girl who lives in Zion.
My blood be toward the people who live in Chaldea,
  says Jerusalem.[d]

[36]*Therefore Yahweh has said this.*

Here am I, arguing the case for you,
  and taking redress for you.[e]

210. Bright, *Jeremiah*, 357.
211. Blayney, *Jeremiah*, 442; see further Vanderhooft, *Neo-Babylonian Empire*, 188–202.

I will wither its sea,
   and dry up its fountain.
[37] *Babylon will become heaps,*
   the abode of jackals, a desolation, something to whistle at,
   with no one living there. [f]

[38] *Together, like cougars* [g] *they roar* [h]—
   they have growled [i] *like lion cubs.*
[39] *When they get hot, I will set out their drink,*
   and get them drunk, in order that they may be merry. [j]
But they will sleep an everlasting sleep
   and not wake up (Yahweh's affirmation).
[40] *I will take them down like lambs for slaughtering,*
   like rams along with goats.

[41] *How Sheshach is being captured,*
   the praise of the entire earth is being seized!
How it is becoming a desolation—
   Babylon among the nations! [k]
[42] *The sea is going up over Babylon—*
   with the noise of its waves it is being covered!
[43] *Its towns are becoming a desolation,*
   a country—desert and steppe,
A country [l] *where no individual lives in them,*
   and no human being passes through them.

[44] *So I will attend to Bel in Babylon* [m]
   and make what he has swallowed come out of his mouth. [n]
Nations will no longer stream to him—
   yes, Babylon's wall is falling. [o]

a. Tg appropriately prefaces v. 34 with "Jerusalem said."

b. The *ketiv* has "us" through v. 34. LXX lacks *rinsed me off*, while Tg "banished" (cf. Vg) derives *hĕdîḥānî* from the more common *nādaḥ* (cf. 50:17) rather than *dûaḥ/dîaḥ* or from a homonym; either way, the translation suggests a paronomasia.

c. Lit. "my violence and my flesh."

d. MT has a section marker here.

e. The *waw*-consecutive continues the participial construction, and in both cola Yahweh emphasizes the point by following the verb with its related noun: "arguing your argument and redressing your redress" (cf. 50:15, 34).

f. The verse reworks 9:11(10); see the translation notes and commentary there. LXX lacks the middle colon.

g. Strictly, "lions"; Jeremiah uses two different words for lions in the two cola.

h. LXX lacks *they roar*. The asyndeton and word order (with the verb at the end of the colon) suggest that the first colon is subordinate to the second; the reverse applies in vv. 41b and 44b.

i. For MT *nāʿărû*, LXX "they were aroused" implies *nĕʿôrû*.

j. LXX "be stupefied" (*NETS*; cf. Vg) for MT *yaʿălōzû* translates in light of the context (cf. *CTAT*, 2:849–50).

k. The *qatal* and *wayyiqtol* verbs are again anticipatory (see the translation note on 50:2); there are further examples in vv. 42–44.

l. LXX lacks *a country*.

m. LXX has simply "to Babylon"; Tg has "to the people who serve Bel in Babylon."

n. *Bel*, *Babel*, and *bilʿô* form a triple assonance.

o. LXX lacks vv. 44b–49a.

This new message takes the form of a protest psalm.

v. 34	Miss Zion protests at Nebuchadrezzar's treatment of her (an opening tricolon and a bicolon)
v. 35	She calls for a corresponding redress to be exacted on Babylon (two self-contained bicola)
vv. 36–44	Yahweh responds
vv. 36–37	An initial commitment to take up Zion's case (after an introduction, two self-contained bicola and a tricolon)
vv. 38–40	A promise to take the animals down (four self-contained bicola)
vv. 41–43	An anticipatory description of the city's fall (five bicola, the last two linked)
v. 44	A closing commitment taking up the terms of the protest (one bicolon)

34 The message begins with a protest such as might appear in a psalm remonstrating at an enemy invasion. Like many such psalms, it takes first-person singular form but speaks on behalf of the community, as v. 35 will make explicit. Again like such psalms, it indicates that "the darkness of trouble" has overwhelmed the community's spirit.[212] *Confounded* suggests as much, being the verb used of occasions when Yahweh confused and bewildered Israel's attackers (Exod 14:24; Josh 10:10; Judg 4:15; 1 Sam 7:10); now the people of God has been on the receiving end of this experience. Those occasions show that being confounded is not just a problem in the minds of its victims. Here, Miss Jerusalem begins with the protest *he consumed me* (*'ākal*), a familiar way to describe a devastating defeat (e.g., 10:25; 50:32). Jeremiah recently used it

---

212. Theodoret, *Ermeneia*, PG 81:752.

with more reference to its literal meaning: other peoples consumed Yahweh's people like sheep (50:7). And he made clear that he meant the image by adding a reference to crunching their bones (50:17). Here he takes it further in more vivid and grisly fashion. Nebuchadrezzar ate up every bit of his victim; to mix the metaphors, he thus turned Jerusalem into an *empty dish*. He embodied the *monster* (*tannin*) standing for supernatural forces of violent and anarchic power that can threaten to overwhelm stability and overwhelm life itself (e.g., Isa 27:1; 51:9).[213] The *treats* with which Nebuchadrezzar thus *filled his belly* were more literally the fine artifacts of the temple. Nebuchadrezzar took some in 597 and more in 587, when he really thus *rinsed me off*, though one can imagine Jeremiah using that hyperbole even in 597. In either context, it's neat that the verb also suggests a paronomasia with another verb meaning sent off into exile (see the translation note).

35 The prayer continues, like a protest psalm, by urging that the attackers be held responsible for their action. Wrong done to another person generates something objective and solid that sits there disrupting and disturbing reality until something is done about it. Even time and the passing of generations may not dissolve it. If the world's proper life is to continue, something has to be done to restore its order and harmony. In the West, people speak of a need to bring closure, which is often a euphemism for retribution. In the First Testament, a standard picture of this need starts from a sense that someone's shed blood sits there crying out about the wrong done to the person (e.g., Gen 4:10; Job 16:18). This blood is against or on the perpetrator or their head (e.g., Lev 20:9; Judg 9:24; 2 Sam 1:16; Ezek 18:13; Jonah 1:14). In her distinctive formulation of this awareness, Miss Jerusalem starts from an alternative picture: the *violence* done to her is on the perpetrator, as Sarah puts it with some irony in Gen 16:5[214] (cf. again Judg 9:24; also Ps 7:16[17]). Abraham (Sarah implies) is responsible for the violence or violation and responsible to do something about it. Here, the formulation of *the girl who lives in Zion*, who speaks in a hendiadys of *the violence done to me and my body*—of the bodily violence done to me—suggests rape, a common reality of war and a recurrent image for the assault of an attacker on a community. The Babylonians raped me, Miss Jerusalem says. You must make them pay for it.

36–37 A protest psalm hopes to receive a response from Yahweh, and this one does. Yahweh might reasonably have replied in snorting fashion to Jerusalem (as he did to some of Jeremiah's own protests) that Jerusalem deserved what happened to it. But the point of the message is to proclaim that calamity is coming on Babylon, and the form of a protest psalm is a

213. R. P. Carroll ("Discombobulations of Time," 77–78) reports that Saddam Hussein was seen in the context of the Gulf War as an embodiment of the Babylonian monster.
214. Kessler, *Battle of the Gods*, 127.

way of doing so. Thus Yahweh works with that form, though in due course he will leave it behind. The psalm's form is related to the appeal of an ordinary person to a king, who is in a position to take action about the matter that the suppliant raises. Here, Yahweh agrees to set about *arguing the case for you and taking redress for you*, the model he assumed in, for example, 50:15, 28, 34. He pictures himself as prosecuting a case in the heavenly cabinet or determining from the chair what the decision must be. He then moves to the traditional imagery of withering and drying up. It has distinctive resonances in connection with Babylon. Babylon sits distinctively astride a major river, surrounded by irrigation canals and streams, as if the vast resources of water lying under the earth's surface bubble up like a fountain. So Yahweh's resolution paints a devastating picture. Following up that threat, he moves on to a familiar hyperbolic description of Babylon's destruction, whose wording makes clear that Jeremiah is again applying to Babylon the threats that Yahweh made to Jerusalem (see the translation note).

38–40 Yahweh reverts to Miss Zion's image of the ravenous beast and runs with it. Babylon is like a pride of hungry lions. They have been out on the prowl and gotten hot. They need a refreshing drink, which he will provide. But he is segueing into the drink imagery of 25:15–29; the Babylonians are now a company of banqueters. He gets them dead drunk and fast asleep, which makes them easy victims for killing, like lambs or rams. "Babylonian lions . . . end up as slaughtered lambs."[215]

41 In another transition, Yahweh returns to a form of speech that can be associated with a lament, though it can also suggest amazement. Here, any suggestion of lament is ironic,[216] but amazement is palpable. Babylon is a city at which the surrounding world marvels. That very fact suggests the danger of its position. It rivals Yahweh in people's eyes and in its own eyes. Yahweh once more describes its fall as if it has already happened—that is, the verbs speak of the event as though it is now past; Babylon is again Sheshach, as in 25:26 (see the translation note and commentary there).

42–43 Yahweh goes on to reverse the significance of water imagery. Babylon did know what an excess of water could be like—it knew what flooding could mean. Judahites were also familiar with the image of the sea as a repository of dynamic but turbulent and riotous energy, like the monster figure of v. 34. And they were familiar with that figure as an image for armies on the rampage overwhelming a country they invaded (e.g., Pss 46; 93; Isa 8:7–8). Yet again, Judah's prospective destiny (e.g., 2:15; 4:7) is also Babylon's.

44 Finally, Yahweh returns once more to Miss Zion's original protest.

215. Allen, *Jeremiah*, 530.
216. Weiser, *Jeremia*, 1:445.

Behind Nebuchadrezzar is Bel, whose name hints at his being a swallower (*bālaʿ*); he swallowed the artifacts of Jerusalem by virtue of the fact that Nebuchadrezzar took them back to Babylon and put them in Bel's temple. It implied that Bel had defeated Yahweh. Yahweh will now reassert himself[217] and ensure that the artifacts return to Jerusalem. Bel's temple now seems like the center of the world, but the world is going to *stream* in a different direction (Isa 2:2). Given the impressive nature of Babylon's wall, it is quite a statement to say that this wall is falling.[218]

8. So Be Mindful of Jerusalem and of Babylon (51:45–58c [LXX 28:45–58c])

⁴⁵*Get out from within it, my people,*
  save, each individual, his life,
  from Yahweh's angry blazing!
⁴⁶*Beware that your mind doesn't become soft or you become afraid*
  at the report that makes itself heard in the country.
The report will come in the year
  and after it in the second year:
Violence in the country
  and ruler against ruler.

⁴⁷*Therefore, there, days are coming*
  when I will attend to Babylon's images.
*Its entire country—it will be shamed,*ᵃ
  and all its people who are run through—they will fall within it.
⁴⁸*Heavens and earth and all that is in them*
  will chant over Babylon.
Because from the north the destroyers will come to it (Yahweh's
    affirmation):
  ⁴⁹*yes, Babylon—regarding the fall of people in Israel who have been run*
      through;
  yes, regarding Babylon—people in the entire earth who have been run
      through have fallen.

⁵⁰*Survivors of the sword, go,*
  don't stand there!
Be mindful of Yahweh from afar,

217. R. P. Carroll, *Jeremiah*, OTL, 848.
218. Thompson, *Jeremiah*, 765.

and Jerusalem—it is to go up into your mind.
51We were shamed, because we heard reviling—
disgrace covered our faces.
Because strangers came
to the sacred places in Yahweh's house.^b

52Therefore, there, days are coming (Yahweh's affirmation)
when I will attend to its images,
and in its entire country the person who has been run through will
groan.
53When Babylon goes up to the heavens,^c
and when it fortifies its strong height,
from me destroyers will come to it (Yahweh's affirmation).^d

54The sound of an outcry from Babylon,
and a great breaking from the country of Chaldea!
55Because Yahweh is destroying Babylon,
and eliminating a loud sound from it.
Their waves^e *will roar like much water—*
the din of their sound will give out.
56Because he is coming upon it,
upon Babylon a destroyer.
Its strong men will be captured—
it will have shattered^f *their bows.*
Because Yahweh is a God of great requital—
he does deal retribution.^g
57I will get its officials and its experts drunk,
its governors and overseers and strong men.
And they will sleep an everlasting sleep
and will not wake up.
(An affirmation of the King,
Yahweh of Armies his name).^h

58a-cYahweh of Armies has said this.

*The great wall*ⁱ *of Babylon, broad—*
it will be totally levelled.^j
Its high gateways—
they will be set on fire.

a. For *tēbôš,* Tg "be dried up" derives the verb from *yābēš* rather than *bûš.*
b. MT has a marker here.

c. Tg refers this colon concretely to building structures with their top in the heavens, in anticipation of the parallel colon and with closer parallel to Gen 11:1–9.

d. MT has a section marker here.

e. Aq, Sym have "its waves," an easier reading.

f. LXX, Vg, Tg implicitly see *ḥittətâ* as intransitive *piel* (cf. GK 52k), which seems implausible. More likely, the verb is impersonal; the implicit subject is the event. Qimchi (in MG) sees Babylon as the subject.

g. The infinitive precedes the finite verb, underlining the factuality of the action. The idiom recurs in v. 58.

h. MT has a section marker here.

i. Since the subsequent adjective *broad* more naturally applies to the wall than to the city, and since the verb that follows is singular, plural *ḥōmôt* is more likely intensive than numerical (Volz, *Jeremia*, 439).

j. The infinitive precedes the finite verb, underlining the factuality of the action.

The form of this new message differs from that of vv. 34–44, but its theme links with it. It implies that the preceding protest is one Judahites need to make, as opposed to one they are actually making. They thus need to listen to Yahweh's response. They are too settled in Babylon. They are not praying that way. The section comprises exhortations followed by declarations, then a closing vision.

vv. 45–46	An exhortation to be mindful and to be prepared to leave (a tricolon, a bicolon, and two linked bicola)
vv. 47–49	A declaration that days are coming, for Babylon's images and people (three bicola and a tricolon)
vv. 50–51	Another exhortation to be mindful and to be prepared to leave (four bicola in two pairs)
vv. 52–53	Another declaration that days are coming, for Babylon's images and fortification (two tricola)
vv. 54–58a	Jeremiah's closing vision of Babylon's fall (nine bicola, then a resumptive introduction and two further bicola)

45 A tricolon thus introduces a recurrent exhortation, beginning from words similar to those of 50:8; 51:6, though adding the appeal to *my people* and the further motivation that they need to escape the threat of *Yahweh's angry blazing*. That phrase again indicates that Yahweh intends to treat Babylon as he threatened to treat Judah (e.g., 4:8, 26). This time, Yahweh will not be angry with Judah, but the expression of his anger will risk anyone in Babylon being victim of collateral damage; the way things work out in the world is that "innocent people" in the wrong place at the wrong time get swallowed up with the guilty (cf. the commentary on 25:8–9a). But on this occasion (as at Sodom) Yahweh tries to get them out of the place before events overwhelm them.

46 Having a *soft mind* can be a virtue (2 Kgs 22:19), but it can mean getting paralyzed by fear (Deut 20:3, 8). "The Jews must not lose their nerve."[219] In the mid-sixth century, the annual reports that Jeremiah speaks of could make knowledgeable people think of Babylonian politics, when Nebuchadrezzar's death in 562 was followed over the next six years by a sequence of kings and assassinations. Josephus quotes Berosus:

> Nabuchodonosor fell sick and died, after a reign of forty-three years, and the realm passed to his son Evilmaraduch. This prince, whose government was arbitrary and licentious, fell a victim to a plot, being assassinated by his sister's husband, Neriglisar, after a reign of two years. On his death Neriglisar, his murderer, succeeded to the throne, and reigned four years. His son, Laborosoardoch, a mere boy, occupied it for nine months, when, owing to the depraved disposition which he showed, a conspiracy was formed against him, and he was beaten to death by his friends. After his murder the conspirators held a meeting, and by common consent conferred the kingdom on Nabonnedos, a Babylonian and one of their gang. In his reign the walls of Babylon abutting the river were magnificently built with baked brick and bitumen.[220]

A later and more imaginative reader might see here the sequence of kingdoms that appear in Daniel, which makes this verse the most interesting in the entire long prophecy about Babylon.[221] But Yahweh may just be commenting more generally on the way "wars and rumors of wars" (Matt 24; Luke 21) characterize human history.[222]

47–49 It's a loose *therefore*, perhaps implying "in light of those facts, pay attention to this message." Attending to Babylon's images suggests attending to the gods they allegedly represent. The vulnerability of the images implies the powerlessness of the gods, and the disaster that comes on both images and gods means the country will be *shamed* by the failure of what it has trusted in. As usual, shame refers not merely to a feeling of being exposed but to the outward results of that exposure. Put crudely, shame means death, whose agent Yahweh reaffirms to be the northern destroyers. The universal *chant over Babylon* could thus have varying implications, including horror and satisfaction. The syntax in v. 49 is elliptical, but the meaning is reasonably clear: Babylon will fall because it has caused so many deaths in Israel. And it will fall because it has caused so many deaths among other nations too. "Op-

219. McKane, *Jeremiah*, 2:1336.
220. Josephus, *Against Apion* 1.20.
221. Duhm, *Jeremia*, 373.
222. Mayer, *Commentary*, 476.

pressed people sigh, requesting a judgment from God, when tyrants and blasphemers seem to themselves to be glorious and think themselves to be highly esteemed. But this judgment of God will speak to everything." Indeed, the tyrants and blasphemers "have been condemned, I say, by the sighs and prayers of people even before the judgment of God is seen and understood."[223]

50 A second sequence of exhortation and promise parallels vv. 45–49. Following the reference to people having *fallen*, those who are rhetorically *survivors of the sword* are the survivors of the carnage Babylon caused in 597 or 587. Jeremiah encouraged them to settle down in Babylon, and once Babylon fell, understandably not many wanted to return to Jerusalem. Verses 45–49 have given one reason why Judahites in Babylon must resist the temptation just to *stand there*, but Jeremiah now gives what one might see as a deeper reason. *From afar* there in Babylon, they are to *be mindful of Yahweh* rather than putting Yahweh and Jerusalem out of mind. The exhortation raises new possibilities about the significance of Ps 137, which refuses to forget Jerusalem and makes a commitment to keep the city in mind and to let it "go up" above any other joy. *Be mindful* and *go up* are the same verbs as in Ps 137:6. While Jer 29 indicates that it's possible to think about Jerusalem too much and not settle down in Babylon, Jer 51 indicates that it's possible not to think about Jerusalem enough and not to be ready to leave.

51 The *we* statements may indicate why people might not want to think about Jerusalem. They are traumatized. Shame, reviling, and disgrace that Yahweh threatened and then imposed (e.g., 24:9) are things people want to forget. In this context, they are distraught at strangers defiling Yahweh's sanctuary not for Yahweh's sake but because of the shame it brought to them.[224] Babylon's destruction will shame Babylon and raise questions about its gods. Jerusalem has already gone through that experience.

52–53 This *therefore* is more straightforward than the one in v. 47, even if the Judahites' concern in v. 51 focused more on themselves than on Yahweh. Yahweh again speaks of attending to the images. Perhaps the order of events in v. 52b is reverse chronological: first they groan, then (having been run through) they die. But Jeremiah's vivid imagination may have the Babylonians continuing to groan over the fate of their city after they die.[225] The subsequent description of Babylon as going up to the heavens parallels Isa 14:13 and suggests overreach in thinking and self-understanding, though it also recalls the story of Babel in Gen 11:1–9; *when it fortifies its strong height* in the parallel colon recalls the building project of which that story speaks.

---

223. Bugenhagen, *In Ieremiam*, 447; cf. Tyler, *Jeremiah*, 448.
224. Rashi, in MG.
225. It might be tempting here to understand *ḥālāl* to mean traumatized (LXX has *traumatiai*! See D. G. Garber, "Vocabulary of Trauma," 309–22).

54–55 Once more, Jeremiah starts again with another anticipatory description of the city's destruction. The poet-prophet "is the one who hears before others hear."[226] *Sound* is the key word here.[227] First, there is *the sound of an outcry*, the cry of pain and protest that will issue from the city when the *great breaking* comes upon it. Its background is that, in *destroying Babylon*, Yahweh will be *eliminating a loud sound from it*, the sound (for instance) of its battle forces (4:29) that roar like the sea (6:23) or the sound of community merrymaking and celebration (7:34). Instead, there is the *sound* of the roaring of the destroyers' *waves*, whose ocean-like breakers with their *din* have overwhelmed the Babylonian ocean. "When Yahweh despoils Babylon (v. 55), the stir and noise associated with the life of a great city will yield to a stillness which is the silence of death."[228]

56–57 And once again, behind the destroyers is the Destroyer. *Captured* and *shattered* recur from 50:2 and in a small way suggest a frame around 50:2–51:58, though the verbs are common—they come also in 50:9, 10, 24, 36; 51:31, 41. More significant are further points of connection with Ps 137:

> Miss Babylon, to be destroyed,
>> the blessings of the one who deals retribution to you,
>> the requital that you have dealt to us!
> The blessings of the one who seizes hold
>> and shatters your babies toward the cliff!

"Destroy," "retribution," "requital," "shatter," "cliff": all are words in common between the psalm and the context in Jeremiah. The prophecy declares that the wish and prayer of the psalm will be fulfilled, or the psalm voices the wish and prayer that the prophecy encourages. The promise about sleep recurs from v. 39, and the verses' promise as a whole is undergirded by the unusually long reassurance about Yahweh's *affirmation*. After the ten references to human kings in Jer 50–51, the chapters almost close with a reminder that Yahweh is the real King.

58a–c One might have expected the reassurance regarding Yahweh's affirmation to mark the end of the messages about Babylon, but actually it is not characteristic for such reassurances to close off a message. While occasionally they do (e.g., 50:30; 51:24, 26), more often they come in the middle of a message (e.g., 50:10, 21, 35, 40; 51:39). And there is no particular reason to see the final pair of bicola as a message on its own. Rather, it is they that

---

226. Brueggemann, *Jeremiah 26–52*, 280.
227. Keown, Scalise, and Smothers, *Jeremiah 26–52*, 372.
228. McKane, *Jeremiah*, 2:1344.

bring vv. 54–58a to a close, with another bold assertion,[229] that the city's *great wall . . . will be totally levelled* and *its high gateways* destroyed.

9. Conclusion (51:58d [LXX 28:58d])

Peoples will toil[a] for emptiness;
   countries—for fire[b] they will get weary.[c]

   a. LXX has "will not toil": that is, the nations' work in attacking Babylon will not be
wasted (R. P. Carroll, *Jeremiah*, OTL, 853).
   b. For MT *bā'ēš*, LXX "in rule" implies *bərō'š*, a slip (*CTAT*, 2:851–53).
   c. MT has a section marker here.

The move to anonymous plural "peoples" and "countries" for the last line in 46:1–51:58 suggests that it closes off the sequence of messages about foreign nations.[230]

58d The line almost corresponds to Hab 2:13:

   Peoples will toil[231] for fire;
      countries—for emptiness they will get weary.[232]

In keeping with the usual pattern, opinions differ on whether Jeremiah is quoting Habakkuk or Habakkuk is quoting Jeremiah or both have a common source—perhaps a proverbial saying[233] worthy of Ecclesiastes that is here applied to a particular context. Either way, the line makes a telling general comment on Babylon in particular and on nations in general. Jeremiah incorporates no suggestion that Judah should take up arms against Babylon or any other nation. He has no thought of Judah taking redress for wrongs that other peoples have done to it. But his framework for thinking about such questions differs from the concern about nonviolence that has become prevalent in some Western thinking over the past century, and he has no instinct toward friendly attitudes to other religions.

---

   229. See the description in Lundbom, *Jeremiah 37–52*, 499.
   230. Volz, *Jeremia*, 441.
   231. Hab 2:13 has the spelling *wəyîgə'û* over against *wəyigə'û* in Jer 51:58.
   232. Hab 2:13 has straightforward *yiqtol yi'āpû* over against the *waw*-consecutive *wəyā'ēpû* in Jer 51:58, where the subject is extraposed (casus pendens; *TTH* 123a).
   233. Thompson, *Jeremiah*, 769.

The worshiping community would publicly re-enact God's involvement in history, God's victory over oppressive regimes, and God's reign on earth. Through ridicule, revel, and affirmation, the worshiping congregation would envision God subverting and disassembling pretentious world powers as a way to carry out divine justice and sovereignty. . . . [The messages'] weapons are rhetoric and imagination not military hardware. They represent the liturgical literature of refugees who find themselves on the margins of society without power, temple, land, or hope.[234]

In this context, the messages declare that Yahweh reigns, that he is involved in contemporary events on the political and military stage, and that he is putting paid to its power structures.[235] They suggest the prayer:

Grant, Almighty God, that since we see that the most opulent kingdoms have not escaped thy hand, we may learn to recumb [recline] only on thine aid, and to submit ourselves to thee, with due humility, so that we may be protected by thy hand, and that this only true confidence may sustain us in all perils, that thou hast undertaken the care of our salvation; and that we may, in the meantime, fight under thy banner with sincerity and uprightness of life, until we shall at length enjoy the fruit of our victory, in the celestial kingdom, through Christ our Lord.—Amen.[236]

10. The Story of the Scroll, and Another Conclusion (51:59–64 [LXX 28:59–64])

[59] The word that Jeremiah the prophet ordered[a] Seraiah ben Neriah, son of Mahseiah, when he went with[b] Zedekiah King of Judah to Babylon in the fourth year of his reign, when Sereiah was accommodation official.[c] [60] Jeremiah wrote down the entire dire fate that would come to Babylon in one document, all these things that are written for Babylon. [61] And Jeremiah said to Seraiah: When you come to Babylon, see that you read out[d] all these things, [62] and say, Yahweh, you yourself spoke regarding this place, about cutting it off so that there will not be in it human being or animal, because it will be a great desolation for all time. [63] And when you have finished reading out this document, you are to tie a stone to it and throw it into the middle of the Euphrates [64] and say, So will Babylon sink and not get up in the face of the dire fate[e] that I am letting come upon it. So they will get weary.

As far as this are Jeremiah's words.[f]

234. Stulman, Jeremiah, 384.
235. Stulman, Jeremiah, 385.
236. Calvin, Jeremiah, 4:165.

a. LXX has "the word that the Lord ordered Jeremiah the prophet to speak to"; the action is undertaken on Yahweh's initiative, not on Jeremiah's (see the commentary), perhaps because it is what one would expect theologically (McKane, *Jeremiah*, 2:1350).

b. For *'et*, Vg, Aq, Sym have "with," but LXX has "from," implying *mē'ēt*; Tg "in/with the commission of" is ambiguous.

c. Lit. "official of rest." For MT *mɘnûḥâ*, LXX, Tg "gift[s]" suggests *mɘnāḥôt/mɘnāḥâ*, "official in charge of the tribute"; Vg "prophecy" suggests *hammaśśā'* as in 1 Chr 15:27 (*BHS*) or suggests that *mɘnûḥâ* implies the spirit of God "resting" on him as in Num 11:25 (HUBP).

d. Lit. "see and read out"; for this idiom, cf. Exod 25:40.

e. For MT *hārā'â*, "the Chaldeans" in the Codex Vaticanus of the Septuagint (LXX^B) implies *kaśdîm*.

f. MT has a marker here. LXX lacks *So they will get weary. As far as this are Jeremiah's words.*

Following the messages about different nations, and specifically the messages about Babylon, is a story about how Jeremiah sends the messages about Babylon to Babylon. While it might be "just a story,"[237] it threatens to deconstruct if it tells of something that never happened. It relates that Jeremiah took action to see that Yahweh implemented his intentions about Babylon; if he did not, the story backfires. Given that many of the messages in Jer 50–51 seem likely to have come from after 587, however, a 594 document would not have contained *all these things that are written for Babylon*—if *all these things* implies the entirety of Jer 50–51. Like other stories in Jeremiah, then, vv. 59–64 are likely to be dramatized fact, a story based on fact, rather than simply history. The story illustrates how a document can become an independent actor in a narrative. Documents can communicate across geographical and temporal distances; they are both fragile and durable, and they exist in both mundane and divine realms. In Jeremiah, texts are rarely devoid of some sense of their performative, effective capacity. They are the stuff of normal, everyday interactions, but they also have the capacity to serve higher purposes. "This mysterious aspect of the written word . . . comes, not from some abstract notion of magical power, but from the power inherent in Yhwh's involvement in that written word."[238]

59 The story refers to something that happened in 594. Zedekiah's going to Babylon that year was perhaps an expression of his loyalty to Nebuchadrezzar, who had put him on the throne in place of Jehoiachin (2 Kgs 24:17). The setting might be the aftermath of the plotting at which Jer 27–28 hints or in the broader context of Babylon being in difficulty with the southwestern

237. So W. McKane, "Jeremiah's Instructions to Seraiah (Jeremiah 51:59–64)," in *Pomegranates and Golden Bells: Studies in Biblical, Jewish, and Near Eastern Ritual, Law, and Literature in Honor of Jacob Milgrom*, ed. D. P. Wright, D. N. Freedman, and A. Hurvitz (Winona Lake, IN: Eisenbrauns, 1995), 697–706.

238. Eggleston, *"See and Read"*, 94, 101.

corner of its empire, near Egypt.[239] LXX plausibly implies that Zedekiah was delivering Judah's taxes; it would be one concrete expression of loyalty. MT likely implies that Seraiah's role involved arranging lodgings for the king and his entourage on the journey—it would take a number of weeks. A seal from Jerusalem bears Seraiah's name (see the commentary on 36:11–14a); 32:12 invites the inference that he was Baruch's brother and that the Mahseiah family might have been a family of scribes.[240]

60 The story concerns a symbolic act, comparable to earlier such acts on Jeremiah's part but with distinctive features. It is an act of some complexity; its several aspects have similar implications, but they work in different ways. First, writing the document puts Yahweh's words into writing and contributes to ensuring that they come about. The commission heightens the contrast between the document's contents and Jeremiah's insistence that Zedekiah must submit to Nebuchadrezzar. It hardly follows that "the dating of this anti-Babylon sign-act to the fourth year of Zedekiah (51:59) clearly indicates that the 'serve Babylon and live' philosophy had met with strong opposition in the years immediately following 597."[241] Setting the oracles against Babylon in this particular year suggests that different perspectives on Babylon are not to be explained merely by attributing them to different people or to the same person at different times. Both the present submission to Babylon and the ultimate doom of Babylon are Yahweh's will.[242] Jeremiah's entrusting Seraiah with his commission does carry massive irony given that the document that he sends is full of declarations that Babylon is going to fall. "How ironic that the diplomatic bag which carried such wealth also contained the book of curses!"[243]

61–62 Reading the document aloud adds to the effectiveness of writing: it becomes something out there in the world—the world where it needs to be implemented. While Seraiah would perhaps read the document in the hearing of the Judahites in Babylon or of the Babylonians themselves (which would be brave, given its contents),[244] the story does not say so, and the reading is not a political act. It's not like the public reading in Jer 36. This reading happens in order for Yahweh to hear it, with an implicit challenge to Yahweh to do as he has said in these messages. This feature of the commission

---

239. See Lipschits, *Fall and Rise of Jerusalem*, 62–65.

240. Lundbom, *Jeremiah 37–52*, 506.

241. Sharp, "Call of Jeremiah," 432

242. P. D. Miller, "Jeremiah," on the passage.

243. R. P. Carroll, *Jeremiah*, OTL, 856.

244. Friebel (*Sign Acts*, 154–69) assumes he would.

fits with one distinctive aspect of the story: that the commission happens on Jeremiah's initiative, not Yahweh's (again, it's possible that Yahweh bade Jeremiah initiate this action, but the story does not say so). The reading is an acted prayer, which makes a link with 51:34–44; Seraiah is to wave the document in Yahweh's face.[245] Whereas Jeremiah's words addressed to Babylon were a speech act, in his commission to Seraiah, "Jeremiah effectually creates a new illocution for Seraiah to perform" as "the audience changes from the hearers of the oracle to God himself when Seraiah prays."[246] Jeremiah refers to Babylon as *this place*, a key phrase in the Jeremiah scroll, which moves from Jerusalem as "this place" (Jer 7) to all the places where Baruch may go (45:5) to Babylon as *this place*.[247] As Jerusalem has been compromised as a sacred space, Babylon has been a kind of interim sacred space.[248] But using the phrase *this place* also links ironically with the transfer of curses in Jeremiah from Jerusalem to Babylon.[249]

63 Seraiah's action is not like the depositing of a document. Nor does it constitute "text destruction" like that in Jer 36.[250] Throwing the document into the river so that it sinks will prevent its destruction, add yet further to the implementing of its declarations, and further guarantee their fulfillment. The city's fate is sealed by the drowning of all the messages that speak about it. "Nothing can now prevent Babylon's defeat."[251]

64a The story compares with other accounts of symbolic acts in Jeremiah that include no account of the act's happening; formally, the story is like a colophon.[252] It exists for the sake of the people who read it, who thereby receive the assurance that Yahweh will fulfill the messages in Jer 50–51. Although the story refers to an event in 594, it carries no implication for when the story was told. It might have been after 587; and within the Jeremiah scroll, it speaks to people living after 587. The last words within the story, *so they will get weary*, make explicit that the closing line in Jeremiah's own

245. Brueggemann, *Jeremiah 26–52*, 284.

246. K. D. Holroyd, "Multiple Speech Act Layers, Jeremiah, and the Future of Studies in Structural Theology," in *Das heilige Herz der Tora: Festschrift für Hendrik* Koorevaar *zu seinem 65. Geburtstag*, ed. S. Riecker and J. Steinberg (Aachen: Shaker, 2011), 90.

247. B. Gosse, "Trois étapes de la rédaction du livre de Jérémie," *ZAW* 111 (1999): 508–29.

248. M. Leuchter, "Sacred Space," 77–99.

249. B. Gosse, "La malédiction contre Babylone de Jérémie 51,59–64 et les rédactions du livre de Jérémie," *ZAW* 98 (1986): 383–99.

250. N. B. Levtow, "Text Production and Destruction in Ancient Israel," in *Social Theory and the Study of Israelite Religion Essays in Retrospect and Prospect*, ed. S. M. Olyan, Resources for Biblical Study 71 (Atlanta: Society of Biblical Literature, 2012), 111–39.

251. R. P. Carroll, *Jeremiah*, OTL, 856.

252. Lundbom, *Jeremiah 37–52*, 502–5.

words in v. 58 indeed applies to the Babylonians. "In the slaughter of Babylon as well as of the rest of the nations in chs. 46–49, Yahweh is able to display the futility of the world's imperial intentions."[253]

64b This closing sentence might be the colophon that originally applied just to Jer 50–51 or to Jer 46–51,[254] but within the Jeremiah scroll, it notes the fact that we are actually at the end of Jeremiah's words; there are none in Jer 52.

253. Diamond, "Jeremiah," 611.

254. See J. R. Lundbom, "Baruch, Seraiah, and Expanded Colophons in the Book of Jeremiah," *JSOT* 36 (1986): 96.

EPILOGUE (52:1-34)

The Jeremiah scroll could have seemed to come to a satisfactory end with 51:64 (which read like an end), as was the case with 45:5 and 36:32, but it did not come to an end at any of these points, almost as if it "resists closure" as an aspect of its links with disaster and trauma.[1] Its readers would certainly not expect a repetition of the account of Jerusalem's fall that appeared in Jer 39, though they might have noticed that the scroll sometimes incorporates more than one account of an event—at least, it contains a story about Jeremiah delivering a message and elsewhere a précis of his words on that occasion. The chapter would be even more surprising to readers who knew the 2 Kings narrative. They would approach the chapter with a sense of déjà vu, wondering what they were expected to take from it.

But Jer 52 forms a frame with Jer 1 around the Jeremiah scroll. With it, the scroll reaches its goal, and there is no reason to see it as a later addition, as if Jer 1–51 once existed without it.[2] Matching the opening chapter and matching the nature of the scroll as a whole, it tells a solemn story of Judah's waywardness and of the calamity that followed, while also affirming that calamity is not Yahweh's last word.

Initially, the chapter reinforces the gloomy tone of the scroll as a whole. Pull up, pull down, wipe out, smash: "Never were four words more fully realized."[3] The chapter "highlights the ultimate tragic irony that the authors face: it vindicates Jeremiah as a true prophet, while at the same time it shows how ineffective all forms of human mediation were in preventing disaster."[4] Following on 51:64b, it answers the question, "What happened, then? Did those words of Jeremiah come true?" In taking up that question, it does not need to make mention of Jeremiah himself. The answer it implies is that Jeremiah's words indeed found some measure of fulfillment, both horribly and encouragingly. Horrifying things happened to the monarchy, to the city, to the temple, and to the people. But in the course of giving an account of these horrors, the chapter incorporates notes of possible encouragement.[5] Not only did the Babylonians leave some people behind in Jerusalem; the number they took to Babylon was minute. The men of battle (which really

1. Cf. K. M. O'Connor, "Terror All Around: Confusion as Meaning-Making," in Diamond and Stulman, *Jeremiah (Dis)placed*, 78.

2. J. Smith argues this point on the basis of the nature of the Greek translation in "Jeremiah 52: Thackeray and Beyond," *Bulletin of the International Organization for Septuagint and Cognate Studies* 35 (2002): 55–96.

3. Wright, *Jeremiah*, 442.

4. C. Patton, "Layers of Meaning," 167.

5. Clements, *Jeremiah*, 268–72.

means all the men) scattered; but the implication is that they did not die. The temple accoutrements and the bronze of items such as the temple pillars went off to Babylon; but they didn't get lost. And finally, the Davidic king who had been taken to Babylon in 597 was released there. So anyone yielding to the temptation to leave the movie theater during the credits would miss something vital and encouraging. The story forms an apposite closure for the scroll insofar as its balance reflects that of Jeremiah's message: much waywardness, much consequential trouble, but a glimmer of hope. Both calamity and reestablishment fall way short of Yahweh's threats and promises, in keeping with the usual pattern. There was no actual annihilation and no genuine renewal. There was frightful calamity but also a hint of extraordinary restoration. There was something, not nothing.

¹*Zedekiah was a man of twenty-one years when he began to reign, and he reigned eleven years in Jerusalem. His mother's name was Hamutal*ᵃ *bat Jeremiah, from Libnah.*ᵇ ²*He did what was dire in Yahweh's eyes in accordance with all that Jehoiakim had done,* ³*because it was directed toward*ᶜ *Yahweh's anger against Jerusalem and Judah, until he threw them out from his presence.*

Zedekiah rebelled against the king of Babylon. ⁴*Then in the ninth year of his reign, in the tenth*ᵈ *month, on the tenth of the month, Nebuchadrezzar King of Babylon came, he and his entire force, against Jerusalem. They camped*ᵉ *against it and built a blockade against it all around.* ⁵*The city came under siege until the eleventh year of King Zedekiah.* ⁶*In the fourth month,*ᶠ *on the ninth of the month, the famine was heavy in the city, and there was no bread for the people of the country.* ⁷*The city broke open and all the men of battle were fleeing. They went out from the city*ᵍ *at night by way of the gateway between the double wall that was opposite the king's garden, with the Chaldeans against the city all around, and they went by the steppes road.* ⁸*But the Chaldean force chased after the king and caught up with Zedekiah*ʰ *in the Jericho steppes; all his force had scattered from him.* ⁹*They captured the king and made him go up to the king of Babylon at Riblah in the region of Hamath,*ⁱ *and he spoke out authoritative decisions*ʲ *with him.* ¹⁰*The king of Babylon slaughtered Zedekiah's sons*ᵏ *before his eyes. All the Judahite officials he also slaughtered at Riblah.*ˡ ¹¹*Zedekiah's eyes he blinded, and he shackled him with bronze chains. The king of Babylon made him come to Babylon and put him in a house of custody*ᵐ *until the day of his death.*ⁿ

¹²*In the fifth month, on the tenth*ᵒ *of the month (it was the nineteenth year of King Nebuchadrezzar King of Babylon),*ᵖ *Nebuzaradan the chief of the guards came—he stood as the king of Babylon's representative*ۊ*—to Jerusalem,* ¹³*and burned Yahweh's house, the king's house, and all the houses in Jerusalem. Every house of a big person*ʳ *he burned in fire.* ¹⁴*All the walls of Jerusalem, all around, the entire Chaldean force that was with the chief of the guards pulled down.* ¹⁵*Some of the poorest elements of the people*ˢ *and the rest of the people who re-*

mained in the city, and the people who had submitted (who had submitted to the king of Babylon) and the rest of the crowd,[t] *Nebuzaradan the chief of the guards made go into exile.* [16]*Some of the poorest elements*[u] *in the country Nebuzaradan*[v] *the chief of the guards let remain as vinedressers and farmworkers.*

[17]*The bronze pillars that belonged to Yahweh's house, the stands, and the bronze sea that was in Yahweh's house, the Chaldeans broke up. They carried all their bronze to Babylon.* [18]*The buckets, the shovels, the trimmers, the throwers, the ladles, and all the bronze articles with which people ministered, they got.* [19]*The bowls, the firepans, the containers, the pots, the lamps, the ladles, and the chalices, what was gold [as] gold and what was silver [as] silver, the chief of the guards got.*[w] [20]*The two pillars, the one sea, and the twelve bronze cattle that were underneath, the stands,*[x] *which King Solomon made for Yahweh's house— there was no weighing their bronze, all these articles.* [21]*The pillars—eighteen cubits*[y] *the height of one pillar, and a line of twelve cubits would go around it; its thickness—four fingers, hollow;*[z] [22]*with a bronze capital on it—the height of one capital five*[aa] *cubits, and lattice work with pomegranates on the capital all around, the whole bronze, and like these for the second pillar with pomegranates.*[bb] [23]*There were ninety-six pomegranates windward;*[cc] *all the pomegranates—a hundred on the lattice work all around.*[dd]

[24]*The chief of the guards got Seraiah the head priest, Zephaniah*[ee] *the second priest, and the three keepers of the threshold,* [25]*and from the city he got*[ff] *an overseer*[gg] *who was appointee over the men of battle, seven*[hh] *people from the heads who were before*[ii] *the king, who were present in the city, the scribe of the army officer*[jj] *who mustered the people of the country, and sixty individuals from the people of the country who were present inside the city.* [26]*Nebuzaradan the chief of the guards got them and made them go to the king of Babylon at Riblah,* [27]*and the king of Babylon struck them down and put them to death*[kk] *at Riblah in the region of Hamath.*

So Judah went into exile from upon its land.[ll] [28]*This is the company that Nebuchadrezzar made go into exile: in the seventh year, 3,023 Judahites;* [29]*in Nebuchadrezzar's eighteenth year, from Jerusalem 832 individuals;* [30]*in Nebuchadrezzar's twenty-third year, Nebuzaradan the chief of the guards made 745 individual Judahites go into exile; all the individuals, 4,600.*[mm]

[31]*Then in the thirty-seventh year of the exile of Jehoiachin*[nn] *King of Judah, in the twelfth month, on the twenty-fifth*[oo] *of the month, Evil-merodach*[pp] *King of Babylon, in the year he began to reign, lifted the head of Jehoiachin King of Judah, let him go from the house of confinement,* [32]*and spoke of good things with him. He put his throne above the throne of the kings who were with him in Babylon,* [33]*so he would change his confinement clothes and eat a meal before him regularly all the days of his life.*[qq] [34]*His provision was given to him as a regular provision from the king of Babylon, a day's allocation on its day, until the day of his death,*[rr] *all the days of his life.*[ss]

The Book of Jeremiah

a. So the *qere*, which corresponds to 2 Kgs 23:31; the *ketiv* implies Hamital (cf. LXX, Vg).

b. A town in the Shephelah; see Josh 10:28–32; 15:42.

c. The expression compares with 32:31 (Thompson, *Jeremiah*, 772); see the translation note there.

d. Some LXX MSS have "eighth" or "ninth."

e. 2 Kgs 25:1 has "he camped."

f. LXX and 2 Kgs 25:3 lack *in the fourth month.*

g. LXX and 2 Kgs 25:4 lack *were fleeing* and *from the city*; 2 Kgs 25:4 also lacks *they went out.*

h. For *Zedekiah*, LXX and 2 Kgs 25:6 have simply "him."

i. LXX has "Diblah" here and elsewhere, and it lacks *in the region of Hamath* (as does 2 Kgs 25:6).

j. 2 Kgs 25:6 has "they spoke out an authoritative decision."

k. 2 Kgs 25:7 has "Zedekiah's sons they slaughtered."

l. 2 Kgs 25:7 lacks this sentence.

m. Lit. "attention house"—that is, punishment house. LXX has "grinding house," with the implication that grinding grain was the prisoners' chief occupation (cf. Judg 16:21); perhaps MT has substituted a more general expression.

n. For this sentence, 2 Kgs 25:7 has simply "He made him come to Babylon."

o. 2 Kgs 25:8 has "seventh."

p. LXX lacks *(it was the nineteenth year of King Nebuchadrezzar King of Babylon).* By the Babylonian Chronicle's method of counting years, it was the eighteenth year (v. 29) (Allen, *Jeremiah*, 540).

q. Lit. "stood before the king of Babylon"; MT's construction is asyndetic or implies an unmarked relative clause. For *ʿāmad*, LXX "standing" implies *ʿōmēd*, while 2 Kgs 25:8 has "servant of the king of Babylon."

r. For MT's *bêt haggādôl* (cf. Tg), LXX, Vg "every big house" implies absolute *bayit* or the idiom whereby an adjective is added in the genitive rather than as an attribute (GK 128w); cf. *bêt gādôl* in 2 Kgs 25:9.

s. 2 Kgs 25:11 lacks *some of the poorest elements of the people.*

t. Taking *ʾāmôn* as an alternative to *hāmôn* (cf. 2 Kgs 25:11), with Vg, Tg, Syr (LXX lacks v. 15). It otherwise occurs only in Prov 8:30, where its meaning is unclear, though one possibility is craftsman or builder—which would fit here.

u. V. 16 thus begins in the same way as v. 15, which may explain LXX's lack of v. 15 as homoioarkton.

v. LXX and 2 Kgs 25:12 lack *Nabuzaradan.*

w. LXX and 2 Kgs 25:14–17 have shorter lists compared with vv. 18–23; on the textual problems, see Holladay, *Commentary on Jeremiah*, 2:437.

x. The more obvious translation "under the stands" (Vg, Aq) makes poor sense; LXX has "under the sea." For the adverbial use of *taḥat*, cf. Gen 49:25 (see *CTAT*, 2:857–59).

y. LXX has "thirty-five cubits." A cubit is roughly half a yard or half a meter.

z. For MT *nābûb*, LXX "around" implies *sābîb.*

aa. Cf. 1 Kgs 7:16; but 2 Kgs 25:17 says "three."

bb. LXX reads "eight pomegranates to the cubit for the twelve cubits."

cc. For MT's puzzling *rûḥâ*, LXX has "the one side."

dd. MT^A has a section marker here.

ee. LXX lacks *Seraiah* and *Zephaniah.*

ff. LXX lacks *from the city he got.*

gg. See the translation note on 29:2.

hh. 2 Kgs 25:19 has "five."

ii. Lit. "who saw the face of."

jj. LXX lacks *officer.*

kk. The double expression adds emphasis (cf. 41:2); LXX lacks *and put them to death.*

ll. LXX lacks *so Judah went into exile from upon its land.* MT^A has a section marker here.

mm. MT has a marker here.

nn. LXX has "Jehoiakim" each time in this verse.

oo. LXX has "twenty-fourth," while 2 Kgs 25:27 has "twenty-seventh."

pp. More precisely, *'ĕwîl-mərōdak*—that is, his name does not include the English word *evil.* In Akkadian, the name would be an alternative to the more familiar Amel-Marduk (see R. H. Sack, *Amēl-Marduk 562–560 B. C.* [Kevelaer: Butzon, 1972]). Either name would mean "man of Marduk," but a Judahite might rejoice that in Hebrew *'ĕwîl-mərōdak* would mean "fool of Marduk" or "Marduk is foolish."

qq. While the two simple *waw* clauses may simply be anomalous (cf. GK 112pp; Duhm, *Jeremia*, 382), they also may indicate the logical connection with what precedes. The subject of the second verb must be Jehoiachin, and probably he is therefore the subject of the first verb. Likewise, *all the days of his life* refers to Jehoiachin's life (cf. v. 34); a reference to Evil-merodach's life would carry some irony, as he was assassinated after a year or two (see the commentary on 51:46).

rr. 2 Kgs 25:30 lacks *until the day of his death.*

ss. LXX lacks *all the days of his life.*

The chapter is one of five First Testament accounts of the fall of Jerusalem and its aftermath. In outline, synoptically, they compare as follows:

	Jer 52 MT	Jer 52 LXX	Jer 37–43	2 Kgs	2 Chr
Zedekiah comes to the throne	52:1–3	52:1	37:1–2	24:18–20	36:11–14
Nebuchadrezzar takes the city	52:4–11	52:4–11	39:1–7	25:1–7	36:15–17
Nebuzaradan destroys the city	52:12–16	52:12–16	39:8–10	25:8–12	36:18–19
The temple pillaged	52:17–23	52:17–23		25:13–18	36:19
Judahite leaders taken to Riblah	52:24–27	52:24–27	39:11–18	25:19–21	
Gedaliah appointed by Nebuzaradan			40:1–43:7	25:22–26	

	Jer 52 MT	Jer 52 LXX	Jer 37–43	2 Kgs	2 Chr
Numbers of people taken to Babylon	52:28–30				36:20–21
Amel-marduk releases Jehoiachin	52:31–34	52:31–34		25:27–30	
Cyrus commissions temple building					36:22–23

First Esdras 1:46–2:7 is another version building on 2 Chr 36 and Ezra 1.[6]

After going different ways for some time, MT and LXX agree that 52:1–34 brings the Jeremiah scroll to a close. Beyond the more significant differences noted by the chart, both the MT and LXX versions of the chapter mostly correspond to the account of the fall of Jerusalem in 2 Kgs 24:18–25:30.[7] "How intertextual can you get?"[8] They also overlap with the narrative in Jer 37–43 (MT and LXX broadly correspond in those chapters, with the usual differences of detail), with significant correspondence in 52:4–16 compared with 39:1–10. While these phenomena must be clues to aspects of the development of the scroll, there is the usual room for disagreement over which version came first, but a comparison of the different versions can draw attention to their respective features.[9] The most noticeable distinctive features of Jer 52 MT are its lack of reference to Gedaliah, its inclusion of the numbers of

6. R. F. Person, "II Kings 24,18–25,30 and Jeremiah 52," *ZAW* 105 (1993): 174–205, provides a Hebrew synopsis of these texts and a retroversion of the Greek texts and compares them; see also R. F. Person, *The Kings-Isaiah and Kings-Jeremiah Recensions*, BZAW 252 (Berlin: de Gruyter, 1997).

7. See the translation notes for detailed differences. P.-M. Bogaert ("Les trois forms de Jérémie 52," in *Tradition of the Text: Studies Offered to Dominique Barthélemy in Celebration of His 70th Birthday*, ed. G. J. Norton and S. Pisano, OBO 109 [Göttingen: Vandenhoeck & Ruprecht, 1991], 1–7), A. Rofé ("Not Exile but Annihilation for Zedekiah's People," in *VIII Congress of the International Organization for Septuagint and Cognate Studies*, ed. L. Greenspoon and O. Munnich, SCS 41 [Atlanta: Scholars, 1995], 165–70), and G. Fischer ("Jeremiah 52," in *X Congress of the International Organization for Septuagint and Cognate Studies*, ed. B. A. Taylor, SCS 51 [Atlanta: Society of Biblical Literature, 2001], 37–48) consider their implications for theories about the relationship of MT and LXX.

8. R. P. Carroll, "Intertextuality and the Book of Jeremiah," in *The New Literary Criticism and the Hebrew Bible*, ed. J. C. Exum and D. J. A. Clines, JSOTSup 143 (Sheffield: JSOT, 1993), 63; cf. R. P. Carroll, "The Book of J," in Diamond, K. M. O'Connor, and Stulman, *Troubling Jeremiah*, 220–43.

9. G. Fischer, "Jeremía 52—ein Schlüssel zum Jeremiabuch," *Bib* 79 (1998): 333–59.

Judahites taken to Babylon, and its lack of reference to Cyrus's commission to Judahites to return to rebuild the temple—which Chronicles can see as fulfilling Yahweh's word to Jeremiah. Related is the fact that Jer 52 and 2 Kgs 25 record the fate of Judahite priestly and military leaders but make no mention of Jeremiah and his fate. The chapter makes no reference to its significance in relation to the fulfillment of Jeremiah's message or his vindication. Like Jer 50–51, it hardly postdates 539; in light of vv. 31–34, a date in the 550s or 540s makes sense, as it does for Jer 50–51.

1 It seems odd that the chapter begins with Zedekiah's accession rather than his rebellion that led to the fall of Jerusalem, or Jehoiakim's reign, or Jehoiachin's accession and deposing (since the chapter closes with Jehoiachin). Jehoiakim had died in 597, and Jehoiachin his son had succeeded him. The likely background to the Babylonians' putting Zedekiah in his place is that Jehoiachin followed (or was assumed to follow) Jehoiakim's policy of courting alliance with Egypt. The Babylonians expected Zedekiah to accept subordination to Babylon, which was also Jeremiah's exhortation.[10] There is a double irony in the Babylonians' changing his name from Mattaniah ("Yah's gift"! 2 Kgs 24:17) to Zedekiah ("Yah my faithfulness"). It was surely not "the intention of the Babylonian ruler . . . in this way to 'show that he was fulfilling the will of the native God of Jerusalem and Judah, both in salvation and judgment'? This is what he actually did. . . . In this situation the prophet saw that another opportunity had been given by God to the people. . . . But Zedekiah did not live up to his name."[11]

2–3a The presence of vv. 2–3 in MT makes for a contrast with LXX. Zedekiah's doing *what was dire in Yahweh's eyes* will have included resistance to Babylon, though Jeremiah's messages have implied that it also involved other forms of unfaithfulness to Yahweh. The explanation that things happened *because it was directed toward Yahweh's anger against Jerusalem and Judah, until he threw them out from his presence* is laconic. It makes links between Zedekiah's action, Yahweh's anger, and Jerusalem's fall, but it leaves their relationship obscure. Did Zedekiah's policies cause Yahweh to act in anger? Or was Jehoiakim's waywardness the cause and Zedekiah's accession and moral or religious stupidity an expression of that anger, and then the immediate cause of the city's fall?[12] Often such questions cannot be answered, only noted. MT simply sets alongside each other on one hand the way Zedekiah

---

10. See, e.g., Lipschits, *Fall and Rise of Jerusalem*, 49–62.

11. Barth, *CD* IV, 1:469, quoting from W. Vischer, *Das Christuszeugnis des Alten Testament* (Munich: Kaiser, 1935–42), 2:535.

12. R. P. Carroll, *Jeremiah*, OTL, 859.

is acting in relation to Yahweh and the way Yahweh will act in the story that follows (there will be no more references to Yahweh except the expression "Yahweh's house") and on the other hand the actions of Zedekiah toward Nebuchadrezzar and the actions of Nebuchadrezzar toward Judah, without commenting on the relationship between them. In isolation, one might universalize the first way of looking at events and affirm a universal supernaturalism or absolutize the second and affirm and reduce history to power. The Jeremiah scroll relativizes each of these perspectives by juxtaposing them with each other and presupposing "intrusion, surprise, discontinuity, gifts, judgment, newness, and ambiguity."[13] Prophets such as Jeremiah

> thought and spoke in a way which was supremely true theologically and supremely realistic politically. But they and their word were a foreign body in their environment. Apart from the fact that they spoke the Word of God, the only point in their favour was that events actually proved them right: that history passed devastatingly over Israel; that first the state of Israel and then that of Judah was completely eliminated; that nothing was left to the men of Israel but the God against whom they had sinned to the last in resisting His judgment, but whose hard hand they could not finally withstand—the covenant God, the Lord of the world, their Judge even as their strength, but as the strength which they had despised . . . [in] their repudiation of their helplessness in face of God, their stubbornness against the only One who could help them.[14]

3b–6 The king's decision to rebel against Yahweh and against Nebuchadrezzar brings calamity on Jerusalem. As usual, the people pay a price for their leadership's action, as in other contexts they benefit from it. In principle, one can hardly fault Judah's desire for independence or desire to determine its own political policies (e.g., to look to Egypt rather than to Babylon). But in this context, in light of events over recent decades, Yahweh has decided that submission to Babylon is an expression of submission to him. Though Nebuchadrezzar is thus unwittingly acting as Yahweh's servant, his own concern lies elsewhere. Keeping control of Judah is one aspect of keeping control of the Levant and its trade routes that he had taken over from the Assyrians[15] and of exercising some authority in relation to Egypt in

13. W. Brueggemann, "The Prophetic Word of God and History," *Int* 48 (1994): 241.
14. Barth, *CD* IV, 1:468–69.
15. H. M. Barstad, "The City State of Jerusalem in the Neo-Babylonian Empire," in *By the Irrigation Canals of Babylon: Approaches to the Study of the Exile*, ed. J. J. Ahn and J. Middlemas, LHBOTS 526 (London: T&T Clark, 2012), 34–48.

this connection. And rebels need to be put in their place to make sure that no other people gets fancy ideas. In itself, a blockade means not attempting to take the city by force but preventing supplies reaching it. It might seem odd for the Babylonians to need to blockade the city for as long as eighteen months, and for Jerusalem to be able to survive such a blockade implies impressive preparation by way of the bringing in of grain and other supplies. But we know from 37:5 that the siege was not continuous; the Babylonians had to interrupt it to pursue other business.

7–11 *The city broke open*[16] sounds more like a breaking from inside than a breaking from outside, and the subsequent account of *all the men of battle . . . fleeing* may suggest that they were the people who finally gave in to the inevitable; they would know that they in particular would get slaughtered if they didn't run for it. The grimmest scene in the First Testament follows, an account that reformulates the one in 39:4–7 (see the commentary there). The death of Zedekiah's sons means that his line will not continue, so that in this context this note initiates the contrast between Zedekiah and Jehoiachin (see vv. 31–34). Likewise, *until the day of his death*, distinctive to Jer 52 compared with 2 Kgs 25:7 as well as Jer 39:7, will make for a contrast with the closing words about Jehoiachin in v. 34: he will be sustained by Babylonian kings *until the day of his death, all the days of his life*.[17] But in the meantime, for Zedekiah, *house of custody* might mean house arrest rather than prison.[18]

12–16 Another month has passed; perhaps the Babylonians were sorting out the people and the plunder before setting about the destruction of the city.[19] Judahites might view what now follows as the grimmest scene in the First Testament. While Nebuchadrezzar could be expressing his wrath toward Jerusalem because its people have wasted his army's energy over the past two years, more importantly he is seeking to ensure that this capital city never counts again. So Nebuzaradan *burned* it *in fire*: so often Jeremiah has talked about burning in fire. The army *pulled* it *down*: Yahweh used this verb in commissioning Jeremiah, and it has recurred since. Some very ordinary people Nebuzaradan *made go into exile*: they could work in Nebuchadrezzar's fields, and he could recoup some of his investment. But some of them he *let remain as vinedressers and tillers*. Their position is less explicit here than it was at 39:10 (see the commentary there). That earlier account makes clearer that it is for their own sake that they are tending vines and other trees rather than providing for the needs of an occupying force, but the repetition in v. 16

---

16. The verb is *niphal*, not *pual* or *hophal* as in 39:2, where see the translation note.
17. Allen, *Jeremiah*, 538.
18. McKane, *Jeremiah*, 2:1365.
19. Lipschits, *Fall and Rise of Jerusalem*, 80.

over against v. 15 suggests that this note is the first of a series of notes of hope running through the chapter. While some ordinary people were subject to forced migration, some were allowed to stay.

17–23 Yet another scene competes for the title as the First Testament's grimmest. The account of the temple building in 1 Kgs 7:15–37 helps to identify the objects v. 17 refers to. The catalog in v. 18 covers *buckets* (*sîr*), in this context containers for ashes (Exod 27:3); *shovels* (*yāʿ*) for sweeping away (*yāʿâ*) burnt logs and ashes; *trimmers* (*məzammeret*) for tending the wicks of lamps; *throwers* (*mizrāq*) from which the blood was tossed (*zāraq*) against the altar; and *ladles* (*kap*) in the shape of the palm of a hand (*kap*), perhaps for burning incense. The catalog goes on in v. 19 to cover *bowls* (*sap*), *firepans* (*maḥtâ*) that would be capable of taking hold (*ḥātâ*) of burning wood, *lamps* (*mənôrâ*), and *flagons* (*mənaqqît*) used in connection with libations (Exod 25:29), and it repeats *throwers*, *pots*, and *ladles* from v. 18. *Pomegranates* were a decorative feature of the temple (1 Kgs 7:18, 20, 42), possibly symbolizing fruitfulness.[20] The lists of temple articles and the account of what happened to them witness to the pain of the community that watched them be destroyed or stolen; it contrasts with the much briefer account in 2 Chr 36:19, whose brevity reflects its origin in a later time when the temple had been rebuilt and was functioning again. Given the plundering in 597, it is surprising that there should be so much to plunder now. It is hard to imagine the Judahite community having had the energy and resources to restore the accoutrements of the temple after 597. So it seems likely that this chapter conflates the various pillagings of the temple as we come to its demise. This possibility may also fit with the overlaps in the lists in vv. 18–19.

24–27 Dramatically, the narrative about these other Judahite leaders (also missing from 2 Chr 36) first lists the people who get arrested then eventually in the last clause relates their fate. This head priest is Seraiah ben Azariah, grandson of Hilkiah (1 Chr 6:13–14 [5:39–40]; for Hilkiah, see 2 Kgs 22); it is a different Seraiah from the ones in 40:8 and 51:59. Zephaniah featured in 29:24–29. Priests exercising oversight at the threshold of the temple would be responsible for safeguarding its sanctity in various ways, but *the keepers of the threshold* stood at the temple door receiving offerings in 2 Kgs 22:4; they were treasurers. The people *present in the city* will be people from elsewhere who took refuge there. *People of the country* sometimes suggests people with power or influence, which would fit here with the fate that overtakes them (see the translation note on 1:18).

28–30 Jer 52 lacks the account of Gedaliah's appointment that appears in 2 Kgs 25:22–26 (the scroll has already treated this development at length in

---

20. Lundbom, *Jeremiah 37–52*, 528.

40:1–43:7) and in its place has a unique list of the numbers of people taken to Babylon in 597, 587, and 582. The numbers are puzzling. Second Kings 24:14 and 16 give figures of 10,000 and 8,000 for 597; maybe 3,023 covers only the men and those larger figures are estimates that include the women and children.[21] Whatever the numbers' historical significance, in this context they convey the impression that the number of people transported to Babylon was small. Jeremiah has often spoken as if "the exile" would mean a wholesale forced migration of the Judahite people analogous to the one presented in 2 Kgs 17 in connection with Ephraim, which is how Western convention has thought of it. In this connection, vv. 28–30 are significant in several ways. They indicate that as usual, Yahweh's action is softer than his threats. They issue the reminder that 587 was not the beginning of exile,[22] and they suggest that the 597 exile was more significant; it was indeed an important break.[23] And they indicate that the exile of 587 was not the last. We know of an exile in 582 only from this passage; the usual guess is that it was a reprisal for the events related in Jer 41, but attempts to answer the question of its significance "are rather like a game of blind man's bluff."[24] As a whole, the small numbers support the notion that the myth of an empty land is indeed a myth—the land was by no means emptied (see the commentary on 42:2–3). Admittedly, in addition to the people transported, no doubt many people had died in the siege. Others had fled, but they could come back, as Jer 40 has indicated. The Babylonians will have intended to put an end to the life of the capital city, but they had no reason to terminate life in what would become the province of Judah. Although "the destruction of Jerusalem and the end of the kingdom of Judah brought about the gravest demographic crisis in the history of the kingdom of Judah,"[25] it did not mean that there was no significant community in Judah after 587, or after 582. Jeremiah 24 in its context could call people left in Jerusalem just bad figs—figs with little potential—and after 587 they are indeed just poor people. But Jer 40 gives a less gloomy picture of the prospects of a community in Judah; they generated the prayers in Lamentations, and archaeological discoveries confirm how they kept life going there.[26] The Jeremiah scroll speaks with more than one voice about the various Judahite communities after 587. According to Jer 24, the Babylonian exiles are good figs, figs with

21. On different possibilities, see Lipschits, *Fall and Rise of Jerusalem*, 59–60.
22. Cf. J. J. Ahn, "Forced Migrations Guiding the Exile," in Ahn and Middlemas, *By the Irrigation Canals*, 173–89.
23. Seitz, *Theology in Conflict*, 101, 202.
24. McKane, *Jeremiah*, 2:1384.
25. Lipschits, *Fall and Rise of Jerusalem*, 270.
26. See Lipschits, *Fall and Rise of Jerusalem*, 102–9.

potential, and Jehoiachin is among them; but there aren't many of them, and Ezekiel doesn't give the impression that they are so insightful or committed. Jeremiah 44 threatens the Egyptian exiles with annihilation, but Jeremiah and Baruch are there, this community made it possible for us to be reading much of Jeremiah's story, and an Egyptian Jewish community flourished over the centuries. Thus "authors from the first generation after the destruction of Jerusalem who lived in Judah, Egypt, and Babylon perceived Babylonian rule, the destruction, the exile, the remnant in Judah, and the status of the House of David in different ways."[27] Indeed, the situation would have been more complicated than that observation necessarily implies. Within Judah, Egypt, and Babylon, authors and ordinary people would have different views on these matters, as the Ezekiel scroll and Lamentations as well as the Jeremiah scroll make clear. Judahites in Babylon and some Judahites in Egypt were not in those places because they chose to go there and saw the future as lying there; they were there because they had been frog-marched to those locations. Differences of perspective on issues such as acceptance of Babylonian authority or the future of the Davidic line would not be simply geographically based.

31 We hear nothing of what happened over the next twenty years. What we do get is a final hopeful coda to the story. Kings such as Evil-merodach sometimes granted an amnesty on their accession, partly to encourage the loyalty of the beneficiaries.[28] The expression *lifted the head* comes only here and in a similar context in Gen 40:13. Bowing the head is a sign of submission or humiliation or shame; you cannot look the other person in the eye. Having one's head lifted is a sign of being restored to acceptability, even to honor. Thus "the sense of an ending offered by ch. 52 is also tinged with the sense of a new beginning."[29] Here, too, Yahweh's threats are harsher than his actions; the release and elevation of Jehoiachin is not what one would have expected on the basis of 22:24–30 (nor is there any indication of a change of heart on Jehoiachin's part). It is a sign that Yahweh may not be finished with Judah and specifically with the line of David; and Jehoiachin's grandson Zerubbabel (1 Chr 3:17–19) will be a leader in Judah half a century later (Ezra 3), even though not a king. The very dating of events by Jehoiachin's exile rather than by the reign of a Babylonian king is suggestive.

32–34 Whereas 22:30 spoke negatively about Jehoiachin's throne, v. 32 now speaks positively. As a passage such as 32:42 spoke of the good Yahweh intended for Judah on the other side of disaster, Evil-merodach now

27. Lipschits, *Fall and Rise of Jerusalem*, 349.
28. Thompson, *Jeremiah*, 784.
29. Diamond, "Jeremiah," 613.

spoke of good things with him. The mention of *the kings who were with him in Babylon* is illumined by a record from Nebuchadrezzar's court (thus from somewhat earlier) that mentions the kings of Tyre, Gaza, Sidon, Arvad, and Ashdod.[30] Eating *regularly* with the king would not imply three meals a day every day. *Regular provision* would cover ordinary life for him and his family. Babylonian administrative records from Nebuchadrezzar's time (thus again from somewhat earlier) record on stone tablets deliveries of oil to various foreigners; the deliveries are quantified by the *sila* (something less than two pints), and they include supplies delivered to Jehoiachin king of Judah and his sons:

> 10 to . . . [Ia]-'-kin, king of Ia . . .
> 2½ sila to [. . . so]ns of the king of Ia-a-ḫu-du
>
> 10 to Ia-ku-ú-ki-nu, the son of the king of Ia-ku-du
> 2½ sila for the 5 sons of the king of Ia-ku-du[31]

Even at this stage, then, we should not think of Jehoiachin as in prison, even if he is under house arrest. And even these records regard him as king of Judah. But Evil-merodach's action would likely relate in some way to his strategy for exercising authority over Judah.[32] Finally, whereas Zedekiah was to be *in a house of custody until the day of his death* (v. 11), Jehoiachin is to be in his reestablished position *until the day of his death.*[33] We have noted that Chronicles lacks an account of Jehoiachin's elevation. Instead, it tells of Yahweh stirring the spirit of Cyrus the Great to commission the rebuilding of the temple in fulfillment of Jeremiah's promise, which it thus sees as the sign that Yahweh has not finished with Judah. It is an indication that Chronicles is written with more hindsight than Jer 52 and that Jer 52 dates from before 539.

> Grant, Almighty God, that as thou hast not only provided for thine ancient Church, by choosing Jeremiah as thy servant, but hast also designed that the fruit of his labors should continue to our age, O grant that we may not be unthankful to thee, but that we may so avail ourselves of so great a benefit, that the fruit of it may appear in us to the glory of thy name;

30. *ANET*, 308.
31. *ANET*, 308.
32. H. M. Barstad, "Empire! '. . . and gave him a seat above the seats of the other kings who were with him in Babylon": Jer. 52.31–34. Fact or Fiction?" in *Open-Mindedness in the Bible and Beyond: A Volume of Studies in Honour of Bob Becking*, ed. M. C. A. Korpel and L. L. Grabbe, LHBOTS 616 (London: T&T Clark, 2015), 11–13.
33. Patton, *Hope for a Tender Sprig*, 81–83.

may we learn so entirely to devote ourselves to thy service, and each of us be so attentive to the work of his calling, that we may strive with united hearts to promote the honor of thy name, and also the kingdom of thine only-begotten Son, until we finish our warfare, and come at length into that celestial rest, which has been obtained for us by the blood of thine only Son.[34]

34. Calvin, *Jeremiah*, 1:33.

Index of Authors

I am grateful to Anna Lo for compiling the Index of Authors and the Index of Scripture and Other Ancient Texts

Index of Subjects

The index mostly covers words or names that occur on more than two or three pages but on less than about fifty.

984

Index of Scripture and Other Ancient Texts

Unless specified, numbers in parentheses indicate the versification in printed Hebrew Bibles where it is different.